D0196022

THE COLLINS POCKET PORTUGUESE DICTIONARY

PORTUGUESE·ENGLISH ENGLISH·PORTUGUESE

General Editor/Organizador
Mike Harland B.A., M.A.

Brazilian Consultant/Assessora Brasileira
Dr Euzi Rodrigues Moraes

COLLINS
London and Glasgow

First published in this edition 1987

© **William Collins Sons & Co. Ltd. 1987**

ISBN 0 00 433207 5

contributors/colaboradores
Betty Wilson, Ana Lúcia Campbell,
Mark Dinneen, Lata Jamieson

consultants/assessores
David Treece, Antonio Fornazaro, John Whitlam

editorial staff/redação
Susan Dunsmore

Printed in Great Britain
Collins Clear-Type Press

INTRODUÇÃO

Quem quiser ler e compreender a língua inglesa encontrará neste dicionário um extenso léxico moderno que abrange uma ampla variedade de locuções de uso corrente. Encontrará também, por ordem alfabética, as abreviaturas, as siglas, os nomes geográficos mais conhecidos e ainda as formas verbais irregulares mais comuns, apontando-se as respectivas raízes, sendo então feita a tradução.

A pessoa que aspirar a comunicar e a expressar-se em língua estrangeira encontrará uma explicação clara e pormenorizada das palavras fundamentais, sendo utilizado um sistema de indicadores que a remeterão para a tradução mais precisa e lhe assinalarão o seu uso correcto.

INTRODUCTION

The user whose aim is to read and understand Portuguese will find a comprehensive and up-to-date wordlist including numerous phrases in current use. He will also find listed alphabetically the main irregular forms with a cross-reference to the basic form where a translátion is given, as well as some of the most common abbreviations, acronyms and geographical names.

The user who wishes to communicate and to express himself in the foreign language will find clear and detailed treatment of all the basic words, with numerous indicators pointing to the appropriate translations, and helping him to use it correctly.

Abbreviations	iv
Pronunciation guide	vi
PORTUGUESE-ENGLISH	1
ENGLISH-PORTUGUESE	181
Verb tables	400
Notes to the user of this dictionary	407
Notes on Portuguese grammar	414
Portuguese verb conjugations	422
The sounds of Portuguese	428
The time, dates and numbers	435

ABREVIATURAS

ABBREVIATIONS

abreviatura	**abr / abbr**	abbreviation
adjetivo	**adj**	adjective
advérbio	**adv**	adverb
administração	**ADMIN**	administration
aeronáutica	**AER / AVIAT**	aeronautics/aviation
agricultura	**AGR**	agriculture
anatomia	**ANAT**	anatomy
arquitetura	**ARQ / ARCH**	architecture
artigo	**art**	article
astronomia/astrologia	**ASTRO**	astronomy/astrology
atributivo	**atr**	attributive
automobilismo	**AUTO / AUT**	automobile
biologia	**BIO / BIOL**	biology
botânico	**BOT**	botany
brasileiro	**Br**	Brazilian
da Grã-Bretanha	**Brit**	British
química	**CHEM**	chemistry
coloquial	**col / fam**	colloquial/familiar
comércio	**COM / COMM**	commerce
composto	**comp**	compound
conjunção	**conj**	conjunction
construção	**CONSTR**	construction
cozinha	**CULIN**	cookery
economia	**ECON**	economics
educação	**EDUC**	education
eletricidade	**ELET / ELEC**	electricity
especialmente	**esp**	especially
exclamação	**excl**	exclamation
feminino	**f**	feminine
ferrovia	**FERRO**	railway
figurado	**fig**	figurative
fotografia	**FOTO**	photography
(verbo inglês) do qual a partícula é invariável	**fus**	(phrasal verb) where the particle is inseparable
geografia/geologia	**GEO**	geography/geology
geralmente	**ger / gen**	generally
invariável	**inv**	invariable
irregular	**irr**	irregular
jurídico	**JUR / LAW**	legal
linguística	**LING**	linguistics
literário	**LIT**	literary
masculino	**m**	masculine
matemática	**MAT / MATH**	mathematics

mecânica	**MEC/MECH**	mechanical
medicina	**MED**	medicine
militar	**MIL**	military
música	**MÚS/MUS**	music
nome	**n**	noun
náutico	**NÁUT/NAUT**	nautical
negativo	**neg**	negative
numeral	**num**	numeral
objeto	**obj**	object
a si mesmo	**o.s.**	oneself
pejorativo	**pej**	pejorative
fotografia	**PHOT**	photography
plural	**pl**	plural
política	**POL**	politics
particípio passado	**pp**	past participle
prefixo	**pref**	prefix
preposição	**prep**	preposition
pronome	**pron**	pronoun
psicologia	**PSICO/PSYCH**	psychology
pretérito	**pt**	past tense
em Portugal	**Pt**	in Portugal
química	**QUÍM**	chemistry
ferrovia	**RAIL**	railway
religião	**REL**	religion
alguém	**sb**	somebody
ensino	**SCOL**	schools, universities
singular	**sg**	singular
algo	**sth**	something
subjuntivo	**subj**	subjunctive
sufixo	**suf**	suffix
tecnologia	**TEC/TECH**	technology
telecomunicações	**TEL**	telecommunications
televisão	**TV**	television
tipografia	**TYP**	typography
dos Estados Unidos	**US**	American
verbo	**vb**	verb
verbo intransitivo	**vi**	verb intransitive
verbo reflexivo	**vr**	verb reflexive
verbo transitivo	**vt**	verb transitive
verbo transitivo/ intransitivo	**vt/i**	verb transitive/ intransitive
marca registrada	**®**	registered trademark
equivalente cultural	**≈**	cultural equivalent

PORTUGUESE PRONUNCIATION

The rules given below refer to Portuguese as spoken in the city and surrounding region of Rio de Janeiro, Brazil.

Consonants

c	[k]	café	c before a o, u is pronounced as in cat
ce, ci	[se, sɪ]	cego	c before e or i, as in receive
ç	[s]	raça	ç is pronounced as s in receive
ch	[ʃ]	chave	ch is pronounced as in shock
d	[d]	data	As in English EXCEPT:
de, di	[dʒɪ]	difícil cidade	d before i and final unstressed e is pronounced as in judge
g	[g]	gado	g before a, o or u, as in gap
ge, gi	[ʒɪ]	gíria	g before e or i, as s in leisure
h		humano	h is always silent in Portuguese
j	[ʒ]	jogo	j is pronounced as s in leisure
l	[w]	total	l after a vowel tends to become w
lh	[ʎ]	trabalho	lh is pronounced like the lli in million
m	[ãw]	cantam	final m preceded by a vowel
	[ĩ]	sim	nasalises the preceding vowel
nh	[ɲ]	tamanho	nh is pronounced like the ni in onion
q	[k]	queijo	q is pronounced as in kick
qu	[kw]	quanto	qu before a or o is pronounced as in quoits
-r-	[r]	compra	r preceded by a consonant (except n) and followed by a vowel is pronounced with a single trill
r-,-r	[x]	rato	initial r, final r, r preceded by a
rr	[x]	bezerro	vowel or n, and rr are pronounced similar to the Scottish ch in loch
s-	[s]	sol	As in English EXCEPT:
-s-	[z]	mesa	intervocalic s is pronounced as in rose
-s-,-s	[ʃ]	escada livros	s preceded or followed by a consonant or finally is pronounced as in sugar
t	[t]	todo	As in English EXCEPT:
te, ti	[tʃɪ]	amante tipo	t followed by i and final unstressed e is pronounced as in cheer
x-	[ʃ]	xarope	initial x is pronounced as in sugar
-x-	[ʃ]	rixa	x in any other position may be
	[ks]	fixo	pronounced as in sugar, axe or sail
	[s]	auxiliar	according to the individual word
z-,-z-	[z]	zangar	As in English EXCEPT:
-z	[ʃ]	cartaz	final z is pronounced as in sugar

Vowels

a, á, à, â	[a]	m*a*ta	*a* is normally pronounced as in f*a*t
ã	[ă]	irmã	*ã* is pronounced as in s*a*ng
e	[e]	v*e*jo	*e* is pronounced either as in
	[ɛ]	dir*e*ta	Scottish gr*ea*t or as in b*e*t, usually
	[ɪ]	fom*e*	depending upon the following sound. Final *e* is pronounced as in m*o*ney
é	[ɛ]	mis*é*ria	*é* is pronounced as in b*e*t
ê	[e]	p*ê*lo	*ê* is pronounced as in Scottish gr*ea*t
i	[ɪ]	v*i*da	*i* is pronounced as in m*ea*n
o	[u]	livr*o*	*o* is pronounced as in f*oo*d when
	[ɔ]	l*o*ja	unstressed, otherwise either as in
	[o]	gl*o*bo	r*o*ck or as in Scottish l*o*w, usually depending upon the next sound
ó	[ɔ]	*ó*leo	*ó* is pronounced as in r*o*ck
ô	[o]	col*ô*nia	*ô* is pronounced as in Scottish l*o*w
u	[u]	l*u*va	*u* is pronounced as in r*u*le. It is
			silent in q*u*e, q*u*i, g*u*e and g*u*i. It is
	[w]	ág*u*a	pronounced *w* in q*u*a, q*u*o and g*u*a
		ag*ü*entar	and when marked with a dieresis

Dipthongs

ãe	[ăj]	mã*e*	nasalised, approximately as in fly*ing*
ai	[aj]	v*ai*	as in r*i*de
ao, au	[aw]	*ao*s, *au*xílio	as in sh*ou*t
ão	[ăw]	v*ão*	nasalised, approximately as in r*ou*nd
ei	[ej]	f*ei*ra	as in Scottish gr*ea*t
eu	[eu]	d*eu*sa	both elements pronounced
oi	[oj]	b*oi*	as in t*oy*
õe	[õj]	avi*õe*s	nasalised, approximately as in 'b*oing*!'

Stress

The rules of stress in Portuguese are as follows:

(a) when a word ends in *a*, *e*, *o*, *m* (except *im*, *um*) or *s* (except *ns*), the second last syllable is stressed: camar*a*da, camar*a*das, p*a*rte, p*a*rtem

(b) when a word ends in *ã*, *i*, *u*, *im*, *um*, *ns* or a consonant other than *m* or *s*, the stress falls on the last syllable: vend*i*, alg*um*, alg*uns*, fal*ar*

(c) when the rules set out in a and b are not applied, an acute or circumflex accent appears over the stressed vowel: ótica, ânimo, inglês

In the phonetic transcription, the symbol ['] precedes the syllable on which the stress falls.

PRONÚNCIA INGLESA

Vogais e ditongos

	Exemplo Inglês	Explicação
ɑː	father	Entre o *a* de padre e o *o* de nó
ʌ	but, come	Aproximadamente como o primeiro *a* de cama
æ	man, cat	Som entre o *a* de lá e o *e* de pé
ə	father, ago	Som parecido com o *e* de que
əː	bird, heard	Entre o *e* aberto e o *o* fechado
ɛ	get, bed	Como em pé
ɪ	it, big	Mais breve do que em si
iː	tea, see	Como em fino
ɔ	hot, wash	Como em pó
ɔː	saw, all	Como o *o* de porte
u	put, book	Som breve e mais fechado do que em burro
uː	too, you	Som aberto como em um
aɪ	fly, high	Como em baile
au	how, house	Como em causa
ɛə	there, bear	Como o *e* de aeroporto
eɪ	day, obey	Como o *ei* de lei
ɪə	here, hear	Como *ia* de companhia
əu	go, note	[ə] seguido de um *u* breve
ɔɪ	boy, oil	Como em bóia
uə	poor, sure	Como *ua* em sua

Consoantes

	Exemplo Inglês	Explicação
d	men*d*ed	Como em con*d*e, an*d*ar
g	*g*et, bi*g*	Como em *g*rande
dʒ	*g*in, *j*udge	Como em a*dj*etivo
ŋ	si*ng*	Como em ci*n*co
h	*h*ouse, *h*e	*h* aspirado
j	*y*oung, *y*es	Como em *i*ogurte
k	*c*ome, mo*ck*	Como em Es*c*ócia
r	*r*ed, t*r*ead	*r* como em pa*r*a, mas pronunciado no céu da boca
s	*s*and, ye*s*	Como em *s*ala
z	ro*s*e, *z*ebra	Como em *z*ebra
ʃ	*sh*e, ma*ch*ine	Como em *ch*apéu
tʃ	*ch*in, ri*ch*	*t* seguido por um *ch*
w	*w*ater, *wh*ich	Como o *u* em q*u*arto
ʒ	vi*s*ion	Como em *j*á
θ	*th*ink, my*th*	Sem equivalente, aproximadamente como um *s* pronunciado entre os dentes
ð	*th*is, *th*e	Sem equivalente, aproximadamente como um *s* pronunciado entre os dentes

b, f, l, m, n, p, t, v pronunciam-se como em português.

O signo * indica que o r final escrito pronuncia-se apenas em inglês britânico quando a palavra seguinte começa por uma vogal. O signo ['] indica a sílaba acentuada.

A

a (a + o = ao; a + a = à; a + os = aos; a + as = às) prep (lugar) at, in, on; (direção) to, towards; (tempo) at; **à direita/esquerda** on the right/left; **ao lado de** beside, at the side of; **~ que horas?** at what time?; **às 5 horas** at 5 o'clock; **à hora** on time; **aos 15 anos** at 15 years of age; **ao vê-lo** when I saw him; **~ cavalo/pé** on horseback/foot; **~ negócios** on business; (maneira): **à força** by force; (sucessão): **dia ~ dia** day by day; **pouco ~ pouco** little by little; **~ como é?** how much is it?; **~ Cr$2000 o quilo** Cr$2000 a kilo; (com verbo): **começou ~ nevar** it started to snow; **aprender ~ falar** to learn to speak; (com infinitivo = gerúndio): **~ correr** running // **art** the // **pron** her; (você) you; (coisa) it; **~ do chapéu azul** the girl/woman in the blue hat.

(a) abr de **assinado** signed.

'aba f (chapéu) brim; (casaco) tail; (montanha) foot.

abacaxi [abaka'ʃi] m (Br) pineapple.

abade/abadessa [a'badʒi/aba'dɛsa] m abbot // f abbess; **abadia** f abbey.

abafadiço/a [abafa'dʒisu/a] adj stifling; (ar) stuffy; (fig) short-tempered; **abafar** vt to suffocate; (col) to pilfer // vi to choke; **abafar-se** vr to wrap up, keep warm.

abaixar [abaj'ʃax] vt to lower; (preço) to reduce; (luz, som) to turn down; **~-se** vr to stoop.

abaixo [a'bajʃu] adv down; **~ de** prep below, under; **~ o governo!** down with the government!; **morro ~** downhill; **rio ~** downstream; **mais ~** further down; **~ e acima** up and down; **~ assinado** undersigned; **deitar ~** to bring down.

abaixo-assi'nado m (documento) petition.

abajur [aba'ʒux] m (Br) lamp(-shade).

aba'lado/a adj loose, shaky; (fig) upset // f flight.

abalançar-se [abalã'saxsi] vr to venture.

aba'lar vt to shake; (fig) to upset // vi to shake; (fugir) to run off; **~-se** vr to be moved.

abali'zado/a adj eminent, distinguished; (opinião) reliable.

a'balo m (GEO) earthquake; (comoção) shock; (ação) shaking.

aba'nar vt to shake, wag; (com leque) to fan.

abandalhar [abãda'ʎax] vt to debase.

abando'nar vt (deixar) to leave, desert; (repudiar) to reject; (renunciar) to abandon, give up; (descuidar) to neglect; **~-se** vr: **~-se a** to abandon o.s. to; **abandono** m (ato) desertion; (estado) neglect.

abarcar [abax'kax] vt (abranger) to include; (conter) to enclose; (monopolizar) to monopolize.

abarro'tado/a adj full; (lugar) crowded, crammed; **abarrotar** vt to fill up; (gente) to crowd, cram; **abarrotar-se** vr to overeat.

abas'tado/a adj wealthy; **abastança** f abundance, surfeit.

abastar'dar vt to degrade; (corromper) to corrupt; **~-se** vr to become corrupt.

abastecer [abaʃtɛ'sex] vt to supply; (motor) to fuel; (AUTO) to fill up; (AER) to refuel; **~-se** vr: **~-se de** to stock up with; **abastecimento** m supply; (comestíveis) provisions pl; (ato) supplying; **abastecimentos** mpl supplies.

aba'ter vt (derrubar) to knock down; (diminuir) to reduce, lessen; **abatido/a** adj depressed, downcast; **abatimento** m (força) weakness; (preço) reduction; (prostração) depression; **fazer um abatimento** to give a discount.

abaulado/a [abaw'ladu/a] adj convex; (estrada) cambered; **abaular-se** vr to bulge.

ab'cesso m tumour; (dentes) abscess.

abdicação [abdʒika'sãw] f abdication; **abdicar** vt/i to abdicate.

ab'dômen m abdomen.

á-bê-'cê m alphabet; (fig) rudiments pl; **o ~ da cozinha** the ABC of cooking.

abeirar [abej'rax] vt to bring near; **~-se** vr: **~-se de** to draw near to.

abelha [a'bɛʎa] f bee; **~-mestra** f queen bee.

abençoar [abẽ'swax] vt to bless.

aberração [abexa'sãw] f aberration; (erro) error.

a'berto/a pp irr de **abrir** // adj open; (livre) clear; (desprotegido) exposed; (sincero) candid, frank // f opening; (clareira) glade; (intervalo) break; **abertura** f opening; (FOTO) aperture; (ELET) socket, outlet (US); (ranhura) gap, crevice.

a'beto m fir tree.

abis'mado/a adj astonished.

a'bismo m abyss, chasm; (fig) depths pl.

abjeção [abʒɛ'sãw] (Pt: -cç-) f degradation; **abjeto/a** (Pt: -ct-) adj abject; (vil) mean.

abnegação [abnɛga'sãw] f self-denial; **abnegado/a** adj unselfish; **abnegar** vt to renounce.

a'bóbada *f* vault; (*telhado*) arched roof.

a'bóbora *f* pumpkin.

abolição [aboli'sãw] *f* abolition; abolir *vt* to abolish, suppress.

abominação [abomina'sãw] *f* abomination; abominar *vt* to loathe, detest.

abo'nar *vt* to guarantee; (*dinheiro*) to advance; ~-se *vr* to boast; abono *m* guarantee; (*JUR*) bail; (*louvor*) praise; abono de família child benefit; em abono da verdade to be absolutely honest.

abor'dar *vt* (*NÁUT*) to board; (*pessoa*) to approach; (*assunto*) to broach, tackle.

aborígene [abo'rɪʒɛnɪ] *adj* native, aboriginal // *m/f* native, aborigine.

aborrecer [aboxe'sex] *vt* (*enfadar*) to annoy; (*maçar*) to bore; ~-se *vr* to get annoyed; (*entediar-se*) to get bored; aborrecido/a *adj* annoying, boring; que aborrecido! how annoying!; aborrecimento *m* dislike; (*enfado*) boredom; que aborrecimento! what a nuisance!

abor'tar *vi* to miscarry, abort // *vt* to abort; aborto *m* (*MED*) miscarriage; (*forçado*) abortion.

abotoar [abo'twax] *vt* to button // *vi* (*BOT*) to bud.

abra'çar *vt* to hug; (*abranger*) to include; ~-se *vr* to embrace; ele abraçou-se a mim he embraced me; abraço *m* embrace, hug; com um abraço (*carta*) with best wishes.

abran'dar *vt* to reduce; (*suavizar*) to soften; ~ a marcha (*AUTO*) to slow down // *vi* to diminish; (*acalmar*) to calm down.

abranger [abrã'ʒex] *vt* to include, comprise; (*alcançar*) to reach.

abra'sar *vt* to burn; (*desbastar*) to erode; (*polir*) to polish // *vi* to be on fire; ~-se *vr* to be consumed with passion.

abre-gar'rafas *m inv* (*Pt*) bottle opener.

abre-'latas *m inv* (*Pt*) can *ou* tin opener.

abre'viar *vt* to abbreviate; (*encurtar*) to shorten; (*texto*) to abridge; abreviatura *f* abbreviation; (*resumo*) précis.

abri'dor *m* (*Br*) opener; ~ de latas tin *ou* can opener; ~ de garrafas bottle opener.

abri'gar *vt* to shelter; (*proteger*) to protect; ~-se *vr* to take shelter; abrigo *m* shelter, cover; abrigo anti-nuclear anti-nuclear shelter.

abril [a'brıw] (*Pt*: A-) *m* April.

a'brir *vt* to open; (*fechadura*) to unlock; (*vestuário*) to unfasten; (*torneiras*) to turn on; (*ELET*, *TV*, *RÁDIO*) to switch on; ~ caminho to force a way through // *vi* to open (up).

abrogação [abroga'sãw] *f* repeal, annulment; abrogar *vt* to repeal, annul.

abrolho [a'broʎu] *m* thorn; ~s *mpl* (*fig*) troubles.

a'brupto/a *adj* abrupt; (*repentino*) sudden; (*íngreme*) steep.

absente'ísta *m/f* absentee.

absen'tismo *m* absenteeism.

ab'side *f* apse; (*relicário*) shrine.

absolu'tismo *m* absolutism; absolutista *adj*, *m/f* absolutist; absoluto/a *adj* absolute; (*puro*) pure.

absol'ver *vt* to absolve; (*JUR*) to acquit; absolvição *f* absolution; (*JUR*) acquittal.

absorção [abzox'sãw] *f* absorption; absorto/a *pp irr de* absorver // *adj* absorbed, engrossed; absorver *vt* to absorb; absorver-se *vr*: absorver-se em to concentrate on.

abstêmio/a [abʃ'temju/a] *adj* abstemious; (*álcool*) teetotal // *m/f* abstainer, teetotaller.

abstenção [abʃtẽ'sãw] *f* abstention; abstencionista *adj*, *m/f* abstainer; abster-se *vr*: abster-se de to abstain *ou* refrain from.

absti'nência *f* abstinence; (*jejum*) fasting.

abstração [abʃtra'sãw] (*Pt*: -cç-) *f* abstraction; (*concentração*) concentration; abstrair *vt* to abstract; (*omitir*) to omit; (*separar*) to separate; abstrair-se *vr* to become distracted; abstrato/a (*Pt*: -ct-) *adj* abstract; (*distraído*) absent-minded.

ab'surdo/a *adj* absurd // *m* nonsense.

abu'lia *f* apathy.

abun'dância [abũ'dãsja] *f* abundance; abundante *adj* abundant; abundar *vi* to abound.

abu'sar *vi* (*exceder-se*) to go too far; ~ de to abuse; abuso *m* abuse; (*JUR*) indecent assault; abuso de confiança breach of trust.

a'butre *m* vulture.

a.C. *abr de* antes de Cristo B.C.

a/c *abr de* ao cuidado de c/o.

aca'bado/a *adj* finished; (*esgotado*) worn out; (*fig*) masterly; acabamento *m* finish.

aca'bar *vt* (*terminar*) to finish, complete; (*levar a cabo*) to accomplish; (*aperfeiçoar*) to complete; (*consumir*) to use up; (*rematar*) to finish off // *vi* to finish, end, come to an end; ~ com to put an end to; ~ de chegar to have just arrived; ~ por to end (up) by; ~-se *vr* (*terminar*) to be over; (*prazo*) to expire; (*esgotar-se*) to run out; acabou-se! that's enough!, it's all over!

acabrunhado/a [akabru'ɲadu/a] *adj* (*abatido*) depressed; (*envergonhado*) ashamed; acabrunhar *vt* (*entristecer*) to distress; (*abater*) to overwhelm.

acade'mia *f* academy; acadêmico/a *adj*, *m/f* academic.

açafrão [asa'frãw] *m* saffron.

a'caime *m* (*Pt*) muzzle.

acaju [aka'ʒu] *m* mahogany.

acalen'tar *vt* to rock to sleep; (*esperanças*) to cherish.

acal'mar vt to calm // vi (vento etc) to abate; **~-se** vr to calm down.

acalo'rado/a adj heated; **acalorar** vt to heat; (fig) to inflame; **acalorar-se** vr (fig) to get heated.

acampa'mento m camping; (MIL) camp, encampment; **acampar** vi to camp.

acanhado/a [aka'ɲadu/a] adj shy; (estreito) cramped, narrow; **acanhamento** m shyness; **acanhar-se** vr to be shy, become shy.

ação [a'sãw] (Pt: -cç-) f action; (ato) act, deed; (movimento) action; (MIL) battle; (enredo) plot; (JUR) lawsuit; (COM) share; **~ ordinária/preferencial** ordinary/ preference share; **~ de graças** thanksgiving.

acare'ar vt to confront.

acariciar [akarɪs'jax] vt to caress; (fig) to cherish.

acarre'tar vt to result in, bring about.

a'caso m chance, accident; **por ~** by chance; **ao ~** at random; **encontrar alguém por ~** to meet sb by chance.

acastanhado/a [akaʃta'ɲadu/a] adj brownish; (cabelo) auburn.

acata'mento m respect; (deferência) deference; **acatar** vt (respeitar) to respect; (honrar) to honour; (lei) to obey.

acaute'lar vt to warn; **~-se** vr to be cautious; **~-se contra** to guard against; **acautele-se!** watch out!

ace'der vi: **~ a** to agree to, accede to.

aceitação [asejta'sãw] f acceptance; (aprovação) approval; **aceitar** vt to accept; **aceitável** adj acceptable.

aceite [a'sejtʃi] (Pt: pp irr de **aceitar**) // adj accepted // m acceptance; **aceito/a** pp irr de **aceitar**.

aceleração [aselera'sãw] f acceleration; (pressa) haste; **acelerado/a** adj (rápido) quick; (apressado) hasty; **acelerador** m accelerator.

acele'rar vt/i to accelerate; **~ o passo** to go faster.

ace'nar vi (com a mão) to wave; (com a cabeça) to nod.

acende'dor m lighter; **acender** vt (cigarro, fogo) to light; (luz) to switch on; (pôr fogo em) to set fire to; (fig) to excite, inflame.

a'ceno m sign, gesture; (com a mão) wave; (com a cabeça) nod.

a'cento m accent; (de intensidade) stress; (sotaque) accent; **acentuação** f accentuation; (ênfase) stress; **acentuado/a** adj (sílaba) stressed; (saliente) conspicuous; **acentuar** vt (marcar com acento) to accent; (salientar) to stress, emphasize.

ace'pipe m tit-bit, delicacy; **~s** mpl (Pt) hors d'œuvres.

a'cerca **~ de** prep about, concerning.

acer'car-se vr: **~ de** to approach, draw near to.

a'cérrimo/a adj (muito acre) very bitter; (defensor) staunch.

acer'tado/a adj (certo) right, correct; (sensato) sensible; **acertar** vt (ajustar) to put right; (relógio) to set; **acertar o caminho** to find the right way // vi to get it right, be right; (adivinhar) to guess right; **acertar no alvo** to hit the mark; **acertar com** to hit upon.

a'cervo m heap; (JUR) estate; **um ~ de** a lot of.

a'ceso/a pp irr de **acender** // adj (luz, gás, TV) on; (fogo) alight; (excitado) excited.

aces'sível adj accessible; (pessoa) approachable; **acesso** m access, entry; (MED) fit, attack; **um acesso de cólera** a fit of anger; **via de acesso** access road.

aces'sório/a adj accessory // m accessory.

ace'tona f nail varnish remover; (QUÍM) acetone.

achado [a'ʃadu] m find, discovery; (pechincha) bargain; (sorte) godsend.

achaque [a'ʃakɪ] m ailment.

achar [a'ʃax] vt (descobrir) to find, discover; (pensar) to think; **acho que sim** I think so; **~-se** vr: **~-se doente** to feel ill, be ill.

achatar [aʃa'tax] vt to squash, flatten.

ache'gar-se vr: **~ a /de** to approach, get closer to.

aci'cate m spur; (fig) incentive.

aciden'tado/a adj (terreno) rough; (viagem) eventful; (vida) chequered // m/f injured person.

aciden'tal adj accidental; **acidente** m accident; (acaso) chance; (MED) fit; **por acidente** by accident.

acidez [asi'deʃ] f acidity; **ácido/a** adj acid; (azedo) sour // m acid.

a'cima adv above; (para cima) up; **rio ~** up river; **passar rua ~** to go up the street; **mais ~** higher up // prep: **~ de** above; (além de) beyond; **~ de 1000 cruzeiros** more than 1000 cruzeiros.

a'cinte m provocation // adv deliberately, on purpose; **acintosamente** adv on purpose.

acionado/a [asju'nadu/a] (Pt: -cc-) pp de **acionar** // m/f (JUR) defendant; **~s** mpl gestures; **acionar** (Pt: -cc-) vt to set in motion; (máquina) to drive, operate; (JUR) to sue.

acionista [asju'nɪʃta] (Pt: -cc-) m/f shareholder.

acir'rar vt to incite, stir up.

aclamação [aklama'sãw] f acclamation; (ovação) applause; **aclamar** vt to acclaim; (aplaudir) to applaud.

aclaração [aklara'sãw] f clarification; (explicação) explanation; **aclarar** vt to explain, clarify // vi to clear up; **aclarar-se** vr to become clear.

aclimação [aklima'sãw] f acclimatization; **aclimar** vt to acclimatize; **aclimar-se** vr to become acclimatized.

'aço m (metal) steel.

acoco'rar-se *vr* to squat, crouch.

a'code *etc vb ver* **acudir.**

acoi'mar *vt* (*multar*) to fine; (*censurar*) to blame; (*tachar*) to brand.

acoi'tar *vt* to shelter, give refuge to.

açoitar [asoj'taʃ] *vt* to whip, lash; **açoite** *m* whip, lash.

aco'lá *adv* over there.

acolchoado/a [akol'ʃwadu/a] *adj* quilted // *m* quilt; **acolchoar** *vt* (*costurar*) to quilt; (*forrar*) to pad; (*estofar*) to upholster.

acolhedor(a) [akoʎe'dox(ra)] *adj* welcoming; (*hospitaleiro*) hospitable; **acolher** *vt* to welcome; (*abrigar*) to shelter; (*aceitar*) to accept; **acolher-se** *vr* to shelter; **acolhida** *f*, **acolhimento** *m* (*recepção*) reception, welcome; (*refúgio*) refuge.

acome'ter *vt* (*atacar*) to attack, assault; **acometimento** *m* (*ataque*) attack.

acomodação [akomoda'sãw] *f* accommodation; (*arranjo*) arrangement; (*adaptação*) adaptation; **acomodar** *vt* (*alojar*) to accommodate; (*arrumar*) to arrange; (*tornar cômodo*) to make comfortable; (*adaptar*) to adapt.

acompanha'mento *m* attendance; (*cortejo*) procession; (*MÚS*) accompaniment; (*CULIN*) side dish; **acompanhante** *m/f* companion; (*MÚS*) accompanist; **acompanhar** *vt* to accompany, go along with; (*MÚS*) to accompany.

aconchegado/a [akõʃe'gadu/a] *adj* snug, cosy; **aconchegar** *vt* to bring near; **aconchegar-se** *vr* to snuggle.

acondiciona'mento *m* packaging; **acondicionar** *vt* to condition; (*empacotar*) to pack; (*embrulhar*) to wrap (up).

aconselhar [akõse'ʎax] *vt* to advise; **~-se** *vr*: **~-se com** to consult; **aconselhável** *adj* advisable.

aconte'cer *vi* to happen, occur; **acontecimento** *m* event.

acor'dar *vt* (*despertar*) to wake (up), awaken; (*provocar*) to arouse // *vi* (*despertar*) to wake up.

acorde [a'kordʒi] *m* chord.

a'cordo *m* agreement; **de ~** agreed; **estar de ~** to agree; **de ~ com** (*pessoa*) in agreement with; (*documento*) in accordance with.

A'çores *mpl*: **os ~** the Azores.

acor'rer *vi* to come running; (*acudir*) to come to sb's aid.

acos'sar *vt* (*perseguir*) to pursue; (*atormentar*) to harass, torment.

acosta'mento *m* hard shoulder, berm (*US*).

acos'tar *vt* to lean against; (*NÁUT*) to bring alongside; **~-se** *vr* to lean back; (*deitar-se*) to lie down.

acostu'mado/a *adj* (*habituado*) used, accustomed; (*habitual*) usual, customary; **acostumar** *vt* to accustom; **acostumar-se** *vr*: **acostumar-se a** to get used to.

acotove'lar *vt* to jostle; **~-se** *vr* to jostle.

açougue [a'sogi] *m* butcher's (shop); **açougueiro** *m* butcher.

acovar'dar-se *vr* (*desanimar*) to lose courage; (*amedrontar-se*) to flinch, cower.

'acre *adj* (*amargo*) bitter; (*violento*) severe, harsh; (*fig*) biting.

acredi'tar *vt* to believe; (*COM*) to credit; (*afiançar*) to guarantee // *vi*: **~ em** to believe in; **acreditável** *adj* credible.

acrescen'tar *vt* (*aumentar*) to increase; (*ajuntar*) to add; **acréscimo** *m* (*aumento*) increase; (*elevação*) rise.

acrian'çado/a *adj* childish.

a'crílico *m* acrylic.

acriso'lar *vt* to refine, purify.

acroba'cia *f* acrobatics *pl*; (*prova*) stunt; **~s aéreas** *fpl* stunt flying; **acrobata** *m/f* acrobat.

a'çúcar *m* sugar; **açucarar** *vt* to sugar; (*adoçar*) to sweeten; **açucareiro** *m* (*vaso*) sugar bowl.

açude [a'sudʒi] *m* dam.

acu'dir *vi* (*acorrer*) to come running; (*ir em socorro*) to go to help; (*responder*) to reply, respond; **~ a** to come to the aid of.

açu'lar *vt* (*incitar*) to incite; **~ um cachorro contra alguém** to set a dog on sb.

acumulação [akumula'sãw] *f* accumulation; (*montão*) heap; **acumulador** *m* accumulator; (*ELET*) battery; **acumular** *vt* to accumulate; (*armazenar*) to store; (*reunir*) to collect.

acusação [akuza'sãw] *f* accusation, charge; (*JUR*) prosecution; **acusar** *vt* to accuse; (*revelar*) to reveal; (*culpar*) to blame; **acusar o recebimento de** to acknowledge receipt of.

a'cústica *f* acoustics *pl*.

a'daga *f* dagger.

adágio [ada'ʒju] *m* adage; (*MÚS*) adagio.

a'damascado/a *adj* (*cor, sabor*) apricot.

adaptabili'dade *f* adaptability; **adaptação** *f* adaptation; **adaptar** *vt* (*modificar*) to adapt; (*acomodar*) to fit; **adaptar-se** *vr*: **adaptar-se a** to adjust to, fit in with.

a'dega *f* cellar.

adejar [ade'ʒax] *vt* (*asas*) to flap // *vi* to flutter; **~ sobre** to hover over.

adelga'çado/a *adj* thin; (*aguçado*) pointed; **adelgaçar** *vt* (*rarefazer*) to attenuate; (*terminar em ponta*) to taper; **adelgaçar-se** *vr* to grow thin.

ade'mais *adv* (*além disso*) besides, moreover.

a'dentro *adv* inside, in; **mata ~** into the woods.

a'depto/a *m/f* follower, adherent.

adequado/a [ade'kwadu/a] *adj* (*suficiente*) adequate; (*apropriado*) appropriate, suitable; **adequar** *vt* to adapt, make suitable.

adere'çar *vt* to adorn, decorate; **~-se**

vr to dress up; **adereço** *m* adornment; **adereços** *mpl* (*teatro*) stage props.

ade'rência *f* adherence; **aderente** *adj* adherent, sticking // *m/f* (*partidário*) supporter; **aderir** *vi* to adhere; (*colar*) to stick.

adesão [adɛ'zãw] *f* adhesion; (*patrocínio*) support; **adesivo/a** *adj* adhesive, sticky // *m* adhesive tape; (*MED*) sticking plaster.

ades'trado/a *adj* skilful, skilled; **adestrar** *vt* to train, instruct; (*cavalo*) to break in.

adeus [a'dewʃ] *excl* goodbye!; **dizer** ~ to say goodbye, bid farewell; ~**inho** *excl* bye!

adia'mento *m* postponement; (*de uma sessão*) adjournment.

adian'tado/a *adj* advanced; (*relógio*) fast; (*col: atrevido*) fresh, insolent; **chegar** ~ to arrive ahead of time; **pagar** ~ to pay in advance.

adianta'mento *m* advancement, progress; (*dinheiro*) advance payment; **adiantar** *vt* to advance; (*relógio*) to put forward; **não adianta (nada)** it's no use (at all).

adi'ante *adv* (*na frente*) in front; (*para a frente*) forward, onward; **mais** ~ further on; (*no futuro*) later on; ~**!** (*continue!*) go on!

adi'ar *vt* to postpone, put off; (*uma sessão*) to adjourn.

adição [adʒi'sãw] *f* addition; (*MAT*) sum; **adicionar** *vt* to add.

a'dicto/a *adj*: ~ **a** addicted to; (*dedicado*) devoted to.

a'dido *m* attaché.

adinheirado/a [adʒiɲej'radu/a] *adj* wealthy, rich.

adita'mento *m* addition.

adivinhação [adʒiviɲa'sãw] *f* (*destino*) fortune-telling; (*conjectura*) guessing; **adivinhar** *vt/i* (*conjecturar*) to guess; (*ler a sorte*) to foretell; **adivinhar o pensamento de alguém** to read sb's mind; **adivinho/a** *m/f* fortune-teller.

adja'cente *adj* adjacent.

adje'tivo *m* adjective.

adjudicação [adʒudʒka'sãw] *f* grant; (*de contratos*) award; (*JUR*) decision; **adjudicar** *vt* to award, grant.

ad'junto/a *adj* joined, attached // *m/f* assistant.

administração [administra'sãw] *f* administration; (*direção*) management; (*comissão*) board; **administrador(a)** *m/f* administrator; (*diretor*) director; (*gerente*) manager; **administrar** *vt* to administer, manage; (*governar*) to govern.

admiração [admira'sãw] *f* (*assombro*) wonder; (*estima*) admiration; **ponto de** ~ (*Pt*) exclamation mark; **admirado/a** *adj* astonished, surprised.

admi'rar *vt* to admire; ~-**se** *vr*: ~-**se de** to be astonished at, be surprised at;

não me admiro! I'm not surprised; **admirável** *adj* (*assombroso*) amazing.

admissão [admi'sãw] *f* admission; (*consentimento para entrar*) admittance; (*escola*) intake.

admi'tir *vt* (*aceitar*) to admit; (*permitir*) to allow; ~ **um empregado** to engage an employee.

admoestação [admwɛʃta'sãw] *f* warning; (*censura*) reprimand.

adoção [adɔ'sãw] (*Pt: -pç-*) *f* adoption.

ado'çar *vt* (*com açúcar*) to sweeten; (*abrandar*) to soften; (*pacificar*) to pacify.

adoe'cer *vi* to fall ill; ~ **de/com** to fall ill with // *vt* to make ill.

adoi'dado/a *adj* crazy.

adoles'cente *adj, m/f* adolescent.

ado'rar *vt* to adore; (*venerar*) to worship; **adorável** *adj* adorable.

adorme'cer *vi* to fall asleep; (*entorpecer-se*) to go numb; **adormecido/a** *adj* sleeping // *m/f* sleeper.

ador'nar *vt* to adorn, decorate; **adorno** *m* (*enfeite*) adornment.

ado'tar (*Pt: -pt-*) *vt* to adopt; **adotivo/a** (*Pt: -pt-*) *adj* (*filho*) adopted.

adquirir [adki'rix] *vt* to acquire; (*obter*) to obtain.

a'drede *adv* on purpose, deliberately.

'adro *m* church forecourt; (*em volta da igreja*) churchyard.

aduana [ad'wana] *f* customs (house); **aduaneiro/a** *adj* customs // *m* customs officer.

adu'bar *vt* to manure; (*comida*) to season, spice; **adubo** *m* (*fertilizante*) fertilizer; (*comida*) seasoning.

adulação [adula'sãw] *f* flattery; **adulador(a)** *adj* flattering // *m/f* flatterer; **adular** *vt* to flatter.

adulteração [adultera'sãw] *f* adulteration; (*contas*) falsification; **adulterador(a)** *m/f* adulterator; **adulterar** *vt* (*vinho*) to adulterate; (*contas*) to falsify // *vi* to commit adultery.

adul'tério *m* adultery; **adúltero/a** *m* adulterer // *f* adulteress.

a'dulto/a *adj* adult, grown up // *m/f* adult.

a'dusto/a *adj* (*chamuscado*) scorched; (*ressequido*) parched; (*queimado*) burnt.

adven'tício/a *adj* (*casual*) accidental; (*estrangeiro*) foreign // *m/f* (*estrangeiro*) foreigner; (*intruso*) upstart.

ad'vento *m* advent, arrival; **o A**~ Advent.

ad'vérbio *m* adverb.

adver'sário *m* adversary, opponent, enemy.

adversi'dade *f* adversity, misfortune; **adverso/a** *adj* adverse, contrary.

adver'tência *f* warning; (*conselho*) advice.

adver'tido/a *adj* prudent; (*informado*) well advised; **advertir** *vt* to warn; (*avisar*) to advise; (*chamar a atenção a*) to draw attention to.

advo'gado *m* lawyer; **advogar** *vt* (*promover*) to advocate; (*JUR*) to plead // *vi* to practise law.

aéreo/a [a'erɪu/a] *adj* air, aerial; **ataque** ~ air raid; **Força A~a** Air Force; **por via** ~a by air mail.

aeromoço/a [aero'mosu/a] (*Br*) *m* steward // *f* air hostess.

aero'nave *f* aircraft.

aero'porto *m* airport.

a'fã *f* (*ardor*) eagerness; (*trabalho*) exertion; (*ânsia*) anxiety.

afabili'dade *f* friendliness, courtesy.

afadi'gar *vt* to tire (out); ~-se *vr* to tire o.s. (out), get tired.

afa'gar *vt* (*acariciar*) to caress, fondle; (*cabelo*) to stroke; (*alisar*) to smooth (down).

afa'mado/a *adj* renowned, famous, celebrated.

afanoso/a [afa'nozu/a] *adj* laborious; (*meticuloso*) painstaking.

afas'tado/a *adj* (*distante*) remote; (*ausente*) away; (*isolado*) secluded; **manter-se** ~ to keep to o.s.; **afastamento** *m* removal, withdrawal; (*distância*) distance.

afas'tar *vt* (*retirar*) to remove; (*apartar*) to keep off, keep away; (*desviar*) to deflect, turn; ~-se *vr* (*ir-se embora*) to move away, go away; (*desviar-se*) to turn, swerve; ~-se do assunto to stray from the subject.

a'fável *adj* courteous, genial.

afa'zer *vt* to accustom; ~-se *vr*: ~-se a to get used to.

afa'zeres *mpl* business *sg*; (*dever*) duties, tasks; ~ domésticos household chores.

afeição [afej'sãw] *f* (*amor*) affection, fondness; (*dedicação*) devotion; **afeiçoado/a** *adj* (*amoroso*) fond; (*devotado*) devoted // *m/f* friend.

afeiçoar-se [afej'swax-sɪ] *vr*: ~ a (*tomar gosto por*) to take a liking to.

afeito/a [a'fejtu/a] *adj*: ~ a accustomed to, used to.

aferi'dor *m* (*de pesos e medidas*) inspector; (*verificador*) checker; (*instrumento*) gauge; **aferir** *vt* (*medir*) to gauge; (*verificar*) to check, inspect; (*comparar*) to compare.

afer'rado/a *adj* obstinate, stubborn.

afer'rar *vt* (*prender*) to secure; (*NÁUT*) to anchor; (*agarrar*) to grasp; ~-se *vr*: ~-se a to cling to.

afetação [afcta'sãw] (*Pt*: **-ct-**) *f* affectation; **afetado/a** (*Pt*: **-ct-**) *adj* (*vaidoso*) conceited, affected; **afetar** (*Pt*: **-ct-**) *vt* to affect; (*fingir*) to pretend, feign.

a'feto/a (*Pt*: **-ct-**) *pp irr* de **afetar** // *adj* affectionate; ~ a fond of // *m* affection, fondness; **afetuoso/a** (*Pt*: **-ct-**) *adj* affectionate, tender.

afi'ado/a *adj* sharp; (*pessoa*) knowing.

afian'çar *vt* (*JUR*) to stand bail for; (*garantir*) to guarantee.

afi'ar *vt* to sharpen.

aficio'nado/a *m/f* fan, enthusiast.

afigu'rar-se *vr* to seem, appear; **afigura-se-me que** it seems to me that.

afilhado/a [afi'ʎadu/a] *m* godson // *f* goddaughter.

afili'ar *vt* to affiliate, admit; ~-se *vr*: ~-se a (*ser inscrito*) to join.

afim [a'fĩ] *adj* (*semelhante*) similar; (*consangüíneo*) akin, related // *m/f* relative, relation.

afinação [afina'sãw] *f* (*MÚS*) tuning, harmony.

afi'nado/a *adj* in tune.

afi'nal *adv* at last, finally; ~ **de contas** after all.

afi'nar *vt* (*MÚS*) to tune // *vi* (*adelgaçar*) to taper.

a'finco *m* tenacity, persistence.

afini'dade *f* affinity.

afirmação [afixma'sãw] *f* affirmation; (*declaração*) statement; **afirmar** *vt/i* tó affirm, assert; (*declarar*) to declare; **afirmativo/a** *adj* affirmative.

afive'lar *vt* to buckle.

afi'xar *vt* (*cartazes*) to stick, post.

aflição [afli'sãw] *f* affliction; (*ansiedade*) anxiety; (*angústia*) distress; (*agonia*) grief.

afligir [afli'ʒix] *vt* to distress; (*inquietar*) to worry; ~-se *vr*: ~-se de to worry about; **aflito/a** *pp irr de* **afligir** // *adj* distressed, upset, anxious.

aflu'ência *f* abundance; (*corrente copiosa*) great flow; (*concorrência*) crowd; **afluente** *adj* copious // *m* tributary.

afluir [a'flwix] *vi* to flow; (*concorrer*) to congregate.

afo'gado/a *adj* drowned // *m* drowned man // *f* drowned woman.

afoga'dor *m* (*Br*: *AUTO*) choke.

afo'gar *vt* to drown // *vi* (*AUTO*) to stall; ~-se *vr* to drown, be drowned.

a'fogo *m* suffocation; (*aflição*) anguish, affliction; (*pressa*) haste.

a'fora *prep* except, apart from // *adv*: **rua** ~ down the street.

afor'rar *vt* (*roupa*) to line; (*poupar*) to save; (*liberar*) to free.

afortu'nado/a *adj* fortunate, lucky.

'África *f* Africa; ~ **do Sul** South Africa; **africano/a** *adj, m/f* African.

a'fronta *f* insult, affront; **afrontar** *vt* to insult; (*ofender*) to offend.

afrouxar [afro'fax] *vt* (*desapertar*) to slacken; (*soltar*) to loosen // *vi* (*soltar-se*) to come loose.

afugentar [afuʒẽ'tax] *vt* to drive off, put to flight.

afun'dar *vt* (*submergir*) to sink; (*cavidade*) to deepen; ~-se *vr* to sink.

agachar-se [aga'ʃax-sɪ] *vr* (*acaçapar-se*) to crouch, squat; (*curvar-se*) to stoop; (*fig*) to cringe.

agar'rar *vt* to seize, grasp; ~-se *vr*: ~-se a to cling to, hold on to.

agasalhado/a [agaza'ʎadu/a] *adj* cosy, snug; (*abrigado*) sheltered; **agasalhar** *vt* (*abrigar*) to shelter; (*acolher*) to welcome; **agasalhar-se** *vr* to wrap o.s. up; **agasalho** *m* wrap, warm clothing.

agas'tar *vt* to irritate; ~**-se** *vr*: ~**-se com** to get angry with.

agatanhar [agata'ɲax] *vt* to scratch.

agência [a'ʒẽsja] *f* agency; (*escritório*) office; ~ **de correio** (*Br*) post office; ~ **de viagens** travel agency.

agenci'ar *vt* to negotiate for; (*procurar*) to obtain.

agenda [a'ʒẽda] *f* agenda; (*caderneta*) diary.

agente [a'ʒẽtʃi] *m* agent; (*de polícia*) policeman.

ágil ['aʒiw] *adj* agile, nimble, active; **agilidade** *f* agility.

agiota [aʒɪ'ota] *m/f* stockjobber; (*usurário*) moneylender; (*interesseiro*) speculator.

agir [a'ʒix] *vi* (*atuar*) to act; (*proceder*) to behave; ~ **bem/mal** to do right/wrong.

agitação [aʒɪta'sãw] *f* agitation; (*perturbação*) disturbance; (*inquietação*) unrest.

agi'tado/a *adj* agitated, disturbed; (*inquieto*) restless; (*mar*) rough; **agitar** *vt* to agitate, disturb; (*sacudir*) to shake; (*a cauda*) to wag; (*mexer*) to stir; (*os braços*) to swing, wave; **agitar-se** *vr* to get upset; (*mar*) to get rough.

aglomeração [aglomera'sãw] *f* gathering; (*multidão*) crowd; **aglomerado** *m*: **aglomerado urbano** city; **aglomerar** *vt* to heap up, pile up; **aglomerar-se** *vr* (*multidão*) to crowd together.

ago'nia *f* agony, anguish; (*ânsia da morte*) death throes *pl*.

agoni'zante *adj* dying // *m/f* dying person; **agonizar** *vi* to be dying; (*afligir-se*) to agonize.

a'gora *adv* now; ~ **mesmo** right now; (*há pouco*) a moment ago; **desde** ~ from now on; **por** ~ for the present; **até** ~ so far, up to now // *excl*: ~**!** come now!, (*Pt*) I don't believe it!; **e** ~ **?** now what? // *conj* now.

a'gosto (*Pt*: A-) *m* August.

agourar [ago'rax] *vt* to predict, foretell; **agouro** *m* omen.

agra'ciar *vt* (*condecorar*) to decorate.

agra'dar *vt* to please; **isso me agrada** I like it; ~**-se** *vr*: ~**-se de** to like, to be pleased with; **agradável** *adj* pleasant.

agrade'cer *vt* to thank, be grateful for; ~ **alguma coisa a alguém** to thank sb for sth; **agradecido/a** *adj* grateful, thankful; **mal agradecido** ungrateful; **agradecimento** *m* gratitude; **agradecimentos** *mpl* thanks.

a'grado *m* (*satisfação*) satisfaction; (*gorjeta*) small gift.

a'grário/a *adj* agrarian.

agravação [agrava'sãw] *f* (*Pt*) aggravation; (: *piora*) worsening; **agravamento** *m* (*Br*) aggravation; **agravante** *adj* aggravating // *f*

aggravating circumstances *pl*; **agravar** *vt* to aggravate, make worse; (*ofender*) to offend // *vi* (*piorar*) to worsen; (*JUR*) to lodge an appeal.

a'gravo *m* (*afronta*) offence; (*JUR*) appeal.

agre'dir *vt* to attack, assault.

agre'gado/a *m/f* (*lavrador*) tenant farmer; (*Br*) living-in servant, retainer // *m* aggregate, sum total; **agregar** *vt* (*juntar*) to collect; (*acrescentar*) to add.

agressão [agre'sãw] *f* aggression; (*ataque*) attack; (*assalto*) assault; **agressivo/a** *adj* aggressive.

a'greste *adj* rural, rustic; (*terreno*) wild, uncultivated; (*rude*) rough; **agrestia** *f* roughness.

a'grícola *adj* agricultural.

agricul'tor *m* farmer; **agricultura** *f* agriculture, farming.

agri'doce *adj* bittersweet.

agrilhoar [agriʎo'ax] *vt* to chain; (*escravizar*) to enslave.

agrono'mia *f* agronomy, agriculture; **agrônomo** *m* agricultural expert.

agru'par *vt* to group; ~**-se** *vr* to group together.

a'grura *f* bitterness.

água ['agwa] *f* water; ~**s** *fpl* (*mar*) sea *sg*; (*chuvas*) rain *sg*; (*maré*) tides; ~ **abaixo** downstream; ~ **acima** upstream; ~ **benta** holy water; ~ **calcária** hard water; ~ **corrente** running water; ~ **doce** fresh water; ~ **leve** soft water; ~ **mineral** mineral water; ~ **oxigenada** peroxide; ~ **potável** drinking water; ~ **salgada** salt water; **fazer** ~ (*NÁUT*) to leak; ~**s paradas são as mais fundas** still waters run deep; ~ **passada não move moinho** let bygones be bygones.

aguaceiro [agwa'sejru] *m* (*chuva*) heavy shower, downpour; (*com vento*) squall.

água-de-colônia ['agwa dʒi kɔ'lonja] *f* eau-de-cologne.

a'guado/a *adj* watery.

água-fur'tada *f* garret, attic.

água-marinha ['agwa-ma'rɪɲa] *f* aquamarine.

aguar [ag'wax] *vt* to water; (*diluir*) to dilute.

aguar'dar *vt* to wait for, await; (*contar com*) to expect // *vi* to wait.

aguar'dente *m* brandy; (*Br*) rum, cachaça.

água'rela *f* watercolour.

aguar'rás *f* turpentine.

agu'çar *vt* (*afiar*) to sharpen; (*estimular*) to excite; ~ **a vista** to keep one's eyes peeled.

agu'deza *f* sharpness; (*perspicácia*) perspicacity; (*som*) shrillness; **agudo/a** *adj* sharp; (*divertido*) witty, penetrating; (*som*) shrill; (*intenso*) acute.

agüentar [agwẽ'tax] *vt* to tolerate, stand, put up with; (*apoiar*) to support // *vi* to last; ~**-se** *vr* to bear up.

aguerrido/a [agɛˈxidu/a] adj warlike, bellicose; (corajoso) courageous.

águia [ˈagja] f eagle; (fig) genius // m (Br) cheat, rogue.

aguilhada [agiˈʎada] f goad; **aguilhão** m (espora) spur, goad; (espigão) spike; (de inseto) sting; (estímulo) stimulus, incentive; **aguilhoar** vt to goad, stimulate.

agulha [aˈguʎa] f (de coser, tricô) needle; (NÁUT) compass; (estrada de ferro) points pl, switch (US); **trabalho de ~** needlework.

agulheiro [aguˈʎejru] m (estojo) needle-case; (almofada) pin cushion; (fabricante) needle-maker.

agulheta [aguˈʎeta] f (bico) nozzle.

ai [aj] excl (suspiro) oh!; (dor) ouch!; **~ de mim!** poor me! // m (suspiro) sigh; (gemido) groan.

aí [aˈi] adv there; (nessa ocasião) then; **por ~** (em lugar indeterminado) somewhere over there, thereabouts; **espera ~!** wait!, hang on a minute!

aia [ˈaja] f (que educa crianças) nursemaid, nanny; (preceptora) governess.

a'inda adv still, yet; (mesmo) even; **~ agora** just now; **~ assim** even so, nevertheless; **~ bem** fortunately, it's a good thing; **~ por cima** on top of all that, in addition; **~ não** not yet // conj: **~ que** even if; **~ quando** even though, even when.

aio [ˈaju] m mentor.

aipo [ˈajpu] m celery.

airado/a [ajˈradu/a] adj (frívolo) frivolous; (leviano) dissolute; **estar ~** (Br) to have a chill.

airoso/a [ajˈrozu/a] adj graceful, elegant; (decoroso) decent.

ajaular [aʒawˈlax] vt to cage (up).

ajeitar [aʒejˈtax] vt (adaptar) to fit, adjust; (arranjar) to arrange, fix; **~-se** vr to adapt.

ajoelhado/a [aʒwɛˈʎadu/a] adj kneeling; (fig) humbled; **ajoelhar-se** vr to kneel (down).

ajuda [aˈʒuda] f help, aid, assistance; (subsídio) grant, subsidy; **sem ~** unaided; **prestar ~ a alguém** to lend sb a hand; **~ de custo** allowance.

ajudante [aʒuˈdãtʃi] m assistant, helper; (MIL) adjutant; **~ de campo** aide-de-camp; **ajudar** vt to help, assist.

ajuizado/a [aʒwiˈzadu/a] adj (sensato) sensible; (sábio) wise; (prudente) discreet; **ajuizar** vt to judge; (supor) to suppose.

ajunta'mento m (reunião) meeting, gathering; **ajuntar** vt (unir) to join, add; (dinheiro) to save up; (documentos) to attach; (reunir) to gather.

ajustagem [aʒuˈtaʒẽ] f (Br: TEC) adjustment.

ajusta'mento m adjustment; (liquidação de contas) settlement; **ajustar** vt (regular) to adjust, fit; (arranjar) to fix; (conta, disputa) to settle; (motor) to tune; (acomodar) to fit; **ajustar um preço** to

agree on a price; **ajustar-se** vr: **ajustar-se a** to conform to; **ajuste** m (acordo) agreement; (liquidação) settlement; (adaptação) adjustment.

'ala f (fileira) row, file; (passagem) aisle; (edifício, exército, ave) wing.

alagação [alagaˈsãw] f flooding; **alagamento** m flooding; (arrasamento) destruction; **alagar** vt to inundate, flood // vi to flood.

alambi'cado/a adj (estilo) pretentious; **alambicar-se** vr (estilo) to become affected; **alambique** m still, retort.

ala'meda f (avenida) avenue; (arvoredo) grove.

'álamo m poplar.

a'lar vt to haul, heave.

a'larde m (ostentação) ostentation; (jactância) boasting; **fazer ~ de** to flaunt, show off; **alardear** vt to show off.

alarga'mento m enlargement; **alargar** vt (ampliar) to extend; (fazer mais largo) to widen, broaden; (afrouxar) to loosen, slacken.

ala'rido m (clamor) outcry; (tumulto) uproar.

a'larma f alarm; (susto) panic; (tumulto) tumult; (vozearia) outcry; **dar o sinal de ~** to raise the alarm; **~ de roubo** burglar alarm; (fogo) fire alarm; **alarmante** adj alarming; **alarmar** vt to alarm; **alarmar-se** vr to be frightened.

a'larme m = **alarma**.

alas'trado/a adj: **~ de** strewn with; **alastrar** vt (espalhar) to scatter; (disseminar) to spread; (lastrar) to ballast; **alastrar-se** vr (epidemia, rumor) to spread.

ala'vanca f lever; (pé-de-cabra) crowbar; **~ de mudanças** gear lever.

al'barda f pack-saddle.

alber'gar vt (hospedar) to provide lodging for; (abrigar) to shelter; (sentimentos) to harbour; **~-se** vr (hospedar-se) to take lodging; (refugiar-se) to take shelter; **albergue** m (estalagem) inn; (refúgio) hospice, shelter; **albergue para jovens** youth hostel; **albergueiro** m innkeeper.

albufeira [awbuˈfejra] f lagoon.

'álbum m album; **~ de recortes** scrapbook.

'alça f (asa) handle; (argola) ring; (fusil) sight.

alcácer [awˈkasɛx] m fortress.

alcachofra [awkaˈʃofra] f artichoke.

alca'çuz m licorice.

al'çada f (jurisdição) jurisdiction; (competência) competence; **isso não é da minha ~** that is beyond my control.

alcan'çar vt (chegar a) to reach, arrive at; (estender) to hand, pass; (obter) to obtain, get; (atingir) to attain; (compreender) to understand // vi (atingir) to reach.

al'cance m reach; (competência) power, competence; (compreensão) understanding; (de tiro, visão) range; **ao ~ de**

within reach/range of; **ao ~ da voz** within earshot; **de grande ~** of great consequence; **fora do ~ da mão** out of reach; **fora do ~ de alguém** beyond sb's grasp.

alcan'til m crag, precipice; **~ado/a** adj (*íngreme*) steep; (*penhascoso*) craggy.

alçapão [awsa'pãw] m trapdoor; (*arapuca*) (bird-)trap.

alça'prema f (*alavanca*) crowbar.

al'çar vt to lift (up); (*edificar*) to erect; **~-se** vr to get up, rise; (*revoltar-se*) to revolt.

alcatéia [awka'teja] f (*de lobos*) pack; (*de ladrões*) gang.

alca'tifa f carpet.

alcatrão [awka'trãw] m tar.

álcool ['awkwɔl] m alcohol; **alcoólico/a** adj, m/f alcoholic.

Alcorão [awko'rãw] m Koran.

alcoviteiro/a [awkovi'tejru/a] m pimp // f procuress.

alcunha [aw'kuɲa] f nickname.

aldeão/aldeã [awdʒi'ãw/awdʒi'ã] m/f villager; **aldeia** f village.

al'draba (Pt: **tranqueta**) f latch; (*de bater*) door knocker; **aldrabão** m (Pt: *vigarista*) swindler; **aldrabar** vt to cheat, swindle.

alecrim [alɛ'krĩ] m rosemary.

alegação [alɛga'sãw] f allegation; **alegar** vt to allege; (*JUR*) to plead.

alego'ria f allegory.

ale'grar vt (*tornar feliz*) to cheer (up), gladden; (*ambiente, etc*) to brighten up; (*animar*) to liven (up); **~-se** vr to be glad; (*embriagar-se*) to get merry ou tight; **alegre** adj (*jovial*) cheerful; (*contente*) happy, glad; (*cores*) bright; (*embriagado*) merry, tight.

ale'grete m (*canteiro*) flowerbed.

ale'gria f joy, happiness.

aleijado/a [alej'ʒadu/a] adj crippled, disabled // m/f cripple; **aleijar** vt (*mutilar*) to maim.

aleitação [alejta'sãw] f, **aleitamento** [alejta'mẽtu] m nursing; (*amamentação*) suckling; **aleitamento materno** breast feeding; **aleitar** vt (*criar a leite*) to nurse; (*amamentar*) to suckle.

aleivosia [alejvo'zia] f (*traição*) treachery; (*calúnia*) slander; **aleivoso/a** adj (*desleal*) treacherous; (*calunioso*) slanderous.

além [a'lẽj] adv (*lá ao longe*) over there; (*mais adiante*) further on; **mais ~** further // prep: **~ de** beyond; (*no outro lado de*) on the other side of; (*para mais de*) over; (*ademais de*) besides; **~ disso** moreover; **~ mar** overseas.

Alemanha [alɛ'maɲa] f Germany; **~ Ocidental/Oriental** West/East Germany; **alemão/mã** adj, m/f German; **os alemães** mpl the Germans // m (*língua*) German.

alen'tado/a adj (*valente*) valiant; (*grande*) great; (*volumoso*) substantial.

alenta'dor(a) adj encouraging; **alentar**

vt to encourage; **alentar-se** vr to cheer up.

a'lento m (*fôlego*) breath; (*ânimo*) courage; **dar ~** to encourage; **tomar ~** to draw breath.

alergia [alɛx'ʒia] f allergy; **alérgico/a** adj allergic.

a'lerta adv on the alert // m alert.

alfa'beto m alphabet.

alface [aw'fasi] f lettuce.

alfaia [aw'faja] f (*móveis*) furniture; (*utensílio*) utensil; (*enfeite*) ornament.

alfaiate [awfa'jatʃi] m tailor.

al'fândega f customs pl, customs house.

alfarra'bista m (*negociante*) second-hand book seller.

alfa'vaca f basil.

alfa'zema f lavender.

alferes [aw'ferɛʃ] m (MIL) second-lieutenant; (*NÁUT*) ensign.

alfi'nete m pin; **~s** mpl pin money; **~ de segurança** safety pin.

al'fombra f carpet.

alforges [aw'fox ʒɛʃ] mpl (*saco*) saddle-bags.

al'forra f (*doença vegetal*) rust.

alfo'rreca f jellyfish.

'alga f seaweed; (*BOT*) alga.

alga'ravia f (*árabe*) Arabic language; (*confusão de vozes*) hubbub; (*linguagem confusa*) gibberish.

alga'rismo m numeral, digit.

alga'zarra f uproar, racket.

álgebra ['awʒebra] f algebra.

algemas [aw'ʒemaʃ] fpl handcuffs.

algeroz [awʒɛ'rɔʃ] m guttering.

algibe [aw'ʒibi] m cistern.

'algo adv somewhat, rather // pron something; (*qualquer coisa*) anything.

algodão [awgo'dãw] m cotton; **~ hidrófilo** cotton wool.

alguém [aw'gẽj] pron someone, somebody; anyone, anybody; **~ quer falar com ela** someone wants to speak to her; **tem** (*Br*)/**há** (*Pt*) **~ aqui?** is there anybody here?

algum(a) [aw'gũ/guma] adj some, any // pron some, one; **~ dia** one day; **~a vez** sometime; **~ tempo** for a while; **~a coisa** something; (*negativa*) **de modo ~** in no way; **coisa ~a** nothing.

al'gures adv somewhere.

alheio/a [a'ʎeju/a] adj (*de outrem*) someone else's; (*estranho*) alien; (*estrangeiro*) foreign; (*impróprio*) inappropriate; **~ a** foreign to.

alho ['aʎu] m garlic; **~-porro** m leek.

a'li adv there; **por ~** over there; (*direção*) that way; **até ~** up to there; **~ por** (*tempo*) round about; **de ~ por diante** from then on; **~ dentro** in there.

ali'ado/a adj allied // m/f ally.

ali'ança f alliance; (*anel*) wedding ring; **aliar** vt to ally; **aliar-se** vr to make an alliance.

ali'ás adv (*além disso*) besides; (*de outro modo*) otherwise; (*contudo*) nevertheless;

(*diga-se de passagem*) incidentally; (*ou seja*) I mean.

'álibi *m* alibi.

ali'cate *m* pliers *pl.*

alicerce [alɪ'sɛxsɪ] *m* (*de edifício*) foundation; (*base*) base.

aliciar [alɪs'jax] *vt* (*seduzir*) to entice; (*subornar*) to bribe.

alienação [alɪena'sãw] *f* alienation; (*de bens*) transfer (of property); ~ **mental** insanity; **alienado/a** *adj* (*demente*) insane; (*bens*) transferred // *m/f* lunatic.

ali'gátor *m* alligator.

aligeirar [alɪʒej'rax] *vt* (*tornar leve*) to lighten; (*apressar*) to quicken; (*mitigar*) to alleviate.

alimentação [alɪmẽta'sãw] *f* (*alimentos*) food; (*ação*) feeding; (*nutrição*) nourishment; (*ELET*) supply; **alimentar** *vt* (*dar alimento*) to feed; **alimentar-se** *vr:* **alimentar-se de** to feed on; **alimento** *m* food; (*nutrição*) nourishment; **alimentos** *mpl* (*JUR*) alimony.

alínea [a'lɪnɪa] *f* (*parágrafo*) paragraph; (*subdivisão de artigo*) sub-heading.

ali'nhado/a *adj* elegant.

alinhamento [alɪɲa'mẽtu] *m* alignment; **alinhar** *vt* to align, line up; **alinhar-se** *vr* (*enfileirar-se*) to form a line.

alinha'var *vt* (*costura*) to tack.

alinho [a'lɪɲu] *m* (*alinhamento*) alignment; (*elegância*) neatness.

ali'sar *vt* (*tornar liso*) to smooth; (*madeira*) to plane.

alista'mento *m* enlistment; **alistar** *vt* (*arrolar*) to enrol; (*MIL*) to recruit; **alistar-se** *vr* to enlist.

alivi'ar *vt* (*mitigar*) to alleviate; (*carga etc*) to lighten; (*pessoa*) to relieve; **alívio** *m* relief, alleviation.

'alma *f* soul; (*pessoa*) person; (*animação*) liveliness; (*caráter*) character.

almejar [awme'ʒax] *vt* to long for, yearn for.

almiran'tado *m* admiralty; **almirante** *m* admiral.

almo'çar *vi* to have lunch // *vt:* ~ **peixe** to have fish for lunch; **almoço** *m* lunch; **pequeno almoço** (*Pt*) breakfast.

almo'creve *m* mule driver.

almo'fada *f* cushion; (*Pt: travesseiro*) pillow.

al'môndega *f* meat ball.

a'lô *excl* (*Br: TEL*) hullo.

alojamento [aloʒa'mẽtu] *m* accommodation; (*habitação*) housing; (*MIL*) billet; **alojar** *vt* to lodge; (*MIL*) to billet; **alojar-se** *vr* to stay.

alon'gar *vt* (*fazer longo*) to lengthen; (*prazo*) to extend; (*prolongar*) to prolong; ~**-se** *vr* (*sobre um assunto*) to dwell.

al'pendre *m* (*telheiro*) shed; (*pórtico*) porch.

'Alpes *mpl:* **os** ~ **the Alps.**

alpi'nismo *m* mountaineering, climbing; **alpinista** *m/f* mountaineer, climber.

al'piste *m* bird seed.

alquebrar [awkɛ'brax] *vt* (*enfraquecer*) to weaken // *vi* (*curvar*) to stoop, be bent double.

alqueive [aw'kejvɪ] *m* fallow land.

alquimia [awkɪ'mɪa] *f* alchemy.

'alta *f ver* **alto.**

altaneiro/a [awta'nejru/a] *adj* (*soberbo*) proud.

al'tar *m* altar; ~**-mor** *m* high altar.

alteração [awtera'sãw] *f* (*mudança*) alteration; (*desordem*) disturbance; (*falsificação*) falsification; **alterar** *vt* (*mudar*) to alter; (*falsificar*) to falsify; **alterar-se** *vr* (*mudar-se*) to become altered; (*enfurecer-se*) to get angry, lose one's temper.

alter'nar *vt/i* to alternate; ~**-se** *vr* to alternate; (*por turnos*) to take turns; **alternativo/a** *adj* alternative; (*ELET*) alternating // *f* alternative; **alterno/a** *adj* alternate.

al'teza *f* (*altura*) height; (*título*) highness.

altisso'nante *adj* high-sounding.

alti'tude *f* altitude.

altivez [awtʃi'veʃ] *f* (*arrogância*) haughtiness; (*nobreza*) loftiness; **altivo/a** *adj* (*arrogante*) haughty; (*elevado*) lofty.

'alto/a *adj* (*elevado*) high; (*de grande estatura*) tall; (*som*) high, sharp; (*GEO*) upper; ~**a noite** dead of night // *adv* (*som*) loudly, aloud // *excl* halt! // *m* (*topo*) top, summit; (*elevação*) height; (*parada*) halt, stop; **do** ~ **from above;** ~**s** *mpl* heights // *f* (*de preços*) rise; (*de hospital*) discharge; (*sociedade*) high society; ~**a fidelidade** high fidelity, hi-fi.

alto-fa'lante *m* loudspeaker.

al'tura *f* height; (*momento*) point, juncture; (*altitude*) altitude; (*profundidade*) depth; (*de um som*) pitch; **nesta** ~ **at the moment; ter 1.80 metros de** ~ **to be 1.80 metres tall; estar à** ~ **de** (*ser capaz de*) to be up to.

a'lude *m* avalanche.

alu'dir *vi:* ~ **a** to allude to, hint at.

alu'gar *vt* (*tomar de aluguel*) to rent, hire; (*dar de aluguel*) to let, rent out; ~**-se** *vr* to let; **aluguel** (*Br*) *m*, **aluguer** (*Pt*) *m* (*ação*) renting, hiring; (*preço*) rent.

aluir [al'wɪx] *vt* (*abalar*) to shake; (*derrubar*) to demolish; (*arruinar*) to ruin // *vi* to collapse; (*ameaçar ruína*) to crumble.

alumi'ar *vt* to light (up); (*ilustrar*) to enlighten // *vi* (*brilhar*) to shine.

alu'mínio *m* aluminium.

a'luno *a m/f* pupil, student; ~ **externo** day pupil; ~ **interno** boarder.

alusão [alu'zãw] *f* allusion.

alu'sivo/a *adj* allusive; (*alegórico*) suggestive.

aluvião [aluvɪ'ãw] *f* (*GEO*) alluvium; (*enchente*) flood.

alvejar [awve'ʒax] *vt* (*tomar como alvo*) to aim at; (*branquear*) to whiten, bleach.

alvena'ria *f* masonry.

alvéolo [aw'veolu] *m* (*ger*) cavity; (*de dentes*) socket.

alvi'trar *vt* to propose, suggest; **alvitre** *m* opinion.

'alvo/a *adj* (*cor*) white; (*puro*) pure // *m* target; **atingir o** ~ to hit the mark.

alvo'rada *f* dawn; **alvorecer** *vi* to dawn.

alvoro'çar *vt* (*agitar*) to stir up; (*entusiasmar*) to excite; ~**-se** *vr* to get excited; **alvoroço** *m* (*agitação*) commotion; (*entusiasmo*) enthusiasm.

al'vura *f* (*brancura*) whiteness; (*pureza*) purity.

'ama *f* (*de leite*) (wet) nurse; (*governanta*) governess.

amabili'dade *f* kindness; (*simpatia*) friendliness.

amachucar [amaʃu'kax] *vt* to crush.

amaci'ar *vt* (*tornar macio*) to soften.

a'mado/a *m/f* beloved, sweetheart; **amador** *m* (*entusiasta*) enthusiast; (*não profissional*) amateur.

amadure'cer *vt/i* (*frutos*) to ripen; (*fig*) to mature.

'âmago *m* (*centro*) heart, core; (*medula*) pith; (*essência*) essence.

amainar [amaj'nax] *vi* (*tempestade*) to abate; (*cólera*) to calm down.

amaldiçoar [amawdʒis'wax] *vt* to curse, swear at.

amalga'mar *vt* to amalgamate; (*combinar*) to fuse, blend.

amamen'tar *vt* to breast-feed.

amaneirado/a [amanej'radu/a] *adj* (*afetado*) affected; (*presumido*) conceited.

amanhã [ama'ɲã] *adv* tomorrow; ~ **de manhã** tomorrow morning; ~ **de tarde** tomorrow afternoon; ~ **à noite** tomorrow night; **depois de** ~ the day after tomorrow // *m* tomorrow.

amanhar [ama'nax] *vt* (*cultivar*) to cultivate; (*preparar*) to prepare.

amanhecer [amaɲe'sex] *vi* (*alvorecer*) to dawn; (*encontrar-se pela manhã*) to be at daybreak; **amanhecemos em Paris** we were in Paris at daybreak // *m* dawn; **ao** ~ at daybreak.

amanho [a'maɲu] *m* (*cultivo*) cultivation; (*arranjo*) arrangement; ~**s** *mpl* tools.

aman'sar *vt* (*animais*) to tame; (*cavalos*) to break in; (*aplacar*) to placate // *vi* to grow tame.

a'mante *m/f* lover; (*apreciador*) enthusiast, lover; **amar** *vt* to love, be in love with.

amare'lado/a *adj* yellowish; (*pele*) sallow; **amarelo/a** *adj* yellow // *m* yellow.

amar'gar *vt* to make bitter; (*fig*) to embitter; **amargo/a** *adj* bitter; **amargura** *f* bitterness.

amar'rar *vt* (*prender*) to tie (up); (*NÁUT*) to moor.

amas'sar *vt* (*pão*) to knead; (*misturar*) to mix; (*amachucar*) to crush.

a'mável *adj* (*afável*) kind.

ama'zona *f* horsewoman // *m*: **o A**~**s**

(*GEO*) the Amazon; **Amazônia** *f*: **a Amazônia** the Amazon region.

ambição [ambi'sãw] *f* ambition; **ambicionar** *vt* (*ter ambição de*) to aspire to; (*desejar*) to crave for; **ambicioso/a** *adj* ambitious.

ambi'destro/a *adj* ambidextrous.

ambiente [ambi'ẽtʃi] *m* atmosphere; (*meio*) environment // *adj* surrounding; **meio** ~ environment; **temperatura** ~ room temperature.

ambigüidade [ambigwi'dadʃi] *f* ambiguity; **ambíguo/a** *adj* ambiguous.

'âmbito *m* (*extensão*) compass; (*campo de ação*) scope, range.

'ambos *adj pl* both; ~ **nós** both of us.

ambu'lância *f* ambulance.

ambu'lante *adj* walking; (*errante*) wandering; **vendedor** ~ street seller // *m* pedlar, street seller.

ambu'latório *m* outpatient department.

ame'aça *f* threat; **ameaçar** *vt* to threaten.

amedron'tar *vt* to scare, intimidate; ~**-se** *vr* to be frightened.

ameigar [amej'gax] *vt* to caress; (*tornar meigo*) to soften.

amêijoa [a'mejʒwa] *f* mussel.

ameixa [a'mejʃa] *f* plum; (*passa*) prune.

amém [a'mẽj] *excl* amen.

a'mêndoa *f* almond; **amendoim** *m* peanut.

ameni'dade *f* wellbeing; **amenidades** *fpl* light conversation.

ameni'zar *vt* (*abrandar*) to soften; (*tornar agradável*) to make pleasant; (*facilitar*) to ease; **ameno/a** *adj* (*agradável*) pleasant; (*suave*) mild, gentle.

A'mérica *f* America; ~ **do Norte/do Sul** North/South America; ~ **Central/Latina** Central/Latin America; **americano/a** *adj*, *m/f* American.

amesquinhar [ameʃki'nax] *vt* to belittle; ~**-se** *vr* (*humilhar-se*) to belittle o.s.; (*tornar-se avarento*) to become stingy.

ames'trar *vt* (*adestrar*) to train; (*um cavalo*) to break in.

ami'anto *m* asbestos.

a'mido *m* starch.

ami'gável *adj* amicable.

a'mígdala *f* tonsil; **amigdalite** *f* tonsillitis.

a'migo/a *adj* (*amistoso*) friendly; **ser** ~ **de** to be friends with // *m/f* friend.

ami'mado/a *adj* (*acariciado*) petted; (*amimalhado*) spoilt.

amimalhar [amima'ʎax] *vt* (*uma criança*) to spoil; **amimar** *vt* to pet, pamper; (*amimalhar*) to spoil.

amis'toso/a *adj* friendly, cordial // *m* (*jogo*) friendly.

amiudar [amju'dax] *vt/i* to repeat; ~ **as visitas** to make frequent visits; **amiúde** *adv* often, frequently.

ami'zade *f* (*relação*) friendship; (*simpatia*) friendliness; **fazer** ~**s** to make friends.

amnésia [am'nɛzja] *f* amnesia.

'amo *m* (*patrão*) master; (*proprietário*) owner.

amodor'rado/a *adj* drowsy; **amodorrar-se** *vr* to become drowsy.

amoe'dar *vt* (*cunhar*) to mint.

amofi'nar *vt* to vex; **~-se** *vr* to fret (over).

amolação [amowa'sãw] *f* nuisance, annoyance; **amolante** *adj* (*Br*) annoying; **amolar** *vt* (*afiar*) to sharpen; (*enfadar*) to annoy.

amol'dar *vt/i* to mould; **~-se** *vr:* **~-se a** (*conformar-se*) to conform to; (*acostumar-se*) to get used to.

amole'cer *vt* (*ger*) to soften; (*o coração*) to melt; (*abrandar-se*) to relent.

amolga'dura *f* dent; **amolgar** *vt* (*entalhar*) to dent; (*esmagar*) to crush.

a'mónia *f*, **amo'níaco** *m* ammonia.

amonto'ar *vt* to pile up, accumulate; **~ riquezas** to amass a fortune.

a'mor *m* love; (*amante*) lover; **fazer ~** to make love; **~ próprio** self-esteem; (*orgulho*) conceit; **por ~ de** for the sake of.

a'mora *f* mulberry; **~ preta** blackberry; **~ silvestre** (*Pt*) blackberry.

amorda'çar *vt/o* to gag.

amo'roso/a *adj* loving, affectionate.

amor-perfeito [amox-pɛx'fejtu] *m* pansy.

amortalhar [amoxta'ʎax] *vt* (*um defunto*) to shroud; (*fig*) to enshroud.

amortece'dor *m* shock-absorber; **amortecer** *vt* (*ger*) to deaden // *vi* to weaken, fade; **amortecido/a** *adj* deadened; (*enfraquecido*) weak.

amortização [amɔrtisa'sãw] *f* payment in instalments.

amos'tra *f* sample.

amoti'nar *vi* to rebel, mutiny.

ampa'rar *vt* (*proteger*) to protect; (*abrigar*) to shelter; (*apoiar*) to support; **~-se** *vr:* **~-se em/contra** (*apoiar-se*) to lean on/against; **amparo** *m* (*apoio*) support; (*proteção*) protection.

am'père *m* (*Br*) ampere, amp.

ampliação [amplia'sãw] *f* (*aumento*) enlargement; (*extensão*) extension; **ampliar** *vt* (*aumentar*) to enlarge.

amplificação [amplifika'sãw] *f* (*aumento*) enlargement; (*som*) amplification; **amplificador** *m* amplifier; **amplificar** *vt* to amplify.

ampli'tude *f* (*TEC*) amplitude; (*espaço*) spaciousness; (*extensão*) extent; **amplo/a** *adj* (*vasto*) ample, spacious; (*numeroso*) numerous.

am'pola *f* (*na pele*) blister; (*MED*) ampoule.

ampu'tar *vt/o* to amputate.

amu'ado/a *adj* sulky; **amuar** *vi* to sulk; **amuo** *m* sulkiness.

anacro'nismo *m* anachronism.

ana'far *vt* to fatten (up).

ana'grama *m* anagram.

anais [a'najʃ] *mpl* annals.

analfabe'tismo *m* illiteracy; **analfabeto/a** *adj, m/f* illiterate.

anali'sar *vt* to analyse; **análise** *f* analysis; **analista** *m/f* analyst; **analítico/a** *adj* analytical.

analogia [analo'ʒia] *f* analogy; **análogo** *adj* analogous.

ana'nás *m* (*Pt*) pineapple.

anão/anã [a'nãw/a'nã] *m/f* dwarf.

anarquia [anax'kia] *f* anarchy; **anarquista** [anax'kiʃta] *m/f* anarchist.

a'nátema *m* anathema.

anato'mia *f* anatomy.

'anca *f* (*de pessoa*) hip; (*de animal*) rump.

ancho/a ['ãʃu/a] *adj* (*largo*) broad; (*vaidoso*) conceited.

anchova [ã'ʃova] *f* anchovy.

ancião/anciã [ãsi'ãw/ãsi'ã] *adj* old, ancient // *m* old man; (*de uma tribo*) elder // *f* old woman.

ancinho [ã'siɲu] *m* rake.

'âncora *f* (*NÁUT*) anchor; (*apoio*) prop, support; **ancoradouro** *m* anchorage; **ancorar** *vt/i* to anchor.

anda'dura *f* gait.

andaime [ã'dajmi] *m* (*ARQ*) scaffolding.

anda'mento *m* (*progresso*) progress; (*movimento*) movement; (*direção*) course; (*MÚS*) tempo; **em ~** in progress.

an'dar *vi* to go; (*ir a pé*) to walk; (*máquina*) to work; (*viajar*) to travel; (*progredir*) to progress; (*estar*) **~ triste** to be sad; **~ a pé/a cavalo** to go on foot/on horseback; **~ de trem/de avião** to travel by train/by plane; **anda! come on!** // *m* (*modo de caminhar*) gait; (*pavimento*) floor, storey (of building); **~ térreo** (*Br*) ground floor.

'Andes *mpl:* **os ~** the Andes.

andorinha [ãdo'riɲa] *f* (*pássaro*) swallow.

andrajos [ã'draʒuʃ] *mpl* rags; **andrajoso/a** *adj* ragged, tattered.

ane'dota *f* anecdote.

anel [a'nɛw] *m* ring; (*elo*) link; (*de cabelo*) curl; **~ de casamento** wedding ring; **~ado/a** *adj* curly.

ane'lante *adj* (*ansioso*) yearning.

ane'lar *vt* to long for // *vi:* **~ por** to long for; **anelo** *m* longing, craving.

ane'mia *f* anaemia; **anêmico/a** *adj* anaemic.

anes'tésico *m* (*MED*) anaesthetic.

ane'xar *vt* to annex; (*juntar*) to attach; **anexo/a** *pp irr de* **anexar** // *adj* attached // *m* annexe.

anfí'bio *m* [ã'fibju/a] *adj* amphibious.

anfiteatro [ãfitʃi'atru] *m* amphitheatre; (*teatro*) dress circle.

anfitrião/anfitriã [ãfitri'ãw/ãfitri'ã] *m* host // *f* hostess.

angari'ar *vt* (*obter*) to obtain; (*atrair*) to attract; **~ votos** to canvass.

angina [ã'ʒina] *f* (*MED*) **~ de garganta** inflammation of the throat; **~ de peito** angina (pectoris).

An'gola *f* Angola; **angolano/a**, **angolense** *adj, m/f* Angolan.

'angra *f* inlet, cove.

angu'lar *adj* angular; **ângulo** *m* angle; (*canto*) corner.

an'gústia *f* (*ansiedade*) anxiety; (*aflição*) anguish; **angustiado/a** *adj* (*ansioso*) anxious; (*atribulado*) troubled; **angustiar** *vt* to distress; **angustioso/a** *adj* distressing.

anho ['aɲu] *m* lamb.

anil [a'niw] *m* (*cor*) indigo; (*lavagem de roupa*) blue powder.

anilha [a'niʎa] *f* (*arco*) ring; (*pia*) washer.

anilho [a'niʎu] *m* (*ilhó*) eyelet.

animação [anima'sãw] *f* (*viveza*) liveliness; (*movimento*) bustle; **animado/a** *adj* (*vivo*) lively; (*alegre*) cheerful; **animador(a)** *adj* encouraging // *m/f* (*Br: TV*) presenter.

animadversão [anımadvɛx'sãw] *f* (*ódio*) hatred, dislike; (*repreensão*) criticism; (*censura*) censure.

animal [ani'maw] *adj* animal; (*sensual*) sensual // *m* animal; (*bruto*) brute; **~ de estimação** pet animal.

ani'mar *vt* (*dar vida*) to liven up; (*encorajar*) to encourage; **~-se** *vr* (*alegrar-se*) to cheer up; **~-se a** (*resolver-se*) to resolve to.

'ânimo *m* (*coragem*) courage; (*espírito*) spirit; (*intenção*) intention; **recobrar ~** to pluck up courage; (*alegrar-se*) to cheer up; **perder o ~** to lose heart // *excl* cheer up!

animosi'dade *f* (*hostilidade*) animosity; (*amargura*) bitterness.

ani'moso/a *adj* (*corajoso*) courageous.

aninhar [ani'ɲax] *vt* (*agasalhar*) to shelter // *vi* to nest; **~-se** *vr* (*aconchegar-se*) to nestle.

aniquilação [anikila'sãw] *f* annihilation; **aniquilar** *vt* to annihilate; (*destruir*) to destroy.

a'nis *m* aniseed.

anis'tia (*Pt:* -mn-) *f* amnesty.

aniver'sário *m* anniversary; **~ de casamento** wedding anniversary; **~ de nascimento** birthday.

anjo ['ãʒu] *m* angel; **~ da guarda** guardian angel.

'ano *m* year; **~ bissexto** leap year; **~ econômico** financial year; **Feliz A~ Novo!** Happy New Year!; **o ~ passado** last year; **o ~ que vem** next year; **por ~ per annum**; **fazer ~s** to have a birthday; **ter dez ~s** to be ten (years old).

anoitecer [anojtɛ'sex] *vi* to grow dark; **ao ~** at nightfall.

anojar [ano'ʒax] *vt* (*enojar*) to sicken; (*molestar*) to annoy; **~-se** *vr:* **~-se de** to become sick of.

anoma'lia *f* anomaly; **anômalo/a** *adj* anomalous.

anoni'mato *m* anonymity; **anônimo/a** *adj* anonymous; (*COM*) **sociedade anônima** limited company, stock company (*US*).

anor'mal [-aw] *adj* abnormal.

anotação [anota'sãw] *f* (*comentário*) annotation; (*nota*) note; **anotar** *vt* (*apontar*) to note down; (*esclarecer*) to annotate.

'ânsia *f* (*ansiedade*) anxiety; (*anelo*) longing; **ter ~s (de vômito)** to feel sick.

ansi'ar *vi:* **~ por** (*desejar alguma coisa*) to yearn for; (*anelar por fazer*) to long to; **ansiedade** *f* (*angústia*) anxiety; (*desejo*) eagerness; **ansioso/a** *adj* (*aflito*) anxious; (*desejoso*) eager.

anta'gônico/a *adj* antagonistic; (*rival*) opposing; **antagonismo** *m* (*hostilidade*) antagonism; (*oposição*) opposition; **antagonista** *m/f* antagonist; (*adversário*) opponent.

an'tártico/a *adj* antarctic // *m* Antarctic.

'ante *prep* (*na presença de*) before; (*em vista de*) in view of, faced with.

ante'braço *m* forearm.

antece'dência *f* (*prioridade*) priority; (*precedência*) precedence; **com ~ in advance**; **antecedente** *adj* (*prévio*) previous; (*precedente*) preceding // *m* antecedent; **antecedentes** *mpl* record *sg*, background *sg*; **anteceder** *vt* to precede, go before.

antecipação [ãtɛsipa'sãw] *f* anticipation; (*pagamento*) advance payment; **com um mês de ~** a month in advance; **antecipadamente** *adv* in advance, beforehand; **pagar antecipadamente** to pay in advance.

anteci'par *vt* to anticipate, forestall; (*adiantar*) to bring forward; (*prognosticar*) to expect; **antecipo** *m* advance payment.

antemão [ãtɛ'mãw] *adv:* **de ~ beforehand**.

an'tena *f* (*BIO*) antenna, feeler; (*TEL*) aerial.

ante'nome *m* Christian name; (*título*) title.

anteontem [ãtɛ'ōtē] *adv* the day before yesterday.

antepa'rar *vt* (*defender*) to shield; (*proteger*) to protect.

ante'paro *m* (*proteção*) screen.

antepas'sados *mpl* ancestors.

ante'por *vt* (*pôr antes*) to put before.

anteri'or *adj* (*prévio*) previous; (*antigo*) former; (*de posição*) front; **~idade** *f* (*prioridade*) priority; (*precedente*) precedent.

'antes *adv* before; (*primeiro*) first; (*ao contrário*) rather; **quanto ~** as soon as possible // *prep:* **~ de** before; **~ de partir** before leaving; **~ do tempo** ahead of time; **~ de tudo** above all // *conj:* **~ que** before.

anti'ácido *adj* antacid // *m* antacid.

antia'éreo/a *adj* anti-aircraft; **abrigo ~** air-raid shelter.

antibi'ótico/a *adj* antibiotic // *m* antibiotic.

antici'clone m anticyclone.
anti'clímax m anticlimax.
anticoncepcio'nal m contraceptive.
anticongelante [ãtʃikõʒe'lãtʃi] m antifreeze.
an'tídoto m antidote.
antigalha [ãtʃi'gaʎa] f (de valor) antique; (de pouco valor) junk.
antiga'mente adv (noutro tempo) formerly; (no passado) in the past; **antigo/a** adj (velho) old, ancient; (anterior) former; (de estilo) antique.
antiguidade [ãtʃigi'dadʒi] f antiquity, ancient times; (de emprego) seniority; ~s fpl (monumentos) ancient monuments; (artigos) antiques.
antilhano/a [ãtʃi'ʎanu/a] adj, m/f West Indian; **Antilhas** fpl: **as Antilhas** the West Indies.
an'tílope m antelope.
antipa'tia f antipathy, dislike; **antipático/a** adj unpleasant; (pessoa) disagreeable.
antiquado/a [ãtʃi'kwadu/a] adj antiquated; (fora de moda) out of date, old-fashioned.
anti-se'mítico/a adj anti-Semitic.
anti-'séptico/a adj antiseptic // m antiseptic.
anti-social [-sosj'aw] adj antisocial.
antítese [ã'tʃitɛz] f antithesis.
antojar [ãto'ʒax] vt to imagine, fancy; **antojo** m (capricho) fancy; (desejo extravagante) craving.
antolhos [ã'toʎuʃ] mpl (pala) eye-shade; (de cavalo) blinkers; (desejos) fancies, whims.
antologia [ãtolo'ʒia] f anthology.
'antro m cave, cavern; (de animal) lair; (ladrões etc) den.
antro'pófago/a m/f cannibal.
antropolo'gia f anthropology; **antropólogo/a** m/f anthropologist.
anu'al adj annual, yearly.
anu'ário m yearbook.
anui'dade f annuity.
anu'ir vi: ~ a to agree to; ~ com to comply with.
anulação [anula'sãw] f (revogação) annulment; (cancelamento) cancellation; **anular** vt (invalidar) to annul; (revogar) to rescind // m ring finger.
anunci'ante m (COM) advertiser; **anunciar** vt to advertise; (noticiar) to report; **anúncio** m (COM) advertisement; (declaração) announcement; (cartaz) poster; **anúncio luminoso** neon sign.
anuvi'ar vt (nublar) to cloud; (obscurecer) to darken; ~-se vr to cloud over; (obscurecer-se) to grow dark.
an'verso m (moeda) obverse.
an'zol m fish-hook; **cair no** ~ to swallow the bait, be tricked.
ao [aw] = a + o, ver a.
aonde [a'õdʒi] adv where . . . to; ~ **vai?** where are you going (to)?
aos [awʃ] = a + os, ver a.
Ap. abr de **apartamento** apartment.

apadrinhar [apadri'ɲax] vt (ser padrinho) to act as godfather to; (: de noivo) to be best man to; (proteger) to protect; (patrocinar) to support.
apa'gado/a adj (fogo) out, extinguished; (luz elétrica) (switched) off; (escuro) dark; (indistinto) faint; **apagar** vt (fogo) to put out, extinguish; (luz elétrica) to switch off; **apagar-se** vr to go out.
apaixonado/a [apajʃo'nadu/a] adj passionate; (parcial) biased; (entusiástico) keen; **ele está** ~ **por ela** he is mad about her; **ele é** ~ **pelo tênis** he's crazy about tennis; **apaixonar-se** vr: **apaixonar-se por** to fall passionately in love with.
apale'ar vt to beat (with a stick).
apalpa'dela f touch; **andar às** ~s to grope one's way; **apalpar** vt to touch, feel; (MED) to examine.
apanhar [apa'ɲax] vt (pegar) to catch; (agarrar) to seize; (levar) to take; (colher) to pick; (juntar) to gather; ~ **em erro** to catch out; ~ **uma constipação** (Pt), ~ **um resfriado** (Br) to catch a cold.
apaniguado/a [apani'gwadu/a] m/f (partidário) follower; (protegido) favourite.
a'para f (de madeira) shaving; (de papel) clipping; (limalha) filing.
apara'dor m sideboard.
apara-'lápis m (Pt) pencil sharpener.
apa'rar vt (cabelo, unhas) to trim, cut; (árvore) to prune; (lápis) to sharpen; (o que cai, se tira) to catch; (pancada) to parry; (alisar) to smooth out.
apa'rato m pomp, show.
apare'cer vi to appear; (apresentar-se) to turn up; (ser publicado) to be published; ~ **em casa de alguém** to drop in on sb, call on sb; **aparecimento** m appearance; (publicação) publication.
aparelhado/a [aparɛ'ʎadu/a] adj (preparado) ready, prepared; (madeira) planed; **aparelhar** vt (preparar) to prepare, get ready; (arrear) to saddle, harness; (NAUT) to rig; **aparelhar-se** vr to get ready.
aparelho [apa'reʎu] m apparatus; (equipamento) equipment; (pesca) tackle, gear; (utensílio) utensil; (máquina) machine; (Br: fone) telephone; ~ **de gesso** plaster cast; ~ **de chá** tea set; ~ **de rádio/TV** radio/TV set.
apa'rência f appearance; (aspecto) aspect; **na** ~ apparently; **manter as** ~s to keep up appearances; **sob a** ~ **de** under the guise of.
aparen'tado/a adj related; **bem** ~ well connected.
aparen'tar vt (fingir) to feign, pretend; (parecer) to look, seem; ~-se vr: ~-se **com** to become related to.
apa'rente adj apparent.
aparição [apari'sãw] f (visão) apparition; (fantasma) ghost.
a'paro m (de caneta) (pen) nib.
apart. abr de **apartamento** apartment.

apar'tado/a adj (remoto) secluded; (distante) distant; **apartamento** m apartment, flat.

apar'tar vt (separar) to separate; (pôr de lado) to set aside; ~-se vr (separar-se) to separate; ~-se de (afastar-se) to go away from; ~-se do assunto to digress.

a'parte m (teatro) aside.

apascen'tar vt to bring to pasture, graze.

apa'tia f apathy; **apático/a** adj apathetic; (indiferente) indifferent.

apavo'rado/a adj terror-stricken; **apavorar** vt to terrify.

apaziguamento [apazɪgwa'mētu] m appeasement; (pacificação) pacification; **apaziguar** vt to appease; (pacificar) to pacify; **apaziguar-se** vr to calm down.

apeadeiro [apɪa'dejru] m (trem) stop, halt.

ape'ar-se vr: ~ de (cavalo) to dismount from.

ape'dido m (Br) newspaper article, statement or advertisement published at request of, or paid for by, the author.

apedrejar [apedre'ʒax] vt to stone.

ape'gado/a adj attached; **apegar-se** vr: **apegar-se a** (aderir) to stick to, cling to; (afeiçoar-se) to become devoted to; **apego** m (afeição) fondness, attachment.

apelação [apela'sãw] f appeal; **apelante** m/f appellant; **apelar** vi to appeal; (JUR) **apelar da sentença** to appeal against the sentence.

apeli'dar vt (Br) to nickname; (Pt) to give a surname to; ~-se vr: ~-se de to go by the name of; **apelido** m (nome de família) surname; (alcunha) nickname.

a'pelo m appeal.

a'penas adv (unicamente) only; (mal) hardly, scarcely // conj (logo que) as soon as; ~ tinha partido quando . . . no sooner had he left when . . .

apêndice [a'pědʒɪsɪ] m appendix; (anexo) supplement; **apendicite** f appendicitis.

aperce'ber-se vr: ~ de to notice, see.

aperfeiçoamento [aperfejswa'mētu] m (perfeição) perfection; (melhoramento) improvement; **aperfeiçoar** vt to perfect; (melhorar) to improve; **aperfeiçoar-se** vr to improve o.s.

aperi'tivo m aperitif.

aperreação [apexɪa'sãw] f (opressão) harassment; **aperreado/a** adj (vexado) harassed; **estar aperreado** (sem dinheiro) to be hard up; **aperrear** vt to dog, harass.

aper'tado/a adj (roupa) tight; (estreito) narrow; (sem dinheiro) hard up.

aper'tar vt (espremer) to squeeze; (unir muito) to pack together; (segurar) to grip; (comprimir) to press; ~ a mão a to shake hands with; ~ o passo to speed up // vi (estreitar) to narrow; (sapatos) to pinch, be tight.

a'perto m (pressão) pressure; (situação difícil) trouble, jam; **um ~ de mão** handshake.

ape'sar prep: ~ de in spite of, despite; ~ disso nevertheless.

apete'cer vt: (Pt) **apetece-me ir ao cinema** I feel like going to the cinema; **apetecível** adj (tentador) tempting; (desejável) desirable.

apetite [ape'tɪtʃɪ] m appetite; (desejo) desire; (ambição) ambition; **apetitoso/a** adj appetizing; (tentador) tempting.

apetrechar [apetre'ʃax] vt to fit out, equip.

ápice ['apɪs] m (cume) summit, top; (vértice) apex; **num ~** (Pt) in a trice.

apiedar-se [apɪe'dax-sɪ] vr: ~ de (ter piedade) to pity; (compadecer-se) to take pity on.

apimen'tado/a adj (picante) peppery; (fig) spicy; **apimentar** vt to pepper, spice.

apinhado/a [apɪ'ɲadu/a] adj crowded; **apinhar** vt (ajuntar) to heap together; **apinhar-se** vr (aglomerar-se) to crowd together.

api'tar vi to whistle; **apito** m whistle.

apla'car vt to placate // vi to calm down; ~-se vr to calm down.

aplainar [aplaj'nax] vt to plane.

apla'nar vt (alisar) to smooth; (nivelar) to level; (dificuldades) to smooth over.

aplaudir [aplaw'dʒɪx] vt to applaud; **aplauso** m applause; (elogio) praise; (aprovação) approval.

aplicação [aplɪka'sãw] f application; (esforço) effort; (costura) appliqué; (da lei) enforcement; **aplicado/a** adj hardworking.

apli'car vt to apply; ~ uma lei to enforce a law; ~-se vr: ~-se a to devote o.s. to, apply o.s. to; **aplicável** adj applicable, relevant.

apo'dar vt (troçar) to taunt, mock; (alcunhar) to nickname; ~ alguém de ladrão to call sb a thief.

apode'rar-se vr: ~ de to seize, take possession of.

a'podo m (alcunha) nickname; (mofa) taunt, jeer.

apodre'cer vt to rot; (corromper) to corrupt // vi to rot, decay; **apodrecimento** m rottenness, decay; (fig) corruption.

apogeu [apo'ʒɛw] m (ASTRO) apogee; (fig) summit, height.

apoiado/a [apo'jadu/a] adj supported; (autorizado) approved; (encostado) leaning // m (aplauso) applause; (aprovação) approval.

apoi'ar vt (sustentar) to support; (fig) to back up; (basear) to base; (uma moção) to second; ~-se vr: ~-se em to lean on, rest on; **apoio** m prop, support; (fig) backing, approval.

apólice [a'pɔlɪs] f (certificado) policy, certificate; (ação) share, bond; ~ de seguro insurance policy.

apologia [apolo'ʒıa] f (elogio) eulogy; (defesa) defence.

aponta'dor m (Br: apara-lápis) pencil sharpener; (capataz) overseer.

aponta'mento m (nota) note; (de uma reunião) minute; (esquema) draft.

apon'tar vt (fusil) to aim; (indicar) to point out to; (dedo) to point; (anotar) to note down; (fazer ponta) to sharpen // vi (aparecer) to begin to appear; (brotar) to sprout; ~ **para** (fazer pontaria) to aim at; ~! take aim!

apoquentar [apokě'tax] vt (afligir) to worry; (aborrecer) to annoy, pester; ~-se vr to worry.

aporre'ar vt to beat.

aporri'nhar vt to pester, annoy.

a'pós prep after; (atrás de) behind // adv afterwards.

aposen'tado/a adj retired; ficar ~ to be retired, be pensioned off; **aposentar** vt (reformar) to retire, pension off; **aposentar-se** vr (reformar-se) to retire; (hospedar-se) to take lodgings.

apo'sento m (quarto) room; (alojamento) lodging.

a'pósito/a adj apposite, appropriate // m (penso) dressing.

apos'sar-se vr: ~ **de** to take possession of, seize.

a'posta f bet; **apostar** vt to bet // vi: **apostar em** to bet on.

a'póstolo m apostle.

a'póstrofe f apostrophe, invocation.

a'póstrofo m apostrophe.

apote'ose f apotheosis.

apoucado/a [apo'kadu/a] adj (mesquinho) mean, base; (escasso) scanty.

apouca'mento m humiliation; **apoucar** vt (rebaixar) to humiliate; (diminuir) to lessen; (desdenhar) to belittle; **apoucar-se** vr to belittle o.s., underrate o.s.; (Br: emagrecer) to waste away.

apra'zar vt (combinar) to arrange, fix // vi: **apraz-me fazer isto** I like doing this.

apreça'dor(a) m/f valuer; **apreçar** vt to value, price.

apreciação [apresıa'sãw] f appreciation; (estimação) estimation; **apreciar** vt to appreciate; (estimar) to value; (gostar de) to enjoy; **apreciativo/a** adj appreciative.

apreci'ável [-ew] adj appreciable; (estimável) estimable; **apreço** m (estima) esteem, regard; (consideração) consideration; **em apreço** in question.

apreender [aprıĕ'dex] vt to apprehend; (tomar) to seize; (entender) to understand, grasp.

apreensão [aprıĕ'sãw] f (percepção) perception; (tomada) seizure, arrest; (receio) apprehension; **apreensivo/a** adj apprehensive.

aprego'ar vt to proclaim, announce; (mercadorias) to cry.

apren'der vt to learn; ~ **de cor** to learn by heart // vi to learn; ~ **a ler** to learn to read.

aprendiz [aprě'dʒıʃ] m apprentice; (principiante) beginner; ~**agem** f apprenticeship.

apresar [apre'zax] vt to take prisoner, capture.

apresentação [aprezěta'sãw] f presentation; (de pessoas) introduction; (porte pessoal) bearing, appearance; **carta de** ~ letter of introduction; **apresentar** vt (expor) to present, show, exhibit; (pessoas) to introduce; **quero apresentar-lhe** may I introduce you to; **apresentar-se** vr (aparecer) to appear, turn up; **apresentar-se a** to introduce o.s. to.

apres'sado/a adj hurried, hasty; **estar** ~ to be in a hurry; **apressar** vt to hurry, hasten; **apressar-se** vr to hurry (up).

apressu'rar vt to hurry, hasten; ~-se vr to hurry (up).

apres'tar vt (aparelhar) to equip, fit out; (aprontar) to get ready; ~-se vr to get ready; **aprestos** mpl (equipamento) equipment, gear; (preparativos) preparations.

aprisio'nado/a adj imprisoned; **aprisionamento** m imprisonment; **aprisionar** vt (cativar) to capture; (encarcerar) to imprison.

apron'tar vt to get ready, prepare; ~-se vr: ~-se para to get ready to.

apropriação [apropria'sãw] f appropriation; (tomada) seizure.

apropri'ado/a adj appropriate, suitable.

apropri'ar vt to appropriate; ~-se vr: ~-se de to seize, take possession of.

aprovação [aprova'sãw] f approval; (louvor) praise; (exame) pass; **aprovado/a** adj approved; **ser aprovado num exame** to pass an exam; **aprovar** vt to approve of; (exame) to pass // vi to pass.

aproveita'mento m use, utilization; (adiantamento) progress.

aproveitar [aprovej'tax] vt (tirar proveito) to profit by; (não desperdiçar) to take advantage of; (utilizar) to use // vi (Pt) to be of use; **não aproveita** it's no use; ~-se vr: ~-se de to make good use of, avail o.s. of; ~-se ao máximo de to make the most of.

aprovisiona'mento m supply, provision; **aprovisionar** vt to supply.

aproximação [aprosıma'sãw] f (estimativa) approximation; (chegada) approach; (proximidade) nearness, closeness; **aproximado/a** adj (cálculo) approximate; (perto) nearby.

aproximar [aprosı'max] vt to bring near; (aliar) to bring together; ~-se vr: ~-se de (acercar-se) to approach, come near.

apru'mado/a adj vertical; (altivo) upright; **aprumo** m vertical position;

aptidão [aptɪ'dãw] *f* aptitude, ability; *(jeito)* knack; **exame de ~** aptitude test; **~ física** physical fitness.

'apto/a *adj* apt; *(idôneo)* suitable; *(capaz)* capable.

apunhalar [apuɲa'lax] *vt* to stab.

apu'pada *f (insulto)* boo, jeer; **apupar** *vt (vaiar)* to boo, jeer at; *(buzinar)* to hoot at; **apupos** *mpl* hooting.

apu'rado/a *adj (escolhido)* select; *(fino)* refined, fine.

apu'rar *vt (purificar)* to purify, refine; *(aperfeiçoar)* to perfect; *(descobrir)* to find out; *(verificar)* to verify; *(dinheiro)* to raise, get; *(votos)* to count; *(caldo)* to thicken.

a'puro *m (elegância)* refinement, elegance; *(miséria)* hardship, difficulty; **estar em ~s** to be in a jam.

aquarela [akwa'rela] *f* water-colour.

aquário [a'kwarju] *m* aquarium; *(zodíaco)* Aquarius.

aquarte'lar *vt (MIL)* to billet, quarter.

a'quático/a *adj* aquatic, water.

aquecedor(a) [akese'dox(ra)] *adj* warming // *m* heater.

aquecer [ake'sex] *vt* to heat, warm; **~-se** *vr* to grow warm, heat up; **aquecimento** *m* heating; **aquecimento central** central heating.

aquedar [ake'dax] *vt* to calm, quieten.

aqueduto [ake'dutu] *m* aqueduct.

aquele, aquela, aqueles, aquelas [a'keli, a'kɛla, a'keliʃ, a'kɛlaʃ] *adj* that, *(pl)* those // *pron* that one, *(pl)* those; **sem mais aquela(s)** without more ado.

aquém [a'kẽj] *adv* on this side; **~ de** on this side of; *(abaixo de)* beneath.

aquentar [akẽ'tax] *vt* to warm, heat; **~-se** *vr* to get warm.

aqui [a'kɪ] *adv (lugar)* here; *(tempo)* now; **eis ~** here is/are, here you have; **por ~ e por ali** here and there; **por ~** hereabouts; *(nesta direção)* this way; **~ mesmo** right here; **daqui em diante** from now on; **daqui a uma semana** a week from now.

aquietar [akɪe'tax] *vt* to calm, quieten; **~-se** *vr* to calm down.

aquilatar [akɪla'tax] *vt (metais)* to value; *(avaliar)* to evaluate.

aquilo [a'kɪlu] *pron* that (thing); **~ que** what.

aquisição [akɪzɪ'sãw] *f* acquisition.

aquoso/a [a'kwozu/a] *adj* aqueous.

ar *m* air; *(semelhança)* look, appearance, aspect; *(aragem)* breeze; *(Pt: AUTO)* choke; **~ condicionado** air conditioning; **ao ~ livre** in the open air; **tomar ~** to go out, get some air; **~es** *mpl* airs; *(clima)* climate *sg*; **dar-se ~es** to put on airs.

'ara *f* altar.

'árabe *adj, m/f* Arab // *m (língua)* Arabic.

a'rábico/a *adj, m/f* Arabian.

a'rado *m* plough.

aragem [a'raʒẽj] *f* breeze.

a'rame *m* wire; **~ farpado** barbed wire.

aranha [a'raɲa] *f* spider.

a'rar *vt* to plough.

arauto [a'rawtu] *m* herald.

arbitra'gem *f* arbitration; *(esporte)* refereeing; **arbitrar** *vt* to arbitrate; *(esporte)* to referee; *(adjudicar)* to award.

arbitrarie'dade *f* arbitrariness; *(ato)* arbitrary act; *(capricho)* capriciousness; **arbitrário/a** *adj* arbitrary; *(caprichoso)* wilful.

ar'bítrio *m (decisão)* decision; *(resolução)* will; **ao ~ de** at the discretion of; **livre ~** free will.

'árbitro *m (juiz)* arbiter; *(JUR)* arbitrator; *(futebol)* referee; *(tênis)* umpire.

ar'busto *m* shrub, bush.

'arca *f (caixa)* chest; *(cofre)* coffer; **~ de Noé** Noah's Ark.

ar'cada *f (série de arcos)* arcade; *(arco)* arch, span.

arcaico/a [ax'kajku/a] *adj* archaic; *(antiquado)* antiquated.

arcanjo [ax'kãʒu] *m* archangel.

ar'car *vt*: **~ com** *(responsabilidades)* to shoulder.

arce'bispo *m* archbishop.

'arco *m (ARQ)* arch; *(MIL, MÚS)* bow; *(ELET, MAT)* arc; *(barril)* hoop.

arco-'íris *m* rainbow.

ar'dente *adj* burning; *(intenso)* fervent; *(apaixonado)* ardent; **arder** *vi* to burn; *(de um golpe)* to smart; *(de uma picada)* to sting; **arder em cólera** to burn with rage; **arder por** to desire passionately.

ar'dido/a *adj (fermentado)* rancid, sour; *(picante)* hot.

ar'dil *m* trick, ruse; **~oso/a** *adj* cunning.

ar'dor *m (paixão)* ardour, passion; **~oso/a** *adj* ardent.

ar'dósia *f* slate.

árduo/a ['axdwu/a] *adj* arduous; *(difícil)* hard, difficult.

área ['arja] *f* area; *(esporte)* penalty area; **~ de serviço** *(pátio)* yard.

areia [a'reja] *f* sand; **~ movediça** quicksand.

arejado/a [are'ʒadu/a] *adj* aired, ventilated; **arejar** *vt* to air, ventilate; **arejar-se** *vr* to get some fresh air.

a'rena *f (contenda)* arena; *(circo)* ring.

a'renga *f harangue; (invectiva)* tirade; **arengar** *vt/i* to harangue.

are'noso/a *adj* sandy.

arenque [a'rẽkɪ] *m* herring.

a'resta *f* edge; *(saliência)* ridge.

ar'fada *f (ofego)* gasp; *(NÁUT)* pitching; **arfar** *vi (ofegar)* to pant, gasp for breath; *(NÁUT)* to pitch.

arga'massa *f* mortar; **argamassar** *vt* to plaster, apply mortar to.

Argélia [ax'ʒɛlja] *f* Algeria; **argelino/a** *adj, m/f* Algerian.

argentino/a [axʒẽ'tʃinu/a] *adj*

Argentinian; (*prateado*) silvery, silver //
m/f Argentinian // *f*: **A~a** Argentina.
argento-vivo [axʒɛtu-'vivu] *m* quick-silver.
argila [ax'ʒila] *f* clay.
ar'gola *f* ring; **~ da porta** door-knocker; **~s** *fpl* (*brincos*) hooped earrings; **argolada** *f* rap, knock.
argúcia [ax'gusja] *f* (*sutileza*) subtlety; (*agudeza*) astuteness; (*piada*) witticism; **arguciar** *vi* to quibble.
argueiro [ax'gejru] *m* (*grânulo*) speck; (*coisa insignificante*) trifle; **fazer de um ~ um cavaleiro** (*Pt*) to make a mountain out of a molehill.
argüente [ax'gwẽtʃi] *m/f* accuser; **argüido** *m* accused.
argüir [ax'gwix] *vt* to accuse; **~ de** to accuse of; **~ por** to blame for // *vi* to argue; (*suplicar*) to plead; (*examinar*) to test, examine.
argumentação [axgumẽta'sãw] *f* argument, controversy; **argumentador(a)** *adj* argumentative // *m/f* arguer.
argumen'tar *vt/i* to argue; **argumento** *m* (*disputa*) argument; (*de obra*) plot, theme; (*sumário*) summary; **como argumento** as an example.
ar'guto/a *adj* (*sutil*) subtle; (*astuto*) shrewd.
ari'ano/a *adj*, *m/f* Aryan.
aridez [ari'deʃ] *f* (*secura*) dryness; (*falta de interesse*) dullness; **árido/a** *adj* (*seco*) arid, dry; (*maçante*) dull, boring.
aristocra'cia *f* aristocracy; **aristocrata** *m/f* aristocrat; **aristocrático/a** *adj* aristocratic.
arit'mético/a *adj* arithmetical // *f* arithmetic.
arlequim [axlɛ'kĩ] *m* harlequin; (*teatro*) buffoon.
'arma *f* arm, weapon; **~ branca** cold steel; **~ de fogo** firearm; **~s** *fpl* (*brasão*) coat of arms; (*profissão militar*) military career; **passar pelas ~s** to shoot, execute.
armação [axma'sãw] *f* (*armadura*) body, frame; (*pesca*) tackle; (*equipamento*) equipment; (*navio*) rigging.
armadilha [axma'dʒiʎa] *f* trap, snare.
ar'mado/a *adj* armed; (*TEC*) reinforced // *f* fleet, navy.
arma'dor *m* (*tapeceiro*) upholsterer; (*NÁUT*) chandler; shipowner; (*agente de funerais*) undertaker.
arma'dura *f* armour; (*ELET*) armature; (*CONSTR*) framework.
arma'mento *m* (*armas*) armament, weapons; (*NÁUT*) equipment.
ar'mar *vt* to arm; (*barraca*) to pitch; (*um aparelho*) to set up; (*preparar*) to prepare; (*NÁUT*) to fit out; **~ uma briga com** to pick a quarrel with; **~ uma armadilha** to set a trap; **~ cavaleiro** to knight.
arma'ria *f* (*MIL*) armoury; (*heráldica*) heraldry.
ar'mário *m* cupboard; (*de roupa*) wardrobe, closet.

armazém [axma'zẽj] *m* (*loja*) store; (*depósito*) warehouse; **~ de secos e molhados** grocery store; **armazenagem** *f* storage; **armazenar** *vt* to store; (*provisões*) to stock.
armeiro [ax'mejru] *m* gunsmith.
'aro *m* (*argola*) ring; (*de óculos*) rim; (*de porta*) frame; **~s** *mpl* outskirts.
a'roma *f* aroma, fragrance; **aromático/a** *adj* aromatic, fragrant.
arpão [ax'pãw] *m* harpoon; **arpoar** *vt* to harpoon.
arquear [axki'ax] *vt* to arch; (*emperrar*) to camber; **~-se** *vr* to bend, arch; (*entortar-se*) to warp.
arqueiro [ax'kejru] *m* archer; (*goleiro*) goalkeeper.
arquejar [axke'ʒax] *vi* to pant, wheeze; **arquejo** *m* panting, gasping.
arqueologia [axkiolo'ʒia] *f* archaeology; **arqueólogo/a** *m/f* archaeologist.
arquétipo [ax'kɛtʃipu] *m* archetype.
arquiban'cada(s) *f(pl)* stalls.
arquiteto/a [axki'tɛtu/a] (*Pt*: -ct-) *m/f* architect; **arquitetura** (*Pt*: -ct-) *f* architecture.
arquivar [axki'vax] *vt* (*depositar*) to file; (*registrar*) to record; **arquivo** *m* archive; (*móvel*) filing cabinet.
arra'baldes *mpl* suburbs.
arraia [a'xaja] *f* (*peixe*) ray; **~ miúda** masses *pl*, rabble.
arrai'al *m* (*povoação*) village; (*Pt*: *festa*) fair.
arrai·gado/a *adj* deep-rooted; (*fig*) ingrained; **arraigar** *vi* to root; **arraigar-se** *vr* (*enraizar-se*) to take root; (*estabelecer-se*) to settle.
arrais [a'xajʃ] *m* (*NÁUT*) skipper.
arran'cada *f* (*puxão*) pull, jerk; (*partida*) get-away; (*investida*) charge; **arrancar** *vt* (*extrair*) to pull up, pull out; (*arrebatar*) to snatch (away); (*fig*) to extract // *vi* to start (off); **arrancar-se** *vr* to run off; **arranco** *m* (*puxão*) pull, jerk; (*partida*) sudden start.
arranha-céu [axaɲa-'sɛw] *m* skyscraper.
arranhadura [axaɲa'dura] *f*, **arranhão** [axa'ɲãw] *m* scratch; **arranhar** *vt* to scratch.
arranjar [axã'ʒax] *vt* (*organizar*) to arrange; (*arrumar*) to tidy (up); (*conseguir*) to get; (*consertar*) to repair; (*conciliar*) to settle; **~ um emprego** to get a job; **~-se** *vr* (*arrumar-se bem*) to get by; (*preparar-se*) to get ready; **~-se sem** to do without; **arranjo** *m* (*disposição*) arrangement; (*negociata*) deal.
arranque [a'xãki] *m* (*AUTO*) starter.
'arras *fpl* (*penhor*) surety; (*doação*) dowry.
arra'sar *vt* (*demolir*) to demolish; (*derrubar*) to raze, level; (*estragar*) to ruin; (*humilhar*) to browbeat; **~-se** *vr* (*humilhar-se*) to humble o.s.

arras'tado/a adj (rasteiro) crawling; (demorado) dragging; (voz) drawling.

arrastão [axas'tãw] m tug, jerk; (rede) dragnet; **arrastar** vt to drag (along); (vento) to sweep (along); (impelir) to drive; arrastar a asa to court // vi to trail; **arrastar-se** vr to crawl; (fig) to grovel; **arrasto** m (ação) dragging; (rede) trawl-net; (TEC) drag.

arrazoado [axa'zwadu] m (JUR) defence; **arrazoar** vt to argue for (a cause) // vi to discuss; (discutir) to argue.

arre'ar vt (cavalo etc) to harness.

arreba'tado/a adj (impetuoso) rash, impetuous; (enlevado) entranced; **arrebatamento** m (impetuosidade) impetuosity; (enlevo) ecstasy.

arreba'tar vt (agarrar) to snatch (away); (levar) to carry off; (enlevar) to entrance; (enfurecer) to enrage; **~-se** vr (entusiasmar-se) to be entranced.

arreben'tado/a adj (falido) broke; (estafado) worn out; **arrebentar** vi (estourar) to explode, burst; **arrebentar-se** vr to be done for.

arrebi'tado/a adj turned-up; (nariz) snub; **arrebitar** vt to turn up.

arrebol [axe'bɔw] m red sky.

arre'cada f earring.

arrecadação [axekada'sãw] f (de impostos etc) collection; (depósito) storehouse; (custódia) custody; **arrecadador** m (de impostos) tax collector; **arrecadar** vt (impostos etc) to collect.

arrecife [axe'sIfI] m reef.

arre'dar vt not to move away, move back; **não ~ pé** not to move, to stand one's ground; **~-se** vr to withdraw.

arre'dio/a adj (cachorro) stray; (gado) runaway, stray; (solitário) solitary; (insociável) unsociable.

arredon'dar vt to round (off); **~ a conta** to make a round sum.

arre'dores mpl suburbs; (cercanias) outskirts.

arrefe'cer vt to cool // vi to cool (off).

arrega'çar vt (mangas) to roll up; (calças) to turn up.

arrega'lar vt to goggle.

arreganhar [axega'ɲax] vt (dentes) to bare (one's teeth).

arreios [a'xejuʃ] mpl harness sg.

arre'lia f (zanga) annoyance; **arreliar** vt to annoy; **arreliar-se** vr to get angry.

arreman'gar vt to roll up; **~-se** vr (aprontar-se) to get ready.

arrema'tar vt (rematar) to conclude; (comprar) to buy by auction; (vender) to sell by auction.

arreme'dar vt to mimic; **arremedo** m mimicry.

arremes'sar vt to throw, hurl; **~-se** vr to hurl o.s.; **arremesso** m (lançamento) throw.

arreme'ter vi to lunge; **~ contra** (acometer) to attack, assail; **arremetida** f attack, onslaught.

arrenda'dor(a) m landlord // f landlady.

arrenda'mento m (ação) renting; (contrato) lease; (preço) rent; **arrendar** vt (dar em arrendamento) to let; (alugar) to rent, hire; **arrendatário/a** m/f tenant.

arrepanhar [axepa'ɲax] vt (arregaçar) to tuck (up); (enrugar) to crease; (arrebatar) to snatch; (economizar) to hoard.

arrepen'der-se vr to repent; (mudar de opinião) to change one's mind; **~ de** to regret, be sorry for; **arrependimento** m repentance, regret.

arrepi'ar vt (amedrontar) to horrify; (cabelo etc) to cause to stand on end; (peixe) to salt; **~-se** vr (sentir calafrios) to shiver; (cabelo) to stand on end; isso me arrepia it gives me goose flesh.

arre'pio m shiver; (de frio) chill; isso me dá ~s it gives me the creeps; **ao ~** the wrong way, against the grain.

ar'resto m (JUR) seizure, confiscation.

arreve'sado/a adj (obscuro) obscure; (intricado) intricate; **arrevesar** vt (pôr ao revés) to turn inside out/upside down; (complicar) to complicate.

arri'ar vt (baixar) to lower; (depor) to lay down // vi (afrouxar) to yield; (desistir) to give up; **~-se** vr (cair) to fall; (vergar) to sag.

ar'riba adv (acima) up, upward(s); (adiante) onward(s).

arribação [axIba'sãw] f (Br: aves) migration; **arribar** vi (recuperar-se) to recuperate.

arri'mar vt to support; **~-se** vr: **~-se a** (apoiar-se) to lean against; **arrimo** m support, prop; **arrimo de família** breadwinner.

arris'cado/a adj risky; (audacioso) daring; **arriscar** vt to risk; (pôr em perigo) to endanger, jeopardize; **arriscar-se** vr to take a risk.

arri'vista m/f upstart; (oportunista) opportunist.

arrochar [axo'ʃax] vt (apertar) to tighten up // vi (ser exigente) to be demanding; **arrocho** m squeeze; (fig) predicament.

arro'gância f arrogance, haughtiness; **arrogante** adj arrogant, haughty.

arro'gar vt to attribute; **~-se** vr to appropriate for o.s.; (atribuir-se) to attribute to o.s.

arroio [a'xɔju] m stream.

arrojado/a [axo'ʒadu/a] adj (temerário) rash; (ousado) daring; **arrojar** vt (lançar) to hurl; **arrojar-se** vr (arremessar-se) to hurl o.s. into; (ousar) to dare to.

arrojo [a'xoʒu] m (ousadia) boldness.

arrola'mento m enrolment; (lista) list; **arrolar** vt to enrol.

arromba'dor m burglar; **arrombamento** m burglary, breaking and entry; **arrombar** vt (abrir à força) to break into.

arros'tar vt to confront, face (up to).

arro'tar vt/i to belch; (alardear) to boast (of).

arrote'ar vt (terreno) to clear; (: cultivar) to cultivate; (educar) to educate.

arrouba'mento m ecstasy, rapture; **arroubar** vt to enrapture, entrance; **arroubo** m ecstasy, rapture.

arroz [a'xoʃ] m rice; ~ **doce**, ~ **de leite** rice pudding; **arrozal** m rice field.

arru'aça f street riot.

arru'ela f (TEC) washer.

arru'gar vt to wrinkle, crease.

arrui'nar vt to ruin; (destruir) to destroy; (estragar) to spoil // vi (estragar-se) to get spoiled, go bad; ~**-se** vr to be ruined.

arrulhar [axu'ʎax] vi (pombos) to coo; **arrulho** m (pombos) cooing.

arrumação [axuma'sãw] f (arranjo) arrangement; (de um quarto etc) tidying up; (de malas) packing; **arrumar** vt (pôr em ordem) to put in order, arrange; (um quarto etc) to tidy up; (malas) to pack; (obter) to get, secure.

arse'nal m (MIL) arsenal; ~ **de Marinha** naval dockyard.

'arte f (ger) art; (habilidade) skill; (ofício) trade, craft; (astúcia) cunning.

arte'fato (Pt: -ct-) m (manufactured) article; (arqueológico) artefact; ~**s de couro** leather goods, leatherware sg.

arteirice [axtej'risi] f cunning, guile; **arteiro/a** adj artful, cunning.

artéria [ax'tɛrja] f (ANAT) artery.

artesa'nato m craftwork, crafts.

artesão/artesã [axte'zãw, arte'zã] m artisan, craftsman // f craftswoman.

'ártico/a adj Arctic // m: o A~ the Arctic.

articulação [axtʃikula'sãw] f articulation; (MED) joint; **articulado/a** adj articulated, jointed; **articular** vt (pronunciar) to articulate; (ligar) to join together.

articu'lista m/f newspaper writer, columnist.

ar'tículo m (ANAT) knuckle; (artigo) article.

artífice [ax'tʃifis] m craftsman; (inventor) inventor // f craftswoman.

artifício [axtʃi'fisju] m (habilidade) skill, art; (astúcia) cunning; **artificioso/a** adj (hábil) skilful; (astucioso) artful.

ar'tigo m article; ~ **de fundo** leading article, editorial; ~**s** mpl goods.

artilharia [axtʃiʎa'ria] f artillery; **artilheiro** m gunner, artilleryman.

artimanha [axtʃi'maɲa] f (ardil) stratagem; (astúcia) cunning.

ar'tista m/f (pintor etc) artist; (de teatro etc) artist; **artístico/a** adj artistic.

ar'trite f (MED) arthritis.

arvo'rar vt (erguer) to raise; (bandeira) to hoist.

'árvore f tree; (TEC) axle, shaft; **arvoredo** m grove.

as art ver **a**.

às = **a** + **as**, ver **a**.

ás m ace.

'asa f wing; (de xícara etc) handle.

asbesto [az'bɛstu] m asbestos.

ascen'dência f (antepassados) ancestry; (domínio) ascendency, sway; **ascendente** adj rising, upward // m (antepassado) ancestor; (domínio) ascendency.

ascen'der vi (subir) to rise, ascend; ~ **a** to amount to; **ascensão** f ascent; (fig) rise; **dia da Ascensão** Ascension Day.

ascen'sor m elevator (US), lift (Brit).

as'ceta m/f ascetic.

'asco m loathing, revulsion; **dar** ~ to be revolting, disgust.

áscua ['aʃkwa] f (brasa) ember; (chispa) spark.

as'falto m asphalt.

asfixia [aʃfik'sia] f suffocation; **asfixiar** vt, **asfixiar-se** vr to suffocate.

Asia ['azja] f Asia; **asiático/a** adj, m/f Asian.

asi'lar vt to give refuge to; ~**-se** vr to take refuge; **asilo** m (refúgio) refuge; (estabelecimento) home, asylum.

asma ['aʒma] f asthma.

asneira [aʒ'nejra] f (tolice) stupidity; (conversa tola) nonsense.

'asno m donkey; (fig) ass.

'aspa f (cruz) cross; ~**s** fpl (chifres) horns; (sinais ortográficos) inverted commas.

as'pargo m asparagus.

as'pecto m (aparência) appearance; (característica) feature; (ponto de vista) point of view; **ter bom** ~ to look well.

aspe'reza f roughness; (severidade) harshness; (rudeza) abruptness.

aspergir [aʃpex'ʒix] vt to sprinkle.

'áspero/a adj rough; (severo) harsh; (difícil) tough; (rude) abrupt.

as'perso/a pp irr de **aspergir** // adj scattered.

aspiração [aʃpira'sãw] f aspiration; (inalação) inhalation; (desejo) longing.

aspira'dor m: ~ **de pó** vacuum cleaner.

aspi'rante m/f applicant, candidate; (MIL) cadet.

aspi'rar vt to breathe in; (sorver) to suck in; (LING) to aspirate // vi: ~ **a** to aspire to.

aspi'rina f aspirin.

asqueroso/a [aʃke'rozu/a] adj disgusting, revolting.

assadeira [asa'dejra] f pan; **assado/a** adj roasted; **carne assada** roast beef // m roast; **assadura** f (skin-)rash.

assal'tante m/f assailant; (arrombador) burglar; **assaltar** vt (atacar) to attack, raid; (assediar) to besiege; (uma casa) to break into; **assalto** m (ataque) attack, raid; (a um banco etc) hold-up; (boxe) round; (a uma casa) burglary, break-in.

assanhado/a [asa'ɲadu/a] adj (enfurecido) furious; (irrequieto) restless; (sexualmente) excited, aroused; **assanhar** vt to enrage, infuriate; (irritar) to inflame; (agitar) to stir up;

(sexualmente) to tease, excite; **assanhar-se** *vr* to fly into a rage.

as'sar *vt* to roast; *(na grelha)* to grill.

assassi'nar *vt* to murder, kill; *(POL)* to assassinate; **assassinato** *m*, **assassínio** *m* murder, killing, assassination; **assassino/a** *m/f* murderer, killer; *(político)* assassin.

assaz [a'saʃ] *adj* enough, sufficient // *adv (suficientemente)* sufficiently; *(muito)* quite, rather.

asse'ado/a *adj (limpo)* clean; *(aspecto)* tidy; *(esmerado)* neat; **assear** *vt* to clean, tidy (up).

assedi'ar *vt (sitiar)* to beseige; *(importunar)* to pester; **assédio** *m* seige; *(insistência)* insistence.

assegu'rar *vt (tornar seguro)* to secure; *(garantir)* to ensure; *(afirmar)* to assure; **~-se** *vr*: **~-se de** to make sure of.

asseio [a'seju] *m (limpeza)* cleanliness; *(esmero)* neatness.

assembléia [asẽ'bleja] *f* assembly; *(reunião)* meeting.

assemelhar [aseme'ʎax] *vt* to liken, compare; **~-se** *vr (ser semelhante)* to be alike; **~-se a** to resemble, look like.

assen'tado/a *adj (baseado)* based; *(firme)* fixed, secure; *(combinado)* agreed.

assenta'dor *m (registrador)* registrar; *(de tijolos)* bricklayer; **assentamento** *m* registration.

assen'tar *vt (fazer sentar)* to seat; *(colocar)* to place; *(estabelecer)* to establish; *(anotar)* to note down; *(decidir)* to decide upon; *(determinar)* to fix, settle // *vi (basear-se)* to be based; *(ficar bem)* to suit; *(pó etc)* to settle; **~-se** *vr* to sit down; **assente** *pp irr de* **assentar** // *adj* agreed, decided.

assenti'mento *m* assent, agreement; **assentir** *vi* to agree.

as'sento *m (móvel)* chair; *(de veículo etc)* seat; *(anotação)* entry, record; *(base)* base; *(ANAT)* bottom; *(residência)* residence.

asses'sor(a) *m/f* adviser.

asses'tar *vt* to aim, point.

asseve'rar *vt* to affirm, assert.

assiduidade [asidwi'dadʒi] *f* assiduousness, diligence; **assíduo/a** *adj* diligent; *(incessante)* constant.

assim [a'sĩ] *adv (deste modo)* like this, in this way, thus; *(portanto)* therefore; *(igualmente)* likewise; **~ ~** so-so; **~ mesmo** in any case; **~ ou assado** in one way or another; **e ~ por diante** and so on // *conj*: **~ como** as well as; **~ que** *(logo que)* as soon as.

assimilação [asimila'sãw] *f* assimilation; **assimilar** *vt* to assimilate; *(apreender)* to take in; *(assemelhar)* to compare.

assina'lado/a *adj (marcado)* marked; *(notável)* notable; *(célebre)* eminent; **assinalar** *vt (marcar)* to mark;

(distinguir) to distinguish; *(especificar)* to point out.

assi'nante *m/f (de jornal etc)* subscriber; **assinar** *vt (nome)* to sign; *(jornal etc)* to subscribe to; *(fixar)* to fix; *(conferir)* to assign; **assinatura** *f (nome)* signature; *(de jornal etc)* subscription; *(teatro)* season ticket.

assis'tência *f (presença)* attendance, presence; *(público)* audience; *(auxílio)* aid, assistance.

assis'tente *adj* assistant // *m/f (pessoa presente)* spectator, onlooker; *(ajudante)* assistant.

assis'tir *vt* to attend, assist // *vi*: **~ a** to attend, be present at.

asso'ar *vt*: **~ o nariz** to blow one's nose; **~-se** *vr (Pt)* to blow one's nose.

assobi'ar *vi* to whistle; **assobio** *m* whistle; *(instrumento)* whistle; *(de vapor)* hiss.

associação [asosja'sãw] *f* association; *(organização)* society; *(parceria)* partnership; **associado/a** *adj*, *m/f* associate, member; *(sócio)* partner; **associar** *vt* to associate; **associar-se** *vr (COM)* to form a partnership; **associar-se a** to associate with.

assola'dor(a) *adj* devastating; **assolar** *vt* to devastate.

asso'mar *vi (aparecer)* to appear; **~ a** *(subir)* to climb to the top of.

assombração [asõbra'sãw] *f (pavor)* dread; *(fantasma)* ghost; **assombrado/a** *adj (sombrio)* shady; *(casa)* haunted; **assombrar** *vt (assustar)* to frighten, startle; *(maravilhar)* to astonish; *(fantasma)* to haunt; **assombrar-se** *vr* to be amazed; **assombro** *m (espanto)* fright; *(pasmo)* astonishment; *(maravilha)* marvel; **assombroso/a** *adj (espantoso)* astonishing, amazing.

assu'mir *vt* to assume // *vi* to take office.

assun'tar *vt (prestar atenção)* to pay attention to; *(verificar)* to find out // *vi (considerar)* to consider.

as'sunto *m (tema)* subject, matter; *(enredo)* plot.

assusta'diço/a *adj* shy, timorous; **assustar** *vt* to frighten, scare, startle; **assustar-se** *vr* to be frightened.

'astro *m* star.

astrologia [aʃtrolo'ʒia] *f* astrology; **astrólogo/a** *m/f* astrologer.

astronauta [aʃtro'nawta] *m/f* astronaut.

astro'nave *f* spacecraft.

astrono'mia *f* astronomy; **astrônomo** *m* astronomer.

as'túcia *f* cunning; *(ardil)* trickery; **astuto/a** *adj* astute; *(esperto)* cunning.

'ata *(Pt: -ct-)* *f (de reunião)* minutes *pl*.

ataca'dista *m/f* wholesaler.

ataca'dor *m (de sapato etc)* lace.

ata'cante *adj* attacking // *m/f* attacker, assailant // *m (futebol)* forward; **atacar** *vt* to attack.

ata'dura *f* bandage.

atalaia [ata'laja] *m* watchman // *f* (*posto de observação*) lookout post; (*sentinela*) lookout, sentry.

atalhar [ata'ʎax] *vt* (*impedir*) to prevent; (*deter*) to stop; (*abreviar*) to shorten // *vi* (*tomar um atalho*) to take a short cut; **atalho** *m* (*caminho*) short cut; (*estorvo*) obstacle.

ataque [a'taki] *m* attack; ~ **aéreo** air raid; ~ **cardíaco** heart attack.

a'tar *vt* to tie (up), fasten; **não** ~ **nem desatar** to waver.

atare'fado/a *adj* busy.

atarra'cado/a *adj* stocky.

atascadeiro [ataʃka'dejru] *m* bog; **atascar-se** *vr* to get bogged down.

ataúde [ata'udʒi] *m* coffin.

atavi'ar *vt* to adorn, decorate; ~**-se** *vr* to get dressed up; **atavio** *m* adornment; (*vestes*) attire.

a'té *prep* (*Pt*: + **a**): (*lugar*) up to, as far as; (*tempo etc*) until, till; ~ **agora** up to now; ~ **certo ponto** to a certain extent; ~ **já** *ou* ~ **logo** see you soon // *conj*: ~ **que** until // *adv* even.

ate'ar *vt* (*fogo*) to kindle; (*fig*) to incite, inflame; ~ **fogo a** to set light to; ~**-se** *vr* (*fogo*) to blaze; (*paixões*) to flare up.

ate'ísmo *m* atheism.

atemori'zar *vt* to frighten; (*intimidar*) to intimidate.

atenção [atẽ'sãw] *f* attention; (*cortesia*) courtesy; (*bondade*) kindness; **prestar** ~ to pay attention; **chamar a** ~ to attract attention; **chamar a** ~ **de alguém** to tell sb off // *excl* be careful!

atenci'oso/a *adj* (*atento*) attentive; (*cortês*) considerate.

aten'der *vt* to attend (to); (*deferir*) to grant; (*telefone etc*) to answer // *vi* (*estar atento*) to pay attention.

aten'tado *m* (*ataque*) attack; (*crime*) crime; (*contra a vida de alguém*) attempt on sb's life; **atentar** *vt* (*empreender*) to undertake // *vi* to make an attempt; **atentar a/em/para** to pay attention to.

a'tento/a *adj* (*atencioso*) attentive; (*cortês*) considerate.

atenuação [atenwa'sãw] *f* reduction, lessening; **atenuante** *adj* extenuating // *m* extenuating circumstances; **atenuar** *vt* (*diminuir*) to reduce, lessen.

aterra'dor/a *adj* terrifying.

aterragem [ate'xaʒej] *f* (*Pt*: **AER**) landing.

ater'rar *vt* (*atemorizar*) to terrify; (*cobrir com terra*) to cover with earth // *vi* (*Pt*: **AER**) to land.

aterrissagem [atexisa'ʒej] *f* (*Br*: **AER**) landing; **aterrissar** *vi* (*Br*: **AER**) to land.

aterrori'zar *vt* to terrorize.

ates'tado/a *adj* certified // *m* certificate; (*JUR*) testimony; **atestar** *vt* (*certificar*) to certify; (*testemunhar*) to bear witness.

ateu/atéia [a'tɛw/a'teja] *adj*, *m/f* atheist.

atiça'dor *m* (*utensílio*) poker; (*pessoa*) instigator; · **atiçar** *vt* (*fogo*) to poke; (*incitar*) to incite.

ati'lado/a *adj* (*esperto*) clever.

ati'nar *vt* (*acertar*) to guess correctly // *vi* to be right; ~ **com** (*solução*) to find.

atingir [atʃĩ'ʒix] *vt* (*chegar*) to reach; (*interessar*) to affect, concern; (*obter*) to attain; (*compreender*) to understand, grasp; (*abranger*) to cover; **atingível** *adj* attainable.

atira'dor *m* marksman; ~ **de tocaia** sniper.

ati'rar *vt* (*lançar*) to throw, fling, hurl // *vi* (*arma*) to shoot; ~ **com** to throw off; ~**-se** *vr*: ~**-se a** (*lançar-se a*) to hurl o.s. at.

ati'tude *f* attitude; (*postura*) position, posture.

ati'var (*Pt*: **-ct-**) *vt* to activate, set in motion; (*apressar*) to hasten; **atividade** (*Pt*: **-ct-**) *f* activity.

a'tivo/a (*Pt*: **-ct-**) *adj* active; (*vivo*) lively // *m* (*COM*) assets *pl*.

at'lântico/a *adj* Atlantic // *m*: **o A**~ the Atlantic.

'atlas *m* atlas.

at'leta *m/f* athlete; **atletismo** *m* athletics *sg*.

atmos'fera *f* atmosphere.

'ato (*Pt*: **-ct-**) *m* act; (*ação*) action; (*cerimônia*) ceremony; (*teatro*) act; ~ **falho** Freudian slip; ~ **público** public ceremony; **em** ~ **contínuo** right away; **no mesmo** ~ at the same time.

à-toa [a'toa] *adj* worthless; **mulher** ~ woman of easy virtue // *adv* to no purpose.

atoleiro [ato'lejru] *m* quagmire; (*fig*) quandary, fix.

a'tômico/a *adj* atomic; **atomizador** *m* atomizer; **átomo** *m* atom.

a'tônito/a *adj* astonished, amazed.

a'tor (*Pt*: **-ct-**) *m* actor.

atordo'ado/a *adj* dazed; **atordo-ador(a)** *adj* stunning; **atordoamento** *m* dizziness; **atordoar** *vt* to daze, stun.

atormenta'dor(a) *adj* tormenting // *m/f* tormentor; **atormentar** *vt* to torment; (*amolar*) to tease; (*importunar*) to plague.

atração [atra'sãw] (*Pt*: **-cç-**) *f* attraction.

atra'car *vt/i* (*NÁUT*) to moor.

atra'ente *adj* attractive.

atraiçoado/a [atrajs'wadu/a] *adj* (*traído*) betrayed; (*desleal*) treacherous; **atraiçoar** *vt* to betray.

atra'ir *vt* to attract; (*atenção*) to catch.

atrapalhação [atrapaʎa'sãw] *f* (*confusão*) confusion; (*embaraço*) embarrassment; **atrapalhar** *vt* (*confundir*) to confuse; (*embaraçar*) to embarrass; **atrapalhar-se** *vr* to get confused.

a'trás *adv* (*lugar*) behind; (*movimento*) back, backwards; (*tempo*) previously // *prep*: ~ **de** behind, after.

atra'sado/a *adj* (*em atraso*) behind; (*país etc*) backward; (*relógio etc*) slow; (*tarde*) late; (*pagamento*) overdue; **atrasar** *vt* (*fazer demorar*) to delay; (*impedir*) to hold back // *vi* (*relógio etc*) to be slow; **atrasar-se** *vr* (*ficar para trás*) to fall behind; (*chegar tarde*) to be late; **atraso** *m* delay; (*de país etc*) backwardness; **em atraso** in arrears; **chegar com atraso** to arrive late.

atra'tivo/a (*Pt*: **-ct-**) *adj* attractive // *m* attraction, appeal; **~s** *mpl* charms.

atra'vés *adv* across // *prep*: **~ de** (*de lado a lado*) across; (*pelo centro de*) through.

atraves'sar *vt* (*cruzar*) to cross; (*pôr ao través*) to put *ou* lay across; (*traspassar*) to pass through; (*impedir*) to block; **~-se** *vr* (*na garganta etc*) to get stuck.

atreito/a [a'trejtu/a] *adj* (*inclinado*) inclined, prone; (*acostumado*) accustomed.

atre'lar *vt* (*cão*) to put on a leash; (*cavalo*) to harness.

atre'ver-se *vr*: **~ a** (*ousar*) to dare to; **atrevido/a** *adj* (*petulante*) impudent; (*corajoso*) bold; **atrevimento** *m* (*ousadia*) boldness; (*insolência*) insolence.

atribuição [atribwi'sãw] *f* attribution; (*privilégio*) privilege; **atribuições** *fpl* rights, powers; **atribuir** *vt* to attribute; (*conferir*) to confer.

atribu'lar *vt* to trouble, distress; **~-se** *vr* to be distressed.

atri'buto *m* attribute; (*qualidade*) characteristic.

'átrio *m* hall; (*pátio*) courtyard.

a'trito *m* (*fricção*) friction; (*desentendimento*) disagreement, difference.

atriz [a'triʃ] (*Pt*: **-ct-**) *f* actress.

atroa'dor(a) *adj* deafening; **atroar** *vt* to shake; (*aturdir*) to stun // *vi* (*retumbar*) to reverberate, thunder.

atrocidade [atrosi'dadʒi] *f* atrocity; (*fig*) outrage.

atropela'mento *m* (*pedestre*) running over; **atropelar** *vt* (*derrubar*) to knock down; (*passar por cima*) to run over; (*empurrar*) to jostle; **atropelo** *m* bustle, scramble; (*confusão*) confusion.

atroz [a'trɔʃ] *adj* (*cruel*) merciless; (*espantoso*) atrocious.

atuação [atwa'sãw] (*Pt*: **-ct-**) *f* acting; (*ação*) action.

atu'al (*Pt*: **-ct-**) *adj* present(-day), current; (*efetivo*) actual; **~idade** (*Pt*: **-ct-**) *f* present (time); **na ~idade** nowadays, these days; **~idades** *fpl* news *sg*.

atuali'zar (*Pt*: **-ct-**) *vt* to modernize, update.

atual'mente (*Pt*: **-ct-**) *adv* now, nowadays.

atu'ar (*Pt*: **-ct-**) *vi* to act; **~ sobre** to influence.

atu'ário (*Pt*: **-ct-**) *m* clerk; (*COM*) actuary.

atulhar [atu'ʎax] *vt* (*encher*) to fill up; (*meter*) to stuff.

atum [a'tũ] *m* tuna fish.

atu'rar *vt* (*soportar*) to endure, put up with // *vi* to endure, last.

atur'dido/a *adj* dazed; (*fig*) astounded; **aturdir** *vt* to stun; (*fig*) to bewilder.

audácia [aw'dasja] *f* boldness; (*insolência*) insolence; **audaz** *adj* daring; (*insolente*) insolent.

audição [awdʒi'sãw] *f* audition; (*concerto*) recital.

audi'ência [awdʒi'ẽsja] *f* audience; (*de tribunal*) session, hearing.

auditor [awdʒi'tox] *m* (*juiz*) judge; (*ouvinte*) listener; **auditório** *m* (*ouvintes*) audience; (*recinto*) auditorium.

auge ['awʒi] *m* climax.

augurar [awgu'rax] *vt* (*felicidades*) to wish; (*ser de bom/mau augúrio*) to augur (well/ill); **augúrio** *m* omen.

aula ['awla] *f* (*Pt*: **sala**) classroom; (*lição*) lesson, class.

aumentar [awmẽ'tax] *vt* (*ger*) to increase; (*ampliar*) to extend; (*com binóculo etc*) to magnify // *vi* to increase; **aumento** *m* increase; (*preços*) rise; (*ampliação*) enlargement; (*crescimento*) growth.

aura ['awra] *f* aura.

áureo/a ['awriu/a] *adj* golden.

auréola [aw'reola] *f* halo.

aurora [aw'rora] *f* dawn.

ausência [aw'zẽsja] *f* absence; (*falta*) lack.

ausen'tar-se *vr* to go/stay away; **ausente** *adj* absent // *m/f* missing person.

austeri'dade *f* austerity; **austero/a** *adj* austere.

aus'tral *adj* southern.

Aus'trália *f* Australia; **australiano/a** *adj, m/f* Australian.

'Áustria *f* Austria; **austríaco/a** *adj, m/f* Austrian.

autenti'car *vt* to authenticate; **autêntico/a** *adj* authentic.

auto ['awtu] *m* (*documento*) document, report; (*automóvel*) car; **~s** *mpl* (*JUR*: *processo*) legal proceedings; (*documentos*) legal papers.

autobiogra'fia *f* autobiography.

autocarro [awto'kaxu] *m* (*Pt*) bus.

autóctone [aw'tɔktonɪ] *adj* indigenous // *m/f* native, aborigine.

autodefesa [awtode'feza] *f* self-defence.

autodeterminação [awtodetɛxmɪna-'sãw] *f* self-determination.

autodo'mínio *m* self-control.

auto-escola [awto-is'kɔla] *f* driving school.

auto-es'trada *f* motorway.

auto'mático/a *adj* automatic.

automobi'lismo *m* motoring; (*esporte*) motor car racing.

automóvel [awto'mɔvɛl] *m* motor car (*Brit*), automobile (*US*).

autono'mia *f* autonomy; (*político*) self

government; **autônomo/a** *adj* autonomous.

au'tor(a) *m* author; (*de um crime*) perpetrator; (*JUR*) plaintiff // *f* authoress.

auto-re'trato *m* self-portrait.

autori'dade *f* authority.

autorização [awtorɪza'sãw] *f* authorization; **autorizar** *vt* to authorize.

auto-serviço [awto-sex'vɪsu] *m* self-service.

auto-sufici'ência *f* self-sufficiency.

auxiliar [awsɪlɪ'ax] *adj* auxiliary // *m/f* assistant // *vt* to help; **auxílio** *m* help, assistance.

Av *abr de* **avenida** avenue.

aval [a'vaw] *m* guarantee; (*COM*) surety.

avalanche [ava'lãʃa] *f* avalanche.

avaliação [avalɪa'sãw] *f* (*cálculo*) valuation, estimate; (*apreciação*) assessment, evaluation; **avaliar** *vt* (*calcular*) to estimate; (*apreciar*) to assess, evaluate.

avan'çada *f* advance; **avançar** *vt* to move forward; (*exceder*) to exceed // *vi* to advance; **avançar o sinal** to drive through a red light; **avanço** *m* advancement; (*progresso*) progress.

avantajado/a [avãta'ʒadu/a] *adj* (*corpulento*) stout.

ava'rento/a *adj* (*cobiçoso*) greedy; (*mesquinho*) mean // *m/f* miser; **avareza** *f* (*cobiça*) greed; (*mesquinhez*) meanness.

ava'ria *f* damage; (*TEC*) breakdown; **avariar** *vt* to damage // *vi* to suffer damage; (*TEC*) to break down.

a'varo/a *adj* (*cobiçoso*) greedy; (*mesquinho*) mean // *m/f* miser.

'ave *f* bird; ~ **de rapina** bird of prey.

aveia [a'veja] *f* oats *pl*.

ave'lã *f* hazelnut.

ave'nida *f* avenue.

aven'tal [-aw] *m* apron; (*de criança*) pinafore.

aven'tar *vt* (*uma idéia etc*) to put forward.

aven'tura *f* adventure; (*proeza*) exploit; **aventurado/a** *adj* daring; **aventurar** *vt* (*ousar*) to risk, venture; **aventurar-se** *vr:* **aventurar-se a** to dare to; **aventureiro/a** *adj* rash // *m/f* adventurer.

averiguação [averɪgwa'sãw] *f* investigation, inquiry; **averiguar** *vt* (*inquirir*) to investigate, ascertain; (*verificar*) to verify.

a'vesso/a *adj* (*contrário*) contrary // *m* wrong side, reverse; **ao** ~ inside out // *fpl:* **às** ~**as** (*inverso*) upside down; (*oposto*) the wrong way round.

avestruz [avɛʃ'truʃ] *m* ostrich.

ave'zar *vt* to accustom; ~**-se** *vr:* ~**-se a** to get used to.

aviação [avɪa'sãw] *f* aviation, flying.

avi'ado/a *adj* (*executado*) ready; (*apressado*) hurried.

avia'dor(a) *m* aviator, airman // *f* airwoman.

avia'mentos *mpl* materials, supplies.

avião [avɪ'ãw] *m* aeroplane; ~ **a jato** jet; ~ **de caça** fighter.

avi'ar *vt* (*receita médica*) to make up.

avidez [avɪ'deʒ] *f* (*cobiça*) greediness; (*desejo*) eagerness; **ávido/a** *adj* (*cobiçoso*) greedy; (*desejoso*) eager.

avil'tar *vt* to debase; ~**-se** *vr* to demean o.s.

avina'grado/a *adj* sour, tasting of vinegar.

a'vir-se *vr* (*conciliar-se*) to reach an understanding; (*arranjar-se*) to manage; (*harmonizar-se*) to get along; **lá se avenha!** that's your problem!

avi'sar *vt* (*advertir*) to warn; (*informar*) to tell, notify; **aviso** *m* (*comunicação*) notice; (*advertência*) warning; (*conselho*) advice.

avis'tar *vt* to glimpse, catch sight of; ~**-se** *vr:* ~**-se com** (*ter entrevista*) to have an interview with.

avi'var *vt* (*animar*) to rouse; (*intensificar*) to intensify, heighten; (*apressar*) to hurry (up) // *vi* to revive, recover.

aviven'tar *vt* (*reviver*) to revive; (*reanimar*) to revitalize.

avizinhar-se [avɪzɪ'ɲaxsɪ] *vr* (*aproximar-se*) to approach, come near.

'avo *m:* **um doze** ~**s** one twelfth.

avô/avó [a'vo/a'vɔ] *m* grandfather // *f* grandmother; **avós** *mpl* grandparents.

avo'engos *mpl* ancestors.

a'vulso/a *adj* separate, detached // *m* single copy.

avul'tado/a *adj* large, bulky; **avultar** *vt* to enlarge, expand // *vi* (*sobressair*) to stand out; (*aumentar*) to increase.

axila [ak'sɪla] *f* armpit.

axioma [asɪ'oma] *m* axiom.

a'záfama *f* bustle; (*pressa*) hurry.

a'zar *m* (*acaso*) chance, fate; (*desgraça*) misfortune.

a'zedo/a *adj* (*sabor*) sour; (*amargo*) bitter; (*fig*) irritable; **azedume** *m* (*sabor*) sourness; (*acrimônia*) bitterness; (*fig*) irritability.

azeite [a'zejtʃɪ] *m* oil.

azeitona [azej'tona] *f* olive.

azenha [a'zɛɲa] *f* water mill.

azeviche [aze'vɪʃɪ] *m* jet.

azevinho [aze'vɪɲu] *m* holly.

a'zia *f* heartburn.

azi'ago/a *adj* (*de mau agouro*) ominous; (*infausto*) ill-fated.

azinhaga [azɪ'ɲaga] *f* (country) lane.

azinheira [azɪ'ɲejra] *f* holm-oak.

'azo *m* (*oportunidade*) opportunity; (*pretexto*) pretext; **dar** ~ **a** to give occasion to.

a'zoto *m* nitrogen.

azougado/a [azo'gadu/a] *adj* (*inquieto*) restless; (*vivo*) lively; (*esperto*) sharp-witted, shrewd; **azougue** *m* quicksilver; (*QUÍM*) mercury.

a'zul *adj* blue; ~ **celeste** sky blue; ~ **marinho** navy blue.

azulejo [azu'leʒu] *m* (glazed) tile.

B

ba'bá f (regular) babysitter.
'baba f saliva, dribble; **babador** m, **babadouro** m bib.
babar [ba'bax] vt to dribble on; **~-se** vr to dribble; **babeiro** m (Pt) bib.
babugem [ba'buʒē] f foam, froth; (restos) left-overs pl.
bacalhau [baka'ʎaw] m (dried) cod.
bacana [ba'kãna] adj inv (col) great, cool, amazing.
bacharel [baʃa'rɛw] m bachelor, graduate; **bacharelar-se** vr to graduate.
ba'cia f basin, bowl; (ANAT) pelvis.
baço/a ['basu/a] adj dull; (metal) tarnished // m (ANAT) spleen.
bactéria [ba'ktɛrja] f germ, bacterium; **~s** fpl bacteria pl.
'báculo m staff; (de bispo) crosier.
badalar [bada'lax] vt/i (sino) to ring, peal; **badalo** m clapper.
bafejar [bafe'ʒax] vt (aquecer com o bafo) to blow on, breathe on; (fortuna) to smile upon.
ba'fio m musty smell.
'bafo m (hálito) (bad) breath; **baforada** f (fumaça) puff.
'baga f (fruta) berry; (gota) drop.
ba'gaço m (de frutos) pulp; (Pt: cachaça) brandy.
bagageiro [baga'ʒejru] m luggage compartment; (Pt) porter; **bagagem** f baggage, luggage.
baga'tela f trinket; (fig) trifle.
'bago m (fruto) berry; (uva) grape; (de chumbo) pellet.
bagulho [ba'guʎu] m (lixo) trash.
ba'gunça f (confusão) mess, shambles.
ba'ía f bay.
bai'lado m dance; (balé) ballet; **bailarino/a** m/f (professional) dancer/ballerina; **baile** m dance; (formal) ball.
bainha [ba'iɲa] f (de arma) sheath; (de costura) hem.
baioneta [bajo'neta] f bayonet; **~ calada** fixed bayonet.
bairro ['bajxu] m district, suburb.
baixa ['bajʃa] f (abaixamento) decrease; (redução de preço) reduction, fall; (diminuição) drop; (em combate) casualty; (do serviço) discharge; **dar ~** to be discharged.
baixada [baj'ʃada] f lowland.
baixa-mar [bajʃa-'max] f low tide.
baixar [baj'ʃax] vt (preço, voz, persianas) to lower; (descer) to take down; **~ a cabeça** to bow // vi to go/come down; (temperatura, preço) to drop, fall; **~ à enfermaria** to go into hospital; **baixeza** f meanness, baseness; **baixinho** adv (em voz baixa) softly, quietly; (em segredo) secretly.
baixo/a ['bajʃu/a] adj low; (pessoa) short, small; (raso) shallow; (chulo) common;

(metal) base // adv low; (em posição baixa) low down; (voz) softly; **em ~** below, downstairs; **para ~** down, downwards // prep: **por ~ de** under, underneath // m (MÚS) bass; (parte inferior) bottom.
'bala f bullet; (Br: doce) sweet; **balaço** m gunshot.
ba'lada f ballad.
ba'lança f scales pl; **~ comercial** balance of trade; (ASTRO) **B~** Libra.
balan'çar vt (fazer oscilar) to swing; (pesar) to weigh (up) // vi (oscilar) to swing; (em cadeira) to rock; **~-se** vr to swing; (navio) to roll.
ba'lanço m (movimento) swinging; (brinquedo) swing; (de navio) rolling; (COM : registro) balance (sheet); (: verificação) audit; **em ~** uncertain.
balão [ba'lãw] m balloon.
ba'lar vi to bleat.
balaus'trada f balustrade.
balbuciar [bawbu'sjax] vt/i to stammer, stutter; (falar de modo confuso) to babble.
balbúrdia [baw'buxdʒja] f uproar, bedlam.
balcão [baw'kãw] m balcony; (de loja) counter; (teatro) circle; **balconista** m/f shop-assistant.
'balda f defect, fault; **baldadamente** adv in vain; **baldado/a** adj unsuccessful, fruitless; **baldar** vt to frustrate, foil.
balde ['bawdʒi] m bucket, pail; **baldeação** f transfer; **baldear** vt (líquido) to decant; (transferir) to transfer.
bal'dio/a adj fallow, uncultivated // m waste land.
baleeira [balɪ'ejra] f whaleboat; **baleeiro** m whaler; **baleia** f whale.
ba'lido m bleating; (um só) bleat.
ba'liza f (estaca) post; (bóia) buoy; (luminosa) beacon; (esporte) goal.
balne'ário m spa, bathing resort.
ba'lofo/a adj (fofo) fluffy; (inchado) puffed up.
balouçar [balo'sax] vt/i (Pt) to swing, sway; **baloiço** m, **balouço** m (de criança) swing; (ação) swinging.
balsa ['bawsa] f raft; (barca) ferry.
'bálsamo m balsam, balm.
'báltico/a adj Baltic // m: **o B~** the Baltic.
balu'arte m rampart, bulwark.
'bamba m/f, adj expert.
'bambo/a adj slack, loose.
bambole'ar vt to swing // vi (pessoa) to sway, totter; (coisa) to wobble.
bam'bu m bamboo.
ba'nana f banana; **bananeira** f banana tree.
'banca f (de trabalho) bench; (escritório) office; (jogo) bank; **~ de jornais** newsstand; **bancada** f row of seats.
ban'cário/a adj bank, banking // m/f banker.
bancar'rota f bankruptcy; **ir à ~** to go bankrupt.

'banco *m (assento)* bench; *(COM)* bank; ~ **de areia** sandbank; ~ **de coral** coral reef.

'banda *f (músicos, grupo, lista)* band; *(lado)* side; *(cinto)* sash; ~ **desenhada** *(Pt)* cartoon; **à** ~ to one side; **pôr de** ~ to put aside.

bandeira [bã'dejra] *f* flag; *(estandarte)* banner; **bandeirante** *m* pioneer; **bandeirinha** *m (esporte)* linesman.

bandeja [bã'deʒa] *f* tray.

ban'dido *m* bandit, outlaw.

'bando *m* band; *(grupo)* group; *(de malfeitores)* gang; *(de ovelhas)* flock; *(de gado)* herd.

bandoleiro [bãdo'lejru] *m* robber, bandit.

banha ['bãɲa] *f* fat; *(de porco)* lard.

banhar [ba'ɲax] *vt (dar banho a)* to bath; *(mergulhar)* to dip; *(lavar)* to wash, bathe; ~**-se** *vr (em banheira)* to have a bath; *(no mar)* to bathe, go for a swim; **banheira** *f* bath; **banheiro** *m* bathroom; *(Pt)* lifeguard; **banhista** *m/f* bather.

banho ['bãɲu] *m (na banheira)* bath; *(de mar)* bathe; *(mergulho)* dip; *(de tinta)* coating; ~ **de sol** sunbathing; ~ **de chuveiro** shower; **tomar** ~ to have a bath; *(de chuveiro)* to have a shower; ~**s de casamento** marriage banns.

banho-maria [baɲu-ma'ria] *m (CULIN)* bain-marie, steamer.

ba'nir *vt* to banish.

banqueiro [bã'kejru] *m* banker; *(diretor)* bank manager.

banquete [bã'ketʃi] *m* banquet, feast.

ban'zar *vt* to surprise, astonish // *vi* to ponder, muse.

banzé [bã'zɛ] *m (col)* rumpus, racket.

baque ['baki] *m* thud, thump; *(contratempo)* disaster.

bar *m* bar; *(estabelecimento)* public house, pub.

bara'funda *f* uproar, tumult.

baralhar [bara'ʎax] *vt (cartas)* to shuffle; *(fig)* to mix up, confuse; **baralho** *m* pack of cards.

barão [ba'rãw] *m* baron.

ba'rata *f* cockroach.

barate'ar *vt* to cut the price of; *(menosprezar)* to belittle; **barato/a** *adj* cheap, inexpensive // *adv* cheaply.

'barba *f* beard; ~**s** *fpl* whiskers; **fazer a** ~ to have a shave.

bar'bante *m (Br)* string.

barbari'dade *f* barbarity, cruelty; *(disparate)* nonsense; **que** ~**!** good heavens!; **barbarismo** *m* barbarism; **bárbaro/a** *adj (cruel)* cruel, savage; *(grosseiro)* rough, crude; *(bacana)* great // *m/f* barbarian.

barba'tana *f* fin.

barbe'ador *m* razor; *(elétrico)* shaver; **barbearia** *f* barber's (shop); **barbeiro** *m* barber.

'barca *f* barge; *(de travessia)* ferry; **barcaça** *f* barge.

'barco *m* boat; *(grande)* ship; ~ **a motor**

motorboat; ~ **a vela** sailing boat; ~ **de remos** rowing boat.

'bardo *m* bard, poet.

barganha [bax'gaɲa] *f* barter, swap; **barganhar** *vt* to swap.

barla'vento *m (NÁUT)* windward; **a** ~ to windward.

ba'rômetro *m* barometer.

baro'nesa *f* baroness.

barqueiro [bax'kejru] *m* boatman.

barra ['baxa] *f* bar, rod; *(faixa)* strip; *(traço)* stroke; *(alavanca)* lever.

bar'raca *f (tenda)* tent; *(de feira)* stall; *(de madeira)* hut; **barracão** *m (tenda)* marquee; *(de madeira)* shed.

barragem [ba'xaʒẽj] *f (represa)* dam; *(impedimento)* barrier.

bar'ranco *m* ravine, gully.

barreira [ba'xejra] *f* barrier; *(cerca)* fence; ~ **do som** sound barrier.

bar'rento/a *adj* muddy.

bar'rete *(Pt)* *m* cap.

barri'cada *f* barricade.

bar'riga *f* belly; ~ **da perna** calf; **fazer** ~ to bulge.

barril [ba'xiw] *m* barrel, cask.

'barro *m* clay; *(lama)* mud.

bar'roco/a *(-axo-]* *adj* baroque; *(ornamentado)* extravagant.

bar'rote *m* beam.

barulhento/a [baru'ʎẽtu/a] *adj* noisy, rowdy; **barulho** *m (ruído)* noise, row; *(tumulto)* din, rumpus.

base ['bazi] *f* base; *(fig)* basis; **sem** ~ groundless; **basear** *vt* to base; **basear-se** *vr*: **basear-se em** to be based on.

básico/a ['baziku/a] *adj* basic.

basquete [baʃ'ketʃi], **basquete'bol** *m* basketball.

bas'tante *adj (suficiente)* enough; *(muito)* quite a lot (of) // *adv (suficientemente)* enough; *(muito)* quite.

bastão [baʃ'tãw] *m* stick.

bas'tar *vi* to be enough, be sufficient; ~ **para** to be enough to; ~**-se** *vr* to be self-sufficient; **basta!** (that's) enough!

bas'tardo/a *adj, m/f* bastard.

basti'dor *m* frame; ~**es** *mpl (teatro)* wings; **nos** ~**es** behind the scenes.

'basto/a *adj (espesso)* thick; *(denso)* dense.

'bata *f (roupão de mulher)* dressing gown; *(de médico)* overall.

batalha [ba'taʎa] *f* battle; **batalhão** *m* battalion; **batalhar** *vi* to battle, fight.

ba'tata *f* potato; ~ **doce** sweet potato; ~**s fritas** chips, French fries *(US)*; **batatinha frita** *f* crisps *pl*.

batedeira [bate'dejra] *f* beater; *(elétrico)* mixer; *(de manteiga)* churn; **batedor** *m* beater; *(polícia)* escort; *(no criquete)* batsman.

'bátega *f* downpour.

ba'tente *m* doorpost; *(aldrava)* knocker; *(col)* job; **no** ~ at work.

bate-'papo *m (Br)* chat.

ba'ter *vt (derrotar, dar pancadas em)* to beat; *(horas)* to strike; *(o pé)* to stamp;

(*trigo*) to thresh; (*porta*) to slam; (*explorar*) to search; (*ovos*) to beat; ~ **uma chapa** to take a picture; ~ **palmas** to clap; ~ **a carteira de alguém** to pick sb's pocket; ~ **um papo** (*Br*) to have a chat // *vi*: ~ **à porta** to knock at the door; **~-se** *vr* to fight.

bate'ria *f* battery; (*MÚS*) percussion; ~ **de cozinha** kitchen utensils *pl*.

ba'tido/a *adj* beaten; (*gasto*) worn, shabby // *m*: ~ **de leite** (*Pt*) milkshake // *f* beat; (*da porta*) slam; (*à porta*) knock; (*da polícia*) raid; (*colisão*) bump; (*bebida*) brandy cocktail.

ba'tina *f* (*REL*) cassock.

ba'tismo (*Pt*: **-pt-**) *m* baptism, christening; **batizar** (*Pt*: **-pt-**) *vt* to baptize, christen; (*vinho*) to dilute.

'batom *m* lipstick.

ba'tucada *f* dance percussion group.

ba'tuta *f* baton.

ba'ú *m* trunk.

baunilha [baw'niʎa] *f* vanilla.

ba'zar *m* bazaar.

ba'zófia *f* boasting, bragging.

beatifi'car *vt* to beatify, bless; **beato/a** *adj* blessed // *f* overpious woman; (*hipócrita*) hypocrite.

bebê [be'be] (*Pt*: **-ê**) *m* baby.

bebedeira [bebe'dejra] *f* (*estado de bêbedo*) drunkenness; **tomar uma** ~ to get drunk; **bêbedo/a** *adj*, *m/f* drunk; **bebedor(a)** *m/f* drinker; (*ébrio*) drunkard; **bebedouro** *m* drinking fountain.

be'ber *vt* to drink; (*absorver*) to drink up, soak up // *vi* to drink; **bebida** *f* drink.

beco ['beku] *m* alley, lane; ~ **sem saída** cul-de-sac.

bedelho [be'deʎu] *m* latch; **meter o** ~ **em** to poke one's nose into.

beiço ['bejsu] *m* lip; **fazer** ~ to pout; **beiçudo/a** *adj* thick-lipped.

beija-flor [bejʒa-'flɔx] *m* hummingbird.

beijar [bej'ʒax] *vt* to kiss; **~-se** *vr* to kiss (one another); **beijo** *m* kiss.

beira ['bejra] *f* (*borda*) edge; (*do rio*) bank; (*orla*) border; ~ **do telhado** eaves; **à** ~ **de** on the edge of; (*ao lado de*) beside, by; (*fig*) on the verge of.

beira-mar [bejra-'max] *f* seaside.

beirar [bej'rax] *vt* (*ficar ao lado de*) to be at the edge of; (*caminhar ao lado de*) to skirt.

beisebol [bejsi'bɔw] *m* baseball.

belas-artes [bɛlaz-'axtʃis] *fpl* fine arts.

beldade [bew'dadʒi], **beleza** [be'leza] *f* beauty; **que beleza!** how lovely!

belga ['bɛwga] *adj*, *m/f* Belgian; **Bélgica** *f* Belgium.

beliche [be'liʃi] *m* bunk.

beliscão [belis'kãw] *m* pinch; **beliscar** *vt* to pinch, nip; (*a comida*) to nibble.

'belo/a *adj* beautiful, lovely.

bem [bɛj] *adv* well; (*muito*) very; (*certamente*) quite; (*cheirar*) good, nice; ~ **ali** right there; ~ **duas horas** a

good two hours // *conj*: ~ **como** as well as // *m* (*ventura*, *utilidade*) good; (*amado*) love; **o** ~ **público** public welfare; **bens** *mpl* goods; **bens de consumo** consumer goods.

bem-aven'turado/a *adj* fortunate.

bem-criado/a [bẽj-kri'adu/a] *adj* well-bred, well-mannered.

bem-disposto/a [bẽj-dʒiʃ'poʃtu/a] *adj* in a good mood.

bem-estar [bẽj-iʃ'tax] *m* comfort, well-being.

bem-me-quer [bẽj-me-'kex] *m* daisy.

bem-vindo/a [bẽj-'vĩdu/a] *adj* welcome.

bênção ['bẽsãw] *f* blessing; **bendito/a** *adj* blessed; **bendizer** *vt* (*louvar*) to praise; (*abençoar*) to bless.

benefi'cência *f* (*bondade*) kindness; (*caridade*) charity.

benefici'ar *vt* (*favorecer*) to benefit; (*melhorar*) to improve; **benefício** *m* (*proveito*) benefit, profit; (*favor*) favour; **benéfico/a** *adj* (*benigno*) beneficial; (*generoso*) generous; (*favorável*) favourable.

bene'mérito/a *adj* (*digno*) worthy; (*ilustre*) distinguished // *m/f* (*pessoa distinta*) distinguished person.

bene'plácito *m* consent, approval.

benevo'lência *f* benevolence, kindness; **benévolo/a** *adj* benevolent, kind.

benfeitor(a) [bẽfej'tox(ra)] *m* benefactor // *f* benefactress.

ben'gala *f* walking stick.

benigni'dade *f* kindness; **benigno/a** *adj* (*bondoso*) kind; (*agradável*) pleasant; (*MED*) benign.

benquisto/a [bẽ'kiʃtu/a] *adj* well-loved, well-liked.

bens *mpl ver* **bem**.

'bento/a *pp irr de* **benzer** // *adj* holy.

benzedeiro/a [bẽzi'dejru/a] *m* sorcerer // *f* sorceress.

ben'zer *vt* to bless; **~-se** *vr* to cross o.s.

'berço *m* cradle; (*lugar de nascimento*) birthplace.

berin'jela [berĩ'ʒela] *f* aubergine, eggplant (*US*).

'berma *f* (*Pt*) hard shoulder, berm (*US*).

ber'rante *adj* flashy, gaudy.

ber'rar *vi* to bellow; (*criança*) to bawl.

besouro [be'zoru] *m* beetle.

'besta *adj* (*tolo*) stupid // *f* (*animal*) beast; (*pessoa*) fool, ass; ~ **de carga** beast of burden; ~ **fera** wild beast; **besteira** [bes'tejra] *f* nonsense, rubbish; **dizer ~s** to talk nonsense.

besti'al [-aw] *adj* bestial; (*repugnante*) repulsive; **~idade** *f* bestiality, brutality.

besun'tar *vt* to smear, daub.

betão [bɔ'tãw] *m* (*Pt*) concrete.

beter'raba [-exa-] *f* beetroot.

be'tume *m* asphalt; (*para colar vidros*) putty.

bexiga [be'ʃiga] *f* (*órgão*) bladder; (*doença*) smallpox; **~s** *fpl* (*sinais*) pock marks.

bezerro/a [be'zexu/a] *m* calf // *f* heifer.

'Bíblia *f* Bible; **bíblico/a** *adj* biblical.

bibliogra'fia *f* bibliography.

biblio'teca *f* library; (*estante*) bookcase; **bibliotecário/a** *m/f* librarian.

'bica *f* spout; (*Pt*) black coffee (*expresso*); **estar na ~** to be about to happen.

bi'cada *f* peck; **bicar** *vt* to peck; (*comida*) to pick at.

bicha ['biʃa] *f* (*lombriga*) worm; (*Pt: fila*) queue; (*Br: homosexual*) gay.

bicho ['biʃu] *m* animal; (*inseto*) insect, bug; (*calouro*) fresher; **matar o ~** to wet one's whistle.

bici'cleta *f* bicycle; (*col*) bike; **andar de ~** to cycle.

'bico *m* (*de ave*) beak; (*ponta*) point; (*de chaleira*) spout; (*boca*) mouth; (*de pena*) nib; (*do peito*) nipple; (*de gás*) jet; **calar o ~** to shut up.

bi'dê [-e] (*Pt: -ê* [-ɛ]) *m* bidet.

bi'ela *f* piston rod.

'bife *m* (beef) steak.

bifurcação [bifuxka'sãw] *f* fork; **bifurcar-se** *vr* to fork, divide.

'bígamo/a *adj* bigamous // *m/f* bigamist.

bi'gode *m* moustache.

bi'gorna *f* anvil.

bijuteria [biʒute'ria] *f* jewellery.

bilha ['biʎa] *f* (*Pt*) jug, jar.

bilhar [bi'ʎax] *m* (*jogo*) billiards *sg*.

bilhete [bi'ʎetʃi] *m* (*entrada, loteria*) ticket; (*cartinha*) note; **~ de ida** single ticket; **~ de ida e volta** return ticket; **~ postal** postcard; **~ de plataforma** platform ticket; **bilheteira** *f* (*Pt*) ticket office; **bilheteiro/a** *m/f* ticket seller; **bilheteria** *f* ticket office; booking office; (*teatro*) box office.

bilíngüe [bi'lĩgwi] *adj* bilingual.

bili'oso/a *adj* bilious, liverish; **bílis** *m* bile; (*fig*) bad temper.

bimen'sal [-aw] *adj* twice-monthly.

bi'nóculo *m* binoculars *pl*; (*para teatro*) opera glasses *pl*.

biogra'fia *f* biography; **biógrafo/a** *m/f* biographer.

biolo'gia *f* biology; **biologista** *m/f* biologist.

bi'ombo *m* (*tapume*) screen.

birra ['bixa] *f* (*teima*) wilfulness, obstinacy; (*aversão*) aversion; **ter ~ com** to dislike, detest.

bis *excl* encore!

bi'sagra *f* hinge.

bisavô/ó [biza'vo/ɔ] *m* great-grandfather // *f* great-grandmother.

bisbilhotar [biʒbiʎo'tax] *vt* to pry into // *vi* to gossip; **bisbilhotice** *f* gossip.

biscoito [biʃ'kojtu] *m* biscuit, cracker (*US*).

bisonho/a [bi'zoɲu/a] *adj* inexperienced // *m* raw recruit.

bis'pado *m* bishopric; **bispo** *m* bishop.

bissexto/a [bi'sɛʃtu/a] *adj*: **ano ~** leap year.

bistu'ri *m* scalpel.

bi'tola *f* gauge; (*padrão*) pattern; (*estalão*) standard.

biva'car *vi* to bivouac; **bivaque** *m* bivouac.

bizar'ria [-axi-] *f* (*galantaria*) gallantry; (*elegância*) elegance; (*pompa*) pomp; **bizarro/a** *adj* (*nobre*) gallant; (*elegante*) elegant, handsome; (*esquisito*) bizarre.

blan'dícia *f* endearment; (*carícia*) caress.

blasfe'mar *vt/i* to blaspheme, curse; **blasfêmia** *f* blasphemy; (*ultraje*) swearing; **blasfemo/a** *adj* blasphemous // *m/f* blasphemer.

blin'dado/a *adj* armoured; **blindagem** *f* armour(-plating).

'bloco *m* block; (*político*) bloc; (*de escrever*) writing pad; **~ de carnaval** carnival troupe; **~ de cilindros** cylinder block.

bloquear [bloki'ax] *vt* to blockade; **bloqueio** *m* blockade.

'blusa *f* (*de mulher*) blouse; **~ de lã** cardigan, pullover; **blusão** *m* jacket.

'boa *f* boa constrictor // *adj ver* **bom**.

bo'ate *f* nightclub.

bo'ato *m* rumour.

bobagem [bo'baʒẽ] *f*, **bobice** [bo'bisi] *f* silliness, nonsense; **deixe de bobagens!** stop being silly!

bo'bina *f* (*para fio*) bobbin; (*ELET*) coil; (*foto*) spool.

'bobo/a *adj* silly, daft // *m/f* fool; **fazer-se de ~** to act the fool // *m* (*de corte*) jester.

boca ['boka] *f* mouth; (*abertura*) opening, entrance; **à ~ pequena** in whispers; **de ~ aberta** open-mouthed, amazed.

bocadinho [boka'dʒiɲu] *m* (*pouco tempo*) a little while; (*pouquinho*) a little bit; **bocado** *m* (*quantidade na boca*) mouthful, bite; (*pedaço*) piece, bit; (*de tempo*) a short while.

bocal [bo'kaw] *m* (*de vaso*) mouth; (*de aparelho*) mouthpiece; (*de cano*) nozzle.

boçal [bo'saw] *adj* stupid, ignorant.

bocejar [bose'ʒax] *vi* to yawn; **bocejo** *m* yawn.

bochecha [bo'ʃeʃa] *f* cheek.

'boda *f* wedding; **~s** *fpl* wedding anniversary *sg*; **~s de prata/ouro** silver/golden wedding *sg*.

bode ['bɔdʒi] *m* goat; **~ expiatório** scapegoat.

bo'dega *f* tavern; (*coisa sem valor*) rubbish.

bofe'tada *f* slap; **bofetão** *m* punch.

boi [boj] *m* ox.

bóia ['bɔja] *f* buoy; (*col*) meal.

bo'iada *f* herd of cattle.

boião [bo'jãw] *m* jar, pot.

boiar [bo'jax] *vt/i* to float.

boico'tar *vt* to boycott; **boicote** *m* boycott.

boieiro [bo'jejru] *m* herdsman.

boina ['bojna] *f* beret.

'bojo *m* (*saliência*) bulge; (*capacidade*)

ability; **bojudo/a** adj bulging; (barrigudo) pot-bellied.

bola ['bɔla] f ball; ~ **de futebol** football; ~ **de gude** marble; ~ **de sabão** soap bubble; **ora ~s!** rubbish!

bolacha [bo'laʃa] f biscuit; (col: bofetada) slap.

bo'lar vt to think up.

boleia [bo'leja] f driver's seat; **dar uma** ~ (Pt) to give a lift.

boletim [bolɛ'tʃĩ] m report; ~ **meteorológico** weather forecast.

bolha ['boʎa] f (na pele) blister; (de ar, sabão) bubble.

boliche [bo'liʃi] m (jogo) bowling, skittles sg.

'Bolívia f Bolivia; **boliviano/a** adj, m/f Bolivian.

bolo ['bolu] m cake; **dar o** ~ to fail to turn up.

bolor [bo'lox] m mould; (nas plantas) mildew; (bafio) mustiness.

bo'lota f acorn.

bolsa ['bowsa] f (saco) bag; (para dinheiro) purse; (de estudos) grant; (COM) stock exchange.

'bolso m pocket.

bom/boa [bõ/'boa] adj good; (bondoso) nice, kind; (MED) well; (tempo) fine; **um** ~ **quarto de hora** a good quarter of an hour; **essa é boa!** that's a good one!; **metido numa boa** in a tight spot; **estar numa boa** (col) to be doing fine; **boa-noite** (ao encontrar-se) goodnight; **boa-tarde** good afternoon, good evening; **boas vindas!** welcome! // excl: ~ ! right!

bomba f (MIL) bomb; (TEC) pump; ~ **atômica/de fumaça/relógio** atomic/smoke/time bomb; ~ **de gasolina** petrol station; ~ **de incêndio** fire engine; **levar** ~ (em exame) to fail.

bombarde'ar vt to bomb, bombard; (fig) to bombard; **bombardeio** m bombing, bombardment.

bombe'ar vt to pump.

bombeiro [bõ'bejru] m fireman; (Br: encanador) plumber; **o corpo de ~s** fire brigade.

bombom ['bõbõ] m sweet.

bom'bordo m (NÁUT) port.

bo'nança f (no mar) fair weather; (fig) calm.

bon'dade f goodness, kindness; **tenha a** ~ **de vir** would you please come.

'bonde m (Br) tram.

bon'doso/a adj kind, good.

bo'né m (chapéu) cap.

bo'neca f doll.

bo'nina f (Pt) daisy.

bo'nito/a adj (belo) pretty; (agradável) nice // m (peixe) tunny.

boquiaberto/a [bokɪa'bɛxtu/a] adj dumbfounded, gaping.

boquilha [bo'kɪʎa] f cigarette holder.

borboleta [boxbo'leta] f butterfly; (Br: roleta) turnstile; **borboletear** vi to flutter, flit.

borbotão [boxbo'tãw] m gush, spurt; **sair aos borbotões** to gush out; **borbotar** vt to pour forth // vi to gush out.

borbulhar [boxbu'ʎax] vi (líquido fervendo) to bubble; (brotar) to sprout; (jorrar) to gush out.

'borco m: **de** ~ (coisa) upside down; (pessoa) face down.

'borda f edge; (do rio) bank; **à** ~ **de** on the edge of.

bor'dado m embroidery.

bordão [box'dãw] m staff; (MÚS) bass string; (arrimo) support.

bor'dar vt to embroider.

bordejar [boxde'ʒax] vi (NÁUT) to tack; (cambalear) to stagger; **bordo** m (ao bordejar) tack; (de navio) side; **a bordo** on board.

'borla f tassel.

bor'nal m haversack.

'borra [-ɔxa] f dregs pl.

borracha [bo'xaʃa] f rubber.

borracho/a [bo'xaʃu/a] adj drunk // m/f drunk(ard).

borrador [boxa'dox] m (caderno) note book; (COM) day book.

borralho [bo'xaʎu] m embers pl; (fig) hearth, fireside.

borrão [bo'xãw] m (escritura) rough draft; (mancha) blot; (esboço) sketch; **borrar** vt to blot; (riscar) to cross out; (pintar) to daub.

bor'rasca f storm; (no mar) squall; **borrascoso/a** adj stormy.

bor'rego m (Pt) lamb.

borri'far vt to sprinkle // vi (chuviscar) to drizzle; **borrifo** m spray; (chuvisco) drizzle.

bosque ['bɔʃkɪ] m wood, forest.

bosquejar [boʃke'ʒax] vt to sketch; **bosquejo** m sketch.

'bossa f (inchaço) swelling; (no crânio) bump; (corcova) hump; **ter** ~ **para** to have an aptitude for.

'bosta f dung.

'bota f boot; ~**s de borracha** wellingtons.

bota-'fora f (despedida) send-off; (de navio) launching.

botânico/a [bo'tãnɪku/a] adj botanical // m/f botanist // f botany.

botão [bo'tãw] m button; (flor) bud.

bo'tar vt to put, place; (Pt: lançar) to throw; ~ **fora** to throw away; ~ **a língua** to stick out one's tongue; ~ **ovos** to lay eggs.

'bote m (barco) boat; (com arma) thrust; (salto) spring; **de um** ~ at one stroke.

botequim [botɛ'kĩ] m bar, café.

bo'tica f pharmacy, chemist's (shop); **boticário/a** m/f pharmacist, chemist.

botija [bo'tʃiʒa] f (earthenware) jug.

'boto/a adj (embotado) blunt; (rombo) dull, stupid.

botoeira [bo'twejra] f button-hole.

boxe ['bɔksɪ] m boxing; ~**ador** m boxer.

bra'beza f wildness; **brabo/a** adj (cavalo) wild; (feroz) fierce.

'braça f (NÁUT) fathom.

bra'çada f armful; (natação) stroke.

bracejar [brasε'ʒax] vi to wave one's arms about.

'braço m arm; (trabalhador) hand; ~ direito (fig) right-hand man; a ~s com struggling with; de ~s cruzados with arms folded; (fig) without lifting a finger; de ~ dado arm-in-arm.

bra'dar vi to shout, yell; **brado** m shout, yell.

braguilha [bra'gıʎa] f flies pl.

bra'mido m bellow, roar; **bramir** vi to bellow, roar.

'branco/a adj white // f white woman // m white man; (espaço) blank; **em** ~ (in) blank; **brancura** f whiteness.

bran'dir vt to brandish.

'brando/a adj (mole) soft; (meigo) gentle, mild; **brandura** f (moleza) softness; (mansidão) gentleness, mildness; **branduras** fpl (carícias) caresses.

branquear [brãkı'ax] vt to whiten; (caiar) to whitewash; (alvejar) to bleach // vi to turn white.

'brasa f hot coal; **em** ~ red-hot; **estar sobre** ~s to be on tenterhooks.

brasão [bra'zãw] m coat of arms; (fig) glory.

braseiro [bra'zejru] m brazier.

Bra'sil [-ıw] m Brazil; **brasileiro/a** adj, m/f Brazilian.

bra'vata f bravado, boasting; **bravatear** vi to boast, brag.

braveza [bra'veza] f (ferocidade) fierceness; (coragem) courage.

bra'vio/a adj (selvagem) wild, untamed.

'bravo/a adj (corajoso) brave; (furioso) angry; (tempestuoso) rough, stormy // m brave man // excl: ~! well done!; **bravura** f courage, bravery.

'breca f: com a ~ ! damn it!; **ser levado da** ~ to be naughty.

bre'car vt (carro) to stop; (reprimir) to curb // vi to brake.

brecha ['brεʃa] f breach; (abertura) opening; (dano) damage; (meio de escapar) loophole.

brejeiro/a [bre'ʒejru/a] adj naughty, mischievous.

brejo ['brεʒu] m marsh, swamp.

brenha ['brεɲa] f (mata) dense wood; (enredamento) tangle, maze.

'breque m (freio) brake.

breu [brew] m tar, pitch; **escuro como** ~ pitch black.

'breve adj short; (leve) light; (rápido) brief; **em** ~ soon, shortly; **para ser** ~ to be brief; **até** ~ see you soon.

brevi'dade f brevity, shortness.

'briga f (luta) fight; (disputa) quarrel.

bri'gada f brigade.

brigão/ona [brı'gãw/ona] adj quarrelsome // m/f brawler, trouble-

maker; **brigar** vi (lutar) to fight; (disputar) to quarrel; (destoar) to clash.

brilhante [brı'ʎãtʃı] adj brilliant // m diamond; **brilhar** vi to shine; **brilho** m (luz viva) brilliance; (esplendor) splendour; (nos sapatos) shine.

brincadeira [brıka'dejra] f (divertimento) fun; (gracejo) joke; **deixe de** ~s! stop fooling!; **fora de** ~ joking apart; **de** ~ for fun; **brincalhão/hona** adj playful // m/f joker, teaser.

brin'car vi (divertir-se) to play, have fun; (gracejar) to joke; **estou brincando** I'm only kidding; ~ **de soldados** to play (at) soldiers; **brinco** m (jóia) earring; (brincadeira) play, fun; (brinquedo) toy.

brin'dar vt (beber) to drink a toast to; (presentear) to give a present to; **brinde** m (saudação) toast; (presente) gift, present.

brinquedo [brı'kedu] m toy.

'brio m (orgulho) pride; (coragem) courage; (ânimo) spirit; **brioso/a** adj (valente) brave; (orgulhoso) proud.

'brisa f breeze.

bri'tânico/a adj British // m/f Briton.

'broca f drill; **brocar** vt to drill, bore.

brocha ['brɔʃa] f (prego) tack.

broche ['brɔʃı] m brooch.

brochura [bro'ʃura] f (de livro) binding; (folheto) brochure, pamphlet.

'brócoli (Pt : **'brócolos**) m broccoli sg.

'bronco/a adj (tosco) rough; (ignorante) ignorant, rough; (rude) coarse // f: **dar uma** ~a to tell off.

bronquite [brõ'kıtʃı] f bronchitis.

'bronze m bronze; ~**ado/a** adj (da cor do bronze) bronze; (pelo sol) suntanned // m suntan.

bronze'ar vt to tan; ~-**se** vr to get a tan.

broquear [brɔkı'ax] vt to drill, bore.

bro'tar vt to produce // vi (manar) to flow; (BOT) to sprout; (nascer) to spring up; **broto** m bud; (fig) youngster.

'broxa f (large) paint brush.

bruços ['brusuʃ]: **de** ~ adv face down.

'bruma f mist, haze; **brumoso/a** adj misty, hazy.

bru'nido/a adj polished; **brunir** vt to polish.

'brusco/a adj brusque; (áspero) rough; (súbito) sudden.

bru'tal [-aw] adj brutal; ~**idade** f brutality.

'bruto/a adj brutish; (grosseiro) coarse; (diamante) uncut; (petróleo) crude; (peso) gross; **em** ~ raw, in the rough // m brute.

bruxa ['bruʃa] f witch; (velha feia) hag; ~**ria** f witchcraft.

Bruxelas [bru'ʃelaʃ] f Brussels.

bruxo ['bruʃo] m magician, wizard.

bruxulear [bruʃul'ax] vi to flicker.

bucha ['buʃa] f wad; ~ **de pão** hunk of bread.

bucho ['buʃu] m stomach.

'buço m down.

bu'dismo *m* Buddhism.

bu'far *vi* to puff, pant; (*com raiva*) to snort.

bufê [bu'fe], bu'fete *m* (*móvel*) sideboard; (*restaurante*) snack bar, buffet bar.

'bufo/a *adj* burlesque // *m* puff; (*palhaço*) buffoon.

bugiganga [buʒi'gãga] *f* trinket; ~s *fpl* knicknacks.

bugio [bu'ʒiu] *m* monkey, ape.

bujão [bu'ʒãw] *m* (*TEC*) cap; ~ de gas gas cylinder.

'bula *f* (*REL*) papal bull; (*MED*) directions for use.

'bulbo *m* bulb.

'bule *m* (*de chá/café*) tea/coffee pot.

bulha [bu'ʎa] *f* (*ruído*) row, noise.

bu'lício *m* (*agitação*) bustle; (*sussurro*) rustling; buliçoso/a *adj* (*vivo*) lively; (*movediço*) restless; (*desenvolto*) boisterous.

bu'lir *vt* to move // *vi* to move, stir; ~ em to touch, meddle with.

'bunda *f* (*col*) bottom, backside.

buquê [bu'ke] *m* bouquet.

bu'raco *m* hole; (*de agulha*) eye.

burburejar [buxburc'ʒax] *vi* (*água etc*) to bubble.

burguês/guesa [bux'geʃ/'geza] *adj* middle-class, bourgeois; burguesia *f* middle class, bourgeoisie.

bu'ril *m* chisel; burilar *vt* to chisel.

'burla *f* trick, fraud; (*zombaria*) mockery; burlar *vt* (*enganar*) to cheat; (*defraudar*) to swindle; (*a lei*) to evade.

burocra'cia *f* bureaucracy; (*excessiva*) red tape; burocrata *m/f* bureaucrat.

burra ['buxa] *f* (*cofre*) safe; (*animal*) she-donkey; (*pessoa*) silly ass, idiot; burrice *f* (*estupidez*) stupidity; (*asneira*) silliness; burro *m* donkey; (*pessoa*) silly ass, idiot; burro/a *adj* stupid.

'busca *f* search; em ~ de in search of; buscar *vt* to look for, search for; ir buscar to fetch, go for; mandar buscar to send for.

'bússola *f* compass.

'busto *m* bust.

bu'zina *f* horn; buzinada *f* toot, hoot; buzinar *vi* to toot, hoot.

'búzio *m* (*concha*) conch; (*corneta*) horn.

C

cá *adv* here, over here; para ~ this way; para lá e para ~ back and forth.

caa'tinga *f* (*Br*) scrub(-land).

ca'baça *f* gourd.

ca'bal [-aw] *adj* (*perfeito*) perfect; (*completo*) complete; (*exato*) exact.

ca'bala *f* (*maquinação*) conspiracy, intrigue; cabalar *vt* (*votos etc*) to canvass (for) // *vi* to plot.

ca'bana *f* hut, shack.

caba'ré *m* (*boate*) night club.

ca'beça *f* (*ANAT*) head; (*inteligência*) intelligence; (*parte mais alta*) top // *m* leader, head.

cabe'çada *f* (*pancada com cabeça*) butt; (*inclinação da cabeça*) nod; (*asneira*) blunder; dar ~s to nod.

cabeçalho [kabe'saʎu] *m* (*de jornal*) headline; (*de livro*) title page; (*título*) title.

cabecear [kabesı'ax] *vt* (*futebol*) to head // *vi* to nod.

cabeceira [kabe'sejra] *f* (*de cama*) head; (*de sepultura*) headstone.

cabe'çudo/a *adj* (*teimoso*) obstinate.

cabeleira [kabe'ʎejra] *f* head of hair; (*postiça*) wig; cabeleireiro/a *m/f* hairdresser; cabelo *m* hair; cabeludo/a *adj* hairy.

ca'ber *vi* (*poder entrar*) to fit, go; cabe a você falar com ele it is up to you to speak to him; cabe-me dizer que I have to say that; não cabe aqui fazer comentários this is not the time or place to comment.

ca'bide *m* (*móvel*) rack; (*gancho*) peg; (*guarda-roupa*) coat hanger.

cabi'mento *m* suitability; ter ~ to be acceptable.

ca'bine *f* cabin; ~ do piloto (*AER*) cockpit; ~ telefônica telephone booth.

cabisbaixo/a [kabiʃ'bajʃu/a] *adj* dispirited, crestfallen.

'cabo *m* (*extremidade*) end; (*de faca, vassoura etc*) handle; (*corda*) rope; (*elétrico etc*) cable; (*GEO*) cape; (*MIL*) corporal; ao ~ de at the end of; de ~ a rabo from end to end; levar a ~ to carry out; dar ~ de to put an end to.

ca'boclo/a (*Br*) *m/f* (*cariboca*) half-breed // *m* (*sertanejo*) backwoodsman; (*habitante do sertão*) peasant(-farmer).

cabo'grama *m* cable(gram).

'cabra *f* goat; ~ cega blind man's buff // *m* (*Br: mulato*) half-caste; (: *capanga*) hired gunhand.

cabreiro/a [ka'brejru/a] *adj* (*col*) suspicious.

ca'bresto *m* (*de cavalos*) halter.

cabri'ola *f* leap.

ca'brito *m* (*ger*) kid.

cabrocha [ka'brɔʃa] *f* mulatto girl.

'caça *f* (*ger*) hunting; (*busca*) hunt; (*animal*) quarry, game; à ~ de in pursuit of // *m* (*AER*) fighter (plane); caçada *f* (*jornada de caçadores*) hunting trip; (*produto de caça*) kill; caçador(a) *m/f* hunter // *m* (*MIL*) rifleman.

ca'çamba *f* (*balde*) bucket.

caça-'minas *m* minesweeper.

ca'çar *vt* to hunt; (*com espingarda*) to shoot.

cacarejar [kakare'ʒax] *vi* (*galinhas etc*) to cackle.

caça'rola *f* (*Pt*) (sauce)pan.

cacau [ka'kaw] *m* cocoa; (*BOT*) cacao.

cacete [ka'setʃı] *adj* tiresome, boring // *m/f* bore // *m* club, stick.

cachaça [ka'ʃasa] *f* (white) rum.

cachecol [kaʃe'kɔw] *m* neck scarf.

cachimbo [ka'ʃĩmbu] *m* pipe.

cacho ['kaʃu] *m* bunch; (*de cabelo*) curl, ringlet.

cachoeira [kaʃ'wejra] *f* waterfall.

cachopa [ka'ʃopa] *f* (*Pt*) girl, lass; **cachopo** *m* (*Pt*) lad.

cachorra [ka'ʃoxa] *f* bitch; (*Pt*) (female) puppy; **cachorrinho/a** *m/f* puppy; **cachorro** *m* dog; (*Pt*) puppy; (*filhote de animal*) cub; (*patife*) rascal; **cachorro quente** hot dog.

cacimba [ka'sĩmba] *f* (*poço*) waterhole; (*chuva miúda*) drizzle.

cacique [ka'siki] *m* chief; (*mandachuva*) local boss.

'caco *m* bit, fragment.

caço'ar *vt* to mock, ridicule // *vi* to joke, jest.

caçoula [ka'sola] *f* pan; (*vaso*) dish.

'cacto *m* cactus.

ca'çula *m/f* youngest child.

'cada *adj inv* each; (*todo*) every; ~ **qual** each one; ~ **semana** each week; ~ **vez mais** more and more; ~ **vez mais barato** cheaper and cheaper.

cada'falso *m* (*forca*) gallows; (*andaime*) scaffold.

ca'dastro *m* (*registro*) register; (*de criminosos*) criminal record.

ca'dáver *m* corpse, dead body.

ca'dê *adv* (*col*) ~ ...? where's ...?, what's happened to ...?

cade'ado *m* padlock.

cadeia [ka'deja] *f* chain; (*prisão*) prison; (*rede*) network.

cadeira [ka'dejra] *f* (*móvel*) chair; ~ **de rodas** wheelchair; ~**s** *fpl* (*ANAT*) hips.

ca'dela *f* (*cão*) bitch.

ca'dência *f* cadence; (*ritmo*) rhythm.

cader'neta *f* (*de apontamentos*) notebook; (*registro de alunos*) school register; (*de banco*) passbook; **caderno** *m* exercise book.

ca'dete *m* cadet.

cadu'car *vi* (*documentos*) to lapse, expire; (*pessoa*) to become senile; **caduco/a** *adj* (*nulo*) invalid, expired; (*decrépito*) decrepit.

cafa'jeste *m/f* (*col*) rogue, yob, thug.

ca'fé *m* coffee; (*estabelecimento*) café; ~ **da manhã** (*Br*) breakfast; **é** ~ **pequeno** it's child's play; **cafeeiro** *m* coffee plant; **cafeicultor** *m* coffee-grower; **cafeteira** *f* (*vaso*) coffee pot; (*máquina*) percolator; **cafezal** *m* coffee plantation; **cafezinho** *m* small black coffee.

ca'fona *adj* in bad taste // *m/f* person of bad taste.

'cágado *m* turtle.

cai'ar *vt* to whitewash.

'caiba *etc vb ver* **caber**.

cãibra ['kãjbra] *f* (*MED*) cramp.

ca'ído/a *adj* (*abatido*) dejected.

caimão [kaj'mãw] *m* alligator.

cai'mento *m* (*vestido*) hang, fall.

cai'pira *m/f* peasant, yokel.

caipi'rinha *f* cocktail of *cachaça*, lemon and sugar.

ca'ir *vi* to fall (down); (*acontecer*) to take place, occur; ~ **bem** to suit, go well with; ~ **em si** to come to one's senses; ~ **de cama** to fall sick; ~ **de quatro** to land on all fours.

cais [kajʃ] *m* (*NÁUT*) quay; (*Pt: FERRO*) platform.

caixa ['kajʃa] *f* box; (*cofre*) safe; (*de uma loja*) cashdesk; ~ **de mudanças** (*Br*), ~ **de velocidades** (*Pt*) gear box; ~ **econômica** savings bank; ~ **postal** P.O. box; ~ **de correio** letter box // *m/f* (*COM: pessoa*) cashier.

caixão [kaj'ʃãw] *m* large box; (*ataúde*) coffin.

caixeira [kaj'ʃejra] *f* saleswoman; **caixeiro** *m* salesman; **caixeiro viajante** commercial traveller.

caixilho [kaj'ʃiʎu] *m* (*moldura*) frame.

caixote [kaj'ʃɔtʃi] *m* packing case; ~ **do lixo** (*Pt*) dustbin, garbage can (*US*).

cajado [ka'ʒadu] *m* staff, crook.

caju [ka'ʒu] *m* cashew nut; ~**eiro** *m* cashew tree.

cal *f* lime; (*para caiar*) whitewash.

calabouço [kala'bosu] *m* dungeon.

ca'lado/a *adj* silent, quiet // *f* (*NÁUT*) draught; **pela** ~**a** stealthily; **na** ~**a da noite** in the dead of night.

cala'frio *m* shiver; **ter** ~**s** to shiver.

cala'mar *m* squid.

calami'dade *f* calamity, disaster; **calamitoso/a** *adj* disastrous.

calão [ka'lãw] *m*: (*baixo*) ~ (*Br*) bad language; (*Pt*) slang.

ca'lar *vt* (*não dizer*) to keep quiet about; (*impor silêncio*) to silence; **cala a boca!** shut up! // *vi*, ~-**se** *vr* to keep silent.

calçadeira [kawsa'dejra] *f* shoe-horn.

calçado/a [kaw'-] *adj* (*rua*) paved // *m* footwear // *f* (*rua*) roadway; (*Br: passeio*) pavement, sidewalk (*US*).

calcanhar [kawka'ɲax] *m* (*ANAT*) heel.

calção [kaw'sãw] *m*, *pl* **calções** [kaw'sõjʃ] shorts *pl*; ~ **de banho** swimming trunks *pl*.

cal'car *vt* (*pisar em*) to tread on; (*espezinhar*) to trample (on).

cal'çar *vt* (*sapatos, luvas*) to put on; (*pavimentar*) to pave.

'calças *fpl* trousers, pants (*US*); ~ **curtas** shorts; **calcinhas** *fpl* panties.

'cálcio *m* calcium.

'calço *m* (*cunha*) wedge.

calcula'dor *m* calculator; **calcular** *vt* (*MAT*) to calculate // *vi* to make calculations; (*supor*) to reckon, guess; **cálculo** *m* calculation; (*MAT*) calculus; (*MED*) stone.

'calda *f* (*de doce*) syrup; **caldear** *vt* (*ligar metais*) to weld, fuse.

caldeira [kaw'dejra] *f* (*CULIN*) boiling pan, kettle; (*TEC*) boiler.

caldeirada [kawdej'rada] *f* (*Pt: guisado*) fish stew.

caldeirão [kawdej'rãw] *m* cauldron; **caldeiro** *m* (*balde*) bucket.

'caldo *m* (*sopa*) soup; (*de fruta*) juice.

calefação [kalεfa'sãw] (*Pt:* -cç-) *f* heating.

calejado/a [kalε'ʒadu/a] *adj* hardened; (*fig*) experienced.

calen'dário *m* calendar.

calha ['kaʎa] *f* (*sulco*) channel; (*para água*) gutter.

calhar [ka'ʎax] *vi* (*convir*) to be suitable, fit; (*acontecer*) to happen; **se ~** (*Pt*) perhaps, maybe.

calhau [ka'ʎaw] *m* stone, pebble.

cali'brar *vt* to gauge, calibrate; **calibre** *m* (*de cano*) bore, calibre; (*fig*) calibre.

'cálice *m* (*copinho*) wine glass; (*REL*) chalice.

'cálido/a *adj* warm.

calma ['kawma] *f* (*serenidade*) calm; (*calor*) heat; **conservar/perder a ~** to keep/lose one's temper // *excl:* **~!** take it easy!

calmante [kaw'mãtʃi] *adj* soothing // *m* (*MED*) sedative; **calmo/a** *adj* calm, tranquil.

'calo *m* callus; (*no pé*) corn.

ca'lor *m* heat; (*agradável*) warmth.

calo'ria *f* calorie; **caloroso/a** *adj* warm; (*entusiástico*) enthusiastic.

ca'lota *f* (*AUTO*) hubcap.

ca'lote *m* (*dívida*) bad debt; (*trapaça*) swindle; **calotear** *vt* (*trapacear*) to swindle.

calouro/a [ka'loru/a] *m/f* (*EDUC*) fresher; (: *US*) freshman; (*noviço*) novice.

ca'lúnia *f* slander; **calunioso/a** *adj* slanderous.

calvície [kaw'visi] *f* baldness; **calvo/a** *adj* bald.

'cama *f* bed; **~ de casal** double bed; **~ de solteiro** single bed.

cama'da *f* layer; (*de tinta*) coat.

'câmara *f* (*ger*) chamber; (*FOTO*) camera; **~ de ar** (*de pneu*) inner tube; **~ municipal** (*Br*) town council; (*Pt*) town hall; **em ~ lenta** in slow motion.

cama'rada *m/f* comrade; (*companheiro*) companion; **~gem** *f* comradeship.

camarão [kama'rãw] *m* shrimp.

camarilha [kama'riʎa] *f* clique; (*política*) lobby group.

camarim [kama'rĩ] *m* (*teatro*) dressing room.

cama'rote *m* (*NÁUT*) cabin; (*teatro*) box.

cam'bada *f* bunch, gang.

cambaio/a [kam'baju/a] *adj* (*de pernas*) bow-legged.

cambale'ante *adj* staggering; **cambalear** *vi* to stagger, reel.

cambalhota [kamba'ʎota] *f* somersault.

cambi'ante *adj* changing, variable // *m* (*cor*) shade; **cambiar** *vt* to change; (*trocar*) to exchange // *vi:* **cambiar de idéia** to change one's mind; **câmbio** *m* (*dinheiro etc*) exchange; (*preço de câmbio*) rate of exchange; **câmbio livre** free trade; **câmbio negro** black market.

cam'bista *m* (*de dinheiro*) money changer; (*Br: de ingressos*) (ticket-)tout.

ca'melo *m* camel; (*fig*) dunce.

came'lô *m* street pedlar.

camião [kami'ãw] *m* (*Pt*) lorry, truck (*US*).

caminhada [kamĩ'nada] *f* walk; **caminhante** *m/f* walker; (*transeunte*) pedestrian.

caminhão [kamĩ'nãw] *m* (*Br*) lorry, truck (*US*).

caminhar [kamĩ'nax] *vi* (*andar*) to go; (*ir a pé*) to walk; (*distâncias*) to travel.

caminho [ka'mĩnu] *m* (*direção*) way; (*vereda*) road, path; **~ de ferro** (*Pt*) railway, railroad (*US*); **a meio ~** halfway (there); **em ~** on the way, en route; **caminhonete** *m* (*AUTO*) van.

camio'neta *f* (*Pt: para passageiros*) coach; (: *comercial*) van.

camio'nista *m/f* (*Pt*) lorry driver, truck driver (*US*).

ca'misa *f* shirt; **~ de dormir** nightshirt; **~ de Vênus** condom, sheath; **camiseta** *f* (*Br*) T-shirt; (*interior*) vest.

cami'sola *f* (*Br*) nightdress; (*Pt: pulôver*) sweater; **~ interior** (*Pt*) vest.

'campa *f* (*de sepultura*) gravestone; (*sino*) bell.

campainha [kampa'ĩna] *f* bell.

cam'pal [-paw] *adj:* **batalha ~** pitched battle; **missa ~** open-air mass.

campa'nário *m* (*torre*) church tower, steeple; (*aldeia*) parish.

campanha [kam'paɲa] *f* (*MIL etc*) campaign; (*planície*) plain.

campeão/campeã [kampɪ'ãw/kampɪ'ã] *m/f* champion; **campeonato** *m* championship.

cam'pestre *adj* rural, rustic.

cam'pina *f* prairie, grassland.

'camping *m* (*Br*) camping; (*lugar*) campsite.

cam'pismo *m* (*Pt*) camping; **parque de ~** campsite; **campista** *m/f* camper.

'campo *m* (*ger*) field; (*fora da cidade*) countryside; (*de esporte*) ground; (*acampamento*) camp; (*alcance*) sphere, scope; (*de tênis*) court; **em ~ aberto** in the open; **pôr em ~** to bring into play.

campo'nês/esa *m* countryman; (*agricultor*) farmer // *f* countrywoman; **campônio/a** *adj*, *m/f* (*pej*) yokel, country bumpkin.

camuflagem [kamu'flaʒẽ] *f* camouflage; **camuflar** *vt* to camouflage.

camun'dongo *m* (*Br*) mouse.

ca'murça *f* chamois (leather).

'cana *f* cane; (*col: cadeia*) jail; (*de açúcar*) sugar cane; **~ de pesca** (*Pt*) fishing rod.

Cana'dá *m* Canada; **canadense** *adj*, *m/f* Canadian.

ca'nal *m* (*ger*) channel; (*de navegação*) canal; (*ANAT*) duct.

canalha [ka'naʎa] *f* rabble, mob // *m/f* wretch, scoundrel.

canalização [kanalıza'sãw] *f* (*água*)

plumbing; (gás) piping; (eletricidade) wiring; **canalizador** m (Pt) plumber; **canalizar** vt to channel; (colocar canos) to lay pipes.

ca'nário m canary.

ca'nastra f (big) basket; (jogo) canasta.

canavi'al m cane field.

canção [kã'sãw] f song; ~ **de ninar** lullaby.

can'cela f gate.

cancela'mento m cancellation; **cancelar** vt to cancel; (invalidar) to annul.

'câncer m cancer.

cancioneiro [kãsjo'nejru] m song book.

'cancro m (Pt) cancer.

candeeiro [kãdʒi'ejru] m (Br) oil-lamp ou gas-lamp; (Pt) lamp.

cande'labro m (castiçal) candlestick; (lustre) chandelier.

can'dente adj white hot; (fig) inflamed.

candi'dato m candidate; **candidatura** f candidature.

candidez [kãdʒi'deʃ] f (inocência) innocence; **cândido/a** adj (ingênuo) naive; (inocente) innocent; (branco) white; **candura** f (simplicidade) simplicity; (inocência) innocence.

ca'neca f mug, tankard.

ca'nela f (especiaria) cinnamon; (ANAT) shin.

ca'neta f pen; ~ **esferográfica** ballpoint pen; **caneta-tinteiro** f fountain pen.

cangaceiro [kãga'sejru] m (Br) bandit.

cangu'ru m kangaroo.

cânhamo ['kaɲamu] m hemp.

canhão [ka'ɲãw] m (MIL) cannon; (GEO) canyon.

canhoto/a [ka'ɲotu/a] adj left-handed // m/f left-handed person // m (de cheque) stub.

ca'niço/a adj (col) skinny // m reed.

ca'nícula f height of the summer; **canicular** adj hot, sultry.

ca'nil [-nɪw] m kennel.

cani'vete m penknife.

canja ['kãʒa] f (sopa) chicken soup; (col) cinch, pushover.

can'jica f maize porridge.

'cano m pipe; (tubo) tube; (de arma de fogo) barrel; ~ **de esgoto** sewer.

ca'noa f canoe.

can'saço m tiredness, weariness; **cansado/a** adj tired, weary; (aborrecido) fed up.

can'sar vt (fatigar) to tire; (irritar) to irritate; (entediar) to bore // vi, ~-**se** vr (ficar cansado) to get tired; **cansativo/a** adj tiring; (tedioso) tedious; **canseira** f (cansaço) weariness; (trabalho árduo) toil.

can'tar vt to sing // m song.

'cântaro m water jug.

cantaro'lar vt to hum.

canteira [kã'tejra] f quarry; **canteiro** m stonemason; (de flores) flower bed.

can'tiga f ballad; (conto) tale; ~ **de ninar** lullaby.

can'til [-tʃɪw] m canteen, flask.

can'tina f canteen.

'canto m (ângulo) corner; (canção) song; **aos quatro** ~**s** to the four corners of the earth; **de** ~ edgeways.

can'tor(a) m/f singer.

canu'dinho m straw.

ca'nudo m tube; (canudinho) straw.

cão [kãw] m, pl **cães** [kãjʃ] dog; (de arma de fogo) hammer.

caos ['kaoʃ] m chaos; **caótico/a** adj chaotic.

'capa f (roupa) cape; (de livro) cover; (envoltório) wrapper.

capa'cete m helmet.

capacho [ka'paʃu] m door mat; (fig) toady.

capaci'dade f capacity; (aptidão) ability, competence.

ca'par vt to castrate, geld.

capataz [kapa'taʃ] m foreman.

capaz [ka'paʃ] adj able, capable.

ca'pela f chapel; **capelão** m (REL) chaplain.

ca'peta m devil.

capim [ka'pĩ] m grass.

capi'tal [-taw] adj capital, principal // m capital, funds pl // f (cidade) capital; ~**ismo** m capitalism; ~**ista** m/f capitalist.

capitane'ar vt to command, head; **capitania** f captaincy; **capitania do porto** port authority; **capitão** m, pl **capitães** captain.

capitulação [kapitula'sãw] f capitulation, surrender.

ca'pítulo m chapter.

ca'pô m (AUTO) bonnet, hood (US).

capoeira [kap'wejra] f (Pt) hencoop; (mata) brushwood; (jogo) foot-fighting dance.

ca'pota f (coberta de automóvel) hood, top.

capo'tar vi to overturn, capsize.

ca'pote m (capa) cloak; (sobretudo) overcoat.

capricho [ka'priʃu] m whim, caprice; (teimosia) obstinacy; (apuro) care; **caprichoso/a** adj capricious; (variável) changeable; (com apuro) meticulous.

cap'tar vt (atrair) to win; (rádio) to pick up; (águas) to collect, dam up; (apanhar) to catch; **captura** f capture; **capturar** vt to capture, seize.

capuz [ka'puʃ] m hood.

cáqui ['kakɪ] adj khaki.

'cara f (de pessoa) face; (de disco) side; (de moeda) face; (aspeto) appearance; **ter boa** ~ to look well; ~ **ou coroa?** heads or tails?; **ser a** ~ **de** (col) to be the spitting image of; **ter** ~ **de** to look (like); **dar de** ~ **com** to bump into // m (col) guy.

cara'bina f rifle.

cara'col [-ow] m snail; (de cabelo) curl.

carac'teres pl of **caráter**.

caracte'rístico/a adj characteristic // f characteristic, feature;

caracterização f characterization; (de ator) make-up; **caracterizar** vt to characterize, typify.

cara'dura adj barefaced, shameless.

cara'melo m caramel; (bala) sweet, candy (US).

caranguejo [karã'geʒu] m crab.

cara'paça f shell.

carapau [kara'paw] m (peixe) jack-fish; (fig) skinny person, beanpole.

carapinha [kara'pɪɲa] f curly hair.

cara'puça f cap; **se a ~ serve if the cap fits.**

ca'ráter m, pl **carac'teres** character; (BIO) characteristic.

cara'vana f caravan.

carboni'zar vt to carbonize; (queimar) to char; **carbono** m carbon.

carbura'dor m carburettor.

car'caça f (esqueleto) carcass; (armação) frame; (de navio) hull.

cárcere ['kaxseri] m prison; **carcereiro** m jailer, warder.

car'comido/a adj worm-eaten; (fig) rotten.

car'dápio m (Br) menu.

cardeal [kaxd3'jaw] adj cardinal // m cardinal.

car'díaco/a adj cardiac.

cardi'nal adj cardinal.

'cardo m thistle.

car'dume m (peixes) shoal.

ca'reca adj bald.

carecer [kare'sex] vi: **~ de** (ter falta) to lack; (precisar) to need; **carência** f (falta) lack, shortage; (necessidade) need; (privação) deprivation; **carente** adj wanting; (pessoa) needy.

cares'tia f expensiveness; (encarecimento) high prices pl; (escassez) scarcity.

ca'reta f grimace; (máscara) mask; **fazer uma ~ to pull a face.**

'carga f (peso) load; (de um navio) cargo; (ato de carregar) loading; (ELET) charge; (dever) duty; (MIL) attack, charge; (reabastecimento) refill; **voltar à ~ to insist.**

'cargo m (responsabilidade) duty, responsibility; (função pública) office.

carica'tura f (desenho) cartoon; (imitação cômica) caricature; **caricaturista** m/f cartoonist.

carícia [ka'risja] f caress.

cari'dade f charity; (bondade) kindness; (esmola) alms pl.

cárie ['karɪ] f (MED) caries; (de dente) tooth decay.

ca'ril [-ɪw] m curry.

carim'bar vt to stamp; (no correio) to postmark; **carimbo** m rubber stamp; (postal) postmark.

carinho [ka'rɪɲu] m affection, fondness; (carícia) caress; **fazer ~ to caress; carinhoso/a adj affectionate.**

cari'oca adj of Rio de Janeiro // m/f native of Rio de Janeiro // m (Pt: café) type of weak coffee.

carita'tivo/a adj charitable.

carmesin [kaxme'sɪ] adj crimson.

carnal [kax'naw] adj carnal; **primo ~ first cousin.**

carnaval [kaxna'vaw] m carnival.

carne ['kaxnɪ] f flesh; (CULIN) meat; **~ moída minced meat; em ~ e osso in flesh and blood.**

carneiro [kax'nejru] m sheep; (macho) ram.

carniça'ria f (matança) slaughter; (açougue) butcher's shop; **carniceiro/a** adj (cruel) cruel; **carnificina** f slaughter; **carnívoro/a** adj carnivorous.

car'nudo/a adj plump, fleshy; (col) beefy.

'caro/a adj dear, expensive; (estimado) dear; **sair ~ to cost a lot // adv dear.**

carochinha [karo'ʃɪɲa] f: **conto da ~ fairy tale.**

ca'roço m (de frutos) stone; (endurecimento) lump.

ca'rola m/f (col) sanctimonious person, obsessive churchgoer.

ca'rona f (Br: viagem gratuita) lift; **viajar de ~ to hitchhike.**

carpinta'ria f carpentry; **carpinteiro** m carpenter; (de teatro) stagehand.

carranca [ka'xa-] f frown, scowl; **carrancudo/a** adj surly; (soturno) sullen; (semblante) scowling.

carra'pato m (insecto) tick; (pessoa) hanger-on.

car'rasco m executioner; (fig) tyrant.

carre'gado/a adj loaded, laden; (semblante) sullen; (céu) dark; **carregador** m porter; **carregamento** m (ação) loading; (carga) load, cargo.

carre'gar vt (veículo, arma) to load; (levar) to carry; (bateria) to charge; (sobrecarregar) to burden; (Pt: apertar) to press.

carreira [ka'xejra] f (ação de correr) run, running; (competição) race; (curso) course; (profissão) career; (trilha) track, route; (fileira) row; (pista de corridas) track, course; **às ~s in a hurry.**

car'reta f cart; (de artilharia) carriage.

carreteiro [kaxe'tejru] m cart driver.

carretel [kaxe'tew] m spool, reel.

carril [ka'xɪw] m (de ferro) rail; (sulco de rodas) rut, track.

carrilhão [kaxɪ'ʎãw] m chime.

carrinha [ka'xɪɲa] f (Pt) van.

carrinho [ka'xɪɲu] m small cart; **~ de criança pram; ~ de mão wheelbarrow.**

carro ['kaxo] m (automóvel) car; (de bois) cart; (de mão) handcart, barrow; (RAIL, TEC) carriage; (caminhão) truck; **~ de corrida racing car; ~ esporte sports car; carroça f cart, waggon.**

carroçe'ria [kaxo-] f (AUTO) bodywork.

carruagem [kaxu'aʒẽ] f carriage, coach.

'carta f letter; (de jogar) card; (mapa) chart; (diploma) diploma; (constituição) charter; **~ aérea airmail letter; ~ registrada registered letter; ~ de**

crédito letter of credit; ~ **de condução** (Pt) driving licence; **dar as** ~**s** to deal.

cartão [kax'tãw] m (Pt: material) cardboard; (bilhete) card; ~ **de visita** (calling) card; ~ **postal** postcard; ~ **de crédito** credit card.

car'taz m poster, bill (US); **ter** ~ to have a good reputation.

carteira [kax'tejra] f (móvel) desk; (para dinheiro) wallet; (num banco) department; ~ **de identidade** identity card; ~ **de motorista** driving licence.

carteiro [kax'tejru] m postman.

cartilagem [kaxtʃi'laʒẽ] f (ANAT) cartilage.

carto'liana f (material) card.

car'tório m registry; (arquivo) archive.

cartucheira [kaxtu'ʃejra] f cartridge belt; **cartucho** m cartridge; (saco de papel) packet.

caruncho [ka'runʃu] m (insecto) woodworm; (podridão) rot.

carvalho [kax'vaʎu] m oak.

carvão [kax'vãw] m coal; (de madeira) charcoal; **carvoeiro** m (comerciante) coal merchant.

'casa f house; (lar) home; (COM) firm; ~ **de botão** buttonhole; ~ **de câmbio** exchange bureau; ~ **de pensão** boarding house; ~ **de saúde** hospital; ~ **da moeda** mint; ~ **de banho** (Pt) bathroom; **em** ~ (at) home; **fora de** ~ out.

ca'saca f dress coat; (col) tails pl; **virar a** ~ to become a turncoat; **casaco** m coat.

casal [ka'zaw] m (par) married couple.

casa'mento m marriage; (boda) wedding; **casar** vt to marry; (combinar) to match (up); **casar-se** vr to get married; (harmonizar-se) to combine well.

'casca f (de árvore) bark; (de banana) skin; (de ferida) scab; (de laranja) peel; (de nozes, ovos) shell; (de milho etc) husk.

cascalho [kaʃ'kaʎu] m (pedra britada) gravel; (na praia) shingle; (entulho) rubble.

cascão [kaʃ'kãw] m crust; (sujeira) grime.

cas'cata f waterfall.

casca'vel m (serpente) rattlesnake.

'casco m (crânio) skull; (pele da cabeça) scalp; (de animal) hoof; (de navio) hull; (para bebidas) empty bottle.

casebre [ka'zɛbri] m hovel, shack.

caseiro/a [ka'zejru/a] adj (produtos) home-made; (pessoa) home-loving // m tenant.

ca'serna f barracks pl.

cas'murro/a adj moody, introverted.

'caso m case; ~ **amoroso** love affair // conj in case, if; **em** ~ **de** in case (of); **em todo** ~ in any case; **fazer pouco** ~ **de** to belittle; **não fazer** ~ **de** to ignore; (não fazer questão de) not to be fussy about; **vir ao** ~ to be relevant.

'caspa f dandruff.

cas'sete m cassette.

cas'sino m casino.

'casta f case; (estirpe) lineage.

castanheira [kaʃta'nejra] f chestnut tree; **castanho/a** adj (Pt) brown // f chestnut; **castanha de caju** cashew nut; **castanha-do-pará** f Brazil nut.

castanholas [kaʃta'nolaʃ] fpl castanets.

cas'telo m castle.

casti'çal [-aw] m candlestick.

casti'ço/a adj pure; (de boa casta) of good stock, pedigree.

casti'dade f chastity.

casti'gar vt to punish; (admoestar) to reprimand; (corrigir) to correct; **castigo** m punishment; (penalidade) penalty.

'casto/a adj chaste, pure.

cas'tor m beaver.

cas'trado/a adj castrated // m eunuch; **castrar** vt to castrate.

casual [kaz'waw] adj accidental; (fortuito) fortuitous; ~**idade** f chance; (acidente) accident; **por** ~**idade** by chance, accidentally.

ca'sulo m (de sementes) pod; (de insectos) cocoon.

'cata f: **à** ~ **de** in search of.

cata'clismo m cataclysm.

cataliza'dor m catalyst.

catalo'gar vt to catalogue; **catálogo** m catalogue; **catálogo telefônico** telephone directory.

cata'plasma f poultice.

cata'pora f (Br) chickenpox.

ca'tar vt to look for, search for; (piolho) to delouse; (recolher) to collect, gather.

cata'rata f (cascata) waterfall; (MED) cataract.

ca'tarro m catarrh; (constipação) cold.

ca'tástrofe f catastrophe.

cata-'vento m weathercock.

catecismo [kate'siʒmu] m catechism.

cate'dral [-aw] f cathedral.

cate'drático/a m/f professor.

cate'goria f category; (social) rank; (qualidade) quality; **de alta** ~ first rate; **categórico/a** adj categorical.

ca'tinga m/f (pessoa) miser // f stench, stink.

cati'vante adj captivating; **cativar** vt (capturar) to capture; (escravizar) to enslave; (fascinar) to captivate; (encantar) to charm; **cativeiro** m captivity; (escravidão) slavery; (cadeia) prison; **cativo/a** m/f (escravo) slave; (prisioneiro) prisoner.

catolicismo [katoli'siʒmu] m catholicism; **católico/a** adj, m/f catholic.

ca'torze num fourteen.

caturrice [katu'xisi] f obstinacy.

caução [kaw'sãw] f security, guarantee; **prestar** ~ to give bail; **sob** ~ on bail.

caucho ['kawʃu] m (árvore) gum tree; (borracha) rubber.

caucionar [kawsjo'nax] vt to guarantee, stand surety for; (JUR) to stand bail for.

cauda ['kawda] f tail; (de vestido) train; (retaguarda) rear.

cau'dal m (dum rio) flow; (torrente) torrent; (cachoeira) waterfall; **caudaloso/a** adj (abundante) abundant; (rio) torrential.

caudilho [kaw'dʒiʎu] m leader, chief.

caule ['kauli] m stalk, stem.

causa ['kawza] f cause; (motivo) motive, reason; (JUR) lawsuit, case; **por ~ de** on account of; **causar** vt to cause, bring about.

cau'tela f caution; (senha) ticket; **~ de penhor** pawn ticket; **cauteloso/a** adj cautious, wary.

'cava f (cova) pit; (de manga) armhole.

ca'vaco m (lenha) firewood; (estilha) splinter; (conversa) chat.

ca'vala f mackerel.

cava'ria f (MIL) cavalry; (equitação) horsemanship; (instituição medieval) chivalry.

cava'riça f stable.

cavaleiro [kava'lejru] m rider, horseman; (cavalheiro) gentleman; (medieval) knight.

cava'lete m stand; (FOTO) tripod; (de pintor) easel; (de mesa) trestle; (do violino) bridge.

cavalheiresco/a [kavaʎej'reʃku/a] adj gentlemanly; (brioso) chivalrous; **cavalheiro** m gentleman; (na dança) partner.

cavalinho [kava'liɲu] m: **~ de pau** rocking horse; **~-de-judeu** m dragonfly; **~-do-mar** m sea horse.

ca'valo m horse; (xadrez) knight; (cartas) jack; **a ~** on horseback; **50 ~s-vapor** 50 horsepower.

ca'var vt to dig; **~ a vida** to earn one's living // vi (animal) to burrow; (fig) to delve.

'cave f (Pt) wine-cellar.

caveira [ka'vejra] f skull.

ca'verna f cavern.

cavi'dade f cavity.

cavilha [ka'viʎa] f (de madeira) peg, dowel; (de metal) bolt.

'cavo/a adj (oco) hollow; (côncavo) concave; **cavouco** m ditch, trench; **cavouqueiro** m navvy.

caxumba [ka'ʃumba] f mumps pl.

c/c abr de **conta corrente** current account.

cear [si'ax] vt to have for supper // vi to dine.

ce'bola f onion; (bolho) bulb.

cecear [sesi'ax] vi to lisp; **ceceio** m lisp.

ce'der vt to give up; (entregar) to hand over; **~ o passo** to give way // vi to give in, concede; (afrouxar) to slacken.

cedilha [se'dʒiʎa] f cedilla.

cedo ['sedu] adv early; (prematuramente) prematurely; (em breve) soon; **mais ~ ou mais tarde** sooner or later; **o mais ~ possível** as soon as possible.

'cedro m cedar.

'cédula f (moeda-papel) banknote; (US)

bill; (eleitoral) ballot paper; (declaração de dívida) I.O.U.; **~ de identidade** identity card.

C.E.E. abr de **Comunidade Econômica Europeia** E.E.C.

ce'gar vt to blind; (ofuscar) to dazzle; **cego/a** adj blind // m blind man // f blind woman; **às cegas** blindly.

cegonha [se'goɲa] f stork.

cegueira [se'gejra] f blindness; (ignorância) ignorance.

ceia ['seja] f evening meal.

ceifa ['sejfa] f (colheita) harvest; **ceifar** vt to reap, harvest; (vidas) to slaughter; **ceifeiro/a** m/f reaper.

'cela f cell.

celebração [selebra'sãw] f celebration; **celebrar** vt to celebrate; (comemorar) to commemorate; (exaltar) to praise.

célebre ['selebri] adj famous, well known; **celebridade** f celebrity.

celeiro [se'lejru] m granary; (depósito) barn.

ce'leste adj celestial, heavenly.

celiba'tário/a adj unmarried; (solteiro) single // m bachelor // f spinster; **celibato** m celibacy.

celo'fane [selo'fani] m cellophane.

'célula f (BIO, ELET) cell.

celu'lar adj cellular.

cem [sẽ] num hundred.

cemi'tério m cemetery, graveyard.

'cena f scene; (palco) stage; **em ~** on the stage; **levar a ~** to stage; **cenário** m (decoração teatral) scenery; (cinema) scenario; (de um acontecimento) scene, setting.

ce'nógrafo/a m/f (teatro) set designer.

cenoura [se'nora] f carrot.

'censo m census.

cen'sor m censor; (crítico) critic; **censura** f (POL etc) censorship; (repreensão) censure, criticism; **censurar** vt (reprovar) to censure; (filme, livro etc) to censor; **censurável** adj blameworthy, reprehensible.

cen'tavo m cent.

centeio [sẽ'teju] m rye.

centelha [sẽ'teʎa] f spark; (fig) flash.

cen'tena f hundred; **às ~s** in hundreds; **centenário/a** adj centenary // m/f centenarian // m centenary, centennial.

cen'tésimo/a adj hundredth // m hundredth part.

cen'tígrado m centigrade.

cen'tímetro m centimetre.

'cento m: **aos ~s** in hundreds; **por ~** per cent.

centopeia [sẽto'peja] f centipede.

cen'tral [-aw] adj central // f (de polícia etc) head office; **~ telefónica** telephone exchange; **~ elétrica** (electric) power station; **~ização** f centralization; **~izar** vt to centralize; **centro** m centre, middle.

'cepa f (cepo) stump.

'cepo m (toco) stump; (toro) log.

'cera f wax.

'cerca f (de madeira, arame) fence; (cerca viva) hedge; (terreno) plot // prep: ~ **de** (mais ou menos) nearly, about.

cer'cado m enclosure, pen.

cerca'nias fpl (arredores) outskirts; (vizinhança) neighbourhood sg.

cer'car vt to enclose; (pôr cerca em) to fence in; (rodear) to surround; (MIL) to besiege.

cercear [sexsɪ'ax] vt (cortar pela base) to cut at the root; (liberdade) to curtail, restrict.

'cerco m encirclement; (lugar cercado) enclosure; (MIL) siege; **pôr** ~ **a** to besiege.

cere'al [-aw] m cereal.

'cérebro m brain; (fig) intelligence.

cereja [se're3a] f cherry; **cerejeira** f cherry tree.

cerimônia [sɛrɪ'monja] f ceremony; **sem** ~ informal; (descortês) rude, offhand; **sem mais** ~**s** without more ado; **cerimonial** adj ceremonial // m etiquette; **cerimonioso/a** adj ceremonious.

cerração [sɛxa'sãw] f (nevoeiro) fog.

cer'rado/a adj shut, closed; (denso) dense, thick // m enclosure; (vegetação) scrub(-land); **cerrar** vt to close, shut.

certame [sex'tami] m (combate) fight; (concurso) contest, competition; (discussão) discussion.

certeiro/a [sex'tejru/a] adj (tiro) well aimed; (acertado) correct.

cer'teza f certainty; **com** ~ certainly, surely; **ter** ~ **de** to be certain of.

certidão [sextʃi'dãw] f certificate.

certifi'cado m (garantia) certificate.

certifi'car vt to certify; (assegurar) to assure; ~**-se** vr: ~**-se de** to make sure of.

'certo/a adj certain, sure; (exato) correct; (combinado) agreed; (um, algum) a certain; **por** ~ certainly; **ao** ~ for certain; **está** ~ okay.

cerveja [sex've3a] f beer; ~**ria** f (fábrica) brewery; (bar) bar, public house.

'cervo/a m (espécie) deer; (macho) stag // f hind.

cerzi'dura f darning; **cerzir** vt to darn.

cessão [sɛ'sãw] f (cedência) surrender; (transferência) transfer.

ces'sar vi to cease, stop; **sem** ~ continually.

'cesta f basket; **cesto** m small basket; (com tampa) hamper; **cesto de vigia** (NÁUT) crow's nest.

ceticismo [setʃi'sɪ3mu] (Pt: -pt-) m scepticism; **cético/a** (Pt: -pt-) adj sceptical // m/f sceptic.

cetim [sɛ'tʃĩ] m satin.

'cetro (Pt: -pt-) m sceptre.

céu [sɛw] m sky; (REL) heaven; (boca) roof.

'ceva f (ação) fattening; (comida para animais) feed; (isca) bait.

ce'vada f barley.

ce'var vt (engordar) to fatten; (alimentar) to feed; (engodar) to bait; ~**-se** vr (saciar-se) to satisfy o.s.; (engordar) to get fat.

chá [ʃa] m tea; (reunião) tea party.

cha'cal [-aw] m jackal.

'chácara f (granja) farm; (casa de campo) country house.

chacinar [ʃasɪ'nax] vt (matar) to slaughter.

cha'cota f (trova) humorous song; (zombaria) mockery; **chacotear** vi: **chacotear de** to make fun of.

chafariz [ʃafa'rɪʃ] m fountain.

cha'furdar vi to wallow.

'chaga f (MED) sore; (: na boca) ulcer; (fig) wound.

cha'lé m chalet.

chaleira [ʃa'lejra] f kettle; (bajulador) crawler, toady.

'chama f flame; **em** ~**s** on fire.

cha'mada f call; (MIL) roll call; (num livro) note; **chamamento** m call; (convocação) summons sg.

cha'mar vt to call; (telefone) to ring, phone; (atenção) to attract; **mandar** ~ to summon, send for // vi to call (out); ~**-se** vr to be called; **chamo-me João** my name is John.

chamariz [ʃama'rɪʃ] m decoy; (pio) bird call; (fig) lure.

chami'né f chimney; (de navio) funnel.

champanha [ʃam'paɲa] m champagne.

cham'pu m shampoo.

chamus'car vt to scorch, singe.

chan'cela f seal, official stamp; **chancelaria** f chancellery.

chantagem [ʃan'taʒẽ] f blackmail; **chantagista** m/f blackmailer.

chão [ʃãw] m ground; (terra) soil.

'chapa f (placa) plate; (eleitoral) list; ~ **de matrícula** (Pt: AUTO) number plate.

chapela'ria f (loja) hatshop; **chapéu** m hat.

chapinha [ʃa'pɪɲa] f: ~ **de garrafa** bottle top.

chapinhar [ʃapɪ'nax] vi to splash.

cha'rada f (quebra-cabeça) puzzle.

'charco m stagnant pond.

charlatão [ʃaxla'tãw] m impostor; (curandeiro) quack.

char'neca f moor, heath.

charrua [ʃa'xua] f (Pt: arado) plough.

cha'ruto m cigar.

chas'sis m (AUTO, ELET) chassis.

chateação [ʃatʃla'sãw] f (maçada) bore; **chatear** vt to bother, annoy; (aborrecer) to bore; **chatice** f (Pt) nuisance; **chato/a** adj (plano) flat, level; (maçante) tiresome // m/f bore.

chave ['ʃavɪ] f key; (ELET) switch; ~ **de porcas** spanner; ~ **inglesa** (monkey) wrench; ~ **de fenda** screwdriver; **chaveiro** m (utensílio) key ring.

'chávena f (Pt) cup.

'chefe m head, chief; (patrão) boss; ~ **de turma** foreman; ~ **de estação**

stationmaster; **chefia** f leadership; **chefiar** vt to lead.

che'gada f arrival.

che'gado/a adj (próximo) near; (íntimo) close, intimate.

che'gar vt (aproximar) to bring near // vi to arrive; (ser suficiente) to be enough; **chega!** that's enough!; ~ **a** (atingir) to reach; (conseguir) to manage (to); ~**-se** vr: ~**-se a** to approach.

cheia ['ʃeja] f flood.

'cheio/a adj full, filled; (repleto) full up; (farto) fed up; ~ **de si** self-important.

cheirar [ʃej'rax] vt to smell // vi: ~ **a** to smell of; **cheiro** m smell; **cheiroso/a** adj scented.

'cheque m cheque, check (US); (xadrez) check; ~ **cruzado** crossed cheque; ~ **em branco** blank cheque; ~**-mate** m checkmate.

chi'ar vi to squeak; (porta) to creak; (vapor) to hiss; (fritura) to sizzle.

chi'bata f (vara) cane.

chicle ['ʃiklɪ], **chi'clete** m (chewing) gum.

chi'cória f chicory.

chi'cote m whip; **chicotear** vt to whip, lash.

'chifre m (corno) horn.

'Chile m Chile; **chileno/a** adj, m/f Chilean.

chilre'ar vi to chirp, twitter; **chilreio** m chirping; **chilro** m chirping.

chimpan'zé m chimpanzee.

'China f China.

chi'nelo m slipper.

chinês/esa [ʃi'neʃ/eza] adj, m/f Chinese.

'chique adj stylish, chic.

chiqueiro [ʃi'kejru] m pigsty.

'chispa f spark; **chispada** f (Br) dash; **chispar** vi to sparkle; (correr) to dash.

'chita f printed cotton, calico.

choça ['ʃosa] f shack, hut.

chocalhar [ʃoka'ʎax] vt/i to rattle; **chocalho** m (mús, brinquedo) rattle; (para animais) bell.

cho'car vt (incubar) to hatch, incubate; (ofender) to shock, offend // vi (carros) to collide, crash; ~**-se** vr (ofender-se) to be shocked.

chocho/a ['ʃoʃu/a] adj hollow, empty.

choco'late m chocolate.

cho'fer m driver.

chofre ['ʃofrɪ] m: **de** ~ all of a sudden.

'chope m draught beer.

'choque m (abalo) shock; (colisão) collision; (MED, ELET) shock; (impacto) impact; (AUTO) crash; (conflito) clash, conflict.

choramin'gar vi to whine, whimper; **choramingas** m/f crybaby.

chorão/rona [ʃo'rãw/rona] m/f crybaby // m (BOT) weeping willow; **chorar** vt/i to weep, cry; **choroso/a** adj tearful.

choupana [ʃo'pana] f shack, hut.

'choupo m poplar.

chouriço [ʃo'risu] m (Br) black pudding; (Pt) spicy sausage.

cho'ver vi to rain; ~ **a cântaros** to rain cats and dogs.

chu'lé m foot odour.

chum'bar vt to fill with lead; (soldar) to solder; (rede) to weight with lead // vi (Pt: reprovar) to fail; **chumbo** m lead; (de caça) gunshot; (Pt: de dente) filling.

chu'par vt to suck; (absorver) to absorb; (parasitar) to sponge on.

chu'peta f (para criança) dummy, pacifier (US).

chur'rasco m barbecue.

chu'tar vt to kick // vi to shoot; **chute** m kick, shot; **chuteira** f football boot.

'chuva f rain; ~**-de-pedra** f hailstorm; **chuveiro** m shower; **chuviscar** vi to drizzle; **chuvisco** m drizzle; **chuvoso/a** adj rainy.

Cª abr **de companhia** Co., company.

cicatriz [sika'triʃ] f scar.

ciciar [sisi'ax] vi to whisper; (rumorejar) to murmur.

cic'lismo m cycling; **ciclista** m/f cyclist.

'ciclo m cycle.

ci'clone m cyclone.

cidadão/cidadã [sida'dãw/sida'dã] m/f citizen; **cidade** f town; (grande) city; **cidadela** f citadel.

ciência [sj'ensja] f science; (erudição) knowledge; **ciente** adj aware, informed; **científico/a** adj scientific; **cientista** m/f scientist.

'cifra f (escrita secreta) cipher; (algarismo) number, figure; **cifrão** m dollar sign.

ci'frar vt to write in code.

ci'gano/a adj, m/f gypsy.

ci'garra [-axa] f cicada; (ELET) buzzer.

cigarreira [siga'xejra] f (estojo) cigarette case; **cigarro** m cigarette.

ci'lada f (emboscada) ambush; (armadilha) trap; (embuste) trick.

ci'líndrico/a adj cylindrical; **cilindro** m cylinder; (rolo) roller.

'cima f: **de** ~ **para baixo** from top to bottom; **para** ~ up // **prep**: **em** ~ **de** on top of; **por** ~ **de** over; **cimeira** f (Pt) summit.

cimen'tar vt to cement; (fig) to strengthen; **cimento** m cement; (fig) foundation; **cimento armado** reinforced concrete.

'cimo m top, summit.

'cinco num five.

ci'nema f cinema, movies pl.

cingir [sin'ʒix] vt (pôr à cintura) to fasten round one's waist; (cercar) to encircle, ring; ~**-se** vr: ~**-se a** (restringir-se) to restrict o.s. to; (chegar-se) to keep close to, hug.

'cínico/a adj cynical; (impúdico) shameless // m/f cynic; **cinismo** m cynicism; (impudência) shamelessness.

cinqüenta [sin'kwenta] num fifty.

'cinta f (banda) sash; (de mulher) girdle.

cinti'lar vi to sparkle, glitter.

'cinto *m* belt; (*faixa*) sash; ~ de segurança safety belt; (*AUTO*) seatbelt.

cin'tura *f* waist; (*linha*) waistline.

'cinza *f* ash, ashes *pl*; cinzeiro *m* ashtray.

cin'zel [-ɛw] *m* chisel; cinzelar *vt* to chisel; (*gravar*) to carve, engrave.

cin'zento/a *adj* grey.

cioso/a [si'ozu/a] *adj* (*zeloso*) zealous.

ci'pó *m* liana, creeper.

ci'preste *m* cypress (tree).

cipri'ota *adj, m/f* Cypriot.

'circo *m* circus.

circuito [six'kwitu] *m* circuit; curto ~ short circuit.

circulação [sixkula'sãw] *f* circulation; (*trânsito*) movement; circular *adj* circular, round // *f* (*carta*) circular // *vi* to circulate; (*trânsito*) to move, flow; circulem! move on!; círculo *m* circle.

circunci'dar *vt* to circumcise; circuncisão *f* circumcision; circunciso/a *adj* circumcised.

circunfe'rência *f* circumference.

circun'flexo/a *adj* circumflex // *m* circumflex.

circun'screver *vt* to circumscribe, limit.

circunspeção [sixkunʃpe'sãw] (*Pt*: -cç-) *f* circumspection; circunspeto/a *adj* cautious; (*sisudo*) serious.

circun'stância *f* circumstance; circunstanciado/a *adj* detailed.

circun'stante *m/f* onlooker, bystander; ~s *mpl* audience.

cir'rose [-ıxo-] *f* cirrhosis.

cirurgia [sirux'ʒia] *f* surgery; ~ plástica/estética plastic surgery; cirurgião *m* surgeon.

cisão [si'zãw] *f* (*divisão*) split, division; (*desacordo*) disagreement.

cisma [si'ʒma] *m* schism // *f* worry; (*suspeita*) suspicion; cismar *vi* to worry; (*LITER: fantasiar*) to daydream; (*Br: suspeitar*) to suspect.

cisne ['siʒni] *m* swan.

cis'terna *f* cistern, tank.

'cisto *m* cyst.

citação [sita'sãw] *f* quotation; (*JUR*) summons *sg*; citar *vt* to quote; (*JUR*) to summon.

ciúme [si'umi] *m* jealousy; ter ~s de to be jealous of; ciumento/a *adj* jealous.

ci'vil [-ıw] *adj* civil; (*cortês*) polite // *m/f* civilian; ~idade *f* politeness.

civilização [sivıliza'sãw] *f* civilization; civilizar *vt* to civilize.

ci'vismo *m* public spirit.

cla'mar *vt* to clamour for // *vi* to cry out, clamour; clamor *m* outcry, uproar; clamoroso/a *adj* noisy.

clandes'tino/a *adj* clandestine; (*ilegal*) underground.

'clara *f* white of egg.

clarabóia [klara'bɔja] *f* skylight.

clarão [kla'rãw] *m* (*cintilação*) flash; (*claridade*) gleam.

clare'ar *vi* (*o dia*) to dawn; (*o tempo*) to clear up, brighten up.

clareira [kla'rejra] *f* (*na mata*) clearing.

cla'reza *f* (*nitidez*) clarity; claridade *f* (*luz*) brightness; clarificação *f* clarification; clarificar *vt* to clarify.

clarim [kla'rı̃] *m* bugle.

clari'nete *m* clarinet; (*pessoa*) clarinetist.

'claro/a *adj* (*gen*) clear; (*luminoso*) bright; (*côr*) light; (*evidente*) clear, evident // *m* (*na escrita*) space; (*clareira*) clearing // *adv* clearly; às claras openly // *excl* of course!

'classe *f* class; ~ média/operária middle/working class.

'clássico/a *adj* classical; (*fig*) classic.

classificação [klasıfika'sãw] *f* classification; classificar *vt* to classify.

claustro ['klawʃtru] *m* cloister.

cláusula ['klawzula] *f* clause.

'clava *f* (*pau*) club.

'clave *f* (*MÚS*) clef.

cla'vícula *f* collar bone.

cle'mência *f* mercy; clemente *adj* merciful.

cleptoma'níaco/a *m/f* kleptomaniac.

'clérigo *m* clergyman; clero *m* clergy.

cli'chê *m* (*FOTO*) plate; (*chavão*) cliché.

cli'ente *m* client; (*loja*) customer; (*de médico*) patient; clientela *f* clientele; (*loja*) customers *pl*; (*de médico*) patients *pl*.

'clima *m* climate.

'clínico/a *adj* clinical // *m* doctor // *f* clinic; (*particular*) practice.

'clipe *m* clip; (*para papéis*) paper clip.

clo'rídrico/a *adj* hydrochloric.

cloro'fórmio *m* chloroform.

'clube *m* club.

coabi'tar *vi* to live together, cohabit.

coação [koa'sãw] (*Pt*: -cç-) *f* coercion.

coa'dor *m* strainer.

coagir [koa'ʒix] *vt* to coerce, compel.

coagu'lar *vt/i* to coagulate; (*sangue*) to congeal, clot; ~-se *vr* to congeal; coágulo *m* clot.

coalhar [koa'ʎax] *vt/i* (*leite*) to curdle; ~-se *vr* to curdle.

coalizão [koalı'zãw] *f* coalition.

co'ar *vt* (*líquido*) to strain.

coa'xar *vi* to croak.

cobaia [ko'baja] *f* guinea pig.

co'berto/a *pp* de cobrir // *adj* covered // *f* cover, covering; (*NÁUT*) deck; cobertor *m* blanket; cobertura *f* covering; (*telhado*) roof; (*apartamento*) penthouse.

cobiça [ko'bısa] *f* greed; (*desejo*) desire; cobiçar *vt* to covet; cobiçoso/a *adj* covetous.

'cobra *f* snake.

cobra'dor *m* collector; (*transporte*) conductor; cobrança *f* collection.

co'brar *vt* to collect; (*cheque*) to cash; (*preço*) to charge; (*reaver*) to get back.

'cobre *m* copper.

co'brir *vt* to cover; (*ocultar*) to hide, conceal; (*proteger*) to protect.

co'cada *f* coconut sweet.

co'çar *vt* to scratch; ~-se *vr* to scratch o.s.; não ter tempo para se ~ to have no time to spare.

cócegas ['kɔsɛgaʃ] *fpl:* fazer ~ to tickle; tenho ~ nos pés my feet tickle.

'coche *m* (*carruagem*) coach.

cochichar [koʃ'ʃax] *vi* to whisper.

cochi'lar *vi* to snooze, doze.

'coco *m* coconut.

'cócoras *fpl:* de ~ squatting.

côdea ['kodja] *f* (*Pt: de pão*) crust; (: *de queijo*) rind.

'código *m* code.

codor'niz *f* quail.

coelho ['kweʎu] *m* rabbit.

coerção [koex'sãw] *f* coercion, compulsion.

coe'rência *f* coherence; coerente *adj* coherent.

coesão [koe'zãw] *f* cohesion.

coetâneo/a [koe'tanju/a] *adj* contemporary.

coexis'tência *f* coexistence; coexistir *vi* to coexist.

'cofre *m* safe; (*caixa*) strongbox.

cogitar [koʒi'tax] *vt/i* to contemplate.

cogu'melo *m* mushroom; ~ venenoso toadstool.

coibição [koibi'sãw] *f* restraint, restriction; coibir *vt* to restrain; coibir de to restrain from; coibir-se *vr:* coibir-se de to abstain from.

coice ['kojsi] *m* kick; (*de arma*) recoil; dar ~s to kick.

coinci'dência *f* coincidence; coincidir *vi* to coincide; (*concordar*) to agree.

coisa ['kojza] *f* thing; (*assunto*) affair; ~ de about.

coitado/a [koj'tadu/a] *adj* poor, wretched; ~! poor thing!

coito ['kojtu] *m* intercourse, coitus.

'cola *f* glue, gum; (*rabo*) tail; (*Br: cópia*) crib.

colaboração [kolabura'sãw] *f* collaboration; colaborar *vi* to collaborate.

co'lapso *m* collapse; ~ cardíaco heart failure.

co'lar *vt* to stick, glue; (*vinho*) to clarify; (*Br: copiar*) to crib; ~ grau to graduate // *m* necklace; ~inho *m* collar.

'colcha *f* bedspread; colchão *m* mattress.

col'chete *m* clasp, fastening; (*parêntese*) square bracket; ~ de gancho hook and eye; ~ de pressão press stud.

coleção [kole'sãw] (*Pt: -cç-*) *f* collection; colecionar (*Pt: -cc-*) *vt* to collect.

co'lega *m/f* colleague.

colégio [ko'lɛʒju] *m* college; (*escola*) (private) school.

'cólera *f* (*ira*) anger; (*fúria*) rage; (*MED*) cholera; colérico/a *adj* (*irado*) angry;

(*furioso*) furious // *m/f* (*MED*) cholera patient.

co'leta (*Pt: -ct-*) *f* collection; coletar (*Pt: -ct-*) *vt* to tax.

co'lete *m* waistcoat, vest (*US*); (*de senhora*) corset; ~ de forças straitjacket; ~ de salvação life jacket, life preserver (*US*).

coletivi'dade (*Pt: -ct-*) *f* community; coletivo/a (*Pt: -ct-*) *adj* collective, joint.

colheita [ko'ʎejta] *f* harvest; (*produto*) crop.

co'lher [ko'ʎex] *vt* (*recolher*) to gather, pick; (*prender*) to catch.

co'lher [ko'ʎex] *f* spoon; colherada *f* spoonful; colherão *m* ladle.

coli'bri *m* hummingbird.

'cólica *f* colic.

coli'dir *vi:* ~ com to collide with, crash into.

coligação [koliga'sãw] *f* coalition.

coligir [koli'ʒix] *vt* to collect.

co'lina *f* hill.

colisão [koli'zãw] *f* collision, crash.

col'mar *vt* to thatch.

colmeia [kow'meja] *f* beehive.

colmilho [kow'miʎu] *m* (*dente*) eye tooth; (*de elefante*) tusk; (*de cão*) fang.

'colo *m* (*pescoço*) neck; (*peito*) bosom; (*regaço*) lap; no ~ on one's lap, in one's arms.

colocação [koloka'sãw] *f* placing; (*emprego*) job, position; colocar *vt* to place, position; (*empregar*) to find a job for; (*COM*) to market.

Co'lômbia *f* Colombia; colombiano/a *adj, m/f* Colombian.

'cólon *m* colon.

co'lônia *f* colony.

colonização [koloniza'sãw] *f* colonization; colonizador(a) *adj* colonizing // *m/f* colonist, settler; colonizar *vt* to colonize; colono *m* settler; (*cultivador*) farmer.

colóquio [ko'lɔkju] *m* conversation; (*congresso*) conference.

colo'rido *m* colouring, colour; colorir *vt* to colour; (*fig*) to disguise.

co'luna *f* column; (*pilar*) pillar; ~ vertebral spine.

com [kõ] *prep* with; (*apesar de*) in spite of; ~ que so, and so; ~ que então! so!

co'madre *f* (*mexeriqueira*) gossip, crony; minha ~ the godmother of my child *ou* the mother of my godchild.

coman'dante *m* commander; (*MIL*) commandant; (*NÁUT*) captain; comandar *vt* to command; comando *m* command; comando a distância remote control.

com'bate *m* combat, fight; (*fig*) battle; combatente *m/f* combatant; combater *vt* to fight, combat // *vi* to fight.

combinação [kõbina'sãw] *f* combination; (*QUÍM*) compound; (*acordo*) arrangement; (*plano*) scheme; (*roupa*) slip; **combinar** vt to combine; (arranjar) to arrange; **combinado!** agreed!

comboio [kõˈboju] m (Pt) train; (de navios) convoy.

combustão [kobuʃˈtãw] f combustion; **combustível** m fuel.

começar [komeˈsax] vt/i to begin, start, commence; **começo** m beginning, start.

co'média f comedy; (teatro) play, drama; **comediante** m (comic) actor // f (comic) actress.

come'dido/a adj moderate; (prudente) prudent; (discreto) discreet; **comedir-se** vr to control o.s.

comemoração [komɛmoraˈsãw] f commemoration, celebration; **comemorar** vt to celebrate, commemorate.

comen'tar vt to comment on; **comentário** m comment, remark; (análise) commentary.

co'mer vt to eat (up); (damas, xadrez) to take, capture // vi to eat; **dar de ~ a** to feed; **~-se** vr: **~-se (de)** to be consumed (with).

comerci'al adj commercial; (relativo ao negócio) business cmp; **comerciante** m/f trader, merchant; **comerciar** vi to trade, do business; **comércio** m commerce; (tráfico) trade; (negócio) business; (fig) dealings pl.

comes'tível adj edible // mpl: **~s** foodstuff.

co'meta m comet.

come'ter vt to commit; **cometimento** m undertaking, commitment.

comichão [komiˈʃãw] f itch, itching.

comício [koˈmisju] m meeting; (assembléia) assembly.

'cômico/a adj comic(al) // m comedian; (de teatro) actor.

co'mida f (alimento) food; (refeição) meal.

co'migo pron with me; with myself.

comilão/lona [komiˈlãw/lona] adj greedy // m/f glutton.

comissão [komiˈsãw] f commission; (comité) committee; **comissário** m commissioner; (COM) agent; **comissário de bordo** purser.

comi'tê m committee.

comi'tiva f retinue.

'como adv as; (assim como) like; (de que maneira) how; **~?** what?, I beg your pardon?; **~ assim?** how come?; **~ que morto** as if dead // excl what!; **~ não!** of course! // conj (porque) as, since; (quando) when; **~ se** as if; **~ quer que** however; **seja ~** for be that as it may.

comoção [komoˈsãw] f (confusão) commotion; **~ nervosa** shock.

comodi'dade f (conforto) comfort; (conveniência) suitability; **cômodo/a** adj (confortável) comfortable; (conveniente) convenient; (próprio) suitable // m (aposento) room // f chest of drawers, bureau (US).

comove'dor(a) adj moving, touching; **comover** vt to move; **comover-se** vr to

be moved; **comovido/a** adj moved, touched.

com'pacto/a adj (comprimido) compact; (espesso) thick; (sólido) solid.

compade'cer vt (ter compaixão de) to pity; (tolerar) to bear; **~-se** vr: **~-se de** to be sorry for, pity; **compadecido/a** adj sympathetic; **compadecimento** m sympathy; (piedade) pity.

com'padre m (col: companheiro) buddy, pal, crony; **meu ~** the godfather of my child ou the father of my godchild.

compaixão [kõpajˈʃãw] m (piedade) compassion, pity; (misericórdia) mercy.

companheiro/a [kõpaˈɲejru/a] m/f (colega) friend; (col) buddy, mate; **~ de trabalho** fellow-worker; **~ de viagem** fellow traveller.

companhia [kõpaˈɲia] f (COM) company, firm; (convivência) company; **fazer ~ a alguém** to keep sb company; **em ~ de** accompanied by, along with.

comparação [kõparaˈsãw] f comparison; **comparar** vt (cotejar) to compare; **comparar a** to liken to; **comparar com** to compare with; **comparar-se** vr: **comparar-se com** to bear comparison with; **comparativo/a** adj comparative; **comparável** adj comparable.

compare'cer vi to appear, show up; **~ a uma reunião** to attend a meeting; **comparecimento** m (presença) attendance.

com'parsa m/f (teatro) extra; (cúmplice) accomplice.

compartilhar [kõpaxtʃiˈʎax] vt (partilhar) to share; **~ de** (participar de) to share in, participate in; **~ com alguém** to share with sb.

comparti'mento m (divisão de móvel/veículo) compartment; (aposento) room; **compartir** vt (dividir) to share out.

compas'sado/a adj (medido) measured; (moderado) moderate; (cadenciado) regular.

com'passo m (instrumento) a pair of compasses; (MÚS) time; (ritmo) beat; **dentro do ~** in time with the music; **fora do ~** out of time.

compatibili'dade f compatibility; **compatível** adj compatible.

compatri'ota m fellow countryman, compatriot // f fellow countrywoman.

compe'lir vt to force, compel.

com'pêndio m (sumário) compendium; (livro de texto) text book.

compenetração [kõpenetraˈsãw] f conviction; **compenetrar-se** vr (convencer-se) to be convinced.

compensação [kõpẽsaˈsãw] f compensation; (de cheques) clearance; **em ~** on the other hand; **compensar** vt (reparar o dano) to make up for, compensate for; (equilibrar) to offset, counterbalance; **compensatório/a** adj compensatory.

compe'tência f (habilidade) competence; (aptidão) ability; **competente** adj (capaz) competent; (idôneo) suitable.

competição [kõpetʃi'sãw] f (rivalidade) competition; (desafio) contest; **competidor(a)** m/f competitor, contestant.

compe'tir vi to compete; (ser da competência de) to be one's responsibility; **compete-lhe decidir** it is up to you to decide; ~ **com** (rivalizar) to compete with, rival; **competitivo/a** adj competitive.

compla'cência f complaisance; **complacente** adj obliging.

compleição [kõplej'sãw] f (estatura) build; (temperamento) temperament, disposition.

complemen'tar adj complementary; **complemento** m complement.

completa'mente adv completely, quite.

comple'tar vt (concluir) to complete, finish; (atingir) to reach; ~ **dez anos** to be ten; **completo/a** adj complete; (cheio) full (up) // m whole; **por completo** completely.

complexi'dade f complexity; **complexo/a** adj complex; (difícil) complicated // m complex.

complicação [kõplika'sãw] f complication; (dificuldade) difficulty; **complicado/a** adj complicated; **complicar** vt to complicate, make difficult; **complicar-se** vr to become complicated; (enredo) to thicken.

compo'nente adj, m component.

com'por vt (MÚS) to compose; (discurso, livro) to write; (arranjar) to arrange; (aliviar) to settle; (imprensa) to set; ~-se vr (tranquilizar-se) to calm down; ~-se **de** to be made up of, be composed of.

com'porta f floodgate; (de canal) lock; ~s fpl wiles.

comporta'mento m behaviour; (conduta) conduct; **mau** ~ (de criança) misbehaviour; (de adulto) misconduct.

compor'tar vt (suportar) to put up with, bear; (conter) to hold; ~-se vr (portar-se) to behave; (ter bons modos) to behave o.s.; ~-se **mal** (criança) to misbehave, behave badly.

composição [kõpozi'sãw] f composition; (imprensa) typesetting; (conciliação) compromise; **compositor(a)** m/f composer; (imprensa) typesetter.

com'posto/a adj (sério) serious; (de muitos elementos) composite, compound; ~ **de** made up of, composed of // m compound.

compos'tura f composure.

com'pota f jam, fruit preserve (US); ~ **de laranja** marmalade.

'compra f purchase; (suborno) bribe; **fazer** ~**s** to go shopping;

comprador(a) m/f buyer, purchaser; **comprar** vt to buy, purchase; (subornar) to bribe.

compreender [kõprien'dex] vt (entender) to understand; (conter em si) to be comprised of, consist of; **compreensão** f understanding, comprehension; **compreensível** adj understandable, comprehensible; **compreensivo/a** adj understanding.

compressão [kõpre'sãw] f compression.

com'prido/a adj long; **ao** ~ lengthways; **comprimento** m length.

compri'mido/a adj compressed // m (pílula) pill; (pastilha) tablet; **comprimir** vt to compress; (apertar) to squeeze; (condensar) to condense.

comprometedor(a) adj compromising.

comprome'ter vt to compromise; (arriscar) to endanger, jeopardize; (empenhar) to pledge; ~-se vr: ~-se **a** to undertake to, promise to; ~-se **com uma moça** to promise to marry a girl.

compro'misso m (promessa) promise; (obrigação) obligation; (hora marcada) appointment; (encontro) engagement, commitment; (acordo) agreement; **sem** ~ without obligation.

comprovação [kõprova'sãw] f proof; (provas) evidence; (ADMIN) receipt, voucher; **comprovar** vt to prove; (confirmar) to confirm.

compul'sivo/a adj compulsive; **compulsório/a** adj compulsory.

compunção [kõpũ'sãw] f compunction.

computação [kõputa'sãw] f computation; **computador(a)** adj (que faz cômputos) computing; (que calcula) calculating // m computer; **computar** vt to compute; (calcular) to calculate; (contar) to count; **cômputo** m computation.

comum [ko'mũ] adj (de todos) common; (habitual) ordinary, usual // m the usual thing; **o** ~ **é partirmos às 8** we usually set off at 8; **fora do** ~ unusual.

comun'gar vi to take communion; ~ **em** (participar em) to share; ~ **com** (unir-se) to commune with; **comunhão** f communion; (REL) Holy Communion; **comunhão de bens** joint ownership.

comunicação [komunika'sãw] f communication; (informações) information; (mensagem) message; **comunicado** m report; (oficial) communiqué.

comuni'car vt (informar) to report; (transmitir) to pass on, communicate; (revelar) to make known; (unir) to join // vi (estabelecer comunicação) to communicate.

comuni'dade f community.

comu'nismo m communism; **comunista** adj, m/f communist.

comu'tar vt (JUR) to commute; (trocar) to exchange.

'**côncavo/a** *adj* concave; (*cavado*) hollow // *m* hollow.

conce'ber *vt* (*ger*) to conceive; (*imaginar*) to conceive of, imagine // *vi* to become pregnant.

conce'der *vt* (*permitir*) to allow; (*outorgar*) to grant; (*admitir*) to admit; (*dar*) to give.

conceição [kõsej'sãw] *f* Immaculate Conception.

conceito [kõ'sejtu] *m* (*idéia*) concept, idea; (*fama*) reputation; (*opinião*) opinion; **conceituado/a** *adj* well thought of, highly regarded.

concelho [kõ'seʌu] *m* (*administração*) council; (*município*) district.

concentração [kõsɛtra'sãw] *f* concentration; **concentrado/a** *adj* concentrated // *m* concentrate.

concen'trar *vt* to concentrate; (*atenção*) to focus; (*reunir*) to bring together; ~-**se** *vr*: ~-**se em** to concentrate on.

concepção [kõsɛp'sãw] *f* (*geração*) conception; (*noção*) idea, concept; (*opinião*) opinion.

concer'tar *vt* (*arranjar*) to fix, put right; (*combinar*) to settle; (*opiniões*) to reconcile; (*uma disputa*) to settle // *vi*: ~ **em** (*concordar*) to agree to.

con'certo *m* (*espetáculo*) concert; (*composição*) concerto; (*acordo*) agreement, harmony.

concessão [kõsɛ'sãw] *f* concession; (*permissão*) permission; (*doação*) grant; **concessionário** *m* concessionaire.

concha ['kõʃa] *f* (*moluscos*) shell; (*para líquidos*) ladle; (*para farinha*) scoop.

conchavar [kõʃa'vax] *vi* (*conluiar-se*) to conspire.

conciliação [kõsɪlɪa'sãw] *f* (*acordo*) compromise; (*harmonização*) reconciliation; **conciliador(a)** *adj* conciliatory // *m/f* conciliator; **conciliar** *vt* (*reconciliar*) to reconcile; **conciliatório/a** *adj* conciliatory.

concílio [kõ'sɪlɪu] *m* (REL) council.

con'ciso/a *adj* brief, concise.

conci'tar *vt* (*estimular*) to stir up, arouse; (*incitar*) to incite.

conclu'dente *adj* (*categórico*) conclusive; (*merecendo fé*) convincing.

concluir [kõ'klwɪx] *vt* (*terminar*) to end, conclude // *vi* (*deduzir*) to conclude; **conclusão** *f* (*término*) end; (*dedução*) conclusion; **chegar a uma conclusão** to come to a decision; **conclusivo/a** *adj* conclusive; (*final*) final.

concor'dância *f* (*acordo*) agreement; (*harmonia*) harmony; **concordar** *vi* to agree; **não concordo!** I disagree!; **concórdia** *f* (*harmonia*) harmony; (*acordo*) agreement; (*paz*) peace.

concor'rência *f* (*competição*) competition; **concorrente** *m/f* (*competidor*) competitor; **concorrer** *vi* (*competir*) to compete; **concorrer para** (*contribuir*) to contribute to.

concreti'zar *vt* to make real; ~-**se** *vr*

(*sonho*) to come true; (*ambições*) to be realized.

con'creto/a *adj* concrete; (*verdadeiro*) real; (*sólido*) solid // *m* concrete; ~ **armado** reinforced concrete.

concupiscência [kõkupɪ'sẽsja] *f* (*desejo de bens*) greed; (*apetite sexual*) lust.

con'curso *m* (*competição*) competition.

concussão [kõku'sãw] *f* concussion.

condão [kõ'dãw] *m* (*dom*) talent; (*poder misterioso*) magic power; **varinha de** ~ magic wand.

'**conde** *m* count.

condecoração [kõdekora'sãw] *f* (*insígnia*) decoration; (*medalha*) medal; **condecorar** *vt* (*dar uma insígnia*) to decorate.

condenação [kõdena'sãw] *f* condemnation; (JUR) conviction; ~ **eterna** damnation; **condenar** *vt* to condemn; (JUR: *sentenciar*) to sentence; (JUR: *declarar culpado*) to convict.

condescen'dência *f* acquiescence, tolerance; **condescender** *vi* (*concordar*) to agree; (*ceder*) to give in; **condescender a/em** to condescend to, deign to.

con'dessa *f* countess.

condição [kõdʒɪ'sãw] *f* condition; (*social*) status; **ter** ~ **para** to be fit to, be able to; **com a** ~ **de que** on condition that, provided that; **condições** *fpl* terms, conditions; **pôr em condições** to put in order.

condicionado/a [kõdʒɪsjo'nadu/a] *adj* conditioned; **ar** ~ air conditioning; **condicional** *adj* conditional; **condicionamento** *m* conditioning.

con'digno/a *adj* (*adequado*) fitting; (*merecido*) due.

condimen'tar *vt* to season; **condimento** *m* seasoning.

condi'zente *adj*: ~ **com** in keeping with; **condizer** *vi*: **condizer com** to match, go well together; **não condizer** to clash.

condo'er-se *vr*: ~ **com** to sympathize with; **condolência** *f* condolence.

condução [kõdu'sãw] *f* (*ato de conduzir*) driving; (*transporte*) transport; (*física*) conduction; **carta de** ~ (Pt) driving licence.

con'duta *f* behaviour; **má** ~ misbehaviour.

con'duto *m* (*tubo*) tube; (*cano*) pipe; (*canal*) channel.

condu'tor *m* (MÚS: ELET) conductor; (*de veículo*) driver; (*guia*) guide; (*chefe*) leader; **conduzir** *vt* (Pt: *veículo*) to drive; (*levar*) to lead; (*guiar*) to guide; (*negócio*) to manage; (*física*) to conduct; **conduzir-se** *vr* to behave.

'**cônego** *m* (REL) canon.

conexão [konɛk'sãw] *f* connection.

confecção [kõfɛk'sãw] *f* making; **roupa de** ~ ready-made clothes *pl*; **confecções** *fpl* manufacturing *sg*;

confeccionar vt (fazer) to make; (fabricar) to manufacture.

confederação [kõfedera'sãw] f confederation; (liga) league.

confede'rar vt to unite; ~-se vr to form an alliance.

confeitar [kõfej'tax] vt (bolo) to ice; **confeitaria** f sweet shop, confectioner's, candy store (US); **confeiteiro/a** m/f confectioner.

confe'rência f conference; (discurso) lecture; **conferencista** m (que fala) speaker; **conferente** m (verificador) checker.

confe'rir vt (verificar) to check; (outorgar) to grant; (título) to confer // vi: ~ com (discutir) to confer with; (estar certo) to tally.

confes'sar vt to confess; ~ alguém (REL) to hear sb's confession; ~-se vr to confess; ~-se culpado (JUR) to plead guilty; **confessionário** m confessional; **confessor** m confessor.

con'fetes mpl confetti.

confi'ado/a adj familiar; (col) cheeky.

confi'ança f confidence; (fé) faith; (atrevimento) familiarity; **de** ~ reliable; **digno de** ~ trustworthy.

confi'ar vt to entrust // vi: ~ **em** (fiar) to trust; (contar) to confide in; (esperar) to hope; ~-se vr to trust.

confi'dência f secret; **em** ~ **in** confidence; **confidencial** adj confidential; **confidente** m confidant // f confidante.

configuração [kõfigura'sãw] f configuration; (forma) shape, form; **configurar** vt to shape, form; **configurar-se** vr to take shape.

confi'nar vt (limitar) to limit; (encerrar) to confine // vi: ~ **com** to border on; ~-se vr: ~-se a to confine o.s. to; **confins** mpl limits, boundaries.

confirmação [kõfixma'sãw] f confirmation; **confirmar** vt to confirm; **confirmar-se** vr (REL) to be confirmed; (realizar-se) to come true.

confiscação [kõfiʃka'sãw] f confiscation, seizure; **confiscar** vt to confiscate, seize.

confissão [kõfi'sãw] f confession.

conflagração [kõflagra'sãw] f conflagration, blaze; **conflagrar** vt to inflame, set alight.

con'flito m (luta) conflict; (guerra) war; (combate) fight; **entrar em** ~ **com** to clash with.

conflu'ente m tributary; **confluir** vi to flow together.

conformação [kõfoxma'sãw] f (resignação) resignation; **conformado/a** adj resigned.

confor'mar vt (formar) to form; ~-se vr: ~-se com to resign o.s. to.

con'forme adj: ~ **com** in agreement with // prep according to, as // conj (logo que) as soon as.

conformi'dade f agreement; (resignação) conformity; **em** ~ **com** in accordance with; **conformista** m/f conformist.

confor'tar vt (consolar) to comfort, console; **confortável** adj comfortable; **conforto** m comfort.

confranger vt (afligir) to torment; ~-se vr to be distressed; **confrangido/a** adj distressed, upset.

confra'ria f fraternity; brotherhood; **confraternizar** vi to fraternize.

confron'tar vt (acarear) to confront; (cotejar) to compare; ~-se vr to face each other.

confun'dir vt (não distinguir) to confuse, mistake; (embaralhar) to mix up; (perturbar) to confuse; ~ **com** to mistake for; ~-se vr to get mixed up, become confused.

confusão [kõfu'zãw] f (tumulto, falta de clareza) confusion; (perplexidade) bewilderment; **que** ~! what a muddle!; **confuso/a** adj (misturado) jumbled, mixed up; (perturbado) confused, bewildered.

congelação [kõʒela'sãw] f (Pt: frio) freezing; (: solidificação) congealing; **congelador** m freezer, deep freeze; **congelamento** m freezing; (ECON) freeze; **congelar** vt (gelar) to freeze; (solidificar) to congeal; **congelar-se** vr to freeze.

con'gênito/a adj congenital.

congestão [kõʒɛʃ'tãw] f congestion; **congestionado/a** adj (olhos) bloodshot; (rosto) flushed; **congestionar-se** vr to flush, go red.

conglomeração [kõglomera'sãw] f conglomeration; **conglomerado** m conglomerate; **conglomerar** vt to heap together; **conglomerar-se** vr (unir-se) to join together, group together.

congraça'mento m confraternization.

congratu'lar vt: ~ **alguém por** to congratulate sb on; ~-se vr: ~-se **com alguém por ter ganho** to congratulate sb on winning.

congregação [kõgrega'sãw] f (REL) congregation; (reunião) gathering; **congregar** vt to assemble; **congregar-se** vr to assemble, gather together.

congres'sista m congressman // f congresswoman; **congresso** m congress.

conhaque [ko'naki] m cognac, brandy.

conhecer [kone'sex] vt to know; (estar consciente de) to be aware of; ~-se vr to get to know one another; **quero conhecê-la** I want to get to know her; **conheci-o no ano passado** I met him last year; **que eu conheça não** not to my knowledge; **conhecido/a** adj known; (célebre) well-known // m/f acquaintance.

conhecimento [koneʃi'mẽtu] m (erudição) knowledge; (compreensão) understanding; (COM) bill of lading; **levar ao** ~ **de alguém** to bring to sb's notice;

ter ~ de to be aware of; tomar ~ de to look into.

coni'vente adj conniving; ser ~ em to connive in.

conjetura [kõʒe'tura] (Pt: -ct-) f conjecture, supposition; fazer ~ sobre to guess (at).

conjugal [kõʒu'gaw] adj conjugal; vida ~ married life; conjugar vt (verbo) to conjugate; (unir) to join; conjugar-se vr to join together; cônjuge m husband // f wife.

conjunção [kõʒũ'sãw] f (união) union; (LING) conjunction.

conjun'tivo m (Pt: LING) subjunctive.

con'junto/a adj joint; em ~ together // m (totalidade) whole; (coleção) collection; (equipe) team; (músicos) group; (roupa) outfit.

conjun'tura f (situação) situation; (momento) juncture.

conjuração [kõʒura'sãw] f plot, conspiracy; conjurado/a m/f conspirator.

conju'rar vt (maquinar) to plot // vi: ~ contra to plot against.

co'nosco (Pt: -nn-) pron with us.

conquanto [kõ'kwantu] conj although, though.

conquista [kõ'kiʃta] f (vitória) conquest; (da ciência) achievement; conquistar vt (subjugar) to conquer; (ganhar) to win, gain; conquistar uma pessoa to win a person over.

consagração [kõsagra'sãw] f (REL) consecration; (homenagem) acclaim; (elogio) praise; consagrado/a adj (estabelecido) established.

consangüíneo/a [kõsã'gwiniu/a] adj related by blood // m/f blood relation.

consciência [kõ'sjẽsja] f (moral) conscience; (percepção) awareness; (senso de responsabilidade) conscientiousness; em sã ~ in all conscience; estar em paz com a ~ to have a clear conscience; consciencioso/a adj conscientious.

consciente [kõsi'ẽtʃi] adj conscious; cônscio/a adj aware.

consecução [kõseku'sãw] f attainment.

conseguinte [kõse'gitʃi] adj: por ~ therefore.

conseguir [kõse'gix] vt (obter) to get, obtain; ~ fazer to manage to do, succeed in doing; não ~ fazer to fail to do.

conselheiro [kõse'ʎejru] m (que aconselha) counsellor, adviser; (POL) councillor.

conselho [kõse'ʎu] m advice; (opinião) opinion; (corporação) council; ~ de guerra court martial; C~ de ministros (POL) Cabinet.

con'senso m consensus; (acordo) agreement.

consenti'mento m consent, permission; consentir vt (admitir) to

allow, permit; (aprovar) to agree to // vi: consentir em to agree to.

conseqüência [kõse'kwẽsja] f (resultado) consequence, result; (importância) importance; por ~ therefore, consequently; em ~ de because of; conseqüente adj consequent.

conser'tar vt to mend, repair.

con'serva f (fruta) preserve; (em vinagre) pickle; fábrica de ~s cannery; conservação f conservation; (vida, alimentos) preservation; conservado/a adj (fruta) preserved; (pessoa) well-preserved; (em vinagre) pickled; conservado em lata tinned, canned.

conserva'dor(a) adj conservative // m/f (POL) conservative; conservar vt (preservar) to preserve, maintain; (reter, manter) to keep, retain; conservar-se vr to keep; conservatório m conservatoire.

consideração [kõsidera'sãw] f consideration; (estima) esteem; (reflexão) thought; tomar em ~ to take into account; considerado/a adj respected, well thought of.

conside'rar vt/i to consider, to think about, reflect on; considerável adj (importante) important; (grande) large, considerable.

consignação [kõsigna'sãw] f consignment; consignar vt (enviar mercadorias) to send, dispatch; (: por navio) to ship; (dedicar) to dedicate.

con'sigo pron (m) with himself; (f) with herself; (pl) with themselves; (com você) with you // vb ver conseguir.

consis'tência f consistency; (firmeza) firmness; (estabilidade) stability.

consis'tente adj (sólido) solid; (espesso) thick; consistir vi: consistir em to be made up of, consist of.

conso'ante f consonant; // prep according to // conj as; ~ prometera as he had promised.

consolação [kõsola'sãw] f consolation; consolar vt to console; consolar-se vr (receber consolação) to console o.s.; (animar-se) to cheer up.

conso'nância f (harmonia) harmony; (concordância) agreement.

consorci'ar vt to join // vi: ~ a to unite with; consórcio m (união) partnership; (COM) consortium.

conspícuo/a [kõ'ʃpikwu/a] adj conspicuous.

conspiração [kõʃpira'sãw] f plot, conspiracy; conspirador(a) m/f plotter, conspirator; conspirar vt to plot // vi to plot, conspire.

con'stância f (perseverança) perseverance; (lealdade) faithfulness; constante adj (invariável) constant, continual; (inalterável) firm; constante de consisting of.

con'star vi: ~ que (ser evidente que) to

be obvious that; ~ **de** to consist of; (*estar escrito*) to be written; **não me constava que ...** I was not aware that ... .

consta'tar *vt* (*verificar*) to verify; (*comprovar*) to prove.

constelação [kõʃtela'sãw] *f* constellation; (*grupo*) cluster; **constelado/a** *adj* (*estrelado*) starry.

consternação [kõʃtexna'sãw] *f* (*desalento*) dismay; (*desolação*) distress; **consternado/a** *adj* (*desalentado*) dismayed.

constipação [kõʃtʃipa'sãw] *f* (*Pt*) cold; **constipado/a** *adj*: **estar constipado** to have a cold; **constipar-se** *vr* to catch a cold.

constitucio'nal *adj* constitutional; **constituição** *f* constitution.

constituir [kõʃtʃi'twix] *vt* (*formar*) to constitute, make up; (*estabelecer*) to establish, set up; (*nomear*) to appoint; **~-se** *vr*: **~-se em** to set o.s. up as.

constrangedor(a) [kõʃtranʒe'dox(ra)] *adj* restricting; **constranger** *vt* (*impedir*) to restrict; (*compelir*) to force, compel; **constrangimento** *m* (*aperto*) restriction; (*violência*) force; (*timidez*) restraint.

construção [kõʃtru'sãw] *f* building, construction; **construir** *vt* to build, construct; **construtivo/a** *adj* constructive; **construtor(a)** *m/f* builder, constructor.

consuetudinário/a [kõswetudʒi-'narju/a] *adj* (*JUR*) usual, customary.

'cônsul *m* consul; **consulado** *m* consulate; **consular** *adj* consular; **consulesa** *f* lady consul; (*esposa*) consul's wife.

con'sulta *f* (*médica*) consultation; **livro de ~** reference book; **horas de ~** consulting hours.

consul'tar *vt* (*médico*) to consult; (*obra*) to refer to; **~ alguém sobre** to ask sb's opinion about; **consultivo/a** *adj* advisory; **consultor(a)** *m/f* adviser, consultant; **consultório** *m* surgery.

consumação [kõsuma'sãw] *f* (*acabamento*) completion; (*realização*) fulfilment; (*bebida/comida*) minimum order; **consumado/a** *adj* (*perfeito*) perfect; (*completo*) complete.

consu'mar *vt* (*completar*) to complete; (*realizar*) to fulfil, carry out.

consumi'dor(a) *adj, m/f* consumer; **consumir** *vt* to consume; (*devorar*) to eat away; (*gastar*) to use up; **consumir-se** *vr* to waste away.

con'sumo *m* consumption; **artigos de ~** consumer goods.

'conta *f* (*cálculo*) count; (*em bar, restaurante*) bill; (*fatura*) invoice; (*COM*) account; (*de colar*) bead; (*responsabilidade*) responsibility; **à ~ de** to the account of; **ajustar ~s com** to settle an account with; **~ corrente** current account; **fazer de ~ que** to

pretend that; **levar em ~** to take into account; **por ~ própria** on one's own account; **prestar ~s** to account for; **sem ~** countless; **não é da sua ~** it's none of your business.

contabili'dade *f* book-keeping, accountancy; (*departamento*) accounts department; **contabilista** *m/f* (*Pt*) accountant.

con'tado/a *adj* (*números*) counted; (*história*) told, related; **dinheiro de ~** (*Pt*) cash payment; **contador(a)** *m/f* (*COM*) accountant; (*narrador*) story-teller // *m* (*TEC: medidor*) meter; **contadoria** *f* audit department; **contagem** *f* (*de números*) counting; (*escore*) score.

contagiar [kõta ʒi'ax] *vt* to infect; **~-se** *vr* to become infected; **contágio** *m* infection; **contagioso/a** *adj* contagious; (*col*) catching.

conta-'gotas *m inv* dropper.

contami'nar *vt* to contaminate; (*contagiar*) to infect; (*viciar*) to corrupt.

con'tanto que *conj* provided that.

conta-quilômetros [kõta-ki'lometruʃ] *m* (*Pt*) speedometer, odometer (*US*).

con'tar *vt* (*números*) to count; (*narrar*) to tell; (*propor*) to intend; (*pesar*) to count, matter; **~ com** to count on, depend on; (*esperar*) to expect; **~ dois anos** to be two years old.

con'tato (*Pt*: -ct-) *m* contact; (*toque*) touch; **pôr-se em ~ com** to get in touch with, contact.

contemplação [kõtẽpla'sãw] *f* contemplation; **contemplar** *vt* to contemplate; (*olhar*) to gaze at // *vi* to meditate; **contemplar-se** *vr* to look at o.s.

contempo'râneo/a *adj, m/f* contemporary.

contempori'zar *vi* (*transigir*) to compromise; (*ganhar tempo*) to play for time.

contenção [kõtẽ'sãw] *f* (*contenda*) quarrel, dispute; (*refreio*) restriction, containment; **contenda** *f* quarrel, dispute.

contenta'mento *m* (*felicidade*) happiness; (*satisfação*) contentment; **contentar** *vt* (*dar prazer*) to please; (*dar satisfação*) to content; **contentar-se** *vr* to be satisfied; **contente** *adj* (*alegre*) happy; (*satisfeito*) pleased, satisfied; **contento** *m*: **a contento** satisfactorily.

con'ter *vt* (*encerrar*) to contain, hold; (*refrear*) to restrain, hold back; **~-se** *vr* to restrain o.s.

contestação [kõtɛʃta'sãw] *f* challenge; (*negação*) denial; **contestar** *vt* (*contrariar*) to dispute, contest, question; (*impugnar*) to challenge; **contestável** *adj* questionable.

conteúdo [kõtʃj'udu] *m* contents *pl*.

con'texto [kõ'teʃtu] *m* context.

con'tido/a *adj* contained; (*reprimido*) restrained, held back.

con'tigo *prep* with you.

contigüidade [kõtʃigwɪ'dadʒɪ] *f* proximity; **contíguo/a** *adj*: **contíguo a** next to; (*próximo*) neighbouring, nearby.

conti'nência *f* chastity; (*militar*) salute; **fazer ~ a** to salute; **continente** *adj* chaste // *m* continent.

contingência [kõtʃɪ'ʒẽsja] *f* eventuality; **contingente** *adj* uncertain; (*condicional*) conditional // *m* quota; (*MIL*) contingent; (*COM*) contingency, reserve.

continuação [kõtʃɪnwa'sãw] *f* continuation.

contin'uar *vt* to continue, carry on // *vi*: **~ a falar** to go on talking, keep on talking; **continue! carry on!**; **continuidade** *f* continuity.

contínuo/a [kõ'tʃɪnwu/a] *adj* (*persistente*) continual; (*sem interrupção*) continuous // *m* office boy.

con'tista *m/f* story writer; **conto** *m* story, tale; (*Pt: dinheiro*) 1000 escudos; **conto-do-vigário** *m* confidence trick.

contorção [kõtɔx'sãw] *f* contortion; (*dos músculos*) twitch; **contorcer** *vt* to twist; **contorcer-se** *vr* to writhe.

contor'nar (*rodear*) to go round; (*ladear*) to skirt; **contorno** *m* (*da terra*) contour; (*da cara*) profile; (*de um esboço*) outline.

'contra *prep* against; (*em troca de*) in exchange for; (*ao contrário de*) contrary to.

contra-almi'rante *m* rear-admiral.

contra-a'taque *m* counterattack.

contrabalan'çar *vt* to counterbalance; (*compensar*) to compensate.

contraban'dista *m/f* smuggler; **contrabando** *m* smuggling; (*artigos*) contraband.

contração [kõtra'sãw] (*Pt:* -cç-) *f* contraction.

contradição [kõtradʒɪ'sãw] *f* contradiction; **contradizer** *vt* to contradict; (*negar*) to deny.

contrafação [kõtrafa'sãw] (*Pt:* -cç-) *f* falsification; (*assinatura*) forgery; **contrafazer** *vt* (*reproduzir*) to copy; (*imitar*) to imitate; (*falsificar*) to counterfeit.

contrafeito/a [kõtra'fejtu/a] *adj* (*acanhado*) uneasy; (*embaraçado*) self-conscious.

contra'forte *m* buttress.

contra'ir *vt* to contract; (*doença*) to catch; (*hábito*) to form; **~ matrimônio** to get married; **~-se** *vr* to shrink.

contra'mestre/tra *m/f* (*fábrica, oficina*) supervisor // *m* (*NÁUT*) boatswain.

contra'peso *m* counterbalance.

contra'por (*opor*) to oppose; **~ a** to set against; **~-se** *vr* to be in opposition.

contraprodu'cente *adj* counter-productive, self-defeating.

contra-revolução [kõtraxevolu'sãw] *f* counter-revolution.

contrari'ar *vt* (*contradizer*) to contradict; (*frustrar*) to frustrate;

(*aborrecer*) to annoy; (*desapontar*) to disappoint; **contrariedade** *f* (*aborrecimento*) annoyance, vexation.

con'trário/a *adj* (*oposto*) contrary; (*desfavorável*) unfavourable, adverse; **pelo ~** on the contrary // *m/f* adversary.

contra-'senso *m* nonsense.

contras'tar *vt* to oppose // *vi* to contrast; **contraste** *m* contrast; (*oposição*) opposition.

contra'tante *adj* contracting // *m/f* contractor; **contratar** *vt* (*serviços*) to contract; (*empregar*) to engage.

contra'tempo *m* (*contrariedade*) setback; (*aborrecimento*) disappointment.

con'trato *m* contract; (*acordo*) agreement.

contravenção [kõtravẽ'sãw] *f* contravention, violation.

contribuição [kõtrɪbwɪ'sãw] *f* contribution; (*imposto*) tax; **contribuinte** *m/f* contributor; (*que paga impostos*) taxpayer; **contribuir** *vt* to contribute // *vi* (*pagar impostos*) to pay taxes.

contris'tar *vt* (*entristecer*) to sadden; (*afligir*) to distress; **~-se** *vr* to become sad.

contro'lar *vt* to control; **controle** *m* control.

contro'vérsia *f* controversy; (*discussão*) debate; **controverso/a** *adj* controversial.

con'tudo *conj* nevertheless, however.

contu'mácia *f* obstinacy; (*JUR*) contempt of court; **contumaz** *adj* obstinate, stubborn.

contun'dente *adj* (*argumento*) cutting; **instrumento ~** blunt instrument; **contundir** *vt* to bruise.

conturbação [kõtuxba'sãw] *f* disturbance, unrest; (*motim*) riot; **conturbado/a** *adj* disturbed; **conturbar** *vt* to disturb; (*amotinar*) to stir up.

contusão [kõtu'zãw] *f* bruise; **contuso/a** *adj* bruised.

convales'cença *f* convalescence; **convalescer** *vi* to convalesce.

convali'dar *vt* (*tornar válido*) to validate.

convenção [kõvẽ'sãw] *f* convention; (*acordo*) agreement.

conven'cer *vt* to convince; (*persuadir*) to persuade; **~-se** *vr*: **~-se de** to be convinced about.

convencio'nal *adj* conventional.

conveni'ência *f* convenience; **conveniente** *adj* convenient, suitable; (*vantajoso*) advantageous.

con'vênio *m* (*reunião*) convention; (*acordo*) agreement; (*pacto*) pact.

con'vento *m* (*de freiras*) convent; (*de frades*) monastery.

con'versa *f* conversation; **~ fiada** idle chatter; **conversação** *f* (*ato*) conversation.

conversão [kõvex'sãw] *f* conversion.

conver'sar *vi* to talk, converse.

conversibili'dade *f* convertibility;

conversível adj convertible // m (automóvel) convertible.

conver'ter vt to convert; **~-se** vr to be converted; **convertido/a** adj converted // m/f convert.

con'vés m (NÁUT) deck.

con'vexo/a adj convex.

convicção [kõvik'sãw] f conviction; (certeza) certainty; **convicto/a** adj (convencido) convinced; (réu) convicted.

convi'dado/a adj invited // m/f guest; **convidar** vt to invite; **convidativo/a** adj attractive.

convin'cente adj convincing.

con'vir vi (ser conveniente) to suit, be convenient; (ficar bem) to be appropriate.

con'vite m invitation.

convi'vência f living together; (familiaridade) familiarity, intimacy; **conviver** vi (viver em comum) to live together; (ter familiaridade) to be on familiar terms; **convívio** m (viver em comum) living together; (familiaridade) familiarity.

convo'car vt to summon, call upon; (reunião) to call, convene.

convulsão [kõvul'sãw] f convulsion; (fig) upheaval; **convulsionar** vt (abalar) to shake; (excitar) to stir up; **convulso/a** adj shaking.

cooperação [koopera'sãw] f cooperation; **cooperar** vi to cooperate; **cooperativo/a** adj cooperative // f (COM) cooperative.

coordenação [kooxdena'sãw] f co-ordination; **coordenar** vt to co-ordinate.

'copa f (duma árvore) top; (dum chapéu) crown; (compartimento) pantry; (taça) cup; **~s** fpl (naipes) hearts.

'cópia f copy; **tirar ~ de** to duplicate; **copiadora** f (máquina) duplicating machine; (loja) photocopying shop; **copiar** vt to copy.

copi'oso/a adj abundant, numerous.

copo ['kɔpu] m (vaso) glass.

coqueiro [ko'kejru] m (BOT) coconut tree.

coqueluche [koke'luʃi] f (MED) whooping cough.

cor f colour; **~-de-rosa** pink; **de ~** coloured; (de memória) by heart.

coração [kora'sãw] m (ANAT) heart; (medula) core; (coragem) courage; (bondade) kindness; **de bom ~** kind-hearted; **de todo o ~** wholeheartedly.

co'rado/a adj ruddy.

coragem [ko'raʒẽ] f courage; (atrevimento) nerve; **corajoso/a** adj courageous.

co'rar vt (tingir) to dye; (roupa) to bleach (in the sun) // vi (ruborizar-se) to blush; (tornar-se branco) to bleach.

cor'cel m steed.

cor'cova f hump; **corcovar** vi (cavalo) to buck; **corcunda** m/f hump; (pessoa) hunchback.

'corda f (cabo) rope, line; (de relógio)

spring; **dar ~ em** to wind up; **roer a ~** to go back on one's word; **~s vocais** vocal chords.

cordão [kox'dãw] m string, twine; (ELET) lead; (fileira) row; **~ de sapato** shoestring.

cordeiro [kox'dejru] m lamb; (fig) sheep.

cordel [kox'dew] m (Pt) string; **literatura de ~** pamphlet literature.

cordial [koxdʒ'jaw] adj cordial // m (bebida) cordial; **~idade** f warmth, cordiality.

coreogra'fia f choreography; **coreógrafo/a** m/f choreographer.

co'reto m bandstand.

co'risco m (faísca) flash.

co'rista m/f chorister // f (no teatro) chorus girl.

corja ['kɔxʒa] f (Pt: canalha) rabble; (bando) gang.

cor'neta f cornet; (MIL) bugle // m bugler; **corneteiro** m bugler; **cornetim** m (MÚS) french horn.

'coro m chorus; (conjunto de cantores) choir.

co'roa f crown; (de flores) garland; (Br: col) fogey, old timer; **coroação** f coronation; **coroar** vt to crown; (premiar) to reward.

coro'nel [-ew] m colonel.

coronha [ko'rɔɲa] f (de um fuzil) butt; (de um revólver) handle.

'corpo m body; (MIL) corps sg; **~ diplomático** diplomatic corps sg; **~ de bombeiros** fire brigade; **lutar ~ a ~** to fight hand to hand.

corpu'lência f stoutness; **corpulento/a** adj stout.

correção [koxɛ'sãw] (Pt: -cç-) f correction; (exatidão) correctness; (castigo) chastisement; **casa de ~** reformatory.

corre'diço/a adj sliding // f (cortina) curtain.

corre'dor(a) m/f runner // m (passagem) corridor, passageway; (cavalo) racehorse.

correia [ko'xeja] f strap; (de máquina) belt; (para cachorro) leash.

correio [ko'xeju] m mail, post; (local) Post Office; (pessoa) courier; (carteiro) postman; **~ aéreo** air mail; **pôr no ~** to post.

cor'rente adj (águas) running; (fluente) flowing; (comum) usual, common; (ano etc) present // f current; (cadeia) chain; **~ de ar** draught.

cor'rer vt to run; (viajar por) to travel across; (cortina) to draw; (examinar) to search; (expulsar) to drive out; (perseguir) to pursue // vi to run, (líquido) to flow, run; (o tempo) to elapse.

correspon'dência f correspondence; **correspondente** adj (que corresponde) corresponding, (apropriado) appropriate // m correspondent.

correspon'der vi: **~ a** (ser apropriado) to suit, be suitable for; (ser igual) to match (up to); (*retribuir*) to reciprocate; ~-se com *vr* to correspond with.

cor'reto/a (*Pt*: -ct-) *adj* correct; (*conduta*) proper.

corre'tor *m* broker; ~ de fundos/de bolsa stockbroker.

cor'rido/a *adj* (*envergonhado*) ashamed; (*expulso*) driven out; (*gasto*) hackneyed // *f* (*ato de correr*) running; (*certame*) race; ~a de cavalos horse race; campo de ~as race course; ~a de touros bull fight.

corrigir [koxɪ'ʒɪx] *vt* to correct; (*censurar*) to reprimand.

corrimão [koxɪ'mãw] *m* handrail.

corriqueiro/a [koxɪ'kejru/a] *adj* hackneyed.

corroboração [koxobora'sãw] *f* confirmation; corroborar *vt* to corroborate, confirm.

corrom'per *vt* to corrupt; (*alimentos*) to turn bad; (*adulterar*) to adulterate.

corrução [koxu'sãw] (*Pt*: -pç-) *f* corruption; (*decomposição*) decay, rot; corrupto/a *adj* corrupt; (*podre*) rotten.

cor'sário *m* (*homem*) pirate; (*navio*) privateer.

'Córsega *f* Corsica.

corta'dura *f* (*corte*) cut; (*entre montes*) gap; cortante *adj* cutting; cortar *vt* to cut; (*eliminar*) to cut out; (*água etc*) to cut off; cortar a palavra a alguém to interrupt sb // *vi* to cut; (*encurtar caminho*) to take a short cut.

'corte *m* cut; (*roupa*) style; (*gume*) cutting edge; (*ferroviário*) cutting; ~ de cabelo haircut // *f* (de um monarca) court; (*namoro*) courtship; fazer a ~ a alguém to court sb; ~s *fpl* (*Pt*) parliament.

cortejo [kox'teʒu] *m* (*procissão*) procession; (*cumprimentos*) greetings *pl*.

cor'tês *adj* polite; cortesão/tesã *adj* courtly // *m* courtier // *f* courtesan; cortesia *f* politeness.

cor'tiça *f* (*matéria*) cork.

cor'tiço *m* (*habitação*) slum tenement.

cor'tina *f* curtain; (*biombo*) screen.

coruja [ko'ruʒa] *f* owl.

corus'car *vi* to sparkle, glitter.

'corvo *m* crow.

co'ser *vt/i* to sew, stitch.

cos'mético/a *adj* cosmetic // *m* cosmetic.

cosmopo'lita *adj* cosmopolitan.

'cospe *etc vb ver* cuspir.

'costa *f* coast, shore; ~s *fpl* back; dar as ~s a to turn one's back on.

cos'tado *m* back; dos quatro ~s through and through.

coste'ar *vt* (*rodear*) to go round; (*gado*) to round up // *vi* to follow the coast.

cos'tela *f* rib.

coste'leta *f* chop, cutlet; ~s *fpl* (*suíças*) side-whiskers.

costu'mado/a *adj* (*usual*) usual; costumar *vt* (*habituar*) to accustom // *vi*

to be accustomed to, be in the habit of; costumava dizer ... he used to say ....

cos'tume *m* custom, habit; (*traje*) costume; de ~ usual(ly); ~s *mpl* behaviour, conduct; costumeiro/a *adj* usual, habitual.

cos'tura *f* sewing, needlework; (*sutura*) seam; sem ~ seamless; costurar *vt/i* to sew; costureira *f* dressmaker.

'cota *f* (*quinhão*) quota, share; (*GEO*) height.

cotação [kota'sãw] *f* (*de preços*) list, quotation; (*consideração*) esteem; ~ bancária bank rate.

cotejar [kote'ʒax] *vt* to compare; cotejo *m* comparison.

cotidi'ano/a *adj* daily.

'coto *m* (*do corpo*) stump; (*de uma vela etc*) stub.

coto'velo *m* (*ANAT*) elbow; (*curva*) bend; falar pelos ~s to talk non-stop.

'coube *etc vb ver* caber.

couraça [ko'rasa] *f* (*para o peito*) breastplate; (*de navio etc*) armour-plate; couraçado *m* (*Pt*) battleship.

couro ['koru] *m* leather; (*de um animal*) hide; ~ cabeludo scalp.

couve ['kovi] *f* cabbage; ~-flor *f* cauliflower.

cova ['kova] *f* (*escavação*) pit; (*caverna*) cavern; (*sepultura*) grave.

co'varde *adj* cowardly // *m/f* coward.

coveiro [ko'vejru] *m* gravedigger.

co'vil *m* den, lair.

covinha [ko'viɲa] *f* dimple.

coxa ['koʃa] *f* thigh; coxear *vi* to limp, hobble.

coxia [ko'ʃia] *f* (*passagem*) aisle, gangway.

coxo/a ['koʃu/a] *adj* lame.

co'zer *vt* to cook; (*em água*) to boil; (*ao forno*) to bake; ~ a bebedeira to sleep it off // *vi* to cook; cozido *m* stew.

cozinha [ko'ziɲa] *f* (*compartimento*) kitchen; (*arte*) cookery; (*modo de cozinhar*) cuisine; cozinhar *vt/i* to cook; cozinheiro/a *m/f* cook.

C.P. *abr de* Caminhos de Ferro Portugueses Portuguese State Railway.

Cr$ *abr de* cruzeiro cruzeiro.

'crânio *m* skull.

craque ['kraki] *m/f* ace, expert // *m* (*jogador de futebol*) soccer star.

'crasso/a *adj* crass.

cra'tera *f* crater.

cra'var *vt* (*prego etc*) to drive (in); (*pedras*) to set; (*com os olhos*) to stare at.

craveiro [kra'vejru] *m* (*BOT*) carnation.

cravelha [kra've⋏a] *f* (*MÚS*) tuning peg.

'cravo *m* (*prego*) nail; (*flor*) carnation.

'creche *f* crèche.

credi'tar *vt* to give credit to, loan; 'crédito *m* credit; a crédito on credit; digno de crédito reliable.

'credo *m* creed // *excl* (*Pt*) heavens!

cre'dor(a) *adj* worthy, deserving // *m* creditor.

creduli'dade *f* credulity; **crédulo/a** *adj* credulous.

'creio *etc vb ver* **crer.**

cremalheira [krema'ʎejra] *f* (*trilho*) rack.

cre'mar *vt* to cremate; **crematório** *m* crematorium.

'creme *adj* cream-coloured // *m* cream; (*doce*) custard; ~ **dental** toothpaste; **cremoso/a** *adj* creamy.

'crença *f* belief.

cren'dice *f* superstition.

'crente *adj* believing // *m/f* believer.

crepitação [krɛpita'sãw] *f* crackling; **crepitar** *vi* to crackle.

crepuscu'lar *adj* twilight; **crepúsculo** *m* dusk, twilight.

crer *vt/i* to think, believe; ~ **em** to believe in.

cres'cente *adj* growing; (*forma*) crescent // *m* crescent; **crescer** *vi* to grow; (*aumentar*) to increase; (*medrar*) to thrive; **crescido/a** *adj* (*pessoa*) grown up; (*grande*) large; **crescimento** *m* growth; (*aumento*) increase.

'crespo/a *adj* (*cabelo*) curly; (*áspero*) rough; (*água*) choppy, rough.

cre'tino *m* cretin, imbecile.

'cria *f* (*animal*) baby animal, young; **criação** *f* creation; (*de animais*) raising, breeding; (*educação*) upbringing; (*animais domésticos*) livestock.

cria'dor(a) *adj* creative // *m/f* creator // *m*: ~ **de gado** cattle breeder.

cri'ança *f* child.

cri'ar *vt* to create; (*crianças*) to bring up; (*animais*) to raise, breed; (*produzir*) to produce; (*amamentar*) to suckle, nurse; **criativo/a** *adj* creative; **criatura** *f* creature; (*indivíduo*) individual.

'crime *m* crime; **criminal** *adj* criminal.

crimi'noso/a *adj, m/f* criminal.

'crina *f* mane.

cri'oulo/a *adj* creole // *m/f* creole; (*Br: negro*) black (person).

cri'sálida *f* chrysalis.

'crise *f* crisis; (*escassez*) shortage; (*MED*) attack, fit.

'crisma *f* (*REL*) confirmation; (*óleo*) holy oil.

cris'mar *vt* (*REL*) to confirm; ~-**se** *vr* (*REL*) to be confirmed.

cri'sol [-ow] *m* crucible; (*fig*) test.

cris'par *vt* (*contrair*) to contract; ~-**se** *vr* to twitch.

'crista *f* (*de monte*) crest; (*de galo*) cock's comb.

cris'tal [-aw] *m* crystal; ~**izar** *vi* to crystallize.

cristan'dade *f* Christianity; **cristão/cristã** *adj, m/f, pl* **-ãos** Christian.

cristia'nismo *m* Christianity; **Cristo** *m* Christ; (*crucifixo*) crucifix.

cri'tério *m* (*norma*) criterion; (*juízo*) judgement.

'crítica *f* criticism; (*artigo*) critique; (*conjunto de críticos*) critics *pl*; **criticar** *vt*

to criticize; (*um livro*) to review; **crítico/a** *adj* critical // *m* critic.

cri'var *vt* (*com balas*) to riddle; (*de perguntas, de insultos*) to bombard with.

crível ['krivew] *adj* credible.

'crivo *m* (*Pt*) sieve.

cro'chê *m* crochet.

croco'dilo *m* crocodile.

'cromo *m* chrome.

'crônico/a *adj* chronic // *f* chronicle; (*coluna de jornal*) newspaper column; **cronista** *m/f* (*de jornal*) columnist; (*historiógrafo*) chronicler.

cronolo'gia *f* chronology; **cronológico/a** *adj* chronological.

croquete [kro'ketʃi] *m* croquette.

cro'qui *m* sketch.

'crosta *f* crust; (*MED*) scab.

cru/'crua *adj* raw; (*não refinado*) crude; (*ignorante*) green.

crucificação [krusifika'sãw] *f* crucifixion; **crucificar** *vt* to crucify; **crucifixo** *m* crucifix.

cruel [kru'ew] *adj* cruel; ~**dade** *f* cruelty.

cru'ento/a *adj* (*sanguinolento*) bloody; (*cruel*) cruel.

'crupe *m* (*MED*) croup.

cruz *f* cross; ~ **gamada** swastika; **C**~ **Vermelha** Red Cross; **cruzado/a** *adj* crossed // *m* crusader; (*moeda*) cruzado // *f* crusade.

cruza'dor *m* (*navio*) cruiser.

cruza'mento *m* (*de estradas*) crossing; (*mestiçagem*) cross breeding; **cruzar** *vt* to cross; (*os braços*) to fold; (*NÁUT*) to cruise; **cruzar-se** *vr* to cross; (*pessoas*) to pass by each other.

cruzeiro [kru'zejru] *m* (*cruz*) (monumental) cross; (*moeda*) cruzeiro; (*viagem de navio*) cruise.

cru'zeta *f* (*régua T*) T square; (*Pt: cabide*) coat hanger.

'cuba *f* vat; (*TEC*) reservoir.

'Cuba *f* Cuba; **cubano/a** *adj, m/f* Cuban.

'cúbico/a *adj* cubic; **cubículo** *m* cubicle; **cubo** *m* cube; (*de roda*) hub.

'cuco *m* cuckoo.

cueca ['kwɛka] *f* (*Br*) underpants; ~**s** (*Pt: para homens*) underpants; (*Pt: para mulheres*) panties.

cueiro [ku'ejru] *m* nappy.

cuidado [kwi'dadu] *m* care; (*preocupação*) worry; **aos** ~**s de** in the care of; **ter** ~ to be careful // *excl*: ~! watch out!; **cuidadoso/a** *adj* careful.

cuidar [kwi'dax] *vi*: ~ **de** to take care of, look after; ~-**se** *vr* to look after o.s.

cujo ['kuʒu] *pron* (*de quem*) whose; (*de que*) of which.

cu'latra *f* (*de arma*) breech.

culi'nário/a *adj* culinary // *f* cookery.

culpa ['kuwpa] *f* fault; (*JUR*) guilt; **ter** ~ **de** to be to blame for; **por** ~ **de** because of; ~**bilidade** *f* guilt; **culpado/a** *adj* guilty // *m/f* culprit.

culpar [kuw'pax] *vt* to blame; (*acusar*) to

accuse; ~-se vr to take the blame; culpável adj guilty.

cultivar [kuwtʃi'vax] vt to cultivate; cultivo m cultivation.

culto/a ['kuwtu/a] adj (que tem cultura) cultured; (civilizado) civilized // m (homenagem) worship; (religião) cult; cultura f culture; (da terra) cultivation; (polidez) refinement; cultural adj cultural.

'cume m top, summit; (fig) climax.

'cúmplice m/f accomplice; cumplicidade f complicity.

cumprimen'tar vt (saudar) to greet; (dar parabéns) to congratulate; cumprimento m (realização) fulfilment; (saudação) greeting; (elogio) compliment; cumprimentos mpl best wishes.

cum'prir vt (desempenhar) to carry out; (promessa) to fulfil; (anos) to reach // vi (convir) to be necessary; ~ a palavra to keep one's word; fazer ~ to enforce; ~-se vr to be fulfilled.

'cúmulo m heap, pile; (auge) height; é o ~! that's the limit!

cunha ['kuɲa] f wedge; (pistolão) connections pl.

cunhado/a [ku'ɲadu/a] m brother-in-law // f sister-in-law.

cunhar [ku'ɲax] vt (moedas) to mint; (palavras) to coin.

cupim [ku'pĩ] m termite.

'cúpula f (ARQ) dome.

'cura f (ato de curar) cure; (tratamento) treatment; (de carnes etc) curing, preservation // m priest; curandeiro m (feiticeiro) healer, medicine man; (charlatão) quack.

cu'rar vt (doença) to cure; (ferida) to treat, heal; (carne etc) to cure, preserve; ~-se vr to get well; curativo/a adj medicinal // m (tratamento) treatment; (penso) dressing.

cu'ringa m (cartas) joker.

curiosi'dade f curiosity; (objeto raro) curio; curioso/a adj curious // m/f snooper, inquisitive person.

curral [ku'xaw] m pen, enclosure.

cur'rículo m curriculum; curriculum vitae m curriculum vitae.

cur'sar vt (aulas) to attend; (cursos) to follow.

cur'sivo m (tipografia) script.

'curso m course; (direção) direction; em ~ (ano etc) current; (processo) in progress.

cur'tir vt (couro) to tan; (tornar rijo) to toughen up; (padecer) to suffer, endure; (col) to enjoy.

'curto/a adj short, brief; (entendimento) narrow; de ~a vista (míope) short-sighted.

curto-circuito [kuxtu-six'kwitu] m short circuit.

'curva f curve, bend; curvar vt to bend, curve; curvar-se vr (abaixar-se) to stoop; curvatura f curvature.

cu'spir vi to spit.

'custa f cost, expense; ~s fpl (JUR) costs; à ~ de at the expense of; custar vi to cost; (ser difícil) to be difficult; custar caro to be expensive; custear vt to bear the cost of.

'custo m cost, price; a ~ with difficulty; a todo ~ at all costs.

cus'tódia f custody.

cus'toso/a adj costly; (difícil) difficult.

cutela'ria f knife-making; cutelo m cleaver, carving knife; cutilada f cut, slash.

'cútis f (pele) skin; (fez) complexion.

D

da = de + a, ver de.

'dádiva f (donativo) donation; (oferta) gift; dadivoso/a adj generous.

'dado/a pp de dar given // m (jogo) die; (fato) fact; ~s mpl (jogo) dice; (fatos) data // ~ que conj supposing that, given that.

da'í adv (= de + aí) (desse lugar) from there; (desse momento) from then; ~ a um mês a month later; ~ por/em diante from then on.

da'li adv (= de + ali) from there.

dal'tônico/a [dawt-] adj colour-blind; daltonismo m colour blindness.

'dama f lady; (xadrez, cartas) queen; ~s fpl draughts, checkers (US).

da'masco m (fruta) apricot; (tecido) damask; damasqueiro m apricot tree.

danação [dana'sãw] f damnation; (travessura) mischief, naughtiness; danado/a adj (condenado) damned; (zangado) furious, angry; (menino) mischievous, naughty; cão danado mad dog.

'dança f (ger) dance; dançar vi to dance; dançarino/a m/f dancer; danceteria f disco(theque).

danifi'car vt (objeto) to damage; daninho/a adj harmful; dano m (moral) harm; (a um objeto) damage; (a uma pessoa) hurt, injury; danoso/a adj (a uma pessoa) harmful; (a uma coisa) damaging.

'dantes adv before, formerly.

da'quele/da'quela = de + aquele/aquela, ver aquele.

daqui [da'ki] adv (= de + aqui) (deste lugar) from here; (deste momento) from now; ~ a pouco soon, in a little while; ~ a uma semana in a week's time; ~ em diante from now on.

da'quilo = de + aquilo, ver aquilo.

dar vt to give; (cartas) to deal; (golpes, horas) to strike; ~ à luz to give birth to; ~ gritos to shout; ~ uma volta/um passeio to go for a walk // vi: ~ certo to turn out right; ~ com (encontrar) to meet, come across; (porta) to slam; ~ de comer/beber a to feed/give a drink to; ~ em (pessoa) to hit, beat up; (lugar) to come to, get to; ~ para to look onto;

~ parte de to report; ~ por to notice; **dá licença?** may I?; **~-se** *vr* (*acontecer*) to happen; **~-se a** (*dedicar-se a*) to devote o.s. to; **~-se bem com** to get on well with; **~-se por vencido** to admit defeat; **não me dou bem com o clima** the climate doesn't suit me; **pouco se me dá** I don't care.

'**dardo** *m* dart; (*grande*) spear.

das = **de + as**, *ver* **de**.

'**data** *f* date; (*época*) time; **de longa ~** of long standing; **datar** *vt* to date // *vi*: **datar de** to date from.

datilogra'far (*Pt*: **-ct-**) *vt* to type; **datilografia** (*Pt*: **-ct-**) *f* typing; **datiló-grafo/a** (*Pt*: **-ct-**) *m/f* typist.

de (*de + o* = *do*; *de + os* = *dos*; *de + a* = *da*; *de + as* = *das*) *prep* of, from; **venho ~ São Paulo** I come from São Paulo; **a casa ~ João** John's house; **um romance ~** a novel by; **tirar a tampa ~** to take the lid off; **o infeliz do homem** the poor man; **um vestido ~ seda** a silk dress; **perto ~** near to; **longe ~** far from; **~ manhã** in the morning; **~ dia** by day; **vestido ~ branco** dressed in white; **um homem ~ cabelo comprido** a man with long hair; **~ dois em dois dias** every other day; **~ trem** by train.

dê *etc vb ver* **dar.**

deão [dʒı'ãw] *m* dean.

debaixo [de'bajʃu] *adv* below, underneath // *prep*: **~ de** under, beneath.

de'balde *adv* in vain.

deban'dada *f* stampede; **em ~** in confusion; **debandar** *vt* to put to flight // *vi* to disperse.

de'bate *m* (*discussão*) debate; (*disputa*) argument; **debater** *vt* to debate; (*discutir*) to discuss; **debater-se** *vr* to struggle.

debe'lar *vt* to put down, suppress.

debi'car *vt* (*caçoar*) to make fun of.

débil ['debıw] *adj, pl* '**débeis** (*pessoa*) weak, feeble; (*luz*) dim, faint // *m*: **~ mental** mental defective, moron; **debi-lidade** *f* weakness; (*luz*) dimness; **debilitar** *vt* to weaken; **debilitar-se** *vr* to become weak, weaken.

debique [de'bıkı] *m* mockery, ridicule.

debi'tar *vt* to debit; (*ELET*) to supply; **débito** *m* debit.

debo'chado/a *adj* mocking // *m/f* mocking person; **debochar** *vt* to mock, make fun of.

debru'çar-se [debru'saxsı] *vr* (*inclinar-se*) to bend over; **~ na janela** to lean out of the window.

debrum [de'brũ] *m* hem.

debulha [de'buʎa] *f* (*trigo*) threshing; **debulhar** *vt* (*grão*) to thresh; (*descascar*) to shell; **debulhar-se** *vr*: **debulhar-se em lágrimas** to burst into tears.

debu'tar *vi* to appear for the first time, make one's début.

'**década** *f* decade.

deca'dência *f* decadence; **decadente** *adj* decadent.

deca'ir *vi* (*cair*) to fall; (*declinar*) to decline; (*cair em decadência*) to decay.

decalcar [-kaw'kax] *vt* to trace; (*fig*) to copy; **decalque** *m* tracing.

de'cano *m* (*membro*) oldest member.

decan'tar *vt* (*líquido*) to decant; (*purificar*) to purify; (*celebrar*) to sing the praises of.

decapi'tar *vt* to behead, decapitate.

decência [de'sèsja] *f* decency.

decênio [de'senju] *m* decade.

de'cente *adj* decent; (*limpo*) clean.

dece'par *vt* to cut off, chop off.

decepção [desep'sãw] *f* disappointment; **decepcionar** *vt* to disappoint, let down.

de'certo *adv* certainly.

deci'dido/a *adj* (*resoluto*) determined; (*resolvido*) decided.

deci'dir *vt* (*determinar*) to decide; (*solucionar*) to resolve; **~-se** *vr*: **~-se a** to make up one's mind to; **~-se por** to decide on, go for.

deci'frar *vt* to decipher; (*adivinhar*) to unravel.

deci'mal [-maw] *adj* decimal // *m* (*número*) decimal; **décimo/a** *adj* tenth // *m* tenth.

decisão [desı'zãw] *f* (*sentença*) decision; (*capacidade de decidir*) decisiveness, resolution; **decisivo/a** *adj* decisive.

declamação [deklama'sãw] *f* (*poema*) recitation; (*pej*) ranting; **declamar** *vt/i* (*poemas*) to recite; (*pej*) to rant.

declaração [deklara'sãw] *f* declaration; (*depoimento*) statement; **~ de amor** proposal; **declarar** *vt* (*anunciar*) to declare; (*designar*) to state; **declarar-se** *vr* to declare o.s.

declinação [deklına'sãw] *f* (*LING*) declension.

decli'nar *vt* (*recusar*) to decline, refuse; (*nomes*) to give // *vi* (*sol*) to sink; **~ de fazer** to decline to do.

de'clive *m* slope, incline.

decolagem [deko'laʒẽ] *f* (*avião*) take-off; **decolar** *vi* to take off.

decomposição [dekõpozı'sãw] *f* (*apodrecimento*) decomposition; (*análise*) dissection; **decompor** *vt* (*analisar*) to analyse; **decompor-se** *vr* to rot, decompose.

decoração [dekora'sãw] *f* decoration; (*teatral*) scenery; **decorar** *vt* to decorate; (*aprender*) to learn by heart; **decorativo/a** *adj* decorative.

de'coro *m* (*decência*) decency; (*dignidade*) decorum; **decoroso/a** *adj* decent, respectable.

decor'rer *vi* (*tempo*) to pass; (*acontecer*) to take place, happen; **~ de** (*originar-se*) to result from.

deco'tado/a *adj* (*roupa*) low-necked; **decotar** *vt* (*vestido*) to cut low; **decote** *m* (*vestido*) low neckline.

decre'scente *adj* decreasing, diminishing; **decrescer** *vi* to decrease, diminish; **decréscimo** *m* decrease, decline.

decre'tar *vt* to decree, order; **decreto** *m* decree, order.

decupli'car *vt* to multiply by ten.

de'curso *m* (*tempo*) course; **no ~ de** in the course of, during.

de'dal *m* thimble; (*quantidade*) thimbleful.

dedeira [de'dejra] *f* (*MÚS*) plectrum.

dedicação [dedʒika'sãw] *f* dedication; (*devotamento*) devotion.

dedi'car *vt* (*poema*) to dedicate; (*tempo, atenção*) to devote; **~-se** *vr*: **~-se a** to devote o.s. to; **dedicatória** *f* (*de obra*) dedication.

dedilhar [dedʒi'ʎax] *vt* (*instrumento*) to finger; (*violão*) to strum.

'dedo *m* finger; (*do pé*) toe; **~ anular** ring finger; **~ indicador** index finger; **~ mínimo** little finger; **~ polegar** thumb.

dedução [dedu'sãw] *f* deduction; **deduzir** *vt* to deduct // *vi* (*concluir*) to deduce, infer.

defa'sado/a *adj* out of step; **defasagem** *f* discrepancy.

defecção [defεk'sãw] *f* defection; (*deserção*) desertion; **defectivo/a** *adj* faulty, defective; (*LING*) defective.

defeito [de'fejtu] *m* defect, flaw; **pôr ~ em** to find fault with; **com ~** broken, out of order; **defeituoso/a** *adj* defective, faulty.

defen'der *vt* (*ger, JUR*) to defend; (*proteger*) to protect; **~-se** *vr*: **~-se de** to stand up against.

defen'sável *adj* defensible; **defensiva** *f* defensive; **ficar na defensiva** to be on the defensive; **defensor(a)** *m/f* defender; (*JUR*) defending counsel.

defe'rência *f* (*condescendência*) deference; (*respeito*) respect.

deferi'mento *m* (*aprovação*) approval; (*concessão*) granting; **deferir** *vt* (*atender a*) to approve; (*conferir*) to grant, bestow // *vi* (*concordar*) to concede; (*acatar*) to defer.

de'fesa *f* defence; (*JUR*) counsel for the defence // *m* (*Pt: futebol*) back.

deficiência [defisi'ẽsja] *f* deficiency; **deficiente** *adj* (*carente*) deficient, lacking; (*imperfeito*) defective.

'déficit *m* deficit.

definhar [defi'ɲax] *vt* to waste away // *vi* (*consumir-se*) to waste away; (*murchar*) to wither.

definição [defini'sãw] *f* definition; **definido/a** *adj* (*demarcado*) defined; (*determinado*) definite; **definir** *vt* (*demarcar*) to define; (*interpretar*) to explain; (*estabelecer*) to establish.

defini'tivo/a *adj* (*absoluto*) definite; (*categórico*) definitive; (*final*) final.

deflação [defla'sãw] *f* deflation.

deformação [defoxma'sãw] *f* (*alteração*) alteration; (*desfiguração*) distortion; **deformar** *vt* to deform; (*deturpar*) to

distort; **deformar-se** *vr* to become deformed; **deformidade** *f* deformity.

defraudação [defrawda'sãw] *f* fraud; (*de dinheiro*) embezzlement; **defraudar** *vt* (*dinheiro*) to embezzle; (*uma pessoa*) to swindle; **defraudar alguém de alguma coisa** to cheat sb of sth.

defron'tar *vt* to face // *vi*: **~ com** to face; (*dar com*) to come face to face with; **~-se** *vr* to face each other.

de'fronte *adv* opposite, facing; **~ de** *prep* opposite, facing.

defu'mado/a *adj* smoked; **defumar** *vt* (*presunto*) to smoke.

de'funto/a *adj* dead, deceased // *m/f* dead person.

degelar [deʒe'lax] *vt* to defrost, thaw // *vi* to thaw out; **degelo** *m* thaw.

degeneração [deʒenera'sãw] *f* degeneration; (*moral*) degeneracy; **degenerar** *vt* to corrupt // *vi* to degenerate; **degenerar-se** *vr* to become depraved.

deglu'tir *vt/i* to swallow.

dego'lar *vt* (*pessoa*) to behead, decapitate; (*pescoço*) to cut the throat of.

degradação [degrada'sãw] *f* degradation; **degradar** *vt* to degrade, debase; **degradar-se** *vr* to demean o.s.

degrau [de'graw] *m* step; (*de escada de mão*) rung.

degre'dar *vt* to exile; **degredo** *m* exile.

degustação [deguʃta'sãw] *f* tasting, sampling; **degustar** *vt* to taste; (*vinho*) to sip.

'dei *etc vb ver* **dar**.

deificar [deifi'kax] *vt* to deify.

dei'tado/a *pp de* **deitar** // *adj* (*estendido*) lying down; (*na cama*) in bed.

deitar [dej'tax] *vt* (*estender*) to lay down; (*na cama*) to put to bed; (*colocar*) to put, place; (*lançar*) to cast; (*Pt: líquido*) to pour; **~ sangue** (*Pt*) to bleed; **~ abaixo** to knock down, flatten; **~ a correr** to start running; **~ uma carta** (*Pt*) to post a letter; **~ fora** (*Pt*) to throw away/out; **~-se** *vr* to lie down; (*na cama*) to go to bed.

deixa ['dejʃa] *f* (*teatro*) cue.

deixar [dej'ʃax] *vt* (*ger*) to leave; (*abandonar*) to abandon; (*permitir*) to let, allow; **~ de lado** to set aside; **~ cair** to drop // *vi*: **~ de** (*parar*) to stop; (*não fazer*) to fail to; **não posso ~ de ir** I must go; **não posso ~ de rir** I can't help laughing.

'dela = **de** + **ela**, *ver* **ela**.

dela'tar *vt* to denounce, inform on; (*revelar*) to reveal; **delator(a)** *m/f* informer.

'dele = **de** + **ele**, *ver* **ele**.

delegação [delega'sãw] *f* delegation.

delega'cia *f* office; **~ de polícia** police station; **delegado/a** *m/f* delegate, representative; **delegar** *vt* to delegate.

deleitar [delej'tax] *vt* to delight; **~-se** *vr*: **~-se com** to enjoy, delight in;

deleite *m* delight; **deleitoso/a** *adj* delightful.

dele'tério/a *adj* harmful.

delfim [dew'fĩ] *m* dolphin.

delgado/a [dewga'-] *adj* thin; (*esbelto*) slim, slender; (*fino*) fine.

deliberação [delibera'sãw] *f* deliberation; (*decisão*) decision.

delibe'rar *vt* to decide, resolve // *vi* to ponder.

delica'deza *f* delicacy; (*cortesia*) kindness; **delicado/a** *adj* delicate; (*frágil*) fragile; (*leve*) light; (*sensível*) sensitive.

de'lícia *f* delight; (*prazer*) pleasure; **delicioso/a** *adj* delightful; (*comida, bebida*) delicious.

delimitação [delimita'sãw] *f* demarcation; **delimitar** *vt* to delimit.

deline'ar *vt* (*esboçar*) to outline; (*planejar*) to plan out.

delinqüência [deli'kwẽsja] *f* delinquency; **delinqüente** *adj, m/f* delinquent, criminal; **delinqüir** *vi* to commit an offence.

deli'rante *adj* delirious; **delirar** *vi* (*com febre*) to be delirious; (*de ódio, prazer*) to go mad, rave; **delírio** *m* (*MED*) delirium; (*êxtase*) ecstasy; (*excitação*) excitement.

de'lito *m* (*crime*) crime; (*pecado*) offence; **apanhar em flagrante ~** to catch red-handed.

de'longa *f* delay; **sem mais ~s** without more ado.

delta ['dɛwta] *f* delta.

dema'gogo *m* demagogue.

demais [de'majʃ] *adv* (*em demasia*) too much; (*muitíssimo*) very much // *pron*: **o ~** the rest (of it); **os ~** *mpl* the rest (of them); **por ~** too much; **já é ~ !** this is too much!; **é bom ~** it is too good.

de'manda *f* (*JUR*) lawsuit; (*disputa*) claim; (*ECON*) demand; **em ~ de** in search of; **demandar** *vt* (*JUR*) to sue; (*buscar*) to search for; (*exigir*) to demand.

demão [de'mãw] *f* (*tinta*) coat, layer.

demarcação [demarxa'sãw] *f* demarcation; **demarcar** *vt* (*delimitar*) to demarcate; (*fixar*) to mark out.

dema'sia *f* excess, surplus; (*imoderação*) lack of moderation; **em ~** too much, in excess; **demasiado/a** *adj* too much; (*pl*) too many // *adv* too much.

de'mência *f* insanity, madness; **demente** *adj* crazy, demented.

demissão [demi'sãw] *f* dismissal; **pedido de ~** resignation; **pedir ~** to resign; **demitir** *vt* to dismiss; (*col*) to sack, fire; **demitir-se** *vr* to resign.

'demo *m* devil.

democra'cia *f* democracy; **democrata** *m/f* democrat; **democrático/a** *adj* democratic.

demolição [demoli'sãw] *f* demolition; **demolir** *vt* to demolish, knock down; (*fig*) to destroy.

demo'níaco/a *adj* devilish; **demônio** *m* devil, demon.

demonstração [demõʃtra'sãw] *f* (*lição prática*) demonstration; (*de amizade*) show, display; (*prova*) proof; **demonstrar** *vt* (*ensinar*) to demonstrate; (*provar*) to prove; (*mostrar*) to show; **demonstrativo/a** *adj* demonstrative.

de'mora *f* delay; (*parada*) stop; **sem ~** at once, without delay.

demo'rar *vt* (*mostrar*) to delay, slow down // *vi* (*permanecer*) to stay; (*tardar a vir*) to be late; **~ a chegar** to be a long time coming; **vai ~ muito?** will it take long?; **~-se** *vr* to stay too long, linger.

dene'grir *vt* to blacken; (*difamar*) to denigrate.

den'goso/a *adj* (*criança*) whining; (*mulher*) coquettish, coy; (*choraminguento*) whimpering.

deno'dado/a *adj* brave, daring.

denominação [denomina'sãw] *f* (*REL*) denomination; (*título*) name.

deno'tar *vt* (*mostrar*) to show, indicate; (*significar*) to signify.

densi'dade *f* density; **denso/a** *adj* (*cerrado*) dense; (*espesso*) thick; (*compacto*) compact; (*fig*) heavy.

den'tado/a *adj* serrated // **f** bite; **dentadura** *f* (set of) teeth; (*artificial*) dentures *pl*; **dental** *adj* dental.

'dente *m* tooth; (*de animal*) fang; (*de elefante*) tusk; (*de alho*) clove; **~ abalado** loose tooth; **~ postiço** false tooth; **falar entre os ~s** to mutter, mumble.

dente-de-le'ão *m* dandelion.

denti'frício *m* toothpaste.

den'tista *m/f* dentist.

'dentro *adv* inside; **aí ~** in there // *prep*: **~ de** inside; (*tempo*) within; **~ de dois dias** in/within two days; **~ em** soon, shortly; **~ em pouco** soon, before long; **de ~ para fora** inside out.

de'núncia *f* denunciation; (*acusação*) accusation; **denunciar** *vt* to denounce, inform against; (*revelar*) to reveal.

depa'rar *vt* (*revelar*) to reveal; (*fazer aparecer*) to present // *vi*: **~ com** to come across, meet.

departa'mento *m* department.

depe'nar *vt* to pluck.

depen'dência *f* dependence; (*edificação*) annexe; (*colonial*) dependency; **dependente** *m/f* dependent; **depender** *vi*: **depender de** to depend on.

dependu'rar *vi* to hang.

depi'lar *vt* to remove hair from; **depilatório** *m* hair-remover.

deplo'rar *vt* to deplore; (*lamentar*) to regret; **deplorável** *adj* deplorable; (*lamentável*) regrettable.

depoimento [depoj'mẽtu] *m* testimony, evidence.

depois [de'pojʃ] *adv* afterwards, next //

prep: ~ **de** after; ~ **de comer** after eating.

de'por *vt* (*rei*) to depose; (*governo*) to overthrow // *vi* (*JUR*) to testify.

deportação [depoxta'sãw] *f* deportation; **deportar** *vt* to deport.

deposição [depozi'sãw] *f* deposition; (*governo*) overthrow.

depositar *vt* to deposit; (*voto*) to cast; ~ **confiança em** to place one's confidence in; ~-**se** *vr* (*líquido*) to form a deposit; **depositário/a** *m/f* trustee // *m* (*fig*) confidant // *f* (*fig*) confidante.

de'pósito *m* deposit; (*armazém*) warehouse, depot; (*de lixo*) dump; (*reservatório*) tank; ~ **de bagagens** left-luggage office.

depravação [deprava'sãw] *f* depravity, corruption; **depravar** *vt* to deprave, corrupt; (*estragar*) to ruin; **depravar-se** *vr* to become depraved.

depre'car *vt* to beg for, pray for // *vi* to plead.

depreciação [depresja'sãw] *f* depreciation; **depreciar** *vt* (*desvalorizar*) to devalue; (*desdenhar*) to belittle; **depreciar-se** *vr* to depreciate, lose value.

depredação [depreda'sãw] *f* depredation; **depredar** *vt* to pillage, plunder.

de'pressa *adv* fast, quickly; (*com pressa*) in a hurry; **vamos** ~ let's hurry.

depressão [deprɛ'sãw] *f* (*ger*) depression; **deprimido/a** *adj* depressed, low; **deprimir** *vt* to depress; **deprimir-se** *vr* to get depressed.

depuração [depura'sãw] *f* purification; **depurar** *vt* to purify.

deputado/a *m/f* deputy; (*agente*) agent; (*político: US*) Representative; (*: Brit*) Member of Parliament, M.P.

'dera *etc vb ver* **dar.**

de'riva *f* drift; **ir à** ~ to drift; **ficar à** ~ to be adrift.

derivação [deriva'sãw] *f* derivation; **derivar** *vt* (*desviar*) to change the course of; (*LING*) to derive // *vi* (*ir à deriva*) to drift; **derivar-se** *vr* (*palavra*) to be derived; (*ir à deriva*) to drift.

derradeiro/a [dexa'dejro/a] *adj* last, final.

derrama'mento *m* spilling; (*sangue, lágrimas*) shedding; **derramar** *vt* to spill; (*sangue, lágrimas*) to shed; (*espalhar*) to scatter; **derramar-se** *vr* to pour out; (*correr*) to flow; **derrame** *m* (*MED*) discharge; (*de sangue*) haemorrhage.

derre'dor *adv/prep:* **em** ~ (**de**) around.

derre'ter *vt* to melt; ~-**se** *vr* to melt; (*neve*) to thaw.

derri'bar *vt ver* **derrubar.**

derro'cada *f* downfall; (*ruína*) collapse.

der'rota *f* defeat, rout; (*NÁUT*) route; **derrotar** *vt* (*vencer*) to defeat; (*em jogo*) to beat.

derru'bar *vt* to knock down; (*destruir*) to destroy; (*demolir*) to pull down.

desaba'far *vt* (*sentimentos*) to give vent to // *vi* to let off steam.

desaba'lado/a *adj* (*excessivo*) excessive; (*precipitado*) headlong.

desa'bar *vi* to fall, tumble down.

desabotoar [dezabot'waʃ] *vt* to unbutton.

desa'brido/a *adj* rude, brusque.

desabro'char *vi* (*flores*) to open, bloom.

desabu'sado/a *adj* (*sem preconceitos*) unprejudiced; (*atrevido*) impudent.

desaca'tar *vt* to disregard; (*desprezar*) to scorn; **desacato** *m* (*falta de respeito*) disrespect; (*desprezo*) disregard.

desa'certo *m* mistake, blunder.

desacor'dado/a *adj* unconscious.

desa'cordo *m* (*falta de acordo*) disagreement; (*desarmonia*) discord.

desacostu'mado/a *adj* unaccustomed.

desacredi'tado/a *adj* discredited; **ficar** ~ to lose one's reputation; **desacreditar** *vt* to discredit; **desacreditar-se** *vr* to lose one's reputation.

desafia'dor(a) *adj* challenging; (*pessoa*) defiant // *m/f* challenger; **desafiar** *vt* (*propor combate*) to challenge; (*afrontar*) to defy.

desafi'nado/a *adj* out of tune; **desafinar** *vt* (*atrapalhar*) to spoil // *vi* to play out of tune.

desa'fio *m* challenge; (*Pt: esporte*) match, game.

desafo'gado/a *adj* (*desimpedido*) clear; (*desembaraçado*) untroubled; **desafogar** *vt* (*libertar*) to free; (*desapertar*) to relieve; (*desabafar*) to give vent to; **desafogo** *m* (*alívio*) relief; (*folga*) leisure.

desafo'rado/a *adj* rude, insolent; **desaforo** *m* insolence, abuse.

desafortu'nado/a *adj* unfortunate, unlucky.

desa'fronta *f* (*satisfação*) redress; (*vingança*) revenge.

desagra'dar *vt* to displease, offend; **desagradável** *adj* unpleasant.

desa'grado *m* displeasure.

desagra'var *vt* (*insulta*) to make amends for; (*pessoa*) to make amends to; ~-**se** *vr* to avenge o.s.; **desagravo** *m* amends *pl.*

desagregação [dezagrega'sãw] *f* (*separação*) separation; (*dissolução*) disintegration; **desagregar** *vt* (*desunir*) to break up, split; (*separar*) to separate; **desagregar-se** *vr* (*desunir-se*) to break up, split; (*separar-se*) to separate.

desa'guar *vt* to drain // *vi* to flow.

desai'roso/a *adj* (*desajeitado*) awkward, clumsy; (*deselegante*) inelegant.

desajeitado/a [dezaʒej'tadu/a] *adj* clumsy, awkward.

desajuizado/a [dezaʒwi'zadu/a] *adj* foolish, unwise.

desalen'tado/a *adj* disheartened;

desalentar vt to discourage; (deprimir) to depress; **desalento** m discouragement.

desalinhado/a [dɛzalɪ'ɲadu/a] adj untidy, disorderly; **desalinho** m untidiness.

desal'mado/a [-awm-] adj cruel, inhuman.

desalojar [dɛzalo'ʒax] vt (expulsar) to oust; ~-se vr to move out.

desamar'rar vt to untie // vi (NÁUT) to cast off.

desa'mor m dislike; (desprezo) disdain.

desampa'rado/a adj (abandonado) abandoned; **desamparar** vt to abandon.

desan'dar vi: ~ a correr to break into a run; ~ a chorar to burst into tears.

desani'mado/a adj (pessoa) depressed, downhearted; (festa) dull; **desanimar** vt (desalentar) to discourage; (deprimir) to depress; **desanimar-se** vr to lose heart; **desânimo** m depression; (desalento) dejection.

desanuvi'ado/a adj unclouded, clear; **desanuviar** vt to clear; **desanuviar-se** vr to clear up; (cabeça) to put one's mind at rest.

desapaixonado/a [dɛzapajʃu'nadu/a] adj dispassionate.

desapare'cer vi to disappear, vanish; **desaparecido/a** adj lost, missing // m missing person; **desaparecimento** m disappearance; (falecimento) death; (perda) loss.

desape'gado/a adj indifferent, detached; **desapegar** vt to detach; **desapego** m indifference, detachment.

desaperce'bido/a adj (desprevenido) unprepared; (desguarnecido) unequipped.

desaper'tar vt (desabotoar) to unfasten; (afrouxar) to loosen.

desapie'dado/a adj pitiless, ruthless.

desaponta'mento m disappointment; **desapontar** vt to disappoint.

desapropri'ar vt (bens) to expropriate; (pessoa) to dispossess.

desapro'var vt (reprovar) to disapprove of; (censurar) to object to.

desaproveitado/a [dɛzaprovej'tadu/a] adj wasted; (terras) undeveloped.

desarma'mento m disarmament; **desarmar** vt to disarm; (desmontar) to dismantle; (bomba) to defuse.

desarmo'nia f discord.

desarraigar [dɛzaxaj'gax] vt to uproot.

desarranjado/a [dɛzaxã'ʒadu/a] adj (intestino) upset; (TEC) out of order; **desarranjar** vt (transtornar) to upset, disturb; (estragar) to mess up; **desarranjo** m (desordem) disorder; (enguiço) breakdown; (col) diarrhoea.

desarru'mado/a adj untidy, messy; (TEC) out of order; **desarrumar** vt to disarrange; (mala) to unpack.

desarticu'lado/a adj dislocated; **desarticular** vt (osso) to dislocate.

desassos'sego m (inquietação) disquiet; (perturbação) restlessness.

desas'trado/a adj (funesto) disastrous; (sem graça) awkward, clumsy; **desastre** m disaster; (acidente) accident; (de avião) crash; **desastroso/a** adj disastrous.

desa'tar vt (botão) to unfasten; (nó) to undo, untie // vi: ~ a chorar to burst into tears; ~ a rir to burst out laughing.

desaten'der vt (não fazer caso de) to pay no attention to, ignore; (desprezar) to be discourteous to // vi: ~ a to ignore.

desati'nado/a adj crazy, wild; **desatinar** vi to behave foolishly; **desatino** m (loucura) madness; ato de desatino folly, foolishness.

desa'vença f (briga) quarrel; (discórdia) disagreement; em ~ at loggerheads.

desavergonhado/a [dɛzavɛxgo'ɲadu/a] adj insolent, impudent, shameless.

desa'vir-se vr: ~ com to fall out with.

desbarata'mento m (derrota) defeat; (desperdício) waste; **desbaratar** vt to ruin; (desperdiçar) to waste, squander; (vencer) to defeat.

desbas'tar vt (cabelo, plantas) to thin (out); (vegetação) to trim; (fig) to polish.

desbo'tar vt to discolour // vi to fade; ~-se vr to fade.

desbrava'dor(a) m/f explorer; **desbravar** vt (terras desconhecidas) to explore.

desca'bido/a adj (impróprio) improper; (inoportuno) inappropriate.

descal'çar vt (sapatos) to take off; ~-se vr to take off one's shoes; **descalço/a** adj barefoot.

desca'mar vt (peixe) to scale.

descam'pado m open country.

descan'sado/a adj (tranquilo) calm, quiet; (vagaroso) slow; fique ~ don't worry; **descansar** vt to rest; (apoiar) to lean // vi (repousar) to rest, relax; **descansar em** (confiar) to trust; **descanso** m (repouso) rest; (alívio) relief; (folga) break; (recreio) relaxation; sem descanso without a pause.

desca'rado/a adj cheeky, impudent; **descaramento** m cheek, impudence.

des'carga f unloading; (vaso sanitário) flushing; (MIL) volley; (ELET) discharge; dar ~ to flush the toilet.

descar'nado/a adj scrawny, skinny.

descaro'çar vt (semente) to seed; (fruto) to stone, core; (algodão) to gin.

descarregadouro [dɛʃkaxɛga'doru] m wharf; **descarregamento** m unloading; (ELET) discharge; **descarregar** vt (carga) to unload; (ELET) to discharge; (aliviar) to relieve; (raiva) to give vent to.

descarrilha'mento m derailment; **descarrilhar** vt to derail // vi to run off the rails; (fig) to go off the rails.

descar'tar vt to discard; ~-se vr: ~-se de to get rid of.

descasca'dor m peeler; **descascar** vt (fruta) to peel; (ervilhas) to shell; (repreender) to tear a strip off // vi: o feijão descascou the skin came off the beans; **a cobra descascou** the snake shed its skin.

descen'dência f descendants pl, offspring pl; **descendente** adj descending, going down // m/f descendant; **descender** vi: **descender de** to descend from.

descentrali'zar vt to decentralize.

descer [dɛʃ'sex] vt (escada) to go/come down; (bagagem) to take down // vi (saltar) to get off; (baixar) to go/come down; ~ **a pormenores** to get down to details.

descer'rar vt (abrir) to open; (revelar) to reveal, disclose.

descida [dɛʃ'sida] f descent; (declive) slope; (abaixamento) fall, drop.

desclassifi'car vt (eliminar) to disqualify; (desacreditar) to discredit.

desco'berto/a adj discovered; (nu) bare, naked; (exposto) exposed; **a ~** openly; **pôr em ~** (conta) to overdraw // f discovery; (invenção) invention; **descobridor(a)** m/f discoverer; (explorador) explorer; **descobrimento** m discovery.

desco'brir vt (tirar cobertura) to uncover; (revelar) to reveal, show; (encontrar) to discover, find; (avistar) to discern; (petróleo) to strike; **~-se** vr to take off one's hat.

desco'lar vt to unstick; (separar) to detach, remove.

descolo'rir vt to discolour // vi to fade.

descompas'sado/a adj (exagerado) out of all proportion; (ritmo) out of step.

descom'por vt (desordenar) to disturb, upset; (afrontar) to abuse; (censurar) to scold, tell off; **descomposto** adj (aspeto) improperly dressed; (transtornado) upset; **descompostura** f (desordem) disarray; (censura) dressing-down.

descompri'mir vt to decompress.

descomu'nal [-aw] adj (fora do comum) unusual; (colossal) huge, enormous.

desconcer'tado/a adj (embaraçado) disconcerted; (em desordem) out of order; **desconcertar** vt (atrapalhar) to confuse, baffle; **desconcertar-se** vr to get upset; **desconcerto** m (desordem) disorder, disarray; (discordância) disagreement.

desco'nexo/a adj (desunido) disconnected, unrelated; (incoerente) incoherent.

desconfi'ado/a adj suspicious, distrustful // m/f suspicious person; **desconfiança** f suspicion, distrust; **desconfiar** vi (julgar) to suspect; **desconfiar de alguém** to distrust sb.

descon'forme adj disagreeing, at variance.

descon'forto m discomfort; (aflição) distress.

descongela'mento m thawing; **descongelar** vt (degelar) to thaw out; **descongelar-se** vr (derreter-se) to melt.

desconhecer [dɛʃkoɲɛ'sex] vt (ignorar) not to know; (não reconhecer) not to

recognise; (um benefício) not to acknowledge; (não admitir) not to accept; **desconhecido/a** adj unknown // m/f stranger; **desconhecimento** m ignorance.

desconjun'tado/a adj disjointed; (ossos) dislocated; **desconjuntar** vt (ossos) to dislocate; **desconjuntar-se** vr to come apart.

desconso'lado/a adj miserable, disconsolate; **desconsolar** vt to sadden, depress; **desconsolar-se** vr to despair.

descon'tar vt (abater) to deduct; (não levar em conta) to discount; (não fazer caso) to make light of.

descontenta'mento m discontent; (desgosto) displeasure; **descontentar** vt (desgostar) to displease; (lei) to go against; (pessoa) to upset; **descontente** adj (não satisfeito) dissatisfied; (infeliz) discontented.

des'conto m discount; **com ~** at a discount.

descontro'lar-se vr (situação) to get out of control; (pessoa) to lose one's self-control.

desco'rar vt to discolour // vi to pale, fade.

descor'tês adj rude, impolite; **descortesia** f rudeness, impoliteness.

desco'ser vt (Pt) (descosturar) to unstitch; (rasgar) to rip apart; **~-se** vr to come apart at the seams.

descostu'rar (Br) ver **descoser**.

des'crédito m discredit.

des'crença f disbelief, incredulity; **descrente** adj sceptical // m/f sceptic; **descrer** vt to disbelieve // vi: **descrer de** to disbelieve in.

descre'ver vt to describe; **descrição** f description; **descritivo/a** adj descriptive; **descrito/a** pp de **descrever**.

descuidado/a [dɛʃkwi'dadu/a] adj careless; **descuidar** vt to neglect // vi: **descuidar de** to neglect, disregard; **descuido** m (falta de cuidado) carelessness; (negligência) neglect; (erro) oversight, slip; **por descuido** inadvertently.

des'culpa f (escusa) excuse; (perdão) pardon; **pedir ~s de alguma coisa a alguém** to apologise to sb for sth.

descul'par vt (justificar) to excuse; (perdoar) to pardon, forgive; **~ alguma coisa a alguém** to forgive sb for sth; **~-se** vr to apologize; **desculpe!** (I'm) sorry, I beg your pardon; **desculpável** adj excusable.

'desde prep from, since; **~ então** from that time, ever since; **~ há muito** for a long time (now); **~ já** at once, right now // conj: **~ que** since.

desdém [dɛʒ'dẽ] m scorn, disdain; **desdenhar** vt to scorn, disdain; **desdenhoso/a** adj disdainful, scornful.

desden'tado/a adj toothless.

des'dita f (*desventura*) misfortune; (*infelicidade*) unhappiness.

desdi'zer vt to contradict; ~-se vr to go back on one's word.

desdo'brar vt (*abrir*) to unfold; (*tropas*) to deploy; (*bandeira*) to unfurl; ~-se vr to unfold; (*pessoa*) to work hard, make a big effort.

des'douro m tarnish, stain.

desejar [dese'ʒax] vt to want, desire; ~ ardentemente to long for; que deseja? what would you like?; desejável adj desirable; desejo m wish, desire.

desejoso/a [deze'ʒozu/a] adj: ~ de alguma coisa wishing for sth; ~ de fazer anxious to do, keen to do.

desemaranhar [dɛzimaraˈnax] vt to disentangle; (*decifrar*) to unravel.

desembainhar [dɛzẽmbajˈnax] vt to unsheathe; (*espada*) to draw.

desembara'çado/a adj (*livre*) free, clear; (*desinibido*) uninhibited, free and easy.

desembara'çar vt (*livrar*) to free; (*desenredar*) to disentangle; ~-se vr to lose one's inhibitions; **desembaraço** m (*viveza*) liveliness; (*facilidade*) ease; (*confiança*) self-assurance.

desemba'rcar vt (*carga*) to unload; (*passageiros*) to put on shore // vi to land, disembark; **desembarque** m landing, disembarkation.

desemboca'dura f river mouth; **desembocar** vi: **desembocar em** (*rio*) to flow into; (*rua*) to lead into.

desembol'sar vt to spend; **desembolso** m expenditure.

desembre'ar vt (AUTO) to declutch.

desembrulhar [dɛzẽbruˈʎax] vt to unwrap; (*esclarecer*) to clear up.

desempaco'tar vt to unpack.

desem'pate m: partida de ~ (*jogo*) play-off, decider.

desempe'nar vt (*endireitar*) to straighten; ~-se vr to stand up straight.

desempenhar [dɛzẽpeˈnax] vt (*cumprir*) to carry out, fulfil; ~ um papel to play a part; **desempenho** m (*cumprimento*) fulfilment; (*teatro*) performance.

desemper'rar vt to loosen.

desempre'gado/a adj unemployed // m/f unemployed person; **desempregar-se** vr to lose one's job; **desemprego** m unemployment.

desencade'ar vt to unleash; (*despertar*) to provoke, trigger off // vi (*chuva*) to pour; ~-se vr to break loose; (*tempestade*) to burst, break out.

desencai'xado/a adj misplaced; **desencaixar** vt to force out of joint; (*deslocar*) to dislodge, gouge out; **desencaixar-se** vr to become dislodged.

desencaminhar [dɛzẽkamiˈnax] vt to lead astray; (*dinheiro*) to embezzle; ~-se vr to go astray.

desencan'tar vt to disenchant; (*desiludir*) to disillusion.

desen'cargo m fulfilment; ~ de consciência clearing of one's conscience; **desencarregar-se** vr (*obrigação*) to discharge o.s.

desenfasti'ar vt to amuse; (*convalescente*) to restore sb's appetite; ~-se vr to amuse o.s.

desenfre'ado/a adj unruly, wild.

desenga'nar vt to disillusion; (*de falsas crenças*) to put sb wise, to open sb's eyes; ~-se vr (*sair de erro*) to realize the truth; (*desiludir-se*) to become disillusioned; **desengano** m disillusionment; (*desapontamento*) disappointment.

desengon'çado/a adj unhinged; (*malseguro*) rickety; (*pessoa*) ungainly.

desengre'nado/a adj out of gear.

desenhar [dezeˈnax] vt to draw; (TEC) to design; ~-se vr (*figurar-se*) to take shape; **desenhista** m/f (TEC) designer; **desenho** m drawing; (*modelo*) design; (*esboço*) sketch; (*plano*) plan; **desenho animado** cartoon.

desenlace [dɛzẽˈlasi] m outcome.

desenre'dar vt to disentangle; (*mistério*) to unravel; ~-se vr to extricate o.s.; **desenredo** m untangling.

desenro'lar vt to unroll; (*narrativa*) to develop; ~-se vr to unfold.

desenten'der vt (*não entender*) to misunderstand; ~-se vr: ~-se com to fall out with; **desentendido/a** adj: fazer-se de desentendido to pretend not to understand; **desentendimento** m misunderstanding.

desenter'rar vt (*cadáver*) to exhume; (*tesouro*) to dig up; (*descobrir*) to bring to light.

desento'ado/a adj discordant; (*desafinado*) out of tune.

desentranhar [dɛzẽtraˈnax] vt to disembowel; (*arrancar*) to draw out.

desentu'pir vt to unblock.

desen'volto/a adj (*desembaraçado*) self-assured, confident; (*desinibido*) uninhibited; **desenvoltura** f (*desembaraço*) self-confidence.

desenvol'ver vt to develop; (*desembrulhar*) to unwrap; ~-se vr to develop; **desenvolvimento** m development; (*crescimento*) growth.

desequilibrado/a [dɛzekiliˈbradu/a] adj unbalanced.

deserção [dezexˈsãw] f desertion; **desertar** vt to desert, abandon // vi to desert; **deserto/a** adj (*desabitado*) deserted; (*solitário*) lonely // m desert.

desespe'rado/a adj desperate; (*furioso*) furious; **desesperança** f despair.

desespe'rar vt to drive to despair; ~-se vr to despair; **desespero** m despair, desperation; (*raiva*) fury.

desfaça'tez f impudence, cheek.

desfal'car vt to embezzle.

desfale'cer vt (enfraquecer) to weaken // vi (enfraquecer) to weaken; (desmaiar) to faint.

desfalque [dɛʃ'fawkɪ] m embezzlement, misappropriation.

desfavo'rável adj unfavourable.

desfa'zer vt (desmanchar) to undo; (dúvidas) to dispel; (agravo) to redress; ~-se vr (desaparecer) to vanish; (derreter-se) to melt; ~-se de (livrar-se) to get rid of.

desfechar [dɛʃfe'ʃax] vt (disparar) to fire; (setas) to shoot; (golpe) to deal; (insultos) to hurl // vi (tempestade) to break; **desfecho** m ending, outcome.

desfeito/a [dɛʃ'fejtu/a] pp de **desfazer** // adj (desmanchado) undone; (dissolvido) dissolved; (derrotado) destroyed; (contrato) broken // f affront, insult.

desfe'rir vt (golpe) to strike; (sons) to emit; (lançar) to throw.

desfi'ar vt to unweave, unravel; ~-se vr to become frayed.

desfigu'rar vt (adulterar) to distort; (tornar feio) to disfigure.

desfiladeiro [dɛʃfila'dejru] m (de montanha) pass.

desfi'lar vi to march past, parade past; **desfile** m parade, procession.

des'forra f (vingança) revenge; (reparação) redress; **tirar** ~ to get even.

desfru'tar vt (deliciar-se com) to enjoy; (parasitar) to sponge on; **desfrute** m (deleite) enjoyment; (zombaria) ridicule, mockery.

desgalhar [dɛʒga'ʎax] vt to prune.

desgar'rado/a adj lost; (navio) off course; **desgarrar-se** vr: **desgarrar-se de** to stray from.

desgas'tar vt to wear away, erode; ~-se vr to become worn away; **desgaste** m wear and tear.

desgos'tar vt (desagradar) to displease; (contrariar) to annoy // vi: ~ **de** to dislike; ~-se vr: ~-se **de** to lose one's liking for; ~-se **com** to take offence at; **desgosto** m (desprazer) displeasure; (pesar) sorrow; (mágoa) pain.

des'graça f (desventura) misfortune; (miséria) misery; (desfavor) disgrace; (desastre) disaster; **desgraçado/a** adj (infeliz) poor, unfortunate; (pobre) poor, miserable // m/f wretch.

desgrenhado/a [dɛʒgre'ɲadu/a] adj dishevelled, tousled.

desidratação [dɛzidrata'sãw] f dehydration; **desidratar** vt to dehydrate.

designação [dɛzigna'sãw] f (indicação) designation; (nomeação) appointment; (escolha) choice; **designar** vt to designate; (nomear) to name, appoint.

designio [de'zigniu] m (propósito) purpose.

desigual [dɛzi'gwaw] adj (terreno) uneven; (combate) unequal.

desilu'dir vt (desenganar) to disillusion; (causar decepção a) to disappoint; ~-se vr to lose one's illusions; **desilusão** f disillusionment, disenchantment.

desimpe'dido/a adj free; **desimpedir** vt (obstáculo) to clear away.

desinchar [dɛzin'ʃax] vt (orgulho) to deflate; (MED) to reduce the swelling of; ~-se vr to become less swollen.

desinfecção [dɛzinfe'sãw] f disinfection; **desinfetante** (Pt: -ct-) adj, m disinfectant; **desinfetar** (Pt: -ct-) vt to disinfect.

desintegração [dɛzintegra'sãw] f disintegration, break-up; **desintegrar** vt to separate; **desintegrar-se** vr to disintegrate, fall to pieces.

desinteres'sado/a adj disinterested, dispassionate, impartial; **desinteressar-se** vr: **desinteressar-se de** to lose interest in; **desinteresse** m (falta de interesse) lack of interest.

desis'tir vi to give up; ~ **de fumar** to stop smoking.

desle'al [-aw] adj disloyal; ~**dade** f disloyalty.

desleixo [dɛʃ'lejʃu] m (negligência) carelessness; (pessoa) slovenliness.

desli'gado/a adj (eletricidade) off; (pessoa) **estar** ~ to be miles away; **desligar** vt (TEC) to disconnect; (desatar) to unfasten, undo; (soltar) to release; (luz, TV) to switch off; (telefone) to hang up; **não desligue** (TEL) hold the line.

desli'zar vi to slide; (por acidente) to slip; (passar de leve) to glide; **deslize** m (lapso) lapse; (escorregadela) slip.

deslo'car vt (mover) to move; (afastar) to remove; (articulação) to dislocate.

deslumbra'mento m dazzle; (fascinação) fascination; **deslumbrar** vt to dazzle; (maravilhar) to amaze; (fascinar) to fascinate.

deslus'trar vt to tarnish; (manchar) to sully.

desmaiado/a [dɛʒma'jadu/a] adj (sem sentidos) unconscious; (pálido) faint; **desmaiar** vi (desfalecer) to faint; (descorar) to turn pale; **desmaio** m (desfalecimento) faint; (desalento) dejection.

desma'mar vt to wean.

desmancha-prazeres [dɛʒmanʃa-pra'zerɪʃ] m/f kill-joy, spoilsport.

desmanchar [dɛzman'ʃax] vt (costura) to undo; (contrato) to break; (noivado) to break off; ~-se vr (costura) to come undone.

desmante'lar vt (demolir) to demolish; (desmontar) to dismantle, take apart.

desmasca'rar vt to unmask.

desmaze'lado/a adj slovenly, untidy.

desme'dido/a adj excessive.

desmen'tido m (negação) denial; (contradição) contradiction; **desmentir** vt (contradizer) to contradict; (negar) to deny.

desmere'cer vt (não merecer) not to deserve; (rebaixar) to belittle.

desmesu'rado/a adj immense, enormous.

desmio'lado/a adj brainless.

desmon'tar vt (máquina) to take to pieces // vi (do cavalo) to dismount, get off.

desmorali'zar vt to demoralize.

desmoro'nar vt to knock down // vi to collapse.

desna'tar vt to skim.

desneces'sário/a adj unnecessary.

des'nível m difference in levels.

desnorte'ado/a adj (perturbado) bewildered, confused; (desorientado) off course; **desnortear** vt to throw off course; (embaraçar) to bewilder; **desnortear-se** vr to lose one's way; (perturbar-se) to become confused.

desnu'dar vt to strip; **~-se** vr to undress.

desnutrição [dɛʒnutrɪ'sãw] f malnutrition.

desobede'cer vt to disobey; **desobediência** f disobedience.

desobri'gar vt to free from doing, excuse from doing.

desocu'pado/a adj (casa) empty, vacant; (disponível) free; (sem trabalho) unemployed; **desocupar** vt (casa) to vacate.

desodo'rante (Pt: -dori'zante) m deodorant.

desolação [dɛzola'sãw] f (de um lugar) desolation; (fig) grief; **desolado/a** adj (lugar) desolate; (fig) distressed; **desolar** vt (afligir) to distress.

deso'nesto adj (sem honestidade) dishonest; (impudico) indecent.

des'onra f dishonour; (descrédito) disgrace; **desonrar** vt (infamar) to disgrace; (mulher) to seduce; **desonrar-se** vr to disgrace o.s.

desordem [dɛz'oxdẽ] f disorder, confusion; **em ~** (casa) untidy.

desorgani'zar vt to disorganize; (dissolver) to break up.

desorientação [dɛzorɪẽta'sãw] f bewilderment, confusion; **desorientar** vt (desnortear) to throw off course; (perturbar) to confuse; **desorientar-se** vr (perder-se) to lose one's way.

deso'ssar vt (galinha) to bone.

de'sova f laying (of eggs); **desovar** vt to lay; (peixe) to spawn.

despachar [dɛʃpa'ʃax] vt (expedir) to dispatch, send off; (atender) to deal with; (matar) to kill; **~-se** vr to hurry (up); **despacho** m (remessa) dispatch; (decisão) decision.

desparafu'sar vt to unscrew.

despeda'çar vt (quebrar) to smash; (rasgar) to tear apart.

despe'dida f (adeus) farewell; (de trabalhador) dismissal.

despe'dir vt (de emprego) to dismiss, sack; (mandar embora) to send away; **~-se** vr: **~-se de** to say goodbye to.

despe'gar vt to detach; **~-se** vr: **~-se**

de to go off, lose one's liking for; **despego** m detachment, indifference.

despeitado/a [dɛʃpej'tadu/a] adj spiteful; (ressentido) resentful; **despeito** m spite; **a despeito de** in spite of, despite.

despejar [dɛʃpe'ʒax] vt (água) to pour; (esvaziar) to empty; (inquilino) to evict; **despejo** m (de casa) eviction; **quarto de despejo** junk room.

despen'car vi to fall down, tumble down.

despenhadeiro [dɛʃpeɲa'dejro] m cliff, precipice.

des'pensa f larder.

desperce'bido/a adj unnoticed.

desperdi'çar vt to waste; (dinheiro) to squander; **desperdício** m waste.

desperta'dor m alarm clock; **despertar** vt (pessoa) to wake; (suspeitas) to arouse; (reminiscências) to revive; (apetite) to whet // vi to wake up, awake; **desperto/a** adj awake.

des'pesa f expense.

des'pido/a adj (nu) naked, bare; (livre) free.

des'pir vt (roupa) to take off; (pessoa) to undress; (despojar) to strip; **~-se** vr to undress.

despis'tar vt to throw off the track, mislead.

despo'jado/a adj (pessoa) unambitious; (lugar) spartan, basic; **despojar** vt (privar) to strip; **despojo** m loot, booty; **despojos mortais** mortal remains.

despon'tar vi to emerge; **ao ~ do dia** at daybreak.

des'porto m (Pt) sport.

despo'sado/a adj, m/f newly-wed; **desposar** vt to marry; **desposar-se** vr to get married.

'déspota m despot; **despotismo** m despotism.

despovo'ado/a adj uninhabited // m wilderness; **despovoar** vt to depopulate.

despre'gar vt to take off, detach; **~ os olhos de** to take one's eyes off; **~-se** vr to free o.s.

despren'der vt (soltar) to loosen; (desatar) to unfasten; (emitir) to emit; **~-se** vr (botão) to come off; (cheiro) to be given off.

despreocu'pado/a adj carefree, unconcerned.

despretensi'oso/a adj unpretentious, modest.

despreve'nido/a adj unprepared, unready; **apanhar ~** to catch unawares.

despre'zar vt (não prezar) to despise, disdain; (recusar) to reject; **desprezível** adj despicable; **desprezo** m scorn, contempt; **dar ao desprezo** to ignore.

desproporção [dɛʃpropox'sãw] f disproportion; **desproporcionado/a** adj disproportionate; (desigual) unequal; **desproporcional** adj disproportionate.

desproposi'tado/a adj (absurdo)

preposterous; **despropósito** *m* nonsense.

despro'vido/a *adj* deprived; ~ **de** without.

desquitar-se [dɛʃkɪ'tax-sɪ] *vr* to get a legal separation; **desquite** *m* legal separation.

desre'grado/a *adj* (*desordenado*) disorderly, unruly; (*devasso*) immoderate; **desregrar-se** *vr* to run riot.

desrespeitar [dɛʃxɛʃpej'tax] *vt* to disrespect; **desrespeito** *m* disrespect; **desrespeitoso/a** *adj* disrespectful.

'desse *etc vb ver* **dar** // = **de** + **esse**.

desse'car *vt* to dry up; ~**-se** *vr* to dry up.

desta'cado/a *adj* outstanding; **destacamento** *m* (*MIL*) detachment.

desta'car *vt* (*MIL*) to detail; ~ **alguma coisa** to make sth stand out; (*fig*) to emphasize sth; ~**-se** *vr* to stand out; (*pessoa*) to be outstanding.

destam'par *vt* to take the lid off.

desta'par *vt* (*descobrir*) to uncover; (*abrir*) to open.

destaque [dɛʃ'takɪ] *m* distinction; pessoa de ~ notable person.

'deste *etc* = **de** + **este**. *ver* **este**.

deste'mido/a *adj* fearless, intrepid.

destempe'rar *vt* (*diluir*) to dilute, weaken; (*perturbar*) to upset.

dester'rar *vt* (*exilar*) to exile; (*fig*) to banish; **desterro** *m* exile.

destilação [dɛʃtʃila'sãw] *f* distillation; **destilar** *vt* to distil; **destilaria** *f* distillery.

desti'nar *vt* to destine; ~ **dinheiro para** to set aside money for; ~**-se** *vr*: ~**-se a** to be intended for, be addressed to; **destinatário/a** *m/f* addressee.

des'tino *m* (*fortuna*) destiny, fate; (*finalidade*) purpose; (*lugar*) destination; **com** ~ **a** bound for; **sem** ~ (*adj*) aimless, (*adv*) aimlessly.

destituição [dɛʃtʃitwi'sãw] *f* (*demissão*) dismissal; **destituir** *vt* (*demitir*) to dismiss; **destituir de** (*privar de*) to deprive of.

desto'ante *adj* (*som*) discordant; (*opiniões*) diverging; **destoar** *vi* (*som*) to jar; (*não condizer*) to be out of keeping.

destran'car *vt* to unbolt.

destra'var *vt* to unlatch.

des'treza *f* (*habilidade*) skill; (*agilidade*) dexterity.

destrin'çar *vt* (*desenredar*) to unravel; (*esmiuçar*) to treat in detail.

'destro/a *adj* (*hábil*) skilful; (*ágil*) agile; (*não canhoto*) right-handed.

destro'çar *vt* (*derrotar*) to destroy; (*quebrar*) to smash, break; (*arruinar*) to ruin, wreck; **destroço** *m* destruction; **destroços** *mpl* wreckage *sg*; (*pedaços*) pieces.

des'tronar *vt* to depose.

destruição [dɛʃtrwi'sãw] *f* destruction;

destruidor(a) *adj* destructive; **destruir** *vt* to destroy.

desu'mano/a *adj* inhuman; (*bárbaro*) cruel.

desunião [dɛzun'jãw] *f* disunity; (*separação*) separation; **desunir** *vt* (*separar*) to separate; (*TEC*) to disconnect; (*fig*) to cause a rift between.

desu'sado/a *adj* (*não usado*) disused; (*incomum*) unusual; **desuso** *m* disuse; **em desuso** out of use.

desvairado/a [dɛʒvaj'radu/a] *adj* (*louco*) crazy, demented; (*desorientado*) bewildered; **desvairar** *vt* to drive mad.

desva'lido/a *adj* (*desamparado*) helpless; (*miserável*) destitute; **desvalorizar** *vt* to devalue; **desvalorizar-se** *vr* to undervalue o.s.

desvane'cer *vt* (*tornar orgulhoso*) to make vain; ~**-se** *vr* to vanish; **desvanecido/a** *adj* faded; (*vaidoso*) vain.

desvantagem [dɛʒvan'taʒẽ] *f* disadvantage.

desva'rio *m* madness, folly.

desve'lar *vt* (*revelar*) to unveil, reveal; ~**-se** *vr* (*ter cuidado*) to be solicitous; **desvelo** *m* (*vigilância*) vigilance; (*cuidado*) devotion.

desven'dar *vt* (*tirar a venda*) to remove the blindfold from; (*revelar*) to disclose.

desven'tura *f* (*desgraça*) misfortune; (*infelicidade*) ، unhappiness; **desventurado/a** *adj* (*desgraçado*) unfortunate; (*infeliz*) unhappy // *m/f* wretch.

desvi'ar *vt* (*veículo*) to divert; (*um golpe*) to ward off; (*dinheiro*) to embezzle; ~ **os olhos** to look away; ~**-se** *vr* (*afastar-se*) to turn away; ~**-se de** (*evitar*) to avoid; ~**-se do assunto** to digress; **desvio** *m* diversion, detour; (*curva*) bend; (*fig*) deviation; (*de dinheiro*) embezzlement; (*FERRO*) siding.

desvirtu'ar *vt* (*fatos*) to misrepresent.

detalhar [deta'ʎax] *vt* to (give in) detail; **detalhe** *m* detail.

detenção [detẽ'sãw] *f* detention; **deter** *vt* (*fazer parar*) to stop; (*prender*) to arrest, detain; (*documento*) to keep; **deter-se** *vr* to stop.

detergente [detɛx'ʒẽtʃi] *m* detergent, soap powder.

deterioração [deterɪora'sãw] *f* deterioration; **deteriorar** *vt* to spoil, damage; **deteriorar-se** *vr* to deteriorate; (*relações*) to worsen.

determinação [detɛxmina'sãw] *f* (*firmeza*) determination; (*decisão*) decision.

determi'nar *vt* (*fixar*) to determine, settle; (*decretar*) to order; (*resolver*) to decide (on); (*causar*) to cause.

detes'tar *vt* to hate, detest; **detestável** *adj* horrible, hateful.

dete'tive (*Pt*: -**ct**-) *m* detective.

de'tidamente *adv* carefully, thoroughly; **detido/a** *adj* (*preso*) under arrest; (*minucioso*) thorough.

deto'nar *vi* to detonate, go off.

de'trás *adv* behind // *prep*: ~ **de** behind; **por** ~ (from) behind.

detri'mento *m*: **em** ~ **de** to the detriment of.

de'trito *m* debris *sg*, remains *pl*, dregs *pl*.

detur'par *vt* (*desfigurar*) to disfigure; (*viciar*) to corrupt; (*adulterar*) to pervert, adulterate.

deus(a) [dew∫(sa)] *m* god; **D**~ **me livre!** God forbid!; **Graças a D**~ thank goodness; **se D**~ **quiser** God willing; **meu D**~**!** good Lord // *f* goddess.

deus-dará [dew∫-da'ra] *adv*: **viver ao** ~ to live from hand to mouth.

deva'gar *adv* slowly; ~**inho** *adv* nice and slowly.

devane'ar *vt* to imagine, dream of // *vi* to daydream; (*divagar*) to wander, digress; **devaneio** *m* daydream.

de'vassa *f* investigation, inquiry.

devassidão [devasi'dãw] *f* debauchery; **devasso/a** *adj* dissolute // *m* lecher.

devas'tar *vt* (*destruir*) to devastate; (*arruinar*) to ruin.

'deve *m* (*débito*) debit; (*coluna*) debit column; **devedor(a)** *adj* owing // *m/f* debtor.

de'ver *m* duty // *vt* to owe // *vi* (*suposição*) **deve (de) estar doente** he must be ill; (*obrigação*) **devo partir às oito** (*have to*) I must go at eight; **você devia ir ao médico** (*ought to*) you should go to the doctor; **ele devia ter vindo** (*ought to have*) he should have come; **que devo fazer?** what shall I do?

de'veras *adv* really, indeed.

devida'mente *adv* properly, duly; **devido/a** *adj* proper; **devido a** due to, owing to; **no devido tempo** in due course.

devoção [devo'sãw] *f* devotion.

devolução [devolu'sãw] *f* devolution; (*restituição*) return; **devolver** *vt* to give back, return; (*COM*) to refund.

devo'rar *vt* to devour, eat up.

devo'tar *vt* to devote; ~-**se** *vr*: ~-**se a** to devote o.s. to; **devoto/a** *adj* devout // *m/f* devotee.

'dez *num* ten.

de'zembro (*Pt*: **D-**) *m* December.

de'zena *f*: **uma** ~ ten; (*dias*) ten days.

dezenove [dezi'nɔvi] (*Pt*: **deza'nove**) *num* nineteen.

dezesseis [dezi'sej∫] (*Pt*: **deza'sseis**) *num* sixteen.

dezessete [dezi'sɛt∫i] (*Pt*: **deza'ssete**) *num* seventeen.

dezoito [de'zojtu] *num* eighteen.

D.F. (*Br*) *abr de* **Distrito Federal** ≈ capital (city).

'dia *m* day; (*claridade*) daylight; ~ **a** ~ day by day; ~ **de anos** (*Pt*) birthday; ~ **de folga** day off; ~ **útil** weekday; **andar em** ~ to be up-to-date; **de** ~ by day; **hoje em** ~ nowadays; **mais** ~ **menos** ~ sooner or later; **no outro** ~

on the next day; **todos os** ~**s every day.**

dia'bético/a *adj*, *m/f* diabetic.

di'abo *m* devil; **dos** ~**s** fiendish; **que** ~**l** damn it!; **por que** ~ **...?** why the devil **...?**; **diabólico/a** *adj* diabolical; **diabrete** *m* imp.

dia'brura *f* prank; ~**s** *fpl* mischief *sg*.

dia'fragma *m* diaphragm.

diagnosti'car *vt* to diagnose; **diagnóstico** *m* diagnosis.

dia'leto (*Pt*: **-ct-**) *m* dialect.

di'álogo *m* dialogue; (*conversa*) talk, conversation.

dia'mante *m* diamond.

di'âmetro *m* diameter.

di'ante *adv* in front // *prep*: ~ **de** before; (*na frente de*) in front of; **daqui em** ~ from now on; **e assim por** ~ and so on; **para** ~ forward; **dianteiro/a** *adj* front // *f* front, vanguard; **tomar a dianteira** to get ahead.

diaposi'tivo *m* (*FOTO*) slide.

di'ário/a *adj* daily // *m* diary; (*jornal*) daily (paper); (*COM*) accounts book; ~ **de bordo** log book // *f* (*de hotel*) daily rate.

diar'réia [dʒia'xeja] *f* diarrhoea.

'dica *f* (*col*) hint.

dicção [dʒik'sãw] *f* diction.

dicionário [dʒisjo'narju] *m* dictionary.

'diesel *adj*: **motor a** ~ diesel motor.

di'eta *f* diet; **fazer** ~ to go on a diet.

difamação [dʒifama'sãw] *f* (*escrita*) libel; (*falada*) slander; **difamar** *vt* to slander, libel.

dife'rença *f* difference; **diferente** *adj* different.

dife'rir *vi*: ~ **de** to differ from.

difícil [dʒi'fisjw] *adj* difficult, hard; **dificilmente** *adv* with difficulty; (*apenas*) hardly; **dificuldade** *f* difficulty; (*aperto*) trouble; **em dificuldades** in trouble; **dificultar** *vt* to make difficult; (*complicar*) to complicate.

difte'ria *f* diphtheria.

difun'dir *vt* (*luz*) to shed, cast; (*espalhar*) to spread; (*notícia*) to broadcast.

'diga *etc vb ver* **dizer**.

digerir [dʒiʒe'rix] *vt* to digest; **digestão** *f* digestion.

'digital [-aw] *adj*: **impressão** ~ fingerprint; **dígito** *m* digit.

dig'nar-se *vr*: ~ **de** to deign to, condescend to; **dignidade** *f* dignity; (*função*) rank; **digno/a** *adj* (*merecedor*) worthy; (*nobre*) dignified.

'digo *etc vb ver* **dizer**.

digressão [dʒigre'sãw] *f* digression.

dilace'rar *vt* to tear to pieces, lacerate.

dilatação [dʒilata'sãw] *f* dilation; **dilatar** *vt* to dilate, expand; (*prolongar*) to prolong; (*retardar*) to delay.

di'lema *m* dilemma.

diligência [dʒili'ʒesja] *f* diligence; (*pesquisa*) inquiry; (*veículo*) stagecoach; **diligente** *adj* hardworking, industrious.

diluir [dʒɪlˈwix] *vt* to dilute.

di'lúvio *m* flood.

dimensão [dʒɪmẽˈsãw] *f* dimension; **dimensões** *fpl* measurements.

diminuição [dʒɪmɪnwɪˈsãw] *f* reduction; **diminuir** *vt* to reduce // *vi* to grow less, diminish; **diminuto/a** *adj* minute, tiny.

Dina'marca *f* Denmark; **dinamarquês/quesa** *adj* Danish // *m/f* Dane.

di'nâmico/a *adj* dynamic; **dinamismo** *m* (*fig*) energy, drive.

dinami'tar *vt* to blow up; **dinamite** *f* dynamite.

'dínamo *m* dynamo.

dinas'tia *f* dynasty.

dinheiro [dʒɪˈɲejru] *m* money; ~ de contado (*Pt*) ready cash; ~ miúdo small change; sem ~ (*col*) penniless, broke.

di'ploma *m* diploma.

diploma'cia *f* diplomacy; **diplomata** *m/f* diplomat; **diplomático/a** *adj* diplomatic; (*discreto*) tactful.

dique ['dʒɪkɪ] *m* dam; (*GEO*) dike.

direção [dʒɪreˈsãw] (*Pt*: -cç-) *f* direction; (*endereço*) address; (*AUTO*) steering; (*administração*) management; (*comando*) leadership; (*diretoria*) board of directors; em ~ a towards.

di'rei *etc vb ver* **dizer**.

direito/a [dʒɪˈrejtu/a] *adj* right-hand; (*reto*) straight; (*justo*) right, just // *m* (*prerrogativa*) right; (*JUR*) law; ter ~ a to have a right to; ~s *mpl* (*alfandegários*) duties; (*de autor*) royalties; livre de ~s duty-free // *f* (*mão*) right hand; (*lado*) right-hand side; (*política*) right wing; mantenha-se à ~a (*AUTO*) keep to the right!; à ~a on the right // *adv* (*em linha reta*) straight; (*bem*) right.

di'reto/a (*Pt*: -ct-) *adj* (*reto*) straight; (*contato*) direct; **trem/comboio** ~ through train; **transmissão** ~a (*TV*) live broadcast; **diretor(a)** (*Pt*: -ct-) *adj* directing, guiding // *m/f* (*COM*) director; (*de jornal*) editor; (*MÚS*) conductor // *m* headmaster // *f* headmistress.

dirigir [dʒɪrɪˈʒix] *vt* to direct; (*COM*) to manage, run; (*veículo*) to drive; (*atenção*) to turn; ~-se *vr*: ~-se a (*falar com*) to speak to, address; (*lugar*) to go to, head for.

diri'mir *vt* (*anular*) to annul, cancel; (*dúvida*) to settle, clear up.

discagem [dʒɪˈkaʒẽ] *f* (*TEL*) dialling; ~ direta direct dialling; **discar** *vt* to dial.

disci'plina *f* discipline; **disciplinar** *vt* to discipline.

dis'cípulo/a *m/f* disciple; (*aluno*) pupil.

'disco *m* disc; (*MÚS*) record; (*de telefone*) dial; ~ voador flying saucer.

discor'dar *vi* to disagree; **discórdia** *f* discord, strife.

discor'rer *vi* (*falar*) to talk, reason; (*vaguear*) to stroll around.

disco'teca *f* record-library; (*danceteria*) discotheque; (*col*) disco.

discre'pância *f* discrepancy; (*desacordo*) disagreement; **discrepar** *vi* to differ from.

dis'creto/a *adj* discreet; (*modesto*) modest; (*prudente*) shrewd; **discrição** *f* discretion, good sense.

discrimi'nar *vt* to discriminate; (*distinguir*) to discern; ~ entre to discriminate between.

discur'sar *vi* (*em público*) to make a speech; (*falar*) to speak; **discurso** *m* speech; (*LING*) discourse.

discussão [dʒɪkuˈsãw] *f* (*debate*) discussion, debate; (*contenda*) argument.

disfar'çar *vt* to disguise; **disfarce** *m* disguise; (*máscara*) mask.

dis'forme *adj* deformed, hideous.

dispa'rar *vt* to shoot, fire // *vi* (*arma*) to go off; (*correr*) to shoot off, bolt.

dispara'tado/a *adj* silly, absurd; **disparate** *m* nonsense, rubbish; (*erro*) blunder.

dis'pêndio *m* expenditure; (*fig*) loss.

dis'pensa *f* exemption; (*REL*) dispensation; **dispensar** *vt* (*desobrigar*) to excuse; (*prescindir de*) to do without; (*conferir*) to grant.

disper'sar *vt* to disperse.

displicência [dʒɪʃplɪˈsensja] *f* (*Br*: *descuido*) negligence, carelessness; **displicente** *adj* careless.

dispo'nível *adj* available; **dispor** *vt* (*arranjar*) to arrange; (*colocar em ordem*) to put in order // *vi*: **dispor de** (*usar*) to have the use of; (*ter*) to have, own; **dispor-se** *vr*: **dispor-se a** to be prepared to, be willing to; **não disponho de tempo para ...** I can't afford the time to ...

disposição [dʒɪpoziˈsãw] *f* (*arranjo*) arrangement; (*humor*) disposition; (*intento*) intention; à sua ~ at your disposal.

disposi'tivo *m* (*mecanismo*) gadget, device.

dis'posto/a *adj* (*arranjado*) arranged, ready; (*inclinado a*) disposed, willing; **estar bem** ~ to be in a good mood; **sentir-se** ~ a fazer to feel like doing.

dis'puta *f* dispute, argument; **disputar** *vt* to dispute; (*lutar por*) to fight over; **disputar uma corrida** to run a race // *vi* (*discutir*) to quarrel, argue; (*competir*) to compete.

'disse *etc vb ver* **dizer**.

disse'car *vt* to dissect.

dissemi'nar *vt* to disseminate; (*espalhar*) to spread.

dissensão [dʒɪsẽˈsãw] *f* dissension, discord.

dissertação [dʒɪsextaˈsãw] *f* dissertation; (*ensaio*) thesis; (*discurso*) lecture; **dissertar** *vi* to speak.

dissi'dente *adj*, *m/f* dissident.

dissimulação [dʒɪsimulaˈsãw] *f* (*fingimento*) pretence; (*disfarce*) disguise; **dissimular** *vt* (*ocultar*) to hide; (*fingir*) to pretend // *vi* to dissemble.

dissipação [dʒɪsɪpa'sãw] *f* waste, squandering; **dissipar** *vt* (*dispersar*) to disperse, dispel; (*malgastar*) to squander, waste; **dissipar-se** *vr* to vanish.

dissolução [dʒɪsolu'sãw] *f* (*dissolvência*) dissolving; (*libertinagem*) debauchery; **dissoluto/a** *adj* dissolute, debauched.

dissol'ver *vt* (*solver*) to dissolve; (*dispersar*) to disperse; (*motim*) to break up.

dissua'dir *vt* to dissuade; ~ **alguém de fazer** to talk sb out of doing, dissuade sb from doing.

dis'tância *f* distance; **a grande** ~ far away; **a** ~ **de 3 quilômetros** 3 kilometres away; **distanciar** *vt* (*afastar*) to distance, set apart; (*colocar por intervalos*) to space out; **distanciar-se** *vr* to move away; **distante** *adj* distant, far-off; (*fig*) aloof; **distar** *vi* to be far away; **o aeroporto dista 10 quilometros da cidade** the airport is 10 kilometres away from the city.

distinção [dʒɪʃtʃɪ'sãw] *f* (*diferença*) difference; (*em exame*) distinction; (*honraria*) honour.

distinguir [dʒɪʃtʃɪgɪx] *vt* (*diferenciar*) to distinguish, differentiate; (*avistar*) to make out; ~-**se** *vr* to stand out; **distintivo/a** *adj* distinctive // *m* (*insígnia*) badge; (*emblema*) emblem; **distinto/a** *adj* (*diferente*) different; (*eminente*) distinguished; (*claro*) distinct.

distração [dʒɪʃtra'sãw] (*Pt*: -cç-) *f* (*alheamento*) absent-mindedness; (*divertimento*) pastime; (*descuido*) oversight; **distraído/a** *adj* absent-minded; (*não atento*) inattentive; **distrair** *vt* (*tornar desatento*) to distract; (*divertir*) to amuse; **distrair-se** *vr* to amuse o.s.

distribuição [dʒɪʃtrɪbwɪ'sãw] *f* distribution; (*de cartas*) delivery; **distribuir** *vt* to distribute; (*repartir*) to share out; (*cartas*) to deliver.

dis'trito *m* district; ~ **eleitoral** constituency.

dis'túrbio *m* disturbance.

di'tado *m* dictation; (*provérbio*) saying.

dita'dor *m* dictator; **ditadura** *f* dictatorship.

di'tame *m* (*da consciência*) dictate; (*regra*) rule; **ditar** *vt* to dictate; (*impor*) to impose.

'dito/a *pp de* dizer; ~ **e feito** no sooner said than done // *m*: ~ **espirituoso** witticism.

di'tongo *m* diphthong.

di'toso/a *adj* (*feliz*) happy; (*venturoso*) lucky.

di'urno/a *adj* day.

diva'gar *vi* (*vaguear*) to wander; ~ **do assunto** to wander off the subject, digress.

divergência [dʒɪvɛx'ʒẽsja] *f* divergence; (*desacordo*) disagreement.

diversão [dʒɪvɛx'zãw] *f* (*divertimento*) amusement; (*passatempo*) pastime.

diversi'dade *f* diversity; **diversificar** *vt* to diversify // *vi* to vary; **diverso/a** *adj* (*diferente*) different; (*pl*) various // *pron*: **diversos** some, several.

diver'tido/a *adj* amusing, funny; **divertimento** *m* amusement, entertainment; **divertir** *vt* to amuse, entertain; **divertir-se** *vr* to enjoy o.s., have a good time.

'dívida *f* debt; (*obrigação*) indebtedness; **contrair** ~**s** to run into debt.

divi'dir *vt* to divide; (*despesas*) to share; ~-**se** *vr* to divide, split up.

di'visa *f* (*emblema*) emblem; (*frase*) slogan; (*MIL*) stripe; ~**s** *fpl* foreign exchange/currency.

divisão [dʒɪvɪ'zãw] *f* division; (*discórdia*) dissension.

divi'sar *vt* (*avistar*) to see, make out.

divisório/a [dʒɪvɪ'zɔrju/a] *adj* (*linha*) dividing // *f* partition.

divorci'ar *vt* to divorce; ~-**se** *vr* to get divorced; **divórcio** *m* divorce.

divul'gar *vt* (*notícias*) to spread; (*segredo*) to divulge; ~-**se** *vr* to leak out.

di'zer *vt* (*exprimir*) to say; (*contar*) to tell; (*falar*) to speak, talk; ~ **bem com** to go well with; **por assim** ~ so to speak; **quer** ~ that is to say; **querer** ~ to mean; ~-**se** *vr* to claim to be; **diz-se que** it is said that // *m* (*dito*) saying.

do = **de** + **o**.

dó *m* (*lástima*) pity; (*MÚS*) do; **ter** ~ **de** to have pity on.

doação [doa'sãw] *f* donation, gift; **doar** *vt* to donate, give.

'dobra *f* pleat; (*de calças*) turn-up; **dobradiço/a** *adj* flexible // *f* hinge.

do'brar *vt* (*duplicar*) to double; (*papel*) to fold; (*joelho*) to bend; (*esquina*) to turn, go round // *vi* (*duplicar-se*) to double; (*sino*) to toll; (*vergar*) to bend; ~-**se** *vr* to double (up); **dobre** *adj* (*fig*) two-faced; **dobro** *m* double.

'doca *f* dock.

doce ['dosɪ] *adj* sweet; (*terno*) gentle // *m* sweet.

docente [do'sẽtʃɪ] *adj* teaching; **o corpo** ~ teaching staff.

dócil ['dosɪw] *adj* docile.

documentação [dokumẽta'sãw] *f* documentation; (*documentos*) papers *pl*; **documento** *m* document.

do'çura *f* sweetness; (*brandura*) gentleness.

doença [do'ẽsa] *f* illness; **doente** *adj* ill, sick // *m/f* sick person; (*cliente*) patient; **doentio/a** *adj* (*pessoa*) sickly; (*clima*) unhealthy; (*curiosidade*) morbid.

do'er *vi* to hurt, ache; (*pesar*) to grieve; ~-**se** *vr* to be offended.

doidice [doj'dʒɪsɪ], **doideira** [doj'dejra] *f* madness, foolishness; **doido/a** *adj* mad, crazy; **doido por mad/crazy about // *m* madman // *f* madwoman.

dois [dojʃ] *num* two.

'dólar *m* dollar.

'dolo *m* fraud.

dolo'rido/a adj painful, sore; (fig) sorrowful.

dom [dõ] m gift; (aptidão) talent, knack; o ~ **da palavra** the gift of the gab.

do'mar vt to tame.

domesti'cado/a adj domesticated; (domado) tame; **doméstico/a** adj domestic, household.

domicílio [domi'silju] m home, residence.

dominação [domina'sãw] f domination; **dominante** adj dominant; (predominante) predominant; **dominar** vt to dominate; (reprimir) to overcome // vi to dominate, prevail; **dominar-se** vr to control o.s.

do'mingo m Sunday.

do'mínio m (poder) power; (dominação) control; (território) domain; (esfera) sphere; ~ **próprio** self-control.

'dona f (proprietária) owner; ~ **de casa** housewife.

'donde adv (Pt) from where; ~ **vem?** where do you come from?

'dono m (proprietário) owner; (chefe) boss.

dor f ache; (aguda) pain; (fig) grief, sorrow; ~ **de cabeça** headache; ~ **de dentes** toothache.

dor'mir vi to sleep; ~ **a sono solto** to sleep soundly; ~ **como uma pedra** to sleep like a log; **hora de** ~ bedtime; **dormitar** vi to doze; **dormitório** m bedroom; (coletivo) dormitory.

'dorso m back.

dos = **de + os**.

dosagem [do'zaʒẽ] m dosage; **dose** f dose; **dose excessiva** overdose.

dotação [dota'sãw] f endowment, allocation; **dotado/a** adj gifted; **dotado de** endowed with; **dotar** vt (favorecer) to endow; (a filha) to give a dowry to; **dote** m dowry; **dotes** mpl gifts.

'dou vb ver **dar**.

dourado/a [do'radu/a] adj golden; (com camada de ouro) gilt, gilded; **dourar** vt to gild.

dou'tor(a) m/f doctor; (licenciado) graduate; **doutorado** m doctorate.

doutrina [do'trina] f doctrine.

doze ['dozi] num twelve.

dragão [dra'gãw] m dragon; (MIL) dragoon.

'drama m (teatro) drama; (peça) play; ~**turgo** m playwright, dramatist.

dre'nar vt to drain.

'droga f drug; (fig) rubbish; **drogado/a** m/f drug addict; **drogaria** f chemist's shop.

dto abr de **direito** on the right.

'duas num ver **dois**.

'dúbio/a adj dubious; (vago) uncertain.

dublagem [du'blaʒẽ] f (filme) dubbing; **dublar** vt to dub.

ducha ['duʃa] f (banho) shower; (MED) douche.

duelo ['dwelu] m duel.

'duna f dune.

dupli'car vt (repetir) to duplicate // vi (dobrar) to double.

duque/duquesa ['duki/du'keza] m duke // f duchess.

duração [dura'sãw] f duration; **de pouca** ~ short-lived; **duradouro/a** adj lasting.

du'rante prep during; ~ **uma hora** for an hour.

du'rar vi to last; **durável** adj lasting.

'durex adj: **fita** ~ ® adhesive tape, sellotape.

du'reza f hardness; (severidade) harshness; **duro/a** adj hard; (som) harsh; (resistente) tough.

'durmo vb ver **dormir**.

'dúvida f doubt; **sem** ~ no doubt; **duvidar** vt to doubt // vi to be uncertain; (hesitar) to hesitate; **duvidoso/a** adj (incerto) doubtful; (indeciso) hesitant; (suspeito) suspicious.

du'zentos/as num two hundred.

'dúzia f dozen.

E

e [i] conj and; ~ **a bagagem?** what about the luggage?

é etc vb ver **ser**.

'ébano m ebony.

'ébrio/a adj drunk // m drunkard.

ebulição [ebuli'sãw] f boiling; (fig) ferment.

eclesi'ástico/a adj ecclesiastical, church // m clergyman.

e'clipse m eclipse.

e'clusa f (de canal) lock; (comporta) floodgate; (represa) dam.

'eco m echo; **ter** ~ to catch on.

ecologia [ekolo'ʒia] f ecology.

econo'mia f economy; (ciência) economics pl; ~**s** fpl savings; **econômico/a** adj (barato) cheap; (que consome pouco) economical; (pessoa) thrifty; (COM) economic; **caixa econômica** savings bank; **economista** m/f economist.

écran m (Pt) screen.

edição [edʒi'sãw] f (publicação) publication; (conjunto de exemplares) edition.

edi'fício m building.

edi'tar vt to publish.

e'dito (Pt: -ct-) m edict, decree.

edi'tor(a) adj publishing; **casa** ~**a** publishing firm // m publisher // f publishers pl; **editorial** adj publishing // m editorial.

edredom [edre'dõ] (Pt: -'dão) m eiderdown.

educação [eduka'sãw] f (ensino) education; (criação) upbringing; (de animais) training; (maneiras) good manners pl; **educar** vt (criar) to bring up; (instruir) to educate; (animal) to train.

efeito [e'fejtu] m effect, result; **fazer** ~ to work; **com** ~ indeed.

eferve'scente adj (bebida) effervescent; (col) fizzy.

efetiva'mente (Pt: -éct-) adv really, in fact; **efetivo/a** (Pt: -ct-) adj effective; (real) actual, real; (funcionário) holding permanent civil service post // m (COM) liquid assets pl; **efetuar** (Pt: -ct-) vt to carry out.

efi'cácia f (de pessoa) efficiency; (de tratamento) effectiveness; **eficaz** adj (pessoa) efficient; (tratamento) effective.

eficiência [efis'jẽsja] f efficiency; **eficiente** adj efficient, competent.

egipcio/a [e'ʒɪpsju/a] adj, m/f Egyptian; Egito (Pt: -pt-) m Egypt.

ego'ísmo m selfishness, egoism; **egoísta** adj selfish, egoistic // m/f egoist.

egrégio/a [e'grɛʒju/a] adj distinguished.

e'gresso m (preso) ex-prisoner; (frade) former monk; (universidade) graduate.

égua ['ɛgwa] f mare.

'ei-lo etc = **eis** + **o**, ver **eis**.

eira ['ejra] f (Pt) threshing floor; **sem ~ nem beira** down and out; **eirado** m terrace.

eis [ejʃ] adv here is, here are pl; **~ aí** there is, there are pl.

ei'vado/a adj contaminated; (fig) full.

eixo ['ejʃu] m (de rodas) axle; (MAT) axis; (de máquina) shaft; **~ de transmissão** drive shaft.

ela ['ɛla] pron (pessoa) she; (coisa) it; (com prep: pessoa) her; (: coisa) it; **~s** fpl they; (com prep) them.

elaboração [elabora'sãw] f (de uma teoria) working out; (preparo) preparation; **elaborar** vt (preparar) to prepare; (fazer) to make.

elastici'dade f elasticity; (flexibilidade) suppleness; **elástico/a** adj elastic; (flexível) flexible; (colchão) springy // m elastic band.

ele ['eli] pron he; (coisa) it; (com prep: pessoa) him; (: coisa) it; **~s** mpl they; (com prep) them.

ele'fante/ta m/f elephant.

ele'gância f elegance; **elegante** adj elegant; (da moda) fashionable.

eleger [ele'ʒex] vt (por votação) to elect; (escolher) to choose.

elegia [ele'ʒia] f elegy.

elegível [ele'ʒivɛw] adj eligible.

eleição [elej'sãw] f (por votação) election; (escolha) choice; **eleito/a** pp irr de **eleger** // adj (por votação) elected; (escolhido) chosen; **eleitor(a)** m/f voter; **eleitorado** m electorate.

elemen'tar adj (simples) elementary; (fundamental) basic, fundamental; **elemento** m element; (parte) component; **elementos** mpl rudiments.

e'lenco m (lista) list; (de atores) cast.

eletrici'dade f (Pt: -ct-) f electricity; **eletricista** (Pt: -ct-) m/f electrician; **elétrico/a** (Pt: -ct-) adj electric // m (Pt) tram; **eletrizar** (Pt: -ct-) vt (fig) to thrill.

e'letro... (Pt: -ct-) pref electro...; **~cutar** vt to electrocute; **eletrodo** (Pt: -éct-) m electrode; **~domésticos** mpl (electrical) household appliances; **eletrônico/a** adj electronic // f electronics sg.

elevação [eleva'sãw] f (ARQ) elevation; (aumento) rise; (ato) raising; (altura) height; **elevador** m lift, elevator; **elevar** vt (levantar) to lift up; (preço) to raise; (exaltar) to exalt; **elevar-se** vr to rise.

elimi'nar vt to remove, eliminate.

e'lite f elite.

'elo m link.

elogiar [eloʒi'ax] vt to praise; **elogio** m praise.

eloqüência [elo'kwẽsja] f eloquence; **eloqüente** adj eloquent; (persuasivo) persuasive.

em [ẽ] (em + o = no; em + a = na; em + essa = nessa; em + os = nos; em + as = nas) prep in; (sobre) on; **~ casa** at home; **~ São Paulo** in São Paulo; **nessa altura** at that time; **~ breve** soon; **nessa ocasião** on that occasion; **tudo aconteceu ~ 6 dias** it all happened in/within six days.

emagrecer [ımagre'sex] vt to make thin // vi to grow thin; (mediante regime) to slim.

ema'nar vi: **~ de** to come from, emanate from.

emanci'par vt to emancipate; **~-se** vr to come of age.

emaranhar [ımara'ɲax] vt to tangle; (complicar) to complicate; **~-se** vr to get entangled; (fig) to get mixed up.

embaci'ado/a adj dull; (vidro) misted.

embaixada [ẽbaj'ʃada] f embassy; **embaixador(a)** m ambassador // f ambassadress; **embaixatriz** f ambassador's wife.

embaixo [ẽbaj'ʃu] adv = **em** + **baixo**, ver **baixo**.

embalagem [ẽba'laʒẽ] f packing; **embalar** vt to pack; (balançar) to rock.

embalsa'mar vt (perfumar) to perfume; (cadáver) to embalm.

embara'çar vt (impedir) to hinder; (complicar) to complicate; (perturbar) to embarrass; **~-se** vr to become embarrassed; **embaraço** m (estorvo) hindrance; (atrapalhação) embarrassment.

embarcação [ẽbaxka'sãw] f vessel; **embarcadiço/a** adj seafaring // m seafarer.

embarca'douro m wharf; **embarcar** vt to embark, put on board; (mercadorias) to ship, stow // vi to go on board, embark.

em'bargo m (de navio) embargo; (JUR) seizure; (impedimento) impediment; **sem ~** nevertheless.

embarque [ẽ'baxkı] m (de pessoas) embarkation; (de mercadorias) shipment.

embasba'cado/a adj gaping, open-mouthed.

embate [ẽ'batʃı] m clash; (choque) shock.

embatu'car *vt* to dumbfound.

embe'ber *vt* to soak up, absorb; ~-**se** *vr*: ~-**se em** to become absorbed in.

embi'car *vi* (*tropeçar*) to stumble; (*NÁUT*) to enter port, dock; (*fig*) ~ **para** to head for; ~ **com** to have an argument with.

embir'rar *vi* to sulk; ~ **em** to persist in; ~ **com** to dislike.

em'blema *m* emblem; (*na roupa*) badge.

emboca'dura *f* (*de rio*) mouth; (*MÚS*) mouthpiece; (*de freio*) bit.

'êmbolo *m* piston.

em'bora *conj* though, although; **ir-se** ~ to go away.

embor'car *vt* to turn upside down.

embor'nal [-aw] *m ver* **bornal.**

embos'cada *f* ambush.

embo'tar *vt* (*lâmina*) to blunt; (*fig*) to deaden, dull.

embreagem [ĕbrɪ'aʒĕ] *f* (*AUTO*) clutch.

embria'gar *vt* to make drunk, intoxicate; ~-**se** *vr* to get drunk; **embriaguez** *f* drunkenness; (*fig*) rapture.

embrião [ĕbrɪ'ãw] *m* embryo.

embro'mar *vt* (*adiar*) to postpone, put off; (*enganar*) to deceive.

embrulhada [ĕbru'ʎada] *f* muddle, mess; **embrulhar** *vt* (*pacote*) to wrap; (*complicar*) to complicate; (*estômago*) to upset; **embrulhar-se** *vr* to get into a muddle; **embrulho** *m* (*pacote*) package, parcel; (*confusão*) mix-up.

embu'çar *vt* to disguise; **embuço** *m* hood; (*disfarce*) disguise.

embur'rar *vi* to sulk.

em'buste *m* (*engano*) deception; (*ardil*) trick; **embusteiro/a** *adj* deceitful // *m/f* cheat; (*mentiroso*) liar; (*impostor*) impostor.

embu'tido/a *adj* (*armário*) built-in.

e'menda *f* correction; (*JUR*) amendment; **emendar** *vt* (*corrigir*) to correct; (*reparar*) to mend; (*injustiças*) to make amends for; (*JUR*) to amend; **emendar-se** *vr* to mend one's ways.

e'menta *f* (*Pt*) menu.

emergência [ɪmɛx'ʒĕsja] *f* (*nascimento*) emergence; (*crise*) emergency; **emergir** *vi* to emerge, appear; (*submarino*) to surface.

emigração [emɪgra'sãw] *f* emigration; (*aves*) migration; **emigrado/a** *adj, m/f* emigrant; **emigrar** *vi* to emigrate; (*aves*) to migrate.

emi'nência *f* eminence; (*altura*) height; **eminente** *adj* eminent, distinguished; (*GEO*) high.

emissão [emɪ'sãw] *f* emission; (*rádio*) broadcast; (*de moeda*) issue; **emissor(a)** *adj* (*moeda-papel*) issuing // *m* (*rádio*) transmitter // *f* (*estação*) broadcasting station; (*empresa*) broadcasting company; **emitir** *vt* (*som*) to give out; (*cheiro*) to give off; (*moeda*) to issue; (*rádio*) to broadcast; (*opinião*) to express.

emoção [emo'sãw] *f* emotion; (*excitação*) excitement; **emocional** *adj* emotional;

emocionante *adj* (*comovente*) moving; (*excitante*) exciting; **emocionar** *vt* (*comover*) to move; (*perturbar*) to upset; (*excitar*) to excite, thrill.

emoldu'rar *vt* to frame.

empaco'tar *vt* to pack, wrap up.

em'pada *f* pie.

empalide'cer *vi* to turn pale.

empa'nar *vt* (*ocultar*) to obscure; (*embaciar*) to dim; (*metal*) to tarnish; (*vidro*) to steam up; (*CULIN*) to batter.

empantur'rar-se *vr* to gorge o.s.

empa'par *vt* to soak; ~-**se** *vr* to get soaked.

emparelhar [ĕpare'ʎax] *vt* to pair; (*equiparar*) to match // *vi*: ~ **com** to be equal to.

empa'tar *vt* (*embaraçar*) to hinder; (*dinheiro*) to tie up; (*no jogo*) to draw, tie; **empate** *m* (*no jogo*) draw; (*no xadrez*) stalemate; (*em negociações*) deadlock.

empavo'nar-se *vr* to strut.

empe'cilho *m* obstacle, (*col*) snag.

empeder'nido/a *adj* hard-hearted.

empe'nar *vt* (*curvar*) to warp, bend.

empenhar [ĕpe'ɲax] *vt* (*objeto*) to pawn; (*palavra*) to pledge; (*empregar*) to exert; (*compelir*) to oblige; ~-**se** *vr*: ~-**se em fazer** to strive to do, do one's utmost to do; **empenho** *m* (*de um objeto*) pawning; (*palavra*) pledging; (*insistência*) determination.

empi'nado/a *adj* (*direito*) upright; (*cavalo*) rearing; (*colina*) steep; **empinar** *vt* to raise, uplift; (*ressaltar*) to thrust out; (*papagaio*) to fly; (*copo*) to empty.

em'plastro *m* (*MED*) plaster.

empobre'cer *vt* to impoverish // *vi* to become poor; **empobrecimento** *m* impoverishment.

em'pola *f* (*na pele*) blister; (*de água*) bubble; **empolado/a** *adj* covered with blisters; (*estilo*) pompous, bombastic.

empol'gante *adj* exciting; **empolgar** *vt* to excite; (*agarrar*) to grasp, seize; (*a atenção*) to grip.

em'pório *m* (*mercado*) market; (*armazém*) department store.

empreende'dor(a) *adj* enterprising // *m/f* entrepreneur; **empreender** *vt* to undertake; **empreendimento** *m* undertaking.

empre'gado/a *m/f* employee; (*em escritório*) clerk // *m* (*Pt: de restaurante*) waiter // *f* (*Br: doméstica*) maid; (*Pt: de restaurante*) waitress; **empregar** *vt* (*pessoa*) to employ; (*coisa*) to use; **empregar-se** *vr* to get a job; **emprego** *m* (*ocupação*) job; (*uso*) use.

empreiteiro [ĕprej'tejru] *m* contractor.

em'presa *f* undertaking; (*COM*) enterprise, firm.

empres'tado/a *adj* on loan; **pedir** ~ to borrow; **emprestar** *vt* to lend; **empréstimo** *m* loan.

empunhar [ĕpu'ɲax] *vt* to grasp, seize.

empurrão [ĕpu'xãw] *m* push, shove; **aos**

empurrões jostling; **empurrar** vt to push, shove.

emude'cer vt to silence // vi to be silent/quiet.

emu'lar vt to emulate.

enamo'rado/a adj (encantar) enchanted; (apaixonado) in love.

encabe'çar vt to head.

encabu'lado/a adj (envergonhado) embarrassed; (acanhado) shy.

encadea'mento m (série) chain; (conexão) link; **encadear** vt to chain together, link together.

encadernação [ēkadɛxna'sãw] f binding; **encadernar** vt to bind.

encaixar [ēkaj'ʃax] vt (colocar) to fit in, set in; (inserir) to insert // vi to fit; **encaixe** m (ato) fitting; (ranhura) groove; (buraco) socket; **encaixotar** vt to pack into boxes.

en'calço [-'kawsu] m pursuit; **ir no ~ de** to pursue.

enca'lhado/a adj stranded; (mercadoria) unsaleable.

encalhar [ēka'ʎax] vi (embarcação) to run aground.

encaminhar [ēkamɪ'ɲax] vt (dirigir) to direct; (no bom caminho) to put on the right path; **~-se** vr: **~-se para/a** to set out for/to.

encana'dor m (Br) plumber; **encanamento** m plumbing.

encane'cido/a adj grey; (cabelo) white.

encan'tado/a adj delighted; **encantador(a)** adj delightful, charming // m enchanter / f enchantress; **encantamento** m (magia) spell; (fascinação) charm; **encantar** vt (enfeitiçar) to bewitch; (cativar) to charm; (deliciar) to delight; **encanto** m (delícia) delight; (fascinação) charm.

encapo'tar vt to cloak, conceal.

encaraco'lar vt/i to curl; **~-se** vr to curl up.

enca'rar vt to face; (olhar) to look at.

encarce'rar vt to imprison.

encare'cer vt (subir o preço) to raise the price of; (louvar) to praise; (exagerar) to exaggerate // vi to go up in price, get dearer; **encarecimento** m (preço) increase.

en'cargo m (responsabilidade) responsibility; (ocupação) job, assignment; (oneroso) burden.

encar'nado/a adj red, scarlet.

encarquilhado/a [ēkaxkɪ'ʎadu/a] adj (fruta) wizened; (rosto) wrinkled.

encarre'gado/a adj: **~ de** in charge of // m/f person in charge; **~ de negócios** chargé d'affaires // m (de operários) foreman.

encarre'gar vt: **~ alguém de alguma coisa** to put sb in charge of sth; **~-se** vr: **~-se de fazer** to undertake to do.

encarrilhar [ēkaxɪ'ʎax] vt to put back on the rails; (fig) to put on the right track.

ence'nar vt (teatro) to stage; (exibir) to show.

ence'rar vt to wax.

encer'rar vt (confinar) to shut in, lock up; (conter) to contain; (concluir) to close.

ence'tar vt to start, begin.

enchente [ē'ʃētʃi] f flood; **encher** vt to fill (up); **encher de/com** to fill up with; **encher-se** vr to fill up; **enchimento** m filling.

enchova [ē'ʃova] f anchovy.

enciclo'pédia f encyclopaedia.

enco'berto/a pp de **encobrir** // adj (escondido) concealed; (céu) overcast; **encobrir** vt to conceal, hide.

encoleri'zar vt to irritate, annoy; **~-se** vr to get angry.

encolher [ēko'ʎex] vt to draw up; (os ombros) to shrug // vi to shrink; **~-se** vr (acanhar-se) to cringe.

enco'menda f order; **feito de ~** made to order, custom-made; **encomendar** vt to order; **encomendar alguma coisa a alguém** to order sth from sb.

encon'trar vt (achar) to find; (inesperadamente) to come across, meet; (dar com) to bump into // vi: **~ com** to bump into; **~-se** vr (achar-se) to be; (ir ter com) to meet; **encontro** m (de pessoas) meeting; (MIL) encounter; **ir (vir) ao encontro de** to go and meet; (aspirações) to meet, fulfil; **ir contra de encontro a** to go against, run contrary to.

encorajar [ēkora'ʒax] vt to encourage.

encor'pado/a adj stout; (vinho) full-bodied; (tecido) closely-woven.

en'costa f slope.

encos'tar vt: **~ em** to lean against; **~-se** vr: **~-se em** to lean against; (deitar-se) to lie down; **encosto** m (arrimo) support; (de cadeira) back.

encres'par vt (o cabelo) to curl; (penas) to ruffle; **~-se** vr (o cabelo) to curl; (água) to ripple; (o mar) to get choppy.

encruzilhada [ēkruzɪ'ʎada] f crossroads sg.

encur'tar vt to shorten.

endere'çar vt (carta) to address; (encaminhar) to direct; **endereço** m address.

endia'brado/a adj devilish; (travesso) mischievous.

endinhei'rado/a adj rich, wealthy, well-off.

endireitar [ēdʒɪrej'tax] vt (objeto) to straighten; (retificar) to put right; (fig) to straighten out; **~-se** vr to straighten up.

endivi'dar-se vr to run into debt.

endoidecer [ēdojde'sex] vt to madden; **~-se** vr to go mad.

endos'sar vt to endorse; **endosso** m endorsement.

endure'cer vt/i to harden; **~-se** vr (fig) to become callous; **endurecido/a** adj hardened; (fig) callous.

energia [enɛx'ʒɪa] f (vigor) energy,

drive; (*TEC*) power, energy; **enérgico/a** *adj* energetic, vigorous.

enevo'ado/a *adj* misty, hazy.

enfa'dar *vt* (*entediar*) to bore; (*incomodar*) to annoy; ~-**se** *vr*: ~-**se de** to get tired of; ~-**se com** (*aborrecer-se*) to get fed up with; **enfado** *m* annoyance; **enfadonho/a** *adj* (*cansativo*) tiresome; (*aborrecido*) boring.

'ênfase *f* emphasis, stress.

enfasti'ado/a *adj* bored; **enfastiar** *vt* (*cansar*) to weary; (*aborrecer*) to bore; **enfastiar-se** *vr*: **enfastiar-se de/com** (*cansar-se*) to get tired of; (*aborrecer-se*) to get bored with.

en'fático/a *adj* emphatic.

enfeitar [ẽfej'tax] *vt* to decorate; ~-**se** *vr* to dress up; **enfeite** *m* decoration.

enfeitiçar [ẽfejtʃi'sax] *vt* to bewitch, cast a spell on.

enferma'ria *f* (*hospital*) infirmary; (*sala*) ward; **enfermeiro/a** *m* male nurse // *f* nurse; **enfermidade** *f* illness; **enfermo/a** *adj* ill, sick // *m/f* sick person, patient.

enferru'jar *vt* to rust, corrode; ~-**se** *vr* to go rusty.

enfe'zar *vt* to stunt; (*enfadar*) to make angry; ~-**se** *vr* to become angry.

enfi'ada *f* (*de pérolas*) string; (*fila*) row; **de** ~ at a stretch; **enfiar** *vt* (*agulha*) to thread; (*pérolas*) to string together; (*vestir*) to slip on // *vi*: **enfiar para** to head for; **enfiar-se** *vr*: **enfiar-se em** to slip into.

enfim [ẽ'fī] *adv* finally, at last; (*em suma*) in short.

enfor'car *vt* to hang; ~-**se** *vr* to hang o.s.

enfraquecer [ẽfrake'sex] *vt* to weaken // *vi* to grow weak.

enfren'tar *vt* (*encarar*) to face; (*confrontar*) to confront; (*arrostar*) to face up to.

enfure'cer *vt* to infuriate; ~-**se** *vr* to get furious.

enga'nar *vt* to deceive; (*desonrar*) to seduce; ~-**se** *vr* (*cair em erro*) to be wrong, be mistaken; (*iludir-se*) to deceive o.s.; ~-**se de paletó** to get the wrong coat; **engano** *m* (*error*) mistake; (*ilusão*) deception; (*logro*) trick; **enganoso/a** *adj* (*mentiroso*) deceitful; (*artificioso*) fake; (*conselho*) misleading; (*aspecto*) deceptive.

engarrafa'mento *m* (*trânsito*) traffic jam; **engarrafar** *vt* to bottle.

engas'gar *vt/i* to choke.

engas'tar *vt* (*jóias*) to set, mount; **engaste** *m* setting, mounting.

enga'tar *vt* (*vagões*) to couple, hitch up; (*AUTO*) to put into gear.

engelhar [ẽʒe'ʎax] *vt/i* (*a pele*) to wrinkle; (*plantas*) to shrivel up.

engen'drar *vt* to engender; (*fig*) to produce.

engenharia [ẽʒeɲa'ria] *f* engineering; **engenheiro** *m* engineer.

engenho [ẽ'ʒeɲu] *m* (*talento*) talent; (*destreza*) skill; (*máquina*) machine; (*moenda*) mill; **engenhoso/a** *adj* clever, ingenious.

englo'bar *vt* to include.

engo'dar *vt* to lure, entice; **engodo** *m* (*para peixe*) bait; (*para pessoas*) lure, enticement.

engo'lir *vt* to swallow.

engo'mar *vt* to starch; (*passar*) to iron.

en'gonço *m* hinge.

engor'dar *vt* to fatten // *vi* to put on weight, get fat.

engra'çado/a *adj* funny, amusing.

engra'dado *m* crate.

engrande'cer *vt* (*aumentar*) to enlarge; (*elevar*) to elevate // *vi* to grow; ~-**se** *vr* (*elevar-se*) to rise; (*ilustrar-se*) to become great.

engraxa'dor *m* (*Pt*) shoe shiner; **engraxar** *vt* to polish; **engraxate** *m* shoe shiner.

engrenagem [ẽgre'naʒẽ] *f* (*AUTO*) gear; **engrenar** *vt* (*AUTO*) to put into gear.

engros'sar *vt/i* (*sopa*) to thicken; (*inchar*) to swell; (*aumentar*) to increase.

enguia [ẽ'gia] *f* eel.

engui'çar [ẽgi'sax] *vi* (*máquina*) to break down; **enguiço** *m* (*má sorte*) bad luck; (*empecilho*) snag; (*desarranjo*) breakdown.

engulho [ẽ'guʎu] *m* nausea.

e'nigma *m* enigma; (*mistério*) mystery.

enjau'lar *vt* to cage, cage up.

enjeitado/a [ẽʒej'tadu/a] *m/f* foundling, waif; **enjeitar** *vt* (*rejeitar*) to reject; (*abandonar*) to abandon.

enjo'ado/a *adj* sick; (*enfastiado*) bored; **enjoar** *vt* to make sick // *vi* to be sick; **enjôo** *m* sickness.

enla'çar *vt* (*atar*) to tie, bind; (*abraçar*) to hug; (*unir*) to link, join; ~-**se** *vr* to be linked; **enlace** *m* link, connexion; (*casamento*) marriage, union.

enlame'ar *vt* to cover in mud; (*reputação*) to besmirch.

enla'tar *vt* to can, tin.

enle'ar *vt* (*atar*) to bind; (*envolver*) to entangle; (*confundir*) to confuse, perplex; **enleio** *m* (*enredo*) entanglement; (*confusão*) confusion.

enle'var *vt* (*deleitar*) to enrapture; (*absorver*) to absorb; **enlevo** *m* (*êxtase*) rapture; (*deleite*) delight.

enlouquecer [ẽloke'sex] *vt* to drive mad // *vi* to go mad.

enlu'tado/a *adj* in mourning; **enlutar-se** *vr* to go into mourning.

enobre'cer *vt* to ennoble.

eno'jado/a *adj* annoyed, fed up; **enojar** *vt* to disgust, sicken; **enojar-se** *vr* to be annoyed.

e'norme *adj* enormous, huge; **enormidade** *f* enormity.

enove'lar *vt* to wind into a ball; (*enrolar*) to roll up.

enquadrar [ẽkwa'drax] *vt* to fit, assimilate.

enquanto [ě'kwãtu] *conj* while; ~ **isso** meanwhile; **por** ~ for the time being; ~ **ele não vem** until he comes.

enraive'cer *vt* to enrage.

enrai'zar *vi* to take root.

enra'scada *f* tight spot, predicament.

enre'dar *vt* (*emaranhar*) to entangle; (*complicar*) to complicate; ~-**se** *vr* to get entangled; **enredo** *m* (*de uma obra*) plot; (*intriga*) intrigue.

enrege'lado/a *adj* (*congelado*) frozen; (*muito frio*) freezing.

enriquecer [ěxike'sex] *vt* to enrich; ~-**se** *vr* to get rich.

enro'lar *vt* to roll up; (*agasalhar*) to wrap // *vi* (*col*) to waffle; ~-**se** *vr* to roll up; (*agasalhar-se*) to wrap up.

enros'car *vt* (*torcer*) to twist, wind (round); ~-**se** *vr* to coil up.

enroquecer [ěxoke'sex] *vt* to make hoarse // *vi* to go hoarse.

enru'gar *vt* (*pele*) to wrinkle; (*testa*) to furrow; (*tecido*) to crease; ~-**se** *vr* to crease.

ensaiar [ěsa'jax] *vt* (*provar*) to test, try out; (*treinar*) to practise; (*teatro*) to rehearse; **ensaio** *m* (*prova*) test; (*tentativa*) attempt; (*treino*) practice; (*teatro*) rehearsal; (*literário*) essay; **ensaio e erro** trial and error.

ensangüentar [ěsãgwě'tax] *vt* to stain with blood.

ense'ada *f* inlet, cove; (*baía*) bay.

ensejo [ě'seʒu] *m* chance, opportunity.

ensimes'mar-se *vr* to be lost in thought.

ensi'nar *vt* to teach; ~ **alguém a patinar** to teach sb to skate; **ensino** *m* teaching, tuition; (*educação*) education.

enso'pado/a *adj* soaked // *m* stew; **ensopar** *vt* to soak, drench.

ensurdece'dor(a) *adj* deafening; **ensurdecer** *vt* to deafen // *vi* to go deaf.

entabu'lar *vt* (*negociação*) to start, open; (*empreender*) to undertake; (*assunto*) to broach; (*conversa*) to strike up.

enta'lar *vt* (*encravar*) to wedge, jam; (*fig*) to put in a fix.

entalhar [ěta'ʎax] *vt* to carve; **entalhe** *m* groove, notch; **entalho** *m* woodcarving.

en'tanto *adv* meanwhile // *conj* (*todavia*) however, nevertheless; **no** ~ (*adv*) meanwhile; (*conj*) yet, however.

então [ě'tãw] *adv* then; **até** ~ up to that time; **desde** ~ ever since; **e** ~? well then?

'ente *m* being.

ente'ado/a *m* stepson // *f* stepdaughter.

enten'der *vt* (*perceber*) to understand; (*pensar*) to think; (*querer dizer*) to mean; **dar a** ~ to imply; **no meu** ~ in my opinion; ~ **de música** to know about music; ~-**se** *vr* (*compreender-se*) to understand one another; ~-**se por** to be meant by; ~-**se com alguém** to get along with sb.

enten'dido/a *adj*: ~ **em** (*conhecedor*) good at; **bem** ~ that is // *m* expert; (*gír*) homosexual, gay; **entendimento** *m* (*intelecto*) intellect; (*compreensão*) understanding; (*juízo*) sense.

enterne'cer *vt* to move, touch; ~-**se** *vr* to be moved.

enter'rar *vt* to bury; (*faca*) to plunge; **enterro** *m* burial; (*funeral*) funeral.

ente'sar *vt* to stiffen; (*esticar*) to stretch; ~-**se** *vr* to stiffen.

enti'dade *f* (*ser*) being; (*corporação*) body; (*coisa que existe*) entity.

entoação [ětoa'sãw] *f* intonation; **entoar** *vt* (*cantar*) to chant.

entonte'cer *vt* to make dizzy // *vi* to become/get dizzy.

entor'nar *vt* to spill; (*fig: copo*) to drink a lot.

entorpe'cente *m* narcotic; **entorpecer** *vt* (*paralisar*) to numb, stupefy; (*retardar*) to slow down; **entorpecimento** *m* numbness; (*torpor*) lethargy.

en'torse *f* sprain.

entor'tar *vt* (*curvar*) to bend; (*empenar*) to warp; ~ **os olhos** to squint.

en'trado/a *adj*: ~ **em anos** (*Pt*) elderly // *f* (*ato*) entry; (*lugar*) entrance; (*TEC*) inlet; (*de casa*) doorway; (*começo*) beginning; (*bilhete*) ticket; (*CULIN*) entrée; (*pagamento inicial*) down payment.

entra'nhado/a *adj* deep-rooted; **entranhar-se** *vr* to penetrate; **entranhas** *fpl* bowels, entrails; (*sentimentos*) feelings; (*centro*) heart.

en'trar *vi* to go/come in, enter; ~ **para um clube** to join a club; ~ **em vigor** to come into force; **deixar** ~ to let in; ~ **bem** (*gír*) to get into trouble.

entra'var *vt* to obstruct, impede.

'entre *prep* (*dois*) between; (*mais de dois*) among(st); ~ **si** to o.s.

entrea'berto/a *adj* half-open; (*porta*) ajar; **entreabrir** *vt* to half open; **entreabrir-se** *vr* (*flores*) to open up.

entrecho'car-se *vr* to collide, crash; (*fig*) to clash.

en'trega *f* (*de mercadorias*) delivery; (*a alguém*) handing over; (*rendição*) surrender; **pagamento contra** ~ C.O.D., cash on delivery; **pronta** ~ speedy delivery; **entregar** *vt* (*dar*) to hand over; (*mercadorias*) to deliver; (*ceder*) to give up; **entregar-se** *vr* (*render-se*) to give o.s. up; (*dedicar-se*) to devote o.s.; **entregue** *pp irr de* **entregar**.

entrela'çar *vt* to entwine.

entrelinha [ětre'liɲa] *f*: **ler nas** ~**s** to read between the lines.

entreme'ar *vt* to intermingle.

entreolhar-se [ětrio'ʎax-si] *vr* to exchange glances.

entre'tanto *adv* meanwhile; **no** ~ in the meantime // *conj* however.

entreteni'mento *m* entertainment; (*distração*) pastime; **entreter** *vt* (*divertir*) to entertain, amuse; (*manter*) to keep up; (*esperanças*) to cherish; **entreter-se** *vr* (*divertir-se*) to amuse o.s.; (*ocupar-se*) to occupy o.s.

entre'vado/a *adj* paralysed, crippled; **entrevar** *vt* to paralyse, cripple.

entre'ver *vt* to glimpse, catch a glimpse of.

entre'vista *f* interview; **entrevistar** *vt* to interview; **entrevistar-se** *vr* to have an interview.

entriste'cer *vt* to sadden, grieve; ~**-se** *vr* to feel sad.

entronca'mento *m* junction.

en'trudo *m* (*Pt*) carnival; (: *REL*) Shrovetide.

entulho [ẽ'tuʎu] *m* rubble, debris *sg*.

entupi'mento *m* blockage; **entupir** *vt* to block, clog; **entupir-se** *vr* to become blocked.

entusias'mar *vt* to fill with enthusiasm; (*animar*) to excite; ~**-se** *vr* to get excited; **entusiasmo** *m* enthusiasm; (*júbilo*) excitement; **entusiasta** *adj* enthusiastic // *m/f* enthusiast.

enume'rar *vt* to enumerate.

enunci'ar *vt* to express, state.

envaidecer [ẽvajde'sex] *vt* to make conceited; ~**-se** *vr* to become conceited.

envelhecer [ẽveʎe'sex] *vt* to age // *vi* to grow old, age.

enve'lope *m* envelope.

envenena'mento *m* poisoning; ~ **do sangue** blood poisoning; **envenenar** *vt* to poison; (*fig*) to corrupt.

envere'dar *vi*: ~ **por um caminho** to follow a road; ~ **para** to head for.

enverga'dura *f* (*asas, velas*) spread; (*avião*) wingspan; (*fig*) scope; **de grande** ~ large-scale.

envergonhado/a [ẽvexgo'ɲadu/a] *adj* ashamed; (*tímido*) shy; **envergonhar** *vt* to shame; (*degradar*) to disgrace; **envergonhar-se** *vr* to be ashamed.

envi'ado/a *m/f* envoy, messenger; **enviar** *vt* to send.

envidra'çar *vt* to glaze.

en'vio *m* sending; (*expedição*) despatch; (*remessa*) remittance; (*de mercadorias*) consignment.

enviuvar [ẽvju'vax] *vi* to be widowed.

en'volto/a *pp irr de* **envolver**; **envolver** *vt* (*embrulhar*) to wrap (up); (*cobrir*) to cover; (*comprometer*) to involve; (*nos braços*) to embrace; **envolver-se** *vr* (*intrometer-se*) to become involved; (*cobrir-se*) to wrap o.s. up.

enxada [ẽ'ʃada] *f* hoe.

enxa'drista *m/f* chess player.

enxaguar [ẽʃag'wax] *vt* to rinse.

enxame [ẽ'ʃami] *m* swarm.

enxaqueca [ẽʃa'keka] *f* migraine.

enxergão [ẽʃex'gãw] *m* (straw) mattress.

enxer'gar *vt* (*avistar*) to catch sight of;

(*divisar*) to make out; (*notar*) to observe, see.

enxer'tar *vt* to graft; (*fig*) to incorporate.

enxó [ẽ'ʃo] *m* adze.

enxofre [ẽ'ʃofri] *m* sulphur.

enxota-'moscas *m* (*Pt*) fly swatter; **enxotar** *vt* (*expulsar*) to drive out.

enxoval [ẽʃo'vaw] *m* (*de noiva*) trousseau; (*de recém-nascido*) layette.

enxovalhar [ẽʃova'ʎax] *vt* (*manchar*) to stain; (*amarrotar*) to crumple; (*reputação*) to blacken; ~**-se** *vr* to disgrace o.s.

enxuga'dor *m* clothes drier; **enxugar** *vt* to dry.

enxur'rada *f* (*de água*) torrent; (*fig*) spate.

enxuto/a [ẽ'ʃutu/a] *adj* dry; (*magro*) slim.

'épico/a *adj* epic // *m* epic poet.

epide'mia *f* epidemic; **epidêmico/a** *adj* epidemic.

Epifa'nia *f* Epiphany.

epilep'sia *f* epilepsy.

e'pílogo *m* epilogue.

episco'pado *m* bishopric.

epi'sódio *m* episode.

e'pístola *f* epistle; (*carta*) letter.

epi'táfio *m* epitaph.

'época *f* time, period; (*da história*) age, epoch; **naquela** ~ at that time; ~ **da colheita** harvest time; **fazer** ~ to be epoch-making.

epopéia [epo'peja] *f* epic.

equa'dor *m* equator; **E**~ *m* Ecuador.

e'quânime *adj* fair; (*caráter*) unbiased, neutral.

eqüidade [ekwi'dadʒi] *f* equity.

equilibrar [ekilı'brax] *vt* to balance; ~**-se** *vr* to balance; **equilíbrio** *m* balance, equilibrium.

equipa [e'kipa] *f* (*Pt*) team.

equipa'mento *m* equipment, kit; **equipar** *vt* (*navio*) to fit out; (*prover*) to equip.

equipa'rar *vt* (*comparar*) to compare; ~**-se** *vr*: ~**-se a** to equal.

equipe [e'kipɪ] *f* (*Br*) team.

equitação [ekita'sãw] *f* (*ato*) riding; (*arte*) horsemanship.

eqüitativo/a [ekwita'tʃivu/a] *adj* fair, equitable.

equivalente [ekiva'lẽtʃi] *adj* equivalent // *m* equivalent; **equivaler** *vi*: **equivaler a** to be the same as, equal.

equivo'cado/a *adj* mistaken, wrong; **equivocar-se** *vr* to make a mistake, be wrong; **equívoco/a** *adj* ambiguous // *m* (*engano*) mistake.

'era *etc vb ver* **ser** // *f* era, age.

e'rário *m* exchequer.

ere'mita *m/f* hermit; **eremitério** *m* hermitage.

e'reto/a (*Pt*: **-ct-**) *adj* upright, erect.

erguer [ex'gex] *vt* (*levantar*) to raise, lift; (*edificar*) to build, erect; ~**-se** *vr* to rise; (*pessoa*) to stand up.

eri'çado/a *adj* bristling; (*cabelos*) on

end; **eriçar-se** *vr* to bristle; (*cabelos*) to stand on end.

'ermo/a *adj* (*solitário*) lonely; (*desabitado*) uninhabited // *m* wilderness.

e'rótico/a *adj* erotic; **erotismo** *m* eroticism.

er'rado/a *adj* wrong, mistaken; **errante** *adj* wandering; **errar** *vt* (*o alvo*) to miss; (*a conta*) to get wrong; **errar o caminho** to lose one's way // *vi* (*vaguear*) to wander, roam; (*enganar-se*) to be wrong, make a mistake.

'erro *m* mistake; **salvo** ~ unless I am mistaken; ~ **de imprensa** misprint; ~ **de pronúncia** mispronunciation; **errôneo/a** *adj* wrong, mistaken; (*falso*) false, untrue.

erudição [erud3ɪ'sãw] *f* erudition, learning; **erudito/a** *adj* learned, scholarly // *m* scholar.

erupção [erup'sãw] *f* eruption; (*na pele*) rash; (*fig*) outbreak.

'erva *f* (*relva*) grass; (*MED*) herb; (*daninha*) weed.

ervilha [ex'vɪʎa] *f* pea.

esbafo'rido/a *adj* breathless, panting.

esbanjar [13ba'3ax] *vt* to squander, waste.

esbar'rar *vi*: ~ **em** to bump into; (*obstáculo*) to come up against; ~**-se** *vr* to jostle one another.

esbel'tez, esbel'teza *f* slenderness; (*elegância*) elegance **esbelto/a** *adj* (*fino*) slender; (*pessoa*) slim; (*elegante*) elegant.

esbo'çar *vt* to sketch; (*delinear*) to outline; **esboço** *m* (*desenho*) sketch; (*primeira versão*) draft.

esbugalhado/a [13buga'ʎadu/a] *adj*: **olhos** ~**s** goggle eyes; **esbugalhar-se** *vr* to goggle, boggle.

esc (*Pt*) *abr de* **escudo**.

escabeche [eʃka'beʃɪ] *m* (*tempero*) marinade, sauce of spiced vinegar and onion; **em** ~ pickled.

esca'broso/a *adj* (*áspero*) rough, rugged; (*indecoroso*) indecent.

escachar [iʃka'ʃax] *vt* to split open.

es'cada *f* (*dentro da casa*) staircase, stairs *pl*; (*fora da casa*) steps *pl*; (*de mão*) ladder; ~ **de caracol** spiral staircase; ~ **de incêndio** fire escape; ~ **rolante** escalator; **escadaria** *f* staircase.

escafan'drista *m/f* deep-sea diver.

es'cala *f* scale; (*NÁUT*) port of call; (*parada*) stop; **fazer** ~ **em** to call at; **sem** ~ non-stop.

esca'lada *f* (*de guerra*) escalation.

escalão [eʃka'lãw] *m* step; (*MIL*) echelon; **escalar** *vt* (*montanha*) to climb; (*muro*) to scale.

escal'dar *vt* to scald; ~**-se** *vr* to scald o.s.

escal'far *vt* (*Pt*: *ovos*) to poach.

es'cama *f* (*de peixe*) scale; (*de tinta*) flake; **escamar** *vt* to scale.

escamote'ar *vt* (*furtar*) to pinch, pilfer; (*empalmar*) to make disappear (by sleight of hand).

escanca'rado/a *adj* wide open.

escandali'zar *vt* to shock; ~**-se** *vr* to be shocked; (*ofender-se*) to be offended; **escândalo** *m* scandal; (*indignação*) outrage; **fazer um escândalo** to make a scene; **escandaloso/a** *adj* shocking, scandalous.

escangalhar [eʃkãga'ʎax] *vt* to break, smash (up); (*a saúde*) to ruin; ~**-se** *vr* to get broken.

escaninho [eʃka'nɪɲu] *m* (*na secretária*) pigeonhole.

escanteio [eʃkan'teju] *m* (*futebol*) corner.

esca'par *vi*: ~ **a/de** to escape from; **deixar** ~ (*uma oportunidade*) to miss; (*palavras*) to blurt out; ~ **por um triz** to have a narrow escape; ~**-se** *vr* to run away, flee.

es'cape *m* (*de gases*) leak; (*AUTO*) exhaust.

escara'muça *f* skirmish.

escaravelho [eʃkara'veʎu] *m* beetle.

escar'late *adj* scarlet; **escarlatina** *f* scarlet fever.

escarne'cer *vt* to mock, make fun of; **escárnio** *m* mockery; (*desprezo*) derision.

escar'pado/a *adj* steep.

escarrapa'char-se *vr* to sprawl.

escar'rar *vt* to spit (up) // *vi* to spit; **escarro** *m* phlegm, spit.

escasse'ar *vt* to skimp on // *vi* to become scarce; **escassez** *f* (*falta*) shortage; **escasso/a** *adj* (*carente*) scarce; (*raro*) rare.

escavação [iʃkava'sãw] *f* digging, excavation; **escavar** *vt* to excavate.

esclare'cer *vt* (*iluminar*) to light up; (*mistério*) to clear up, explain; ~**-se** *vr* to become clear, be explained; **esclarecimento** *m* explanation.

escoadouro [iʃkoa'doru] *m* drain; (*cano*) drainpipe; **escoar** *vt* to drain off // *vi* to drain away; **escoar-se** *vr* to seep out.

esco'cês/esa *adj* Scottish // *m* Scot, Scotsman // *f* Scotswoman; **Escócia** *f* Scotland.

es'col *m* best; **de** ~ of excellence.

es'cola *f* school; ~ **superior** college; **escolar** *adj* school // *m* pupil, schoolboy // *f* schoolgirl.

escolha [iʃ'koʎa] *f* choice; **escolher** *vt* to choose, select.

escolho [iʃ'koʎu] *m* reef; (*obstáculo*) obstacle; (*risco*) pitfall.

es'colta *f* escort; **escoltar** *vt* to escort.

es'combros *mpl* ruins, debris *sg*.

esconde-es'conde *m* hide-and-seek; **esconder** *vt* to hide, conceal; **esconder-se** *vr* to hide; **esconderijo** *m* hiding place; (*de bandidos*) hideout; **escondidas** *fpl*: **às escondidas** secretly.

esconju'rar *vt* (*o Demônio*) to exorcize; (*afastar*) to keep off; (*amaldiçoar*) to curse // *vi* (*suplicar*) to beg.

es'copo *m* aim, purpose.

es'cora f prop, support; (cilada) ambush.
es'cória f (de metal) dross; a ~ da humanidade the scum of the earth.
escoriação [eʃkorja'sãw] f abrasion, scratch.
escorpião [iʃkoxpi'ãw] m scorpion; (ASTRO) Scorpio.
escorrega'dela f slip; (erro) mistake, slip; escorregadi(ç)o/a adj slippery; escorregar vi to slip; (errar) to slip up; (decorrer) to slip by.
escor'rer vt (fazer correr) to drain (off); (verter) to pour out // vi (pingar) to drip; (correr em fio) to trickle.
esco'teiro m scout.
escotilha [eʃko'tʃiʎa] f hatch, hatchway.
es'cova f brush; ~ de dentes toothbrush; escovar vt to brush.
escrava'tura f (tráfico) slave trade; (escravidão) slavery; escravidão f slavery; escravizar vt to enslave; escravo/a adj captive // m/f slave.
escre'vente m/f clerk; escrever vt/i to write; escrever à máquina to type; escrevinhar vt to scribble.
es'crito/a pp de escrever // adj: ~ à mão handwritten // m piece of writing; dar por ~ to put in writing // f writing; (pessoal) handwriting; escritor(a) m/f writer; (autor) author.
escri'tório m office; (em casa) study.
escri'tura f (JUR) deed; (caligrafia) handwriting; as Sagradas E~s the Scriptures.
escrituração [eʃkritura'sãw] f bookkeeping; escriturar vt (contas) to register, enter up; (documento) to draw up; escriturário/a m/f clerk/clerkess.
escrivaninha [eʃkriva'niɲa] f writing desk.
escrivão/vã [eʃkri'vãw/vã] m/f registrar, recorder.
es'crúpulo m scruple; (inquietação da consciência) prick of conscience; sem ~ unscrupulous; escrupuloso/a adj scrupulous; (cuidadoso) careful.
escru'tínio m (votação) poll; (apuração de votos) counting; (exame atento) scrutiny; ~ secreto secret ballot.
escudeiro [eʃku'dejru] m squire.
es'cudo m shield; (moeda) Portuguese coin.
esculhambação [eʃkuʎaba'sãw] f (col) mess; esculhambado/a adj (descuidado) shabby, slovenly; (estragado) messed up, knackered; esculhambar vt to mess up; (criticar) to criticise, give stick.
escul'pir vt/i to carve; (gravar) to engrave.
escul'tor(a) m sculptor // f sculptress; escultura f sculpture.
es'cuma f (Pt) foam; (: em cerveja) froth.
es'cuna f (NÁUT) schooner.
es'curas fpl: às ~ in the dark.
escure'cer vt to darken, get dark; ao ~ at dusk; escuridão f (trevas) darkness; escuro/a adj (sombrio) dark; (dia)

overcast; (pessoa) swarthy; (negócios) shady // m darkness.
es'cusa f excuse; escusado/a adj unnecessary; é escusado fazer isso there's no need to do that; escusar vt (desculpar) to excuse, forgive; (não precisar de) not to need; escusar-se vr (desculpar-se) to apologise; escusar-se de fazer to refuse to do.
escu'tar vt to listen to // vi to listen, hear.
esface'lar vt (destruir) to destroy.
esfaimado/a [iʃfaj'madu/a] adj famished, ravenous.
esfal'far vt to tire out, exhaust; ~-se vr to tire o.s. out.
esfaquear [iʃfaki'ax] vt to stab.
esfarra'pado/a adj ragged, in tatters; esfarrapar vt to tear to pieces.
es'fera f sphere; (globo) globe; esférico/a adj spherical.
esfero'gráfica m ballpoint pen.
esfinge [eʃ'fiʒi] f sphinx.
esfo'lar vt to skin; (arranhar) to graze; (cobrar demais a) to overcharge, fleece.
esfome'ado/a adj famished, starving.
esfor'çado/a adj (enérgico) energetic; (forte) strong; (valoroso) brave; esforçar-se vr: esforçar-se para to try hard to, strive to; esforço m effort; (coragem) courage; (TEC) stress; fazer esforços to try hard.
esfre'gar vt to rub; (com água) to scrub.
esfri'ar vt to cool, chill; ~-se vr to grow cold; (fig) to cool off.
esfu'mar vt to tone down, soften; ~-se vr to fade away.
esgalhar [izga'ʎax] vt to prune.
esga'nado/a adj (sufocado) choked; (voraz) greedy; (avaro) grasping; esganar vt to strangle, choke.
esgarava'tar vt (arranhar) to scratch; (fig) to delve into.
esgo'tado/a adj (exausto) exhausted; (consumido) used up; (livros) out of print; os ingressos estão ~s the tickets are sold out; esgotamento m exhaustion; esgotar vt (vazar) to drain, empty; (consumir) to use up; (cansar) to exhaust; esgotar-se vr (cansar-se) to become exhausted; (mercadorias) to be sold out.
es'goto m drain; (público) sewer.
es'grima f (esporte) fencing; esgrimir vi to fence.
esgueirar-se [izgej'rax-si] vr to slip away, sneak off.
esguelha [ez'geʎa] f slant; de ~ obliquely, sideways.
esguichar [ezgi'ʃax] vt to squirt // vi to squirt out.
esguio/a [ez'giu/a] adj (pessoa) lanky; (pessoa, objeto) slender.
esma'gar vt to crush; (vencer) to overpower.
es'malte m enamel; (de unhas) nail varnish.
esme'rado/a adj careful, neat; (bem acabado) polished.

esme'ralda *f* emerald.

esme'rar-se *vr* to do one's best; **esmero** *m* (great) care.

esmigalhar-se [ɛʒmɪgaˈʎax-sɪ] *vr* to crumble.

esmiuçar [ɛʒmjuˈsax] *vt* (*pão*) to crumble; (*examinar*) to examine in detail.

'esmo *m*: **andar a** ~ to walk aimlessly; **falar a** ~ to prattle.

esmo'er *vt* to munch, chew.

es'mola *f* alms *pl*; (*col*) thrashing; **pedir** ~s to beg.

esmore'cer *vt* to discourage // *vi* (*desanimar-se*) to lose heart.

es'nobe *adj* snobbish; (*col*) stuck-up // *m/f* snob; **esnobismo** *m* snobbery.

esp'acial [-aw] *adj* spatial, space; **nave** ~ space-ship.

es'paço *m* space; (*tempo*) period; ~ **para 3 pessoas** room for 3 people; **a** ~**s** from time to time; **espaçoso/a** *adj* spacious, roomy.

es'pada *f* sword; ~**s** *fpl* (*no baralho*) spades; **espadarte** *m* swordfish.

es'pádua *f* shoulder blade.

espairecer [ɛʃpajreˈsex] *vt* to amuse, entertain; ~**-se** *vr* to relax.

espal'dar *m* (*chair*) back.

espalhafato [ɛʃpaʎaˈfatu] *m* din, commotion.

espalhar [ɪʃpaˈʎax] *vt* to scatter, spread (around); (*luz*) to shed.

espana'dor *m* duster; **espanar** *vt* to dust.

espan'car *vt* to beat up, thrash.

espanhol(a) [ɛʃpaˈɲol(a)] *adj* Spanish // *m/f* Spaniard // *m* (*língua*) Spanish.

espan'talho *m* scarecrow; **espantar** *vt* (*causar medo a*) to frighten; (*admirar*) to amaze, astonish; (*afugentar*) to frighten away; **espantar-se** *vr* (*admirar-se*) to be amazed; (*assustar-se*) to be frightened; **espanto** *m* (*medo*) fright, fear; (*admiração*) amazement; **espantoso/a** *adj* (*admirável*) amazing; (*assustador*) frightening.

espara'drapo *m* (sticking) plaster.

espargir [ɛʃpaxˈʒɪx] *vt* (*líquido*) to sprinkle; (*flores*) to scatter; (*luz*) to shed.

esparra'mar *vt* (*líquido*) to splash; (*espalhar*) to scatter.

es'pasmo *m* spasm, convulsion.

espaven'tar *vt* to frighten; **espavorir** *vt* to terrify.

especi'al [-aw] *adj* special; **em** ~ especially; ~**idade** *f* (*particularidade*) speciality; (*ramo de atividades*) specialisation; ~**ista** *m/f* specialist; (*perito*) expert; ~**-izar-se** *vr*: ~**-izar-se em** to specialize in.

especia'ria *f* spice.

es'pécie [ɛʃˈpɛsɪ] *f* (*BIO*) species *sg*; (*tipo*) sort, kind; **causar** ~ to take aback; **pagar em** ~ to pay in kind.

especifi'car *vt* to specify; **específico/a** *adj* specific.

es'pécime *m* specimen.

especi'oso/a *adj* (*argumento*) specious; (*enganoso*) deceptive.

especta'dor(a) *m/f* (*testemunha*) onlooker; (*ao futebol*) spectator; (*no teatro*) member of the audience; ~**es** *mpl* audience *sg*.

es'pectro *m* ghost, phantom; (*FÍSICA*) spectrum.

especu'lar *vi* to speculate.

espelho [ɛʃˈpeʎu] *m* mirror; (*fig*) model; ~ **retrovisor** (*AUTO*) rearview mirror.

espe'lunca *f* (*caverna*) den; (*local sujo*) hovel; (*casa de jogo*) gambling den.

es'pera *f* (*demora*) wait; (*expectativa*) expectation; **à** ~ **de** waiting for; **à minha** ~ waiting for me; **esperança** *f* (*confiança*) hope; (*expectativa*) expectation; **esperar** *vt* (*aguardar*) to wait for; (*desejar*) to hope for; (*contar com*) to expect // *vi* to wait; (*desejar*) to hope; (*contar com*) to expect; **espero que sim/não** I hope so/not; **fazer alguém esperar** to keep sb waiting.

es'perma *f* sperm.

espertalhão/lhona [ɛʃpɛxtaˈʎãw/ʎona] *m/f* crook, swindler; **esperteza** *f* cleverness, cunning; **esperto/a** *adj* clever.

es'pesso/a *adj* thick; **espessura** *f* thickness.

espetacu'lar (*Pt*: -ct-) *adj* spectacular; **espetáculo** (*Pt*: -ct-) *m* (*teatral*) show; (*vista*) sight; (*cena ridícula*) spectacle; **dar espetáculo** to make a spectacle of o.s.

espe'tar *vt* (*carne*) to put on a spit; (*cravar*) to stick; (*fixar*) to fix; **espetinho** *m* skewer; **espeto** *m* spit.

espia [ɛʃˈpɪa], **espião** [ɛʃpɪˈãw] *m/f* spy; **espiar** *vt* (*observar*) to spy on; (*uma ocasião*) to watch out for // *vi* to spy, watch.

espichar [ɛʃpɪˈʃax] *vt* (*couro*) to stretch out; (*pescoço*) to stick out // *vi* (*deitar-se*) to stretch out; (*col: morrer*) to kick the bucket.

es'piga *f* (*de milho*) ear; **espigueiro** *m* granary.

espi'nafre *m* spinach.

espin'garda *f* shotgun, rifle; ~ **de ar comprimido** air rifle.

espinha [ɛʃˈpɪɲa] *f* (*de peixe*) bone; (*na pele*) pimple; (*coluna vertebral*) spine; **espinhar** *vt* (*picar*) to prick; (*irritar*) to irritate, annoy.

espinheiro [ɛʃpɪˈɲejro] *m* bramble bush; **espinhento/a** *adj* pimply; **espinho** *m* thorn; (*de animal*) spine; **espinhoso/a** *adj* (*planta*) prickly, thorny; (*fig*) difficult; (*problema*) thorny.

espionagem [ɛʃpɪoˈnaʒẽ] *f* spying, espionage; **espionar** *vt* to spy on // *vi* to spy, snoop.

espi'ral [-aw] *adj*, *f* spiral.

es'pírita *m/f* spiritualist.

es'pírito *m* spirit; (*álcool*) spirits *pl*; **E~ Santo** Holy Spirit; **espirituoso/a** *adj* (*vivo*) lively; (*dito*) witty.

espir'rar vi to sneeze; (jorrar) to spurt out; (riso) to burst out; **espirro** m sneeze.

es'plêndido / a adj splendid; **esplendor** m splendour.

espo'leta f (de arma) fuse.

espoli'ar vt to plunder; **espólio** m (herança) estate, property; (roubado) booty, spoils pl.

esponja [eʃ'põʒa] f sponge; (parasita) sponger.

espon'sais mpl (contrato) engagement sg; (cerimônia) wedding ceremony sg.

espon'tâneo / a adj spontaneous.

es'pora f spur.

espo'rádico / a adj sporadic.

esporão [eʃpo'rãw] m (de galo) spur; (ARQ) buttress; **esporear** vt (picar) to spur on; (fig) to incite.

es'porte m (Br) sport; **esportista** adj sporting // m sportsman // f sportswoman; **esportivo / a** adj sporting.

espo'sar vt to marry; (causa) to defend; **esposo / a** m husband // f wife.

espraiar [eʃpra'jax] vt/i to spread; (dilatar) to expand.

espreguiçar-se [eʃpregi'sax-si] vr to stretch.

espreitar [eʃprej'tax] vt (espiar) to spy on; (observar) to observe, watch.

espre'mer vt (fruta) to squeeze; (roupa molhada) to wring out.

es'puma f foam; (de cerveja) froth, head; (de sabão) lather; **espumante** adj frothy, foamy; (vinho) sparkling.

es'púrio / a adj spurious, bogus.

esquadra [eʃ'kwadra] f (NÁUT) fleet; (MIL) squadron; (da polícia) police station.

esquadrão [eʃkwa'drãw] m, **esquadrilha** [eʃkwa'driʎa] f squadron.

esquadrinhar [eʃkwadri'nax] vt to scrutinize.

esquadro [eʃ'kwadru] m set square.

esqualidez [eʃkwali'deʃ] f squalor; **esquálido / a** adj squalid, filthy.

esquecer [eʃke'sex] vt/i to forget; **~-se** vr: **~-se de** to forget; **esquecidiço / a** adj forgetful; **esquecido / a** adj forgotten; (esquecidiço) forgetful; **esquecimento** m (falta de memória) forgetfulness; (olvido) oblivion.

esque'leto m skeleton; (arcabouço) framework.

es'quema m (resumo) outline; (plano) scheme; (esboço) diagram.

esquen'tar vt to heat (up), warm (up).

esquerdo / a [eʃ'kexdu/a] adj left // f left; à **~a de** on the left.

esqui [eʃ'ki] m (patim) ski; (esporte) skiing; **~ aquático** water skiing; **esquiar** vi to ski.

esquilo [eʃ'kilu] m squirrel.

esquina [eʃ'kina] f corner.

esquisito / a [eski'situ/a] adj strange, odd.

esquivar-se [eʃki'vax-si] vr: **~ de** to escape from, get away from; **esquivo / a** adj aloof, standoffish.

esq° abr ver **esquerdo**.

esse, essa, esses, essas ['esi, 'esa, 'esiʃ, 'esaʃ] adj, pron (sg) that; (pl) those.

es'sência f essence; **essencial** adj essential // m: **o essencial** the main thing.

estabele'cer vt to establish, set up; **~-se** vr to establish o.s., set o.s. up; **estabelecimento** m establishment; (casa comercial) business.

estabili'dade f stability.

es'tábulo m cow-shed.

es'taca f post, stake; **estacada** f (defensiva) stockade; (fileira de estacas) fencing.

estação [eʃta'sãw] f station; (do ano) season; **~ balneária** seaside resort; **~ rodoviária** coach station.

esta'car vt to prop up // vi to stop short, halt.

estaciona'mento m (ato) parking; (lugar) parking place; **estacionar** vt to park // vi to park; (não mover) to remain stationary; **estacionário / a** adj (veículo) stationary; (COM) slack.

es'tada f stay.

es'tádio m stadium.

esta'dista m statesman // f stateswoman; **estado** m state; **estado civil** marital status; **em bom estado** in good condition; **estado maior** staff; **Estados Unidos (da América)** United States (of America), U.S.A.

esta'far vt to tire out, fatigue; **~-se** vr to tire o.s. out.

esta'fermo m (Pt) scarecrow; (: col) nincompoop.

estagiário / a [eʃtaʒi'arju/a] m/f probationer; (professor) student teacher; (médico) junior doctor; **estágio** m (de professor) probationary period; **fazer um estágio** (como professor) to be a student teacher; (como médico) to be a junior doctor; (aprendizado) to be on an apprenticeship.

estagnação [eʃtagna'sãw] f stagnation; **estagnado / a** adj stagnant; **estagnar-se** vr to stagnate.

estalagem [eʃta'laʒẽ] f inn.

esta'lar vt (quebrar) to break; (os dedos) to snap // vi (fender-se) to split, crack; (crepitar) to crackle; (uma guerra) to break out; **~ de fome** to be dying of hunger.

estaleiro [eʃta'lejru] m shipyard.

esta'lido, esta'lo m (do chicote) crack; (dos dedos) snap; (dos lábios) smack; **~ de trovão** thunderclap; (de foguete) bang.

es'tampa f (figura impressa) print; (ilustração) picture; **estampado / a** adj printed // m (tecido) print; **estampar** vt (imprimir) to print; (marcar) to stamp.

estam'pido m bang.

estampilha [eʃtam'piʎa] f (TESOURO) stamp.

estan'car vt (sangue) to staunch; (fazer cessar) to stop; (a sede) to quench // vi (*esgotar*) to run dry; ~**-se** *vr* (*parar*) to stop.

es'tância *f* (*fazenda*) ranch, farm; (*versos*) stanza; ~ **hidromineral** spa resort; **estancieiro** *m* rancher, farmer.

estan'darte *m* standard, banner.

estanho [ɛʃ'taɲu] *m* (*metal*) tin.

estanque [ɛʃ'tãkı] *adj* watertight.

es'tante *f* (*armário*) bookcase; (*suporte*) stand.

es'tar *vi* (*estado temporário*) to be; ~ **fazendo**, ~ **a fazer** (*Pt*) to be doing; ~ **bem** to be all right; **está bem** OK; ~ **bem com** to be on good terms with; ~ **calor/frio** (*o tempo*) to be hot/cold; ~ **com fome/sede/medo** to be hungry/thirsty/afraid; ~ **doente** to be ill; ~ **em casa** to be in; ~ **na hora de fazer** to be time to do; ~ **para conversas** to be in the mood for talking; ~ **para fazer** to be about to do; ~ **por alguma coisa** to be in favour of sth; ~ **por fazer** to be still to be done.

es'tático/a *adj* static // *f* (*TEC*) static.

esta'tística *f* statistic; (*ciência*) statistics *sg*.

estati'zar *vt* to nationalize.

es'tátua *f* statue.

esta'tura *f* stature; (*altura*) height.

esta'tuto *m* (*JUR*) statute; (*de cidade*) bye-law; (*de associação*) rule.

es'tável *adj* stable.

este ['ɛʃtʃi] *m* east.

este, esta, estes, estas ['ɛʃtʃi, 'ɛʃta, 'ɛʃtʃiʃ, 'ɛʃtaʃ] *adj* (*sg*) this; (*pl*) these // *pron* this one; (*pl*) these.

e'steio *m* prop, support; (*NÁUT*) stay.

esteira [ɛʃ'tejra] *f* mat; (*de navio*) wake; (*rumo*) path.

es'teja *etc vb ver* estar.

esten'der *vt* to extend; (*mapa*) to spread out; (*massa*) to roll out; (*roupa molhada*) to hang out; ~ **a mão** to hold out one's hand; ~ **a mesa** to lay the table; ~**-se** *vr* (*dilatar-se*) to stretch; (*epidemia*) to spread; (*no chão*) to lie down.

esteno-dacti'lógrafo/a *m/f* shorthand typist; **estenografia** *f* shorthand.

e'stepe *m* spare tyre.

es'terco *m* manure, dung.

es'tereo... *pref* stereo; ~**fônico/a** *adj* stereophonic; (*col*) stereo; ~**tipar** *vt* to stereotype; **estereótipo** *m* stereotype.

es'téril [-rıw] *adj* sterile; (*fig*) futile.

ester'lino/a *adj* sterling; **libra** ~**a** pound sterling // *m* sterling.

es'tético/a *adj* aesthetic // *f* aesthetics *sg*; (*beleza*) beauty.

es'teve *vb ver* estar.

esti'agem *f* dry season; **estiar** *vi* (*não chover*) to stop raining; (*o tempo*) to clear up.

esti'bordo *m* starboard.

esti'car *vt* (*uma corda*) to stretch, tighten; (*a perna*) to stretch out; ~**-se** *vr* to stretch out.

es'tigma *m* (*marca*) mark, scar; (*fig*)

stigma; ~**tizar** *vt* (*marcar*) to brand; (*fig*) to stigmatize.

estilha'çar *vt* to splinter; (*despedaçar*) to shatter; **estilhaço** *m* fragment, chip, splinter.

es'tilo *m* style; (*TEC*) stylus.

es'tima *f* esteem; (*afeto*) affection; **estimação** *f* (*respeito*) esteem, estimation; (*afeição*) affection; **animal de estimação** pet animal; **estimar** *vt* (*apreciar*) to appreciate; (*avaliar*) to value; (*ter estima a*) to have a high regard for; (*calcular aproximadamente*) to estimate; **estimatura** *f* estimate.

estimu'lante *adj* stimulating // *m* stimulant; **estimular** *vt* to stimulate; (*excitar*) to excite; (*animar*) to encourage; **estímulo** *m* stimulus; (*ânimo*) encouragement; (*incitamento*) provocation.

es'tio *m* summer.

estipulação [ɛʃtipula'sãw] *f* stipulation; (*condição*) condition; **estipular** *vt* to stipulate.

esti'rar *vt* to stretch (out); ~**-se** *vr* to stretch.

es'tirpe *f* stock, lineage.

es'tive *etc vb ver* estar.

esto'cada *f* stab, thrust.

esto'car *vt* to stock.

estofa'dor *m* upholsterer; **estofar** *vt* to upholster; (*acolchoar*) to pad, stuff; **estofo** *m* (*tecido*) material; (*para acolchoar*) padding, stuffing.

es'tóico *adj* stoic(al); (*impassível*) impassive.

estojo [ɛʃ'toʒu] *m* case; ~ **de unhas** manicure set; ~ **de ferramentas** tool kit.

e'stola *f* stole.

es'tólido/a *adj* stupid.

es'tômago *m* stomach; **ter** ~ **para** to tolerate.

estonte'ar *vt* to stun, daze.

estoque [ɛʃ'tɔkı] *m* (*COM*) stock.

es'tore *m* (*Pt*) blind.

es'tória *f* story.

estor'ninho [ɛʃtox'niɲu] *m* starling.

estor'var *vt* to hinder, obstruct; (*fig*) to bother, disturb; ~ **alguém de fazer** to prevent sb from doing; **estorvo** *m* hindrance, obstacle; (*fig*) bother, nuisance.

estou'rar [ɛʃto'rax] *vi* to explode; (*pneu*) to burst; (*escândalo*) to blow up; **estouro** *m* explosion; **ser um estouro** (*col*) to be great.

estou'vado/a *adj* rash, foolhardy.

es'trábico/a *adj* cross-eyed; **estrabismo** *m* squint.

es'trada *f* road; ~ **de ferro** (*Br*) railway, railroad (*US*); ~ **de rodagem** (*Br*) motorway, freeway (*US*); ~ **de terra** dirt road.

es'trado *m* (*tablado*) platform.

estra'gar *vt* (*uma festa*) to spoil; (*arruinar*) to ruin, wreck; (*desperdiçar*) to waste; **estrago** *m* (*destruição*) destruction; (*desperdício*) waste; (*dano*) damage; **os estragos da guerra** the ravages of war.

estrangeiro/a [ɛʃtrã'ʒejru/a] *adj* foreign // *m/f* foreigner; **no ~** abroad.

estrangula'dor *m* strangler; (*TEC*) throttle; **estrangulamento** *m* (*AUTO*) bottleneck; **estrangular** *vt* to strangle, choke.

estranhar [ɛʃtra'ɲax] *vt* to be surprised at; **~ os visitantes** to be shy with visitors; **estranhei o clima** the climate did not agree with me; **estranho/a** *adj* strange, odd; (*influências*) outside // *m* (*desconhecido*) stranger; (*de fora*) outsider.

estratagema [ɛʃtrata'ʒema] *m* (*MIL*) stratagem; (*ardil*) trick.

estra'tégia *f* strategy; **estratégico/a** *adj* strategic.

es'trato *m* layer, stratum.

estre'ar *vt* (*vestido, peça*) to wear/put on for the first time; (*veículo*) to use for the first time; (*filme*) to show for the first time.

estrebuchar [ɛʃtrebu'ʃax] *vi* to struggle; (*ao morrer*) to shake (in death throes).

estréia [ɛʃ'treja] *f* (*de artista*) debut; (*de uma peça*) first night; (*abertura*) opening; **é a ~ do meu carro** it's the first time I've used my car.

estreitar [ɛʃtrej'tax] *vt* (*reduzir*) to narrow; (*roupa*) to take in; (*abraçar*) to hug // *vi* (*estrada*) to narrow; **~-se** *vr* (*rua*) to narrow; (*laços de amizade*) to deepen; **estreiteza** *f* narrowness; (*de roupa*) tightness; **estreiteza de pontos de vista** narrowmindedness; **estreito/a** *adj* narrow; (*apertado*) tight; (*saia*) straight; (*amizade*) close // *m* strait.

es'trela *f* star; **estrelado/a** *adj* (*céu*) starry; (*ovo*) fried; **estrela-do-mar** *f* starfish; **estrelar** *vt* (*ovos*) to fry.

estreme'cer *vt* (*sacudir*) to shake // *vi* (*vibrar*) to shake; (*tremer*) to tremble; (*horrorizar-se*) to shudder; **estremecimento** *m* (*sacudida*) shaking, trembling; (*tremor*) tremor; (*amizade*) deep friendship.

es'trepito *m* din, racket; (*fig*) fuss; **estrepitoso/a** *adj* noisy, rowdy; (*fig*) sensational.

es'tria *f* groove.

estri'bar *vt* to base; **~-se** *vr*: **~-se em** to be based on.

estribilho [ɛʃtri'biʎu] *m* (*MÚS*) chorus; (*na conversa*) catchphrase.

es'tribo *m* (*de cavalo*) stirrup; (*degrau*) step; (*plataforma*) platform; (*apoio*) support.

estri'dente *adj* (*penetrante*) shrill, piercing; (*dissonante*) grating.

es'trito/a *adj* (*rigoroso*) strict; (*restrito*) restricted.

es'trofe *f* stanza.

estron'dar *vi* to boom; (*fig*) to resound; **estrondo** *m* (*de trovão*) rumble; (*de*

armas) din; **estrondo sônico** sonic boom.

estropi'ar *vt* (*aleijar*) to maim, cripple; (*fatigar*) to wear out, exhaust; (*texto*) to mutilate; (*pronunciar mal*) to mispronounce.

es'trume *m* manure.

estru'tura *f* structure.

estu'ário *m* estuary.

estu'dante *m/f* student; **estudantil** *adj* student; **estudar** *vt* to study.

es'túdio *m* studio.

estudi'oso/a *adj* studious; **estudo** *m* study.

es'tufa *f* (*fogão*) stove, heater; (*de plantas*) greenhouse; **estufadeira** *f* (*Pt*) stewpot; **estufado** *m* (*Pt*) stew.

es'tulto/a *adj* foolish, silly.

estupefação [ɛʃtupefa'sãw] (*Pt*: -cç-) *f* numbness; (*fig*) amazement, astonishment; **estupefato/a** (*Pt*: -ct-) *adj* (*entorpecido*) numb; (*pasmado*) speechless.

estu'pendo/a *adj* wonderful; (*col*) fantastic, terrific.

estupi'dez *f* stupidity; (*asneira*) piece of nonsense; **estúpido/a** *adj* stupid, silly // *m/f* idiot.

estu'prar *vt* to rape; **estupro** *m* rape.

estuque [ɛʃ'tuki] *m* stucco; (*massa*) plaster.

es'túrdia *f* prank, silliness.

estur'rar *vt* (*torrar*) to scorch; (*queimar*) to burn.

esvae'cer-se *vr* to fade away, vanish.

esva'ir-se *vr* to vanish, disappear; **~ em sangue** to lose a lot of blood.

esvazi'ar *vt* to empty.

esvoa'çar *vi* to flutter.

e'tapa *f* (*fase*) stage.

eterni'dade *f* eternity; **eterno/a** *adj* eternal.

'ético/a *adj* ethical // *f* ethics *pl*.

etiqueta [ɛtʃi'keta] *f* (*maneiras*) etiquette; (*rótulo*) label, tag.

'étnico/a *adj* ethnic.

eu [ew] *pron* I.

E.U.A. *abr de* **Estados Unidos da América** U.S.A., United States of America.

eucaristia [ewkariʃ'tʃia] *f* Holy Communion.

eufe'mismo *m* euphemism.

eufo'ria *f* euphoria.

Eu'ropa *f* Europe; **europeu/péia** *adj, m/f* European.

euta'násia *f* euthanasia.

evacu'ar *vt* to evacuate; (*sair de*) to leave; (*MED*) to discharge // *vi* to defecate.

eva'dir *vt* to evade; (*col*) to dodge; **~-se** *vr* to escape.

evangelho [evã'ʒeʎu] *m* gospel; **evangélico/a** *adj* evangelical.

evaporação [evapora'sãw] *f* evaporation; **evaporar** *vt/i* to evaporate // *vi* (*desaparecer*) to vanish; **evaporar-se** *vr* (*desaparecer*) to vanish.

evasão [eva'sãw] *f* escape, flight; (*fig*) evasion; **evasivo/a** *adj* evasive // *f* excuse.

e'vento *m* (*acontecimento*) event; (*eventualidade*) eventuality; **eventual** *adj* fortuitous, accidental; **eventualidade** *f* eventuality.

evi'dência *f* evidence, proof; **evidenciar** *vt* (*comprovar*) to prove; (*mostrar*) to show; **evidenciar-se** *vr* to be evident, be obvious; **evidente** *adj* obvious, evident.

evi'tar *vt* to avoid; (*impedir*) to prevent.

evo'car *vt* to evoke; (*o passado*) to recall.

evolução [evolu'sãw] *f* (*desenvolvimento*) development; (*MIL*) manoeuvre; (*movimento*) movement; (*BIO*) evolution; **evoluir** *vi* to evolve.

exacer'bar *vt* (*irritar*) to irritate, annoy; (*agravar*) to aggravate, worsen.

exage'rar *vt/i* to exaggerate; **exagero** *m* exaggeration.

exalar [εza'lax] *vt* (*odor*) to give off.

exal'tado/a *adj* (*fanático*) fanatical; (*apaixonado*) overexcited; **exaltar** *vt* (*elevar*) to exalt; (*louvar*) to praise; (*excitar*) to excite; (*irritar*) to annoy; **exaltar-se** *vr* (*excitar-se*) to get worked up; (*arrebatar-se*) to get carried away.

exame [ɪ'zamɪ] *m* examination, exam; **fazer um ~** to take an exam; **examinar** *vt* to examine.

exangue [ɪ'zãgɪ] *adj* (*sem sangue*) bloodless; (*exausto*) exhausted.

exantema [ɪzan'tema] *m* (*MED*) rash.

exaspe'rar *vt* to exasperate; **~-se** *vr* to get exasperated.

exatidão [ɪzatʃi'dãw] (*Pt*: -ct-) *f* (*precisão*) accuracy; (*perfeição*) correctness; **exato/a** (*Pt*: -ct-) *adj* (*certo*) right, correct; (*preciso*) exact.

exaurir [ɪzaw'rix] *vt* (*esgotar*) to exhaust, drain; **~-se** *vr* (*cansar-se*) to become exhausted; (*águas*) to run dry; **exausto/a** *pp irr de* **exaurir** // *adj* exhausted.

exceção [ɪʃse'sãw] (*Pt*: -pç-) *f* exception.

exceder [ɪʃse'dex] *vt* to exceed; (*superar*) to surpass; **~ em peso/brilho** to outweigh/outshine; **~-se** *vr* (*exagerar*) to go too far; (*cansar-se*) to overdo things.

exce'lência *f* excellence; **por ~** par excellence; **Vossa E~** Your Excellency; **excelente** *adj* excellent.

excentrici'dade *f* eccentricity; **excêntrico/a** *adj*, *m/f* eccentric.

excepcio'nal [-aw] *adj* (*extraordinário*) exceptional; (*especial*) special.

exces'sivo/a *adj* excessive; **excesso** *m* excess; (*COM*) surplus.

ex'ceto (*Pt*: -pt-) *prep* except for, apart from; **excetuar** (*Pt*: -pt) *vt* to except, make an exception of.

excitação [ɪʃsita'sãw] *f* excitement; **excitado/a** *adj* excited; (*estimulado*) aroused; **excitar** *vt* to excite; (*estimular*) to arouse; **excitar-se** *vr* to get excited.

exclamação [εʃklama'sãw] *f* exclamation; **exclamar** *vi* to exclaim.

excluir [εʃ'klwɪx] *vt* to exclude; (*deixar fora*) to leave out, shut out; **exclusivo/a** *adj* exclusive; **para uso exclusivo de** for the sole use of.

excomun'gar *vt* to excommunicate.

excursão [εʃkux'sãw] *f* trip, outing; (*em grupo*) excursion; **~ a pé** hike; **excursionista** *m/f* tourist; (*para o dia*) day-tripper; (*a pé*) hiker.

execução [ezeku'sãw] *f* execution; (*de música*) performance; **executante** *m/f* player, performer; **executar** *vt* to execute; (*MÚS*) to perform.

execu'tivo/a *adj*, *m/f* executive; **executor(a)** *m* executor; (*verdugo*) executioner.

exemplar [izẽ'plax] *adj* exemplary // *m* model, example; (*BIO*) specimen; (*livro*) copy; **exemplo** *m* example; **por exemplo** for example, for instance.

exéquias [ɪ'zekjaʃ] *fpl* funeral rites.

exercer [izer'sex] *vt* to exercise; (*influência, pressão*) to exert; (*função*) to perform; (*profissão*) to practise; **exercício** *m* (*ginástica*) exercise; (*de medicina*) practice; (*MIL*) drill; (*COM*) financial year; **exercitar** *vt* (*profissão*) to practise; (*direitos, músculos*) to exercise; (*adestrar*) to train.

exército [ɪ'zexsitʊ] *m* army.

exibição [ɪzibɪ'sãw] *f* display; **exibir** *vt* to show, display; **exibir-se** *vr* to show off.

exigência [ɪzɪ'ʒẽsja] *f* demand; **exigente** *adj* demanding; **exigir** *vt* to demand.

exíguo/a [ε'zɪgwu/a] *adj* (*diminuto*) small; (*escasso*) scanty.

exilado/a [εzɪ'ladu/a] *adj* exiled // *m/f* exile; **exilar** *vt* to exile; (*pessoa indesejável*) to deport; **exilar-se** *vr* to go into exile; **exílio** *m* exile; (*forçado*) deportation.

exímio/a [ε'zɪmju/a] *adj* (*eminente*) famous, distinguished; (*excelente*) excellent.

eximir [εzɪ'mɪx] *vt*: **~ de** to exempt from; **~-se** *vr*: **~-se de** to avoid, shun.

existência [ɪzɪ'ʃtẽsja] *f* existence; (*ser*) being; **existir** *vi* to exist, be.

êxito ['εzitʊ] *m* (*resultado*) result; (*bom sucesso*) success; **ter ~** to succeed, be successful; **não ter ~** to fail, be unsuccessful.

exonerar [εzone'rax] *vt* (*demitir*) to dismiss; **~ de uma obrigação** to free from an obligation.

exorcismar [εzoxsiʒ'max] *vt* to exorcise; **exorcismo** *m* exorcism; **exorcizar** *vt* to exorcise.

exortação [εzoxta'sãw] *f* exhortation; (*advertência*) warning; **exortar** *vt* (*animar*) to urge on; (*aconselhar*) to advise.

exótico/a [ε'zotʃiku/a] *adj* exotic.

expan'dir *vt* to expand; (*vela*) to unfold; (*espalhar*) to spread; **~-se** *vr* (*dilatar-se*) to expand; ~-se com alguém to be frank with sb; **expansão** f expansion, spread; (de alegria) effusiveness; **expansivo/a** adj (pessoa) outgoing.

expecta'tiva f (esperança) expectation; (perspectiva) prospect.

expedição [ɛʃpedʒiˈsãw] f (viagem) expedition; (de mercadorias) despatch; (por navio) shipment.

expediente [ɛʃpeˈdʒjẽtʃi] m expedient; (serviço) day's work; (correspondência) correspondence; (horas) ~ do escritório office hours pl; **expedir** vt (enviar) to send, despatch; (decreto) to issue.

expe'dito/a adj prompt, speedy.

expe'lir vt (invasor) to expel; (fazer sair) to throw out.

experi'ência f (prática) experience; (prova) experiment, test; em ~ on trial.

experimen'tado/a adj (perito) experienced; (testado) tried; (provado) tested; **experimentar** vt (comida) to taste; (vestido) to try on; (pôr à prova) to try out, test; (conhecer pela experiência) to experience; (sofrer) to suffer, undergo; **experimento** m (científico) experiment.

expi'ar vt to atone for.

expi'rar vt (ar) to exhale, breathe out // vi (morrer) to die; (terminar) to end.

expla'nar vt to explain.

explicação [ɛʃplikaˈsãw] f explanation; (Pt: lição) private lesson; **explicar** vt to explain.

expli'cito/a adj explicit, clear.

explo'dir vi to explode, blow up.

exploração [ɛʃploraˈsãw] f (de um país) exploration; (abuso) exploitation; (de uma fábrica) running; **explorar** vt (região) to explore; (mina) to work, run; (ferida) to probe; (enganar) to exploit; (uma situação) to make the most of.

explosão [ɛʃploˈzãw] f explosion, blast; (fig) outburst; **explosivo/a** adj explosive; (pessoa) hot-headed // m explosive.

ex'por vt to expose; (a vida) to risk; (teoria) to explain; (mercadorias) to display; (quadros) to exhibit; ~-se vr to expose o.s.

exportação [ɛʃpoxtaˈsãw] f (ato) export(ing); (mercadorias) exports pl; **exportador(a)** adj exporting // m/f exporter; **exportar** vt to export.

exposição [ɛʃposiˈsãw] f (exibição) exhibition; (explicação) explanation; (declaração) statement; (narração) account; (FOTO) exposure; **expositor(a)** m/f exhibitor.

expressão [ɛʃpreˈsãw] f expression; **expressar** vt to express; **expresso/a** adj (manifesto) definite, clear; (ordem, carta) express // m express.

expri'mir vt to express; ~-se vr to express o.s.

expropri'ar vt to dispossess, expropriate.

expug'nar vt to take by storm.

expulsão [ɛʃpulˈsãw] f expulsion; **expulsar** vt to expel; (inimigo) to drive out; (botar fora) to throw out.

expur'gar vt to expurgate.

'êxtase m ecstasy.

extensão [ɛʃtẽˈsãw] f extension; (de uma empresa) expansion; (terreno) expanse; (tempo) length, duration; (alcance) extent; **extenso/a** adj (amplo) wide; (comprido) long; por **extenso** in full.

extenuado/a [ɛʃtenˈwadu/a] adj (esgotado) worn out; **extenuante** adj exhausting; (debilitante) debilitating; **extenuar** vt to exhaust; (debilitar) to weaken.

exteri'or adj (de fora) outside, exterior; (aparência) outward; (comércio) foreign // m (da casa) outside; (aspecto) outward appearance; do ~ (do estrangeiro) from abroad.

extermi'nar vt (inimigo) to wipe out, exterminate; (acabar com) to do away with; **extermínio** m extermination, wiping out.

exter'nato m day school; **externo/a** adj external; (aparente) outward; aluno **externo** day pupil.

extinguir [ɛʃtʃĩˈgix] vt (fogo) to put out, extinguish; (um povo) to wipe out; (sede) to quench; ~-se vr (fogo, luz) to go out; (BIO) to become extinct; **extinto/a** adj (fogo) extinguished; (língua) dead; (animal) extinct; **extintor** m (fire) extinguisher.

extir'par vt (desarraigar) to uproot; (corrupção) to eradicate.

extorquir [ɛʃtoxˈkix] vt to extort; **extorsão** f extorsion.

'extra adj extra // m/f extra person; (teatro) extra.

extração [ɛʃtraˈsãw] (Pt: -cç-) f extraction; (de loteria) draw.

extra'ir vt to extract, take out.

extraordi'nário/a adj extraordinary; (despesa) extra; (reunião) special; horas ~as overtime sg.

extrater'restre adj extraterrestial.

ex'trato (Pt: -ct-) m extract; (resumo) summary; (banco) statement.

extrava'gância f (prodigalidade) extravagance; **extravagante** adj (pródigo) extravagant; (roupa) outlandish; (conduta) wild.

extrava'sar vi to overflow.

extravi'ado/a adj lost, missing; **extraviar** vt (perder) to mislay; (pessoa) to lead astray; (dinheiro) to embezzle // vi to get lost; **extraviar-se** vr to get lost; **extravio** m (perda) loss; (roubo) embezzlement; (fig) deviation.

extre'mado/a adj (coragem) outstanding.

extremi'dade f extremity; (do dedo) tip; (fim) end; (orla) edge; **extremo/a** adj extreme; (longe) far.

extre'moso/a adj fond, loving.

extrover'tido/a m/f extrovert.

exube'rância f exuberance;

exuberante adj (abundante) abundant, plentiful; (animado) exuberant.

exumar [ezu'max] vt (corpo) to exhume; (fig) to dig up.

ex-voto [es-'votu] m votive offering.

F

'fábrica f factory; ~ **de conservas** cannery.

fabricação [fabrika'sãw] f manufacture; (produção) production; **fabricante** m/f manufacturer; **fabricar** vt to manufacture, make; (inventar) to fabricate.

'fábula f fable; (conto) tale; (Br) fortune; **fabuloso/a** adj fabulous.

'faca f knife; **facada** f stab, cut.

façanha [fa'saɲa] f exploit, deed.

facção [fak'sãw] f faction; **faccioso/a** adj factious.

face ['fasi] f (rosto) face; (bochecha) cheek; **em** ~ **de** in view of; **fazer** ~ **a** to face up to.

fachada [fa'ʃada] f facade, front.

facho ['faʃu] m torch.

fácil ['fasiw] adj easy; **facilidade** f ease; (jeito) dexterity; **facilitar** vt to facilitate, make easy; (fornecer) to provide.

fa'cínora m criminal.

'faço etc vb ver **fazer**.

'facto m (Pt) fact; **de** ~ in fact.

facul'dade f faculty; (poder) power; **facultar** vt (permitir) to allow; (conceder) to grant; **facultativo/a** adj optional // m doctor.

'fada f fairy.

fa'dado/a adj fated, destined, doomed; **bem** ~ fortunate; **fadar** vt to destine; (condenar) to doom.

fa'diga f fatigue; (trabalho) toil.

fa'dista m/f singer of 'fado' // m ruffian; (ocioso) layabout // f prostitute; **fado** m fate; (canção) traditional song of Portugal.

fagueiro/a [fa'gejru/a] adj (encantador) sweet; (contente) happy.

fagulha [fa'guʎa] f spark.

faia ['faja] f beech (tree).

faina ['fajna] f toil, work; (tarefa) task.

faisão [faj'sãw] m pheasant.

fa'ísca f spark; (brilha) flash; **faiscar** vi to sparkle; (cintilar) to flash.

faixa ['fajʃa] f (cinta) belt; (tira) strip; (área) zone; (AUTO: pista) lane; (Br: para pedestres) zebra crossing, crosswalk (US).

fa'juto/a adj (col) kitsch.

'fala f speech; (conversa) conversation; (dito) remark; **chamar às** ~**s** to call to account; **sem** ~ speechless.

falácia [fal'asja] f fallacy.

fala'dor(a) adj talkative // m/f chatterbox; **falante** adj garrulous, talkative.

fa'lar vt/i to speak, talk; ~ **com** to talk to; **por** ~ **em** speaking of; **sem** ~ **em**

apart from; ~ **pelos cotovelos** to talk one's head off.

falaz [fa'laʃ] adj deceptive, misleading; (falso) false.

falcão [faw'kãw] m falcon.

fale'cer vi to die; (faltar) to be lacking; **falecido/a** adj dead // m/f deceased; **falecimento** m death.

fa'lência f bankruptcy; **abrir** ~ to declare o.s. bankrupt; **levar à** ~ to bankrupt.

falhar ['faʎax] vi to fail; (não acertar) to miss; (errar) to be wrong; **falho/a** adj faulty // f (defeito, GEO etc) fault; (lacuna) omission.

fa'lido/a adj, m/f bankrupt; **falir** vi to fail; (COM) to go bankrupt.

fal'sário/a [faw-] m/f forger; **falsear** vt to forge, falsify; **falsidade** f falsehood; (fingimento) pretence; (engano) deceit.

falsifi'car vt to forge, falsify; (adulterar) to adulterate; (desvirtuar) to misrepresent; **falso/a** adj false; (fraudulento) dishonest; (errôneo) wrong; **pisar em falso** to miss one's step, put a foot wrong.

'falta f (carência) lack; (ausência) absence; (defeito) fault; (futebol) foul; **por/na** ~ **de** for lack of; **sem** ~ without fail; **ter** ~ **de** to lack, be in need of; **fazer** ~ to be lacking, be needed.

fal'tar vi (escassear) to be lacking, be wanting; (falhar) to fail; ~ **ao trabalho** to be absent from work; ~ **à palavra** to break one's word; **falta pouco para** ... it won't be long until ....

'falto/a adj lacking, deficient.

'fama f (renome) fame; (reputação) reputation; **ter** ~ **de generoso** to be said to be generous.

fa'mélico/a adj starving.

fa'mília f family; **familiar** adj (da família) family cmp; (conhecido) familiar; **familiaridade** f familiarity; (semcerimônia) informality.

fa'minto/a adj hungry; (fig) eager.

fa'moso/a adj famous.

fa'nático/a adj fanatical // m/f fanatic; **fanatismo** m fanaticism.

fanfarrão/rona [fãfa'xãw/'xona] adj boastful // m/f braggart; (valentão) bully.

fani'quito m fit of nervousness.

fanta'sia f fantasy; (imaginação) imagination; (capricho) fancy; (traje) fancy dress; **fantasiar** vt to imagine // vi to daydream; **fantasiar-se** vr to dress up.

fan'tasma m ghost; (alucinação) illusion; (ameaça) spectre; **fantástico/a** adj fantastic; (ilusório) imaginary; (incrível) unbelievable.

fantoche [fã'toʃi] m puppet.

'farda f uniform.

'fardo m bundle; (carga) load; (fig) burden.

fa'rei etc vb ver **fazer**.

farejar [fare'ʒax] vt to smell (out), sniff

(out); (*procurar*) to seek; (*adivinhar*) to sense // *vi* to sense.

farfalhar [faxfa'ʎax] *vi* to rustle; (*fanfarrear*) to boast; **farfalhice** *f* showiness; **farfalhudo/a** *adj* ostentatious.

farinha [fa'rɪɲa] *f* (manioc) flour.

farmacêutico/a [farma'sewtʃiku/a] *adj* pharmaceutical // *m/f* chemist, pharmacist; **farmácia** *f* chemist's (shop), pharmacy.

'faro *m* sense of smell; (*fig*) flair.

fa'rofa *f* (CULIN) side dish based on manioc flour.

fa'rol [-ow] *m* lighthouse; (AUTO) headlight; **~eiro** *m* lighthouse keeper; (*col*) braggart; **~etes traseiros** *mpl* rear lights.

'farpa *f* barb; (*estilha*) splinter; (*rasgão*) tear; **farpado/a** *adj* barbed.

'farra *f* binge, spree.

far'rapo *m* rag; (*pedaço*) tatter.

'farsa *f* farce; **farsante** *m/f* joker.

far'tar *vt* to satiate, fill up; (*enfastiar*) to tire, sicken; **~-se** *vr* to gorge o.s.; **~-se de** (*cansar-se*) to get fed up with; **farto/a** *adj* full, satiated; (*abundante*) plentiful; (*cansado*) fed up; **cabeleira farta** full head of hair, shock of hair.

fartum [fax'tũ] *m* stench.

far'tura *f* abundance, plenty.

fas'cículo *m* (*de publicação*) instalment.

fasci'nante *adj* fascinating; **fascinar** *vt* to fascinate; (*encantar*) to charm.

fas'cismo *m* fascism; **fascista** *adj, m/f* fascist.

fase ['fazɪ] *f* phase; (*etapa*) stage.

fastidi'oso/a,   fasti'ento/a   *adj* tedious; (*enfadonho*) annoying.

fastígio [faʃ'tʃiʒju] *m* peak, summit; (*fig*) height.

fas'tio *m* lack of appetite; (*repugnância*) disgust; (*tédio*) boredom.

fatal [fa'taw] *adj* fatal; (*decisivo*) fateful; (*inevitável*) inescapable; **~idade** *f* (*destino*) fate; (*desgraça*) disaster.

fa'tia *f* slice.

fa'tídico/a *adj* fateful.

fati'gante   *adj*   tiring;   (*aborrecido*) tiresome; **fatigar** *vt* to tire; (*aborrecer*) to bore; **fatigar-se** *vr* to get tired.

'fato *m* fact; (*sucesso*) event; (Pt: *traje*) suit; **~ de banho** (Pt) swimming costume; **de ~** in fact, really.

fa'tor (Pt: -ct-) *m* factor; (*agente*) agent.

'fátuo/a *adj* (*vão*) fatuous.

fa'tura (Pt: -ct-) *f* bill, invoice; **faturar** (Pt: -ct-) *vt* to invoice.

'fava *f* (broad) bean; **mandar alguém às ~s** to send sb packing.

fa'vela *f* slum, shanty town.

fa'vor *m* favour; **a ~ de** in favour of; **em ~ de** on behalf of; **por ~** please; **faça o ~ de ...** would you be so good as to ..., kindly ...; **~ecer** *vt* to favour; (*beneficiar*) to benefit; **~ito/a** *adj, m/f* favourite.

faxina [fa'ʃina] *f* (*gravetos*) brushwood;

(*limpeza*) cleaning (up); **faxineira** *f* (*pessoa*) cleaner.

fa'zenda *f* farm; (*de café*) plantation; (*de gado*) ranch; (*propriedade*) property; (*pano*) cloth, fabric; (ECON) treasury, exchequer; **fazendeiro** *m* (*de café*) plantation-owner; (*de gado*) rancher, ranch-owner.

fa'zer *vt* (*ger*) to make; (*executar*) to do; (TEC) to produce, manufacture; (*obrigar*) to force, compel // *vi* (*portar-se*) to act, behave; **~-se** *vr* (*tornar-se*) to become; **~-se de** to pretend to be; **~ água** to leak; **~ as vezes de** to replace; **~ anos** to celebrate one's birthday; **~ caso de** to take notice of; **~ com que** to cause, see to it that; **~ de** to act as; **~ perguntas** to ask (questions); **~ bem/mal** to act rightly/wrongly; **faz frio/calor** it's cold/hot; **faz um ano** a year ago; **faz um ano que** it is a year since; **não faz mal** never mind; **tanto faz** it's all the same.

'fé *f* faith; (*crença*) belief; (*confiança*) trust; **de boa/má ~** in good/bad faith; **dar ~ de** (*notar*) to notice; (*testificar*) to bear witness to.

feal'dade *f* ugliness.

'febre *f* fever; (*fig*) excitement; **~ do feno** hay fever; **~ amarela** yellow fever; **~ palustre** malaria; **febril** *adj* feverish.

fe'chado/a *adj* shut, closed; **noite ~a** well into the night.

fechadura [feʃa'dura] *f* (*porta*) lock.

fechar [fe'ʃax] *vt* to close, shut; (*concluir*) to finish, conclude; (*luz, torneira*) to turn off; **~ à chave** to lock // *vi* to close (up), shut; **~-se** *vr* to close, shut; (*pessoa*) to withdraw.

fecho ['feʃu] *m* fastening; (*trinco*) latch; (*término*) close, closing; **~ ecler** zip fastener.

'fécula *f* starch.

fecun'dar *vt* to fertilize, make fertile; **fecundo/a** *adj* fertile; (*produtivo*) fruitful.

fe'der *vi* to stink.

federação [fɪdera'sãw] *f* federation.

fede'ral *adj* federal.

fe'dor *m* stench; **fedorento/a** *adj* stinking.

feição [fej'sãw] *f* form, shape; (*caráter*) nature; (*modo*) manner; **à ~** favourably; **feições** *fpl* (*face*) features.

feijão [fej'ʒãw] *m* beans *pl*.

feio/a ['feju/a] *adj* ugly; (*ameaçador*) grim; **fazer ~** to make a bad impression.

feira ['fejra] *f* fair; (*mercado*) market.

feitiçaria [fejtʃisa'ria] *f* witchcraft, magic; **feiticeiro/a** *adj* bewitching, enchanting // *m* wizard // *f* witch; **feitiço** *m* charm, spell.

feitio [fej'tʃu] *m* shape, pattern; (*caráter*) nature, manner; (TEC) workmanship.

feito/a ['fejtu/a] *pp* de **fazer** // *adj* (*terminado*) finished, ready; **~!** agreed!;

~ **a mão** hand-made; **homem** ~ grown man // m act, deed; (façanha) feat; **de** ~ in fact.

feitor(a) [fej'tox(ra)] m/f administrator; (capataz) supervisor.

feixe ['fejʃi] m bundle, bunch; (TEC) beam.

fel ['fɛw] m bile, gall; (fig) bitterness.

felici'dade f happiness; (sorte) good luck; (êxito) success; ~**s** fpl congratulations; **felicitações** fpl congratulations, best wishes; **felicitar** vt to congratulate.

fe'liz adj happy; (afortunado) fortunate; (próspero) successful.

fel'pudo/a adj fuzzy, downy.

feltro ['fewtru] m felt.

'fêmea f (BIO, BOT) female; (mulher) woman; **feminino/a** adj feminine; (BIO) female.

'fenda f slit, crack; (GEO) fissure; **fender** vt/i to split, crack.

fene'cer vi to die; (terminar) to come to an end.

'feno m hay.

fenome'nal [-aw] adj phenomenal; (espantoso) amazing; (pessoa) brilliant; **fenômeno** m phenomenon.

'féretro m (andor) bier.

feri'ado m holiday; **férias** fpl holidays, vacation sg; **de férias** on holiday.

fe'rida f wound, injury; (ofensa) insult; **ferir** vt to injure, wound; (ofender) to offend.

fermen'tar vt to ferment; (fig) to excite // vi to ferment; **fermento** m yeast; **fermento em pó** baking powder.

'fero/a adj fierce // f (wild animal; (fig: pessoa cruel) beast; (pessoa irascível) hot-tempered person; (pessoa talentosa) dab-hand, whizz kid; **ferocidade** f fierceness, ferocity; **feroz** adj fierce, ferocious; (cruel) cruel.

fer'rado/a adj (cavalgadura) shod; (sem saída) done for; ~ **no sono** sound asleep; **ferradura** f horseshoe.

ferra'menta f tool; (caixa de ferramentas) tool kit.

ferrão [fɛ'xãw] m goad; (de inseto) sting.

fer'rar vt to spike; (cavalo) to shoe; (gado) to brand; ~**-se** vr (col) to make a mess of, bungle, botch.

ferreiro [fe'xejru] m blacksmith.

ferrenho/a [fe'xeɲu/a] adj inflexible; (fig) stubborn.

'férreo/a adj iron; (duro) hard; (fig) intransigent.

fer'rete m branding iron; (fig) stigma.

'ferro m iron; ~ **de passar** iron; ~ **batido** wrought iron; ~ **fundido** cast iron; ~ **velho** scrap metal; **de** ~ (pessoa) sturdy; **a** ~ **e fogo** at all costs; ~**s** mpl shackles, chains.

ferrolho [fɛ'xoʎu] m (trinco) bolt.

ferro'via f railway, railroad (US).

ferrugem [fe'xuʒẽ] f rust; (BOT) blight.

fértil ['fɛxtʃiw] adj fertile, fruitful; **fertilidade** f fertility; (abundância) fruitfulness; **fertilizante** adj fertilizing // m fertilizer; **fertilizar** vt to fertilize.

fer'vente adj boiling; (fervoroso) fervent; **ferver** vt to boil // vi to boil; (espumar) to seethe; (fig) to rage; **fervilhar** vi (ferver) to simmer; (pulular) to swarm.

fer'vor m fervour; ~**oso/a** adj zealous, fervent.

'festa f (reunião) party; (conjunto de ceremônias) festival; **dia de** ~ public holiday; ~**s** fpl caresses; **boas** ~**s** (Natal) Merry Christmas; (ano novo) Happy New Year; **festejar** vt (celebrar) to celebrate; (acolher) to welcome, greet; (acariciar) to caress; **festejo** m (festividade) festivity; (carícias) caresses pl.

festim [feʃ'tʃĩ] m (banquete) banquet; (festa particular) party.

festi'val [-aw] m festival; **festividade** f festivity; **festivo/a** adj festive; **dia festivo** public holiday.

fe'tiche m fetish.

'fétido/a adj (malcheiroso) foul; (podre) rotten.

'feto m (MED) foetus; (BOT) fern.

feudal [few'daw] adj feudal; ~**ismo** m feudalism.

fevereiro [feve'rejru] (Pt: **F**-) m February.

fez vb ver **fazer**.

'fezes fpl (borra) dregs; (excremento) excrement sg.

fiação [fja'sãw] f spinning; (fábrica) textile mill.

fi'ado/a adj (a crédito) on credit; **comprar/vender** ~ to buy/sell on credit // f (fileira) row, line.

fia'dor(a) m/f (JUR) guarantor; (COM) backer.

fi'ambre m cold meat; (presunto) ham.

fiança [fi'ãsa] f surety, guarantee; (JUR) bail; **prestar** ~ **por** to stand bail for.

fi'apo m thread.

fi'ar vt (algodão etc) to spin; (confiar) to entrust; (vender a crédito) to sell on credit; ~**-se** vr: ~**-se em** to trust.

fi'asco m fiasco.

'fibra f fibre.

fi'car vi (permanecer) to stay, remain; (sobrar) to be left; (tornar-se) to become; (estar situado) to be; (durar) to last; (parar) to stop; (escuro) to grow dark; ~ **cego/surdo** to go blind/deaf; ~ **com** (guardar) to keep; ~ **com raiva/medo** to get angry/frightened; ~ **de** to agree to; ~ **por fazer** to be still to be done; ~ **bom** to recover; ~ **bem** to suit; **esta saia não fica bem para você** that skirt doesn't suit you.

ficção [fik'sãw] f fiction.

ficha ['fiʃa] f token; (de fichário) (index) card; (fig) record; (ELET) plug; **fichar** vt to file, index; **fichário** m (móvel) filing cabinet; (caixa) card index; (caderno) file; **ficheiro** m (Pt) ver **fichário**.

fictício/a [fik'tʃisju/a] adj fictitious.

fi'dalgo m nobleman.

fide'digno/a adj trustworthy.

fideli'dade f (lealdade) loyalty; (exatidão) exactness; **fiel** adj (leal) faithful; (exato) accurate; (que não falha) reliable.

'figa f talisman; **duma ~** damned; **fazer ~s a** to exorcise, give a thumb between two fingers to.

'fígado m liver; **de maus ~s** bad-tempered, vindictive.

'figo m fig; **figueira** f fig tree.

fi'gura f figure; (forma) form, shape; (gramática) figure of speech; (aspecto) appearance; **figurante** m/f (cinema) extra; **figurão** m V.I.P.; **figurar** vi (fazer parte) to figure, appear.

'fila f row, line; (Br: fileira de pessoas) queue; **em ~** in a row; **fazer ~** to form a line, queue.

filan'tropo m philanthropist.

fi'lar vt (agarrar) to seize; (col: pedir/obter gratuitamente) to scrounge.

filate'lia f philately.

fi'lé m (bife) steak; (peixe) fillet.

fi'leira f file, row, line; **~s** fpl military service.

fi'lete m fillet; (de parafuso) thread.

filho/a ['fiʌu/a] m son; **~ da mãe** son of a gun, creep; **~s** mpl children; (pe animais) young // f daughter; **filhote** m young; (cachorro) pup(py).

fili'al [-jaw] f (sucursal) branch.

Fili'pinas fpl: **as ~** the Philippines.

filmagem [fiw'maʒẽ] f filming; **filmar** vt to film; **filme** m film.

filoso'fia f philosophy; **filósofo/a** m/f philosopher.

filtrar [fiw'trax] vt to filter; **~-se** vr (líquidos) to filter; (infiltrar-se) to infiltrate; **filtro** m (TEC) filter.

fim [fĩ] m end; (motivo) aim, purpose; **a ~ de** in order to; **por ~** finally; **ter por ~** to aim at; **no ~ das contas** after all; **pôr ~ a** to put an end to; **sem ~** endless; **~ de semana** weekend.

'fímbria f (franja) fringe; (de vestido) hem.

fi'nado/a adj, m/f deceased.

final [fi'naw] adj final, last // m end; (MÚS) finale; **~izar** vt to finish, conclude.

fi'nanças fpl finance sg; **financeiro/a** adj financial // m financier; **financiamento** m financing; **financiar** vt to finance; **financista** m/f financier.

fi'nar-se vr (consumir-se) to waste away; (morrer) to die.

fin'car vt (cravar) to drive in; (fixar) to fix.

fin'dar vt/i to end, finish.

fi'neza f fineness; (gentileza) kindness.

fingimento [fiʒi'mẽtu] m pretence; **fingir** vt (inventar) to invent, make up; (simular) to feign // vi to pretend; **fingir-se vr: fingir-se de** to pretend to be.

finlan'dês/esa adj Finnish // m/f Finn // m (língua) Finnish; **Finlândia** f Finland.

'fino/a adj (ger) fine; (delgado) slender; (educado) polite; (astuto) shrewd; (som,

voz) shrill; **finório/a** adj crafty, sly; **finura** f fineness; (magreza) slenderness; (elegância) finesse.

'fio m thread; (BOT) fibre; (ELET) wire; (telefônico) line; (de líquido) trickle; (gume) edge.

'firma f (assinatura) signature; (COM) firm, company.

fir'mar vt (tornar firme) to secure, make firm; (assinar) to sign; (estabelecer) to establish; (basear) to base; **~-se** vr: **~-se em** (basear-se) to rest on, be based on; **firme** adj firm; (estável) stable; (sólido) solid; (constante) steady; (cor) fast; **firmeza** f firmness; (estabilidade) stability; (constância) steadiness.

fis'cal [-aw] m supervisor; (aduaneiro) customs officer; (de impostos) tax inspector; **~izar** vt (supervisionar) to supervise; (examinar) to inspect, check.

fis'gar vt to catch; (enfeitiçar) to captivate.

'físico/a adj physical // m/f (cientista) physicist // m (corpo) physique // f physics sg.

'fita f (tira) strip, band; (de seda, algodão) ribbon, tape; (filme) film; (para máquina de escrever) ribbon; (magnética, adesiva) tape; **~ métrica** tape measure; **~ elástica** rubber band.

fi'tar vt (com os olhos) to stare at, gaze at; **fito/a** adj fixed // m aim, intention.

fi'vela f buckle.

fixar [fik'sax] vt to fix; (pegar) to stick, fasten; (data) to set; (atenção) to concentrate on; (estabelecer) to fix; **~ os olhos em** to stare at; **~ residência** to set up house, settle down; **~-se** vr: **~-se em** to notice; **fixo/a** adj fixed; (firme) firm; (permanente) permanent; (cor) fast.

fiz etc vb ver **fazer**.

fla'grante adj flagrant; **apanhar em ~** to catch red-handed.

flame'jante adj flaming; **flamejar** vi to blaze.

fla'nela f flannel.

'flash m (FOTO) flash.

flauta ['flawta] f flute.

flecha ['fleʃa] f arrow.

fleugma ['flewma] f, **'fleuma** f phlegm.

fle'xível adj flexible.

'floco m (de neve) snowflake; **~ de milho** cornflake.

flor f flower; (o melhor) cream, pick; **em ~** in bloom; **a fina ~** the elite; **a ~ de** on the surface of; **~escente** adj (BOT) in flower; (próspero) flourishing; **~escer** vi (BOT) to flower; (prosperar) to flourish.

flo'resta f forest.

flu'ência f fluency; **fluente** adj fluent; **fluido/a** adj fluid // m fluid; **fluir** vi to flow.

fluores'cente adj fluorescent; **lâmpada ~** fluorescent light.

flutu'ar vi to float.

fluxo ['fluksu] *m* (*corrente*) flow; (*ELET*) flux; ~**grama** *f* flow chart.

'foca *f* (*animal*) seal.

focali'zar *vt* to focus (on).

focinho [fo'sɪɲu] *m* snout.

'foco *m* focus; (*farol*) light.

'fofo/a *adj* soft, spongy.

fogão [fo'gãw] *m* stove, cooker.

'foge *etc vb ver* **fugir**.

'fogo *m* fire; (*fig*) ardour; ~**s de artifício** fireworks; **a ~ lento** on a low flame; **à prova de ~** fireproof; **abrir ~** to open fire; **pôr ~ a** to set fire to; **pegar ~** to catch fire; **fazer ~** to make a fire.

fo'goso/a *adj* fiery.

fogo-'fátuo *m* will-o'-the-wisp.

fogueira [fo'gejra] *f* bonfire; **morrer na ~** to be burnt at the stake.

foguete [fo'getʃɪ] *m* rocket.

foi *vb ver* **ir** *ou* **ser**.

foice ['fɔjsɪ] *f* scythe.

fol'clore *m* folklore; **folclórico/a** *adj* folkloric.

'fole *m* bellows *sg*.

'fôlego *m* breath; (*folga*) breathing space; **perder o ~** to lose one's breath.

'folga *f* (*descanso*) rest, break; (*espaço livre*) clearance; **dia de ~** rest day; **folgado/a** *adj* (*pessoa*) easy going; (*roupa*) loose, slack; **folgar** *vt* to loosen, slacken // *vi* (*descansar*) to rest, relax; (*divertir-se*) to have fun, amuse o.s.; **folgar em** to enjoy.

folha ['fɔʎa] *f* leaf; (*de papel, de metal*) sheet; (*página*) page; (*de faca*) blade; ~ **de estanho** tinfoil; **folhagem** *f* foliage; **folhear** *vt* to leaf through; **folheto** *m* booklet, pamphlet.

fo'lia *f* revelry, merriment.

'fome *f* hunger; (*escassez*) famine; (*avidez*) longing; **passar ~** to go hungry; **ter ~** to be hungry.

fomen'tar *vt* to instigate, promote; **fomento** *m* (*MED*) fomentation; (*estímulo*) promotion.

'fone *m* telephone, phone; (*peça do telefone*) receiver.

'fonte *f* (*nascente*) spring; (*chafariz*) fountain; (*origem*) source; (*ANAT*) temple; **de ~ limpa** from a reliable source.

for *etc vb ver* **ir** *ou* **ser**.

'fora *adv* out, outside // *prep* (*exceto*) apart from; ~ **de** outside; ~ **de si** beside o.s. // *excl*: ~! get out!

foragido/a [fora'ʒidu/a] *adj* (*fugitivo*) fugitive.

forasteiro/a [foraʃ'tejru/a] *adj* (*alheio*) alien // *m/f* stranger; (*de outro país*) foreigner.

'forca *f* gallows *pl*.

força ['foxsa] *f* (*energia física*) strength; (*TEC*, *ELET*) power; (*esforço*) effort; (*coerção*) force; **à ~** by force; **à ~ de** by dint of; **dar (uma) ~ a** to back up, encourage; **fazer ~** to try (hard); **por ~** of necessity.

for'cado *m* pitchfork.

forçado/a [fox'sadu/a] *adj* forced; (*afetado*) false; **forçar** *vt* to force; (*olhos, voz*) to strain; **forçar-se** *vr*: **forçar-se a** to force o.s. to; **forcejar** *vi* (*esforçar-se*) to strive; (*lutar*) to struggle; **forçoso/a** *adj* (*necessário*) necessary; (*vigoroso*) forceful.

forja ['foxʒa] *f* forge; **forjar** *vt* to forge.

'forma *f* form, shape; (*molde*) mould; (*maneira*) manner, way; (*MED*) fitness; **desta ~** in this way; **de tal ~ que** in such a way that; **de qualquer ~** anyway; **da mesma ~** likewise; **de outra ~** otherwise.

formação [foxma'sãw] *f* formation; (*antecedentes*) background; **formado/a** *adj* (*modelado*) formed; **ser formado de** to consist of // *m/f* graduate.

formal [fox'maw] *adj* formal; ~**idade** *f* formality.

formão [fox'mãw] *m* chisel.

for'mar *vt* to form; (*constituir*) to constitute, make up; (*educar*) to train, educate; ~**-se** *vr* (*tomar forma*) to form; (*EDUC*) to graduate; **formatura** *f* (*MIL*) formation; (*EDUC*) graduation.

formi'dável *adj* (*temível*) formidable; (*extraordinário*) tremendous, great, excellent.

for'miga *f* ant; **formigar** *vi* (*ser abundante*) to abound; (*sentir comichão*) to itch; **formigueiro** *m* ants' nest; (*multidão*) throng, swarm.

for'moso/a *adj* (*belo*) beautiful; (*esplêndido*) superb; **formosura** *f* beauty.

'fórmula *f* formula; **formular** *vt* to formulate; **formular votos** to express one's hopes/wishes; **formulário** *m* form.

fornalha [fox'naʎa] *f* furnace.

forne'cer *vt* to supply, provide.

'forno *m* (*CULIN*) oven; (*TEC*) furnace; **alto ~** blast furnace.

'foro *m* forum; (*JUR*) Court of Justice; ~**s** *mpl* privileges; **de ~ íntimo** personal, private.

forra ['fɔxa] *f*: **ir à ~** (*col*) to get one's own back.

forragem [fo'xaʒẽ] *f* fodder.

for'rar *vt* (*cobrir*) to cover; (: *interior*) to line; (*de papel*) to paper; **forro/a** *adj* freed // *m* (*cobertura*) covering; (*teto*) ceiling; (*roupa*) lining.

fortale'cer *vt* to strengthen; **fortaleza** *f* strength; (*coragem*) fortitude; (*forte*) fortress; **ser uma fortaleza** to be as strong as an ox; **forte** *adj* strong; (*pancada*) hard; (*chuva*) heavy; (*comida*) rich; (*som*) loud // *adv* strongly; (*som*) loud(ly) // *m* (*fortaleza*) fortress; **fortificar** *vt* to fortify.

fortuito/a [fox'twitu/a] *adj* accidental.

for'tuna *f* (*sorte*) fortune, (good) luck; (*riqueza*) fortune, wealth.

'fosco/a *adj* (*sem brilho*) dull; (*opaco*) opaque.

'fósforo *m* (*QUÍM*) phosphorous; (*pau de fósforo*) match.

'fossa *f* pit.

'fóssil [-sıw] *m, pl* **'fósseis** fossil.

'fosso *m* trench, ditch; (*de uma fortaleza*) moat.

'foto *f* photo.

foto'cópia *f* photocopy; **fotocopiadora** *f* photocopier; **fotocopiar** *vt* to photocopy.

fotogra'far *vt* to photograph; **fotografia** *f* photography; (*uma foto*) photography; **fotógrafo/a** *m/f* photographer.

foz *f* river mouth.

fração [fra'sãw] (*Pt:* -cç-) *f* fraction.

fracas'sar *vi* to fail; **fracasso** *m* failure.

'fraco/a *adj* weak.

'frade *m* (*REL*) friar; (: *monge*) monk.

'fraga *f* crag, rock.

fra'gata *f* (*NÁUT*) frigate.

frágil ['fraʒɪw] *adj, pl* **frágeis** ['fraʒejs] (*débil*) fragile; (*quebradiço*) breakable; **fragilidade** *f* fragility; (*de uma pessoa*) frailty.

frag'mento *m* fragment.

fra'grância *f* (*aroma*) fragrance; (*perfume*) perfume; **fragrante** *adj* fragrant.

'fralda [-awda] *f* (*da camisa*) shirt tail; (*para bebê*) nappy, diaper (*US*); (*de montanha*) foot.

frambo'esa *f* raspberry.

França ['frãsa] *f* France; **francês/esa** *adj* French // *m* (*língua*) French; (*pessoa*) Frenchman // *f* Frenchwoman.

'franco/a *adj* (*sincero*) frank; (*isento*) free; **entrada** ~**a** free admission; ~ **de porte** post paid // *m* franc.

frangalho [frã'gaʎu] *m* (*trapo*) rag, tatter; (*pessoa*) wreck; **em** ~**s** in tatters.

'frango *m* chicken.

franja ['frãʒa] *f* fringe.

franquear [frãki'ax] *vt* (*caminho*) to clear; (*isentar de imposta*) to exempt from duties.

franqueza [frã'keza] *f* frankness.

franquia [frã'kia] *f* (*para cartas*) postage; (*isenção*) exemption.

fran'zir *vt* (*preguear*) to pleat; (*enrugar*) to wrinkle, crease; (*sobrancelhas*) to frown; (*lábios*) to curl.

fraqueza [fra'keza] *f* weakness.

'frasco *m* flask.

'frase *f* sentence; ~ **feita** set phrase.

fra'tura (*Pt:* -ct-) *f* fracture, break.

fraude ['frawdʒı] *f* fraud, deception; **fraudulento/a** *adj* fraudulent.

fre'ar (*Br*) *vt* (*conter*) to curb, restrain // *vi* (*veículo*) to brake.

freguês/guesa [fre'geʃ/'geza] *m/f* (*cliente*) customer; (*Pt*) parishioner; **freguesia** (*clientes*) customers *pl*; (*Pt*) parish.

frei [frej] *m* friar, monk; (*título*) Brother.

freio ['freju] *m* (*Br: veículo*) brake; (*cavalo*) bridle; (*bocado do freio*) bit; (*fig*) check; ~ **de mão** handbrake.

freira ['frejra] *f* nun.

freixo ['frejʃu] *m* (*BOT*) ash.

fre'mente *adj* (*que estremece*) trembling; (*violento*) raging; **fremir** *vi* (*bramar*) to roar; (*tremer*) to tremble; **frêmito** *m* (*rumor*) murmur; (*vibração*) tremor; (*bramido*) roaring; (*emoção*) thrill; **frêmito cardíaco** palpitation (of the heart).

frene'si *m* frenzy; **frenético/a** *adj* frantic, frenzied.

'frente *f* (*de objeto*) front; (*rosto*) face; (*fachada*) facade; ~ **a** ~ face to face; **em** ~ **de** opposite; **à** ~ **de** at the front of; **para a** ~ ahead, forward.

freqüência [fre'kwẽsja] *f* frequency; **com** ~ often, frequently; **freqüentar** *vt* to frequent, attend regularly; **frequente** *adj* frequent.

'fresco/a *adj* (*frio*) cool; (*novo*) fresh; (*col: efeminado*) camp // *m* (*ar*) fresh air; (*arte*) fresco // *f:* **ir tomar a** ~**a** to get some fresh air; **frescura** *f* freshness; (*frialdade*) coolness; (*col: pieguice*) slush; **que frescura!** how fussy/stuffy!

'fresta *f* gap, slit.

fre'tar *vt* (*alugar*) to hire, charter; **frete** *m* (*carregamento*) freight, cargo; (*tarifa*) freightage.

frial'dade *f* coldness; (*indiferença*) indifference, coolness.

fricção [frik'sãw] *f* friction; (*ato*) rubbing; (*MED*) massage.

frieira [fri'ejra] *f* chilblain.

fri'eza *f* coldness; (*indiferença*) coolness.

frigideira [friʒi'dejra] *f* frying pan; **frigir** *vt* to fry; **no frigir dos ovos** when it comes down to it.

frigo'rífico *m* (*Pt*) refrigerator, fridge (*col*); (: *congelador*) freezer.

frincha ['friʃa] *f* chink, slit.

'frio/a *adj* cold // *m* coldness; **estou com** ~ I'm cold; **faz** ~/**está fazendo** ~ it's cold.

fri'sar *vt* (*encrespar*) to curl; (*salientar*) to emphasise.

fri'tar *vt* to fry; **frito/a** *adj* fried; (*col*) **estar frito** to be done for.

'frívolo/a *adj* frivolous.

fronha ['frona] *f* pillowcase.

frontão [frõ'tãw] *m* gable.

'fronte *f* (*ANAT*) forehead, brow.

fronteira [frõ'tejra] *f* frontier, border; **fronteiriço** *adj* frontier *cmp.*

'frota *f* fleet.

frouxo/a ['froʃu/a] *adj* loose, slack; (*fraco*) weak; (*indolente*) lax; (*col: impotente*) impotent.

frus'trar *vt* to frustrate.

'fruta *f* fruit; **fruteira** *f* fruit bowl; **frutífero/a** *adj* (*proveitoso*) fruitful; (*árvore*) fruit-bearing; **fruto** *m* (*BOT*) fruit; (*resultado*) result, product; **dar fruto** to bear fruit.

'fuga *f* flight, escape; (*de gás etc*) leak; **fugaz** *adj* fleeting; **fugir** *vi* to flee, escape; **fugitivo/a** *adj, m/f* fugitive.

fui *vb ver* **ir** *ou* **ser.**

fu'lano/a *m/f* so-and-so.

'fulcro *m* fulcrum.

ful'gor *m* brilliance.

fuligem [fu'lɪʒẽ] f soot.

fulmi'nante adj (devastador) devastating; (palavras) scathing.

fu'maça f (Br: de fogo) smoke; (: de gás) fumes pl; **fumador(a)** m/f (Pt) smoker; **fumante** m/f smoker; **fumar** vt/i to smoke.

'fumo m (Pt: de fogo) smoke; (Pt: de gás) fumes pl; (Br: tabaco) tobacco; ~s mpl conceit.

função [fũ'sãw] f function; (ofício) duty; (papel) role; (espetáculo) performance; **funcionamento** m functioning, working; **pôr em funcionamento** to set going, start; **funcionar** vi to function; (máquina) to work, run.

funcio'nário/a m/f official; (público) civil servant.

'funda f sling; (MED) truss.

fundação [fũda'sãw] f foundation; **fundamental** adj fundamental, basic; **fundamentar** vt (argumento) to substantiate; (basear) to base; **fundamento** m (CONSTR) foundation; (motivo) motive; **sem fundamento** groundless; **fundar** vt to establish, found; (basear) to base.

funde'ar vi to anchor.

fundição [fũdʒi'sãw] f fusing; (fábrica) foundry; **fundir** vt to fuse; (metal) to smelt, melt down; (COM) to merge; (em molde) to cast; **fundir a cuca** to set one's head spinning; **fundir-se** vr (derreter-se) to melt; (confundir-se) to merge, fuse.

'fundo/a adj deep; (fig) profound // m (do mar) bottom; (profundidade) depth; (base) basis; (parte traseira) back; (de quadro) background; (de dinheiro) fund; **a ~ deep(ly), thorough(ly); no ~ in essence; ~s mpl (COM) funds.

'fúnebre adj funeral cmp, funereal; **funeral** m funeral; **funerário/a** adj funeral cmp; **casa funerária** undertakers pl.

fu'nesto/a adj (fatal) fatal; (infausto) disastrous.

fun'gar vt/i to sniff.

fu'nil [-nɪw] m funnel.

furacão [fura'kãw] m hurricane.

furão [fu'rãw] m ferret.

fu'rar vt (perfurar) to bore, perforate; (penetrar) to penetrate; (frustrar) to foil; ~ **uma greve** to break a strike.

furgão [fux'gãw] m van; **furgoneta** f (Pt) van.

'fúria f fury, rage; **furibundo/a** adj furious; **furioso/a** adj furious.

'furo m hole; (num pneu) puncture; (de reportagem) scoop.

fu'ror m fury, rage; **fazer ~** to be all the rage.

fur'tar vt/i to steal; ~-se vr: ~-se a to avoid, evade; **furtivo/a** adj furtive, stealthy; **furto** m theft.

fu'rúnculo m (MED) boil.

fusão [fu'zãw] f fusion; (aliança) union, merger; (derretimento) melting.

'fusco/a adj dark, dusky.

fu'sível [-ɪvew] m (ELET) fuse.

'fuso m (TEC) spindle; ~ **horário** time zone.

fusti'gar vt (espancar) to beat; (açoitar) to flog, whip; (castigar) to punish.

fute'bol m football; ~ **de salão** five-a-side football; ~ **totó** table football.

fútil ['futʃɪw] adj futile; (insignificante) trivial; **futilidade** f futility.

fu'trica f gossip.

fu'turo/a adj future // m future.

fu'zil [-ɪw] m (arma) rifle; **fuzilar** vt to shoot.

G

ga'bar vt to praise; ~-se vr: ~-se de to boast about.

gabar'dina (Pt: -'dine) raincoat; (pano) gabardine.

gabi'nete m (COM) office; (escritório) study; (de ministros) cabinet.

ga'bola adj boastful.

'gado m livestock; (reses) cattle.

gafanhoto [gafa'notu] m grasshopper, locust.

gaguejar [gage'ʒax] vi to stammer, stutter.

gai'ato/a adj mischievous.

gaiola [ga'jola] f (para pássaro) cage; (cadeia) jail.

gaita ['gajta] f: ~ **de boca** harmonica; ~ **de foles** bagpipes pl.

gaivota [gaj'vota] f seagull.

gajo ['gaʒu] m (Pt: col) guy, fellow.

'gala f (traje) full dress; (festa) gala.

ga'lã m (ator) leading man; **galantear** vt to court, woo; **galanteio** m wooing.

galão [ga'lãw] m (MIL) stripe; (medida) gallon; (Pt: café) white coffee.

ga'láxia m galaxy.

ga'lé f (NÁUT) galley // m galley slave.

ga'lego/a adj Galician // m/f (col) foreigner.

ga'lera f (NÁUT) galley.

gale'ria f gallery; (varanda) veranda.

'Gales m: **País de ~** Wales; **galês/esa** adj Welsh //m Welshman; (língua) Welsh // f Welshwoman.

gal'gar vt (saltar) to leap over; (subir) to climb up.

gal'go m greyhound.

galhardia [gaʎax'dʒia] f (elegância) elegance; (valor) bravery; (galantaria) dash.

galheteiro [gaʎe'tejru] m cruet stand.

galho ['gaʎu] m (de árvore) branch; (galhada) antler; (gir) hassle, problem; **quebrar um/o ~** to patch it up, sort it out.

galinha [ga'liɲa] f hen; (covarde) coward; **galo** m cock, rooster; (inchação) bump.

galo'par vi to gallop; **galope** m gallop.

galvani'zar vt to galvanize.

'gama f (MÚS) scale; (fig) range; (animal) doe; **gamo** m (fallow) deer.

'gana f (desejo) craving, desire; (ódio) hate; ter ~s de to have a good mind to.

gancho ['gãʃu] m hook.

gan'grena f gangrene.

ganhador(a) [gaɲa'dox(ra)] adj winning // m/f winner.

ganha-pão [gaɲa-'pãw] m living, livelihood.

ganhar [ga'ɲax] vt to win; (salário) to earn; (adquirir) to gain, get; (um lugar) to reach; ~ a vida to earn a living // vi (vencer) to win; ganho/a pp de ganhar // m (lucro) profit, gain; ganhos mpl (ao jogo) winnings.

ga'nir vi to yelp, squeal.

'ganso/a m gander // f goose.

garagem [ga'raʒẽ] f garage.

garan'tia f guarantee; garantir vt to guarantee; (responsabilizar-se por) to vouch for.

garatujar [garatu'ʒax] vt to scribble, scrawl.

'garbo m (elegância) elegance; garboso/a a adj (enérgico) dashing; (elegante) elegant.

garço/a ['gaxsu/a] adj bluish green // f heron.

garçom [gax'sõ] m (Br) waiter.

garçonete [gaxso'netʃi] f (Br) waitress.

'garfo m fork.

gargalhada [gaxga'ʎada] f burst of laughter; rir às ~s to roar with laughter.

gar'ganta f (ANAT) throat; (GEO) gorge, ravine.

gargarejar [gaxgare'ʒax] vi to gargle; gargarejo m (ato) gargling; (líquido) gargle.

garim'peiro m prospector.

ga'roa f drizzle; garoar vi to drizzle.

ga'roto/a m youngster, kid; (Pt: café) coffee with milk // f girl.

'garra f claw; (de ave) talon; ~s fpl (posse) clutches.

gar'rafa f bottle; ~ térmica (Br) thermos flask.

gar'rido/a adj (elegante) smart; (brilhante) bright.

garrulice [gaxu'lisi] f chatter, prattle; gárrulo/a adj (palrador) chattering, prattling; (ave) twittering.

ga'rupa f (de cavalo) hindquarters pl; (alforje) saddle pack; (moto) back seat.

'gás m gas; ~ lacrimogêneo tear gas.

gaso'lina f petrol, gas(oline) (US); posto de ~ petrol station, gas station (US).

ga'sosa f (Pt) fizzy drink, soda pop (US).

gas'tar vt (dinheiro, tempo) to spend; (energias) to use up; (deteriorar) to wear out; (desperdiçar) to waste; ~-se vr (deteriorar-se) to wear out; gasto/a pp de gastar // adj (dinheiro, tempo, energias) spent; (frase) trite; (deteriorado) worn out // m (despesa) expenditure; (quebra) waste; gastos mpl expenses; (custo) costs.

gatilho [ga'tʃiʎu] m trigger.

gatinhar [gatʃi'ɲax] vi to crawl;

gatinhas fpl: andar de gatinhas (Br) to go on all fours.

'gato/a m cat; (de carpinteiro) clamp; (gatuno) thief; ~ montês wildcat // f cat; andar de ~as (Pt) to go on all fours.

ga'tuno m thief.

ga'veta f drawer.

gavião [gavi'ãw] m hawk.

'gaza f, 'gaze f gauze.

ga'zeta f (jornal) newspaper, gazette; fazer ~ (Pt) to play truant.

geada [ʒi'ada] f frost.

geladeira [ʒela'dejra] f (Br) refrigerator, icebox (US); gelado/a adj frozen // m (Pt : sorvete) ice cream; gelar vt (congelar) to freeze; (vinho etc) to chill // vi to freeze.

gelatina [ʒela'tʃina] f gelatine.

geléia [ʒe'leja] f jelly, jello (US); (compota) jam.

geleira [ʒe'lejra] f (GEO) glacier.

gelo ['ʒelu] m ice; quebrar o ~ to break the ice.

gelosia [ʒelo'zia] f (estore) blind; (janela) lattice window.

gema ['ʒema] f (de ovo) yolk; (pedra preciosa) gem; (BOT) bud; ser da ~ to be genuine.

gêmeo/a ['ʒemju/a] adj, m/f twin.

gemer [ʒe'mex] vi to groan, moan; gemido m groan, moan.

genebra [ʒe'nebra] f (Pt: gim) gin.

general [ʒene'raw] m (MIL) general; ~idade f generality; ~ização f generalization; ~izar vi to generalize; ~izar-se vr to become general, spread.

gênero ['ʒeneru] m (espécie) type, kind; (literatura) genre; (BIO) genus; (gramática) gender; ~s mpl goods; (alimentícios) foodstuffs.

generosi'dade f generosity; generoso/a adj generous.

gênese ['ʒenɛz] f origin, beginning.

ge'nética f genetics sg.

gengibre [ʒẽ'ʒibri] m ginger.

gengiva [ʒẽ'ʒiva] f (ANAT) gum.

genial [ʒeni'aw] adj inspired; (idéia) brilliant; (prazenteiro) cheerful; gênio m (temperamento) nature; (humor) temper; (pessoa inspirada) genius; de bom gênio good-natured; de mau gênio bad-tempered.

genro ['ʒẽxu] m son-in-law.

gente ['ʒẽtʃi] f (pessoas) people pl; ~ grande grown-ups pl; tem ~ batendo a porta there's somebody knocking at the door; ser ~ (de importância) to be somebody; a ~ (indeterminado) we, one.

gentil [ʒẽ'tʃiw] adj (esbelto) graceful; (cortês) polite; ~eza f (delicadeza) kindness; (elegância) elegance.

gentio/a [ʒẽ'tʃiu/a] adj, m/f heathen.

genuíno/a [ʒen'winu/a] adj genuine.

geogra'fia f geography.

geolo'gia f geology.

geome'tria f geometry.

geração [ʒera'sãw] f (da família)

generation; (formação) creation; (produção) production; **gerador(a)** adj productive // m/f (produtor) producer // m (TEC) generator.

geral [ʒeˈraw] adj general; **em ~** generally; **o ~ dos homens** most men; **~ mente** adv generally, usually.

gerar [ʒeˈrax] vt (produzir) to produce; (eletricidade) to generate.

gerência [ʒeˈrẽsja] f management; **gerente** m manager; **gerir** vt to manage, run.

germe [ˈʒɛxmɪ] m (embrião) embryo; (micróbio) germ; (fig) origin; **germinar** vi (semente) to germinate; (fig) to develop.

gesso [ˈʒesu] m plaster (of Paris).

gesticular vi to make gestures, gesture; **gesto** m gesture.

giba [ˈʒɪba] f hump; (NÁUT) jib.

gigante/a adj gigantic, huge // m giant.

gilete f (Br: lâmina) razor blade; (: aparelho) razor.

gim [ʒĩ] m gin.

ginásio [ʒɪˈnazju] m (para ginástica) gymnasium; (escola) secondary school; **ginástica** f gymnastics sg.

ginja [ˈʒɪʒa] f (Pt) morello cherry; **ginjinha** f cherry brandy.

gira-discos [ʒɪraˈdʒɪʃkus] m (Pt) record-player.

girafa f giraffe.

girar [ʒɪˈrax] vt/i to turn, rotate; (como pião) to spin.

girassol [ʒɪraˈsow] m sunflower.

giratório/a adj revolving.

gíria [ˈʒɪrɪa] f (calão) slang; (jargão) jargon.

giro [ˈʒɪru] m turn; **dar um ~** to go for a walk; (em veículo) to go for a spin; **que ~!** (Pt) terrific!

giz [ʒɪʃ] m chalk.

glacê [glaˈse] m icing.

glacial [-jaw] adj icy.

glândula f gland.

global [-aw] adj (total) total, entire; **preço ~** overall price; **globo** m globe.

glória f glory; **gloriar-se** vr: **gloriar-se de** to boast of; **glorificar** vt to glorify; **glorioso/a** adj glorious.

glosa f comment; **glosar** vt to comment on; (criticar) to criticize; (conta) to cancel; (contestar) to take issue with, query.

glossário m glossary.

glutão/tona [gluˈtãw/tɔna] adj greedy // m/f glutton.

goela f gullet; (garganta) throat.

goiaba f guava.

gol [gow] m (Pt: **golo**) m goal; **marcar um ~** to score a goal.

gola f collar; **~ rulê** polo neck.

gole [ˈgolɪ] m gulp, swallow; **de um só ~** at one gulp.

goleiro [goˈlejru] m (Br) goalkeeper.

golfar [gowˈfax] vt (vomitar) to spit up; (emitir) to throw out // vi to spurt out.

golfe [ˈgowfɪ] m golf; **campo de ~** golf course; **golfista** m/f golfer.

golfo m gulf.

golpe [ˈgowpɪ] m blow; (de mão) smack; (de punho) punch; **~ de estado** coup d'état; **de um só ~** at a stroke; **golpear** vt to beat, hit; (com navalha) to stab; (com o punho) to punch.

goma f (cola) gum, glue; (de roupa) starch.

gomo m (de laranja) slice.

gonzo m hinge.

gorar vt to frustrate, thwart // vi to fail, go wrong.

gordo/a adj (pessoa) fat; (gordurento) greasy; (carne) fatty; **gordura** f fat; (derretida) grease; (obesidade) fatness; **gordurento/a** adj (ensebado) greasy; (gordo) fatty; **gorduroso/a** adj (cabelo) greasy, oily.

gorila m gorilla.

gorjear [goxˈʒjax] vi to chirp, twitter; **gorjeio** m twittering, chirping.

gorjeta [gorˈʒeta] f tip, gratuity.

gorro m cap; (boina) beret.

gostar vi: **~ de** to like; **~ mais de** to prefer; **gosto** m taste; (prazer) pleasure; **a seu gosto** to one's liking; **de bom/mau gosto** in good/bad taste; **gostoso** m (col: homem) dish; **gostoso/a** adj (comida) tasty; (ambiente) pleasant; (delicioso) lovely, gorgeous // (col: mulher) cracker.

gota f drop; (de suor) bead; **~ a ~** drop by drop; **goteira** f (cano) gutter; (buraco) leak; **gotejar** vi to drip.

gótico/a adj Gothic.

governa dor(a) m/f governor; **governar** vt (um país) to govern, rule; (dirigir) to manage; (barco) to steer; **governo** m (do país) government; (controle) control; (NÁUT) steering; **governo da casa** housekeeping.

gozado/a adj funny; **gozar** vt to enjoy; (col) to make fun of // vi to enjoy o.s.; (col: sexo) to come, have an orgasm; **gozar de** to enjoy; (Pt: rir) to make fun of; **gozo** m (prazer) pleasure; (uso) enjoyment, use.

Grã-Bretanha [grã-breˈtaɲa] f Great Britain.

graça [ˈgrasa] f grace; (elegância) charm; (gracejo) joke; (humor) wit; **de ~** free, for nothing; **sem ~** dull, boring; **ter ~** to be funny; **~ s a** thanks to; **gracejar** vi to joke; **gracejo** m joke; **gracioso/a** adj charming; (divertido) funny.

grade [ˈgradʒɪ] f (no chão) grating; (grelha) grill; (de embalagem) crate; (na janela) bars pl.

grado/a adj (importante) important // m: **de bom/mau ~** willingly/unwillingly.

graduação [gradwaˈsãw] f graduation; (divisão) division; (posição) rank; **curso de ~** degree course; **gradual** adj gradual; **graduar** vt to graduate; **graduar-se** vr to graduate.

'gráfico/a adj graphic // m (MAT) graph; (diagrama) diagram, chart.

grã-fino/a [grã-'finu/a] m/f aristocrat; (col) snob.

gra'fite f (lápis) lead; (escritura) graffiti.

gralha ['graʎa] f jay; (Pt) rook.

'grama m (peso) gramme // f (Br: capim) grass; gramado m (Br) lawn; gramar vt to plant/sow with grass; (Pt: col) to be fond of // vi (Pt: col) to cry out.

gra'mática f grammar.

grampe'ar vt to staple; (Br: TEL) to bug; grampo m staple; (no cabelo) hairgrip; (de carpinteiro) clamp.

'grana f (col) money, dough.

gra'nada f (MIL) shell; (pedra) garnet; ~ de mão hand grenade.

'grande adj big, large; (alto) tall; (fig) great; grandeza f (tamanho) size; (fig) greatness; grandioso/a adj magnificent, grand.

gra'nel m granary; a ~ (COM) in bulk.

gra'nito m (GEO) granite.

gra'nizo m hail; chover ~ to hail.

granja ['grãʒa] f farm; (de galinhas) chicken farm.

granjear [grãʒi'ax] vt (simpatia, amigos) to win, gain.

grão ['grãw] m, pl grãos ['grãwʃ] grain; (semente) seed; (de café) bean.

gras'nar vi (corvo) to caw; (pato) to quack; (rã) to croak.

gratidão [gratʃi'dãw] f gratitude.

gratificação [gratʃifika'sãw] f (gorjeta) tip; (bônus) bonus; gratificante adj rewarding; gratificar vt (dar gorjeta) to tip.

'grátis adv free, for nothing.

'grato/a adj (agradável) pleasant; ficar ~ a alguém por (agradecido) to be grateful to sb for.

gratuito/a [gra'twitu/a] adj (grátis) free; (infundado) gratuitous.

grau [graw] m (ger) degree; (nível) level; (escolar) class.

gravação [grava'sãw] f (em madeira) carving; (TEC) recording; gravador m tape recorder.

gra'var vt (madeira) to carve; (metal) to engrave; (na memória) to fix; (TEC) to record.

gra'vata f tie; ~ borboleta bow tie.

grave ['gravi] adj (sério) serious; (trágico) grave.

'grávida adj pregnant.

gravi'dade f gravity.

gravi'dez f pregnancy.

gra'vura f (em madeira) engraving; (estampa) print.

graxa ['graʃa] f (para sapatos) polish; (lubrificante) grease.

'grego/a adj, m/f Greek.

grei [grej] f (rebanho) flock; (congregação) congregation.

grelha ['grɛʎa] f grill; (de fornalha) grate; grelhado/a adj grilled // m (prato) grill; grelhar vt to grill.

'grêmio m (associação) guild; (clube) club.

'greta f crack; gretado/a adj cracked.

'greve f strike; fazer ~ to go on strike; ~ de fome hunger strike; ~ branca go-slow; grevista m/f striker.

gri'fado/a adj in italics; grifar vt to italicize; (sublinhar) to underline; (fig) to emphasize.

grilhão [gri'ʎãw] m chain; grilhões mpl (fig) fetters.

'grilo m cricket; (AUTO) squeak; (col) problem; qual é o ~? what's the matter?

grim'par vi to climb; (AUTO) to seize up.

gri'nalda f garland.

gri'par-se vr to catch flu; gripe f flu, influenza.

'grisalho/a adj (cabelo) grey.

'grita f uproar; gritante adj glaring, gross, blatant; gritar vt/i to shout, yell; gritaria f shouting, din; grito m shout; (de espanto) scream; (de dor) cry; (de animal) call; dar um grito to cry out.

groselha [gro'zeʎa] f (red)currant.

grosseiro/a [gro'sejru/a] adj (incivil) rude; (piada) crude; grosseria f rudeness; fazer uma grosseria to be vulgar.

'grosso/a adj (denso) thick; (áspero) rough; (voz) deep; a ~ modo roughly // m (do exército) the main body; o ~ de the bulk of // f gross; grossura f thickness.

gro'tesco/a adj grotesque.

'grua f (MEC) crane.

gru'dar vt/i to glue, stick; grude f glue.

grunhido [gru'ɲidu] m grunt; grunhir vi (porco) to grunt; (tigre) to growl; (resmungar) to grumble.

'grupo m group; (TEC) unit, set; ~ sanguíneo blood group.

'gruta f grotto.

guarda ['gwaxda] f (polícia) policewoman; (vigilância) guarding; (de objeto) safekeeping; estar de ~ to be on guard; pôr-se em ~ to be on one's guard // m (MIL) guard; (polícia) policeman.

guarda-chuva [gwaxda-'ʃuva] m umbrella.

guarda-'costas m inv (NÁUT) coastguard boat; (capanga) bodyguard.

guardanapo [gwaxda'napu] m napkin.

guardar [gwax'dax] vt to guard; (conservar) to keep; (vigiar) to watch over; ~ silêncio to keep quiet; ~-se vr (defender-se) to protect o.s.; ~-se de (acautelar-se) to guard against.

guarda-redes [gwaxda-'xedʒis] m (Pt) goalkeeper.

guarda-roupa [gwaxda-'xopa] m (armário) wardrobe; (público) cloakroom.

guarda-'sol m sunshade, parasol.

guarida [gwa'rida] f refuge.

guarnecer [gwaxne'sex] vt (prover) to provide; (MIL) to garrison; (adornar) to trim; **guarnição** f (MIL) garrison; (NÁUT) crew; (de roupa) trimming; (CULIN) garnish.

'**gude** m (jogo) marbles pl; **bola de** ~ marble.

guelra ['gɛlra] f (de peixe) gill.

guerra ['gɛxa] f war; (luta) struggle; ~ **nuclear** nuclear warfare; ~ **fria** cold war; **fazer** ~ to wage war; **após** ~ post-war; **guerrear** vi to wage war; **guerreiro/a** adj (lutando) fighting; (belicoso) warlike // m warrior; **guerrilha** f (luta) guerrilla warfare; (tropa) guerrilla band; **guerrilheiro/a** adj, m/f guerrilla.

guia ['gia] f (conselho) guidance; (COM) permit, bill of lading // m guide; (livro) guidebook; **guiar** vt (orientar) to guide; (AUTO) to drive; (avião) to pilot; **guiar-se** vr: **guiar-se por** to go by.

guidom [gi'dõ] (Pt: -dão) m handlebar.

guilhotina [giʌo'tʃina] f guillotine.

guinada [gi'nada] f (NÁUT) lurch; (virada) swerve; (dor) sharp pain.

guin'char vt (carro) to tow.

guincho ['gĩʃu] m (de animal, rodas) squeal; (de pessoa) shriek.

guin'dar vt to hoist, lift; (fig) to raise, promote; **guindaste** m hoist, crane.

'**guisa** f: **a** ~ **de** like, by way of.

gui'sado m stew.

gui'tarra f guitar.

'**gula** f gluttony, greed; **guloseima** f delicacy, titbit; **guloso/a** adj greedy.

'**gume** m cutting edge; (fig) sharpness.

gutu'ral adj guttural.

H

NB: initial H is always silent in Portuguese.

h abr de **hora** hour.

há vb ver **haver**.

'**hábil** [-IW] adj, pl '**hábeis** (inteligente) clever; (competente) capable; (destro) able, skilful; **habilidade** f (destreza) skill, ability; (inteligência) cleverness; **habilidoso/a** adj skilful, clever.

habilitação [abilita'sãw] f (aptidão) eligibility, qualification; **habilitações** fpl (JUR) documentary evidence sg; (conhecimentos) qualifications pl; **habilitar** vt to prepare.

habitação [abita'sãw] f dwelling, residence; (BIO) habitat; **habitante** m/f inhabitant; **habitar** vt (viver em) to live in; (povoar) to inhabit // vi to live.

'**hábito** m habit; (social) custom; **habitual** adj usual.

habitu'ar vt: ~ **alguém a** to get sb used to, accustom sb to; ~**-se** vr: ~**-se a** to get used to.

'**haja** etc vb ver **haver**.

'**hálito** m breath.

ham'búrguer m hamburger.

harmo'nia f harmony; (paz) peace; (acordo) agreement; **harmonioso/a** adj harmonious.

'**harpa** f harp.

'**hasta** f: ~ **pública** auction.

'**haste** f (de bandeira) flagpole; (TEC) shaft, rod; **hastear** vt to raise, hoist.

haurir [aw'rix] vt (esgotar) to drain, exhaust; (aspirar) to inhale; (beber) to suck up.

ha'ver vb auxiliar to have // vb impessoal: **há** there is, (pl) there are; **há muita gente** there are a lot of people; **deve** ~ there must be; **há cinco dias que não o vejo** I haven't seen him for five days; **há um ano que ela chegou** it's a year since she came; **há muito tempo** long ago; ~ **de** (futuro): **há de ver** you will see; **haja o que houver** come what may; **o que é que há?** what's the matter? // m (COM) credit; **haveres** mpl property sg, possessions.

hec'tare m hectare.

hedi'ondo/a adj vile, revolting; (crime) heinous.

'**hei** vb ver **haver**.

hélice ['ɛlis] f propeller.

heli'cóptero m helicopter.

hemis'fério m hemisphere.

hemorragia [emoxa'ʒia] f haemorrhage; ~ **nasal** nosebleed.

hemor'roidas fpl haemorrhoids, piles.

'**hera** f ivy.

he'rança f inheritance; (fig) heritage.

her'dade f (Pt) large farm.

her'dar vt: ~ **de** to inherit from; ~ **a** to bequeath to; **herdeiro/a** m heir // f heiress.

herege [e'reʒi] m/f heretic; **heresia** f heresy; **herético/a** adj heretical.

her'mético/a adj airtight.

he'rói [e'roj] m hero; **heróico/a** adj heroic; **heroína** f heroine; **heroísmo** m heroism.

'**herpes** m herpes sg.

hesitação [ezita'sãw] f hesitation; **hesitar** vi to hesitate.

heterossexual [eteroscks'wal] adj heterosexual.

hi'ato m (intervalo) interval, gap; (LING) hiatus.

'**híbrido/a** adj hybrid.

hidráulico/a [i'drawliku/a] adj hydraulic; **instalação** ~**a** water-works sg.

hidravião [idravi'ãw] m seaplane.

hidre'létrico/a (Pt: -ct-) adj hydroelectric.

'**hidro...** pref hydro..., water...; **hidrófilo/a** adj absorbent; **hidrofobia** f rabies sg; **hidrogênio** m hydrogen.

hiena ['jena] f hyena.

hierarquia [jerax'kia] f hierarchy.

'**hífen** m hyphen.

higiene [i'ʒjeni] f hygiene; **higiênico/a** adj (MED) hygienic, sanitary; **papel higiênico** toilet paper.

'**hino** m hymn; ~ **nacional** national anthem.

hipertensão [ɪpɛxtẽ'sãw] f high blood pressure.

'hípico/a adj (atr) horse; **hipismo** m horse racing.

hip'nose f hypnosis; **hipnotisar** vt to hypnotize.

hipocri'sia f hypocrisy; **hipócrita** adj hypocritical // m/f hypocrite.

hi'pódromo m racecourse.

hipo'teca f mortgage.

hipótese [ɪ'pɔtez] f hypothesis; **na ~ de** in the event of; **em ~ alguma** under no circumstances; **hipotético/a** adj hypothetical.

hirto/a ['ɪxtu/a] adj stiff, rigid.

his'pânico/a adj Hispanic.

histe'ria f hysteria.

his'tória f (o passado) history; (conto) story, tale; (mentira) fib; **~ da carochinha** nursery tale; **historiador(a)** m/f historian; **histórico/a** adj historical; (fig) historic; **historieta** f anecdote, very short story.

hoje ['oʒɪ] adv today; (atualmente) now(adays); **~ à noite** tonight; **~ de manhã** this morning; **de ~ a uma semana** in a week's time; **de ~ em diante** from now on; **~ em dia** nowadays.

holan'dês/esa adj Dutch // m Dutchman; (língua) Dutch // f Dutchwoman.

holo'fote m searchlight.

homem ['omẽ] m man; (a humanidade) mankind; **~ do povo** man in the street; **~ de bem** honest man; **~ de estado** statesman; **~ de negócios** businessman; **~-rã** m frogman.

homenagem [ome'naʒẽ] f (feudal) homage; (respeito) honour, respect.

homi'cida adj (pessoa) homicidal // m/f murderer; **homicídio** m murder; **homicídio involuntário** manslaughter.

homizi'ado/a adj in hiding // m/f fugitive; **homiziar** vt (dar abrigo) to shelter; (esconder) to hide.

homossexual [omosɛks'wal] adj homosexual; (col) gay // m homosexual.

honesti'dade f honesty; (decência) decency; (pureza) purity, virtue; **honesto/a** adj (íntegro) honest; (virtuoso) virtuous.

hono'rário/a adj honorary // mpl: **~s** fees.

'honra f honour; (castidade) virtue; **em ~ de** in honour of; **honradez** f honesty; (de pessoa) integrity; **honrado/a** adj honest; (respeitado) honourable; **honrar** vt to honour; **honroso/a** adj honourable.

hóquei ['ɔkej] m hockey.

'hora f (ger) time; (específica) hour; **~ de dormir** bedtime; **~s vagas** spare time; **a que ~s?** when?, at what time?; **que ~s são?** what time is it?; **são duas ~s** it's two o'clock; **bem na ~** just in time; **chegar na ~** to be on time; **dar ~s** to strike the hour; **de última ~** last-minute; **fazer ~** to kill time;

marcar ~ to make an appointment; **meia ~** half an hour; **altas ~s** in the small hours; **na ~ "H"** in the nick of time; **horário/a** adj hourly; **100 km horários** 100 kilometres an hour // m timetable.

horizon'tal adj horizontal; **horizonte** m horizon.

ho'róscopo m horoscope.

hor'rendo/a adj horrendous, frightful; **horripilante** adj horrifying, hair-raising; **horripilar** vt to horrify; **horrível** adj awful, horrible.

hor'ror m horror; **que ~!** how awful!; **~izar** vt to horrify, frighten; **~izar-se** vr to be horrified; **~oso/a** adj ghastly, appalling.

'horta f vegetable garden; **~ liças** fpl vegetables.

hortelã [ɔxte'la] f mint; **~ pimenta** peppermint.

hortelão/loa [ɔxte'lãw/loa] m/f (Pt) (market) gardener.

hospedagem [oʃpe'daʒẽ] f lodging; **hospedar** vt to put up, lodge; **hospedar-se** vr to stay, lodge; **hospedaria** f inn; **hóspede** m (amigo) guest; (estrangeiro) lodger; **hospedeiro/a** adj hospitable, welcoming // m (de hospedaria) landlord; (em casa) host // f (de hospedaria) landlady; (em casa) hostess; (Pt: de bordo) air hostess.

hospi'tal m hospital.

hospitaleiro/a [oʃpɪta'lejru/a] adj hospitable; **hospitalidade** f hospitality.

'hóstia f Host, wafer.

hos'til adj hostile; **~idade** f hostility.

ho'tel m hotel; **~eiro/a** adj hotel cmp // m hotelier; **rede ~eira** hotel chain.

'houve etc vb ver **haver**.

humani'dade f (os homens) man(kind); (compaixão) humanity; **humanitário/a** adj humanitarian; (benfeitor) humane; **humano/a** adj human; (bondoso) humane.

'húmido/a adj (Pt) ver **úmido**.

humil'dade f humility; **humilde** adj humble; (pobre) poor; **humilhação** f humiliation; **humilhar** vt to humiliate.

hu'mor m (disposição) mood, temper; (graça) humour; **de bom/mau ~** in a good/bad mood; **~ismo** m humour; **~ístico/a** adj humorous.

'húngaro/a adj, m/f Hungarian.

I

iate ['jatʃɪ] m yacht; **iatismo** m yachting.

i'bérico/a adj, m/f Iberian; **ibero-americano** adj, m/f Ibero American.

içar [ɪ'sax] vt to hoist, raise.

icterícia [ɪkte'rɪsja] f jaundice.

'ida f going, departure; **~ e volta** round trip, return.

i'dade f age; **ter cinco anos de ~** to be five (years old); **de meia ~** middle-aged; **de menor ~** under age; **a I~ Média** the Middle Ages.

ide'al [-aw] adj (perfeito) ideal; (imaginário) imaginary // m ideal; ~ista m/f idealist; ~izar vt to idealize; (planejar) to devise, create.

ide'ar vt (imaginar) to imagine, think up; idéia f idea; (mente) mind; mudar de idéia to change one's mind; não ter idéia to have no idea; não faço idéia I can't imagine.

'idem pron ditto.

i'dêntico/a adj identical; identidade f identity; carteira de identidade identity card; identificação f identification; identificar vt to identify; identificar-se vr: identificar-se com to identify with.

ideologia [Idʒiolo'ʒia] f ideology; ideológico/a adj ideological.

idi'oma m language.

idi'ota adj idiotic // m/f idiot; idiotice f idiocy.

idio'tismo m (LING) idiom.

i'dólatra adj idolatrous // m idolater // f idolatress; idolatrar vt to idolize; idolatria f idolatry; ídolo m idol.

idoneidade [Idonej'dadʒi] f suitability; (competência) competence; ~ moral moral probity; idôneo/a adj (conveniente) suitable, fit; (pessoa) able, capable.

i'doso/a adj elderly, old.

ignição [Igni'sãw] f ignition.

igno'mínia f disgrace, ignominy; ignominioso/a adj ignominious.

igno'rado/a adj (desconhecido) unknown; (obscuro) obscure; ignorância f ignorance; ignorante adj ignorant, uneducated // m/f ignoramus; ignorar vt not to know, be unaware of; ignoto/a adj (lit) unknown.

igreja [I'greʒa] f church.

igual [I'gwaw] adj equal; (superfície, temperatura) even; em partes iguais in equal parts; ser ~ a to be the same as, be like // m/f equal; igualar vt (fazer igual) to make equal; (nivelar) to level // vi: igualar a to be equal to, be the same as; igualdade f (paridade) equality; (uniformidade) evenness, uniformity.

igualha [I'gwaʎa] f: gente de minha ~ my equals; da mesma ~ of the same ilk.

iguaria [Igwa'ria] f (CULIN) delicacy.

ilação [Ila'sãw] f inference, deduction.

ile'gal [-aw] adj illegal.

ile'gítimo/a adj illegitimate.

ilegível [Ile'ʒivew] adj illegible.

i'leso/a adj unhurt.

ilha ['iʎa] f island.

ilharga [I'ʎaxga] f (ANAT) side; (de animal) flank.

i'lhéu/i'lhoa m/f islander.

i'lícito/a adj illicit.

ilimi'tado/a adj unlimited.

i'lógico/a adj illogical; (absurdo) absurd.

ilu'dir vt (enganar) to deceive; (a lei) to evade; ~-se vr to deceive o.s.

iluminação [Ilumina'sãw] f lighting; (fig)

enlightenment; iluminar vt to light up; (fig) to enlighten.

ilusão [Ilu'zãw] f illusion; (quimera) delusion; (burla) trick; ~ de ótica optical illusion; ilusionista m/f conjurer; ilusório/a adj (enganoso) deceptive.

ilustração [Iluʃtra'sãw] f (figura) illustration; (saber) learning; ilustrado/a adj (com gravuras) illustrated; (instruído) learned; ilustrar vt (com gravuras) to illustrate; (instruir) to instruct; (explicar) to explain; ilustrar-se vr (distinguir-se) to excel; (instruir-se) to inform o.s.; ilustre adj famous, illustrious.

'imã (Pt: i'man) m magnet.

imagem [I'maʒẽ] f image; (semelhança) likeness; (visual) picture; imaginação f imagination; imaginar vt to imagine; (supor) to suppose; imaginário/a adj imaginary; imaginativo/a adj imaginative.

ima'turo/a adj immature; (fruta) unripe.

imba'tível adj invincible.

imbe'cil adj stupid // m/f imbecile, half-wit; ~idade f stupidity.

imbri'car vt, ~-se vr to overlap.

imbuir [Ĩ'bwix] vt: ~ de (sentimentos) to imbue with.

imediações [Imedʒia'sõjʃ] fpl vicinity sg, neighbourhood sg.

imediata'mente adv immediately, right away; imediato/a adj immediate; (seguinte) next; imediato a next to; de imediato straight away // m second-in-command.

imensi'dade f immensity; imenso/a adj immense, huge.

imere'cido/a adj undeserved.

imigração [Imigra'sãw] f immigration; imigrante adj, m/f immigrant; imigrar vi to immigrate.

imiscuir-se [Imiʃ'kwix-si] vr to meddle, interfere.

imitação [Imita'sãw] f imitation, copy; imitar vt to imitate, copy.

imobi'liário/a adj property cmp; real estate (US) // f estate agency.

imo'lar vt to sacrifice.

imo'ral adj immoral.

imor'tal adj immortal; ~izar vt to immortalize.

i'móvel adj (parado) motionless, still; (não movediço) immovable // m property.

impaciência [Impas'jẽsja] f impatience; impacientar-se vr to lose one's patience; impaciente adj impatient; (inquieto) anxious.

im'pacto (Pt: im'pacte) m impact.

impalu'dismo m malaria.

'impar adj (números) odd.

imparci'al [-jaw] adj fair, impartial; ~idade f impartiality.

im'pávido/a adj (lit) fearless, intrepid.

impe'cável [-avew] adj perfect, impeccable.

impe'dido/a adj hindered; (estrada)

blocked; (futebol) offside; (Pt: TEL) engaged // m (MIL) batman; **impedir** vt (obstruir) to obstruct; (estrada) to block; (movimento) to impede; **impedir alguém de fazer** to prevent sb from doing.

impe'lir vt to drive (on); (obrigar) to force, impel.

impene'trável [-avew] adj impenetrable; (fig) incomprehensible.

impeni'tente adj unrepentant.

impen'sado/a adj (imprevidente) thoughtless; (sem cálculo) unpremeditated; (imprevisto) unforeseen.

impera'dor m emperor; **imperar** vi to reign, rule; (fig) to prevail; **imperativo/a** adj (urgente) imperative // m necessity; **imperatriz** f empress.

impercep'tível [-ivew] adj imperceptible; (diminuto) slight.

imperdo'ável [-avew] adj unforgivable, inexcusable.

impere'cível [-ivew] adj imperishable.

imperfeição [impɛxfej'sãw] f imperfection; (falha) flaw; **imperfeito/a** adj imperfect; (inacabado) unfinished; (defeituoso) faulty.

imperi'al [-jaw] adj imperial; **~ismo** m imperialism.

impe'rícia f (inabilidade) incompetence; (inexperiência) inexperience.

im'pério m empire; **imperioso/a** adj (dominador) domineering; (urgente) pressing, urgent.

imperme'ável [-avew] adj impervious; (à água) waterproof // m raincoat.

imperti'nência f impertinence; (despropósito) irrelevance; **impertinente** adj (alheio) irrelevant; (insolente) impertinent.

impessoal [impɛs'waw] adj impersonal.

'ímpeto m (TEC) impetus; (furor) force; (de cólera) surge, rush; **agir com ~** to act on impulse.

impetuosi'dade f impetuosity; (veemência) vehemence; **impetuoso/a** adj (pessoa) headstrong, impetuous; (ato) rash, hasty.

impie'dade f irreverence; (crueldade) cruelty.

impla'cável [-avew] adj (pessoa) unforgiving; (destino, doença) relentless.

impli'car vt (envolver) to implicate; (dar a entender) to imply; **~ com** (contender) to pick a quarrel with; **~-se** vr (meterse) to get involved.

im'plícito adj implicit; (subentendido) implied.

implo'rar vt to beg, implore.

impo'nente adj impressive, imposing.

impopu'lar adj unpopular.

im'por vt to impose; (respeito) to command; **~-se** vr to make one's influence felt.

importação [impoxta'sãw] f (ato) importing; (mercadorias) imports pl; **importador(a)** adj import cmp // m/f importer.

impor'tância f importance; (de dinheiro)

sum, amount; **não tem ~** it doesn't matter, never mind; **importante** adj important // m : **o importante** the main/important thing; **importar** vt (COM) to import; (trazer) to bring in // vi to matter, be important; **não me importo** I don't care; **não importa!** never mind!; **importar em** to add up to, amount to.

im'porte m (total) amount; (custo) cost.

importu'nar vt to bother, annoy; **importuno/a** adj (maçante) annoying; (inoportuno) inopportune.

impossibili'dade f impossibility; **impossibilitar** vt to make impossible; **impossível** adj impossible; (insuportável) insufferable.

im'posto/a pp de **impor** // m tax; **~ de renda** (Br) income tax; **~ predial** rates pl.

impos'tor m impostor; **impostura** f deception.

impo'tência f impotence; **impotente** adj impotent; (fraco) powerless.

imprati'cável adj impracticable.

impre'ciso/a adj vague.

impreg'nar vt to impregnate.

im'prensa f (a arte) printing; (máquina, jornalistas) press; (casa) printer's.

imprescin'dível [-dʒivew] adj essential, indispensable.

impressão [impre'sãw] f (sensação) impression; (imprensa) printing; (marca) imprint; **~ digital** fingerprint; **impressionante** adj impressive; (comovente) moving; **impressionar** vt (afetar) to impress; (comover) to move // vi to be impressive; **impresso/a** pp irr de **imprimir** // adj printed // m (para preencher) form; (folheto) leaflet; **impressos** mpl printed matter; **impressor** m printer; **impressora** f printing machine.

impre'visto/a adj unexpected, unforeseen.

impri'mir vt to print; (marca) to stamp; (infundir) to instil; **~-se** vr to be stamped, be impressed.

'ímprobo/a adj (desonesto) dishonest; (árduo) arduous.

improce'dente adj groundless, unjustified.

improfícuo/a [impro'fikwu/a] adj useless, futile.

impro'pério m insult.

improprie'dade f (inoportunidade) unsuitability; (incorreção) incorrectness, impropriety; **impróprio/a** adj (inadequado) unsuitable; (errado) wrong; (conduta) improper.

impro'vável [-avew] adj unlikely.

improvi'dência f (imprudência) rashness; (descuido) carelessness; **improvidente** adj (esbanjador) thriftless; (negligente) careless.

improvi'sado/a adj improvised, impromptu; **improvisar** vt/i to improvise; (*teatro*) to ad-lib; **improviso** *m* impromptu talk; **de improviso** suddenly; **falar de improviso** to talk off the cuff.

impru'dência *f* imprudence; (*irreflexão*) rashness; **imprudente** *adj* (*irrefletido*) rash.

impu'dência *f* impudence; (*col*) cheek; **impudente** *adj* (*sem-vergonha*) shameless; (*descarado*) impudent; (*lascivo*) lewd.

impu'dico/a *adj* (*sem-vergonha*) shameless; (*lascivo*) lewd.

impug'nar *vt* (*refutar*) to refute; (*opor-se a*) to oppose.

impulsio'nar *vt* (*impelir*) to drive, impel; (*estimular*) to urge.

impul'sivo/a *adj* impulsive; **impulso** *m* (*ímpeto*) thrust, push; (*estímulo*) urge, impulse.

im'pune *adj* unpunished; **~mente** *adv* with impunity; **impunidade** *f* impunity.

impu'reza *f* impurity; (*despudor*) indecency; **impuro/a** *adj* impure; (*sensual*) lewd.

imputação [ɪmputa'sãw] *f* accusation; **imputar** *vt* (*atribuir*) to attribute; **imputar alguma coisa a alguém** to blame sb for sth; **imputável** *adj* attributable.

imun'dície *f* filth; **imundo/a** *adj* filthy.

i'mune *adj*: **~ a** immune to/from; **imunidade** *f* immunity.

imu'tável [-avew] *adj* fixed, unalterable, unchanging.

inaba'lável [-avew] *adj* unshakeable.

in'ábil [-abɪw] *adj* (*desajeitado*) clumsy; (*incapaz*) incapable; **inabilidade** *f* (*incompetência*) incompetence; (*falta de destreza*) clumsiness; **inabilitar** *vt* (*incapacitar*) to incapacitate; (*em exame*) to disqualify.

inabi'tável *adj* uninhabitable.

inaca'bável *adj* interminable, unending.

inação [ɪna'sãw] (*Pt*: **-cç-**) *f* (*inércia*) inactivity; (*irresolução*) indecision.

inaceitável [ɪnasej'tavew] *adj* unacceptable.

inaces'sível *adj* inaccessible.

inadequado/a [ɪnadɛ'kwadu/a] *adj* (*impróprio*) unsuitable.

inadmis'sível *adj* inadmissible.

inadquirível [ɪnadkɪ'rivew] *adj* unobtainable.

inadver'tência *f* oversight; **inadvertido/a** *adj* unintentional.

ina'lar *vt* to inhale, breathe in.

inalte'rável *adj* unchangeable; (*impassível*) imperturbable.

inanição [ɪnanɪ'sãw] *f* starvation.

inani'mado/a *adj* (*morto*) lifeless; (*sem vida*) inanimate.

inaptidão [ɪnaptʃɪ'dãw] *f* inability; **inapto/a** *adj* (*incapaz*) unfit, incapable; (*inadequado*) unsuited.

inatingível [ɪnatʃĩ'ʒivew] *adj* unattainable.

inativi'dade (*Pt*: **-ct-**) *f* inactivity; (*de*

funcionário) unemployment, redundancy; **inativo/a** (*Pt*: **-ct-**) *adj* inactive; (*inerte*) inert; (*aposentado*) retired.

i'nato/a *adj* innate, inborn.

inaudito/a [ɪnaw'dʒɪtu/a] *adj* unheard-of.

inauguração [ɪnawgura'sãw] *f* inauguration; (*de exposição*) opening; **inaugurar** *vt* to inaugurate; (*exposição*) to open.

incalcu'lável *adj* incalculable.

incan'sável *adj* tireless, untiring.

incapaci'dade *f* (*inaptidão*) incapacity; (*incompetência*) incompetence; **incapacitar** *vt* (*inabilitar*) to make unfit; (*estropiar*) to disable; **incapaz** *adj* : **incapaz de fazer** unable to do, incapable of doing; **incapaz para** unfit for.

inçar [ĩ'sax] *vt* to infest.

incauto/a [ĩ'kawtu/a] *adj* (*imprudente*) rash; (*crédulo*) unsuspecting.

incendi'ar *vt* to set fire to; (*fig*) to inflame; **~-se** *vr* to catch fire; **incendiário/a** *adj* incendiary; (*fig*) inflammatory // *m/f* agitator; **incêndio** *m* fire; **incêndio premeditado** arson.

in'censo *m* incense.

incen'tivo *m* incentive.

incer'teza *f* uncertainty; (*dúvida*) doubt; **incerto/a** *adj* uncertain; (*duvidoso*) doubtful.

inces'sante *adj* incessant.

inchado/a [ĩ'ʃadu/a] *adj* swollen; (*fig*) conceited; **inchar** *vt* to swell; (*inflar*) to blow up // *vi* to swell; **inchar-se** *vr* to swell (up); (*fig*) to become conceited.

inci'dente *m* incident.

incine'rar *vt* to burn; (*cadáver*) to cremate.

incisão [ĩsɪ'zãw] *f* (*corte*) cut; (*MED*) incision; **incisivo/a** *adj* cutting, sharp; (*fig*) incisive // *m* incisor.

incitação [ĩsɪta'sãw] *f*, **incita'mento** *m* incitement; **incitar** *vt* to incite; (*instigar*) to rouse.

inci'vil *adj* rude, ill-mannered.

incle'mência *f* harshness, rigour; (*tempo*) inclemency; **inclemente** *adj* severe, harsh; (*tempo*) inclement.

inclinação [ĩklɪna'sãw] *f* (*propensão*) inclination; (*da terra*) slope; (*simpatia*) liking; **~ da cabeça** nod; **inclinado/a** *adj* : **estar inclinado/pouco inclinado a** to be inclined/loath to; **inclinar** *vt* (*objeto*) to tilt; (*cabeça*) to nod; (*conversa*) to turn // *vi* (*terra*) to slope; (*objeto*) to tilt; **inclinar para** (*propensão*) to incline towards; **inclinar-se** *vr* (*objeto*) to tilt; (*dobrar o corpo*) to bow, stoop.

'ínclito/a *adj* illustrious, renowned.

incluir [ĩ'klwɪx] *vt* to include; (*conter*) to incorporate; (*pôr dentro*) to enclose; **inclusão** *f* inclusion.

inclusive [ĩklu'zɪvɪ] *adj* inclusive // *prep* including; (*até*) up to // *adv* inclusively; **incluso/a** *adj* included; (*em carta*) enclosed.

incoerente [Ikoe'rētʃI] *adj* incoherent.

in'cógnito/a *adj* unknown // *adv* incognito // *f* unknown quantity; (*MAT*) unknown.

inco'lor *adj* colourless.

incólume [I'kolumI] *adj* safe and sound; (*ileso*) unharmed.

incomensu'rável *adj* immense.

incomo'dar *vt* (*molestar*) to bother, trouble; (*irritar*) to annoy; **~-se** *vr* to bother, put o.s. out; **não se incomode!** never mind!; **incômodo/a** *adj* (*desconfortável*) uncomfortable; (*importuno*) annoying; (*inoportuno*) inconvenient // *m* (*indisposição*) ailment; (*maçada*) nuisance, trouble; (*amolação*) inconvenience.

incompa'rável *adj* incomparable.

incompatibili'dade *f* incompatibility; **incompatível** *adj* incompatible.

incompe'tência *f* incompetence; **incompetente** *adj* incompetent.

incom'pleto/a *adj* incomplete, unfinished.

incompreen'sível *adj* incomprehensible.

incomuni'cável *adj* (*preso*) in solitary confinement.

inconce'bível *adj* inconceivable; (*incrível*) incredible.

inconcili'ável *adj* irreconcilable; (*incompatível*) incompatible.

inconclu'dente *adj* inconclusive.

incondicio'nal [-aw] *adj* unconditional; (*apoio*) wholehearted; (*partidário*) staunch.

inconfi'dência *f* disloyalty; (*JUR*) treason; **inconfidente** *adj* disloyal // *m* conspirator.

inconfun'dível [-dʒIvew] *adj* unmistakeable.

incongru'ente *adj* incongruous.

inconsciência [Ikõ'sjēsja] *f* unconsciousness; (*irreflexão*) thoughtlessness; **inconsciente** *adj* unconscious; (*involuntário*) unwitting; (*irresponsável*) irresponsible.

inconseqüente [Ikõse'kwētʃI] *adj* inconsistent; (*contraditório*) illogical.

inconsis'tente *adj* (*contraditório*) inconsistent; (*fraco*) weak.

incons'tante *adj* fickle.

incontes'tável *adj* undeniable.

inconti'nência *f* (*sensual*) licentiousness; (*MED*) incontinence; **incontinente** *adj* (*sensual*) licentious; (*MED*) incontinent.

inconveni'ência *f* unsuitability, inappropriateness; (*descortesia*) impoliteness; **inconveniente** *adj* (*impróprio*) unsuitable, inappropriate; (*indecoroso*) impolite // *m* difficulty, problem; **qual é o inconveniente?** what's wrong with it?

incorpo'rar *vt* to incorporate; (*juntar*) to add; (*COM*) to merge; **~-se** *vr* : **~-se a/em** to join.

incorreção [Ikoxɛ'sãw] (*Pt*: **-cç-**) *f* (*erro*) inaccuracy.

incor'rer *vi* : **~ em** to incur.

incor'reto/a (*Pt*: **-ct-**) *adj* (*errado*) wrong, incorrect; (*pessoa*) bad-mannered; (*ação*) improper.

incorrigível [IkɔxI'ʒIvew] *adj* incorrigible.

incorru'tível (*Pt*: **-pt-**) *adj* incorruptible.

increduli'dade *f* incredulity; (*ceticismo*) scepticism; **incrédulo/a** *adj* incredulous; (*cético*) sceptical // *m/f* sceptic.

incre'mento *m* (*desenvolvimento*) growth; (*acréscimo*) increase.

incrível [I'krIvew] *adj* incredible.

incru'ento/a *adj* (*lit*) bloodless.

incrus'tar *vt* to encrust; (*inserir*) to inlay.

incuba'dora *f* incubator; **incubar** *vt* (*ovos*) to incubate; (*plano*) to hatch.

incul'car *vt* to impress (upon sb); (*aconselhar*) to recommend.

incul'par *vt* (*censurar*) to blame; (*acusar*) to accuse.

in'culto/a *adj* (*pessoa*) uncultured, uneducated; (*terreno*) uncultivated.

incum'bir *vt* : **~ alguém de** to put sb in charge of // *vi* : **~ a alguém** to be sb's duty; **~-se** *vr*: **~-se de** to undertake, take charge of.

incu'rável *adj* incurable.

incursão [Ikux'zãw] *f* (*invasão*) raid, attack; (*penetração*) foray.

incu'tir *vt* to instil, inspire.

indagação [Idaga'sãw] *f* (*pesquisa*) investigation; (*busca*) search; (*JUR*) inquiry; **indagar** *vt* (*investigar*) to investigate; (*averiguar*) to ascertain // *vi* : **indagar de** to inquire about.

inde'cente *adj* indecent, improper; (*obsceno*) obscene.

indecisão [Idesi'zãw] *f* indecision; (*hesitação*) hesitation; **indeciso/a** *adj* (*irresoluto*) undecided, hesitant; (*indistinto*) vague.

indeco'roso/a *adj* indecent, improper.

indefe'rido/a *adj* refused, rejected; **indeferir** *vt* (*desatender*) to reject; (*requerimento*) to turn down.

inde'feso/a *adj* undefended; (*fraco*) defenceless.

indefi'nido/a *adj* indefinite; (*vago*) vague, undefined.

inde'lével [-ew] *adj* indelible.

indenização [IdenIza'sãw] (*Pt*: **-mn-**) *f* compensation; (*COM*) indemnity; **indenizar** (*Pt*: **-mn-**) *vt* (*compensar*) to compensate; (*gastos*) to reimburse // *vi*: **indenizar de** to compensate for.

indepen'dência *f* independence; **independente** *adj* independent; (*auto-suficiente*) self-sufficient.

indese'jável *adj* undesirable.

'Índia *f* India; **indiano/a** *adj*, *m/f* Indian.

indicação [IndʒIka'sãw] *f* indication; (*sinal*) sign; (*sugestão*) hint; (*de* *termômetro*) reading; **indicador** *m* indicator; (*TEC*) gauge; (*dedo*) index finger; (*ponteiro*) pointer; **indicar** *vt* (*mostrar*) to show, indicate; (*apontar*) to point to; (*termômetro*) to register.

índice ['ɪndʒɪsɪ] *m* (*de livro*) index; (*dedo*) index finger.

indício [ɪn'dʒɪsju] *m* (*sinal*) sign; (*vestígio*) trace; (*sugestão*) clue.

indife'rença *f* indifference; (*apatia*) apathy; **indiferente** *adj* indifferent; (*apático*) apathetic; **isso me é indiferente** it's all the same to me.

indígena [ɪn'dʒɪʒena] *adj, m/f* native; (*índio*) Indian.

indigência [ɪndʒɪ'ʒɛsja] *f* poverty; (*fig*) lack, need.

indigestão [ɪndʒɪʒe∫'tãw] *f* indigestion; **indigesto/a** *adj* indigestible; (*aborrecido*) dull, boring.

indignação [ɪndʒɪgna'sãw] *f* indignation; **indignado/a** *adj* indignant; **indignar** *vt* to anger, incense; **indignar-se** *vr*: **indignar-se com** to get indignant about.

indigni'dade *f* indignity; (*ultraje*) outrage; **indigno/a** *adj* (*não merecedor*) unworthy; (*desprezível*) disgraceful, despicable.

'índio/a *adj, m/f* (*da América*) Indian.

indi'reto/a (*Pt*: **-ct-**) *adj* indirect; (*olhar*) sidelong; (*procedimento*) roundabout // *f* insinuation.

indis'creto/a *adj* indiscreet; (*sem tato*) tactless; **indiscrição** *f* indiscretion; (*falta de diplomacia*) tactlessness; (*ato*) blunder, gaffe.

indiscu'tível *adj* indisputable.

indispen'sável *adj* essential, vital // *m* essentials *pl*.

indispo'nível *adj* unavailable.

indis'por *vt* to disturb, upset; (*saúde*) to make ill; **~-se** *vr* : **~-se com um amigo** to fall out with a friend; **indisposição** *f* sickness; **indisposição gástrica** stomach upset; **indisposto/a** *adj* (*doente*) unwell, poorly.

indis'tinto/a *adj* indistinct; (*vago*) vague.

individual [ɪndʒɪvɪ'dwaw] *adj* individual; **indivíduo** *m* individual, person.

indi'zível *adj* (*extraordinário*) unspeakable; (*indescritível*) indescribable.

in'dócil [-ɪw] *adj* (*rebelde*) unruly, wayward; (*incontentável*) difficult, restless.

'índole *f* (*temperamento*) nature; (*tipo*) sort, type.

indo'lência *f* laziness, indolence.

indo'mável [-avew] *adj* (*animal*) untameable; (*coragem*) indomitable; (*criança*) unmanageable, unruly; **indómito/a** *adj* untamed, wild.

indulgência [ɪndul'ʒɛsja] *f* (*clemência*) forgiveness; (*perdão*) pardon; (*REL*) indulgence.

indul'tar *vt* to pardon; (*JUR*) to reprieve; **indulto** *m* pardon; (*anistia*) amnesty; (*REL*) dispensation.

in'dústria *f* industry; **industrial** *adj* industrial // *m/f* industrialist; **industrioso/a** *adj* (*laborioso*) hardworking, industrious; (*hábil*) clever, skilful.

indu'zir *vt* to induce; **~ a** to persuade to; **~ em erro** to lead astray.

in'édito/a *adj* (*livro*) unpublished; (*incomum*) unheard of, rare.

ine'fável *adj* indescribable.

inefi'caz *adj* ineffective; (*inútil*) useless; **ineficiência** *f* inefficiency.

ine'gável *adj* (*lit*) undeniable.

inelu'tável *adj* inescapable, inevitable.

i'népcia *f* ineptitude; **inepto** *f a adj* inept, incompetent.

inequívoco/a [ɪne'kɪvoku/a] *adj* (*evidente*) clear; (*inconfundível*) unmistakeable.

i'nércia *f* (*torpor*) lassitude, lethargy; (*FÍSICA*) inertia.

ine'rente *adj* inherent.

in'erme *adj* (*lit*: *não armado*) unarmed; (*desprotegido*) defenceless.

in'erte *adj* still, motionless; (*FÍSICA*) inert.

inesgo'tável *adj* inexhaustible; (*superabundante*) boundless, abundant.

inespe'rado/a *adj* unexpected, unforeseen.

inesquecível [ɪne∫ke'sɪvew] *adj* unforgettable.

inesti'mável *adj* invaluable.

inevi'tável *adj* inevitable.

inexatidão [ɪnezat∫ɪ'dãw] (*Pt*: **-ct-**) *f* inaccuracy; **inexato/a** (*Pt*: **-ct-**) *adj* inaccurate.

inexpug'nável *adj* (*fortaleza*) impregnable; (*invencível*) invincible.

infa'lível *adj* infallible; (*inevitável*) inevitable.

in'fame *adj* (*notório*) notorious; (*detestável*) vile, shocking; **infâmia** *f* (*má fama*) notoriety; (*desonra*) disgrace; (*vileza*) villainy.

in'fância *f* infancy, childhood.

infanta'ria *f* infantry.

in'fante *m* (*filho dos reis*) prince; (*soldado*) foot soldier; **infantil** *adj* (*ingênuo*) childlike; (*pueril*) childish; (*para crianças*) children's *cmp*.

infati'gável *adj* untiring.

infausto/a [ɪ'faw∫tu/a] *adj* unlucky.

infecção [ɪfɛk'sãw] *f* infection; (*contaminação*) contamination; **infeccionar** *vt* (*ferida*) to infect; (*contaminar*) to contaminate; **infeccioso/a** *adj* infectious.

infelici'dade *f* unhappiness; (*desgraça*) misfortune; **infeliz** *adj* (*triste*) unhappy; (*infausto*) unfortunate; (*sem sorte*) unlucky; **infelizmente** *adv* unfortunately.

inferi'or *adj* (*em valor*) inferior; (*mais baixo*) lower // *m* inferior, subordinate; **~idade** *f* inferiority.

infe'rir *vt* to infer, deduce.

in'ferno *m* hell.

infes'tar vt (bandidos) to overrun; (ratos) to infest.

infe'tar (Pt: -ct-) vt to infect, contaminate.

infideli'dade f infidelity, unfaithfulness; (REL) disbelief; **infiel** adj (desleal) disloyal; (marido) unfaithful; (texto) inaccurate // m/f unbeliever.

'ínfimo/a adj lowest.

infini'dade f infinity; **uma ~ de** countless; **infinito/a** adj infinite // m infinity.

inflação [ifla'sãw] f inflation; **inflacionário/a** adj inflationary.

infla'mar vt (MED) to inflame; (fig) to excite; **~-se** vr to catch fire; (avermelhar-se) to go red; (fig) to get excited.

in'flar vt to inflate, blow up; **~-se** vr to swell (up).

infle'xível adj stiff, rigid; (fig) unyielding.

infligir [ifli'ʒix] vt: **~ alguma coisa a alguém** to inflict sth upon sb.

influ'ência f influence; **influenciar** vt to influence; **influente** adj influential.

influir [i'flwix] vi: **~ em** to influence, have an influence on.

influxo [i'fluksu] m influx; (preemar) high tide.

informação [ifoxma'sãw] f (comunicação) report; (MIL) intelligence; (JUR) inquiry; **informações** fpl information sg; **pedir informações sobre** to ask about, inquire about.

informal [ifox'maw] adj informal.

infor'mante m informant; (JUR) informer; **informar** vt to inform; **informar alguém de** to let sb know about // vi: **informar de** to report on, tell about; **informar-se** vr: **informar-se de** to find out about, inquire about.

in'forme adj shapeless // m report, statement.

infor'túnio m misfortune.

infração [ifra'sãw] (Pt: -cç-) f breach, infringement; (futebol) foul; **~ de trânsito** traffic offence; **infrator(a)** (Pt: -ct-) m/f offender, law breaker.

infringir [ifrĩ'ʒix] vt to infringe, contravene.

infru'tífero/a adj fruitless.

infun'dado/a adj groundless, unfounded.

infun'dir vt to infuse; (terror) to strike; (incutir) to instil.

ingente [ĩ'ʒẽtʃi] adj huge, enormous.

ingenuidade [ĩʒenwi'dadʒi] f (simplicidade) ingenuousness; **in-gênuo/a** adj (inocente) ingenuous.

ingerência [ĩʒe'rẽsja] f interference.

ingerir [ĩʒe'rix] vt to ingest; (engolir) to swallow.

Ingla'terra f England; **inglês/esa** adj English // m Englishman; (língua) English // f Englishwoman.

ingratidão [igratʃi'dãw] f ingratitude;

ingrato/a adj (mal agradecido) ungrateful; (desagradável) unpleasant.

ingredi'ente m ingredient.

'íngreme adj steep.

ingres'sar vi: **~ em** to enter, go into; (um clube) to join; **ingresso** m (entrada) entry; (admissão) admission; (bilhete) ticket.

inhaca [i'ɲaka] f (fedor) stink; (má sorte) bad luck.

ini'bir vt to inhibit; **~ de** to prevent from.

inici'al [-jaw] adj initial, first // f initial; **iniciar** vt to initiate; (começar) to begin, start; **iniciativa** f initiative; **início** m beginning; **de/no início** at first.

ini'migo/a adj, m/f enemy; **inimizade** f enmity, hatred.

iníquo/a [i'nikwa] adj iniquitous.

injeção [ĩʒe'sãw] (Pt: -cç-) f injection; **injetado/a** (Pt: -ct-) adj (olhos) bloodshot; **injetar** (Pt: -ct-) vt to inject.

injúria [ĩ'ʒurja] f (insulto) insult; (agravo) offence; (dano) harm; **injuriar** vt (insultar) to insult; (causar dano) to harm; **injurioso/a** adj insulting; (ofensivo) offensive.

injustiça [ĩʒuʃ'tʃisa] f injustice; **injusto/a** adj unfair, unjust.

ino'cência f innocence; **inocente** adj innocent; (ingênuo) simple, naïve // m/f (idiota) simpleton.

inocu'lar vt to inoculate.

inócuo/a [i'nɔkwu/a] adj harmless.

inofen'sivo/a adj harmless, inoffensive.

inopi'nado/a adj unexpected.

inopor'tuno/a adj inconvenient, inopportune.

in'óspito/a adj inhospitable.

inovação [inova'sãw] f innovation; **inovar** vt to innovate.

inoxi'dável adj: **aço ~** stainless steel.

inquebran'tável [ĩkebrã'tavew] adj unbreakable; (amizade) firm.

inquérito [ĩ'kɛritu] m inquiry; (JUR) inquest.

inquietação [ĩkjeta'sãw] f (preocupação) anxiety, uneasiness; (agitação) restlessness; **inquietar** vt to worry, disturb; **inquietar-se** vr to worry, bother; **inquieto/a** adj (ansioso) anxious, worried; (agitado) restless.

inquilino/a [ĩki'linu/a] m/f tenant.

inquirição [ĩkiri'sãw] f (indagação) investigation; (inquisição) interrogation; (JUR) cross-examination; **inquirir** vt (JUR) to cross-examine // vi to enquire.

insaciável [ĩsas'javew] adj insatiable.

insa'lubre adj unhealthy.

insani'dade f madness, insanity.

insatis'feito/a adj dissatisfied, unhappy.

inscre'ver vt to inscribe; (aluno) to enrol, register; **~-se** vr to enrol; **inscrição** f (legenda) inscription; (em escola) enrolment, registration.

insegu'rança *f* insecurity; **inseguro/a** *adj* insecure.

insensa'tez *f* folly, madness; **insensato/a** *adj* unreasonable, foolish.

insensibili'dade *f* insensitivity; (*indiferença*) callousness; **insensível** *adj* insensitive; (*dormente*) numb; (*despropositado*) nonsensical.

inse'rir *vt* to insert, put in.

inseti'cida (*Pt: -ct-*) *m* insecticide; **inseto** (*Pt: -ct-*) *m* insect.

insidi'oso/a *adj* insidious.

in'signe *adj* distinguished, eminent.

in'sígnia *f* (*sinal distintivo*) badge; (*emblema*) emblem; (*bandeira*) ensign.

insignifi'cante *adj* insignificant.

insinuação [ɪnsɪnwaˈsãw] *f* insinuation; (*sugestão*) hint; **insinuante** *adj* ingratiating; **insinuar** *vt* to insinuate, imply; **insinuar-se** *vr*: **insinuar-se por/entre** to slip into; **insinuar-se na confiança de alguém** to worm one's way into sb's confidence.

in'sípido/a *adj* insipid.

insis'tência *f* insistence; (*obstinação*) persistence; **insistir** *vi*: **insistir em** (*perseverar*) to persist in; (*exigir*) to insist on; (*fig: sublinhar*) to stress.

inso'frido/a *adj* impatient, restless.

insolação [ɪnsolaˈsãw] *f*: **pegar uma ~** to get sunstroke.

inso'lência *f* insolence; **insolente** *adj* insolent.

in'sólito/a *adj* unusual.

inso'lúvel *adj* insoluble.

insol'vência *f* insolvency.

inson'dável *adj* unfathomable.

in'sônia *f* insomnia.

in'sosso/a *adj* unsalted; (*sem sabor*) tasteless.

inspeção [ɪnʃpeˈsãw] (*Pt: -cç-*) *f* inspection, check; **inspecionar** (*Pt: -cc-*) *vt* (*oficialmente*) to inspect; (*observar*) to examine; (*conferir*) to check; **inspetor(a)** (*Pt: -ct-*) *m/f* inspector.

inspiração [ɪnʃpɪraˈsãw] *f* inspiration; **inspirar** *vt* to inspire; (*MED*) to inhale; **inspirar-se** *vr* to be inspired.

instalação [ɪnʃtalaˈsãw] *f* installation; **~ hidráulica** waterworks *sg*; **instalar** *vt* (*equipamento*) to install; (*estabelecer*) to set up; **instalar-se** *vr* (*numa cadeira*) to install o.s.; (*alojar-se*) to settle in.

in'stância *f* (*pedido urgente*) urgent request; (*pedido insistente*) entreaty, adjuration; (*JUR*) **tribunal de primeira ~** magistrate's court; **em última ~** as a last resort.

instan'tâneo/a *adj* instant, instantaneous // *m* (*FOTO*) snapshot; **instante** *m* instant, moment; **nesse instante** just a moment ago.

in'star *vt* to urge; **~ com alguém para que faça algo** to urge sb to do sth // *vi* (*estar iminente*) to be imminent, be about to happen; (*ser urgente*) to be urgent; (*insistir*) to insist.

instaurar [ɪnʃtawˈrax] *vt* to establish, set up.

in'stável *adj* unstable; (*tempo*) unsettled.

insti'gar *vt* (*incitar*) to urge; (*provocar*) to provoke.

in'stinto *m* instinct; **por ~** instinctively.

instituição [ɪnʃtʃitwɪˈsãw] *f* institution; **instituir** *vt* to institute; (*fundar*) to establish, found; **instituto** *m* (*escola*) institute; (*instituição*) institution.

instrução [ɪnʃtruˈsãw] (*Pt: -cç-*) *f* instruction; (*erudição*) learning; **instruído/a** *adj* educated; **instruir** *vt* to instruct; (*adestrar*) to train; (*educar*) to teach.

instru'mento *m* instrument; (*ferramenta*) implement.

instru'tor(a) (*Pt: -ct-*) *m* instructor; (*esporte*) coach // *f* instructress.

insubordi'nado/a *adj* unruly; **insubordinar-se** *vr* to rebel; (*NÁUT*) to mutiny.

insuficiência [ɪnsufisˈjɛsja] *f* shortage; (*MED*) deficiency; **insuficiente** *adj* (*não bastante*) insufficient.

insu'flar *vt* to blow up, inflate; (*fig*) to instil.

insu'lar *vt* (*TEC*) to insulate.

insu'lina *f* insulin.

insul'tar *vt* to insult; **insulto** *m* insult.

insupe'rável *adj* (*árduo*) insurmountable; (*excelente*) unsurpassable.

insupor'tável *adj* unbearable.

insurgente [ɪnsuxˈʒetʃi] *adj* rebellious // *m/f* rebel; **insurgir-se** *vr* to rebel, revolt; **insurreição** *f* rebellion, insurrection.

insus'peito/a [ɪnsuʃˈpejta/a] *adj* unsuspected; (*imparcial*) impartial.

insusten'tável *adj* untenable.

intangível [ɪntãˈʒɪvew] *adj* intangible.

in'tato/a (*Pt: -ct-*) *adj* intact; (*ileso*) unharmed; (*fig*) untouched.

inte'gral [-aw] *adj* whole; **pão ~** wholemeal bread // *f* (*MAT*) integral; **integrar** *vt* to unite, combine; (*MAT, RAÇAS*) to integrate.

integri'dade *f* integrity; **íntegro/a** *adj* entire; (*reto*) upright, honest.

inteiramente [ɪntejraˈmetʃi] *adv* entirely, completely.

inteirar [ɪntejˈrax] *vt* (*completar*) to complete; **~ alguém de** to inform sb about/of; **~-se** *vr*: **~-se de** to find out about; **inteireza** *f* entirety; (*integridade*) integrity; **inteiro/a** *adj* (*total*) whole, entire; (*ileso*) unharmed; (*não quebrado*) undamaged.

inte'lecto *m* intellect; **intelectual** *adj, m/f* intellectual.

inteligência [ɪnteliˈʒesja] *f* intelligence; **inteligente** *adj* intelligent, clever; **inteligível** *adj* intelligible.

intem'périe *f* bad weather.

intenção [ɪnteˈsãw] *f* intention; **segundas intenções** ulterior motives; **ter a ~ de** to intend to; **inten-**

cionado/a adj: bem intencionado well-meaning; mal intencionado ill-intentioned; intencional adj intentional, deliberate.

inten'dência f (Pt) management, administration.

intensi'dade f intensity; intenso/a adj intense; (emoção) deep; (impressão) vivid.

inten'tar vt to try, attempt; (JUR) ~ uma ação contra to sue; intento m aim, purpose.

interca'lar vt to insert.

inter'câmbio m (troca) exchange.

interce'der vi: ~ por to intercede on behalf of; intercessão f intercession.

interco'stal adj, pl interco'stais (MED) intercostal.

interdição [ĩtexdʒi'sãw] f prohibition, ban; interditado/a adj prohibited, forbidden; interdito/a adj prohibited, forbidden // m prohibition, ban; (JUR) injunction.

interes'sante adj interesting; interessar vt to interest, be of interest to; interessar-se vr: interessar-se em/por to take an interest in, be interested in; interesse m interest; (próprio) self-interest; (proveito) advantage; no interesse de for the sake of; interesseiro/a adj self-seeking.

interfe'rência f interference; interferir vi: interferir em to interfere in; (rádio) to jam.

ínterim [ˈĩterĩ] m interim; nesse ~ in the meantime.

inte'rino/a adj temporary, interim.

interi'or adj inner, inside; (COM) domestic, internal // m inside, interior; (coração) heart; (do país) no ~ inland, in the country; Ministério do I~ Home Office.

interjeição [ĩtexʒej'sãw] f interjection.

intermedi'ário/a adj intermediary // m (COM) middleman; intermédio m intermediary; (intervenção) intervention; por intermédio de by means of, through; (pessoa) through the intervention of.

intermi'nável adj endless.

intermissão [ĩtexmi'sãw] f interval; intermitente adj intermittent.

internacio'nal adj international.

inter'nar vt to intern; (aluno) to put into boarding school; (doente) to put into hospital; internato m boarding school; interno/a adj internal, interior; (do país) domestic // m/f (aluno) boarder; (em hospital) intern.

interpe'lar vt to challenge; (pessoa) to question.

inter'por vt to put in, interpose; ~-se vr to intervene.

interpretação [ĩtexpreta'sãw] f interpretation; (teatro) performance; interpretar vt to interpret; (um papel) to play, perform; intérprete m/f interpreter; (teatro) performer, artist.

interrogação [ĩtexoga'sãw] f ques-tioning, interrogation; ponto de ~ question mark; interrogar vt to question, interrogate; interrogatório m cross-examination.

interrom'per vt to interrupt; (parar) to stop; (ELET) to cut off; ~-se vr to break off, pause; interrupção f interruption; (intervalo) break; interruptor m (ELET) switch.

interseção [ĩtexse'sãw] (Pt: -cç-) f intersection.

interur'bano/a adj: telefonema ~ trunk call.

inter'valo m interval; (descanso) break; a ~s every now and then.

intervenção [ĩtexvẽ'sãw] f intervention; (MED) operation; intervir vi to intervene; (tomar parte) to participate.

intes'tino/a adj (interno) internal; (nacional) domestic // m intestine.

inti'mar vt to announce; (JUR) to summon; ~ alguém a fazer to order sb to do.

intimi'dade f intimacy; (vida privada) private life; (familiaridade) familiarity; íntimo/a adj intimate; (sentimentos) innermost; (amigo) close; (vida) private; no íntimo at heart // m/f close friend.

intole'rância f intolerance; intolerável adj intolerable, unbearable.

intoxicação [ĩtɔksika'sãw] f poisoning.

intransigente [ĩtrãsi'ʒẽtʃi] adj uncompromising; (rígido) strict.

intransi'tável adj impassable.

intrepi'dez f courage, bravery; intrépido/a adj daring, intrepid.

intri'cado/a adj intricate.

in'triga f intrigue; (enredo) plot; ~ amorosa (Pt) love affair; intrigante m/f troublemaker // adj intriguing; intrigar vt to intrigue.

in'trínseco/a adj intrinsic.

introdução [ĩtrodu'sãw] f introduction; introduzir vt to introduce; (prego) to insert; introduzir-se vr to get into.

introme'ter-se vr to interfere, meddle; intrometido/a adj interfering; (col) nosey // m/f busybody.

intrujão [ĩtru'ʒãw] m swindler; intrujar vt to trick, swindle.

in'truso/a m/f intruder.

intuição [ĩtwi'sãw] f intuition; intuito m (intento) intention; (fim) aim, purpose.

intumescência [ĩtume'sẽsja] f swelling; intumescer-se vr to swell (up); intumescido/a adj swollen.

inume'rável adj, i'número/a adj countless, innumerable.

inundação [ĩũda'sãw] f (enchente) flood; (ato) flooding; inundar vt to flood; (fig) to inundate.

inusi'tado/a adj unusual.

inútil [ĩ'nutʃiw] adj useless; (esforço) futile; ser ~ to be of no use, be no good; inutilidade f uselessness; inutilizar vt to make useless, render useless; inutilizar-

se *vr* to become useless; **inutilmente** *adv* in vain.

inva'dir *vt* to invade.

in'válido/a *adj, m/f* invalid.

invari'ável *adj* invariable; *(constante)* constant.

invasão [ɪnvaˈzãw] *f* invasion; **invasor(a)** *adj* invading // *m/f* invader.

inveja [ɪnˈveʒa] *f* envy; *(ciúme)* jealousy; **invejar** *vt* to envy; *(cobiçar: bens)* to covet // *vi* to be envious; **invejoso/a** *adj* envious.

invenção [ɪnvěˈsãw] *f* invention; **inventar** *vt* to invent; *(uma história)* to make up.

inven'tário *m* inventory.

inven'tiva *f* inventiveness; **inventor(a)** *m/f* inventor.

in'verno *m* winter.

inveros'símil *(Pt: -osí-) adj* unlikely, improbable.

inversão [ɪnvexˈsãw] *f* reversal, inversion; *(COM)* investment; **inverso/a** *adj* inverse; *(oposto)* opposite; *(ordem)* reverse; **ao inverso de** contrary to; **inversor(a)** *m/f* investor; **inverter** *vt* (*COM*) to invest; *(mudar)* to alter; *(colocar às avessas)* to turn upside down, invert; **inverter a marcha** *(AUTO)* to reverse.

in'vés *m* wrong side; **ao ~** on the contrary; **ao ~ de** contrary to.

investigação [ɪnveʃtʃigaˈsãw] *f* investigation; *(estudo)* research; **investigar** *vt* to investigate; *(examinar)* to examine; *(estudar)* to research into.

investi'mento *m* investment; **investir** *vt* to invest; **investir contra** *(atacar)* to attack; **investir alguém no cargo de presidente** to install sb in the presidency // *vi* : **investir com** to set upon, attack.

in'victo/a *adj* unconquered.

invi'sível *adj* invisible.

invo'car *vt* to invoke, call on.

in'vólucro *m* *(cobertura)* covering; *(envoltório)* wrapping.

iodo [ˈjodu] *m* iodine.

ioga [ˈjɔga] *f* yoga.

iogurte [joˈgurtʃi] *m* yogurt.

ir *vi* to go; **~ a cavalo/a pé** to ride/walk; **~ de avião/de carro** to fly/drive; **~ ter com** *(Pt)* to meet; **~ bem** to be all right; *(harmonizar)* to go well; **~ buscar** to fetch, go and get; **~ falando** to keep on talking; **~ melhor** *(de saúde)* to be feeling better; **~ morrendo** to be dying; **como vai?** how are you?; **~-se** *vr* : **~-se embora** to go away.

'ira *f* anger, rage; **irado/a** *adj* angry, irate.

Irã [ɪˈrã] *(Pt:* **Irão***) m* Iran; **iraniano/a** *adj, m/f* Iranian.

ira'scível *adj* irritable, short-tempered.

'íris *m* iris.

Ir'landa *f* Ireland; **irlandês/esa** *adj* Irish

// *m* Irishman; *(língua)* Irish // *f* Irishwoman.

irmã [ɪxˈmã] *f* sister; **irmanar** *vt* to join together, unite; **irmandade** *f* brotherhood; *(confraternidade)* fraternity; **irmão** *m* brother.

iro'nia *f* irony; **irônico/a** *adj* ironic(al).

'irra! *excl (Pt)* damn!

irradi'ar *vt (luz)* to radiate; *(espalhar)* to spread; *(rádio)* to broadcast, transmit // *vi* to radiate; *(rádio)* to be on the air; **~-se** *vr (propagar-se)* to spread; *(rádio)* to be transmitted.

irre'al *adj* unreal.

irreconcili'ável *adj* irreconcilable.

irrefle'tido/a *adj* rash, thoughtless.

irremedi'ável *adj (sem remédio)* incurable; *(sem esperança)* hopeless.

irresis'tível *adj* irresistible; *(desejo)* overwhelming.

irrespon'sável *adj* irresponsible.

irri'gar *vt* to irrigate.

irri'sório/a *adj* derisory, ludicrous.

irri'tar *vt* to irritate; *(agastar)* to annoy; **~-se** *vr* to get angry, get annoyed.

'isca *f (pesca)* bait; *(fig)* lure, bait.

isenção [ɪzěˈsãw] *f* exemption; **isentar** *vt* to exempt; *(livrar)* to free; **isento/a** *adj (dispensado)* exempt; *(livre)* free.

Is'lã *m* Islam.

Is'lândia *f* Iceland.

iso'lado/a *adj (separado)* isolated; *(solitário)* lonely; **isolamento** *m* isolation; *(MED)* isolation ward; *(ELET)* insulation; **isolar** *vt* to isolate; *(ELET)* to insulate.

isqueiro [ɪʃˈkejru] *m* (cigarette) lighter.

Isra'el *m* Israel; **israelense** *adj, m/f* Israeli.

'isso *pron* that, that thing; **~ mesmo** exactly; **por ~** therefore, so; **só ~?** is that all?

'istmo *m* isthmus.

'isto *pron* this, this thing; **~ é** that is, namely.

I'tália *f* Italy; **italiano/a** *adj, m/f* Italian.

i'tálico *m* italics *pl.*

itine'rário *m (plano)* itinerary; *(caminho)* route; *(livro)* guidebook.

Iugoslávia [jugoʃˈlavia] *f* Yugoslavia.

J

já [ʒa] *adv (de antemão)* already; *(agora)* now; *(sem demora)* right now, at once; *(em pouco tempo)* soon; **até ~** (good)bye; **desde ~** from now on; **é para ~** it won't be a minute; **~ esteve na Inglaterra?** have you ever been to England?; **~ não** no longer, no more; **~ não vem** he doesn't come any more; **~ que** now that, since; **~ se vê** of course; **~ vou** I'm coming.

jaça [ˈʒasa] *f* fault, imperfection.

jaca'ré *m* alligator.

jacente [ʒaˈsětʃi] *adj* lying; *(herança)* unclaimed.

jacinto [ʒa'sĩtu] m hyacinth.

jac'tância f boasting; **jactar-se** vr: jactar-se de to boast about.

ja'ez m harness; (categoria) sort.

jaguar [ʒa'gwax] m jaguar.

ja'gunço m hired gun(man), bandit.

ja'leco m jacket.

jamais [ʒa'majʃ] adv never; (com palavra negativa) ever; **ninguém ~ veio** nobody ever came.

ja'manta f juggernaut.

janeiras [ʒa'nejraʃ] fpl (canções) carols; (presentes) New Year's gifts.

janeiro [ʒa'nejru] (Pt: J-) m January.

jan'ela f window.

jan'gada f raft, float.

ja'nota m dandy.

'janta f dinner.

jan'tar m supper; (ceia) dinner // vt to have for supper // vi to dine.

Japão [ʒa'pãw] m Japan; **japonês/esa** adj, m/f Japanese.

jaqueta [ʒa'keta] f jacket.

jardim [ʒax'dʒĩ] m garden; **~ zoológico** zoo; **~-de-infância** m kindergarten; **jardineiro/a** m/f gardener // f (móvel) flower-stand; (ônibus) open bus; (professora) kindergarten teacher.

jargão [ʒax'gãw] m (gíria profissional) jargon.

'jarra f jar.

jar'rete m hamstring.

'jarro m jug.

jasmim [ʒaʒ'mĩ] m jasmine.

jato ['ʒatu] (Pt: -ct-) m jet; (líquido) gush; (luz) stream.

jaula ['ʒawla] f cage.

java'li m wild boar.

ja'zer vi to lie; **jazigo** m grave; (monumento) tomb; (GEO) deposit.

jeito ['ʒejtu] m (maneira) way, manner; (aspecto) appearance; (propensão) skill, knack; **a ~** conveniently, handily; **falta de ~** clumsiness; **ter ~ de** to look like; **jeitoso/a** adj (hábil) skilful; (elegante) handsome; (apropriado) suitable.

jejuar [ʒe'ʒwax] vi to fast; **jejum** m fast.

jerarquia [ʒerax'kia] f ver **hierarquia.**

je'rico m donkey; **idéia de ~** stupid idea.

je'suíta m Jesuit; **Jesus** m Jesus.

jibóia [ʒi'bɔja] f boa (constrictor).

'jipe m jeep.

joalheiro [ʒoa'ʎejru] m jeweller; **joalheria** f jeweller's (shop).

joão-ninguém [ʒwãw-nĩ'gẽj] m (a) nobody.

jo'coso/a adj jocular, humorous.

joelho [ʒo'eʎu] m knee; **de ~s** kneeling.

joga'dor(a) m/f player; (jogador de azar) gambler; **jogar** vt to play; (fazer apostas) to gamble; (atirar) to fling, throw; **jogo** m play; (partida) game; (de azar) gamble; **jogo de palavras** pun, play on words; **em jogo** at stake.

jóia ['ʒɔja] f jewel.

jor'nada f (viagem) day's journey; (dia de trabalho) working day.

jor'nal m newspaper; **~ falado** news bulletin; **~eiro** m (day) labourer; **~ista** m journalist, newspaperman // f newspaperwoman.

jor'rar vi to gush, spurt out; **jorro** m jet; (fig) stream, flood.

jovem ['ʒɔvẽ] adj young // m young man, youth // f young woman, girl.

jovi'al adj jovial, cheerful.

'juba f (de leão) mane.

jubilação [ʒubila'sãw] f jubilation; (aposentadoria) retirement; **jubilar** vt (aposentar) to retire, pension off // vi to rejoice; **jubilar-se** vr to retire.

jubileu [ʒubi'lew] m jubilee.

'júbilo m rejoicing.

judeu/judia [ʒu'dew/ʒu'dʒja] adj Jewish // m Jew // f Jewess; **judiação** f maltreatment; **judiaria** f (crueldade) ill treatment.

judica'tura f (cargo) office of judge; (magistratura) judicature; **judicial** adj, **judiciário/a** adj judicial; **judicioso/a** adj judicious, wise.

'jugo m yoke; (fig) oppression.

juiz(a) ['ʒuiʃ(za)] m/f judge // m (árbitro) referee; **juizo** m judgement; (parecer) opinion; (siso) common sense; **Juizo Final** Day of Judgement, doomsday; **perder o juizo** to lose one's mind.

julga'mento m judgement; (audiência) trial; (sentença) sentence; **julgar** vt to judge; (achar) to think.

julho ['ʒuʎu] (Pt: J-) m July.

ju'mento/a m/f donkey.

junco m reed, rush.

junho ['ʒuɲu] (Pt: J-) m June.

'juntar vt to join, connect; (ajuntar) to bring together, unite; **junto/a** adj joined; (chegado) near; **ir juntos** to go together; **junto a/de** near/next to // f (comissão) board, committee, commission; (articulação) joint; **juntura** f join; (articulação) joint.

'jura f oath; **jurado/a** m/f juror; **juramento** m oath, vow; **jurar** vt/i to swear.

júri ['ʒuri] m jury.

ju'rídico/a adj legal.

jurisdição [ʒuriʃdʒi'sãw] f jurisdiction; **jurisprudência** f jurisprudence; **jurista** m/f jurist.

'juro m (ECON) interest.

justeza [ʒuʃ'teza] f rightness; (precisão) exactness, precision.

justiça [ʒuʃ'tʃisa] f justice; (eqüidade) fairness; **com ~** justly, fairly.

justiceiro/a [ʒuʃtʃi'sejru/a] adj upright; (equitativo) impartial.

justificação [ʒuʃtʃifĩka'sãw] f justification; **justificar** vt to justify.

justo/a ['ʒuʃtu/a] adj just, fair, right; (exato) exact; (apertado) tight.

juve'nil [-īw] adj youthful; **juventude** f youth; (jovialidade) youthfulness; (jovens) young people pl.

L

L *abr de* **Largo** (*endereços*) Square.
lá *adv* there; ~ **fora** outside; ~ **em baixo** down there; **por** ~ (*direção*) that way, over there; (*situação*) over there.
lã [lã] *f* wool.
laba'reda *f* flame; (*fig*) ardour.
'labia *f* lip; **ter** ~ to have the gift of the gab.
'lábio *m* lip.
labi'rinto *m* labyrinth, maze.
la'bor *m* work, labour.
labora'tório *m* laboratory.
labori'oso/a *adj* (*diligente*) hardworking; (*árduo*) laborious.
la'buta *f* toil, drudgery; **labutar** *vi* to toil; (*esforçar-se*) to struggle, strive.
'laca *f* lacquer.
lacaio [la'kaju] *m* lackey.
la'çar *vt* to bind, tie; **laço** *m* knot; (*laçada*) bow; (*armadilha*) snare; (*fig*) bond, tie.
la'cónico/a *adj* laconic.
la'craia *f* centipede.
la'crar *vt* to seal (with wax).
'lacrau *m* scorpion.
'lacre *m* sealing wax.
lacri'moso/a *adj* tearful.
'lácteo/a *adj* milky; **via** ~**a** Milky Way.
la'cuna *f* gap; (*omissão*) omission.
ladainha [lada'iɲa] *f* litany.
lade'ar *vt* (*flanquear*) to flank.
ladeira [la'dejra] *f* slope, hillside.
la'dino/a *adj* cunning, crafty.
'lado *m* side; (*MIL*) flank; (*rumo*) direction; **ao** ~ **de** beside; **de** ~ sideways; **pôr de** ~ to set aside; **por outro** ~ on the other hand; **de um** ~ **para outro** back and forth.
'ladra *f* thief.
ladrão [la'drãw] *m* thief, robber.
la'drar *vi* to bark.
ladrilho [la'driʎu] *m* tile.
la'gar *m* fruit press.
la'garta *f* caterpillar.
la'garto *m* lizard.
'lago *m* lake; **lagoa** *f* pool, pond.
la'gosta *f* lobster; **lagostim** *m* crayfish.
'lágrima *f* tear; (*gota*) drop.
la'guna *f* lagoon.
laia ['laja] *f* kind, sort, type.
laivo ['lajvu] *m* (*mancha*) stain; (*nódoa*) spot; ~**s** *mpl* smattering.
'laje *f* paving stone, flagstone; **lajear** *vt* to pave.
'lama *f* mud; ~**çal** *m* quagmire, mud patch; ~**cento/a** *adj* muddy.
lambão/bona [lam'bãw/'bona] *adj* greedy, gluttonous; (*desmazelado*) sloppy.
lam'ber *vt* to lick.
lamen'tar *vt* to lament; (*sentir*) to regret; **lamentável** *adj* regrettable; (*deplorável*) deplorable; **lamento** *m* lament; (*gemido*) moan.
'lâmina *f* (*chapa*) sheet; (*placa*) plate; (*de faca*) blade.

'lâmpada *f* lamp; ~ **elétrica** light bulb; **lampião** *m* lantern; (*de rua*) street lamp.
lança ['lãsa] *f* lance, spear.
lançadeira [lãsa'dejra] *f* shuttle.
lança'mento *m* throwing; (*NÁUT, COM*) launching; **lançar** *vt* to throw, fling; (*NÁUT, COM*) to launch; (*MED*) to vomit; **lance** *m* (*acontecimento*) incident; (*crise*) emergency; (*aventura*) exploit; (*impulso*) fit; (*esporte*) stroke, shot; (*leilão*) bid; (*de escada*) flight.
lancha ['lãʃa] *f* launch; ~ **torpedeira** torpedo boat.
lanche ['lãʃi] *m* snack.
lanchonete [lãʃo'netʃi] *f* (*Br*) snack bar.
langui'dez *f* languor, listlessness; **lânguido/a** *adj* languid; (*sem energia*) listless.
la'nhar *vt* to slash, gash; (*fig: estropiar*) to murder; **lanho** *m* slash, gash.
lan'terna *f* lantern.
lanter'ninha *m/f* (*Br*) usher(ette).
la'nudo/a *adj* woolly; **lanugem** *f* down, fluff.
'lapa *f* (*abrigo*) cave, grotto.
la'pela *f* lapel.
lapi'dar *vt* (*apedrejar*) to stone; (*jóias*) to cut; (*aperfeiçoar*) to polish, refine; **lápide** *f* tombstone.
'lápis *m* pencil; **lapiseira** *f* propelling pencil; (*caixa*) pencil case.
'lapso *m* lapse; (*de tempo*) interval; (*erro*) slip.
lar *m* hearth, fireside; (*casa*) home.
laranja [la'rãʒa] *f* orange; **laranjada** *f* orangeade; **laranjal** *m* orange grove; **laranjeira** *f* orange tree.
la'rápio *m* thief.
lareira [la'rejra] *f* hearth, fireside.
'larga *f*: **à** ~ lavishly, generously; **dar** ~**s a** to give free rein to; **largada** *f* (*corrida*) start; **largar** *vt* to let go of, release; (*conceder*) to concede, give up // *vi* to leave, depart.
'largo/a *adj* wide, broad; (*amplo*) extensive; **ao** ~ at a distance, far off; **fazer-se ao** ~ to put out to sea; **passar de** ~ **sobre** to overlook, ignore; **mede 5 metros de** ~ it is 5 metres wide // *m* (*praça*) square; **largueza** *f* liberality; **largura** *f* width, breadth.
laringe [la'rĩʒi] *f* larynx.
larva *f* larva, grub.
'lasca *f* (*de madeira*) splinter, chip; (*de pedra*) chip; (*fatia*) slice.
lascivo/a [la'sivu/a] *adj* lewd.
lassidão [lasi'dãw], **lassi'tude** *f* lassitude, weariness.
'lástima *f* pity, compassion; (*desgraça*) misfortune; **lastimar** *vt* to lament; **lastimar-se** *vr* to complain, be sorry for o.s.; **lastimoso/a** *adj* (*lamentável*) pitiful; (*plangente*) mournful.
'lastro *m* ballast.
'lata *f* tin, can; (*material*) tin-plate; ~ **de lixo** rubbish bin, garbage can (*US*).
la'tada *f* trellis.
latão [la'tãw] *m* brass.

'látego *m* whip.

latejar [latɛˈʒax] *vi* to throb, beat; **latejo** *m* throbbing, beat.

la'tente *adj* latent, hidden.

late'ral *adj* side, lateral // *f* (*futebol*) sideline // *m* (*futebol*) throw-in.

la'tido *m* bark(ing), yelp(ing).

lati'fúndio *m* large estate.

latim [laˈtʃĩ] *m* (*LING*) Latin; **gastar o seu ~** to waste one's breath.

la'tino/a *adj* Latin; **~-americano/a** *adj*, *m/f* Latin-American.

la'tir *vi* to bark, yelp.

lati'tude *f* latitude; (*largura*) breadth; (*fig*) scope.

'lato/a *adj* broad.

latrocínio [latroˈsĩju] *m* armed robbery.

laudo [ˈlawdu] *m* (*JUR*) decision, findings *pl*.

laure'ado/a *adj* honoured // *m* laureate; **laurel** *m* laurel wreath; (*fig*) prize, reward.

lauto/a [ˈlawtu/a] *adj* sumptuous; (*abundante*) lavish, abundant.

'lava *f* lava.

la'vabo *m* washbasin; **~s** (*Pt*) toilets; **lavadora** *f* washing machine; **lavadouro** *m* washing place.

lavagem [laˈvaʒẽ] *f* washing; (*restos*) slops *pl*; **~ a seco** dry cleaning; **~ cerebral** brainwashing; **lavanderia** *f* laundry; **lavar** *vt* to wash; **lavar a seco** to dry clean.

la'vatório *m* (*Pt*) washbasin.

lavoura [laˈvora] *f* tilling; (*agricultura*) farming; (*terreno*) plantation.

'lavra *f* ploughing; (*mina*) mine; **ser da ~ de** to be the work of; **lavrador** *m* farmer; **lavrar** *vt* to work; (*esculpir*) to carve; (*redigir*) to draw up.

laxante [laˈʃãtʃi] *adj*, *m* laxative.

leal [liˈaw] *adj* loyal; **~dade** *f* loyalty.

leão [leˈãw] *m* lion.

'lebre *f* hare.

lecionar [lɛsjoˈnax] (*Pt*: **-cc-**) *vt* to teach, instruct.

legação [legaˈsãw] *f* legation; **legado** *m* envoy, legate; (*herança*) legacy, bequest.

le'gal *adj* legal, lawful; (*col*) great, fine; **~idade** *f* legality, lawfulness; **~izar** *vt* to legalize; (*autenticar*) to authenticate.

le'gar *vt* to bequeath, leave; **legatário/a** *m/f* legatee.

legenda [leˈʒẽda] *f* inscription; (*letreiro*) caption; (*cinema*) subtitle.

legião [leʒiˈãw] *f* legion.

legislação [leʒizlaˈsãw] *f* legislation; **legislar** *vi* to legislate.

legiti'mar *vt* to legitimize; **legítimo/a** *adj* legitimate; (*justo*) rightful; (*autêntico*) genuine.

legível [leˈʒivew] *adj* legible, readable.

légua [ˈlɛgwa] *f* league.

le'gume *m* vegetable.

lei [lej] *f* law; (*regra*) rule; (*metal*) standard.

leigo/a [ˈlejgu/a] *adj* (*REL*) lay, secular; (*fig*) ignorant // *m* layman.

leilão [lejˈlãw] *m* auction.

'leio *etc vb ver* **ler**.

leitão [lejˈtãw] *m* sucking pig.

leite [ˈlejtʃi] *m* milk; **~ em pó** powdered milk; **~ desnatado** skimmed milk; **~ de magnésia** milk of magnesia; **leiteira** *f* (*para ferver*) milk pan; (*para servir*) milk jug; **leiteria** *f* dairy.

'leito *m* (*ger*) bed; (*camada*) layer.

lei'tor(a) *m/f* reader; **leitura** *f* reading.

'lema *m* motto; (*POL*) slogan.

lem'brança *f* recollection, memory; (*presente*) souvenir; **~s** *fpl* : **~s a sua mãe!** regards to your mother!; **lembrar** *vt* (*fazer recordar*) to remind; (*ter memória de*) to recall; **lembrar-se** *vr* : **lembrar-se de** to remember.

'leme *m* rudder; (*NÁUT*) helm; (*fig*) control.

'lenço *m* handkerchief; (*de pescoço*) headscarf.

len'çol [-ow] *m* sheet; **em maus lençóis** in a fix.

'lenda *f* legend; **lendário/a** *adj* legendary.

'lêndea *f* (*piolho*) nit.

lenha [ˈleɲa] *f* firewood; **~dor** *m* woodcutter; **lenho** *m* (*madeira*) log; (*material*) timber.

leni'tivo/a *adj* soothing // *m* palliative; (*alívio*) relief.

'lente *f* lens *sg*; **~s de contato** *fpl* contact lenses.

lentidão [lẽtʃiˈdãw] *f* slowness.

lentilha [lẽˈtʃiʎa] *f* lentil.

'lento/a *adj* slow.

le'oa *f* lioness.

leo'pardo *m* leopard.

'lepra *f* leprosy; **leproso/a** *adj* leprous // *m/f* leper.

leque [ˈlɛki] *m* fan.

ler *vt* to read.

'lerdo/a *adj* slow, sluggish; (*tolo*) dull, stupid.

lés *m* : **de ~ a ~** (*Pt*) from one end to the other.

lesão [leˈzãw] *f* lesion; (*fig*) injury; (*JUR*) violation; **lesar** *vt* to injure; (*JUR*) to violate.

'lésbica *f* lesbian.

lesma *f* slug; (*fig*) sluggard.

'leso/a *adj* injured, wounded; (*tolhido*) paralytic, palsied; (*idiota*) daft; (*prejudicado*) wronged; **crime de ~a majestade** high treason.

'leste *m* east.

le'tal [-aw] *adj* lethal.

letargia [letaxˈʒia] *f* lethargy.

le'tivo/a (*Pt*: **-ct-**) *adj* school *cmp*; **ano ~** academic year.

'letra *f* letter; (*caligrafia*) handwriting; (*de canção*) lyrics *pl*; **~ de câmbio** (*COM*) bill of exchange; **~ de imprensa** print; **ao pé da ~** literally, word for word; **letrado/a** *adj* learned, erudite // *m/f* scholar.

letreiro [let'rejru] *m* sign, notice; (*inscrição*) inscription; (*legenda*) caption.

léu [lɛw] *m*: **ao ~** (*à vontade*) at random, aimlessly.

'leva *f* (*NÁUT*) weighing anchor; (*MIL*) levy; (*alistamento*) recruitment.

le'vado/a *adj* mischievous.

levanta'mento *m* lifting, raising; (*revolta*) uprising, rebellion; (*arrolamento*) survey.

levan'tar *vt* to lift, raise; (*apanhar*) to pick up; (*suscitar*) to arouse; **~ vôo** (*AER*) to take off; **~-se** *vr* to get up, stand up; (*rebelar-se*) to rebel.

le'vante *m* east; (*revolta*) revolt.

le'var *vt* to take; (*portar*) to bear, carry; (*tirar*) to take away; (*tempo*) to pass, spend; (*roupa*) to wear; **~ a mal** to take amiss; **~ a cabo** to carry out; **~ adiante** to go ahead with; **~ uma vida feliz** to lead a happy life; **~ em conta** to take into account.

'leve *adj* light; (*insignificante*) slight; **(ao) de ~** lightly, softly.

le'vedo *m*, **leve'dura** *f* yeast.

levian'dade *f* frivolity; **leviano/a** *adj* frivolous; (*inconstante*) fickle.

'léxico *m* dictionary, lexicon.

'le'zíria *f* (*Pt*) marshland.

lha(s) = lhe + a(s).

lhaneza [ʎa'neza] *f* frankness; (*singeleza*) simplicity; (*afabilidade*) amiability; **lhano/a** *adj* frank; (*simples*) straightforward; (*amável*) amiable.

lhe *pron* (*a ele*) to him; (*a ela*) to her; (*a você*) to you; **~s** *pl* (*a eles/elas*) to them; (*a vocês*) to you.

lho(s) = lhe + o(s).

'lia *f* dregs *pl*, sediment.

li'ame *m* tie, bond.

liba'nês/esa *adj* Lebanese; **Líbano** *m*: **o Líbano** the Lebanon.

li'belo *m* satire, lampoon; (*JUR*) formal indictment.

li'bélula *f* dragonfly.

libe'ral *adj* generous; (*tolerante*) liberal // *m/f* liberal; **~idade** *f* liberality; **~ismo** *m* liberalism.

libe'rar *vt* to free, release.

liber'dade *f* freedom; **~ condicional** probation; **~ sob palavra** parole; **pôr em ~** to set free; **libertador** *m* liberator; **libertar** *vt* to free.

liber'tino/a *adj* loose-living // *m/f* libertine.

li'berto/a *pp irr de* **libertar.**

libidi'noso/a *adj* lecherous, lustful.

'libra *f* pound; **~ esterlina** pound sterling; **L~** (*ASTRO*) Libra.

lição [li'sãw] *f* lesson.

licença [li'sēsa] *f* (*ger*) licence, license (*US*); (*permissão*) permission; (*MIL*) leave; **em ~** on leave; **com ~** excuse me; **dá ~?** may I?; **licenciado/a** *m/f* graduate; **licenciar** *vt* to license; **licenciar-se** *vr* (*EDUC*) to graduate; **licenciatura** *f* degree.

licenci'oso/a *adj* licentious.

liceu [li'sew] *m* (*Pt*) secondary school.

licitação [lisita'sãw] *f* auction; **licitante** *m/f* bidder; **licitar** *vt* (*pôr em leilão*) to put up for auction.

'lícito/a *adj* lawful; (*justo*) fair, just; (*permissível*) permissible.

li'cor *m* liqueur; (*líquido*) liquor.

'lida *f* toil; **lidar** *vi* to toil; (*lutar*) to strive, struggle.

'liga *f* league; (*de meias*) garter, suspender; (*QUÍM*) alloy.

ligação [liga'sãw] *f* connection; **ligado/a** *adj* (*TEC*) connected; (*luz, rádio etc*) on.

liga'dura *f* bandage; (*MÚS*) ligature.

li'gar *vt* to tie, bind; (*unir*) to join, connect; (*abrir*) to switch on; **~ importância a** to pay attention to; **~ para** to telephone, ring up.

ligeireza [liʒej'reza] *f* lightness; (*rapidez*) swiftness; (*agilidade*) nimbleness; **ligeiro/a** *adj* light; (*de importância*) slight; (*rápido*) quick, swift; (*ágil*) nimble.

li'lás *adj, m* lilac.

'lima *f* (*BOT*) lime; (*ferramenta*) file.

limão [li'mãw] *m* lemon.

li'mar *vt* to file; (*fig*) to polish.

limeira [li'mejra] *f* lime tree.

limi'ar *m* threshold.

limitação [limita'sãw] *f* limitation, restriction; **limitar** *vt* to limit, restrict; **limitar-se** *vr*: **limitar-se a** to limit o.s. to; **limitar-se com** to border on; **limite** *m* limit, boundary.

'limo *m* (*BOT*) water weed; (*lodo*) slime.

limoeiro [lim'wejru] *m* lemon tree; **limonada** *f* lemonade.

limpa'dor *m*: **~ de pára-brisas** windscreen wiper, windshield wiper (*US*); **limpar** *vt* to clean; (*enxugar*) to wipe; (*polir*) to shine, polish; (*fig*) to clean up; **limpeza** *f* cleanliness; (*esmero*) neatness; (*ato*) cleaning; (*fig*) clean-up.

'limpo/a *pp irr de* **limpar** // *adj* (*COM*) net, clear; (*fig*) pure; **passar a ~** to make a fair copy; **tirar a ~** to find out the truth about, clear up.

'lince *m* lynx; **ter olhos de ~** to have eyes like a hawk.

linchar [lĩ'ʃax] *vt* to lynch.

'lindo/a *adj* pretty, lovely; (*fig*) fine.

língua ['lĩgwa] *f* tongue; (*linguagem*) language; **dar com a ~ nos dentes** to let the cat out of the bag; **estar na ponta da ~** to be on the tip of one's tongue.

linguado [lĩ'gwadu] *m* (*peixe*) sole.

linguagem [lĩ'gwaʒẽ] *f* language; (*falada*) speech.

linguarudo/a [lĩgwa'rudu/a] *adj* gossiping.

lingüeta [lĩ'gweta] *f* (*balança*) pointer; (*fechadura*) bolt.

lingüiça [lĩ'gwisa] *f* sausage.

lingüista [lĩ'gwiʃta] *m/f* linguist; **lingüística** *f* linguistics *sg*.

linha ['lĩɲa] *f* line; (*fio*) cord, thread; (*ELET*) cable, wire; (*fila*) row; **~ de**

montagem assembly line; ~ **reta** straight line.

linhaça [lɪˈnasa] f linseed.

linhagem [lɪˈnaʒẽ] f lineage.

linho [ˈlɪnu] m linen; (planta) flax.

li'nóleo m linoleum.

líquen [ˈlɪkɐn] m lichen.

liquidação [lɪkɪdaˈsãw] f liquidation; (venda) clearance sale; **liquidar** vt to liquidate; (conta) to settle; **líquido/a** adj liquid, fluid; (COM) net // m liquid.

'lira f lyre; (moeda) lira; **lírico/a** adj lyric(al).

'lírio m lily.

li'rismo m lyricism.

Lis'boa f Lisbon; **lisboeta** adj Lisbon cmp // m/f inhabitant ou native of Lisbon.

'liso/a adj smooth; (tecido) plain; (cabelo) straight.

lisonja [lɪˈzõʒa] f flattery; **lisonjear** vt to flatter; **lisonjeiro/a** adj flattering.

'lista f list; (listra) stripe; (tira) strip; (Pt: menu) menu; ~ **telefônica** telephone directory.

'listra f stripe.

lite'rário/a adj literary; **literato** m (escritor) writer; **literatura** f literature.

liti'gar vt to contend, fight // vi to go to law; **litígio** m (JUR) lawsuit; (contenda) dispute.

'lito'ral [-aw] adj coastal // m coast, seaboard.

'litro m litre, liter (US).

'lívido/a adj livid.

livra'mento m release; ~ **condicional** parole; **livrar** vt to release, liberate; (salvar) to save; **Deus me livre!** Heaven forbid; **livrar-se** vr to escape; **livrar-se de** to get rid of.

livra'ria f bookshop.

'livre adj free; (lugar) unoccupied; (desimpedido) clear, open; (natural) spontaneous; **ao ar** ~ in the open air; ~ **de impostos** tax-free.

livreiro/a [lɪˈvrejru] m bookseller; **livro** m book; **livro de bolso** pocket-sized book; **livro de consulta** reference book; **livro de mercadorias** stock book; **livro de cheques** (Pt) cheque book, check book (US).

lixa [ˈlɪʃa] f sandpaper; (unhas) nail-file; (peixe) dogfish.

lixo [ˈlɪʃu] m rubbish, garbage (US).

lobisomem [lobɪˈsomẽ] m werewolf; **lobo** m wolf; **lobo-marinho** m sea-lion.

lobri'gar vt to glimpse.

'lóbulo m ear lobe.

locação [lokaˈsãw] f lease.

local [loˈkaw] adj local // m site, place; ~**idade** f (zona) locality; (sítio) location; ~**izar** vt to locate; (situar) to place.

loção [loˈsãw] f lotion.

locomoção [lokomoˈsãw] f locomotion; **locomotiva** f railway engine, locomotive.

locução [lokuˈsãw] f (frase) expression.

'lodo m mud, slime.

lógico/a [ˈlɔʒɪku/a] adj logical // f logic.

'logo adv (imediatamente) right away, at once; (após) then; (mais tarde) later; ~, ~ **straightaway**, without delay; ~ **mais** in a while, shortly; ~ **no começo** right at the start // conj so; ~ **que** as soon as; **até** ~! cheerio!

lo'grar vt to achieve; (obter) to get, obtain; (alcançar) to attain; ~ **fazer** to manage to do.

'logro m enjoyment; (engano) fraud.

loiro/a [ˈlojru/a] adj ver **louro/a**.

loja [ˈlɔʒa] f shop; (maçônica) lodge; **lojista** m/f shopkeeper.

'lomba f ridge; (ladeira) slope; **lombada** f (de animal) back; (de livro) spine; **lombar** adj lumbar; **lombo** m back; (pedaço de carne) loin.

'lona f canvas.

'Londres m London; **londrino/a** adj London cmp // m/f Londoner.

longe [ˈlõʒɪ] adv far, far away; **ao** ~ in the distance; **de** ~ from afar; ~ **dos olhos, ~ de coração** out of sight, out of mind // prep: ~ **de** far from // mpl : ~**s** (indícios) traces; **longínquo/a** adj distant, remote.

longitude [lõʒɪˈtudʒɪ] f (GEO) longitude; **longo/a** adj long; **ao longo de** along, alongside.

'lontra f otter.

loquaz [loˈkwaʃ] adj talkative.

lotação [lotaˈsãw] f capacity; (vinho) blending; ~ **completa/esgotada** (teatro) sold out.

'lote m (porção) portion, share; (grupo) batch; (leilão) lot; (terreno) plot; **loteria** f lottery.

louça [ˈlosa] f china; (conjunto) crockery; ~ **de barro** earthenware; **lavar a** ~ to do the washing up.

louça'nia f elegance.

louco/a [ˈloku/a] adj crazy, mad; ~ **varrido** raving mad; ~ **de** mad with; ~ **por** crazy about // m/f lunatic, mad person; **loucura** f madness; (ato) crazy act.

louro/a [ˈloru/a] adj blond, fair // m laurel; (CULIN) bay leaf.

'lousa f flagstone; (tumular) gravestone; (quadro-negro) blackboard; (portátil) slate.

louva-a-deus [lova-a-ˈdɛwʃ] m inv praying mantis.

lou'var vt to praise; **louvável** adj praiseworthy; **louvor** m praise.

lua [ˈlua] f moon; **estar no mundo da** ~ to have one's head in the clouds; **lua-de-mel** f honeymoon; **luar** m moonlight.

lubrifi'cante m lubricant; **lubrificar** vt to lubricate.

luci'dez f lucidity, clarity; **lúcido/a** adj lucid.

'lúcio m (peixe) pike.

lu'crar vt (aproveitar) to profit from/by; (gozar) to enjoy // vi to gain; **lucro** m gain; (COM) profit.

ludibri'ar vt to dupe, deceive; (escarnecer) to mock, deride.

lu'fada f gust (of wind).

lu'gar m place; (espaço) space, room; (ocasião) opportunity; **em ~ de** instead of; **dar ~ a** to give rise to; **~ comum** commonplace; **em primeiro ~** in the first place; **em todo ~** everywhere; **~ejo** m village.

'lúgubre adj mournful; (escuro) gloomy.

'lula f squid.

'lume m fire; (luz) light; **trazer a ~** to bring to light; **vir a ~** to become known; **dar a ~** to publish.

lumi'nária f lamp, lantern; **~s** fpl illuminations; **luminoso/a** adj luminous, bright; (claro) clear.

lu'nar adj lunar // m (na pele) mole.

lu'neta f eye-glass; (telescópio) telescope.

'lupa f magnifying glass.

lupa'nar m brothel.

'lúpulo m (BOT) hop.

lusco-'fusco m (anoitecer) dusk; (amanhecer) daybreak; (luz) twilight.

lusi'tano/a, 'luso/a adj Portuguese, Lusitanian.

lus'trar vt to polish, clean; **lustre** m gloss, sheen; (fig) lustre; (luminária) chandelier; **lustro** m polish, shine; (tempo) lustrum, five-year period.

'luta f fight, struggle; (contenda) contest; **~ livre** wrestling; **lutar** vi to fight, struggle; (luta livre) to wrestle.

'luto m mourning; (dó) grief; **de ~** in mourning.

'luva f glove; **assentar como uma ~** to fit like a glove; **~s** fpl (recompensa) reward sg.

luxo ['luʃu] m luxury; **de ~** de luxe; **poder dar-se o ~ de** to afford; **luxuoso/a** adj luxurious; **luxúria** f lust; (BOT) lushness.

luz f light; **dar à ~** to give birth to; **sair à ~** to be published; **à ~ de** in view of; **~idio/a** adj shining, glossy; **luzir** vi to shine, gleam; (fig) to be successful.

Lx.a abr de **Lisboa.**

M

ma pron = **me** + **a**.

má adj ver **mau.**

'maca f stretcher.

maçã [ma'sã] f apple; **~ do rosto** cheekbone.

macacão [maka'kãw] m (de trabalhador) overalls pl; (da moda) jump-suit.

ma'caco m monkey; (MEC) jack; (fato) **~** (Pt) overalls pl.

ma'çada f (pancada) blow with a club; (coisa sem interesse) bore; (coisa enfadonha) nuisance.

maca'dame m tarmac.

maça'dor/a adj (Pt: sem interesse) boring; (: cansativo) tedious.

maça'neta f knob.

ma'çante adj (Br) ver **maçador(a).**

mação [ma'sãw] m (maçom) (free)mason.

macaquear [makake'ax] vt to imitate, ape.

ma'çar vt to bore.

macarrão [maka'xãw] m macaroni; (ger) pasta.

machado [ma'ʃadu] m axe.

machão [ma'ʃãw] m tough guy, he-man; (mulher) butch woman.

machete [ma'ʃetʃi] m machete.

macho ['maʃu] adj male; (fig) virile, manly // m male.

machucar [maʃu'kax] vt to crush; (contusão) to bruise; (cereais) to mash; (ferir) to injure, hurt.

maciço/a [ma'sisu/a] adj (espesso) thick; **ouro ~** solid gold; **uma dose ~a** a massive dose // m (GEO) massif.

macieira [masi'ejra] f apple tree.

macilento/a [masi'lẽtu/a] adj gaunt, haggard.

macio/a [ma'siu/a] adj (brando) soft; (liso) smooth.

'maço m (de folhas) bundle; (de cigarros) packet.

maçona'ria f freemasonry.

má-criação [ma-kria'sãw] f rudeness, bad manners pl.

'mácula f stain, blemish.

ma'cumba f black magic, voodoo.

madeira [ma'dejra] f wood; (pau) stick; **~ compensada** plywood; **de ~** wooden; **~s** fpl (MÚS) woodwind // m Madeira wine; **madeiro** m (lenho) log; (viga) beam.

madeixa [ma'dejʃa] f (de cabelo) lock; **~s** fpl tresses.

ma'draço/a adj idle // m/f loafer, idler.

ma'drasta f stepmother.

'madre f (freira) nun; (superiora) mother superior.

madres'silva f honeysuckle.

madrinha [ma'drɪɲa] f godmother.

madru'gada f (early) morning; (alvorada) dawn, daybreak; **duas horas da ~** two in the morning; **madrugador(a)** m/f early riser; (fig) early bird; **madrugar** vi to get up early; (fig) to get ahead; (aparecer cedo) to be early.

madu'rar vt/i (fruta) to ripen; (fig) to mature; **madureza** f (fruta) ripeness; (pessoa) maturity; **maduro/a** adj (fruta) ripe; (fig) mature.

mãe [mãj] f mother.

maestro/maestrina [ma'ɛʃtru/maeʃ'trina] m (compositor) composer; (de orquestra) conductor // f (de orquestra) conductress.

maga'refe m (Pt) butcher, slaughterer.

maga'zine m magazine; (armazém) store.

magia [ma'ʒia] f magic; **mágico/a** adj magic // m/f magician.

magis'tério m (ensino) teaching; (profissão) teaching profession; (professorado) teachers pl.

magis'trado m magistrate; **magistral**

adj magisterial; (*fig*) masterly; magistratura *f* magistracy.

mag'nânimo/a *adj* magnanimous.

mag'nata, mag'nate *m* magnate, tycoon.

mag'nético/a *adj* magnetic; **magnetizar** *vt* to magnetize; (*fascinar*) to mesmerize.

mag'nífico/a *adj* splendid, magnificent.

magni'tude *f* magnitude; **magno/a** *adj* (*grande*) great; (*importante*) important.

'mago *m* magician; **os reis ~s** the Three Wise Men, the Three Kings.

'mágoa *f* (*tristeza*) sorrow, grief; (*fig: desagrado*) hurt; **magoado/a** *adj* hurt; **magoar** *vt* (*ferir*) to hurt, injure; (*fig*) to hurt, wound.

magrinho/a [ma'grɪɲu/a] *adj* thin; (*pej*) skinny; **magro/a** *adj* (*pessoa*) thin; (*carne*) lean.

maio ['maju] (*Pt*: **M-**) *m* May.

maiô [ma'jo] *m* (*Br*) swimsuit.

maionese [majo'nezɪ] *f* mayonnaise.

maior [ma'jɔx] *adj* (*comparativo: de tamanho*) bigger; (*: de importância*) greater; (*superlativo: de tamanho*) biggest; (*: superior*) greatest; **~ de idade** of age, adult; **~ de 21 anos** over 21 // *m* adult; **~ al** *m* chief, leader.

maioria [majo'ria] *f* majority; **a ~ de** most of; **maioridade** *f* adulthood; **atingir a maioridade** to come of age.

mais [majʃ] *adv* more; (*com palavra negativa ou interrogativa*) any more // *adj* more; (*superlativo*) most // *m*: **o ~** the rest // *prep* plus, as well as; **~ de** more than; **~ nada** nothing else; **~ dois** two more; **~ ou menos** more or less; **~ uma vez** once more; **a ~** too much; **alguém/ninguém ~** somebody/nobody else; **cada vez ~** more and more; **por ~ que** however much; **quanto ~ ganha, ~ gasta** the more he earns, the more he spends.

mai'sena *f* cornflower.

maiúscula [ma'juʃkula] *f* capital letter.

majes'tade *f* majesty; **majestoso/a** *adj* majestic.

ma'jor *m* (*MIL*) major.

mal *m, pl* **'males** (*maldade*) evil; (*dano*) harm; (*MED*) illness; (*desgraça*) trouble, misfortune; **falar ~ de** to speak ill of; **fazer ~ a** to harm, hurt; **fazer ~ em** to be wrong to; **levar a ~** to take offence at; **não faz ~** never mind // *adv* badly; (*dificilmente*) hardly; **estar ~** to be ill // *conj* (*logo que*) no sooner had they **tiveram de partir no sooner had they** arrived than they had to leave.

'mala *f* suitcase; (*Br*: *AUTO*) boot, trunk (*US*); **~s** *fpl* luggage *sg*; **fazer as ~s** to pack.

malaba'rismo *m* juggling; **malabarista** *m/f* juggler.

malan'dragem *f* (*preguiça*) idleness; (*velhacaria*) villainy, double-dealing; **malandro/a** *adj* idle // *m/f* (*patife*) spiv,

rogue, scoundrel; (*preguiçoso*) idler, layabout.

ma'lária *f* malaria.

mal-arru'mado/a *adj* untidy.

malbara'tar *vt* (*dissipar*) to squander, waste.

malcri'ado/a *adj* ill-mannered, rude.

mal'dade *f* evil, wickedness.

maldição [mawdʒi'sãw] *f* curse; **maldito/a** *adj* damned, accursed; **maldizente** *m/f* slanderer; **maldizer** *vt* to curse.

mal'doso/a *adj* wicked; (*fig*) malicious.

maledicência [maledʒi'sẽsja] *f* slander; **maledicente** *m/f* slanderer.

ma'léfico/a *adj* (*pessoa*) malicious; (*coisa*) harmful, injurious.

mal-enten'dido/a *adj* misunderstood // *m* misunderstanding.

mal-es'tar *m* (*doença*) indisposition, discomfort; (*inquietação*) uneasiness.

ma'leta *f* small suitcase, grip.

malevolência [malevo'lẽsja] *f* malice, spite; **malévolo/a** *adj* malicious, spiteful.

malfa'dado/a *adj* unlucky.

malfeito/a [mal'fejtu/a] *adj* poorly made; (*disforme*) misshapen; (*injusto*) wrong, unjust; **malfeitor** *m* malefactor; (*facínora*) criminal.

malha ['maʎa] *f* mesh; (*no tricô*) stitch; (*suéter*) sweater; (*de ginástica*) leotard; **fazer ~** (*Pt*) to knit; **artigos de ~** knitwear; **~ perdida** ladder, run.

malhado/a [ma'ʎadu/a] *adj* spotted, mottled, dappled.

malhar [ma'ʎar] *vt* (*cereais*) to thresh; (*bater*) to beat, strike; (*fig*) to deride, knock.

malho ['maʎu] *m* (*maço*) mallet; (*grande*) sledgehammer.

mal-humo'rado/a *adj* grumpy, sullen.

malícia [ma'lisja] *f* (*má índole*) wickedness; (*astúcia*) slyness; (*esperteza*) cleverness; (*brejeirice*) mischievousness; (*intenção: maldosa*) spite(fulness); (*: satírica*) sarcasm; **malicioso/a** *adj* wicked; (*astuto*) sly; (*brejeiro*) mischievous; (*sarcástico*) spiteful, sarcastic.

maligni'dade *f* malice, spite; (*MED*) malignancy; **maligno/a** *adj* (*maléfico*) evil, malicious; (*danoso*) harmful; (*MED*) malignant.

malmequer [mawme'kex] *m* marigold.

malo'grado/a *adj* (*frustrado*) abortive, frustrated; (*sem êxito*) unsuccessful; (*infeliz*) unlucky; **malograr** *vt* (*planos*) to spoil, upset; (*frustrar*) to thwart, frustrate; **malograr-se** *vr* (*planos*) to fall through; (*fracassar*) to fail; **malogro** *m* failure.

ma'lote *m* (*small*) case; (*serviço*) express courier.

mal-pas'sado/a *adj* underdone; (*bife*) rare.

malquerença [mawke'rẽsa] *f* ill will, enmity.

mal'quisto/a adj disliked; (odiado) hated.

malsão/sã [maw'sãw/'sã] adj (doentio) sickly; (insalubre) unhealthy; (nocivo) harmful.

'malta f (Pt) gang, mob; (: col) lot.

'malte m malt.

maltrapilho/a [mawtra'piʎu/a] adj in rags, ragged // m/f ragamuffin.

maltra'tar vt to ill-treat; (insultar) to abuse; (estragar) to ruin, damage.

ma'luco/a adj crazy, daft // m madman // f madwoman; **maluquice** f madness; (bobagem) silliness.

mal'vado/a adj wicked.

malversação [mawvexsa'sãw] f (dinheiro) embezzlement; **malversar** vt (administrar mal) to mismanage; (dinheiro) to embezzle, misappropriate.

'mama f breast; **mamadeira** f (Br) feeding bottle.

mamãe [ma'mãj] f mum, mummy.

mamão [ma'mãw] m papaya.

ma'mar vt to suck; (fig) to take in; (empresa) to milk (dry); **mamilo** m nipple.

'mana f sister.

ma'nada f herd, drove.

manancial [manã'sjaw] m spring; (fig) source.

man'car vt to cripple // vi to limp.

mancebo [mã'sebu] m young man, youth.

mancha ['mãʃa] f (nódoa) stain; (na pele) mark, spot; (em pintura) blotch; **sem ~** (reputação) spotless; **manchar** vt (sujar) to dirty; (enodoar) to stain, mark.

'manco/a adj crippled, lame; (defeituoso) defective, faulty.

man'dado m (ordem) order; (JUR) writ, injunction; **~ de prisão/busca** warrant for arrest/search warrant; **mandamento** m order, command; (REL) commandment; **mandante** m instigator.

mandão/dona [mã'dãw/'dɔna] adj bossy, domineering // m/f bossy person.

man'dar vt (ordenar) to order; (enviar) to send; **~ buscar/chamar** to send for; **~ embora** to send away; **~ fazer um vestido** to have a dress made; **~ que alguém faça/~ alguém fazer** to tell sb to do // vi to be in charge.

manda'tário m (delegado) delegate; (representante) representative, agent; **mandato** m (autorização) mandate; (ordem) order.

man'díbula f jaw.

man'dinga f witchcraft.

mandi'oca f cassava, manioc.

'mando m (comando) command; (poder) power; **a ~ de** by order of.

mandrião/driona [mãdri'ãw/dri'ona] adj (Pt) lazy // m/f idler, lazybones sg; **mandriar** vi to idle, loaf about.

maneira [ma'nejra] f (modo) way; (estilo) style, manner; **à ~ de** like; **de ~ que** so that; **de ~ alguma** not at all; **~s** fpl manners.

manejar [mane'ʒax] vt (instrumento) to handle; (máquina) to work; **manejável** adj manageable; **manejo** m handling.

manequim [mane'kĩ] m model; (boneco) dummy.

ma'neta adj one-handed.

'manga f sleeve; (fruta) mango; (filtro) filter; (mangueira) hose; (aguaceiro) cloudburst.

man'gar vi: **~ com/de** to tease, make fun of.

mangue ['mãgi] m mud-flat, swamp; (planta) mangrove.

mangueira [mã'gejra] f hose(pipe); (árvore) mango tree.

manha ['maɲa] f (malícia) guile, craftiness; (ardil) trick; (mau hábito) habit; (choro) whining.

manhã [ma'ɲã] f morning; **de ~** in the morning.

manhoso/a [ma'ɲozu/a] adj (ardiloso) crafty, sly; (esperto) smart, clever; (choroso) whining.

ma'nia f (MED) mania; (obsessão) obsession, craze; (paixão) passion.

mania'tar vt to tie the hands of; (algemar) to handcuff.

manicômio [mani'komiu] m asylum, mental hospital.

mani'cura f, **mani'cure** f (tratamento) manicure; (pessoa) manicurist.

manie'tar vt ver **maniatar**.

manifestação [manifeʃta'sãw] f demonstration, display; (expressão) expression, declaration; (política) demonstration; **manifestar** vt (revelar) to show, display; (declarar) to express, declare; **manifestar-se** vr to appear; (patentear-se) to be obvious, be evident; **manifesto/a** adj obvious, clear // m manifesto.

manilha [ma'niʎa] f (ceramic) drain-pipe.

manipu'lar vt to manipulate; (manejar) to handle.

mani'vela f (ferramenta) crank.

manjar [mã'ʒar] m food, dish; (iguaria) delicacy, titbit; (Br) coconut and milk pudding; **~ branco** blancmange.

manjedoura [mãʒe'dora] f manger, crib.

manjericão [mãʒeri'kãw] m basil.

'mano m brother.

ma'nobra f manoeuvre; (de trens) shunting; (fig) trick; **manobrar** vt to manoeuvre; (acionar) to operate, work // vi to manoeuvre; (fazer funcionar) to work; (planejar) to scheme.

manquejar [mãke'ʒax] vi to limp.

mansão [mã'sãw] f mansion; (morada) residence.

mansidão [mãsi'dãw] f gentleness, meekness; **manso/a** adj (brando) gentle; (águas) calm; (animal) tame.

'manta f (cobertor) blanket; (xale) shawl; (de viajar) travelling rug.

manteiga [mã'tejga] f butter; **manteigueira** f butter dish.

man'ter vt to maintain; (uma família) to support; (a palavra) to keep; (princípios) to abide by; **~-se** vr (sustentar-se) to support o.s.; (permanecer) to remain; (aguentar) to hold on; **~-se firme** to stand firm.

mantilha [mã'tʃiʎa] f mantilla; (véu) veil.

manti'mentos mpl provisions.

'manto m cloak; (de cerimônia) robe.

manual [man'waw] adj manual // m handbook; (compêndio) manual.

manufa'tura (Pt: -ct-) f manufacture; (fábrica) factory.

manus'crito/a adj handwritten // m manuscript.

manuse'ar vt (manejar) to handle; (livro) to leaf through.

manutenção [manute̶'sãw] f maintenance.

mão [mãw] f, pl irr: **mãos** [mãwʃ] hand; (de animal) paw; (de pintura) coat; **à ~** by hand; (perto) at hand; **feito à ~** handmade; **contra a ~** on the wrong side of the road; **dar a ~ a** to shake hands with; **de mãos dadas** hand in hand; **de segunda ~** second-hand; **pôr mãos à obra** to set to work; **ter uma ~ (boa) para** to be good at.

mão-de-obra [mãw-dʒɪ-'ɔbra] f (trabalho) workmanship; (trabalhadores) labour.

'mapa m map; (gráfico) chart.

maquilagem [makɪ'laʒẽ] f make-up; (ato) making up; **maquilar-se** vr to put on one's make-up.

máquina ['makɪna] f machine; (de trem) engine; (fig) machinery; **~ de calcular** calculator; **~ fotográfica/de filmar** camera; **~ de escrever** typewriter; **~ de lavar roupa** washing-machine.

maquinação [makɪna'sãw] f machination, plot.

maquinal [makɪ'naw] adj mechanical, automatic; **maquinaria** f machinery; **maquinismo** m mechanism; (máquinas) machinery; **maquinista** m engine driver.

'mar m sea; **em alto ~** on the high seas; **por ~** by sea; **cair no ~** to fall overboard; **fazer-se ao ~** to set sail.

maracu'já m passionflower; (fruto) passion fruit.

ma'rasmo m debilitation; (caquexia) wasting away; (apatia) apathy.

mara'tona f marathon.

maravilha [mara'vɪʎa] f marvel, wonder; **às mil ~s** wonderfully; **maravilhar** vt to amaze, astonish; **maravilhar-se** vr: **maravilhar-se de** to be astonished at, be amazed at; **maravilhoso/a** adj marvellous, wonderful.

'marca f mark; (COM) make, brand; (carimbo) stamp; **~ de fábrica** trademark; **marcação** f marking; (em jogo) scoring; (de instrumento) reading; (teatro) action; **marcar** vt to mark; (animal) to brand; (delimitar) to demarcate; (observar) to keep an eye on; (hora, data) to fix, set; (Pt: discar) to dial; (num jogo) to score; **marcar uma consulta** to make an appointment.

marceneiro [maxse'nejru] m cabinet-maker, joiner.

marcha ['maxʃa] f (a pé) walking; (em cortejo) march; (de acontecimentos) course; (passo) pace, step; (AUTO) gear; **~ à ré** (Br), **~ atrás** (Pt) reverse (gear); **pôr-se em ~** to set off; **marchar** vi (ir) to go; (andar a pé) to walk; (MIL) to march.

'marco m landmark; (de janela) frame; (fig) frontier.

março ['maxsu] (Pt: **M-**) m March.

ma'ré f tide; **~ alta/baixa** high/low tide; **marear** vt to make seasick // vi to be seasick.

marechal [mare'ʃaw] m marshal.

marfim [max'fĩ] m ivory.

marga'rida f daisy.

marga'rina f margarine.

margem ['maxʒẽ] f (borda) edge; (do rio) bank; (de impresso) margin; (fig: tempo) time; (: lugar) space; **a ~ de** alongside; **dar ~ a** to give an opportunity to.

ma'ricas m (Pt) (col) queer, gay.

ma'rido m husband.

marinheiro [marɪ'nejru] m seaman, sailor; **marinho/a** adj sea, marine // f navy; (pintura) seascape; **marinha mercante** merchant navy.

mari'ola m messenger; (patife) scoundrel // f wrapped tablet of banana candy.

mari'onete f puppet.

mari'posa f moth; (col) prostitute.

ma'risco m shellfish.

ma'rítimo/a adj sea, maritime; **pesca ~a** sea fishing.

marme'lada f quince jam; (col) double-dealing; **marmelo** m quince.

mar'mita f (vaso) pot.

'mármore m marble; **marmóreo/a** adj marble.

ma'roto/a m/f rogue, rascal; (criança) naughty boy/girl.

marquês/quesa [max'keʃ/'keza] m marquis // f marchioness.

mar'reco m duck.

Mar'rocos m Morocco.

marrom [ma'xõ] adj brown.

marroquim [maxo'kĩ] m morocco leather.

'marte m Mars.

marte'lar vt to hammer (on); **martelo** m hammer.

'mártir m martyr; **martírio** m martyrdom; (fig) torment.

marujo [ma'ruʒu] m sailor.

marulhar [maru'ʎax] vi (agitar-se) to surge; (de encontro a alguma coisa: forte) to crash, pound; (: brando) to lap; (produzir ruído) to roar; **marulho** m surge; (agitação) tossing; (fig) noise, hubbub.

mar'xista adj, m/f Marxist.

mas conj but // pron = **me + as**.

mas'car vt to chew.

'máscara f mask; **sob a ~ de** under the guise of; **mascarado/a** adj masked; **mascarar** vt to mask; disguise.

mascu'lino/a adj masculine; (BIO) male; **roupa ~a** a men's clothes pl.

mas'morra f dungeon.

masoquista [maso'kiʃta] m/f masochist.

'massa f (física) mass; (de tomate) paste; (CULIN) dough; **as ~s** the masses; **em ~ en masse**; **~ de vidraceiro** putty.

massa'crar vt to massacre; **massacre** f massacre.

massagem [ma'saʒẽ] f massage.

mas'sudo/a adj bulky; (espesso) thick.

masti'gar vt to chew; (palavras) to mumble, mutter.

mastim [maʃ'tʃĩ] m watchdog.

'mastro m (NÁUT) mast; (para bandeira) flagpole.

mastur'bar-se vr to masturbate.

'mata f forest, wood.

mata-bicho [mata-'biʃu] m tot of brandy, snifter.

mata-borrão [mata-bo'xãw] m blotting paper.

mata'dor(a) m/f killer // m (em tourada) matador; **matadouro** m slaughterhouse.

mata'gal m bush; (brenha) thicket, undergrowth.

ma'tança f massacre; (de reses) slaughter(ing); **matar** vt to kill; (a sede) to quench; (aula) to skip; **matar-se** vr to kill o.s.

'mate adj matt // m (chá) maté tea; **xeque ~** checkmate.

mate'mático/a adj mathematical // m/f mathematician // f mathematics sg, maths sg.

ma'téria f matter; (TEC) material; (escolar: assunto) subject; **em ~ de** on the subject of.

materi'al adj material; (corporal) physical // m material; (TEC) equipment; **~ humano** manpower; **~ismo** m materialism; **~ista** adj materialistic // m/f materialist.

matéria-'prima f raw material.

mater'nal adj motherly, maternal; **escola ~** nursery school; **maternidade** f motherhood, maternity; (hospital) maternity hospital; **materno/a** adj motherly, maternal; (língua) mother.

matilha [ma'tʃiʎa] f (cães) pack; (chusma) rabble.

mati'nal adj morning.

ma'tiz m shade; (combinação de cores) blend (of colours); **matizar** vt (colorir) to tinge, colour; (combinar cores) to blend.

'mato m scrubland, bush; (floresta) forest; (o campo) country.

ma'traca f rattle; **falar como uma ~** to talk nineteen to the dozen; **matraquear** vi to rattle, clatter; (tagarelar) to chatter, rabbit on.

matreiro/a [ma'trejru/a] adj cunning, crafty.

ma'trícula f (lista) register; (inscrição) registration; (pagamento) enrolment fee; (PT: AUTO) registration number; (US) license plate number; **chapa de ~** numberplate; (US) license plate; **matricular** vt, **matricular-se** vr to enrol, register.

matri'mônio m marriage.

ma'triz f (MED) womb; (fonte) source; (molde) mould; (COM) head office; **igreja ~** mother church.

maturi'dade f maturity.

matu'tino/a adj morning // m morning paper.

mau/má [maw/ma] adj bad; (malvado) evil, wicked.

mau-olhado [maw-o'ʎadu] m evil eye.

mavi'oso/a adj tender, soft; (som) sweet.

maxila [mak'sila] f, **maxi'lar** m jawbone.

máxime ['maksime] adv especially.

máximo/a ['masimu/a] adj (maior que todos) greatest; **o ~ cuidado** the greatest of care // m maximum; (o cúmulo) peak; **no ~** at most // f maxim, saying.

maxixe [ma'ʃiʃi] m gherkin; (Br: dança) 19th-century dance.

ma'zela f (ferida) sore spot; (doença) illness; (fig) blemish.

me pron (direto) me; (indireto) (to) me; (reflexivo) (to) myself.

me'ada f skein, hank.

me'ado m middle; **em ~(s) de Julho** in mid-July.

me'cânico/a adj mechanical; **broca ~a** a power drill // m mechanic // f (ciência) mechanics sg; (mecanismo) mechanism; **mecanismo** m mechanism.

mecha ['meʃa] f (de vela) wick; (cabelo) tuft; (tingida) highlight; (MED) swab; **mechar** vt (cabelo) to put highlights in.

'meço etc vb ver **medir**.

medalha [me'daʎa] f medal.

'média f average; **em ~** on average.

mediação [medʒia'sãw] f mediation; **por ~ de** through; **medianeiro** m mediator; **mediano/a** adj medium, average; (medíocre) mediocre.

medi'ante prep by (means of), through; **mediar** vt to mediate (for) // vi (ser mediador) to mediate; **a distância que medeia entre** the distance between.

medicação [medʒika'sãw] f treatment; **medicamento** m medicine.

medição [medʒi'sãw] f measurement.

medi'cina f medicine; **médico/a** adj medical // m/f doctor.

me'dida f measure; (medição) measurement; (moderação) prudence; **à ~ que** while, as; **tomar ~s** to take steps; **tomar as ~s de** to measure; **feito sob ~** made to measure; **medidor** m: **medidor de pressão** pressure gauge; **medidor de gás** gas meter.

'médio/a adj (lugar) middle, mid; (no

meio-termo) medium; (*mediano*) average // f average.

me'díocre *adj* mediocre; **mediocridade** f mediocrity.

me'dir *vt* to measure; (*pesar*) to weigh up; (*avaliar*) to judge // *vi* to measure; ~-se *vr* (*competir*) to vie.

medi'tar *vt* (*pensar em*) to think over // *vi* to meditate.

mediter'râneo/a *adj* Mediterranean // m: o M~ the Mediterranean.

'médium m (*pessoa*) medium.

'medo m fear; com ~ afraid; **ter ~ de** to be afraid of; **medonho/a** *adj* terrible, awful.

me'drar *vi* to thrive, flourish.

me'droso/a *adj* (*com medo*) frightened; (*tímido*) timid.

me'dula f marrow.

me'dusa f jellyfish.

meia ['meja] f stocking; (*curta*) sock // *adj ver* meio; ~-calça f tights *pl*, panty hose (*US*).

meia-i'dade f middle age.

meia-noite [meja-'nojtʃi] f midnight.

meigo/a ['mejgu/a] *adj* gentle; (*voz*) sweet; **meiguice** f gentleness, sweetness.

meio/a ['meju/a] *adj* half; ~ **quilo** half a kilo; **uma hora e** ~**a** half past one // *adv* half, rather; ~ **morto** half-dead // m (*ponto*) middle; (*ambiente*) environment; (*método*) means *pl*, way; **cortar ao** ~ to cut in half.

meio-dia [meju-'dʒia] m midday, noon.

mel m honey; **melaço** m molasses *pl*; **melado/a** *adj* (*cor*) honey-coloured; (*pegajoso*) sticky // m (*melaço: US*) molasses; (: *Brit*) treacle.

melancia [melã'sia] f watermelon.

melan'cólico/a *adj* sad, melancholy.

melão [me'lãw] m melon.

me'lena f long hair; (*juba*) mane.

melhor [me'ʎɔx] *adj, adv* (*comparativo*) better; (*superlativo*) best; ~ **que nunca** better than ever; **quanto mais** ~ the more the better; **seria** ~ **começarmos** we had better begin; **tanto** ~ so much the better; **melhora** f, **melhoramento** m improvement; **melhorar** *vt* to improve, make better // *vi* to improve, get better.

meli'ante m scoundrel; (*vagabundo*) tramp.

melin'drar *vt* to offend, hurt; ~-se *vr* to take offence, be hurt; **melindroso/a** *adj* (*sensível*) sensitive, touchy; (*problema, situação*) tricky.

melo'dia f melody; (*composição*) tune.

melo'drama m melodrama; **melodramático/a** *adj* melodramatic.

me'loso/a *adj* sweet; (*fig*) corny.

'melro m blackbird.

'membro m member; (*do corpo*) limb; **membrudo/a** *adj* big; (*fig*) robust.

memo'rando m (*aviso*) note; (*COM: comunicação*) memorandum.

me'mória f memory; **de** ~ by heart; ~**s** *fpl* (*de autor*) memoirs.

menção [mẽ'sãw] f mention, reference; ~ **honrosa** honours, distinction; **fazer** ~ **de sair** to make as if to leave, begin to leave; **mencionar** *vt* to mention.

mendi'cância f begging; **mendigar** *vt* to beg for // *vi* to beg; **mendigo/a** m/f beggar.

mene'ar *vt* (*corpo, cabeça*) to shake; (*quadris*) to swing; **meneio** m (*balanço*) swaying.

me'nino/a m boy // f girl; (*olhos*): ~**a dos olhos** pupil.

menopausa [meno'pawza] f menopause.

me'nor *adj* (*mais pequeno: comparativo*) smaller; (: *superlativo*) smallest; (*mais jovem: comparativo*) younger; (: *superlativo*) youngest; (*o mínimo*) the least, slightest; (*de* ~ *idade*) under age; **não tenho a** ~ **idéia** I haven't the slightest idea // m/f juvenile, young person; ~ **abandonado** abandoned child.

'menos *adj* (*comparativo: sg*) less; (: *pl*) fewer; (*superlativo: sg*) least; (: *pl*) fewest // *adv* (*comparativo*) less; (*superlativo*) least // *prep* except // m: o ~ the least; **a** ~ (*faltando*) missing; **a** ~ **que** unless; **ao/pelo/quando** ~ at least; **mais ou** ~ more or less; **de/por que** ~ than.

menospre'zar *vt* to underrate; (*desprezar*) to despise, scorn; **menosprezo** m contempt, disdain.

mensageiro/a [mẽsa'ʒejru/a] *adj, m/f* messenger; **mensagem** f message.

men'sal *adj* monthly; ~**idade** f monthly payment; ~**mente** *adv* monthly.

menstruação [mẽʃtrua'sãw] f period, menstruation; **menstruar** *vi* to menstruate, have a period; **mênstruo** m period, menstruation.

men'tal *adj* mental; ~**idade** f mentality; (*a mente*) mind; **mente** f mind; **de boa mente** willingly.

mente'capto/a *adj* mad, crazy // m/f fool, idiot.

men'tir *vi* to lie; **mentira** f lie; (*ato*) lying; **parece mentira que** it seems incredible that; **mentiroso/a** *adj* lying; (*enganoso*) deceitful // m/f liar.

me'nu m menu.

mer'cado m market; **M**~ **Comum** Common Market; ~ **negro/paralelo** black market; **mercador** m merchant, trader; **mercadoria** f commodity; **mercadorias** *fpl* goods.

mer'cante *adj, m/f* merchant; **mercantil** *adj* mercantile, commercial.

mercê [mex'se] f (*favor*) favour; (*perdão*) mercy; **à** ~ **de** at the mercy of.

mercearia [mexsea'ria] f grocer's (shop); **merceeiro** m grocer.

merce'nário/a *adj, m* mercenary.

mer'cúrio m mercury.

merecer [mere'sex] *vt* to deserve, merit; (*valer*) to be worth // *vi* to deserve;

merecido/a adj deserved; (justo) just, due; **merecimento** m desert; (valor, talento) merit.

me'renda f snack; (no campo) picnic; ~ **escolar** free school meal; **merendar** vt to have as a snack // vi to have a snack; **merendeira** f (funcionária) dinner-lady; (lancheira) lunch-bag/box.

merengue [me'rēgi] m meringue.

mergulhar [mexgu'ʎax] vt to dip in, immerse // vi (para nadar) to dive; (penetrar) to plunge; **mergulho** m dip(ping), immersion; (em natação) dive.

meridio'nal adj southern.

'mérito m merit; (valor) worth, value.

'mero/a adj mere.

'mês m month; (salário) month's pay.

'mesa f table; (COM) board; **pôr/tirar** a ~ to lay/clear the table.

me'sada f monthly allowance; (criança) pocket-money.

'mescla f mixture; **mesclar** vt to mix (up); (cores) to blend.

me'seta f plateau, tableland.

'mesmo/a adj same; **eu** ~ I myself; **este** ~ **homem** this very man; **ele** ~ **o fez** he did it himself; **o Rei** ~ the King himself; **continuar na** ~**a** to be just the same; **dá no** ~ or **na** ~**a** it's all the same // m: **o** ~ **the same** (thing) // adv (até) even; **aqui/agora/hoje** ~ right here/right now/this very day; ~ **que** even if; **é** ~ it's true; **isso** ~! exactly!

mesquinho/a [meʃ'kiɲu/a] adj (avaro) mean, miserly.

mesquita [meʃ'kita] f mosque.

messias [me'siaʃ] m Messiah.

mes'tiço/a adj half-caste, of mixed race; (animal) crossbred // m/f half-caste; (animal) half-breed.

'mestre/'mestra adj master- cmp; **chave mestra** master key; **obra mestra** masterpiece // m master; (chefe: de fábrica) manager; (: de operários) foreman; **de** ~ masterful, masterly // f (professora) mistress; **mestria** f mastery; (habilidade) expertise; **com mestria** to perfection.

me'sura f (cumprimento) bow; (cortesia) courtesy.

'meta f (corrida de cavalos) finishing post; (regata) finishing line; (gol) goal; (alvo) aim; (fim) end.

me'tade f half; (meio) middle; ~ **de uma laranja** half an orange.

me'táfora f metaphor.

me'tal m, pl **me'tais** metal; ~ **sonante** hard cash; **metais** (MÚS) brass sg; **metálico/a** adj (som) metallic; (de metal) metal; ~**urgia** f metallurgy.

mete'oro m meteor.

me'ter vt (colocar) to put; (implicar) to involve; (introduzir) to introduce; ~ **na cabeça** to take it into one's head; ~**-se** vr (esconder-se) to hide; (intrometer-se) to get involved in; ~**-se na cama** to get into bed; ~**-se com** (provocar) to pick a quarrel with; ~**-se a médico** to set o.s. up as a doctor.

me'tódico/a adj methodical; **método** m method.

metralhadora [metraʎa'dora] f sub-machine gun.

'métrico/a adj metric; **metro** m metre, meter (US).

me'trô (Br), **'metro** (Pt) m (FERRO) underground, subway (US).

me'trópole f metropolis; (capital) capital; **metropolitano/a** adj metropolitan // m (FERRO) underground, subway (US).

meu/minha [mew/'miɲa] adj my; **um amigo** ~ a friend of mine // pron mine.

mexer [me'ʃex] vt (mover) to move; (a cabeça) to nod, shake; (misturar) to mix, stir; (ovos) to scramble // vi (mover) to move; ~ **em** to meddle with; ~ **com** (comerciar) to deal in; (provocar) to annoy, tease; ~**-se** vr to move, budge; (apressar-se) to get a move on; **mexa-se!** get going!, budge yourself!

mexericar [meʃeri'kax] vi to gossip; **mexeriqueiro/a** adj gossiping // m/f gossip, busybody.

mexicano/a [meʃi'kanu/a] adj, m/f Mexican; **México** m Mexico.

mexido [me'ʃidu/a] adj (papéis) mixed up; (agitado) restless; **ovos** ~**s** scrambled eggs // f mess, disorder.

mexilhão [meʃi'ʎãw] m mussel.

mezinha [me'ziɲa] f home-made remedy.

mi'ar vi to miaow; **miau** m miaow.

mi'cróbio m germ, microbe.

micro'fone m microphone.

micro'onda f microwave.

micros'cópio m microscope.

migalha [mi'gaʎa] f crumb; ~**s** fpl scraps.

migração [migra'sāw] f migration; **migrar** vi to migrate; **migratório/a** adj migratory; **aves migratórias** birds of passage.

mijar [mi'ʒax] vi to urinate; ~**-se** vr to wet o.s.

mil num thousand; **dois** ~ two thousand.

mi'lagre m miracle; **milagroso/a** adj miraculous.

milha ['miʎa] f mile.

milhão [mi'ʎãw] m million.

milhar [mi'ʎax] m thousand.

milharal [miʎa'raw] m maize field; **milho** m maize, corn (US).

mi'lícia f (MIL) militia; (: vida) military life; (: força) military force.

mi'límetro m millimetre, millimeter (US).

milio'nário/a adj, m/f millionaire.

mili'tante adj, m/f militant; **militar** adj military // m soldier // vi (POL) to be an active member.

mim [mĩ] pron me; (reflexivo) myself.

mi'mado/a adj (acariciado) petted; (animalhado) spoilt; **mimar** vt to pamper, spoil; **mimo** m (presente) gift;

(carícia) caress sg; (de criança) spoiling; (coisa delicada) delicacy; **mimoso/a** adj (delicado) delicate; (terno) tender, loving, sweet; (acustumado a mimos) spoilt.

'mina f mine; (fig: de riquezas) gold mine; (: de informações) mine of information; **minar** vt to mine; (fig) to undermine; **mineiro/a** adj mining; (de Minas Gerais) from Minas Gerais // m miner; **mineral** adj mineral // m mineral; **minério** m ore.

'míngua f: **à ~ de** for want of; **minguante** adj waning // m wane, decline; **quarto minguante** (ASTRO) last quarter; **minguar** vi (diminuir) to decrease, dwindle; (faltar) to run short.

minha ['mɪɲa] adj, pron ver **meu**.

minhoca [mɪ'ɲɔka] f (earth)worm.

minia'tura adj, f miniature.

'mínimo/a adj minimum; **a ~a atenção** the slightest attention // m minimum, least; **no ~** at least.

minissaia [mɪnɪ'saja] f miniskirt.

minis'tério m ministry; **M~ do Exterior/da Fazenda** Foreign Office/Treasury; **ministro** m minister.

mino'rar vt to lessen, reduce; **minoria** f minority.

minuci'oso/a adj (indivíduo) thorough; (explicação) detailed.

mi'núsculo/a adj minute, tiny; **letra ~a** small letter.

mi'nuta f (rascunho) rough draft; (CULIN) **à ~** cooked to order.

mi'nuto m minute.

mi'olo m (de pão) inside; (polpa) pulp; (de maçã) core; **~s** mpl (fig) brains.

míope ['mɪopɪ] adj short-sighted; **miopia** f short-sightedness.

'mira f (de fuzil) sight; (objetivo) aim, purpose; **à ~ de** on the lookout for; **ter em ~** to keep an eye on.

mi'rada f look; **miradouro** m viewpoint, belvedere.

miragem [mɪ'raʒẽ] f mirage.

mira'mar m sea view.

mi'rante m viewpoint, belvedere.

mi'rar vt to look at; (observar) to watch; (fig: apontar para) to aim at; **~ para** to look onto; **~-se** vr to look at o.s.

mir'rar vt/i, **mir'rar-se** vr to wither, dry up.

misce'lânea f (miscellany; (fig) mixture.

mise'rável adj (lastimável) miserable, wretched; (avaro) stingy, mean; (insignificante) paltry; (lugar) squalid; (infame) despicable // m (indigente) wretch; (coitado) poor thing; (perverso) rotter; **miséria** f (estado lastimável) misery; (pobreza) poverty; (avareza) stinginess; **uma miséria** (dinheiro) a pittance; **misericórdia** f (compaixão) pity, compassion; (graça) mercy.

'missa f (REL) mass.

missão [mɪ'sãw] f mission.

'misse f beauty queen.

míssil ['mɪsjw] m missile.

missio'nário m missionary.

mis'ter m (trabalho) occupation, job; (profissão) profession; (propósito) purpose; **ser ~** to be necessary.

mis'tério m mystery.

'místico/a adj, m/f mystic.

'misto/a adj mixed; (confuso) mixed up // m mixture; **misto-quente** m toasted cheese and ham sandwich.

mis'tura f (ato) mixing; (conjunto) mixture; (QUÍM) compound; **misturar** vt to mix, blend; **misturar-se** vr: **misturar-se com** to mix in with, mingle with.

'mito m myth.

miudezas [mju'dezaʃ] fpl minutiae; (bugigangas) odds and ends; **miúdo/a** adj (pequeno) tiny, minute; (cuidadoso) thorough; **dinheiro miúdo** small change // m/f (Pt: criança) youngster, kid; **miúdos** mpl (dinheiro) change sg; (de aves) giblets.

mixórdia [mɪ'ʃɔxdʒɪa] f mess, jumble.

mo pron = **me** + **o**.

mó f (de moinho) millstone; (para afiar) grindstone; **moagem** f grinding.

mobi'lar vt (Pt) to furnish; **mobília** f furniture; **mobiliar** vt (Br) to furnish; **mobiliário** m furnishings pl.

mobili'zar vt to mobilize.

'moça f ver **moço**.

moção [mo'sãw] f motion.

mochila [mo'ʃɪla] f rucksack.

mocho/a ['moʃu/a] adj hornless // m (ave) owl.

mocidade [mosɪ'dadʒɪ] f youth; (os moços) young people; **moço/a** adj young; (da juventude) youthful // m young man, lad; **moço de bordo** ordinary seaman; **moço de cavalariça** groom // f girl, young woman.

'moda f fashion; (estilo) style; **estar na ~** to be in fashion, be all the rage; **fora da ~** old-fashioned; **sair da ~** to go out of fashion.

mode'lar vt to model; **modelo** m model; (costura) pattern.

mode'rado/a adj moderate; (clima) mild; **moderar** vt to moderate; (violência) to control, restrain; (velocidade) to reduce; **moderar-se** vr to calm down.

moderni'zar vt to modernize; **moderno/a** adj modern; (atual) present-day; **modernoso/a** adj newfangled.

mo'déstia f modesty; **modesto/a** adj modest; (simples) simple, plain.

'módico/a adj moderate; (preço) reasonable.

modifi'car vt to modify, alter.

mo'dismo m idiom.

mo'dista f dressmaker.

'modo m (maneira) way, manner; (LING) mood; (MÚS) mode; **~s** mpl manners; **~ de pensar** way of thinking; **de ~ que** so (that); **de ~ nenhum** in no way; **de qualquer ~** anyway, anyhow; **tenha ~s!** behave yourself!

mo'dorra f (sonolência) drowsiness; (letargia) lethargy.

mo'eda f (uma) coin; (dinheiro) money; **uma ~ de 10p** a 10p piece; **~ corrente** currency; **pagar na mesma ~** to give tit for tat.

mo'er vt (café) to grind; (cana) to crush; (bater) to beat; (cansar) to tire out.

mo'far vi to get mouldy; **~ de** to mock, scoff at.

mo'fino/a adj (covarde) cowardly; (doentio) sickly; (avarento) stingy.

'mofo m (BOT) mould; (cheiro) mustiness.

'mogno m mahogany.

mo'ído/a pp de **moer** // adj (café) ground; (carne) minced; (cansado) tired out; **moinho** m mill; (de café) grinder.

moita ['mojta] f thicket.

'mola f (TEC) spring.

mo'lar m molar (tooth).

mol'dar vt to mould; (metal) to cast; **molde** m mould; (de papel) pattern; (fig) model; **moldura** f (de pintura) frame.

'mole adj (macio, fofo) soft; (fraco) weak, flabby; (fácil) easy; (pessoa) easy-going, soft, listless.

mo'lécula f molecule.

moles'tar vt to bother; (desgostar) to annoy; (incomodar) to put out; **~-se** vr (aborrecer-se) to be annoyed; (magoar-se) to be hurt; **moléstia** f (doença) illness; **molesto/a** adj (incômodo) troublesome; (aborrecido) annoying; (molestado) troubled.

molhado/a [mo'ʎada/a] adj wet, damp; **molhar** vt (umedecer) to wet; (: de leve) to moisten, dampen; (meter) to dip; **molhar-se** vr to get wet.

molhe ['moʎi] m (Pt) jetty; (: cais) wharf, quay.

molho ['moʎu] m (de chaves) bunch; (de trigo) sheaf; (CULIN) sauce; (: de salada) dressing; (: de carne) gravy; **pôr de ~** to soak.

momen'tâneo/a adj momentary; **momento** m moment; (TEC) momentum; **a todo momento** constantly; **de um momento para outro** suddenly; **no momento em que** just as.

mo'narca m/f monarch, ruler; **monarquia** f monarchy.

mo'nástico/a adj monastic.

monção [mõ'sãw] f monsoon.

mon'dar vt (Pt: ervas daninhas) to weed; (árvores) to prune; (fig) to weed out.

monge ['mõʒi] m monk; **monja** f nun.

'mono m/f monkey, ape.

mono'pólio m monopoly; **monopolizar** vt to monopolize.

monoto'nia f monotony; **monótono/a** adj monotonous.

'monstro m adj monster; (fig) fantastic // m monster; **monstruoso/a** adj monstrous.

'monta f: **de pouca ~** trivial, of little account.

montagem [mõ'taʒẽ] f assembly; (ARQ)

---

erection; (cinema) montage; (teatro) production.

montanha [mõ'taɲa] f mountain; **~-russa** f roller coaster; **montanhês/esa** adj mountain // m/f highlander; **montanhoso/a** adj mountainous.

mon'tante m total, sum.

montão [mõ'tãw] m heap, pile.

mon'tar vt (subir a) to mount, get on; (cavalgar) to ride; (peças) to assemble, put together; (loja, máquina) to set up // vi: **~ a/em** (animal) to get on; (cavalgar) to ride; (despesa) to come to; **montaria** f (caçada) hunting; (cavalgadura) mount; (sela) side-saddle.

'monte m hill; (montão) heap, pile; (de gente) crowd.

'montra f (Pt) shop window.

monumen'tal [-taw] adj monumental; (fig) magnificent, splendid; **monumento** m monument.

mo'rada f home, residence; (Pt: endereço) address; **morador(a)** m/f (de casa) resident; (de casa alugada) tenant; (habitante) inhabitant.

moral [mo'raw] adj moral // f (ética) ethics pl; (conclusão) moral // m morale; **~izar** vi to moralize.

mo'rango m strawberry.

mo'rar vi to live, reside.

'mórbido/a adj (malsão) unhealthy; (doente) sickly.

morcego [mɔx'segu] m (BIO) bat.

mor'cela f black pudding.

mor'daça f (de animal) muzzle; (fig) gag; **mordaz** adj biting; (corrosivo) caustic; (sarcástico) scathing.

morde'dura f bite; **morder** vt to bite; (penetrar em) to bite into; (corroer) to corrode; **morder a língua** to bite one's tongue; **morder-se** vr: **morder-se de inveja** to be green with envy.

mo'reno/a adj dark(-skinned); (de cabelos) brunette // f brunette; (cor) brown.

mor'fina f morphine.

mor'gado/a m (Pt: herdeiro) heir; (filho mais velho) eldest son; (propriedade) entailed estate // f heiress.

mori'bundo/a adj dying.

morigerado/a [moriʒe'radu/a] adj upright.

morma'cento/a adj sultry.

'morno/a adj lukewarm, tepid.

mo'roso/a adj slow, sluggish.

mor'rer vi to die; (luz, cor) to fade; (fogo) to die down; (AUTO) to stall; **~ por** to be mad about; **~ de rir** to die laughing.

'morro m hill.

morta'dela f salami.

mor'tal adj mortal; (letal) deadly.

mortalha [mox'taʎa] f shroud.

mortali'dade f mortality; **mortandade** f slaughter; **morte** f death.

morteiro [mox'tejru] m mortar.

mortiço/a [mox'tʃisu/a] adj (morrediço)

dying; (*embaciado*) dull; (*desanimado*) lifeless; (*luz*) dimming; **mortífero/a** *adj* deadly, lethal; **mortificar** *vt* (*torturar*) to torture; (*afligir*) to annoy, torment.

'**morto/a** *pp irr de* **matar** *ou* **morrer** // *adj* (*cor*) dull; (*exausto*) exhausted; (: *col*) done in; **estar** ~ to be dead; **ser** ~ to be killed; **estar** ~ **de inveja** to be green with envy; **estar** ~ **por, estar** ~ **de vontade de** to be dying to // *m* dead man; (*cadáver*) corpse, dead body // f dead woman.

mos *pron* = **me** + **os**.

mosaico [mo'sajku] *m* mosaic.

'**mosca** f fly.

Moscou [moʃ'ko] *m* Moscow.

mosquiteiro [moʃki'tejru] *m* mosquito net; **mosquito** *m* mosquito.

'**mossa** f dent; (*fig*) impression.

mos'tarda f mustard.

mosteiro [moʃ'tejru] *m* monastery; (*de monjas*) convent.

'**mosto** *m* (*vinho*) must.

'**mostra** f (*exibição*) display; (*sinal*) sign, indication; **dar** ~**s de** to show signs of; ~ **dor** *m* (*de relógio*) face, dial; **mostrar** *vt* to show; (*mercadorias*) to display; (*provar*) to prove; **mostrar-se** *vr* to appear, seem.

'**mote** *m* (*frase*) motto; (*tema*) theme.

motejar [mote'ʒax] *vt* to taunt, mock // *vi*: ~ **de** (*gracejar*) to jeer at, make fun of; **motejo** *m* mockery, derision; (*dito*) joke.

motim [mo'tʃĩ] *m* riot, revolt; (*militar*) mutiny.

moti'var *vt* (*causar*) to cause, bring about; (*estimular*) to motivate; **motivo** *m* (*causa*) cause, reason; (*fim*) motive; (*MÚS*) motif.

'**moto** *m*: **de** ~ **próprio** of one's own accord.

'**moto** f, **motoci'cleta** f, **moto'ciclo** (*Pt*) *m* motorbike; **motoneta** f (*motor-*)scooter; **motoniveladora** f bulldozer.

mo'tor/mo'triz *adj* driving // *m* motor, engine; ~ **de arranque** starter (*motor*); ~ **de explosão** internal combustion engine; **motorista** *m/f* driver; **motorizado/a** *adj* motorized.

mouco/a ['moku/a] *adj* deaf, hard of hearing.

move'diço/a *adj* easily moved; (*instável*) unsteady; **areia** ~**a** quicksand; **móvel** *adj* movable // *m* (*peça de mobília*) piece of furniture; **móveis** *mpl* furniture *sg*; **bens móveis** personal property.

mo'ver *vt* to move; (*cabeça*) to shake; (*causar*) to cause; (*acionar*) to drive; ~ **uma ação** to start a lawsuit; ~-**se** *vr* to move; **movimento** *m* movement; (*TEC*) motion; (*na rua*) activity, bustle.

mu'ar *m/f* mule.

'**muco** *m* mucus.

muçulmano/a [musul'manu/a] *adj, m/f* Moslem.

mu'dança f change; (*de casa*) move;

(*AUTO*) gear; **mudar** *vt* to change; (*deslocar*) to move // *vi* (*ave*) to moult; **mudar de roupa/de conversa** to change clothes/the conversation; **mudar de casa** to move (house); **mudar-se** *vr* (*de casa*) to move (away); (*transformar-se*) to change.

'**mudo/a** *adj* dumb; (*calado, cinema*) silent; (*telefone*) dead.

mugir [mu'ʒix] *vi* (*vaca*) to moo, low.

muito/a ['mwĩtu/a] *adj* a lot of; (*em frase negativa ou interrogativa: sg*) much, (: *pl*) many // *adv* a lot; (+ *adjetivo*) very; ~ **admirado** much admired; (+ *comparativo*) ~ **melhor** a lot/much/far better; (*de tempo*) long; ~ **depois** long after; **há** ~ a long time ago; ~**as vezes** often; **por** ~ **que** however much // *pron* a lot; (*em frase negativa ou interrogativa*) much.

'**mula** f mule.

mu'lato/a *adj, m/f* mulatto.

mu'leta f crutch; (*fig*) support.

mulher [mu'ʎex] f woman; (*esposa*) wife.

'**multa** f fine; **levar uma** ~ to get fined; **multar** *vt* to fine.

multidão [multʃi'dãw] f (*grande afluência*) crowd; **uma** ~ **de** (*muitos*) lots of.

multilate'ral *adj* multilateral.

multipli'car *vt* (*MAT*) to multiply; (*aumentar*) to increase.

mun'dano/a *adj* worldly; **mundial** *adj* worldwide; (*guerra, recorde*) world // *m* (*campeonato*) world championship; **o mundial de futebol** the World Cup.

'**mundo** *m* world; **todo o** ~ everybody; **um** ~ **de** lots of, a great many; **correr o** ~ to see the world.

munheca [mu'ɲeka] f wrist.

munição [muni'sãw] f (*de armas*) ammunition; (*chumbo*) shot; (*MIL*) munitions *pl*, supplies *pl*.

município [mu'nisɪpju] *m* town council, corporation; (*cidade*) town; (*condado*) county.

mu'nir *vt*: ~ **de** to provide with, supply with.

muralha [mu'raʎa] f (*de fortaleza*) rampart; (*muro*) wall.

murchar [mur'ʃax] *vt* (*BOT*) to wither // *vi* (*BOT*) to wither, wilt; (*fig*) to fade.

murmuração [muxmura'sãw] f muttering; (*maledicência*) gossiping; **murmurar** *vi* (*segredar*) to murmur, whisper; (*queixar-se*) to mutter, grumble; (*água*) to ripple; (*folhagem*) to rustle; **murmúrio** *m* whispering; (*queixa*) grumbling; (*água*) rippling; (*folhagem*) rustling; (*maledicência*) gossiping.

'**muro** *m* wall.

'**murro** *m* punch, sock.

'**músculo** *m* muscle.

museu [mu'sew] *m* museum.

'**musgo** *m* moss; **musgoso/a** *adj* mossy.

musi'cal [-kaw] *adj, m* musical; **músico/a** *adj* musical // *m/f* musician // f music.

mutação [muta'sãw] *f* change, alteration; (*BIO*) mutation.

muti'lar *vt* to mutilate; (*pessoa*) to maim.

mutu'ário *m* borrower; **mútuo/a** *adj* mutual // *m* loan.

N

na = **em** + **a**.

'nabo *m* turnip.

nação [na'sãw] *f* nation.

'nácar *m* mother-of-pearl; (*cor*) pink, pearly.

nacio'nal [-naw] *adj* national; ~**idade** *f* nationality; ~**ismo** *m* nationalism; ~**ista** *m/f* nationalist; ~**izar** *vt* to nationalize.

'naco *m* piece, chunk.

'nada *pron* nothing; **não dizer** ~ to say nothing, not to say anything // *m* nothingness; (*pessoa*) nonentity // *adv* not at all, in no way; **antes de mais** ~ first of all; **de/por** ~! not at all!

nada'dor(a) *m/f* swimmer; **nadar** *vi* to swim.

'nádegas *fpl* buttocks.

'nado *m*: ~ **de peito** breaststroke; ~ **de costas** backstroke; **a** ~: **atravessar a** ~ to swim across.

naipe ['najpɪ] *m* (*cartas*) suit (of cards); (*categoria*) order.

namo'rado/a *m* boyfriend // *f* girlfriend; **namorar** *vt* (*ser namorado de*) to be going out with, court, woo; **namoricar** *vt* to flirt with; **namoro** *m* courtship; (*amistade*) relationship.

não [nãw] *adv* not; (*resposta*) no; ~ **sei** I don't know; ~ **muito** not much; ~ **só ... mas também** not only ... but also; **agora** ~ not now // *excl*: ~! no!

não- *pref*: ~**alinhado/a** *adj* non-aligned; ~**conformista** *adj, m/f* non-conformist.

narci'sista *adj* narcissistic; **narciso** *m* (*BOT*) narcissus; (*pessoa*) vain man; **narciso-dos-prados** *m* daffodil.

nar'cótico/a *adj, m* narcotic.

nari'gudo/a *adj* big-nosed; **narina** *f* nostril; **nariz** *m* nose; **meter o nariz em** to poke one's nose into; **torcer o nariz para** to turn one's nose up at.

narração [naxa'sãw] *f* narration; (*relato*) account; **narrar** *vt* to narrate, recount; **narrativo/a** *adj* narrative // *f* narrative; (*história*) story.

nas = **em** + **as**.

nasal [na'zaw] *adj* nasal; ~**ização** *f* nasalization.

nascença [na'sẽsa] *f* birth; (*fig*) origin; **nascente** *adj* nascent // *m* East, Orient // *f* (*fonte*) spring.

nas'cer *vi* to be born; (*plantas*) to sprout; (*o sol*) to rise // *m*: ~ **do sol** sunrise; **nascido/a** *adj* born; **nascimento** *m* birth; (*fig*) origin; (*estirpe*) descent.

'nata *f* (*CULIN*) cream.

natação [nata'sãw] *f* swimming.

natal [na'taw] *adj* (*relativo ao nascimento*)

natal; (*lugar*) native; **cidade** ~ home town; **terra** ~ birthplace // *m*: **N**~ Christmas; ~**ício/a** *adj*: **aniversário** ~**ício** birthday // *m* birthday; ~**idade** *f*: **índice de** ~**idade** birth rate; **natividade** *f* nativity.

na'tivo/a *adj* native; (*natural*) natural // *m/f* native.

'NATO *f* (*Pt*) NATO.

'nato/a *adj* born.

natu'ral [-aw] *adj* natural // *m* (*nativo*) native; (*índole*) nature; ~**idade** *f* naturalness; ~**ização** *f* naturalization; ~**izar-se** *vr* to become naturalized; ~**mente** *adv* naturally.

natu'reza *f* nature; (*espécie*) kind, type; ~ **morta** still life; **por** ~ by nature.

nau [naw] *f* ship; (*de guerra*) warship; **naufragar** *vi* to be shipwrecked; (*fig*: *malograr-se*) to fail; **naufrágio** *m* shipwreck; (*fig*) failure; **náufrago/a** *m/f* castaway, shipwrecked person.

náusea ['nawsea] *f* nausea; **sentir** ~**s** to feel sick; **nauseabundo/a** *adj*, **nauseante** *adj* nauseating, sickening.

náutico/a ['nawtʃiku/a] *adj* nautical // *f* seamanship.

navalha [na'vaʎa] *f* (*de barba*) razor; (*faca*) knife.

'nave *f* (*de igreja*) nave; (*navio*) ship; ~ **espacial** spaceship.

navegação [navega'sãw] *f* navigation, sailing; ~ **aérea** air traffic; ~ **costeira** coastal shipping; **navegador** *m* navigator; **navegar** *vt* (*navio*) to sail; (*avião*) to fly // *vi* (*viajar em navio*) to sail (*: em avião*) to fly; (*dirigir o rumo*) to navigate; **navegável** *adj* navigable.

na'vio *m* ship; ~ **a vela** sailing boat; ~ **de carreira** liner; ~ **de guerra** warship; ~ **petroleiro** oil tanker.

'nazi (*Pt*), **na'zista** (*Br*) *adj, m/f* Nazi.

ne'blina *f* fog, mist; **nebuloso/a** *adj* foggy, misty; (*céu*) cloudy; (*fig*) vague // *f* (*ASTRO*) nebula.

neces'sário/a *adj* necessary; **necessidade** *f* need, necessity; (*pobreza*) poverty, need; **ter necessidade de** to need; **necessitado/a** *adj* needy, poor; **necessitar** *vt* to need, require // *vi* to be in need.

necrologia [nɛkrolo'ʒia] *f* obituary column; **necrológio** *m* obituary; **necrópole** *f* cemetery; **necrotério** *m* mortuary, morgue (*US*).

'néctar *m* nectar.

'nédio/a *adj* (*luzidio*) glossy, sleek; (*rechonchudo*) plump.

neerlandês/esa [neexlã'deʃ/eza] *adj* Dutch // *m* Dutchman // *f* Dutchwoman; **Neerlândia** *f* the Netherlands *pl*.

ne'fando/a *adj* atrocious, heinous.

ne'fasto/a *adj* (*de mau agouro*) ominous; (*trágico*) tragic.

ne'gaça *f* lure, bait; **negacear** *vt* (*atrair*) to entice; (*provocar*) to provoke.

negação [nega'sãw] *f* negation; (*recusa*) refusal, denial; **negar** *vt* (*recusar*) to refuse; (*desmentir*) to deny; **negar-se** *vr*: **negar-se a** to refuse to; **negativo/a** *adj* negative // *m* (*TEC, FOTO*) negative // *f* (*LING*) negative; (*recusa*) denial; **negável** *adj* deniable.

negligência [negli'ʒẽsja] *f* negligence, carelessness; **negligente** *adj* negligent, careless.

negociação [negosia'sãw] *f* negotiation; (*transação*) transaction; **negociante** *m* businessman; (*comerciante*) merchant // *f* businesswoman; **negociar** *vt/i* (*diplomacia etc*) to negotiate; (*comerciar*) to trade; **negociável** *adj* negotiable.

negócio [ne'gɔsju] *m* (*COM*) business; (*transação*) deal, transaction; (*col: coisa*) thing; (*assunto*) affair, business; **homem de** ~**s** businessman; **a** ~**s** on business.

negreiro [ne'grejru] *m* slave-trader.

'negro/a *adj* black; (*medonho*) dreadful // *m* black man, Negro // *f* black woman, Negress; **negrura** *f* blackness.

nem [nẽj] *conj* nor, neither; ~ **sequer** not even; ~ **que** not even if; ~ **bem** hardly; ~ **um só** not a single one; ~ **estuda** ~ **trabalha** he neither studies nor works.

ne'nê *m*, **ne'ném** *m* baby.

nenhum(a) [ne'ɲu/'ɲuma] *adj* no, not any // *pron* (*nem um só*) none, not one; (*de dois*) neither.

ne'núfar *m* water lily.

neologismo [neolo'ʒiʒmu] *m* neologism.

neozelan'dês/esa *adj* New Zealand *cmp* // *m/f* New Zealander.

'nervo *m* (*ANAT*) nerve; (*fig*) energy, strength; ~**sidade** *f* nervousness; (*energia nervosa*) nervous energy; ~**sismo** *m* (*nervosidade*) nervousness; (*irritabilidade*) irritability; **nervoso/a** *adj* nervous; (*irritável*) irritable; (*excitável*) excitable; **nervudo/a** *adj* (*Pt: robusto*) robust.

néscio/a ['nɛsju/a] *adj* (*ignorante*) ignorant; (*insensato*) foolish.

'nessa = **em** + **essa**.

'nesse = **em** + **esse**.

'neto/a *m* grandson; ~**s** *mpl* grandchildren // *f* granddaughter.

neuralgia [newraw'ʒia] *f* neuralgia; **neurose** *f* neurosis; **neurótico/a** *adj*, *m/f* neurotic.

neutrali'dade *f* neutrality; **neutralizar** *vt* to neutralize; (*anular*) to counteract; **neutro/a** *adj* neuter.

nêutron ['newtrõ] (*Pt*: **neu'trão**) *m* neutron.

ne'vada *f* snowfall; **nevar** *vi* to snow; **nevasca** *f* snowstorm; **neve** *f* snow.

'névoa *f* fog, mist; **nevoeiro** *m* thick fog.

nexo ['nɛksu] *m* connection, link; **sem** ~ disconnected, incoherent.

Nica'rágua *f* Nicaragua; **nicaragüense** *adj*, *m/f* Nicaraguan.

nicho ['niʃu] *m* niche.

'nimbo *m* (*GEO*) halo; (*nuvem*) rain cloud.

'nímio/a *adj* excessive.

ni'nar *vt* to sing to sleep.

ninguém [nĩ'gẽj] *pron* nobody, no-one; **não vi** ~ I saw no-one, I didn't see anybody; ~ **mais** nobody else.

ninhada [nĩ'ɲada] *f* brood.

ninharia [niɲa'ria] *f* (*bagatela*) trifle.

ninho ['niɲu] *m* (*de aves*) nest; (*toca*) lair; (*lar*) home.

níquel ['nikɛw] *m* nickel; **niquelar** *vt* (*TEC*) to nickel-plate.

'nisso, 'nisto = **em** + **isso, isto**.

niti'dez *f* (*clareza*) clarity; (*brilho*) brightness; (*imagem*) sharp. **nítido/a** *adj* bright; (*limpo*) clear.

ni'trato *m* nitrate.

nitrogênio [nitro'ʒenju] *m* nitrogen.

'nível *m* level; ~ **de vida** standard of living; ~ **do mar** sea level; **ao** ~ **de** level with; **nivelar** *vt* (*terreno etc*) to level; (*arrasar*) to flatten; **nivelar-se** *vr*: **nivelar-se com** to be equal to.

no = **em** + **o**.

nó *m* knot; (*de uma questão*) crux; ~ **corredio** slipknot; ~ **na garganta** lump in the throat; ~**s dos dedos** knuckles.

'nobre *adj*, *m* noble; **nobreza** *f* nobility.

noção [no'sãw] *f* notion; ~ **vaga** inkling.

nocivo/a [no'sivu/a] *adj* harmful.

noc'tâmbulo *m* (*sonâmbulo*) sleep-walker.

'nódoa *f* spot; (*mancha*) stain.

nogueira [no'gejra] *f* (*árvore*) walnut tree; (*madeira*) walnut.

noitada [noj'tada] *f* (*noite inteira*) whole night; (*noite de divertimento*) a night out; **noite** *f* night; **à/de noite** at night.

noivado [noj'vadu] *m* (*compromisso de casamento*) engagement; **noivo/a** *m* (*prometido*) fiancé; (*recém-casado*) bridegroom; **noivos** *mpl* (*prometidos*) engaged couple; (*recém-casados*) newlyweds // *f* (*prometida*) fiancée; (*recém-casada*) bride.

nojento/a [no'ʒẽtu/a] *adj* nauseating, disgusting; **nojo** *m* (*náusea*) nausea; (*repulsa*) loathing; (*luto*) mourning.

'no-la = **nos** + **a**; **no-lo** = **nos** + **o**; **no-las** = **nos** + **as**; **no-los** = **nos** + **os**.

'nome *m* name; (*fama*) fame; (*LING*) noun; ~ **de batismo** Christian name; **em** ~ **de** in the name of; **nomeação** *f* nomination; (*para um cargo*) appointment; **nomeada** *f* fame; **nomeadamente** *adv* namely; **nomear** *vt* to nominate; (*conferir um cargo*) to appoint; (*dar nome a*) to name; **nomenclatura** *f* nomenclature.

'nono/a *adj* ninth.

'nora *f* daughter-in-law; (*Pt: de tirar água*) waterwheel.

nor'deste *m* northeast; **o N**~ Northeast; **nordestino/a** *adj* northeastern // *m/f* Northeasterner.

'nórdico/a *adj* Nordic.

'norma *f* standard, norm; (*regra*) rule; **como** ~ as a rule.

normal [nox'maw] *adj* normal; (*natural*)

natural, usual; ~**idade** f normality; ~**izar-se** vr to return to normal.

noro'este adj northwest, northwestern // m northwest.

'norte adj northern, north // m north; (fig: direção) bearing, direction.

norte-ameri'cano/a adj, m/f (North) American.

Noruega [nor'wega] f Norway; **norueguês/esa** adj, m/f Norwegian.

nos [nuʃ] pron (direto) us; (indireto) us, to us, for us; (reflexivo) (to) ourselves; (recíproco) (to) each other // = **em + os**.

nós [nɔʃ] pron we; ~ **mesmos** ourselves; **para** ~ for us.

'nosso/a adj our // pron ours; **um amigo** ~ a friend of ours.

nostalgia [noʃtal'ʒia] f nostalgia; (saudades da pátria etc) homesickness.

'nota f note; (escolar) mark; (conta) bill; (cédula) banknote; **digno de** ~ noteworthy; ~**bilidade** f notability; (pessoa) notable; ~**ção** f notation.

no'tar vt (reparar em) to notice, note; **é de** ~ **que** it is to be noted that; **fazer** ~ to call attention to; ~**-se** vr to be obvious.

no'tário m notary.

no'tável adj notable, remarkable.

notícia [no'tʃisja] f (informação) piece of news; ~**s** fpl news sg; **pedir** ~**s de** to inquire about; **ter** ~**s de** to hear from; **noticiar** vt to announce, report; **noticiário** m (de jornal) news section; (cinema) newsreel; (rádio etc) news bulletin.

notificação [notʃifika'sãw] f notification; **notificar** vt to notify, inform.

notorie'dade f renown, fame; **notório/a** adj well-known, evident.

no'turno/a (Pt: -ct-) adj nocturnal, nightly // m (trem) night train.

'nova f piece of news; ~**s** fpl news sg.

nova'mente adv again.

no'vato/a adj inexperienced, raw // m/f (principiante) beginner, novice; (EDUC) fresher.

'nove num nine; ~**centos/as** num nine hundred.

no'vela f short novel, novella; (rádio, televisão) soap-opera.

no'velo m (bola de fio) ball of thread.

no'vembro (Pt: N-) m November.

no'venta num ninety.

noviciado [novis'jadu] m (REL) novitiate; **noviço** m (REL) novice.

novi'dade f novelty; (notícia) piece of news; **sem** ~ without incident; ~**s** fpl news sg.

novilho/a [no'viʎu/a] m young bull // f heifer.

'novo/a adj new; (jovem) young; (adicional) further; **de** ~ again // f nova.

noz f walnut, nut; ~ **moscada** nutmeg.

nu/'nua adj naked, bare; ~ **em pelo** stark naked // m/f nude.

nu'blado/a adj cloudy, overcast; **nublar** vt to darken; **nublar-se** vr to cloud over.

'nuca f nape (of the neck).

nucle'ar adj nuclear; **núcleo** m nucleus sg; (centro) centre.

nu'dez f nakedness, nudity; **nudismo** m nudism.

nuli'dade f nullity, invalidity; (pessoa) nonentity; **nulo/a** adj null, void; (inepto) inept.

numeração [numera'sãw] f numbering, numbers pl; **numeral** m numeral; **numerar** vt to number; (contar) to enumerate, count.

nume'rário m cash, money.

nu'mérico/a adj numerical; **número** m number; (de jornal) issue; **sem número** countless; **numeroso/a** adj numerous.

'nunca adv never; ~ **mais** never again; **como** ~ as never before; **quase** ~ hardly ever.

núpcias ['nupsiaʃ] fpl nuptials, wedding sg.

nutrição [nutri'sãw] f nutrition; **nutrido/a** adj (bem alimentado) well-nourished; (robusto) robust; **nutrimento** m nourishment; **nutrir** vt to nourish, feed; (proteger) to nurture; (alentar) to encourage; **nutritivo/a** adj nourishing.

nuvem ['nuvẽj] f cloud; (insetos) swarm; **pôr nas nuvens** to praise to the skies; **cair das nuvens** (espantar-se) to be astounded.

O

o art ver **a**.

oásis [o'asiʃ] m oasis.

obcecação [obseka'sãw] f obfuscation; (obstinação) obstinacy; **obcecar** vt to blind.

obedecer [obede'sex] vi: ~ **a** to obey; **obediência** f obedience; **obediente** adj obedient.

obesi'dade f obesity; **obeso/a** adj obese.

óbice ['obisi] m obstacle.

'óbito m demise, death.

objeção [obʒe'sãw] (Pt: -cç-) f objection; **pôr objeções a** to object to; **objetar** (Pt: -ct-) vt to object.

obje'tivo/a (Pt: -ct-) adj objective // m objective, aim; **sem** ~ aimlessly.

ob'jeto (Pt: -ct-) m (coisa) object; (causa) motive; (propósito) aim.

oblíquo/a [o'blikwu/a] adj oblique, slanting; (olhar) sidelong.

obo'é m oboe.

'obra f (ger) work; (ARQ) building, construction; (teatro) play; ~ **prima** masterpiece; **em** ~**s** under repair; **O**~**s Públicas** Public Works; **obrar** vt to work; (produzir) to produce; (causar) to cause, bring about // vi to act, work; **obreiro/a** adj working // m/f worker.

obrigação [obriga'sãw] f obligation, duty; (COM) bond; **obrigado/a** adj (*compelido*) obliged, compelled; (*agradecido*) grateful // *excl*: **obrigado!** thanks!; **obrigar** *vt* to oblige, compel; **obrigar-se** *vr*: **obrigar-se a fazer algo** to undertake to do sth; **obrigatório/a** *adj* compulsory, obligatory.

obsceni'dade *f* obscenity; **obsceno/a** *adj* obscene.

obscure'cer *vt* to obscure; **~-se** *vr* to get dark; **obscuridade** *f* obscurity; (*falta de luz*) darkness; **obscuro/a** *adj* dark; (*fig*) obscure.

obse'dar *vt*, **obsedi'ar** *vt* to obsess.

obsequiar [obsekɪ'ax] *vt* (*presentear*) to give presents to; (*tratar com agrados*) to treat kindly; **obséquio** *m* favour, kindness; **obsequioso/a** *adj* obliging, courteous.

observação [obsɛxva'sãw] *f* observation; (*comentário*) remark, comment; **observador(a)** *adj* observant // *m/f* observer; **observância** *f* observance; **observar** *vt* to observe; (*notar*) to notice; **observatório** *m* observatory.

obsessão [obsɛ'sãw] *f* obsession.

obso'leto/a *adj* obsolete.

obs'táculo *m* obstacle; (*dificuldade*) hindrance, drawback.

obs'tante: **não ~** *conj* nevertheless, however // *prep* in spite of, notwithstanding.

obs'tar *vi*: **~ a** to hinder, obstruct; (*opor-se*) to oppose.

obs'tetra *m/f* obstetrician; **obstetrícia** *f* obstetrics *sg*: **obstétrico/a** *adj* obstetric.

obstinação [obʃtʃɪna'sãw] *f* obstinacy; **obstinado/a** *adj* obstinate, stubborn; **obstinar-se** *vr* to be obstinate; **obstinar-se em** (*porfiar em*) to persist in.

obstrução [obʃtru'sãw] *f* obstruction; **obstruir** *vt* to obstruct; (*impedir*) to impede.

obtenção [obtẽ'sãw] *f* acquisition; (*consecução*) attainment; **obter** *vt* to obtain, get; (*ganhar*) to gain.

obturação [obtura'sãw] *f* (*dum dente*) filling; **obturador** *m* (*FOTO*) shutter; **obturar** *vt* to stop up, plug; (*dente*) to fill.

ob'tuso/a *adj* (*ger*) obtuse; (*pessoa*) thick, slow, dull.

'óbvio/a *adj* obvious.

ocasião [okazɪ'ãw] *f* (*oportunidade*) opportunity, chance; (*momento*) occasion, time; (*causa*) cause; **ocasionar** *vt* to cause, bring about.

o'caso *m* (*do sol*) sunset; (*ocidente*) the west; (*decadência*) decline.

oceano [ose'anu] *m* ocean.

ocidental [osɪdẽ'taw] *adj* western; **ocidente** *m* west.

ócio ['osju] *m* (*folga*) leisure, rest; (*preguiça*) idleness; **ociosidade** *f* idleness; **ocioso/a** *adj* idle.

'oco/a *adj* hollow, empty; (*fútil*) vain, futile // *m* hollow.

ocorrência [oko'xẽsja] *f* incident, event; (*circunstância*) circumstance; **ocorrer** *vi* to happen, occur; (*vir ao pensamento*) to come to mind.

ocu'lar *adj* ocular; **oculista** *m/f* optician; **óculo** *m* spyglass; **óculos** *mpl* glasses, spectacles; **óculos de proteção** goggles.

ocul'tar *vt* to hide, conceal; **oculto/a** *adj* (*escondido*) hidden; (*desconhecido*) unknown; (*secreto*) secret.

ocupação [okupa'sãw] *f* occupation; **ocupado/a** *adj* (*pessoa*) busy; (*lugar*) occupied; (*Br: telefone*) engaged; **ocupar** *vt* to occupy; **ocupar-se** *vr*: **ocupar-se de/com/em** to concern o.s. with; (*cuidar*) to look after.

odi'ar *vt* to hate; **ódio** *m* hate, hatred; **odioso/a** *adj* hateful; (*mau*) nasty.

o'dor *m* smell; **~ífero/a** *adj* fragrant.

'odre *m* wineskin.

o'este *m* west.

ofe'gante *adj* breathless, panting; **ofegar** *vi* to pant, puff.

ofen'der *vt* to offend; (*ferir*) to hurt, injure; **~-se** *vr* to take offence; **ofensa** *f* (*injúria*) insult, abuse; (*lesão*) injury; **ofensivo/a** *adj* (*ofensivo*) aggressive // *f* (*MIL*) offensive.

oferecer [ofere'sex] *vt* to offer, present; (*propor*) to propose; **~-se** *vr* (*ocorrer*) to occur; (*pessoa*) to offer o.s., volunteer; **oferecimento** *m* offer; **oferta** *f* (*oferecimento*) offer; (*dádiva*) gift; **a oferta e a demanda** (*COM*) supply and demand.

oficial [ofɪs'jaw] *adj* official // *m* official; (*MIL*) officer.

ofi'cina *f* workshop; **~ mecânica** garage.

ofício [o'fɪsju] *m* (*profissão*) profession, trade; (*REL*) service; (*carta*) official letter; **bons ~s** good offices; **oficioso/a** *adj* (*de fontes oficiais*) unofficial.

of'tálmico/a *adj* ophthalmic.

ofus'car *vt* (*obscurecer*) to darken; (*deslumbrar*) to dazzle.

oitavo/a [ɔj'tavu/a] *adj* eighth // *m* eighth; **oitenta** *num* eighty; **oito** *num* eight; **oitocentos/as** *num* eight hundred.

o'lá *excl* hello!

ola'ria *f* pottery!

ole'ado *m* oil cloth.

oleiro [o'lejru] *m* potter; (*de tijolos*) brickmaker.

'óleo *m* (*lubricante*) oil; **~ combustível** fuel oil; **~ de rícino** castor oil; **pintura a ~** oil painting; **oleoso/a** *adj* oily; (*gorduroso*) greasy.

ol'fato *m* sense of smell.

olhada [o'ʎada] *f* glance, look; **olhar** *vt* to look at; (*observar*) to watch; (*ponderar*) to consider; (*cuidar de*) to look after; **olhar fixamente** to stare at // *vi* to look; **olhar para** to look at; **olhar por** to look after; **olhar-se** *vr* (*pessoas*) to look at one another // m look, glance; **olhar fixo** stare.

olheiras [o'ʎejras] fpl dark rings under the eyes.

olho ['oʎu] m eye; (vista) eyesight; **a ~s vistos** before one's very eyes; **~ por ~** an eye for an eye; **num abrir e fechar de ~s** in a flash; **não pregar ~** not to sleep a wink; **ver com bons ~s** to approve of.

oligarquia [oligax'kia] f oligarchy.

olim'píada f: **as O~s** the Olympics.

oli'val, oli'vedo m olive grove; **oliveira** f olive tree.

ol'meiro, 'olmo m elm.

o'lor m fragrance; **~oso/a** adj fragrant.

olvi'dar vt to forget.

om'breira f (de porta) doorpost; (de roupa) shoulder pad.

'ombro m shoulder; **encolher os ~s/dar de ~s** to shrug one's shoulders.

ome'leta (Pt), **ome'lete** (Br) f omelette, omelet (US).

omissão [omi'sãw] f (falta) omission; (descuido) neglect; **omisso/a** adj (negligente) neglectful; **omitir** vt to omit.

omo'plata f shoulder blade.

onça ['õsa] f (peso) ounce; (animal) jaguar; **~-parda** f puma.

'onda f wave; **~ sonora/luminosa** sound/light wave; **~ curta/média/longa** short/medium/long wave; **~ de calor** heat wave; **ir na ~** to be taken in.

'onde adv where // conj where, in which; **por ~** through which; **por ~?** which way?; **~ quer que** wherever.

onde'ado/a adj wavy // m (cabelo) wave; **ondeante** adj waving, undulating; **ondear** vt to wave // vi to wave; (água) to ripple; (serpear) to meander, wind; **ondulação** f undulation; **ondulado/a** adj wavy; **ondulante** adj waving, undulating.

one'rar vt to burden, weigh down; **oneroso/a** adj onerous.

'ônibus m (Br) bus.

onipo'tência (Pt: **omn-**) f omnipotence; **onipotente** (Pt: **omn-**) adj omnipotent.

o'nívoro/a (Pt: **omn-**) adj omnivorous.

'ônix m onyx.

ontem ['õtẽ] adv yesterday; **~ à noite** last night; **~ à tarde** yesterday afternoon.

'ONU f abr de **Organização das Nações Unidas** UNO, United Nations Organization.

'onze num eleven.

o'paco/a adj opaque; (obscuro) dark.

o'pala f opal; (tecido) fine muslin.

opção [op'sãw] f option, choice; (preferência) first claim, right.

'ópera f opera; **~ bufa** comic opera.

operação [opera'sãw] f operation; (COM) transaction; **operador(a)** m/f operator; (cirurgião) surgeon; (num cinema) projectionist; (dum filme) camera operator; **operar** vt (produzir) to produce, bring about; (MED) to operate on // vi (agir) to act, function; **operar-se** vr (suceder) to take place; (MED) to have an operation.

ope'rário/a adj working; **classe ~a** working class // m/f worker.

opi'nar vt (julgar) to think // vi (dar o seu parecer) to express an opinion; **opinião** f opinion.

'ópio m opium.

o'píparo/a adj (lit) splendid, lavish.

opo'nente adj opposing // m/f opponent; **opor** vt to oppose; (resistência) to put up, offer; **opor-se** vr (fazer objeção) to object; (resistir) to resist.

oportuni'dade f opportunity; **oportunismo** m opportunism; **oportunista** m/f opportunist; **oportuno/a** adj (momento) opportune, right; (conveniente) convenient, suitable.

oposição [opozi'sãw] f opposition; **em ~ a** against; **oposto/a** adj (contrário) opposite; (em frente) facing, opposite; (antagônico) opposed, contrary.

opressão [opre'sãw] f oppression; **opressivo/a** adj oppressive; **opressor(a)** m/f oppressor; **oprimir** vt to oppress.

o'próbrio m (infâmia) ignominy; (lit: desonra) shame.

op'tar vi (escolher) to choose; **~ por** to opt for.

opu'lência f opulence; **opulento/a** adj opulent.

o'púsculo m pamphlet, booklet.

'ora adv now; **de ~ em diante** from now on; **por ~** for the time being // conj now; (pois bem) well; **~ sim, ~ não** first yes, then no // excl well now!; **~ essa!** the very idea!, come off it!; **~ bem** now then; **~ viva!** hello there!

oração [ora'sãw] f (reza) prayer; (discurso) speech; (LING) sentence.

o'ráculo m oracle.

ora'dor(a) m/f (aquele que fala) speaker; (pregador) preacher.

o'ral adj oral.

orango'tango m orang-utan.

o'rar vi (REL) to pray.

'orbe m orb, sphere; **órbita** f orbit.

orçamento [oxsa'mẽtu] m (finanças) budget; (avaliação) estimate.

ordeiro/a [ox'dejru/a] adj peaceable, law-abiding.

ordem ['oxdẽ] f (ger) order; (mandado) command; **~ do dia** agenda; **de primeira** ~ first-rate; **por ~** in order, in turn; **até nova ~** until further notice; **pôr em ~** to arrange, tidy; **às suas ordens** at your service.

ordenação [oxdena'sãw] f (REL) ordination; (lei) decree.

orde'nado/a adj (posto em ordem) in order; (metódico) orderly // m salary, wages pl.

orde'nança m (MIL) orderly // f (regulamento) ordinance.

orde'nar vt to arrange, put in order; ~-**se** vr (REL) to be ordained.

ordenhar [oxde'ɲax] vt to milk.

ordi'nário/a adj ordinary; (comum) usual; (medíocre) mediocre; (mal-educado) coarse, vulgar; **de** ~ usually.

orelha [o'reʎa] f (ANAT) ear; (aba) flap; **orelhão** m open telephone kiosk.

orfa'nato m orphanage; **órfão/órfã** m/f orphan.

or'gânico/a adj organic; **organismo** m organism; (entidade) organization.

orga'nista m/f organist.

organização [oxganiza'sãw] f organization; **organizar** vt to organize.

órgão ['oxgãw] m organ.

or'gasmo m orgasm.

orgia [ox'ʒia] f orgy.

orgulhar-se [oxgu'ʎax-si] vr: ~ **de** to be proud of; **orgulho** m pride; (arrogância) arrogance; **orgulhoso/a** adj proud; (soberbo) haughty.

orientação [orjēta'sãw] f (direção) direction; (posição) position; (tendência) tendency; (EDUC) training, guidance.

orien'tal adj eastern.

orien'tar vt (situar) to orientate; (dirigir) to direct; (informar) to guide; ~-**se** vr to get one's bearings.

ori'ente m: **O**~ the East; **Extremo O**~ Far East; **O**~ **Médio/Próximo** Middle/Near East.

orifício [ori'fisju] m hole, opening.

origem [o'riʒē] f (procedência) origin; (ascendência) lineage, descent; **lugar de** ~ birthplace; **original** adj (novo) original; (estranho) strange, odd; **originalidade** f originality; **originar** vt to originate, start; **originar-se** vr to arise; **originário/a** adj (proveniente) native.

ori'undo/a adj (procedente) arising from; (natural) native of.

'orla f (borda) edge, border; (de roupa) hem; (faixa) strip; ~ **marítima** seafront.

ornamen'tar vt to decorate, adorn; **ornamento** m adornment, decoration; **ornar** vt to adorn, decorate; **ornato** m (adorno) ornament; (ornamento) decoration.

ornitologia [oxnitolo'ʒia] f ornithology; **ornitologista** m/f ornithologist.

orquestra [ox'kɛʃtra] f orchestra; ~ **de câmara/sinfônica** chamber/symphony orchestra.

orquídea [ox'kidea] f orchid.

ortodo'xia f orthodoxy; **ortodoxo/a** adj orthodox.

ortogra'fia f spelling.

ortope'dia f orthopaedics sg.

orvalhar [ox'vaʎax] vt to sprinkle with dew; **orvalho** m dew.

os art ver **a**.

oscilação [osila'sãw] f (movimento) oscillation; (flutuação) fluctuation; (vacilação) hesitation; **oscilar** vi

(balançar-se) to sway, swing; (hesitar) to hesitate.

'osso m bone; (dificuldade) predicament; **um** ~ **duro de roer** a hard nut to crack; **ossudo/a** adj bony.

osten'sivo/a adj ostensible, apparent.

ostentação [oʃtēta'sãw] f ostentation; (exibição) display, show; **ostentar** vt to show; (alardear) to show off, flaunt; **ostentoso/a** adj ostentatious, showy.

'ostra f oyster.

ostra'cismo m ostracism.

'OTAN f abr de **Organização do Tratado do Atlântico Norte** NATO, North Atlantic Treaty Organization.

'ótico/a (Pt: -pt-) adj optical // m/f optician // f optics sg.

'ótimo/a (Pt: -pt-) adj excellent, splendid // excl great!, super!

ou [o] conj or; ~ **este** ~ **aquele** either this one or that one; ~ **seja** in other words.

'ouço etc vb ver **ouvir**.

ourela [o'rela] f edge, border.

ouriço [o'risu] m (europeu) hedgehog; (do Brasil) coendou; (casca) shell; (col: animação) riot; ~ **do mar** sea urchin.

ourives [o'rivɛʃ] m inv (fabricante) goldsmith; (vendedor) jeweller; ~**aria** f (arte) goldsmith's art; (loja) jeweller's (shop); **ouro** m gold; (cartas) diamonds; **de ouro** golden; **ouropel** m tinsel.

ousa'dia f daring; **ousar** vt/i to dare.

outeiro [o'tejru] m hill.

ou'tono m autumn.

ou'torga f granting, concession; **outorgar** vt (dar) to grant; (conceder) to concede.

outrem [o'trē] pron inv (sg) somebody else; (pl) other people.

outro/a [o'tru/a] adj (sg) another; (pl) other // pron another (one); ~**s** others; ~ **a coisa** something else; ~ **qualquer** any other; **de** ~ **modo/de** ~**a maneira** otherwise; ~ **tanto** the same again.

ou'trora adv formerly; (antigamente) a long time ago.

outrossim [otro'sī] adv likewise, moreover.

ou'tubro (Pt: **O**-) m October.

ouvido [o'vidu] m (ANAT) ear; (sentido) hearing; **de** ~ by ear; **dar** ~ **s a** to listen to; **ouvinte** m/f listener; **ouvir** vt to hear; (escutar) to listen to; (missa) to attend; **ouvir dizer que ...** to hear that ...; **ouvir falar de** to hear of.

ovação [ova'sãw] f ovation, acclaim.

o'val f oval; **ovalado/a** adj oval.

o'vário m ovary.

ovelha [o'veʎa] f sheep.

'ovo m egg; ~**s cozidos duros** hard-boiled eggs; ~**s escalfados** (Pt)/**pochê** (Br) poached eggs; ~**s estrelados/fritos** fried eggs; ~**s mexidos** scrambled eggs; ~**s quentes** soft-boiled eggs; **ovulação** f ovulation; **óvulo** m ovum.

oxalá [oʃaˈla] *excl* if only it were so!, some hope! // *conj* let's hope ..., if only ...!; ~ **ele venha hoje!** let's hope he comes today!

oxidação [oksıdaˈsãw] *f* oxidation; *(ferrugem)* rusting; **oxidar** *vi* to rust; **óxido** *m* oxide; **óxido de carbônio** carbon monoxide; **oxigenar** *vt* to oxygenate; *(cabelo)* to bleach; **oxigênio** *m* oxygen.

o'zônio *m* ozone.

P

pá *f* shovel; *(de remo, hélice)* blade; ~ **de lixo** dustpan; ~ **mecânica** bulldozer // *m (Pt)* pal, mate.

pa'cato/a *adj (pessoa)* peace-loving; *(lugar)* peaceful.

pachorrento/a [paʃoˈxẽtu/a] *adj* slow, sluggish.

paciência [pasiˈjẽsja] *f* patience; *(perseverança)* endurance; *(cartas)* patience; **ter** ~ to be patient; ~ we'll just have to put up with it!; **paciente** *adj* patient; *(resignado)* resigned // *m/f* patient.

pacificação [pasıfıkaˈsãw] *f* pacification; **pacificar** *vt* to pacify, calm (down); **pacificar-se** *vr* to calm down; **pacífico/a** *adj (pessoa)* peace-loving; *(sossegado)* peaceful; **Oceano Pacífico** Pacific Ocean; **pacifismo** *m* pacifism; **pacifista** *m/f* pacifist.

'paço *m* palace; *(fig)* court.

pa'cote *m* packet; *(embrulho)* parcel.

'pacto *m* pact; *(ajuste)* agreement; **pactuar** *vt* to agree on // *vi* to make a pact *ou* an agreement.

pada'ria *f* bakery, baker's (shop).

padecer [padeˈsex] *vt* to suffer; *(suportar)* to put up with, endure; **padecimento** *m* suffering; *(dor)* pain.

padeiro [paˈdejru] *m* baker; *(entregador de pão)* breadman.

padrão [paˈdrãw] *m (oficial)* standard; *(medida)* gauge; *(desenho)* pattern; *(modelo)* model; ~ **da vida** standard of living.

pa'drasto *m* stepfather; **padre** *m* priest; **O Santo Padre** the Holy Father; **padrinho** *m (REL)* godfather; *(de noivo)* best man; *(de duelo)* second; *(fig)* sponsor.

padroeiro/a [padroˈejru/a] *m* patron; *(santo)* patron saint // *f* patroness; *(santa)* patron saint.

padronização [padronızaˈsãw] *f* standardization; **padronizar** *vt* to standardize.

'paga *f* payment; *(soldo)* pay; **em** ~ **de** in return for; ~**dor(a)** *adj* paying // *m (quem paga)* payer; *(de soldada)* pay clerk; *(de banco)* teller; ~**mento** *m* payment.

pagão/pagã [paˈgãw/paˈgã] *adj, m/f* pagan.

pa'gar *vt* to pay; *(compras, pecados)* to pay for; *(o que devia)* to pay back; *(recompensar)* to reward; ~ **a prestações** to pay hire purchase *ou* in instalments; ~ **à vista** *(Br)*/**a pronto** *(Pt)* to pay on the spot, pay at the time of purchase; ~ **dinheiro** *(Br)*/**de contado** *(Pt)* to pay cash; **a** ~ unpaid.

página [ˈpaʒına] *f (folha)* page.

'pago/a *pp* de **pagar** // *adj* paid; *(fig)* even // *m* pay.

pa'gode *m* pagoda; *(fig)* fun, high jinks *pl.*

pai [paj] *m* father; ~**s** *mpl* parents.

painel [pajˈnɛw] *m (numa parede)* panel; *(quadro)* picture; *(AUTO)* dashboard; *(de avião)* instrument panel.

paio [ˈpaju] *m* pork sausage.

paiol [paˈjɔw] *m* storeroom; *(celeiro)* barn; *(de pólvora)* powder magazine; ~ **de carvão** coal bunker.

pairar [pajˈrax] *vi* to hover; *(embarcação)* to lie to.

país [paˈiʃ] *m* country; *(região)* land; ~ **encantado** fairyland; ~ **natal** native land; **paisagem** *f* scenery; *(o campo)* countryside; *(pintura)* landscape; **paisano/a** *adj* civilian // *m/f (não militar)* civilian; *(compatriota)* fellow countryman; **à paisana** *(soldado)* in civvies; *(policial)* in plain clothes.

paixão [pajˈʃãw] *f* passion; **paixoneta** *f* crush.

pajem [ˈpaʒẽ] *m (moço)* page.

'pala *f (de boné)* peak; *(em automóvel)* sun visor; *(de vestido)* yoke.

palácio [paˈlasju] *m* palace; ~ **da justiça** courthouse.

pala'dar *m* taste.

pala'dino *m (medieval, fig)* champion.

palanque [paˈlãkı] *m (estrado)* stand.

pa'lavra *f* word; *(fala)* speech; *(promessa)* promise; *(direito de falar)* right to speak; ~! honestly!; ~**s cruzadas** crossword (puzzle); **cortar a** ~ **a alguém** to cut sb short; **dirigir a** ~ **a** to address; **em poucas** ~**s** briefly; **pedir a** ~ to ask permission to speak; **palavrão** *m (obsceno)* swearword; **palavreado** *m* babble, gibberish; *(loquacidade)* smooth talk.

'palco *m (teatro)* stage.

pa'lerma *adj* silly, stupid; *(col)* daft // *m/f* fool.

pales'tino/a *adj, m/f* Palestinian // *f:* **P~a** Palestine.

pa'lestra *f (conversa)* chat, talk; *(conferência)* talk.

pa'leta *f* palette.

pale'tó *m* coat, jacket.

palha [ˈpaʎa] *f* straw; *(fig)* trifle; **por dá cá aquela** ~ *(Pt)* for no obvious reason.

palhaço [paˈʎasu] *m* clown.

palheiro [paˈʎejru] *m* hayloft; *(monte de feno)* haystack; **palhoça** *f* thatched hut.

pali'ar *vt (disfarçar)* to disguise, gloss

over; (*atenuar*) to mitigate, extenuate; **paliativo/a** *adj* palliative.

pali'çada *f* fence; (*militar*) stockade; (*para torneio*) enclosure.

pali'dez *f* paleness; **pálido/a** *adj* pale.

'pálio *m* canopy.

pali'tar *vt* to pick // *vi* to pick one's teeth.

pa'lito *m* stick; (*para os dentes*) toothpick.

'palma *f* (*folha*) palm leaf; (*da mão*) palm; **bater ~s** to clap; **palmada** *f* slap; **palmeira** *f* palm tree; **palmo** *m* (hand) span; **palmo a palmo** inch by inch.

pal'pável *adj* tangible; (*fig*) obvious.

'pálpebra *f* eyelid.

palpitação [pawpɪta'sãw] *f* beating, throbbing; **palpitacões** *fpl* palpitations; **palpitante** *adj* beating, throbbing; (*fig: emocionante*) thrilling; (: *de interesse atual*) sensational; **palpitar** *vi* (*coração*) to beat; (*comover-se*) to shiver; **palpite** *m* (*intuição*) hunch; (*turfe*) tip.

pal'rar *vi* to chatter, prattle.

pa'lude *m* marsh, swamp; **paludismo** *m* malaria; **palustre** *adj* (*terra*) marshy; (*aves*) marsh-dwelling.

Pana'má *m* Panama; **panamenho/a** *adj* Panamanian.

'pança *f* belly, paunch.

pan'cada *f* (*no corpo*) blow, hit; (*choque*) knock; (*relógio*) stroke; **~ d'água** downpour; **dar uma ~ com a cabeça** to bang one's head; **dar ~ em alguém** to hit sb; **levar uma ~** to get hit.

pan'çudo/a *adj* fat, potbellied.

'pândega *f* merrymaking, good time.

pan'deiro *m* tambourine.

pa'nela *f* (*de barro*) pot; (*de metal*) pan; **~ de pressão** pressure cooker.

pan'fleto *m* pamphlet.

'pânico/a *m* panic; **em ~** panic-stricken.

panificação [panɪfɪka'sãw] *f* (*fabricação*) bread-making; (*padaria*) bakery; **panificadora** *f* baker's.

'pano *m* cloth; (*teatro*) curtain; (*largura de tecido*) width; (*de parede*) panel; (*mancha no corpo*) blemish; **~ de cozinha** dishcloth; **~ de pratos** teacloth; **~ de pó** duster.

pano'rama *m* (*vista*) view; (*fig: observação*) survey.

panqueca [pã'kcka] *f* pancake.

panta'nal [-aw] *m* swampland; **pântano** *m* marsh, swamp; **pantanoso/a** *adj* marshy, swampy.

pan'tera *f* panther.

panto'mima *f* pantomime.

pão [pãw] *m*, *pl* **pães** [pãjʃ] bread; **um ~ a loaf**; **~ de carne** meat loaf; **~ de forma** sliced loaf; **~ caseiro** homemade bread; **~ torrado** toast; **ganhar o ~** to earn a living; **~-de-ló** *m* sponge cake; **~zinho** *m* roll.

'papa *m* Pope // *f* (*cozida*) mush, pap; **não ter ~s na língua** to be outspoken, not to mince one's words.

papagaio [papa'gaju] *m* parrot; (*de papel*) kite.

papai [pa'paj] *m* dad, daddy; **P~ Noel** Santa Claus, Father Christmas.

pa'palvo *m* simpleton.

papa-'moscas *f inv* (*BIO*) flycatcher.

papari'car *vt* to pamper; **paparicos** *mpl* (*mimos*) pampering *sg*.

pa'pel *m* paper; (*no teatro*) part, role; **fazer um ~** to play a part; **~ aéreo** airmail paper; **~ carbono/de embrulho** carbon paper/wrapping paper; **~ de escrever/de alumínio** writing paper/tinfoil; **~ higiênico** toilet paper; **~ de parede** wallpaper; **~ de seda/transparente** tissue paper/tracing paper; **~ usado** waste paper; **~ada** *f* pile of papers; (*burocracia*) red tape.

papelão [pape'lãw] *m* cardboard; (*fig*) fiasco; **papelaria** *f* stationer's (shop); **papelzinho** *m* scrap of paper.

'papo *m* (*de ave*) crop; **bater ~** (*Br*) to chat, have a chat.

papoula [pa'pola] *f* poppy.

paquete [pa'ketʃɪ] *m* steamship.

par *adj* (*igual*) equal; (*número*) even // *m* pair; (*casal*) couple; (*pessoa na dança*) partner; (*nobre*) peer; **abrir de ~ em ~** to open wide; **sem ~** incomparable; **abaixo de ~** (*COM, GOLFE*) below below par.

'para *prep* for; (*direção*) to, towards; **bom ~ comer** good to eat; **~ não ser ouvido** so as not to be heard; **~ quê?** what for?, why?; **ir ~ São Paulo** to go to São Paulo; **ir ~ casa** to go home; **~ com** (*atitude*) towards; **de lá ~ cá** since then; **~ a semana** next week; **estar ~** to be about to // *conj*: **~ que** so that, in order that.

parabéns [para'bẽʃ] *mpl* congratulations; (*aniversário*) happy birthday; **dar ~ a** to congratulate.

pa'rábola *f* parable; (*MAT*) parabola.

pára-'brisa *m* windscreen; (*US*) windshield.

pára-choques [para-'ʃɔkɪʃ] *m inv* (*AUTO: exterior*) bumper; (: *interior*) shock absorber.

pa'rada *f* stop; (*COM*) stoppage; (*militar, colegial*) parade.

paradeiro [para'dejru] *m* whereabouts; (*COM*) slump.

para'doxo *m* paradox.

para'fina *f* paraffin.

pa'ráfrase *f* paraphrase.

para'fusar *vt* to screw in // *vi*: **~** (*meditar*) to ponder; **parafuso** *m* screw.

paragem [pa'raʒẽ] *f* stop; **~ de eléctrico** (*Pt*) tram stop; **paragens** *fpl* (*lugares*) places, parts.

pa'rágrafo *m* paragraph.

para'íso *m* paradise.

paralele'pípedo *m* paving stone.

para'lelo/a *adj* parallel // *m* (*GEO, comparação*) parallel // *f* parallel line; **~as** *fpl* (*esporte*) parallel bars.

para'lisar vt to paralyse; (trabalho) to bring to a standstill; ~-se vr to become paralysed; (fig) to come to a standstill; **paralisia** f paralysis; **paralítico/a** adj, m/f paralytic.

para'mento m (adorno) ornament; ~s mpl (vestes) vestments; (de igreja) hangings.

paramili'tar adj paramilitary.

para'nóico/a adj, m/f paranoid, paranoiac.

parapeito [para'pejtu] m (muro) wall, parapet; (da janela) windowsill.

pára-quedas [para-'kedaʃ] m inv parachute; a **pára-quedista** m/f parachutist // m (MIL) paratrooper.

pa'rar vi to stop; (ficar) to stay // vt to stop; **fazer** ~ (deter) to stop; ~ **na cadeia** to end up in jail; ~ **de fazer** to stop doing.

pára-raios [para-'xajoʃ] m inv lightning conductor.

para'sita adj parasitic // m parasite; **parasito** m parasite.

parceiro/a [pax'fejru/a] m/f partner.

par'cela f piece, bit; (de terra) plot.

parce'ria f partnership.

parci'al adj (eclipse) partial; (juiz) biased; ~**idade** f (preconceito) bias, prejudice; (paixão) partiality; (partido) party, faction.

'parco/a adj (escasso) scanty; (que economiza) thrifty.

par'dal m sparrow.

'pardo/a adj (cinzento) grey; (castanho) brown.

pare'cer m (opinião) opinion; **de bom** ~ good-looking // vi (ter a aparência de) to look, seem; (ter semelhança com) to look like, seem like; ~**-se** vr to look alike, resemble each other; ~**-se com o pai** to take after one's father; **ao que parece** apparently; **parece-me que** I think that, it seems to me that; **que lhe parece?** what do you think?; **parecido/a** adj alike, similar; **parecido com** like.

pa'rede f wall; (greve) strike.

parelha [pa'reʎa] f (de cavalos) team; (par) pair; (de pessoas) couple.

pa'rente/a m/f relative, relation; **parentela** f relations pl; **parentesco** m relationship; (fig) connection.

pa'rêntese m parenthesis; (na escrita) bracket.

pari'dade f (igualdade) equality; (de câmbio) parity.

pa'rir vt to give birth to // vi to give birth; (mulher) to have a baby.

parlamen'tar adj parliamentary; **parlamento** m parliament.

'pároco m parish priest.

pa'ródia f parody; **parodiar** vt (imitar) to copy; (fazer paródia de) to mimic, parody.

paróquia [pa'rokja] f (REL) parish; **paroquiano/a** m/f parishioner.

paro'xismo m fit, attack; ~**s** mpl death throes.

parque ['paxkɪ] m (de caça) reserve; (público) park; ~ **industrial** industrial estate; ~**amento** m (Pt) parking.

par'reira f trellised vine.

'parte f part; (quinhão) share; (lado) side; (papel) role; ~ **interna** inside; **a maior** ~ **de** most of; **a maior** ~ **das vezes** most of the time; **à** ~ (separadamente) apart; (além de) apart from; **em grande** ~ to a great extent; **em** ~ **alguma** nowhere; **por toda (a)** ~ everywhere; **pôr de** ~ to set aside; **tomar** ~ **em** to take part in; **dar** ~ to inform of.

parteira [pax'tejra] f midwife.

participação [paxtʃɪsɪpa'sãw] f participation; (comunicação) announcement, notification; ~ **nos lucros** profit-sharing; **participante** m/f participant; **participar** vt to announce, notify of // vi: **participar de** (tomar parte) to participate in, take part in; (compartilhar) to share in.

parti'cípio m participle.

particu'lar adj (especial) particular, special; (privativo, pessoal) private // m particular; **em** ~ in private; ~**es** mpl details; ~**izar** vt (especificar) to specify; (detalhar) to give details of; ~**izar-se** vr to distinguish o.s.; ~**mente** adv privately.

parti'dário/a adj partisan // m/f (esporte) supporter, follower; (POL) partisan.

par'tido/a adj broken // m (POL) party; (para casamento) catch; (em jogo) handicap; **tirar** ~ **de** to profit from; **tomar o** ~ **de** to side with // f (saída) departure; (esporte) game, match; (COM: quantidade) lot; (: remessa) shipment; (em corrida) start; **perder a** ~**a** to lose.

partilha [pax'tʃiʎa] f share; **partilhar** vt to share; (distribuir) to share out.

par'tir vt (quebrar) to break; (dividir) to divide, split // vi (pôr-se a caminho) to set off, set out; (ir-se embora) to leave, go away; ~ **de** (começar) to start; (originar) to arise from; ~**-se** vr (quebrar-se) to break; **a** ~ **de** (starting) from.

'parto m (child)birth; **estar em trabalho de** ~ to be in labour.

'parvo/a adj stupid, silly // m/f fool, idiot; **parvoíce** f silliness, stupidity.

'Páscoa f Easter; (dos judeus) Passover.

pas'mado/a adj amazed, astonished; **pasmar** vt to amaze, astonish; **pasmar-se** vr: **pasmar-se com** to be amazed at.

pas'palho m simpleton.

pasquim [paʃ'kĩ] m (jornal) satirical newspaper.

'passa f (de uva) raisin; (de ameixa) prune.

pas'sada f (passo) step; **dar uma** ~ **em** to call in at.

passadeira [pasa'dejra] f (tapete) stair carpet; (mulher) ironing woman; (Pt:

para peões) zebra crossing, crosswalk (*US*).

passa'diço/a *adj* passing // *m* (*NÁUT*) bridge.

pas'sado/a *adj* (*decorrido*) past; (*antiquado*) old-fashioned; (*fruto*) bad; (*peixe*) off; **o ano ~** last year; **bem ~a** (*carne*) well done // *m* past.

passa'dor *m* (*coador*) strainer; (*filtro*) filter; (*de macarrão*) colander; (*de cabelo*) pin, grip.

passageiro/a [pasa'ʒejru/a] *adj* (*transitório*) passing; (*local*) busy // *m* passenger.

passagem [pa'saʒē] *f* passage; (*preço de condução*) fare; (*bilhete*) ticket; **~ de nível** level crossing; **~ de ida e volta** return trip ticket, round trip ticket (*US*); **~ subterrânea** subway; **~ de pedestres** pedestrian crossing; **de ~** in passing.

passa'porte *m* passport.

pas'sar *vt* to pass; (*ponte, rio*) to cross; (*exceder*) to go beyond, exceed; (*coar: farinha*) to sieve; (*: líquido*) to strain; (*: café*) to percolate; (*a ferro*) to iron; (*tarefa*) to set; (*telegrama*) to send; (*o tempo*) to spend; (*bife*) to cook; (*a outra pessoa*) to pass on; **~ por cima** to overlook // *vi* to pass; (*na rua*) to go past; (*tempo*) to go by; (*fruta*) to go off; (*terminar*) to be over; (*ser admissível*) to pass; (*mudar*) to change; **~ bem** (*de saúde*) to be well; **como está passando?** how are you?; **não ~ de** to be only; **~ sem** to do without; **~ por casa de** to call in on; **~ pela cabeça** to occur to; **~ a ser** to become; **~-se** *vr* (*acontecer*) to go on, happen; (*desertar*) to go over; (*tempo*) to go by.

passa'rela *f* footbridge; (*para modelos*) catwalk.

'pássaro *m* bird.

passa'tempo *m* pastime; (*diversão*) amusement; **como ~** for fun.

pas'sável *adj* passable, so-so, all right.

'passe *m* (*licença*) pass.

passe'ar *vt* to take for a walk; (*exibir*) to show off // *vi* to go for a walk; **~ a cavalo** to go for a ride; **passeata** *f* stroll; (*marcha coletiva*) protest march; **passeio** *m* walk; (*calçada*) pavement; **dar um passeio** to go for a walk; **um passeio de automóvel** drive.

pas'sivo/a *adj* passive // *m* (*COM*) liabilities (*pl*).

'passo *m* step; (*medida*) pace; (*ruído dos passos*) footstep; (*sinal de pé*) footprint; **apertar o ~** to hurry up; **a cada ~** constantly; **ceder o ~** to give way; **dar um ~** to take a step; **marcar ~** to mark time.

'pasta *f* paste; (*de couro*) briefcase; (*de cartolina*) folder; (*de ministro*) portfolio; **~ dentifrícia/de dentes** toothpaste.

pastagem [paʃ'taʒē] *f* pasture; **pastar** *vt* to graze on // *vi* to graze.

pas'tel *m* pie; (*desenho*) pastel drawing;

~aria *f* (*loja*) cake shop; (*comida*) pastry.

pastilha [paʃ'tiʎa] *f* (*MED*) tablet; (*doce*) pastille; (*TEC. informática*) chip.

'pasto *m* (*erva*) grass; (*terreno*) pasture; **casa de ~** (*Pt*) cheap restaurant, diner.

pas'tor(a) *m* shepherd; (*REL*) clergyman, pastor // *f* shepherdess.

'pata *f* (*pé de animal*) foot, paw; (*ave*) duck; **meter a ~** to put one's foot in it; **patada** *f* kick.

pata'mar *m* (*de escada*) landing.

pa'tente *adj* obvious, evident // *f* (*COM*) patent; (*MIL: título*) commission; **altas ~s** high-ranking officers; **patentear** *vt* to show, reveal; (*COM*) to patent; **patentear-se** *vr* to be shown, be evident.

pa'terno/a *adj* fatherly, paternal; **casa ~a** family home.

pa'teta *adj* stupid, daft // *m/f* idiot.

pa'tético/a *adj* pathetic, moving.

pa'tíbulo *m* gallows.

pa'tife *m* scoundrel, rogue.

patim [pa'tʃĩ] *m* skate; **~ de rodas** roller skate; **patinação** *f* skating; (*lugar*) skating rink; **patinar** *vi* to skate; (*AUTO: derrapar*) to skid.

patinhar [patʃi'nax] *vi* (*como um pato*) to dabble; (*em lama*) to splash about, slosh.

'pátio *m* (*de uma casa*) patio, backyard; (*espaço cercado de edifícios*) courtyard; (*de escola*) playground; (*MIL*) parade ground; **~ de recreio** playground.

'pato *m* duck; (*macho*) drake.

patranha [pa'traɲa] *f* fib, story.

patrão [pa'trãw] *m* (*COM*) boss; (*dono de casa*) master; (*proprietário*) landlord; (*NÁUT*) skipper.

'pátria *f* native land, homeland.

patri'mônio *m* (*herança*) inheritance; (*fig*) heritage; (*bens*) property.

patri'ota *m/f* patriot; **patriótico/a** *adj* patriotic; **patriotismo** *m* patriotism.

pa'troa *f* (*mulher do patrão*) boss's wife; (*dona de casa*) lady of the house; (*proprietária*) landlady.

patroci'nar *vt* to sponsor; (*apoiar*) to support; **patrocínio** *m* sponsorship, backing.

patrulha [pa'truʎa] *f* patrol.

patus'cada *f* good time, spree; **andar em ~s** to live it up.

pau [paw] *m* (*madeira*) wood; (*vara*) stick; (*viga*) beam; **de ~** wooden; **~ de bandeira** flagpole; **a meio ~** (*bandeira*) at half-mast; **~s** *mpl* (*cartas*) clubs; **levar ~** (*em exame*) to fail.

pa'ul *m* marsh, swamp.

pau'lada *f* blow (with a stick).

paulatina'mente *adv* gradually; **paulatino/a** *adj* slow, gradual.

paulifi'car *vt* to annoy, bother.

pau'pérrimo/a *adj* poverty-stricken.

pausa ['pawza] *f* pause; (*intervalo*) break; (*descanso*) rest; **pausado/a** *adj* (*lento*) slow; (sem pressa) leisurely; (cadenciado) measured.

pauta ['pawta] f (linha) (guide)line; (MÚS) staff; (lista) list; (folha) ruled paper; (indicações) guidelines; **sem ~** (papel) plain; **pautado/a** adj (papel) ruled.

pavão/voa [pa'vãw/'voa] m peacock // f peahen.

pavilhão [pavi'ʎãw] m (tenda) tent; (de madeira) hut; (em exposição) stand; (bandeira) flag; **~ de isolamento** isolation ward.

pavi'mento m (chão, andar) floor; (da rua) road surface.

pa'vio m wick.

pavone'ar vt (ostentar) to show off // vi (caminhar) to strut; **~-se** vr to show off.

pa'vor m dread, terror; **ter ~ de** to be terrified of; **~oso/a** adj dreadful, terrible.

paz f peace; (sossego) peacefulness; **fazer as ~es** to make up, be friends again.

pé m (de pessoa) foot; (da mesa) leg; (fig: base) footing; (de alface) head; (milho, café) plant; **ir a ~** to walk, go on foot; **ao ~ de** near, by; **a água dá ~** (natação) you can touch the bottom; **em ~** standing (up); **em ~ de guerra** on a war footing; **pôr-se em ~** to stand up.

peão [pɪ'ãw] m (Pt) pedestrian; (MIL) foot soldier; (xadrez) pawn; (trabalhador) farm labourer.

'peça f (pedaço) piece; (AUTO) part; (aposento) room; (logro) trick; (teatro) play; (serviço) **pago por ~** piecework; **~ de roupa** garment.

pe'cado m sin; **pecador(a)** m/f sinner, wrongdoer; **pecaminoso/a** adj sinful; **pecar** vi to sin; (cometer falta) to do wrong; **pecar por excesso de zelo** to be overzealous.

pechincha [pe'ʃiʃa] f (vantagem) godsend; (coisa barata) bargain; **pechinchar** vi to bargain, haggle.

'peço etc vb ver **pedir**.

peçonha [pe'soɲa] f poison.

pecu'ária f cattle-raising.

peculi'ar adj (especial) special, peculiar; (particular) particular.

pe'cúlio m (acumulado) savings pl; (bens) wealth.

pe'daço m piece, bit; **esperar um ~ to** wait a bit; **aos ~s** in pieces.

pedágio [pe'daʒju] m (Br: pagamento) toll; (: posto) tollbooth.

pe'dal m pedal; **pedalar** vt to pedal // vi to pedal; (andar de bicicleta) to cycle.

pe'dante adj pedantic // m/f pedant.

pederneira [pedex'nejra] f flint.

pedes'tal m pedestal.

pe'destre m (Br) pedestrian.

pedi'atra m/f paediatrician, pediatrician (US); **pediatria** f paediatrics (sg), pediatrics (sg) (US).

pedi'curo/a m/f chiropodist, podiatrist (US).

pe'dido m (COM) order; (solicitação) request; **~ de casamento** proposal (of

marriage); **~ de demissão** resignation; **~ de informação** inquiry.

pedinchar [pedĩ'ʃax] vt to beg for // vi to beg.

pe'dir vt to ask for; (COM: comida) to order; (demandar) to demand; **~ alguma coisa a alguém** to ask sb for sth // vi to ask; **~ a alguém que faça to ask sb to do; ~ desculpa** to apologize; **~ emprestado** to borrow; **~ 100 cruzeiros por algo** to ask 100 cruzeiros for sth; **~ para vir** to ask to come.

'pedra f stone; (rochedo) rock; (de granizo) hailstone; (de açúcar) lump; **~ de amolar** grindstone; **pedregal** m stony ground; **pedregoso/a** adj stony, rocky; **pedreira** f quarry; **pedreiro** m stonemason.

pedre'gulho m gravel.

pega ['pega] f (briga) quarrel // f ['pega] magpie; (Pt: moça) bird; (: meretriz) tart.

pegada [pe'gada] f (do pé) footprint; (no futebol) save; (vestígio) track, trace.

pega'diço/a adj (viscoso) sticky; (MED) infectious, catching; **pegado/a** adj (colado) stuck; (unido) together; **a casa pegada** the house next door.

pe'gar vt (selos) to stick (on); (agarrar) to take hold of; (doença, fogo, fugitivo, peixe) to catch; **ir ~** (buscar) to go and get; (compreender) to take in; **~ um emprego** to get a job; **~ uma rua** to take a street; **~ fogo a** to set fire to // vi (aderir) to stick; (planta) to take; (moda) to catch on; (doença) to be contagious; (motor) to start; **~ em** (segurar) to grab, pick up; **~ com** (casa) to be next door to; **~ a fazer** to start to do; **~-se** vr (aderir) to stick; (brigar) to have a fight, quarrel.

peitilho [pej'tʃiʎu] m shirt front; **peito** m (ANAT) chest; (de ave, mulher) breast; (fig) courage; **dar o peito a um bebê** to breastfeed a baby.

peitoril [pejto'riw] m windowsill.

peixaria [pejʃa'ria] f fishmonger's; **peixe** m fish; **peixeiro/a** m fishmonger // f fishwife.

pe'jar-se vr to be ashamed; **pejo** m shame; **ter pejo** to be ashamed.

pejora'tivo/a adj pejorative.

'pela = **por** + **a**.

pe'lado/a adj (sem pele) skinned; (sem pêlo) shorn; (fruta) peeled; (nu) bare; (sem dinheiro) broke.

'pélago m (mar alto) high seas pl, ocean; (abismo) depths pl; (fig) abyss.

pe'lar vt (tirar a pele) to skin; (tirar o pêlo) to cut the hair of; (fruta) to peel; (fig) to fleece; **~-se** vr: **~-se por** to be crazy about, adore.

'pelas = **por** + **as**.

pele ['pelɪ] f skin; (couro) leather; (como agasalho) fur (coat).

peleja [pele'ʒa] f (luta) fight; (briga) quarrel; **pelejar** vi (lutar) to fight;

(*discutir*) to quarrel; **pelejar pela paz** to struggle for peace.

pele-vermelha [pelɪ-vexˈmeʎa] *m/f* redskin.

pe'lica *f* kid (leather).

peli'cano *m* pelican.

pe'lícula *f* film; (*de pele*) film of skin.

pe'lintra *adj* (*Pt*) shabby; (: *pobre*) penniless.

'pelo = **por** + **o.**

'pêlo *m* hair; (*de animal*) fur, coat; **em ~** stark naked; **montar em ~** to ride bareback.

'pelos = **por** + **os.**

pelotão [peloˈtāw] *m* platoon, squad.

pe'lúcia *f* plush.

pe'ludo/a *adj* hairy.

'pena *f* (*pluma*) feather; (*de caneta*) nib; (*escrita*) writing; (*castigo*) punishment; (*sofrimento*) suffering; (*piedade*) pity; (*mágoa*) grief, sadness; **~ capital** capital punishment; **cumprir ~** to serve a term in jail; **que ~!** what a shame!; **ter ~ de** to feel sorry for; **valer a ~** to be worthwhile; **não vale a ~** it's not worth it; **sob ~ de** under penalty of.

pe'nal *adj* penal; **~idade** *f* penalty; (*castigo*) punishment; **impor uma ~idade a** to penalize.

'pênalti *m* (*futebol*) penalty.

pe'nar *vt* to grieve // *vi* to suffer.

pen'dência *f* dispute, quarrel.

pen'dente *adj* (*pendurado*) hanging; (*por decidir*) pending; (*inclinado*) sloping; **~ de** (*dependente*) dependent on // *m* pendant.

pen'der *vt* to hang // *vi* to hang; (*estar para cair*) to sag, droop; **~ de** (*estar pendurado*) to hang from; **~ para** (*inclinar*) to lean towards; (*ter tendência para*) to tend to; **~ a** (*estar disposto a*) to be inclined to.

'pêndulo *m* pendulum.

pendu'rado/a *adj* hanging; **pendurar** *vi*: **pendurar de** to hang from.

pe'nedo *m* rock, boulder.

peneira [peˈnejra] *f* (*da cozinha*) sieve; (*do jardim*) riddle; **peneirar** *vt* to sift, sieve; (*chover*) to drizzle.

pe'netra *m/f* gate-crasher; **penetração** *f* (*ato*) penetration, entering; (*perspicácia*) insight, sharpness; **penetrante** *adj* (*olhar*) searching; (*ferida*) deep; (*pessoa*) sharp; (*som*) penetrating; piercing; **penetrar** *vt* (*entrar: com dificuldade*) to get into, penetrate; (: *em segredo*) to steal into; (*espada*) to pierce; (*compreender*) to understand.

penha [ˈpeɲa] *f* (*rocha*) rock; (*penhasco*) cliff; **penhasco** *m* cliff, crag.

penhor [peˈɲox] *m* pledge; **casa de ~es** pawnshop; **dar em ~** to pawn; **~adamente** *adv* gratefully; **~ado/a** *adj* pawned; **penhorar** *vt* (*dar em penhor*) to pledge, pawn; (*pegar*) to confiscate; (*fig*) to put under an obligation.

penici'lina *f* penicillin.

pe'nínsula *f* peninsula; **peninsular** *adj* peninsular.

'pênis *m* penis.

peni'tência *f* (*contrição*) penitence; (*expiação*) penance; **penitenciária** *f* prison, penitentiary; **penitente** *adj* repentant // *m/f* penitent.

pe'noso/a *adj* (*assunto, tratamento*) painful; (*trabalho*) hard.

pen'sado/a *adj* deliberate, intentional; **pensador(a)** *m/f* thinker; **pensamento** *m* thought; (*ato*) thinking; (*mente*) thought, mind; (*opinião*) way of thinking; (*idéia*) idea.

pensão [pẽˈsāw] *f* (*casa*) boarding house; (*comida*) board; **~ completa** full board; **~ de aposentadoria** (*retirement*) pension.

pen'sar *vi* to think; (*imaginar*) to imagine; **~ em** to think of/about; **~ fazer** (*ter intenção*) to intend to do, be thinking of doing; **~ sobre** (*meditar*) to ponder over // *vt* (*ferimento*) to dress; **pensando bem** on second thoughts; **~ alto** to think out loud; **pensativo/a** *adj* thoughtful, pensive.

pensio'nista *m/f* pensioner; (*que mora em pensão*) boarder.

'penso *m* (*tratamento*) treatment, care; (*Pt: de ferimento*) dressing.

'pente *m* comb; **~adeira** *f* dressing table; **~ado** *m* (*arranjo de cabelo*) hairdo; (*estilo*) hair style; **pentear** *vt* to comb; (*arranjar o cabelo*) to do, style; **pentear-se** *vr* (*com um pente*) to comb one's hair; (*arranjar o cabelo*) to do one's hair.

pente'costes *m* Whitsuntide.

pente-'fino *m* fine-tooth comb.

penugem [peˈnuʒē] *f* (*de ave*) down; (*pêlo*) fluff.

pe'núltimo/a *adj* last but one.

pe'numbra *f* (*ao cair da tarde*) twilight, dusk; (*sombra*) shadow; (*meia-luz*) half-light.

pe'núria *f* poverty.

pe'pino *m* cucumber.

pe'pita *f* (*de ouro*) nugget.

pequenez [pekeˈneʃ] *f* smallness; (*infância*) infancy; (*fig: mesquinhez*) meanness; **pequeno/a** *adj* small, little // *m* boy // *f* girl; (*namorada*) girlfriend.

Pequim [peˈkĩ] *m* Peking.

'pêra *f* pear.

pe'ralta *adj* naughty // *m* dandy, fop; (*menino*) naughty child.

pe'rante *prep* before, in the presence of.

per'calço *m* (*dificuldade*) difficulty; (*estorvo*) drawback; (*transtorno*) hitch.

perce'ber *vt* (*por meio dos sentidos*) to perceive; (*compreender*) to understand; (*ver*) to see; (*um som*) to hear; (*ver ao longe*) to make out; (*dinheiro: receber*) to receive.

percentagem [pexsēˈtaʒē] *f* percentage.

percepção [pexsɛpˈsāw] *f* perception; (*compreensão*) understanding; **per-**

ceptível adj perceptible, noticeable; (som) audible.

percevejo [pexse've3u] m (inseto) bug; (prego) drawing pin.

percor'rer vt (viajar por) to travel (across/over); (passar por) to go through, traverse; (investigar) to search through; **percurso** m (espaço percorrido) distance (covered); (trajeto) route; (viagem) journey; **fazer o percurso entre** to travel between.

percussão [pexku'sãw] f (MÚS) percussion; **percutir** vt to strike.

'perda f loss; (dano) damage; (desperdício) waste.

perdão [pex'dãw] m pardon, forgiveness; ~! sorry!

per'der vt (ficar sem) to lose; (o tempo) to waste; (trem, oportunidade) to miss // vi to lose; ~-se vr (extraviar-se) to get lost; (arruinar-se) to be ruined; (desaparecer) to disappear; **perdição** f perdition, ruin; **perdido/a** adj lost; (imoral) depraved; **perdido por** (apaixonado) desperately in love with.

perdigão [pexd3i'gãw] m (macho) partridge.

perdigueiro [pexd3i'gejru] m (cachorro) pointer, setter.

per'diz f partridge.

perdo'ar vt (desculpar) to forgive, pardon; (justificar) to excuse; (dívida) to spare.

perdu'lário/a adj wasteful // m/f spendthrift.

perdu'rar vi (durar muito) to last a long time; (continuar a existir) to still exist.

pere'cer vi to perish; (morrer) to die; (acabar) to come to nothing.

peregrinação [peregrina'sãw] f (viagem) long tour, travels pl; (REL) pilgrimage; **peregrinar** vi (viajar) to travel; (REL) to go on a pilgrimage; **peregrino/a** adj (estranho) strange; (de beleza rara) exquisite; (raro) rare // m/f pilgrim.

pereira [pe'rejra] f pear tree.

peremp'tório/a adj (final) final, (decisivo) decisive.

perene [pe'reni] adj (perpétuo) everlasting; (BOT) perennial.

perfa'zer vt (completar o número de) to make up.

perfeição [pexfej'sãw] f perfection; **perfeitamente** adv perfectly // excl: **perfeitamente!** exactly!; **perfeito/a** adj perfect; (completo) complete.

per'fídia f treachery; **pérfido/a** adj treacherous.

per'fil m (do rosto) profile; (silhueta) silhouette, outline; (ARQ) (cross) section; **de** ~ in profile; **perfilar** vt (soldados) to line up; (aprumar) to straighten up; **perfilar-se** vr to stand to attention.

perfu'mar vt, **perfu'mar-se** vr to put perfume on; **perfume** m perfume; (cheiro) scent.

perfura'dor(a) m borer, drill; (de papel) punch // f punch machine; **perfurar** vt (o chão) to drill a hole in; (papel) to punch (a hole in); **perfuratriz** f drill.

pergaminho [pexga'miɲu] m parchment; (diploma) diploma.

per'gunta f question; **fazer uma** ~ **a alguém** to ask sb a question; **perguntar** vt to ask; (interrogar) to question; **perguntar alguma coisa a alguém** to ask sb sth // vi: **perguntar por alguém** to ask after sb; **perguntar-se** vr to wonder.

perícia [pe'risja] f (conhecimento) expertise; (destreza) skill; **pericial** adj expert.

periferia f periphery; (da cidade) outskirts pl; **periférico/a** adj peripheral; **estrada periférica** ring road // m (informática) peripheral.

pe'rífrase f circumlocution.

pe'rigo m danger; **correr** ~ to be in danger; **perigoso/a** adj dangerous; (arriscado) risky.

peri'ódico/a adj periodic; (chuvas) occasional; (doença) recurrent // m (revista) magazine, periodical; (jornal) (news)paper; **período** m period; (estação) season; **período letivo** term (time).

peripécia [peri'pɛsja] f unexpected event, incident.

periquito [peri'kitu] m parakeet.

peri'scópio m periscope.

pe'rito/a adj: ~ **em** (destro) skilful at, clever at; (sabedor) expert at // m/f expert; ~ **em matéria de** expert in.

perju'rar vi to commit perjury; **perjúrio** m perjury; **perjuro/a** m/f perjurer.

permanecer [pexmane'sex] vi (num lugar) to stay; (continuar a ser) to remain, keep; ~ **parado** to keep still; **permanência** f (estada) stay; (constância) permanence; (continuidade) continuance; **permanente** adj (dor) constant; (cor) fast; (residência, pregas) permanent // m (cartão) pass // f perm.

permeio [pex'meju] adv: **de** ~ **in** between.

permissão [pexmi'sãw] f permission, consent; **permitir** vt to allow, permit; (conceder) to grant; **permitir a alguém fazer** to let sb do, allow sb to do.

per'muta f (troca) exchange; (de coisas colecionadas) swap, swapping; **permutação** f (MAT) permutation; (troca) exchange; **permutar** vt to exchange; (col) to swap.

'perna f leg.

pernicioso/a [pexnisi'ozu/a] adj (nocivo) harmful; (mau) bad; (MED) malignant.

per'nil m (de animal) haunch; (CULIN) leg.

pernoi'tar vi to spend the night.

'pérola f pearl.

pero'rar vi to make a speech, hold forth.

perpas'sar vi to pass by.

perpendicu'lar adj perpendicular; **ser** ~ **a** to be at right angles to.

perpetração [pexpetra'sãw] *f* perpetration; **perpetrar** *vt* to perpetrate, commit.

perpe'tuar *vt* to perpetuate; **perpetuidade** *f* eternity; **perpétuo/a** *adj* perpetual; (*eterno*) eternal; **prisão perpétua** life imprisonment.

perplexi'dade *f* confusion, bewilderment; **perplexo/a** *adj* (*confuso*) bewildered, puzzled; (*indeciso*) uncertain.

perquirir [pexki'rix] *vt* to probe, investigate.

perscru'tar *vt* to scrutinize, examine.

perseguição [pexsegi'sãw] *f* pursuit; (*REL, POL*) persecution; **perseguidor(a)** *m/f* pursuer; (*REL, POL*) persecutor; **perseguir** *vt* (*seguir*) to pursue; (*moça*) to chase after; (*REL*) to persecute; (*importunar*) to harass, pester.

perseve'rança *f* (*insistência*) persistence; (*constância*) perseverance; **perseverante** *adj* persistent; **perseverar** *vi* to persevere; **perseverar em** (*conservar-se firme*) to persevere in; **perseverar corajoso** to remain brave; **perseverar em erro** to keep on doing wrong.

persi'ana *f* Persian blind.

persig'nar-se *vr* to cross o.s.

persis'tente *adj* persistent; **persistir** *vi* to persist; **persistir em** to persist in; **persistir calado** to keep quiet.

personagem [pexso'naʒẽ] *m/f* famous person, celebrity; (*teatro*) character; **personalidade** *f* personality.

perspec'tiva *f* (*na pintura*) perspective; (*panorama*) view; (*probabilidade*) prospect; **em ~** expected, in prospect.

perspi'cácia *f* insight, perceptiveness; **perspicaz** *adj* (*que observa*) observant; (*que vê bem*) keen-sighted; (*fig*) shrewd.

persuadir [pexswa'dʒix] *vt* to persuade; (*convencer*) to convince; **~ alguém de que/alguém a fazer** to persuade sb that/sb to do; **~-se** *vr* to convince o.s., make up one's mind; **persuasão** *f* persuasion; (*convicção*) conviction.

perten'cente *adj* belonging; **~ a** (*pertinente*) pertaining to; **pertencer** *vi*: **pertencer a** to belong to; (*referir-se*) to concern; **pertences** *mpl* (*de uma pessoa*) belongings.

perti'nácia *f* obstinacy; **pertinaz** *adj* (*persistente*) persistent; (*obstinado*) obstinate; **pertinente** *adj* (*referente*) relevant; (*apropriado*) appropriate.

'perto/a *adj* nearby // *adv* (*não longe*) near; **~ da casa** near or close to the house; **conhecer de ~** to know very well; **de ~** closely; **~ de 100 cruzeiros** about 100 cruzeiros.

perturbação [pextuxba'sãw] *f* (*angústia*) distress; (*desordem*) upset; (*MED*) trouble; (*POL*) disturbance; **perturbado/a** *adj* upset; (*desvairado*) delirious; **perturbar** *vt* (*o sossego*) to disturb; (*pessoa*) to upset, trouble.

pe'ru *m* turkey.

Pe'ru *m* Peru; **peruano/a** *adj, m/f* Peruvian.

perversão [pexvex'sãw] *f* perversion; **perversidade** *f* perversity; **perverso/a** *adj* perverse; (*malvado*) wicked; **perverter** *vt* (*corromper*) to corrupt, pervert; **pervertido/a** *adj* perverted // *m/f* pervert.

pesa'delo *m* nightmare.

pe'sado/a *adj* heavy; (*trabalho*) hard; (*estilo*) dull, boring; (*andar*) slow; (*piada*) coarse; (*comida*) stodgy; (*ar*) sultry.

pêsames ['pesamĩʃ] *mpl* condolences, sympathy *sg*.

pe'sar *vt* to weigh; (*fig*) to weigh up // *vi* to weigh; (*ser pesado*) to be heavy; (*influir*) to carry weight; (*causar mágoa*) to hurt, grieve; **~ sobre** (*recair*) to fall upon; **em que pese** despite; **~-oso/a** *adj* (*triste*) sorrowful, sad; (*arrependido*) regretful, sorry.

'pesca *f* (*ato*) fishing; (*os peixes*) catch; **ir à ~** to go fishing; **pescada** *f* whiting; **~dor(a)** *m* fisherman // *f* fisherwoman; **~dor à linha** angler; **pescar** *vt* (*peixe*) to catch; (*tentar apanhar*) to fish for; (*retirar como que pescando*) to fish out; (*um marido*) to catch, get // *vi* to fish; (*Br: col*) to understand.

pes'coço *m* neck.

'peso *m* weight; (*ônus*) burden; (*prestígio*) importance; **~ bruto/líquido** gross/net weight; **em ~** in full force.

pesqueiro/a [peʃ'kejru/a] *adj* fishing.

pesquisa [peʃ'kiza] *f* inquiry, investigation; (*científica*) research; **~ de mercado** market research.

'pêssego *m* peach.

pessi'mista *adj* pessimistic // *m/f* pessimist; **péssimo/a** *adj* very bad, awful.

pes'soa *f* person; **~s** *fpl* people; **em ~** personally; **pessoal** *adj* (*particular, íntimo*) personal; (*individual*) individual // *m* personnel *pl*, staff *pl*; (*col*) people, folk.

pes'tana *f* eyelash; **pestanejar** *vi* to blink; (*piscar*) to wink.

'peste *f* (*epidemia*) epidemic; (*bubônica*) plague; (*fig*) pest, nuisance; **pestífero/a** *adj* (*nocivo*) noxious, poisonous; **pestilência** *f* plague; (*epidemia*) epidemic.

'peta *f* lie; (*col*) fib.

'pétala *f* petal.

petição [petʃi'sãw] *f* (*rogo*) request; (*documento*) petition; **peticionário/a** *m/f* petitioner; (*JUR*) plaintiff.

petis'car *vt* to nibble at, peck at // *vi* to have a nibble; **petisco** *m* savoury, titbit.

pe'tiz *m* (*Pt*) boy.

petrechos [pe'treʃuʃ] *mpl* equipment *sg*; (*MIL*) stores, equipment; (*da cozinha*) utensils.

petrifi'car *vt* (*de medo*) to petrify; (*tornar duro*) to harden; (*assombrar*) to stupefy; **~-se** *vr* to be petrified.

petroleiro/a [petro'lejru/a] *adj* oil *cmp*,

petroleum *cmp // m (navio)* oil tanker; **petróleo** *m* oil, petroleum; **petróleo bruto** crude oil.

petu'lância *f* impertinence; *(col)* cheek; **petulante** *adj* impudent, cheeky.

peúga ['pjuga] *f (Pt)* sock.

pevide [pe'vɪdɪ] *f (Pt: de melão)* seed; *(: de maçã)* pip.

p. ex. *abr de* **por exemplo** e.g. (for example).

'pia *f* wash basin; *(da cozinha)* sink; ~ **batismal** font.

pi'ada *f* joke.

pia'nista *m/f* pianist; **piano** *m* piano.

pião [pɪ'ãw] *m (brinquedo)* top.

pi'ar *vi* to cheep; *(coruja)* to hoot.

picadeiro [pɪka'dejru] *m (circo)* ring.

pica'dinho *m* mince.

'picado/a *adj (por agulha)* pricked; *(por abelha)* stung; *(por cobra, mosquito)* bitten; *(irritado)* cross // *m (carne)* mince // *f (de agulha)* prick; *(de abelha)* sting; *(de mosquito, cobra)* bite; *(de avião)* dive; *(de navalha)* stab; *(atalho)* path, trail.

pi'cante *adj (tempero)* hot; *(piada)* risqué, blue; *(comentário)* saucy.

pica-pau [pɪka-'paw] *m* woodpecker.

pi'car *vt (agulha)* to prick; *(abelha)* to sting; *(mosquito)* to bite; *(pássaro)* to peck; *(um animal)* to goad; *(carne)* to mince; *(papel)* to shred; *(fruta)* to chop up; *(irritar)* to nettle; *(a língua)* to burn // *vi (a isca)* to take the bait; *(produzir coceira)* to sting; ~-**se** *vr* to be offended.

pica'resco/a *adj* comic, ridiculous.

pica'reta *f* pickaxe.

'pícaro/a *adj* crafty, cunning.

pi'çarra *f* shale.

'pico *m (de monte)* peak; *(espinho)* thorn; *(Pt: um pouco)* a bit; **mil e** ~ just over a thousand; **meio-dia e** ~ just after midday.

pico'lé *m* iced lolly.

pico'tar *vt* to perforate.

pic'tórico/a *adj* pictorial.

piedade [pɪe'dadʒɪ] *f (devoção)* piety; *(compaixão)* pity; **ter** ~ **de** to have pity on; **piedoso/a** *adj (REL)* pious; *(compassivo)* merciful.

piegas ['pjegaʃ] *adj inv* sentimental; *(col)* soppy // *m/f* softy; **pieguice** *f* sentimentality.

pigarrear [pɪgaxɪ'ax] *vi* to clear one's throat; **pigarro** *m (col)* a frog in one's throat.

pig'mento *m* pigment.

pigmeu/pigméia [pɪg'mɛw/pɪg'meja] *adj, m/f* pigmy.

pilão [pɪ'lãw] *m (de monte)* crusher; *(rural)* mortar; **pilar** *vt* to pound, crush // *m* pillar.

pilha ['pɪʎa] *f (eletroquímica)* battery; *(monte)* pile, heap; *(informática)* stack.

pilhagem [pɪ'ʎaʒẽ] *f (ato)* pillage; *(objetos)* plunder, booty; **pilhar** *vt (saquear)* to plunder, pillage; *(conseguir)* to get (hold of); *(roubar)* to rob; *(apanhar)* to catch.

pilhéria [pɪ'ʎɛrja] *f* joke; **pilheriar** *vi* to joke, jest.

pilotagem [pɪlo'taʒẽ] *f* flying; **escola de** ~ flying school; **pilotar** *vt (avião)* to fly; *(navio)* to steer; **piloto** *m (de avião)* pilot; *(de navio)* first mate; *(motorista)* (racing) driver; *(chama)* pilot light; **piloto automático** automatic pilot.

'pílula *f* pill; **a** ~ **anticoncepcional** the pill.

pi'menta *f (CULIN)* pepper; ~-**do-reino** *f* black pepper; **pimentão** *m (BOT)* pepper; **pimentão verde** green pepper; **pimenteira** *f* pepper plant.

pimpão/pona [pɪ'pãw/'pona] *(Pt) adj* smart, flashy // *m/f* show-off.

pimpolho [pɪ'poʎu] *m (rebento)* shoot; *(criança)* youngster.

pinaco'teca *f* art gallery.

pi'náculo *m* pinnacle, summit.

pinça ['pɪsa] *f (pequena)* tweezers *pl*; *(de casa)* tongs *pl*; *(MED)* forceps *pl*.

'pincaro *m* summit, peak.

pincel [pɪ'sɛw] *m* brush; *(para pintar)* paintbrush; ~ **de barba** shaving brush; ~**ada** *f* (brush) stroke.

'pinga *f (gota)* drop; *(Pt: trago)* drink; *(cachaça)* rum; **pingar** *vi* to drip; *(começar a chover)* to start to rain.

pingente [pɪ'ʒẽtʃɪ] *m* pendant; *(brinco)* earring.

'pingo *m (gota)* drop; *(ortografia)* dot; ~ **de gente** *(col)* scrap of nothing.

pingue-pongue [pɪgɪ-'põgɪ] *m* ping-pong.

pingüim [pɪ'gwĩ] *m* penguin.

pinha ['pɪɲa] *f* pine cone; **pinhal** *m* pine wood; **pinheiro** *m* pine (tree); **pinho** *m* pine.

'pino *m (peça)* pin; **a** ~ upright; **o sol está a** ~ the sun is at its height.

'pinta *f (mancha)* spot; *(aparência)* appearance, looks *pl*.

pin'tar *vt* to paint; *(descrever)* to describe; ~-**se** *vr* to put on one's make-up // *vi* to paint; *(col)* to appear, turn up; ~ **o sete** to paint the town red.

pintarroxo [pɪta'xoʃu] *m* linnet; *(Pt)* robin.

'pinto *m* chick.

pin'tor(a) *m/f* painter; **pintura** *f* painting; *(do rosto)* make-up; *(quadro)* picture; **pintura a óleo** oil painting; **pintura rupestre** cave painting.

'pio/a *adj (devoto)* pious; *(caridoso)* charitable // *m* cheep, chirp.

piolho [pɪ'oʎu] *m* louse.

pioneiro/a [pɪo'nejru/a] *adj* pioneering // *m* pioneer.

pi'or *adj, adv (comparativo)* worse; *(superlativo)* worst // *m*: **o** ~ worst of all; **piora** *f* worsening; **piorar** *vt* to make worse, worsen // *vi* to get worse.

'pipa *f* barrel, cask; *(de papel)* kite.

pipa'rote *m (com o dedo)* flick.

pique ['pɪkɪ] *m (lança)* pike; *(sabor)* piquancy; *(jogo)* hide and seek; **a** ~

vertically, steeply; a ~ **de** on the verge of; **ir a** ~ to sink.

piquenique [pɪke'nɪkɪ] *m* picnic; **fazer** ~ to have a picnic.

piquete [pɪ'ketʃɪ] *m* (*MIL*) squad; (*em greve*) picket.

pi'râmide *f* pyramid.

pi'rata *m* pirate; (*sedutor*) lady-killer; ~**ria** *f* piracy.

pires ['pɪrɪʃ] *m inv* saucer.

piri'lampo *m* glow worm.

pirotec'nia *f* pyrotechnics *sg*, art of making fireworks.

pirueta [pɪr'weta] *f* pirouette.

piru'lito *m* (*Br*) lollipop.

pi'sada *f* (*passo*) footstep; (*rastro*) footprint; **pisar** *vt* (*andar por cima de*) to tread on; (*uvas*) to tread, press; (*esmagar, subjugar*) to crush; (*café*) to pound // *vi* (*andar*) to step, tread; (*acelerar*) to put one's foot down.

pisca'dela *f* (*involuntária*) blink; (*sinal*) wink; **pisca-piscas** *fpl* (*AUTO*) indicators; **piscar** *vt* to blink; (*dar sinal*) to wink; (*estrelas*) to twinkle.

pis'cina *f* swimming pool; (*col*) baths *pl*; (*para peixes*) fish pond.

'piso *m* floor.

'pista *f* (*vestígio*) track, trail; (*indicação*) clue; (*de corridas*) track; (*de aviões*) runway; (*de equitação*) ring; (*de estrada*) lane; (*de dança*) (dance) floor.

pistão [pɪʃ'tãw] *m* piston.

pis'tola *f* (*arma*) pistol; (*para tinta*) spray gun.

pi'tada *f* (*porção*) pinch.

pi'tar *vt/i* to smoke; **piteira** *f* cigarette-holder.

pi'toresco/a *adj* picturesque.

'placa *f* plate; (*AUTO*) number plate, license plate (*US*); ~ **de sinalização** roadsign.

placi'dez *f* peacefulness, serenity; **plácido/a** *adj* (*sereno*) calm; (*manso*) placid.

plagiar [plaʒɪ'ax] *vt* to plagiarize; **plágio** *m* plagiarism.

plaina ['plajna] *f* (*instrumento*) plane.

'plana *f*: **de primeira** ~ first-class.

plana'dor *m* glider.

pla'nalto *m* tableland, plateau.

pla'nar *vi* to glide.

plane'ar (*Pt*), **plane'jar** (*Br*) *vt* to plan; (*edifício*) to design.

pla'neta *m* planet.

plangente [plã'ʒetʃɪ] *adj* plaintive, mournful.

planície [pla'nɪsɪ] *f* plain.

planifi'car *vt* (*programar*) to plan out; (*uma região*) to make a plan of.

'plano/a *adj* (*terreno*) flat, level; (*liso*) smooth // *m* (*projeto, mapa*) plan; (*MAT*) plane; ~ **diretor** master plan; **em primeiro/em último** ~ in the foreground/background.

'planta *f* (*BIO*) plant; (*do pé*) sole; (*plano*) plan.

plantação [plãta'sãw] *f* (*ato*) planting;

(*terreno*) planted land; **plantar** *vt* (*um vegetal*) to plant; (*semear*) to sow; (*casas*) to put up; (*estabelecer*) to set up; **plantar-se** *vr* to plant o.s., stand.

pla'nura *f* plain.

plaquê [pla'ke] *m* (*Pt*) gold plate.

plas'mar *vt* to mould, shape.

'plástico/a *adj* plastic // *m* plastic // *f* modelling.

plata'forma *f* platform.

'plátano *m* plane tree.

platéia [pla'teja] *f* (*teatro etc*) stalls *pl*.

pla'tina *f* platinum; **platinado/a** *adj* platinum *cmp*; **loura platinada** platinum blonde // *mpl*: **platinados** points.

plausível [plaw'zɪvɛw] *adj* credible, plausible.

'plebe *f* common people, populace; **plebeu/béia** *adj* plebeian // *m/f* pleb; **plebiscito** *m* referendum, plebiscite.

'plectro *m* (*MÚS*) plectrum.

pleitear [plejtʃɪ'ax] *vt* (*JUR*: *causa*) to plead; (*contestar*) to contest; **pleito** *m* lawsuit, case; (*fig*) dispute.

ple'nário/a *adj* plenary; **plenilúnio** *m* full moon; **plenitude** *f* plenitude, fullness; **pleno/a** *adj* full; (*completo*) complete; **em pleno dia** in broad daylight.

pleurisia [plɛwrɪ'zɪa] *f* pleurisy.

'plinto *m* plinth.

'pluma *f* feather; **plumagem** *f* plumage.

plu'ral [-aw] *adj*, *m* plural.

pluto'crata *adj* plutocratic // *m/f* plutocrat.

plu'tônio *m* plutonium.

pluvi'al [-jaw] *adj* pluvial, rain *cmp*.

pneu ['pnew] *m* tyre, tire (*US*); ~**mático/a** *adj* pneumatic // *m* tyre, tire (*US*).

pneumonia [pnewmo'nɪa] *f* pneumonia.

pó [pɔ] *m* (*partículas*) powder; (*sujeira*) dust; ~ **de arroz** face powder.

'pobre *adj* poor // *m/f* poor person; **os** ~**s** the poor; **pobreza** *f* poverty.

poça ['posa] *f* puddle, pool; ~ **de sangue** pool of blood.

poção [po'sãw] *f* potion.

pocilga [po'sɪwga] *f* pigsty.

poço ['posu] *m* (*de água*) well; (*de mina*) shaft.

'poda *f* pruning; ~**deira** *f* pruning knife; **podar** *vt/i* to prune.

po'der *vt* (*ser capaz de*) to be able to, be capable of, can; (*ter o direito de*) to be allowed to, may; **pode ser que** it may be that; **não pode deixar de fazer isso** he can't help doing it; **até não mais** ~ with all one's might; **não posso com ele** I cannot cope with him // *m* power; (*autoridade*) authority; ~ **aquisitivo** purchasing power; **poderio** *m* might, power; **poderoso/a** *adj* mighty, powerful.

'podre *adj* rotten, putrid; (*fig*) rotten, corrupt; **podridão** *f* decay, rottenness.

poeira [po'ejra] f dust; **poeirento/a** adj dusty.

po'ema m poem.

po'ente m west; (do sol) setting.

poesia [poe'zia] f poetry; (poema) poem; **poeta** m poet; **poético/a** adj poetic; **poetisa** f poetess.

pois [pojʃ] adv well (then); (portanto) so; (Pt: assentimento) yes; ~ **bem/** ~ **então** well then; ~ **é** that's right; ~ **não!** (Br) of course!; ~ **não?** (Pt) isn't it?, aren't you?, didn't they? etc // conj as, since, because.

po'laco/a (Pt) adj Polish // m/f Pole // m (língua) Polish.

po'lar adj polar; ~**idade** f polarity; ~**izar** vt to polarize.

'poldro/a m colt // f filly.

pole'gada f inch; **polegar** m thumb.

poleiro [po'lejru] m perch.

po'lêmica f controversy, dispute.

'pólen m pollen.

po'lia f pulley.

po'lícia f police, police force // m (Pt) policeman, constable; **agente de** ~ police constable; ~ **rodoviária** traffic police; **policial** adj police cmp; **novela** ou **romance policial** detective story // m (Br) policeman, constable // f (Br) policewoman.

poli'dez f good manners pl, politeness; **polido/a** adj (lustrado) polished, shiny; (cortês) well-mannered, polite.

poli'éster m polyester.

poli'glota adj, m/f polyglot.

poli'mento m (lustração) polishing; (finura) refinement.

'pólio, poliomielite [poliomie'litʃi] f polio(myelitis).

po'lir vt to polish.

poli'técnica f (escola) polytechnic.

po'lítico/a adj political; (astuto) crafty // m/f politician // f politics sg; (programa) policy; (astúcia) cunning.

'pólo m (GEO, ELET) pole; (esporte) polo; ~ **aquático** water polo.

polo'nês/esa adj Polish // m/f Pole // m (língua) Polish.

'polpa f pulp.

poltrão/trona [pol'trãw/'trona] adj cowardly // m/f coward // f armchair, easy chair.

poluição [polwi'sãw] f pollution; **poluir** vt to pollute.

polvilhar [powvi'ʎax] vt to sprinkle, powder; **polvilho** m powder.

'polvo m octopus.

'pólvora f gunpowder.

po'mada f pomade, ointment; (vaidade) vanity.

po'mar m orchard.

'pomba f dove; **pombal** m dovecote; **pombo** m pigeon.

'pomo m (fruto) fruit; ~ **de discórdia** bone of contention; ~-**de-Adão** m Adam's apple.

'pompa f pomp, ceremony; **pomposo/a** adj ostentatious, pompous.

poncho ['põʃu] m poncho, cape.

ponderação [põdera'sãw] f consideration, meditation; **ponderado/a** adj prudent, well-considered; **ponderar** vt to consider, weigh up // vi to meditate, muse.

'ponho etc vb ver **pôr**.

'ponta f point, tip; (extremidade) end; (um pouco) touch; ~ **esquerda** (futebol) outside-left; ~ **de cigarro** cigarette end; **na** ~ **da língua** on the tip of one's tongue; **na(s)** ~**(s) dos pés** on tiptoe; **ponta-cabeça** f: **de ponta-cabeça** upside down; **pontada** f (dor) twinge.

pontão [põ'tãw] m pontoon.

ponta'pé m kick; **dar** ~ **em** to kick.

ponta'ria f aim; **fazer** ~ to take aim.

ponte ['põtʃi] f (ger) bridge; ~ **aérea** air shuttle, airlift; ~ **levadiça** drawbridge; ~ **suspensa/pênsil** suspension bridge.

ponte'ado/a adj stippled, dotted // m stipple; **pontear** vt (pontilhar) to dot, stipple; (dar pontos) to sew, stitch.

ponteiro/a [põ'tejru/a] m (indicador) pointer; (de relógio) hand; (MÚS. plectro) plectrum // f ferrule, tip.

pontia'gudo/a adj sharp, pointed.

pontifi'cado m pontificate; **pontífice** m pontiff, Pope.

pontilhar [põtʃi'ʎax] vt to dot, stipple; **linha pontilhada** dotted line.

pontinha [põ'tʃina] f (um pouco) bit, touch.

'ponto m point; (sinal) dot, speckle; (pontuação) full stop; (jogo) point; (objetivo) aim, object; (teatro) prompter; (lugar) spot, place; ~ **morto** (AUTO) neutral; **em** ~ prompt, on the dot; ~ **e vírgula** semicolon; ~ **de interrogação/exclamação** question/exclamation mark; ~ **de vista** point of view; ~ **de ônibus** (Br) bus stop; ~ **de táxi** (Br) taxi stand; **até certo** ~ to a certain extent.

pontuação [põtwa'sãw] f punctuation.

pontual [põ'twaw] adj punctual; ~**idade** f punctuality.

pon'tuar vt to punctuate.

'popa f stern, poop; **à** ~ astern, aft.

pope'lina f poplin.

popu'laça f mob, rabble; **população** f population; **popular** adj (estimado) popular; (do povo) of the people; (comum) common, current; **popularidade** f popularity; **popularizar** vt to popularize, make popular; **popularizar-se** vr to become popular.

pôquer ['pokex] m (jogo) poker.

por [pox] (por + o = pelo; por + a = pela; por + os = pelos; por + as = pelas) prep (a fim de) in order to; (a favor de) for; (por causa de) out of, because of, from; (meio) by; (troca) (in exchange) for; (através de) through, by; **soubemos disso** ~ **carta** we learnt about it by letter; **viemos pelo parque** we came through the park; **faço isso** ~ **ela** I do it for her;

pelas duas horas about two o'clock; ~ **aqui** this way; ~ **isso** therefore; ~ **cento** per cent; ~ **mais difícil que seja** however difficult it is; ~ **Deus!** for heaven's sake!; ~ **escrito** in writing; ~ **fora / ~ dentro** outside/inside; ~ **exemplo** for example; ~ **ano** yearly; ~ **mês** monthly; ~ **semana** weekly; ~ **dia** daily; **está** ~ **acontecer** it is about to happen, it is yet to happen; ~ **que** (Br) why; ~ **quê?** (Br) why?

pôr [pox] vt to put; (colocar) to place; (roupas) to put on; (dúvidas) to raise; (ovos) to lay; ~ **furioso** to infuriate; ~ **de lado** to set aside; **~-se** vr (sol) to set; **~-se de pé** to stand up; **~-se a caminho** to set off.

porão [po'rãw] m (NÁUT) hold; (casa) basement.

porção [pox'sãw] f portion, piece; **uma** ~ **de** a lot of.

porcaria f filth; (fig) mess; (coisa ruim) rubbish // excl: ~! damn!

porcelana f porcelain, china.

porco / a adj filthy // m (BIO) pig, hog; (carne) pork // f (BIO) sow; (TEC) nut; **porco-espinho** m porcupine; **porco-montês** m wild boar.

porém [po'rẽ] conj however, nevertheless.

porfia f (altercação) dispute, wrangle; (obstinação) stubbornness, obstinacy; **porfiado / a** adj (disputado) hotly disputed; (obstinado) stubborn, obstinate; **porfiar** vt (questionar) to dispute; **porfiar em** (obstinar-se) to persist in.

pormenor m detail; **~izar** vt to detail.

pornografia f pornography; **pornográfico / a** adj pornographic.

poro m pore; **poroso / a** adj porous.

porquanto conj since, seeing that.

porque [ˈpoxke] conj because, since; (interrogativo: Pt) why; **porquê** adv why; **porquê?** (Pt) why? // m reason, motive.

porta f (dum edifício) door, doorway; (dum jardim) gate; ~ **giratória** revolving door; **a ~s fechadas** behind closed doors.

porta-aviões [poxta-avi'õjʃ] m inv aircraft carrier.

porta-chaves [poxta-'ʃaviʃ] m inv keyholder.

portador(a) m/f bearer; **ao** ~ (COM) payable to bearer.

portagem [pox'taʒẽ] f (Pt) toll.

portal [-aw] m doorway.

portaló m (NÁUT) gangway.

porta-luvas m inv (AUTO) glove compartment.

porta-malas m inv (AUTO) boot, trunk (US).

porta-moedas [poxta-'mwedaʃ] m (Pt) purse.

portanto conj so, therefore.

portar vt to carry; **~-se** vr to behave.

portaria f (dum edifício) entrance hall;

(recepção) reception desk; (do governo) edict, decree.

porta-seios [poxta-'sejuʃ] m inv bra, brassiere.

portátil [pox'tatʃiw] adj portable.

porta-voz m (pessoa) spokesman // f (pessoa) spokeswoman.

porte m (transporte) transport; (custo) freight charge, carriage; (NÁUT) tonnage, capacity; (atitude) bearing; ~ **pago** post paid.

porteiro / a [pox'tejru/a] m/f caretaker.

portento m wonder, marvel; **portentoso / a** adj amazing, marvellous.

pórtico m porch, portico.

portinhola [poxtʃi'ɲola] f (de carruagem) door.

porto m (do mar) port, harbour; (vinho) port; **P~** Oporto; ~ **de escala** port of call.

português / guesa [portu'geʃ/'geza] adj, m/f Portuguese // m (língua) Portuguese.

porvir m future.

pôs vb ver **pôr**.

posar vi (FOTO) to pose.

pós-datar vt to postdate.

pós-escrito m postscript.

posição [pozi'sãw] f (lugar) position; (social) standing, status.

positivo / a adj, m positive.

pospor vt to put after; (adiar) to postpone.

possante adj powerful, strong.

posse [ˈposi] f possession, ownership; **~s** fpl possessions, belongings; **tomar** ~ to take office; **tomar** ~ **de** to take possession of; **possessão** f possession; **possessivo / a** adj possessive; **possesso / a** adj possessed, crazed.

possibilidade f possibility; (oportunidade) chance; **~s** fpl means; **possibilitar** vt to make possible, permit; **possível** adj possible, feasible; **fazer todo o possível** to do one's best.

posso etc vb ver **poder**.

possuidor(a) [poswi'dox(ra)] m/f owner, possessor; **possuir** vt to own, possess; (usufruir) to enjoy; (posto) to hold.

posta f (pedaço) piece, slice; (correio) post, mail; **postal** adj postal // m postcard.

poste m pole, post.

postergar vt (adiar) to postpone.

posteridade f posterity.

posterior adj (mais tarde) subsequent, later; (traseiro) rear, back // m posterior, bottom; **~mente** adv later, subsequently.

postiço / a [poʃ'tʃisu/a] adj false, artificial; **dentes ~s** false teeth.

posto / a pp de **pôr** // adj put, placed; **sol** ~ sunset // m post, position; (emprego) job; ~ **de gasolina** service/petrol station // conj: ~ **que** although.

postu'lado *m* postulate, assumption; **postular** *vt* (*pedir*) to request.

'póstumo/a *adj* posthumous.

pos'tura *f* (*posição*) posture, position; (*atitude*) attitude.

po'tassa *f* potash; **potássio** *m* potassium.

po'tável *adj* drinkable; **água** ~ drinking water.

'pote *m* jug, pitcher; **chover a** ~**s** (*Pt*) to rain cats and dogs.

potência [po'tēsja] *f* power, strength; (*nação*) power; **potencial** *adj* potential, latent // *m* potential; **potente** *adj* powerful, potent.

'potro/a *m* (*cavalo*) colt, foal // *f* filly, foal.

pouca-vergonha [poka-vex'goɲa] *f* shameful behaviour, disgrace.

pouco/a ['pouka] *adj* (*sg*) little; (*pl*) few // *adv* not much, little // *m* a little; **há** ~ **tempo** a short time ago; ~**as vezes** rarely; ~ **a** ~ gradually, bit by bit; **por** ~ almost; **aos** ~**s** gradually; ~**chino/a** *adj*: **um** ~**chinho/a** (*Pt*) very little // *m* a little bit.

pou'par *vt* to save; (*economizar*) to economize on; (*vida*) to spare.

pousada [po'zada] *f* inn, resting place; **pousar** *vt* to place, set down; (*mão*) to rest, place // *vi* to rest; (*pássaros*) to perch.

'povo *m* people; (*raça*) people, race; **póvoa** *f* (*aldeia*) village, hamlet; **povoação** *f* (*vila*) town, settlement; (*habitantes*) population; (*ato de povoar*) settlement, colonization; **povoado/a** *adj* populated // *m* village, settlement; **povoar** *vt* (*de habitantes*) to people, populate; (*de animais etc*) to stock.

praça ['prasa] *f* (*largo*) square; (*mercado*) market; (*soldado*) soldier; **sentar** ~ to enlist; ~ **de touros** bull ring; ~ **forte** stronghold.

'prado *m* meadow, grassland; (*Br:* hipódromo*) racecourse.

'praga *f* (*maldição*) curse; (*coisa importuna*) pest, plague; (*desgraça*) calamity.

prag'mático/a *adj* (*prático*) pragmatic.

praguejar [prage'ʒax] *vt/i* to curse.

praia ['praja] *f* beach, seashore.

prancha ['prãʃa] *f* plank; (*NÁUT*) gangplank.

prante'ar *vt* to mourn // *vi* to weep; **pranto** *m* weeping.

'prata *f* silver; **prateado/a** *adj* silver-plated; (*brilhante*) silvery.

prateleira [prate'lejra] *f* (*de livros*) shelf.

prati'cante *adj* practising // *m/f* apprentice; **praticar** *vt* (*fazer*) to practise, perform; (*crime*) to commit, perpetrate; **praticável** *adj* practical, feasible; **prático/a** *adj* practical // *m/f* expert // *m* (*NÁUT*) pilot // *f* (*ato de praticar*) practice; (*experiência*) experience, know-how; (*costume*) habit, custom.

'prato *m* (*louça*) plate, dish; (*comida*) dish; (*coberta*) course; ~**s** *mpl* (*MÚS*) cymbals.

praxe ['praksi] *f* custom, usage.

prazenteiro/a [prazē'tejru/a] *adj* cheerful, pleasant; **prazer** *m* pleasure; **muito prazer em conhecê-lo** pleased to meet you.

'prazo *m* term, period; (*vencimento*) expiry date, time limit; **a curto/longo** ~ short-/long-term; **comprar a** ~ to buy on hire purchase *ou* in instalments.

prea'mar *f* (*Br*) high tide, high water.

pre'âmbulo *m* preamble, introduction.

pre'cário/a *adj* precarious, insecure.

preca'tado/a *adj* cautious; **precatar-se** *vr* to take precautions, be careful; **quando mal se precata** when least expected.

precaução [prekaw'sãw] *f* precaution.

preca'ver-se *vr* to be on one's guard; (*guardar-se*) to take precautions; **precavido/a** *adj* cautious.

prece ['presi] *f* prayer.

prece'dência *f* precedence; **preceder** *vt* to precede.

preceito [pre'sejtu] *m* precept, ruling; **preceituar** *vt* to decree, prescribe.

precep'tor *m* tutor, instructor.

preciosidade [presiozi'dadʒi] *f* (*qualidade*) preciousness; (*coisa*) treasure; **preciosismo** *m* preciosity; **precioso/a** *adj* (*valioso*) precious, valuable; (*afetado*) over-refined.

precipício [presi'pisju] *m* precipice; (*fig*) abyss.

precipitação [presipita'sãw] *f* haste; (*imprudência*) rashness; **precipitado/a** *adj* hasty; (*imprudente*) rash; **precipitar** *vt* (*apressar*) to hurry, precipitate; (*lançar*) to hurl down; **precipitar-se** *vr* to hurry.

precisão [presi'zãw] *f* (*exatidão*) precision, exactness; (*falta*) need, necessity; **precisar** *vt* (*especificar*) to specify, state in detail; (*faltar*) to want, need; **preciso ir** I have to go // *vi*: **precisar de** to need; **preciso/a** *adj* (*exato*) precise, exact; (*necessário*) necessary, imperative; **é preciso ir** you must go.

pre'claro/a *adj* famous, illustrious.

preço ['presu] *m* price; (*custo*) cost; (*valor*) value; ~ **por atacado/a varejo** wholesale/retail price; ~ **de ocasião** bargain price; ~ **de venda** sale price.

precoce [pre'kɔsi] *adj* precocious; (*antecipado*) early; **precocidade** *f* (*talento*) precociousness.

preconce'bido/a *adj* preconceived; **preconceito** *m* prejudice, bias.

preconi'zar *vt* to extol.

precur'sor(a) *m/f* (*predecessor*) precursor, forerunner; (*mensageiro*) herald.

preda'dor *m* predator; **predatório/a** *adj* predatory.

predeces'sor *m* predecessor.

predesti'nado/a adj predestined.
predetermi'nado/a adj predetermined.
predi'al adj property cmp, real-estate cmp; **imposto** ~ domestic rates.
predição [predʒɪ'sãw] f prediction, forecast.
predileção [predʒɪlɛ'sãw] (Pt: -cç-) f preference, predilection; **predileto/a** (Pt: -ct-) adj favourite.
'prédio m building; ~ **de apartamentos** block of flats.
predis'por vt to predispose.
predi'zer vt to predict, forecast.
predomi'nância f predominance, prevalence; **predominar** vi to predominate, prevail; **predomínio** m predominance, supremacy.
preeminência [prɪemɪ'nɛsja] f pre-eminence, superiority; **preeminente** adj pre-eminent, superior.
preencher [prɪe'ʃex] vt (minuta) to fill in/out, complete; (necessidade) to fulfil, meet.
pré-fabri'cado/a adj prefabricated.
prefácio [pre'fasju] m preface.
prefeito [pre'fejtu] m mayor; **prefeitura** f town hall.
prefe'rência f preference; **de** ~ preferably; **preferir** vt to prefer; **preferível** adj preferable.
pre'fixo m (LING) prefix.
'prega f pleat, fold.
prega'dor m preacher; **pregão** m proclamation, cry; **pregões** mpl marriage banns; **pregar** vt/i (um sermão) to preach; (anunciar) to proclaim.
pregar [prɛ'gax] vt (com prego) to nail; (fixar) to pin, fasten; (cosendo) to sew; ~ **uma peça** to play a trick; ~ **os olhos em** to fix one's eyes on; **não** ~ **olho** not to sleep a wink; **prego** m nail.
pregoeiro [pre'gwejru] m (proclamador) town crier; (num leilão) auctioneer.
preguear [pregɪ'ax] vt to pleat, fold.
preguiça [pre'gɪsa] f laziness; (animal) sloth; **preguiçoso/a** adj lazy.
preia-mar [preja-'max] f (Pt) high tide, high water.
preito ['prejtu] m homage, tribute; **render** ~ **a** to pay homage to.
prejudi'car vt to damage, prejudice; **prejuízo** m (dano) damage, harm; (parcialidade) prejudice.
pre'lado m prelate.
preleção [prelɛ'sãw] (Pt: -cç-) f lecture.
prelimi'nar adj preliminary // f (partida) preliminary.
'prelo m (printing) press; **no** ~ **in the press.**
pre'lúdio m (prólogo) prelude; (MÚS) overture.
prema'turo/a adj premature.
premedi'tado/a adj premeditated; **premeditar** vt to premeditate.
pre'mente adj pressing; **premer** vt to press; (espremer) to squeeze.
premi'ado/a adj prize-winning;

premiar vt to award a prize to; (pagar) to reward; **prêmio** m prize; (seguros) premium.
pre'mir vt ver **premer.**
pre'missa f premise.
'prenda f gift, present; (em jogo) forfeit; ~**s** fpl talents, accomplishments; **prendado/a** adj gifted, talented.
prende'dor m fastener; ~ **de roupa** clothes peg; ~ **de papéis** paper clip; **prender** vt (pregar) to fasten, fix; (capturar) to arrest, capture; (agarrar) to catch, seize; **prender-se** vr to get caught, stick.
prenhe ['prɛɲɪ] adj pregnant; **prenhez** f pregnancy.
pre'nome m first name, Christian name.
'prensa f (ger) press; **prensar** vt to press, compress.
prenunci'ar vt to predict, foretell; **prenúncio** m forewarning, sign.
preocupação [preokupa'sãw] f (envolvimento) preoccupation; (inquietação) worry, concern; **preocupar** vt (absorver) to preoccupy; (inquietar) to worry; **preocupar-se** vr: **preocupar-se com** to worry about, be worried about.
preparação [prepara'sãw] f preparation; **preparar** vt to prepare, arrange; **preparar-se** vr: **preparar-se para** to prepare to ou for; **preparativos** mpl preparations, arrangements.
preponde'rância f preponderance, predominance.
preposição [prepozɪ'sãw] f preposition.
prerroga'tiva f prerogative, privilege.
'presa f (na guerra) spoils pl; (vítima) prey; (dente de animal) fang.
pres'bita adj long-sighted.
presbi'tério m presbytery.
presbi'tia f, **presbi'tismo** m long-sightedness.
presciência [pre'sɪesja] f foreknowledge, foresight; **presciente** adj far-sighted, prescient.
prescin'dir vi: ~ **de algo** to do without sth; **prescindível** adj dispensable.
prescre'ver vt to prescribe // vi to expire; **prescrição** f order, rule.
presença [pre'zẽsa] f presence; (comparecimento) attendance; (porte) bearing, air; ~ **de espírito** presence of mind; **presenciar** vt to witness, be present at; **presente** adj present; **ter presente** to bear in mind // m (oferta) gift, present; (tempo) present; (LING) present (tense); **os presentes** those present; **presentemente** adv at present.
pre'sépio m Nativity scene, crib.
preservação [prezexva'sãw] f preservation; **preservar** vt to preserve, protect; **preservativo** m preservative; (anticoncepcional) sheath.
presi'dência f (de um país) presidency; (de uma assembléia) chairmanship, presidency; **assumir a** ~ to take the chair; **presidente** m (de um país)

president; (*de uma assembléia*) chairman, president.

presidi'ário *m* convict; **presídio** *m* (*prisão*) military prison; (*praça de guerra*) fortress.

presi'dir *vt* to preside over // *vi* to preside.

presilha [prɛ'ziʎɐ] *f* fastener.

'preso/a *adj* (*em prisão*) imprisoned; (*capturado*) under arrest, captured; (*atado*) bound, tied // *m/f* prisoner.

'pressa *f* haste, hurry; (*rapidez*) speed; (*urgência*) urgency; **à(s) ∼(s)** hurriedly; **dar-se ∼** to hurry (up); **estar com ∼** to be in a hurry.

pressagiar [prɛsaʒi'ax] *vt* to foretell, presage; **presságio** *m* omen, sign.

pressão [prɛ'sãw] *f* pressure; **∼ sanguínea** blood pressure.

pressenti'mento *m* premonition, presentiment; **pressentir** *vt* to sense, have a premonition of.

pressu'posto *m* (*conjetura*) presupposition.

pressu'roso/a *adj* (*apressado*) hurried, in a hurry; (*zeloso*) keen, eager.

prestação [prɛʃta'sãw] *f* instalment; **prestamista** *m/f* moneylender; (*comprador*) person paying hire purchase; **prestar** *vt* to give, render; (*servir*) to be of use; (*emprestar*) to lend; **prestar-se** *vr*: **prestar-se a** to be suitable for; **prestar atenção** to pay attention; **prestar juramento** to take an oath; **não presta para nada** it's absolutely useless.

prestes ['prɛʃtʃiʃ] *adj inv* ready, about; **∼ a partir** about to leave; **presteza** *f* (*prontidão*) willingness, promptness; (*agilidade*) nimbleness, agility.

prestidigitação [prɛʃtʃidiʒita'sãw] *f* sleight of hand, conjuring, magic tricks; **prestidigitador** *m* conjurer, magician.

pre'stígio *m* (*reputação*) prestige, reputation; **prestigioso/a** *adj* prestigious, eminent.

'préstimo *m* use, usefulness; **sem ∼** useless, worthless; **∼s** *mpl* favours, services.

presu'mido/a *adj* vain, self-important; **presumir** *vt* to presume, suppose; (*entender*) to assume; **presunção** *f* (*suposição*) presumption; (*vaidade*) conceit, self-importance; **presunçoso/a** *adj* vain, self-important.

pre'sunto *m* (*cured*) ham.

preten'dente *m/f* claimant; (*candidato*) candidate, applicant; (*galanteador*) suitor; **pretender** *vt* (*desejar*) to want to; (*tencionar*) to intend; (*esperar conseguir*) to hope to get; **pretensão** *f* (*reivindicação*) claim; (*vaidade*) pretention; (*aspiração*) aim, aspiration; **pretensões** *fpl* (*presunção*) pretentiousness; **pretensioso/a** *adj* pretentious.

prete'rir *vt* to ignore, disregard.

pre'térito/a *adj* past, bygone // *m* (LING) preterite.

pretexto [pre'teʃtu] *m* pretext, excuse; **a ∼ de** on the pretext of.

pretidão [pretʃi'dãw] *f* blackness, darkness; **preto/a** *adj* black; **pôr o preto no branco** to put it down in writing // *m* black man, Negro // *f* black woman, Negress.

prevalecer [prevale'sex] *vi* to prevail, predominate; **∼ sobre** to outweigh; **∼-se** *vr*: **∼-se de** (*aproveitar-se*) to take advantage of.

prevari'car *vi* (*faltar ao dever*) to fail in one's duty; (*proceder mal*) to misbehave.

prevenção [prevẽ'sãw] *f* (*ato de evitar*) prevention; (*preconceito*) prejudice; (*cautela*) caution; **prevenido/a** *adj* (*cauteloso*) cautious, wary; (*avisado*) forewarned; **prevenir** *vt* (*evitar*) to prevent; (*avisar*) to warn; (*antecipar-se*) to anticipate; (*preparar*) to prepare; **prevenir-se** *vr* (*acautelar-se*) to take precautions; (*equipar-se*) to equip o.s.; **preventivo/a** *adj* preventive.

pre'ver *vt* to foresee.

previa'mente *adj* previously.

previ'dência *f* (*previsão*) foresight; (*precaução*) precaution; **∼ social** social welfare.

'prévio/a *adj* previous, prior; (*preliminar*) preliminary.

previsão [previ'zãw] *f* (*antevisão*) foresight; (*prognóstico*) forecast; **meteorológica** weather forecast; **previsto/a** *adj* foreseen.

pre'zado/a *adj* esteemed; (*numa carta*) dear; **prezar** *vt* to value highly, esteem; **prezar-se** *vr* (*ter dignidade*) to have self-respect; **prezar-se de** (*orgulhar-se*) to pride o.s. on.

pri'mado *m* (*primazia*) primacy; **primar** *vi* to excel, stand out.

pri'mário/a *adj* primary.

prima'vera *f* spring; (*planta*) primrose.

pri'maz *m* primate; **primazia** *f* primacy; (*prioridade*) priority; (*superioridade*) superiority.

primeiro/a [pri'mejru/a] *adj* first; (*fundamental*) fundamental, prime; **∼ ministro** prime minister; **em ∼ lugar** first of all // *adv* first // *f* (AUTO) first gear.

primi'tivo/a *adj* primitive; (*original*) original.

'primo/a *m/f* cousin; **∼ co-irmão** first cousin; **∼ segundo** second cousin // *m* (*número*) prime number.

primo'génito/a *adj* first-born.

pri'mor *m* excellence, perfection; **com ∼** to perfection; **é um ∼** it's perfect.

primordial [-ox'dʒjaw] *adj* (*original*) original; (*principal*) principal, fundamental.

primo'roso/a *adj* excellent, exquisite.

prin'cesa *f* princess.

princi'pado *m* principality.

princi'pal [-aw] adj principal, main // m (chefe) head, principal.

príncipe ['prĩsɪpɪ] m prince.

principi'ante m beginner; **principiar** vt to begin.

princípio [prĩ'sɪpju] m (começo) beginning, start; (origem) origin; (moral) principle; ~s mpl rudiments; no ~ in the beginning; por ~ on principle.

pri'or m (sacerdote) parish priest; (de convento) prior.

priori'dade f priority.

prisão [prɪ'zãw] f (encarceramento) imprisonment; (cadeia) prison, jail; (detenção) arrest; **ordem de ~** warrant for arrest; **~ perpétua** life imprisonment; **~ de ventre** constipation; **prisioneiro/a** m/f prisoner.

'prisma f prism.

privação [prɪva'sãw] f deprivation; (penúria) want, hardship; **privacidade** f privacy; **privações** fpl hardship sg; **privado/a** adj (particular) private; (carente) deprived; **privar** vt to deprive // vi: **privar com** to be on intimate terms with; **privativo/a** adj peculiar to; (particular) private.

privilegiado/a [prɪvɪleʒɪ'adu/a] adj privileged; (distinto) distinguished; **privilégio** m privilege.

pró [prɔ] adv for, in favour // m advantage; **os ~s e os contras** the pros and cons.

'proa f prow, bow; (fig) conceit.

probabili'dade f probability, likelihood; **~s** fpl odds; **segundo todas as ~s** in all probability.

probi'dade f integrity, uprightness.

pro'blema m problem; **problemático/a** adj problematic.

'probo/a adj honest.

proce'dência f (origem) origin, source; **procedente** adj (oriundo) derived from, rising from; (lógico) logical; **proceder** vi (ir adiante) to proceed; (comportar-se) to act, behave; (JUR) to take legal action; **proceder a** to carry out; **proceder de** to originate from, arise from // m conduct; **procedimento** m (comportamento) conduct, behaviour; (processo) procedure; (JUR) legal action, trial.

procela [pro'sela] f storm, tempest; **proceloso/a** adj stormy.

proces'sar vt (proceder contra) to take proceedings against, prosecute; (verificar) to check, verify; **processo** m process; (procedimento) procedure; (JUR) lawsuit, legal proceedings.

procissão [prosɪ'sãw] f procession.

proclamação [proklama'sãw] f proclamation; **proclamar** vt to proclaim.

procriação [prokrɪa'sãw] f procreation; **procriar** vt/i to procreate.

pro'cura f search; (COM) demand; **em ~ de** in search of; **~ção** f power of

attorney; (documento) letter of attorney; **por ~ção** by proxy; **~dor** m (advogado) attorney; (mandatário) agent; **P~dor Geral da República** Attorney General; **procurar** vt (buscar) to look for, seek; (esforçar-se) to try to, aim at; (ir visitar) to call on, go and see.

prodigali'zar vt (gastar excessivamente) to squander; (dar com profusão) to lavish.

prodígio [pro'dʒɪʒju] m prodigy; **prodigioso/a** adj prodigious, marvellous.

'pródigo/a adj (perdulário) wasteful; (generoso) lavish; **filho ~** prodigal son.

produção [produ'sãw] f production; (volume de produção) output; (produto) product; **produtividade** f productivity; **produtivo/a** adj productive; (rendoso) profitable; **produto** m product; (produção) production; (renda) proceeds pl, profit; **produtos alimentícios** foodstuffs; **produzir** vt to produce; (ocasionar) to cause, bring about.

proemi'nência f prominence; (protuberância) protuberance; **proeminente** adj prominent.

pro'eza f exploit, feat.

profanação [profana'sãw] f sacrilege, profanation; **profanar** vt to desecrate, profane; **profano/a** adj profane; (secular) secular // m layman // f laywoman.

profecia [profe'sɪa] f prophecy.

profe'rir vt to utter; **~ um discurso** to make a speech.

profes'sar vt (declarar) to profess // vi (REL) to take religious vows; **professor(a)** m/f teacher; **professor titular** (Br)/**catedrático** (Pt) university professor; **professorado** m (professores) teaching staff; (classe) teaching profession.

pro'feta m prophet; **profetizar** vt/i to prophesy, predict.

proficiência [profɪsɪ'ẽsja] f proficiency, competence; **proficiente** adj proficient, competent.

proficuo/a [pro'fɪkwa/a] adj useful, advantageous.

profissão [profɪ'sãw] f (ofício) profession; (declaração) declaration; **profissional** adj professional.

pro'fundas fpl depths; **profundidade** f depth; **tem 4 metros de profundidade** it is 4 metres deep; **profundo/a** adj deep; (complexo) profound.

profusão [profu'zãw] f profusion, abundance; **profuso/a** adj (abundante) profuse, abundant.

progênie [pro'ʒenɪ] (Pt: **progénie** [-ɛ-]) f (ascendência) lineage; (prole) offspring, progeny; **progenitor** m ancestor; (pai) father.

prognosti'car vt to predict, forecast // vi (MED) to make a prognosis; **prognóstico** m prediction, forecast; (MED) prognosis.

pro'grama m programme; (TEC:

informática) program; **programação** *f* program(m)ing; **programar** *vt* to program(me), schedule.

progre'dir *vi* to progress, make progress; **progressista** *adj, m/f* progressive; **progressivo/a** *adj* progressive; (*gradual*) gradual; **progresso** *m* progress.

proibição [proɪbɪ'sãw] *f* prohibition, ban; **proibir** *vt* to prohibit, forbid; "**proibido fumar**" "no smoking".

projeção [proʒe'sãw] (*Pt: -cç-*) *f* projection; (*arremesso*) throwing; (*proeminência*) prominence; **projetar** (*Pt: -ct-*) *vt* (*ger*) to project; (*arremessar*) to throw; (*planejar*) to plan; **projetar-se** *vr* (*lançar-se*) to hurl o.s.; (*sombra etc*) to fall; (*delinear-se*) to stand out; (*prolongar-se*) to stretch; **projétil** (*Pt: -ct-*) *m* projectile, missile; (*MIL*) missile; **projetista** (*Pt: -ct-*) *m/f* planner; (*engenheiro projetista*) designer; **projeto** (*Pt: -ct-*) *m* plan, project; **projeto de lei** bill; **projetor** (*Pt: -ct-*) *m* (*cinema*) projector; (*holofote*) searchlight.

prol *m* advantage; **em ~ de** on behalf of, for the benefit of.

'prole *f* offspring, progeny.

proletari'ado *m* proletariat; **proletário/a** *adj, m/f* proletarian.

proliferação [prolɪfera'sãw] *f* proliferation; **proliferar** *vi* to proliferate; **prolífico/a** *adj* prolific.

prolixo/a [pro'lɪksu/a] *adj* long-winded, tedious.

'prólogo *m* prologue.

prolongação [prolõga'sãw] *f* extension; **prolongado/a** *adj* prolonged; **pro-longamento** *m* extension; **prolongar** *vt* (*tornar mais longo*) to extend, lengthen; (*adiar*) to prolong; **prolongar-se** *vr* to extend.

pro'messa *f* promise; **prometedor(a)** *adj* promising; **prometer** *vt* to promise // *vi* (*ter potencial*) to show promise; **prometido/a** *adj* promised // *m* fiancé // *f* fiancée.

promiscuidade [promɪʃkwɪ'dadʒɪ] *f* (*mistura desordenada*) disorder, confusion; (*~ sexual*) promiscuity; **promíscuo/a** *adj* (*misturado*) disorderly, mixed up; (*comportamento sexual*) promiscuous.

promissão [promɪ'sãw] *f* promise; **terra da ~** Promised Land; **promissor(a)** *adj* promising.

promoção [promo'sãw] *f* promotion; (*COM*) publicity (campaign).

promon'tório *m* headland, promontory.

promo'tor(a) *adj* promoting // *m* promoter; (*JUR*) prosecutor; **~ público** public prosecutor; **promover** *vt* (*dar impulso a*) to promote; (*causar*) to cause; (*elevar a cargo superior*) to promote.

promul'gar *vt* (*lei etc*) to promulgate; (*tornar público*) to declare publicly.

pro'nome *m* pronoun.

prontidão [prõtʃɪ'dãw] *f* (*estar preparado*) readiness; (*rapidez*) promptness, speed;

pronto/a *adj* (*preparado*) ready; (*rápido*) quick, speedy; (*sem dinheiro*) broke // *adv* promptly // *excl*: **pronto!** right!, that's it!; **pronto-socorro** *m* emergency hospital; (*Pt: reboque*) towtruck.

prontuário [prõ'twarju] *m* (*manual*) handbook; (*policial*) record.

pro'núncia *f* pronunciation; (*JUR*) indictment; **pronunciamento** *m* proclamation, pronouncement; **pronunciar** *vt* to pronounce; (*discurso*) to make, deliver; (*JUR*) to indict; **pronunciar mal** to mispronounce; **pronunciar-se** *vr* (*expressar opinião*) to express one's opinion.

propagação [propaga'sãw] *f* propagation; **propaganda** *f* (*política*) propaganda; (*COM*) advertising; **propagar** *vt* to propagate.

propensão [propẽ'sãw] *f* inclination, tendency; **propenso/a** *adj* inclined; **ser propenso a** to be inclined to, have a tendency to.

propiciar [propɪsɪ'ax] *vt/i* (*tornar favorável*) to favour; (*proporcionar*) to provide; **propício/a** *adj* (*favorável*) favourable, propitious; (*adequado*) appropriate.

pro'pina *f* (*gorjeta*) tip; (*Pt: cota*) fee.

pro'por *vt* to propose, put forward; (*um problema*) to pose; **~-se** *vr* (*pretender*) to intend.

proporção [propox'sãw] *f* proportion; **proporções** *fpl* dimensions; **proporcionado/a** *adj* proportionate; **proporcionar** *vt* (*dar*) to provide, give; (*adaptar*) to adjust, adapt.

proposição [propozɪ'sãw] *f* proposition, proposal.

pro'pósito *m* purpose, aim; **a ~** by the way; (*oportunamente*) suitably; **a ~ de** with regard to; **de ~** on purpose.

pro'posta *f* proposal; (*oferecimento*) offer.

propria'mente *adv* properly, exactly; **~ dito** strictly speaking.

proprie'dade *f* property; (*direito de proprietário*) ownership; (*particularidade*) attribute, quality; (*o que é apropriado*) appropriateness, propriety; **~ imobiliária** real estate; **proprietário/a** *m* owner, proprietor; (*de casa alugada*) landlord; (*de jornal*) publisher // *f* owner; (*de estalagem etc*) landlady.

'próprio/a *adj* own, of one's own; (*mesmo*) very, selfsame; (*conveniente*) proper; (*caraterístico*) characteristic; (*depois de pronome*) -self; **eu ~** I myself; **ele ~** he himself; **mora em casa ~a** he lives in a house of his own; **por si ~** of one's own accord; **o ~ homem** the very man.

propulsão [propul'sãw] *f* propulsion; **~ a jato** jet propulsion; **propulsor(a)** *adj* propelling // *m* propellor.

prorrogação [proxoga'sãw] *f* extension; (*COM*) deferment; (*JUR*) stay; **prorrogar** *vt* to extend, prolong.

prorrom'per *vi* to burst out, break out.

'prosa *f* prose; (*conversa*) chatter; (*tagarelice*) boasting, bragging; **ter boa ~ to** have the gift of the gab; **prosador(a)** *m/f* prose writer; **prosaico/a** *adj* prosaic; (*trivial*) dull, humdrum.

proscénio [pro'senju] *m* proscenium.

proscre'ver *vt* to prohibit, ban; (*expulsar*) to banish, exile; **proscrição** *f* proscription; (*proibição*) prohibition, ban; (*desterro*) exile; **proscrito** *m* (*criminoso*) outlaw; (*desterrado*) exile.

pro'sélito *m* convert.

pros'pecto *m* (*vista*) outlook, prospect; (*impresso*) prospectus; **prospector** *m* prospector.

prospe'rar *vi* to prosper, thrive; **prosperidade** *f* prosperity; (*bom êxito*) success; **próspero/a** *adj* prosperous, thriving; (*bem sucedido*) successful; (*favorável*) favourable.

prossecução [proseku'sãw] *f* (*Pt*) continuation; **prosseguimento** *m* continuation; **prosseguir** *vt* (*continuar*) to continue, carry on with; (*seguir*) to follow // *vi* to continue, go on.

prostituição [proʃtitwi'sãw] *f* prostitution; **prostituir** *vt* to prostitute; **prostituir-se** *vr* (*desonrar-se*) to debase o.s.; (*tornar-se prostituta*) to become a prostitute; **prostituta** *f* prostitute.

prostração [proʃtra'sãw] *f* prostration; (*cansaço*) exhaustion; (*desalento*) dejection; **prostrar** *vt* (*derrubar*) to knock down, throw down; (*enfraquecer*) to tire out; **prostrar-se** *vr* to prostrate o.s.; (*humilhar-se*) to humble o.s.

protago'nista *m/f* protagonist.

proteção [prote'sãw] (*Pt*: -cç-) *f* protection; (*amparo*) support, backing; **protecionismo** (*Pt*: -cc-) *m* protectionism; **proteger** *vt* to protect; **protegido/a** *adj* protected // *m* protégé // *f* protégée.

prote'ína *f* protein.

prote'lar *vt* to postpone, put off.

prote'stante *adj, m/f* Protestant; **protestantismo** *m* Protestantism; **protestar** *vt* to protest; (*declarar*) to declare, affirm // *vi* to protest, object; **protesto** *m* (*queixa*) protest; (*declaração*) affirmation.

protetor(a) [prote'tox(ra)] (*Pt*: -ct-) *adj* protective, protecting // *m/f* protector.

proto'colo *m* protocol.

pro'tótipo *m* prototype.

'prova *f* proof; (*ensaio*) test, trial; (*EDUC: exame*) examination; (*sinal*) sign; (*de comida, bebida*) taste; (*de roupa*) fitting; (*tipografia*) proof; **à ~ on** trial; **à ~ de bala/fogo/água** bulletproof/fire-proof/waterproof; **pôr à ~ to** put to the test; **provação** *f* (*sofrimento*) hardship, suffering; **provar** *vt* (*comprovar*) to prove; (*comida*) to taste; (*roupa*) to try on // *vi* to try.

pro'vável *adj* probable, likely.

prove'dor(a) *m/f* (*fornecedor*) provider; (*COM*) supplier.

proveito [pro'vejtu] *m* (*ganho*) profit; (*vantagem*) advantage; **em ~ de** for the benefit of; **tirar ~ de** to benefit from; **proveitoso/a** *adj* profitable, advantageous.

proveniência [proven̄i'ẽsja] *f* source, origin; **proveniente** *adj*: **proveniente de** coming from, originating from.

pro'ver *vt* (*fornecer*) to provide, supply; (*vaga*) to fill // *vi*: **~ a** to take care of, see to.

pro'vérbio *m* proverb.

pro'veta *f* test tube.

provi'dência *f* providence; **~s** *fpl* measures, steps; **tomar ~s** to take steps; **providenciar** *vt* (*prover*) to provide; (*tomar providências*) to take steps, arrange // *vi* (*tomar providências*) to make arrangements; (*prover*) to make provision; **providenciar para que** to see to it that; **providente** *adj* provident; (*prudente*) prudent, careful.

pro'vido/a *adj* (*fornecido*) supplied, provided; (*cheio*) full up, fully stocked.

'próvido/a *adj* provident; (*prudente*) prudent, careful.

provi'mento *m*: **dar ~** (*JUR*) to grant a petition.

pro'víncia *f* province; **provinciano/a** *adj* provincial.

pro'vir *vi*: **~ de** to come from, derive from.

provisão [provi'zãw] *f* (*abastecimento*) provision, supply; **provisões** *fpl* provisions; **provisório/a** *adj* provisional, temporary.

provocação [provɔka'sãw] *f* provocation; **provocador(a)** *adj*, pro-**vocante** *adj* provocative, provoking; **provocar** *vt* to provoke; (*ocasionar*) to cause; (*atrair*) to tempt, attract; (*estimular*) to rouse, stimulate.

proximi'dade *f* proximity, nearness; **~s** *fpl* neighbourhood, vicinity.

próximo/a ['prɔsimu/a] *adj* (*perto*) near, close; (*seguinte*) next; (*vizinho*) neighbouring; **~ a/de** near to, close to; **futuro ~** next, coming // *m* fellow man.

pru'dência *f* (*sabedoria*) wisdom; (*cautela*) care, prudence; **prudente** *adj* sensible, prudent.

'prumo *m* plumb line; (*NÁUT*) lead; **a ~** perpendicularly, vertically.

pru'rido *m* (*comichão*) itch; (*fig*) yearning, desire.

pseudônimo [psew'donimu] *m* pseudonym.

psicanálise [psika'nalizɪ] *f* psychoanalysis; **psicanalítico/a** *adj* psychoanalytic(al).

psicologia [psikolo'ʒia] *f* psychology; **psicológico/a** *adj* psychological; **psicólogo/a** *m/f* psychologist; **psicopata** *m/f* pyschopath; **psicose** *f* psychosis.

psiquiatra [psɪkɪ'atra] *m/f* psychiatrist; **psiquiatria** *f* psychiatry; **psiquiátrico/a** *adj* psychiatric.

'pua *f* sharp point; (*de broca*) bit; (*de galo de briga*) spur.

puber'dade *f* puberty.

publicação [publɪka'sãw] *f* publication; **publicar** *vt* (*editar*) to publish; (*divulgar*) to divulge; (*proclamar*) to announce; (*popularizar*) to make well known; **publicidade** *f* publicity; (*COM*) advertising; **publicitário/a** *adj* publicity *cmp*; (*COM*) advertising *cmp*; **público/a** *adj* public // *m* public (*cinema, teatro etc*) audience.

'púcaro *m* (*Pt*) jug, mug.

'pude *etc vb ver* **poder**.

'púdico/a *adj* bashful, shy.

pudim [pu'dʒĩ] *m* pudding; ~-**flã** *m* (*Pt*) crème caramel.

pu'dor *m* bashfulness, modesty; **atentado ao** ~ indecent assault.

puerícia [pue'rɪsja] *f* childhood; **puericultura** *f* child care; **pueril** *adj* puerile; **puerilidade** *f* childishness, foolishness.

pugilato [puʒɪ'lato] *m* boxing, fighting; **pugilismo** *m* boxing; **pugilista** *m* boxer.

'pugna *f* fight, struggle; **pugnar** *vi* (*lutar*) to struggle; (*pelejar*) to fight.

pujança [pu'ʒãsa] *f* vigour, strength; (*de vegetação*) vigorous growth; **na** ~ **da vida** in the prime of life; **pujante** *adj* vigorous, powerful.

pu'lar *vi* to jump, leap; ~ **de alegria** to jump for joy.

'pulga *f* flea; **pulgão** *m* greenfly.

pulha ['puʎa] *m* rat, creep.

pulmão [pul'mãw] *m* lung; **pulmonar** *adj* pulmonary, lung *cmp*.

'pulo *m* leap, jump; **dar** ~**s de contente** to be delighted; **dar um** ~ **até** to pay a flying visit to; **aos** ~**s by leaps and bounds; **de um** ~ at one bound.

pu'lôver *m* (*Br*) pullover.

'púlpito *m* pulpit.

pulsação [pulsa'sãw] *f* pulsation, beating; (*MED*) pulse; **pulsar** *vi* (*palpitar*) to pulsate, throb.

pulseira [pul'sejra] *f* bracelet.

'pulso *m* (*ANAT*) wrist; (*MED*) pulse; (*fig*) vigour, energy; **obra de** ~ work of great importance; **homem de** ~ energetic man; **tomar o** ~ **de alguém** to take sb's pulse.

pulu'lar *vi* to swarm, teem.

pulveriza'dor *m* (*para líquidos etc*) spray, spray gun; **pulverizar** *vt* to pulverize; (*reduzir a pó*) to grind; (*líquido*) to spray.

punção [pũ'sãw] *m* (*instrumento*) punch // *f* (*MED*) puncture.

pundo'nor *m* dignity, self-respect.

pungente [pũ'ʒẽtʃi] *adj* (*acre*) sharp, pungent; (*doloroso*) painful.

punguista [pũ'gɪʃta] *m* pickpocket.

'punha *etc vb ver* **pôr**.

pu'nhado *m* handful.

punhal [pu'ɲaw] *m* dagger; ~**ada** *f* stab.

punho ['puɲu] *m* fist; (*de manga*) cuff; (*de espada*) hilt; **de seu próprio** ~ in one's own handwriting.

punição [punɪ'sãw] *f* punishment; **punir** *vt* to punish.

'pupilo/a *m* (*tutelado*) ward; (*aluno*) pupil // *f* (*ANAT*) pupil; (*tutelada*) ward.

pu'rê *m* purée; ~ **de batatas** mashed potatoes.

pu'reza *f* purity; (*nitidez*) clarity.

'purga *f* (*MED*) purgative; **purgação** *f* purge; (*purificação*) purification; **purgante** *m* purgative; **purgar** *vt* to purge; (*purificar*) to purify; **purgativo/a** *adj*, *m* purgative; **purgatório** *m* purgatory.

purificação [purɪfɪka'sãw] *f* purification; **purificar** *vt* to purify; (*refinar*) to refine; **purista** *m/f* purist; **puritanismo** *m* puritanism; **puritano/a** *adj* (*atitude*) puritanical; (*seita*) puritan // *m/f* puritan; **puro/a** *adj* pure; (*límpido*) clear; (*limpo*) clean; (*verdadeiro*) genuine; (*completo*) complete, absolute; (*casto*) chaste.

'púrpura *f* purple; **purpúreo/a** *adj* (*cor*) crimson.

puru'lento/a *adj* festering, suppurating.

pus *m* pus, matter.

pus *etc vb ver* **pôr**.

pusi'lânime *adj* fainthearted; (*covarde*) cowardly.

'puta *f* whore, prostitute.

putrefação [putrefa'sãw] (*Pt*: -cç-) *f* rotting, putrefaction; **pútrido/a** *adj* putrid, rotten.

puxador [puʃa'dox] *m* handle, knob; **puxão** *m* tug, jerk; **puxar** *vt* to pull; (*sacar*) to pull out; (*provocar*) to provoke; (*assunto*) to bring up; **puxar a** to take after; **puxa-saco** *m* creep, crawler, toady.

Q

quadra ['kwadra] *f* (*de rua*) block; (*estrofe*) quatrain; (*campo de esportes*) court; (*período*) time, period; (*jogos*) four; **quadrado/a** *adj* square; (*fig*) stupid // *m* square; **quadrar** *vt* to square, make square // *vi*: **quadrar a** (*ser conveniente*) to suit; (*adaptar-se*) to fit, agree with; **quadriculado/a** *adj* squared; (*desenho decorativo*) checkered; **papel quadriculado** squared paper.

quadril [kwa'drɪw] *m* hip, haunch.

quadrilha [kwa'drɪʎa] *f* gang; (*dança*) square dance.

qua'drinhos [kwa'drɪɲuʃ] *mpl*: **história em** ~ (*Br*) cartoon.

quadro ['kwadru] *m* (*pintura*) painting; (*lista*) list; (*tabela*) chart, table; (*TEC*) painel) panel; (*pessoal*) staff; (*teatro*) scene; ~ **de avisos** bulletin board; ~

negro blackboard; ~ **de reserva** (MIL) reserve list.

'quádruplo / a adj quadruple.

qual [kwaw] pron, pl **quais** [kwajʃ] which; ~ **deles** which of them; **o** ~ which; (pessoa: sujeito) who; (pessoa: objeto) whom; **seja** ~ **for** whatever/whichever it may be; **cada** ~ each one; ~ **é? / ~ é a tua?** what are you up to? // conj as, like; ~ **seja** such as; **tal** ~ just like // excl nonsense!; ~ **nada!/ ~ o quê!** no such thing!

qualidade [kwali'dadʒɪ] f quality; **na** ~ **de** in the capacity of.

qualificação [kwalifika'sãw] f qualification; **qualificado / a** adj qualified; **qualificar** vt to qualify; **qualificar de / como** to classify as, regard as; **qualificar-se** vr to qualify.

qualquer [kwaw'kɛx] adj, pl **quais'quer** [kwaj'kɛx] any // pron any; (pessoa) anyone, anybody; ~ **dos dois** either; ~ **outro** any other; ~ **dia** any day; ~ **que seja** whichever it may be; (pessoa) whoever it may be; **um disco** ~ any record at all, any record you like.

quando ['kwãdu] adv when // conj when; (interrogativo) when?; (se) if, even if; (ao passo que) whilst; **ainda** ~ even though; ~ **muito** at most; ~ **menos** at least; ~ **quer que** whenever; **de** ~ **em** ~ / **de vez em** ~ now and then; **desde** ~? how long?, since when?; ~ **mais não seja** if for no other reason.

quantia [kwã't∫ia] f sum, amount; **quantidade** f quantity, amount.

quanto / a ['kwãtu/a] adj, pron all that, as much as; (interrogativo: sg) how much?; (: pl) **quantos / as** how many? // adv: ~ **tempo?** how long?; ~ **custa?** how much does it cost?; ~ **a as** regards; **a mim** as for me; ~ **antes** as soon as possible; ~ **mais cedo melhor** the sooner the better; ~ **mais trabalha, mais ganha** the more he works, the more he earns; **tudo** ~ everything that, as much as; ~ **sofria!** how he suffered!

quão [kwãw] adv how.

quarenta [kwa'rẽta] num forty.

quarentão [kwarẽ'tãw] m man in his forties.

quaren'tena f quarantine.

quaren'tona f woman in her forties.

quaresma [kwa'rɛʒma] f Lent.

quarta-feira ['kwaxta-fejra] f Wednesday; ~ **de cinzas** Ash Wednesday.

quarteirão [kwaxtej'rãw] m (de casas) block; (número) quarter-century.

quartel [kwax'tɛw] m (MIL) barracks sg; (quarta parte) quarter; (dum século) quarter-century; ~-**general** m headquarters pl.

quarteto [kwax'tetu] m (MÚS) quartet.

quarto / a ['kwaxtu/a] adj fourth // m (quarta parte) quarter; (aposento) room; (MIL) watch; (anca) haunch; ~ **de banho** bathroom; ~ **de dormir**

bedroom; ~ **de casal** double bedroom; ~ **de solteiro** single room; ~ **crescente / minguante** (ASTRO) first/last quarter // f quarter; (cântaro) pitcher; (MÚS) fourth.

quartzo ['kwaxtsu] m quartz.

quase ['kwazɪ] adv almost, nearly.

quatro ['kwatru] num four; ~**centos / as** num four hundred.

que [kɪ] pron (sujeito) who, that; (: coisa) which, that; (complemento) whom, that; (: coisa) which, that; (interrogativo: coisa) what?, which?; **o** ~ (coisa) what; (pessoa) he who; (interrogativo) what?, which?; ~ **não** other than, but; **nada** ~ **fazer** nothing to do; ~ **nem** (Br: col) like // conj that // adj which, what; ~ **jornal?** what newspaper?; ~ **pena!** what a pity!; **do** ~ than; **mais do** ~ **pensa** more than you think; **não há nada** ~ **fazer** there's nothing to be done.

quê [ke] m something; (complicação) complication; **tem seus** ~**s** it has its drawbacks; **não tem de** ~ don't mention it; **para** ~? what for?; **por** ~? why?

quebra ['kɛbra] f break, rupture; (COM) bankruptcy; **de** ~ as a bonus, extra; ~-**cabeça** m puzzle, problem; (jogo) jigsaw puzzle; **quebradiço / a** adj fragile, breakable; **quebrado / a** adj (partido) broken; (cansado) exhausted; (COM) bankrupt // f (vertente) slope; (barranco) ravine, gully; (curva) bend.

quebra-'galho adj inv makeshift // m stopgap.

quebra-gelo [kɛbra-'ʒelu] m (NÁUT) icebreaker.

quebra-luz [kɛbra-'luʃ] m lampshade.

quebra-mar [kɛbra-'max] m breakwater, sea wall.

quebra-nozes [kɛbra-'nozɪʃ] m inv nutcrackers pl.

quebrantar [kɛbrã'tax] vt (quebrar) to break; (debilitar) to weaken, wear out; ~-**se** vr (tornar-se fraco) to grow weak; **quebranto** m (fraqueza) weakness; (mau-olhado) blight, evil eye.

quebrar [ke'brax] vt (romper) to break; (debilitar) to weaken // vi (COM) to go bankrupt; ~-**se** vr (romper-se) to get broken.

queda ['kɛda] f fall; (decadência) decline; (ruína) downfall; (tendência) inclination; ~-**d'água** f waterfall.

queijada [kej'ʒada] f cheesecake; (coletivo) a lot of cheese; **queijo** m cheese.

queima ['kejma] f burning; (COM) clearance sale; **queimado / a** adj burnt; (zangado) angry; **queimado do sol** sunburnt; **queimadura** f burn; **queimadura do sol** sunburn; **queimar** vt to burn, scorch; (com líquido) to scald; (bronzear a pele) to tan; (murchar) to wither; (mercadorias) to sell cheaply // vi to burn; (estar quente) to be burning hot; **queimar-se** vr (pessoa) to burn o.s.;

(*incendiar-se*) to burn down; (*zangar-se*) to get angry; ~-**roupa** *f*: à ~-**roupa** point-blank; (*MIL*) at point-blank range.

'**queira** *etc vb ver* **querer**.

queixa ['kejʃa] *f* complaint; (*lamentação*) lament; (*gemido*) moan.

queixada [kej'ʃada] *f* (*de animal*) jaw.

queixar-se [kej'ʃax-sɪ] *vr* to complain; (*soltar gemidos*) to wail; ~ **de** to complain about.

queixo ['kejʃu] *m* (*barba*) chin; (*maxilar*) jaw; **de** ~ **caído** open-mouthed.

queixoso/a [kej'ʃozu/a] *adj* complaining; (*magoado*) doleful // *m* (*JUR*) plaintiff; **queixume** *m* complaint; (*lamentação*) lament; (*gemido*) moan.

quem [kēj] *pron* who, whom; (*interrogativo*) who?, whom?; ~ **quer que** whoever; **seja** ~ **for** whoever it may be; **de** ~ **whose**; ~ **é?** who is it?, who is there?

quente ['kētʃɪ] *adj* hot; (*fig*) fiery, ardent; **quentura** *f* heat, warmth.

quer [kɛx] *conj* either, or; ~ **chova** ~ **não** whether it rains or not; ~ **queiras**, ~ **não** whether you like it or not; **onde** ~ **que** wherever; **quando** ~ **que** whenever; **quem** ~ **que** whoever.

querela [ke'rɛla] *f* dispute; (*JUR*) complaint, accusation; **querelado** *m* (*JUR*) defendant; **querelador(a)** *m/f*, **querelante** *m/f* (*JUR*) plaintiff; **querelar** *vt* (*JUR*) to prosecute, sue // *vi*: **querelar contra/de** (*queixar-se*) to lodge a complaint against; **querelar-se** *vr* to complain.

querença [ke'rēsa] *f* liking, affection.

querer [ke'rex] *vt* (*desejar*) to want, wish; (*ter afeição*) to be fond of; ~ **bem a** to love; ~ **mal a** to hate; ~ **dizer** to mean; **sem** ~ unintentionally; **querido/a** *adj* dear // *m/f* darling.

quermesse [kex'mɛsɪ] *f* church fête.

querosene [kero'zɛnɪ] *m* kerosene oil.

quesito [ke'zitu] *m* (*questão*) query, question; (*requisito*) requirement.

questão [kɛʃ'tãw] *f* (*pergunta*) question, inquiry; (*assunto*) matter, question; (*contenda*) dispute, quarrel; **fazer** ~ **de** to insist on; **questionar** *vi* to question, argue // *vt* to question, call into question; **questionário** *m* questionnaire.

quiçá [kɪ'sa] *adv* perhaps.

quieto/a [kɪ'etu/a] *adj* still, quiet; **quietude** *f* calm, tranquillity.

quilate [kɪ'latʃɪ] *m* carat; (*fig*) excellence.

quilha ['kiʎa] *f* (*NÁUT*) keel; ~ **corrediça** centreboard.

quilo ['kilu] *m* kilo; ~**grama** *m* kilogramme; **quilômetro** *m* kilometre; ~**watt** *m* kilowatt.

quimera [kɪ'mera] *f* chimera; **quimérico/a** *adj* fantastic.

químico/a ['kɪmiku/a] *adj* chemical // *m/f* chemist // *f* chemistry.

quina ['kina] *f* (*canto*) corner; (*em jogos*) five; **de** ~ edgeways, edgewise (*US*).

quinhão [kɪ'ɲãw] *m* share, portion.

quinhentista [kɪɲē'tʃɪʃta] *adj* sixteenth century *cmp*; **quinhentos/as** *num* five hundred.

quinina [kɪ'nina] *f* quinine.

qüinquagenário/a [kwĩkwaʒe-'narju/a] *adj* in his/her fifties.

quinquilharias [kĩkɪʎa'riaʃ] *fpl* odds and ends; (*miudezas*) knicknacks, trinkets.

quinta-feira [kĩta-'fejra] *f* Thursday.

quintal [kĩ'taw] *m* back yard; (*jardim*) back garden.

quinteiro [kĩ'tejru] *m* (*Pt*) farmer.

quinto/a ['kĩtu/a] *adj*, *m* fifth // *f* estate; (*terreno cultivado*) farm.

quinze ['kĩzɪ] *num* fifteen; **duas e** ~ **a** quarter past two; ~ **para as sete a** quarter to seven; **quinzena** *f* fortnight; (*salário*) fortnight's wages.

quiosque [kɪ'ɔʃkɪ] *m* (*Pt: com jornais*) newsstand; (: *com comida/bebida*) food/drink stand.

quiromante [kɪro'mãtʃɪ] *m/f* palmist, fortune teller.

'**quis** *etc vb ver* **querer**.

quisto ['kɪʃtu] *m* cyst.

quitação [kɪta'sãw] *f* (*de dívidas*) discharge, remission; (*recibo*) receipt.

quitanda [kɪ'tãda] *f* (*loja*) grocer's (shop); **quitandeiro** *m* (*numa loja*) grocer; (*vendedor de hortaliças*) greengrocer.

quitar [kɪ'tax] *vt* (*dívida*) to pay off; (*desquitar-se*) to separate from; **quite** *adj* (*livre*) free; (*com um credor*) squared up; (*igualado*) even.

quociente [kwo'sjētʃɪ] *m* quotient; ~ **de inteligência**, (**Q.I.**) intelligence quotient, (I.Q.).

quota ['kwota] *f* quota; (*porção*) share, portion.

quotidiano/a [kwotʃɪ'dʒanu/a] *adj* (*usual*) everyday.

R

R *abr de* **Rua** street.

rã *f* frog.

ra'bada *f* (*rabo*) tail; (*fig*) tail end.

raba'nada *f* (*fatia*) French toast.

raba'nete *m* radish.

ra'bino *m* rabbi.

rabis'car *vt* (*escrever mal, às pressas*) to scribble // *vi* to doodle; (*escrever mal*) to scribble.

'**rabo** *m* (*cauda*) tail; (*col*) bottom; ~-**de-cavalo** *m* ponytail.

rabu'gento/a *adj* sulky, grumpy.

'**raça** *f* race; (*de animal*) breed; **de** ~ thoroughbred; (*pessoa*) of character, of breeding.

ração [xa'sãw] *f* ration.

racha ['xaʃa] *f* (*fenda*) split; (*greta*) crack /// *m* (*col*) scrap.

rachador [xaʃa'dox] *m* woodcutter; **rachadura** *f* (*fenda*) crack; **rachar** *vt* (*objeto, despesas*) to split; (*lenha*) to chop

// *vi*, **rachar-se** *vr* to split; (*cristal*) to crack; **frio de rachar** bitter cold.

racial [xa'sjaw] *adj* racial.

raciocinar [xasiosi'nax] *vi* to reason; **raciocínio** *m* reasoning; **racional** *adj* rational; **racionalizar** *vt* to rationalize.

racionamento [xasjona'mẽtu] *m* rationing; **racionar** *vt* (*distribuir*) to ration out; (*limitar a venda de*) to ration.

racismo [xa'siʒmu] *m* racialism, racism; **racista** *adj*, *m/f* racist.

ra'dar *m* radar.

radiação [xadʒia'sãw] *f* radiation; (*raio*) ray; **radiador** *m* radiator; **radiante** *adj* radiant; (*de alegria*) overjoyed.

radical [xadʒi'kaw] *adj* radical // *m* radical; (*LING*) root; **radicar-se** *vr* to take root; (*fixar residência*) to settle down.

rádio ['xadʒju] *m* radio; (*QUÍM*) radium; **radioamador** *m* radio ham.

radioa'tivo/a (*Pt*: -ct-) *adj* radioactive.

radiodifusão [xadʒjodʒifu'zãw] *f* broadcasting; **radiodifusora** *f* radio station; **radioemissora** *f* radio broadcasting station.

radiogra'far *vt* to X-ray; **radiografia** *f* X-ray.

radio'grama *m* cablegram.

radiojornal [xadʒjoʒux'naw] *m* radio news.

radi'oso/a *adj* radiant, brilliant; (*fig: radiante*) radiant; (: *alegre*) overjoyed.

radiotera'pia *f* radiotherapy.

radiouvinte [xadʒjo'vĩtʃi] *m/f* listener.

ra'gu *m* stew, ragoût.

raia ['raja] *f* (*risca*) line; (*fronteira*) boundary; (*limite*) limit; (*de corrida*) track; (*peixe*) ray, skate; **chegar às ~s** to reach the limit; **raiado/a** *adj* striped.

raiar [xa'jax] *vi* (*brilhar*) to shine; (*madrugada*) to dawn; (*aparecer*) to appear.

rainha [xa'iɲa] *f* queen.

raio ['xaju] *m* (*de sol*) ray; (*de luz*) beam; (*de roda*) spoke; (*relâmpago*) flash of lightning; (*distância*) range; (*MAT*) radius; **~s X** X-rays.

raiva ['xajva] *f* rage, fury; (*MED*) rabies *sg*; **ter ~ de** to hate; **raivoso/a** *adj* furious; (*MED*) rabid, mad.

raiz [xa'iʃ] *f* root; (*origem*) source; **~ quadrada** square root; **criar raízes** to put down roots.

rajada [xa'ʒada] *f* (*vento*) gust; (*de tiros*) burst.

ra'lado/a *adj*: **pão ~** breadcrumbs *pl*; **ralador** *m* grater; **ralar** *vt* (*coco*) to grate; (*pão*) to crumble; (*fig*) to annoy.

ra'lé *f* the common people, rabble.

rale'ar *vt/i* to thin out.

ralhar [xa'ʎax] *vi* to scold; **~ com alguém** to tell sb off.

'ralo/a *adj* thin, sparse // *m* (*de regador*) rose, nozzle; (*ralador*) grater.

'rama *f* branches *pl*, foliage; **em ~** raw; **pela ~** superficially; **ramada** *f* branches *pl*, foliage; **ramagem** *f*

branches *pl*, foliage; **ramal** *m* (*FERRO*) branch line; (*telefônico*) extension; (*AUTO*) branch (road).

ramalhete [xama'ʎetʃi] *m* bouquet, posy.

ramifi'car-se *vr* to branch out; **ramo** *m* branch; (*profissão, negócios*) line; (*de flores*) bunch; **Domingo de Ramos** Palm Sunday.

'rampa *f* ramp; (*ladeira*) slope.

ran'çar *vi* to go rancid.

rancheiro [xã'ʃejru] *m* cook; **rancho** *m* (*grupo*) group, band; (*cabana*) hut; (*MIL*) mess.

ran'cor *m* (*ressentimento*) bitterness; (*ódio*) hatred; **~oso/a** *adj* bitter, resentful; (*odiento*) hateful.

ran'çoso/a *adj* rancid; (*cheiro*) musty.

ranger [xã'ʒex] *vi* to creak // *vt*: **~ os dentes** to grind one's teeth; **rangido** *m* creak.

ranho ['xaɲu] *m* (*col*) snot; **ranhoso/a** *adj* (*col*) snotty.

ranhura [xa'ɲura] *f* groove; (*para moeda*) slot.

ra'núnculo *m* buttercup.

rapace [xa'pasi] *adj* rapacious // *f* bird of prey; **rapacidade** *f* rapacity, rapaciousness.

rapadeira [xapa'dejra] *f* scraper.

rapa'pé *m* bowing and scraping; (*lisonja*) flattery.

ra'par *vt* to scrape; (*barbear*) to shave; (*o cabelo*) to crop; **~ a alguém** (*roubar*) to steal from sb; (*col*) to pinch from sb.

rapa'riga (*Pt*) *f* girl; (*Br*) young woman.

ra'paz *m* boy; (*col*) lad; **~iada** *f* (*grupo*) gang of lads.

ra'pé *m* snuff.

rapi'dez *f* speed, rapidity; **rápido/a** *adj* quick, fast // *adv* fast, quickly // *m* (*trem*) express.

ra'pina *f* robbery; **ave de ~** bird of prey.

ra'poso/a *m/f* (*fig*) crafty person // *m* fox // *f* vixen.

rap'sódia *f* rhapsody.

rap'tar *vt* to kidnap; **rapto** *m* kidnapping; **raptor** *m* kidnapper.

raqueta [xa'keta] *f* (*Pt*), **raquete** [xa'ketʃi] *f* (*Br*) (*de tênis*) racquet; (*de pingue-pongue*) bat.

raquítico/a [xa'kitʃiku/a] *adj* (*franzino*) stunted, puny; (*fig*) poor, feeble; **raquitismo** *m* rickets *sg*.

rara'mente *adv* rarely, seldom; **rarear** *vt* to make scarce // *vi* to become scarce; (*cabelos*) to thin; **raridade** *f* rarity; **raro/a** *adj* rare; (*ralo*) thin // *adv* rarely, seldom.

ra'sante *adj* (*vôo*) low-flying.

ra'sar *vt* (*nivelar*) to level; (*tocar de leve: a pele*) to graze; (: *as ondas*) to skim; (*encher*) to fill to the brim; **~-se** *vr* to fill up.

rascunhar [xaʃku'ɲax] *vt* to draft, make a rough copy of; **rascunho** *m* rough copy, draft.

ras'gado/a adj (roupa) torn, ripped; (cumprimentos) effusive; (gesto) generous; **rasgão** m tear, rip; **rasgar** vt to tear, rip; (destruir) to tear up, rip up; **rasgar-se** vr to split; **rasgo** m (rasgão) tear, rip; (risco) stroke; (ação) feat; (ímpeto) burst; (da imaginação) flight.

'raso/a adj (liso) flat, level; (sapato) flat; (não fundo) shallow; (baixo) low; **soldado** ~ private.

'raspa f (de madeira) shaving; (de metal) filing; ~**deira** f scraper; **raspão** m scratch, graze; **tocar de raspão** to graze; **raspar** vt (limpar, tocar) to scrape; (alisar) to file; (ferir) to graze; (arranhar) to scratch; (pêlos) to shave; (apagar) to rub out; **raspar-se** vr to clear off, sneak off.

rasteiro/a [xaʃ'tejru/a] adj (que se arrasta) crawling; (planta) creeping; (a pouca altura) low-lying; (ordinário) common // f (pernada) trip; **dar uma** ~**a em** to trip up; **rastejar** vi (com dificuldade) to crawl; (furtivamente) to creep.

rastilho [xaʃ'tʃiʎu] m (de pólvora) fuse.

'rasto m (vestígio) trace; (sinal) sign; (pista) track, trail; **andar de** ~**s** to crawl; **levar de** ~**s** to drag along.

ratão [xa'tãw] m rat; **ratazana** f (Pt) rat.

rate'ar vt (dividir) to share // vi (motor) to break down.

ratifi'car vt to confirm, ratify.

'rato m rat; (Pt: rato pequeno) mouse; (ladrão) thief; ~ **de biblioteca** bookworm; ~**eira** f rat trap; (pequena) mousetrap.

razão [xa'zãw] f (juízo, motivo) reason; (bom senso) common sense; (raciocínio, argumento) reasoning, argument; (conta) account; (MAT) ratio // m (COM) ledger; à ~ **de** at the rate of; **em** ~ **de** on account of; **dar** ~ **a alguém** to support sb; **ter** ~/**não ter** ~ to be right/be wrong; **razoar** vi (raciocinar) to reason; (falar) to talk; **razoável** adj reasonable; (moderado, justo) fair.

r/c (Pt) abr de **rés-do-chão** ground floor, first floor (US).

ré f ver **réu**; (AUTO) reverse gear; **dar marcha a** ~ to reverse, back up.

reabastecer [xiabaʃte'sex] vt (AUTO) to refuel; (mercadorias) to restock.

reabili'tar vt (restituir) to restore the reputation of; (condenado) to rehabilitate.

rea'brir vt to reopen.

reação [xia'sãw] (Pt: -cç-) f reaction; ~ **em cadeia** chain reaction; **reacionário/a** adj reactionary; **reagir** vi to react; **reagir a** (resistir) to resist; (protestar) to rebel against.

re'al adj real; (de rei) royal.

realçar [xeaw'sax] vt to accentuate, emphasize; (fig, com maquilagem) to highlight; **realce** m (destaque) emphasis; (mais brilho) highlight; **dar realce a** to enhance.

realejo [xea'leʒu] m barrel organ.

rea'leza f royalty.

realidade [xeali'dadʒi] f reality; **na** ~ really, in fact.

realimentação [xealimẽta'sãw] f (ELET) feedback.

realização [xealiza'sãw] f fulfilment; (de projeto) execution, carrying out; (transformação em dinheiro) conversion into cash; **realizar** vt (um objetivo) to achieve; (projeto) to carry out; (ambições) to fulfill; (reunião) to hold; (negócios) to transact; **realizar-se** vr (acontecer) to take place; (sonhos) to come true.

realmente [xeaw'mẽtʃi] adv really, actually.

reani'mar vt to revive; (encorajar) to encourage; ~**-se** vr (pessoa) to cheer up.

reaparecer [xeapare'sex] vi to reappear.

rea'tar vt (continuar) to resume, take up again; (nó) to retie.

rea'tor (Pt: -ct-) m reactor.

rea'ver vt to recover, get back.

rebaixa [xe'bajʃa] f reduction; **rebaixar** vt (tornar mais baixo) to lower; (o preço de) to lower the price of; (humilhar) to put down, humiliate // vi to drop; **rebaixar-se** vr to demean o.s.

rebanho [xe'baɲu] m (de carneiros, fig) flock; (de gado, elefantes) herd.

rebarba'tivo/a adj (pessoa) disagreeable, unpleasant.

rebate [xe'batʃi] m (sinal) alarm; (COM) discount; ~ **falso** false alarm; **rebater** vt (um golpe) to ward off; (acusações) to refute; (COM) to discount; (futebol) to kick back.

rebe'lar-se vr to rebel, revolt; **rebelde** adj rebellious; (indisciplinado) unruly, wild // m/f rebel; **rebeldia** f rebelliousness; (fig: obstinação) stubbornness; (: oposição) defiance; **rebelião** f rebellion.

rebentão [xebē'tãw] m offshoot; (criança) offspring; **rebentar** vi (guerra) to break out; (brotar) to sprout; **rebentar de alegria** to burst with happiness; **rebento** m shoot; (filho) offspring.

rebite [xe'bitʃi] m (TEC) rivet.

rebo'ar vi to resound, echo.

reboca'dor m (embarcação) tug(boat); (de paredes) plasterer; **rebocar** vt (paredes) to plaster; (veículo mal estacionado) to tow away; (dar reboque a) to tow; **reboco** m plaster.

rebo'lar vt (os quadris) to swing // vi, ~**-se** vr to roll over; (bambolear-se) to sway; (fig) to work hard.

re'bolo m (mó) grindstone; (cilindro) cylinder.

reboque [xe'bɔki] m (ato) tow; (cabo) towrope; (Br: camionete) towtruck; **carro** ~ trailer; **a** ~ in tow.

re'bordo m rim, edge.

rebu'çado m (Pt) sweet, candy (US).

rebu'liço m commotion, hubbub.

rebus'cado/a adj affected; **rebuscar** vt (buscar) to search carefully for.

re'cado m (mensagem) message; **mandar** ~ to send word; **menino de** ~s errand boy.

reca'ída f relapse.

recalci'trante adj recalcitrant.

reca'mado/a adj embroidered.

recambiar [xekã'bjax] vt to send back.

re'canto m (lugar aprazível) corner, nook; (esconderijo) hiding place.

recapitu'lar vt to sum up, recapitulate.

reca'tado/a adj (modesto) modest; (reservado) reserved; **recatar-se** vr to become withdrawn; (ocultar-se) to hide; **recato** m (modéstia) modesty.

recauchutado/a [xekawʃu'tadu/a] adj: **pneumático** ~ (AUTO) retread, remould.

recear [xese'ax] vt to fear // vi to be afraid.

recebe'dor(a) m/f receiver; (de impostos) collector; **receber** vt to receive; (hóspedes) to take in; (convidados) to entertain; (acolher bem) to welcome // vi to entertain, have guests; **recebimento** m (Br) reception; (: de uma carta) receipt; **acusar o recebimento de** to acknowledge receipt of.

receio [xe'seju] m fear.

receita [xe'sejta] f (renda) income; (do Estado) revenue; (MED) prescription; (culinária) recipe; **receitar** vt to prescribe.

recém [xe'sẽ] adv recently, newly; ~-**chegado/a** m/f newcomer; ~-**nascido/a** m/f newborn child.

recen'der vt: ~ **um cheiro** to give off a smell // vi to smell; ~ **a** to smell of.

recenseamento [xesẽsɪa'mẽtu] m census; **recensear** vt to take a census of.

recente [xe'sẽtʃi] adj recent; (novo) new, fresh.

receoso/a [xesɪ'ozu/a] adj (medroso) frightened, fearful; (tímido) timid, shy.

recepção [xesep'sãw] f reception; (de uma carta) receipt; **acusar a** ~ **de** (Pt) to acknowledge receipt of; **recepcionista** m/f receptionist.

recep'táculo m receptacle.

recep'tar vt to receive; **receptivo/a** adj receptive; (acolhedor) welcoming; **receptor** m/f receiver.

recheado/a [xeʃɪ'adu/a] adj (ave) stuffed; (empada, bolo) filled; (cheio) full, crammed; **recheio** m (para carne assada) stuffing; (de empada, de bolo) filling; (o conteúdo) contents pl.

rechonchudo/a [xeʃõ'ʃudu/a] adj chubby, plump.

re'cibo m (documento) receipt.

reci'diva f recurrence.

recife [xe'sifi] m reef.

re'cinto m (espaço fechado) enclosure; (lugar) area.

recipiente [xesipɪ'ẽtʃi] m container, receptacle.

recipro'car vt (trocar) to exchange; **reciproco/a** adj reciprocal.

'récita f (teatral) performance; **recitação** f recitation; **recital** m recital; **recitar** vt (declamar) to recite.

reclamação [xeklama'sãw] f (queixa) complaint; (protesto) protest; (JUR) claim; **reclamante** m/f claimant; **reclamar** vt (exigir) to demand; (herança) to claim // vi: **reclamar contra** to complain about; **reclame** m, **reclamo** m (anúncio) advertisement; (queixa) complaint.

recli'nar vt, **recli'nar-se** vr to rest, lean; (deitar-se) to lie down.

reclusão [xeklu'sãw] f (isolamento) seclusion; (encarceramento) imprisonment; (prisão) prison.

reco'brar vt to recover, get back; ~-**se** vr to recover.

recolher [xeko'ʎex] vt (dados, mensalidades) to collect; (gado, roupa) to bring in; (juntar) to gather together; (abrigar) to give shelter to; (notas antigas) to withdraw; ~-**se** vr (ir para casa) to go home; (deitar-se) to go to bed; (retrair-se) to withdraw; (concentrar-se) to meditate; **recolhido/a** adj (lugar) secluded; (retraído) withdrawn; **recolhimento** m (vida retraída) retirement; (contemplação) meditation.

recomendação [xekomẽda'sãw] f recommendation; (conselho) advice; (advertência) warning; **recomendações** fpl regards; **recomendar** vt (aconselhar) to recommend, advise; **recomendar alguém a alguém** to remember sb to sb, give sb's regards to sb.

recom'pensa f (prêmio) reward; (indenização) recompense; **recompensar** vt (premiar) to reward; (indenizar) to compensate for.

recom'por vt (reorganizar) to reorganize; (restabelecer) to restore.

reconcili'ar vt to reconcile; ~-**se** vr to become reconciled.

re'côndito/a adj (escondido) hidden; (ignorado) unknown.

reconfor'tar vt to invigorate; ~-**se** vr to be invigorated.

reconhecer [xekoɲe'sex] vt to recognize; (admitir) to realise, admit; (MIL) to reconnoitre; (assinatura) to witness; **reconhecido/a** adj recognized; (agradecido) grateful, thankful; **reconhecimento** m recognition; (gratidão) gratitude; (MIL) reconnaissance.

reconquista [xekõ'kɪʃta] f reconquest.

reconside'rar vt/i to reconsider.

reconstituinte [xekõʃtʃi'twĩtʃi] m tonic.

reconstru'ir vt to rebuild, reconstruct.

recordação [xekoxda'sãw] f (reminiscência) memory; (coisa) souvenir, memento; **recordar** vt (lembrar) to remember; **recordar-se** *vr*: **recordar-se de** to remember.

re'corde *adj inv* record *cmp* // *m* record; **em tempo ~** in record time; **bater um ~** to break a record.

recor'rer *vi*: **~ a** (*para socorro*) to run to, turn to; (*valer-se*) to resort to; **~ da sentença** (*JUR*) to appeal against the sentence.

recor'tar *vt* to cut out; **~-se** *vr* to be silhouetted; **recorte** *m* (*ato*) cutting out; (*de jornal*) cutting, clipping; **álbum de recortes** scrapbook.

recos'tar *vt* to lean, rest; **~-se** *vr* to lean back; (*deitar-se*) to lie down.

recreação [xekrea'sãw] *f* fun, recreation; **por sua alta ~** just for fun; **recrear** *vt* to entertain, amuse; **recrear-se** *vr* to have fun; **recreativo/a** *adj* recreational; **recreio** *m* recreation; (*divertimento*) amusement, fun; **hora de recreio** break; (*escola*) playtime; **viagem de recreio** trip, outing.

recri'ar *vt* to recreate.

recriminação [xekrimina'sãw] *f* recrimination; **recriminar** *vt* to reproach, reprove.

recrudes'cência *f* worsening; **recrudescer** *vi* to grow worse, worsen; **recrudescimento** *m* worsening.

re'cruta *m/f* recruit; **~mento** *m* recruitment.

récua ['xɛkwa] *f* (*de mulas*) pack, train; (*de cavalos*) drove.

recu'ar *vt/i* to move back.

recuperação [xekupera'sãw] *f* recovery; **recuperar** *vt* to recover; (*tempo perdido*) to make up for; (*reabilitar*) to rehabilitate; **recuperar-se** *vr*: **recuperar-se de** to recuperate from.

re'curso *m* resort; (*JUR*) appeal; **~s** *mpl* (*meios*) means; (: *financeiros*) resources; **em último ~** as a last resort.

re'cusa *f* refusal; (*negação*) denial; **recusar** *vt* (*não aceitar*) to refuse; (*negar*) to deny; (*rejeitar*) to reject; **recusar-se** *vr*: **recusar-se a** to refuse to.

redação [xeda'sãw] (*Pt*: **-cç-**) *f* (*escolar*) composition, essay; (*de jornal*) editing; (*redatores*) editorial staff; (*lugar*) editorial office.

redargüir [xedax'gwix] *vi* to retort.

reda'tor(a) (*Pt*: **-ct-**) *m/f* journalist; (*revisor*) editor; **~-chefe** *m/f* editor in chief.

rede ['xedʒi] *f* net; (*de salvamento*) safety net; (*de cabelos*) hairnet; (*de dormir*) hammock; (*cilada*) trap; (*FERRO. TEC*) network.

'rédea *f* rein; **dar ~ larga a** to give free rein to.

redemoinho [xedemo'iɲu] *m* ver **remoinho**.

redenção [xedẽ'sãw] *f* redemption; **redentor(a)** *adj* redeeming // *m/f* redeemer.

redigir [xedʒi'ʒix] *vt* (*escrever*) to compose, write.

re'dil *m* (*Pt*) sheepfold.

redo'brar *vt* to fold again; (*aumentar*) to increase; (*sinos*) to ring out // *vi* (*aumentar*) to increase; (*sinos*) to ring out.

redon'deza *f* roundness; (*arredores*) vicinity; **redondo/a** *adj* round; (*gordo*) plump.

re'dor *m*: **ao/em ~ (de)** around, round about.

redução [xedu'sãw] *f* reduction; (*MED. ossos*) setting.

redun'dância *f* redundancy; **redundar** *vi*: **redundar em** (*resultar em*) to result in.

re'duto *m* stronghold.

redu'zido/a *adj* reduced; (*limitado*) limited; (*pequeno*) small; **reduzir** *vt* to reduce; (*dinheiro*) to convert; (*MED*) to set; (*abreviar*) to abridge; **reduzir-se** *vr*: **reduzir-se a** to be reduced to.

reembolsar [xiẽbol'sax] *vt* to reimburse; (*depósito*) to refund; **reembolso** *m* refund, repayment; **reembolso postal** cash on delivery, C.O.D.

refa'zer *vt* (*fazer novamente*) to redo, repeat; (*consertar*) to repair, fix; (*restaurar*) to restore; (*nutrir*) to build up; **~-se** *vr* (*MED*) to recover.

re'fego *m* (*dobra*) fold; (*num vestido*) pleat.

refeição [xefej'sãw] *f* meal.

refei'tório *m* dining hall, refectory.

refém [xe'fẽ] *m* hostage.

refe'rência *f* reference; **com ~ a** with reference to, about.

referen'dar *vt* to countersign, endorse.

referendum [xefe'rẽdũ] *m* (*POL*) referendum.

refe'rente *adj*: **~ a** concerning, regarding.

refe'rido/a *adj* aforesaid, already mentioned; **referir** *vt* (*contar*) to relate, tell; **referir-se** *vr*: **referir-se a** to refer to.

refeste'lar-se *vr* (*recostar-se*) to stretch out, lean back; (*comprazer-se*) to enjoy o.s.

refi'nado/a *adj* refined; (*completo*) absolute; **refinamento** *m* refinement; **refinar** *vt* to refine; (*fig*) to perfect, polish; **refinaria** *f* refinery.

refle'tido/a (*Pt*: **-ct-**) *adj* reflected; (*prudente*) thoughtful; **refletir** (*Pt*: **-ct-**) *vt* (*espelhar*) to reflect; (*som*) to echo; **refletir em** (*pensar*) to consider, think about; **refletir-se** *vr* to be reflected; **refletor(a)** (*Pt*: **-ct-**) *adj* reflecting // *m* reflector.

reflexão [xeflɛk'sãw] *f* reflection; (*contemplação*) thought, contemplation; **reflexivo/a** *adj* reflexive.

re'flexo/a *adj* (*luz*) reflected; (*ação*) reflex // *m* reflection; (*MED*) reflex; (*cópia*) copy.

refluxo [xe'fluksu] *m* ebb.

refo'gado m (*tempero*) sautéed seasonings; (*prato*) stew; **refogar** vt to stew in seasoning.

refor'çado/a adj strengthened; (*forte*) strong; (*ARQ*) reinforced; **reforçar** vt (*fazer mais forte*) to strengthen; (*revigorar*) to invigorate; **reforçar-se** vr to grow stronger; **reforço** m reinforcement.

re'forma f (*agrária*) reform; (*ARQ*) renovation; (*REL*) reformation; (*aposentadoria*) retirement; **reformado/a** adj (*Pt, MIL*) retired; **reformar** vt (*ARQ*) to rebuild, renovate; (*modificar*) to change, alter; (*aposentar*) to retire; (*sentença*) to commute; **reformar-se** vr (*militar*) to retire; (*prisioneiro*) to reform, mend one's ways.

reforma'tório m approved school, borstal.

refrão [xe'frãw] m (*cantado*) refrain; (*provérbio*) saying.

refra'tário/a (*Pt:* **-ct-**) adj (*desobediente*) difficult, unmanageable; (*TEC*) heat-resistant.

refre'ar vt (*frear*) to check; (*dominar*) to restrain; ~ **a língua** to mind one's language, mince one's words; ~**-se** vr to restrain o.s.

re'frega f fight.

refres'cante adj refreshing; **refrescar** vt (*refrigerar*) to cool; (*restaurar*) to refresh // vi to cool down; **refrescar-se** vr to be refreshed; **refresco** m (*bebida*) cool drink.

refrigerador [xefrizera'dox] m refrigerator; (*col*) fridge; **refrigerante** m cool drink, soft drink; **refrigerar** vt to keep cool; (*consolar*) to comfort, console; **refrigério** m solace, consolation.

refugiado/a [xefuʒi'adu/a] m/f refugee; **refugiar-se** vr to take refuge, seek shelter; **refúgio** m refuge.

re'fugo m waste, rubbish, garbage (*US*); (*coisa inútil*) reject.

reful'gência f brilliance; **refulgir** vi to shine out.

refun'dir vt (*ouro*) to recast; (*escrito*) to revise; ~**-se** vr (*derreter-se*) to melt.

refutação [xefuta'sãw] f refutation; **refutar** vt to refute.

reg abr de **regimento, regular**.

regº abr de **regulamento**.

'rega f watering; (*irrigação*) irrigation.

re'gaço m (*colo*) lap.

rega'dor m watering can.

rega'lado/a adj (*encantado*) delighted; (*confortável*) comfortable // adv comfortably; **regalar** vt (*causar prazer*) to delight; **regalar alguém com algo** to give sb sth, present sb with sth; **regalar-se** vr (*divertir-se*) to enjoy o.s.; (*alegrar-se*) to be delighted.

rega'lia f privilege.

re'galo m (*presente*) present; (*prazer*) pleasure, treat.

re'gar vt (*aguar*) to water; (*molhar*) to sprinkle; (*comida*) to wash down.

re'gata f regatta.

regate'ar vt (*o preço*) to haggle over, bargain for // vi to haggle; **regateio** m haggling.

re'gato m brook, stream.

regência [xe'ʒẽsja] f regency; (*LING*) government; (*MÚS*) conducting.

regeneração [xeʒenera'sãw] f regeneration; **regenerar** vt to regenerate; (*prisioneiro*) to reform.

regente [xe'ʒẽtʃi] m (*POL*) regent; (*de orquestra*) conductor; (*de banda*). leader; **reger** vt to govern, rule; (*orquestra*) to conduct; **reger uma cadeira** (*EDUC*) to hold a chair.

região [xeʒi'ãw] f region.

re'gime m (*POL*) regime; (*de motor*) speed, r.p.m.; (*dieta*) diet; **fazer** ~ **to** go on a diet.

regi'mento m (*MIL*) regiment; (*regras*) regulations pl, rules pl.

régio/a ['xɛʒju/a] adj (*real*) royal; (*digno do rei*) regal.

regional [xɛʒio'naw] adj regional.

registra'dor(a) (*Pt:* **regista'dor(a)**) m/f registrar, recorder; **caixa registradora** cash register; **registrar** (*Pt:* **registar**) vt to register, record; **registro** (*Pt:* **registo**) m (*ato*) registration; (*livro*) register; (*contador*) meter; (*MÚS*) range; **registro civil** registry office.

'rego m (*para água*) ditch; (*de arado*) furrow.

regozi'jar vt to gladden, cheer up; ~**-se** vr to be delighted, rejoice; **regozijo** m joy, delight.

'regra f rule; **sair da** ~ to step out of line; **em** ~ as a rule, usually; ~**s** fpl (*MED*) periods.

regres'sar vi to come ou go back, return; **regresso** m return.

régua ['xɛgwa] f ruler; ~ **de calcular** slide rule.

regueira [xe'gejra] f drainage ditch.

regula'dor(a) adj regulating // m regulator; **regulamento** m rules pl, regulations pl.

regu'lar adj regular; (*estatura*) average, medium; (*normal*) normal, usual; (*razoável*) not bad // vt (*regrar*) to control; (*regularizar*) to regulate; (*ajustar*) to adjust // vi to function; ~**-se** vr: ~**-se por** to be guided by; ~**idade** f regularity; ~**izar** vt (*pôr em ordem*) to sort out, settle; (*regular*) to regularize.

rei [xej] m king.

reimpri'mir vt to reprint.

reinado [xej'nadu] m reign; **reinar** vi to reign; (*fig*) to prevail.

reincidir [xeĩsi'dʒix] vi to relapse.

reino ['xejnu] m kingdom.

reinte'grar vt (*em emprego*) to reinstate; (*reconduzir*) to return, restore.

reite'rar vt/i to reiterate, repeat.

reitor [xej'tox] m (*pároco*) rector; (*de uma universidade*) vice-chancellor, president (*US*).

reivindi'car vt (exigir) to claim.

rejeição [xeʒej'sãw] f rejection; **rejeitar** vt to reject; (recusar) to refuse.

rejuvenes'cer vt to rejuvenate // vi to be rejuvenated; **~-se** vr to be rejuvenated.

relação [xela'sãw] f relation; (ligação) connection, relationship; (MAT) ratio; (lista) list; **com/em ~ a** regarding, with reference to; **relações públicas** public relations, P.R.; **relacionar** vt (pôr em lista) to make a list of; (ligar) to connect; **relacionar-se** vr: **relacionar-se com** (ligar-se) to be connected with, have to do with; (conhecer) to become acquainted with.

re'lâmpago m lightning; (clarão) flash of lightning; **passar como um ~** to flash past; **relampaguear** vi, **relampejar** vi to flash; **relampagueava** the lightning flashed.

re'lance m glance; **olhar de ~ to** glance at.

rela'tar vt to give an account of.

rela'tivo/a adj relative.

re'lato m (relatório) account, report; (história) story; **relatório** m report.

relaxação [xelaʃa'sãw] f relaxation; (desleixo) slovenliness; **relaxado/a** adj relaxed; (frouxo) slack; (desleixado) slovenly, sloppy; **relaxamento** m relaxation; (desleixo) slovenliness; **relaxar** vt (afrouxar) to loosen, relax; (moderar) to moderate // vi (afrouxar) to slacken; (enfraquecer) to weaken; **relaxar-se** vr (afrouxar-se) to relax; (desleixar-se) to become lax; **relaxe** m relaxation.

rele'gar vt to relegate.

re'lento m: **ao ~** out of doors.

reles ['xɛliʃ] adj inv common, vulgar.

rele'vante adj outstanding, notable; **relevar** vt (tornar saliente) to emphasize; (atenuar) to relieve; (desculpar) to pardon, forgive; **relevo** m relief; (fig) prominence, importance; **pôr em relevo** to emphasize.

reli'cário m reliquary, shrine.

religião [xelɪ'ʒjãw] f religion; **religioso/a** adj religious // m monk // f nun.

relinchar [xelĩ'ʃax] vi to neigh; **relincho** m (som) neigh; (ato) neighing.

relíquia [xe'lɪkja] f relic; **~ de família** family heirloom.

relógio [xe'lɔʒju] m clock; (de gás) meter; **~ despertador** alarm clock; **~ de pulso** (wrist)watch; **relojoeiro** m watchmaker.

relu'tância f reluctance.

relu'zente adj brilliant, shining; **reluzir** vi to gleam, shine.

'relva f grass; (terreno gramado) lawn; **relvado** m (Pt) lawn.

rem abr de **remetente** sender.

remanes'cente adj leftover // m surplus; (de comida) leftovers pl.

re'manso m stillness, quiet; (água) backwater.

re'mar vt/i to row.

rema'tado/a adj (concluído) completed; (fig) complete; **rematar** vt to finish off; **remate** m (fim) end, conclusion; (acabamento) finishing touch; (ARQ) coping; (cume) peak.

remedi'ado/a adj comfortably off; **remediar** vt (emendar) to put right, repair; **remédio** m (medicamento) medicine; (recurso) remedy; (ajuda) help; (JUR) recourse; **não tem remédio** it can't be helped; **que remédio?** what else can one do?

reme'lento/a adj bleary-eyed.

remen'dar vt to mend; (com pano) to patch; **remendo** m repair; (de pano) patch.

re'messa f (COM) shipment, dispatch; (de dinheiro) remittance; **remetente** m/f (de carta) sender; (COM) shipper; **remeter** vt (expedir) to send, dispatch; (dinheiro) to remit; (entregar) to hand over; **remeter-se** vr: **remeter-se a** (referir-se) to refer to.

reme'xer vt (papéis) to rummage through; (líquidos) to stir (up); (misturar) to mess about.

reminiscência [xemɪnɪ'sẽsja] f reminiscence.

re'mir vt (coisa penhorada, REL) to redeem; (livrar) to free; (compensar) to make up for; **~-se** vr (pecador) to redeem o.s.

remissão [xemɪ'sãw] f (perdão) forgiveness; (compensação) payment; (num livro) cross-reference.

re'misso/a adj remiss, careless.

re'mível adj redeemable.

'remo m (de embarcação) oar; (esporte) rowing.

remo'çar vt to rejuvenate; **~-se** vr to be rejuvenated.

remo'inho m (ato) whirling, swirling; (na água) eddy, whirlpool; (de vento) whirlwind.

remon'tar vt (elevar) to raise; (tornar a armar) to re-assemble; **~ o vôo** to soar // vi (recuar) to go back; (em cavalo) to remount.

remoque [xe'mɔkɪ] m gibe, taunt; **remoquear** vi to taunt.

remor'der vt (morder) to bite again and again; (atormentar) to distress, torture; (cismar em) to brood over.

re'morso m remorse.

re'moto/a adj remote, far off.

remo'ver vt (mover) to move; (transferir) to transfer; (demitir) to dismiss; (retirar) to remove.

remuneração [xemunera'sãw] f remuneration; (pagamento) payment; **remunerador(a)** adj remunerative; **remunerar** vt to remunerate; (premiar) to reward.

'rena f reindeer.

re'nal adj renal, kidney cmp.

renascença [xena'sĕsa] *f* rebirth; *(fig)* revival; **a R~** the Renaissance; **renascer** *vi* to be reborn; *(fig)* to be revived.

'renda *f* income; *(nacional)* revenue; *(tecido)* lace; **~ bruta/líquida** gross/net income; **imposto de ~** income tax; **rendado/a** *adj* lace-trimmed; *(com aspecto de renda)* lacy // *m* lacework.

rendeiro/a [xĕ'dejru/a] *m/f* tenant // *f* lacemaker.

ren'der *vt (produzir)* to produce, yield; *(preço)* to fetch; *(graças)* to give; *(guarda)* to relieve // *vi (dar lucro)* to pay; **~-se** *vr (capitular)* to surrender; **rendição** *f* surrender; **rendido/a** *adj* subdued; **rendimento** *m (renda)* income; *(lucro)* profit; *(juro)* interest; *(produtividade)* productivity, output; *(duma máquina)* efficiency; **rendoso/a** *adj* profitable.

rene'gado/a *adj, m/f* renegade; **renegar** *vt (renunciar)* to renounce; *(detestar)* to hate; *(trair)* to betray; *(negar)* to deny.

renhido/a [xe'ɲidu/a] *adj* hard-fought; *(batalha)* bloody.

reni'tência *f* obstinacy; **renitente** *adj* obstinate, stubborn.

re'nome *m* fame, renown; **de ~** renowned.

renovação [xenova'sãw] *f* renewal; *(ARQ)* renovation; **renovador** *m*: **renovador de ar** ventilator; **renovar** *vt* to renew; *(restaurar)* to renovate // *vi* to be renewed.

re'novo *m* sprout, shoot.

rentabili'dade *f* profitability.

rente ['xĕtʃi] *adj (cabelo)* close-cropped; *(casa)* nearby // *adv* close.

renúncia [xe'nũsja] *f* renunciation; *(de cargo)* resignation; **renunciar** *vt* to give up, renounce // *vi* to resign.

reorgani'zar *vt* to reorganize.

reparação [xepara'sãw] *f (conserto)* mending, repairing; *(fig)* amends *pl*, reparation; **reparar** *vt (consertar)* to repair; *(forças)* to restore; *(compensar)* to compensate for, make amends for; *(observar)* to notice // *vi*: **reparar em** to notice; **não repare em** pay no attention to; **repare em** *(olhar)* look at; **reparo** *m (conserto)* repair; *(crítica)* criticism; *(observação)* observation; *(ajuda)* help; *(defesa)* defence.

repartição [xepartʃi'sãw] *f (ato)* distribution; *(COM)* department, office; **repartir** *vt (distribuir)* to distribute; *(dar em porções)* to share out; **repartir-se** *vr (dividir-se)* to divide; *(espalhar-se)* to spread.

repas'sar *vt (passar de novo)* to go over again; *(lição)* to revise, go over.

repatri'ar *vt* to repatriate; **~-se** *vr* to go back home.

repelão [xepe'lãw] *m* push, shove; **de ~** brusquely.

repe'lente *adj, m* repellent; **repelir** *vt* to drive away, repel.

re'pente *m* outburst; **de ~** suddenly; **repentino/a** *adj* sudden.

repercussão [xepexku'sãw] *f* repercussion; **repercutir** *vt (som)* to echo // *vi (som)* to reverberate, echo; **repercutir-se** *vr*: **repercutir-se (em)** to have repercussions (on).

reper'tório *m (lista)* list; *(coleção)* collection, catalogue; *(de livro)* index; *(teatro)* repertoire.

repetição [xepetʃi'sãw] *f* repetition; **repetido/a** *adj* repeated; **repetidas vezes** repeatedly, again and again; **repetir** *vt* to repeat; *(vestido)* to wear again; **repetir-se** *vr* to be repeated.

repi'car *vt (sinos)* to ring; *(carne)* to mince; *(legumes)* to chop // *vi (sinos)* to ring (out).

repim'pado/a *adj (refestelado)* lolling; *(satisfeito)* full up.

repique [xe'piki] *m* peal.

repi'sar *vt (assunto)* to repeat (: insistir) to harp on; *(uvas)* to tread.

re'pleto/a *adj* replete, full up.

'réplica *f (cópia)* replica; *(contestação)* reply, retort; **replicar** *vt* to answer, reply to // *vi* to reply, answer back.

repolho [xe'poʎu] *m* cabbage.

repon'tar *vi (aparecer)* to appear.

re'por *vt* to put back, replace.

reportagem [xepox'taʒĕ] *f (ato)* reporting; *(noticiário)* report; *(repórteres)* reporters *pl*; **reportar** *vt (o pensamento)* to take back; **reportar-se** *vr*: **reportar-se a** to refer to; **repórter** *m/f* reporter.

reposteiro [xepoʃ'tejru] *m (de porta)* curtain.

repou'sar *vi* to rest; **repouso** *m* rest.

repreender [xepriĕ'dex] *vt* to reprimand; *(col)* to tell off; **repreensão** *f* rebuke, reprimand; **repreensível** *adj* reprehensible.

re'presa *f* dam.

repre'sália *f* reprisal.

representação [xeprezĕta'sãw] *f* representation; *(escrita)* petition; *(teatro)* performance; **representante** *m* representative; **representativo/a** *adj* representative; **representar** *vt* to represent; *(teatro)* to play; **representar um anjo** to play the part of an angel // *vi (JUR: queixa)* to make a complaint.

repressão [xepre'sãw] *f* repression; **reprimir** *vt* to repress; *(lágrimas)* to keep back.

'réprobo/a *adj, m/f* reprobate.

reprodução [xeprodu'sãw] *f* reproduction; **reproduzir** *vt* to reproduce; *(repetir)* to repeat; **reproduzir-se** *vr* to breed, multiply; *(repetir-se)* to be repeated.

reprovação [xeprova'sãw] *f* disapproval; *(em exame)* failure; **reprovar** *vt (condenar)* to disapprove of; *(aluno)* to fail.

'réptil *m* reptile.

'repto m challenge, provocation.

re'pública f republic; **republicano/a** adj, m/f republican.

repudi'ar vt to repudiate, reject; (a esposa) to divorce; (abandonar) to disown; **repúdio** m rejection.

repug'nância f repugnance; **repugnante** adj repugnant, repulsive; **repugnar** vt (enojar) to be repugnant to // vi to be repulsive; **repugnar a alguém** to disgust sb.

re'pulsa f (ato) rejection; (sentimento) repugnance; (fig) rebuff; (física) repulsion; **repulsivo/a** adj repulsive.

reputação [reputa'sãw] f reputation; **reputar** vt to consider, regard as.

repuxar [xepu'ʃax] vt (puxar) to tug; (esticar) to pull tight; **repuxo** m (de água) fountain; (de arma) kick, recoil.

requebrado [reke'bradu] m (rebolado) swing, sway; **requebrar** vt (menear) to wiggle, swing; **requebrar-se** vr to wiggle, swing.

requeijão [xekej'ʒãw] m cottage cheese.

requeimar [xekej'max] vt (fogo) to scorch; (sol) to burn; (picar) to burn.

requentar [xekẽ'tax] vt to reheat, warm up.

requerente [xeke'rẽtʃi] m/f (JUR) petitioner; **requerer** vt (emprego) to apply for; (pedir) to request, ask for; (exigir) to require, call for; (JUR) to petition for; **requerimento** m application; (pedido) request; (petição) petition.

requintado/a [xekî'tadu/a] adj refined, elegant; **requinte** m refinement, elegance; (cúmulo) height.

requisição [xekızı'sãw] f request, demand; **requisitar** vt to make a request for; (MIL) to requisition; **requisito** m requirement.

requisitório [xekızı'torju] m official indictment.

rês [xeʃ] f head of cattle; **reses** fpl cattle, livestock sg.

rescin'dir vt (contrato) to rescind.

rés-do-'chão m (Pt: andar térreo) ground floor, first floor (US).

resenha [xe'zeɲa] f (relatório) report; (resumo) summary; **resenhar** vt (livro) to review.

re'serva f reserve; (para hotel, fig) reservation; **reservado/a** adj reserved; (retraído) standoffish; **reservar** vt (guardar) to keep back; (mesa) to book, reserve; **reservar-se** vr to save o.s.; **reservatório** m (lago) reservoir.

resfole'gar vi to pant.

resfri'ado/a (Br) adj: estar ~ to have a cold // adj cold, chill; **resfriar** vt to cool, chill // vi, **resfriar-se** vr (pessoa) to catch (a) cold.

resga'tar vt (prisioneiro) to ransom; (salvar) to rescue; (retomar) to get back, recover; (dívida) to pay off; (remir) to redeem; **resgate** m (livramento) rescue, recovery; **pagar um resgate** to pay a ransom.

resguardar [xe3gwax'dax] vt to protect; ~-se vr: ~-se de to guard against; **resguardo** m protection; (cuidado) care.

resi'dência f house, residence; **residente** adj, m/f resident; **residir** vi to live, reside.

resíduo [xe'zɪdwu] m residue.

resignação [xezɪgna'sãw] f resignation; **resignado/a** adj resigned; **resignar-se** vr: **resignar-se com** to resign o.s. to.

re'sina f resin.

resis'tência f resistance; (de atleta) stamina; **resistente** adj resistant; (calçado) hard-wearing, strong; **resistente a traças** mothproof; **resistir** vi: **resistir a** (não ceder) to resist; (sobreviver) to survive; **resistir ao uso** to wear well; (durar) to last.

'resma f ream.

resmun'gar vt/i to mutter, mumble.

resolução [xezolu'sãw] f resolution; (coragem) courage; (de um problema) solution; **resoluto/a** adj resolute.

resol'ver vt (problema) to solve; (questão) to resolve; (decidir) to decide // vi: ~ **em** (transformar) to turn into; ~-se vr: ~-se a (decidir) to make up one's mind to, decide to.

respec'tivo/a adj respective.

respeitar [xeʃpej'tax] vt to respect; **respeitável** adj (venerável) respected; (digno de respeito) respectable; (importante) considerable; **respeito** m respect; **a respeito de/com respeito a** as to, as regards; **dizer respeito a** to concern; **faltar ao respeito a** to be rude to; **respeitos** mpl regards; **respeitoso/a** adj respectful.

respin'gar vt/i to splash, spatter.

respiração [xeʃpira'sãw] f breathing; (hálito) breath; (MED) respiration; **respirador** m respirator; **respirar** vt/i to breathe; (folgar) to have a respite; **respiro** m (abertura) vent.

resplande'cente adj resplendent; **resplandecer** vi to gleam, shine (out); **resplendor** m brilliance; (fig) splendour; (: fama) glory.

respondão/dona [xeʃpõ'dãw/'dona] adj cheeky, insolent; **responder** vt to answer // vi to answer; **responder por** to be responsible for, answer for.

responsabili'dade f responsibility; **responsabilizar-se** vr: **responsabilizar-se por** to take responsibility for, take charge of; **responsável** adj: **responsável por** responsible for // m person responsible ou in charge.

res'posta f answer, reply.

resquício [xeʃ'kisju] m (vestígio) trace.

res'saca f (refluxo) undertow; (contra o litoral) surf; (fig) hangover.

ressaibo [xɪ'sajbu] m (mau sabor) unpleasant taste; (fig) trace.

ressal'tar vt to emphasize // vi to stand out.

res'salva f (proteção) safeguard; (MIL) exemption certificate; (correção) correction; (restrição) qualification.

ressar'cir vt (pagar) to compensate; (compensar) to compensate for; ~ alguém de to compensate sb for.

resse'car vt, **resse'car-se** vr to dry up.

ressen'tido/a adj (ofendido) hurt, resentful; **ressentimento** m resentment; **ressentir-se** vr: ressentir-se de (ser ofendido) to resent, be hurt by; (sofrer) to suffer from, feel the effects of.

ressequido/a [xesɛˈkidu/a] adj parched; (seco) dried up.

resso'ar vi to resound; (ecoar) to echo; **ressonância** f resonance; (eco) echo.

ressurgimento [xesuxʒiˈmẽtu] m resurgence, revival.

ressurreição [xesuxejˈsãw] f resurrection.

ressusci'tar vt to revive, resuscitate.

restabele'cer vt to re-establish, restore; ~-se vr to recover, recuperate.

res'tante m rest; **restar** vi to remain, be left; não lhe resta nada he has nothing left; resta-me comprar o chapéu I still have the hat to buy.

restauração [xeʃtawraˈsãw] f restoration; (dente) filling.

restaurante [xeʃtawˈrãtʃi] m restaurant.

restaurar [xeʃtawˈrax] vt to restore; (recuperar) to recover; (renovar) to renew.

'réstia f (de cebolas) string; (luz) ray.

restituição [xeʃtʃitwiˈsãw] f restitution, return; (dinheiro) repayment; **restituir** vt to return, give back; (dinheiro) to repay; (restaurar) to restore; (repor) to put back.

'resto m rest, remainder; de ~ besides; ~s mpl remains, scraps.

restolho [xeʃˈtoʎu] m stubble; (resto) remains pl.

restrição [xeʃtɾiˈsãw] f restriction; **restringir** vt to restrict; (diminuir) to reduce; **restrito/a** adj restricted; (diminuído) reduced.

resul'tado m result; dar ~ to succeed; **resultar** vi to result; (evidenciar-se) to turn out to be.

resu'mido/a adj abbreviated, abridged; (curto) concise; **resumir** vt to abbreviate; (simbolizar) to epitomize; (sintetizar) to sum up; (reduzir) to reduce; **resumir-se** vr: resumir-se a to consist in/of; **resumo** m summary, résumé; em resumo in short, briefly.

resva'lar vt to slide, slip.

retaguarda [xɛtaˈgwaxda] f rearguard; (posição) rear.

retalhar [xeta'ʎax] vt to cut up; (separar) to divide; (despedaçar) to shred; (ferir) to slash; **retalho** m piece; (sobra) scrap, shred; **vender a retalho** (Pt) to sell retail; **colcha de retalhos** patchwork quilt.

retar'dar vt to hold up, slow down; (atrasar) to postpone; **retardatário/a** m/f latecomer.

retenção [xetẽˈsãw] f retention; **reter** vt (guardar) to retain; (deter) to stop, detain; **reter-se** vr to restrain o.s.

rete'sar vt to tighten; (esticar) to stretch.

reti'cência f reticence, reserve; ~s fpl suspension points; **reticente** adj reticent.

retidão [xetʃiˈdãw] (Pt: -ct-) f rectitude; (justeza) soundness; (de linha) straightness.

retifica'dor (Pt: -ct-) m rectifier; **retifi'car** (Pt: -ct-) vt to rectify.

reti'nir vi (ferros) to clink; (campainha) to ring, jingle; (ressoar) to resound.

reti'rada f withdrawal, retreat; **bater em** ~ to beat a retreat; **retirado/a** adj isolated; (recluso) solitary; **retirar** vt to withdraw; (retratar) to take back // vi to withdraw, retire; (MIL) to retreat; **retiro** m retreat.

'reto/a (Pt: -ct-) adj straight; (vertical) upright; (justo) fair; (honesto) honest, upright // m rectum.

reto'car vt (pintura) to touch up; (aperfeiçoar) to perfect; **retoque** m finishing touch.

retorcer [xetox'sex] vt to twist; ~-se vr to wriggle, writhe.

re'tórica f rhetoric.

re'torno m return; (COM) barter, exchange.

retorquir [xetox'kix] vi to retort, reply.

retrac'tar vt (Pt) to retract, recant.

retra'ído/a adj retracted; (fig) reserved, timid; **retraimento** m withdrawal; (contração) contraction; (fig) timidity, shyness; **retrair-se** vr to withdraw, retire; (recuar) to draw back.

retratação [xetrataˈsãw] (Pt: -ct-) f retraction; **retratar** vt (fazer o retrato) to portray, depict; (retirar) to retract, recant; **retrato** m portrait; (FOTO) photo; (sósia) spitting image.

retribuição [xetribwiˈsãw] f reward, recompense; (pagamento) remuneration; **retribuir** vt to reward, recompense; (corresponder) to requite; (pagar) to remunerate; (hospitalidade) to return.

retroce'der vi to retreat, fall back; (decair) to decline.

retru'car vi to retort, reply.

retum'bância f resonance; **retumbar** vi to resound, echo; (ribombar) to rumble, boom.

réu/ré [xɛw/xɛ] m/f defendant; (culpado) culprit, criminal; ~ de morte condemned man.

reumatismo [xɛwmaˈtʃiʒmu] m rheumatism.

reunião [xiuˈnjãw] f meeting; (ato) reunion; **reunir** vt to bring together; (juntar) to join, unite; **reunir-se** vr to meet, gather together.

revelação [xeveˈlasãw] f revelation; (FOTO) development; **revelar** vt to reveal; (*mostrar*) to show; (*FOTO*) to develop; **revelar-se** *vr* to turn out to be.

reve'lia *f* default; **à** ~ by default; **à** ~ **de** without the knowledge or consent of.

re'ver *vt* to see again; (*examinar*) to scrutinize; (*revisar*) to check, revise.

reverde'cer *vt/i* to turn green again.

reve'rência *f* reverence, respect; (*ato*) bow; (: *de mulher*) curtsey; **reverenciar** *vt* to revere, venerate; (*obedecer*) to obey; **reverendo/a** *adj* venerable // *m* priest, clergyman; **reverente** *adj* reverent, reverential.

reversão [xevex'sāw] *f* reversion; **reversível** *adj* reversible; **reverso** *m* reverse; (*oposto*) opposite; **o reverso da medalha** (*fig*) the other side of the coin.

re'vés *m* reverse; (*infortúnio*) setback, mishap; **ao** ~ on the contrary; **ao** ~ **de** contrary to; **de** ~ obliquely, aslant; (*olhar*) askance.

reves'tir *vt* to put on; (*tapar*) to cover; ~**-se** *vr*: ~**-se de** (*assumir*) to assume, take on.

reve'zar *vt* to relieve // *vi* to take turns, rotate; (*alternar*) to alternate.

revigo'rar *vt* to refresh, reinvigorate.

revi'rada *f* about-turn, change of direction; **revirar** *vt* to turn round; (*atrapalhar*) to throw into confusion; **revirar os olhos** to roll one's eyes; **reviravolta** *f* about-turn, U-turn.

revisão [xevi'zāw] *f* revision; ~ **de provas** proofreading; **revisar** *vt* to revise; (*rever*) to check; **revisor** *m* (*FERRO*) ticket inspector; (*de provar*) proofreader.

re'vista *f* (*ger*) review; (*MIL*) inspection; (*publicação*) journal, magazine; (*teatro*) revue; **passar em** ~ to review; (*inspecionar*) to inspect, go over.

revo'gar *vt* to revoke, repeal; (*anular*) to cancel.

re'volta *f* revolt, revolution; **revoltar** *vt* to disgust; **revoltar-se** *vr* to rebel, revolt; **revolto/a** *pp irr de* **revolver** // *adj* turbulent; (*agitado*) troubled; (*cabelo*) dishevelled; (*mar*) rough; (*desarrumado*) untidy.

revolução [xevolu'sāw] *f* revolution; **revolucionar** *vt* to revolutionize; **revolucionário/a** *adj*, *m/f* revolutionary.

revol'ver *vt* (*mexer*) to stir; (*olhos*) to roll // *vi* (*girar*) to revolve, rotate.

re'vólver *m* revolver, gun.

re'zar *vt* (*missa*) to say // *vi* to pray.

'ria *f* estuary, river mouth.

riacho [ri'aʃu] *m* stream, brook.

ri'balta *f* (*teatro*) footlights *pl*.

ribanceira [xibā'sejra] *f* (*margem*) steep river bank; (*rampa*) steep slope; (*precipício*) cliff.

ribeira [xi'bejra] *f* riverside; (*riacho*) stream; **ribeirão** *m* (*Br*) stream; **ribeirinho/a** *adj* riverside *cmp*; **ribeiro** *m* brook, stream, creek (*US*).

ribom'bar *vi* to rumble, boom; (*ressoar*) to resound.

ricaço [xi'kasu] *m* plutocrat, very rich man.

rícino ['xisinu] *m* castor-oil plant; **óleo de** ~ castor oil.

'rico/a *adj* rich, wealthy; (*abundante*) fertile; (*opulento*) sumptuous; (*Pt: lindo*) beautiful; (: *excelente*) splendid.

ridiculari'zar,   ridiculi'zar *vt* to ridicule; **ridículo/a** *adj* ridiculous.

'rifa *f* raffle, lottery.

rifão [xi'fāw] *m* proverb, saying.

ri'far *vt* to raffle; (*col: abandonar*) to dump.

rigidez [xiʒi'deʃ] *f* rigidity, stiffness; (*austeridade*) severity, strictness; (*inflexibilidade*) inflexibility; **rígido/a** *adj* rigid, stiff; (*fig*) strict, severe.

ri'gor *m* rigidity; (*severidade*) harshness, severity; (*exatidão*) precision; **a** ~ strictly speaking; **de** ~ essential, obligatory; **no** ~ **do inverno in the depths of winter; ~oso/a** *adj* rigorous; (*severo*) harsh; (*exigente*) demanding; (*minucioso*) precise, accurate.

rijo/a ['xiʒu/a] *adj* tough, hard; (*rigoroso*) cruel, severe; (*robusto*) sturdy, strong.

rim [xĩ] *m* kidney; **rins** *mpl* small of the back *sg*.

'rima *f* rhyme; (*poema*) verse, poem; **rimar** *vt* to put into verse // *vi* to rhyme; **rimar com** to agree with, tally with.

'rímel ® *m* mascara.

rinchar [xĩ'ʃax] *vi* to neigh, whinny.

rinoceronte [xinɔse'rõtʃi] *m* rhinoceros.

'rio *m* river.

'ripa *f* lath, slat.

riqueza [xi'keza] *f* wealth, riches *pl*; (*qualidade*) richness; (*fartura*) abundance; (*fecundidade*) fertility.

rir *vi* to laugh; ~ **de** to laugh at; **risada** *f* (*riso*) laughter; (*gargalhada*) guffaw.

'risca *f* stroke; (*decor*) stripe; (*cabelo*) parting; **à** ~ to the letter, exactly; **riscar** *vt* to score, mark; (*apagar*) to score out; (*desenhar*) to draw, trace; (*acender*) to light; **risco** *m* scratch; (*desenho*) drawing, sketch; (*perigo*) risk.

ri'sível *adj* laughable, ridiculous; **riso** *m* laughter; (*gargalhada*) laugh; **risonho/a** *adj* laughing, smiling; (*contente*) cheerful, happy.

'ríspido/a *adj* (*rude*) sharp, curt; (*áspero*) harsh.

'riste *m*: **em** ~ (*dedo*) pointing; (*orelhas*) pointed.

'rítmico/a *adj* rhythmic(al); **ritmo** *m* rhythm.

'rito *m* rite; (*seita*) cult; **ritual** *adj*, *m* ritual.

ri'val *adj*, *m/f* rival; ~**idade** *f* rivalry; ~**izar** *vt* to rival // *vi*: ~**izar com** to compete with, vie with.

rixa ['xiʃa] *f* quarrel, fight.

robuste'cer *vt* to strengthen; ~**-se** *vr* to become stronger; **robusto/a** *adj* strong, robust.

'roça f plantation; (*mato*) clearing; (*campo*) country; **roçado** m clearing; **roçar** vt (*terreno*) to clear; (*atritar*) to graze // vi: **roçar em/por** to graze, brush against; **roceiro** m (*lavrador*) peasant; (*caipira*) country bumpkin.

rocha ['xɔʃa] f rock; (*penedo*) crag; **rochedo** m crag, cliff.

'roda f wheel; (*círculo*) circle; (*grupo*) ring; **~ dentada** cog(wheel); **alta ~** high society; **em/à ~ de** round, around; **rodagem** f: **estrada de rodagem** trunk/major road; **rodar** vt (*fazer girar*) to turn, spin; (*rolar*) to roll // vi to roll; (*girar*) to turn; (*AUTO*) to drive; **roda-viva** f bustle, commotion.

rode'ar vt to go round; (*circundar*) to encircle, surround; **rodeio** m circumlocution; (*subterfúgio*) subterfuge; (*gado*) round-up; **fazer rodeios** to beat about the bush; **sem rodeios** plainly, frankly.

ro'dela f (*pedaço*) slice.

'rodo m rake; **a ~** in abundance.

rodopi'ar vi to whirl around, swirl.

roedor(a) [xoe'dox(ra)] adj gnawing // m rodent; **roer** vt to gnaw, nibble; (*enferrujar*) to corrode.

ro'gado pp de **rogar**; **fazer-se de ~** to play hard to get; **rogar** vi to ask, request; **rogar a alguém que . . .** to beg sb to . . .; **rogo** m request;-**a rogo de** at the request of.

rol m roll, list.

'rola f (turtle-)dove.

ro'lar vt/i to roll.

rol'dana f pulley.

roldão [xol'dãw] m confusion; **de ~** headlong, pell-mell.

ro'leta f roulette; (*borboleta*) turnstile.

rolha ['xoʎa] f cork; (*fig*) gag (on free speech).

ro'liço/a adj plump, chubby.

'rolo m (*de papel etc*) roll; (*cilindro*) roller.

'Roma f Rome.

ro'mã f pomegranate.

romagem [xo'maʒẽ] f pilgrimage.

ro'mance m (*novela*) novel; (*conto*) story; (*amor*) romance; **~ policial** detective story; **romanceado/a** adj exaggerated, fanciful; **romancista** m/f novelist.

ro'mânico/a adj (*LING*) Romance; (*ARQ*) romanesque; **romano/a** adj, m/f Roman.

ro'mântico/a adj romantic; **romantismo** m romanticism.

roma'ria f (*peregrinação*) pilgrimage; (*festa*) festival.

'rombo m (*abertura*) opening, hole; (*MAT*) rhombus; (*desfalque*) embezzlement.

romeiro/a [xo'mejru/a] m/f pilgrim.

ro'meno/a adj, m/f Rumanian // m (*língua*) Rumanian.

rom'pante m (*arrogância*) arrogance; (*impetuosidade*) rashness, impetuousness.

rom'per vt/i to break; (*rasgar*) to tear; (*relações*) to break off; **rompimento** m

breaking; (*fenda*) break; (*interrupção*) rupture, breaking-off.

ron'car vi (*ressonar*) to snore; (*estrondar*) to roar.

'ronco m (*de sono*) snore; (*de motor*) roar; (*grunhir*) grunt.

'ronda f patrol, beat; **fazer a ~** to go the rounds; **rondar** vt to patrol, go the rounds of; (*vaguear*) to prowl, hang around // vi to prowl about, lurk.

ronqueira [xõ'kejra] f wheeze.

ronrom [xõ'xõ] m purring; **ronronar** vi to purr.

roque ['xɔkɪ] m (*xadrez*) rook, castle; (*MÚS*) rock.

ror m: **um ~ de** (*col*) a lot of, loads of.

rosa ['xɔza] f rose // adj rose-coloured, pink; **rosado/a** adj rosy, pink; **~-dos-ventos** f inv compass.

ro'sário m rosary.

rosbife [xɔʃ'biʃ] m roast beef.

'rosca f spiral, coil; (*de parafuso*) thread; (*pão*) ring-shaped loaf.

roseira [xo'zejra] f rosebush.

roséola [xo'zeola] f rash.

ros'nar vi (*murmurar*) to mutter, mumble; (*cão*) to growl, snarl.

ros'sio m (*Pt*) large square.

'rosto m (*cara*) face; (*frontispício*) title page.

'rota f route, course.

rotação [xota'sãw] f rotation.

roteiro [xo'tejru] m (*itinerário*) itinerary; (*ordem*) schedule; (*guia*) guidebook; (*de filme*) script.

ro'tina f routine; **rotineiro/a** adj routine.

'roto/a pp irr de **romper** // adj broken; (*rasgado*) torn.

'rótula f (*ANAT*) kneecap.

'rótulo m label, tag.

roubar [xo'bax] vt to steal, rob; **~ algo a alguém** to steal sth from sb; **roubo** m theft, robbery.

rouco/a ['roku/a] adj hoarse.

roupa ['xopa] f clothes pl, clothing; **~ de baixo**, **~ branca** underclothes pl, underwear; **~ de cama** bedclothes pl, bed linen; **~-gem** f clothes pl, apparel; (*fig*) appearance; **roupão** m dressing gown.

rouquidão [xokɪ'dãw] f hoarseness.

rouxinol [xoʃi'nɔl] m nightingale.

roxo/a ['xoʃu/a] adj purple, violet.

'rua f street // excl: **~!** get out!, clear off!

ru'béola f (*MED*) German measles.

ru'bi m ruby.

ru'bor m blush; (*fig*) shyness, bashfulness; **~izar** vi to blush.

ru'brica f (*título*) rubric, title; (*teatro*) stage directions pl; (*firma*) signed initials pl; **rubricar** vt to initial.

'ruço/a adj grey, dun.

'rude adj rough, unpolished; **rudeza** f roughness, crudity.

rudi'mento m rudiment; **~s** mpl rudiments, first principles.

ru'ela f lane, alley.

ru'far vt (tambor) to beat.

rufião [xu'fjãw] m pimp.

'ruga f (na pele) wrinkle; (na roupa) crease.

'rúgbi m rugby.

rugido [xu'ʒidu] m roar; **rugir** vi to roar, bellow.

ru'goso/a adj (pele) wrinkled; (roupa) creased.

ruído ['xwidu] m noise, din; **ruidoso/a** adj noisy.

ruim [xu'ĩ] adj (malvado) wicked, evil; (inútil) useless; (ordinário) awful; (mau) bad.

ruína ['xwina] f (restos) ruin; (decadência) downfall, destruction.

ruindade [xwĩ'dadʒi] f wickedness, evil.

ruir [xu'ix] vi to collapse, go to ruin.

ruivo/a ['xwivu/a] adj red-haired // m/f redhead.

rum m rum.

rumi'nar vt/i to ruminate, chew the cud; (fig) to meditate, ponder.

'rumo m course, bearing; ~ **a** bound for; **sem** ~ adrift.

ru'mor m (ruído) noise; (notícia) rumour, report; ~**ejar** vi to murmur; (folhas) to rustle; (água) to ripple.

rup'tura f break, rupture.

ru'ral adj rural, rustic.

'rusga f (briga) quarrel, row.

'russo/a adj, m/f Russian // m (língua) Russian.

'rústico/a adj rustic; (rude) rough, crude.

ruti'lar vi to shine, glitter.

S

S. abr de **Santo** / **Santa** / **São** Saint.

sã adj ver **são**.

'sábado m Saturday.

sabão [sa'bãw] m soap.

sabe'dor(a) adj (consciente) aware, informed; **sabedoria** f (razão) wisdom; (sensatez) common sense; (erudição) learning.

sa'ber vt (ter conhecimento de) to know; (ter capacidade para) to know how to, be able to; ~ **de cor e salteado** to know off by heart; **ele sabe nadar?** can he swim? // vi to taste; ~ **a** a taste of // m knowledge, learning; **a** ~ namely; **sabichão/chona** m/f know-it-all, smart aleck; **sábio/a** adj wise, learned // m/f scholar, learned person.

sabo'nete m toilet soap.

sa'bor m taste, flavour; **ao** ~ **de** at the mercy of; **saborear** vt to relish, savour; ~**oso/a** adj tasty, delicious.

sabota'dor m saboteur; **sabotagem** f sabotage; **sabotar** vt to sabotage.

sabugueiro [sabu'gejru] m elder, elderberry.

sabur'rento/a adj (língua) furry.

'saca f sack, bag.

sa'car vt to take out, pull out; (dinheiro)

to withdraw; (esporte) to serve; (col) to understand.

saca'rina f saccharine, saccharin (US).

saca-rolhas [saka'-xoʎaʃ] m inv corkscrew.

sacerdócio [sasex'dosju] m priesthood; **sacerdote** m priest.

saciar [sa'sjax] vt (satisfazer) to satisfy; (fartar) to satiate; (sede) to quench.

'saco m sack, bag; ~ **de dormir** sleeping bag; **encher o** ~ **a** (Br: col) to annoy, pester // excl: ~! (Br: col) damn!.

sacra'mento m sacrament.

sacrifi'car vt to sacrifice; **sacrifício** m sacrifice.

sacrilégio [sakri'lɛʒju] m sacrilege; **sacrílego/a** adj sacrilegious.

sacristão [sakri'ʃtãw] m sacristan, sexton; **sacristia** f sacristy; **sacro/a** adj sacred; (santo) holy.

sacudi'dela f shake, jolt; **sacudido/a** adj shaken; (movimento) rapid, quick; **sacudir** vt to shake, jolt.

sa'dio/a adj healthy; (saudável) wholesome.

sa'fado/a adj (gasto) worn out; (descarado) shameless, barefaced // m rogue; **safar** vt (extrair) to pull out; **safar-se** vr to escape.

sa'fira f sapphire.

'safra f harvest; (produto) crop.

sagacidade [sagasi'dadʒi] f shrewdness; (astúcia) cleverness; **sagaz** adj shrewd, clever.

sa'grado/a adj sacred, holy.

saguão [sa'gwãw] m (pátio) yard, patio; (entrada) foyer, lobby.

saia ['saja] f skirt.

saibro ['sajbru] m gravel.

sa'ída f (porta) exit, way out; (partida) departure; (venda) outlet, sale; **de** ~ firstly; **sair** vi (ir para fora) to go out; (vir para fora) to come out; (partir) to leave, depart; (pessoa) to set out; **sair bem** to turn out well, be successful; **sair de** to leave; **sair-se** vr: **sair-se bem/mal de** to be successful/unsuccessful in.

sal m salt; (graça) wit, sparkle.

'sala f (large) room; (num edifício público) hall; (numa casa) lounge, drawing room; ~ **de espera** waiting room; ~ **de estar** living room.

sa'lada f salad; (fig) confusion, mix up.

salão [sa'lãw] m large room, hall; **de** ~ (jogos) indoor; (anedota) proper, acceptable.

sa'lário m wages pl, salary.

sal'dar vt (contas) to settle; **saldo** m balance; (sobra) surplus; (fig) result.

saleiro [sa'lejru] m salt cellar; **salgado/a** adj salty, salted; (picante) saucy, risqué; **salgar** vt to salt.

salgueiro [sal'gejru] m willow; ~ **chorão** weeping willow.

sali'ência f prominence, projection; **salientar** vt to point out; (acentuar) to stress, emphasise; **saliente** adj jutting out, prominent; (evidente) clear, conspicuous; (importante) outstanding.

salitre [sa'litrɪ] m saltpetre, nitre.

sa'liva f saliva; (cuspe) spittle.

salmão [sal'mãw] m salmon.

'salmo m psalm.

salmoura [saw'mora] f brine, pickle.

sa'lobro / a adj salty, brackish.

saloio [sa'lɔju] m (Pt: camponês) country bumpkin.

salpi'car vt to splash; (polvilhar) to sprinkle.

'salsa f parsley.

salseira [sawsejra] f sauce boat.

salsicha [saw'siʃa] f sausage.

sal'tar vt to jump (over), leap (over) // vi to jump, leap; (mergulhar) to dive; (omitir) to skip, miss out; ~ à vista to be obvious.

salteador [sawtʃja'dox] m highwayman.

saltim'banco m charlatan.

salti'tar vt (brincar) to skip.

'salto m jump, leap; (mergulho) dive; (de calçado) heel; ~ em altura high jump; dar um ~ to jump, leap; ~-mortal m somersault.

salubre [sa'lubrɪ] adj healthy, salubrious.

salu'tar adj salutary, beneficial.

'salva f salvo, salute; (de palmas) round; (bandeja) tray, salver; (BOT) sage.

salvação [sawva'sãw] f salvation; **salvador** m saviour; **salvados** mpl salvage; (COM) salvaged goods.

salvaguarda [sawva'gwaxda] f protection, safeguard.

sal'var vt (livrar) to save, rescue; (objetos, de ruína) to salvage; **salva-vidas** m inv (bóia) lifebuoy; (pessoa) lifeguard; **barco salva-vidas** lifeboat; **salvo / a** adj safe; **a salvo** in safety; **pôr-se a salvo** to run to safety // prep except, save; **todos salvo ele** all except him; **salvo-conduto** m safe-conduct.

'samba f samba; **sambar** vi to dance the samba.

sa'nar vt to cure; (remediar) to remedy; **sanatório** m sanatorium; **sanável** adj curable; (remediável) remediable.

sanção [sã'sãw] f sanction; **sancionar** vt to sanction; (autorizar) to authorize.

san'dália f sandal.

sandes f (Pt) sandwich.

san'dice f foolishness, lunacy.

sanduíche [sand'wiʃɪ] m (Br) sandwich.

saneamento [sanıa'mẽtu] m sanitation; **sanear** vt (corrupção) to clean up; (drenar) to drain.

sa'nefa f pelmet.

san'grar vt/i to bleed; **sangrento / a** adj bloody; (manchado de sangue) bloodstained.

sangue [sã'gɪ] m blood; ~-frio m cold-bloodedness; **sanguessuga** f leech, bloodsucker; **sanguinário / a** adj bloodthirsty, cruel; **sanguíneo / a** adj sanguine; (atr) blood-; (tez) ruddy; **vaso sanguíneo** blood vessel.

sanha ['saɲa] f rage, fury.

sani'dade f (saúde) healthiness; **sanita** f (Pt) toilet, lavatory; **sanitário / a** adj hygienic, sanitary; **vaso sanitário** toilet, lavatory (bowl); **sanitários** mpl toilets.

santi'dade f holiness, sanctity; **sua S~** His Holiness (the Pope); **santificar** vt to sanctify, make holy.

'santo / a adj holy, sacred; **dia ~** holy day; **todo o ~ dia** the whole day long // f/m saint; **santuário** m shrine, sanctuary.

são / sã [sãw / sã] adj (sadio) healthy, sound; (salubre) wholesome; ~ e salvo safe and sound.

sapa'ria f shoe shop; **sapateiro** m shoemaker, cobbler; **sapato** m shoe.

sa'peca adj forward, flirtatious.

sapi'ência f wisdom, learning.

'sapo m toad.

saque ['sakɪ] m (COM) draft, bill; (esporte) serve; (pilhagem) plunder, pillage; **saquear** vt to pillage, plunder.

sara'banda f (dança) saraband.

saracote'ar vi to shake one's hips.

saraiva [sa'rajva] f hail; **saraivada** f hailstorm; **saraivar** vi to hail.

sa'rampo m measles pl.

sarapin'tado / a adj spotted, speckled.

sa'rar vt to cure, heal // vi to recover, be cured.

sarau [sa'raw] m soirée, social evening.

'sarça f (BOT) bramble (bush).

sar'casmo m sarcasm; **sarcástico / a** adj sarcastic.

'sarda f freckle.

sardinha [sax'dʒɪɲa] f sardine; **como ~ em lata** (apertado) like sardines.

sar'dônico / a adj sardonic, sarcastic.

sargento [sax'ʒẽtu] m sergeant.

sarilho [sa'riʎu] m winch, reel; (fig) confusion, mix-up.

sarja ['saxʒa] f (tecido) serge.

sarjeta [sar'ʒeta] f gutter.

'sarna f scabies sg.

'sarro m (de vinho) tartar, deposit; **tirar um ~** (col) to pet, neck.

Sa'tã m, Sata'nás m Satan, the Devil.

satélite [sa'tɛlɪtʃɪ] m satellite; (fig) hanger-on.

'sátira f satire.

satisfação [satʃɪʃfa'sãw] f satisfaction; (recompensa) reparation; **satisfazer** vt to satisfy.

satu'rar vt to saturate, soak.

saudação [sawda'sãw] f greeting.

saudade [saw'dadʒɪ] f (desejo ardente) longing, yearning; (lembrança nostálgica) homesickness, nostalgia; **ter ~s de** (desejar) to long for; (sentir falta de) to miss; **deixar ~s** to be greatly missed; **dá ~s a Maria** give Mary my regards.

saudar [saw'dax] vt (cumprimentar) to greet; (dar as boas vindas) to welcome.

saudável [saw'davɛw] adj healthy, wholesome; **saúde** f health; (brinde) toast; **beber à saúde de** to drink to, toast; **casa de saúde** hospital; **vender saúde** to be bursting with health.

saudoso/a [saw'dozu/a] *adj* (*nostálgico*) nostalgic; (*da família ou terra natal*) homesick; (*de uma pessoa*) longing.

sauna ['sawna] *f* sauna.

sazo'nado/a *adj* ripe, mature.

se [sɪ] *conj* if, whether; ~ **bem que** even though // *pron* (*ger*) oneself; (*m*) himself; (*f*) herself; (*coisa*) itself; (*você*) yourself; (*vocês*) yourselves; (*eles/elas*) themselves; (*reciprocamente*) each other; **diz-~ que** ... it is said that ...; **sabe-~ que** it is known that ... .

sé [sɛ] *f* cathedral; **Santa S~** Holy See.

sê [se] *vb ver* **ser**.

seara [sɪ'ara] *f* (*campo de cereais*) wheat *ou* corn field; (*campo cultivado*) tilled field.

sebe ['sɛbɪ] *f* (*Pt*) fence; ~ **viva** hedge.

se'bento/a *adj* (*sujo*) dirty, filthy; (*gordurento*) greasy.

'sebo *m* fat, tallow; (*livraria*) secondhand bookshop.

'seca *adj ver* **seco**.

seca'dor *m* drier.

seção [se'sãw] (*Pt*: **-cç-**) *f* section.

se'car *vt* to dry; (*tornar murcho*) to parch // *vi* to dry (up); (*plantas*) to wither.

secessão [sesɪ'sãw] *f* secession.

'seco/a *adj* (*árido*) arid; (*alimentos*) dried; (*ríspido*) curt, brusque; (*desejoso*) eager; **pôr em** ~ (*embarcação*) to run aground // *f* (*estiagem*) drought // *mpl* : ~**s e molhados** groceries; **armazém de** ~**s e molhados** grocery store.

secre'taria *f* (*local*) general office, secretary's office; (*ministério*) ministry; **secretário/a** *m/f* secretary// *f* (*mesa*) writing desk.

se'creto/a *adj*, *m* secret.

sec'tário/a *adj* sectarian // *m/f* follower; **sectarismo** *m* sectarianism.

secu'lar *adj* (*leigo*) secular, lay; (*muito antigo*) age-old; **século** *m* (*cem anos*) century; (*época*) age.

secun'dar *vt* (*apoiar*) to support, back up.

secun'dário/a *adj* secondary.

se'cura *f* dryness; (*fig*) coldness.

'seda *f* silk; **papel de** ~ tissue paper; **bicho da** ~ silkworm.

seda'tivo/a *adj*, *m* sedative.

sede ['sedʒɪ] *f* thirst; (*fig*) craving; **ter** ~ to be thirsty; **matar a** ~ to quench one's thirst // ['sedʒɪ] *f* (*de empresa, instituição*) headquarters *sg*; (*de governo*) seat; (*REL*) see, diocese.

seden'tário/a *adj* sedentary.

se'dento/a *adj* thirsty; (*fig*) eager, avid.

sedição [sedʒɪ'sãw] *f* sedition; **sedicioso/a** *adj* seditious.

sedi'mento *m* sediment.

sedução [sedu'sãw] *f* seduction; (*atração*) allure, charm; **sedutor(a)** *adj* seductive; (*tentador*) alluring // *m/f* seducer; **seduzir** *vt* to seduce; (*fascinar*) to fascinate, entice; (*desencaminhar*) to lead astray.

'sega *f* harvest, reaping; ~**deira** *f*

(*foice*) scythe; (*máquina*) harvester; ~**dor** *m* harvester, reaper; **segar** *vt* (*ceifar*) to harvest, reap.

seg'mento *m* segment; (*divisão*) section.

segre'dar *vt* to whisper; **segredo** *m* secret; (*silêncio, sigilo*) secrecy; (*discrição*) discretion; **em segredo** in private.

segregação [segrega'sãw] *f* segregation; **segregar** *vt* to segregate, separate.

seguido/a [se'gɪdu/a] *adj* following; (*contínuo*) continuous, consecutive; **três dias** ~**s** three days running; **em** ~**a** (*depois*) afterwards; next; (*imediatamente*) immediately, right away; **seguidor(a)** *m/f* follower.

seguimento [segɪ'mɛtu] *m* continuation; **dar** ~ **a** to proceed with; **em** ~ **de** after; **seguinte** *adj* next, following; **seguir** *vt* to follow; (*vir depois*) to come after; (*perseguir*) to pursue; (*continuar*) to continue // *vi* to follow (on); (*continuar*) to continue, carry on; **logo a seguir** next; **seguir-se** *vr* to follow, ensue; (*resultar*) to result.

segunda-feira [segũda-'fejra] *f* Monday.

se'gundo/a *adj* second; ~ **tempo** (*futebol*) second half // *prep* according to // *conj* as; ~ **disse** as he said, from what he said // *m* second // *f* (*MÚS*) second; (*AUT*) second (gear); **de** ~**a** second-rate; **de** ~**a mão** second-hand.

segura'mente *adv* surely.

segu'rança *f* safety; (*proteção*) security; (*confiança*) confidence; (*certeza*) certainty; **com** ~ assuredly; **segurar** *vt* (*tornar seguro*) to secure, fix; (*agarrar*) to seize, take hold of; (*garantir*) to guarantee, ensure; (*COM*) to insure; **seguro/a** *adj* (*livre de perigo*) safe; (*livre de risco*) secure; (*certo*) certain, sure; (*firme*) firm, secure; (*confiável*) reliable; (*avaro*) stingy; (*tempo*) settled // *m* (*COM*) insurance; **seguro de vida** life insurance; **apólice de seguro** insurance policy; **fazer seguro** to take out an insurance policy.

sei *vb ver* **saber**.

seio ['seju] *m* breast, bosom; (*âmago*) heart; (~ *paranasal*) sinus; **no** ~ **de** in the heart of.

seis [sejʃ] *num* six; ~**centos/as** *num* six hundred.

seita ['sejta] *f* sect.

seiva ['sejva] *f* sap; (*fig*) vigour, vitality.

seixo ['sejʃu] *m* pebble.

'seja *etc vb ver* **ser**.

'sela *f* saddle.

se'lar *vt* (*carta*) to stamp; (*pôr selo em*) to mark with a seal, stamp; (*cavalo*) to saddle; (*fechar*) to shut, seal; (*concluir*) to conclude; (*confirmar*) to confirm.

seleção [selɛ'sãw] (*Pt*: **-cç-**) *f* selection, choice; (*equipe*) team, squad; **selecionado** (*Pt*: **-cc-**) *m* (*equipe*) team; **selecionar** (*Pt*: **-cc-**) *vt* to select, choose.

se'letivo/a (Pt: -ct-) adj selective; seleto/a (Pt: -ct-) adj select, choice // f anthology.

selim [se'lῖ] m saddle.

'selo m (postal, estampilha) stamp; (carimbo, sinete) seal.

'selva f jungle, forest.

selvagem [sɛw'vaʒẽ] adj (silvestre) wild; (feroz) savage, fierce; (não domesticado) wild.

sem [sẽ] prep without.

se'máforo m (AUTO) traffic lights pl; (FERRO) signal.

se'mana f week; semanal adj weekly; semanário m weekly (publication).

sem'blante m face; (fig) appearance, look.

seme'ar vt to sow; (fig) to spread; (espalhar) to scatter.

semelhança [semeˈʎãsa] f similarity, resemblance; a ~ de like; semelhante adj similar, resembling; (tal) such // f fellow creature; semelhar vi to seem like, resemble.

'sêmen m semen.

se'mente f seed; sementeira f sowing, spreading.

semes'tral adj half-yearly; semestre m six months; (EDUC) semester.

semicírculo [semiˈsixkulu] m semicircle.

semiconsciente [semicõ'sjẽtʃi] adj semiconscious.

semifi'nal f semifinal; ~ista m/f semifinalist.

semi'nário m (EDUC, congresso) seminar; (REL) seminary.

sempi'terno/a adj everlasting, eternal.

sempre ['sẽpri] adv always; (na verdade) really, actually; (ainda) still, yet; você ~ vai? (Pt) are you still going?; para ~ forever; ~ que whenever; como ~ as always; a história de ~ the same old story; para todo o ~ for ever and ever; quase ~ nearly always.

sem-vergonha [sẽ-vɛxˈgoɲa] m/f (pessoa) shameless person; sem-vergonhice f shamelessness.

se'nado m senate; senador(a) m/f senator.

senão [seˈnãw] conj otherwise, if not; (mas sim) but, but rather; ~ quando when suddenly; ~ que/também but also // prep (exceto) except, save // m flaw, defect.

'senda f path.

senha ['seɲa] f (sinal) sign; (palavra de passe) password; (recibo) receipt, voucher; (Pt: bilhete) ticket, voucher.

senhor(a) [seˈɲox(ra)] m (homem) man; (cavalheiro) gentleman; (feudal) lord; (dono) owner; (tratamento) Mr.; (tratamento respeitoso) sir; (: carta) Ilustríssimo (Il.ᵐᵒ) S~; (Pt) Excelentíssimo (Ex.ᵐᵒ) S~ Dear Sir; Nosso S~ Our Lord; o ~ you; ~ de si cool, collected // f (mulher) lady; (esposa) wife; (tratamento) Mrs.; (tratamento

respeitoso) madam; (: carta) Excelentíssima (Ex.ᵐᵃ) S~a Dear Madam; Nossa S~a Our Lady; a ~a you.

senho'ria f (proprietária) landlady; senhorial adj (atr) manor-, manorial; senhoril adj lordly; senhorinha f ver senhorita; senhorio m (autoridade) domination, control; (proprietário) landlord; senhorita f Miss; (mulher jovem) young lady.

se'nil adj senile; ~idade f senility.

sensabo'ria f (insipidez) insipidity, dullness; (col) unpleasantness.

sensação [sẽsa'sãw] f sensation, feeling; causar ~ to cause a sensation; sensacional adj sensational.

sensa'tez f good sense; sensato/a adj sensible, level-headed.

sensibilidade [sẽsibiliˈdadʒi] f sensitivity, sensibility; sensibilizar vt to touch, move; sensibilizar-se vr to be moved; sensitivo/a adj psychic; sensível adj sensitive; (perceptível) perceptible; (considerável) considerable; sensivelmente adv perceptibly, markedly.

'senso m sense; (juízo) judgement; ~ comum ou bom ~ common sense; sensual adj sensual, sensuous.

sen'tar vt to seat // vi to sit; ~-se vr to sit down.

sen'tença f (JUR) sentence; sentenciar vt (julgar) to pass judgement on; (pronunciar sentença) to sentence.

sen'tido/a adj (magoado) grieved, sorrowful; (triste) sad // excl: ~! attention! // m sense; (significação) sense, meaning; (direção) direction; ~ único (Pt: sinal) one-way; perder/recobrar os ~s to lose/recover consciousness; em certo ~ in a sense; sem ~ meaningless.

sentimen'tal adj sentimental; ~ismo m sentimentalism; sentimento m sentiment, feelings pl; (pesar) grief; sentimentos mpl condolences.

senti'nela f sentry, guard; estar de ~ to be on guard duty; render ~ to relieve the guard.

sen'tir vt to feel; (perceber) to perceive, sense; (lamentar) to regret; (ressentir-se) to be offended by; ~ a falta de to miss // vi (ter sensibilidade) to feel; (ter pesar) to grieve; ~-se vr to feel; (imaginar-se) to imagine o.s. to be, feel like.

sen'zala f slave quarters.

separação [separaˈsãw] f separation; (parede) partition; separado/a adj separate, separated; em separado separately, apart; separar vt to separate; (dividir) to divide; separar-se vr to separate; (dividir-se) to be divided; (afastar-se) to leave, depart; separata f offprint; separatismo m separatism.

'séptico/a adj septic.

se'pulcro m tomb; sepultar vt (enterrar)

to bury; (*esconder*) to hide, conceal; **sepultura** *f* grave, tomb.

sequaz [se'kwaʃ] *m* (*seguidor*) follower, adherent.

seqüela [se'kwela] *f* sequel; (*conseqüência*) consequence.

seqüência [se'kwẽsja] *f* sequence, succession.

sequer [se'kɛx] *adv* at least; **nem ~** not even.

seqüestra'dor(a) *m/f* sequestrator; (*raptor*) kidnapper; (*de avião etc*) hijacker; **seqüestrar** *vt* (*bens*) to seize, confiscate; (*raptar*) to kidnap; (*avião etc*) to hijack; **seqüestro** *m* seizure; (*rapto*) abduction, kidnapping.

sequioso/a [sekɪ'ozu/a] *adj* (*sedento*) thirsty; (*desejoso*) eager.

séquito ['sɛkɪtu] *m* retinue, suite.

ser *vi* to be; **~ de** (*provir de*) to be from, come from; (*feito de*) to be made of; (*pertencer a*) to belong to; **a não ~ que** unless; **pode ~** it may be; **que horas são?** what time is it?; **é uma hora** it is one o'clock; **~ feito de** to have become of; **o que é feito dele?** what has become of him?; **seja... seja....** whether... or....; **ou seja** that is to say; **era uma vez** once upon a time; **será que...?** I wonder if...? // *m* being.

serão [se'rãw] *m* (*trabalho noturno*) night work; (*horas extraordinárias*) overtime; (*sarau*) evening party; **fazer ~** to work overtime.

sereia [se'reja] *f* (*sirena*) siren; (*figura mitológica*) mermaid.

sere'nar *vt* (*acalmar*) to calm (down) // *vi* (*tornar-se sereno*) to calm down; **~-se** *vr* to grow calm; **serenidade** *f* calmness, tranquillity; **sereno/a** *adj* calm; (*tempo*) fine, clear // *m* (*relento*) damp night air; (*chuva*) drizzle; **no sereno** in the open.

seri'ado/a *adj* in a series, serialised // *m* (*filme*) serial; **série** *f* series sg; (*seqüência*) sequence, succession; (*EDUC*) grade; (*categoria*) category; **em série** (*filme etc*) serial *cmp*; **produção em série** mass production.

seriedade [serje'dadʒɪ] *f* seriousness; (*aplicação*) diligence; (*honradez*) honesty, sincerity.

se'ringa *f* syringe.

serin'gal *m* rubber plantation; **seringalista** *m* rubber plantation owner; **seringueira** *f* rubber tree; **seringueiro** *m* rubber tapper.

'sério/a *adj* serious; (*sincero*) sincere, honest; (*aplicado*) diligent; **a ~** seriously; **levar a ~** to take seriously.

sermão [sex'mãw] *m* sermon.

se'rôdio/a *adj* late, belated.

serpeante [sexpɪ'ãtʒɪ] *adj* wriggling; (*fig*) winding, meandering; **serpear** *vi* (*como serpente*) to wriggle; (*fig*) to wind, meander; **serpente** *f* snake; (*pessoa*) snake in the grass; **serpentear** *vi* ver **serpear**.

serpen'tina *f* (*conduto*) coil; (*fita de papel*) streamer.

'serra *f* (*montanha*) mountain range; (*TEC*) saw; **subir a ~** to lose one's temper; **serragem** *f* (*pó*) sawdust.

serralheiro [sexa'ʎejru] *m* locksmith.

serra'nia *f* mountain range; **serrano/a** *adj* highland // *m/f* highlander.

ser'rar *vt* to saw, cut; **serraria** *f* sawmill.

sertanejo/a [sexta'neʒu/a] *adj* rustic, country // *m/f* inhabitant of the backlands // *m* backwoodsman; **sertão** *m* backlands, bush (country).

ser'vente *m/f* (*criado*) servant; (*operário*) assistant; **~ de pedreiro** bricklayer's labourer.

servi'çal *adj* obliging, helpful // *m/f* (*criado*) servant; (*trabalhador*) wage earner; **serviço** *m* service; (*de chá etc*) set; **serviço ativo** (*MIL*) active duty; **serviço doméstico** housework; **serviço militar** military service; **serviços públicos** public utilities; **prestar serviço** to help, be of help; **estar de serviço** to be on duty.

servidão [sexvɪ'dãw] *f* servitude, serfdom; **servido/a** *adj* served; (*usado*) worn; **servido de** (*provido*) supplied with, provided with; **está servido almoçar?** would you care to join us for lunch?; **servidor** *m* (*criado*) servant; (*funcionário*) employee; **servil** *adj* servile; **servir** *vt* to serve // *vi* to serve; (*ser útil*) to be useful; (*ajudar*) to help; (*ficar bem*) to suit; **servir-se** *vr* (*tomar para si*) to serve o.s.; **servir-se de** to use, make use of; **servo/a** *m/f* (*feudal*) serf; (*criado*) servant.

sessão [sɛ'sãw] *f* session; (*reunião*) meeting; (*de cinema*) showing.

ses'senta *num* sixty.

'sesta *f* siesta, nap.

'seta *f* arrow, dart.

sete ['sɛtʃɪ] *num* seven; **~centos/as** *num* seven hundred.

se'tembro (*Pt*: **S-**) *m* September.

se'tenta *num* seventy.

setentrio'nal *adj* northern.

'sétimo/a *adj* seventh.

se'tor (*Pt*: **-ct-**) *m* sector.

seu/sua [sew/'sua] *adj* (*dele*) his; (*dela*) her; (*duma coisa*) its; (*deles, delas*) their; (*de você, vocês*) your // *pron* (*dele*) his; (*dela*) hers; (*deles, delas*) theirs; (*de você, vocês*) yours.

severi'dade *f* severity, harshness; **severo/a** *adj* severe, harsh.

sevícias [se'vɪsjaʃ] *fpl* (*maus tratos*) ill treatment; (*desumanidade*) inhumanity, cruelty.

'sexo *m* sex.

sexta-feira [sɛʃta-'fejra] *f* Friday; **S~ Santa** Good Friday.

sexto/a ['sɛʃtu/a] *adj* sixth.

sexual [sɛks'waw] *adj* sexual; **~idade** *f* sexuality.

sezão [se'zãw] *f* (*febre*) (intermittent) fever; (*malária*) malaria.

s.f.f. *abr de* **se faz favor** please.

si *pron* oneself; (*m*) himself; (*f*) herself; (*coisa*) itself; (*você*) yourself, you; (*vocês*) yourselves; (*pl*) themselves.

siamês / esa [sɪa'meʃ/eza] *adj* Siamese.

sibi'lar *vi* to hiss; (*assobiar*) to whistle.

si'cário *m* hired assassin.

si'crano *m* what's-his-name, so-and-so.

siderúrgico / a [sɪde'ruxʒɪku/a] *adj* iron and steel *cmp*; **usina ~a** steel works // *f* the steel industry.

'sidra *f* cider.

sifão [sɪ'fãw] *m* syphon; (*soda*) soda.

'siga *etc vb ver* **seguir**.

sigilo [sɪ'ʒɪlu] *m* secret; (*silêncio, segredo*) secrecy; **guardar ~ sobre** to keep secret; **~oso/a** *adj* secret.

signa'tário *m* signatory.

significação [sɪgnɪfɪka'sãw] *f* significance; **significado** *m* meaning; **significar** *vt* to mean, signify; **significativo/a** *adj* significant; **signo** *m* sign.

'sigo *vb ver* **seguir**.

'sílaba *f* syllable.

silenci'ar *vt* (*pessoa*) to silence; (*escândalo*) to hush up // *vi* to remain silent; **silêncio** *m* silence, quiet; **silencioso/a** *adj* silent, quiet // *m* (*AUTO*) silencer.

silhueta [sɪ'ʎweta] *f* silhouette.

silício [sɪ'lɪsju] *m* silicon.

'silo *m* silo.

'silva *f* bramble bush.

sil'var *vi* to hiss; (*assobiar*) to whistle.

silvestre [sɪl'vɛʃtrɪ] *adj* wild.

sim [sĩ] *adv* yes; **creio que ~** I think so; **isso ~** that's it!; **pelo ~, pelo não** just in case; **claro que ~** of course // *m* consent; **dar o ~** to consent.

sim'bólico/a *adj* symbolic; **simbolismo** *m* symbolism; **simbolizar** *vt* to symbolise; **símbolo** *m* symbol.

sime'tria *f* symmetry; **simétrico/a** *adj* symmetrical.

simi'lar *adj* similar; **~idade** *f* similarity.

simpa'tia *f* (*inclinação*) liking; (*afeto*) affection; (*afinidade*) affinity, fellow feeling; **simpático/a** *adj* (*agradável*) nice, pleasant; (*amável*) kind; **simpatizante** *adj* sympathising // *m/f* sympathiser; **simpatizar** *vi*: **simpatizar com** to take a liking to; (*causa*) to sympathise with.

simples ['sĩplɛʃ] *adj inv* simple; (*único*) single; (*de fácil compreensão*) simple, easy; (*mero*) mere, simple; (*ingênuo*) naïve; **simplicidade** *f* simplicity; (*ingenuidade*) naïveté; (*modéstia*) plainness; (*naturalidade*) naturalness; **simplificar** *vt* to simplify; **simplório/a** *adj* gullible // *m/f* fool, simpleton.

simulação [sɪmula'sãw] *f* simulation; (*fingimento*) pretence, sham; **simulacro** *m* (*imitação*) imitation; (*fingimento*) pretence, sham; (*ídolo*) idol; **simulado/a** *adj* simulated, pretend; **simular** *vt* to simulate.

simultaneamente [sɪmultanɪa'mẽtʃɪ] *adv* simultaneously; **simultâneo/a** *adj* simultaneous.

'sina *f* fate, destiny.

sina'goga *f* synagogue.

si'nal *m, pl* **sinais** [sɪ'najʃ] sign, signal; (*da pele*) mole, birthmark; (*indício*) indication; (*presságio*) omen; (*penhor*) deposit, guarantee; **~ de tráfego** traffic light; **~ rodoviário** road sign; **fazer ~** to signal; **dar de ~** to give as a deposit; **~eira** *f* traffic signal; **~eiro** *m* (*FERRO*) signalman; **~ização** *f* (*ato*) signalling; (*para motoristas*) traffic signs *pl*; (*FERRO*) signals *pl*; **~izar** *vi* to signal.

sinceridade [sɪserɪ'dadʒɪ] *f* sincerity; **sincero/a** *adj* sincere.

síncope ['sɪkopɪ] *f* faint, fainting fit.

sincroni'zar *vt* to synchronize.

sindi'cal *adj* union *cmp*, trade union *cmp*; **~ista** *m/f* trade unionist; **sindicato** *m* (*de trabalhadores*) trade union; (*financeiro*) syndicate; **síndico** *m* syndic; (*de condomínio*) manager; (*de massa falida*) receiver.

sineiro [sɪ'nejru] *m* bell-ringer; (*fabricante*) bellmaker.

sinfo'nia *f* symphony; **sinfônico/a** *adj* symphonic.

singeleza [sɪʒe'leza] *f* (*simplicidade*) simplicity; **singelo/a** *adj* simple.

sin'grar *vt* to sail.

singu'lar *adj* singular; (*extraordinário*) exceptional; (*bizarro*) odd, peculiar; **~idade** *f* strangeness, peculiarity; **~izar** *vt* (*distinguir*) to single out; **~izar-se** *vr* to stand out, distinguish o.s.

sinis'trado *m* injured party; **sinistro/a** *adj* left; (*fig*) sinister // *m* disaster, accident.

'sino *m* bell.

si'nônimo/a *adj* synonymous // *m* synonym.

sinopse [sɪ'nɔpsɪ] *f* synopsis.

'sinta *etc vb ver* **sentir**.

sintaxe [sɪ'tasɪ] *f* syntax.

'síntese *f* synthesis; **em ~** in short; **sintético/a** *adj* (*resumido*) summarized; (*artificial*) synthetic; **sintetizar** *vt* to synthesize; (*resumir*) to summarize.

sin'toma *m* symptom; **sintomático/a** *adj* symptomatic.

sintoni'zar *vt* (*rádio*) to tune (in) // *vi*: **~ com** to get on with.

sinuosidade [sɪnwozɪ'dadʒɪ] *f* (*ondulação*) winding; **sinuoso/a** *adj* winding, wavy.

si'rena *f* siren.

si'ri *m* crab.

'sirvo *vb ver* **servir**.

'siso *m* good sense; **dente do ~** wisdom tooth.

sis'tema *m* system; (*método*) method; **sistemático/a** *adj* systematic.

si'sudo/a *adj* serious, sober.

siti'ar *vt* to besiege, lay siege to; **sítio** *m* (*lugar*) place, location; (*MIL*) siege; (*propriedade rural*) small farm.

situação [sɪtwa'sãw] *f* situation, position;

(*posição social*) standing; **situado/a** *adj* situated; **estar situado** to be situated; **situar** *vt* (*pôr*) to place, put; (*edifício*) to situate, locate.

só [sɔ] *adj* (*desacompanhado*) alone; (*único*) single; (*solitário, desamparado*) solitary, alone; **um ~** only one; **a ~s** alone // *adv* only, just; **não ~ ... mas também** ... not only ... but also ....

soalheiro/a [swaˈʎejru/a] *adj* sunny // *f* heat of the sun // *m* sunny spot.

soalho [ˈswaʎu] *m* (wooden) floor.

so'ar *vi* to sound; (*cantar*) to sing; (*horas*) to strike; **~ a** to sound like, seem like.

sob *prep* under; **~ pena de** on pain of; **~ minha palavra** on my word; **~ juramento** on oath; **~ emenda** subject to correction.

'sobe *etc vb ver* **subir**.

sobejar [sobeˈʒax] *vi* (*superabundar*) to be more than enough, abound; (*restar*) to be left over; **sobejo/a** *adj* abundant; (*imenso*) immense // *mpl*: **sobejos** remains, leftovers.

sobera'nia *f* sovereignty; **soberano/a** *adj* sovereign; (*fig*) supreme // *m/f* sovereign.

so'berbo/a *adj* (*arrogante*) haughty, arrogant; (*magnífico*) magnificent, splendid // *f* haughtiness, arrogance.

'sobra *f* surplus, remnant; **de ~** spare, extra; (*demasiado*) in abundance; **ficar de ~** to be left over; **~s** *fpl* leftovers, remains.

sobra'çar *vt* (*levar debaixo do braço*) to carry under one's arm.

so'brado *m* (*andar*) floor; (*casa*) house (of two or more storeys).

sobrance'ar *vt* to tower above; **sobranceiro/a** *adj* (*acima de*) lofty, towering; (*proeminente*) prominent; (*arrogante*) haughty, arrogant.

sobrancelha [sobrãˈseʎa] *f* eyebrow; **franzir as ~s** to frown.

so'brar *vi* to be left over, remain; **ficar sobrando** (*pessoa*) to be left out; **sobram-me cinco** I have five left.

sobre [ˈsobri] *prep* on; (*por cima de*) above, over; (*acima de*) on top of, above; (*a respeito de*) about, concerning; (*além de*) as well as, besides.

sobreaviso [sobriaˈvizu] *m*: **de ~** alert, on one's guard.

sobre'capa *f* (*de livro*) cover.

sobre'carga *f* (*carga excessiva*) excess load, overloading; **sobrecarregar** *vt* (*carregar em demasia*) to overload; (*oprimir*) to oppress.

sobrecenho [sobreˈseɲu] *m* frown, scowl.

sobre-hu'mano/a *adj* superhuman.

sobreiro [soˈbrejru] *m* cork oak.

sobrele'var *vt* (*exceder em altura*) to tower above, rise above; (*levantar*) to raise; (*dominar*) to overcome // *vi* (*destacar-se*) to stand out; **~-se** *vr* to stand out.

sobre'maneira [sobremaˈnejra] *adv* exceedingly, extraordinarily.

sobre'mesa *f* dessert.

sobre'modo *adv* exceedingly.

sobrenatu'ral *adj* supernatural.

sobrenome [sobreˈnomi] *m* (*Br*) surname, family name.

sobrepe'liz *f* surplice.

sobre'por *vt* (*pôr em cima*) to put on top, lay on top; (*adicionar*) to add; (*antepor*) to put first, value more; **~-se** *vr*: **~-se a** (*pôr-se sobre*) to cover, go on top of; (*sobrevir*) to follow, succeed; (*fig*) to overcome.

sobrepujar [sobrepuˈʒax] *vt* (*exceder em altura*) to rise above; (*superar*) to excel, surpass; (*vencer*) to overcome.

sobrescri'tar *vt* to address; **sobrescrito** *m* (*envelope*) envelope; (*endereço*) address.

sobressa'ir *vi* to stand out.

sobressa'lente *adj* spare, surplus // *m* spare.

sobressal'tar *vt* (*surpreender*) to startle; (*atemorizar*) to frighten; **~-se** *vr* to be startled; **sobressalto** *m* shock; (*susto*) scare, shock; **de sobressalto** suddenly.

sobretaxa [sobreˈtaʃa] *f* surcharge.

sobre'tudo *m* overcoat // *adv* above all, especially.

sobre'vir *vi* (*suceder*) to occur, arise; **~ a** (*seguir*) to follow (on from).

sobrevi'vência *f* survival; **sobrevivente** *adj* surviving // *m/f* survivor; **sobrevi'ver** *vi* to survive; **sobreviveu ao seu pai** he survived his father.

sobriedade [sobrieˈdadʒi] *f* sobriety, soberness; (*comedimento*) moderation, restraint.

sobrinho/a [soˈbriɲu/a] *m* nephew // *f* niece.

'sóbrio/a *adj* sober; (*moderado*) moderate, restrained.

sobrolho [soˈbroʎu] *m* eyebrow; **~ carregado** scowl; **carregar o ~** to scowl; **franzir o ~** to frown.

so'capa *f*: **à ~** furtively, on the sly.

so'car *vt* (*esmurrar*) to hit, strike; (*calcar*) to crush, pound.

soca'var *vt* (*escavar*) to excavate.

social [soˈsjaw] *adj* social; (*pessoa*) sociable; **~ismo** *m* socialism; **~ista** *adj, m/f* socialist; **~izar** *vi* to socialize; **sociável** *adj* sociable.

sociedade [sosjeˈdadʒi] *f* society; (*COM*) company; **~ anônima** joint-stock *ou* limited company; **sócio** *m* (*COM*) partner, associate; (*membro dum clube*) member; **sócio comanditário** (*COM*) silent partner.

sociologia [sosjoloˈʒia] *f* sociology; **sociológico/a** *adj* sociological; **sociólogo/a** *m/f* sociologist.

'soco *m* (*golpe*) blow, punch.

soço'brar *vt* (*afundar*) to sink, wreck // *vi* (*naufragar*) to sink, founder.

socor'rer *vt* to help, assist; (*salvar*) to

rescue; **~-se** *vr*: **~-se de** to resort to, have recourse to; **socorro** *m* help, assistance; **ir em socorro de** to come to the aid of; **primeiros socorros** first aid *sg* // *excl*: **socorro!** help!

'soda *f* (*cáustica*) caustic soda; (*para bebidas*) soda water.

so'fá *m* sofa, settee; **~-cama** *m* studio couch.

so'fisma *m* sophism; (*col*) trick; **sofismar** *vt* to swindle, cheat.

'sôfrego/a *adj* (*ávido*) greedy; (*impaciente*) impatient.

so'frer *vt* (*padecer*) to suffer; (*agüentar*) to bear, put up with; (*experimentar*) to go through, experience // *vi* to suffer; **sofrido/a** *adj* long-suffering, patient; **sofrimento** *m* suffering; (*paciência*) endurance; **sofrível** *adj* bearable; (*razoável*) passable, moderate.

'sogro/a *m* father-in-law // *f* mother-in-law.

soja ['soʒa] *f* soya.

sol *m* sun; (*luz*) sunshine, sunlight; **ao/no ~** in the sun; **fazer ~** to be sunny; **de ~ a ~** from dawn to dusk.

'sola *f* (*de calçado ou pé*) sole.

sola'var *vt* (*escavar*) to dig into; (*fig: arruinar*) to undermine, destroy.

so'lar *adj* solar // *m* manor house.

sola'vanco *m* jolt, bump; **andar aos ~s** to jog along.

'solda *f* solder.

sol'dado *m* soldier; **~ raso** private soldier; **~ de chumbo** toy soldier.

solda'dor *m* welder; **soldar** *vt* to solder, weld; (*fig*) to unite, amalgamate.

'soldo *m* (MIL) pay.

soleira [so'lejra] *f* (*duma porta*) doorstep, threshold.

solene [so'lenɪ] *adj* solemn; **solenidade** *f* solemnity; **solenizar** *vt* to solemnize.

sole'trar *vt* to spell out; (*ler devagar*) to read out slowly.

solha ['soʎa] *f* plaice.

solicitação [solɪsɪta'sãw] *f* request; **solicitações** *fpl* (*apelo*) inducement *sg*, appeal *sg*; **solicitar** *vt* to ask for, seek; (*emprego*) to apply for.

so'lícito/a *adj* (*diligente*) diligent; (*prestimoso*) helpful; **solicitude** *f* great care; (*boa vontade*) concern, thoughtfulness.

solidão [solɪ'dãw] *f* solitude, isolation; (*sem amigos, parentes etc*) loneliness; (*lugar*) wilderness, desert.

solidariedade [solɪdarje'dadʒɪ] *f* solidarity; **solidário/a** *adj* (*manifestando simpatia*) sympathetic; (*partilhando responsabilidade*) jointly responsible; **solidarizar-se** *vt* to sympathize.

soli'dez *f* solidity, strength; **sólido/a** *adj* solid.

solilóquio [solɪ'lokju] *m* soliloquy.

so'lista *m/f* soloist.

soli'tário/a *adj* lonely, solitary // *m* hermit; (*jóia*) solitaire.

'solo *m* (*terreno*) ground, earth; (MÚS) solo.

sol'tar *vt* (*tornar livre*) to set free; (*desatar*) to loosen, untie; (*afrouxar*) to slacken, loosen; (*emitir*) to emit; (*grito, risada*) to let out; **~-se** *vr* (*desprender-se*) to come loose; (*escapar*) to escape.

solteiro/a [sol'tejru/a] *adj* unmarried, single // *m* bachelor // *f* single woman, spinster; **solteirona** *f* old maid.

'solto/a *pp irr de* **soltar** // *adj* loose; (*livre*) free; (*sozinho*) alone; **à ~a** freely; **verso ~** blank verse; **intestino ~** loose bowels, diarrhoea; **dormir a sono ~** to sleep like a log; **soltura** *f* looseness; (*liberdade*) release, discharge.

solução [solu'sãw] *f* solution.

solu'çar *vi* (*chorar*) to sob; (MED) to hiccup.

solucionar [solusjo'nax] *vt* to solve.

so'luço *m* (*pranto*) sob; (MED) hiccup.

so'lúvel *adj* soluble.

solvência *f* solvency; **solver** *vt* (*resolver*) to solve; (*pagar*) to pay.

som [sõ] *m* sound; (MÚS) tone; (Br: col: equipamento*) hi-fi, stereo; **sem tom nem ~** without rhyme or reason; **ao ~ de** (MÚS) to the accompaniment of.

'soma *f* sum, total; **somar** *vt* (*adicionar*) to add (up); (*chegar a*) to add up to, amount to // *vi* to add up.

'sombra *f* shadow; (*como proteção*) shade; (*fantasma*) ghost; (*indício*) trace, sign; (*capanga*) henchman, bodyguard; **à ~ de** in the shade of; (*sob a proteção de*) under the protection of; **fazer ~ a** to outshine; **nem por ~s** not a chance; **sem ~ de dúvida** without a shadow of a doubt; **sombreado/a** *adj* shady; **sombrear** *vt* to shade; **sombrinha** *f* parasol, sunshade; (Br) lady's umbrella; **sombrio/a** *adj* (*escuro*) shady, dark; (*triste*) gloomy.

'some *etc vb ver* **sumir.**

so'menos *adj* inferior, poor; **de ~ importância** unimportant.

somente [sɔ'mẽtʃɪ] *adv* only, merely; **tão ~** only.

'somos *vb ver* **ser.**

sonambu'lismo *m* sleepwalking; **sonâmbulo/a** *adj* sleepwalking // *m/f* sleepwalker.

so'nata *f* sonata.

'sonda *f* (*instrumento*) plummet, sounding lead; (MED) probe; (*de petróleo*) drill; **sondagem** *f* (NÁUT) sounding; (*para petróleo*) drilling; (*para minerais*) boring; (*de opinião, mercado*) survey; **sondar** *vt* (NÁUT) to sound, probe; (*explorar*) to explore, probe; (*opinião etc*) to sound out, take a survey of.

so'neca *f* nap, snooze.

sone'gar *vt* (*ocultar*) to conceal, withhold; (*surripiar*) to steal, pilfer; (*deixar de pagar*) to dodge.

so'neto *m* sonnet.

sonhador(a) [soɲa'dox(ra)] *adj* dreamy, dreaming // *m/f* dreamer; **sonhar** *vi* to dream; **sonhar com** to dream about; **sonho** m dream; (CULIN) doughnut; **sonho acordado** daydream.

'sono m sleep; **estar com ~ /ter ~** to be sleepy; **pegar no ~** to fall asleep; **~lência** f drowsiness; **~lento/a** adj sleepy, drowsy.

so'noro/a adj sonorous; (ressonante) resonant, resounding.

'sonso/a adj sly, artful.

'sopa f soup; (coisa fácil) pushover, cinch; **em ~** soaked.

so'papo m slap, cuff.

so'pé m foot, bottom.

sopeira [so'pejra] f (CULIN) soup dish.

sope'sar vt (tomar o peso de) to weigh in one's hand; (equilibrar) to balance in one's hand; (aguentar o peso de) to bear, support.

sopi'tar vt (fazer dormir) to make sleepy; (acalmar) to calm (down), appease; (debilitar) to weaken; (conter) to curb, repress.

so'prar vt to blow; (encher de ar) to blow up; (apagar um fogo, vela etc) to blow out; (dizer em voz baixa) to whisper // vi to blow; **sopro** m blow, puff; (de vento) gust; (hálito) breath; (no coração) murmur; **instrumento de sopro** wind instrument.

'sórdido/a adj sordid; (sujo) dirty; (obsceno) indecent, dirty; (mesquinho) miserly.

'sorna (Pt) adj lazy; (maçador) pestering // f (preguiça) laziness, sluggishness // m/f (pessoa) idler.

'soro m (MED) serum; (do leite) whey.

'sóror f (REL) sister.

sorrateiro/a [soxa'tejru/a] adj sly, sneaky.

sorri'dente adj smiling; **sorrir** vi to smile; **sorriso** m smile.

sorte ['sɔxtʃi] f (fortuna) luck; (casualidade) chance; (destino) fate, destiny; (condição) lot; (género) sort, kind; **desta ~** so, thus; **de ~ que** so that; **dar ~** to bring good luck; **tentar a ~** to try one's luck; **ter ~** to be lucky; **tirar a ~** to draw lots; **~ grande** big prize; **sortear** vt to draw lots for; (rifar) to raffle; (MIL) to draft; **sorteio** m draw; (rifa) raffle; (MIL) draft.

sor'tido/a adj (abastecido) supplied, stocked; (variado) varied, assorted.

sortilégio [soxtʃi'lɛʒju] m (bruxaria) sorcery; (encantamento) charm, fascination.

sorti'mento m assortment, stock; **sortir** vt (abastecer) to supply, stock; (variar) to vary, mix.

sorum'bático/a adj gloomy, melancholy.

sorvedouro [soxve'doru] m whirlpool; (abismo) chasm.

sor'ver vt to sip; (inalar) to inhale; (tragar) to swallow up; (absorver) to soak up, absorb; **sorvete** m (Br) ice cream; **sorvo** m sip.

'sósia m/f double; (col) spitting image.

soslaio [soʒ'laju] adv: **de ~** sideways, obliquely; **olhar algo de ~** to squint at sth.

sosse'gado/a adj peaceful, calm; **sossegar** vt to calm, quieten // vi to rest; **sossego** m peacefulness, calm.

sotaina [so'tajna] f cassock, soutane.

sótão ['sɔtãw] m attic, loft.

sotaque [so'taki] m (fala) accent.

sota'vento m (NÁUT) lee; **a ~** to leeward.

soter'rar vt to bury.

so'turno/a adj sad, gloomy.

sou vb ver **ser**.

'soube etc vb ver **saber**.

soutien [su'tʃjã] m bra(ssiere).

'sova f beating, thrashing.

so'vaco m armpit.

so'var vt (golpear) to beat, thrash; (massa) to knead.

so'vela f awl.

sovi'ético/a adj, m/f Soviet.

so'vina m/f miser, skinflint.

sozinho/a [sɔ'ziɲu/a] adj (all) alone, by oneself.

Sr. abr de **senhor** Mr.

Sr.ª abr de **senhora** Mrs.

Sr.ª abr de **senhorita** Miss.

sua ['sua] adj, pron ver **seu**.

su'ado/a adj hard-earned; **suar** vi to sweat, perspire // vt to slave over, strive for.

suave ['swavɪ] adj (brando) soft; (benigno) mild; (terno) gentle; (sem dificuldades) smooth; (encantador) suave; **suavidade** f (brandura) softness; (ternura) gentleness; (amenidade) mildness; (encanto) charm; **suavizar** vt to soften.

subal'terno/a adj inferior, subordinate // m (MIL) subaltern.

subarren'dar vt (Pt) to sublet.

subconsciência [subcõ'sjẽsja] f subconscious; **subconsciente** adj, m subconscious.

subdesenvol'vido/a adj underdeveloped; **subdesenvolvimento** m underdevelopment.

'súdito m (Pt) ver **súdito**.

subenten'der vt to understand, assume.

su'bido/a adj (alto) high, lofty; (nobre) noble // f ascent, climb; (ladeira) slope; (de preços) rise; **subir** vi to go up, ascend, climb; (preços) to rise; **subir a** (montar) to mount, get on to // vt (levantar) to raise; (uma ladeira) to climb, go up.

'súbito/a adj sudden; **de ~** suddenly.

subjetivo/a [subʒɛ'tʃivu/a] (Pt: **-ct-**) adj subjective.

subjugar [subʒu'gax] vt to subjugate, subdue; (dominar) to overpower.

sublevação [subleva'sãw] f (up)rising, revolt; **sublevar** vt to stir up in revolt; **sublevar-se** vr to revolt, rebel.

sublime [su'blimɪ] adj sublime, noble.

sublinhar [subli'ɲax] vt (pôr linha debaixo

de) to underline; (*destacar*) to emphasise, stress.

subloca'tário *m* sub-tenant.

suba'rino/a *adj* underwater // *m* submarine.

submergir [submɛx'ʒix] *vt*, **submergir-se** *vr* to submerge.

subme'ter *vt* (*subjugar*) to subdue; (*entregar*) to submit; ~-se *vr*: ~-se a to submit to; (*operação*) to undergo.

submissão [submi'sãw] *f* submission; **submisso/a** *adj* submissive, docile.

subordi'nar *vt* to subordinate.

subor'nar *vt* to bribe; **suborno** *m* bribery.

sub-reptício/a [sub-xɛp'tʃisju/a] *adj* surreptitious.

subscre'ver *vt* (*assinar*) to sign; (*concordar*) to agree with; ~-se *vr* to sign one's name; **subscrição** *f* subscription.

subsecre'tário/a *m/f* under-secretary.

subseqüente [subse'kwẽtʃi] *adj* subsequent, following.

subsidi'ário/a *adj* subsidiary // *f* (*COM*) subsidiary (company); **subsídio** *m* subsidy; (*ajuda*) aid; **subsídios** *mpl* data, information.

subsis'tência *f* (*sustento*) subsistence; (*meio de vida*) livelihood.

subs'tância *f* substance; **substantivo/a** *adj* substantive // *m* noun.

substituir [subʃtʃi'twix] *vt* to substitute, replace; **substituto/a** *adj*, *m/f* substitute.

subterfúgio [subtɛx'fuʒju] *m* subterfuge, trick.

subter'râneo/a *adj* subterranean, underground.

sub'til *adj* (*Pt*) *ver* sutil.

sub'título *m* subtitle.

subtra'ir *vt* (*furtar*) to steal, embezzle; (*deduzir*) to subtract.

subur'bano/a *adj* suburban; **subúrbio** *m* suburb.

subvenção [subvẽ'sãw] *f* subsidy, grant; **subvencionar** *vt* to subsidize.

subver'sivo/a *adj*, *m/f* subversive; **subverter** *vt* to subvert.

su'cata *f* scrap metal.

sucedâneo/a [suse'danju/a] *adj* substitute // *m* (*substância*) substitute.

suce'der *vi* (*acontecer*) to happen, occur; ~ a (*acontecer a*) to befall; (*seguir*) to succeed, follow; **sucedido/a** *adj*: **bem sucedido** successful // *m* event, occurrence; **sucessão** *f* succession; **sucessivo/a** *adj* successive; **sucesso** *m* event, occurrence; **sucessor(a)** *m/f* successor.

súcia ['susja] *f* gang, band.

sucinto/a [su'sĩtu/a] *adj* concise, succinct.

'suco *m* (*Br*) juice; **suculento/a** *adj* succulent, juicy.

sucum'bir *vi* (*render*) to succumb, yield; (*morrer*) to die, perish.

sucur'sal *f* (*COM*) branch.

su'dário *m* shroud.

sudeste [su'dɛʃtʃi] *adj* southeast // *m* the South East.

'súdito (*Pt*: **-bd-**) *m* (*de rei etc*) subject.

sudoeste [sud'wɛʃtʃi] *adj* southwest // *m* the South West.

Suécia ['swɛsja] *f* Sweden; **sueco/a** *adj* Swedish // *m/f* Swede // *m* (*língua*) Swedish.

sueste ['swɛʃtʃi] *adj* southeast // *m* the South East.

suéter ['swɛtɛx] *m* (*Br*) sweater.

suficiência [sufis'jẽsja] *f* (*quantidade suficiente*) sufficiency; (*aptidão*) competence; **suficiente** *adj* sufficient, enough.

sufixo [su'fiksu] *m* suffix.

sufo'cante *adj* (*calor*) sweltering, oppressive; **sufocar** *vt/i* to suffocate, choke.

sufrágio [su'fraʒju] *m* suffrage, vote.

su'gar *vt* to suck; (*fig*) to extort.

sugerir [suʒe'rix] *vt* to suggest; **sugestão** *f* suggestion; (*indireta*) hint.

suíças ['swisaʃ] *fpl* sideburns.

suicida [swi'sida] *m/f* suicidal person; (*morto*) suicide, a person who has committed suicide; **suicidar-se** *vr* to commit suicide; **suicídio** *m* suicide.

suíço/a ['swisu/a] *adj*, *m/f* Swiss // *f*: S~a Switzerland.

suíno ['swinu] *m* pig, hog.

su'jar *vt* to soil, dirty.

sujeição [suʒej'sãw] *f* subjection.

sujeira [su'ʒejra] *f* (*Br*) *ver* sujidade.

suje'tar *vt* to subdue, subject; ~-se *vr* to submit; **sujeito/a** *adj* subjected; (*exposto*) subject, liable // *m* (*LING*) subject; (*homem*) guy, fellow // *f* (*mulher*) woman.

sujidade [suʒi'dadə] *f* (*Pt*) (*estado*) dirtiness; (*porcaria*) filth, dirt.

sujo/a ['suʒu/a] *adj* dirty, filthy.

sul *adj inv* south, southern // *m* the south.

sul'car *vt* to plough; **sulco** *m* (*rego de arado*) furrow; (*ruga*) wrinkle.

'suma *f* summary; **em** ~ in short.

suma'mente *adv* extremely.

su'mário/a *adj* (*breve*) brief, concise; (*JUR*) summary // *m* summary.

sumiço [su'misu] *m* disappearance; **dar** ~ a to spirit away; **levar** ~ to disappear.

su'mido/a *adj* faint, indistinct; (*olhos*) sunken; (*voz*) low.

sumidouro [sumi'doru] *m* (*esgoto*) drain.

su'mir *vt* (*submergir*) to submerge; (*esconder*) to hide; ~-se *vr* to disappear, vanish.

'sumo *m* (*Pt*) juice.

'sumo/a *adj* extreme; (*superior*) supreme.

'sumula *f* summary.

'sunga *f* swimming trunks; (*suporte*) jock strap, athletic support.

suntuoso/a [sũ'twozu/a] (*Pt*: **-umpt-**) *adj* sumptuous.

su'or *m* sweat, perspiration.

superaquecer [superake'sex] *vi* to overheat.

supe'rar *vt* (*dominar*) to overcome; (*exceder*) to exceed, surpass; **superávit** *m* (*COM*) surplus.

superestru'tura *f* superstructure.

superficial [supɛxfis'jaw] *adj* superficial; **superfície** *f* (*parte externa*) surface; (*extensão*) area.

su'pérfluo/a *adj* superfluous, unnecessary.

superinten'dente *m* superintendent, supervisor.

superi'or *adj* (*melhor*) superior; (*mais elevado*) higher; ~ **a** above; (*além de*) beyond // *m* superior; (*REL*) superior, abbot; **superiora** *f* mother superior.

superla'tivo/a *adj* superlative // *m* superlative.

supermer'cado *m* supermarket.

superpo'tência *f* superpower.

superpovoado/a [supɛxpov'wadu/a] *adj* overpopulated.

superprodução [supɛxprodu'sãw] *f* overproduction.

super'sônico/a *adj* supersonic.

superstição [supɛxʃtʃi'sãw] *f* superstition; **supersticioso/a** *adj* superstitious.

supervi'sar, supervisio'nar *vt* to supervise.

suplan'tar *vt* to supplant, supersede.

suple'mento *m* supplement.

su'plente *m/f* substitute.

'súplica *f* supplication, plea; **suplicante** *m* supplicant; (*JUR*) plaintiff; **suplicar** *vt* to plead, beg.

suplício [su'plisju] *m* torture.

su'por *vt* to suppose.

supor'tar *vt* to hold up, support; (*tolerar*) to bear, tolerate; **suportável** *adj* bearable, tolerable; **suporte** *m* support, stand.

suposição [supozi'sãw] *f* supposition, presumption; **suposto/a** *adj* supposed, would-be // *m* assumption.

suprema'cia *f* supremacy; **supremo/a** *adj* supreme, highest.

supressão [supre'sãw] *f* suppression; (*omissão*) omission.

supri'mento *m* supply.

supri'mir *vt* to suppress; (*omitir*) to omit, delete.

su'prir *vt* to supply, provide; (*substituir*) to make up for, take the place of.

sur'dina *f* (*MÚS*) mute; **em** ~ stealthily, on the quiet.

'surdo/a *adj* deaf; (*som*) muffled, dull // *m/f* deaf person; ~**-mudo/a** *adj* deaf and dumb // *m/f* deaf-mute.

surgir [sux'ʒix] *vi* (*emergir*) to emerge, appear; (*sair*) to come out, emerge; (*levantar-se*) to arise.

surpreendente [suxpriě'dětʃi] *adj* surprising, amazing; **surpreender** *vt* to surprise, amaze; (*pegar de surpresa*) to

take unawares; **surpresa** *f* surprise; **de surpresa** by surprise.

'surra *f* beating, thrashing; **surrado/a** *adj* worn out; **surrar** *vt* to beat, thrash; (*couro*) to tan, cure.

sur'tir *vt* to produce, bring about; ~ **bem** to turn out well.

suscetível [susɛ'tʃivɛw] *adj*, **susceptível** [susɛp'tʃivɛw] *adj* susceptible.

suscitar [susi'tax] *vt* to excite, stir up; ~ **dúvidas** to raise doubts.

suspeitar [suʃpej'tax] *vt/i* to suspect; (*desconfiar*) to distrust; **suspeito/a** *adj* suspect, suspicious // *f* suspicion; **suspeitoso/a** *adj* distrustful, suspicious.

suspen'der *vt* (*pendurar*) to hang; (*interromper*) to suspend, stop; (*adiar*) to adjourn, defer; **suspensão** *f* suspension; (*interrupção*) interruption, stoppage; **suspensórios** *mpl* braces, suspenders (*US*).

suspicácia [suʃpi'kasja] *f* distrust, suspicion; **suspicaz** *adj* (*suspeito*) suspect; (*desconfiado*) suspicious.

suspi'rar *vi* to sigh; ~ **por algo** to long for sth; **suspiro** *m* sigh; (*doce*) meringue.

sussur'rar *vt/i* to whisper; **sussurro** *m* whisper.

sus'tância *f* (*força*) strength; (*comida*) nourishment.

sus'tar *vt/i* to stop.

susten'tar *vt* to sustain; (*objeto*) to hold up, support; (*manter*) to maintain; **sustento** *m* food, sustenance; **suster** *vt* to support, hold up; (*reprimir*) to restrain, hold back.

'susto *m* fright, scare.

sutiã [su'tʃjã] *m* bra(ssiere).

su'til (*Pt*: **-bt-**) *adj* subtle; (*fino*) fine, delicate; ~**eza** *f* subtlety; (*finura*) fineness, delicacy.

T

ta = **te** + **a**.

tabaca'ria *f* tobacconist's (shop); **tabaco** *m* tobacco.

ta'bela *f* table, chart; (*lista*) list; **por** ~ indirectly.

tabelião [tabel'jãw] *m* notary public.

ta'berna *f* tavern, bar; **taberneiro/a** *m/f* (*dono*) publican.

tabique [ta'biki] *m* partition.

ta'blado *m* stage, platform.

ta'bu *adj*, *m* taboo.

'tábua *f* (*madeira*) plank, board; (*MAT*) list, table.

tabuleiro [tabu'lejru] *m* tray; (*xadrez*) board.

tabu'leta *f* (*letreiro*) sign, signboard.

'taça *f* cup.

tacanho/a [ta'kaɲu/a] *adj* mean, niggardly; (*de idéias curtas*) narrow-minded.

tacha ['taʃa] *f* (*prego*) tack; **tachar** *vt* to find fault with; **tachar de** to brand as.

'tácito/a adj tacit, implied; **taciturno/a** adj taciturn, reserved.

'taco m (de bilhar) cue; (de golfe, hóquei) club, stick; (bucha) plug, wad.

taga'rela adj talkative; // m/f chatterbox; **tagarelar** vi to chatter, gossip; **tagarelice** f chat, chatter, gossip.

taipa ['tajpa] f mud wall.

tal adj such; ~ **e coisa** this and that; **um** ~ **de Sr. X** a certain Mr. X; **que** ~? what do you think?; (Pt) how are things?; ~ **pai**, ~ **filho** like father, like son // adv so, as; ~ **como** just as; ~ **qual** just so, just as it is // pron such a thing.

'tala f (MED) splint.

ta'lante m: **a seu** ~ at will.

talão [ta'lãw] m (de recibo) stub; ~ **de cheques** cheque book.

'talco m talc; **pó de** ~ (Pt) talcum powder.

ta'lento m talent; (aptidão) ability.

talha ['taʎa] f (corte) carving; (vaso) pitcher; (NÁUT) tackle; **talhada** f slice.

talhão [ta'ʎãw] m plot, patch.

talhar [ta'ʎax] vt to cut, slice; (esculpir) to carve // vi (coalhar) to curdle; **talhe** m cut, shape.

talher [ta'ʎex] m item of cutlery; (lugar) place (at table); ~**es** mpl cutlery.

talho ['taʎu] m (corte) cutting, slicing; (Pt: açougue) butcher's (shop).

'talo m stalk, stem; (ARQ) shaft.

talude [ta'ludʒi] m slope, incline.

tal'vez adv perhaps, maybe; ~ **tenha razão** maybe you're right.

ta'manco m clog, wooden shoe.

tamanho/a [ta'maɲu/a] adj so big, so great // m size; **em** ~ **natural** life-size.

'tâmara f (fruto) date.

também [tã'bẽj] adv also, too, as well; (aliás) besides.

tam'bor m drum; **tamboril** m, **tamborim** m tambourine.

'tampa f lid; (de garrafa) cap; **tampão** m cover; (rolha) stopper, plug.

'tanga f loincloth; **estar de** ~ (col) to be broke.

tanger [tã'ʒex] vt (MÚS) to play; (sinos) to ring; (cordas) to pluck; ~ **a** (dizer respeito) to concern; **no que tange a** as regards, with respect to.

tange'rina f tangerine.

tangível [tã'ʒivew] adj tangible.

tanoeiro [tan'wejru] m cooper.

tanque [ˈtãki] m (reservatório, MIL) tank.

'tanto/a adj (sg) so much; (: + interrogativa/negativa) as much; (pl) so many; (: + interrogativa/negativa) as many; **vinte e** ~**s** twenty-odd; ~ **como** as much as // adv so much; ~ **melhor/pior** so much the better/the more's the pity; ~ **se me dá** it's all the same to me; ~ ... **como** ... both ... and ...; ~ **mais** ... **quanto mais** ... the more ... the more ....

tão [tãw] adv so; ~ **rico quanto** as rich as; ~**-só** adv only.

'tapa f slap.

ta'par vt to cover; (garrafa) to cork.

tapeça'ria f tapestry, wall hanging.

tapete [ta'petʃi] m carpet, rug.

tapume [ta'pumi] m fencing, boarding; (cerca viva) hedge.

taquigrafia [takigra'fia] f shorthand.

tar'dança f delay, slowness; **tardar** vi to delay, be slow; (chegar tarde) to be late; **sem mais tardar** without delay; **ele tardou a vir** he was long in coming // vt to delay; **tarde** f (dia) afternoon; (quase noite) evening // adv late; **tardinha** f late afternoon; **tardio/a** adj late.

ta'refa f task, job.

ta'rifa f tariff.

ta'rimba f bunk; (fig) army life; **ter** ~ to be an old hand; **tarimbado/a** adj experienced.

tartamude'ar vi to stammer, stutter; **tartamudo/a** m/f stammerer, stutterer.

tarta'ruga f turtle.

tas = **te** + **as**.

'tasca f (Pt) cheap eating place.

'tático/a (Pt: -ct-) adj tactical // f tactics pl.

'tato (Pt: -ct-) m (sentido) touch; (prudência) tact.

ta'tu m armadillo.

tatuagem [ta'twaʒẽ] f tattoo.

tauromaquia [tawroma'kia] f bullfighting.

tavão [ta'vãw] m horsefly.

taxa ['taʃa] f (imposto) tax; (preço) fixed price, fee; ~ **de câmbio** exchange rate; ~ **de juros** interest rate; **taxar** vt (fixar o preço de) to fix the price of; (lançar impostos sobre) to tax.

'táxi m taxi, cab.

'tcheco/a adj, m/f Czech; **Tcheco-Eslováquia** f Czechoslovakia.

te pron you.

tear [tʃ'ax] m loom.

teatral [tʃia'traw] adj theatrical; **teatro** m theatre, theater (US); (obras) plays pl, dramatic works pl.

tecelão/lã [tese'lãw/'lã] m/f weaver; **tecer** vt to weave; (fig) to contrive, devise; **tecido** m cloth, material; (MED) tissue.

'tecla f (MÚS, máquina de escrever) key; **teclado** m keyboard.

'técnico/a adj technical // m/f technician; (especialista) expert // f technique.

'tédio m tedium; (aborrecimento) boredom; **tedioso/a** adj tedious; (aborrecido) boring.

teia ['teja] f (enredo) intrigue, plot; ~ **de aranha** spider's web.

teimar [tej'max] vi: ~ **em** to insist on; (persistir) to persist in; **teimoso/a** adj obstinate, persistent.

teixo ['tejʃu] m yew.

tela ['tela] f (tecido) fabric, material; (de pintar) canvas; (cinema, televisão) screen.

tele... ['tɛli] pref tele...; ~**comando** m remote control; ~**comunicação** f telecommunications *pl*; **~férico** *m* cable car; **~fonar** *vt/i* to telephone, phone; (*col*) to ring; **~fone** *m* phone, telephone; **~fonema** *m* phone call; **~fónico/a** *adj* telephone *cmp*; **~fonista** *m/f* telephonist; **~grafar** *vt/i* to telegraph, wire; **~grama** *m* telegram, cable; **~guiado/a** *adj* remote-controlled; **~impressor** *m* teleprinter; **telêmetro** *m* rangefinder; **~objetiva** (*Pt*: -ct-) *f* telephoto lens; **~pático/a** *adj* telepathic; **~scópico/a** *adj* telescopic; **~scópio** *m* telescope; **~spetador(a)** (*Pt*: -ct-) *m/f* viewer; **~tipista** *m/f* teletypist; **~tipo** *m* teletype; **~visão** *f* television; **~visar** *vt* to televise; **~visor** *m* (*aparelho*) television (set), TV (set).

telex ['tɛlɛks] *m* telex.

telha ['teʎa] *f* tile; **ter uma ~ de menos** to have a screw loose; **telhado** *m* roof; **telhudo/a** *adj* crazy.

'tema *m* theme; (*assunto*) subject.

te'mer *vt* to fear, be afraid of.

teme'rário/a *adj* reckless, foolhardy; **temeridade** *f* recklessness, foolhardiness.

teme'roso/a *adj* fearful, afraid; **temível** *adj* fearsome, terrible; **temor** *m* fear, dread.

'têmpera *f* (*de metais*) tempering; (*caráter*) temperament; (*pintura*) distemper, tempera; **temperado/a** *adj* (*metal*) tempered; (*clima*) temperate; **temperamento** *m* temperament, nature; **temperar** *vt* (*metal*) to temper, harden; (*comida*) to season.

tempera'tura *f* temperature.

tem'pero *m* seasoning, flavouring.

tempestade [tēpɛʃ'tadʒɪ] *f* storm, tempest; **~ em copo de agua** storm in a teacup; **tempestuoso/a** *adj* stormy; (*fig*) tempestuous.

'templo *m* temple; (*igreja*) church.

'tempo *m* (*no relógio*) time; (*meteorológico*) weather; (*gramática*) tense; **bom/mau ~** fine/bad weather; **a ~** on time; **ao mesmo ~** at the same time; **de ~ em ~** from time to time; **no ~ da onça/há muito ~** a long time ago; **levar ~** to take time; **temporada** *f* season; (*espaço*) spell; **temporal** *adj* secular, worldly // *m* storm, gale; **temporário/a** *adj* temporary, provisional.

tenaci'dade *f* tenacity; **tenaz** *adj* tenacious; (*teimoso*) stubborn // *f* tongs *pl*.

tencio'nar *vt/i* to intend, plan.

'tenda *f* (*barraca*) tent; (*de mercado*) stall.

ten'dência *f* tendency, inclination; **tendencioso/a** *adj* tendentious, biassed; **tender** *vi* to tend to, have a tendency to.

tene'broso/a *adj* dark, gloomy.

tenente [te'nètʃɪ] *m* lieutenant.

'tênia *f* tapeworm.

'tênis *m* (*jogo*) tennis; (*sapatos*) training shoes; **tenista** *m/f* tennis player.

'tenro/a *adj* tender; (*brando*) soft; (*delicado*) delicate; (*novo*) young.

tensão [tē'sãw] *f* (*ger*) tension; (*pressão*) pressure, strain; (*rigidez*) tightness; (*TEC*) stress; (*ELET.* *voltagem*) voltage; **tenso/a** *adj* tense; (*sob pressão*) under stress, strained.

'tenta *f* (*MED*) probe.

tentação [tēta'sãw] *f* temptation.

ten'táculo *m* tentacle.

tenta'dor(a) *adj* tempting; (*sedutor*) inviting // *m* tempter // *f* temptress; **tentar** *vt/i* (*intentar*) to try, attempt; (*seduzir*) to tempt, entice; **tentativa** *f* try, attempt.

tente'ar *vt* (*sondar*) to probe; (*apalpar*) to grope (for).

'tento *m* attention, care; (*casino*) chip; (*ponto*) point; (*futebol*) goal.

tênue ['tenuɪ] *adj* tenuous; (*fino*) thin; (*delicado*) delicate; **tenuidade** *f* tenuousness.

teologia [tʃɪolo'ʒɪa] *f* theology; **teólogo** *m* theologian.

te'or *m* (*conteúdo*) tenor; (*sentido*) meaning, drift; (*norma*) system; (*QUÍM*) grade.

teo'ria *f* theory; **teórico/a** *adj* theoretical.

'tépido/a *adj* tepid, lukewarm.

ter *vt* to have; (*na mão*) to hold; (*considerar*) to consider; (*conter*) to hold, contain; (*possuir*) to have, possess; **~ fome** to be hungry; **~ frio/calor** to be cold/hot; **~ razão** to be right; **ela tem 5 anos** she is 5 years old; **tem 10 metros de largura** it is 10 metres wide; **~ que/de** to have to, must; **~ o que dizer/fazer** to have something to say/do; **~ a ver com** to concern, have to do with; **tem telefone aqui?** is there a phone here?; **ir ~ com** (*Pt*) to (go and) meet; **~-se** *vr*: **~-se por** to consider o.s.

terça-feira [tɛxsa-'fejra] *f* Tuesday; **~ gorda** Shrove Tuesday.

terceiro/a [tɛx'sejra] *adj* third; **terço** *m* third (part).

tergiversar [tɛxʒɪvɛx'sax] *vi* to prevaricate, evade the issue.

ter'mal *adj* thermal; **termas** *fpl* spa *sg*, hot springs.

terminação [tɛxmɪna'sãw] *f* (*LING*) ending; **terminal** *adj* terminal // *m* (*de rede, ELET*) terminal; **terminantemente** *adv* categorically, expressly; **terminar** *vt/i* to finish, end; **término** *m* (*fim*) end, termination.

termite [tɛx'mɪtʃɪ] *f* termite.

'termo *m* (*fim*) end, termination; (*limite*) limit, boundary; (*prazo*) period; (*vocábulo*) term, expression; (*Pt*: *garrafa*) (thermos) flask; **~ médio** average; **pôr ~ a** to put an end to.

ter'mômetro *m* thermometer.

'terno/a *adj* gentle, tender // *m* (*de pessoas*) trio, threesome; (*em cartas*) three; (*Br: roupa*) suit; **ternura** *f* gentleness, tenderness.

'terra *f* (*mundo*) earth, world; (*pátria*) homeland; (*solo*) ground; (*terreno*) soil, earth; ~ **firme** dry land; **terraço** *m* terrace; **terramoto** *m* (*Pt*) earthquake; **terreiro** *m* yard, square; **terremoto** *m* earthquake.

ter'reno *m* ground, land; (*porção de terra*) plot of land; (*GEO*) terrain; (*terra*) soil; **térreo/a** *adj* ground level *cmp*; **andar térreo** (*Br*) ground floor, first floor (*US*); **terrestre** *adj* terrestrial, land *cmp*; (*mundano*) worldly.

ter'rina *f* tureen.

terri'tório *m* territory; (*distrito*) district, region.

ter'rível *adj* terrible, dreadful; **terror** *m* terror, dread; **terrorismo** *m* terrorism; **terrorista** *m/f* terrorist.

ter'túlia *f* gathering (of friends).

tesão [te'zãw] *m* (*col*) randiness; (*pessoa*) turn-on.

tese ['tezɪ] *f* thesis; (*proposição*) proposition, theory.

'teso/a *adj* (*tenso*) tense, taut; (*hirto*) erect, upright; (*imóvel*) immovable; (*col*) **estar** ~ to be broke *ou* skint.

tesoura [te'zora] *f* scissors *pl*; (*fig*) backbiter; **uma** ~ a pair of scissors.

tesoureiro/a *m/f* [tezo'rejru/a] treasurer; **tesouro** *m* treasure; (*COM*) treasury, exchequer.

'testa *f* brow, forehead; **à** ~ **de** at the head of; ~-**de-ferro** *f* figurehead, dummy.

testa'mento *m* will, testament; **Velho/Novo T** ~ Old/New Testament.

teste ['tɛʃtʃɪ] *m* test, exam.

testemunha [teʃtʃɪ'muɲa] *f* witness; ~ **ocular** eyewitness; **testemunhar** *vi* to testify // *vt* to give evidence of, reveal; **testemunho** *m* evidence, testimony; **dar testemunho** to give evidence.

tes'tudo/a *adj* big-headed; (*fig*) stubborn, headstrong.

'teta *f* teat, nipple.

'teto (*Pt: -ct-*) *m* ceiling; (*telhado*) roof.

'tétrico/a *adj* gloomy, dismal; (*horrível*) horrible, frightening.

teu/tua [tew/'tua] *adj* your // *pron* yours.

'teve *vb ver* **ter**.

te'vê *f* telly.

'têxtil *m, pl* **têxteis** textile.

texto ['teʃtu] *m* text.

tex'tura *f* texture.

texugo [te'ʃugu] *m* badger.

tez *f* complexion; (*pele*) skin.

ti *pron* you.

'tia *f ver* **tio**.

'tíbia *f* shinbone.

tibi'eza *f* tepidness; (*fig*) half-heartedness; **tíbio/a** *adj* tepid, lukewarm; (*fig*) unenthusiastic.

'tifo *m* typhoid, typhus.

tigela [tʃɪ'ʒela] *f* bowl.

tigre ['tʃɪgrɪ] *m* tiger; **tigresa** *f* tigress.

tijolo [tʃɪ'ʒolu] *m* brick.

til *m* tilde.

timão [tʃɪ'mãw] *m* (*NÁUT*) helm, tiller.

timbre ['tʃɪmbrɪ] *m* insignia, emblem; (*selo*) stamp; (*MÚS*) tone, timbre.

time ['tʃɪmɪ] *m* (*Br*) team.

timi'dez *f* shyness, timidity; **tímido/a** *adj* shy, timid.

timoneiro [tʃɪmo'nejru] *m* helmsman, coxswain.

'tímpano *m* eardrum; (*MÚS*) kettledrum.

'tina *f* (*banheira*) tub; (*vasilha*) vat.

tingir [tʃɪ'ʒix] *vt* to dye; (*fig*) to tinge.

'tinha *etc vb ver* **ter**.

ti'nir *vi* to jingle, tinkle.

'tino *m* (*juízo*) discernment, judgement; (*intuição*) intuition; **perder o** ~ to lose one's senses; **ter** ~ **para algo** to have a flair for sth.

'tinta *f* (*de pintar*) paint; (*de escrever*) ink; (*para tingir*) dye, stain; (*vestígio*) hint, touch; **tinteiro** *m* inkwell; **tinto/a** *adj* dyed, stained; **vinho tinto** red wine; **tintura** *f* dye; (*vestígio*) hint, touch; **tinturaria** *f* dyer's; (*lavanderia*) launderette; (*: a seco*) dry-cleaners.

'tio/a *m* uncle // *f* aunt.

'típico/a *adj* typical, characteristic; **tipo** *m* (*ger*) type; (*de imprensa*) print; (*classe*) kind; (*homem*) guy, chap; **tipografia** *f* printing, typography; (*estabelecimento*) printing office, printer's; **tipógrafo** *m* printer.

tique ['tʃɪkɪ] *m* habit, idiosyncrasy; (*MED*) twitch, tic.

'tira *f* strip; (*Br: col*) cop.

'tiracolo *m*: **a** ~ slung from the shoulder.

'tirada *f* (*de caminho, tempo*) stretch; **tiragem** *f* (*dum livro*) edition.

tira-'manchas *m inv* stain remover.

tira'nia *f* tyranny.

ti'rano/a *adj* tyrannical // *m* tyrant.

tirante [tʃɪ'ratʃɪ] *m* (*de arreio*) trace; (*MEC*) driving rod; (*viga*) tie beam // *prep* except; **tirar** *vt* (*retirar*) to remove, take away; (*sacar*) to take out, draw; (*puxar*) to pull; (*roupa*) to take off, remove; **sem tirar nem pôr** exactly, precisely; **tirar uma fotografia** to take a photograph.

tiri'tar *vi* to shiver.

'tiro *m* (*disparo*) shot; (*ato de disparar*) shooting, firing; (*de bois*) team; ~ **ao alvo** target practice; **sair o** ~ **pela culatra** (*fig*) to backfire.

tirocínio [tʃɪro'sinju] *m* apprenticeship, training.

tiroteio [tʃɪro'teju] *m* shooting, exchange of shots.

'tísico/a *adj* consumptive // *f* consumption.

tis'nar *vt* to smudge; (*enegrecer*) to blacken.

'títere ['tʃɪterɪ] *m* puppet.

titube'ar *vi* (*cambalear*) to totter, stagger; (*vacilar*) to hesitate.

titu'lar *adj* titular // *m* holder; (*POL*) minister // *vt* to title; **título** *m* title;

(COM) bond, certificate; *(universitário)* degree; **a título de** by way of, as.

'tive *etc vb ver* **ter.**

to = **te** + **o.**

'toa *f* towrope; **à ~** at random.

to'ada *f* tune, melody; *(boato)* rumour.

toalha [to'aʎa] *f* towel; **~ de mesa** tablecloth.

to'ar *vi* to sound, resound.

'toca *f* burrow, hole; *(refúgio)* hiding place.

toca-'discos *m inv (Br)* record-player.

tocante [to'kãtʃi] *adj* moving, touching; **no ~ a** regarding, concerning; **tocar** *vt* to touch, feel; *(MUS)* to play; *(campainha)* to ring; *(comover)* to move, touch; **pelo que me toca** as far as I am concerned; **tocar em algo** to touch upon sth.

'toco *m* tree stump; *(cigarro)* stub.

toda'via *adv* yet, still, however.

'todo/a *adj* all; *(inteiro)* whole, entire; *(cada)* every; **a ~a velocidade** at full speed; **~a a gente** *(Pt)*, **~ o mundo** *(Br)* everyone, everybody; **em ~a a parte** everywhere; **~s nós** all of us; **~s os dias** *ou* **~ dia** every day; **~ o dia** all day // *m* whole; **ao ~** altogether; **de ~** completely; **todos** *mpl* everybody *sg*, everyone *sg*; **~-poderoso/a** *adj* almighty, all-powerful // *m*: **o T~-poderoso** the Almighty.

'toga *f* toga; *(EDUC)* gown.

toicinho [toj'siɲu] *m* bacon fat.

tojo [to'ʒu] *m* gorse.

'toldo *m* awning, sun blind.

toleima [to'lejma] *f* folly, stupidity.

tole'rância *f* *(liberalidade)* broadmindedness, tolerance; *(indulgência)* toleration, forbearance; **tolerante** *adj* broadminded, understanding; **tolerar** *vt* *(permitir)* to tolerate, allow; *(aguentar)* to put up with, bear; **tolerável** *adj* tolerable, bearable; *(admissível)* passable.

tolher [to'ʎex] *vt* to impede, hinder.

tolice [to'lisi] *f* stupidity, foolishness; **tolo/a** *adj* foolish, mad, stupid.

tom [tõ] *m* tone; *(inflexão)* intonation; *(cor)* shade.

to'mada *f* capture; *(ELET)* socket; **tomar** *vt* to take; *(capturar)* to capture, seize; *(decisão)* to make; *(bebida)* to take, have; **tomar-se** *vr*: **tomar-se de** to be overcome with.

tomate [to'matʃi] *m* tomato.

tom'bar *vi* to fall down, tumble down // *vt* to knock down, knock over; *(conservar un edifício)* to list; **tombo** *m* *(queda)* tumble, fall; *(registro)* archives *pl*, records *pl*.

tomilho [to'miʎu] *m* thyme.

'tomo *m* tome, volume.

'tona *f* surface; **vir à ~** to come to the surface; *(fig)* to come to light.

to'nel *m* cask, barrel.

tone'lada *f* ton; **tonelagem** *f* tonnage.

'tônico/a *adj* tonic; **nota ~a** keynote;

acento ~ stress // *f* tonic; **tonificante** *adj* invigorating.

toninha [to'niɲa] *f* porpoise.

'tono *m* air, melody; *(TEC)* tone.

ton'teira *f* *(tontice)* nonsense; *(vertigem)* dizziness; **tontice** *f* stupidity, nonsense; **tonto/a** *adj* stupid, silly; *(zonzo)* dizzy, lightheaded; **às tontas** impulsively; **tontura** *f* dizziness, lightheadedness.

to'par *vt* to meet, come across; *(col)* to fancy, agree to; **você topa um sorvete?** do you fancy an ice cream?; **~ com** to meet, come across.

tope ['tɔpi] *m (cimo)* summit, top.

'tópico/a *adj* topical // *m* topic; *(tema)* subject.

'topo *m* *(cimo)* top, summit; *(extremidade)* end, extremity.

toque ['tɔki] *m* *(contato)* touch, contact; *(instrumento musical)* playing; *(campainha)* ringing; *(corneta)* bugle call; *(vestígio)* trace, touch.

toranja [to'rãʒa] *f* grapefruit.

torção [tox'sãw] *m* twist, twisting; *(MED)* sprain.

torce'dura *f* twist; *(torção)* sprain; **torcer** *vt* to twist; *(direção)* to turn; *(produzir torção em)* to sprain; *(desvirtuar)* to distort, misconstrue; *(esporte)* to support; **torcer-se** *vr* to squirm, writhe.

torcida [tox'sida] *f* *(mecha)* wick; *(esporte: ato de torcer)* supporting; *(: adeptos)* supporters.

'tordo *m* thrush.

tor'menta *f* storm.

tor'mento *m* torment, torture; *(angústia)* anguish.

tormen'toso/a *adj* stormy, tempestuous.

tor'nado *m* tornado.

tor'nar *vi* *(voltar)* to return, go back; **~ a fazer algo** to do sth again // *vt* to render, make; **~-se** *vr* to become.

torne'ar *vt* to turn (on a lathe), shape.

torneio [tox'neju] *m* tournament.

torneira [tox'nejra] *f* tap, faucet *(US)*.

torniquete [toxni'ketʃi] *m* *(MED)* tourniquet; *(Pt: roleta)* turnstile.

'torno *m* lathe; **em ~ de** around, about.

torno'zelo *m* ankle.

torpe ['toxpi] *adj* obscene, vile.

tor'pedo *m* torpedo.

tor'peza *f* obscenity, vileness.

tor'rada *f* toast; **torradeira** *f* toaster.

torrão [to'xãw] *m* turf, sod; *(terra)* soil, land; *(de açúcar)* lump; **~ natal** native land.

tor'rar *vt* *(pão)* to toast; *(café)* to roast; *(plantação)* to parch.

torre ['toxi] *f* tower; *(duma igreja)* steeple, tower; *(xadrez)* castle, rook; **~ de vigia** watchtower.

torrefação [toxefa'sãw] *(Pt: -cç-)* *f* coffee-roasting house.

torrente [to'xẽtʃi] *f* torrent.

tor'resmo *m* crackling.

'tórrido/a *adj* torrid.

'torta *f* pie, tart.

'torto/a adj twisted, crooked; **a ~ e a direito** recklessly, indiscriminately; **tortuoso/a** adj winding.

tor'tura f torture; (fig) anguish, agony; **torturar** vt to torture; (fig) to torment.

torvelinho [torve'liɲu] m (vento) whirlwind; (água) whirlpool.

tos = te + os.

tosão [to'zãw] m fleece; **tosar** vt (ovelha) to shear; (cabelo) to crop.

'tosco/a adj rough, unpolished; (grosseiro) coarse, crude.

tosquiar [toʃki'ax] vt (ovelha) to shear, clip.

tosse ['tosi] f cough; **~ convulsa** ou **comprida** whooping cough; **tossir** vi to cough.

'tosta f (Pt) toast; **~ mista** toasted cheese and ham sandwich; **tostado/a** adj toasted; (pelo sol) tanned; **tostar** vt to toast; **tostar-se** vr to get tanned, get sunburnt.

to'tal adj total, complete // m total; **~idade** f totality, entirety; **~itário/a** adj totalitarian.

touca ['toka] f bonnet; (de freira) veil.

touca'dor m (penteadeira) dressing table.

toupeira [to'pejra] f mole; (fig) numbskull, idiot.

tou'rada f bullfight; **tourear** vi to fight (bulls); **touro** m bull; **pegar a touro a unha** to take the bull by the horns; **praça de touros** bullring.

'tóxico/a adj poisonous, toxic; **toxicômano/a** m/f drug addict.

trabalhador(a) [trabaʎa'dox(ra)] adj hard-working, industrious // m/f worker, labourer; **trabalhar** vi to work, labour; (máquina) to work, function // vt (máquina) to work, operate; (o solo) to till, work; **trabalhista** adj labour; **Partido Trabalhista** Labour Party; **trabalho** m work, labour; (emprego) occupation, job; **trabalho braçal** manual work; **trabalhos forçados** hard labour, forced labour; **trabalhoso/a** adj laborious, arduous.

'traça f moth.

tra'çado m sketch, plan.

tração [tra'sãw] (Pt: -cç-) f traction, pull.

tra'çar vt to draw; (delinear) to trace, outline; **traço** m (linha) line, dash; (de lápis) stroke; (vestígio) trace, vestige; (caráter) feature, trait.

tradição [tradʒi'sãw] f tradition; **tradicional** adj traditional.

tradução [tradu'sãw] f translation; **tradutor(a)** m/f translator; **traduzir** vt to translate.

'tráfego m (trânsito) traffic.

trafi'cante m/f trafficker, dealer; **traficar** vi to trade, deal; **tráfico** m traffic.

tra'gar vt to swallow; (fumaça) to inhale; (suportar) to tolerate.

tragédia [tra'ʒedʒja] f tragedy;

trágico/a adj tragic; **tragicomédia** f tragicomedy.

'trago m mouthful, gulp; (dose) shot // vb ver **trazer**.

traição [trai'sãw] f treason, treachery; (deslealdade) betrayal, disloyalty; **traiçoeiro/a** adj treacherous; (infiel) disloyal; **traidor(a)** m traitor // f traitress.

traineira [traj'nejra] f trawler.

tra'ir vt to betray, be disloyal to.

trajar [tra'ʒax] vt to wear; **~-se** vr: **~-se de preto** to be dressed in black; **traje** m dress, clothes pl; **traje de banho** bathing costume; **traje de noite** evening gown; **traje a rigor** evening dress; **traje de passeio** informal dress.

trajeto [tra'ʒetu] (Pt: -ct-) m course, path; **trajetória** (Pt: -ct-) f trajectory, path.

tralha ['traʎa] f fishing net; (col) junk.

'trama f (tecido) woof; (enredo) scheme, plot; **tramar** vt (tecer) to weave; (intrigar) to scheme, plot.

trambolhão [trambo'ʎãw] m tumble; **andar aos trambolhões** to stumble along; **trambolho** m encumbrance.

trâmite ['tramitʃi] m path; (fig) course; **~s** mpl (fig) procedure sg; (JUR) channels.

tramóia [tra'mɔja] f (fraude) swindle, trick; (trama) plot, scheme.

tramon'tana f Pole star; **perder a ~** to lose one's bearings.

trampolim [trampo'lĩ] m trampoline; (de piscina) diving board; (fig) springboard.

trampoli'nagem f trick, swindle; **trampolineiro** m trickster, swindler; **trampolinice** f trick, swindle.

'tranca f (de uma porta) bolt.

'trança f (cabelo) lock; (galão) braid; **~s** fpl plaits.

tran'car vt (porta) to bar, bolt.

tranqüilidade [trãkwili'dadʒi] f tranquillity; (paz) peacefulness; (calma) calm; **tranqüilizar** vt to calm, quieten; **tranqüilo/a** adj tranquil; (quieto) quiet; (calmo) calm; (pacífico) peaceful.

'transa f (Br: namoro) affair.

transação [trãza'sãw] (Pt: -cç-) f transaction, deal.

tran'sado/a adj: **bem ~** well made.

transat'lântico/a adj transatlantic // m (transatlantic) liner.

transbor'dar vi to overflow; **transbordo** m (de viajantes) change, transfer.

transcor'rer vi to elapse, go by.

transe ['trãzi] m ordeal; (lance) plight; **a todo ~** at all costs.

transeunte [trãz'jũtʃi] m/f passer-by, pedestrian.

transfe'rir vt to transfer.

transfigu'rar vt to transfigure, transform.

transformação [trãʃfoxma'sãw] f transformation; **transformador** m

(*ELET*) transformer; **transformar** *vt* to transform, change.

'**trânsfuga** *m* (*desertor*) deserter; (*político*) renegade, turncoat.

transfusão [trãʃfuˈzãw] *f* transfusion; ~ **de sangue** blood transfusion.

transgre'dir *vt* to transgress, infringe; **transgressão** *f* transgression, infringement.

transição [trãziˈsãw] *f* transition, change.

tran'sido/a *adj* numb, benumbed.

transigente [trãziˈʒetʃi] *adj* willing to compromise; **transigir** *vi* to compromise, make concessions.

transi'tar *vt* (*percorrer*) to go through // *vi*: ~ **por** to move about/through; **transitável** *adj* (*caminho*) passable; **transitivo/a** *adj* (*LING*) transitive; **trânsito** *m* transit, passage; (*na rua: veículos*) traffic; (: *pessoas*) flow; **transitório/a** *adj* transitory, passing.

transmissão [trãʒmiˈsãw] *f* (*RÁDIO, TV*) transmission, broadcast; (*transferência*) transfer; **transmitir** *vt* (*RÁDIO, TV*) to broadcast, transmit; (*transferir*) to transfer.

transparente [trãʒpaˈretʃi] *adj* transparent; (*roupa*) seethrough; (*evidente*) clear, obvious.

transpi'rar *vi* (*suar*) to perspire, sweat; (*divulgar-se*) to become known, transpire.

transplan'tar *vt* to transplant; **transplante** *m* transplant.

trans'por *vt* to cross over, span; (*inverter*) to transpose.

transpor'tar *vt* (*levar*) to transport, carry; (*enlevar*) to entrance, enrapture; ~-**se** *vr* to be entranced; **transporte** *m* transport, conveyance; (*COM*) haulage; (*contas*) amount carried forward; (*êxtase*) rapture, delight.

transtor'nar *vt* to upset; ~-**se** *vr* to get upset; **transtorno** *m* upset, disturbance.

transver'sal *adj* transverse, cross.

transvi'ado/a *adj* wayward, erring; **transviar** *vt* to lead astray; **transviar-se** *vr* to go astray.

tra'paça *f* swindle, fraud; **trapaceiro/a** *adj* crooked, cheating // *m/f* swindler, cheat.

trapalhada [trapaˈʎada] *f* confusion, mix up; **trapalhão/lhona** *m/f* bungler, blunderer.

'**trapo** *m* rag, cloth.

traquéia [traˈkeja] *f* windpipe.

traquinas [traˈkinaʃ] *adj* *inv* mischievous.

tra'rei *etc vb ver* **trazer**.

trás *prep, adv* after, behind; **para** ~ backwards; **por** ~ **de** behind; **traseiro/a** *adj* back, rear // *m* (*ANAT*) bottom, behind // *f* rear.

trasla'dar *vt* to remove, transfer; (*copiar*) to transcribe; **traslado** *m* (*cópia*) copy; (*deslocamento*) removal, transference.

traspas'sar *vt* (*atravessar*) to cross; (*penetrar*) to pierce, penetrate; (*exceder*) to exceed, overstep; (*transferir*) to transmit, transfer; (*Pt: sublocar*) to sublet; **traspasse** *m* transfer; (*sublocação*) sublease, sublet.

traste ['traʃtʃi] *m* (*ger*) piece of junk; (*móvel*) old piece of furniture; (*fig*) rogue, rascal.

tra'tado *m* treaty, pact; (*obra*) treatise.

trata'mento *m* treatment; (*título*) title.

tratante [traˈtãtʃi] *m* crook, swindler.

tra'tar *vt* to treat; (*tema*) to deal with, cover; ~ **com** (*COM*) to deal with; ~ **de** (*assunto*) to discuss, attend to; ~ **por** to address as; **de que se trata?** what is it about?; **trata-se de** it is a question of; **tratável** *adj* treatable; (*afável*) approachable, amenable; **trato** *m* (*tratamento*) treatment; (*contrato*) agreement, contract; **maus tratos** illtreatment.

tra'tor (*Pt: -ct-*) *m* tractor.

trautear [trawteˈax] *vt* to hum; (*col*) to annoy, pester // *vi* to hum.

travão [traˈvãw] *m* (*Pt*) brake; **travar** *vt* (*roda*) to lock; (*iniciar*) to engage in; (*conversa*) to strike up; **travar amizade com** to become friendly with, make friends with // *vi* (*Pt*) to brake.

trave ['travi] *f* beam, crossbeam; (*esporte*) crossbar.

tra'vés *m* slant, incline; **de** ~ across, sideways; **olhar de** ~ to look sideways (at); **travessa** *f* crossbeam, crossbar; (*rua*) lane, alley; **travessão** *m* (*de balança*) bar, beam; (*pontuação*) dash.

travesseiro [traveˈsejru] *m* pillow; **consultar o** ~ to sleep on it, think it over.

traves'sia *f* (*viagem*) journey, crossing.

tra'vesso/a *adj* mischievous, naughty; (*atravessado*) cross, transverse; **travessura** *f* mischief, prank.

'**travo** *m* bitterness, sourness.

tra'zer *vt* to bring; (*roupa*) to wear; (*causar*) to bring about, cause; ~ **à memória** to bring to mind.

trecho ['treʃu] *m* (*extrato*) passage; (*parte*) stretch.

trégua ['tregwa] *f* truce; (*descanso*) respite, rest.

treinar [trejˈnax] *vt*, **treinar-se** *vr* to train; **treino** *m* training.

'**trela** *f* (*correia*) lead, leash; (*col: conversa*) chat; **dar** ~ **a** to chat with; (*encorajar*) to lead on.

trem [trẽj] *m* train; **trens** *mpl* (*col*) gear *sg*, belongings *pl*; (*Pt: carruagem*) carriage, coach; ~ **de carga** freight train; ~ **correio** mail train; ~ **de cozinha** kitchen utensils *pl*; ~ **de aterrissagem** (*avião*) landing gear.

treme'dal *m* bog, quagmire.

tremeli'car *vi* to tremble, shiver.

tremelu'zir *vi* to twinkle, glimmer.

tre'mendo/a *adj* (*formidável*) tremendous, enormous; (*terrível*) terrible, awful; **tremer** vi to shudder, quake; **tremor** m tremor, trembling.

trempe ['trẽpɪ] f tripod.

tremu'lar vi (bandeira) to flutter, wave; (luz) to glimmer, flicker; **trêmulo/a** adj shaky, trembling.

'**trena** f tape-measure.

tre'nó m sledge, sleigh.

trens mpl ver **trem**.

trepadeira [trɛpa'dejra] f creeper, climbing plant; **trepar** vt to climb // vt/i (col) to screw.

trepidação [trɛpɪda'sãw] f shaking; **trepidar** vi to tremble, shake.

três num three.

tresan'dar vt (fazer andar para trás) to turn back; (transtornar) to upset // vi to stink, reek.

tresloucado/a [treʒlo'kadu/a] adj crazy, deranged.

tresmalhar [treʒma'ʎax] vt (deixar fugir) to let escape; (dispersar) to scatter, disperse // vi to stray.

trespa'ssar vt ver **traspassar**; **trespasse** m ver **traspasse**.

'**trevas** fpl darkness sg; (estupidez) ignorance.

'**trevo** m clover.

treze ['trezɪ] num thirteen.

tre'zentos/as num three hundred.

triangular [trɪãgu'lax] adj triangular; **triângulo** m triangle.

'**tribo** f tribe.

tribulação [tribula'sãw] f tribulation, affliction.

tri'buna f platform, rostrum; (REL) pulpit; **tribunal** m court; (comissão) tribunal.

tribu'tar vt (impor impostos a) to tax; (render) to render; **tributo** m tribute.

tri'cô m knitting; **tricotar** vt/i to knit.

'**trigo** m wheat; **trigueiro/a** adj dark, swarthy.

tri'lar vi to warble, trill.

trilhado/a [trɪ'ʎadu/a] adj (pisado) well-worn, well-trodden; **trilhar** vt (vereda) to tread, wear; **trilho** m (Br: FERRO) rail; (vereda) path, track.

trimestre [trɪ'mɛʃtrɪ] m (período) term, quarter; (pagamento) quarterly payment.

tri'nado m warbling, singing.

tri'ncar vt to crunch; (morder) to bite // vi to crunch.

trinchar [trɪ'ʃax] vt to carve.

trincheira [trɪ'ʃejra] f (escavação) trench; (barreira) barrier.

'**trinco** m latch.

trindade [trɪ'dadʒɪ] f trinity; ~**s** fpl angelus sg.

'**trinta** num thirty.

'**trio** m trio.

'**tripa** f gut, intestine; ~**s** fpl bowels, guts; (CULIN) tripe sg; **comer a ~ forra** to gorge o.s.; **fazer das ~s coração** to pluck up courage.

tri'pé m tripod.

tripulação [tripula'sãw] f crew;

tripulante m crew member; **tripular** vt to man.

'**trismo** m lockjaw.

triste ['triʃtʃɪ] adj sad, unhappy; (sombrio) miserable, wretched; **tristeza** f sadness, unhappiness; (mágoa) melancholy.

tritu'rar vt (moer) to grind; (argumento) to destroy, tear to pieces.

triunfar [triũ'fax] vi to triumph, win; **triunfo** m victory, triumph.

trivi'al adj (comum) common(place), ordinary; (insignificante) trivial, trifling.

triz m: **por um ~** by the skin of one's teeth; **escapar por um ~** to have a narrow escape.

'**troca** f exchange, swap; **em ~ de** in exchange for.

'**troça** f ridicule, mockery; **fazer ~ de** to make fun of.

troca'dilho m pun, play on words.

tro'car vt to exchange, swap; (substituir) to change, replace; ~ **dinheiro** to change money.

tro'çar vt to ridicule, make fun of; **trocista** m/f joker, wag.

'**troco** m (dinheiro) change; (réplica) retort, rejoinder; **a ~ de** in exchange for.

'**troço** m (pedaço) piece, portion; (Br: coisa inútil) thingummyjig; (: coisa) thing.

troféu [tro'fɛw] m trophy.

'**tromba** f (do elefante) trunk; (de outro animal) snout; ~-**d'água** f waterspout.

trom'beta f (MÚS) trumpet, bugle; **trombone** m (MÚS) trombone; **trompa** f (MÚS) horn.

tronchar [trõ'ʃax] vt to cut off, chop off.

'**tronco** m (de árvore) trunk; (de corpo) torso, trunk; (de família) lineage; (: fig) stock.

'**trono** m throne.

'**tropa** f troop, gang; (MIL) troop; (exército) army; **ir para a ~** (Pt) to join the army.

trope'çar vi to stumble, trip; (fig) to blunder; ~ **em dificuldades** to meet with difficulties; **tropeço** m obstacle, hindrance; **pedra de tropeço** stumbling block.

'**trôpego/a** adj shaky, unsteady.

tro'pel m (ruído) uproar, tumult; (confusão) confusion, throng; (estrépito de pés) stamping of feet; **tropelia** f tumult, confusion.

tropi'cal adj tropical; **trópico** m tropic.

tro'tar vi to trot; **trote** m trot.

trouxa ['troʃa] f bundle of clothes; (col: pessoa) sucker.

'**trouxe** etc vb ver **trazer**.

'**trova** f ballad, folksong; ~**dor** m troubadour, minstrel.

trovão [tro'vãw] m clap of thunder; **trovejar** vi to thunder; **trovoada** f thunderstorm; **trovoar** vi to thunder.

truão [tru'ãw] m clown, buffoon.

truci'dar vt to butcher, slaughter.

trun'car vt to chop off, cut off; (texto) to mutilate.

'trunfo *m* trump card.

truque ['trukɪ] *m* (*ardil*) trick, dodge; (*publicitário*) gimmick.

'truta *f* trout.

tu *pron* (*Pt*) you; **tua** *adj, pron ver* **teu**.

tubarão [tuba'rãw] *m* shark.

tu'bérculo *m* tuber.

tuberculose [tubɛxku'lozɪ] *f* tuberculosis, T.B.

'tubo *m* tube, pipe; ~ **de ensaio** test tube.

tu'cano *m* toucan.

'tudo *pron* all, everything; ~ **quanto** everything that; **antes de** ~ first of all.

tufão [tu'fãw] *m* typhoon, hurricane.

'tufo *m* tuft.

tu'gúrio *m* (*cabana*) hut, shack; (*refúgio*) shelter.

tulha ['tuʎa] *f* (*arca*) bin, store; (*celeiro*) granary.

tu'lipa *f* tulip.

'tumba *f* (*sepultura*) tomb; (*lápide*) tombstone.

tu'mido/a *adj* (*dilatado*) swollen.

tu'mor *m* tumour.

tu'multo *m* tumult, uproar; **tumultuar** *vt* to rouse, incite; **tumultuoso/a** *adj* tumultuous; (*revolto*) stormy.

'tunda *f* thrashing, beating; (*fig*) dressing-down.

'túnel *m* tunnel.

'túnica *f* tunic.

'turba *f* throng, crowd; ~ **multa** mob.

turbante [tux'bãtʃɪ] *m* turban.

tur'bar *vt* (*escurecer*) to darken, cloud; (*perturbar*) to upset, perturb; ~-**se** *vr* (*inquietar-se*) to be troubled *ou* upset.

turbilhão [tuxbɪ'ʎãw] *m* (*de vento*) whirlwind; (*de água*) whirlpool.

turbu'lência *f* turbulence; **turbulento/a** *adj* turbulent, stormy.

'turco/a *adj* Turkish // *m/f* Turk // *m* (*língua*) Turkish.

'turfa *f* peat.

túrgido/a ['tuxʒɪdu/a] *adj* swollen, bloated.

tu'rismo *m* tourism; (*indústria*) tourist industry; **turista** *m/f* tourist; **turístico/a** *adj* tourist *cmp*.

'turma *f* group, gang; (*turno*) shift.

'turno *m* shift, period of work; **por** ~**s** alternately, by turns, in turn.

Tur'quia [tux'kia] *f* Turkey.

'turra *f* (*disputa*) argument, dispute; **andar às** ~**s** to be at loggerheads.

tur'var *vt* (*tornar opaco*) to cloud, obscure; (*escurecer*) to darken; ~-**se** *vr* to become clouded; **turvo/a** *adj* (*opaco*) clouded, muddy.

tu'tano *m* (*ANAT*) marrow.

tu'tela *f* protection, guardianship; **tutelar** *adj* protecting, guardian; **anjo tutelar** guardian angel // *vt* to watch over, protect; **tutor(a)** *m/f* guardian.

TV *abr de* **televisão**.

U

'úbere *m* udder.

ubiqüidade [ubɪkwɪ'dadʒɪ] *f* ubiquity; **ubíquo/a** *adj* ubiquitous.

'ufa *excl* whew!

ufa'nar-se *vr* to boast; ~ **de** to take pride in, pride o.s. on.

'ufanismo *m* (*Br*) boastful nationalism, chauvinism.

uísque (*Pt*: **whisky**) ['wɪʃkɪ] *m* whisky, whiskey (*US*).

uivar [wɪ'vax] *vi* to howl; **uivo** *m* howl.

'úlcera *f* ulcer; **ulcerar** *vi* to ulcerate.

ulterior [ulterɪ'ox] *adj* (*além*) further, farther; (*depois*) later, subsequent; ~**mente** *adv* later on, subsequently.

ultimação [ultʃɪma'sãw] *f* conclusion, finishing; **ultimamente** *adv* (*há pouco*) recently, lately; **ultimar** *vt* to finish, bring to a conclusion; **ultimar-se** *vr* to come to a conclusion; **ultimato** *m* ultimatum; **último/a** *adj* final, last; (*mais recente*) latest; (*fig*) final, extreme; **por último** finally; **a(s) última(s)** the latest news; **estar nas últimas** to be on one's last legs.

ultrajar [ultra'ʒax] *vt* to insult, offend; **ultraje** *m* insult, offence.

ultra'mar *m* overseas; (*tinta*) ultramarine; ~**ino/a** *adj* overseas *cmp*; (*azul*) ultramarine.

ultrapas'sar *vt* (*atravessar*) to cross, go beyond; (*exceder*) to exceed, surpass; (*transgredir*) to overstep; (*AUTO*) to overtake.

ultra-som [ultra-'sõ] *m* ultrasound; **ultra-sônico/a** *adj* ultrasonic; (*MED*) ultrasound *cmp*; **ultra-sonografia** *f* ultrasound scanning.

ulu'lar *vi* to howl, wail.

um(a) [ũ/'uma] *art, pl* **uns/umas** [ũs/'umas] (*sg*) a; (*antes de vogal ou 'h' mudo*) an; (*pl*) some // **num one** // *pron* one; ~ **e outro** both; ~ **a** ~ one by one; ~ **ao outro** one another; (*entre dois*) each other; **à uma** at the same time; (*aproximadamente*): ~ **5** about 5.

um'bigo *m* navel.

um'bral *m* (*limiar*) threshold.

umede'cer *vt* to moisten, wet; ~-**se** *vr* to get wet; **umidade** *f* dampness; (*clima*) humidity; **úmido/a** *adj* wet, moist; (*roupa*) damp; (*clima*) humid.

unânime [u'nanɪmɪ] *adj* unanimous; **unanimidade** *f* unanimity.

unção [ũ'sãw] *f* anointing.

undécimo/a [ũ'dɛsɪmu/a] *adj* eleventh // *m* (*fração*) eleventh.

ungir [ũ'ʒɪx] *vt* to rub with ointment; (*REL*) to anoint; **ungüento** *m* ointment.

unha ['uɲa] *f* nail; (*garra*) claw; **com** ~**s e dentes** tooth and nail; **ser** ~ **e carne com** to be hand in glove with; **unhada** *f* scratch.

união [unɪ'ãw] *f* union; (*ato*) joining;

(unidade) unity; **(casamento)** marriage; **(TEC)** joint; **a U~ Soviética** the Soviet Union.

unica'mente adv only; **único/a** adj only; **(sem igual)** unique; **(só um)** single; **mão única** **(sinal)** one-way.

uni'dade f **(TEC)** unit; **(fig)** unity; **unido/a** adj joined, linked; **(fig)** united; **manter-se unidos** to stick together; **unificar** vt to unite; **unificar-se** vr to join together.

uni'forme adj uniform; **(semelhante)** alike, similar; **(superfície)** even // m uniform; **uniformidade** f uniformity; **uniformizar** vt to standardize; **(pessoa)** to put into uniform; **uniformizar-se** vr to put on one's uniform.

unilate'ral adj unilateral.

u'nir vt **(juntar)** to join together; **(pessoas, fig)** to unite; **(misturar)** to mix together; **(atar)** to tie together; **~-se** vr to join together.

u'níssono m: **em ~** in unison.

univer'sal adj universal; **(geral)** general; **(mundial)** worldwide.

universi'dade f university; **universitário/a** adj university cmp // m/f **(professor)** lecturer; **(aluno)** university student.

uni'verso m universe.

'uno/a adj one, in one.

un'tar vt **(esfregar)** to rub; **(engordurar)** to grease, oil; **(MED)** to rub with ointment; **unto** m fat, lard; **untuoso/a** adj greasy; **untura** f **(REL)** anointing; **(unguento)** ointment.

urânio [u'ranju] m uranium.

urbani'dade f courtesy, politeness.

urba'nismo m town planning; **urbanização** f urbanization; **urbano/a** adj **(da cidade)** city, urban; **(cortês)** polite; **urbe** f city.

ur'dir vt **(tecer)** to weave; **(aranha)** to spin; **(fig: vingança)** to plot; **(: conspiração)** to hatch.

urgência [ux'ʒẽsja] f urgency; **(pressa)** speed, haste; **com toda ~** as quickly as possible; **urgente** adj urgent; **entrega urgente** special delivery; **urgir** vi to be urgent; **(tempo)** to be pressing // vt **(tornar necessário)** to necessitate.

u'rina f urine; **urinar** vi to urinate, pass water.

'urna f urn; **~ eleitoral** ballot box.

ur'rar vt/i to roar.

'urso m bear; **~-branco** m polar bear.

URSS [uexces'esɪ] f: **a ~** the USSR.

urti'cária f nettle rash; **urtiga** f nettle.

uru'bu m vulture.

Uruguai [uru'gwaj] m: **o ~** Uruguay; **uruguaio/a** adj, m/f Uruguayan.

urze ['uxzɪ] m heather.

u'sado/a adj used; **(roupa)** worn; **(gasto)** worn out; **~ a (acostumado)** accustomed to; **(uso)** usage; **usar** vt **(servir-se de)** to use; **(vestir)** to wear; **(gastar com o uso)** to wear out // vi: **usar de** to use.

u'sina f **(fábrica)** factory; **(de energia)** plant; **(de açúcar)** mill.

'uso m **(emprego)** use; **(utilização)** usage; **(prática)** practice; **(moda)** fashion; **usual** adj usual; **(comum)** common; **usuário** m user; **usuário do telefone** telephone subscriber.

usufruir [uzu'frwɪx] vt to enjoy the benefits of; **usufruto** m enjoyment; **(JUR)** usufruct.

u'sura f usury; **usurário** m usurer.

usur'par vt to seize; **(trono)** to usurp.

utensílio [utẽ'sɪlju] m utensil.

'útero m womb, uterus.

'útil adj, pl **úteis** ['utejʃ] useful; **(benéfico)** helpful; **dias úteis** weekdays, working days; **utilidade** f usefulness; **(vantagem)** advantage; **utilizar** vt to use; **utilizar-se** vr: **utilizar-se de** to make use of.

uto'pia f Utopia; **utópico/a** adj Utopian.

'uva f grape.

V

v abr de **volt**.

vá etc vb ver **ir**.

'vaca f cow; **carne de ~** beef.

va'cância f vacancy; **vacante** adj vacant.

vaci'lar vi **(hesitar)** to hesitate.

va'cina f vaccine; **vacinar** vt to vaccinate.

vacuidade [vakwɪ'dadʒɪ] f emptiness.

vacum [va'kũ] adj: **gado ~** cattle.

vácuo ['vakwu] m vacuum; **(fig)** void; **(espaço)** space.

vade'ar vt to wade through.

vadiação [vadʒɪa'sãw], **vadiagem** [vadʒɪ'aʒẽ] f vagrancy; **vadiar** vi to lounge about; **(não trabalhar)** to idle about; **vadio/a** adj **(ocioso)** idle, lazy; **(errante)** wandering; **(vagabundo)** vagrant // m idler; **(vagabundo)** vagabond, vagrant.

'vaga f **(onda)** wave; **(vacância)** vacancy; **(lugar livre)** place.

vagabun'dar vi to wander about, roam about; **vagabundo/a** adj **(errante)** wandering; **(ocioso)** idle; **(barato)** cheap, worthless** // m/f tramp.

vagão [va'gãw] m **(de passageiros)** carriage; **(de cargas)** wagon; **~-leito** m **(Pt)** sleeping car.

va'gar vi to wander about, roam about; **(barco)** to drift; **(ficar vago)** to be vacant; **~oso/a** adj slow; **(sem pressa)** leisurely.

vagem ['vaʒẽ] f green bean; **(invólucro)** pod.

vagido [va'ʒɪdu] m wail.

vagina [va'ʒɪna] f vagina.

'vago/a adj **(indeterminado)** vague; **(desocupado)** vacant, free; **horas ~as** spare time; **vaguear** vi to wander, roam; **(passear)** to ramble.

vai etc vb ver **ir**.

'vaia f booing; **vaiar** vt/i to boo, hiss.

vaidade [vaj'dadʒɪ] f vanity; (futilidade) futility; **vaidoso/a** adj vain, conceited.

vaivém [vaj'vɛj] m coming and going, to-and-fro; **vaivens** mpl (fig) ups and downs.

'vala f ditch; ~ **comum** common grave.

vale ['valɪ] m valley; (poético) vale; (escrito) voucher; ~ **postal** postal order; (reconhecimento de dívida) I.O.U.

valentão/tona [valẽ'tãw/'tona] adj tough // m/f bully; (col) show-off; **valente** adj brave; (forte) strong; **valentia** f courage, bravery; (proeza) feat.

va'ler vi (ser igual em valor, merecer) to be worth; (ser válido) to be valid; (ter valor) to count; (significar) to mean; (ser útil) to be useful; (socorrer) to help; ~ **a pena** to be worthwhile; **não vale a pena** it isn't worth it; ~ **por** (equivaler) to be equal to; **para** ~ (muito) very much, a lot; **vale dizer** in other words; ~**-se** vr: ~**-se de** to use, make use of.

va'leta f gutter.

valete [va'letʃɪ] m (no jogo) jack.

va'lia f value; **de** ~ valuable; **validade** f validity; **validar** vt to validate, make valid.

'válido/a adj valid; **valioso/a** adj valuable.

va'lise f case, grip.

va'lor m value, worth; (coragem) courage; (preço) price; (importância) importance; **dar** ~ **a** to value; **sem** ~ worthless; **no** ~ **de** to the value of; ~**es** mpl (dum exame) marks; (COM) securities.

valorização [valorɪza'sãw] f increased value; **valorizar** vt to value; (aumentar o valor) to raise the value of; **valorizar-se** vr to go up in value.

valo'roso/a adj brave.

'valsa f waltz.

'válvula f valve.

vam'piro m vampire.

vanda'lismo m vandalism; **vândalo** m vandal.

vanglori'ar-se vr: ~ **de** to boast of/about.

vanguarda [vã'gwaxda] f vanguard, forefront; (arte) avant-garde.

vantagem [vã'taʒẽ] f advantage; (ganho) profit, benefit; **vantajoso/a** adj advantageous; (lucrativo) profitable; (proveitoso) beneficial.

vão/vã [vãw/vã] adj (fútil) futile; **em** ~ in vain // m (intervalo) space; (abertura) opening.

va'por m steam, vapour; (navio) steamer; **cozer no** ~ to steam; ~**oso/a** adj steamy, misty; (transparente) transparent, seethrough.

vaqueiro [va'kejru] m cowboy, cowhand.

'vara f (pau) stick; (TEC) rod; (JUR) jurisdiction; (de porcos) herd; **salto de** ~ pole vault.

va'randa f verandah; (balcão) balcony.

varão [va'rãw] adj male // m man, male; (de ferro) rod.

varapau [vara'paw] m (pessoa) beanpole.

va'rar vt (furar) to pierce; (passar) to cross // vi to beach, run aground.

varejeira [vare'ʒejra] f bluebottle.

varejista [vare'ʒɪʃta] m/f (Br) retailer; **varejo** m (Br: COM) retail trade; **loja de varejo** retail store.

variação [varɪa'sãw] f variation, change; **variado/a** adj varied, assorted; **variar** vt/i to vary; (mudar) to change; (diversificar) to diversify; **variável** adj variable.

varicela [varɪ'sela] f chicken pox.

variedade [varɪe'dadʒɪ] f variety; ~**s** fpl (teatro) variety show sg.

varinha [va'rɪɲa] f wand; ~ **de condão** magic wand.

'vário/a adj (diverso) varied; (pl) various, several; (COM) sundry.

va'ríola f smallpox.

varizes [va'rizɪʃ] fpl varicose veins.

varo'nil adj manly, virile.

varrão [va'xãw] m boar.

var'rer vt to sweep; (sala) to sweep out; (folhas) to sweep up.

várzea ['vaxzɪa] f meadow, field.

'vasa f slime.

vase'lina f vaseline.

vasilha [va'ziʎa] f (para líquidos) jug; (para alimentos) dish, container; (barril) barrel.

'vaso m pot; (para flores) vase; (NÁUT) vessel; ~ **sanitário** toilet (bowl); ~ **sanguíneo** blood vessel.

vassoura [va'sora] f brush, broom.

vastidão [vaʃtʃi'dãw] f vastness, immensity; **vasto/a** adj vast, huge.

vatici'nar vt/i to foretell, prophesy; **vaticínio** m prophecy.

vau [vaw] m ford, river crossing; (NÁUT) beam.

'vaza f (no jogo) trick.

vaza'mento m leak.

va'zante f ebb tide.

vazão [va'zãw] f flow; (saída) outlet; **dar** ~ **a** (expressar) to give vent to; (COM) to clear; **vazar** vt (tornar vazio) to empty; (entornar) to spill; (verter) to pour out // vi to empty; (pouco a pouco) to leak; (a maré) to go out; **vazio/a** adj empty; (pessoa) empty-headed, frivolous // m vacuum; (espaço) void.

veado/a [vɪ'adu/a] m deer; (Br: col) gay; **carne de** ~ venison // f hind.

ve'dado/a adj (proibido) forbidden; (fechado) enclosed; **vedar** vt (proibir) to ban, prohibit; (sangue) to stop the flow of; (burraco) to stop up.

ve'deta f (atriz) star; (NÁUT) speedboat.

ve'dete f (atriz) star.

veemência [vɪe'mẽsja] f vehemence; (paixão) passion; (vigor) vigour; **veemente** adj vehement; (intenso) intense; (fervoroso) fervent.

vegetação [veʒeta'sãw] f vegetation;

vegetal adj vegetable cmp, plant cmp // m vegetable; **vegetariano/a** adj, m/f vegetarian.

veia ['veja] f (MED, BOT) vein; **não estou com ~** I'm not in the mood.

ve'ículo m vehicle; (fig: meio) means sg.

veio ['veju] m (de rocha) vein; (na mina) seam; (madeira) grain; (eixo) shaft // vb ver **vir**.

'veja etc vb ver **ver**.

'vela f candle; (AUTO) spark plug; (NÁUT) sail; **fazer-se à/de ~** to set sail.

ve'lar vt (ocultar) to hide; (vigiar) to keep watch over; (um doente) to sit up with // vi (não dormir) to stay up; (vigiar) to keep watch.

veleidade [velej'dadʒi] f whim, fancy; (inconstância) fickleness.

veleiro [ve'lejru] m (navio) sailing ship.

ve'leta f weather vane.

velhaco/a [ve'ʎaku/a] adj crooked // m crook.

velharia [vɛʎa'rɪa] f (coisa) old-fashioned thing; **velhice** f old age; **velho/a** adj old // m old man // f old woman.

velocidade [velosɪ'dadʒi] f speed, velocity; (Pt: AUTO) gear; **velocímetro** m speedometer.

ve'lódromo m cycle track.

ve'loz adj fast.

ve'ludo m velvet; **~ cotelê** corduroy.

vence'dor(a) adj winning // m/f winner, victor; **vencer** vt (num jogo) to beat; (dominar) to overcome, master // vi (num jogo) to win; (conseguir o seu fim) to win through; **vencer-se** vr (prazo) to run out; (promissória) to become due; **vencimento** m (COM) expiry; (data) expiry date; (salário) salary; **dar vencimento a** to cope with.

'venda f sale; (pano) blindfold; **à ~** on sale, for sale.

ven'dar vt to blindfold.

venda'val m gale; (fig) tumult.

ven'dável adj marketable; **vendedor** m seller; **vender** vt to sell; **vender por atacado/a varejo** to sell wholesale/retail; **vender fiado/a prestações** to sell on credit/in instalments; **vendilhão** m pedlar.

ve'neno m poison; (fig, de serpente) venom; **venenoso/a** adj poisonous; (fig) venomous.

veneração [venera'sãw] f reverence; **venerar** vt to revere; (REL) to worship.

ve'néreo/a adj venereal.

'venha etc vb ver **vir**.

'vênia f (desculpa) forgiveness; (licença) permission; **venial** adj venial, forgivable.

'venta f nostril.

venta'nia f gale; **ventar** vi: **venta** the wind is blowing.

'ventas fpl nose sg.

ventilação [vẽtʃila'sãw] f ventilation; **ventilador** m ventilator; (elétrico) fan;

ventilar vt to ventilate; (roupa, sala) to air; (fig) to discuss.

'vento m wind; (brisa) breeze; **~inha** f (cata-vento) weathercock; (grimpa) weather vane; (Pt: AUTO) fan; **~sidade** f flatulence, wind; **ventoso/a** adj windy.

'ventre m belly; (útero) womb.

ventríloquo [vẽ'trɪlokwu] m ventriloquist.

ven'tura f (boa sorte) luck; (felicidade) happiness; (destino) fortune.

ver vt to see; (olhar para) to look at // vi to see; **~-se** vr (achar-se) to be, find o.s.; (duas pessoas) to meet; **~-se com** to settle accounts with; **a meu ~** in my opinion; **bem se vê que** it's obvious that; **já se vê** of course; **não tenho nada que ~ com isto** it is nothing to do with me, it is none of my concern.

veraci'dade f truthfulness.

verane'ar vi to spend the summer; **veraneio** m summer holidays pl; **verão** m summer.

ve'raz adj truthful.

'verba f (JUR) clause; (nota) note; (alocação de recursos) allocation, allowance; (quantia) sum; **verbal** adj verbal.

ver'bete m (num dicionário) entry.

'verbo m verb; **verboso/a** adj wordy, verbose.

ver'dade f truth; **na ~** in fact; **é ~** it's true; **verdadeiro/a** adj true; (genuíno) real.

'verde adj green; (fruta) unripe; (fig) immature // m green; **~jar** vi to turn green; **verdor** m greenness; (BOT) greenery; (fig) inexperience.

ver'dugo m executioner.

ver'dura f (BOT) greenery; (cor verde) greenness; **~s** fpl (CULIN) greens, green vegetables.

verea'dor m councillor; **vereança** f (cargo) office of councillor; (tempo) period of office.

ve'reda f path.

vere'dicto m verdict.

'verga f (vara) stick; (de metal) rod.

vergão [vex'gãw] m weal.

ver'gar vt (curvar) to bend // vi to bend; (com um peso) to sag.

vergas'tar vt to whip.

vergel [vex'ʒɛw] m orchard.

vergonha [vex'goɲa] f shame; (timidez) embarrassment; (honra) sense of shame; **é uma ~** it's disgraceful; **ter ~ de** to be ashamed of; **ter ~ de fazer** to be ashamed of doing; (ser tímido) to be too shy to do; **sem ~** cheeky, brazen; **vergonhoso/a** adj shameful; (indecoroso) disgraceful.

ver'gôntea f shoot; (fig) offspring.

ve'rídico/a adj true, truthful.

verificação [verifɪka'sãw] f (exame) checking; (confirmação) verification; **verificar** vt to check; (confirmar) to verify; **verificar-se** vr (acontecer) to happen; (realizar-se) to come true.

'verme *m* worm.

vermelho/a [vex'mɛʎu/a] *adj* red.

ver'mute *m* vermouth.

ver'náculo/a *adj, m* vernacular.

ver'niz *m* varnish; (*couro*) patent leather; (*fig*) whitewash.

veros'símil *adj* (*provável*) likely, probable; (*crível*) credible.

ver'rina *f* violent attack, diatribe.

ver'ruga *f* wart.

ver'sado/a *adj*: ~ **em** clever at, good at.

versão [vex'zãw] *f* version; (*tradução*) translation; **versar** *vi*: **versar sobre** to be about, concern.

ver'sátil *adj* versatile.

verse'jar *vt* to write verses; **verso** *m* verse; (*linha*) line of poetry; (*da página*) other side, reverse; **vide verso** see over.

ver'tente *f* slope.

ver'ter *vt* to pour out; (*por acaso*) to spill; (*traduzir*) to translate; (*lágrimas, sangue*) to shed // *vi*: ~ **de** to spring from.

verti'cal *adj* (*TEC*) vertical; (*de pé*) upright, standing.

'vértice *m* apex.

vertigem [vex'tʃiʒẽ] *f* dizziness; **vertiginoso/a** *adj* dizzy, giddy; (*velocidade*) frenetic.

'vesgo/a *adj* cross-eyed.

'vespa *f* wasp.

'véspera *f* the day before; ~ **de Natal** Christmas Eve; ~**s** *fpl* (*REL*) vespers; **estar nas** ~**s de** to be about to; **vespertino/a** *adj* evening.

'veste *f* garment; (*REL*) vestment, robe; **vestiário** *m* (*em casa*) cloakroom; (*esporte*) changing room; (*de ator*) dressing room.

vestibu'lar *m* college entrance exam.

ves'tíbulo *m* hall(-way), vestibule; (*teatro*) foyer.

ves'tido/a *adj* dressed // *m* (*roupa*) dress; **vestidura** *f* (*REL*) robe.

vestígio [veʃ'tʃiʒju] *m* (*pista*) track; (*sinal*) sign, trace.

ves'tir *vt* (*uma criança*) to dress; (*pôr roupa*) to put on; (*trajar roupa*) to wear; (*comprar roupa para*) to clothe; (*fazer roupa para*) to make clothes for // *vt*, ~**-se** *vr* to dress; (*de manhã*) to get dressed; (*fantasiar-se*) to dress up; **vestuário** *m* clothing.

ve'tar *vt* to veto; (*proibir*) to forbid.

vetera'no/a *adj, m/f* veteran.

veteri'nário/a *adj* veterinary // *m/f* vet(erinary surgeon).

'veto *m* veto.

ve'tusto/a *adj* ancient; (*honrado*) time-honoured.

véu [vɛw] *m* veil.

ve'xar *vt* (*molestar*) to annoy, upset; (*envergonhar*) to put to shame; ~**-se** *vr* to become ashamed.

vez *f* time; (*turno*) turn; **uma** ~ once; **alguma** ~ ever; **algumas** ~**es**, **às** ~**es** sometimes; ~ **por outra** sometimes; **cada** ~ **mais/menos** more and more/less and less; **desta** ~ this time; **de** ~ once and for all; **de** ~ **em quando** from time to time; **em** ~ **de** instead of; **fazer as** ~**es de** (*pessoa*) to stand in for; (*coisa*) to replace; **mais uma** ~ again, once more; **raras** ~**es** seldom; **uma** ~ **que** since.

'via *f* road, route; (*meio*) way; (*documento*) copy; ~ **férrea** railway line; **em** ~**s de** about to; **por** ~ **aérea** by air; **por** ~ **das dúvidas** just in case; **por** ~ **de regra** generally // *prep* via, by way of.

viação [vɪa'sãw] *f* transport; (*companhia de ônibus*) bus/coach company.

via'duto *m* viaduct.

viageiro/a [vɪa'ʒejru/a] *adj* travelling; **viagem** *f* journey, trip; **viajens** *fpl* travels; **viagem de ida e volta** return trip, round trip; **viagem de núpcias** honeymoon; **viajante** *adj* travelling // *m* traveller; (*COM*) commercial traveller; **viajar** *vi* to travel; **viandante** *m* traveller.

via'tura *f* vehicle.

vi'ável *adj* (*fig*) feasible; (*MED*) viable.

'víbora *f* viper.

vibração [vɪbra'sãw] *f* vibration; **vibrante** *adj* vibrant; (*discurso*) stirring; **vibrar** *vt* (*brandir*) to brandish; (*fazer oscilar*) to vibrate; (*cordas*) to strike // *vi* to vibrate, shake; (*som*) to echo.

vicejar [vise'ʒax] *vi* to flourish.

vice-presidente [vɪsɪ-prezɪ'dẽtʃi] *f* vice president.

vice-rei [vɪsɪ-'xej] *m* viceroy.

vici'ado/a *adj* addicted; (*ar*) foul // *m/f* addict; **um** ~ **em entorpecentes** a drug addict; **viciar** *vt* (*criar vício em*) to make addicted; (*falsificar*) to falsify; (*estragar*) to spoil; (*corromper*) to corrupt; **viciar-se** *vr* to become addicted; **vício** *m* vice; (*defeito*) failing; (*costume*) bad habit; (*em entorpecentes*) addiction; **vicioso/a** *adj* (*defeituoso*) defective; (*círculo*) vicious.

vicissi'tude *f* vicissitude; ~**s** *fpl* ups and downs.

vi'çoso/a *adj* (*plantas*) luxuriant; (*fig*) exuberant.

'vida *f* life; (*duração*) lifetime; (*fig*) vitality; **com** ~ alive; **ganhar a** ~ to earn one's living; **modo de** ~ way of life; **para toda a** ~ forever; **sem** ~ dull, lifeless.

vi'deira *f* grapevine.

vi'draça *f* window pane; **vidraçaria** *f* glazier's; (*fábrica*) glass factory; (*conjunto de vidraças*) glasswork; **vidraceiro** *m* glazier; **vidraria** *f* (*fábrica*) glass factory; (*artigos*) glassware; (*arte*) glassmaking; **vidreiro** *m* glazier, glassmaker; **vidro** *m* glass.

vi'ela *f* alley.

vi'er *etc vb ver* **vir**.

vi'és *m* slant; (*costura*) bias strip; **ao/de** ~ diagonally.

vi'este *vb ver* **vir**.

'viga f beam; (de ferro) girder.

viga'rice [viga'risi] f swindle.

vi'gário m vicar.

viga'rista m swindler, confidence trickster.

vigência [vi'ʒēsja] f validity; **durante a ~ da lei** while the law is in force; **vigente** adj in force, valid.

vigia [vi'ʒia] f (ato) watching; (NÁUT) porthole; **de ~** on watch // m night watchman; **vigiar** vt to watch, keep an eye on; (velar por) to keep watch over // vi to be on the lookout.

vigilância f vigilance; **vigilante** adj vigilant; (atento) alert.

vi'gor m energy; **em ~** in force; **entrar / pôr em ~** to take effect/put into effect; **vigorar** vi to be in force; **~oso / a** adj vigorous.

vil adj vile, low.

'vila f town; (casa) villa.

vila'nia f villainy; **vilão / vilã** m/f (patife) villain.

vi'leza f vileness; (ação) mean trick.

vilipendi'ar vt to revile; (desprezar) to despise.

vim vb ver **vir**.

vime ['vimi] m wicker.

vi'nagre m vinegar.

'vinco m (em tecido) crease; (sulco) furrow.

'vínculo m bond, tie.

'vinda f arrival; **dar as boas ~s** to welcome.

vindi'car vt to vindicate.

vin'dima f grape harvest; **vindimar** vt (fig) to harvest // vi to gather grapes.

vindouro / a [vĩ'doru/a] adj future, coming // s mpl future generations.

vinga'dor(a) adj avenging // m/f avenger; **vingança** f vengeance, revenge; **vingar** vt to avenge // vi (ter êxito) to be successful; (crescer) to grow; **vingar-se** vr: **vingar-se de** to take revenge on; **vingativo / a** adj vindictive.

'vinha vb ver **vir**.

vinha ['viɲa] f vineyard; **vinhedo** m vineyard; **vinho** m wine; **vinícola** adj inv wine-producing.

vi'nil m vinyl.

vinte ['vĩtʃi] num twenty; **vintém** m: **sem vintém** penniless; **vintena** f twenty, a score.

violação [viola'sāw] f violation; **~ da lei** lawbreaking.

violão [vio'lāw] m guitar.

vio'lar vt to violate; (a lei) to break.

vio'lência f violence; **violentar** vt to force; (mulher) to rape; **violento / a** adj violent; (intenso) intense; (furioso) furious.

vio'leta f violet.

vio'lino m violin.

vir vi to come; **~ a ser** to become; **a semana que vem** next week; **~ abaixo** to collapse; **mandar ~** to send for; **o sol vinha nascendo** the sun was rising.

viração [vira'sāw] f breeze.

vi'rada f turning; (momento de virar) turning-point; (guinada) swerve; **viragem** f turn; (fig) swing; **virar** vt to turn; (página) to turn over; (esquina) to turn; (bolsos) to turn inside out; (copo) to empty; **virar de cabeça para baixo** to turn upside down // vi (mudar) to change; **virar do avesso** to turn inside out; **virar para** to face; **virar-se** vr to turn; (voltar-se) to turn round.

vira'volta f reversal, turnabout.

virgem ['virʒē] adj (puro) pure; (não usado) unused; (: cassete) blank // f virgin.

'vírgula f comma; (decimal) point.

vi'ril adj virile.

virilha [vi'riʎa] f groin.

virili'dade f virility.

virtualmente [virtwal'mētʃi] adv virtually.

virtude [vir'tudʒi] f virtue; **em ~ de** owing to, because of; **virtuoso / a** adj virtuous // m virtuoso.

viru'lência f virulence; **virulento / a** adj virulent.

'vírus m virus.

visão [vi'zãw] f vision; (MED) eyesight; **visar** vt (um alvo) to aim at; (ter em vista) to have in view; (documento) to stamp.

'visco m mistletoe; (fig) bait.

vis'conde m viscount.

vis'coso / a adj sticky, viscous.

viseira [vi'zejra] f visor.

visibili'dade f visibility.

visio'nário / a adj, m/f visionary.

vi'sita f visit, call; (pessoa) visitor; **fazer uma ~** to visit; **ter ~s** to have company; **~ de médico** flying visit; **visitar** vt to visit, call on; (inspecionar) to inspect.

visível [vi'zivɛw] adj visible.

vislum'brar vt to glimpse, catch a glimpse of; **vislumbre** m (sinal) glimpse; (idéia) hint, inkling.

'visto / a pp de **ver** // adj seen; **~ que** since; **está ~ que** of course // m (em passaporte) visa; (em documento) stamp // f sight; (MED) eyesight; (panorama) view; (braguilha) fly; **à ~a de** in view of; **~a curta** shortsightedness; **pagamento à ~a** cash payment; **conhecer de ~a** to know by sight; **dar na ~a** to be striking; **dar uma ~a de olhos em** to glance at; **fazer ~a grossa a** to turn a blind eye to; **pôr à ~a** to show; **ter em ~a** to have in mind.

visto'ria f inspection.

vis'toso / a adj handsome, eye-catching.

vi'tal adj vital; (essencial) essential; **~ício / a** adj for life; **~idade** f vitality.

vita'mina f vitamin.

vi'tela f calf; (carne) veal.

viticul'tura f vine growing.

'vítima f victim.

vi'tória f victory, win; **vitorioso / a** adj winning, victorious.

'vítreo / a adj (feito de vidro) glass; (com o

aspeto de vidro) glassy; **vitrina** f, **vitrine** f shop window; (armário) glass case.

vi'trola f gramophone.

vitupe'rar vt (insultar) to insult, abuse; **vitupério** m (insulto) abuse.

viuvez [vju've∫] f widowhood; **viúvo/a** adj widowed // m widower // f widow.

'viva m cheer; ~! hurray!; ~ o rei! long live the king!

vivaci'dade f vivacity; (energia) vigour; **vivaz** adj (animado) lively.

viveiro [vi'vejru] m nursery.

vi'venda f (casa) residence.

vi'ver vi to live; ~ de pão/de seu trabalho to live on bread/by one's work.

'víveres mpl provisions.

vivifi'car vt to give life to.

vivissecção [vivisek'sãw] f vivisection.

'vivo/a adj alive, living; (cheiro) strong; (cor) bright; (animado) lively // m: **os** ~s the living; **televisionar ao** ~ to televise live.

vizinhança [vizi'nãsa] f neighbourhood; **vizinho/a** adj neighbouring; (perto) nearby // m/f neighbour.

voa'dor/a adj flying; (veloz) swift; **voar** vi to fly; (explodir) to blow up, explode; **fazer voar (pelos ares)** (dinamitar) to blow up, blast.

vocabu'lário m vocabulary; **vocábulo** m (palavra) word; (termo) term.

vocação [voka'sãw] f vocation, calling.

vo'cal adj vocal.

você [vo'se] pron you.

vocife'rar vt/i to shout, yell.

'vodca f vodka.

'voga f (NÁUT) rowing; (moda) fashion; (popularidade) popularity; **em** ~ popular, fashionable.

vo'gal f (LING) vowel // m/f (votante) voting member.

vo'gar vi to row; (boiar) to float; (importar) to matter; (estar na moda) to be popular.

vo'lante adj (móvel) mobile // m (AUTO) steering wheel; (motorista) driver; (impresso para apostas) betting slip.

vo'látil adj volatile.

voleibol [volej'bɔw] m volleyball.

volição [voli'sãw] f volition.

volt m volt.

'volta f turn; (regresso) return; (curva) bend, curve; (circuito) lap; (passeio) stroll; (resposta) retort; **passagem de ida e** ~ return ticket, round trip ticket (US); **dar uma** ~ to go for a walk; **estar de** ~ to be back; **na** ~ **do correio** by return (post); **por** ~ **de** about, around.

voltagem [vol'taʒẽ] f voltage.

vol'tar vt/i to return, go/come back; ~ **a fazer** to do again; ~ **a si** to come to; ~-**se** vr to turn; (ir de regresso) to turn back.

volubili'dade f fickleness.

vo'lume m (livro, som) volume; (tamanho) bulk; (pacote) package; **volumoso/a** adj bulky, big; (som) loud.

volun'tário/a adj voluntary // m/f volunteer.

voluntari'oso/a adj headstrong.

voluptuoso/a [volup'twozu/a] adj voluptuous.

vo'lúvel adj fickle, changeable.

vol'ver vt to turn // vi to go/come back.

vomi'tar vt/i to vomit; (fig) to pour out; **vômito** m (ato) vomiting; (efeito) vomit.

von'tade f will; (desejo) wish; **má** ~ ill will; **à** ~ (as much) as you like; **com** ~ with pleasure; **esteja à** ~ make yourself at home; **ter** ~ **de fazer** to feel like doing.

vôo (Pt: **voo**) ['vou] m flight; **levantar** ~ to take off.

voragem [vo'raʒẽ] f abyss, gulf; (turbilhão) whirlpool.

vo'raz adj voracious, greedy.

vórtice ['voxt∫isi] m whirlpool; (de ar) whirlwind.

vós [vɔ∫] pron you.

vos [vu∫] pron you, to you.

'vosso/a adj your // pron: (o) ~ yours.

votação [vota'sãw] f vote, ballot; (ato) voting; **votante** m/f voter; **votar** vt (eleger) to vote for; (dedicar) to devote; (prometer) to make a vow of // vi to vote; **votar-se** vr: **votar-se a** to dedicate o.s. to; **voto** m vote; (promessa) vow; **fazer votos por** to wish for; **fazer votos que** to hope that.

vou vb ver **ir**.

vovô [vo'vo] m grandad.

vovó [vo'vɔ] f grandma.

voz f voice; (grito) cry; (boato) rumour; **a meia** ~ in a whisper; **dar** ~ **de prisão a alguém** to tell sb he is under arrest; **de viva** ~ orally; **ter** ~ **ativa** to be an authority; **em** ~ **alta** aloud; ~**earia** f, ~**eario** m shouting, hullabaloo.

vulcão [vul'kãw] m volcano.

vul'gar adj (comum) common, (reles) cheap; ~**idade** f commonness; (ação) vulgarity; ~**izar** vt to popularize; (abandalhar) to cheapen; **vulgo** m common people pl // adv commonly known as.

vulne'rável adj vulnerable.

'vulto m (corpo) figure, form; (volume) mass; (fig) importance; (pessoa importante) important person.

X

Initial x is pronounced [∫].

xá [∫a] m shah.

'xácara f ballad.

xa'drez m (jogo) chess; (tabuleiro) chessboard; (tecido) checked cloth // adj check(ered).

xale ['∫ali] m shawl.

xam'pu m shampoo.

xa'rá m (Br) namesake.

xaro'pada f cough syrup; (col) boring talk; **xarope** m syrup.

xelim [ʃe'lĩ] *m* shilling.
xenofo'bia *f* xenophobia.
xeque [ʃɛkɪ] *m* (*xadrez*) check; ~-**mate** *m* checkmate.
xere'tar *vi* to poke one's nose in.
xe'rez *m* sherry.
'xícara *f* (*Br*) cup.
xilo'fone *m* xylophone.
xin'gar *vt* (*insultar*) to abuse; ~ **alguém de algo** to call sb sth.
xis *m* (letter) x.
xixi [ʃi'ʃi] *m*: **fazer** ~ to wee, have a wee.
xo'dó *m* flirting; (*pessoa*) sweetheart.

Z

'zaga *f* (*futebol*) fullback position; **zagueiro** *m* fullback.
'zanga *f* (*cólera*) anger; (*irritação*) annoyance; **zangado/a** *adj* angry; (*aborrecido*) annoyed.
zangão [zã'gãw] *m* (*inseto*) drone.
zan'gar *vt* to annoy, irritate; ~-**se** *vr* (*aborrecer-se*) to get annoyed; ~-**se com** to get cross with.
za'rolho/a *adj* blind in one eye.
Zé *abr de* **José** Joe.
'zebra *f* zebra; (*fig*) silly ass; (*jogo*) collapse, surprise result.
zela'dor *m* caretaker; **zelar** *vt* to look after; **zelo** *m* devotion, zeal; **zeloso/a** *adj* zealous; (*diligente*) hard-working.
zênite ['zenɪtʃɪ] *m* zenith.
zé-povinho [zɛ-po'viɲu] *m* the man in the street; (*o povo*) the masses *pl*; (*ralé*) riffraff.
'zero *m* zero, nothing; (*esporte*) nil; ~ **à esquerda** nonentity, a nobody.
ziguezague [zɪgɪ'zagɪ] *m* zigzag.
'zinco *m* zinc; **folha de** ~ corrugated iron.
'zíper *m* zip.
zo'ar *vi* to buzz, drone.
zo'díaco *m* zodiac.
zom'bar *vi*: ~ **de** to make fun of; **zombaria** *f* mockery, ridicule.
'zona *f* area; (*parte*) part; (*GEO*) zone.
'zonzo/a *adj* dizzy.
zôo ['zou] *m* zoo; **zoológico/a** *adj* zoological; **jardim zoológico** zoo; **zoólogo** *m* zoologist.
'zorra *f* (*col*) mess.
zum *m* zoom.
zum'bido *m* buzz(ing); (*de tráfego*) hum; **zumbir** *vi* to buzz; (*motor*) to hum.
zu'nido *m* (*vento*) whistling; (*inseto*) whir, buzz; **zunir** *vi* (*vento*) to whistle; (*seta*) to whizz; (*bala*) to zip; (*inseto*) to buzz.
zunzum [zũ'zũ] *m* buzz(ing); (*boato*) rumour.
zur'rapa *f* rough wine; (*col*) plonk.
zur'rar *vi* to bray.

ENGLISH - PORTUGUESE
INGLÊS - PORTUGUÊS

A

a, an [eɪ, ə, æn] *art* um(a); **3 a day/week** 3 por dia/semana; **10 km an hour** 10 km por hora.

A.A. *n abbr of* **Automobile Association**; **Alcoholics Anonymous.**

aback [ə'bæk] *adv*: **to be taken ~** ficar surpreendido, sobressaltar-se.

abandon [ə'bændən] *vt* abandonar, deixar; (*renounce*) renunciar a // *n* abandono, desamparo; (*wild behaviour*) desenfreamento.

abashed [ə'bæʃt] *adj* envergonhado.

abate [ə'beɪt] *vi* abater; (*lessen*) diminuir; (*calm down*) acalmar-se.

abattoir ['æbətwɑ:ʲ] *n* matadouro.

abbey ['æbɪ] *n* abadia, mosteiro.

abbot ['æbət] *n* abade *m*.

abbreviate [ə'bri:vɪeɪt] *vt* abreviar, resumir; **abbreviation** [-'eɪʃən] *n* (*short form*) abreviatura; (*act*) abreviação *f*.

abdicate ['æbdɪkeɪt] *vt* abdicar, renunciar a // *vi* abdicar, renunciar ao trono; **abdication** [-'keɪʃən] *n* abdicação *f*.

abdomen ['æbdəmən] *n* abdômen *m*.

abduct [æb'dʌkt] *vt* raptar; **~ion** [-'dʌkʃən] *n* rapto, seqüestro.

aberration [æbə'reɪʃən] *n* aberração *f*.

abet [ə'bet] *vt* (*incite*) incitar; (*aid*) ser cúmplice de.

abeyance [ə'beɪəns] *n*: **in ~** (*law*) em desuso; (*matter*) suspenso.

abhor [əb'hɔ:ʲ] *vt* detestar, odiar; **~rent** *adj* detestável, repugnante.

abide [ə'baɪd] *pt, pp* **abode** *or* **abided** *vt* agüentar, suportar; **to ~ by** *vt fus* cumprir, ater-se a.

ability [ə'bɪlɪtɪ] *n* habilidade *f*, capacidade *f*; (*talent*) talento.

ablaze [ə'bleɪz] *adj* em chamas, ardendo, em chamas (*Pt*), a arder.

able ['eɪbl] *adj* capaz; (*skilled*) talentoso; **to be ~ to do sth** poder fazer alguma coisa; **~-bodied** *adj* são/sã; **ably** *adv* habilmente.

abnormal [æb'nɔ:məl] *adj* anormal; **~ity** [-'mælɪtɪ] *n* anormalidade *f*.

aboard [ə'bɔ:d] *adv* a bordo // *prep* a bordo de.

abode [ə'bəud] *pt, pp of* **abide** // *n* residência, domicílio.

abolish [ə'bɒlɪʃ] *vt* abolir, suprimir; **abolition** [æbəu'lɪʃən] *n* abolição *f*, supressão *f*.

abominable [ə'bɒmɪnəbl] *adj* abominável, detestável.

aborigine [æbə'rɪdʒɪnɪ] *n* aborígene *m*, primitivo.

abort [ə'bɔ:t] *vt* abortar; **~ion** [ə'bɔ:ʃən] *n* aborto; **to have an ~ion** fazer um aborto; **~ive** *adj* abortivo, fracassado.

abound [ə'baund] *vi* abundar.

about [ə'baut] *prep* (*subject*) acerca de, sobre; (*place*) em redor de, por // *adv* quase, mais ou menos; **to walk ~ the town** andar pela cidade; **it takes ~ 10 hours** leva mais ou menos 10 horas; **at ~ 2 o'clock** aproximadamente às duas; **to be ~ to** estar a ponto de; **what or how ~ doing this?** que tal se fizermos isso?; **~ turn** *n* meia-volta.

above [ə'bʌv] *adv* em/por cima, acima // *prep* sobre, acima de, por cima de; **mentioned ~** acima mencionado; **~ all** sobretudo; **~ board** *adj* legítimo, limpo.

abrasion [ə'breɪʒən] *n* (*on skin*) esfoladura; **abrasive** [ə'breɪzɪv] *adj* abrasivo.

abreast [ə'brest] *adv* lado a lado; **to keep ~ of** estar a par de.

abridge [ə'brɪdʒ] *vt* resumir, abreviar.

abroad [ə'brɔ:d] *adv* (*to be*) no estrangeiro; (*to go*) ao estrangeiro.

abrupt [ə'brʌpt] *adj* (*sudden*) brusco, inesperado; (*gruff*) áspero; **~ly** *adv* bruscamente.

abscess ['æbsɪs] *n* abscesso.

abscond [əb'skɒnd] *vi* fugir, esconder-se.

absence ['æbsəns] *n* ausência.

absent ['æbsənt] *adj* ausente; **~ee** [-sən'ti:] *n* ausente *m/f*; **~eeism** [-'ti:ɪzəm] *n* absenteísmo; **~-minded** *adj* distraído.

absolute ['æbsəlu:t] *adj* absoluto; **~ly** [-'lu:tlɪ] *adv* absolutamente.

absolve [əb'zɒlv] *vt*: **to ~ sb (from)** absolver *or* perdoar alguém (de).

absorb [əb'zɔ:b] *vt* absorver; **to be ~ed in a book** estar absorvido num livro; **~ent** *adj* absorvente; **~ing** *adj* absorvente, cativante.

abstain [əb'steɪn] *vi*: **to ~ (from)** abster-se (de).

abstention [əb'stenʃən] *n* abstenção *f*, desistência.

abstinence ['æbstɪnəns] *n* abstinência, sobriedade *f*.

abstract ['æbstrækt] *adj* abstrato (*Pt*: -ct-) // *n* resumo.

absurd [əb'sɜ:d] *adj* absurdo, ridículo; **~ity** *n* absurdo, disparate *m*.

abundance [ə'bʌndəns] *n* abundância; **abundant** [-dənt] *adj* abundante.

abuse [ə'bju:s] *n* (*insults*) insultos *mpl*, injúrias *fpl*; (*misuse*) abuso // *vt* [ə'bju:z] (*ill-treat*) maltratar; (*take advantage of*) abusar de; **abusive** *adj* ofensivo.

abysmal [ə'bɪzməl] *adj* abismal; (*ignorance etc*) profundo, abissal.

abyss [ə'bɪs] n abismo.

academic [ækə'dɛmɪk] adj acadêmico, universitário; (pej: issue) teórico.

academy [ə'kædəmɪ] n (learned body) academia; (school) instituto, academia, colégio.

accede [æk'siːd] vi: to ~ to (request) consentir (em), aceder a; (throne) subir a.

accelerate [æk'sɛləreɪt] vt acelerar // vi apressar-se; **acceleration** [-'reɪʃən] n aceleração f; **accelerator** n acelerador m.

accent ['æksɛnt] n (gen) acento; (pronunciation) sotaque m.

accept [ək'sɛpt] vt aceitar; (approve) aprovar; (permit) admitir; ~able adj aceitável, admissível; ~ance n aceitação f, aprovação f.

access ['æksɛs] n acesso, entrada; to have ~ to ter acesso para; ~ible [-'sɛsəbl] adj acessível.

accessory [æk'sɛsərɪ] n acessório; toilet accessories npl artigos mpl de toilette.

accident ['æksɪdənt] n acidente m; (chance) casualidade f; by ~ (unintentionally) sem querer; (by coincidence) por acaso; ~al [-'dɛntl] adj acidental; ~ally [-'dɛntəlɪ] adv sem querer, casualmente; ~-prone adj com tendência para sofrer/causar acidente.

acclaim [ə'kleɪm] vt aclamar, aplaudir // n aclamação f, aplausos mpl.

acclimatize [ə'klaɪmətaɪz] vt: to become ~d aclimatar-se, habituar-se.

accommodate [ə'kɔmədeɪt] vt acomodar, alojar, hospedar; (reconcile) conciliar; (oblige, help) comprazer; (adapt) to ~ one's plans to acomodar seus projetos a; **accommodating** adj complacente, serviçal.

accommodation [əkɔmə'deɪʃən] n, **accommodations** (US) [əkɔmə'deɪʃənz] npl alojamento, acomodação f; (space) lugar m (Br), sítio (Pt).

accompaniment [ə'kʌmpənɪmənt] n acompanhamento; **accompany** [-nɪ] vt acompanhar.

accomplice [ə'kʌmplɪs] n cúmplice m/f.

accomplish [ə'kʌmplɪʃ] vt (finish) acabar, alcançar; (achieve) realizar, levar a cabo; ~ed adj ilustre, talentoso; ~ment n (ending) conclusão f; (bringing about) realização f; (skill) talento, habilidade f.

accord [ə'kɔːd] n acordo // vt conceder // vi concordar; of his own ~ por sua iniciativa; ~ance n: in ~ance with de acordo com; ~ing to prep segundo; (in accordance with) conforme; ~ingly adv (thus) por conseguinte, consequentemente.

accordion [ə'kɔːdɪən] n acordeão m.

accost [ə'kɔst] vt dirigir-se a.

account [ə'kaunt] n (COMM) conta; (report) relato; of little ~ sem importância; on his own ~ por sua

conta; on no ~ de modo nenhum; on ~ of por causa de; to take into ~, take ~ of levar em conta; to ~ for prestar contas de; (answer for) justificar; (explain) explicar; ~able adj responsável.

accountancy [ə'kauntənsɪ] n contabilidade f; **accountant** [-tənt] n contador(a) (Br), contabilista m/f (Pt).

accumulate [ə'kjuːmjuleɪt] vt acumular, amontoar // vi acumular-se; **accumulation** [-'leɪʃən] n acumulação f.

accuracy ['ækjurəsɪ] n exatidão (Pt: -ct-) f, precisão f; **accurate** [-rɪt] adj (number) exato (Pt: -ct-); (answer) correto (Pt: -ct-); (shot) exato (Pt: -ct-), preciso.

accusation [ækju'zeɪʃən] n acusação f; **accuse** [ə'kjuːz] vt acusar; (blame) culpar; **accused** [ə'kjuːzd] n culpado a.

accustom [ə'kʌstəm] vt acostumar; ~ed adj: ~ed to acostumado a.

ace [eɪs] n ás m.

ache [eɪk] n dor f // vi doer; my head ~s doi-me a cabeça.

achieve [ə'tʃiːv] vt (reach) alcançar; (realize) realizar; (victory, success) obter; ~ment n (completion) realização f; (success) sucesso.

acid ['æsɪd] adj ácido; (bitter) azedo // n ácido; ~ity [ə'sɪdɪtɪ] n acidez f.

acknowledge [ək'nɔlɪdʒ] vt reconhecer; (letter) acusar o recebimento de (Br), acusar a recepção de (Pt); (fact) admitir; ~ment n reconhecimento, notificação f de recebimento.

acne ['æknɪ] n acne f.

acorn ['eɪkɔːn] n bolota.

acoustic [ə'kuːstɪk] adj acústico; ~s npl acústica sg.

acquaint [ə'kweɪnt] vt: to ~ sb with sth (warn) avisar alguém de alguma coisa; (inform) pôr alguém ao corrente de alguma coisa; to be ~ed with (person) conhecer; (fact) saber; ~ance n conhecimento; (person) conhecido/a.

acquiesce [ækwɪ'ɛs] vi: to ~ in aquiescer em, concordar com.

acquire [ə'kwaɪə*] vt adquirir; (achieve) alcançar; **acquisition** [ækwɪ'zɪʃən] n aquisição f; **acquisitive** [ə'kwɪzɪtɪv] adj cobiçoso.

acquit [ə'kwɪt] vt absolver; to ~ o.s. well desempenhar-se bem; ~tal n absolvição f.

acre ['eɪkə*] n acre m.

acrimonious [ækrɪ'məunɪəs] adj (remark) mordaz; (argument) acrimonioso.

acrobat ['ækrəbæt] n acrobata m/f; ~ics [ækrəu'bætɪks] npl acrobacia sg.

across [ə'krɔs] prep (on the other side of) no outro lado de; (crosswise) através de // adv transversalmente, de um lado ao outro; to run/swim ~ atravessar correndo/a nado; ~ from em frente de.

act [ækt] n ação (Pt: -çç-) f; (THEATRE) ato (Pt: -ct-); (in music-hall etc) número; (LAW) lei f // vi (machine) funcionar; (person) agir; (*THEATRE*) representar; (*pretend*) fingir; (*take action*) tomar medidas // *vt* (*part*) representar; **to ~ as** fazer-se de; **~ing** *adj* interino // *n*: **to do some ~ing** ser ator/atriz.

action ['ækʃən] *n* ação (*Pt*: -cç-) *f*; (*MIL*) batalha, combate *m*; (*LAW*) processo judicial; **to take ~** proceder.

activate ['æktɪveɪt] *vt* (*mechanism*) ativar (*Pt*: -ct-).

active ['æktɪv] *adj* ativo (*Pt*: -ct-); (*volcano*) em atividade; **activity** [-'tɪvɪtɪ] *n* atividade (*Pt*: -ct-) *f*.

actor ['æktə*] *n* ator (*Pt*: -ct-) *m*; **actress** [-trɪs] *n* atriz (*Pt*: -ct-) *f*.

actual ['æktjuəl] *adj* real, existente; **~ly** *adv* realmente, de fato (*Pt*: -ct-).

acupuncture ['ækjupʌŋktʃə*] *n* acupuntura.

acute [ə'kju:t] *adj* (*gen*) agudo.

ad [æd] *n abbr of* **advertisement**.

A.D. *adv abbr of* **Anno Domini** d.C. (depois de Cristo).

Adam ['ædəm] *n* Adão; **~'s apple** *n* pomo-de-Adão (*Br*), maçã-de-Adão *f* (*Pt*).

adamant ['ædəmənt] *adj* inflexível.

adapt [ə'dæpt] *vt* adaptar; (*reconcile*) acomodar // *vi*: **to ~** (**to**) adaptar-se (a); **~able** *adj* (*device*) ajustável; (*person*) adaptável; **~ation** [ædæp'teɪʃən] *n* adaptação *f*, ajustamento; **~er** *n* (*ELEC*) adaptador *m*.

add [æd] *vt* acrescentar; (*figures: also: ~ up*) somar // *vi*: **to ~ to** (*increase*) aumentar; **it doesn't ~ up** isto não soma.

adder ['ædə*] *n* víbora.

addict ['ædɪkt] *n* (*enthusiast*) dedicado/a; (*to drugs etc*) viciado/a; **~ed** [ə'dɪktɪd] *adj*: **to be(come) ~ed to** ser (ficar) viciado em; **addiction** [ə'dɪkʃən] *n* (*enthusiasm*) dedicação *f*; (*dependence*) vício.

adding machine ['ædɪŋməʃi:n] *n* máquina de somar.

addition [ə'dɪʃən] *n* (*adding up*) adição *f*; (*thing added*) soma; **in ~** além disso; **in ~ to** além de; **~al** *adj* adicional.

additive ['ædɪtɪv] *n* aditivo.

address [ə'drɛs] *n* endereço; (*speech*) discurso // *vt* (*letter*) endereçar; (*speak to*) dirigir-se a, dirigir a palavra a; **~ee** [ædrɛ'si:] *n* destinatário/a.

adenoids ['ædɪnɔɪdz] *npl* adenóides *fpl*.

adept ['ædɛpt] *adj*: **~ at** hábil *or* competente em.

adequate ['ædɪkwɪt] *adj* (*apt*) adequado; (*enough*) suficiente.

adhere [əd'hɪə*] *vi*: **to ~ to** aderir a; (*fig: abide by*) manter-se fiel a; (: *hold to*) apegar-se a; **adherent** *n* partidário/a.

adhesive [əd'hi:zɪv] *adj*, *n* adesivo.

adjacent [ə'dʒeɪsənt] *adj*: **~ to** adjacente a, contíguo a.

adjective ['ædʒɛktɪv] *n* adjetivo (*Pt*: -ct-).

adjoining [ə'dʒɔɪnɪŋ] *adj* adjacente, contíguo.

adjourn [ə'dʒə:n] *vt* adiar; (*session*) suspender // *vi* encerrar a sessão.

adjudicate [ə'dʒu:dɪkeɪt] *vi* adjudicar; **adjudicator** *n* juiz *m*, árbitro.

adjust [ə'dʒʌst] *vt* (*change*) ajustar; (*arrange*) arranjar; (*machine*) regular // *vi*: **to ~** (**to**) adaptar-se (a); **~able** *adj* ajustável; **~ment** *n* regulação *f*; (*engine*) regulagem *f*; (*of prices, wages*) reajuste *m*.

adjutant ['ædʒətənt] *n* ajudante *m*.

ad-lib [æd'lɪb] *vt/i* improvisar; **ad lib** *adv* à vontade.

administer [əd'mɪnɪstə*] *vt* dirigir; (*justice*) administrar; **administration** [-'treɪʃən] *n* administração *f*; (*government*) governo; **administrative** [-trətɪv] *adj* administrativo; **administrator** [-treɪtə*] *n* administrador(a) *m/f*.

admirable ['ædmərəbl] *adj* admirável.

admiral ['ædmərəl] *n* almirante *m*; **A~ty** *n* Ministério da Marinha, Almirantado.

admiration [ædmə'reɪʃən] *n* admiração *f*.

admire [əd'maɪə*] *vt* admirar; **admirer** *n* admirador(a) *m/f*.

admission [əd'mɪʃən] *n* (*entry*) entrada; (*enrolment*) admissão *f*; (*confession*) confissão *f*.

admit [əd'mɪt] *vt* admitir; (*permit*) permitir; (*acknowledge*) reconhecer; (*accept*) aceitar; **to ~ to** confessar; **~tance** *n* entrada; **~tedly** *adv* evidentemente.

admonish [əd'mɔnɪʃ] *vt* repreender; (*advise*) avisar.

ado [ə'du:] *n*: **without (any) more ~** sem mais cerimônias.

adolescence [ædəu'lɛsns] *n* adolescência; **adolescent** [-'lɛsnt] *adj*, *n* adolescente *m/f*.

adopt [ə'dɔpt] *vt* adotar (*Pt*: -pt-); **~ed** *adj* adotivo (*Pt*: -pt-); **~ion** [ə'dɔpʃən] *n* adoção (*Pt*: -pç-) *f*.

adore [ə'dɔ:*] *vt* adorar.

adorn [ə'dɔ:n] *vt* adornar, enfeitar.

adrenalin [ə'drɛnəlɪn] *n* adrenalina.

Adriatic [eɪdrɪ'ætɪk] *n*: **the ~** (**Sea**) o (Mar) Adriático.

adrift [ə'drɪft] *adv* à deriva; **to come ~** desprender-se.

adult ['ædʌlt] *n* (*gen*) adulto.

adulterate [ə'dʌltəreɪt] *vt* adulterar.

adulterer *n* adúltero; **adulteress** *n* adúltera; **adultery** [ə'dʌltərɪ] *n* adultério.

advance [əd'vɑ:ns] *n* (*gen*) avanço; (*money*) adiantamento, empréstimo; (*MIL*) avançada // *vt* (*develop*) desenvolver, promover; (*lend*) emprestar // *vi* avançar; **in ~** com antecedência; (*pay*) adiantado; **~d** *adj* avançado; (*EDUC: studies*) adiantado; **~d in years** de idade avançada; **~ment** *n* avanço, progresso; (*in rank*) promoção *f*, ascensão *f*.

advantage [əd'vɑ:ntɪdʒ] *n* vantagem *f*; (*tennis*) a favor de; **to take ~ of** (*use*) aproveitar-se de; (gain by) tirar proveito de; ~ous [æd vən'teɪdʒəs] adj vantajoso, favorável.

advent ['ædvənt] n vinda, chegada; A~ Advento.

adventure [əd'vɛntʃə*] n aventura; adventurer n aventureiro; adventurous [-tʃərəs] adj venturoso.

adverb ['ædvə:b] n advérbio.

adversary ['ædvəsərɪ] n adversário/a.

adverse ['ædvə:s] adj adverso, contrário; ~ to contrário a.

adversity [əd'və:sɪtɪ] n adversidade f.

advert ['ædvə:t] n abbr of advertisement anúncio.

advertise ['ædvətaɪz] vi anunciar, fazer propaganda; (in newspaper etc) publicar um anúncio // vt anunciar; ~ment [əd'və:tɪsmənt] n anúncio; advertising n publicidade f, anúncios mpl.

advice [əd'vaɪs] n conselhos mpl; (a piece of ~) conselho; (notification) aviso; to take legal ~ consultar um advogado.

advisable [əd'vaɪzəbl] adj aconselhável.

advise [əd'vaɪz] vt aconselhar; (inform) informar; adviser n conselheiro; (business adviser) consultor m; advisory adj consultivo.

advocate ['ædvəkeɪt] vt (argue for) defender; (give support to) advogar, recomendar // n [-kɪt] advogado.

aerial ['ɛərɪəl] n antena // adj aéreo.

aeronautics [ɛərə'nɔ:tɪks] n aeronáutica sg.

aeroplane ['ɛərəpleɪn] n avião m.

aerosol ['ɛərəsɔl] n aerossol m.

aesthetic [i:s'θɛtɪk] adj estético; ~s estética sg.

afar [ə'fɑ:*] adv: from ~ de longe.

affable ['æfəbl] adj afável, simpático.

affair [ə'fɛə*] n negócio; (also: love ~) caso; that is my ~ isso é comigo.

affect [ə'fɛkt] vt afetar (Pt: -ct-), tocar; (move) comover; ~ation [æfɛk'teɪʃən] n afetação (Pt: -ct-) f; ~ed adj afetado (Pt: -ct-).

affection [ə'fɛkʃən] n afeto (Pt: -ct-), afeição f; ~ate adj afetuoso (Pt: -ct-), carinhoso.

affiliated [ə'fɪlɪeɪtɪd] adj filial.

affinity [ə'fɪnɪtɪ] n afinidade f.

affirmation [æfə'meɪʃən] n afirmação f.

affirmative [ə'fə:mətɪv] adj afirmativo.

affix [ə'fɪks] vt (signature) apor; (stamp) afixar, colar.

afflict [ə'flɪkt] vt afligir; to be ~ed with sofrer de; ~ion [ə'flɪkʃən] n aflição f, dor f.

affluence ['æfluəns] n riqueza, opulência; affluent [-ənt] adj rico, opulento.

afford [ə'fɔ:d] vt (provide) fornecer, dar; can we ~ it? temos dinheiro para comprar isso?

affront [ə'frʌnt] n afronta, ofensa.

afield [ə'fi:ld] adv: far ~ muito longe.

afloat [ə'fləut] adv (floating) flutuando; (at sea) no mar.

afoot [ə'fut] adv: there is something ~ está acontecendo algo (Br), algo está-se a passar (Pt).

aforesaid [ə'fɔ:sɛd] adj supracitado, referido.

afraid [ə'freɪd] adj: to be ~ of (person) ter medo de; (thing) recear; to be ~ to ter medo de, temer; I am ~ that lamento que.

afresh [ə'frɛʃ] adv de novo, outra vez.

Africa ['æfrɪkə] n África; ~n adj, n africano/a.

aft [ɑ:ft] adv a ré.

after ['ɑ:ftə*] prep (time) depois de; (place, order) atrás de; day ~ day dia após dia; time ~ time repetidas vezes // adv depois, atrás // conj depois que; what are you ~? o que você quer?; who are you ~? quem procura?; to ask ~ sb perguntar por alguém; ~ all afinal de contas; ~ you! passe primeiro!; ~birth n placenta; ~-effects npl consequências, resultados; ~life n vida após a morte; ~math n consequências fpl, resultados mpl; ~noon n tarde f; ~-shave (lotion) n loção f após-barba; ~thought n reflexão f; ~wards adv depois, mais tarde; immediately ~wards logo depois.

again [ə'gɛn] adv outra vez, de novo; to do sth ~ voltar a fazer algo; ~ and ~ repetidas vezes; now and ~ de vez em quando.

against [ə'gɛnst] prep (opposed) contra, em oposição a; (close to) junto de/a.

age [eɪdʒ] n (gen) idade f; (old ~) velhice f; (period) época; to be under ~ ser menor de idade // vi envelhecer-se // vt envelhecer; to come of ~ atingir a maioridade; it's been ~s since ... há muito tempo que não ...; ~d adj ['eɪdʒɪd] velho, idoso // adj [eɪdʒd]: ~d 10 de 10 anos de idade; ~ group n faixa etária; ~less adj (eternal) eterno; (ever young) sempre jovem; ~ limit n idade f mínima/máxima.

agency ['eɪdʒənsɪ] n agência; through or by the ~ of por meio de.

agenda [ə'dʒɛndə] n ordem f do dia, programa m.

agent ['eɪdʒənt] n (gen) agente m/f; (representative) representante m/f.

aggravate ['ægrəveɪt] vt agravar; (annoy) irritar; aggravation [-'veɪʃən] n irritação f.

aggregate ['ægrɪgeɪt] n (whole) conjunto; (collection) agregado.

aggression [ə'grɛʃən] n agressão f; aggressive [ə'grɛsɪv] adj agressivo; (zealous) ativo (Pt: -ct-).

aggrieved [ə'gri:vd] adj ofendido, aflito.

aghast [ə'gɑ:st] adj horrorizado; to be ~ espantar-se.

agile ['ædʒaɪl] adj ágil.

agitate ['ædʒɪteɪt] vt (shake) agitar; (trouble) perturbar; to ~ for fazer agitação em prol de or a favor de;

agitation [-ʃən] n agitação f; **agitator** n agitador(a) m/f.

ago [ə'gəu] adv: **2 days** ~ há 2 dias; **not long** ~ há pouco tempo; **how long** ~? há quanto tempo?

agog [ə'gɔg] adj (anxious) ansioso; (excited) excitado.

agonizing ['ægənaizɪŋ] adj (pain) agudo; (suspense) angustiante.

agony ['ægənɪ] n (pain) dor f; (distress) angústia; **to be in** ~ sofrer dores terríveis.

agree [ə'gri:] vt (price) combinar, ajustar // vi (statements etc) combinar; **to** ~ **(with)** (person) concordar (com), estar de acordo (com); **to** ~ **to do** aceitar fazer; **to** ~ **to sth** consentir algo; **to** ~ **that** (admit) admitir; **garlic doesn't** ~ **with me** não me dou bem com o alho; ~**able** adj agradável; (person) simpático; (willing) disposto; ~**d** adj (time, place) combinado; ~**ment** n acordo; (COMM) contrato; **in** ~**ment** de acordo, conforme.

agricultural [ægrɪ'kʌltʃərəl] adj agrícola; **agriculture** ['ægrɪkʌltʃə*] n agricultura.

aground [ə'graund] adv: **to run** ~ encalhar.

ahead [ə'hɛd] adv adiante de; ~ **of** à frente de; (fig: schedule etc) antes de; ~ **of time** antes do tempo; **to go** ~ **(with)** prosseguir (com); **to be** ~ **of sb** (fig) ter vantagem sobre alguém; **go right** or **straight** ~ continue sempre em frente.

aid [eɪd] n ajuda, auxílio // vt ajudar, auxiliar; **in** ~ **of** em benefício de; **to** ~ **and abet** (JUR) ser cúmplice de.

aide [eɪd] n (person) ajudante m/f.

ailment ['eɪlmənt] n doença, achaque m.

aim [eɪm] vt (gun, camera) apontar; (missile, remark) dirigir; (blow) apontar // vi (also: **take** ~) apontar // n pontaria; (objective) propósito, meta; **to** ~ **at** (objective) visar; **to** ~ **to do** pretender fazer; ~**less** adj sem propósito; ~**lessly** adv ao acaso, sem rumo.

air [ɛə*] n ar m; (appearance) aparência, aspeto (Pt: -ct-) // vt arejar; (grievances, ideas) discutir // cmp (currents, attack etc) aéreo; ~**borne** adj (in the air) no ar; (MIL) aéreo; ~-**conditioned** adj com ar condicionado; ~-**conditioning** n ar condicionado; ~**craft** n, pl inv avião m; ~**craft carrier** n porta-aviões m inv; **A**~ **Force** n Força Aérea, Aviação f; ~**gun** n espingarda de ar comprimido; ~ **hostess** n aeromoça (Br), hospedeira (Pt); ~ **letter** n carta aérea; ~**lift** n ponte aérea; ~**line** n linha aérea; ~**liner** n avião m de passageiros; ~**lock** n entupimento de ar; ~**mail** n: **by** ~**mail** por avião, via aérea; ~**plane** n (US) avião f; ~**port** n aeroporto; ~ **raid** n ataque m aéreo; ~**sick** adj: **to be** ~**sick** enjoar-se (no avião); ~**strip** n pista (de aterrissar); ~**tight** adj hermético; ~**y** adj (room) arejado, ventilado; (manners) ligeiro, delicado.

aisle [aɪl] n (of church) nave f; (of theatre) corredor m, coxia.

ajar [ə'dʒɑ:*] adj entreaberto.

akin [ə'kɪn] adj: ~ **to** parecido com.

alarm [ə'lɑ:m] n alarme m; (anxiety) inquietação f // vt alarmar, inquietar; ~ **clock** n despertador m; ~**ing** adj alarmante.

Albania [æl'beɪnɪə] n Albânia.

album ['ælbəm] n álbum m; (record) L.P., álbum.

alcohol ['ælkəhɔl] n álcool m; ~**ic** [-'hɔlɪk] adj, n alcoólico; ~**ism** n alcoolismo.

alcove ['ælkəuv] n alcova.

alderman ['ɔ:ldəmən] n, pl -**men** vereador m.

ale [eɪl] n cerveja.

alert [ə'lɔ:t] adj atento; (sharp) esperto // n alerta, alarme m; **to be on the** ~ estar de sobreaviso or alerta // vt espertar, alertar.

algebra ['ældʒɪbrə] n álgebra.

Algeria [æl'dʒɪərɪə] n Algéria; ~**n** adj, n argelino.

alias ['eɪlɪəs] adv também chamado // n outro nome, pseudônimo.

alibi ['ælɪbaɪ] n álibi m.

alien ['eɪlɪən] n estrangeiro // adj: ~ **to** estranho a, alheio a; ~**ate** vt alienar; ~**ation** [-'neɪʃən] n alienação f.

alight [ə'laɪt] adj aceso // vi apear.

align [ə'laɪn] vt alinhar; ~**ment** n alinhamento.

alike [ə'laɪk] adj igual, parecido // adv igualmente, do mesmo modo; **to look** ~ parecer-se.

alimony ['ælɪmənɪ] n (payment) pensão f alimentícia, sustento.

alive [ə'laɪv] adj (gen) vivo; (lively) ativo (Pt: -ct-).

alkali ['ælkəlaɪ] n álcali m.

all [ɔ:l] adj todo; (pl) todos/as // pron tudo; (pl: pessoas) todos // adv tudo, completamente; ~ **alone** completamente só; **not at** ~ em absoluto, absolutamente não; ~ **the time** / his life todo o tempo/toda a sua vida; ~ **five** todos os cinco; ~ **of them** todos eles; ~ **of us went** todos nós fomos; **not as hard as** ~ **that** não tão difícil assim; ~ **in** ~ ao todo; **it's** ~ **the same** dá no mesmo.

allay [ə'leɪ] vt (fears) acalmar; (pain) aliviar.

allegation [ælɪ'geɪʃən] n alegação f, afirmação f.

allege [ə'lɛdʒ] vt alegar, afirmar.

allegiance [ə'li:dʒəns] n lealdade f.

allegory ['ælɪgərɪ] n alegoria.

allergic [ə'lə:dʒɪk] adj: ~ **to** alérgico a; **allergy** ['ælədʒɪ] n alergia.

alleviate [ə'li:vɪeɪt] vt aliviar.

alley ['ælɪ] n (street) viela, beco; (in garden) passeio.

alliance [ə'laɪəns] n aliança; **allied** ['ælaɪd] adj aliado; (related) aparentado.

alligator ['æligeitə*] n aligátor m, jacaré m.

all-in ['ɔ:lin] adj (also adv: charge) tudo incluído; ~ **wrestling** n luta livre.

alliteration [əlitə'reiʃən] n aliteração f.

all-night ['ɔ:l'nait] adj (café) aberto toda a noite; (party) que dura toda a noite.

allocate ['æləkeit] vt (share out) distribuir; (devote) designar; **allocation** [-'keiʃən] n (of money) repartição f; (distribution) distribuição f.

allot [ə'lɔt] vt distribuir, repartir; ~**ment** n distribuição f, partilha; (garden) lote m.

all-out ['ɔ:laut] adj (effort etc) máximo; **all out** adv com todas suas forças; (speed) a toda a velocidade.

allow [ə'lau] vt (practice, behaviour) permitir, deixar; (sum to spend etc) dar, conceder; (a claim) admitir; (sum, time estimated) conceder; (concede) to ~ that reconhecer que; to ~ sb to do permitir a alguém fazer; to ~ for vt fus levar em conta; ~**ance** n (gen) concessão f; (payment) pensão f, subsídio; (discount) desconto; **family** ~**ance** abono de família; to make ~**ances for** levar em consideração.

alloy ['ælɔi] n liga; (mix) mistura.

all: ~ **right** adv (well) bem; (correct) correto (Pt: -ct-); (as answer) está bem!; ~-**round** adj (gen) completo; (view) geral, amplo; (person) consumado; ~-**time** adj (record) de todos os tempos.

allude [ə'lu:d] vi: to ~ to aludir a.

alluring [ə'ljuəriŋ] adj tentador(a), sedutor(a).

allusion [ə'lu:ʒən] n alusão f.

ally ['ælai] n aliado // vr [ə'lai]: to ~ o.s. **with** aliar-se com.

almighty [ɔ:l'maiti] adj onipotente (Pt: -mn-), todo-poderoso.

almond ['ɑ:mənd] n (fruit) amêndoa; (tree) amendoeira.

almost ['ɔ:lməust] adv quase.

alms [ɑ:mz] npl esmolas fpl, esmola sg.

aloft [ə'lɔft] adv em cima, no alto.

alone [ə'ləun] adj só, sozinho // adv só, somente; to **leave sb** ~ deixar alguém em paz; to **leave sth** ~ não tocar em algo; **let** ~ sem falar em.

along [ə'lɔŋ] prep por, ao longo de // adv: **is he coming** ~ **with us?** ele vem con(n)osco?; **he was limping** ~ **ia** coxeando; ~ **with** junto com, em companhia de; ~**side** prep ao lado de // adv (NAUT) encostado.

aloof [ə'lu:f] adj afastado, separado // adv: to **stand** ~ afastar-se.

aloud [ə'laud] adv em voz alta.

alphabet ['ælfəbet] n alfabeto; ~**ical** [-'betikəl] adj alfabético.

alpine ['ælpain] adj alpino, alpestre.

Alps [ælps] npl: the ~ os Alpes.

already [ɔ:l'redi] adv já.

alright ['ɔ:l'rait] adv = **all right**.

also ['ɔ:lsəu] adv também.

altar ['ɔltə*] n altar m.

alter ['ɔltə*] vt alterar, modificar // vi alterar-se, modificar-se; (worsen) alterar-se; ~**ation** [ɔltə'reiʃən] n alteração f, modificação f.

alternate [ɔl'tɔ:nit] adj alternado; on ~ **days** em dias alternados // vi ['ɔltə:neit] alternar-se; ~**ly** adv alternadamente; **alternating** [-'neitiŋ] adj (current) alternado.

alternative [ɔl'tɔ:nətiv] adj alternativo // n alternativa; ~**ly** adv: ~**ly one could** ... por outro lado se podia ...

alternator ['ɔltə:neitə*] n (AUT) alternador m.

although [ɔ:l'ðəu] conj embora; (given that) se bem que.

altitude ['æltitju:d] n altitude f.

alto ['æltəu] n (female) contralto f; (male) alto.

altogether [ɔ:ltə'geðə*] adv totalmente, de todo; (on the whole, in all) no total, ao todo.

aluminium [ælju'miniəm], **aluminum** [ə'lu:minəm] (US) n alumínio.

always ['ɔ:lweiz] adv sempre.

am [æm] vb see **be**.

a.m. adv abbr of **ante meridiem** da manhã.

amalgamate [ə'mælgəmeit] vi amalgamar-se, unir-se // vt amalgamar, unir; **amalgamation** [-'meiʃən] n (COMM) amalgamação f, união f.

amass [ə'mæs] vt acumular, amontoar.

amateur ['æmətə*] n amador(a) m/f.

amaze [ə'meiz] vt assombrar, espantar; ~**ment** n assombro, espanto.

Amazon ['æməzən] n (GEO) o Amazonas m.

ambassador [æm'bæsədə*] n embaixador m.

amber ['æmbə*] n âmbar m; at ~ (AUT) em amarelo.

ambidextrous [æmbi'dekstrəs] adj ambidestro.

ambiguity [æmbi'gjuiti] n ambiguidade f; (of meaning) duplo sentido; **ambiguous** [-'bigjuəs] adj ambíguo.

ambition [æm'biʃən] n ambição f; **ambitious** [-ʃəs] adj ambicioso; (plan) grandioso.

ambivalent [æm'bivələnt] adj ambivalente; (pej) equívoco.

amble ['æmbl] vi (gen: ~ **along**) andar a furta-passo, caminhar.

ambulance ['æmbjuləns] n ambulância.

ambush ['æmbuʃ] n emboscada // vt emboscar; (fig) atacar de surpresa.

amenable [ə'mi:nəbl] adj: ~ to (advice etc) acessível a.

amend [ə'mend] vt (law, text) emendar; (habits) corrigir; ~**ment** n emenda, correção (Pt: -cç-); ~**s** npl: to make ~**s (for)** compensar, reparar.

amenities [ə'mi:nitiz] npl atrações (Pt: -cç-) fpl, comodidades fpl.

America [ə'merikə] n América, os Estados Unidos mpl; ~**n** adj, n americano/a.

amiable ['eɪmɪəbl] adj (kind) amável, simpático; (hearty) caloroso.

amicable ['æmɪkəbl] adj amigável, amigo.

amid(st) [ə'mɪd(st)] prep entre, no meio de.

amiss [ə'mɪs] adv: to take sth ~ levar alguma coisa a mal.

ammonia [ə'məʊnɪə] n amoníaco.

ammunition [æmju'nɪʃən] n munição f.

amnesia [æm'niːzɪə] n amnésia.

amnesty ['æmnɪstɪ] n anistia (Pt: -mn-).

amok [ə'mɔk] adv: to run ~ enlouquecer-se.

among(st) [ə'mʌŋ(st)] prep entre, no meio de.

amoral [æ'mɔrəl] adj amoral.

amorous ['æmərəs] adj amoroso; (in love) apaixonado, enamorado.

amount [ə'maʊnt] n (gen) quantidade f; (of bill etc) quantia, importância, montante m // vi: to ~ to (reach) chegar a; (total) montar a; (be same as) equivaler a, significar.

amp(ere) ['æmp(ɛə*)] n ampère m.

amphibian [æm'fɪbɪən] n anfíbio; **amphibious** [-bɪəs] adj anfíbio.

amphitheatre ['æmfɪθɪətə*] n anfiteatro.

ample ['æmpl] adj (spacious) amplo, extenso; (abundant) abundante; (enough) suficiente.

amplifier ['æmplɪfaɪə*] n amplificador m.

amplify ['æmplɪfaɪ] vt amplificar, aumentar; (explain) explicar.

amputate ['æmpjuteɪt] vt amputar, cortar.

amuck [ə'mʌk] adv = amok.

amuse [ə'mjuːz] vt divertir; (distract) distrair, entreter; ~ment n diversão f, divertimento; (pastime) passatempo; (laughter) riso.

an [æn, ən, n] art see a.

anaemia [ə'niːmɪə] n anemia; **anaemic** [-mɪk] adj anêmico; (fig) insípido.

anaesthetic [ænɪs'θetɪk] n anestésico; **anaesthetist** [æ'niːsθɪtɪst] n anestesista m/f.

analgesic [ænæl'dʒiːsɪk] adj, n analgésico.

analogy [ə'nælədʒɪ] n analogia.

analyse, analyze (US) ['ænəlaɪz] vt analizar; **analysis** [ə'næləsɪs], pl -ses [-siːz] n análise f; **analyst** [-lɪst] n analista m/f; **analytic(al)** [-lɪtɪk(əl)] adj analítico.

anarchist ['ænəkɪst] adj, n anarquista m/f; **anarchy** [-kɪ] n anarquia.

anatomy [ə'nætəmɪ] n anatomia.

ancestor ['ænsɪstə*] n antepassado; **ancestry** [-trɪ] n ascendência, linhagem f.

anchor ['æŋkə*] n âncora // vi ancorar, fundear // vt (fig) segurar, amarrar; to weigh ~ levantar âncoras; ~age n ancoradouro.

anchovy ['æntʃəvɪ] n enchova.

ancient ['eɪnʃənt] adj antigo, velho.

and [ænd] conj e; ~ so on e assim por diante; try ~ come tente vir; better ~ better cada vez melhor.

Andes ['ændiːz] npl: the ~ os Andes.

anecdote ['ænɪkdəʊt] n anedota.

anemia n (US) see anaemia.

anesthetic n (US) see anaesthetic.

anew [ə'njuː] adv de novo, outra vez.

angel ['eɪndʒəl] n anjo.

anger ['æŋgə*] n cólera, zanga // vt irritar, zangar.

angina [æn'dʒaɪnə] n angina (de peito).

angle ['æŋgl] n ângulo; from their ~ do ponto de vista deles.

angler ['æŋglə*] n pescador m de vara (Br), pescador m à linha (Pt).

Anglican ['æŋglɪkən] adj, n anglicano/a.

angling ['æŋglɪŋ] n pesca à vara (Br), pesca à linha (Pt).

Anglo- [æŋgləʊ] pref anglo-; ~Saxon adj anglo-saxão.

angrily ['æŋgrɪlɪ] adv com zanga, zangadamente.

angry ['æŋgrɪ] adj zangado; to be ~ with sb/at sth estar zangado com alguém/algo; to get ~ zangar-se.

anguish ['æŋgwɪʃ] n (physical) dor f, sofrimento; (mental) angústia.

angular ['æŋgjulə*] adj (shape) angular; (features) anguloso.

animal ['ænɪməl] n animal m; (insect) bicho // adj animal.

animate ['ænɪmeɪt] vt (enliven) animar; (encourage) encorajar; ~d adj animado.

animosity [ænɪ'mɔsɪtɪ] n animosidade f.

aniseed ['ænɪsiːd] n erva-doce f, anis f.

ankle ['æŋkl] n tornozelo.

annex ['æneks] n (also: annexe) (building) anexo // vt [æ'neks] (territory) anexar; (document) ajuntar.

annihilate [ə'naɪəleɪt] vt aniquilar.

anniversary [ænɪ'vɜːsərɪ] n aniversário.

annotate ['ænəʊteɪt] vt anotar.

announce [ə'naʊns] vt anunciar; ~ment n anúncio; (official) comunicação f; **announcer** n (RADIO, TV) locutor(a) m/f.

annoy [ə'nɔɪ] vt aborrecer, irritar; don't get ~ed! não se aborreça; ~ance n aborrecimento; (thing) moléstia; ~ing adj aborrecido; (person) importuno.

annual ['ænjuəl] adj anual // n (BOT) anual f; (book) anuário; ~ly adv anualmente, cada ano.

annuity [ə'njuːɪtɪ] n anuidade f or renda anual.

annul [ə'nʌl] vt anular, cancelar; (law) revogar; ~ment n anulação f, revogação f.

annum ['ænəm] n see per.

anoint [ə'nɔɪnt] vt ungir.

anomaly [ə'nɔməlɪ] n anomalia.

anonymity [ænə'nɪmɪtɪ] n anonimato; **anonymous** [ə'nɔnɪməs] adj anônimo.

anorak ['ænəræk] n anoraque m (Br), anorak m (Pt).

anorexia [ænə'reksɪə] n (MED) anorexia.

another [ə'nʌðə*] adj: ~ book (one

more) outro livro; (*a different one*) um outro livro, um livro diferente // *pron* outro; *see also* one.

answer ['ɑ:nsə*] *n* resposta; (*to problem*) solução *f* // *vi* responder, contestar // *vt* (*reply to*) responder a; (*problem*) resolver; **to ~ the phone** atender o telefone; **in ~ to your letter** em resposta *or* respondendo à sua carta; **to ~ the bell** *or* **the door** atender à porta; **to ~ back** *vi* replicar, retrucar; **to ~ for** *vt fus* responder por, responsabilizar-se por; **to ~ to** *vt fus* (*description*) corresponder a; (*needs*) satisfazer; **~able** *adj*: **~able to sb for sth** responsável perante alguém por algo.

ant [ænt] *n* formiga.

antacid [æn'æsɪd] *adj* antiácido.

antagonist [æn'tægənɪst] *n* antagonista *m/f*, adversário/a; **~ic** [-'nɪstɪk] *adj* antagônico, hostil; (*opposed*) oposto, contrário; **antagonize** [-naɪz] *vt* contrariar, hostilizar.

Antarctic [ænt'ɑ:ktɪk] *n*: **the ~** o Antártico; **~a** *n* Antártica.

antelope ['æntɪləup] *n* antílope *m*.

antenatal ['æntɪ'neɪtl] *adj* pré-natal; **~ clinic** clínica pré-natal.

antenna [æn'tɛnə], *pl* **~e** [-ni:] *n* antena.

anthem ['ænθəm] *n*: **national ~** hino nacional.

anthology [æn'θɒlədʒɪ] *n* antologia.

anthropologist [ænθrə'pɒlədʒɪst] *n* antropologista *m/f*, antropólogo/a; **anthropology** [-dʒɪ] *n* antropologia.

anti... [ænti] *pref* anti...; **~-aircraft** *adj* anti-aéreo.

antibiotic [æntibaɪ'ɒtɪk] *adj*, *n* antibiótico.

anticipate [æn'tɪsɪpeɪt] *vt* antecipar; (*foresee*) prever; (*expect*) esperar; (*forestall*) antecipar-se a; (*look forward to*) aguardar, esperar; **anticipation** [-'peɪʃən] *n* antecipação *f*; (*hope*) expectativa.

anticlimax [æntɪ'klaɪmæks] *n* desapontamento.

anticlockwise [æntɪ'klɒkwaɪz] *adv* em sentido anti-horário.

antics ['æntɪks] *npl* bobices *fpl*; (*of child*) travessuras.

anticyclone [æntɪ'saɪkləun] *n* anticiclone *m*.

antidote ['æntɪdəut] *n* antídoto, remédio.

antifreeze ['æntɪfri:z] *n* anticongelante *m*.

antihistamine [æntɪ'hɪstəmi:n] *n* antihistamínico.

antiquated ['æntɪkweɪtɪd] *adj* antiquado.

antique [æn'ti:k] *n* antiguidade *f*, antigualha // *adj* antigo; **~ dealer** *n* antiquário; **~ shop** *n* loja de antiguidades.

antiquity [æn'tɪkwɪtɪ] *n* antiguidade *f*.

antiseptic [æntɪ'sɛptɪk] *adj*, *n* antiséptico.

antisocial [æntɪ'səuʃəl] *adj* anti-social.

antlers ['æntləz] *npl* esgalhos *mpl*, chifres *mpl*.

anus ['eɪnəs] *n* ânus *m*.

anvil ['ænvɪl] *n* bigorna.

anxiety [æŋ'zaɪətɪ] *n* (*worry*) inquietude *f*; (*eagerness*) ânsia; (*MED*) ansiedade *f*.

anxious ['æŋkʃəs] *adj* (*worried*) inquieto; (*keen*) desejoso; **~ly** *adv* ansiosamente.

any ['ɛnɪ] *adj* (*in negative and interrogative sentences* = *some*) algum/a; (*negative sense*) nenhum/a; (*no matter which*) qualquer; (*each and every*) todo; **I haven't ~ money/books** não tenho dinheiro/livros; **have you ~ butter / children?** tem manteiga/filhos?; **at ~ moment** a qualquer momento; **in ~ case** em todo o caso; **at ~ rate** de qualquer modo // *pron* algum, nenhum; (*anybody*) alguém; (*in negative and interrogative sentences*): **I haven't ~** não tenho nenhum; **have you got ~?** tem algum?; **can ~ of you sing?** algum de vocês sabe cantar? // *adv* (*in negative sentences*) nada; (*in interrogative and conditional constructions*) algo; **I can't hear him ~ more** não consigo mais ouvi-lo; **do you want ~ more soup?** quer mais sopa?; **~body** *pron* qualquer um, qualquer pessoa; (*in interrogative sentences*) alguém; (*in negative sentences*): **I don't see ~body** não vejo ninguém; **~how** *adv* de qualquer modo; (*carelessly*) descuidamente; **~one** = **~body**; **~thing** *pron* algo, qualquer coisa; (*in negative sentences*) nada; (*everything*) tudo; **~time** *adv* (*at any moment*) a qualquer momento; (*whenever*) não importa quando; **~way** *adv* de qualquer modo; **~where** *adv* em qualquer parte; (*negative sense*) em parte nenhuma; (*everywhere*) em *or* por toda a parte; **I don't see him ~where** não o vejo em parte nenhuma.

apart [ə'pɑ:t] *adv* à parte, separado; **10 miles ~** separados por 10 milhas; **~ from** *prep* além de, à parte de.

apartheid [ə'pɑ:teɪt] *n* apartheid *m*.

apartment [ə'pɑ:tmənt] *n* (*US*) apartamento; (*room*) quarto; **~ house** *n* (*US*) quarteirão *m*.

apathetic [æpə'θɛtɪk] *adj* apático, indiferente; **apathy** ['æpəθɪ] *n* apatia, indiferença.

ape [eɪp] *n* macaco // *vt* macaquear, imitar.

aperitif [ə'pɛrɪtɪv] *n* aperitivo.

aperture ['æpətʃjuə*] *n* orifício; (*PHOT*) abertura.

apex ['eɪpɛks] *n* ápice *m*; (*fig*) cume *m*.

aphrodisiac [æfrəu'dɪzɪæk] *adj*, *n* afrodisíaco.

apiece [ə'pi:s] *adv* cada um, por cabeça.

apologetic [əpɒlə'dʒɛtɪk] *adj* (*tone, letter*) apologético, cheio de desculpas.

apologize [ə'pɒlədʒaɪz] *vi*: **to ~ (for sth to sb)** desculpar-se (de algo a alguém); **apology** [-dʒɪ] *n* desculpa, apologia.

apostle [ə'pɒsl] *n* apóstolo.
apostrophe [ə'pɒstrəfi] *n* apóstrofo.
appal [ə'pɔːl] *vt* horrorizar; ~**ling** *adj*
pavoroso; (*awful*) horrível.
apparatus [æpə'reɪtəs] *n* aparelho.
apparent [ə'pærənt] *adj* aparente;
(*obvious*) claro; ~**ly** *adv* aparentemente,
pelo(s) visto(s).
apparition [æpə'rɪʃən] *n* aparição *f*;
(*ghost*) fantasma *m*.
appeal [ə'piːl] *vi* (*LAW*) apelar // *n* (*LAW*)
apelação *f*; (*request*) pedido; (*plea*)
súplica; (*charm*) atração *f* (Pt: -cç-); to
~ **for** suplicar, solicitar; to ~ **to** (*subj:
person*) suplicar a; (*subj: thing*) atrair,
agradar; to ~ **to sb for mercy** pedir
misericórdia a alguém; **it doesn't ~ to
me** não me atrai; ~**ing** *adj* (*nice*)
atraente; (*touching*) comovedor(a),
comovente.
appear [ə'pɪə*] *vi* aparecer; (*LAW*)
apresentar-se, comparecer; (*publication*)
ser publicado; (*seem*) parecer; **it would
~ that** pareceria que; ~**ance** *n*
aparência; (*look, aspect*) aspecto.
appease [ə'piːz] *vt* (*pacify*) apaziguar;
(*satisfy*) satisfazer.
appendicitis [əpendɪ'saɪtɪs] *n* apendicite
f.
appendix [ə'pendɪks], *pl* -**dices** [-dɪsiːz]
n apêndice *m*.
appetite ['æpɪtaɪt] *n* apetite *m*; (*fig*)
desejo, sede *f*.
appetizing ['æpɪtaɪzɪŋ] *adj* apetitoso.
applaud [ə'plɔːd] *vt/i* aplaudir; **applause**
[-ɔːz] *n* aplausos *mpl*.
apple ['æpl] *n* maçã *f*; ~ **tree** *n*
macieira.
appliance [ə'plaɪəns] *n* (*TEC*) aparelho;
home ~**s** eletrodomésticos (Pt: -ect-)
mpl.
applicable [ə'plɪkəbl] *adj* aplicável;
(*relevant*) apropriado.
applicant [ə'plɪkənt] *n* candidato,
concorrente *m/f*, requerente *m/f*.
application [æplɪ'keɪʃən] *n* aplicação *f*;
(*for a job, a grant etc*) candidatura,
requerimento; ~ **form** *n* formulário.
apply [ə'plaɪ] *vt*: to ~ (**to**) aplicar (a) //
vi: to ~ **to** apresentar-se a; (*be suitable
for*) ser aplicável a; (*be relevant to*) dizer
respeito a; to ~ **for** (*permit, grant, job*)
solicitar, pedir; to ~ **the brakes** frear
(*Br*), travar (*Pt*); to ~ **o.s. to** aplicar-se
a, dedicar-se a.
appoint [ə'pɔɪnt] *vt* (*to post*) nomear;
(*date, place*) marcar; ~**ment** *n*
(*engagement*) encontro, marcação *f*;
(*date*) compromisso; (*act*) nomeação *f*;
(*post*) cargo.
apportion [ə'pɔːʃən] *vt* repartir,
distribuir; (*blame*) pôr.
appraisal [ə'preɪzl] *n* avaliação *f*,
estimativa.
appreciable [ə'priːʃəbl] *adj* apreciável,
notável.
appreciate [ə'priːʃɪeɪt] *vt* (*like*) apreciar,
estimar; (*be grateful for*) agradecer;

(*assess*) avaliar, apreciar; (*be aware of*)
compreender, perceber // *vi* (*COMM*)
valorizar-se; **appreciation** [-'eɪʃən] *n*
apreciação *f*, estima.
appreciative [ə'priːʃɪətɪv] *adj* (*person*)
agradecido; (*comment*) elogioso.
apprehend [æprɪ'hend] *vt* perceber,
compreender; (*arrest*) prender.
apprehension [æprɪ'henʃən] *n*
compreensão *f*, apreensão *f*; (*fear*)
receio; **apprehensive** [-'hensɪv] *adj*
apreensivo, receoso.
apprentice [ə'prentɪs] *n* aprendiz *m/f*;
~**ship** *n* aprendizagem *f*.
approach [ə'prəʊtʃ] *vi* aproximar-se //
vt aproximar-se de; (*ask, apply to*) dirigir-se a
// *n* aproximação *f*; (*access*) acesso;
(*proposal*) proposição *f*; ~**able** *adj*
(*person*) tratável; (*place*) acessível.
appropriate [ə'prəʊprɪeɪt] *vt* (*take*)
apropriar-se de; (*allot*): to ~ **sth for**
destinar algo a // *adj* [-rɪɪt] (*apt*)
apropriado, próprio; (*relevant*)
adequado.
approval [ə'pruːvəl] *n* aprovação *f*; **on**
~ (*COMM*) à prova.
approve [ə'pruːv] *vt* aprovar; ~**d
school** *n* reformatório.
approximate [ə'prɒksɪmɪt] *adj*
aproximado // *vt* [-meɪt] aproximar;
approximation [-'meɪʃən] *n*
aproximação *f*.
apricot ['eɪprɪkɒt] *n* damasco.
April ['eɪprəl] *n* abril (Pt: A-) *m*; ~
Fool's Day *n* Dia *m* da mentira;
Primeiro-de-abril *m*.
apron ['eɪprən] *n* avental *m*.
apt [æpt] *adj* (*suitable*) adequado;
(*appropriate*) apropriado; (*likely*): ~ **to
do** estar sujeito a fazer.
aptitude ['æptɪtjuːd] *n* aptidão *f*, talento.
aqualung ['ækwəlʌŋ] *n* aparelho
respiratório autônomo.
aquarium [ə'kweərɪəm] *n* aquário *m*.
Aquarius [ə'kweərɪəs] *n* Aquário.
aquatic [ə'kwætɪk] *adj* aquático.
aqueduct ['ækwɪdʌkt] *n* aqueduto.
Arab ['ærəb] *n* árabe *m/f*.
Arabia [ə'reɪbɪə] *n* Arábia; ~**n** *adj* árabe.
Arabic ['ærəbɪk] *n* arábico.
arable ['ærəbl] *adj* cultivável.
arbitrary ['ɑːbɪtrərɪ] *adj* arbitrário.
arbitrate ['ɑːbɪtreɪt] *vi* arbitrar;
arbitration [-'treɪʃən] *n* arbitragem *f*;
arbitrator *n* árbitro.
arc [ɑːk] *n* arco.
arcade [ɑː'keɪd] *n* arcada; (*round a
square*) arcos *mpl*; (*passage with shops*)
galeria.
arch [ɑːtʃ] *n* arco; (*vault*) abóbada // *vt*
arquear, curvar.
archaeologist [ɑːkɪ'ɒlədʒɪst] *n*
arqueólogo; **archaeology** [-dʒɪ] *n*
arqueologia.
archaic [ɑː'keɪɪk] *adj* arcaico.
archbishop [ɑːtʃ'bɪʃəp] *n* arcebispo.

arch-enemy ['ɑ:tʃ'ɛnimi] *n* arqui-inimigo.

archer ['ɑ:tʃə*] *n* arqueiro, flecheiro; **~y** *n* tiro de arco.

archetype ['ɑ:kitaip] *n* arquétipo.

archipelago [ɑ:kɪ'pɛligəu] *n* arquipélago.

architect ['ɑ:kitɛkt] *n* arquiteto (*Pt*: -ct-); **~ural** [-'tɛktʃərəl] *adj* arquitetônico (*Pt*: -ctó-); **~ure** *n* arquitetura (*Pt*: -ct-).

archives ['ɑ:kaivz] *npl* arquivo *sg*.

archway ['ɑ:tʃwei] *n* arco.

Arctic ['ɑ:ktik] *adj* ártico (*Pt*: -ct-) // *n*: the **~** o Ár(c)tico.

ardent ['ɑ:dənt] *adj* (*passionate*) ardente, apaixonado; (*fervent*) fervoroso; **ardour** ['ɑ:də*] *n* ardor *m*; fervor *m*.

arduous ['ɑ:djuəs] *adj* (*gen*) árduo; (*journey*) difícil.

are [ɑ:*] *vb see* **be**.

area ['ɛəriə] *n* (*gen*) área; (*MAT*) superfície *f*, extensão *f*; (*zone*) zona, região *f*.

arena [ə'ri:nə] *n* arena; (*of circus*) picadeiro (*Br*), pista (*Pt*); (*for bullfight*) arena (*Br*), praça (*Pt*).

aren't [ɑ:nt] = **are not**.

Argentina [ɑ:dʒən'ti:nə] *n* Argentina; **Argentinian** [-'tiniən] *adj*, *n* argentino/a.

argue ['ɑ:gju:] *vi* (*quarrel*) discutir; (*reason*) argumentar; **to ~ that** sustentar que; **argument** *n* (*reasons*) argumento; (*quarrel*) discussão *f*; (*debate*) debate *m*; **argumentative** [-'mɛntətiv] *adj* discutidor(a).

aria ['ɑ:riə] *n* (*MUS*) ária.

arid ['ærid] *adj* árido.

Aries ['ɛəriz] *n* Áries *m*.

arise [ə'raiz], *pt* **arose**, *pp* **arisen** [ə'rizn] *vi* (*rise up*) levantar-se, erguer-se; (*emerge*) surgir; **to ~ from** resultar de.

aristocracy [æris'tɔkrəsi] *n* aristocracia; **aristocrat** ['æristəkræt] *n* aristocrata *m/f*.

arithmetic [ə'riθmətik] *n* aritmética.

ark [ɑ:k] *n*: Noah's A~ *n* arca de Noé.

arm [ɑ:m] *n* (*ANAT*) braço; (*weapon*) arma // *vt* armar; **~s** *npl* (*weapons*) armas *fpl*; (*HERALDRY*) brasão *m*; **~s race** *n* carreira armamentista; **~ in ~** de braço dado; **~band** *n* faixa de braço, braçadeira; (*for swimming*) bóia de braço; **~chair** *n* poltrona; **~ed** *adj* armado; **~ed robbery** *n* assalto à mão armada; **~ful** *n* braçada.

armistice ['ɑ:mistis] *n* armistício.

armour ['ɑ:mə*] *n* armadura; **~ed car** *n* carro blindado; **~y** *n* arsenal *m*.

armpit ['ɑ:mpit] *n* sovaco.

army ['ɑ:mi] *n* exército.

aroma [ə'rəumə] *n* aroma; **~tic** [ærə'mætik] *adj* aromático.

arose [ə'rəuz] *pt of* **arise**.

around [ə'raund] *adv* em volta; (*in the area*) perto // *prep* em redor de, em volta de; (*fig: about*) cerca de.

arouse [ə'rauz] *vt* despertar.

arrange [ə'reindʒ] *vt* arranjar;

(*programme*) organizar; **~ment** *n* arranjo; (*agreement*) acordo; **~ments** *npl* (*plans*) planos *mpl*, medidas *fpl*; (*preparations*) preparativos *mpl*.

arrears [ə'riəz] *npl* atrasos *mpl*; **to be in ~ with one's rent** atrasar o aluguel.

arrest [ə'rɛst] *vt* prender, deter; (*sb's attention*) chamar, prender // *n* detenção *f*, prisão *f*; **under ~** preso.

arrival [ə'raivəl] *n* chegada; **new ~** recém-chegado.

arrive [ə'raiv] *vi* chegar.

arrogance ['ærəgəns] *n* arrogância; **arrogant** [-gənt] *adj* arrogante.

arrow ['ærəu] *n* flecha, seta.

arsenal ['ɑ:sinl] *n* arsenal *m*.

arsenic ['ɑ:snik] *n* arsênico.

arson ['ɑ:sn] *n* incêndio premeditado.

art [ɑ:t] *n* arte *f*; (*craft*) artes *fpl*; (*skill*) habilidade *f*, jeito; (*technique*) técnica; **A~s** *npl* (*EDUC*) Letras *fpl*; **~ gallery** *n* museu *m* de belas artes; (*small and private*) galeria de arte.

artery ['ɑ:təri] *n* (*MED*) artéria; (*fig*) estrada principal.

arthritis [ɑ:'θraitis] *n* artrite *f*.

artichoke ['ɑ:titʃəuk] *n* alcachofra; **Jerusalem ~** topinambo.

article ['ɑ:tikl] *n* artigo, objeto (*Pt*: -ct-); (*in newspaper*) artigo; (*LAW: training*): **~s** *npl* contrato de aprendizagem *sg*.

articulate [ɑ:'tikjulit] *adj* articulado // *vt* [-leit] articular, pronunciar; **~d lorry** *n* caminhão (*Pt*: camião) *m* articulado, jamanta.

artificial [ɑ:ti'fiʃəl] *adj* artificial; (*teeth etc*) postiço, falso; **~ respiration** *n* respiração *f* artificial.

artillery [ɑ:'tiləri] *n* artilharia.

artisan ['ɑ:tizæn] *n* artesão/sã.

artist ['ɑ:tist] *n* artista *m/f*; (*MUS*) intérprete *m/f*; **~ic** [ɑ:'tistik] *adj* artístico; **~ry** *n* arte *f*, maestria.

artless ['ɑ:tlis] *adj* (*innocent*) natural, simples; (*clumsy*) desajeitado.

as [æz, əz] *conj* (*cause*) como, já que; (*time: moment*) quando; (*duration*) enquanto; (*manner*) como, conforme; (*in the capacity of*) como; **~ big ~** tão grande como; **twice ~ big ~** duas vezes maior que; **~ she said como ela disse; **~ if** *or* **though** como se; **~ for** *or* **to that** quanto a isso; **~ or so long ~** *conj* desde que, contanto que; **~ much/many ~** tanto/s ... como; **~ soon ~** *conj* logo que, assim que; **~ such** *adv* como tal; **~ well** *adv* também; **~ well ~** *conj* assim como; *see also* **such**.

asbestos [æz'bɛstəs] *n* asbesto, amianto.

ascend [ə'sɛnd] *vt* ascender, subir; **~ancy** *n* predomínio, ascendência.

ascent [ə'sɛnt] *n* subida; (*slope*) rampa; (*promotion*) ascensão *f*.

ascertain [æsə'tein] *vt* averiguar, verificar.

ascetic [ə'sɛtik] *adj* ascético.

ascribe [ə'skraıb] vt: to ~ sth to atribuir algo a.

ash [æʃ] n cinza; (tree) freixo.

ashamed [ə'ʃeımd] adj envergonhado; to be ~ of ter vergonha de.

ashen ['æʃn] adj cinzento.

ashore [ə'ʃɔ:*] adv em terra.

ashtray ['æʃtreı] n cinzeiro.

Asia ['eıʃə] n Ásia; ~n, ~tic [eısı'ætık] adj, n asiático/a.

aside [ə'saıd] adv de parte, de lado.

ask [ɑ:sk] vt (question) perguntar; (demand) exigir; (invite) convidar; to ~ sb sth perguntar algo a alguém; to ~ sb to do sth pedir a alguém para fazer algo; to ~ sb about sth perguntar a alguém sobre algo; to ~ (sb) a question fazer uma pergunta (a alguém); to ~ sb out to dinner convidar alguém para jantar; to ~ for vt fus pedir.

askance [ə'skɑ:ns] adv: to look ~ at sb olhar alguém de soslaio.

askew [ə'skju:] adv torto, de esguelha.

asleep [ə'sli:p] adj adormecido, dormindo; to fall ~ adormecer.

asparagus [əs'pærəgəs] n aspargo (Pt: esp-).

aspect ['æspεkt] n aspecto, aparência; (direction in which a building etc faces) orientação f.

aspersions [əs'pɜ:ʃənz] npl: to cast ~ on difamar, caluniar.

asphalt ['æsfælt] n asfalto; (place) pista asfaltada.

asphyxiate [æs'fıksıeıt] vt asfixiar, sufocar // vi asfixiar-se, sufocar-se; **asphyxiation** [-'eıʃən] n asfixia, sufocação f.

aspiration [æspə'reıʃən] n (fig) aspiração f, ambição f.

aspire [əs'paıə*] vi: to ~ to aspirar a.

aspirin ['æsprın] n aspirina.

ass [æs] n jumento, burro; (col) estúpido.

assailant [ə'seılənt] n assaltante m/f, atacante m/f.

assassin [ə'sæsın] n assassino; ~ate vt assassinar; ~ation [-'neıʃən] n assassinato, assassínio.

assault [ə'sɔ:lt] n (gen: attack) assalto // vt assaltar, atacar; (sexually) agredir, violar.

assemble [ə'sεmbl] vt reunir; (TECH) montar // vi reunir-se.

assembly [ə'sεmblı] n (meeting) reunião f, assembleia; (people) congregação f; (construction) montagem f; ~ line n linha de produção.

assent [ə'sεnt] n assentimento, aprovação f // vi consentir, assentir.

assert [ə'sɜ:t] vt afirmar; (claim etc) fazer valer; ~ion [ə'sɜ:ʃən] n afirmação f.

assess [ə'sεs] vt avaliar; (tax, damages) fixar; (property etc: for tax) taxar; ~ment n avaliação f; ~or n avaliador(a) m/f; (of tax) avaliador(a) do fisco.

asset ['æsεt] n bem m; (quality) vantagem f; ~s npl (funds) ativo (Pt: -ct-) sg, fundos mpl.

assiduous [ə'sıdjuəs] adj assíduo.

assign [ə'saın] vt (date) fixar; (task) designar; (resources) destinar; (property) transmitir; ~ment n designação f; (task) tarefa.

assimilate [ə'sımıleıt] vt assimilar.

assist [ə'sıst] vt ajudar; (progress etc) auxiliar; ~ance n ajuda, auxílio; (welfare) subsídio; ~ant n. assistente m/f, auxiliar m/f; (also: shop ~ant) balconista m/f.

assizes [ə'saızız] npl sessão f de tribunal superior.

associate [ə'səuʃıt] adj associado // n colega m/f; (in crime) cúmplice m/f; (member) sócio // (vb: [-ʃıeıt]) vt associar // vi: to ~ with sb associar-se com alguém.

association [əsəusı'eıʃən] n associação f; (COMM) sociedade f.

assorted [ə'sɔ:tıd] adj sortido, variado.

assortment [ə'sɔ:tmənt] n sortimento.

assume [ə'sju:m] vt (suppose) supor, presumir; (responsibilities etc) assumir; (attitude, name) adotar (Pt: -pt-), tomar.

assumption [ə'sʌmpʃən] n (supposition) suposição f, presunção f; (act) assunção f.

assurance [ə'ʃuərəns] n garantia; (confidence) confiança; (certainty) certeza; (insurance) seguro.

assure [ə'ʃuə*] vt assegurar.

asterisk ['æstərısk] n asterisco.

astern [ə'stɜ:n] adv à popa; (direction) à ré.

asteroid ['æstərɔıd] n asteróide m.

asthma ['æsmə] n asma; ~tic [æs'mætık] adj, n asmático/a.

astonish [ə'stɔnıʃ] vt assombrar, espantar; ~ment n assombro, espanto.

astound [ə'staund] vt assombrar, espantar.

astray [ə'streı] adv: to go ~ perder-se; to lead ~ desencaminhar.

astride [ə'straıd] adv escarrapachado // prep a cavalo ou montado sobre.

astrologer [əs'trɔlədʒə*] n astrólogo; **astrology** [-dʒı] n astrologia.

astronaut ['æstrənɔ:t] n astronauta m/f.

astronomer [əs'trɔnəmə*] n astrônomo; **astronomical** [æstrə'nɔmıkəl] adj astronômico; (fig) enorme; **astronomy** [-mı] n astronomia.

astute [əs'tju:t] adj astuto, esperto.

asylum [ə'saıləm] n (refuge) asilo, refúgio; (hospital) manicômio.

at [æt] prep em, a; ~ the top no cimo; ~ 4 o'clock às quatro; ~ £1 a kilo a uma libra o quilo; ~ night à noite; ~ a stroke de um golpe; two ~ a time de dois em dois; ~ times às vezes.

ate [eıt] pt of **eat**.

atheist ['eıθııst] n ateu/atéia.

Athens ['æθınz] n Atenas f.

athlete ['æθli:t] n atleta m/f.

athletic [æθ'letɪk] adj atlético; ~s n atletismo sg.

Atlantic [ət'læntɪk] n: the ~ (Ocean) o (Oceano) Atlântico.

atlas ['ætləs] n atlas m.

atmosphere ['ætməsfɪə*] n atmosfera; (fig) ambiente m.

atom ['ætəm] n átomo; ~ic [ə'tɔmɪk] adj atômico; ~(ic) bomb n bomba atômica; ~izer ['ætəmaɪzə*] n atomizador m, pulverizador m.

atone [ə'təʊn] vi: to ~ for expiar.

atrocious [ə'trəʊʃəs] adj (very bad) atroz; (fig) horrível, detestável.

atrocity [ə'trɔsɪtɪ] n atrocidade f.

attach [ə'tætʃ] vt (gen) (document, letter) juntar; ~ed adj (letter) junto; to be ~ed to sb/sth (to like) ter afeição por alguém/algo.

attaché [ə'tæʃeɪ] n adido; ~ case n pasta.

attachment [ə'tætʃmənt] n (tool) acessório; (love): ~ (to) afeição f (por).

attack [ə'tæk] vt (MIL) atacar; (criminal) agredir, assaltar; (task etc) empreender // n ataque m, assalto; (on sb's life) atentado; **heart** ~ ataque de coração or cardíaco; ~er n agressor(a) m/f, assaltante m/f.

attain [ə'teɪn] vt (also: ~ to) alcançar, atingir; (achieve) conseguir; ~ments npl dotes mpl, talento sg.

attempt [ə'tempt] n tentativa; (attack) atentado // vt tentar, intentar.

attend [ə'tend] vt assistir a; (patient) tratar; to ~ to vt fus (needs, affairs etc) ocupar-se de; (speech etc) prestar atenção a; (customer) atender a; ~ance n comparecimento; (people present) assistência; ~ant n servidor(a) m/f; (THEATRE) arrumador(a) m/f // adj concomitante.

attention [ə'tenʃən] n atenção f // excl (MIL) sentido!; for the ~ of... (ADMIN) atenção...

attentive [ə'tentɪv] adj atento; (polite) cortês.

attest [ə'test] vi: to ~ to atestar.

attic ['ætɪk] n sótão m.

attitude ['ætɪtjuːd] n (gen) atitude f; (disposition) disposição f.

attorney [ə'tɔːnɪ] n (lawyer) advogado; (having proxy) procurador m; **A~ General** n (Brit) procurador da coroa; (US) procurador geral.

attract [ə'trækt] vt atrair; (attention) chamar; **attraction** [ə'trækʃən] n (gen pl) atrativos mpl; (amusements) atrações fpl; (PHYSICS) atração (Pt: -cç-) f; (fig: towards sth) atração (por algo); ~ive adj atraente.

attribute ['ætrɪbjuːt] n atributo // vt [ə'trɪbjuːt]: to ~ sth to atribuir or imputar algo a.

aubergine ['əʊbəʒiːn] n berinjela.

auburn ['ɔːbən] adj castanho-avermelhado.

auction ['ɔːkʃən] n (also: sale by ~)

leilão m // vt leiloar; ~eer [-'nɪə*] n leiloeiro/a.

audacious [ɔː'deɪʃəs] adj audaz, atrevido; (pej) descarado; **audacity** [ɔː'dæsɪtɪ] n audácia, atrevimento; (pej) descaramento.

audible ['ɔːdɪbl] adj audível.

audience ['ɔːdɪəns] n auditório, público; (interview) entrevista.

audio-visual [ɔːdɪəʊ'vɪzjʊəl] adj audiovisual.

audit ['ɔːdɪt] vt fazer a auditoria de.

audition [ɔː'dɪʃən] n audição f.

auditor ['ɔːdɪtə*] n auditor(a) m/f.

auditorium [ɔːdɪ'tɔːrɪəm] n auditório.

augment [ɔːg'ment] vt aumentar // vi aumentar-se.

augur ['ɔːgə*] vi: it ~s well é de bom augúrio.

August ['ɔːgəst] n agosto (Pt: A-).

aunt [ɑːnt] n tia; ~ie, ~y n diminutive of aunt.

au pair ['əʊ'peə*] n (also: ~ girl) au pair f.

aura ['ɔːrə] n emanação f; (atmosphere) ambiente m.

auspices ['ɔːspɪsɪz] npl: under the ~ of sob os auspícios de.

auspicious [ɔːs'pɪʃəs] adj propício.

austere [ɔs'tɪə*] adj austero; (manner) severo; **austerity** [ɔ'sterɪtɪ] n austeridade f.

Australia [ɔs'treɪlɪə] n Austrália; ~n adj, n australiano/a.

Austria ['ɔstrɪə] n Áustria; ~n adj, n austríaco/a.

authentic [ɔː'θentɪk] adj autêntico.

author ['ɔːθə] n autor(a) m/f.

authoritarian [ɔːθɔrɪ'teərɪən] adj autoritário.

authoritative [ɔː'θɔrɪtətɪv] adj autorizado; (manner) autoritário.

authority [ɔː'θɔrɪtɪ] n autoridade f; the authorities npl as autoridades.

authorize ['ɔːθəraɪz] vt autorizar.

auto ['ɔːtəʊ] n (US) carro, automóvel m.

autobiography [ɔːtəbaɪ'ɔgrəfɪ] n autobiografia.

autocratic [ɔːtə'krætɪk] adj autocrático.

autograph ['ɔːtəgrɑːf] n autógrafo // vt (photo etc) autografar.

automatic [ɔːtə'mætɪk] adj automático // n (gun) pistola automática.

automation [ɔːtə'meɪʃən] n automação f.

automaton [ɔː'tɔmətən] n, pl -mata [-tə] n autômato.

automobile ['ɔːtəməbiːl] n (US) carro, automóvel m.

autonomous [ɔː'tɔnəməs] adj autônomo.

autopsy ['ɔːtɔpsɪ] n autópsia.

autumn ['ɔːtəm] n outono.

auxiliary [ɔːg'zɪlɪərɪ] adj, n auxiliar m/f.

Av. abbr of **avenue**.

avail [ə'veɪl] vt: to ~ o.s. of aproveitar, valer-se de // n: to no ~ em vão, inutilmente.

availability [əveɪlə'bɪlɪtɪ] n disponibilidade f.

available [ə'veɪləbl] adj disponível; (usable) utilizável.

avalanche ['ævəlɑːnʃ] n avalanche, alude m.

avant-garde ['ævãŋ'gɑːd] adj de vanguarda.

avaricious [ævə'rɪʃəs] adj avarento, avaro.

Ave. abbr of **avenue.**

avenge [ə'vendʒ] vt vingar.

avenue ['ævənjuː] n avenida; (path) caminho.

average ['ævərɪdʒ] n média, termo médio // adj (mean) médio; (ordinary) vulgar, comum // vt calcular a média de; on ~ em média; to ~ out vt tirar a média // vi: to ~ out at resultar como média, ser por regra geral.

averse [ə'vɜːs] adj: to be ~ to sth / doing ser avesso or pouco disposto a algo/a fazer algo; **aversion** [ə'vɜːʃən] n aversão f, repugnância.

avert [ə'vɜːt] vt prevenir; (blow, one's eyes) desviar.

aviary ['eɪvɪərɪ] n aviário, viveiro de aves.

aviation [eɪvɪ'eɪʃən] n aviação f.

avid ['ævɪd] adj ávido.

avocado [ævə'kɑːdəʊ] n (also: ~ pear) abacate m.

avoid [ə'vɔɪd] vt evitar, esquivar-se de; ~able adj evitável; ~ance n evitação f.

await [ə'weɪt] vt esperar, aguardar.

awake [ə'weɪk] adj acordado // (vb: pt **awoke**, pp **awoken** or **awaked**) vt despertar, acordar // vi despertar, acordar; ~ning n despertar m.

award [ə'wɔːd] n (prize) prêmio, condecoração f; (LAW) sentença; (act) concessão f // vt (prize) outorgar, conceder; (LAW: damages) adjudicar.

aware [ə'wɛə*] adj consciente; (informed) informado; to become ~ of reparar em, saber; ~ness n consciência; (knowledge) conhecimento.

awash [ə'wɔʃ] adj inundado.

away [ə'weɪ] adv (gen) fora; (far ~) muito longe; **two kilometres** ~ a dois quilômetros de distância; **two hours** ~ **by car** a duas horas de carro; **the holiday was two weeks** ~ faltavam duas semanas para as férias; ~ **from** longe de; **he's** ~ **for a week** está ausente uma semana; **to take** ~ vt levar; **to work/pedal** ~ trabalhar/pedalar sem parar; **to fade** ~ desvanecer-se; (sound) apagar-se; ~ **match** n (SPORT) jogo de fora.

awe [ɔː] n temor m respeitoso; ~-**inspiring**, ~**some** adj imponente; ~-**struck** adj pasmado.

awful ['ɔːfəl] adj terrível, horrível; ~**ly** adv (very) muito.

awhile [ə'waɪl] adv por algum tempo, um pouco.

awkward ['ɔːkwəd] adj (clumsy) desajeitado; (shape) incômodo; (problem)

difícil; (embarrassing) embaraçoso, delicado.

awning ['ɔːnɪŋ] n toldo.

awoke [ə'wəʊk], **awoken** [-kən] pt, pp of **awake.**

awry [ə'raɪ] adv: to be ~ estar de viés or de esguelha; **to go** ~ sair mal.

axe, ax (US) [æks] n machado // vt (employee) despedir; (project etc) parar; (jobs) reduzir.

axiom ['æksɪəm] n axioma m.

axis ['æksɪs], pl **axes** [-siːz] n eixo.

axle ['æksl] n eixo.

ay(e) [aɪ] excl (yes) sim; **the ayes** npl os que votam a favor.

Aztec ['æztɛk] adj, n asteca m/f.

B

B.A. abbr of **Bachelor of Arts** Licenciado/Bacharel m em Letras.

babble ['bæbl] vi balbuciar.

baboon [bə'buːn] n babuíno.

baby ['beɪbɪ] n criança, bebê m/f; ~ **carriage** n (US) carrinho de bebê; ~**ish** adj infantil; ~-**sit** vi tomar conta de crianças; ~-**sitter** n baby-sitter m/f.

bachelor ['bætʃələ*] n solteiro; (EDUC) bacharel m.

back [bæk] n (of person) costas fpl; (of animal) lombo; (of hand) dorso; (of house, car, train) parte f de trás; (of chair) encosto; (of page) verso; (of coin) reverso; (FOOTBALL) zagueiro (Br); defesa m (Pt) // vt (also: ~ **up**) apoiar; (horse: at races) apostar em; (car) recuar or fazer marcha-à-ré (Pt: marcha atrás) // vi (car etc) recuar // adj (in compounds) de trás; ~ **seats/wheels** (AUT) assentos mpl/rodas fpl de trás; ~ **payments** pagamentos atrasados mpl; ~ **rent** aluguel m atrasado // adv (not forward) para trás; (returned): **he's** ~ ele voltou; **he ran** ~ recuou correndo; (restitution): **throw the ball** ~ devolva a bola; **can I have it** ~? pode devolvê-lo?; (again): **he called** ~ chamou de novo; **to** ~ **down** vi desistir; **to** ~ **out** (of) vi (promise) não cumprir (com).

back: ~**ache** n dor f nas costas; ~**bencher** n membro do parlamento sem liderança; ~**biting** n difamação f; ~**bone** n coluna vertebral; ~**cloth** n pano de fundo; ~**date** vt (letter) pôr data atrasada em; ~**dated pay rise** aumento de vencimento com efeito retroativo; ~**er** n partidário; (COMM) promotor m; ~**fire** n (AUT) retorno de chama // vi (plans) falhar; ~**gammon** n gamão m; ~**ground** n fundo; (of events) antecedentes mpl; (basic knowledge) bases fpl; (experience) conhecimentos mpl, experiência; **family** ~**ground** origem f, antecedentes mpl; ~**hand** n (TENNIS: also: ~**hand stroke**) revés m; ~**handed** adj (fig) ambíguo, insincero; ~**hander** n (bribe) suborno; (Pt) peita;

~ing n (fig) apoio; ~lash n reação (Pt: -cç-) f; ~log n: ~log of work atrasos mpl; ~ number n (of magazine etc) número atrasado; ~ pay n pagamento atrasado; ~side n (col) traseiro; ~stage adv nos bastidores; ~stroke n nado de costas; ~ward adj (movement) para trás; (person, country) atrasado; (shy) tímido; ~wards adv (move, go) para trás; (read a list) às avessas; (fall) de costas; ~water n (fig) lugar m atrasado; ~yard n quintal m.

bacon ['beɪkən] n toucinho, bacon m.

bacteria [bæk'tɪərɪə] npl bactérias fpl.

bad [bæd] adj mau; (serious) grave; (meat, food) estragado; to go ~ estragar-se.

badge [bædʒ] n emblema m; (of policeman) crachá m.

badger ['bædʒə*] n texugo.

badly ['bædlɪ] adv (work, dress etc) mal; ~ wounded gravemente ferido; he needs it ~ faz-lhe grande falta; to be ~ off (for money) estar com pouco dinheiro.

badminton ['bædmɪntən] n badminton m.

bad-tempered ['bæd'tɛmpəd] adj mal humorado; (temporary) de mau humor.

baffle ['bæfl] vt (puzzle) confundir.

bag [bæg] n saco, bolsa; (handbag) bolsa; (satchel) sacola; (case) mala; (of hunter) caça // vt (col: take) apanhar; ~ful n saco cheio; ~gage n bagagem f; ~gage checkroom n (US) depósito da bagagem; ~gy adj largo; ~pipes npl gaita de foles.

bail [beɪl] n fiança // vt (prisoner: gen: give ~ to) libertar sob fiança; (boat: also: ~ out) esgotar a água de; to ~ sb out tirar alguém da prisão sob fiança; see also bale.

bailiff ['beɪlɪf] n oficial m de justiça (Br), oficial m de diligências (Pt).

bait [beɪt] n isca, engodo // vt iscar, cevar.

bake [beɪk] vt cozer ao forno // vi (cook) cozer-se; (be hot) fazer um calor terrível; ~d beans npl feijão m cozido; baker n padeiro; ~ry n (for bread) padaria; (for cakes) confeitaria; baking n (act) cozimento; (batch) fornada; baking powder n fermento em pó.

balance ['bæləns] n equilíbrio; (scales) balança; (COMM) balanço; (remainder) resto, saldo // vt equilibrar; (budget) nivelar; (account) fazer o balanço; (compensate) contrabalançar; ~ of trade/payments balança do comércio/de pagamentos; ~d adj (personality, diet) equilibrado; ~ sheet n balanço geral.

balcony ['bælkənɪ] n (open) varanda; (closed) galeria.

bald [bɔːld] adj calvo, careca; ~ness n calvície f.

bale [beɪl] n (AGR) fardo; to ~ out (of a plane) atirar-se de pára-quedas; to ~ sb

out of a difficulty ajudar alguém a sair dum problema.

baleful ['beɪlful] adj (look) triste; (sinister) funesto, sinistro.

ball [bɔːl] n (gen) bola; (dance) baile m.

ballad ['bæləd] n balada.

ballast ['bæləst] n lastro.

ballerina [bælə'riːnə] n bailarina.

ballet ['bæleɪ] n balé m, bailado; ~ dancer n bailarino/a.

balloon [bə'luːn] n balão m; bola de soprar; ~ist n aeronauta m/f.

ballot ['bælət] n votação f; ~ box n urna; ~ paper n cédula eleitoral.

ball-point pen ['bɔːlpɔɪnt'-] n (caneta) esferográfica.

ballroom ['bɔːlrum] n salão m de baile.

balmy ['bɑːmɪ] adj (breeze, air) suave, fragrante; (col) = barmy.

Baltic ['bɔːltɪk] n: the ~ (Sea) o (Mar) Báltico.

balustrade ['bæləstreɪd] n balaustrada.

bamboo [bæm'buː] n bambu m.

ban [bæn] n proibição f, interdição f // vt proibir, interditar; (exclude) excluir.

banal [bə'nɑːl] adj banal, vulgar.

banana [bə'nɑːnə] n banana.

band [bænd] n (group) bando, banda; (gang) quadrilha, bando; (strip) faixa, cinta; (at a dance) orquestra; (MIL) banda; to ~ together vi juntar-se, associar-se.

bandage ['bændɪdʒ] n atadura (Br), ligadura (Pt) // vt enfaixar.

bandit ['bændɪt] n bandido; one-armed ~ caça-níqueis m inv (Br), máquina de tragar (Pt).

bandstand ['bændstænd] n coreto.

bandwagon ['bændwægən] n: to jump on the ~ (fig) aderir.

bandy ['bændɪ] vt (jokes, insults) trocar.

bandy-legged ['bændɪ'lɛgd] adj cambaio, de pernas tortas.

bang [bæŋ] n estalo; (of door) estrondo; (blow) pancada // vt bater com força; (door) fechar com violência // vi produzir estrondo; to ~ upon bater com força em.

banger ['bæŋə*] n (car: gen: old ~) calhambeque m, lata-velha.

bangle ['bæŋgl] n bracelete m, pulseira.

banish ['bænɪʃ] vt desterrar, exilar, banir.

banister(s) ['bænɪstə(z)] n(pl) corrimão m.

banjo ['bændʒəu], pl ~es or ~s n banjo.

bank [bæŋk] n (COMM) banco; (of river, lake) borda, margem f; (of earth) rampa, ladeira // vi (AVIAT) ladear-se; to ~ on vt fus contar com; to ~ with ter a conta com; ~ account n conta bancária; ~er n banqueiro; B~ holiday n feriado nacional; ~ing n transações fpl bancárias; ~note n nota; ~ rate n (Br) taxa bancária.

bankrupt ['bæŋkrʌpt] n falido/a, quebrado/a // adj falido, quebrado; to go ~ falir; to be ~ estar falido/

quebrado; ~**cy** n falência; (fraudulent) bancarrota.

banner ['bænə*] n bandeira; (in demonstration) estandarte m.

banns [bænz] npl proclamas fpl.

banquet ['bæŋkwɪt] n banquete m.

baptism ['bæptɪzəm] n batismo (Pt: -pt-).

baptize [bæp'taɪz] vt batizar (Pt: -pt-).

bar [ba:*] n (gen, MUS) barra; (of window etc) tranca; (of soap) sabão m; (fig: hindrance) obstáculo; (prohibition) impedimento; (pub) bar m; (counter: in pub) balcão m // vt (road) obstruir; (window) trancar; (person) excluir; (activity) proibir; **behind** ~**s** na prisão; **the B**~ (LAW) (profession) a advocacia; (people) o corpo de advogados; ~ **none** sem exceção (Pt: -pç-).

barbaric [ba:'bærɪk] adj bárbaro.

barbarous ['ba:bərəs] adj bárbaro.

barbecue ['ba:bɪkju:] n churrasco.

barbed wire ['ba:bd-] n arame m farpado.

barber ['ba:bə*] n barbeiro, cabeleireiro.

barbiturate [ba:'bɪtjurɪt] n barbitúrico.

bare [bɛə*] adj nu; (head) descoberto // vt desnudar, descobrir; **to** ~ **one's teeth** mostrar os dentes; ~**back** adv em pêlo, sem arreios; ~**faced** adj descarado; ~**foot** adj, adv descalço; ~**ly** adv apenas, mal.

bargain ['ba:gɪn] n contrato, negócio; (good buy) pechincha // vi negociar; (haggle) regatear; **into the** ~ ainda por cima.

barge [ba:dʒ] n barcaça; **to** ~ **in** vi entrar sem permissão; **to** ~ **into** vt fus (collide with) atropelar; (interrupt) intrometer-se em.

baritone ['bærɪtəun] n barítono.

bark [ba:k] n (of tree) casca; (of dog) latido // vi ladrar, latir.

barley ['ba:lɪ] n cevada.

barmaid ['ba:meɪd] n garçonete f (Br), empregada (de bar) (Pt).

barman ['ba:mən] n garçom m (Br), empregado (de bar) (Pt).

barmy ['ba:mɪ] adj (col) maluco.

barn [ba:n] n celeiro.

barnacle ['ba:nəkl] n craca f.

barometer [bə'rɔmɪtə*] n barômetro.

baron ['bærən] n barão m; ~**ess** n baronesa.

barracks ['bærəks] npl quartel m, caserna.

barrage ['bæra:ʒ] n (MIL) fogo de barragem; (dam) barragem f.

barrel ['bærəl] n barril m, barrica; (of gun) cano.

barren ['bærən] adj (sterile) estéril; (land) árido.

barricade [bærɪ'keɪd] n barricada // vt barricar.

barrier ['bærɪə*] n barreira; (obstacle) obstáculo.

barring ['ba:rɪŋ] prep exceto (Pt: -pt-), salvo.

barrister ['bærɪstə*] n advogado/a.

barrow ['bærəu] n (cart) carrinho (de mão).

bartender ['ba:tɛndə*] n (US) garçom m (Br), empregado (de bar) (Pt).

barter ['ba:tə*] vt: **to** ~ **sth for sth** trocar algo por algo.

base [beɪs] n base f // vt: **to** ~ **sth on** basear or fundamentar algo em // adj baixo, inferior; ~**ball** n beisebol m; ~**ment** n porão m, subsolo.

bash [bæʃ] vt (col: with fist) dar soco or murro em; (: with object) acertar.

bashful ['bæʃful] adj tímido, envergonhado.

bashing ['bæʃɪŋ] n (col) surra.

basic ['beɪsɪk] adj básico; ~**ally** adv fundamentalmente, basicamente.

basil ['bæzl] n manjericão m.

basin ['beɪsn] n (vessel) bacia, tigela; (dock, GEO) bacia; (also: **wash**~) pia.

basis ['beɪsɪs] n, pl **-ses** [-si:z] n base f.

bask [ba:sk] vi: **to** ~ **in the sun** pegar sol (Br), tomar o sol (Pt).

basket ['ba:skɪt] n cesto; (with handle) cesta; ~**ball** n basquete(bol) m; ~**work** n obra de verga, trabalho de vime.

Basque [bæsk] adj, n basco/a; ~ **Country** País m Basco.

bass [beɪs] n (MUS) baixo; (fish) robalo, perca.

bassoon [bə'su:n] n fagote m.

bastard ['ba:stəd] n bastardo/a.

baste [beɪst] vt (CULIN) untar.

bastion ['bæstɪən] n baluarte m.

bat [bæt] n (ZOOL) morcego; (for ball games) bastão m; (for cricket, baseball) bastão; (for table tennis) raquete f; **he didn't** ~ **an eyelid** ele nem pestanejou.

batch [bætʃ] n (of bread) fornada; (pile of papers) monte m; (lot) remessa.

bated ['beɪtɪd] adj: **with** ~ **breath** contendo a respiração.

bath [ba:θ, pl ba:ðz] n (~**tub**) banho, banheira; (also: ~) banho, piscina // vt banhar; **to have a** ~ tomar um banho; ~**chair** n cadeira de rodas.

bathe [beɪð] vi banhar-se // vt banhar, lavar; **bather** n banhista m/f.

bathing ['beɪðɪŋ] n banho; ~ **cap** n touca de banho; ~ **costume** n (woman's) maiô m (Br), fato de banho (Pt); ~ **trunks** npl calção m (de banho) (Br), calções mpl de banho (Pt).

bath: ~**mat** n tapete m de borracha; ~**room** n banheiro (Br), casa de banho (Pt); ~**s** npl piscina sg; ~ **towel** n toalha de banho.

baton ['bætən] n (MUS) batuta.

battalion [bə'tælɪən] n batalhão m.

batter ['bætə*] vt espancar, bater // n massa; ~**ed** adj (hat, pan) amassado, muito usado.

battery ['bætərɪ] n bateria; (of torch) pilha.

battle ['bætl] n batalha; (fig) luta // vi lutar; ~**field** n campo de batalha; ~**ments** npl ameias fpl; ~**ship** n couraçado.

bawdy ['bɔːdɪ] adj indecente; (joke) imoral.

bawl [bɔːl] vi gritar, berrar.

bay [beɪ] n (GEO) baía; (BOT) louro // vi ladrar; **to hold sb at ~** manter alguém a distância.

bayonet ['beɪənɪt] n baioneta.

bay window ['beɪ-] n janela saliente.

bazaar [bə'zɑː*] n bazar m.

bazooka [bə'zuːkə] n bazuca.

b. & b., B. & B. abbr of **bed and breakfast** cama e café da manhã (Br), cama e pequeno almoço (Pt).

BBC n abbr of **British Broadcasting Corporation.**

B.C. adv abbr of **before Christ** antes de Cristo, a.c.

be [biː], pt **was, were,** pp **been** vi (of permanent place/state) ser; (of temporary place/condition) estar; **I am English** sou inglês; **I am tired** estou cansado; **how are you?** como está?; **who is it?** quem é?; **it is raining** está chovendo (Br), está a chover (Pt); **I am warm** estou com calor; **it is cold** está frio; **where is the bank?** onde é o banco?; **how much is it?** quanto é or custa?; **he is four (years old)** tem quatro anos; **2 and 2 are 4** dois e dois são quatro; **where have you been?** onde tem estado?, onde você estava?

beach [biːtʃ] n praia // vt puxar para a terra or praia, encalhar.

beacon ['biːkən] n (lighthouse) farol m; (marker) guia.

bead [biːd] n (necklace) conta; (of sweat) gota.

beak [biːk] n bico.

beaker ['biːkə*] n copo com bico.

beam [biːm] n (ARCH) viga; (of light) raio; (NAUT) través m // vi brilhar; (smile) sorrir; **~ing** adj (sun, smile) radiante.

bean [biːn] n feijão m; **runner ~** vagem f (Br), feijão m verde (Pt); **broad ~** fava; **coffee ~** grão m de café.

bear [bɛə*] n urso // (vb: pt **bore,** pp **borne**) vt (weight etc) levar; (cost) pagar; (responsibility) ter; (endure) suportar, aguentar; (stand up to) resistir a; (children) ter, dar à luz // vi: **to ~ right/left** virar à direita/à esquerda; **~able** adj suportável, tolerável.

beard [bɪəd] n barba; **~ed** adj barbado.

bearing ['bɛərɪŋ] n porte m, comportamento; (position) posição f; (connection) relação f; (ball) **~** rolamento de esferas; **~s** npl orientação f; **to take a ~** orientar-se; **to find one's ~s** encontrar o rumo.

beast [biːst] n besta, animal m; (col) bruto, selvagem m; **~ly** adj bestial; (awful) horrível.

beat [biːt] n (of heart) batida; (MUS) ritmo, compasso; (of policeman) ronda // (vb: pt **beat,** pp **beaten**) vt (hit) golpear; (eggs) bater; (defeat) vencer, derrotar; (better) ultrapassar; (drum) tocar; (rhythm) marcar // vi (heart) bater; **to ~ about**

the bush fazer rodeios; **to ~ it** ir embora; **to ~ off** vt repelir; **to ~ up** vt (col: person) dar uma sova em; **~er** n (for eggs, cream) batedeira; **~ing** n batida; (of person) sova, surra.

beautiful ['bjuːtɪful] adj belo, lindo, formoso; **~ly** adv maravilhosamente, lindamente; **beautify** [-faɪ] vt embelezar.

beauty ['bjuːtɪ] n beleza, formosura; (person) beldade f, beleza; **~ salon** n salão m de beleza; **~ spot** n 'sinal' m (de beleza na pele); (TOURISM) lugar m de beleza excepcional.

beaver ['biːvə*] n castor m.

becalmed [bɪ'kɑːmd] adj parado devido à calmaria.

became [bɪ'keɪm] pt of **become.**

because [bɪ'kɔz] conj porque; **~ of** prep por causa de.

beck [bɛk] n: **to be at the ~ and call of** estar às ordens de.

beckon ['bɛkən] vt (also: **~ to**) chamar com sinais, acenar para.

become [bɪ'kʌm] (irr: like come) vt (suit) favorecer a // vi (+ noun) fazer-se, tornar-se; (+ adj) tornar-se, ficar; **to ~ fat** engordar, ficar gordo.

becoming [bɪ'kʌmɪŋ] adj (behaviour) decoroso; (clothes) favorecedor(a), elegante.

bed [bɛd] n cama; (of flowers) canteiro; (of coal, clay) camada, base f; **to go to ~** ir dormir; **single/double ~** cama de solteiro/de casal; **~clothes** npl roupa sg de cama; **~ding** n roupa de cama.

bedlam ['bɛdləm] n confusão f.

bedraggled [bɪ'dræɡld] adj molhado, ensopado; (dirty) enlameado.

bed: ~ridden adj acamado; **~room** n quarto de dormir; **~side** n: **at sb's ~side** à cabeceira de alguém; **~sit(ter)** n kitinete f, kitchinete f; **~spread** n colcha.

bee [biː] n abelha.

beech [biːtʃ] n faia.

beef [biːf] n carne f de vaca; **roast ~** rosbife m.

bee: ~hive n colméia; **~line** n: **to make a ~line for** ir direto a.

been [biːn] pp of **be.**

beer [bɪə*] n cerveja.

beetle ['biːtl] n besouro.

beetroot ['biːtruːt] n beterraba.

before [bɪ'fɔː*] prep (of time) antes de; (of space) diante de // conj antes que // adv (time) antes, anteriormente; (space) diante, adiante; **the week ~** a semana anterior; **I've never seen it ~** nunca vi isso antes.

befriend [bɪ'frɛnd] vt fazer amizade com; fazer-se amigo de.

beg [bɛɡ] vi pedir, rogar; (as beggar) pedir esmola // vt pedir, rogar por; (entreat) suplicar.

began [bɪ'ɡæn] pt of **begin.**

beggar ['bɛɡə*] n mendigo.

begin [bɪ'ɡɪn], pt **began,** pp **begun** vt/i

começar, principiar; **~ner** *n* principiante *m/f;* **~ning** *n* princípio, começo.

begrudge [bɪ'grʌdʒ] *vt:* **to ~** sb sth invejar algo de alguém.

begun [bɪ'gʌn] *pp of* begin.

behalf [bɪ'hɑːf] *n:* **on ~** of em nome de, em favor de.

behave [bɪ'heɪv] *vi* (*person*) portar-se, comportar-se; (*thing*) funcionar; (*well: also:* **~ o.s.**) comportar-se (bem); **behaviour, behavior** (*US*) *n* comportamento, conduta.

behind [bɪ'haɪnd] *prep* atrás de // *adv* atrás, detrás, para trás // *n* traseiro; **~ time** atrasado.

behold [bɪ'həʊld] (*irr: like* hold) *vt* contemplar.

beige [beɪʒ] *adj* bege.

being ['biːɪŋ] *n* (*state*) existência; (*entity*) ser *m;* **to come into ~** nascer, aparecer.

belated [bɪ'leɪtɪd] *adj* atrasado, tardio.

belch [beltʃ] *vi* arrotar // *vt* (*gen:* **~ out:** *smoke etc*) vomitar.

belfry ['belfrɪ] *n* campanário.

Belgian ['beldʒən] *adj, n* belga *m/f.*

Belgium ['beldʒəm] *n* Bélgica.

belie [bɪ'laɪ] *vt* desmentir, contradizer.

belief [bɪ'liːf] *n* (*opinion*) opinião *f;* (*trust, faith*) fé *f;* (*acceptance as true*) crença, convicção *f.*

believable [bɪ'liːvəbl] *adj* crível, acreditável.

believe [bɪ'liːv] *vt/i* crer, acreditar; **believer** *n* crente *m/f,* fiel *m/f;* (*POL*) partidário/a.

belittle [bɪ'lɪtl] *vt* diminuir, depreciar.

bell [bel] *n* sino; (*small, door*) campainha; (*animal's, on toy*) guizo, sininho.

belligerent [bɪ'lɪdʒərənt] *adj* (*at war*) beligerante; (*fig*) agressivo.

bellow ['beləʊ] *vi* berrar, mugir; (*person*) bramar // *vt* (*orders*) gritar, berrar.

bellows ['beləʊz] *npl* fole *m.*

belly ['belɪ] *n* barriga, ventre *m.*

belong [bɪ'lɒŋ] *vi:* **to ~** to pertencer a; (*club etc*) ser sócio de; **~ings** *npl* bens *mpl.*

beloved [bɪ'lʌvɪd] *adj, n* querido, amado.

below [bɪ'ləʊ] *prep* abaixo de, debaixo de // *adv* em baixo; **see ~** ver abaixo.

belt [belt] *n* cinto; (*MED*) faixa; (*TECH*) correia, cinta // *vt* (*thrash*) surrar; **~way** *n* (*US*) via circular.

bench [bentʃ] *n* banco; **the B~** (*LAW*) tribunal *m;* (*people*) magistratura.

bend [bend] *pt, pp* **bent** *vt* dobrar, curvar; (*leg, arm*) dobrar // *vi* dobrar-se, inclinar-se // *n* (*in road*) curva; (*in pipe, river*) ângulo, curva; **to ~ down** *vi* dobrar-se; **to ~ over** *vi* inclinar-se.

beneath [bɪ'niːθ] *prep* abaixo de, em baixo de (*Br*), debaixo de (*Pt*); (*unworthy of*) indigno de // *adv* em baixo.

benefactor ['benɪfæktə*] *n* benfeitor(a) *m/f.*

beneficial [benɪ'fɪʃəl] *adj* proveitoso, benéfico.

benefit ['benɪfɪt] *n* benefício, proveito; (*profit*) bonificação *f;* (*money*) subsídio // *vt* beneficiar, aproveitar // *vi:* **he'll ~ from it** ele há-de beneficiar-se disso.

Benelux ['benɪlʌks] *n* Benelux *m.*

benevolent [bɪ'nevələnt] *adj* benévolo.

bent [bent] *pt, pp of* bend // *n* inclinação *f;* **to have a ~** for ter queda para // *adj:* **to be ~ on** estar empenhado em.

bequeath [bɪ'kwiːð] *vt* legar.

bequest [bɪ'kwest] *n* legado.

bereaved [bɪ'riːvd] *n:* **the ~** os enlutados *mpl;* **bereavement** ['riːvmənt] *n* privação *f,* luto.

beret ['bereɪ] *n* boina.

berm [bɜːm] *n* (*US*) acostamento (*Br*), berma (*Pt*).

berry ['berɪ] *n* baga.

berserk [bə'sɜːk] *adj:* **to go ~** perder as estribeiras.

berth [bɜːθ] *n* (*bed*) cama; (*cabin*) beliche *m;* (*for ship*) ancoradouro // *vi* ancorar, prover com beliche.

beseech [bɪ'siːtʃ] *pt, pp* **besought** ['sɔːt] *vt* suplicar.

beset [bɪ'set] *pt, pp* **beset** *vt* assediar; (*person*) acossar.

beside [bɪ'saɪd] *prep* junto de, ao lado de, ao pé de; **to be ~ o.s. (with anger)** estar fora de si.

besides [bɪ'saɪdz] *adv* além disso // *prep* (*as well as*) além de; (*except*) salvo, exceto (*Pt:* -pt-).

besiege [bɪ'siːdʒ] *vt* (*town*) sitiar, pôr cerco a; (*fig*) assediar.

best [best] *adj* melhor // *adv* o melhor; **the ~ part of** (*quantity*) a maior parte de; **at ~** quando muito; **to make the ~ of** sth tirar o maior partido possível de algo; **to the ~ of my knowledge** que eu saiba; **to the ~ of my ability** o melhor que eu puder; **~ man** *n* padrinho de casamento.

bestow [bɪ'stəʊ] *vt* outorgar; (*affection*) dar, oferecer.

bestseller ['best'selə*] *n* sucesso de vendagem, best-seller *m.*

bet [bet] *n* aposta // *vt/i, pt, pp* **bet** *or* **betted** apostar, jogar.

betray [bɪ'treɪ] *vt* trair, atraiçoar; (*denounce*) delatar; **~al** *n* traição *f.*

better ['betə*] *adj, adv* melhor // *vt* melhorar; (*go above*) superar // *n:* **to get the ~ of** levar vantagem sobre, levar a melhor; **you had ~ do it** é melhor você fazer isso; **he thought ~ of it** pensou melhor, mudou de opinião; **to get ~** melhorar(-se); (*MED*) recuperar-se; **~ off** *adj* em melhor situação.

betting ['betɪŋ] *n* jogo, aposta; **~ shop** *n* agência de apostas.

between [bɪ'twiːn] *prep* no meio de, entre; **~ you and me** cá entre nós, aqui entre nós // *adv* no meio.

beverage ['bevərɪdʒ] *n* bebida.

bevy ['bɛvɪ] *n*: **a ~ of** um grupo/bando de.

beware [bɪ'wɛə*] *vi*: **to ~ (of)** precaver-se (de), ter cuidado (com) // *excl* cuidado!

bewildered [bɪ'wɪldəd] *adj* perturbado, perplexo.

bewitching [bɪ'wɪtʃɪŋ] *adj* feiticeiro, encantador(a), sedutor(a).

beyond [bɪ'jɔnd] *prep* (*in space*) além de; (*exceeding*) acima de, fora de; (*above*) superior a; **~ doubt** fora de dúvida; **~ repair** irreparável; **~ reach** fora do alcance // *adv* além, mais longe.

bias ['baɪəs] *n* (*prejudice*) preconceito, prevenção *f*; (*preference*) inclinação *f*; **~(s)ed** *adj* (*against*) preconceituoso (contra); (*towards*) parcial.

bib [bɪb] *n* babadouro, babador *m*.

Bible ['baɪbl] *n* Bíblia.

bibliography [bɪblɪ'ɔgrəfɪ] *n* bibliografia.

bicker ['bɪkə*] *vi* discutir.

bicycle ['baɪsɪkl] *n* bicicleta.

bid [bɪd] *n* (*at auction*) oferta, lance *m*; (*attempt*) tentativa // (*vb*: *pt* **bade** [bæd] *or* **bid**, *pp* **bidden** ['bɪdn] *or* **bid**) *vi* fazer uma oferta, (*COMM*) licitar, fazer uma licitação // *vt* mandar, ordenar; **to ~ sb good day** desejar bom dia a alguém; **~der** (*COMM*) licitante *m*; **the highest ~der** quem oferece mais; **~ding** *n* (*at auction*) lance *m*; (*COMM*) licitação *f*; (*order*) ordem *f*.

bide [baɪd] *vt*: **to ~ one's time** esperar o momento adequado.

bidet ['biːdeɪ] *n* bidê *m*.

bier [bɪə*] *n* féretro.

big [bɪg] *adj* grande; (*important*) importante; (*error*) grave.

bigamy ['bɪgəmɪ] *n* bigamia.

bigheaded ['bɪg'hɛdɪd] *adj* vaidoso.

bigot ['bɪgət] *n* fanático, intolerante *m/f*; **~ed** *adj* fanático, intolerante; **~ry** *n* fanatismo, intolerância.

bike [baɪk] *n* bicicleta.

bikini [bɪ'kiːnɪ] *n* biquíni *m*.

bile [baɪl] *n* bílis *f*.

bilingual [baɪ'lɪŋgwəl] *adj* bilíngüe.

bill [bɪl] *n* (*account*) conta; (*invoice*) fatura (*Pt*: -ct-); (*POL*) projeto (*Pt*: -ct-) de lei; (*US*: *banknote*) bilhete *m*, nota; (*of bird*) bico; **stick no ~s** é proibido afixar cartazes.

billet ['bɪlɪt] *n* alojamento.

billfold ['bɪlfəuld] *n* (*US*) carteira para notas.

billiards ['bɪlɪədz] *n* bilhar *m*.

billion ['bɪlɪən] *n* (*Brit*:=*1,000,000,000,000*) trilhão *m*; (*US*:=*1,000,000,000*) bilhão *m*.

billy goat ['bɪlɪ-] *n* bode *m*.

bin [bɪn] *n* (*gen*) caixa; **bread/litter ~** cesta de pão/lata de lixo.

bind [baɪnd], *pt*, *pp* **bound** *vt* atar, ligar; (*wound*) enfaixar; (*book*) encadernar; (*oblige*) obrigar; **~ing** *adj* (*contract*) sujeitante.

binge [bɪndʒ] *n* bebedeira, farra.

bingo ['bɪŋgəu] *n* bingo.

binoculars [bɪ'nɔkjuləz] *n* binóculo *msg*.

bio... [baɪə] *pref*: **~chemistry** *n* bioquímica; **~graphy** [baɪ'ɔgrəfɪ] *n* biografia; **~logical** *adj* biológico; **~logy** [baɪ'ɔlədʒɪ] *n* biologia.

birch [bəːtʃ] *n* bétula; (*cane*) vara de vidoeiro.

bird [bəːd] *n* ave *f*, pássaro; (*col*: *girl*) menina, moça; **~cage** *n* gaiola; **~'s eye view** *n* vista aérea *or* geral; **~watcher** *n* ornitófilo.

birth [bəːθ] *n* nascimento; (*MED*) parto; **to give ~ to** dar à luz; **~ certificate** *n* certidão *m* de nascimento; **~ control** *n* controle *m* de natalidade; (*methods*) métodos *mpl* anticoncepcionais; **~day** *n* aniversário (*Br*), dia *m* de anos (*Pt*); **~place** *n* lugar *m* de nascimento; **~rate** *n* índice *m* de natalidade.

biscuit ['bɪskɪt] *n* bolacha, biscoito.

bisect [baɪ'sɛkt] *vt* dividir ao meio.

bishop ['bɪʃəp] *n* bispo.

bit [bɪt] *pt of* **bite** // *n* pedaço, bocado; (*of horse*) freio; **a ~ of** um pouco de; **a ~ mad** um pouco *or* meio doido; **~ by ~** pouco a pouco.

bitch [bɪtʃ] *n* (*dog*) cadela, cachorra.

bite [baɪt], *pt* **bit**, *pp* **bitten** *vt/i* morder; (*insect etc*) picar // *n* mordedura; (*insect ~*) picadura; (*mouthful*) bocado; **let's have a ~ (to eat)** vamos comer algo.

biting ['baɪtɪŋ] *adj* cortante; (*wind*) penetrante; (*sharp*) mordaz.

bitten ['bɪtn] *pp of* **bite**.

bitter ['bɪtə*] *adj* amargo; (*wind, criticism*) cortante, penetrante; (*battle*) encarniçado // *n* (*beer*) cerveja amarga; **~ness** *n* amargor *m*; (*anger*) rancor *m*.

bizarre [bɪ'zɑː*] *adj* esquisito.

blab [blæb] *vi* chocalhar, dar à língua, dar/bater com a língua nos dentes // *vt* (*also*: **~ out**) revelar, chocalhar.

black [blæk] *adj* (*colour*) negro, preto; (*dark*) escuro, sombrio // *n* negro, preto; (*colour*) cor *f* preta // *vt* (*shoes*) lustrar (*Br*), engraxar (*Pt*); (*INDUSTRY*) boicotar; **to give sb a ~ eye** dar um soco em alguém (no olho); (*col*) engraxar alguém; **~ and blue** *adj* contuso, contundido; **~berry** *n* amora preta (*Br*), amora silvestre (*Pt*); **~bird** *n* melro; **~board** *n* quadro(-negro); **~currant** *n* groselha negra; **~en** *vt* enegrecer; (*fig*) denegrir; **~ jack** *n* (*US*) vinte-e-um *m*; **~leg** *n* fura-greve *m*; **~list** *n* lista negra; **~mail** *n* chantagem // *vt* fazer chantagem a; **~mailer** *n* chantagista *m/f*; **~ market** *n* mercado *or* câmbio negro; **~out** *n* blecaute *m*; (*fainting*) desmaio; **~smith** *n* ferreiro.

bladder ['blædə*] *n* bexiga.

blade [bleɪd] *n* folha; (*cutting edge*) lâmina; **a ~ of grass** uma folha de relva.

blame [bleɪm] *n* culpa // *vt*: **to ~ sb for sth** culpar alguém por algo; **to be to ~** ter a culpa; **~less** *adj* (*person*) inocente.

bland [blænd] *adj* suave; (*taste*) brando.

blank [blæŋk] *adj* em branco; (*shot*) sem bala; (*look*) sem expressão // *n* lacuna, espaço em branco; (*cartridge*) cartucho sem bala; bala de festim.

blanket ['blæŋkɪt] *n* cobertor *m*, manta // *vt* cobrir, tapar.

blare [blɛə*] *vi* (*horn*) buzinar.

blasé ['blɑːzeɪ] *adj* indiferente.

blasphemy ['blæsfɪmɪ] *n* blasfêmia.

blast [blɑːst] *n* (*of wind*) rajada; pé-de-vento *m*; (*of whistle*) toque *m*; (*of explosive*) explosão *f*, sopro; (*force*) choque *m* // *vt* (*blow up*) fazer voar; (*blow open*) abrir com uma carga explosiva; ~ **furnace** *n* alto forno; ~-**off** *n* (*SPACE*) lançamento.

blatant ['bleɪtənt] *adj* descarado.

blaze [bleɪz] *n* (*fire*) fogo; (*flames*) chamas *fpl*; (*fig*) explosão *f* // *vi* (*fire*) arder; (*fig*) resplandecer // *vt*: **to** ~ **a trail** (*fig*) abrir (um) caminho.

blazer ['bleɪzə*] *n* casaco esportivo, blazer *m*.

bleach [bliːtʃ] *n* (*also*: **household** ~) água sanitária // *vt* (*linen*) branquear; ~**ed** *adj* (*hair*) oxigenado; (*linen*) alvejante.

bleak [bliːk] *adj* (*countryside*) desolado; (*prospect*) desanimador(a).

bleary-eyed ['blɪərɪ'aɪd] *adj* de olhos injetados (*Pt*: -ct-).

bleat [bliːt] *vi* balir.

bleed [bliːd], *pt*, *pp* **bled** [blɛd] *vt/i* sangrar.

blemish ['blɛmɪʃ] *n* mancha, falha.

blend [blɛnd] *n* mistura // *vt* misturar // *vi* (*colours etc*) combinar-se, misturar-se.

bless [blɛs], *pt*, *pp* **blessed** or **blest** [blɛst] *vt* abençoar; ~**ing** *n* bênção *f*; (*advantage*) benefício, vantagem *f*.

blew [bluː] *pt of* **blow**.

blight [blaɪt] *vt* (*hopes etc*) frustrar, gorar.

blimey ['blaɪmɪ] *excl* (*col*) meu Deus!

blind [blaɪnd] *adj* cego // *n* (*for window*) persiana *f* // *vt* cegar; (*dazzle*) deslumbrar; ~ **alley** *n* beco-sem-saída *m*; ~ **corner** *n* canto oculto; ~**fold** *n* venda // *adj*, *adv* com os olhos vendados, às cegas // *vt* vendar os olhos a; ~**ly** *adv* às cegas, cegamente; ~**ness** *n* cegueira; ~ **spot** *n* ponto cego.

blink [blɪŋk] *vi* piscar; (*light*) cintilar, piscar; ~**ers** *npl* (*AUT*) luzes *fpl* intermitentes, faróis *mpl* pisca-pisca, pisca-pisca *m*; (*horse*) antolhos *mpl*.

blinking ['blɪŋkɪŋ] *adj* (*col*): **this** ~... este danado..., este infame...

bliss [blɪs] *n* felicidade *f*; (*fig*) êxtase *m*.

blister ['blɪstə*] *n* (*on skin*) bolha, empola // *vi* (*paint*) empolar-se; ~**ing** *adj* (*heat*) causticante.

blithe [blaɪð] *adj* alegre.

blithering ['blɪðərɪŋ] *adj* (*col*): **this** ~ **idiot** esta besta quadrada.

blitz [blɪts] *n* bombardeio aéreo.

blizzard ['blɪzəd] *n* nevasca.

bloated ['bləʊtɪd] *adj* inchado.

blob [blɒb] *n* (*drop*) gota; (*stain*, *spot*) mancha.

block [blɒk] *n* bloco; (*in pipes*) entupimento; (*of buildings*) quarteirão *m* // *vt* (*gen*) obstruir, bloquear; (*progress*) impedir; ~**ade** [-'keɪd] *n* bloqueio // *vt* bloquear; ~**age** *n* estorvo, obstrução *f*; ~ **of flats** *n* prédio de apartamentos; ~ **letters** *npl* letras *fpl* maiúsculas.

bloke [bləʊk] *n* (*col*) cara *m* (*Br*), gajo (*Pt*).

blond(e) [blɒnd] *adj*, *n* louro/a.

blood [blʌd] *n* sangue *m*; ~ **donor** *n* doador(a) *m/f* de sangue; ~ **group** *n* grupo sanguíneo; ~ **hound** *n* sabujo; ~ **pressure** *n* pressão *f* sanguínea; ~**shed** *n* matança; ~**shot** *adj* injetado (*Pt*: -ct-); ~**stained** *adj* manchado de sangue; ~**stream** *n* corrente *f* sanguínea; ~**thirsty** *adj* sanguinário; ~ **transfusion** *n* transfusão *f* de sangue; ~**y** *adj* sangrento, miserável, desgraçado; (*col!*): **this** ~**y...** essa droga de ..., esse maldito de ...; ~**y strong/good** (*col!*) forte/bom para burro or à beça; ~**y-minded** *adj* (*col*) espírito de porco.

bloom [bluːm] *n* flor *f*; (*fig*) florescimento, viço // *vi* florescer; ~**ing** *adj* (*col*): **this** ~**ing...** esse maldito..., esse miserável....

blossom ['blɒsəm] *n* flor *f* // *vi* florescer; (*fig*) desabrochar-se.

blot [blɒt] *n* borrão *m* // *vt* secar; (*ink*) manchar; **to** ~ **out** *vt* (*view*) apagar, ocultar.

blotchy ['blɒtʃɪ] *adj* (*complexion*) cheio de manchas.

blotting paper ['blɒtɪŋ-] *n* mata-borrão *m*.

blouse [blauz] *n* blusa.

blow [bləʊ] *n* golpe *m* // (*vb*: *pt* **blew**, *pp* **blown** [bləʊn]) *vi* soprar // *vt* (*glass*) soprar; (*fuse*) queimar; (*instrument*) tocar; **to** ~ **one's nose** assoar o nariz; **to** ~ **away** *vt* levar, arrancar; **to** ~ **down** *vt* derrubar; **to** ~ **off** *vt* levar; **to** ~ **out** *vi* apagar; **to** ~ **over** *vi* passar, ser esquecido; **to** ~ **up** *vi* explodir; (*fig*) perder a paciência // *vt* dinamitar; (*tyre*) encher; (*PHOT*) ampliar; ~**lamp** *n* maçarico; ~-**out** *n* (*of tyre*) furo, estouro.

blubber ['blʌbə*] *n* óleo de baleia // *vi* (*pej*) chorar.

blue [bluː] *adj* azul; ~ **film/joke** filme/anedota picante; **to have the** ~**s** estar deprimido or (*col*) na fossa; ~**bell** *n* campainha (*Br*), campânula; ~**bottle** *n* varejeira azul; ~ **jeans** *npl* jeans *msg* (*Br*), jeans *mpl* (*Pt*); ~**print** *n* anteprojeto (*Pt*: -ct-).

bluff [blʌf] *vi* enganar, mentir // *n* blefe *m*; (*crag*) penhasco.

blunder ['blʌndə*] *n* erro crasso, asneira, disparate *m* // *vi* cometer um erro crasso.

blunt [blʌnt] *adj* boto, embotado; (*person*)

franco, direto (Pt: -ct-) // vt embotar;
~ness n (of person) franqueza, rudeza.
blur [blə:*] n borrão m, nebulosidade f //
vt borrar, nublar.
blurt [blə:t]: ~ out vt (say) deixar
escapar, dizer impensadamente.
blush [blʌʃ] vi corar, ruborizar-se // n
rubor m, vermelhidão f.
blustering ['blʌstərɪŋ] adj (person)
fanfarrão/rona.
blustery ['blʌstərɪ] adj (weather)
borrascoso, tormentoso.
board [bɔ:d] n tábua; (on wall) quadro;
(for chess etc) tabuleiro; (committee)
junta, conselho; (in firm) diretoria (Pt:
-ct-), conselho administrativo // vt (ship)
embarcar; (train) embarcar em; full ~
pensão f completa; to go by the ~ (fig)
ficar abandonado; to ~ up vt (door)
guarnecer de tábuas; ~ and lodging n
pensão f; ~**er** n hóspede m/f; (SCOL)
interno; ~**ing house** n pensão m; ~**ing
pass** n (US) cartão m de embarque;
~**ing school** n internato; ~ **room** n
gabinete   m   da   diretoria   da
administração.
boast [bəust] vi gabar-se, jactar-se // vt
ostentar // n jactância, bazófia; ~**ful** adj
vaidoso, jactancioso.
boat [bəut] n barco, bote m; (big) navio;
~**er** n (hat) chapéu m de palha; ~**ing** n
(esporte) remo; ~**man** n barqueiro;
~**swain** ['bəusn] n contramestre m.
bob [bɔb] vi (boat, cork on water: also: ~
up and down) balouçar-se; to ~ up vi
aparecer, surgir // n (col) = **shilling.**
bobbin ['bɔbɪn] n (of sewing machine)
bobina, carretel m.
bobby ['bɔbɪ] n (col) policial m/f (Br),
polícia m (Pt).
bobsleigh ['bɔbsleɪ] n bob m, trenó f
duplo.
bodice ['bɔdɪs] n corpete m.
bodily ['bɔdɪlɪ] adj corpóreo, corporal //
adv (in person) em pessoa; (lift) em peso.
body ['bɔdɪ] n corpo; (corpse) cadáver m;
(of car) carroçaria; (fig: society)
conjunto; (fig: quantity) parte f principal;
in a ~ todos juntos; ~**guard** n guarda-
costas m inv; ~**work** n carroçaria.
bog [bɔg] n pântano, atoleiro // vt: to
get ~**ged down** (fig) atolar-se.
boggle ['bɔgl] vi: **the mind** ~**s** (wonder)
não dá para imaginar; (innuendo) nem
quero pensar.
bogus ['bəugəs] adj falso; (person) fingido,
farsante.
boil [bɔɪl] vt ferver; (eggs) cozinhar // vi
ferver // n (MED) furúnculo; **to come to
the** ~ começar a ferver; **to** ~ **down
to** (fig) reduzir-se a; ~**er** n caldeira;
~**er suit** n macacão m; ~**ing point** n
ponto de ebulição.
boisterous ['bɔɪstərəs] adj (noisy)
barulhento; (excitable) agitado; (crowd)
turbulento.
bold [bəuld] adj (brave) valente, audaz;
(excessively) atrevido; (pej) descarado;

(outline, colour) forte; ~**ness** n arrojo,
coragem   f;   (cheek)   audácia,
descaramento.
Bolivia [bə'lɪvɪə] n Bolívia; ~**n** adj, n
boliviano/a.
bollard ['bɔləd] n (AUT) poste m.
bolster ['bəulstə*] n travesseiro; **to** ~
up vt reforçar; (fig) sustentar.
bolt [bəult] n (lock) trinco, ferrolho; (with
nut) parafuso, cavilha // vt (door) fechar
a ferrolho, trancar; (food) engolir // vi
fugir; (horse) disparar.
bomb [bɔm] n bomba // vt bombardear;
~**ard** [-'bɑ:d] vt bombardear; (fig)
assediar;   ~**ardment** [-'bɑ:dmənt] n
bombardeio.
bombastic [bɔm'bæstɪk] adj empolado;
(person) pomposo.
bomb: ~ **disposal** n desmontagem f de
explosivos; ~**er** n (AVIAT) bombardeiro;
~**shell** n granada de artilharia; (fig)
bomba.
bona fide ['bəunə'faɪdɪ] adj genuíno,
autêntico.
bond [bɔnd] n (binding promise) título;
(FINANCE) obrigação f; (link) vínculo,
laço.
bondage [bɔndɪdʒ] n escravidão f.
bone [bəun] n osso; (of fish) espinha // vt
tirar as espinhas de, desossar; ~-**dry**
adj completamente seco; ~ **idle** adj
preguiçoso.
bonfire ['bɔnfaɪə*] n fogueira.
bonnet ['bɔnɪt] n boina; (Brit: of car) capô
f.
bonus ['bəunəs] n bônus m, prêmio.
bony ['bəunɪ] adj (arm, face, MED: tissue)
ossudo; (meat) cheio de ossos; (fish)
cheio de espinhas.
boo [bu:] vt apupar, vaiar.
booby trap ['bu:bɪ-] n armadilha com
bomba.
book [buk] n livro; (notebook) caderno;
(of stamps etc) livro; (COMM): ~**s** as
contas // vt reservar; (driver) contratar;
~**case** n estante f para livros; ~**ing
office** n (RAIL, THEATRE) bilheteria; (Pt)
bilheteira; ~-**keeping** n escrituração f,
contabilidade   f;   ~**let** n livrinho,
brochura; ~**maker** n book(maker) m
(Br), agenciador m de apostas (Pt);
~**seller** n livreiro; ~**shop** n livraria;
~ **stall** n banca de livros.
boom [bu:m] n (noise) barulho, estrondo;
(in prices etc) aumento rápido; (ECON)
fase f ou aumento de prosperidade.
boomerang ['bu:məræŋ] n bumerangue
m.
boon [bu:n] n benefício.
boost [bu:st] n estímulo // vt estimular;
~**er** n (MED) revacinação f.
boot [bu:t] n bota; (Brit: of car) mala (Br),
porta-bagagem m (Pt) // vt dar pontapé
em; **to** ~ (in addition) ainda por cima.
booth [bu:ð] n (at fair) barraca, tenda;
(telephone ~, voting ~) cabine f.
booty ['bu:tɪ] n despojos mpl, pilhagem f.

booze [bu:z] (col) n bebedeira, bebida alcoólica // vi embebedar-se.

border ['bɔːdə*] n margem f, borda; (of a country) fronteira // adj fronteiriço; to ~ on vt fus limitar-se com; (fig) chegar às raias de; ~iine n (fig) fronteira.

bore [bɔː*] pt of bear // vt (hole) furar, perfurar; (person) aborrecer // n (person) chato, maçante; (of gun) calibre m; what a ~! que chateação! (Br), que saco! (Br), que maçada! (Pt); ~dom n aborrecimento, tédio.

boring ['bɔːrɪŋ] adj chato, aborrecido, maçante.

born [bɔːn] adj: to be ~ nascer; I was ~ in 1960 nasci em 1960.

borne [bɔːn] pp of bear.

borough ['bʌrə] n município.

borrow ['bɔrəu] vt: to ~ sth (from sb) pedir algo emprestado a alguém.

borstal ['bɔːstl] n reformatório (de menores).

bosom ['buzəm] n peito; (fig) seio; ~ friend n amigo do peito or íntimo.

boss [bɔs] n chefe m/f; (employer) patrão/troa m/f; (agriculture, industry etc) capataz m // vt dar ordens a, mandar; ~y adj mandão/dona.

bosun ['bəusn] n contramestre m.

botanist ['bɔtənɪst] n botânico; **botany** [-nɪ] n botânica.

botch [bɔtʃ] vt (also: ~ up) estropiar, atamancar.

both [bəuθ] adj, pron ambos, os dois; ~ of us went, we ~ went nós dois fomos, ambos fomos // adv: ~ A and B tanto A como B.

bother ['bɔðə*] vt (worry) preocupar; (disturb) incomodar, molestar // vi (gen: ~ o.s.) preocupar-se; to ~ doing dar-se ao trabalho de fazer; to ~ about preocupar-se com // n: what a ~! que chateação! (Br), que maçada! (Pt).

bottle ['bɔtl] n garrafa; (small) frasco; (baby's) mamadeira (Br), biberão m (Pt) // vt engarrafar; to ~ up vt conter, refrear; ~neck n (traffic) engarrafamento; (bottle) gargalo; ~-opener n abridor m (de garrafas) (Br), abre-garrafas m inv (Pt).

bottom ['bɔtəm] n (of box, sea) fundo; (buttocks) traseiro; (col) bunda; (of page, list) pé m // adj (low) inferior, mais baixo; (last) último; ~less adj sem fundo; (fig) insondável.

bough [bau] n ramo.

bought [bɔːt] pt, pp of buy.

boulder ['bəuldə*] n pedregulho, matacão m.

bounce [bauns] vi (ball) saltar, quicar; (cheque) ser devolvido // vt fazer saltar // n (rebound) salto.

bound [baund] pt, pp of bind // n (leap) pulo, salto; (gen pl: limit) limites mpl // vi (leap) pular, saltar // adj: ~ by limitado por; to be ~ to do sth (obliged) ter a obrigação de fazer algo; (likely) na certa ir fazer algo; out of ~s

entrada proibida, fora dos limites; ~ for com destino a.

boundary ['baundrɪ] n limite m, fronteira.

boundless ['baundlɪs] adj ilimitado.

bouquet ['bukeɪ] n (of flowers) ramalhete m; (of wine) aroma m.

bout [baut] n (of malaria etc) ataque m; (: outbreak) surto; (BOXING etc) combate m.

bow [bəu] n (knot) laço; (weapon, MUS) arco // n [bau] (of the head) reverência; (NAUT) proa // vi [bau] curvar-se, fazer uma reverência; (yield): to ~ to or before ceder ante, submeter-se a.

bowels [bauəlz] npl intestinos mpl, tripas fpl.

bowl [bəul] n tigela; (for washing) bacia; (ball) bola de madeira // vi (CRICKET) arremessar a bola; ~s n jogo de boliche.

bow-legged ['bəulegɪd] adj cambaio, de pernas tortas.

bowler ['bəulə*] n (CRICKET) lançador m (da bola); (also: ~ hat) chapéu-coco m.

bowling ['bəulɪŋ] n (game) boliche m; ~ alley n pista de boliche; ~ green n gramado (Pt: relvado) para boliches.

bow tie ['bəu-] n gravata-borboleta.

box [bɔks] n (also: cardboard ~) caixa, caixote m; (for jewels) estojo; (for money) cofre m; (THEATRE) camarote m // vt encaixotar // vi (SPORT) boxear; ~er n (person) boxeador m, pugilista; (dog) boxer m; ~ing n (SPORT) boxe m, pugilismo; B~ing Day n Dia de Santo Estêvão, 26 de dezembro; ~ing gloves npl luvas fpl de boxe; ~ing ring n ringue m de boxe; ~ office n bilheteria (Br), bilheteira (Pt); ~room n quarto pequeno.

boy [bɔɪ] n (young) menino, garoto; (older) moço, rapaz m; (servant) criado.

boycott ['bɔɪkɔt] n boicote m, boicotagem f // vt boicotar.

boyfriend ['bɔɪfrɛnd] n namorado.

boyish ['bɔɪʃ] adj de menino, pueril.

B.R. abbr of **British Rail.**

bra [brɑː] n sutiã (Pt: soutien) m.

brace [breɪs] n reforço, braçadeira; (on teeth) aparelho; (tool) arco de pua // vt firmar, reforçar; ~s npl suspensórios mpl; to ~ o.s. (fig) recobrar ânimo.

bracelet ['breɪslɪt] n pulseira.

bracing ['breɪsɪŋ] adj tonificante.

bracken ['brækən] n samambaia (Br), feto (Pt).

bracket ['brækɪt] n (TECH) suporte m; (group) classe f, grupo; (also: brace ~) chave f; (also: round ~) parêntese m; (gen: square ~) colchete m // vt (group) agrupar.

brag [bræg] vi gabar-se.

braid [breɪd] n (trimming) galão m; (of hair) trança.

Braille [breɪl] n braile m.

brain [breɪn] n cérebro; ~s npl inteligência, miolos mpl; ~child n idéia original; ~wash vt fazer uma lavagem cerebral a; ~**wave** n inspiração f, ideia maravilhosa; ~**y** adj inteligente or muito esperto.

braise [breɪz] vt estufar.

brake [breɪk] n (on vehicle) freio (Br), travão m (Pt) // vt/i frear (Br), travar (Pt); ~ **drum** n tambor m de freio (Pt: de travão); ~ **fluid** n óleo de freio (Pt: dos travões).

bramble ['bræmbl] n amora-preta.

branch [brɑːntʃ] n ramo, galho; (fig) ramificação f, seção (Pt: -çc-) f; (road) ramal m; (COMM) sucursal f, filial f // vi (also: ~ **out**) ramificar-se; (fig) desenvolver-se, ampliar-se.

brand [brænd] n marca; (iron) ferro de marcar // vt (cattle) marcar com ferro quente.

brandish ['brændɪʃ] vt brandir.

brand-new ['brænd'njuː] adj novo em folha, completamente novo.

brandy ['brændɪ] n conhaque m.

brash [bræʃ] adj (rough) grosseiro; (cheeky) descarado.

brass [brɑːs] n latão m; ~ **band** n banda de música.

brassiere ['bræsɪə*] n sutiã (Pt: soutien) m.

brat [bræt] n (pej) pirralho, fedelho, malcriado.

bravado [brə'vɑːdəu] n bravata.

brave [breɪv] adj valente, corajoso // n guerreiro pele-vermelha // vt (challenge) desafiar; (resist) encarar; ~**ry** n coragem f, bravura.

brawl [brɔːl] n briga, rixa // vi brigar.

brawn [brɔːn] n força; (meat) patê m de carne; ~**y** adj musculoso, carnudo.

bray [breɪ] n zurro, ornejo // vi zurrar, ornejar.

brazen ['breɪzn] adj descarado // vt: to ~ **it out** defender-se descaradamente.

brazier ['breɪzɪə*] n braseiro.

Brazil [brə'zɪl] n Brasil m; ~**ian** adj, n brasileiro/a.

breach [briːtʃ] vt abrir brecha em // n (gap) brecha; (breaking): ~ **of contract** inadimplência (Br), inadimplemento (Pt); ~ **of the peace** perturbação f da ordem pública.

bread [brɛd] n pão m; ~ **and butter** n pão com manteiga; (fig) ganha-pão m, sustento // adj comum e corrente; ~**crumbs** npl migalhas fpl; (CULIN) farinha de rosca.

breadth [brɛtθ] n largura; (fig) amplitude f.

breadwinner ['brɛdwɪnə*] n arrimo de família.

break [breɪk], pt **broke**, pp **broken** vt (gen) quebrar, partir; (split) romper; (promise) quebrar; (word) faltar a; (fall) amortecer; (journey) interromper; (law) violar, transgredir; (record) bater; (news) revelar // vi quebrar-se, partir-se; (storm) estalar // n (gap) abertura; (crack) fenda; (fracture) fratura (Pt: -ct-); (breakdown) ruptura, rompimento; (rest)

descanso; (time) intervalo; (at school) recreio; (chance) oportunidade f; (escape) evasão f, fuga; **to** ~ **down** vt (figures, data) analisar; (undermine) acabar com // vi desarranjar-se; (TECH: parar) enguiçar; (MED) sofrer um colapso; (AUT) avariar-se; (person) desatar a chorar; **to** ~ **even** vi sair sem ganhar nem perder; **to** ~ **free** or **loose** vi escapar-se, libertar-se; **to** ~ **in** vt (horse etc) domar; (US: car) fazer a rodagem de // vi (burglar) forçar uma entrada; **to** ~ **into** vt fus (house) arrombar; **to** ~ **off** vi (speaker) parar-se, deter-se; (branch) partir; **to** ~ **open** vt (door etc) abrir com esforço, forçar; **to** ~ **out** vi estalar, rebentar; **to** ~ **out in spots** aparecer coberto de manchas; **to** ~ **up** vi romper-se // vt romper; (intervene) intervir em; ~**able** adj quebradiço, frágil; ~**age** n (COMM) quebra; ~**down** n (AUT) avaria; (in communications) interrupção f; (machine) enguiço; (MED: also: **nervous** ~**down**) esgotamento nervoso; ~**down lorry** (Brit) n reboque m (Br), pronto socorro (Pt); ~**er** n onda grande.

breakfast ['brɛkfəst] n café m da manhã (Br), pequeno almoço (Pt).

break: ~**through** n ruptura; (fig) avanço, irrupção f; ~**water** n quebra-mar m.

breast [brɛst] n (of woman) peito, seio; (chest) peito; ~-**stroke** n nado de peito.

breath [brɛθ] n fôlego, hálito, respiração f; **out of** ~ ofegante, sem fôlego; ~**alyser** n bafômetro.

breathe [briːð] vt/i respirar; (noisily) ressonar; **breather** n pausa.

breath: ~**less** adj sem fôlego, ofegante; ~**taking** adj empolgante.

breed [briːd], pt, pp **bred** [brɛd] vt criar, gerar // vi reproduzir-se, procriar-se // n raça, casta; ~**er** n (person) criador(a) m/f; ~**ing** n (of person) educação f.

breeze [briːz] n brisa, aragem f.

breezy ['briːzɪ] adj ventoso; (person) despreocupado, animado.

brevity ['brɛvɪtɪ] n brevidade f.

brew [bruː] vt (tea) fazer; (beer) fermentar // vi fazer-se, preparar-se; (fig) armar-se; ~**er** n cervejeiro; ~**ery** n cervejaria.

bribe [braɪb] n suborno // vt subornar; ~**ry** n suborno.

brick [brɪk] n tijolo; ~**layer** n pedreiro; ~**works** n fábrica de tijolos.

bridal ['braɪdl] adj nupcial.

bride [braɪd] n noiva; ~**groom** n noivo; **bridesmaid** n dama de honra.

bridge [brɪdʒ] n ponte f; (NAUT) ponte de comando; (CARDS) bridge m // vt (river) lançar uma ponte sobre; ~**head** n cabeça-de-ponte f.

bridle ['braɪdl] n cabeçada, freio // vt enfrear; (fig) refrear, conter; ~ **path** n senda.

brief [briːf] adj breve, curto // n (LAW)

causa // vt (*inform*) informar; (*instruct*) instruir; ~s npl (*for men*) cueca sg (*Br*), cuecas fpl (*Pt*); (*for women*) calcinha sg (*Br*), cuecas fpl (*Pt*); ~**case** n pasta; ~**ing** n (*PRESS*) instruções fpl.

brigade [bri'geid] n (*MIL*) brigada.

brigadier [brigǝ'diǝ*] n general m de brigada, brigadeiro.

bright [brait] adj claro, brilhante; (*weather*) resplandescente; (*person: clever*) esperto, inteligente; (: *lively*) alegre, animado; (*colour*) vivo; ~**en** vt (*room*) tornar mais alegre // vi (*weather*) clarear; (*person: gen*: ~**en up**) animar-se, alegrar-se.

brilliance ['briljǝns] n brilho, claridade f; **brilliant** [-ǝnt] adj brilhante; (*clever*) inteligente, esperto.

brim [brim] n borda; (*of hat*) aba; ~**ful** adj cheio até as bordas; (*fig*) repleto.

brine [brain] n (*CULIN*) salmoura.

bring [briŋ], pt, pp **brought** vt (*thing*) trazer; (*person*) conduzir; **to ~ about** vt ocasionar, produzir; **to ~ back** vt trazer de volta; (*return*) devolver; **to ~ down** vt baixar; (*price*) reduzir; **to ~ forward** vt adiantar; **to ~ in** vt (*harvest*) recolher; **to ~ off** vt (*task, plan*) conseguir; **to ~ out** vt (*object*) tirar; **to ~ round** vt (*unconscious person*) fazer voltar a si; (*convince*) convencer, ganhar; **to ~ up** vt (*person*) educar, criar; (*carry up*) subir; (*question*) introduzir.

brink [briŋk] n borda.

brisk [brisk] adj vigoroso; (*speedy*) rápido; (*trade*) ativo (*Pt*: -ct-).

brisket ['briskit] n carne f de vaca para assar.

bristle ['brisl] n cerda // vi eriçar-se; **to ~** with estar cheio de.

Britain ['britǝn] n Grã-Bretanha.

British ['britiʃ] adj britânico; **the ~** npl os Britânicos; **the ~ Isles** npl as Ilhas Britânicas.

Briton ['britǝn] n britânico.

brittle ['britl] adj quebradiço, frágil.

broach [brǝutʃ] vt (*subject*) abordar, tocar em.

broad [brɔːd] adj amplo, largo; (*accent*) carregado; **in ~ daylight** em pleno dia; ~**cast** n transmissão f // (vb: pt, pp ~**cast**) vt (*RADIO, TV*) transmitir // vi falar ou tocar pelo rádio; ~**casting** n radiodifusão f, transmissão f; ~**en** vt alargar // vi alargar-se, ampliar-se; ~**ly** adv em geral; ~**-minded** adj tolerante, liberal.

brochure ['brǝuʃjuǝ*] n folheto, brochura.

broil [brɔil] vt (*US*) grelhar.

broke [brǝuk] pt of **break** // adj (*col*) sem um vintém, duro.

broken ['brǝukǝn] pp of **break** // adj: ~ **leg** perna quebrada; **in ~ English** num inglês mascavado; ~**-hearted** com o coração partido.

broker ['brǝukǝ*] n corretor(a) m/f.

bronchitis [brɔŋ'kaitis] n bronquite f.

bronze [brɔnz] n bronze m.

brooch [brǝutʃ] n broche m.

brood [bruːd] n ninhada; (*children*) filhos mpl; (*pej*) prole f // vi (*hen*) chocar; (*obsessively*) cismar, parafusar, matutar.

brook [bruk] n arroio, ribeiro.

broom [brum] n vassoura; (*BOT*) giesta; ~**stick** n cabo de vassoura.

Bros. abbr of **Brothers**.

broth [brɔθ] n caldo.

brothel ['brɔθl] n bordel m.

brother ['brʌðǝ*] n irmão m; ~**-in-law** n cunhado.

brought [brɔːt] pt, pp of **bring**.

brow [brau] n fronte f; (*forehead*) testa; (*of hill*) cimo, cume m.

brown [braun] adj marrom (*Br*), castanho (*Pt*); (*hair*) castanho; (*tanned*) bronzeado, moreno // n (*colour*) cor f castanha // vt tostar; (*tan*) bronzear; (*CULIN*) dourar; ~**ie** n menina 'Girl Guide', fadinha de bandeirante.

browse [brauz] vi (*among books*) folhear livros.

bruise [bruːz] n hematoma m, contusão f // vt magoar, contundir.

brunette [bruː'net] n morena.

brunt [brʌnt] n: **the ~ of** o ímpeto de; (*greater part*) a maior parte de.

brush [brʌʃ] n escova; (*for painting, shaving etc*) pincel m; (*BOT*) mato rasteiro; (*quarrel*) escaramuça // vt escovar; (*gen*: ~ **past**, ~ **against**) tocar ao passar, roçar; **to ~ aside** vt afastar, não fazer caso de; **to ~ up** vt (*knowledge*) retocar, revisar; ~**wood** n (*bushes*) mato; (*sticks*) lenha, gravetos mpl.

brusque [bruːsk] adj brusco, áspero.

Brussels ['brʌslz] n Bruxelas; ~ **sprout** n couve-de-bruxelas f.

brutal ['bruːtl] adj brutal; ~**ity** [-'tæliti] n brutalidade f.

brute [bruːt] n bruto; (*person*) animal m.

B.Sc. abbr of **Bachelor of Science** licenciado/a em ciências.

bubble ['bʌbl] n bolha (*Br*), borbulha (*Pt*) // vi borbulhar; ~ **gum** n chiclete m (de bola) (*Br*), pastilha elástica (*Pt*).

buck [bʌk] n macho; (*US: col*) dólar m // vi corcovear; **to pass the ~** fazer o jogo do empurra; **to ~ up** vi (*cheer up*) animar-se, cobrar ânimo.

bucket ['bʌkit] n balde m.

buckle ['bʌkl] n fivela // vt afivelar // vi torcer-se, cambar-se.

bud [bʌd] n broto, rebento; (*of flower*) botão m // vi brotar, desabrochar; (*fig*) florescer.

Buddhism ['budizm] n budismo.

budding ['bʌdiŋ] adj em botão, nascente.

buddy ['bʌdi] n (*US*) camarada m, companheiro.

budge [bʌdʒ] vt mover; (*fig*) fazer ceder // vi mexer-se.

budgerigar ['bʌdʒǝrigɑː*] n periquito.

budget ['bʌdʒit] n orçamento.

budgie ['bʌdʒi] *n* = **budgerigar.**

buff [bʌf] *adj* (*colour*) cor *f* de camurça // *n* (*enthusiast*) entusiasta *m/f*.

buffalo ['bʌfələu], *pl* ~ *or* ~**es** *n* búfalo.

buffer ['bʌfə*] *n* pára-choque *m*.

buffet ['bufei] *n* (*bar*) bar *m*, cafeteria; (*food*) bufê *m* // *vt* ['bʌfit] (*strike*) esbofetear; (*wind etc*) fustigar; ~ **car** *n* vagão-restaurante *m*.

buffoon [bə'fu:n] *n* bufão *m*.

bug [bʌg] *n* (*insect*) percevejo; (: *gen*) bicho; (*fig: germ*) micróbio; (*spy device*) microfone *m* oculto; (*tap*) escuta clandestina; (*machine for tapping*) aparelho de escuta // *vt* (*fam*) maçar, enfadar; (*spy on*) escutar, grampear.

bugle ['bju:gl] *n* trompa, corneta.

build [bild] *n* (*of person*) talhe *m*, estatura // *vt, pt, pp* **built** construir, edificar; ~**er** *n* construtor *m*; (*contractor*) contratista *m/f*; empreiteiro/a *m/f*; ~**ing** *n* (*act of*) construção *f*; (*habitation, offices*) edifício, prédio; (*habitation*) edifício, prédio; ~**ing society** *n* sociedade *f* imobiliária, financiadora; **to** ~ **up** *vt* (*MED*) fortalecer; (*stocks*) acumular.

built [bilt] *pt, pp of* **build** // *adj*: ~-**in** (*cupboard*) embutido; (*device*) interior, incorporado, embutido; ~-**up** (*area*) urbanizado.

bulb [bʌlb] *n* (*BOT*) bulbo; (*ELEC*) lâmpada.

Bulgaria [bʌl'gɛəriə] *n* Bulgária; ~**n** *adj, n* búlgaro/a.

bulge [bʌldʒ] *n* bojo, saliência // *vi* inchar-se; (*pocket etc*) fazer bojo.

bulk [bʌlk] *n* (*mass*) massa, volume *m*; (*major part*) parte *f* principal, grosso; **in** ~ (*COMM*) a granel; **the** ~ **of** a maior parte de; ~**head** *n* anteparo; ~**y** *adj* volumoso; (*person*) corpulento.

bull [bul] *n* touro; ~**dog** *n* buldogue *m*.

bulldozer ['buldəuzə*] *n* escavadora.

bullet ['bulit] *n* bala; ~**proof** *adj* à prova de balas; ~ **wound** *n* ferida de bala.

bulletin ['bulitin] *n* boletim *m*; ~ **board** *n* (*US*) quadro de anúncios.

bullfight ['bulfait] *n* tourada; ~**er** *n* toureiro; ~**ing** *n* os touros *mpl*; (*art of* ~*ing*) tauromaquia.

bullion ['buljən] *n* ouro *or* prata em barras.

bullock ['buløk] *n* boi *m*, novilho.

bull's-eye ['bulzai] *n* centro do alvo, mosca (do alvo) (*Br*).

bully ['buli] *n* fanfarrão *m*, valentão *m* // *vt* intimidar, tiranizar.

bum [bʌm] *n* (*col: backside*) traseiro, bunda; (*tramp*) vagabundo, vadio.

bumblebee ['bʌmblbi:] *n* (*ZOOL*) mamangaba.

bump [bʌmp] *n* (*blow*) choque *m*, embate *m*, baque *m*; (*jolt*) sacudida; (*on head*) galo, inchaço; (*sound*) baque *m* // *vt* (*strike*) bater contra, dar encontrão em // *vi* dar sacudidas; **to** ~ **into** *vt fus* chocar-se com/contra, colidir com; (*person*) dar

com; ~ **er** *n* (*Brit*) pára-choque *m* // *adj*: ~ **er crop/harvest** grande safra.

bumpy ['bʌmpi] *adj* (*road*) cheio de altos e baixos; (*journey*) cheio de solavancos.

bun [bʌn] *n* pão *m* doce (*Br*), pãozinho (*Pt*); (*of hair*) coque *m*.

bunch [bʌntʃ] *n* (*of flowers*) ramo; (*of keys*) molho; (*of bananas*) cacho; (*of people*) grupo.

bundle ['bʌndl] *n* (*gen*) trouxa; (*tied up*) embrulho; (*of sticks*) feixe *m*; (*of papers*) maço // *vt* (*also:* ~ **up**) embrulhar, atar; (*put*): **to** ~ **sth/sb into** meter algo/alguém às pressas em.

bung [bʌŋ] *n* tampão *m*, batoque *m* // *vt* abatocar; (*throw: gen:* ~ **into**) botar em.

bungalow ['bʌŋgələu] *n* bangalô *m*, chalé *m*.

bungle ['bʌŋgl] *vt* estropear, estragar, fazer mal feito.

bunion ['bʌnjən] *n* joanete *m*.

bunk [bʌŋk] *n* besteira, disparate *m*; ~ **beds** *npl* beliche *msg*.

bunker ['bʌŋkə*] *n* (*coal store*) carvoeira; (*MIL*) abrigo, casamata; (*GOLF*) obstáculo bunker *m*.

bunny ['bʌni] *n* (*also:* ~ **rabbit**) coelhinho.

bunting ['bʌntiŋ] *n* bandeiras *fpl*.

buoy [bɔi] *n* bóia; **to** ~ **up** *vt* fazer boiar; (*fig*) sustentar, animar; ~**ant** *adj* flutuante; (*person*) alegre.

burden ['bə:dn] *n* carga; (*fig*) fardo // *vt* carregar.

bureau [bjuə'rəu], *pl* ~**x** [-z] *n* (*furniture*) secretária, escrivaninha; (*office*) escritório, agência.

bureaucracy [bjuə'rɔkrəsi] *n* burocracia; **bureaucrat** ['bjuərəkræt] *n* burocrata *m/f*.

burglar ['bə:glə*] *n* ladrão/ladrona *m/f*; ~ **alarm** *n* alarme *m* contra ladrões; ~**y** *n* roubo; **burgle** ['bə:gl] *vt* assaltar.

burial ['bɛriəl] *n* enterro; ~ **ground** *n* cemitério.

burlesque [bə:'lɛsk] *n* paródia.

burly ['bə:li] *adj* robusto, forte.

burn [bə:n], *pt, pp* **burned** *or* **burnt** *vt* queimar; (*house*) incendiar // *vi* queimar-se, arder, incendiar-se; (*sting*) arder, picar // *n* queimadura; **to** ~ **down** *vt* incendiar; ~**er** *n* (*gas*) bico de gás, fogo; ~**ing** *adj* ardente.

burp [bə:p] (*col*) *n* arroto // *vi* arrotar.

burrow ['bʌrəu] *n* toca, lura // *vt* fazer uma toca, cavar.

bursar ['bə:sə*] *n* tesoureiro; (*student*) bolsista (*Br*), bolseiro (*Pt*); ~**y** *n* (*grant*) bolsa.

burst [bə:st], *pt, pp* **burst** *vt* (*balloon, pipe*) arrebentar; (*banks etc*) romper // *vi* rebentar-se, romper-se; (*tyre*) furar-se; (*bomb*) explodir // *n* (*gen*) estouro *m*, rebentamento; (*explosion*) explosão *f*; (*shots*) rajada; **a** ~ **of energy** uma explosão de energia; **to** ~ **into flames** incendiar-se de repente; **to** ~ **into laughter** cair na gargalhada; **to** ~ **into**

tears desatar a chorar; **to be ~ing with** estar estourando de; **to ~ into** vt fus (room etc) irromper em; **to ~ open** vi abrir-se de repente.

bury ['bɛrɪ] vt enterrar; (body) enterrar, sepultar.

bus [bʌs] n ônibus m (Br), autocarro (Pt).

bush [buʃ] n arbusto, mata; (scrub land) sertão m; **to beat about the ~** falar com rodeios (Br), fazer rodeios (Pt); **~y** adj (thick) espesso, denso.

busily ['bɪzɪlɪ] adv atarefadamente.

business ['bɪznɪs] n (matter) negócio; (trading) comércio, negócios mpl; (firm) empresa, casa; (occupation) profissão f; (affair) assunto; **it's my ~ to...** encarrego-me de...; **it's none of my ~** eu não tenho nada com isto; **that's my ~** isso é cá comigo; **he means ~** fala a sério; **~like** adj eficiente, metódico; **~man** n homem m de negócios, comerciante m/f.

bus-stop ['bʌsstɔp] n ponto de ônibus (Br), paragem f de autocarro (Pt).

bust [bʌst] n (ANAT) busto // adj (broken) partido, rasgado; **to go ~** falir.

bustle ['bʌsl] n animação f, movimento // vi apressar-se, andar azafamado; **bustling** adj (town) animado, movimentado.

busy ['bɪzɪ] adj ocupado, atarefado; (shop, street) animado, movimentado; (TEL) ocupado (Br), impedido (Pt) // vr: **to ~ o.s. with** ocupar-se em; **~body** n intrometido.

but [bʌt] conj mas, porém // prep exceto (Pt: -pt-), menos; **nothing ~** só, somente; **~ for** sem, se não fosse; **~ finished** quase acabado, tudo menos acabado.

butane ['bju:teɪn] n butano.

butcher ['butʃə*] n açougueiro (Br), homem do talho (Pt) // vt chacinar; (cattle etc for meat) abater e carnear; **~'s (shop)** n açougue m (Br), talho (Pt).

butler ['bʌtlə*] n mordomo.

butt [bʌt] n (cask) tonel m; (for rain) barril m; (thick end) cabo, extremidade f; (of gun) coronha; (of cigarette) toco (Br), ponta (Pt); (fig: target) alvo // vt dar cabeçadas contra, marrar.

butter ['bʌtə*] n manteiga // vt untar com manteiga; **~ bean** n fava; **~cup** n botão-de-ouro m, ranúnculo.

butterfly ['bʌtəflaɪ] n borboleta.

buttocks ['bʌtəks] npl nádegas fpl.

button ['bʌtn] n botão m // vt abotoar; **~hole** n casa de botão, botoeira; (flower) flor f na lapela // vt obrigar a ouvir.

buttress ['bʌtrɪs] n contraforte m; (fig) apoio, esteio.

buxom ['bʌksəm] adj (baby) saudável; (woman) rechonchudo.

buy [baɪ], pt, pp bought vt comprar // n compra; **to ~ sb sth/sth from sb** comprar algo para alguém/algo a alguém; **~er** n comprador(a) m/f.

buzz [bʌz] n zumbido; (col: phone call) telefonema m // vi zumbir.

buzzard ['bʌzəd] n abutre m, urubu m.

buzzer ['bʌzə*] n sirene f; (doorbell) campainha.

by [baɪ] prep por; (beside) perto de, ao pé de, junto a; (according to) segundo, de acordo com; (before): **~ 4 o'clock** antes das quatro // adv see pass, go etc; **~ bus/car** de ônibus/carro; **paid ~ the hour** pago por hora; **~ night/day** de noite/dia; **(all) ~ oneself** (completamente) só, sozinho; **~ the way** a propósito; **~ and large** em geral; **~ and ~** logo, mais tarde.

bye(-bye) ['baɪ('baɪ)] excl até logo (Br), tchau (Br), adeus (Pt).

by(e)-law ['baɪlɔ:] n lei f de município.

by-election ['baɪɪlɛkʃən] n eleição f parcial.

bygone ['baɪgɔn] adj passado, antigo // n: **let ~s be ~s** que passou passou, águas passadas não movem moinhos.

bypass ['baɪpɑ:s] n via secundária, desvio // vt evitar.

by-product ['baɪprɔdʌkt] n subproduto, produto derivado.

bystander ['baɪstændə*] n circunstante m/f, observador(a) m/f, curioso.

byword ['baɪwɔ:d] n: **to be a ~ for** ser conhecido por.

C

C. abbr of **centigrade**.

C.A. abbr of **chartered accountant**.

cab [kæb] n táxi m; (of truck) cabine m.

cabaret ['kæbəreɪ] n cabaré m.

cabbage ['kæbɪdʒ] n repolho (Br), couve f (Pt).

cabin ['kæbɪn] n cabana; (on ship) camarote m; **~ cruiser** n lancha a motor com cabine.

cabinet ['kæbɪnɪt] n (POL) conselho de ministros; (furniture) armário; (also: **display ~**) armário com vitrina; **~-maker** n marceneiro.

cable ['keɪbl] n cabo; (telegram) cabograma m // vt enviar cabograma; **~-car** n trem m funicular.

cackle ['kækl] vi cacarejar.

cactus ['kæktəs], pl **-ti** [-taɪ] n cacto.

caddie ['kædɪ] n caddie m.

cadet [kə'dɛt] n (MIL) cadete m.

cadge [kædʒ] vt filar; **cadger** n filante m/f.

Caesarean (section) [si:'zɛərɪən] n cesariana.

café ['kæfeɪ], **cafeteria** [kæfɪ'tɪərɪə] n café m.

caffein(e) ['kæfi:n] n cafeína.

cage [keɪdʒ] n gaiola, jaula // vt engaiolar, enjaular.

cagey ['keɪdʒɪ] adj (col) cuidadoso, reservado.

Cairo ['kaırǝu] n Cairo.

cajole [kǝ'dʒǝul] vt lisonjear.

cake [keɪk] n (large) bolo; (small) bolinho, queque m; (of soap) sabonete m; ~**d with** empastado de.

calamitous [kǝ'læmıtǝs] adj calamitoso; **calamity** [-ıtı] n calamidade f.

calcium ['kælsıǝm] n cálcio.

calculate ['kælkjuleıt] vt calcular; **calculating** adj (clever) matreiro, calculista; (devious) esperto; **calculation** [-'leıʃǝn] n cálculo; **calculator** n calculador m.

calculus ['kælkjulǝs] n cálculo.

calendar ['kælǝndǝ*] n calendário; ~ **month/year** mês m/ano civil.

calf [kɑːf], pl **calves** n (of cow) bezerro, vitela; (of other animals) cria; (also: ~**skin**) pele f ou couro de bezerro; (ANAT) barriga-da-perna.

calibre, caliber (US) ['kælıbǝ*] n calibre m.

call [kɔːl] vt/i chamar; (telephone) telefonar a, ligar para; (visit: also: ~ **in**, ~ **round**) fazer uma visita // n (shout) chamada; (TEL) telefonema m; (of bird) canto; (appeal) chamamento, apelo; **to** ~ **for** vt fus (demand) pedir, exigir; (fetch) ir buscar; **to** ~ **off** vt (cancel) cancelar; **to** ~ **on** vt fus (visit) visitar; (turn to) recorrer a; **to** ~ **out** vi gritar, bradar; **to** ~ **up** vt (MIL) chamar às fileiras; ~**box** n cabine f telefônica; ~**er** n visita m/f; (TEL) chamador m; ~ **girl** n prostituta; ~**ing** n vocação f, profissão f.

callous ['kælǝs] adj insensível, cruel.

calm [kɑːm] n calma, tranqüilidade f // vt acalmar, tranqüilizar // adj (gen) tranqüilo; (sea) calmo, sereno; ~**ly** adv tranqüilamente, com calma; ~**ness** n tranqüilidade f; **to** ~ **down** vi acalmar-se, tranqüilizar-se // vt acalmar, tranqüilizar.

calorie ['kælǝrı] n caloria.

calve [kɑːv] vi parir.

calves [kɑːvz] pl of **calf**.

camber ['kæmbǝ*] n (of road) abaulamento.

Cambodia [kæm'bǝudjǝ] n Camboja.

came [keɪm] pt of **come**.

camel ['kæmǝl] n camelo.

cameo ['kæmıǝu] n camafeu m.

camera ['kæmǝrǝ] n máquina fotográfica; (CINEMA, TV) câmara; **in** ~ em câmara; ~**man** n camaraman m.

camouflage ['kæmǝflɑːʒ] n camuflagem f // vt camuflar.

camp [kæmp] n campo, acampamento // vi acampar // adj afetado (Pt: -ct-), afeminado.

campaign [kæm'peɪn] n (MIL, POL etc) campanha // vi fazer campanha.

camp: ~**bed** n cama de campanha; ~**er** n campista m/f; (vehicle) reboque m; ~**ing** n camping m (Br), campismo (Pt); **to go** ~**ing** fazer camping (Br),

fazer campismo (Pt); ~**site** n camping (Br), parque m de campismo (Pt).

campus ['kæmpǝs] n cidade f universitária.

can [kæn] auxiliary vb (gen) poder; (know how to) saber; **I** ~ **swim** sei nadar // n (of oil, water) lata // vt enlatar; (preserve) conservar em latas.

Canada ['kænǝdǝ] n Canadá m; **Canadian** [kǝ'neıdıǝn] adj, n canadense m/f.

canal [kǝ'næl] n canal m.

canary [kǝ'nɛǝrı] n canário; **C**~ **Islands** npl (Ilhas) Canárias fpl.

cancel ['kænsǝl] vt cancelar; (train) cancelar; (appointment) anular; (cross out) riscar, invalidar; ~**lation** [-'leıʃǝn] n cancelamento, anulação f.

cancer ['kænsǝ*] n câncer m (Br), cancro (Pt); **C**~ (ASTRO) câncer.

candid ['kændıd] adj franco, sincero, cândido/a.

candidate ['kændıdeıt] n candidato.

candle ['kændl] n vela; (in church) círio; ~**stick** n (also: ~ **holder**) (single) castiçal m; (bigger, ornate) candelabro, lustre m.

candour ['kændǝ*] n franqueza.

candy ['kændı] n açúcar m cristalizado; (US) bala (Br), rebuçado (Pt).

cane [keɪn] n (BOT) cana; (stick) vara, bengala // vt (SCOL) castigar (com bengala).

canine ['kænaın] adj canino.

canister ['kænıstǝ*] n caixa, lata.

cannabis ['kænǝbıs] n cânhamo, maconha.

canned [kænd] adj em lata, enlatado.

cannibal ['kænıbǝl] n canibal m/f; ~**ism** n canibalismo.

cannon ['kænǝn], pl ~ or ~**s** n canhão m; ~**ball** n bala (de canhão).

cannot ['kænɔt] = **can not**.

canny ['kænı] adj astuto.

canoe [kǝ'nuː] n canoa; ~**ing** n (SPORT) canoagem f; ~**ist** n canoísta m/f.

canon ['kænǝn] n (clergyman) cónego; (standard) cânone m.

canonize ['kænǝnaız] vt canonizar.

can opener ['kænǝupnǝ*] n abridor m de latas (Br), abre-latas m inv (Pt).

canopy ['kænǝpı] n dossel m; (ARCH) baldaquino.

can't [kænt] = **can not**.

cantankerous [kæn'tæŋkǝrǝs] adj rabujento, irritável.

canteen [kæn'tiːn] n cantina; (bottle) cantil m; (of cutlery) jogo (de talheres).

canter ['kæntǝ*] n meio galope // vi ir a meio galope.

canvas ['kænvǝs] n (gen) lona; (painting) tela; (NAUT) velas fpl; **under** ~ (camping) em barracas.

canvass ['kænvǝs] vt (POL) pedir votos de.

canyon ['kænjǝn] n canhão m, garganta, desfiladeiro.

cap [kæp] n gorro; (peaked) boné m; (of

pen) tampa; (of bottle) tampa; (MED)
diafragma m // vt rematar; (outdo)
superar; (FOOTBALL) escalar (para a
equipe nacional).

capability [keɪpə'bɪlɪtɪ] n capacidade f;
capable ['keɪpəbl] adj capaz.

capacity [kə'pæsɪtɪ] n capacidade f;
(position) posição f.

cape [keɪp] n capa; (GEO) cabo.

caper ['keɪpə*] n (CULIN: gen: ~s)
alcaparra; (prank) asneira, travessura.

capital ['kæpɪtl] n (also: ~ city) capital
f; (money) capital m; (also: ~ letter)
maiúscula; ~**ism** n capitalismo; ~**ist**
adj, n capitalista m/f; ~ **punishment** n
pena de morte.

capitulate [kə'pɪtjuleɪt] vi capitular,
render-se; **capitulation** [-'leɪʃən] n
capitulação f, rendição f.

capricious [kə'prɪʃəs] adj caprichoso.

Capricorn ['kæprɪkɔːn] n Capricórnio.

capsize [kæp'saɪz] vti emborcar, virar.

capstan ['kæpstən] n cabrestante m.

capsule ['kæpsjuːl] n cápsula.

captain ['kæptɪn] n capitão m // vt
capitanear, ser o capitão de.

caption ['kæpʃən] n (heading) título; (to
picture) legenda.

captivate ['kæptɪveɪt] vt cativar,
fascinar.

captive ['kæptɪv] adj, n cativo; **captivity**
[-'tɪvɪtɪ] n cativeiro.

capture ['kæptʃə*] vt prender,
aprisionar; (place) tomar; (attention)
captar, chamar // n captura, tomada;
(thing taken) presa.

car [kɑː*] n carro, automóvel m; (RAIL)
vagão m.

carafe [kə'ræf] n garrafa de mesa.

caramel ['kærəməl] n caramelo.

carat ['kærət] n quilate m.

caravan ['kærəvæn] n reboque m, trailer
m; (of camels) caravana.

caraway ['kærəweɪ] n: ~ **seed**
sementes fpl de alcaravia.

carbohydrate [kɑːbəu'haɪdreɪt] n
hidrato de carbono; (food) carboidrato.

carbon ['kɑːbən] n carbono; ~ **copy** n
cópia de papel carbono; ~ **paper** n
papel m carbono.

carburettor, **carburetor** (US)
[kɑːbju'retə*] n carburador m.

carcass ['kɑːkəs] n cadáver m de animal,
carcaça.

card [kɑːd] n carta, bilhete m; (visiting ~,
post~ etc) cartão m, bilhete m; ~**board**
n cartão, papelão m; ~ **game** n jogo de
cartas.

cardiac ['kɑːdɪæk] adj cardíaco.

cardigan ['kɑːdɪgən] n casaco de lã,
cardigã m.

cardinal ['kɑːdɪnl] adj cardeal; (MAT)
cardinal // n (REL) cardeal m; (MAT)
número cardinal.

card index n fichário.

care [kɛə*] n (gen) cuidado; (worry)
preocupação f, ansiedade f; (charge)
encargo, custódia // vi: to ~ **about**

preocupar-se com, ter interesse em; **in
sb's** ~ a cargo de alguém; **to take** ~
to cuidar-se or ter o cuidado de; **to take**
~ **of** vt cuidar de; **to** ~ **for** vt fus cuidar
de; (like) gostar de; **I don't** ~ não me
importa.

career [kə'rɪə*] n carreira // vi (also: ~
along) correr a toda velocidade.

carefree ['kɛəfriː] adj despreocupado.

careful ['kɛəful] adj cuidadoso; (cautious)
cauteloso; **(be)** ~**l** tenha cuidado!; ~**ly**
adv com cuidado, cuidadosamente.

careless ['kɛəlɪs] adj descuidado;
(heedless) desatento; ~**ly** adv sem
cuidado, sem preocupação; ~**ness** n
descuido, falta de atenção.

caress [kə'rɛs] n carícia // vt acariciar.

caretaker ['kɛəteɪkə*] n curador(a) m/f,
guarda m/f, zelador(a) m/f.

car-ferry ['kɑːferɪ] n barca para carros
(Br), barco de passagem (Pt).

cargo ['kɑːgəu], pl ~**es** n
carregamento, carga; (freight) frete m.

Caribbean [kærɪ'biːən] n: the ~ (Sea)
Mar m das Antilhas, Mar das Caraíbas.

caricature ['kærɪkətjuə*] n caricatura.

carnal ['kɑːnl] adj carnal.

carnation [kɑː'neɪʃən] n cravo.

carnival ['kɑːnɪvəl] n carnaval m.

carnivore ['kɑːnɪvɔː*] n carnívoro.

carol ['kærəl] n: **(Christmas)** ~ cântico
de Natal.

carp [kɑːp] n (fish) carpa; **to** ~ **at** vt fus
queixar-se de.

car park n estacionamento.

carpenter ['kɑːpɪntə*] n carpinteiro;
• **carpentry** [-trɪ] n carpintaria.

carpet ['kɑːpɪt] n tapete m // vt atapetar;
~ **slippers** npl chinelos mpl.

carriage ['kærɪdʒ] n carruagem f; coche
m; (RAIL) vagão m; (for goods) transporte
m; (bearing) porte m; ~**way** n (part of
road) pista; **dual** ~**way** pista-dupla.

carrier ['kærɪə*] n carregador(a) m/f,
transportador(a) m/f; (company)
empresa de transportes; ~ **bag** n saco,
sacola.

carrot ['kærət] n cenoura.

carry ['kærɪ] vt (gen) levar; (transport)
transportar; (a motion, bill) aprovar;
(involve: responsibilities etc) implicar // vi
(sound) transportar; **to** ~ **on** vi
(continue) seguir, continuar; (fam:
complain) queixar-se, protestar // vt
prosseguir, continuar; **to** ~ **out** vt
(orders) cumprir; (investigation) levar a
cabo, realizar.

cart [kɑːt] n carroça, carreta; (US: for
lugguage) carrinho // vt transportar (em
carroça).

cartilage ['kɑːtɪlɪdʒ] n cartilagem f.

cartographer [kɑː'tɔgrəfə*] n
cartógrafo.

carton ['kɑːtən] n (box) caixa (de
papelão); (of yogurt) pote m.

cartoon [kɑː'tuːn] n (PRESS) caricatura,
cartum m; (comic strip) história em
quadrinhos (Br), banda desenhada (Pt);

(*film*) desenho animado; ~ist *n* caricaturista *m/f*, cartunista *m/f*.

cartridge ['kɑːtrɪdʒ] *n* cartucho.

carve [kɑːv] *vt* (*meat*) trinchar; (*wood, stone*) cinzelar, esculpir; (*on tree*) gravar; **to ~ up** dividir, repartir; **carving** *n* (*in wood etc*) escultura, obra de talha *or* de entalhe; **carving knife** *n* trinchante *m*, faca-de-trinchar *f*.

car wash *n* lavagem *f* de carros.

cascade [kæs'keɪd] *n* cascata, queda d'água; (*fig*) cachoeira // *vi* cascatear, cair em cascata.

case [keɪs] *n* (*container*) caixa; (*MED*) caso; (*for jewels etc*) estojo; (*LAW*) causa judicial, processo; (*also*: **suit~**) mala; **in ~ (of)** em caso (de); **in any ~** em todo o caso; **just in ~** (*conj*) se por acaso; (*adv*) por via das dúvidas; **to make a good ~** ter bons argumentos.

cash [kæʃ] *n* dinheiro (em espécie) // *vt* cobrar, descontar; **to pay (in) ~** pagar em dinheiro; **~ on delivery** reembolsar contra entrega; **~book** *n* livro-caixa *m*; **~desk** *n* caixa.

cashew [kæ'ʃuː] *n* (*also*: **~ nut**) caju *m*.

cashier [kæ'ʃɪə*] *n* caixa *m/f*.

cashmere [kæʃ'mɪə*] *n* caxemira, cachemira.

cash register *n* caixa-registradora.

casing ['keɪsɪŋ] *n* cobertura; (*of boiler etc*) revestimento.

casino [kə'siːnəu] *n* casino.

cask [kɑːsk] *n* barril *m*, casco.

casket ['kɑːskɪt] *n* cofre *m*, guarda-joias; (*US: coffin*) caixão *m*.

casserole ['kæsərəul] *n* panela de ir ao forno; (*food*) ensopado (*Br*) no forno, guisado (*Pt*) no forno.

cassette [kæ'sɛt] *n* cassete *m*; ~ **player** *n* gravador *m*.

cassock ['kæsək] *n* sotaina, batina.

cast [kɑːst], *pt, pp* **cast** *vt* (*throw*) lançar, atirar; (*skin*) mudar, perder; (*metal*) fundir; (*THEATRE*) dar o papel (a) // *vi* (*FISHING*) lançar // *n* (*THEATRE*) elenco; (*mould*) forma, molde *m*; (*also*: **plaster ~**) gesso; **to ~ away** *vt* desperdiçar; **to ~ down** *vt* abater, desalentar; **to ~ loose** soltar; **to ~ one's vote** votar; **to ~ off** *vi* (*NAUT*) soltar o cabo.

castanets [kæstə'nɛts] *npl* castanholas *fpl*.

castaway ['kɑːstəwəɪ] *n* náufrago.

caste [kɑːst] *n* casta.

casting vote ['kɑːstɪŋ-] *n* voto decisivo, voto de minerva.

cast iron *n* ferro fundido.

castle ['kɑːsl] *n* castelo; (*CHESS*) torre *f*.

castor ['kɑːstə*] *n* (*wheel*) rodízio; ~ **oil** *n* óleo de rícino; ~ **sugar** *n* açúcar *m* branco refinado.

castrate [kæs'treɪt] *vt* castrar.

casual ['kæʒjul] *adj* (*by chance*) fortuito; (*irregular*: *work etc*) eventual, incerto; (*unconcerned*) despreocupado; (*informal*: *clothes*) esportivo, sem cerimônia; ~**ly** *adv* casualmente, sem refletir.

casualty ['kæʒjultɪ] *n* vítima *f* ferido; (*dead*) morto; (*MIL*) baixa; **casualties** *npl* perdas *fpl*.

cat [kæt] *n* gato; ~'s **eye** *n* (*Brit*: *AUTO*) olho de gato.

Catalan ['kætəlæn] *adj*, *n* catalão/lã *m/f*.

catalogue, catalog (*US*) ['kætələg] *n* catálogo // *vt* catalogar.

Catalonia [kætə'ləunɪə] *n* Catalunha.

catalyst ['kætəlɪst] *n* catalisador *m*.

catapult ['kætəpʌlt] *n* catapulta.

cataract ['kætərækt] *n* (*also* *MED*) catarata.

catarrh [kə'tɑː*] *n* catarro.

catastrophe [kə'tæstrəfɪ] *n* catástrofe *f*; **catastrophic** [kætə'strɔfɪk] *adj* catastrófico.

catch [kætʃ], *pt, pp* **caught** *vt* (*gen*) pegar, apanhar; (*arrest*) deter; (*grasp*) agarrar; (*breath*) pegar; (*person*: *by surprise*) pegar, surpreender; chamar; (*MED*) pegar (*Br*), apanhar (*Pt*); (*also*: ~ **up**) alcançar // *vi* (*fire*) pegar fogo; (*in branches etc*) prender-se // *n* (*fish etc*) pesca; (*act of catching*) captura; (*trick*) manha, armadilha; (*of lock*) trinco, lingüeta; **to ~ on** *vi* (*understand*) entender (*Br*), perceber (*Pt*); (*grow popular*) virar moda; **to ~ sight of** ver; **to ~ up** *vi* equiparar-se.

catch: ~**ing** *adj* (*MED*) contagioso; ~**ment area** *n* área de influência; ~**phrase** *n* cliché *m*, slogan *m*; ~**y** *adj* (*tune*) atraente.

catechism ['kætɪkɪzəm] *n* (*REL*) catecismo.

categoric(al) [kætɪ'gɔrɪk(əl)] *adj* categórico, terminante.

categorize ['kætɪgəraɪz] *vt* classificar; **category** [-rɪ] *n* categoria, classe *f*.

cater ['keɪtə*] *vi*: **to ~ for** fornecer comida a; (*needs*) atender a; (*consumers*) satisfazer; ~**er** *n* fornecedor *m*, abastecedor *m*; ~**ing** *n* serviço de bufê; (*trade*) abastecimento.

caterpillar ['kætəpɪlə*] *n* lagarta; ~ **track** *n* lagarta.

cathedral [kə'θiːdrəl] *n* catedral *f*.

catholic ['kæθəlɪk] *adj* católico; **C~** *adj*, *n* (*REL*) católico/a.

cattle ['kætl] *npl* gado *sg*.

catty ['kætɪ] *adj* malicioso, rancoroso.

Caucasus ['kɔːkəsəs] *n* Cáucaso.

caught [kɔːt] *pt, pp of* **catch**.

cauliflower ['kɔlɪflauə*] *n* couve-flor *f*.

cause [kɔːz] *n* causa, motivo, razão *f* // *vt* causar; (*provoke*) provocar.

causeway ['kɔːzweɪ] *n* (*road*) calçada; (*embankment*) banqueta.

caustic ['kɔːstɪk] *adj* cáustico; (*fig*) mordaz.

caution ['kɔːʃən] *n* cautela, prudência; (*warning*) aviso // *vt* acautelar, avisar.

cautious ['kɔːʃəs] *adj* cauteloso, prudente, precavido; ~**ly** *adv* com cautela; ~**ness** *n* cautela, prudência.

cavalier [kævə'lɪə*] *adj* arrogante, descortês.

cavalry ['kævəlrɪ] n cavalaria.
cave [keɪv] n caverna, gruta; **to ~ in** vi dar de si; (roof etc) ceder; **~man** n troglodita m, homem m das cavernas; **~woman** n troglodita f, mulher f das cavernas.
cavern ['kævən] n caverna.
caviar(e) ['kævɪɑː*] n caviar m.
cavity ['kævɪtɪ] n buraco, cavidade f.
cavort [kə'vɔːt] vi cabriolar.
caw [kɔː] vi grasnar.
CBI n abbr of **Confederation of British Industries**.
cc abbr of **cubic centimetres**; carbon copy.
cease [siːs] vt/i cessar; **~fire** n cessar-fogo m; **~less** adj contínuo, incessante; **~lessly** adv sem parar, sem cessar.
cedar ['siːdə*] n cedro.
cede [siːd] vt ceder.
ceiling ['siːlɪŋ] n teto (Pt: -ct-); (fig) limite m.
Celsius ['sɛlsɪəs] adj (US) = **centigrade**.
celebrate ['sɛlɪbreɪt] vt celebrar // vi celebrar, festejar; **~d** adj célebre; **celebration** [-'breɪʃən] n celebração f; festa.
celebrity [sɪ'lɛbrɪtɪ] n celebridade f.
celery ['sɛlərɪ] n aipo.
celestial [sɪ'lɛstɪəl] adj (of sky) celeste; (divine) celestial.
celibacy ['sɛlɪbəsɪ] n celibato.
cell [sɛl] n cela; (BIOL) célula; (ELEC) pilha.
cellar ['sɛlə*] n porão m; (for wine) adega.
'cello ['tʃɛləʊ] n violoncelo.
cellophane ['sɛləfeɪn] n celofane m.
cellular ['sɛljʊlə*] adj celular.
cellulose ['sɛljʊləʊs] n celulose f.
Celt [kɛlt, sɛlt] adj, n celta m/f; **~ic** adj celta.
cement [sə'mɛnt] n cimento // vt cimentar; (fig) cimentar, fortalecer.
cemetery ['sɛmɪtrɪ] n cemitério.
cenotaph ['sɛnətɑːf] n cenotáfio.
censor ['sɛnsə*] n censor // vt (cut) cortar, expurgar; **~ship** n censura.
censure ['sɛnʃə*] vt censurar.
census ['sɛnsəs] n censo.
cent [sɛnt] n (US: coin) centavo, cêntimo; see also **per**.
centenary [sɛn'tiːnərɪ] n centenário.
centi... [sɛntɪ] pref: **~grade** adj centígrado; **~litre** n centilitro; **~metre** n centímetro; **~pede** n centopéia.
central ['sɛntrəl] adj central; **C~ American** adj centroamericano; **~ heating** n aquecimento central; **~ize** vt centralizar.
centre ['sɛntə*] n centro; **~-forward** n (SPORT) centro-avante m, centro; **~-half** n (SPORT) centromédio.
century ['sɛntjʊrɪ] n século; **20th ~** século vinte.

ceramic [sɪ'ræmɪk] adj cerâmico; **~s** n cerâmica sg.
cereal ['sɪrɪəl] n cereal m.
ceremony ['sɛrɪmənɪ] n cerimônia.
certain ['sɜːtən] adj (gen) certo; **for ~** com certeza; **~ly** adv certamente, com certeza; **~ty** n certeza, segurança.
certificate [sə'tɪfɪkɪt] n certificado; **certified public accountant** n (US) = chartered accountant.
certify ['sɜːtɪfaɪ] vt certificar.
cervix ['sɜːvɪks] n cerviz f.
cessation [sə'seɪʃən] n cessação f, suspensão f.
cf. abbr = **compare**.
chafe [tʃeɪf] vt (rub) roçar; (wear) gastar; (irritate) irritar.
chaffinch ['tʃæfɪntʃ] n tentilhão m.
chagrin ['ʃægrɪn] n desgosto, mortificação f.
chain [tʃeɪn] n (gen) corrente f; (of shops) cadeia // vt (also: ~ up) encadear; **~ reaction** n reação (Pt: -cç-) f em cadeia; **~ store** n magazine m (Br), grande armazém f (Pt).
chair [tʃɛə*] n cadeira; (armchair) poltrona; (of university) cátedra // vt (meeting) presidir; **~lift** n teleférico; **~man** n presidente m.
chalet ['ʃæleɪ] n chalé m.
chalice ['tʃælɪs] n cálice m.
chalk [tʃɔːk] n (GEO) greda; (for writing) giz m.
challenge ['tʃælɪndʒ] n desafio // vt desafiar, reptar; (statement, right) disputar, contestar; **to ~ sb to do sth** desafiar alguém para fazer algo; **challenger** n (SPORT) competidor(a) m/f; **challenging** adj desafiante; (tone) de desafio.
chamber ['tʃeɪmbə*] n sala, câmara; **~ of commerce** câmara de comércio; **~maid** n arrumadeira (Br), empregada (Pt); **~ music** n música de câmara.
chamois ['ʃæmwɑː] n camurça.
champagne [ʃæm'peɪn] n champanha f (Br), champanhe m (Pt).
champion ['tʃæmpɪən] n campeão/peã m/f; **~ship** n campeonato.
chance [tʃɑːns] n (luck) sorte f; (opportunity) oportunidade, ocasião f; (likelihood) possibilidade f; (risk) risco; (concession) chance f // vt arriscar // adj fortuito, casual; **to ~ it** arriscar-se; **to take a ~** arriscar-se; **by ~** por acaso.
chancel ['tʃɑːnsəl] n coro, capela-mor f.
chancellor ['tʃɑːnsələ*] n chanceler m; (Brit) **C~ of the Exchequer** n Ministro das Finanças.
chandelier [ʃændə'lɪə*] n candelabro.
change [tʃeɪndʒ] vt (gen) mudar, trocar; (replace) substituir; (gear, clothes, house) mudar de, trocar de; (exchange) trocar; (transform) transformar // vi (gen) mudar(-se); (trains) fazer baldeação (Br), mudar (Pt); **to ~ into** transformar-se em // n câmbio, modificação f, transformação f; (coins)

trocado; (*money returned*) troco; **for a ~** para variar; **~able** *adj* (*weather*) variável, instável; **~less** *adj* imutável; **~over** *n* (*to new system*) mudança.

changing ['tʃeɪndʒɪŋ] *adj* variável; **~ room** *n* vestiário.

channel ['tʃænl] *n* (*TV*) canal *m*; (*of river*) leito; (*of sea*) canal, estreito; (*groove*) ranhura; (*fig: medium*) meio, via // *vt* canalizar; **the (English) C~** o Canal da Mancha; **the C~ Islands** Ilhas Anglo-Normandas *fpl*.

chant [tʃɑːnt] *n* cântico // *vt* cantar; (*fig*) entoar.

chaos ['keɪɔs] *n* caos *m*; **chaotic** [keɪ'ɔtɪk] *adj* caótico.

chap [tʃæp] *n* (*col: man*) sujeito (*Br*), tipo (*Pt*) // *vi* (*skin*) rachar(-se).

chapel ['tʃæpəl] *n* capela.

chaperon ['ʃæpərəun] *n* mulher *f* acompanhante.

chaplain ['tʃæplɪn] *n* capelão *m*.

chapter ['tʃæptə*] *n* capítulo.

char [tʃɑː*] *vt* (*burn*) tostar, queimar // *n* = **charlady**.

character ['kærɪktə*] *n* caráter (*Pt: -ct-*) *m*, natureza, qualidade *f*; (*in novel, film*) personagem *f*; (*role*) papel *m*; **~istic** [-'rɪstɪk] *adj* característico // *n* característica; **~ize** *vt* caracterizar.

charade [ʃə'rɑːd] *n* charada.

charcoal ['tʃɑːkəul] *n* carvão *m* de lenha; (*ART*) carvão.

charge [tʃɑːdʒ] *n* carga; (*LAW*) encargo, acusação *f*; (*cost*) preço, custo; (*responsibility*) encargo; (*task*) incumbência // *vt* (*LAW: with*) acusar (de); (*gun, battery*) carregar; (*MIL: enemy*) atacar; (*price*) cobrar; (*customer*) pedir; (*sb with task*) encarregar // *vi* atacar, precipitar-se; (*make pay*) cobrar; **~s** *npl*: **bank ~s** taxas cobradas pelo banco; **free of ~** grátis; **to reverse the ~s** (*TEL*) telefonar a cobrar; **to take ~ of** encarregar-se de; **to be in ~ of** estar a cargo de *or* encarregado de; **how much do you ~?** quanto você cobra?; **to ~ an expense (up) to sb's account** pôr a despesa na conta de alguém.

charitable ['tʃærɪtəbl] *adj* caritativo.

charity ['tʃærɪtɪ] *n* (*gen*) caridade *f*; (*sympathy*) compaixão *f*; (*organization*) organização *f* de caridade.

charlady ['tʃɑːleɪdɪ] *n* mulher *f* de limpezas, faxineira.

charm [tʃɑːm] *n* charme *m*, encanto, atrativo (*Pt: -ct-*); (*spell*) feitiço; (*object*) amuleto // *vt* encantar, enfeitiçar; **~ing** *adj* encantador(a), simpático, charmoso.

chart [tʃɑːt] *n* quadro; (*graph*) gráfico; (*map*) mapa *m* // *vt* fazer um gráfico de; (*course*) traçar.

charter ['tʃɑːtə*] *vt* (*plane*) fretar, alugar; (*ship*) fretar // *n* (*document*) carta, alvará *m*; **~ed accountant** *n* perito contador; **~ flight** *n* vôo *m* charter *or* fretado.

charwoman ['tʃɑːwumən] *n* = **charlady**.

chase [tʃeɪs] *vt* (*follow*) perseguir; (*hunt*) caçar, dar caça a // *n* perseguição *f*, caça; **to ~ after** correr atrás.

chasm ['kæzəm] *n* abismo.

chassis ['ʃæsɪ] *n* chassi *m*.

chaste [tʃeɪst] *adj* casto; **chastity** ['tʃæstɪtɪ] *n* castidade *f*.

chat [tʃæt] *vi* (*also:* **have a ~**) conversar, bater papo (*Br*), cavaquear (*Pt*) // *n* conversa, bate-papo *m* (*Br*), cavaqueira (*Pt*).

chatter ['tʃætə*] *vi* (*person*) falar; (*teeth*) tiritar // *n* (*of birds*) chilro; (*of people*) tagarelice *m*; **~box** *n* tagarela *m/f*, falador(a) *m/f*.

chatty ['tʃætɪ] *adj* (*style*) informal; (*person*) conversador(a).

chauffeur ['ʃəufə*] *n* chofer *m*, motorista *m/f*.

cheap [tʃiːp] *adj* barato; (*trick*) de mau gosto; (*poor quality*) barato, de pouca qualidade // *adv* barato; **to ~en** *vt* baixar o preço de, rebaixar; **to ~en o.s.** rebaixar-se; **~ly** *adv* barato, por baixo preço.

cheat [tʃiːt] *vi* trapacear; (*at cards*) roubar (*Br*), fazer batota (*Pt*); (*in exam*) colar (*Br*), cabular (*Pt*) // *vt* defraudar, enganar // *n* fraude *f*; (*person*) trapaceiro/a; **~ing** *n* trapaça.

check [tʃek] *vt* (*examine*) controlar; (*facts*) verificar; (*count*) contar; (*halt*) impedir, deter; (*restrain*) parar, refrear // *n* (*inspection*) controle *m*, inspeção (*Pt: -cç-*) *f*; (*curb*) freio; (*bill*) conta; (*obstacle*) impedimento, estorvo; (*token*) ficha, talão *m*; (*pattern: gen*) xadrez *m*; **to ~ in** *vi* (*in hotel*) registrar-se (*Pt:* registar-se); (*in airport*) apresentar-se // *vt* (*luggage*) entregar; **to ~ out** *vi* (*of hotel*) pagar a conta e sair; **to ~ up** *vi*: **to ~ up on sth** verificar algo; **to ~ up on sb** investigar alguém; **~ing account** *n* (*US*) conta corrente; **~mate** *n* xeque-mate *m*; **~out** *n* caixa; **~point** *n* (ponto de) controle *m*; **~up** *n* (*MED*) check-up *m*; (*of machine*) revisão.

cheek [tʃiːk] *n* bochecha; (*impudence*) descaramento; **~bone** *n* maçã *f* do rosto; **~y** *adj* insolente, descarado.

cheer [tʃɪə*] *vt* dar vivas a, aplaudir; (*gladden*) alegrar, animar // *vi* aplaudir, gritar com entusiasmo // *n* grito (de aplauso); **~s** *npl* aplausos *mpl*; **~s!** saúde!; **to ~ up** *vi* animar-se, alegrar-se // *vt* alegrar, animar; **~ful** *adj* alegre; **~fulness** *n* alegria; **cheerio** *excl* tchau (*Br*), adeus (*Pt*); **~less** *adj* triste, sombrio.

cheese [tʃiːz] *n* queijo.

chef [ʃef] *n* cozinheiro-chefe *m/f*.

chemical ['kemɪkəl] *adj*, *n* químico.

chemist ['kemɪst] *n* farmacêutico; (*scientist*) químico; **~ry** *n* química; **~'s (shop)** *n* farmácia.

cheque [tʃek] *n* cheque *m*; **~book** *n*

talão m de cheques (Br), livro de cheques (Pt).

chequered ['tʃɛkəd] adj (fig) variado, acidentado.

cherish ['tʃɛrɪʃ] vt (love) querer, apreciar; (protect) cuidar; (hope etc) acalentar.

cherry ['tʃɛrɪ] n cereja.

chess [tʃɛs] n xadrez m; ~board n tabuleiro (de xadrez), ~man n peça, pedra (de xadrez).

chest [tʃɛst] n (ANAT) peito; (box) caixa, cofre m; ~ of drawers n cômoda.

chestnut ['tʃɛsnʌt] n castanha; ~ (tree) n castanheiro.

chew [tʃu:] vt mastigar; ~ing gum n chiclete m (Br), pastilha elástica (Pt).

chic [ʃik] adj elegante, chique.

chick [tʃik] n pinto, pintainho; (fam) menina.

chicken ['tʃikin] n galinha; (food) galinha, frango; ~pox n catapora (Br), varicela (Pt).

chickpea ['tʃikpi:] n grão-de-bico m.

chicory ['tʃikərɪ] n chicória.

chief [tʃi:f] n chefe m/f // adj principal; ~ly adv principalmente.

chiffon ['ʃifon] n gaze f.

chilblain ['tʃilblein] n frieira.

child [tʃaild], pl ~ren ['tʃildrən] n criança; (offspring) filho; ~birth n parto; ~hood n infância, meninice f; ~ish adj infantil, pueril; ~like adj próprio (de criança); ~ minder n cuidadora de crianças.

Chile ['tʃili] n Chile m; ~an adj, n chileno/a.

chill [tʃil] n frio; (MED) resfriamento // vt esfriar; (CULIN) semi-congelar; ~y adj frio.

chime [tʃaim] n (peal) repique m, som m // vi repicar, soar.

chimney ['tʃimni] n chaminé f; ~ sweep n limpador m de chaminés.

chimpanzee [tʃimpæn'zi:] n chimpanzé m.

chin [tʃin] n queixo.

china ['tʃainə] n porcelana; (gen) louça fina.

China ['tʃainə] n China; **Chinese** [tʃai'ni:z] adj chinês/esa; the Chinese os Chineses // n (LING) chinês m.

chink [tʃiŋk] n (opening) fresta, abertura; (noise) tinir m.

chip [tʃip] n (gen pl: CULIN) batata frita; (of wood) lasca; (of glass, stone) lasca, pedaço; (at poker) ficha // vt (cup, plate) lascar; to ~ in vi interromper; (contribute) compartilhar as despesas.

chiropodist [ki'rɔpədist] n pedicuro.

chirp [tʃə:p] vi chilrar, piar; (cricket) chilrear.

chisel ['tʃizl] n (for wood) formão m; (for stone) cinzel m.

chit [tʃit] n talão m.

chitchat ['tʃittʃæt] n palestra, bisbilhotice f.

chivalrous ['ʃivəlrəs] adj cavalheiresco; **chivalry** [-rɪ] n cavalaria.

chives [tʃaivz] npl cebolinha sg.

chlorine ['klɔ:ri:n] n cloro.

chock [tʃɔk]: ~-a-block, ~-full adj abarrotado, apinhado.

chocolate ['tʃɔklit] n chocolate m.

choice [tʃɔis] n seleção (Pt: -çç-) f, escolha; (preference) preferência // adj seleto (Pt: -ct-), escolhido.

choir ['kwaiə*] n coro; ~boy n menino de coro.

choke [tʃəuk] vi sufocar-se; (on food) engasgar-se // vt afogar, sufocar; (block) obstruir // n (AUT) afogador m (Br), ar m (Pt); **choker** n (necklace) colar m curto.

cholera ['kɔlərə] n cólera.

choose [tʃu:z], pt **chose**, pp **chosen** vt escolher; (team) selecionar (Pt: -cc-).

chop [tʃɔp] vt (wood) cortar, talhar; (CULIN: also: ~ up) cortar em pedaços; (meat) picar // n golpe m; (CULIN) costeleta; ~s npl (jaws) boca sg, beiços mpl; ~py adj (sea) agitado; ~sticks npl pauzinhos mpl, palitos mpl.

choral ['kɔ:rəl] adj coral.

chord [kɔ:d] n (MUS) acorde m.

chore [tʃɔ:*] n tarefa; (routine task) trabalho de rotina.

choreographer [kɔri'ɔgrəfə*] n coreógrafo/a.

chorister ['kɔristə*] n corista m/f.

chortle ['tʃɔ:tl] vi rir, gargalhar.

chorus ['kɔ:rəs] n coro; (repeated part of song) estribilho.

chose [tʃəuz], **chosen** ['tʃəuzn] pt, pp of **choose.**

Christ [kraist] n Cristo.

christen ['krisn] vt batizar (Pt: -pt-); ~ing n batismo (Pt: -pt-).

Christian ['kristiən] adj, n cristão/tã m/f; ~ity [-'ænitɪ] n cristianismo; ~ name n nome m de batismo (Pt: -pt-).

Christmas ['krisməs] n Natal m; **Merry** ~! Feliz Natal!; ~ **Eve** n véspera do Natal.

chrome [krəum], **chromium** ['krəumiəm] n cromo.

chromosome ['krəuməsəum] n cromossomo.

chronic ['krɔnik] adj crônico.

chronicle ['krɔnikl] n crônica.

chronological [krɔnə'lɔdʒikəl] adj cronológico.

chrysanthemum [kri'sænθəməm] n crisântemo.

chubby ['tʃʌbi] adj roliço.

chuck [tʃʌk] vt jogar (Br), deitar (Pt); to ~ out vt (thing) jogar fora (Br), deitar fora (Pt); (person) expulsar; to ~ (up) vt abandonar.

chuckle ['tʃʌkl] vi rir.

chug [tʃʌg] vi andar fazendo ruído da descarga; to ~ along vi (fig) ir manejando.

chum [tʃʌm] n camarada m, amigo.

chunk [tʃʌŋk] n pedaço, naco.

church [tʃɔ:tʃ] n igreja; ~**yard** n adro, cemitério.

churlish ['tʃə:lɪʃ] adj grosseiro, rude.

churn [tʃə:n] n (for butter) batedeira; (for milk) lata, vasilha // vt bater, agitar.

chute [ʃu:t] n (also: rubbish ~) despejador m; (children's slide) rampa, tobogã m.

chutney ['tʃʌtnɪ] n conserva picante.

CID n abbr of Criminal Investigation Department Brigada de Investigação Criminal.

cider ['saɪdə*] n sidra.

cigar [sɪ'gɑ:*] n charuto.

cigarette [sɪgə'rɛt] n cigarro; ~ **case** n cigarreira; ~ **end** n ponta de cigarro; ~ **holder** n piteira (Br), boquilha (Pt).

Cinderella [sɪndə'rɛlə] n Gata Borralheira.

cinders ['sɪndəz] npl cinzas fpl.

cine [sɪnɪ]: ~-**camera** n câmara cinematográfica; ~-**film** n filme m cinematográfico.

cinema ['sɪnəmə] n cinema m.

cinnamon ['sɪnəmən] n canela.

cipher ['saɪfə*] n cifra.

circle ['sə:kl] n círculo; (in cinema) balcão m // vi dar voltas // vt (surround) rodear, cercar; (move round) dar a volta.

circuit ['sə:kɪt] n circuito; (tour) volta; (track) pista; (lap) volta; ~**ous** [sə:'kjuɪtəs] adj tortuoso, indireto (Pt: -ct-).

circular ['sə:kjulə*] adj circular // n circular f.

circulate ['sə:kjuleɪt] vi circular // vt pôr em circulação, espalhar; **circulation** [-'leɪʃən] n circulação f; (of newspaper) tiragem f.

circumcise ['sə:kəmsaɪz] vt circuncidar.

circumference [sə'kʌmfərəns] n circunferência.

circumspect ['sə:kəmspɛkt] adj circunspeto (Pt: -ct-), prudente.

circumstances ['sə:kəmstənsɪz] npl circunstâncias fpl; (financial condition) situação f econômica.

circus ['sə:kəs] n circo; (roundabout) rotunda, praça circular.

cistern ['sɪstən] n tanque m, reservatório; (in toilet) caixa d'água.

cite [saɪt] vt citar.

citizen ['sɪtɪzn] n (POL) cidadão/dã m/f; (resident) habitante m/f; ~**ship** n cidadania.

citrus fruit ['sɪtrəs-] n citrinos mpl.

city ['sɪtɪ] n cidade f; **the C**~ centro financeiro de Londres.

civic ['sɪvɪk] adj cívico, municipal.

civil ['sɪvɪl] adj civil; (polite) delicado, cortês; (defence) passivo; (well-bred) educado; ~ **engineer** n engenheiro civil; **C**~ **Service** administração f pública; ~**ian** [sɪ'vɪlɪən] adj civil, paisano // n civil m/f, paisano/a.

civilization [sɪvɪlaɪ'zeɪʃən] n civilização f.

civilized ['sɪvɪlaɪzd] adj civilizado.

claim [kleɪm] vt exigir, reclamar; (rights etc) reivindicar; (assert) pretender // vi (for insurance) reclamar // n reclamação f; (LAW) direito; (pretension) pretensão f; ~**ant** n (ADMIN, LAW) reclamante m/f.

clairvoyant [klɛə'vɔɪənt] n clarividente m/f.

clam [klæm] n molusco.

clamber ['klæmbə*] vi trepar.

clammy ['klæmɪ] adj (cold) frio e úmido; (sticky) pegajoso.

clamp [klæmp] n grampo // vt segurar; **to** ~ **down on** vt fus suprimir, proibir.

clan [klæn] n clã m.

clang [klæŋ] n retintim m, som metálico // vi retinir.

clap [klæp] vi aplaudir // vt (put) pôr; **to** ~ **hands** bater palmas // n (of hands) palmas; (of thunder) trovoada; ~**ping** n aplausos mpl.

claret ['klærət] n clarete m.

clarification [klærɪfɪ'keɪʃən] n esclarecimento; **clarify** ['klærɪfaɪ] vt esclarecer, aclarar, clarificar.

clarinet [klærɪ'nɛt] n clarinete m.

clarity ['klærɪtɪ] n claridade f.

clash [klæʃ] n colisão f; (fig) choque m // vi (meet) encontrar-se; (battle) chocar; (disagree) entrar em conflito, ter uma desavença.

clasp [klɑ:sp] n fecho; (on jewels) fivela // vt afivelar; (hand) apertar; (embrace) abraçar.

class [klɑ:s] n (gen) classe f // adj de classe // vt classificar.

classic ['klæsɪk] adj clássico // n (work) obra clássica; ~**al** adj clássico.

classification [klæsɪfɪ'keɪʃən] n classificação f; **classify** ['klæsɪfaɪ] vt classificar.

class: ~**mate** n colega m/f de aula; ~**room** n sala de aula.

clatter ['klætə*] n ruído, estrépito; (of hooves) barulho de casco // vi fazer barulho or ruído.

clause [klɔ:z] n cláusula; (LING) oração f.

claustrophobia [klɔ:strə'fəubɪə] n claustrofobia.

claw [klɔ:] n (of cat) pata, unha; (of bird of prey) garra; (of lobster) pinça; (TECH) unha // vt: **to** ~ **at** arranhar; (tear) rasgar.

clay [kleɪ] n argila.

clean [kli:n] adj limpo; (clear) nítido, bem definido // vt limpar; **to** ~ **out** vt limpar; **to** ~ **up** vt limpar, assear; ~-**cut** adj (person) alinhado; ~**er** n (person) faxineiro/a; ~**ing** n (gen) limpeza; (clothes) lavagem f; ~**liness** ['klɛnlɪnɪs] n limpeza; ~-**shaven** adj sem barba, de cara raspada.

cleanse [klɛnz] vt limpar; **cleanser** n limpador m; (for face) creme m de limpeza; **cleansing department** n departamento de limpeza.

clear [klɪə*] adj claro; (road, way) limpo, livre; (complete) completo // vt (space) despejar, limpar; (LAW: suspect) absolver; (obstacle) salvar, passar sobre; (debt) liquidar // vi (gen) esclarecer-se, aclarar-se; (fog etc) clarear-se // adv: ~ of a salvo de; to ~ up vt limpar; (mystery) resolver, esclarecer; ~ance n (removal) despejo; (permission) permissão f; ~-cut adj bem definido, nítido; ~ing n (in wood) clareira; ~ing bank n câmara de compensação; ~ly adv claramente; ~way n (Brit) estrada onde não se pode estacionar.

cleaver ['kliːvə] n cutelo (de açougueiro).

clef [klɛf] n (MUS) clave f.

clemency ['klɛmənsɪ] n clemência.

clench [klɛntʃ] vt apertar, cerrar.

clergy ['kləːdʒɪ] n clero; ~man n clérigo, pastor m.

clerical ['klɛrɪkəl] adj clerical.

clerk [klɑːk, (US) kləːrk] n caixeiro, empregado/a m/f.

clever ['klɛvə*] adj (mentally) inteligente, esperto; (deft, crafty) hábil; (device, arrangement) engenhoso.

cliché ['kliːʃeɪ] n clichê m, frase f feita.

click [klɪk] vt (tongue) estalar; (heels) bater.

client ['klaɪənt] n cliente m/f; ~ele [kliːɑːnˈtɛl] n clientela.

cliff [klɪf] n penhasco.

climate ['klaɪmɪt] n clima m; (fig) ambiente m.

climax ['klaɪmæks] n clímax m, ponto culminante; (sexual) clímax.

climb [klaɪm] vi subir, trepar // vt (stairs) subir; (tree) trepar em; (hill) escalar // n subida; ~er n alpinista m/f; ~ing n alpinismo.

clinch [klɪntʃ] vt (deal) fechar; (argument) decidir, resolver.

cling [klɪŋ], pt, pp **clung** [klʌŋ] vi: to ~ to pegar-se a, aderir a; (of clothes) agarrar-se a, ajustar-se a.

clinic ['klɪnɪk] n clínica; ~al adj clínico.

clink [klɪŋk] vi tinir.

clip [klɪp] n (for hair) prendedor m, fivela; (also: **paper** ~) mola, clipe m; (clamp) fecho // vt (cut) cortar; (shorten) aparar; (clamp) grampear; ~pers npl (for gardening) podadeira sg; (for hair) máquina sg; (for nails) tesoura sg para cortar unhas; ~ping n recorte m.

clique [kliːk] n panelinha.

cloak [kləuk] n capa, manto // vt (fig) encobrir; ~room n vestiário; (WC) lavatórios mpl.

clock [klɔk] n relógio; (in taxi) taxímetro; (fam) cara; ~wise adv em sentido horário; ~work n mecanismo de relógio // adj de corda.

clog [klɔg] n tamanco, soco // vt entupir // vi entupir-se, emperrar.

cloister ['klɔɪstə*] n claustro.

close adj, adv and derivatives [kləus] adj próximo, perto; (print, weave) denso, compacto; (friend) íntimo; (connection) estreito; (examination) detalhado, minucioso; (weather) abafado; (atmosphere) sufocante; (room) mal arejado // adv

perto, próximo // vb and derivatives [kləuz] vt (shut) fechar, encerrar; (end) acabar, concluir // vi (shop etc) fechar-se; (end) concluir-se, terminar-se // n (end) fim m, conclusão f, terminação f; to ~ down vi fechar-se definitivamente; ~d adj (shop etc) fechado; ~d shop n estabelecimento industrial só para empregados sindicalizados; ~ly adv (exactly) fielmente; (carefully) rigorosamente.

closet ['klɔzɪt] n (cupboard) armário; (WC) retrete m, privada.

close-up ['kləusʌp] n primeiro plano.

closure ['kləuʒə*] n (close-down) encerramento, fechamento; (end) fim m.

clot [klɔt] n (gen: blood ~) coágulo; (fam: idiot) imbecil m/f // vi (blood) coagular-se, coalhar-se.

cloth [klɔθ] n (material) tecido, fazenda; (rag) pano, trapo.

clothe [kləuð] vt vestir; (fig) revestir; ~s npl roupa sg; ~s brush n escova (para a roupa); ~s line n corda (para estender a roupa); ~s peg, ~s pin (US) n pregador m; **clothing** n = clothes.

cloud [klaud] n nuvem f; ~burst n aguaceiro; ~y adj nublado; (liquid) turvo.

clout [klaut] vt dar uma bofetada em.

clove [kləuv] n cravo; ~ of garlic dente m de alho.

clover ['kləuvə*] n trevo.

clown [klaun] n palhaço // vi (also: ~ about, ~ around) fazer palhaçadas.

club [klʌb] n (society) clube m; (weapon) cacete m; (also: **golf** ~) taco // vt esbordoar // vi: to ~ together cotizar-se; ~s npl (CARDS) paus mpl; ~ car n (US) vagão-restaurante m; ~house n sede f do clube.

cluck [klʌk] vi cacarejar.

clue [kluː] n sinal m; (in crosswords) indício, pista; I haven't a ~ não faço idéia.

clump [klʌmp] n (of trees) grupo.

clumsy ['klʌmzɪ] adj (person) desajeitado; (movement) deselegante, mal-feito.

cluster ['klʌstə*] n grupo; (BOT) cacho, ramo // vi agrupar-se, apinhar-se.

clutch [klʌtʃ] n (grip, grasp) alcance m, garra; (AUT) embreagem f; (Pt: embraiagem); (pedal) pedal m de embreagem (Pt: embraiagem) // vt empunhar, pegar em.

clutter ['klʌtə*] vt abarrotar, encher desordenadamente.

Co. abbr of county; company.

c/o abbr of care of a/c, aos cuidados de.

coach [kəutʃ] n (bus) ônibus m (Br), autocarro (Pt); (horse-drawn) carruagem f, coche m; (of train) vagão m; (SPORT) treinador m, instrutor m // vt (SPORT) treinar; (student) preparar, ensinar.

coagulate [kəuˈægjuleɪt] vi coagular-se.

coal [kəul] n carvão m; ~ face n frente f

de carvão; **~field** n região f carbonífera.

coalition [kəuə'lɪʃən] n coalizão f.

coal: **~man,** **~ merchant** n carvoeiro; **~mine** n mina de carvão.

coarse [kɔːs] adj grosso, áspero; (vulgar) grosseiro, ordinário.

coast [kəust] n costa, litoral m // vi (AUT) ir em ponto morto; **~al** adj costeiro, litorâneo; **~er** n embarcação f costeira, barco de cabotagem; **~guard** n guarda costeira; **~line** n litoral m.

coat [kəut] n (jacket) casaco; (overcoat) sobretudo; (of animal) pelo, lã f; (of paint) demão f, camada // vt cobrir, revestir; **~ of arms** n brasão m; **~ hanger** n cabide m; **~ing** n camada, mão f.

coax [kəuks] vt persuadir com meiguice.

cob [kɔb] n see **corn.**

cobbler ['kɔblə] n sapateiro.

cobbles ['kɔblz], **cobblestones** ['kɔblstəunz] npl pedras arredondadas fpl.

cobra ['kəubrə] n cobra.

cobweb ['kɔbweb] n teia de aranha.

cocaine [kə'keɪn] n cocaína.

cock [kɔk] n (rooster) galo; (male bird) macho // vt (gun) engatilhar; **~atoo** n cacatua; **~erel** n frango, galo pequeno.

cockle ['kɔkl] n berbigão m.

cockpit ['kɔkpɪt] n (in aircraft) cabina.

cockroach ['kɔkrəutʃ] n barata.

cocktail ['kɔkteɪl] n coquetel (Pt: cocktail) m; **~ cabinet** n móvel-bar m; **~ party** n coquetel (Pt: cocktail) m.

cocoa ['kəukəu] n cacau m; (drink) chocolate m.

coconut ['kəukənʌt] n coco.

cocoon [kə'kuːn] n casulo.

cod [kɔd] n bacalhau m.

code [kəud] n código; (cipher) cifra; **codify** vt codificar.

coerce [kəu'əːs] vt forçar, obrigar; **coercion** [-'əːʃən] n coerção f.

coexistence [kəuɪg'zɪstəns] n coexistência.

coffee ['kɔfɪ] n café m; **~ bean** n grão m de café; **~ grounds** npl borras fpl de café; **~pot** n cafeteira.

coffin ['kɔfɪn] n caixão m.

cog [kɔg] n dente m; **~wheel** n roda dentada.

cognac ['kɔnjæk] n conhaque m.

coherent [kəu'hɪərənt] adj coerente.

coil [kɔɪl] n rolo; (rope) corda enrolada; (ELEC) bobina; (contraceptive) D.I.U. m // vi enrolar-se, espiralar-se.

coin [kɔɪn] n moeda // vt (word) cunhar, criar; **~age** n cunhagem f; **~-box** n caixa de moedas, cofrinho.

coincide [kəuɪn'saɪd] vi coincidir; (agree) estar de acordo; **coincidence** [kəu'ɪnsɪdəns] n coincidência.

coke [kəuk] n (coal) coque m; (drink) coca-cola f.

colander ['kɔləndə*] n coador m, passador m.

cold [kəuld] adj frio // n frio; (MED) resfriado (Br), constipação f (Pt); it's ~

está frio; **to be ~** estar com frio; **to catch ~** resfriar-se (Br), apanhar constipação (Pt); **to ~-shoulder** tratar com frieza; **~ly** adv friamente; **~ sore** n herpes m labial.

coleslaw ['kəulslɔː] n salada de repolho cru.

colic ['kɔlɪk] n cólica.

collaborate [kə'læbəreɪt] vi colaborar; **collaboration** [-'reɪʃən] n colaboração f.

collage [kɔ'lɑːʒ] n colagem f.

collapse [kə'læps] vi (gen) cair, tombar; (MED) desmaiar // n (gen) queda, ruína; (MED) colapso; **collapsible** adj dobrável.

collar ['kɔlə*] n (of coat, shirt) colarinho, gola; **~bone** n clavícula.

collate [kɔ'leɪt] vt cotejar.

colleague ['kɔliːg] n colega m/f.

collect [kə'lɛkt] vt reunir; (as a hobby) colecionar (Pt: -cc-); (call and pick up) recolher; (wages, debts) cobrar; (donations, subscriptions) colher // vi reunir-se, colecionar-se (Pt: -cc-); **~ion** [kə'lɛkʃən] n coleção (Pt: -cç-) f; (of people) reunião f, grupo; (of donations) arrecadação f; (of post) coleta.

collective [kə'lɛktɪv] adj coletivo (Pt: -ct-).

collector [kə'lɛktə*] n colecionador (Pt: -cc-) m; (of taxes etc) cobrador m.

college ['kɔlɪdʒ] n colégio; (faculty) faculdade f.

collide [kə'laɪd] vi chocar, colidir.

collie ['kɔlɪ] n cão m pastor.

collision [kə'lɪʒən] n choque m.

colloquial [kə'ləukwɪəl] adj familiar, coloquial.

colon ['kəulən] n (sign) dois pontos; (MED) cólon m.

colonel ['kəːnl] n coronel m.

colonial [kə'ləunɪəl] adj colonial.

colonize ['kɔlənaɪz] vt colonizar.

colony ['kɔlənɪ] n colônia.

colossal [kə'lɔsl] adj colossal.

colour, color (US) ['kʌlə*] n cor f // vt colorir; (with crayons) colorir, pintar; (dye) tingir // vi (blush) corar; **~s** npl (of party, club) cores fpl; **~-blind** adj daltônico; **~ed** adj colorido; **~eds** npl gente f de cor; **~ film** n filme m colorido; **~ful** adj colorido; (personality) vivo, animado; **~ing** n colorido; **~less** adj sem cor, pálido; **~ scheme** n combinação f de cores; **~ television** n televisão f a cores.

colt [kəult] n potro.

column ['kɔləm] n coluna; **~ist** ['kɔləmnɪst] n cronista m/f.

coma ['kəumə] n coma m.

comb [kəum] n pente m; (ornamental) pente; (of cock) crista // vt (hair) pentear; (area) vascular.

combat ['kɔmbæt] n combate m // vt combater.

combination [kɔmbɪ'neɪʃən] n (gen) combinação f.

combine [kəm'baɪn] vt combinar; (qualities) reunir // vi combinar-se // n ['kɔmbaɪn] (*ECON*) associação f; (*pej*) monopólio; ~ (**harvester**) *n* ceifeiro.

combustion [kɔm'bʌstʃən] *n* combustão f.

come [kʌm], *pt* **came**, *pp* **come** *vi* vir; **to ~ about** *vi* suceder, acontecer; **to ~ across** *vt fus* (*person*) topar com; (*thing*) encontrar; **to ~ away** *vi* ir-se embora; **to ~ back** *vi* voltar; **to ~ by** *vt fus* (*acquire*) conseguir; **to ~ down** *vi* baixar; (*plane*) descer; (*crash*) desabar; (*buildings*) desmoronar-se; **to ~ forward** *vi* apresentar-se; **to ~ in** *vi* entrar; (*train*) chegar; (*fashion*) entrar na moda; **to ~ in for** *vt fus* (*criticism etc*) merecer; **to ~ into** *vt fus* (*money*) herdar; **to ~ off** *vi* (*button*) desprender-se, soltar-se; (*attempt*) realizar-se; **to ~ on** *vi* (*pupil, undertaking*) avançar, fazer progressos // *vt* (*find*) encontrar; ~ **on!** vamos!, venha!; **to ~ out** *vi* sair, aparecer; (*be revealed*) revelar-se; **to ~ out for/against** declarar-se por/ contra; **to ~ to** *vi* voltar a si; (*total*) somar; **to ~ up** *vi* subir; (*sun*) aparecer; (*problem*) surgir; **to ~ up against** *vt fus* (*resistance, difficulties*) tropeçar com; **to ~ up with** *vt fus* (*idea*) propor, sugerir; **to ~ upon** *vt fus* encontrar, achar; ~**back** *n* (*THEATRE*) reaparição f.

comedian [kɔ'miːdɪən] *n* cômico, **comédienne** [-'ɛn] *n* cômica.

comedown ['kʌmdaun] *n* (*fam*) revés *m*, humilhação f.

comedy ['kɔmɪdɪ] *n* comédia.

comet ['kɔmɪt] *n* cometa *m*.

comfort ['kʌmfət] *n* comodidade f, conforto; (*well-being*) bem-estar *m*; (*solace*) consolo; (*relief*) alívio // *vt* confortar, aliviar; ~**able** *adj* confortável; ~**er** *n* (*US*) edredom (*Pt*: -dão) *m*.

comic ['kɔmɪk] *adj* (*also*: ~**al**) cômico // *n* (*magazine*) revista em quadrinhos (*Br*), revista de banda desenhada (*Pt*); ~ **strip** *n* história em quadrinhos (*Br*), banda desenhada (*Pt*).

coming ['kʌmɪŋ] *n* vinda, chegada // *adj* que vem, vindouro; ~(**s**) **and going(s)** *n*(*pl*) vaivém *m*, azáfama.

comma ['kɔmə] *n* vírgula.

command [kɔ'mɑːnd] *n* ordem f, mandado; (*MIL: authority*) comando; (*mastery*) domínio // *vt* (*troops*) mandar; (*give orders to*) mandar, ordenar; (*dispose of*) dispor de; (*deserve*) merecer; ~**eer** [kɔmən'dɪə*] *vt* requisitar; ~**er** *n* (*MIL*) comandante *m/f*, chefe *m/f*.

commando [kɔ'mɑːndəu] *n* comando.

commemorate [kɔ'mɛmɔreɪt] *vt* comemorar; **commemoration** [-'reɪʃən] *n* comemoração f; **commemorative** [-rətɪv] *adj* comemorativo.

commence [kɔ'mɛns] *vt/i* começar, iniciar.

commend [kɔ'mɛnd] *vt* (*praise*) elogiar, louvar; (*recommend*) recomendar; (*entrust*) encomendar; ~**ation**

[kɔmɛn'deɪʃən] *n* elogio, louvor *m*, recomendação f.

commensurate [kɔ'mɛnʃərɪt] *adj* igual (*with* a).

comment ['kɔmɛnt] *n* comentário // *vi* fazer comentários, comentar; ~**ary** ['kɔmɔntɔrɪ] *n* comentário; ~**ator** ['kɔmɔnteɪtə*] *n* comentarista *m/f*.

commerce ['kɔmɔːs] *n* comércio.

commercial [kɔ'mɔːʃəl] *adj* comercial // *n* (*TV*) anúncio (comercial); ~ **break** *n* intervalo publicitário; ~**ize** *vt* comercializar.

commiserate [kɔ'mɪzɔreɪt] *vi*: **to ~ with** comiserar-se de, condoer-se de.

commission [kɔ'mɪʃən] *n* (*fee*) comissão f; (*act*) incumbência // *vt* (*MIL*) dar patente oficial; (*work of art*) encomendar; (*artist*) incumbir; **out of** ~ fora do serviço ativo (*Pt*: -ct-); ~**aire** [kɔmɪʃɔ'nɛɔ*] *n* porteiro; ~**er** *n* comissário.

commit [kɔ'mɪt] *vt* (*act*) cometer; (*to sb's care*) entregar; **to ~ o.s. (to do)** comprometer-se (de fazer); **to ~ suicide** suicidar-se; ~**ment** *n* compromisso.

committee [kɔ'mɪtɪ] *n* comitê *m*.

commodity [kɔ'mɔdɪtɪ] *n* mercadoria.

common ['kɔmɔn] *adj* (*gen*) comum; (*pej*) ordinário // *n* terrenos baldios *mpl*; **the C~s** a Câmara dos Comuns; **in ~** em comum; ~ **er** *n* plebeu/béia *m/f*; ~ **law** *n* lei f consuetudinária; ~**ly** *adv* geralmente; **C~ Market** *n* Mercado Comum; ~**place** *adj* vulgar, trivial // *n* lugar-comum *m*; ~**room** *n* sala comum; ~ **sense** *n* bom senso; **the C~wealth** *n* Comunidade f Britânica.

commotion [kɔ'mɔuʃən] *n* tumulto, confusão f.

communal ['kɔmjuːnl] *adj* comunal.

commune ['kɔmjuːn] *n* (*group*) comuna // *vi* [kɔ'mjuːn]: **to ~ with** conversar com.

communicate [kɔ'mjuːnɪkeɪt] *vt* comunicar // *vi*: **to ~ (with)** comunicar-se com.

communication [kɔmjuːnɪ'keɪʃən] *n* comunicação f; ~ **cord** *n* sinal *m* de alarme.

communion [kɔ'mjuːnɪən] *n* (*also*: **Holy C~**) comunhão f.

communiqué [kɔ'mjuːnɪkeɪ] *n* comunicado.

communism ['kɔmjunɪzəm] *n* comunismo; **communist** *adj*, *n* comunista *m/f*.

community [kɔ'mjuːnɪtɪ] *n* comunidade f; (*large group*) multidão f; (*locals*) vizinhança; ~ **centre** *n* centro social.

commute [kɔ'mjuːt] *vi* viajar diariamente // *vt* comutar; **commuter** *n* viajante *m/f* habitual.

compact [kɔm'pækt] *adj* compacto; (*style*) sólido, (*packed*) apertado // *n* ['kɔmpækt] (*pact*) pacto; (*for powder*) estojo.

companion [kəm'pænɪən] *n* companheiro/a; ~**ship** *n* companhia.

company ['kʌmpənɪ] *n* (*gen*) companhia; (*COMM*) sociedade *f*, companhia; **to keep sb** ~ fazer companhia a alguém; **limited** ~ sociedade *f* limitada.

comparable ['kɔmpərəbl] *adj* comparável.

comparative [kəm'pærətɪv] *adj* comparativo.

compare [kəm'pɛə*] *vt* comparar; (*set side by side*) cotejar // *vi:* **to** ~ **with** comparar-se com; **comparison** [-'pærɪsn] *n* comparação *f*; **in comparison with** em comparação com, comparado com.

compartment [kəm'pɑ:tmənt] *n* (*also RAIL*) compartimento.

compass ['kʌmpəs] *n* bússola; ~**es** *npl* compasso *sg*.

compassion [kəm'pæʃən] *n* compaixão *f*; ~**ate** *adj* compassivo.

compatible [kəm'pætɪbl] *adj* compatível.

compel [kəm'pɛl] *vt* obrigar; ~**ling** *adj* (*fig: argument*) convincente.

compendium [kəm'pɛndɪəm] *n* compêndio.

compensate ['kɔmpənseɪt] *vt* compensar // *vi:* **to** ~ **for** compensar; **compensation** [-'seɪʃən] *n* (*for loss*) indenização *f* (*Pt: -mn-) f*.

compère ['kɔmpɛə*] *n* apresentador(a) *m/f*.

compete [kəm'pi:t] *vi* (*take part*) competir, concorrer; (*vie with*) competir (com), fazer competição (com).

competence ['kɔmpɪtəns] *n* competência, capacidade *f*; **competent** [-ənt] *adj* competente, capaz.

competition [kɔmpɪ'tɪʃən] *n* (*contest*) concurso; (*ECON*) concorrência; (*rivalry*) competição *f*.

competitive [kəm'pɛtɪtɪv] *adj* (*ECON*) competitivo; (*spirit*) competidor(a), de rivalidade.

competitor [kəm'pɛtɪtə*] *n* (*rival*) competidor(a) *m/f*; (*participant*) concorrente *m/f*.

compile [kəm'paɪl] *vt* compilar, compor.

complacency [kəm'pleɪsnsɪ] *n* satisfação *f* consigo mesmo, complacência; **complacent** [-ənt] *adj* vaidoso.

complain [kəm'pleɪn] *vi* (*gen*) queixar-se; ~**t** *n* (*gen*) queixa; (*JUR*) querela; (*MED*) queixa, doença.

complement ['kɔmplɪmənt] *n* complemento; (*esp ship's crew*) tripulação *f*; ~**ary** [kɔmplɪ'mɛntərɪ] *adj* complementar.

complete [kəm'pli:t] *adj* (*full*) completo; (*finished*) acabado // *vt* (*fulfil*) completar; (*finish*) acabar; (*a form*) preencher; ~**ly** *adv* completamente; **completion** [-ʃən] *n* (*gen*) conclusão *f*, término; (*of contract etc*) realização *f*.

complex ['kɔmplɛks] *adj* complexo // *n* (*gen*) complexo.

complexion [kəm'plɛkʃən] *n* (*of face*) cor *f*, tez *f*; (*fig*) aspecto.

complexity [kəm'plɛksɪtɪ] *n* complexidade *f*.

compliance [kəm'plaɪəns] *n* (*submission*) submissão *f*; (*agreement*) conformidade *f*; **in** ~ **with** de acordo com; **compliant** [-ənt] *adj* complacente, submisso.

complicate ['kɔmplɪkeɪt] *vt* complicar; ~**d** *adj* complicado; **complication** [-'keɪʃən] *n* complicação *f*.

compliment *n* ['kɔmplɪmənt] (*formal*) cumprimento; (*praise*) elogio; ~**s** *npl* cumprimentos *mpl*; **to pay sb a** ~ elogiar alguém; ~**ary** [-'mɛntərɪ] *adj* lisonjeiro; (*free*) gratuito.

comply [kəm'plaɪ] *vi:* **to** ~ **with** cumprir com.

component [kəm'pəunənt] *adj* componente // *n* (*TECH*) peça.

compose [kəm'pəuz] *vt* compor; **to be** ~**d of** compor-se de; **to** ~ **o.s.** tranqüilizar-se; ~**d** *adj* calmo; **composer** *n* (*MUS*) compositor(a) *m/f*.

composite ['kɔmpəzɪt] *adj* composto.

composition [kɔmpə'zɪʃən] *n* composição *f*.

compost ['kɔmpost] *n* adubo.

composure [kəm'pəuʒə*] *n* serenidade *f*, calma.

compound ['kɔmpaund] *n* (*CHEM, LING*) composto; (*enclosure*) recinto // *adj* (*gen*) composto; (*fracture*) complicado.

comprehend [kɔmprɪ'hɛnd] *vt* compreender; **comprehension** [-'hɛn-ʃən] *n* compreensão *f*.

comprehensive [kɔmprɪ'hɛnsɪv] *adj* (*broad*) extenso; (*general*) abrangente; (*INSURANCE*) contra todo risco, global; ~ (*school*) *n* escola secundária de amplo programa.

compress [kəm'prɛs] *vt* comprimir // *n* ['kɔmprɛs] (*MED*) compressa; ~**ion** [-'prɛʃən] *n* compressão *f*.

comprise [kəm'praɪz] *vt* (*also:* **be** ~**d of**) compreender, constar de.

compromise ['kɔmprəmaɪz] *n* (*agreement*) compromisso, acordo; (*midpoint*) meio-termo // *vt* comprometer // *vi* chegar a um meio-termo.

compulsion [kəm'pʌlʃən] *n* compulsão *f*.

compulsive [kəm'pʌlsɪv] *adj* maníaco; (*PSYCH*) compulsório.

compulsory [kəm'pʌlsərɪ] *adj* obrigatório.

computer [kəm'pju:tə*] *n* computador *m*; ~**ize** *vt* informatizar; ~ **programmer** *n* programador(a) *m/f*; ~ **programming** *n* programação *f*; ~ **science** *n* informática; **computing** *n* informática.

comrade ['kɔmrɪd] *n* camarada *m/f*; ~**ship** *n* camaradagem *f*.

con [kɔn] *vt* enganar // *n* vigarice *f*.

concave [kɔn'keɪv] *adj* côncavo.

conceal [kən'si:l] *vt* ocultar.

concede [kən'si:d] *vt* conceder // *vi* ceder, conceder.

conceit [kən'si:t] *n* presunção *f*; ~ed *adj* presunçoso.

conceivable [kən'si:vəbl] *adj* concebível.

conceive [kən'si:v] *vt/i* conceber.

concentrate ['kɔnsəntreit] *vi* concentrar-se // *vt* concentrar.

concentration [kɔnsən'treiʃən] *n* concentração *f*; ~ **camp** *n* campo de concentração.

concept ['kɔnsɛpt] *n* conceito.

conception [kən'sɛpʃən] *n* (idea) conceito, ideia; (BIOL) concepção *f*.

concern [kən'sə:n] *n* (matter) assunto; (COMM) empresa; (anxiety) preocupação *f* // vt dizer respeito a; **to be** ~ed (about) interessar-se (por); preocupar-se (com); ~ing prep sobre, a respeito de, acerca de.

concert ['kɔnsət] *n* concerto; ~ **hall** *n* sala de concertos; ~ **master** *n* (US) primeiro violino de uma orquestra.

concertina [kɔnsə'ti:nə] *n* concertina.

concerto [kən'tʃə:təu] *n* concerto.

concession [kən'sɛʃən] *n* concessão *f*; **tax** ~ incentivo fiscal.

conciliation [kənsɪlɪ'eiʃən] *n* conciliação *f*; **conciliatory** [-'sɪliətrɪ] *adj* conciliador(a).

concise [kən'sais] *adj* conciso.

conclude [kən'klu:d] *vt* (finish) acabar, concluir; (treaty etc) firmar; (agreement) chegar a; (decide) chegar à conclusão de; **conclusion** [-'klu:ʒən] *n* conclusão *f*; **conclusive** [-'klu:sɪv] *adj* conclusivo, decisivo.

concoct [kən'kɔkt] *vt* (gen) confeccionar; (plot) fabricar, tramar.

concrete ['kɔnkri:t] *n* concreto (Br), betão *m* (Pt) // *adj* concreto.

concur [kən'kə:*] *vi* estar de acordo, concordar.

concurrently [kən'kʌrntlɪ] *adv* ao mesmo tempo.

concussion [kən'kʌʃən] *n* concussão *f* cerebral.

condemn [kən'dɛm] *vt* condenar; ~ation [kɔndɛm'neiʃən] *n* (gen) condenação *f*; (blame) censura.

condensation [kɔndɛn'seiʃən] *n* condensação *f*.

condense [kən'dɛns] *vi* condensar-se // *vt* condensar, abreviar; ~d milk *n* leite *m* condensado.

condescend [kɔndɪ'sɛnd] *vi* condescender, dignar-se; ~ing *adj* condescendente.

condition [kən'dɪʃən] *n* condição *f* // vt condicionar; **on** ~ **that** com a condição (de) que.

condolences [kən'dəulənsɪz] *npl* pêsames *mpl*.

condone [kən'dəun] *vt* admitir, aceitar.

conducive [kən'dju:sɪv] *adj*: ~ **to** conducente para/a.

conduct ['kɔndʌkt] *n* conduta, comportamento // *vt* [kən'dʌkt] (lead)

conduzir; (manage) levar, dirigir; (MUS) reger // *vi* (MUS) reger uma orquestra; **to** ~ **o.s.** comportar-se; ~or *n* (of orchestra) regente *m*; (on bus) cobrador *m*; (RAIL) revisor *m*; (ELEC) condutor *m*; ~ress *n* (on bus) cobradora.

cone [kəun] *n* cone *m*; (for ice-cream) casquinha.

confectioner [kən'fɛkʃənə*] *n* confeiteiro (Br), pasteleiro (Pt); ~'s (shop) *n* confeitaria (Br), pastelaria (Pt); (sweet shop) confeitaria; ~y *n* (cakes) bolos *mpl*; (sweets) doces *mpl*.

confederation [kɔnfedə'reiʃən] *n* confederação *f*.

confer [kən'fə:*] *vt*: **to** ~ **on** outorgar a // *vi* conferenciar.

conference ['kɔnfərns] *n* (meeting) congresso.

confess [kən'fɛs] *vt* confessar // *vi* confessar-se; ~ion [-'fɛʃən] *n* confissão *f*; ~ional [-'fɛʃənl] *n* confessionário; ~or *n* confessor *m*.

confetti [kən'fɛtɪ] *n* confete *m*.

confide [kən'faid] *vi*: **to** ~ **in** confiar em, fiar-se em.

confidence ['kɔnfɪdns] *n* (gen) confiança; (secret) confidência; ~ **trick** *n* conto do vigário; **confident** *adj* confiante, convicto; **confidential** [kɔnfɪ'dɛnʃəl] *adj* confidencial; (secretary) de confiança.

confine [kən'fain] *vt* (limit) limitar; (shut up) encarcerar; ~d *adj* (space) reduzido, retido; ~ment *n* (prison) prisão *f*; (enclosure) reclusão *f*; (MED) parto; ~s ['kɔnfainz] *npl* confins *mpl*.

confirm [kən'fə:m] *vt* confirmar; ~ation [kɔnfə'meiʃən] *n* confirmação *f*; ~ed *adj* inveterado.

confiscate ['kɔnfɪskeit] *vt* confiscar; **confiscation** [-'keiʃən] *n* confiscação *f*.

conflict ['kɔnflɪkt] *n* conflito // *vi* [kən'flɪkt] (opinions) divergir; ~ing *adj* (views) divergente; (interests) oposto; (account) discrepante.

conform [kən'fɔ:m] *vi* conformar-se; ~ **to** ajustar-se a, acomodar-se a; ~ist *n* conformista *m/f*.

confound [kən'faund] *vt* frustrar; ~ed *adj* maldito.

confront [kən'frʌnt] *vt* (problems) enfrentar; (enemy, danger) defrontar-se com; ~ation [kɔnfrən'teiʃən] *n* confrontação *f*.

confuse [kən'fju:z] *vt* (perplex) desconcertar; (mix up) confundir; ~d *adj* confuso; (person) perplexo; **confusing** *adj* confuso; **confusion** [-'fju:ʒən] *n* confusão *f*.

congeal [kən'dʒi:l] *vi* (freeze) congelar-se; (coagulate) coagular-se.

congenial [kən'dʒi:nɪəl] *adj* simpático, agradável.

congenital [kən'dʒɛnɪtl] *adj* congênito.

congested [kən'dʒɛstɪd] *adj* (gen) congestionado; **congestion** [-'dʒɛstʃən] *n* congestão *f*.

conglomeration [kənglɔmə'reiʃən] n conglomeração f, aglomeração f.

congratulate [kən'grætjuleit] vt felicitar; **congratulations** [-'leiʃənz] npl parabéns mpl.

congregate ['kɔŋgrigeit] vi reunir-se; **congregation** [-'geiʃən] n (in church) os fiéis mpl; (assembly) congregação f, reunião f.

congress ['kɔŋgrɛs] n congresso; ~**man** n (US) deputado.

conical ['kɔnikl] adj cônico.

conifer ['kɔnifə*] n conífera; ~**ous** [kə'nifərəs] adj (forest) conífero.

conjecture [kən'dʒɛktʃə*] n conjetura (Pt: -ct-).

conjugal ['kɔndʒugl] adj conjugal.

conjugate ['kɔndʒugeit] vt conjugar.

conjunction [kən'dʒʌŋkʃən] n conjunção f.

conjure ['kʌndʒə*] vi fazer truques; to ~ **up** vt (ghost, spirit) fazer aparecer, invocar; (memories) evocar; **conjurer** n mágico, prestidigitador(a) m/f; **conjuring trick** n mágica.

conk [kɔŋk]: ~ **out** vi (col) pifar.

con man ['kɔn-] n vigarista m.

connect [kə'nɛkt] vt juntar, unir; (ELEC) ligar, conectar; (fig) relacionar, unir // vi: to ~ **with** (train) conectar com; ~**ion** [-ʃən] n ligação f, união f; (ELEC, RAIL) conexão f; (TEL) comunicação f; (fig) relação f.

connive [kə'naiv] vi: to ~ **at** ser conivente em.

connoisseur [kɔni'sə*] n conhecedor(a) m/f, apreciador(a) m/f.

connotation [kɔnə'teiʃən] n conotação f.

conquer ['kɔŋkə*] vt (gen) conquistar; (enemy) vencer; (feelings) dominar; ~**or** n conquistador m.

conquest ['kɔŋkwɛst] n conquista.

cons [kɔnz] npl see **pro.**

conscience ['kɔnʃəns] n consciência.

conscientious [kɔnʃi'ɛnʃəs] adj consciencioso; (objection) de consciência.

conscious ['kɔnʃəs] adj consciente; ~**ness** n consciência.

conscript ['kɔnskript] n recruta m/f; ~**ion** [kən'skripʃən] n serviço militar obrigatório.

consecrate ['kɔnsikreit] vt consagrar.

consecutive [kən'sɛkjutiv] adj sucessivo, seguido.

consensus [kən'sɛnsəs] n consenso.

consent [kən'sɛnt] n consentimento // vi: to ~ **to** consentir em.

consequence ['kɔnsikwəns] n conseqüência.

consequently ['kɔnsikwɔntli] adv por conseguinte.

conservation [kɔnsə'veiʃən] n conservação f.

conservative [kən'sɔːvətiv] adj conservador; (cautious) moderado; **C**~ adj, n conservador(a) m/f.

conservatory [kən'sɔːvətri] n conservatório; (greenhouse) estufa.

conserve [kən'sɔːv] vt conservar // n conserva.

consider [kən'sidə*] vt (gen) considerar; (take into account) levar em consideração; (study) estudar, examinar; ~**able** adj considerável; (sum) importante.

considerate [kən'sidərit] adj atencioso, delicado; **consideration** [-'reiʃən] n consideração f; (reward) remuneração f.

considering [kən'sidəriŋ] prep em vista de.

consign [kən'sain] vt consignar; ~**ment** n consignação f.

consist [kən'sist] vi: to ~ **of** consistir em.

consistency [kən'sistənsi] n (of person etc) coerência, solidez f; (thickness) consistência.

consistent [kən'sistənt] adj (person) compatível, coerente; (even) constante.

consolation [kɔnsə'leiʃən] n consolação f, consolo.

console [kən'səul] vt consolar // n ['kɔnsəul] consolo.

consolidate [kən'sɔlideit] vt consolidar.

consommé [kən'sɔmei] n consomê m, caldo.

consonant ['kɔnsənənt] n consoante f.

consortium [kən'sɔːtiəm] n consórcio.

conspicuous [kən'spikjuəs] adj (visible) visível; (garish etc) berrante; (outstanding) notável.

conspiracy [kən'spirəsi] n conspiração f, trama.

conspire [kən'spaiə*] vi conspirar.

constable ['kʌnstəbl] n polícia m/f; **chief** ~ chefe m de polícia.

constabulary [kən'stæbjuləri] n polícia (distrital).

constant ['kɔnstənt] adj (gen) constante; (loyal) leal, fiel.

constellation [kɔnstə'leiʃən] n constelação f.

consternation [kɔnstə'neiʃən] n consternação f.

constipated ['kɔnstipeitəd] adj com prisão de ventre.

constituency [kən'stitjuənsi] n (POL) distrito eleitoral; **constituent** [-ənt] n (POL) eleitor(a) m/f; (part) componente m.

constitute ['kɔnstitjuːt] vt constituir.

constitution [kɔnsti'tjuːʃən] n constituição f; ~**al** adj constitucional.

constrain [kən'strein] vt obrigar; ~**ed** adj: to feel ~**ed** to... sentir-se compelido a...; ~**t** n (force) força, coação f (Pt: -cç-); (confinement) confinamento; (shyness) acanhamento.

constrict [kən'strikt] vt apertar, constringir.

construct [kən'strʌkt] vt construir; ~**ion** [-ʃən] n construção f; ~**ive** adj construtivo.

construe [kən'struː] vt interpretar.

consul ['kɔnsl] n cônsul m/f; ~**ate** ['kɔnsjulɪt] n consulado.

consult [kən'sʌlt] vt/i consultar; ~**ant** n (MED) (médico) especialista m/f; (other specialist) assessor m; ~**ation** [kɔnsəl'teɪʃən] n consulta; ~**ing room** n consultório.

consume [kən'sju:m] vt (eat) comer; (drink) beber; (fire etc, COMM) consumir; **consumer** n consumidor(a) m/f; **consumer goods** npl bens mpl de consumo; **consumer society** n sociedade f de consumo.

consummate ['kɔnsʌmeɪt] vt consumar.

consumption [kən'sʌmpʃən] n consumo.

cont. abbr of **continued**.

contact ['kɔntækt] n contato (Pt: -act-); (col) pistolão m // vt entrar/pôr-se em conta(c)to com; **he has good** ~**s** tem boas relações; ~ **lenses** npl lentes fpl de conta(c)to.

contagious [kən'teɪdʒəs] adj contagioso.

contain [kən'teɪn] vt conter; **to** ~ **o.s.** conter-se; ~**er** n recipiente m; (for shipping etc) container m, cofre m de carga.

contaminate [kən'tæmɪneɪt] vt contaminar; **contamination** [-'neɪʃən] n contaminação f.

cont'd abbr of **continued**.

contemplate ['kɔntəmpleɪt] vt (gen) contemplar; (expect) contar com; (intend) pretender, pensar; **contemplation** [-'pleɪʃən] n contemplação f.

contemporary [kən'tempərərɪ] adj, n contemporâneo.

contempt [kən'tempt] n desprezo; ~**ible** adj desprezível; ~**uous** adj desdenhoso.

contend [kən'tend] vt (argue) afirmar // vi (struggle) lutar; ~**er** n contendor(a) m/f.

content [kən'tent] adj (happy) contente; (satisfied) satisfeito // vt contentar, satisfazer // n ['kɔntent] conteúdo; ~**s** npl conteúdo sg; ~**ed** adj contente, satisfeito.

contention [kən'tenʃən] n contenda; (argument) argumento.

contentment [kən'tentmənt] n contentamento.

contest ['kɔntest] n contenda; (competition) concurso // vt [kən'test] (dispute) disputar; (legal case) defender; (POL) ser candidato a; ~**ant** [kən'testənt] n competidor(a) m/f; (in fight) adversário/a m/f.

context ['kɔntekst] n contexto.

continent ['kɔntɪnənt] n continente m; **the** C~ o continente europeu; ~**al** [-'nentl] adj continental.

contingency [kən'tɪndʒənsɪ] n contingência; **contingent** [-ənt] n contingente m.

continual [kən'tɪnjuəl] adj contínuo; ~**ly** adv constantemente.

continuation [kəntɪnju'eɪʃən] n

prolongamento; (after interruption) continuação f.

continue [kən'tɪnju:] vi prosseguir, continuar // vt seguir, persistir em; (start again) recomeçar.

continuity [kɔntɪ'njuɪtɪ] n continuidade f.

continuous [kən'tɪnjuəs] adj contínuo.

contort [kən'tɔ:t] vt retorcer; ~**ion** [-'tɔ:ʃən] n contorção f; ~**ionist** [-'tɔ:ʃənɪst] n contorcionista m/f.

contour ['kɔntuə*] n contorno; (also: ~ line) curva de nível.

contraband ['kɔntrəbænd] n contrabando.

contraception [kɔntrə'sepʃən] n anticoncepção f; **contraceptive** [-'septɪv] adj, n anticoncepcional f.

contract ['kɔntrækt] n contrato // (vb: [kən'trækt]) vi (COMM): **to** ~ **to do sth** comprometer-se por contrato para fazer algo; (become smaller) contrair-se, encolher-se // vt contrair; ~**ion** [-ʃən] n contração (Pt: -cç-) f; ~**or** n contratante m/f.

contradict [kɔntrə'dɪkt] vt (deny) desmentir; (be contrary to) contradizer; ~**ion** [-ʃən] n contradição f.

contralto [kɔn'træltəu] n contralto.

contraption [kən'træpʃən] n (pej) geringonça.

contrary ['kɔntrərɪ] adj, n contrário.

contrast ['kɔntrɑ:st] n contraste m // vt [kən'trɑ:st] contrastar, comparar; ~**ing** adj oposto.

contravene [kɔntrə'vi:n] vt opor-se a; (law) infringir.

contribute [kən'trɪbju:t] vt contribuir // vi: **to** ~ **to** (gen) contribuir para; (newspaper) escrever para; **contribution** [kɔntrɪ'bju:ʃən] n (money) contribuição f; (to debate) intervenção f; (to journal) colaboração f; **contributor** n (to newspaper) colaborador(a) m/f.

contrive [kən'traɪv] vt (invent) idealizar; (carry out) efetuar (Pt: -ct-); (plot) tramar // vi: **to** ~ **to do** chegar a fazer.

control [kən'trəul] vt (gen) controlar; (traffic etc) dirigir; (machinery) regular; (temper) dominar // n (command) controle m, autoridade f; (of car) direção f (Br), condução f (Pt); (check) freio, controle; ~**s** npl mando sg; ~ **panel** n painel m de instrumentos; ~ **room** n sala de comando; ~ **tower** n (AVIAT) torre f de controle.

controversial [kɔntrə'və:ʃl] adj discutível; **controversy** ['kɔntrəvə:sɪ] n controvérsia.

convalesce [kɔnvə'les] vi convalescer; **convalescence** n convalescença; **convalescent** adj, n convalescente m/f.

convector [kən'vektə*] n (heater) aquecedor m de convecção.

convene [kən'vi:n] vt convocar // vi reunir-se.

convenience [kən'vi:nɪəns] n (comfort) comodidade f; (advantage) vantagem f, conveniência; **at your ~** quando lhe convier; **public ~** sanitários mpl (Br), lavabos mpl (Pt); **convenient** [-ənt] adj cômodo; (useful) útil; (place) acessível; (time) oportuno, conveniente.

convent ['kɔnvənt] n convento; **~ school** n colégio de freiras.

convention [kən'venʃən] n convenção f; (meeting) assembléia; **~al** adj convencional.

converge [kən'vəːdʒ] vi convergir.

conversant [kən'vəːsnt] adj: **to be ~ with** estar familiarizado com.

conversation [kɔnvə'seiʃən] n conversação f, conversa; **~al** adj (familiar) familiar; (talkative) loquaz.

converse ['kɔnvəːs] n inverso // vi [kən'vəːs] conversar; **~ly** [-'vəːsli] adv pelo contrário, inversamente.

conversion [kən'vəːʃən] n conversão f; **~ table** n tábua de conversão.

convert [kən'vəːt] vt (REL, COMM) converter; (alter) transformar; // n ['kɔnvəːt] convertido **~ible** adj conversível // n conversível m.

convex ['kɔn'veks] adj convexo.

convey [kən'vei] vt (gen) levar; (thanks) comunicar; (idea) exprimir; **~or belt** n correia transportadora.

convict [kən'vikt] vt (gen) condenar; (sentence) declarar culpado // n ['kɔnvikt] presidiário; **~ion** [-ʃən] n condenação f; (belief) fé f, convicção f.

convince [kən'vins] vt convencer; **convincing** adj convincente.

convoy ['kɔnvɔi] n escolta.

convulse [kən'vʌls] vt convulsionar; (laughter) fazer morrer de rir; **convulsion** [-'vʌlʃən] n convulsão f; (laughter) ataque m, acesso.

coo [kuː] vi arrulhar.

cook [kuk] vt (gen) cozinhar; (stew etc) guisar; (meal) preparar // vi cozer; (person) cozinhar // n cozinheiro/a; **~er** n fogão m; **~ery** n (dishes) cozinha; (art) arte f culinária; **~ery book** n livro de receitas; **~ie** n (US) bolacha, biscoito; **~ing** n cozinha.

cool [kuːl] adj fresco; (not hot) tépido; (not afraid) calmo; (unfriendly) frio // vt esfriar // vi arrefecer-se; **~ness** n frescura; (hostility) frieza; (indifference) indiferença.

coop [kuːp] n galinheiro, capoeira // vt: **to ~ up** (fig) confinar.

co-op ['kəuɔp] n abbr of **Cooperative (Society)**.

cooperate [kəu'ɔpəreit] vi cooperar, colaborar; **cooperation** [-'reiʃən] n cooperação f, colaboração f; **cooperative** [-rətiv] adj cooperativo // n cooperativa.

coordinate [kəu'ɔːdineit] vt coordenar; **coordination** [-'neiʃən] n coordenação f.

cop [kɔp] n (col) polícia m.

cope [kəup] vi: **to ~ with** poder com; (problem) estar à altura de.

co-pilot ['kəu'pailət] n co-piloto.

copious ['kəupiəs] adj copioso, abundante.

copper ['kɔpə*] n (metal) cobre m; (col: policeman) polícia m; **~s** npl moedas fpl de pouco valor.

coppice ['kɔpis], **copse** [kɔps] n bosquete m.

copulate ['kɔpjuleit] vi copular-se; **copulation** [-'leiʃən] n cópula.

copy ['kɔpi] n cópia; (of book etc) exemplar m; (of writing) originais mpl // vt copiar; **~right** n direitos mpl de autor, direitos autorais mpl.

coral ['kɔrəl] n coral m; **~ reef** n recife m de coral.

cord [kɔːd] n corda; (ELEC) cordão m, cabo; (fabric) veludo cotelê.

cordial ['kɔːdiəl] adj, n cordial m.

cordon ['kɔːdn] n cordão m; **to ~ off** vt isolar.

corduroy ['kɔːdərɔi] n veludo cotelê.

core [kɔː*] n (gen) centro, núcleo; (of fruit) caroço // vt descaroçar.

coriander [kɔri'ændə*] n coentro.

cork [kɔːk] n rolha; (tree) cortiça; **~screw** n saca-rolhas m inv.

cormorant ['kɔːmərnt] n cormorão m, corvo marinho.

corn [kɔːn] n (wheat) trigo; (US: maize) milho; (cereals) grão m, cereal m; (on foot) calo; **~ on the cob** (CULIN) espiga de milho.

corned beef ['kɔːnd-] n carne f de boi enlatada.

corner ['kɔːnə*] n (gen) ângulo; (outside) esquina; (inside) canto; (in road) curva; (FOOTBALL) corner m // vt (trap) encurralar; (COMM) monopolizar // vi (in car) dobrar a esquina; **~stone** n pedra angular.

cornet ['kɔːnit] n (MUS) cornetim m; (of ice-cream) casquinha.

cornflour n, **cornstarch** (US) n ['kɔːnflauə*, 'kɔːnstɑːtʃ] n farinha de milho.

Cornwall ['kɔːnwəl] n Cornualha.

corny ['kɔːni] adj (col) velho, gasto.

corollary [kə'rɔləri] n corolário.

coronary ['kɔrənəri] n: **~ (thrombosis)** trombose f.

coronation [kɔrə'neiʃən] n coroação f.

coroner ['kɔrənə*] n magistrado que investiga mortes suspeitas.

coronet ['kɔrənit] n coroa aberta, diadema.

corporal ['kɔːpərl] n cabo // adj corpóreo.

corporate ['kɔːpərit] adj corporativo.

corporation [kɔːpə'reiʃən] n (of town) junta; (COMM) corporação f.

corps [kɔː*], pl **corps** [kɔːz] n corpo.

corpse [kɔːps] n cadáver m.

corpuscle ['kɔːpʌsl] n corpúsculo.

corral [kə'rɑːl] n curral m.

correct [kə'rekt] adj (accurate) justo, exato (Pt: -ct-); (proper) correto (Pt: -ct-) // vt corrigir; **~ion** [-ʃən] n correção (Pt:

-cç-) f, retificação (Pt: -ct-); (erasure) emenda.

correlate ['kɔrileit] vt correlacionar.

correspond [kɔris'pɔnd] vi (write) escrever-se; (be equal to) corresponder; ~**ence** n correspondência; ~**ence course** n curso por correspondência; ~**ent** n correspondente m/f; ~**ing** adj correspondente.

corridor ['kɔridɔ:*] n corredor m, passagem f.

corroborate [kə'rɔbəreit] vt corroborar.

corrode [kə'rəud] vt corroer // vi corroer-se; **corrosion** [-'rəuʒən] n corrosão f.

corrugated ['kɔrəgeitid] adj ondulado; ~ iron n chapa ondulada or corrugada.

corrupt [kə'rʌpt] adj corrompido; (person) venal, corrupto // vt corromper; (bribe) subornar; ~**ion** [-ʃən] n corrupção f.

corset ['kɔ:sit] n espartilho.

Corsica ['kɔ:sikə] n Córsega.

cortège [kɔ:'te:ʒ] n séquito, cortejo.

cortisone ['kɔ:tizəun] n cortisona.

cosh [kɔʃ] n cassetete m.

cosiness ['kəuzinis] n conforto; (atmosphere) aconchego, conforto.

cos lettuce [kɔs-] n alface m (cos).

cosmetic [kɔz'metik] n cosmético.

cosmic ['kɔzmik] adj cósmico.

cosmonaut ['kɔzmɔnɔ:t] n cosmonauta m/f.

cosmopolitan [kɔzmə'pɔlitn] adj cosmopolita.

cosmos ['kɔzmɔs] n cosmo.

cost [kɔst] n (gen) custo; (price) preço; ~**s** npl custas fpl // vi, pt, pp **cost** custar, valer // vt custar; **at the** ~ **of** à custa de; **how much does it** ~? quanto custa?

co-star ['kəustɑ:*] n co-estrela m/f.

Costa Rican ['kɔstə'ri:kən] adj costarriquenho.

costly ['kɔstli] adj (expensive) caro, custoso; (valuable) suntuoso.

cost price n preço de custo.

costume ['kɔstju:m] n traje m; (also: **swimming** ~) (woman's) maiô m (Br), fato de banho (Pt); (man's) calção msg (de banho) (Br), calções mpl de banho (Pt).

cosy ['kəuzi] adj cômodo; (atmosphere) aconchegante; (life) folgado, confortável.

cot [kɔt] n (child's) cama (de criança), berço.

cottage ['kɔtidʒ] n casa de campo; (rustic) cabana; ~ **cheese** n ricota.

cotton ['kɔtn] n algodão m; (thread) fio, linha; **to** ~ **on to** vt (col) perceber; ~ **wool** n, ~ **batting** (US) n algodão (hidrófilo).

couch [kautʃ] n sofá m.

cough [kɔf] vi tossir // n tosse f; **to** ~ **up** vt expelir; ~ **drop** n pastilha para a tosse.

could [kud] pt of **can**; ~**n't** = **could not**.

council ['kaunsl] n conselho; **city** or **town** ~ câmara municipal; ~ **estate** n conjunto residencial subvencionado pelo governo; ~ **house** n casa popular; ~**lor** n vereador(a) m/f.

counsel ['kaunsl] n (advice) conselho; (lawyer) advogado // vt aconselhar; ~**lor** n (US) conselheiro.

count [kaunt] vt (gen) contar; (include) incluir // vi contar // n (gen) conta; (of votes) contagem f; (nobleman) conde m; (sum) total m, soma; **to** ~ **on** vt fus contar com; **that doesn't** ~! isso não vale!; ~**down** n contagem f regressiva.

counter ['kauntə*] n (in shop) balcão m; (in games) ficha, pedra // vt contrariar; (blow) parar; (attack) n contra-ataque // adv: ~ **to** contrário a; ~**act** vt opor-se a, neutralizar; ~**attack** n contra-ataque m // vi contra-atacar; ~**balance** n contrapeso; ~**-espionage** n contra-espionagem f.

counterfeit ['kauntəfit] n falsificação f // vt falsificar // adj falso, falsificado.

counterfoil ['kauntəfɔil] n canhoto (Br), talão m (Pt).

counterpart ['kauntəpɑ:t] n contrapartida; (of person) sósia m/f.

counter-revolution [kauntərevə'lu:ʃən] n contra-revolução f.

countersign ['kauntəsain] vt referendar.

countess ['kauntis] n condessa.

countless ['kauntlis] adj inumerável.

country ['kʌntri] n país m; (native land) pátria; (as opposed to town) campo; (region) região f, terra; ~ **dancing** n dança regional; ~ **house** n casa de campo; ~**side** n campo, paisagem f.

county ['kaunti] n condado, distrito; ~ **town** n capital f do condado.

coup [ku:] pl ~**s** [-z] n golpe m; ~ **d'état/de grâce** golpe de estado/de graça.

coupé ['ku:pei] n cupê m.

couple ['kʌpl] n (of things, people) par m; (married ~) casal m // vt (ideas, names) unir, juntar; (machinery) ligar, juntar; **a** ~ **of** um par de.

coupling ['kʌpliŋ] n (RAIL) engate m.

coupon ['ku:pɔn] n cupom (Pt: -pão) m; (pools ~) talão m.

courage ['kʌridʒ] n valentia, coragem f; ~**ous** [kə'reidʒəs] adj corajoso, valente.

courier ['kuriə*] n correio, mala; (for tourists) guia m/f, agente m/f de turismo.

course [kɔ:s] n (direction) direção (Pt: -cç-) f, caminho; (of river, ESCOL) curso; (of ship) rumo; (of bullet) trajetória (Pt: -ect-); (fig) procedimento; (GOLF) campo; (part of meal) prato; **of** ~ adv claro, naturalmente; **of** ~! claro!, evidentemente!; **in due** ~ oportunamente, no devido tempo.

court [kɔ:t] n (royal) corte f; (LAW)

tribunal *m*, sessão *f* de tribunal; (*TENNIS*) quadra // *vt* (*woman*) cortejar, namorar; (*danger etc*) procurar; **to take to ~** demandar, levar ao tribunal.

courteous ['kɔːtɪəs] *adj* cortês/esa.

courtesan [kɔːtɪ'zæn] *n* cortesã *f*.

courtesy ['kɔːtəsɪ] *n* cortesia; **by ~ of** com permissão de.

court-house ['kɔːthaus] *n* (*US*) palácio de justiça.

courtier ['kɔːtɪə*] *n* cortesão *m*.

court: ~-martial, *pl* **~s-martial** *n* conselho de guerra // *vt* submeter a conselho de guerra; **~room** *n* sala de tribunal; **~yard** *n* pátio.

cousin ['kʌzn] *n* primo/a *m/f*; **first ~** primo/a irmão/mã.

cove [kəuv] *n* angra, enseada.

covenant ['kʌvənənt] *n* convênio.

cover ['kʌvə*] *vt* (*gen*) cobrir; (*with lid*) tapar; (*chairs etc*) revestir; (*distance*) percorrer; (*include*) abranger; (*protect*) abrigar; (*journalist*) investigar; (*issues*) tratar // *n* (*gen*) coberta; (*lid*) tampa; (*for chair etc*) capa; (*for bed*) cobertor *m*; (*envelope*) envelope *m*; (*for book*) capa, forro; (*of magazine*) capa; (*shelter*) abrigo; (*insurance*) cobertura; **under ~** (*indoors*) abrigado; **under ~ of** sob o abrigo de; (*fig*) sob capa de; **to ~ up for sb** encobrir a alguém; **~age** *n* alcance *m*; **~ charge** *n* couvert *m*; **~ing** *n* cobertura, invólucro; **~ing letter** *n* carta de cobertura.

covet ['kʌvɪt] *vt* cobiçar.

cow [kau] *n* vaca // *vt* intimidar.

coward ['kauəd] *n* covarde *m/f*; **~ice** [-ɪs] *n* covardia; **~ly** *adj* covarde.

cowboy ['kaubɔɪ] *n* vaqueiro.

cower ['kauə*] *vi* encolher-se (de medo).

cowshed ['kauʃɛd] *n* estábulo.

coxswain ['kɔksn] *n* (*abbr*: **cox**) timoneiro/a *m/f*.

coy [kɔɪ] *adj* tímido.

coyote [kɔɪ'əutɪ] *n* coiote *m*.

cozy ['kəuzɪ] *adj* (*US*) = **cosy**.

crab [kræb] *n* caranguejo; **~ apple** *n* maçã ácida.

crack [kræk] *n* rachadura; (*noise*) estalo; (*fam*) pancada // *vt* estalar, quebrar; (*nut*) partir, descascar; (*safe*) forçar; (*whip etc*) estalar; (*knuckles*) estalar, partir; (*joke*) soltar // *adj* (*expert*) excelente; **to ~ up** *vi* (*MED*) sofrer um colapso nervoso; **~er** *n* (*biscuit*) biscoito; (*Christmas*) busca-pé-surpresa *m*.

crackle ['krækl] *vi* crepitar; **crackling** *n* (*of fire*) crepitação *f*; (*of leaves etc*) estalidos *mpl*; (*of pork*) torresmo.

cradle ['kreɪdl] *n* berço.

craft [krɑːft] *n* (*skill*) arte *f*; (*trade*) ofício; (*cunning*) astúcia; (*boat*) barco.

craftsman ['krɑːftsmən] *n* artífice *m*, artesão *m*; **~ship** *n* artesanato.

crafty ['krɑːftɪ] *adj* astuto.

crag [kræg] *n* penhasco; **~gy** *adj* escarpado.

cram [kræm] *vt* (*fill*) encher, abarrotar; **~med** *adj* abarrotado.

cramp [kræmp] *n* (*MED*) cãibra; (*TECH*) grampo // *vt* (*limit*) restringir; (*annoy*) estorvar; **~ed** *adj* apertado, confinado.

crampon ['kræmpən] *n* gato *m* de ferro.

crane [kreɪn] *n* (*TECH*) guindaste *m*; (*bird*) grou *m*.

crank [kræŋk] *n* manivela; (*person*) excêntrico; **~shaft** *n* eixo de manivelas.

cranky ['kræŋkɪ] *adj* (*eccentric*) excêntrico; (*bad-tempered*) irritadiço.

cranny ['krænɪ] *n see* **nook**.

crash [kræʃ] *n* (*noise*) estrondo; (*of cars etc*) choque *m*, batida; (*of plane*) desastre *m* de avião; (*COMM*) falência, quebra // *vt* (*plane*) espatifar // *vi* (*plane*) cair; (*two cars*) colidir, bater; (*fall noisily*) cair (com estrondo); **~ course** *n* curso intensivo; **~ helmet** *n* capacete *m*; **~ landing** *n* aterrissagem *f* forçada (*Br*), aterragem forçosa (*Pt*).

crate [kreɪt] *n* caixote *m*; (*old car*) lata-velha; (*of beer*) engradado.

crater ['kreɪtə*] *n* cratera.

cravat(e) [krə'væt] *n* gravata.

crave [kreɪv] *vt*: **to ~ for** ansiar por; **craving** *n* (*of pregnant woman*) desejo.

crawl [krɔːl] *vi* (*gen*) arrastar-se; (*child*) engatinhar; (*vehicle*) arrastar-se a passo de tartaruga // *n* rastejo; (*SWIMMING*) crawl *m*.

crayfish ['kreɪfɪʃ] *n, pl inv* lagostim *m*.

crayon ['kreɪən] *n* lápis *m* de cera, crayon *m*.

craze [kreɪz] *n* mania; (*fashion*) moda.

crazy ['kreɪzɪ] *adj* (*person*) louco, maluco, doido; (*idea*) disparatado.

creak [kriːk] *vi* chiar, ranger; (*door etc*) ranger.

cream [kriːm] *n* (*of milk*) nata; (*gen*) creme *m*; (*fig*) a fina flor // *adj* (*colour*) creme; **~ cake** *n* bolo de creme; **~ cheese** *n* ricota (*Br*), queijo creme (*Pt*); **~y** *adj* cremoso.

crease [kriːs] *n* (*fold*) dobra, vinco; (*in trousers*) vinco; (*wrinkle*) ruga // *vt* (*fold*) dobrar, vincar; (*wrinkle*) amassar, enrugar // *vi* (*wrinkle up*) amassar-se, enrugar-se.

create [kriː'eɪt] *vt* criar; **creation** [-ʃən] *n* criação *f*; **creative** *adj* criativo; **creator** *n* criador(a) *m/f*.

creature ['kriːtʃə*] *n* (*animal*) animal *m*, bicho; (*living thing*) criatura.

crèche, creche [krɛʃ] *n* creche *f*.

credentials [krɪ'dɛnʃlz] *npl* credenciais *fpl*.

credibility [krɛdɪ'bɪlɪtɪ] *n* credibilidade *f*.

credible ['krɛdɪbl] *adj* crível.

credit ['krɛdɪt] *n* (*gen*) crédito; (*merit*) mérito, honra // *vt* (*believe*) acreditar // *adj* creditício; **~s** *npl* (*CINEMA*) crédito; **~able** *adj* louvável; **~ card** *n* cartão *m* de crédito; **~or** *n* credor(a) *m/f*.

credulity [krɪ'djuːlɪtɪ] *n* credulidade *f*.

creed [kriːd] *n* credo.

creek [kri:k] n enseada; (US) riacho.

creep [kri:p] pt, pp **crept** vi (animal) rastejar; (person) andar na ponta dos pés; (plant) trepar; ~**er** n trepadeira; ~**y** adj (frightening) horripilante.

cremate [krɪ'meɪt] vt cremar; **cremation** [-ʃən] n cremação f.

crematorium [krɛmə'tɔːrɪəm], pl **-ria** [-rɪə] n crematório.

creosote ['krɪəsəut] n creosoto.

crêpe [kreɪp] n (fabric) crepe m; (paper) papel crepom m; ~ **bandage** n atadura de crepe.

crept [krɛpt] pt, pp de **creep.**

crescent ['krɛsnt] n meia-lua; (street) rua semicircular.

cress [krɛs] n agrião m.

crest [krɛst] n (of bird) crista; (of hill) cimo, topo; (of helmet) cimeira; (of coat of arms) timbre m; ~**fallen** adj abatido.

Crete [kri:t] n Creta.

crevasse [krɪ'væs] n fenda.

crevice ['krɛvɪs] n fenda, greta.

crew [kru:] n (of ship etc) tripulação f; (gang) bando, quadrilha; (MIL) guarnição f; ~**cut** n corte m à escovinha; ~**neck** n gola arredondada.

crib [krɪb] n manjedoira, presépio; (US: cot) berço // vt (col) plagiar.

crick [krɪk] n (in neck) cãibra.

cricket ['krɪkɪt] n (insect) grilo; (game) criquete m, cricket m.

crime [kraɪm] n crime m; (less serious) delito; **criminal** ['krɪmɪnl] n criminoso // adj criminal; (law) penal; **the Criminal Investigation Department (CID)** Brigada de Investigação Criminal.

crimson ['krɪmzn] adj inv carmesim.

cringe [krɪndʒ] vi agachar-se, encolher-se.

crinkle ['krɪŋkl] vt enrugar.

cripple ['krɪpl] n coxo, aleijado // vt aleijar, inutilizar.

crisis ['kraɪsɪs], pl **-ses** [-si:z] n crise f.

crisp [krɪsp] adj fresco; (cooked) torrado; (hair) crespo; (manner) seco; ~**s** npl batatas fritas (em pacote).

criss-cross ['krɪskrɔs] adj cruzado.

criterion [kraɪ'tɪərɪən], pl **-ria** [-rɪə] n critério.

critic ['krɪtɪk] n (gen) crítico/a m/f; (paper) crítico; ~**al** adj (gen) crítico; (illness) grave; ~**ally** adv (ill) gravemente; ~**ism** ['krɪtɪsɪzm] n crítica; ~**ize** ['krɪtɪsaɪz] vt criticar.

croak [krəuk] vi (frog) coaxar; (raven) crocitar // n grasnido.

crochet ['krəuʃeɪ] n crochê m.

crockery ['krɔkərɪ] n louça.

crocodile ['krɔkədaɪl] n crocodilo.

crocus ['krəukəs] n açafrão-da-primavera m.

croft [krɔft] n pequena chácara; ~**er** n arrendatário.

croissant ['krwasã] n croissant m.

crone [krəun] n velha encarquilhada.

crony ['krəunɪ] n camarada m/f, compadre m.

crook [kruk] n (fam) vigarista m/f; (of shepherd) cajado; (of arm) curva; ~**ed** ['krukɪd] adj torto; (path) tortuoso; (action) desonesto.

crop [krɔp] n (species) colheita; (quantity) safra // vt cortar, ceifar; **to** ~ **up** vi aparecer, surgir.

croquet ['krəukeɪ] n croquet m, croquê m.

croquette [krə'kɛt] n croquete m.

cross [krɔs] n cruz f // vt (street etc) cruzar, atravessar // adj zangado, mal-humorado; **to** ~ **o.s.** persignar-se; **to** ~ **out** vt riscar; **to** ~ **over** vi cruzar-se; ~**bar** n travessa; (SPORT) barra transversal; ~**country (race)** n corrida pelo campo; ~**-examination** n interrogatório; ~**-examine** vt interrogar; ~**-eyed** adj vesgo; ~**ing** n (road) cruzamento; (rail) passagem f de nível; (sea-passage) travessia; (also: **pedestrian** ~**ing**) faixa (para pedestres) (Br), passadeira (Pt); ~ **purposes** npl: **to be at** ~ **purposes** não entender-se; ~**-reference** n referência remissiva; ~**roads** n encruzilhada; ~ **section** n corte m transversal; (of population) grupo representativo; ~**walk** n (US) faixa (para pedestres) (Br), passadeira (Pt); ~**wind** n vento costal; ~**word** n palavras cruzadas fpl.

crotch [krɔtʃ] n (of garment) fundilho.

crotchet ['krɔtʃɪt] n (MUS) semínima.

crotchety ['krɔtʃɪtɪ] adj (person) rabugento.

crouch [krautʃ] vi agachar-se.

croupier ['kru:pɪə] n crupiê m/f.

crow [krəu] n (bird) corvo; (of cock) canto, cocoricó m // vi (cock) cantar, cocoricar.

crowbar ['krəubɑ:*] n alavanca, pé-de-cabra m.

crowd [kraud] n multidão f; (SPORT) público; (unruly) tropel m; (common herd) turba, vulgo // vt (gather) amontoar; (fill) encher // vi (gather) reunir-se; (pile up) amontoar-se; ~**ed** adj (full) cheio; (well-attended) concorrido.

crown [kraun] n (of head) topo, alta; (of hat) copa; (of hill) cume m // vt coroar; ~ **jewels** npl jóias fpl reais; ~ **prince** n príncipe m herdeiro.

crucial ['kru:ʃl] adj decisivo.

crucifix ['kru:sɪfɪks] n crucifixo; ~**ion** [-'fɪkʃən] n crucificação f; **crucify** [-faɪ] vt crucificar.

crude [kru:d] adj (materials) bruto; (fig: basic) grosseiro; (: vulgar) vulgar; ~ **(oil)** n óleo cru.

cruel ['kruəl] adj cruel; ~**ty** n crueldade f.

cruet ['kru:ɪt] n galheta.

cruise [kru:z] n cruzeiro, viagem f marítima // vi (ship) fazer um cruzeiro; (car) circular lentamente; **cruiser** n cruzador m.

crumb [krʌm] n migalha.

crumble ['krʌmbl] vt esmigalhar // vi (gen) desintegrar-se; (building) desmoronar-se; **crumbly** adj friável.

crumpet ['krʌmpɪt] n bolo leve.

crumple ['krʌmpl] vt (paper) enrugar; (material) amarrotar.

crunch [krʌntʃ] vt (food etc) mastigar // n (fig) crise f; **~y** adj crocante.

crusade [kruː'seɪd] n cruzada.

crush [krʌʃ] n (people) esmagamento; (crowd) aglomeração f; (drink): **lemon ~** limonada // vt (gen) esmagar; (paper) amassar; (cloth) enrugar; (fruit) espremer; **~ing** adj (burden) esmagador(a).

crust [krʌst] n côdea; (MED) crosta.

crutch [krʌtʃ] n muleta.

crux [krʌks] n ponto crucial.

cry [kraɪ] vi chorar; (shout) gritar // n grito.

crypt [krɪpt] n cripta.

cryptic ['krɪptɪk] adj enigmático, secreto.

crystal ['krɪstl] n cristal m; **~-clear** adj cristalino, claro; **crystallize** vt cristalizar // vi cristalizar-se.

cub [kʌb] n filhote m.

Cuba ['kjuːbə] n Cuba; **~n** adj, n cubano/a.

cubbyhole ['kʌbɪhəul] n esconderijo.

cube [kjuːb] n cubo // vt (MATH) elevar ao cubo; **~ root** n raiz f cúbica; **cubic** adj cúbico.

cubicle ['kjuːbɪkl] n cubículo.

cuckoo ['kuku:] n cuco; **~ clock** n relógio de cuco.

cucumber ['kjuːkʌmbə*] n pepino.

cuddle ['kʌdl] vt abraçar // vi abraçar-se; **cuddly** adj fofo.

cue [kjuː] n (snooker) taco; (THEATRE etc) deixa.

cuff [kʌf] n (of shirt, coat etc) punho; (blow) bofetada; **off the ~** adv improvisado; **~links** npl abotoaduras fpl.

cuisine [kwɪ'ziːn] n cozinha.

cul-de-sac ['kʌldəsæk] n beco sem saída.

culinary ['kʌlɪnərɪ] adj culinário.

cull [kʌl] vt (flowers) escolher; (select) selecionar (Pt: -cc-); (kill) matar seletivamente.

culminate ['kʌlmɪneɪt] vi: **to ~ in** terminar em; **culmination** [-'neɪʃən] n culminação f, auge m.

culpable ['kʌlpəbl] adj culpável.

culprit ['kʌlprɪt] n culpado/a m/f, acusado/a m/f.

cult [kʌlt] n culto.

cultivate ['kʌltɪveɪt] vt (also fig) cultivar; **cultivation** [-'veɪʃən] n cultivo; (fig) cultura.

cultural ['kʌltʃərəl] adj cultural.

culture ['kʌltʃə*] n (also fig) cultura; **~d** adj culto.

cumbersome ['kʌmbəsəm] adj pesado, incômodo.

cumulative ['kjuːmjulətɪv] adj cumulativo.

cunning ['kʌnɪŋ] n astúcia // adj astuto.

cup [kʌp] n xícara (Br), chávena (Pt); (prize, event) taça.

cupboard ['kʌbəd] n armário; (for crockery) guarda-louça.

Cupid ['kjuːpɪd] n Cupido.

cupola ['kjuːpələ] n cúpula.

cup-tie ['kʌptaɪ] n jogo eliminatório.

cur [kəː] n cão m vadio, vira-latas m inv; (person) patife m/f.

curable ['kjuərəbl] adj curável.

curate ['kjuərɪt] n coadjutor m.

curator [kjuə'reɪtə*] n diretor (Pt: -ct-) m, curador m.

curb [kəːb] vt refrear // n meio-fio.

curdle ['kəːdl] vi coalhar.

curds [kəːdz] npl coalho.

cure [kjuə*] vt curar // n tratamento, cura.

curfew ['kəːfjuː] n hora de recolher.

curio ['kjuərɪəu] n antiguidade f.

curiosity [kjuərɪ'ɔsɪtɪ] n curiosidade f; **curious** ['kjuərɪəs] adj curioso.

curl [kəːl] n anel m, caracol m // vt (hair) frisar, encrespar; (paper) enrolar; (lip) torcer // vi: **to ~ up** frisar-se, enrolar-se; (person) encaracolar-se; (fam) rir até morrer; **~er** n rolo, bobe m; **~y** adj frisado, crespo.

currant ['kʌrnt] n passa de corinto; (black, red) groselha.

currency ['kʌrnsɪ] n dinheiro, moeda.

current ['kʌrnt] n (ELEC) corrente f; (in river) correnteza // adj corrente, atual (Pt: -ct-); **~ account** n conta corrente; **~ affairs** npl atualidades (Pt: -ct-) fpl; **~ly** adv a(c)tualmente.

curriculum [kə'rɪkjuləm] pl **~s** or **-la** [-lə] n programa m de estudos; **~ vitae** n curriculum vitae m.

curry ['kʌrɪ] n caril m // vt: **to ~ favour with** captar simpatia de; **~ powder** n pós mpl de caril, curry m.

curse [kəːs] vi xingar (Br), praguejar (Pt) // vt amaldiçoar, xingar (Br) // n maldição f; (swearword) palavrão m (Br), baixo calão m (Pt).

cursory ['kəːsərɪ] adj rápido, superficial.

curt [kəːt] adj seco, brusco.

curtail [kəː'teɪl] vt (visit etc) abreviar, encurtar; (expenses etc) reduzir.

curtain ['kəːtn] n cortina; (THEATRE) pano; **~ ring** n argola.

curts(e)y ['kəːtsɪ] n mesura, reverência // vi fazer reverência.

curve [kəːv] n curva // vt encurvar, torcer // vi encurvar-se, torcer-se; (road) fazer (uma) curva.

cushion ['kuʃən] n almofada; (SNOOKER) tabela // vt (seat) escorar com almofada; (shock) amortecer.

custard ['kʌstəd] n (for pouring) nata, creme m.

custodian [kʌs'təudɪən] n guarda m/f.

custody ['kʌstədɪ] n custódia; **to take into ~** deter.

custom ['kʌstəm] n costume m; (COMM) clientela; **~ary** adj costumeiro.

customer ['kʌstəmə*] n cliente m/f.

custom-made ['kʌstəm'meɪd] adj (US) feito sob medida or sob encomenda.

customs ['kʌstəmz] npl alfândega sg; ~ **duty** n imposto alfandegário; ~ **officer** n inspetor (Pt: -ct-) da alfândega.

cut [kʌt], pt, pp **cut** vt cortar; (price) baixar; (record) gravar; (reduce) reduzir // vi cortar; (intersect) interceptar-se // n (gen) corte m; (in skin) corte, golpe m; (with sword) corte; (of knife) incisão f; (in salary etc) redução f; (of meat) fatia, corte; **power** ~ corte; **to** ~ **a tooth** estar com um dente nascendo; **to** ~ **down** vt (tree) derrubar; (reduce) abater; **to** ~ **off** vt (gen) cortar; (retreat) impedir; (troops) cercar; **to** ~ **out** vt (shape) recortar; (delete) suprimir; ~ **through** vi abrir caminho; ~**back** n redução f.

cute [kju:t] adj bonitinho, gracinha; (shrewd) astuto.

cuticle ['kju:tɪkl] n cutícula.

cutlery ['kʌtləri] n cutelaria, talheres mpl.

cutlet ['kʌtlɪt] n costeleta.

cut: ~**out** n figura para recortar; ~**price** adj, ~**rate** (US) adj a preço reduzido; ~**throat** n assassino // adj impiedoso, feroz.

cutting ['kʌtɪŋ] adj (gen) cortante; (remark) mordaz // n (PRESS) recorte m; (RAIL) corte m.

cwt abbr of **hundredweight**.

cyanide ['saɪənaɪd] n cianeto.

cyclamen ['sɪkləmən] n cíclame m.

cycle ['saɪkl] n ciclo; (bicycle) bicicleta // vi andar de bicicleta; **cycling** n ciclismo; **cyclist** n ciclista m/f.

cyclone ['saɪkləun] n ciclone m.

cygnet ['sɪgnɪt] n cisne novo.

cylinder ['sɪlɪndə*] n cilindro; ~ **block** n bloco de cilindros; ~ **capacity** n capacidade f cilíndrica; ~ **head** n cilíndrico; ~**head gasket** n culatra.

cymbals ['sɪmblz] npl pratos mpl.

cynic ['sɪnɪk] n cínico/a; ~**al** adj cínico, sarcástico; ~**ism** ['sɪnɪsɪzəm] n cinismo.

cypress ['saɪprɪs] n cipreste m.

Cypriot ['sɪprɪət] adj, n cipriota m/f.

Cyprus ['saɪprəs] n Chipre f.

cyst [sɪst] n cisto; ~**itis** n cistite f.

czar [zɑ:*] n czar m.

Czech [tʃek] adj, n tcheco/a.

Czechoslovakia [tʃekəslə'vækɪə] n Tchecoslováquia.

D

dab [dæb] vt (eyes, wound) tocar (de leve); (paint, cream) aplicar de leve // n (of paint) pincelada; (of liquid) gota; (amount) pequena quantidade f.

dabble ['dæbl] vi: **to** ~ **in** interessar-se por.

dad [dæd], **daddy** ['dædɪ] n papai m; **daddy-long-legs** n pernilongo.

daffodil ['dæfədɪl] n narciso-dos-prados m.

daft [dɑ:ft] adj bobo, besta.

dagger ['dægə*] n punhal m, adaga; **to look** ~**s at sb** olhar feio para alguém.

daily ['deɪlɪ] adj diário, cotidiano // n (paper) diário; (domestic help) diarista (Br), mulher f a dias (Pt) // adv diariamente, cada dia.

dainty ['deɪntɪ] adj delicado; (tasteful) elegante, gracioso.

dairy ['dɛərɪ] n leiteria // adj de laticínios; ~ **farm** n fazenda de gado leiteiro; ~ **produce** n laticínios mpl.

daisy ['deɪzɪ] n margarida.

dale [deɪl] n vale m.

dam [dæm] n represa, barragem f // vt represar.

damage ['dæmɪdʒ] n dano, prejuízo; (to machine) avaria // vt danificar, prejudicar; ~**s** npl (LAW) indenização f por danos.

damn [dæm] vt condenar; (curse) maldizer // n (col): **I don't give a** ~ estou me lixando // adj (col) (que) droga de; ~ **(it)!** (que) droga!; ~**ing** adj (evidence) grave, sério.

damp [dæmp] adj úmido, molhado // n umidade f // vt (also: ~**en**) (cloth, rag) molhar; (enthusiasm etc) jogar água fria em; ~**ness** n umidade f.

damson ['dæmzən] n ameixa pequena.

dance [dɑ:ns] n dança, (party) baile m // vi dançar; ~ **hall** n salão m de baile; **dancer** n dançarino/a; (professional) bailarino/a; **dancing** n dança.

dandelion ['dændɪlaɪən] n dente-de-leão m.

dandruff ['dændrəf] n caspa.

Dane [deɪn] n dinamarquês/esa m/f.

danger ['deɪndʒə*] n perigo; (risk) risco; ~**!** (on sign) perigo!; **to be in** ~ **of** correr o risco de; ~**ous** adj perigoso; ~**ously** adv perigosamente.

dangle ['dæŋgl] vt balançar // vi pender balançando.

Danish ['deɪnɪʃ] adj, n dinamarquês/esa m/f.

dare [dɛə*] vt: **to** ~ **sb to do sth** desafiar alguém a fazer algo // vi: **to** ~ **(to) do sth** atrever-se a fazer algo; ~**devil** n intrépido, atrevido; **daring** adj atrevido, ousado // n atrevimento, audácia.

dark [dɑ:k] adj (gen) escuro; (complexion) moreno; (hair) escuro; (cheerless) triste, sombrio; (fig) secreto, escondido // n (gen) escuro; (night) trevas fpl; **to be left in the** ~ **about** (fig) ser deixado no escuro sobre; **after** ~ depois de escurecer; ~**en** vt escurecer; (colour) fazer mais escuro // vi escurecer-se; (sky) anuviar-se; ~ **glasses** npl óculos mpl escuros; ~**ness** n escuridão f, trevas fpl; ~ **room** n câmara escura.

darling ['dɑ:lɪŋ] adj, n querido/a.

darn [dɑ:n] vt remendar, cerzir.

dart [dɑ:t] n (gen) dardo; (in game)

flecha, dardo // vi precipitar-se; **to ~ away/along** ir-se, seguir precipitadamente; **~board** n alvo; **~s** n jogo de dardos.

dash [dæʃ] n (*sign*) hífen m; (: *long*) travessão m; (*rush*) correria // vt (*throw*) arremessar; (*hopes*) frustrar // vi precipitar-se, ir depressa; **to ~ away or off** vi sair apressado; **~board** n painel m de instrumentos; **~ing** adj arrojado.

data ['deɪtə] npl dados mpl; **~ processing** n processamento de dados.

date [deɪt] n (*day*) data; (*with friend*) encontro; (*fruit*) tâmara; (*tree*) tamareira // vt datar; **to ~** adv até agora; **out of ~** desatualizado; **up to ~** moderno, em dia, **~d** adj antiquado.

daub [dɔːb] vt borrar.

daughter ['dɔːtə*] n filha; **~-in-law** n nora.

daunting ['dɔːntɪŋ] adj desalentador(a).

dawdle ['dɔːdl] vi (*waste time*) perder tempo; (*go slow*) andar devagar.

dawn [dɔːn] n madrugada, amanhecer m // vi (*day*) amanhecer; (*fig*): **it ~ed on him that ...** começou a perceber que... .

day [deɪ] n dia m; (*working ~*) jornada, dia útil; **the ~ before** véspera; **the following ~** o dia seguinte; **by ~** de dia; **~break** n amanhecer m; **~dream** n fantasia, devaneio // vi devanear; **~light** n luz f (de dia); **~time** n dia // adj de dia, diurno.

daze [deɪz] vt (*stun*) aturdir // n: **in a ~** aturdido.

dazzle ['dæzl] vt deslumbrar; **dazzling** adj deslumbrante.

dead [dɛd] adj (*gen*) morto; (*deceased*) falecido; (*telephone*) cortado; (*ELEC*) sem corrente // adv (*gen*) totalmente; (*exactly*) absolutamente; **~ tired** morto de cansado; **to stop ~** estacar; **the ~** os mortos mpl; **~en** vt (*blow, sound*) amortecer; (*make numb*) anestesiar; **~end** n beco sem saída; **~ heat** n (SPORT) empate m; **~line** n prazo final; **~lock** n impasse m, beco sem saída; **~ly** adj mortal, fatal; **~pan** adj sem expressão.

deaf [dɛf] adj surdo; **~-aid** n aparelho para a surdez; **~en** vt ensurdecer; **~ening** adj ensurdecedor(a); **~ness** n surdez f; **~-mute** n surdo-mudo.

deal [diːl] n (*agreement*) acordo; (*business*) transação (Pt: -cç-) f, negócio; (CARDS) mão f // vt, pt, pp **dealt** [dɛlt] (*gen*) dar; **a great ~ (of)** bastante, muito; **to ~ in** tratar com; **to ~ with** vt (*people*) tratar com; (*problem*) ocupar-se de; (*subject*) tratar de; (COMM) negociar com; (*punish*) castigar; **~er** n negociante m/f; (CARDS) carteador m, banqueiro; **~ings** npl transações (Pt: -cç-) fpl; (*relations*) relações fpl.

dear [dɪə*] adj querido; (*expensive*) caro // n: **my ~** meu querido/minha querida // excl: **~ me!** Meu Deus!; **D~ Sir/Madam** (*in letter*) Ilmo. Senhor/Exma. Senhora (Br), Exmo.

Senhor/Exma. Senhora (Pt); **~ly** adv (*love*) ternamente; (*pay*) caro.

death [dɛθ] n morte f; **~bed** n leito de morte; **~ certificate** n certidão f de óbito; **~ duties** npl (*Brit*) impostos mpl sobre inventário; **~ly** adj mortal; (*silence*) profundo; **~ penalty** n pena de morte; **~ rate** n (índice f de) mortalidade f.

debar [dɪ'bɑː*] vt (*exclude*) excluir.

debase [dɪ'beɪs] vt degradar.

debate [dɪ'beɪt] n debate m // vt debater.

debauchery [dɪ'bɔːtʃərɪ] n libertinagem f.

debit ['dɛbɪt] n débito // vt: **to ~ a sum to sb or to sb's account** lançar uma quantia ao débito de alguém or à conta de alguém.

debris ['dɛbriː] n escombros mpl.

debt [dɛt] n dívida; **to be in ~** ter dívidas; **~or** n devedor(a) m/f.

début ['deɪbjuː] n estréia.

decade ['dɛkeɪd] n década.

decadence ['dɛkədəns] n decadência.

decay [dɪ'keɪ] n decadência; (*of building*) ruína; (*fig*) deterioração f; (*rotting*) podridão f; (*of tooth*) cárie f // vi (*rot*) apodrecer-se; (*fig*) decair.

deceased [dɪ'siːst] adj defunto, falecido.

deceit [dɪ'siːt] n engano; **~ful** adj enganador(a).

deceive [dɪ'siːv] vt enganar.

decelerate [diː'sɛləreɪt] vt moderar a marcha de, desacelerar // vi diminuir a velocidade.

December [dɪ'sɛmbə*] n dezembro (Pt: D-).

decency ['diːsənsɪ] n decência.

decent ['diːsənt] adj (*proper*) decente; (*person*) honesto, amável.

decentralize [diː'sɛntrəlaɪz] vt descentralizar.

deception [dɪ'sɛpʃən] n engano, fraude f; **deceptive** [-tɪv] adj enganador(a).

decibel ['dɛsɪbɛl] n decibel m.

decide [dɪ'saɪd] vt (*person*) decidir; (*question, argument*) resolver // vi decidir; **to ~ on sth** decidir-se por algo; **~d** adj (*resolute*) decidido; (*clear, definite*) claro, definido; **~dly** [-dɪdlɪ] adv decididamente.

deciduous [dɪ'sɪdjuəs] adj decíduo, caduco.

decimal ['dɛsɪməl] adj decimal // n decimal m; **~ point** n vírgula de decimais.

decimate ['dɛsɪmeɪt] vt dizimar.

decipher [dɪ'saɪfə*] vt decifrar.

decision [dɪ'sɪʒən] n decisão f.

decisive [dɪ'saɪsɪv] adj decisivo; (*conclusive*) terminante; (*manner*) categórico.

deck [dɛk] n (NAUT) coberta; (*of bus*) andar m; (*of cards*) baralho; **~chair** n cadeira de lona.

declaration [dɛklə'reɪʃən] n declaração f; **declare** [dɪ'klɛə*] vt (*gen*) declarar.

decline [dɪ'klaɪn] n declínio, decadência;

(*lessening*) diminuição *f*, baixa // *vt* recusar // *vi* decair, diminuir; (*fall*) baixar.

declutch ['di:'klʌtʃ] *vi* debrear.

decode [di:'kəud] *vt* decifrar.

decompose [di:kəm'pəuz] *vi* decompor-se; **decomposition** [di:kɔmpə'zɪʃən] *n* decomposição *f*.

decontaminate [di:kɔn'tæmɪneɪt] *vt* descontaminar.

décor ['deɪkɔ:*] *n* decoração *f*; (*THEATRE*) cenário.

decorate ['dekəreɪt] *vt* ornamentar, decorar; (*paint*) pintar; (*paper*) decorar com papel; **decoration** [-'reɪʃən] *n* decoração *f*, adorno; (*act*) decoração; (*medal*) condecoração *f*; **decorator** *n* (*painter*) pintor *m*.

decoy ['di:kɔɪ] *n* engodo.

decrease ['di:kri:s] *n* diminuição *f* // (*vb*: [di:'kri:s]) *vt* diminuir, reduzir // *vi* reduzir-se.

decree [dɪ'kri:] *n* decreto; ~ **nisi** *n* ordem *f* provisória de divórcio.

decrepit [dɪ'krepɪt] *adj* decrépito.

dedicate ['dedɪkeɪt] *vt* dedicar; **dedication** [-'keɪʃən] *n* (*devotion*) dedicação *f*; (*in book*) dedicatória.

deduce [dɪ'dju:s] *vt* deduzir.

deduct [dɪ'dʌkt] *vt* deduzir; (*from wage etc*) descontar; ~**ion** [dɪ'dʌkʃən] *n* redução *f*, dedução *f*; (*conclusion*) conclusão *f*, dedução *f*.

deed [di:d] *n* feito, ato (*Pt*: -ct-); (*feat*) façanha; (*LAW*) escritura, título.

deem [di:m] *vt* julgar.

deep [di:p] *adj* (*gen*) profundo; (*voice*) baixo, grave; (*person*) fechado; **to take a** ~ **breath** respirar fundo // *adv*: **the spectators stood 20** ~ os espectadores formaram-se em 20 fileiras; **to be 4 metres** ~ ter 4 metros de profundidade; ~**en** *vt* aprofundar // *vi* (*mystery*) aumentar; ~**-freeze** *n* congelador *m*; ~**-fry** *vt* fritar em recipiente fundo; ~**-sea diving** *n* pesca submarina; ~**-seated** *adj* (*beliefs*) arraigado; ~**-set** *adj* (*eyes*) fundo.

deer [dɪə*] *n, pl inv* veado, cervo; ~**skin** *n* camurça, pele *f* de cervo.

deface [dɪ'feɪs] *vt* desfigurar, deformar.

defamation [defə'meɪʃən] *n* difamação *f*.

default [dɪ'fɔ:lt] *vi* não pagar; (*SPORT*) não comparecer // *n*: **by** ~ (*LAW*) à revelia; (*SPORT*) por ausência; ~**er** *n* (*in debt*) devedor(a) *m/f* insolvente.

defeat [dɪ'fi:t] *n* derrota // *vt* derrotar, vencer; (*fig: efforts*) frustrar; ~**ist** *adj, n* derrotista *m/f*.

defect ['di:fekt] *n* defeito // *vi* [dɪ'fekt] desertar; ~**ive** [dɪ'fektɪv] *adj* (*gen*) defeituoso; (*person*) retardado mental.

defence [dɪ'fens] *n* defesa; ~**less** *adj* indefeso.

defend [dɪ'fend] *vt* defender; ~**ant** *n* acusado/a; (*in civil case*) réu/ré *m/f*; ~**er** *n* defensor(a) *m/f*.

defensive [dɪ'fensɪv] *adj* defensivo; **on the** ~ na defensiva.

defer [dɪ'fɔ:*] *vt* (*postpone*) adiar; **to** ~ **to** submeter-se a; ~**ence** ['defərəns] *n* deferência, respeito.

defiance [dɪ'faɪəns] *n* desafio, desrespeito; **in** ~ **of** sem respeito por; a despeito de; **defiant** [-ənt] *adj* (*insolent*) desafiante, insolente; (*challenging*) desafiador(a).

deficiency [dɪ'fɪʃənsɪ] *n* (*lack*) falta; (*defect*) defeito; **deficient** [-ənt] *adj* (*lacking*) deficiente; (*incomplete*) incompleto; (*defective*) imperfeito; (*mentally*) anormal; **deficient in** falto de, carente de.

deficit ['defɪsɪt] *n* déficit *m*.

defile [dɪ'faɪl] *vt* sujar, profanar.

define [dɪ'faɪn] *vt* definir.

definite ['defɪnɪt] *adj* (*fixed*) definitivo; (*clear, obvious*) claro, categórico; **he was** ~ **about it** ele foi categórico; ~**ly** *adv* claramente.

definition [defɪ'nɪʃən] *n* definição *f*.

definitive [dɪ'fɪnɪtɪv] *adj* definitivo.

deflate [di:'fleɪt] *vt* (*gen*) esvaziar; (*person*) fazer perder o rebolado.

deflect [dɪ'flekt] *vt* desviar.

deform [dɪ'fɔ:m] *vt* deformar; ~**ed** *adj* deformado; ~**ity** *n* deformidade *f*.

defraud [dɪ'frɔ:d] *vt* defraudar; **to** ~ **sb of sth** defraudar alguém de algo.

defrost [di:'frɔst] *vt* (*fridge*) descongelar; ~**er** *n* (*US*) desembaçante *m* de pára-brisa.

deft [deft] *adj* destro, hábil.

defunct [dɪ'fʌŋkt] *adj* extinto, morto.

defuse [di:'fju:z] *vt* tirar o estopim *or* a espoleta de.

defy [dɪ'faɪ] *vt* (*resist*) opor-se a; (*challenge*) desafiar; (*order*) desobedecer.

degenerate [dɪ'dʒenəreɪt] *vi* degenerar // *adj* [dɪ'dʒenərɪt] degenerado.

degradation [degrə'deɪʃən] *n* degradação *f*; **degrading** [dɪ'greɪdɪŋ] *adj* degradante.

degree [dɪ'gri:] *n* grau *m*; (*SCOL*) diploma *m*, título; ~ **in maths** grau em matemática.

dehydrated [di:haɪ'dreɪtɪd] *adj* desidratado; (*milk*) em pó.

de-ice [di:'aɪs] *vt* (*windscreen*) descongelar.

deign [deɪn] *vi*: **to** ~ **to do** dignar-se a fazer.

deity ['di:ɪtɪ] *n* divindade *f*, deidade *f*.

dejected [dɪ'dʒektɪd] *adj* abatido, desanimado; (*face*) triste; **dejection** [-ʃən] *n* desânimo.

delay [dɪ'leɪ] *vt* demorar, atrasar; (*trains*) atrasar // *vi* retardar-se // *n* demora, atraso; **without** ~ sem demora, sem atraso.

delegate ['delɪgɪt] *n* delegado/a // *vt* ['delɪgeɪt] delegar; **delegation** [-'geɪʃən] *n* delegação *f*.

delete [dɪ'li:t] *vt* eliminar, riscar.

deliberate [dɪ'lɪbərɪt] *adj* (*intentional*)

intencional; (*slow*) pausado, lento // vi
[dɪ'lɪbəreɪt] deliberar; **~ly** adv (*on purpose*) de propósito; (*slowly*) lentamente.

delicacy ['dɛlɪkəsɪ] n delicadeza; (*choice food*) iguaria.

delicate ['dɛlɪkɪt] adj (*gen*) delicado; (*fragile*) frágil; (*skilled*) fino.

delicatessen [dɛlɪkə'tɛsn] n loja especializada em comida exótica.

delicious [dɪ'lɪʃəs] adj delicioso, saboroso.

delight [dɪ'laɪt] n (*feeling*) prazer m, deleite m; (*object*) encanto; **to take ~ in** deleitar-se com; **~ful** adj encantador(a), delicioso.

delinquency [dɪ'lɪŋkwənsɪ] n delinquência; **delinquent** [-ənt] adj, n delinquente m/f.

delirious [dɪ'lɪrɪəs] adj delirante; **delirium** [-ɪəm] n delírio.

deliver [dɪ'lɪvə*] vt (*distribute*) distribuir; (*hand over*) entregar; (*message*) comunicar; (*speech*) proferir; (*blow*) dar, desfechar; (*MED*): **to be ~ed** dar à luz; **~y** n entrega; (*distribution*) distribuição f; (*of speaker*) enunciação f; (*MED*) parto; (*saving*) libertação f; **to take ~y of** receber.

delta ['dɛltə] n delta m.

delude [dɪ'luːd] vt enganar.

deluge ['dɛljuːdʒ] n dilúvio // vt inundar.

delusion [dɪ'luːʒən] n ilusão f, erro.

de luxe [dəˈlʌks] adj de luxo.

delve [dɛlv] vi: **to ~ into** investigar, pesquisar.

demand [dɪ'mɑːnd] vt (*gen*) exigir, pedir; (*rights*) reclamar // n (*gen*) exigência, pedido; (*claim*) reclamação f; (*ECON*) procura; **to be in ~** ser muito solicitado; **on ~** à vista; **~ing** adj (*boss*) exigente; (*work*) absorvente.

demarcation [diːmɑːˈkeɪʃən] n demarcação f.

demean [dɪ'miːn] vt: **to ~ o.s.** rebaixar-se.

demeanour [dɪ'miːnə*] n conduta, comportamento.

demented [dɪ'mɛntɪd] adj demente, doido.

demister [diːˈmɪstə*] n (*AUT*) desembaçante m de pára-brisa.

democracy [dɪ'mɒkrəsɪ] n democracia; **democrat** ['dɛməkræt] n democrata m/f; **democratic** [dɛmə'krætɪk] adj democrático.

demolish [dɪ'mɒlɪʃ] vt demolir, derrubar; **demolition** [dɛmə'lɪʃən] n demolição f, destruição f.

demonstrate ['dɛmənstreɪt] vt demonstrar // vi manifestar-se; **demonstration** [-'streɪʃən] n (*POL*) manifestação f; (*proof*) prova, demonstração f; **demonstrator** n (*POL*) manifestante m/f.

demoralize [dɪ'mɒrəlaɪz] vt desmoralizar.

demote [dɪ'məut] vt rebaixar de posto.

demure [dɪ'mjuə*] adj recatado.

den [dɛn] n (*of animal*) covil m; (*study*) aposento privado, cantinho.

denial [dɪ'naɪəl] n (*refusal*) negativa; (*of report etc*) desmentido; **self-~** abnegação f.

denim ['dɛnɪm] n brim m, zuarte m; **~s** npl jeans msg (*Br*), jeans mpl (*Pt*).

Denmark ['dɛnmɑːk] n Dinamarca.

denomination [dɪnɒmɪ'neɪʃən] n valor m, denominação f; (*REL*) seita.

denominator [dɪ'nɒmɪneɪtə*] n denominador m.

denote [dɪ'nəut] vt indicar, significar.

denounce [dɪ'nauns] vt denunciar.

dense [dɛns] adj (*thick*) denso, espesso; (: *foliage etc*) denso; (*stupid*) estúpido, bronco; **~ly** adv: **~ly populated** com grande densidade de população.

density ['dɛnsɪtɪ] n densidade f.

dent [dɛnt] n amolgadura, depressão f // vt (*also*: **make a ~ in**) amolgar, dentar.

dental ['dɛntl] adj dental; **~ surgeon** n odontólogo.

dentist ['dɛntɪst] n dentista m/f; **~ry** n odontologia.

dentures ['dɛntʃəz] npl dentadura sg.

deny [dɪ'naɪ] vt (*gen*) negar; (*report*) desmentir.

deodorant [diː'əudərənt] n desodorante m (*Br*), desodorizante m (*Pt*).

depart [dɪ'pɑːt] vi ir-se, partir; (*train*) sair; **to ~ from** (*fig: differ from*) afastar-se de.

department [dɪ'pɑːtmənt] n departamento; (*COMM*) seção (*Pt*: -cç-) f; (*POL*) repartição f; **~ store** n magazine m (*Br*), grande armazém m (*Pt*).

departure [dɪ'pɑːtʃə*] n partida, ida; (*of train*) saída; **a new ~** nova orientação; **~s board**, **~ board** (*US*) n horário de saídas.

depend [dɪ'pɛnd] vi: **to ~ on** depender de; (*rely on*) contar com; **it ~s** depende; **~able** adj (*person*) de confiança, seguro; **~ence** n dependência; **~ant**, **~ent** n dependente m/f.

depict [dɪ'pɪkt] vt (*in picture*) pintar; (*describe*) representar.

depleted [dɪ'pliːtɪd] adj depauperado.

deplorable [dɪ'plɔːrəbl] adj deplorável, lamentável; **deplore** [dɪ'plɔː*] vt deplorar, lamentar.

deploy [dɪ'plɔɪ] vt dispor.

depopulation [ˈdiːpɒpjuːleɪʃən] n despovoamento.

deport [dɪ'pɔːt] vt deportar; **~ation** [-'teɪʃən] n deportação f; **~ment** n comportamento.

depose [dɪ'pəuz] vt depor.

deposit [dɪ'pɒzɪt] n (*gen*) depósito; (*CHEM*) sedimento; (*of ore, oil*) depósito // vt (*gen*) depositar; **~ account** n conta de depósito a prazo; **~or** n depositante m/f.

depot ['dɛpəu] n (*storehouse*) armazém m; (*for vehicles*) garagem f, parque m.

depraved [dɪ'preɪvd] *adj* depravado, viciado; **depravity** [-'prævɪtɪ] *n* depravação *f*, vício.

depreciate [dɪ'priːʃɪeɪt] *vi* depreciar-se, desvalorizar-se; **depreciation** [-'eɪʃən] *n* depreciação *f*.

depress [dɪ'prɛs] *vt* deprimir; (*press down*) apertar; ～**ed** *adj* deprimido; ～**ing** *adj* triste, desanimador(a); ～**ion** [dɪ'prɛʃən] *n* depressão *f*.

deprivation [dɛprɪ'veɪʃən] *n* privação *f*; (*loss*) perda.

deprive [dɪ'praɪv] *vt*: **to** ～ **sb of** privar alguém de; ～**d** *adj* pobre.

depth [dɛpθ] *n* (*gen*) profundidade *f*; (*of room etc*) comprimento; **in the** ～**s of** nas profundezas de.

deputation [dɛpju'teɪʃən] *n* delegação *f*.

deputize ['dɛpjutaɪz] *vi*: **to** ～ **for sb** substituir alguém.

deputy ['dɛpjutɪ] *adj*: ～ **head** diretor(a) (*Pt*: -ct-) adjunto/a *m/f* // *n* substituto/a, suplente *m/f*; (*POL*) deputado/a; (*agent*) representante *m/f*.

derail [dɪ'reɪl] *vt*: **to be** ～**ed** descarrilhar-se; ～**ment** *n* descarrilhamento.

deranged [dɪ'reɪndʒd] *adj* (*person*) louco, transtornado.

derelict ['dɛrɪlɪkt] *adj* abandonado.

deride [dɪ'raɪd] *vt* ridicularizar, zombar de; **derision** [-'rɪʒən] *n* irrisão *f*, escárnio.

derivative [dɪ'rɪvətɪv] *n* derivado // *adj* derivado; (*work*) pouco original.

derive [dɪ'raɪv] *vt* derivar // *vi*: **to** ～ **from** derivar-se de.

dermatitis [dəːmə'taɪtɪs] *n* dermatite *f*; **dermatology** [-'tɔlədʒɪ] *n* dermatologia.

derogatory [dɪ'rɔgətərɪ] *adj* pejorativo.

derrick ['dɛrɪk] *n* guindaste *m*, torre *f* de perfurar.

descend [dɪ'sɛnd] *vt/i* descer, baixar; **to** ～ **from** descer de; ～**ant** *n* descendente *m/f*.

descent [dɪ'sɛnt] *n* descida; (*GEO*) declive *m*, ladeira; (*origin*) descendência.

describe [dɪs'kraɪb] *vt* descrever; **description** [-'krɪpʃən] *n* descrição *f*; (*sort*) classe *f*, espécie *f*; **descriptive** [-'krɪptɪv] *adj* descritivo.

desecrate ['dɛsɪkreɪt] *vt* profanar.

desert ['dɛzət] *n* deserto // (*vb*: [dɪ'zəːt]) *vt* abandonar // *vi* (*MIL*) desertar; ～**er** *n* desertor *m*; ～**ion** [dɪ'zəːʃən] *n* deserção *f*.

deserve [dɪ'zəːv] *vt* merecer; **deserving** *adj* (*person*) digno; (*action, cause*) meritório.

design [dɪ'zaɪn] *n* (*sketch*) desenho, esboço; (*layout, shape*) plano, modelo; (*pattern*) projeto (*Pt*: -ct-); (*intention*) propósito, intenção *f* // *vt* (*gen*) desenhar; (*plan*) projetar (*Pt*: -ct-).

designate ['dɛzɪgneɪt] *vt* (*point to*) apontar; (*appoint*) nomear; (*destine*) designar // *adj* ['dɛzɪgnɪt] designado;

designation [-'neɪʃən] *n* (*appointment*) nomeação *f*; (*name*) designação *f*.

designer [dɪ'zaɪnə*] *n* (*ART*) artista *m/f* gráfico/a; (*TECH*) desenhista *m/f*, projetista *m/f*; (*fashion* ～) estilista *m/f*.

desirable [dɪ'zaɪərəbl] *adj* (*proper*) desejável; (*attractive*) atraente.

desire [dɪ'zaɪə*] *n* desejo // *vt* desejar.

desk [dɛsk] *n* (*in office*) secretária *f*; (*for pupil*) carteira *f*; (*in hotel, at airport*) recepção *f*.

desolate ['dɛsəlɪt] *adj* (*place*) deserto; (*person*) desolado; **desolation** [-'leɪʃən] *n* (*of place*) desolação *f*; (*of person*) aflição *f*.

despair [dɪs'pɛə*] *n* desespero // *vi*: **to** ～ **of** desesperar-se de.

despatch [dɪs'pætʃ] *n*, *vt* = **dispatch**.

desperate ['dɛspərɪt] *adj* desesperado; ～**ly** *adv* desesperadamente; (*very*) terrivelmente, gravemente.

desperation [dɛspə'reɪʃən] *n* desespero, desesperança; **in** ～ desesperado.

despicable [dɪs'pɪkəbl] *adj* desprezível.

despise [dɪs'paɪz] *vt* desprezar.

despite [dɪs'paɪt] *prep* apesar de, a despeito de.

despondent [dɪs'pɔndənt] *adj* abatido, desanimado.

dessert [dɪ'zəːt] *n* sobremesa; ～**spoon** *n* colher *f* de sobremesa.

destination [dɛstɪ'neɪʃən] *n* destino.

destiny ['dɛstɪnɪ] *n* destino.

destitute ['dɛstɪtjuːt] *adj* indigente, necessitado.

destroy [dɪs'trɔɪ] *vt* (*gen*) destruir; (*finish*) acabar com; ～**er** *n* (*NAUT*) contratorpedeiro.

destruction [dɪs'trʌkʃən] *n* destruição *f*; (*fig*) ruína; **destructive** [-tɪv] *adj* destrutivo, destruidor(a).

detach [dɪ'tætʃ] *vt* separar; (*unstick*) desprender; ～**able** *adj* separável; (*TECH*) desmontável; ～**ed** *adj* (*attitude*) imparcial, objetivo (*Pt*: -ct-); (*house*) independente, isolado; ～**ment** *n* (*gen*) separação *f*; (*MIL*) destacamento; (*fig*) obje(c)tividade *f*, imparcialidade *f*.

detail ['diːteɪl] *n* detalhe *m* // *vt* (*gen*) detalhar; (*MIL*) destacar; **in** ～ pormenorizado, em detalhe; ～**ed** *adj* detalhado.

detain [dɪ'teɪn] *vt* deter; (*in captivity*) prender.

detect [dɪ'tɛkt] *vt* (*gen*) descobrir; (*MED, POLICE*) identificar; (*MIL, RADAR, TECH*) detectar; ～**ion** [dɪ'tɛkʃən] *n* descobrimento, identificação *f*; ～**ive** *n* detetive (*Pt*: -ect-) *m*; ～**ive story** *n* romance *m* policial; ～**or** *n* detetor (*Pt*: -tect-) *m*.

détente [deɪ'tɑːnt] *n* distensão *f* de relações.

detention [dɪ'tɛnʃən] *n* detenção *f*, prisão *f*.

deter [dɪ'təː*] *vt* (*discourage*) desanimar; (*dissuade*) dissuadir; (*prevent*) impedir.

detergent [dɪ'təːdʒənt] *n* detergente *m*.

deteriorate [dɪ'tɪərɪəreɪt] vi deteriorar-se; **deterioration** [-'reɪʃən] n deterioração f.

determination [dɪtə:mɪ'neɪʃən] n (gen) determinação f; (resolve) resolução f.

determine [dɪ'tə:mɪn] vt (gen) determinar; (limits etc) definir; (dispute) resolver; ~d adj (person) resoluto, decidido.

deterrent [dɪ'terənt] n dissuasivo.

detest [dɪ'test] vt detestar; ~able adj detestável.

detonate ['detəneɪt] vi explodir, estalar // vt detonar; **detonator** n detonador m.

detour ['di:tuə*] n desvio.

detract [dɪ'trækt] vt: to ~ from tirar prazer de, depreciar.

detriment ['detrɪmənt] n: to the ~ of em detrimento de; ~al [detrɪ'mentl] adj (to) prejudicial (a).

devaluation [dɪvælju'eɪʃən] n desvalorização f; **devalue** [-'vælju:] vt desvalorizar.

devastate ['devəsteɪt] vt devastar; **he was ~d by** the news as notícias deixaram-no desolado; **devastating** adj devastador(a); (fig) assolador(a).

develop [dɪ'veləp] vt (gen) desenvolver; (PHOT) revelar; (disease) contrair; (engine trouble) começar a ter // vi desenvolver-se; (advance) progredir; (appear) aparecer; ~ing country país m em desenvolvimento; ~ment n desenvolvimento; (advance) progresso; (of affair, case) desenvolvimento, progresso; (of land) urbanização f.

deviate ['di:vɪeɪt] vi desviar-se; **deviation** [-'eɪʃən] n desvio.

device [dɪ'vaɪs] n (scheme) estratagema m, plano; (apparatus) aparelho, mecanismo.

devil ['devl] n diabo, demônio; ~ish adj diabólico.

devious ['di:vɪəs] adj intricado, indireto (Pt: -ct-); (person) indire(c)to.

devise [dɪ'vaɪz] vt idear, inventar.

devoid [dɪ'vɔɪd] adj: ~ of destituído de.

devote [dɪ'vəut] vt: to ~ sth to dedicar algo a; ~d adj (loyal) leal, fiel; **the book is ~d to politics** o livro trata de política; **devotee** [devəu'ti:] n adepto/a, entusiasta m/f.

devotion [dɪ'vəuʃən] n dedicação f; (REL) devoção f.

devour [dɪ'vauə*] vt devorar.

devout [dɪ'vaut] adj devoto.

dew [dju:] n orvalho.

dexterity [deks'terɪtɪ] n destreza.

diabetes [daɪə'bi:ti:z] n diabete f; **diabetic** [-'betɪk] adj, n diabético.

diagnose [daɪəg'nəuz] vt diagnosticar; **diagnosis** [-'nəusɪs] pl -ses [-'nəusi:z] n diagnóstico.

diagonal [daɪ'ægənl] adj diagonal // n diagonal f.

diagram ['daɪəgræm] n diagrama m, esquema m.

dial ['daɪəl] n disco // vt (number) discar

(Br), marcar (Pt); ~ling code, ~ code (US) n código; ~ling tone, ~ tone (US) n sinal de discar (Br), sinal de marcar (Pt).

dialect ['daɪəlekt] n dialeto (Pt: -ct-).

dialogue ['daɪələg] n diálogo.

diameter [daɪ'æmɪtə*] n diâmetro.

diamond ['daɪəmənd] n diamante m; ~s npl (CARDS) ouros mpl.

diaper ['daɪəpə*] n (US) fralda.

diaphragm ['daɪəfræm] n diafragma m.

diarrhoea, diarrhea (US) [daɪə'ri:ə] n diarréia.

diary ['daɪərɪ] n (daily account) diário; (book) agenda.

dice [daɪs] n, pl inv dados mpl // vt (CULIN) cortar em cubos.

dictate [dɪk'teɪt] vt ditar; ~s ['dɪkteɪts] npl ditames mpl; **dictation** [-'teɪʃən] n ditado.

dictator [dɪk'teɪtə*] n ditador m; ~ship n ditadura.

diction ['dɪkʃən] n dicção f.

dictionary ['dɪkʃənrɪ] n dicionário.

did [dɪd] pt of **do**.

die [daɪ] vi morrer; to ~ away vi (sound, light) extinguir-se lentamente; to ~ down vi (gen) apagar-se; (wind) abrandar; to ~ out vi desaparecer, apagar-se.

diesel ['di:zəl]: ~ engine n motor m Diesel; ~ (oil) n óleo diesel.

diet ['daɪət] n dieta; (restricted food) regime m // vi (also: be on a ~) estar de dieta, fazer regime.

differ ['dɪfə*] vi (be different) ser diferente de, diferenciar-se de; (disagree) discordar; ~ence n diferença; (quarrel) desacordo; ~ent adj diferente; ~entiate [-'renʃieɪt] vt distinguir // vi diferenciar-se; to ~entiate between distinguir entre; ~ently adv de outro modo, de forma diferente.

difficult ['dɪfɪkəlt] adj difícil; ~y n dificuldade f.

diffidence ['dɪfɪdəns] n timidez f; **diffident** [-ənt] adj tímido.

diffuse [dɪ'fju:s] adj difuso // vt [dɪ'fju:z] difundir.

dig [dɪg] pt, pp **dug** vt (hole) cavar; (garden) cultivar; (coal) escavar; (nails etc) cravar // n (prod) pontada; (archaeological) escavação f; (remark) indireta (Pt: -ct-); to ~ in vi cavar trincheiras; to ~ into (savings) consumir; to ~ out vi (hole) escavar; (fig) estudar com afinco; to ~ up vt desenterrar; (plant) arrancar.

digest [daɪ'dʒest] vt (food) digerir; (facts) assimilar // n ['daɪdʒest] sumário; ~ion [dɪ'dʒestʃən] n digestão f.

digital ['dɪdʒɪtəl] adj digital.

dignified ['dɪgnɪfaɪd] adj grave, sério; (action) honrado.

dignity ['dɪgnɪtɪ] n dignidade f.

digress [daɪ'gres] vi: to ~ from afastar-se de; ~ion [daɪ'greʃən] n digressão f.

digs [dɪgz] *npl* (*Brit: col*) pensão *f*, alojamento.

dilapidated [dɪ'læpɪdeɪtɪd] *adj* arruinado, estragado.

dilate [daɪ'leɪt] *vt* dilatar // *vi* dilatar-se.

dilemma [daɪ'lɛmə] *n* dilema *m*.

diligent [dɪlɪʤənt] *adj* diligente.

dilute [daɪ'lu:t] *vt* diluir // *adj* diluído.

dim [dɪm] *adj* (*light*) fraco; (*sight*) turvo; (*outline*) indistinto; (*stupid*) burro; (*room*) escuro // *vt* (*light*) abaixar; (*US: AUT*) abaixar os faróis.

dime [daɪm] *n* (*US*) moeda de dez centavos.

dimension [dɪ'mɛnʃən] *n* dimensão *f*.

diminish [dɪ'mɪnɪʃ] *vi* diminuir(-se).

diminutive [dɪ'mɪnjʊtɪv] *adj* diminuto // *n* (*LING*) diminutivo.

dimly ['dɪmlɪ] *adv* fracamente; (*not clearly*) indistintamente.

dimple ['dɪmpl] *n* covinha.

din [dɪn] *n* zoeira.

dine [daɪn] *vi* jantar; **diner** *n* (*person*) comensal *m/f*; (*RAIL*) = **dining car**.

dinghy ['dɪŋgɪ] *n* dingue *m*, bote *m*; **rubber ~** bote de borracha.

dingy ['dɪnʤɪ] *adj* (*room*) escuro; (*dirty*) sujo; (*dull*) descolorido.

dining ['daɪnɪŋ]: **~ car** *n* vagão–restaurante *m*; **~ room** *n* sala de jantar.

dinner ['dɪnə] *n* (*evening meal*) jantar *m*; (*lunch*) almoço; (*public*) jantar *m*, banquete *m*; **~ jacket** *n* smoking *m*; **~ party** *n* jantar; **~ time** *n* hora de jantar *or* almoçar.

diocese ['daɪəsɪs] *n* diocese *f*.

dip [dɪp] *n* (*slope*) inclinação *f*; (*in sea*) mergulho // *vt* (*in water*) molhar; (*ladle etc*) meter; (*AUT: lights*) abaixar // *vi* mergulhar-se.

diphtheria [dɪf'θɪərɪə] *n* difteria.

diploma [dɪ'pləʊmə] *n* diploma *m*.

diplomacy [dɪ'pləʊməsɪ] *n* diplomacia; **diplomat** ['dɪpləmæt] *n* diplomata *m/f*; **diplomatic** [dɪplə'mætɪk] *adj* diplomático.

dipstick ['dɪpstɪk] *n* (*AUT*) vara de metal graduada para indicar o nível de óleo.

dire [daɪə*] *adj* terrível, extremo.

direct [daɪ'rɛkt] *adj* (*gen*) direto (*Pt: -ct-*) // *vt* dirigir; **can you ~ me to...?** pode indicar-me onde fica...?

direction [dɪ'rɛkʃən] *n* direção (*Pt: -cç-*) *f*; **~s** *npl* (*advice*) ordens *fpl*, instruções *fpl*; **~s for use** modo de usar.

directly [dɪ'rɛktlɪ] *adv* (*in straight line*) diretamente (*Pt: -ect-*); (*at once*) imediatamente.

director [dɪ'rɛktə*] *n* diretor (*Pt: -ct-*) *m*; **managing ~** dire(c)tor gerente.

directory [dɪ'rɛktərɪ] *n* (*TEL*) lista (telefônica).

dirt [dɜ:t] *n* sujeira (*Br*), sujidade (*Pt*); **~-cheap** *adj* baratíssimo; **~y** *adj* sujo; (*joke*) indecente // *vt* sujar; (*stain*) manchar; **~y trick** *n* golpe *m* baixo, sujeira.

disability [dɪsə'bɪlɪtɪ] *n* incapacidade *f*; **disabled** [dɪs'eɪbld] *adj* incapacitado.

disadvantage [dɪsəd'vɑ:ntɪʤ] *n* desvantagem *f*, inconveniente *m*.

disagree [dɪsə'gri:] *vi* (*differ*) discordar; (*be against, think otherwise*): **to ~ (with)** não estar de acordo (com); **~able** *adj* desagradável; **~ment** *n* (*gen*) desacordo; (*quarrel*) briga.

disallow ['dɪsə'laʊ] *vt* (*goal*) anular, não admitir.

disappear [dɪsə'pɪə*] *vi* desaparecer; **~ance** *n* desaparição *f*.

disappoint [dɪsə'pɔɪnt] *vt* desapontar, decepcionar; (*hopes*) frustrar; **~ing** *adj* decepcionante **~ment** *n* decepção *f*, desapontamento.

disapproval [dɪsə'pru:vəl] *n* desaprovação *f*.

disapprove [dɪsə'pru:v] *vi*: **to ~ of** desaprovar.

disarm [dɪs'ɑ:m] *vt* desarmar; **~ament** *n* desarmamento; **~ing** *adj* encantador(a).

disaster [dɪ'zɑ:stə*] *n* desastre *m*; **disastrous** *adj* desastroso.

disband [dɪs'bænd] *vt* dissolver // *vi* debandar.

disbelief [dɪsbə'li:f] *n* incredulidade *f*.

disc, disk (*US*) [dɪsk] *n* disco.

discard [dɪs'kɑ:d] *vt* (*old things*) desfazer-se de; (*fig*) descartar.

discern [dɪ'sɜ:n] *vt* perceber; **~ing** *adj* perspicaz.

discharge [dɪs'tʃɑ:ʤ] *vt* (*duties*) cumprir, desempenhar; (*patient*) dar alta a; (*employee*) despedir; (*soldier*) licenciar; (*defendant*) pôr em liberdade // *n* ['dɪstʃɑ:ʤ] (*ELEC*) descarga; (*dismissal*) despedida; (*of duty*) desempenho; (*of debt*) pagamento, resgate *m*.

disciple [dɪ'saɪpl] *n* discípulo/a.

discipline ['dɪsɪplɪn] *n* disciplina // *vt* disciplinar.

disclaim [dɪs'kleɪm] *vt* negar.

disclose [dɪs'kləʊz] *vt* revelar; **disclosure** [-'kləʊʒə*] *n* revelação *f*.

disco ['dɪskəʊ] *n abbr of* **discothèque**.

discoloured [dɪs'kʌləd] *adj* descorado, desbotado.

discomfort [dɪs'kʌmfət] *n* desconforto; (*unease*) inquietação *f*; (*physical*) mal-estar *m*.

disconcert [dɪskən'sɜ:t] *vt* desconcertar.

disconnect [dɪskə'nɛkt] *vt* (*gen*) separar; (*ELEC etc*) desligar.

discontent [dɪskən'tɛnt] *n* descontentamento; **~ed** *adj* descontente.

discontinue [dɪskən'tɪnju:] *vt* interromper; (*payments*) suspender.

discord ['dɪskɔ:d] *n* discórdia; (*MUS*) dissonância; **~ant** [dɪs'kɔ:dənt] *adj* dissonante.

discothèque ['dɪskəʊtɛk] *n* discoteca.

discount [*n* 'dɪskaʊnt] *n* desconto // *vt* [dɪs'kaʊnt] descontar.

discourage [dɪs'kʌrɪʤ] *vt* desanimar;

(*oppose*) desencorajar; **discouraging** *adj* desanimador(a).

discourteous [dɪs'kɔːtɪəs] *adj* descortês.

discover [dɪs'kʌvə*] *vt* descobrir; ~**y** *n* descobrimento, descoberta.

discredit [dɪs'krɛdɪt] *vt* desacreditar.

discreet [dɪ'skriːt] *adj* (*tactful*) discreto; (*careful*) circunspeto (*Pt*: -ct-), prudente; ~**ly** *adv* discretamente.

discrepancy [dɪ'skrɛpənsɪ] *n* (*difference*) diferença; (*disagreement*) discrepância.

discretion [dɪ'skrɛʃən] *n* (*tact*) discrição *f*; (*care*) prudência, circunspeção (*Pt*: -çç-) *f*.

discriminate [dɪ'skrɪmɪneɪt] *vi*: to ~ **between** fazer distinção entre; to ~ **against** discriminar contra; **discriminating** *adj* acurado; **discrimination** [-'neɪʃən] *n* (*discernment*) discernimento; (*bias*) discriminação *f*.

discuss [dɪ'skʌs] *vt* (*gen*) discutir; (*a theme*) tratar de; ~**ion** [dɪ'skʌʃən] *n* discussão *f*.

disdain [dɪs'deɪn] *n* desdém *m* // *vt* desdenhar.

disease [dɪ'ziːz] *n* doença, enfermidade *f*.

disembark [dɪsɪm'bɑːk] *vt/i* desembarcar.

disengage [dɪsɪn'geɪdʒ] *vt* soltar; (*clutch*) desprender.

disentangle [dɪsɪn'tæŋgl] *vt* desenredar.

disfigure [dɪs'fɪgə*] *vt* disfigurar.

disgrace [dɪs'greɪs] *n* ignomínia; (*downfall*) queda; (*shame*) vergonha, desonra // *vt* desonrar; ~**ful** *adj* vergonhoso; (*behaviour*) escandaloso.

disgruntled [dɪs'grʌntld] *adj* descontente, mal-humorado.

disguise [dɪs'gaɪz] *n* disfarce *m* // *vt* disfarçar; **in** ~ disfarçado.

disgust [dɪs'gʌst] *n* repugnância // *vt* repugnar a, dar nojo em; ~**ing** *adj* repugnante, nojento.

dish [dɪʃ] *n* (*gen*) prato; **to do** *or* **wash the** ~**es** lavar os pratos; **to** ~ **up** *vt* servir; **to** ~ **out** *vt* servir, repartir; ~**cloth** *n* pano de prato *or* de louça.

dishearten [dɪs'hɑːtn] *vt* desalentar.

dishevelled [dɪ'ʃɛvəld] *adj* despenteado, desgrenhado.

dishonest [dɪs'ɒnɪst] *adj* (*person*) desonesto, desleal; (*means*) fraudulento; ~**y** *n* desonestidade *f*.

dishonour [dɪs'ɒnə*] *n* desonra; ~**able** *adj* desonroso.

dish towel [dɪʃ'haʊtl] *n* (*US*) pano de prato.

dishwasher ['dɪʃwɒʃə*] *n* máquina de lavar louça/pratos.

disillusion [dɪsɪ'luːʒən] *vt* desiludir.

disinfect [dɪsɪn'fɛkt] *vt* desinfetar (*Pt*: -ct-); ~**ant** *n* desinfe(c)tante *m*.

disintegrate [dɪs'ɪntɪgreɪt] *vi* desagregar-se, desintegrar-se.

disinterested [dɪs'ɪntrəstɪd] *adj* desinteressado.

disjointed [dɪs'dʒɔɪntɪd] *adj* desconexo.

disk [dɪsk] *n* (*US*) = **disc.**

dislike [dɪs'laɪk] *n* antipatia, aversão *f* // *vt* antipatizar com, não gostar de.

dislocate ['dɪsləkeɪt] *vt* deslocar.

dislodge [dɪs'lɒdʒ] *vt* desentocar; (*enemy*) desalojar.

disloyal [dɪs'lɔɪəl] *adj* desleal.

dismal ['dɪzml] *adj* (*dark*) sombrio; (*depressing*) deprimente; (*depressed*) deprimido; (*very bad*) horrível.

dismantle [dɪs'mæntl] *vt* desmontar, desmantelar.

dismay [dɪs'meɪ] *n* consternação *f* // *vt* consternar.

dismiss [dɪs'mɪs] *vt* (*worker*) despedir; (*official*) demitir; (*idea*) descartar; (*LAW*) liberar; (*possibility*) rejeitar // *vi* (*MIL*) mandar fora de forma; ~**al** *n* despedida, demissão *f*.

dismount [dɪs'maʊnt] *vi* desmontar.

disobedience [dɪsə'biːdɪəns] *n* desobediência; **disobedient** [-ənt] *adj* desobediente.

disobey [dɪsə'beɪ] *vt* desobedecer.

disorder [dɪs'ɔːdə*] *n* desordem *f*; (*rioting*) tumulto; (*MED*) indisposição *f*; (*disease*) doença; ~**ly** *adj* (*untidy*) desordenado; (*meeting*) tumultuado; (*conduct*) escandaloso.

disorganized [dɪs'ɔːgənaɪzd] *adj* desorganizado.

disorientated [dɪs'ɔːrɪɛnteɪtəd] *adj* desorientado.

disown [dɪs'əʊn] *vt* repudiar.

disparaging [dɪs'pærɪdʒɪŋ] *adj* depreciativo.

disparity [dɪs'pærɪtɪ] *n* desigualdade *f*.

dispatch [dɪs'pætʃ] *vt* despachar; (*kill*) liquidar, matar // *n* (*sending*) remessa; (*speed*) rapidez *f*, urgência; (*PRESS*) comunicado; (*MIL*) parte *f*.

dispel [dɪs'pɛl] *vt* dissipar.

dispensary [dɪs'pɛnsərɪ] *n* dispensário, farmácia.

dispense [dɪs'pɛns] *vt* dispensar; **to** ~ **with** *vt fus* prescindir de; **dispenser** *n* (*container*) distribuidor *m* automático; **dispensing chemist** *n* farmacêutico/a.

dispersal [dɪs'pɜːsl] *n* dispersão *f*; **disperse** [-'pɜːs] *vt* dispersar // *vi* dispersar-se.

displace [dɪs'pleɪs] *vt* (*shift*) deslocar; ~**d person** *n* (*POL*) destituído; ~**ment** *n* deslocamento.

display [dɪs'pleɪ] *n* (*exhibition*) exposição *f*; (*MIL*) parada; (*of feeling*) manifestação *f*; (*pej*) ostentação *f*, espetáculo (*Pt*: -ct-) // *vt* expor, manifestar; (*ostentatiously*) ostentar.

displease [dɪs'pliːz] *vt* (*offend*) ofender; (*annoy*) desagradar; (*be unpleasant to*) desgostar; ~**d with** descontente com; **displeasure** [-'plɛʒə*] *n* desgosto.

disposable [dɪs'pəʊzəbl] *adj* descartável.

disposal [dɪs'pəʊzl] *n* (*sale*) venda; (*arrangement*) disposição *f*; (*of rubbish*) destruição *f*; **at one's** ~ à disposição de alguém.

dispose [dɪs'pəʊz] *vt*: **to** ~ **of** (*time,*

money) dispor de; (*unwanted goods*) desfazer-se de; (*throw away*) jogar fora (*Br*), tirar fora (*Pt*); ~d *adj*: ~d to do disposto a fazer; **disposition** [-'zɪʃən] *n* disposição *f*.

disproportionate [dɪsprə'pɔːʃənət] *adj* desproporcionado.

disprove [dɪs'pruːv] *vt* refutar.

dispute [dɪs'pjuːt] *n* disputa; (*verbal*) discussão *f*; (*also*: **industrial** ~) contenda, disputa // *vt* (*argue*) discutir; (*question*) questionar.

disqualification [dɪskwɔlɪfɪ'keɪʃən] *n* inabilitação *f*, incapacitação *f*; (*SPORT, from driving*) desqualificação *f*.

disqualify [dɪs'kwɔlɪfaɪ] *vt* (*SPORT*) desclassificar; **to** ~ **sb for sth/from doing sth** desqualificar alguém para algo/de fazer algo.

disregard [dɪsrɪ'gaːd] *vt* desconsiderar; (*ignore*) não fazer caso de.

disrepair [dɪsrɪ'pɛə*] *n*: **to fall into** ~ ficar dilapidado.

disreputable [dɪs'rɛpjutəbl] *adj* (*person*) de má fama; (*behaviour*) vergonhoso.

disrespectful [dɪsrɪ'spɛktful] *adj* desrespeitoso.

disrupt [dɪs'rʌpt] *vt* (*plans*) desfazer; (*conversation*) interromper; ~ion [-'rʌpʃən] *n* transtorno, interrupção *f*.

dissatisfaction [dɪssætɪs'fækʃən] *n* descontentamento; **dissatisfied** [-'sætɪsfaɪd] *adj* descontente.

dissect [dɪ'sɛkt] *vt* dissecar.

dissent [dɪ'sɛnt] *n* desacordo.

disservice [dɪs'səːvɪs] *n*: **to do sb a** ~ prejudicar alguém.

dissident ['dɪsɪdnt] *adj, n* dissidente *m/f*.

dissipate ['dɪsɪpeɪt] *vt* dispersar; (*waste*) dissipar, desperdiçar.

dissociate [dɪ'səuʃɪeɪt] *vt* dissociar, separar.

dissolute ['dɪsəluːt] *adj* dissoluto.

dissolve [dɪ'zɔlv] *vt* dissolver // *vi* dissolver-se.

dissuade [dɪ'sweɪd] *vt*: **to** ~ **sb (from)** dissuadir alguém (de).

distance ['dɪstns] *n* distância; **in the** ~ ao longe.

distant ['dɪstnt] *adj* distante; (*manner*) afastado, reservado.

distaste [dɪs'teɪst] *n* repugnância; ~ful *adj* repugnante, desagradável.

distil [dɪs'tɪl] *vt* destilar; ~lery *n* destilaria.

distinct [dɪs'tɪŋkt] *adj* (*different*) distinto; (*clear*) claro; (*unmistakeable*) nítido; **as** ~ **from** diferente de, fazendo distinção de; ~ion [dɪs'tɪŋkʃən] *n* distinção *f*; ~ive *adj* distintivo; ~ly *adv* claramente.

distinguish [dɪs'tɪŋgwɪʃ] *vt* distinguir; ~ed *adj* (*eminent*) eminente, distinto; ~ing *adj* (*feature*) distinto.

distort [dɪs'tɔːt] *vt* alterar; ~ion [dɪs'tɔːʃən] *n* deformação *f*; (*of sound*) deturpação *f*.

distract [dɪs'trækt] *vt* distrair; (*attention*)

desviar; (*bewilder*) aturdir; ~ed *adj* distraído; ~ion [dɪs'trækʃən] *n* distração (*Pt*: -cç-) *f*; (*confusion*) aturdimento, perplexidade *f*; (*amusement*) divertimento.

distraught [dɪs'trɔːt] *adj* desesperado, louco.

distress [dɪs'trɛs] *n* (*anguish*) angústia; (*misfortune*) desgraça; (*want*) miséria; (*pain*) dor *f*; (*danger*) perigo // *vt* (*cause anguish*) afligir; (*pain*) doer; ~ing *adj* aflitivo, angustioso; ~ **signal** *n* sinal *m* de socorro.

distribute [dɪs'trɪbjuːt] *vt* (*gen*) distribuir; (*share out*) repartir; **distribution** [-'bjuːʃən] *n* distribuição *f*; **distributor** *n* (*AUT*) distribuidor *m*; (*COMM*) distribuidor(a).

district ['dɪstrɪkt] *n* (*of country, ADMIN*) distrito; (*of town*) bairro; ~ **nurse** *n* (*US*) promotor *m* público; ~ **nurse** *n* (*Brit*) enfermeira do distrito.

distrust [dɪs'trʌst] *n* desconfiança // *vt* desconfiar de.

disturb [dɪs'təːb] *vt* (*gen*) perturbar; (*bother*) incomodar; (*interrupt*) interromper; (*upset*) transtornar; (*disorganize*) atrapalhar; ~ance *n* (*gen*) perturbação *f*; (*political etc*) distúrbio; (*violence*) agitação *f*; (*of mind*) transtorno; ~ing *adj* perturbador(a), inquietante.

disuse [dɪs'juːs] *n*: **to fall into** ~ cair em desuso.

disused [dɪs'juːzd] *adj* desusado, abandonado.

ditch [dɪtʃ] *n* fosso; (*irrigation* ~) rego // *vt* (*col*) desfazer-se de.

dither ['dɪðə*] *vi* vacilar.

ditto ['dɪtəu] *adv* idem, o mesmo.

divan [dɪ'væn] *n* divã *m*.

dive [daɪv] *n* (*from board*) salto; (*underwater, of submarine*) mergulho; (*AVIAT*) picada // *vi* saltar; mergulhar; picar; **diver** *n* (*SPORT*) saltador(a) *m/f*; (*underwater*) mergulhador(a) *m/f*.

diverge [daɪ'vəːdʒ] *vi* divergir.

diverse [daɪ'vəːs] *adj* diversos/as, vários/as.

diversify [daɪ'vəːsɪfaɪ] *vt* diversificar.

diversion [daɪ'vəːʃən] *n* (*AUT*) desvio; (*distraction, MIL*) diversão *f*.

diversity [daɪ'vəːsɪtɪ] *n* diversidade *f*.

divert [daɪ'vəːt] *vt* (*turn aside*) desviar; (*amuse*) divertir.

divest [daɪ'vɛst] *vt*: **to** ~ **sb of sth** privar alguém de algo.

divide [dɪ'vaɪd] *vt* dividir; (*separate*) separar // *vi* dividir-se; (*road*) bifurcar-se; ~d **highway** *n* (*US*) pista-dupla.

dividend ['dɪvɪdɛnd] *n* dividendo; (*fig*) lucro.

divine [dɪ'vaɪn] *adj* divino.

diving ['daɪvɪŋ] *n* (*SPORT*) salto; (*underwater*) mergulho; ~ **board** *n* trampolim *m*; ~ **suit** *n* escafandro.

divinity [dɪ'vɪnɪtɪ] *n* divindade *f*; (*SCOL*) teologia.

division [dɪ'vɪʒən] *n* divisão *f*; (*sharing*

out) repartição *f*; (*disagreement*) discórdia; (*POL*) votação *f*.

divorce [dɪ'vɔːs] *n* divórcio // *vt* divorciar-se de; ~**d** *adj* divorciado; **divorcee** [-'siː] *n* divorciado/a.

divulge [daɪ'vʌldʒ] *vt* divulgar, revelar.

D.I.Y. *adj*, *n abbr of* **do-it-yourself.**

dizziness ['dɪzɪnɪs] *n* vertigem *f*, tontura.

dizzy ['dɪzɪ] *adj* (*person*) tonto; (*height*) vertiginoso; **to feel** ~ sentir-se tonto, sentir-se atordoado.

DJ *n abbr of* **disc jockey.**

do [duː] *pt* **did**, *pp* **done** *vt/i* (*gen*) fazer; (*speed*) ir a; (*THEATRE*) representar // *n* (*col*) festa; **he didn't laugh** ele não riu; **she swims better than I** ~ ela nada melhor que eu; **he laughed, didn't he?** ele riu, não foi?; **that will** ~! basta!, chega!; **to make** ~ **with** contentar-se com; ~ **you agree?** concorda?; **to** ~ **one's hair** (*comb*) pentear-se; (*style*) fazer um penteado; **will it** ~? dá?, chega?, serve?; **to** ~ **well** prosperar, ter êxito; **to** ~ **without** sth prescindir de algo; **to** ~ **away with** *vt fus* (*kill*) exterminar; (*suppress*) suprimir; **to** ~ **up** *vt* (*laces*) atar; (*room*) arrumar, renovar.

docile ['dəʊsaɪl] *adj* dócil.

dock [dɔk] *n* (*NAUT*) doca, estaleiro; (*LAW*) banco (dos réus); ~**s** *npl* estaleiros *mpl*, porto // *vi* (*arrive*) chegar; (*enter* ~) entrar no estaleiro; (*pay etc*) deduzir; ~**er** *n* trabalhador *m* portuário, estivador *m*; ~**yard** *n* estaleiro.

doctor ['dɔktə*] *n* médico; (*Ph.D. etc*) doutor/a *m/f* // *vt* (*fig*) tratar, falsificar; (*drink etc*) falsificar ~'**s office** *n* (*US*) consultório.

doctrine ['dɔktrɪn] *n* doutrina.

document ['dɔkjumənt] *n* documento; ~**ary** [-'mentəri] *adj* documental // *n* documentário; ~**ation** [-'teɪʃən] *n* documentação *f*.

dodge [dɔdʒ] *n* (*of body*) evasiva; (*fig*) trapaça // *vt* (*gen*) esquivar-se de, evitar; (*blow*) furtar-se a.

dodgems ['dɔdʒəmz] *npl* carros *mpl* de choque.

dodgy ['dɔdʒɪ] *adj* arriscado.

dog [dɔg] *n* cachorro, cão *m* // *vt* seguir os passos de; ~ **biscuits** *npl* biscoitos *mpl* de cachorro; ~ **collar** *n* coleira de cachorro; (*fig*) gola de padre.

dogged ['dɔgɪd] *adj* tenaz, persistente.

dogma ['dɔgmə] *n* dogma *m*; ~**tic** [-'mætɪk] *adj* dogmático.

doings ['duːɪŋz] *npl* (*events*) acontecimentos *mpl*; (*acts*) atos (*Pt*: -ct-) *mpl*.

do-it-yourself [duːɪtjɔːˈself] *adj* do tipo faça-você-mesmo.

doldrums ['dɔldrəmz] *npl*: **to be in the** ~ (*person*) estar abatido; (*business*) estar parado or estagnado.

dole [dəʊl] *n* (*Brit*) (*payment*) subsídio de desemprego; **on the** ~ desempregado; **to** ~ **out** *vt* repartir.

doleful ['dəʊlful] *adj* triste, lúgubre.

doll [dɔl] *n* boneca; **to** ~ **o.s. up** embonecar-se (*Br*), ataviar-se (*Pt*).

dollar ['dɔlə*] *n* dólar *m*.

dolphin ['dɔlfɪn] *n* golfinho.

domain [də'meɪn] *n* território, propriedade *f*; (*empire*) domínio.

dome [dəʊm] *n* (*ARCH*) cúpula; (*shape*) abóbada.

domestic [də'mestɪk] *adj* (*gen*) doméstico; (*national*) nacional; (*home-loving*) caseiro; (*internal*: *trade*) doméstico; (: *strife*) interno; ~**ated** *adj* domesticado; (*home-loving*) caseiro.

dominant ['dɔmɪnənt] *adj* dominante.

dominate ['dɔmɪneɪt] *vt* dominar; **domination** [-'neɪʃən] *n* dominação *f*.

domineering [dɔmɪ'nɪərɪŋ] *adj* dominante, mandão/dona.

dominion [də'mɪnɪən] *n* domínio.

domino ['dɔmɪnəʊ], *pl* ~**es** *n* peça de dominó; ~**es** *n* (*game*) dominó *msg*.

donate [də'neɪt] *vt* doar; **donation** [də'neɪʃən] *n* doação *f*.

done [dʌn] *pp of* **do.**

donkey ['dɔŋkɪ] *n* burro.

donor ['dəʊnə*] *n* doador(a) *m/f*.

don't [dəʊnt] = **do not.**

doom [duːm] *n* (*fate*) sorte *f*; (*death*) morte *f* // *vt*: **to be** ~**ed to failure** estar destinado ao fracasso.

door [dɔː*] *n* porta; (*entry*) entrada; **next** ~ na casa ao lado; ~ **bell** *n* campainha; ~ **handle** *n* maçaneta (*Br*), puxador *m* (*Pt*); (*of car*) maçaneta; ~ **knocker** *n* aldrava; ~**man** *n* (*in hotel*) porteiro; ~**mat** *n* capacho; ~**step** *n* degrau *m* da porta.

dope [dəʊp] *n* (*col*: *person*) imbecil *m/f* // *vt* (*horse etc*) dopar.

dopey ['dəʊpɪ] *adj* (*dizzy*) zonzo.

dormant ['dɔːmənt] *adj* inativo (*Pt*: -ct-); (*latent*) latente.

dormitory ['dɔːmɪtrɪ] *n* dormitório.

dormouse ['dɔːmaʊs], *pl* -**mice** [-maɪs] *n* rato (de campo).

dosage ['dəʊsɪdʒ] *n* dose *f*.

dose [dəʊs] *n* dose *f* // *vt*: **to** ~ **o.s.** medicar-se.

doss house ['dɔs-] *n* pensão *f* barata, pensão *f* de malta (*Pt*).

dot [dɔt] *n* ponto; ~**ted with** salpicado de; **on the** ~ em ponto.

dote [dəʊt]: **to** ~ **on** *vt fus* adorar, idolatrar.

double ['dʌbl] *adj* duplo // *adv* (*twice*): **to cost** ~ custar o dobro // *n* (*gen*) dobro // *vt* dobrar; (*efforts*) duplicar // *vi* duplicar-se; **at the** ~ em passo acelerado; ~**s** *n* (*TENNIS*) duplas *fpl*; ~ **bass** *n* contrabaixo; ~ **bed** *n* cama de casal; ~ **bend** *n* curva dupla; ~**-breasted** *adj* trespassado; ~**cross** *vt* (*trick*) enganar; (*betray*) atraiçoar; ~**decker** *n* ônibus *m* de dois andares (*Br*), autocarro *m* de dois andares (*Pt*); ~ **room** *n* quarto de casal; **doubly** *adv* duplamente.

doubt [daut] n dúvida // vt duvidar; (suspect) desconfiar de; to ~ that duvidar que; **there is no ~ that** não há dúvida que; ~**ful** adj duvidoso; (person) desconfiado; ~**less** adv sem dúvida;

dough [dəu] n massa; ~**nut** n sonho (Br), bola de Berlim (Pt).

dove [dʌv] n pomba; ~**tail** vi (fig) encaixar-se.

dowdy ['daudɪ] adj desalinhado; (inelegant) deselegante, pouco elegante.

down [daun] n (fluff) lanugem f; (feathers) penugem f // adv abaixo; (~wards) para baixo; (on the ground) por terra // prep por, abaixo // vt (col: drink) beber; (: food) devorar; ~ **with X!** abaixo X!; ~**at-heel** adj descuidado, desmazelado; (appearance) deselegante; ~**cast** adj abatido; ~**fall** n queda, ruína; ~**hearted** adj desanimado; ~**hill** adv: **to go** ~**hill** ir morro abaixo; ~ **payment** n depósito, sinal m; ~**pour** n aguaceiro; ~**right** adj (clear) categórico; (out-and-out) completo, definitivo; ~**stairs** adv (below) (lá) em baixo; (~wards) para baixo; ~**stream** adv água ou rio abaixo; ~**to-earth** adj prático, realista; ~**town** adv no centro da cidade; ~**ward** adj, adv, ~**wards** adv para baixo.

dowry ['daurɪ] n dote m.

doz. abbr of **dozen**.

doze [dəuz] vi dormitar; **to ~ off** vi cochilar.

dozen ['dʌzn] n dúzia.

Dr. abbr of **doctor**; **drive**.

drab [dræb] adj monótono, desinteressante.

draft [drɑ:ft] n (first copy) rascunho; (COMM) saque m, letra; (US: call-up) recrutamento // vt (plan) redigir; (conscript) recrutar; (write roughly) esboçar; (US) = **draught**.

drag [dræg] vt arrastar; (river) dragar // vi arrastar-se pelo chão // n (col) chatice f (Br), maçada (Pt); **to ~ on** vi arrastar-se.

dragonfly ['drægənflaɪ] n libélula.

drain [dreɪn] n cano (de esgoto); (in street) sarjeta; (source of loss) escoamento; (loss) perda; (on resources) sorvedouro // vt (land, marshes) escoar; (MED) drenar; (reservoir) esvaziar; (fig) esgotar // vi escorrer; ~**age** n (act) drenagem f (MED, AGR) dreno; (sewage) esgoto; ~**ing board**, ~**board** (US) n escorredor m; ~**pipe** n cano de esgoto.

dram [dræm] n (drink) trago.

drama ['drɑ:mə] n (art) teatro; (play) drama m; ~**tic** [drə'mætɪk] adj dramático; ~**tist** ['dræmətɪst] n dramaturgo.

drank [dræŋk] pt of **drink**.

drape [dreɪp] vt ornar, cobrir // vi cair; ~**s** npl (US) cortinas fpl.

drastic ['dræstɪk] adj (measure) severo; (change) drástico; (forceful) enérgico.

draught [drɑ:ft] n (of air) corrente f; (drink) trago; (NAUT) calado; (beer) chope m; ~**s** n jogo de damas; **on** ~ (beer) de barril; ~**board** n tabuleiro de damas.

draughtsman ['drɑ:ftsmən] n desenhista m, projetista (Pt: -ect-) m.

draw [drɔ:] pt **drew**, pp **drawn** vt (pull) puxar, tirar; (take out) retirar; (attract) atrair; (picture) desenhar; (money) tirar, receber // vi (SPORT) empatar // n (SPORT) empate m; (lottery) sorteio; (attraction) atração (Pt: -çç-) f; **to ~ near** vi aproximar-se, **to ~ out** vi (lengthen) esticar, alargar; **to ~ up** vi (stop) parar(-se) // vt (document) redigir; ~**back** n inconveniente m, desvantagem f; ~**bridge** n ponte f levadiça.

drawer [drɔ:*] n gaveta.

drawing ['drɔ:ɪŋ] n desenho; ~ **board** n tábua (do desenhista), prancheta; ~ **pin** n tachinha (Br), pionés m (Pt); ~ **room** n sala de visitas.

drawl [drɔ:l] n fala arrastada.

drawn [drɔ:n] pp of **draw**.

dread [drɛd] n medo, temor m // vt temer, recear, ter medo de; ~**ful** adj terrível.

dream [dri:m] n sonho // vt/i, pt, pp **dreamed** or **dreamt** [drɛmt] sonhar; ~**er** n sonhador(a) m/f; ~**y** adj (distracted) sonhador(a), distraído; (music) sentimental.

dreary ['drɪərɪ] adj monótono, maçante.

dredge [drɛdʒ] vt dragar; **dredger** n (ship) draga; (also: **sugar dredger**) polvilhador m.

dregs [drɛgz] npl lia sg.

drench [drɛntʃ] vt encharcar; **to get** ~**ed** molhar-se, encharcar-se.

dress [drɛs] n vestido; (clothing) roupa // vt vestir; (wound) pensar; (CULIN) preparar, temperar // vi vestir-se; **to ~ up** vi vestir-se com elegância; (in fancy dress) fantasiar-se; ~ **circle** n balcão m nobre; ~**er** n (furniture) aparador m; (: US) cômoda de espelho; ~**ing** n (MED) penso; (CULIN) molho; ~**ing gown** n roupão m; ~**ing room** n (THEATRE) camarim m; (SPORT) vestiário; ~**ing table** n penteadeira (Br), toucador m (Pt); ~**maker** n costureira, modista; ~**making** n (arte f da) costura; ~ **rehearsal** n ensaio geral; ~ **shirt** n camisa social.

drew [dru:] pt of **draw**.

dribble ['drɪbl] vi gotejar, pingar; (baby) babar(-se) // vt (ball) driblar.

dried [draɪd] adj (gen) seco; (milk) em pó.

drift [drɪft] n (of current etc) velocidade f; (of sand etc) monte m; (distance off course) deriva; (meaning) intenção f // vi (boat) derivar; (sand, snow) amontoar-se; ~**wood** n madeira flutuante.

drill [drɪl] n furador m; (bit, of dentist) broca; (for mining etc) broca, furador m; (MIL) exercícios militares // vt furar,

brocar // vi (for oil) perfurar; ~**ing rig** n torre f de perfurar.

drink [drɪŋk] n bebida // vt/i, pt **drank**, pp **drunk** beber; **to have a** ~ tomar uma bebida; ~**er** n bebedor(a) m/f; ~**ing water** n água potável.

drip [drɪp] n (act) gotejar m; (one ~) gota, pingo; (MED) gota a gota m // vi gotejar, pingar; ~-**dry** adj (shirt) de lavar e vestir; ~**ping** n gordura; ~**ping wet** adj encharcado.

drive [draɪv] n passeio (de automóvel); (journey) viagem f; (also: ~**way**) entrada; (energy) energia, vigor m; (PSYCH) impulso; (SPORT) tiro, golpe m // (vb: pt **drove**, pp **driven** ['drɪvn]) vt conduzir; (car) dirigir (Br), guiar (Pt); (urge) fazer trabalhar; (by power) impelir; (nail) cravar; (push) empurrar; (TECH: motor) acionar (Pt: -cc-) // vi (AUT: at controls) dirigir (Br), guiar (Pt); (: travel) passear de carro; **left-/right-hand** ~ direção f à esquerda/direita.

driver ['draɪvə*] n motorista m/f; (of taxi, bus) chofer m, motorista; ~'s **license** n (US) carteira de motorista (Br), carta de condução (Pt).

driving ['draɪvɪŋ] n automobilismo; ~ **instructor** n instrutor(a) m/f de auto-escola (Pt: de condução); ~ **lesson** n aula de direção (Pt: de condução); ~ **licence** n (Brit) carteira de motorista (Br), carta de condução (Pt); ~ **mirror** n retrovisor m; ~ **school** n auto-escola f; ~ **test** n exame m de motorista.

drizzle ['drɪzl] n chuvisco // vi chuviscar.

drone [drəun] n zumbido; (male bee) zangão m.

drool [dru:l] vi babar(-se); **to** ~ **over** sth babar por algo.

droop [dru:p] vi pender; (fig) decair, esmorecer.

drop [drɔp] n (of water) gota; (lessening) quebrada, baixa; (fall) queda; (of cliff) escarpa, declive m // vt (allow to fall) deixar cair; (voice, eyes, price) baixar; (set down from car) deixar (saltar/descer); (omit) omitir // vi cair; (price, temperature) baixar; (wind) parar; **to** ~ **off** vi (sleep) adormecer // vt (passenger) deixar (saltar); **to** ~ **out** vi (withdraw) retirar-se; ~-**out** n pessoa que abandona o trabalho/os estudos, etc; ~**per** n conta-gotas m inv; ~**pings** npl fezes fpl (de animal).

drought [draut] n seca.

drove [drəuv] pt of **drive**.

drown [draun] vt afogar // vi afogar-se.

drowsy ['drauzi] adj sonolento; **to be** ~ ter sono.

drudgery ['drʌdʒəri] n trabalho monótono e árduo.

drug [drʌg] n remédio, medicamento; (narcotic) droga // vt drogar; ~ **addict** n drogado/a; ~**gist** n (US) farmacêutico/a; ~**store** n (US) drogaria.

drum [drʌm] n tambor m; (large) bombo;

(for oil, petrol) tambor, barril m; ~**s** npl bateria sg // vi tocar tambor; (with fingers) tamborilar; ~**mer** n baterista m; ~**stick** n (MUS) baqueta; (of chicken) perna.

drunk [drʌŋk] pp of **drink** // adj bêbado // n (also: ~**ard**) bêbado/a; ~**en** adj bêbado; ~**enness** n embriaguez f.

dry [draɪ] adj seco; (day) sem chuva; (climate) árido, seco // vt secar; (tears) limpar // vi secar; **to** ~ **up** vi secar completamente; (in speech) calar-se; (dishes) enxugar (a louça); ~-**cleaner's** n lavanderia; ~-**cleaning** n lavagem f a seco; ~**er** n secador m; ~**ness** n secura; ~ **rot** n putrefação f fungosa.

dual ['djuəl] adj dual, duplo; ~-**control** adj duplo comando; ~ **nationality** n dupla nacionalidade f; ~-**purpose** adj de duplo uso.

dubbed [dʌbd] adj (CINEMA) dublado.

dubious ['dju:biəs] adj duvidoso; (reputation, company) suspeitoso.

duchess ['dʌtʃis] n duquesa.

duck [dʌk] n pato // vi mergulhar-se, abaixar-se repentinamente; ~**ling** n patinho.

duct [dʌkt] n conduto, canal m.

dud [dʌd] n (shell) bomba falhada; (object, tool): **it's a** ~ não presta // adj: ~ **cheque** cheque m sem cobertura.

due [dju:] adj (proper) devido; (expected) esperado; (fitting) conveniente, oportuno // n (debt) dívida; (desert) aquilo que foi merecido // adv: ~ **north** exatamente (Pt: -act-) ao norte; ~**s** npl (for club, union) jóia sg; (in harbour) direitos mpl; **in** ~ **course** no devido tempo; ~ **to** devido a.

duel ['djuəl] n duelo.

duet [dju:'ɛt] n dueto.

dug [dʌg] pt, pp of **dig**.

duke [dju:k] n duque m.

dull [dʌl] adj (light) sombrio; (slow) lento; (boring) enfadonho; (sound, pain) surdo; (weather, day) escuro // vt (pain, grief) aliviar; (mind, senses) entorpecer.

duly ['dju:li] adv devidamente; (on time) no devido tempo.

dumb [dʌm] adj mudo; (stupid) estúpido; ~**founded** [dʌm'faundid] adj pasmado.

dummy ['dʌmi] n (tailor's model) manequim m; (for baby) chupeta // adj falso, postiço.

dump [dʌmp] n (heap) montão m; (place) depósito de lixo; (col) chiqueiro; (MIL) depósito // vt (put down) depositar, descarregar; (get rid of) desfazer-se de; (goods) inundar o mercado com; ~**ing** n (ECON) dumping m; (of rubbish): 'no ~**ing**' 'proibido jogar lixo' (Br), 'proibido deitar lixo' (Pt).

dumpling ['dʌmplɪŋ] n bolinho cozido.

dunce [dʌns] n burro, ignorante.

dune [dju:n] n duna.

dung [dʌŋ] n estrume m.

dungarees [dʌŋgə'ri:z] npl macacão msg.

dungeon ['dʌndʒən] n calabouço.

dupe [dju:p] n (victim) otário/a, trouxa m/f // vt enganar.

duplicate ['dju:plɪkət] n duplicado // vt ['dju:plɪkeɪt] duplicar; (on machine) reproduzir; in ~ em duplicata; **duplicator** n duplicador m.

durable ['djuərəbl] adj durável.

duration [djuə'reɪʃən] n duração f.

duress [djuə'rɛs] n: under ~ sob coação.

during ['djuərɪŋ] prep durante.

dusk [dʌsk] n crepúsculo, anoitecer m.

dust [dʌst] n pó m, poeira f // vt (furniture) limpar o pó de; (cake etc): to ~ **with** polvilhar com; ~**bin** n (Brit) lata de lixo; ~**er** n espanador m de pó, pano de pó; ~ **jacket** n sobrecapa; ~**man** n (Brit) lixeiro; ~**y** adj empoeirado.

Dutch [dʌtʃ] adj holandês/esa // n (LING) holandês m; ~**man/woman** n holandês/esa m/f.

duty ['dju:tɪ] n dever m; (tax) taxa; (customs) taxa alfandegária; on ~ de serviço; (at night etc) de plantão, de guarda; off ~ de folga; ~-**free** adj livre de impostos; ~-**free shop** duty-free f.

dwarf [dwɔ:f], pl **dwarves** [dwɔ:vz] n anão/anã m/f // vt ananicar.

dwell [dwɛl], pt, pp **dwelt** [dwɛlt] vi morar; **to** ~ **on** vt fus estender-se sobre; ~**ing** n residência.

dwindle ['dwɪndl] vi minguar, diminuir.

dye [daɪ] n tinta // vt tingir.

dying ['daɪɪŋ] adj moribundo, agonizante; (moments) final; (words) último.

dynamic [daɪ'næmɪk] adj dinâmico; ~**s** n, npl dinâmica sg.

dynamite ['daɪnəmaɪt] n dinamite f.

dynamo ['daɪnəməu] n dínamo m.

dynasty ['dɪnəstɪ] n dinastia f.

E

each [i:tʃ] det cada inv // pron cada um; ~ **other** um ao outro; **they hate** ~ **other** (eles) se odeiam; **they have 2 books** ~ eles têm 2 livros cada um.

eager ['i:gə*] adj (gen) ávido; (hopeful) desejoso; (ambitious) ambicioso; **to be** ~ **to do sth** ansiar por fazer algo; **to be** ~ **for** ansiar por.

eagle ['i:gl] n águia.

ear [ɪə*] n orelha; (MUS) ouvido; (of corn) espiga; ~**ache** n dor f de ouvidos; ~**drum** n tímpano.

earl [ə:l] n conde m.

early ['ə:lɪ] adv (gen) cedo; (before time) a tempo, com antecedência // adj (gen) prematuro; (reply) pronto; (first) primeiro; (work) juvenil; **have an** ~ **night** vá para cama cedo; **in the** ~ **or** ~ **in the spring/19th century** no princípio da primavera/do século dezenove; **as** ~ **as possible** o mais cedo possível.

earmark ['ɪəmɑ:k] vt (keep) reservar (for para); (intend) destinar (for para); (mark) assinalar.

earn [ə:n] vt (gen) ganhar; (salary) receber; (interest) ganhar; (praise) merecer.

earnest ['ə:nɪst] adj sério; **in** ~ adv a sério.

earnings ['ə:nɪŋz] npl (personal) vencimentos mpl, salário sg, ordenado sg; (company) lucro sg.

ear: ~**phones** npl fones mpl de ouvido; ~**ring** n brinco; ~**shot** n: **within** ~**shot** ao alcance do ouvido or da voz.

earth [ə:θ] n (gen) terra; (ELEC) fio terra; **what on** ~! que diabo! // vt (ELEC) ligar à terra; ~**enware** n louça de barro; ~**quake** n terremoto; ~**y** adj (fig: vulgar) grosseiro; (: sensual) sensual.

earwig ['ɪəwɪg] n lacrainha.

ease [i:z] n (gen) facilidade f; (relief) alívio; (calm) tranqüilidade f; (relaxed state) comodidade f // vt facilitar; (loosen) soltar; (relieve: pressure) afrouxar; (weight) aliviar; (help pass): **to** ~ **sth in/out** meter/tirar algo com cuidado; **at** ~! (MIL) descansar!; **to be at** ~ estar à vontade; **to** ~ **off or up** vi (gen) acalmar-se; (at work) deixar de trabalhar tanto; (wind) baixar; (rain) moderar-se.

easel ['i:zl] n cavalete m.

east [i:st] n leste m, este m // adj oriental, do leste // adv para o leste; **the E**~ o Oriente.

Easter ['i:stə*] n Páscoa.

easterly ['i:stəlɪ] adj (to the east) para o leste; (from the east) do leste.

eastern ['i:stən] adj do leste, oriental.

East Germany n Alemanha Oriental.

eastward(s) ['i:stwəd(z)] adv ao leste.

easy ['i:zɪ] adj (gen) fácil; (simple) simples; (slow) lento, pacato; (comfortable) folgado, cômodo; (relaxed) natural, complacente // adv: **to take it or things** ~ (not worry) levar as coisas com calma; (go slowly) ir devagar; (rest) descansar; ~ **chair** n espreguiçadeira, poltrona; ~ **going** adj pacato, fácil.

eat [i:t], pt **ate**, pp **eaten** ['i:tn] vt (gen) comer; (supper) jantar; **to** ~ **into, to** ~ **away at** vt fus corroer; ~**able** adj comestível.

eau de Cologne [əudəkə'ləun] n (água de) Colônia.

eaves [i:vz] npl beira sg, beiral msg.

eavesdrop ['i:vzdrɔp] vi escutar às escondidas (on sb alguém).

ebb [ɛb] n maré f // vi baixar; (fig: also: ~ **away**) declinar; ~ **tide** n baixa-mar f, maré f vazante.

ebony ['ɛbənɪ] n ébano m.

eccentric [ɪk'sɛntrɪk] adj, n excêntrico.

ecclesiastical [ɪkli:zɪ'æstɪkəl] adj eclesiástico.

echo ['ɛkəu], pl ~**es** n eco // vt (sound) ecoar, repetir // vi ressoar, repetir.

eclipse [ɪ'klɪps] *n* eclipse *m* // *vt* eclipsar.

ecology [ɪ'kɔlədʒɪ] *n* ecologia.

economic [i:kə'nɔmɪk] *adj* econômico; *(proposition etc)* rentável; **~al** *adj* econômico; **~s** *n* economia; **economist** [ɪ'kɔnəmɪst] *n* economista *m/f*.

economize [ɪ'kɔnəmaɪz] *vi* economizar, poupar.

economy [ɪ'kɔnəmɪ] *n* economia.

ecstasy ['ɛkstəsɪ] *n* êxtase *m*; **ecstatic** [-'tætɪk] *adj* extasiado.

ecumenical [i:kju'mɛnɪkl] *adj* ecumênico.

eczema ['ɛksɪmə] *n* eczema *m*.

edge [ɛdʒ] *n* (of knife etc) fio; (of object) borda; (of lake etc) margem *f* // *vt* (SEWING) embainhar; **on ~** (fig) = **edgy; to ~ away from** afastar-se pouco a pouco de; **~ways** *adv*: **he couldn't get a word in ~ways** não pôde entrar na conversa; **edging** *n* (SEWING) debrum *m*; (of path) borda.

edgy ['ɛdʒɪ] *adj* nervoso, inquieto.

edible ['ɛdɪbl] *adj* comestível.

edict ['i:dɪkt] *n* édito.

edifice ['ɛdɪfɪs] *n* edifício.

edit ['ɛdɪt] *vt* (be editor of) dirigir; (cut) cortar, redigir; **~ion** [ɪ'dɪʃən] *n* (gen) edição *f*; (number printed) tiragem *f*; **~or** *n* redator(a) (Pt: -ct-) *m/f*; (of newspaper) diretor (Pt: -ct-) *m*; (of book) organizador(a) *m/f* da edição; **~orial** [-'tɔːrɪəl] *adj* editorial // *n* editorial *m*.

educate ['ɛdjukeɪt] *vt* (gen) educar; (instruct) instruir.

education [ɛdju'keɪʃən] *n* educação *f*; (schooling) ensino; (SCOL) pedagogia; **~al** *adj* (policy etc) educacional; (teaching) docente; (instructive) educativo.

EEC *n abbr of* **European Economic Community** Comunidade *f* Econômica Européia.

eel [i:l] *n* enguia.

eerie ['ɪərɪ] *adj* (strange) estranho; (mysterious) misterioso.

effect [ɪ'fɛkt] *n* efeito // *vt* efetuar (Pt: -ct-), levar a cabo; **~s** *npl* bens *mpl*; **to take ~** (drug) fazer efeito; **in ~** na realidade; **~ive** *adj* (gen) eficaz; (striking) impressionante; (real) efetivo (Pt: -ct-); **to become ~ive** entrar em vigor; **~iveness** *n* eficácia.

effeminate [ɪ'fɛmɪnɪt] *adj* efeminado.

effervescent [ɛfə'vɛsnt] *adj* efervescente.

efficiency [ɪ'fɪʃənsɪ] *n* (gen) eficiência; (of machine) rendimento.

efficient [ɪ'fɪʃənt] *adj* eficiente.

effigy ['ɛfɪdʒɪ] *n* efígie *f*.

effort ['ɛfət] *n* esforço; **to make an ~ to** esforçar-se para; **~less** *adj* com desenvoltura.

effrontery [ɪ'frʌntərɪ] *n* descaramento.

effusive [ɪ'fjuːsɪv] *adj* efusivo.

e.g. *adv abbr of* **exempli gratia** por exemplo.

egg [ɛg] *n* ovo; **hard-boiled ~** ovo cozido; **soft-boiled ~** ovo quente; **poached ~** ovo pochê (Br), ovo escalfado (Pt); **fried ~** ovo estrelado or frito; **scrambled ~s** ovos mexidos; **to ~ on** *vt* incitar; **~cup** *n* oveiro, taça para ovos quentes; **~plant** *n* (US) beringela; **~shell** *n* casca de ovo.

ego ['iːgəu] *n* ego; **~ism** *n* egoísmo; **~ist** *n* egoísta *m/f*.

Egypt ['iːdʒɪpt] *n* Egito (Pt: -pt-); **~ian** [ɪ'dʒɪpʃən] *adj*, *n* egípcio/a.

eiderdown ['aɪdədaun] *n* edredom (Pt: -dão) *m*.

eight [eɪt] *num* oito; **eighteen** *num* dezoito; **eighth** *adj*, *n* oitavo; **~y** *num* oitenta.

Eire ['ɛərə] *n* Eire *m*.

either ['aɪðə*] *det* (each) cada; (any) qualquer; (both) ambos, um ou outro; **on ~ side** de ambos os lados // *pron*: **~ (of them)** cada um/qualquer/ambos (deles); **I don't like ~** não gosto nem de um nem do outro // *adv* também não; **no, I don't ~** eu também não // *conj*: **~ yes or no** ou sim ou não.

eject [ɪ'dʒɛkt] *vt* expelir; (tenant) despejar; **~or seat** *n* assento ejetor (Pt: -ct-).

eke [iːk]: **to ~ out** *vt* (money) economizar; (food) economizar em; (add to) complementar.

elaborate [ɪ'læbərɪt] *adj* complicado; (decorated) rebuscado // (vb: [ɪ'læbəreɪt]) *vt* elaborar // *vi* entrar em detalhes.

elapse [ɪ'læps] *vi* decorrer.

elastic [ɪ'læstɪk] *adj*, *n* elástico; **~ band** *n* tira de borracha, elástico.

elated [ɪ'leɪtɪd] *adj*: **to be ~** rejubilar-se; **elation** [ɪ'leɪʃən] *n* exaltação *f*.

elbow ['ɛlbəu] *n* cotovelo.

elder ['ɛldə*] *adj* mais velho // *n* (tree) sabugueiro; (person) o mais velho; (of tribe) ancião; (of church) presbítero; **~ly** *adj* idoso, de idade // *n*: **the ~ly** as pessoas de idade, os idosos.

eldest ['ɛldɪst] *adj* mais velho // *n* o mais velho.

elect [ɪ'lɛkt] *vt* eleger; **to ~ to do** optar por fazer // *adj*: **the president ~** o presidente eleito; **~ion** [ɪ'lɛkʃən] *n* eleição *f*; **~ioneering** [ɪlɛkʃə'nɪərɪŋ] *n* campanha eleitoral; **~or** *n* eleitor(a) *m/f*; **~oral** *adj* eleitoral; **~orate** *n* eleitorado.

electric [ɪ'lɛktrɪk] *adj* elétrico (Pt: -ct-); **~al** *adj* elé(c)trico; **~ blanket** *n* cobertor *m* elé(c)trico; **~ chair** *n* cadeira elé(c)trica; **~ cooker** *n* fogão *m* elé(c)trico; **~ fire** *n* aquecimento elé(c)trico.

electrician [ɪlɛk'trɪʃən] *n* eletricista (Pt: -ct-) *m/f*.

electricity [ɪlɛk'trɪsɪtɪ] *n* eletricidade (Pt: -ct-) *f*.

electrify [ɪ'lɛktrɪfaɪ] *vt* (RAIL) eletrificar (Pt: -ct-); (audience) eletrizar (Pt: -ct-).

electro... [ɪlɛktrəu] *pref:* ~**cute** [-kju:t] *vt* eletrocutar (*Pt:* -ctr-); **electrode** [ɪˈlɛktrəud] *n* eletrodo (*Pt:* eléctrodo); ~**magnetic** *adj* eletromagnético (*Pt:* -ctr-).

electron [ɪˈlɛktrɔn] *n* elétron (*Pt:* electrão) *m*.

electronic [ɪlɛkˈtrɔnɪk] *adj* eletrônico (*Pt:* -ct-); ~**s** *n* eletrônica (*Pt:* -ct-).

elegance [ˈɛlɪɡəns] *n* elegância; **elegant** [-ɡənt] *adj* elegante.

element [ˈɛlɪmənt] *n* (*gen*) elemento; **to brave the ~s** enfrentar intempérie; ~**ary** [-ˈmɛntərɪ] *adj* (*gen*) elementar; (*primitive*) rudimentar; (*school, education*) primário.

elephant [ˈɛlɪfənt] *n* elefante *m*.

elevate [ˈɛlɪveɪt] *vt* (*gen*) elevar; (*in rank*) promover.

elevation [ɛlɪˈveɪʃən] *n* elevação *f*; (*land*) eminência; (*height*) altura.

elevator [ˈɛlɪveɪtəʳ] *n* (*US*) elevador *m*.

eleven [ɪˈlɛvn] *num* onze; ~**ses** *npl* refeição *f* leve da manhã; ~**th** *adj* décimo-primeiro.

elf [ɛlf], *pl* **elves** [ɛlvz] *n* elfo, duende *m*.

elicit [ɪˈlɪsɪt] *vt:* **to** ~ (**from**) arrancar (de), eliciar (de).

eligible [ˈɛlɪdʒəbl] *adj* elegível, apto; **to be** ~ **for sth** ter qualificações para algo.

eliminate [ɪˈlɪmɪneɪt] *vt* eliminar; (*strike out*) suprimir; (*suspect*) eliminar, excluir; **elimination** [-ˈneɪʃən] *n* eliminação *f*, exclusão *f*.

élite [eɪˈliːt] *n* elite *f*.

elm [ɛlm] *n* olmo.

elocution [ɛləˈkjuːʃən] *n* elocução *f*.

elongated [ˈiːlɔŋɡeɪtɪd] *adj* alongado.

elope [ɪˈləup] *vi* fugir (de casa) com namorado; ~**ment** *n* fuga do lar paterno.

eloquence [ˈɛləkwəns] *n* eloqüência; **eloquent** [-wənt] *adj* eloqüente.

else [ɛls] *adv* outro, mais; **something** ~ outra coisa; **somewhere** ~ em outro lugar (*Br*), noutro sítio (*Pt*); **everywhere** ~ por todo o lado (menos aqui); **where** ~? onde mais?; **what** ~ **can we do?** que mais podemos fazer?; **or** ~ senão; **there was little** ~ **to do** não havia outra coisa a fazer; **somebody** ~ **spoke** ninguém mais falou; ~**where** *adv* (*be*) em outro lugar (*Br*), noutro sítio (*Pt*); (*go*) para outro lugar (*Br*), a outro sítio (*Pt*).

elucidate [ɪˈluːsɪdeɪt] *vt* esclarecer, elucidar.

elude [ɪˈluːd] *vt* (*gen*) iludir; (*blow*) esquivar; (*pursuer*) escapar de, esquivar-se de.

elusive [ɪˈluːsɪv] *adj* esquivo; (*answer*) evasivo.

emaciated [ɪˈmeɪsɪeɪtɪd] *adj* emaciado, macilento.

emanate [ˈɛməneɪt] *vi* emanar, provir.

emancipate [ɪˈmænsɪpeɪt] *vt* emancipar; ~**d** *adj* emancipado;

emancipation [-ˈpeɪʃən] *n* emancipação *f*, liberação *f*.

embalm [ɪmˈbɑːm] *vt* embalsamar.

embankment [ɪmˈbæŋkmənt] *n* aterro; (*riverside*) dique *m*.

embargo [ɪmˈbɑːɡəu], *pl* ~**es** *n* embargo, proibição *f*.

embark [ɪmˈbɑːk] *vi* embarcar // *vt* embarcar; **to** ~ **on** (*fig*) empreender, começar; ~**ation** [ɛmbɑːˈkeɪʃən] *n* (*people, goods*) embarque *m*.

embarrass [ɪmˈbærəs] *vt* embaraçar, constranger; **to be** ~**ed financially** estar com dificuldades financeiras; ~**ing** *adj* embaraçoso, constrangedor(a); ~**ment** *n* embaraço, constrangimento; (*financial*) dificuldades *fpl*.

embassy [ˈɛmbəsɪ] *n* embaixada.

embed [ɪmˈbɛd] *vt* (*gen*) embutir; (*teeth etc*) cravar.

embellish [ɪmˈbɛlɪʃ] *vt* embelezar; (*fig*) adornar.

embers [ˈɛmbəz] *npl* brasa *sg*, borralho *sg*, cinzas *fpl*.

embezzle [ɪmˈbɛzl] *vt* desviar; ~**ment** *n* desvio.

embitter [ɪmˈbɪtəʳ] *vt* amargar; (*fig*) azedar, acirrar; ~**ed** *adj* amargurado.

emblem [ˈɛmbləm] *n* emblema *m*.

embody [ɪmˈbɔdɪ] *vt* (*features*) incorporar; (*ideas*) incluir.

embossed [ɪmˈbɔst] *adj* realçado; ~ **with** ornado com relevos de.

embrace [ɪmˈbreɪs] *vt* abraçar, dar um abraço em; (*include*) abarcar, abranger; (*adopt: idea*) adotar (*Pt:* -pt-) // *vi* abraçar-se // *n* abraço.

embroider [ɪmˈbrɔɪdəʳ] *vt* bordar; (*fig: story*) florear; ~**y** *n* bordado.

embryo [ˈɛmbrɪəu] *n* (*also fig*) embrião *m*.

emerald [ˈɛmərəld] *n* esmeralda.

emerge [ɪˈmɜːdʒ] *vi* (*gen*) sair, aparecer; (*arise*) surgir; **emergence** *n* surgimento, aparecimento.

emergency [ɪˈmɜːdʒənsɪ] *n* (*event*) emergência; (*crisis*) crise *f*; (*need*) necessidade *f* urgente; **in an** ~ em caso de urgência; **state of** ~ estado de emergência; ~ **exit** *n* saída de emergência; ~ **landing** *n* aterrissagem *f* forçada (*Br*), aterragem *f* forçosa (*Pt*); ~ **meeting** reunião *f* extraordinária.

emery [ˈɛmərɪ]: ~ **board** *n* lixa de unhas; ~ **paper** *n* lixa or papel *m* de esmeril.

emetic [ɪˈmɛtɪk] *n* emético.

emigrant [ˈɛmɪɡrənt] *n* emigrante *m/f*.

emigrate [ˈɛmɪɡreɪt] *vi* emigrar; **emigration** [-ˈɡreɪʃən] *n* emigração *f*.

eminence [ˈɛmɪnəns] *n* eminência; **eminent** [-ənt] *adj* eminente.

emission [ɪˈmɪʃən] *n* emissão *f*.

emit [ɪˈmɪt] *vt* (*gen*) emitir; (*smoke*) soltar; (*smell*) exalar; (*sound*) produzir.

emotion [ɪˈməuʃən] *n* emoção *f*; ~**al** *adj*

(person) sentimental, emotivo; (scene) comovente; ~ally adv emocionalmente.

emotive [ɪ'məʊtɪv] adj que sensibiliza.

emperor ['ɛmpərə*] n imperador m.

emphasis ['ɛmfəsɪs], pl -ses [-siːz] n ênfase f.

emphasize ['ɛmfəsaɪz] vt (word, point) enfatizar, acentuar; (feature) salientar.

emphatic [ɛm'fætɪk] adj (strong) enérgico; (unambiguous, clear) enfático; ~ally adv com ênfase.

empire ['ɛmpaɪə*] n império.

empirical [ɛm'pɪrɪkl] adj empírico.

employ [ɪm'plɔɪ] vt empregar; ~ee [-'iː] n empregado/a; ~er n empregador(a) m/f, patrão/troa m/f; ~ment n (gen) emprego; (work) trabalho; ~ment agency n agência de empregos; ~ment exchange n bolsa de trabalho.

empower [ɪm'paʊə*] vt: to ~ sb to do sth autorizar alguém para fazer algo.

empress ['ɛmprɪs] n imperatriz f.

emptiness ['ɛmptɪnɪs] n vazio, vácuo.

empty ['ɛmptɪ] adj vazio; (place) deserto; (house) desocupado; (threat) vão/vã // n (bottle) vazio // vt esvaziar; (place) evacuar // vi esvaziar-se; (place) ficar deserto; ~-handed adj de mãos vazias.

emulate ['ɛmjʊleɪt] vt emular.

emulsion [ɪ'mʌlʃən] n emulsão f.

enable [ɪ'neɪbl] vt: to ~ sb to do sth (allow) permitir que alguém faça algo; (prepare) capacitar alguém para fazer algo.

enact [ɪn'ækt] vt (law) pôr em vigor, aprovar; (play) representar; (role) fazer.

enamel [ɪ'næməl] n esmalte m.

enamoured [ɪ'næməd] adj: to be ~ of (person) estar apaixonado por; (activity etc) ser louco por; (idea) encantar-se com.

encased [ɪn'keɪst] adj: ~ in (enclosed) encaixado em; (covered) coberto de.

enchant [ɪn'tʃɑːnt] vt encantar; ~ing adj encantador(a).

encircle [ɪn'sɜːkl] vt (gen) cercar, circundar; (waist) rodear.

encl. abbr of enclosed anexo, junto.

enclose [ɪn'kləʊz] vt (land) cercar; (with letter etc) anexar (Br), enviar junto (Pt); please find ~d segue junto.

enclosure [ɪn'kləʊʒə*] n cercado; (COMM) documento anexo.

encore [ɔŋ'kɔː*] excl bis!, outra! // n bis m.

encounter [ɪn'kaʊntə*] n encontro // vt encontrar, topar com; (difficulty) enfrentar.

encourage [ɪn'kʌrɪdʒ] vt encorajar, animar; (growth) estimular; ~ment n estímulo; (of industry) fomento.

encroach [ɪn'krəʊtʃ] vi: to ~ (up)on (gen) invadir; (time) ocupar.

encrusted [ɪn'krʌstəd] adj: ~ with incrustado de.

encumber [ɪn'kʌmbə*] vt: to be ~ed with (carry) estar carregado de; (debts) estar sobrecarregado de.

encyclop(a)edia [ɛnsaɪkləʊ'piːdɪə] n enciclopédia.

end [ɛnd] n (gen, also aim) fim m; (of table) ponta; (of street) final m; (SPORT) ponta // vt acabar, terminar; (also: bring to an ~, put an ~ to) acabar com, pôr fim a // vi terminar, acabar; in the ~ ao fim, por fim, finalmente; on ~ (object) na ponta; to stand on ~ (hair) arrepiar-se; for hours on ~ por horas a fio; to ~ up vi: to ~ up in terminar em; (place) ir parar em.

endanger [ɪn'deɪndʒə*] vt pôr em perigo.

endear [ɪn'dɪə*] vt: to ~ o.s. to sb conquistar a afeição de alguém, cativar alguém; ~ing adj simpático, atrativo (Pt: -ct-); ~ment n carinho, meiguice f.

endeavour [ɪn'dɛvə*] n esforço; (attempt) tentativa; (striving) empenho // vi: to ~ to do esforçar-se para fazer; (try) tentar fazer.

ending ['ɛndɪŋ] n fim m, conclusão f; (of book) desenlace m; (LING) terminação f.

endless ['ɛndlɪs] adj interminável, infinito.

endorse [ɪn'dɔːs] vt (cheque) endossar; (approve) aprovar; ~ment n (on driving licence) descrição f das multas.

endow [ɪn'daʊ] vt (provide with money) dotar; (: institution) fundar; to be ~ed with ser dotado de.

endurance [ɪn'djʊərəns] n resistência; **endure** vt (bear) agüentar, suportar; (resist) resistir // vi (last) durar; (resist) resistir.

enemy ['ɛnəmɪ] adj, n inimigo.

energetic [ɛnə'dʒɛtɪk] adj energético.

energy ['ɛnədʒɪ] n energia.

enforce [ɪn'fɔːs] vt (LAW) fazer cumprir; ~d adj forçoso.

engage [ɪn'geɪdʒ] vt (attention) chamar; (worker) contratar; (clutch) engrenar // vi (TECH) engrenar com; to ~ in dedicar-se a, ocupar-se com; ~d adj (phone) ocupado (Br), impedido (Pt); (toilet) ocupado; (betrothed) noivo; to get ~d ficar noivo; he is ~d in research dedica-se à pesquisa; ~d tone n sinal m de ocupado (Br), sinal de impedido (Pt); ~ment n (appointment) encontro; (battle) combate m; (to marry, period) noivado; ~ment ring n aliança de noivado.

engaging [ɪn'geɪdʒɪŋ] adj atraente, simpático.

engender [ɪn'dʒɛndə*] vt engendrar, gerar.

engine ['ɛndʒɪn] n (AUT) motor m; (RAIL) locomotiva; ~ driver n maquinista m.

engineer [ɛndʒɪ'nɪə*] n engenheiro; (US: RAIL) maquinista m; ~ing n engenharia.

England ['ɪŋglənd] n Inglaterra.

English ['ɪŋglɪʃ] adj inglês/esa // n (LING) inglês m; the ~ os ingleses; ~man/woman n inglês/esa m/f.

engrave [ɪn'greɪv] vt gravar; **engraving** n gravura, gravação f.

engulf [ɪn'gʌlf] vt engolfar, tragar.

enhance [ɪn'hɑ:ns] vt (gen) aumentar; (beauty) realçar.

enigma [ɪ'nɪgmə] n enigma m; ~tic [ɛnɪg'mætɪk] adj enigmático.

enjoy [ɪn'dʒɔɪ] vt (like) gostar de; (have: health, privilege) desfrutar de; (food) comer com gosto; to ~ o.s. divertir-se; ~able adj (pleasant) agradável; (amusing) divertido; ~ment n (joy) prazer m; (use) gozo.

enlarge [ɪn'lɑ:dʒ] vt aumentar; (broaden) estender, alargar; (PHOT) ampliar // vi: to ~ on (subject) desenvolver, estender-se sobre; ~ment n (PHOT) ampliação f.

enlighten [ɪn'laɪtn] vt (inform) informar, instruir; ~ed adj (cultured) culto; (knowledgeable) bem informado; (tolerant) compreensivo; ~ment n esclarecimento; (HISTORY): the E~ment o Século das Luzes.

enlist [ɪn'lɪst] vt alistar; (support) conseguir, aliciar // vi alistar-se.

enmity ['ɛnmɪtɪ] n inimizade f.

enormity [ɪ'nɔ:mɪtɪ] n enormidade f; **enormous** [-məs] adj enorme.

enough [ɪ'nʌf] adj: ~ time/books bastante tempo/bastantes livros // n: have you got ~? você tem bastante? // adv: big ~ suficientemente grande; he has not worked ~ não tem trabalhado bastante; ~! basta!, chega!; that's ~, thanks chega, obrigado; I've had ~ of him estou farto dele; ... which, funnily ~ ... o que, por estranho que pareça ... .

enquire [ɪn'kwaɪə*] vt/i = **inquire**.

enrage [ɪn'reɪdʒ] vt enfurecer, enraivecer.

enrich [ɪn'rɪtʃ] vt enriquecer.

enrol [ɪn'rəul] vt inscrever; (SCOL) matricular // vi inscrever-se, matricular-se; ~ment n inscrição f; matrícula..

en route [ɔn'ru:t] adv (on the way) no caminho; ~ to a caminho de.

ensign ['ɛnsaɪn] n (flag) bandeira; (MIL) insígnia; (US: NAUT) guarda-marinha m.

enslave [ɪn'sleɪv] vt escravizar.

ensue [ɪn'sju:] vi seguir-se; (result) resultar; (happen) acontecer.

ensure [ɪn'ʃuə*] vt assegurar.

entail [ɪn'teɪl] vt (imply) supor; (result in) acarretar.

entangle [ɪn'tæŋgl] vt enredar, emaranhar; ~ment n emaranhado.

enter ['ɛntə*] vt (room) entrar em; (club) ficar or fazer-se sócio de; (army) alistar-se em; (sb for a competition) inscrever; (write down) anotar, apontar // vi entrar; to ~ for vt fus apresentar-se para; to ~ into vt fus (relations) estabelecer; (plans) fazer parte de; (debate) tomar parte em; (agreement) chegar a, firmar; to ~ (up)on vt fus (career) entrar para.

enteritis [ɛntə'raɪtɪs] n enterite f.

enterprise ['ɛntəpraɪz] n empresa;

(spirit) iniciativa; **free** ~ livre iniciativa; **private** ~ iniciativa privada; **enterprising** adj empreendedor(a).

entertain [ɛntə'teɪn] vt (amuse) divertir, entreter; (receive: guest) receber (em casa); (idea) acolher; (plan) estudar; ~er n artista m/f; ~ing adj divertido; ~ment n (amusement) diversão f; (show) espetáculo (Pt: -ct-); (party) festa.

enthralled [ɪn'θrɔ:ld] adj encantado, cativado.

enthusiasm [ɪn'θu:zɪæzəm] n entusiasmo.

enthusiast [ɪn'θu:zɪæst] n entusiasta m/f; ~ic [-'æstɪk] adj entusiástico; to be ~ic about entusiasmar-se por.

entice [ɪn'taɪs] vt atrair, tentar; (seduce) seduzir; **enticing** adj sedutor(a), tentador(a).

entire [ɪn'taɪə*] adj inteiro, completo; (total) total, todo; ~ly adv totalmente; ~ty [ɪn'taɪərətɪ] n: in its ~ty na sua totalidade.

entitle [ɪn'taɪtl] vt: to ~ sb to sth dar a alguém direito a algo; ~d adj (book) intitulado; to be ~d to ter direito de fazer.

entourage [ɔntu'rɑ:ʒ] n séquito.

entrails ['ɛntreɪlz] npl entranhas fpl.

entrance ['ɛntrəns] n entrada // vt [ɪn'trɑ:ns] encantar, fascinar; to gain ~ to (university etc) ser admitido em; ~ examination n exame m de admissão; (university) exame vestibular (Br); ~ fee n jóia.

entrant ['ɛntrənt] n participante m/f.

entreat [ɛn'tri:t] vt rogar, suplicar; ~y n rogo, súplica.

entrée ['ɔntreɪ] n (CULIN) entrada.

entrenched [ɛn'trɛntʃd] adj entrincheirado.

entrepreneur [ɔntrəprə'nə:] n empresário; (of works) empreiteiro.

entrust [ɪn'trʌst] vt: to ~ sth to sb confiar algo a alguém.

entry ['ɛntrɪ] n entrada; (permission to enter) acesso; (in register) registro, assentamento; (in account) lançamento; (dictionary) verbete m; ~ form n formulário de inscrição; no ~ entrada proibida; (AUT) contramão f (Br).

enumerate [ɪ'nju:məreɪt] vt enumerar.

enunciate [ɪ'nʌnsɪeɪt] vt pronunciar; (principle etc) enunciar.

envelop [ɪn'vɛləp] vt envolver.

envelope ['ɛnvələup] n envelope m.

envious ['ɛnvɪəs] adj invejoso; (look) de inveja.

environment [ɪn'vaɪərnmənt] n meio ambiente m; ~al [-'mɛntl] adj ambiental.

envisage [ɪn'vɪzɪdʒ] vt (foresee) prever; (imagine) conceber, imaginar.

envoy ['ɛnvɔɪ] n emissário.

envy ['ɛnvɪ] n inveja // vt ter inveja de; to ~ sb sth invejar alguém por algo, cobiçar algo de alguém.

enzyme ['ɛnzaɪm] n enzima.

ephemeral [ɪ'fɛmərl] adj efêmero.

epic ['ɛpɪk] *n* epopéia // *adj* épico.

epidemic [ɛpɪ'dɛmɪk] *n* epidemia.

epilepsy ['ɛpɪlɛpsɪ] *n* epilepsia; **epileptic** [-'lɛptɪk] *adj*, *n* epilético/a (*Pt*: -pt-).

episode ['ɛpɪsəud] *n* episódio.

epistle [ɪ'pɪsl] *n* epístola.

epitaph ['ɛpɪtɑ:f] *n* epitáfio.

epitome [ɪ'pɪtəmɪ] *n* epítome *m*; **epitomize** *vt* epitomar, resumir.

epoch ['iːpɔk] *n* época.

equable ['ɛkwəbl] *adj* uniforme, igual; (*character*) tranqüilo, calmo.

equal ['iːkwl] *adj* (*gen*) igual; (*treatment*) equitativo, equivalente // *n* igual *m/f* // *vt* ser igual a; **to be ~ to** (*task*) estar à altura de; **~ity** [iː'kwɔlɪtɪ] *n* igualdade *f*; **~ize** *vt/i* igualar; (*SPORT*) empatar; **~izer** *n* gol (*Pt*: golo) *m* de empate; **~ly** *adv* igualmente; (*share etc*) por igual.

equanimity [ɛkwə'nɪmɪtɪ] *n* equanimidade *f*.

equate [ɪ'kweɪt] *vt*: **to ~ sth with** equiparar algo com; **equation** [ɪ'kweɪʃən] *n* (*MATH*) equação *f*.

equator [ɪ'kweɪtə*] *n* equador *m*; **~ial** [ɛkwə'tɔːrɪəl] *adj* equatorial.

equilibrium [iːkwɪ'lɪbrɪəm] *n* equilíbrio.

equinox ['iːkwɪnɔks] *n* equinócio.

equip [ɪ'kwɪp] *vt* (*gen*) equipar; (*person*) prover, munir; **to be well ~ped** estar bem preparado *or* equipado; **~ment** *n* equipamento.

equitable ['ɛkwɪtəbl] *adj* equitativo.

equivalent [ɪ'kwɪvəlnt] *adj* equivalente; **to be ~ to** ser equivalente a // *n* equivalente *m*.

equivocal [ɪ'kwɪvəkl] *adj* equívoco; (*open to suspicion*) ambíguo.

era ['ɪərə] *n* era, época.

eradicate [ɪ'rædɪkeɪt] *vt* erradicar, extirpar.

erase [ɪ'reɪz] *vt* apagar; **eraser** *n* borracha (de apagar).

erect [ɪ'rɛkt] *adj* erguido, ereto (*Pt*: -ct-) // *vt* erigir, levantar; (*assemble*) montar.

erection [ɪ'rɛkʃən] *n* construção *f*; (*assembly*) montagem *f*; (*structure*) edifício; (*MED*) ereção (*Pt*: -cç-) *f*.

ermine ['ɔːmɪn] *n* arminho.

erode [ɪ'rəud] *vt* (*GEO*) causar erosão; (*salary*) corroer; **erosion** [ɪ'rəuʒən] *n* erosão *f*, corrosão *f*.

erotic [ɪ'rɔtɪk] *adj* erótico; **~ism** [ɪ'rɔtɪsɪzm] *n* erotismo.

err [ɔː*] *vi* errar, enganar-se; (*REL*) pecar.

errand ['ɛrnd] *n* recado, missão *f*; **~ boy** *n* mensageiro.

erratic [ɪ'rætɪk] *adj* errático; (*uneven*) irregular.

erroneous [ɪ'rəunɪəs] *adj* errôneo.

error ['ɛrə*] *n* engano, erro.

erupt [ɪ'rʌpt] *vi* entrar em erupção; (*MED*) causar erupção; (*fig*) explodir; **~ion** [ɪ'rʌpʃən] *n* erupção *f*; (*fig*) explosão *f*.

escalate ['ɛskəleɪt] *vi* estender-se, intensificar-se; **escalation** [-'leɪʃən] *n* escalada, intensificação *f*.

escalator ['ɛskəleɪtə*] *n* escada rolante.

escapade [ɛskə'peɪd] *n* peripécia.

escape [ɪ'skeɪp] *n* (*gen*) fuga; (*from duties*) escapatória; (*from chase*) fuga, evasão *f* // *vi* (*gen*) escapar; (*flee*) fugir, evadir-se; (*leak*) vazar, escapar // *vt* evitar, fugir de; (*consequences*) fugir de; **to ~ from** (*place*) escapar de; (*person*) escapulir de; (*clutches*) livrar-se de; **escapism** *n* escapismo, fuga à realidade.

escort ['ɛskɔːt] *n* acompanhante *m/f*; (*MIL, NAUT*) escolta // *vt* [ɪ'skɔːt] acompanhar; (*MIL, NAUT*) escoltar.

Eskimo ['ɛskɪməu] *n* esquimó *m/f*.

especially [ɪ'spɛʃlɪ] *adv* (*gen*) especialmente; (*above all*) sobre tudo; (*particulary*) em particular.

espionage ['ɛspɪɑnɑːʒ] *n* espionagem *f*.

esplanade [ɛsplə'neɪd] *n* (*by sea*) avenida beira-mar, esplanada.

espouse [ɪ'spauz] *vt* (*cause*) abraçar.

Esquire [ɪ'skwaɪə*] *n* (*abbr* Esq.): J. Brown, ~ Sr. J. Brown.

essay ['ɛseɪ] *n* (*SCOL*) ensaio.

essence ['ɛsns] *n* essência.

essential [ɪ'sɛnʃl] *adj* (*necessary*) indispensável; (*basic*) essencial; **~ly** *adv* essencialmente.

establish [ɪ'stæblɪʃ] *vt* estabelecer; (*facts*) verificar; (*proof*) demonstrar; (*relations*) fundar; **~ed** *adj* (*business*) com boa reputação; (*staff*) fixo; **~ment** *n* estabelecimento; **the E~ment** *n* a classe dirigente.

estate [ɪ'steɪt] *n* (*land*) fazenda (*Br*), propriedade *f* (*Pt*); (*property*) proprie-dade; (*inheritance*) herança; (*POL*) estado; **~ housing** *n* urbanização *f*; **~ industrial** ~ zona industrial; **~ agent** *n* corretor *m* de imóveis (*Br*), agente *m/f* imobiliário (*Pt*); **~ car** *n* (*Brit*) perua (*Br*), canadiana (*Pt*).

esteem [ɪ'stiːm] *n*: **to hold sb in high ~** estimar muito alguém // *vt* estimar.

estimate ['ɛstɪmət] *n* estimativa; (*assessment*) avaliação *f*, cálculo; (*COMM*) orçamento // *vt* [-meɪt] estimar, avaliar, calcular; **estimation** [-'meɪʃən] *n* estimação *f*, opinião *f*; (*esteem*) apreço.

estrange [ɪ'streɪndʒ] *vt* alienar.

estuary ['ɛstjuərɪ] *n* estuário.

etching ['ɛtʃɪŋ] *n* água-forte *f*.

eternal [ɪ'tɔːnl] *adj* eterno.

eternity [ɪ'tɔːnɪtɪ] *n* eternidade *f*.

ether ['iːθə*] *n* éter *m*.

ethical ['ɛθɪkl] *adj* ético; (*honest*) honrado; **ethics** ['ɛθɪks] *n* ética // *npl* moral *f*.

ethnic ['ɛθnɪk] *adj* étnico.

etiquette ['ɛtɪkɛt] *n* etiqueta.

eucalyptus [juːkə'lɪptəs] *n* eucalipto.

euphemism ['juːfəmɪzm] *n* eufemismo.

euphoria [juː'fɔːrɪə] *n* euforia.

Europe ['juərəp] *n* Europa; **European** [-'piːən] *adj*, *n* europeu/péia.

euthanasia [ju:θə'neɪzɪə] n eutanásia.

evacuate [ɪ'vækjueɪt] vt evacuar; **evacuation** [-'eɪʃən] n evacuação f.

evade [ɪ'veɪd] vt evadir, evitar.

evaluate [ɪ'væljueɪt] vt avaliar; (value) determinar o valor de; (evidence) interpretar.

evangelist [ɪ'vændʒəlɪst] n evangelista m/f; (preacher) evangelizador(a) m/f.

evaporate [ɪ'væpəreɪt] vi evaporar-se // vt evaporar; **~d milk** n leite m evaporado; **evaporation** [-'reɪʃən] n evaporação f.

evasion [ɪ'veɪʒən] n evasão f, fuga; (fig) evasiva; **evasive** [-sɪv] adj evasivo.

eve [i:v] n: **on the ~ of** na véspera de.

even ['i:vn] adj (level) plano; (smooth) liso; (speed, temperature) uniforme; (number) par; (nature) equilibrado; (SPORT) igual // adv até, mesmo, ainda; **~ more** ainda mais; **~ so** mesmo assim; **never ~** nem sequer; **not ~** nem; **~ he was there** até ele esteve ali; **~ if** mesmo que; **~ on Sundays** até nos domingos; **to ~ out** vi nivelar-se; **to get ~ with sb** ficar quite com alguém.

evening ['i:vnɪŋ] n noite f; (before six) tarde f; (dusk) anoitecer m; (event) noitada; **in the ~** à noite; **~ class** n aula noturna (Pt: -ct-); **~ dress** n traje m de rigor (Br), traje de cerimônia (Pt); (woman's) vestido de noite.

event [ɪ'vɛnt] n acontecimento; (SPORT) prova; **in the ~ of** no caso de (que); **~ful** adj tumultuado, cheio de acontecimentos; (game etc) cheio de emoção, agitado.

eventual [ɪ'vɛntʃuəl] adj (last) final; (resulting) definitivo; **~ity** [-'ælɪtɪ] n eventualidade f; **~ly** adv (finally) finalmente; (in time) por fim.

ever ['ɛvə*] adv já, alguma vez; (in negative) nunca, jamais; (at all times) alguma vez; **the best ~** o melhor que já se viu; **have you ~ seen it?** você alguma vez já viu isto?; **better than ~** melhor que nunca; **~ since** adv desde então // conj depois que; **~green** n sempre-verde f; **~lasting** adj eterno, perpétuo.

every ['ɛvrɪ] det (each) cada; (all) todo; **~ day** todo dia; **~ other car** cada dois carros; **~ now and then** de vez em quando; **~ 3 weeks** de 3 em 3 semanas; **~body** pron todos mpl, todo mundo (Br), toda a gente (Pt); **~day** adj (daily) diário; (usual) corrente; (common) comum; (routine) rotineiro; **~one =** **~body**; **~thing** pron tudo; **~where** adv (be) em todo lugar (Br), em toda a parte (Pt); (go) todo lugar (Br), a toda a parte (Pt).

evict [ɪ'vɪkt] vt expulsar; **~ion** [ɪ'vɪkʃən] n expulsão f, despejo.

evidence ['ɛvɪdəns] n (proof) prova(s); (of witness) testemunho, depoimento; (facts) dados mpl, evidência; **to give ~** testemunhar, prestar depoimento.

evident ['ɛvɪdənt] adj evidente; **~ly** adv naturalmente, evidentemente.

evil ['i:vl] adj mau/má; (influence) funesto; (smell) horrível // n mal m, maldade f; **~doer** n malfeitor(a) m/f.

evocative [ɪ'vɔkətɪv] adj evocativo, sugestivo.

evoke [ɪ'vəuk] vt evocar.

evolution [i:və'lu:ʃən] n evolução f, desenvolvimento.

evolve [ɪ'vɔlv] vt desenvolver // vi desenvolver-se.

ewe [ju:] n ovelha.

ex-... [ɛks] pref ex....

exact [ɪg'zækt] adj exato (Pt: -ct-) // vt: **to ~ sth (from)** exigir algo (de); **~ing** adj exigente; (conditions) difícil; **~itude** n exatidão (Pt: -ct-) f; **~ly** adv exatamente (Pt: -act-); (time) em ponto.

exaggerate [ɪg'zædʒəreɪt] vt/i exagerar; **exaggeration** [-'reɪʃən] n exagero.

exalted [ɪg'zɔ:ltɪd] adj exaltado, elevado.

exam [ɪg'zæm] n abbr of **examination.**

examination [ɪgzæmɪ'neɪʃən] n (gen) exame m; (LAW) inquirição f; (inquiry) investigação f.

examine [ɪg'zæmɪn] vt (gen) examinar; (inspect) inspecionar (Pt: -cc-); (SCOL, LAW: person) interrogar; (at customs: luggage) revistar; **examiner** n inspetor(a) (Pt: -ct-) m/f, examinador(a) m/f.

example [ɪg'zɑ:mpl] n exemplo; (copy) exemplar m; **for ~** por exemplo.

exasperate [ɪg'zɑ:spəreɪt] vt exasperar, irritar; **exasperating** adj irritante.

excavate ['ɛkskəveɪt] vt escavar; **excavation** [-'veɪʃən] n escavação f.

exceed [ɪk'si:d] vt exceder; (number) ser superior a; (speed limit) ultrapassar; (limits) ir além de; (powers) exceder-se em; (hopes) superar; **~ingly** adv extremamente, muitíssimo.

excel [ɪk'sɛl] vi sobressair, distinguir-se.

excellence ['ɛksələns] n excelência.

Excellency ['ɛksələnsɪ] n: **His ~** Sua Excelência.

excellent ['ɛksələnt] adj excelente.

except [ɪk'sɛpt] prep (also: **~ for**, **~ing**) exceto (Pt: -pt-), a não ser // vt excetuar (Pt: -pt-), excluir; **~ if/when** a menos que, a não ser que; **~ that** exce(p)to que; **~ion** [ɪk'sɛpʃən] n exceção (Pt: -pç-) f; **to take ~ion to** ressentir-se de; **~ional** [ɪk'sɛpʃənl] adj excepcional.

excerpt ['ɛksɜ:pt] n trecho, citação f.

excess [ɪk'sɛs] n excesso; (COMM) excedente m; **~ baggage** n excesso de bagagem; **~ fare** n sobretaxa de excesso; **~ive** adj excessivo.

exchange [ɪks'tʃeɪndʒ] n permuta, câmbio; (of goods, of ideas) troca; (also: **telephone ~**) estação f telefônica (Br), central f telefónica (Pt) // vt trocar, permutar.

exchequer [iks'tʃɛkə*] n Ministério da Fazenda.

excise ['ɛksaiz] n imposto de consumo // vt [ɛk'saiz] cortar (fora).

excite [ik'sait] vt (stimulate) excitar; (awaken) despertar; (move) entusiasmar; **to get ~d** entusiasmar-se; **~ment** n emoções fpl; (anticipation) expectativa; (agitation) agitação f; **exciting** adj emocionante, empolgante.

exclaim [ik'skleim] vi exclamar; **exclamation** [ɛksklə'meiʃən] n exclamação f; **exclamation mark** n ponto de exclamação.

exclude [ik'sklu:d] vt excluir; (except) excetuar (Pt: -pt-); **exclusion** [ik'sklu:ʒən] n exclusão f.

exclusive [ik'sklu:siv] adj exclusivo; (club, district) privativo; ~ **of tax** sem incluir os impostos; **~ly** adv unicamente.

excommunicate [ɛkskə'mju:nikeit] vt excomungar.

excrement ['ɛkskrəmənt] n excremento.

excrete [ik'skri:t] vi excretar.

excruciating [ik'skru:ʃieitiŋ] adj (ex)cruciante, torturante.

excursion [ik'skə:ʃən] n excursão f.

excusable [ik'skju:zəbl] adj perdoável, excusável.

excuse [ik'skju:s] n desculpa, escusa; (evasion) pretexto // vt [ik'skju:z] desculpar, perdoar; **to ~ sb from doing sth** dispensar alguém de fazer algo; ~ **me!** (calling attention) desculpe!; (asking permission) (com) licença; **if you will ~ me** com a sua licença.

execute ['ɛksikju:t] vt (plan) realizar; (order) cumprir; (person) executar; **execution** n realização f; execução f; **executioner** n verdugo, carrasco.

executive [ig'zɛkjutiv] n (COMM, POL) executivo // adj executivo.

executor [ig'zɛkjutə*] n executor m; (JUR) testamenteiro.

exemplary [ig'zɛmpləri] adj exemplar.

exemplify [ig'zɛmplifai] vt exemplificar.

exempt [ig'zɛmpt] adj: ~ **from** isento de // vt: **to ~ sb from** dispensar or isentar alguém de; **~ion** [ig'zɛmpʃən] n isenção f; dispensa; (immunity) imunidade f.

exercise ['ɛksəsaiz] n exercício // vt exercer; (right) valer-se de; (dog) levar para passear // vi fazer exercício; ~ **book** n caderno.

exert [ig'zə:t] vt exercer; **to ~ o.s.** esforçar-se, empenhar-se; (overdo things) trabalhar demasiado; **~ion** n esforço.

exhaust [ig'zɔ:st] n (pipe) escape m, exaustor m; (fumes) escapamento (de gás) // vt esgotar; **~ion** [ig'zɔ:stʃən] n exaustão f; **nervous ~ion** esgotamento nervoso; **~ive** adj exaustivo.

exhibit [ig'zibit] n (ART) obra exposta; (LAW) objeto (Pt: -ct-) exposto // vt (show) manifestar, mostrar; (emotion) demonstrar; (film) apresentar; (paintings) expor; **~ion** [ɛksi'biʃən] n exposição f; **~ionist** [ɛksi'biʃənist] n exibicionista m/f.

exhilarating [ig'ziləreitiŋ] adj estimulante, tônico.

exhort [ig'zɔ:t] vt exortar.

exile ['ɛksail] n exílio; (person) exilado // vt desterrar, exilar.

exist [ig'zist] vi existir; (live) viver; **~ence** n existência; (life) vida; **~ing** adj existente, atual (Pt: -ct-).

exit ['ɛksit] n saída.

exonerate [ig'zɔnəreit] vt: **to ~ from** exonerar de.

exorcize ['ɛksɔ:saiz] vt exorcizar.

exotic [ig'zɔtik] adj exótico.

expand [ik'spænd] vt (widen) ampliar; (number) aumentar // vi (trade, gas, etc) expandir-se; (metal) dilatar-se.

expanse [ik'spæns] n extensão f; (of wings) envergadura.

expansion [ik'spænʃən] n (of town) desenvolvimento; (of trade) expansão f.

expatriate [ɛks'pætriət] n expatriado.

expect [ik'spɛkt] vt (gen) esperar; (count on) contar com; (suppose) supor // vi: **to be ~ing** estar grávida; **~ant mother** n (mulher f) grávida; **~ation** [ɛkspɛk'teiʃən] n esperança, expectativa.

expedience [ik'spi:diəns], **expediency** [ik'spi:diənsi] n conveniência; **expedient** adj conveniente, oportuno // n expediente m, recurso.

expedition [ɛkspə'diʃən] n expedição f.

expel [ik'spɛl] vt expelir; (SCOL) expulsar.

expend [ik'spɛnd] vt gastar; (use up) consumir; **~able** adj prescindível; **~iture** n gasto, despesa.

expense [ik'spɛns] n gasto, despesa; (high cost) custo; **~s** npl (COMM) despesas fpl; **at the ~ of** à custa de; **~ account** n relatório de despesas.

expensive [ik'spɛnsiv] adj caro, custoso.

experience [ik'spiəriəns] n experiência // vt experimentar; (suffer) sofrer; **~d** adj experimentado, experiente.

experiment [ik'spɛrimənt] n experimento, experiência // vi fazer experiências; **~al** [-'mɛntl] adj experimental.

expert ['ɛkspə:t] adj hábil, perito // n perito; (specialist) especialista m/f; **~ise** [-'ti:z] n perícia.

expire [ik'spaiə*] vi (gen) expirar; (end) terminar; (run out) vencer; **expiry** n expiração f; término; vencimento.

explain [ik'splein] vt explicar; (clarify) esclarecer; (demonstrate) expor; **explanation** [ɛksplə'neiʃən] n explicação f; **explanatory** [ik'splænətri] adj explicativo.

explicit [ik'splisit] adj explícito.

explode [ik'spləud] vi estourar, explodir; (with anger) rebentar // vt detonar, fazer explodir.

exploit ['ɛksplɔit] n façanha // vt

[ɪk'splɔɪt] explorar; ~**ation** [-'teɪʃən] n exploração f.

exploration [ɛksplɔ'reɪʃən] n exploração f; **exploratory** [ɪk'splɔrətrɪ] adj (fig: talks) exploratório, de pesquisa.

explore [ɪk'splɔ:*] vt explorar; (fig) examinar, pesquisar; **explorer** n explorador(a) m/f.

explosion [ɪk'splɔuʒən] n explosão f; **explosive** [-sɪv] adj, n explosivo.

exponent [ɪk'spəunənt] n representante m/f, expoente m/f.

export [ɛk'spɔ:t] vt exportar // n ['ɛkspɔ:t] exportação f // cmp de exportação; ~**ation** [-'teɪʃən] n exportação f; ~**er** n exportador(a) m/f.

expose [ɪk'spəuz] vt expor; (unmask) desmascarar; ~**d** adj exposto; (position) desabrigado.

exposure [ɪk'spəuʒə*] n exposição f; (PHOT) revelação f; (: shot) fotografia; **to die from** ~ (MED) morrer de frio; ~ **meter** n fotômetro.

expound [ɪk'spaund] vt expor, explicar.

express [ɪk'sprɛs] adj (definite) expresso, explícito; (letter etc) urgente // n (train) rápido // adv (send) por via urgente or expressa // vt exprimir, expressar; ~**ion** [ɪk'sprɛʃən] n expressão f; ~**ive** adj expressivo; ~**ly** adv expressamente; ~**way** n rodovia (Br), auto-estrada (Pt).

expulsion [ɪk'spʌlʃən] n expulsão f.

exquisite [ɛk'skwɪzɪt] adj (dress) bonito, refinado.

extend [ɪk'stɛnd] vt (visit, street) prolongar; (building) aumentar; (offer) oferecer // vi (land) estender-se.

extension [ɪk'stɛnʃən] n extensão f; (building) acréscimo, expansão f; (TEL) ramal m (Br), extensão f (Pt); (of deadline) prolongamento, prorrogação f.

extensive [ɪk'stɛnsɪv] adj (gen) extenso; (broad) vasto, amplo; (frequent) geral, comum; **he's travelled** ~**ly** ele já viajou muito.

extent [ɪk'stɛnt] n (breadth) extensão f; (scope) alcance m; **to some** ~ até certo ponto; **to the** ~ **of...** a ponto de...; **to such an** ~ **that...** a tal ponto que...; **to what** ~? até que ponto?

exterior [ɛk'stɪərɪə*] adj exterior, externo // n exterior m; (appearance) aspecto.

exterminate [ɪk'stə:mɪneɪt] vt exterminar; **extermination** [-'neɪʃən] n extermínio.

external [ɛk'stə:nl] adj externo, exterior; ~**ly** adv por fora.

extinct [ɪk'stɪŋkt] adj extinto; ~**ion** [ɪk'stɪŋkʃən] n extinção f.

extinguish [ɪk'stɪŋgwɪʃ] vt extinguir; ~**er** n extintor m.

extort [ɪk'stɔ:t] vt arrancar à força, extorquir; ~**ion** [ɪk'stɔ:ʃən] n extorsão f; ~**ionate** [ɪk'stɔ:ʃnət] adj extorsivo, excessivo.

extra ['ɛkstrə] adj adicional; (excessive) de mais, extra; (bonus: payment)

extraordinário // adv (in addition) adicionalmente // n (addition) extra m, suplemento; (THEATRE) figurante m/f; (newspaper) edição f extra.

extra... [ɛkstrə] pref extra....

extract [ɪk'strækt] vt tirar, extrair; (confession) arrancar, obter // n ['ɛkstrækt] extrato (Pt: -ct-).

extradite ['ɛkstrədaɪt] vt (from country) extraditar; (to country) obter a extradição de; **extradition** [-'dɪʃən] n extradição f.

extramarital [ɛkstrə'mærɪtl] adj extramatrimonial.

extramural [ɛkstrə'mjuərl] adj externo; (course) de extensão universitária.

extraordinary [ɪk'strɔ:dnrɪ] adj extraordinário; (odd) estranho.

extravagant [ɪk'strævəgənt] adj (lavish) extravagante; (wasteful) gastador(a), esbanjador(a); (price) exorbitante; (praise) excessivo; (odd) excêntrico, estranho.

extreme [ɪk'stri:m] adj (poverty etc) extremo; (case) excessivo // n extremidade f; ~**ly** adv muito, extremamente; **extremist** adj, n extremista m/f.

extremity [ɪk'strɛmətɪ] n extremidade f, ponta; (need) apuro, necessidade f.

extricate ['ɛkstrɪkeɪt] vt livrar.

extrovert ['ɛkstrəvə:t] n extrovertido.

exuberant [ɪg'zju:bərnt] adj (person) eufórico; (style) exuberante.

exude [ɪg'zju:d] vt ressumar.

exult [ɪg'zʌlt] vi regozijar-se.

eye [aɪ] n olho // vt olhar, observar; **to keep an** ~ **on** vigiar, ficar de olho em; ~**ball** n globo ocular; ~**bath** n recipiente m para lavar o olho; ~**brow** n sobrancelha; ~**brow pencil** n lápis m de sobrancelha; ~**catching** adj de chamar a atenção; ~**drops** npl gotas fpl para os olhos; ~**glasses** n (US) óculos mpl; ~**lash** n cílio; ~**lid** n pálpebra; ~**opener** n revelação f, grande surpresa; ~**shadow** n sombra de olhos; ~**sight** n vista, visão f; ~**sore** n monstruosidade f; ~**wash** n (fig) disparates mpl, maluquices fpl; ~ **witness** n testemunha f ocular.

eyrie ['ɪərɪ] n ninho de ave de rapina.

F

F. abbr of **Fahrenheit**.

fable ['feɪbl] n fábula.

fabric ['fæbrɪk] n tecido, pano.

fabrication [fæbrɪ'keɪʃən] n maquinação f.

fabulous ['fæbjuləs] adj fabuloso.

façade [fə'sɑ:d] n fachada.

face [feɪs] n (ANAT) cara, rosto; (of clock) mostrador m; (side, surface) superfície f // vt (person) encarar; (building) dar para, ter frente para; **to lose** ~ perder o prestígio; **in the** ~ **of** (difficulties etc) diante de, à vista de; **on the ~ of** it a julgar pelas aparências, à primeira vista; **~ to ~** cara a cara; **to ~ up to** vt fus enfrentar; **~ cloth** n toalha de rosto; **~ cream** n creme m facial; **~ lift** n operação f plástica; **~ powder** n pó m de arroz; **~-saving** adj para salvar as aparências.

facet ['fæsɪt] n faceta.

facetious [fə'siːʃəs] adj engraçado, faceto.

face value ['feɪs'vælju:] n (of stamp) valor m nominal; **to take sth at ~** (fig) aceitar as aparências de algo.

facial ['feɪʃəl] adj facial.

facile ['fæsaɪl] adj superficial.

facilitate [fə'sɪlɪteɪt] vt facilitar.

facilities [fə'sɪlɪtɪz] npl facilidades fpl, instalações fpl.

facing ['feɪsɪŋ] prep de frente para // adj em frente.

fact [fækt] n fato (Pt: -ct-); **in ~** realmente, na verdade.

faction ['fækʃən] n facção f.

factor ['fæktə*] n fator (Pt: -ct-) m.

factory ['fæktərɪ] n fábrica.

factual ['fæktjuəl] adj real, fatual (Pt: -ct-).

faculty ['fækəltɪ] n faculdade f; (US: teaching staff) corpo docente.

fade [feɪd] vi desbotar; (sound, hope) desvanecer-se; (light) apagar-se; (flower) murchar.

fag [fæg] n (col: cigarette) cigarro; **~ end** n ponta de cigarro, guimba; **~ged out** adj (col) estafado.

fail [feɪl] vt (candidate) reprovar; (exam) não passar em, ser reprovado em // vi (person) fracassar; (business) falir; (supply) acabar-se; (engine) falhar; (voice) falhar; (patient) enfraquecer-se; **to ~ to do sth** (neglect) deixar de fazer algo; (be unable) não poder fazer algo; **without ~** sem falta; **~ing** n defeito // prep na/à falta de; **~ure** ['feɪljə*] n fracasso; (person) fracassado; (mechanical etc) falha.

faint [feɪnt] adj fraco; (recollection) vago; (mark) indistinto; (dizzy) tonto // n desmaio // vi desmaiar; **~-hearted** adj pusilânime; **~ly** adv indistintamente, vagamente; **~ness** n fraqueza.

fair [fɛə*] adj justo; (colour) louro, claro; (weather) bom; (good enough) suficiente; (sizeable) considerável // adv (play) limpo // n feira; (funfair) parque m de diversões; **~ly** adv (justly) com justiça; (equally) com imparcialidade; (quite) bastante; **~ness** n justiça; (impartiality) imparcialidade f.

fairy ['fɛərɪ] n fada; **~ tale** n conto de fadas.

faith [feɪθ] n fé f; (trust) confiança; (sect) religião f; **~ful** adj fiel; **~fully** adv fielmente; **yours ~fully** atenciosamente.

fake [feɪk] n (painting etc) falsificação f; (person) impostor(a) m/f // adj falso // vt

fingir; (painting etc) falsificar; **his illness is a ~** sua doença é fingimento or um embuste.

falcon ['fɔːlkən] n falcão m.

fall [fɔːl] n queda; (US: autumn) outono // vi, pt fell, pp fallen ['fɔːlən] cair; (price) baixar; **~s** npl (waterfall) cascata, queda d'água; **to ~ flat** vi (on one's face) cair de cara no chão; (plan) falhar; **to ~ back** vi retroceder; **to ~ back on** vt fus (remedy etc) recorrer a; **to ~ backwards** vi cair de costas; **to ~ behind** vi ficar para trás; **to ~ down** vi (person) cair; (building) desabar; (hopes) cair por terra; **to ~ for** vt fus (trick) deixar-se enganar por; (person) enamorar-se de; **to ~ in** vi (roof) ruir; (MIL) alinhar-se; **to ~ off** vi cair; (diminish) declinar, diminuir; **to ~ out** vi (friends etc) brigar; (MIL) sair da fila; **to ~ through** vi (plan, project) falhar, fracassar.

fallacy ['fæləsɪ] n (error) erro; (lie) mentira, falácia.

fallible ['fæləbl] adj falível.

fallout ['fɔːlaʊt] n chuva radioativa (Pt: -ct-); **~ shelter** n refúgio contra chuva radioa(c)tiva.

false [fɔːls] adj (gen) falso; (hair, teeth etc) postiço; (disloyal) desleal, traidor(a); **~hood** n (lie) mentira; (falseness) falsidade f; **~ly** adv falsamente; (accuse) com falsidade; **~ teeth** npl dentadura postiça sg.

falter ['fɔːltə*] vi vacilar.

fame [feɪm] n fama.

familiar [fə'mɪlɪə*] adj familiar; (well-known) conhecido; (tone) íntimo; **to be ~ with** (subject) estar familiarizado com; **~ity** [fəmɪlɪ'ærɪtɪ] n familiaridade f; **~ize** [fə'mɪlɪəraɪz] vr: **to ~ize o.s. with** familiarizar-se com.

family ['fæmɪlɪ] n família; **~ business** n negócio familiar; **~ doctor** n médico da família.

famine ['fæmɪn] n fome f.

famished ['fæmɪʃt] adj faminto.

famous ['feɪməs] adj famoso, célebre; **~ly** adv (get on) maravilhosamente.

fan [fæn] n leque m; (ELEC) ventilador m; (person) fã (Pt: fan) m/f; (SPORT) torcedor(a) m/f (Br), adepto (Pt) // vt abanar; (fire, quarrel) atiçar; **to ~ out** vi espalhar-se.

fanatic [fə'nætɪk] n fanático/a; **~al** adj fanático.

fan belt ['fænbelt] n correia do ventilador (Br), correia da ventoinha (Pt).

fanciful ['fænsɪful] adj (gen) fantástico; (imaginary) imaginário.

fancy ['fænsɪ] n (whim) capricho; (taste) inclinação f, gosto; (imagination) imaginação f // adj (decorative) ornamental; (luxury) luxuoso; (as decoration) como decoração // vt (feel like, want) desejar, querer; (imagine) imaginar; (think) crer; **to take a ~ to**

tomar gosto por; **it took** *or* **caught my** ~ **gostei disso; to** ~ **that...** imaginar que...; **he fancies her** ele gosta dela; ~ **dress** *n* fantasia; ~**-dress ball** *n* baile *m* à fantasia.

fang [fæŋ] *n* presa.

fantastic [fæn'tæstɪk] *adj* fantástico.

fantasy ['fæntəzɪ] *n* fantasia.

far [fɑ:*] *adj* (*distant*) distante, longe // *adv* (*also* ~ **away,** ~ **off**) longe; ~ **better** muito melhor; ~ **from** longe de; **by** ~ **de** longe; **go as** ~ **as the farm** vá até a (*Pt*: à) fazenda; **as** ~ **as I know** que eu saiba; **how** ~ **?** até onde?; (*fig*) até que ponto?; **the F**~ **East** O Extremo Oriente; ~**away** *adj* remoto, distante.

farce [fɑ:s] *n* farsa; **farcical** *adj* farsante.

fare [fɛə*] *n* (*on trains, buses*) preço (da passagem); (*in taxi*: *cost*) tarifa; (: *passenger*) passageiro; (*food*) comida.

farewell [fɛə'wɛl] *excl, n* adeus *m*.

farm [fɑ:m] *n* fazenda (*Br*), quinta (*Pt*) // *vt* cultivar; ~**er** *n* fazendeiro, agricultor *m*; ~**hand** *n* lavrador *m*, trabalhador *m* rural; ~**house** *n* casa da fazenda (*Br*), casa da quinta (*Pt*); ~**ing** *n* (*gen*) agricultura; (*tilling*) cultura; ~**land** *n* terra de cultivo; ~ **worker** *n* = ~**hand**; ~**yard** *n* curral *m*.

far-sighted ['fɑ:'saɪtɪd] *adj* previdente.

fart [fɑ:t] (*col!*) *n* peido // *vi* soltar um peido.

farther ['fɑ:ðə*] *adv* mais distante, mais afastado.

farthest ['fɑ:ðɪst] *superlative of* **far.**

fascinate ['fæsɪneɪt] *vt* fascinar; **fascination** [-'neɪʃən] *n* fascinação *f*.

fascism ['fæʃɪzəm] *n* fascismo; **fascist** [-ɪst] *adj, n* fascista *m/f*.

fashion ['fæʃən] *n* moda; (*manner*) maneira // *vt* amoldar; **in** ~ na moda; **out of** ~ fora da moda; ~**able** *adj* na moda, elegante; ~ **show** *n* desfile *m* de modas.

fast [fɑ:st] *adj* rápido; (*dye, colour*) firme, permanente; (*clock*): **to be** ~ estar adiantado; ~ **asleep** profundamente adormecido // *adv* rapidamente, depressa; (*stuck, held*) firmemente // *n* jejum *m* // *vi* jejuar.

fasten ['fɑ:sn] *vt* fixar, prender; (*coat*) fechar; (*belt*) apertar, atar // *vi* prender-se, fixar-se; ~**er,** ~**ing** *n* (*gen*) presilha, fecho; (*of door etc*) fechadura; **zip** ~ *m* fecho ecler (*Pt*: éclair).

fastidious [fæs'tɪdɪəs] *adj* (*fussy*) meticuloso; (*demanding*) exigente.

fat [fæt] *adj* gordo; (*meat*) com muita gordura; (*greasy*) gorduroso // *n* (*on person*) gordura; (*lard*) banha, gordura.

fatal ['feɪtl] *adj* (*gen*) fatal; (*injury*) mortal; (*consequence*) funesto; ~**ism** *n* fatalismo; ~**ity** [fə'tælɪtɪ] *n* (*road death etc*) vítima *m/f*; ~**ly** *adv*: ~**ly injured** mortalmente ferido.

fate [feɪt] *n* destino; (*of person*) sorte *f*; ~**ful** *adj* fatídico.

father ['fɑ:ðə*] *n* pai *m*; ~**hood** *n* paternidade *f*; ~**-in-law** *n* sogro; ~**ly** *adj* paternal.

fathom ['fæðəm] *n* braça // *vt* (*NAUT*) sondar; (*unravel*) penetrar, deslindar; (*understand*) compreender.

fatigue [fə'ti:g] *n* fatiga, cansaço.

fatten ['fætn] *vt/i* engordar.

fatty ['fætɪ] *adj* (*food*) gorduroso // *n* (*fam*) gorducho/a.

faucet ['fɔ:sɪt] *n* (*US*) torneira.

fault [fɔ:lt] *n* (*error*) defeito, falta; (*blame*) culpa; (*defect*: *in character*) defeito; (*in manufacture*) imperfeição *f*; (*GEO*) falha // *vt* criticar; **it's my** ~ é minha culpa; **to find** ~ **with** criticar, queixar-se de; **at** ~ culpado; ~**less** *adj* (*action*) impecável; (*person*) irrepreensível; ~**y** *adj* imperfeito, defeituoso.

fauna ['fɔ:nə] *n* fauna.

faux pas ['fəu'pɑ:] *n* passo em falso; (*gaffe*) gafe *f*.

favour, favor (*US*) ['feɪvə*] *n* favor *m*; (*support*) apoio; (*approval*) aprovação *f* // *vt* (*proposition*) favorecer, aprovar; (*person etc*) favorecer; (*assist*) auxiliar; **to ask a** ~ **of** pedir um favor a; **to do sb a** ~ fazer favor a alguém; **to find** ~ **with** cair nas boas graças de; **in** ~ **of** em favor de; ~**able** *adj* favorável; ~**ite** [-rɪt] *adj,* *n* favorito; ~**itism** *n* favoritismo.

fawn [fɔ:n] *n* cervo novo, cervato // *adj* (*also:* ~**-coloured**) castanho-claro.

fear [fɪə*] *n* medo, temor *m* // *vt* ter medo de, temer; **for** ~ **of** com medo de; ~**ful** *adj* medonho, terrível; (*cowardly*) medroso; (*awful*) terrível; ~**less** *adj* (*gen*) sem medo, intrépido; (*bold*) audaz.

feasible ['fi:zəbl] *adj* praticável, factível.

feast [fi:st] *n* banquete *m*; (*REL*: *also*: ~ **day**) festa // *vt/i* banquetear-se.

feat [fi:t] *n* façanha, feito.

feather ['fɛðə*] *n* pena; ~**-weight** *n* (*BOXING*) peso-pena *m*.

feature ['fi:tʃə*] *n* (*gen*) característica; (*ANAT*) feição, traço; (*article*) artigo // *vt* (*subj*: *film*) apresentar // *vi* figurar; ~**s** *npl* (*of face*) feições *fpl*; ~ **film** *n* filme *m* de longa metragem.

February ['fɛbruərɪ] *n* fevereiro (*Pt*: F-).

fed [fɛd] *pt, pp of* **feed.**

federal ['fɛdərəl] *adj* federal; **federation** [-'reɪʃən] *n* federação *f*.

fed-up [fɛd'ʌp] *adj*: **to be** ~ estar (de saco) cheio (*Br*), estar farto (*Pt*).

fee [fi:] *n* taxa (*Br*), propina (*Pt*); (*school*) matrícula; (*of club*) jóia; (*of doctor, lawyer*) honorários *mpl*.

feeble ['fi:bl] *adj* fraco, débil; ~**-minded** *adj* imbecil.

feed [fi:d] *n* (*gen*) comida; (*of baby*) alimento infantil; (*of animal*) ração *f* // *vt, pt, pp* **fed** (*gen*) alimentar; (*baby*: *breastfeed*) amamentar; (*animal*) dar de comer a; (*data, information*): **to** ~ **into** introduzir em; **to** ~ **on** *vt fus* alimentar-se de; ~**ing bottle** *n* mamadeira.

feel [fi:l] n (sensation) sensação f; (sense of touch) tato (Pt: -ct-) // vt, pt, pp **felt** tocar, apalpar; (cold, pain etc) sentir; (think, believe) crer, acreditar; **to ~ hungry/cold** ter fome/frio (Pt); estar com fome/frio (Br); **to ~ lonely/better** sentir-se só/melhor; **it ~s soft** é macio; **to ~ like** (want) querer; **to ~ about** or **around** apalpar, tatear (Pt: -ct-); **~er** n (of insect) antena; **to put out ~ers** (fig) sondar opiniões; **~ing** n (gen) sensação f; (foreboding) pressentimento; (opinion) opinião f; (emotion) sentimento.

feet [fi:t] pl of **foot**.

feign [feɪn] vt fingir.

feline ['fi:laɪn] adj felino.

fell [fɛl] pt of **fall** // vt (tree) lançar por terra, derrubar.

fellow ['fɛləu] n (gen) camarada m/f; (fam) cara m (Br), tipo (Pt); (of learned society) membro; **~ students** colegas m/fpl de curso; **~ citizen** n concidadão/dã m/f; **~ countryman** n compatriota m/f; **~ men** npl semelhantes mpl; **~ship** n amizade f; (grant) bolsa de estudo.

felony ['fɛlənɪ] n crime m.

felt [fɛlt] pt, pp of **feel** // n feltro; **~-tip pen** n caneta pilot ® (Br), caneta de feltro (Pt).

female ['fi:meɪl] n (woman) mulher f; (ZOOL) fêmea // adj feminino.

feminine ['fɛmɪnɪn] adj feminino.

feminist ['fɛmɪnɪst] n feminista.

fence [fɛns] n cerca // vt (also: ~ **in**) cercar // vi esgrimir; **fencing** n (sport) esgrima.

fend [fɛnd] vi: **to ~ for o.s.** defender-se sozinho.

fender ['fɛndə*] n guarda-fogo m; (US: AUT) pára-choque m; (: RAIL) limpa-trilhos m inv.

ferment [fə'mɛnt] vi fermentar // n ['fə:mɛnt] (fig) agitação f; **~ation** [-'teɪʃən] n fermentação f.

fern [fə:n] n samambaia (Br), feto (Pt).

ferocious [fə'rəuʃəs] adj feroz; **ferocity** [-'rɔsɪtɪ] n ferocidade f.

ferret ['fɛrɪt] n furão m // vt: **to ~ out** descobrir, desentocar.

ferry ['fɛrɪ] n (small) barco (de travessia); (ship) barca // vt transportar em barca.

fertile ['fə:taɪl] adj fértil; (BIOL) fecundo; **fertility** [fə'tɪlɪtɪ] n fertilidade f, fecundidade f; **fertilize** ['fə:tɪlaɪz] vt fertilizar, fecundar; (AGR) adubar; **fertilizer** n adubo, fertilizante m.

fervent ['fə:vənt] adj ardente, apaixonado.

fester ['fɛstə*] vi inflamar-se.

festival ['fɛstɪvəl] n (REL) festa; (ART, MUS) festival m.

festive ['fɛstɪv] adj festivo; **the ~ season** (Christmas) a época do Natal.

festivities [fɛs'tɪvɪtɪz] npl festas fpl, festividades fpl.

fetch [fɛtʃ] vt ir buscar, trazer; (sell for) alcançar.

fetching ['fɛtʃɪŋ] adj atraente.

fête [feɪt] n festa.

fetish ['fɛtɪʃ] n fetiche m.

fetters ['fɛtəz] npl grilhões mpl.

feud [fju:d] n (hostility) inimizade f; (quarrel) disputa, rixa.

feudal ['fju:dl] adj feudal; **~ism** n feudalismo.

fever ['fi:və*] n febre f; **~ish** adj febril.

few [fju:] adj (not many) poucos; (some) alguns; **a ~** adj uns poucos // pron alguns; **~er** adj menos; **~est** adj os/as menos.

fiancé [fɪ'ã:ŋseɪ] n noivo; **~e** n noiva.

fiasco [fɪ'æskəu] n fiasco.

fibre, fiber (US) ['faɪbə*] n fibra; **~-glass** n fibra de vidro.

fickle ['fɪkl] adj inconstante.

fiction ['fɪkʃən] n (gen) ficção f; **~al** adj de ficção; **fictitious** [fɪk'tɪʃəs] adj fictício.

fiddle ['fɪdl] n (MUS) violino; (cheating) fraude f, embuste m; (swindle) trapaça // vt (accounts) falsificar; **to ~ with** vt fus brincar com; **fiddler** n violinista m/f.

fidelity [fɪ'dɛlɪtɪ] n fidelidade f.

fidget ['fɪdʒɪt] vi estar irrequieto; **~y** adj inquieto, nervoso.

field [fi:ld] n (gen, ELEC) campo; (fig) esfera, especialidade f; (competitors) competidores mpl; (entrants) concorrentes mpl; **~ glasses** npl binóculo msg; **~ marshal** n marechal-de-campo m; **~work** n trabalho de campo.

fiend [fi:nd] n demônio; **~ish** adj diabólico.

fierce [fɪəs] adj feroz; (wind, attack) violento; (heat) intenso; (fighting, enemy) feroz, violento.

fiery ['faɪərɪ] adj (burning) ardente; (temperament) apaixonado.

fifteen [fɪf'ti:n] num quinze.

fifth [fɪfθ] adj, n quinto.

fiftieth ['fɪftɪɪθ] adj qüinquagésimo.

fifty ['fɪftɪ] num cinqüenta.

fig [fɪg] n figo.

fight [faɪt] n (gen) briga; (MIL) combate m; (struggle) luta // (vb: pt, pp **fought**) vt lutar contra; (cancer, alcoholism) combater // vi brigar, lutar; **~er** n combatente m/f; (fig) lutador(a) m/f; (plane) caça m; **~ing** n (gen) luta, briga; (battle) batalha.

figment ['fɪgmənt] n: **a ~ of the imagination** um produto da imaginação.

figurative ['fɪgjurətɪv] adj figurado.

figure ['fɪgə*] n (DRAWING, MATH) figura, desenho; (number, cipher) número, cifra; (outline) forma; (of woman) corpo // vt (esp US) imaginar // vi (appear) figurar; **to ~ out** vt (understand) compreender; **~head** n (NAUT) carranca de proa; (fig) chefe m nominal; **~ skating** n movimentos mpl de patinação.

file [faɪl] n (tool) lixa; (dossier) dossiê m,

pasta; (*folder*) pasta de papéis; (*row*) fila, coluna // *vt* lixar; (*papers*) arquivar; (*LAW: claim*) apresentar, dar entrada em; (*store*) arquivar; **to ~ in/out** *vi* entrar/sair em fila; **to ~ past** *vt fus* desfilar em frente de/ante; **filing** *n* arquivamento; **filing cabinet** *n* fichário, arquivo.

fill [fɪl] *vt* encher // *n*: **to eat one's ~** encher-se, fartar-se de comer; **to ~ in** *vt* preencher; **to ~ up** *vt* encher (até a borda) // *vi* (*AUT*) abastecer o carro.

fillet ['fɪlɪt] *n* filete *m*, filé *m*.

filling ['fɪlɪŋ] *n* (*CULIN*) recheio; (*for tooth*) obturação *f* (*Br*), chumbo (*Pt*); **~ station** *n* posto de gasolina.

film [fɪlm] *n* filme *m* // *vt* (*scene*) rodar, filmar // *vi* filmar; **~ star** *n* astro, estrela de cinema.

filter ['fɪltə*] *n* filtro // *vt* filtrar; **~ tip** *n* filtro // *adj* com filtro.

filth [fɪlθ] *n* sujeira (*Br*), sujidade *f* (*Pt*); **~y** *adj* sujo; (*language*) indecente, obsceno.

fin [fɪn] *n* (*gen*) barbatana.

final ['faɪnl] *adj* (*last*) final, último; (*definitive*) definitivo // *n* (*SPORT*) final *f*; **~s** *npl* (*SCOL*) exames *mpl* finais.

finale [fɪ'nɑːlɪ] *n* final *m*.

final: ~ist *n* (*SPORT*) finalista *m/f*; **~ize** *vt* concluir, completar; **~ly** *adv* (*lastly*) finalmente, por fim; (*eventually*) por fim; (*irrevocably*) definitivamente.

finance [faɪ'næns] *n* (*money*) fundos *mpl*; **~s** *npl* finanças *fpl* // *vt* financiar; **financial** [-'nænʃəl] *adj* financeiro; (*economic*) econômico; **financier** *n* (*gen*) financista *m/f*; (*investor*) investidor/a *m/f*.

find [faɪnd], *pt*, *pp* **found** *vt* (*gen*) encontrar, achar; (*come upon*) descobrir // *n* achado, descoberta; **to ~ sb guilty** (*LAW*) declarar alguém culpado; **to ~ out** *vt* descobrir; **~ings** *npl* (*LAW*) veredito *sg*, decisão *fsg*; (*of report*) recomendações *fpl*.

fine [faɪn] *adj* (*delicate*) fino; (*good*) bom/boa; (*small, thin*) delgado; (*beautiful*) bonito // *adv* (*well*) bem // *n* (*LAW*) multa // *vt* (*LAW*) multar; **to be ~** (*weather*) estar bom; **~ arts** *npl* belas artes *fpl*.

finery ['faɪnərɪ] *n* enfeites *mpl*.

finesse [fɪ'nɛs] *n* sutileza (*Pt*: -bt-).

finger ['fɪŋɡə*] *n* dedo // *vt* (*touch*) manusear; (*MUS*) dedilhar; **little/index ~** dedo mínimo/indicador; **~nail** *n* unha; **~print** *n* impressão *f* digital; **~tip** *n* ponta do dedo.

finicky ['fɪnɪkɪ] *adj* (*fussy*) afetado (*Pt*: -ct-), meticuloso.

finish ['fɪnɪʃ] *n* (*end*) fim *m*; (*goal*) remate *m*; (*polish etc*) polimento // *vt/i* terminar, concluir; **to ~ off** *vt* acabar; (*kill*) liquidar; **to ~ third** chegar no terceiro lugar; **~ing line** *n* linha de chegada, meta.

finite ['faɪnaɪt] *adj* finito.

Finland ['fɪnlənd] *n* Finlândia.

Finn [fɪn] *n* finlandês/esa *m/f*; **~ish** *adj* finlandês/esa // *n* (*LING*) finlandês *m*.

fiord [fjɔːd] *n* fiorde *m*.

fir [fɜː*] *n* abeto.

fire ['faɪə*] *n* (*gen*) fogo; (*accidental*) incêndio // *vt* (*gun*) disparar; (*set fire to*) incendiar; (*excite*) exaltar; (*interest*) despertar; (*dismiss*) despedir // *vi* incendiar-se; **on ~** em chamas; **~ alarm** *n* alarme *m* de incêndio; **~arm** *n* arma de fogo; **~ brigade** *n* (corpo de) bombeiros *mpl*; **~ engine** *n* carro de bombeiro; **~ escape** *n* escada de incêndio; **~ extinguisher** *n* extintor *m* de incêndio; **~man** *n* bombeiro; **~place** *n* lareira; **~proof** *adj* à prova de fogo; **~side** *n* lugar *m* junto à lareira; **~ station** *n* quartel *m* do corpo de bombeiros; **~wood** *n* lenha; **~works** *npl* fogos *mpl* de artifício.

firing ['faɪərɪŋ] *n* (*MIL*) tiros *mpl*, tiroteio; **~ squad** *n* pelotão *m* de fuzilamento.

firm [fɜːm] *adj* firme // *n* firma; **~ly** *adv* firmemente; **~ness** *n* firmeza.

first [fɜːst] *adj* primeiro // *adv* (*before others*) primeiro; (*when listing reasons etc*) em primeiro lugar // *n* (*person: in race*) primeiro/a; (*AUT*) primeira; **at ~** a/no princípio; **~ of all** antes de tudo, antes de mais nada; **~-aid kit** *n* estojo de pronto socorro; **~-class** *adj* de primeira classe; **~-hand** *adj* de primeira mão; **~ly** *adv* primeiramente, em primeiro lugar; **~ name** *n* primeiro nome *m*; **~-rate** *adj* de primeira categoria.

fir tree *n* abeto.

fiscal ['fɪskəl] *adj* fiscal.

fish [fɪʃ] *n*, *pl inv* peixe *m* // *vt/i* pescar; **to go ~ing** ir pescar; **~erman** *n* pescador *m*; **~ery** *n* pescaria; **~ing boat** *n* barco de pesca; **~ing line** *n* linha de pesca; **~ing rod** *n* vara (de pesca); **~ing tackle** *n* apetrechos *mpl* (de pesca); **~ market** *n* mercado de peixe; **~monger** *n* peixeiro; **~monger's (shop)** *n* peixaria; **~y** *adj* (*fig*) suspeito.

fission ['fɪʃən] *n* fissão *f*.

fissure ['fɪʃə*] *n* fenda, fissura.

fist [fɪst] *n* punho.

fit [fɪt] *adj* (*MED, SPORT*) em (boa) forma; (*proper*) adequado, apropriado // *vt* (*clothes*) caber em; (*try on: clothes*) experimentar, provar; (*facts*) enquadrar-se *or* condizer com; (*accommodate*) ajustar, adaptar; (*correspond exactly*) encaixar em // *vi* (*clothes*) servir; (*in space, gap*) caber; (*correspond*) encaixar-se // *n* (*MED*) ataque *m*; **~ to bom** para; **~ for** adequado para; **this dress is a good ~** este vestido tem um bom corte; **to ~ in** *vi* (*gen*) encaixar-se; (*fig: person*) dar-se bem (com todos); **to ~ out** (*also: ~ up*) *vt* equipar; **~ful** *adj* espasmódico, intermitente; **~ment** *n* móvel *m*; **~ness** *n* (*MED*) saúde *f*, boa forma; (*of remark*) conveniência; **~ter** *n* ajustador *m*, montador *m*; **~ting** *adj* próprio, apropriado // n (of dress) prova; ~tings npl instalações fpl, acessórios mpl.

five [faiv] num cinco; **fiver** n (Brit: col) nota de cinco libras.

fix [fiks] vt (secure) fixar, colocar; (arrange) arranjar; (mend) consertar // n: **to be in a** ~ estar em apuros; ~**ed** [fikst] adj (prices etc) fixo; ~**ture** ['fikstʃə*] n coisa fixa; (furniture) móvel m fixo; (SPORT) desafio, encontro.

fizz [fiz] vi efervescer.

fizzle ['fizl] ~ **out** vi fracassar, falhar.

fizzy ['fizi] adj (drink) gasoso; (gen) efervescente.

fjord [fjɔːd] = **fiord**.

flabbergasted ['flæbəgaːstid] adj pasmado.

flabby ['flæbi] adj frouxo; (fat) fláccido.

flag [flæg] n bandeira; (stone) laje f // vi acabar-se, descair; **to** ~ **sb down** fazer sinais a alguém para que pare; ~**pole** n mastro de bandeira.

flagrant ['fleigrənt] adj flagrante.

flair [flɛə*] n aptidão f, inclinação f especial.

flake [fleik] n (of rust, paint) lasca; (of snow, soap powder) floco // vi (also: ~ **off**) lascar, descamar-se.

flamboyant [flæm'bɔiənt] adj (dress) espalhafatoso; (person) extravagante.

flame [fleim] n chama.

flamingo [flə'miŋgəu] n flamingo.

flammable ['flæməbl] adj inflamável.

flan [flæn] n torta.

flank [flæŋk] n flanco; (of person) lado // vt ladear.

flannel ['flænl] n (also: **face** ~) pano; (fabric) flanela; (col) disparate m; ~**s** npl calças fpl de flanela.

flap [flæp] n (of pocket) aba; (of envelope) dobra; (of table) aba; (wing movement) bater m // vt (wings) bater // vi (sail, flag) ondular.

flare [flɛə*] n fogacho, chama; (MIL) sinal m luminoso; (in skirt etc) folga; **to** ~ **up** vi chamejar; (fig: person) encolerizar-se; (: revolt) irromper.

flash [flæʃ] n relâmpago; (also: **news** ~) notícias fpl de última hora; (PHOT) flash m // vt (light, headlights) piscar; (torch) acender // vi brilhar, relampejar; **in a** ~ num instante; **he** ~**ed by** or **past** passou como um raio; ~**back** n flashback m; ~ **bulb** n lâmpada de flash; ~**er** n (AUT) pisca-pisca m.

flashy ['flæʃi] adj (pej) espalhafatoso.

flask [flɑːsk] n frasco; (also: **vacuum** ~) garrafa térmica.

flat [flæt] adj chato, plano; (smooth) liso; (tyre) vazio; (beer) choco; (MUS) desafinado // n (apartment) apartamento; (MUS) bemol m; (AUT) pneu m furado; ~**ly** adv terminantemente; ~**ness** n (of land) chateza, lisura; ~**ten** vt (also: ~**ten out**) aplanar; (smooth out) alisar; (demolish) derrubar; (col) esmagar.

flatter ['flætə*] vt adular, lisonjear; ~**er** n adulador(a) m/f; ~**ing** adj lisonjeiro; ~**y** n bajulação f.

flatulence ['flætjuləns] n flatulência.

flaunt [flɔːnt] vt ostentar, pavonear.

flavour, flavor (US) ['fleivə*] n sabor m, gosto // vt condimentar, aromatizar; ~**ed with** com sabor de; ~**ing** n condimento.

flaw [flɔː] n defeito; ~**less** adj impecável.

flax [flæks] n linho; ~**en** adj de cor de linho.

flea [fliː] n pulga; ~**pit** n (cinema) pulgueiro.

flee [fliː], pt, pp **fled** [fled] vt fugir de, abandonar // vi desaparecer, fugir.

fleece [fliːs] n velo; (wool) lã f // vt (col) pelar, depenar.

fleet [fliːt] n (gen, of lorries etc) frota; (of ships) esquadra.

fleeting ['fliːtiŋ] adj fugaz.

Flemish ['flɛmiʃ] adj flamengo.

flesh [flɛʃ] n carne f; (of fruit) polpa; **of** ~ **and blood** de carne e osso.

flew [fluː] pt of **fly**.

flex [flɛks] n fio // vt (muscles) flexionar; ~**ibility** [-'biliti] n flexibilidade f; ~**ible** adj flexível.

flick [flik] n pancada leve; (with finger) piparote m; (with whip) chicotada // vt dar pancada leve em; **to** ~ **through** vt fus folhear.

flicker ['flikə*] vi (light) tremeluzir; (flame) tremular // n tremulação f.

flier ['flaiə*] n voador(a) m/f.

flight [flait] n vôo m; (escape) fuga; (also: ~ **of steps**) lance m; **to take** ~ fugir, pôr-se em fuga; **to put to** ~ pôr em fuga; ~ **deck** n (AVIAT) cabine f do piloto.

flimsy ['flimzi] adj (thin) delgado, franzino; (weak) débil.

flinch [flintʃ] vi acovardar-se.

fling [fliŋ], pt, pp **flung** vt lançar.

flint [flint] n pederneira; (in lighter) pedra.

flip [flip] vt (turn over) dar a volta em; (throw) jogar; **to** ~ **a coin** tirar cara ou coroa.

flippant ['flipənt] adj petulante, pouco sério.

flirt [fləːt] vi flertar // n namorador(a) m/f, paquerador(a) m/f; ~**ation** [-'teiʃən] n namoro, paquera.

flit [flit] vi esvoaçar.

float [fləut] n bóia; (in procession) carro alegórico // vi flutuar; (swimmer) boiar // vt (gen) fazer flutuar; (company) lançar.

flock [flɔk] n (of sheep) rebanho; (of birds) bando; (of people) multidão f.

flog [flɔg] vt açoitar; (col) vender.

flood [flʌd] n enchente f, inundação f; (of words, tears etc) torrente m // vt inundar; ~**ing** n inundação f; ~**light** n refletor (Pt: -ct-) m, holofote m.

floor [flɔː*] n chão m; (storey) andar m;

(of sea) fundo; (dance ~) pista de dança // vt (fig) confundir, pasmar; **ground ~** (Brit), **first ~** (US) andar térreo (Br), rés-do-chão m (Pt); **first ~** (Brit), **second ~** (US) primeiro andar; ~**board** n tábua de assoalho.

flop [flɔp] n fracasso // vi (fail) fracassar.

floppy ['flɔpi] adj frouxo.

flora ['flɔːrə] n flora; **floral** ['flɔːrl] adj floral.

florid ['flɔrɪd] adj (style) florido.

florist ['flɔrɪst] n florista m/f; ~'s (shop) n florista, floricultura.

flounce [flauns] n babado, debrum m; to ~ **out** vi sair indignada.

flounder ['flaundə*] vi atrapalhar-se.

flour ['flauə*] n farinha.

flourish ['flʌrɪʃ] vi florescer; ~**ing** adj próspero.

flout [flaut] vt (law) desrespeitar; (offer) desprezar.

flow [fləu] n (movement) fluxo, circulação f; (direction) curso; (tide) corrente f // vi correr, fluir; (blood) circular.

flower ['flauə*] n flor f // vi florescer, florir; ~ **bed** n canteiro; ~**pot** n vaso; ~**y** adj florido.

flown [fləun] pp of **fly**.

flu [fluː] n (col) gripe f.

fluctuate ['flʌktjueɪt] vi flutuar; **fluctuation** [-'eɪʃən] n flutuação f.

fluent ['fluːənt] adj (speech) fluente; he speaks ~ French, he's ~ in French ele fala francês fluentemente; ~**ly** adv fluentemente.

fluff [flʌf] n felpa, penugem f; ~**y** adj macio, fofo.

fluid ['fluːɪd] adj, n fluido.

fluke [fluːk] n (col) sorte f.

flung [flʌŋ] pt, pp of **fling**.

fluorescent [fluə'resnt] adj fluorescente.

fluoride ['fluəraɪd] n fluoreto.

flurry ['flʌrɪ] n (of snow) lufada; (haste) agitação f; ~ **of activity** muita atividade (Pt: -ct-).

flush [flʌʃ] n (on face) rubor m; (plenty) abundância f // vt lavar com água // vi ruborizar-se // adj: ~ **with** rente com; to ~ **the toilet** dar descarga; ~**ed** adj ruborizado, corado.

flustered ['flʌstəd] adj atrapalhado.

flute [fluːt] n flauta.

flutter ['flʌtə*] n agitação f; (of wings) bater m de asas; (fam: bet) aposta // vi agitar-se, esvoaçar.

flux [flʌks] n fluxo; **in a state of ~** mudando continuamente.

fly [flaɪ] n (insect) mosca; (on trousers: also: **flies**) braguilha // (vb: pt **flew**, pp **flown**) vt (gen) fazer voar; (plane) pilotar; (cargo) transportar (de avião); (distances) percorrer // vi voar; (passengers) ir de avião; (escape) fugir; (flag) hastear; to **let ~** descarregar, desafogar; ~**ing** n (activity) voar m // adj: ~**ing visit** visita de médico; **with** ~**ing colours** brilhantemente; ~**ing**

saucer n disco voador; ~**over** n (Brit: bridge) viaduto; ~**past** n desfile m aéreo; ~**sheet** n (for tent) duplo teto (Pt: -ct-).

foal [fəul] n potro.

foam [fəum] n espuma // vi espumar; ~ **rubber** n espuma de borracha.

fob [fɔb] vt: to ~ **sb off** oferecer o falso como verdadeiro a alguém.

focal ['fəukəl] adj focal.

focus ['fəukəs], pl ~**es** n foco // vt (field glasses etc) enfocar; to ~ **on** enfocar, focalizar; **in/out of** ~ enfocado/ desenfocado or em foco/fora de foco.

fodder ['fɔdə*] n forragem f.

foe [fəu] n inimigo.

foetus ['fiːtəs] n feto.

fog [fɔg] n nevoeiro; ~**gy** adj: **it's ~gy** está nevoento.

foil [fɔɪl] vt frustrar // n folha metálica; (also: **kitchen ~**) folha or papel m de alumínio; (FENCING) florete m.

fold [fəuld] n (bend, crease) dobra, vinco, prega; (of skin) ruga; (AGR) redil m, curral m // vt dobrar; to ~ **up** vi (map etc) dobrar; (business) abrir falência // vt (map etc) dobrar; ~**er** n (for papers) pasta; (brochure) folheto; ~**ing** adj (chair, bed) dobrável.

foliage ['fəuliːdʒ] n folhagem f.

folk [fəuk] npl gente f // adj popular, folclórico; ~**s** npl (family) família sg, parentes mpl; (people) a gente; ~**lore** ['fəuklɔː*] n folclore m; ~**song** n canção f popular or folclórica.

follow ['fɔləu] vt seguir // vi seguir; (result) resultar; he ~**ed suit** ele fez o mesmo; to ~ **up** vt (letter) responder a; (offer) levar adiante; (case) acompanhar; ~**er** n seguidor(a) m/f; (POL) partidário/a; ~**ing** adj seguinte // n séquito, adeptos mpl.

folly ['fɔlɪ] n loucura.

fond [fɔnd] adj (loving) amoroso, carinhoso; **to be ~ of** gostar de.

fondle ['fɔndl] vt acariciar.

fondness ['fɔndnɪs] n (for things) gosto, afeição f; (for people) carinho.

font [fɔnt] n pia batismal (Pt: -pt-).

food [fuːd] n comida; ~ **mixer** n batedeira; ~ **poisoning** n intoxicação f (alimentar); ~**stuffs** npl comestíveis mpl.

fool [fuːl] n tolo; (CULIN) puré m de frutas com creme // vt enganar // vi (gen: ~ **around**) brincar; (waste time) perder tempo; ~**hardy** adj temerário; ~**ish** adj bobo; (stupid) burro; (careless) imprudente; ~**proof** adj (plan etc) infalível.

foot [fut], pl **feet** n pé m; (measure) pé (= 304 mm); (of animal) pata // vt (bill) pagar; **on ~** a pé; ~**ball** n bola; (game) futebol m; ~**baller** n futebolista m; ~**brake** n freio de pé (Br), travão m de pé (Pt); ~**bridge** n passarela; ~**hills** npl contraforte msg; ~**hold** n apoio para pés; ~**ing** n (fig) posição f; **to lose**

one's ~ing escorregar; on an equal ~ing em pé de igualdade; ~lights npl ribalta sg; ~man n lacaio; ~note n nota de rodapé or ao pé da página; ~path n senda, vereda, caminho; (pavement) calçada; ~sore adj com os pés doloridos; ~step n passo; ~wear n calçados mpl.

for [fɔː*] prep (gen) para; (as, in exchange for, because of) por; (during) durante; (in spite of) apesar de // conj pois, porque; it was sold ~ 100 pesetas foi vendido por 100 pesetas; what ~? para quê?; what's it ~? para que serve?; he was away ~ 2 years esteve fora 2 anos; he went ~ the paper foi pegar o jornal; ~ sale vende-se.

forage ['fɔrɪdʒ] n forragem f.

foray ['fɔreɪ] n incursão f.

forbid [fə'bɪd], pt forbad(e) [fə'bæd], pp forbidden [fə'bɪdn] vt proibir; ~ding adj (gloomy) lúgubre; (severe) severo.

force [fɔːs] n força // vt forçar; to ~ o.s. to forçar-se a; the F~s npl Forças Armadas; in ~ em vigor; ~d [fɔːst] adj forçado; ~ful adj forçoso.

forceps ['fɔːseps] npl fórceps m inv.

forcibly ['fɔːsəblɪ] adv à força.

ford [fɔːd] n vau m // vt vadear.

forearm ['fɔːrɑːm] n antebraço.

foreboding [fɔː'bəudɪŋ] n presságio.

forecast ['fɔːkɑːst] n prognóstico // vt (irr: like cast) prognosticar.

forefathers ['fɔːfɑːðəz] npl antepassados mpl.

forefinger ['fɔːfɪŋgə*] n (dedo) indicador m.

forego = forgo.

foregone ['fɔːgɒn] adj: it's a ~ conclusion é uma conclusão inevitável.

foreground ['fɔːgraund] n primeiro plano.

forehead ['fɔrɪd] n testa.

foreign ['fɔrɪn] adj estrangeiro; (trade) exterior; ~er n estrangeiro; ~ exchange n câmbio (de moeda estrangeira); F~ Minister n Ministro das Relações Exteriores; F~ Office n Ministério das Relações Exteriores.

foreleg ['fɔːleg] n perna dianteira.

foreman ['fɔːmən] n capataz m; (in construction) contramestre m.

foremost ['fɔːməust] adj principal.

forensic [fə'rɛnsɪk] adj forense.

forerunner ['fɔːrʌnə*] n precursor(a) m/f.

foresee [fɔː'siː] (irr: like see) vt prever; ~able adj previsível.

foresight ['fɔːsaɪt] n previsão f.

forest ['fɔrɪst] n floresta.

forestall [fɔː'stɔːl] vt prevenir.

forestry ['fɔrɪstrɪ] n silvicultura.

foretaste ['fɔːteɪst] n (gen) antegosto, antegozo; (sample) amostra.

foretell [fɔː'tɛl] (irr: like tell) vt predizer, profetizar.

forever [fə'rɛvə*] adv para sempre.

foreword ['fɔːwəd] n prefácio.

forfeit ['fɔːfɪt] n prenda, perda; (fine) multa // vt perder (direito a).

forgave [fə'geɪv] pt of forgive.

forge [fɔːdʒ] n forja; (smithy) ferraria // vt (signature, money) falsificar; (metal) forjar; to ~ ahead vi avançar constantemente; forger n falsificador(a) m/f; ~ry n falsificação f.

forget [fə'gɛt], pt forgot, pp forgotten vt esquecer // vi esquecer; ~ful adj esquecido; ~fulness n (gen) esquecimento; (thoughtlessness) descuido; (oblivion) falta de memória.

forgive [fə'gɪv], pt forgave, pp forgiven vt perdoar; to ~ sb for sth perdoar algo a alguém; ~ness n perdão m.

forgo [fɔː'gəu] (irr: like go) vt (give up) renunciar a; (go without) abster-se de.

forgot [fə'gɒt] pt of forget.

forgotten [fə'gɒtn] pp of forget.

fork [fɔːk] n (for eating) garfo; (for gardening) forquilha; (of roads) bifurcação f // vi (road) bifurcar-se; to ~ out vt (col: pay) desembolsar; ~ed [fɔːkt] adj (lightning) em ziguezague; ~-lift truck n empilhadeira.

form [fɔːm] n forma; (SCOL) série f; (questionnaire) formulário // vt formar; in top ~ em plena forma.

formal ['fɔːməl] adj (offer, receipt) oficial; (person etc) cerimonioso; (occasion, dinner) formal; (dress) a rigor (Br), de cerimônia (Pt); ~ity [-'mælɪtɪ] n cerimônia; ~ities npl formalidades fpl; ~ly adv oficialmente, formalmente.

format ['fɔːmæt] n formato.

formation [fɔː'meɪʃən] n formação f.

formative ['fɔːmətɪv] adj (years) formativo.

former ['fɔːmə*] adj anterior; (earlier) antigo; (ex) ex; the ~ ... the latter ... aquele ... este ...; ~ly adv antigamente.

formidable ['fɔːmɪdəbl] adj terrível, temível.

formula ['fɔːmjulə] n fórmula.

formulate ['fɔːmjuleɪt] vt formular.

forsake [fə'seɪk], pt forsook [fə'suk], pp forsaken [fə'seɪkən] vt (gen) abandonar; (plan) renunciar a.

fort [fɔːt] n forte m.

forte ['fɔːtɪ] n forte m.

forth [fɔːθ] adv para adiante; back and ~ de cá para lá; and so ~ e assim por diante; ~coming adj próximo, que está para aparecer; (character) comunicativo; (book) a ser publicado; ~right adj franco.

fortieth ['fɔːtɪɪθ] adj quadragésimo.

fortification [fɔːtɪfɪ'keɪʃən] n fortificação f; fortify ['fɔːtɪfaɪ] vt fortalecer.

fortitude ['fɔːtɪtjuːd] n fortaleza.

fortnight ['fɔːtnaɪt] n quinzena; ~ly adj quinzenal // adv quinzenalmente.

fortress ['fɔːtrɪs] n fortaleza.

fortuitous [fɔː'tjuːɪtəs] adj fortuito.

fortunate ['fɔːtʃənɪt] adj: to be ~ ter

sorte; **it is ~ that...** é uma sorte que...; **~ly** adv afortunadamente, felizmente.

fortune ['fɔ:tʃən] n sorte f; (wealth) fortuna; **~-teller** n adivinho/a.

forty ['fɔ:tɪ] num quarenta.

forum ['fɔ:rəm] n foro.

forward ['fɔ:wəd] adj (movement) para a frente; (position) avançado; (front) dianteiro; (not shy) imodesto, presunçoso // n (SPORT) atacante m // vt (letter) remeter; (career) promover; **to move ~ avançar; ~(s)** adv para a frente.

fossil ['fɔsl] n fóssil m.

foster ['fɔstə*] vt fomentar; **~ brother** n irmão m de criação; **~ child** n filho adotivo (Pt: -pt-); **~ mother** n mãe f ado(p)tiva.

fought [fɔ:t] pt, pp of **fight**.

foul [faul] adj (gen) sujo, porco; (weather) horrível; (smell etc) nojento // n (FOOTBALL) falta // vt (dirty) sujar; (block) entupir; (football player) cometer uma falta contra; **~ play** n (SPORT) jogada suja; (LAW) crime m.

found [faund] pt, pp of **find** // vt (establish) fundar; **~ation** [-'deɪʃən] n (act) fundação f; (basis) base f; (also: **~ation cream**) creme m base; **~ations** npl (of building) alicerces mpl.

founder ['faundə*] n fundador(a) m/f // vi afundar-se.

foundry ['faundrɪ] n fundição f.

fountain ['fauntɪn] n fonte f; **~ pen** n caneta-tinteiro.

four [fɔ:*] num quatro; **on all ~s** de quatro; **~-poster** n cama com colunas; **~some** ['fɔ:səm] n grupo de quatro pessoas; **~teen** num catorze; **~teenth** adj décimo-quarto; **~th** adj quarto.

fowl [faul] n ave f (doméstica).

fox [fɔks] n raposo // vt confundir, enganar; **~trot** n foxtrote m.

foyer ['fɔɪeɪ] n vestíbulo.

fracas ['fræka:] n desordem f, rixa.

fraction ['frækʃən] n fração (Pt: -cç-) f.

fracture ['fræktʃə*] n fratura (Pt: -ct-) // vt fraturar (Pt: -ct-).

fragile ['frædʒaɪl] adj frágil.

fragment ['frægmənt] n fragmento; **~ary** adj fragmentário.

fragrance ['freɪgrəns] n fragrância; **fragrant** [-ənt] adj fragrante, perfumado.

frail [freɪl] adj (fragile) frágil, quebradiço; (weak) delicado.

frame [freɪm] n (gen) estrutura f; (body) corpo; (TECH) armação f; (of picture, door) moldura; (of spectacles: also: **~s**) armação f, aro // vt encaixilhar; (reply) formular; (fam) incriminar; **~ of mind** n estado de espírito; **~work** n armação f.

France [frɑ:ns] n França.

franchise ['fræntʃaɪz] n (POL) direito de voto, privilégio.

frank [fræŋk] adj franco // vt (letter) franquear; **~ly** adv francamente; **~ness** n franqueza.

frantic ['fræntɪk] adj frenético.

fraternal [frə'tə:nl] adj fraterno; **fraternity** [-nɪtɪ] n (club) fraternidade f; (US) clube m de estudantes; (guild) confraria; **fraternize** ['frætənaɪz] vi confraternizar.

fraud [frɔ:d] n fraude m; (person) impostor(a) m/f; **~ulent** adj fraudulento.

fraught [frɔ:t] adj: **~ with** repleto de.

fray [freɪ] n combate m, luta // vi esfiapar-se; **tempers were ~ed** estavam com os nervos em frangalhos.

freak [fri:k] n (person) anormal m/f; (event) anomalia; (thing) aberração f.

freckle ['frekl] n sarda.

free [fri:] adj (gen) livre; (not fixed) solto; (gratis) gratuito; (unoccupied) livre; (liberal) generoso // vt (prisoner etc) pôr em liberdade; (jammed object) soltar; **(of charge)** adv grátis; **~dom** ['fri:dəm] n liberdade f; **~-for-all** n quebra-quebra m; **~ kick** n (tiro) livre m; **~lancer** n free-lance m/f; **~ly** adv livremente; **~mason** n maçom m; **~ trade** n mercado livre; **~way** n (US) auto-estrada; **~wheel** vi ir em ponto morto; **~ will** n livre arbítrio; **of one's own ~ will** por sua própria vontade.

freeze [fri:z] pt **froze**, pp **frozen** vi gelar-se, congelar-se // vt gelar; (prices, food, salaries) congelar // n geada, congelamento; **freezer** n congelador m, freezer m (Br).

freezing ['fri:zɪŋ] adj gelado; **~ point** n ponto de congelamento; **3 degrees below ~** 3 graus abaixo de zero.

freight [freɪt] n (goods) carga; (money charged) frete m; **~ car** n (US) vagão m de carga.

French [frentʃ] adj francês/esa // n (LING) francês m; **the ~** os franceses; **~ fried (potatoes)** npl batatas fpl fritas; **~man/woman** n francês/esa m/f; **~ window** n porta-janela, janela de batente.

frenzy ['frenzɪ] n frenesi m.

frequency ['fri:kwənsɪ] n freqüência; **frequent** [-ənt] adj freqüente // vt [frɪ'kwent] freqüentar; **frequently** [-əntlɪ] adv freqüentemente, a miúdo.

fresco ['freskəu] n fresco.

fresh [freʃ] adj (gen) fresco; (new) novo; (water) doce; **~en** vi (wind, air) tornar-se mais forte; **to ~en up** vi (person) lavar-se, refrescar-se; **~ly** adv (newly) novamente; (recently) recentemente; **~ness** n frescura.

fret [fret] vi afligir-se.

friar ['fraɪə*] n frade m; (before name) frei m.

friction ['frɪkʃən] n fricção f.

Friday ['fraɪdɪ] n sexta-feira f.

fridge [frɪdʒ] n geladeira (Br), frigorífico (Pt).

friend [frend] n amigo; **~liness** n simpatia; **~ly** adj simpático; **~ship** n amizade f.

frieze [fri:z] n friso.

frigate ['frɪgɪt] n fragata.

fright [fraɪt] n susto; **to take ~** assustar-se; **~en** vt assustar; **~ening** adj assustador(a); **~ful** adj assustador(a), horrível; **~fully** adv terrivelmente.

frigid ['frɪdʒɪd] adj (MED) frígido, frio; **~ity** [frɪ'dʒɪdɪtɪ] n frialdade f; (MED) frigidez f.

frill [frɪl] n babado.

fringe [frɪndʒ] n franja; (edge: of forest etc) orla, margem f; **~ benefits** npl benefícios mpl adicionais.

frisky ['frɪskɪ] adj alegre, brincalhão/lhona.

fritter ['frɪtə*] n bolinho frito; **to ~ away** vt desperdiçar.

frivolous ['frɪvələs] adj frívolo.

frizzy ['frɪzɪ] adj frisado.

fro [frəu] see **to**.

frock [frɔk] n vestido.

frog [frɔg] n rã f; **~man** n homem-rã m.

frolic ['frɔlɪk] vi brincar.

from [frɔm] prep de; **~ January (on)** a partir de janeiro; **~ what he says** pelo que ele diz.

front [frʌnt] n (foremost part) parte f dianteira; (of house) fachada; (promenade: also: **sea ~**) orla marítima; (MIL, POL, METEOROLOGY) frente f; (fig: appearances) aparências fpl // adj dianteiro, da frente; **in ~ (of)** em frente (de); **~al** adj frontal; **~ door** n porta principal; **~ier** ['frʌntɪə*] n fronteira; **~ page** n primeira página; **~ room** n (Brit) salão m, sala de estar; **~-wheel drive** n tração (Pt: -cç-) f dianteira.

frost [frɔst] n (gen) geada; (visible) gelo; **~bite** n enregelamento; **~ed** adj (glass) fosco; **~y** adj (window) coberto de geada; (welcome) glacial.

froth [frɔθ] n espuma.

frown [fraun] n olhar m carrancudo, cara amarrada // vi franzir as sobrancelhas, amarrar a cara.

froze [frəuz] pt of **freeze**.

frozen ['frəuzn] pp of **freeze**.

frugal ['fru:gəl] adj frugal.

fruit [fru:t] n, pl inv fruto; (to eat) fruta; **~erer** n fruteiro; **~erer's (shop)** n fruteiro (Br), frutaria (Pt); **~ful** adj proveitoso; **~ion** [fru:'ɪʃən] n: **to come to ~** ion realizar-se; **~ machine** n caça-níqueis m inv (Br), máquina de jogo (Pt).

frustrate [frʌs'treɪt] vt frustrar; **~d** adj frustrado; **frustration** [-'treɪʃən] n frustração f.

fry [fraɪ], pt, pp **fried** vt fritar; **small ~** gente f insignificante; **~ing pan** n frigideira.

ft. abbr of **foot, feet**.

fuchsia ['fju:ʃə] n fúcsia.

fuel [fjuəl] n (for heating) combustível m; (coal) carvão m; (wood) lenha; (for propelling) carburante m; **~ oil** n óleo combustível; **~ tank** n depósito de combustível.

fugitive ['fju:dʒɪtɪv] n fugitivo.

fulfil [ful'fɪl] vt (function) cumprir com; (condition) satisfazer; (wish, desire) realizar; **~ment** n satisfação f; realização f.

full [ful] adj cheio; (fig) completo, pleno; (complete) completo; (information) detalhado // adv: **~ well** perfeitamente; **I'm ~** estou satisfeito; **~ employment** pleno emprego; **~ fare** passagem f completa; **a ~ two hours** duas horas completas; **at ~ speed** a toda a velocidade; **in ~** (reproduce, quote) integralmente; **~-length** adj (portrait) de corpo inteiro; **~ moon** n lua cheia; **~-sized** adj (portrait etc) em tamanho natural; **~ stop** n ponto (final); **~-time** adj (work) de tempo completo or integral // n (SPORT) final m; **~y** adv completamente; **~y-fledged** adj (teacher, barrister) diplomado.

fumble ['fʌmbl]: **to ~ with** vt fus atrapalhar-se com.

fume [fju:m] vi fumegar; (be angry) estar com raiva; **~s** npl gases mpl.

fumigate ['fju:mɪgeɪt] vt fumigar.

fun [fʌn] n (amusement) divertimento; (joy) alegria; **to have ~** divertir-se; **for ~** de brincadeira; **to make ~ of** vt fus fazer troça de, zombar de.

function ['fʌŋkʃən] n função f // vi funcionar; **~al** adj funcional.

fund [fʌnd] n provisão f, fundos mpl; (source, store) fonte f; **~s** npl fundos mpl.

fundamental [fʌndə'mentl] adj fundamental.

funeral ['fju:nərəl] n (burial) enterro; (ceremony) exéquias fpl; **~ service** n missa fúnebre.

funfair ['fʌnfɛə*] n parque m de diversões.

fungus ['fʌŋgəs], pl **-gi** [-gaɪ] n fungo.

funnel ['fʌnl] n funil m; (of ship) chaminé m.

funnily ['fʌnɪlɪ] adv: **~ enough** por incrível que pareça.

funny ['fʌnɪ] adj engraçado, divertido; (strange) esquisito, estranho.

fur [fə:*] n pele f; (in kettle etc) depósito, crosta; **~ coat** n casaco de peles.

furious ['fjuərɪəs] adj furioso; (effort) violento; **~ly** adv com fúria.

furlong ['fə:lɔŋ] n oitava parte de uma milha.

furlough ['fə:ləu] n (US) licença.

furnace ['fə:nɪs] n forno.

furnish ['fə:nɪʃ] vt mobilar (Pt), mobiliar (Br); (supply) fornecer; **~ings** npl mobília, equipamento.

furniture ['fə:nɪtʃə*] n mobília, móveis mpl; **piece of ~** móvel m; **~ polish** n cera de lustrar móveis.

furrier ['fʌrɪə*] n peleiro.

furrow ['fʌrəu] n sulco.

furry ['fə:rɪ] adj peludo.

further ['fə:ðə*] adj (new) novo, adicional; (place) mais longe // adv mais

adiante; (*more*) mais; (*moreover*) além disso // *vt* promover, adiantar; ~ **education** *n* educação *f* superior; ~**more** [fə:ðə'mɔ:*] *adv* além disso.
furthest ['fə:ðist] *superlative of* **far**.
furtive ['fə:tiv] *adj* furtivo.
fury ['fjuəri] *n* fúria.
fuse, fuze (*US*) [fju:z] *n* fusível *m*; (*for bomb etc*) mecha // *vt* (*metal*) fundir; (*fig*) unir // *vi* fundir-se; unir-se; (*ELEC*): **to ~ the lights** queimar as luzes; ~ **box** *n* caixa de fusíveis.
fuselage ['fju:zəla:ʒ] *n* fuselagem *f*.
fusion ['fju:ʒən] *n* fusão *f*.
fuss [fʌs] *n* (*noise*) rebuliço; (*dispute*) espalhafato; (*complaining*) protesto; (*ceremony*) cerimônias *fpl*; **to make a ~** criar caso; ~**y** *adj* (*person*) exigente, meticuloso.
futile ['fju:tail] *adj* fútil, inútil; **futility** [-'tiliti] *n* inutilidade *f*.
future ['fju:tʃə*] *adj* (*gen*) futuro; (*coming*) vindouro // *n* futuro; **futuristic** [-'ristik] *adj* futurístico.
fuzzy ['fʌzi] *adj* (*PHOT*) indistinto; (*hair*) frisado, encrespado.

G

gabble ['gæbl] *vi* tagarelar.
gable ['geibl] *n* cumeeira.
gadget ['gædʒit] *n* aparelho; (*in kitchen*) pequeno utensílio.
Gaelic ['geilik] *n* (*LING*) gaélico.
gag [gæg] *n* (*on mouth*) mordaça; (*joke*) piada // *vt* amordaçar.
gaiety ['geiiti] *n* alegria.
gaily ['geili] *adv* alegremente.
gain [gein] *n* lucro, ganho // *vt* ganhar // *vi* (*watch*) adiantar-se; **to ~ by sth** tirar proveito de algo; **to ~ on sb** aproximar-se de alguém.
gait [geit] *n* modo de andar.
gala ['gɑ:lə] *n* festa, gala.
galaxy ['gæləksi] *n* galáxia.
gale [geil] *n* (*wind*) ventania.
gallant ['gælənt] *adj* valente; (*towards ladies*) galante; ~**ry** *n* valentia; (*courtesy*) galanteria.
gall-bladder ['gɔ:lblædə*] *n* vesícula biliar.
gallery ['gæləri] *n* galeria; (*also:* **art ~**) galeria de arte.
galley ['gæli] *n* (*ship's kitchen*) cozinha; (*ship*) galé *f*.
gallon ['gæln] *n* galão *m* (4.543 *litros*).
gallop ['gæləp] *n* galope *m* // *vi* galopar.
gallows ['gæləuz] *n* forca *sg*.
gallstone ['gɔ:lstəun] *n* cálculo biliar.
gamble ['gæmbl] *n* (*risk*) risco; (*bet*) aposta // *vt*: **to ~ on** apostar em; (*fig*) confiar em // *vi* jogar, arriscar; (*COMM*) especular; **gambler** *n* jogador(a) *m/f*; **gambling** *n* jogo.
game [geim] *n* (*gen*) jogo; (*match*) encontro; (*of cards, of football*) partida; (*HUNTING*) caça // *adj* valente; (*ready*): **to**

be ~ for anything topar qualquer parada; ~ **bird** *n* ave *f* de caça; ~**keeper** *n* guarda-caça *m*.
gammon ['gæmən] *n* (*bacon*) toucinho (defumado); (*ham*) presunto.
gang [gæŋ] *n* gangue *f*, grupo; (*of workmen*) turma // *vi*: **to ~ up on sb** conspirar contra alguém.
gangrene ['gæŋgri:n] *n* gangrena.
gangster ['gæŋstə*] *n* gângster *m*.
gangway ['gæŋwei] *n* (*in theatre etc*) passagem *f*, coxia; (*on ship*) passadiço; (*on dock*) portaló *m*.
gaol [dʒeil] = **jail**.
gap [gæp] *n* brecha, fenda; (*in trees, traffic*) abertura; (*in time*) intervalo.
gape [geip] *vi* estar or ficar boquiaberto; **gaping** *adj* (*hole*) muito aberto.
garage ['gæra:ʒ] *n* garagem *f*.
garbage ['gɑ:bidʒ] *n* lixo; ~ **can** *n* (*US*) lata de lixo.
garbled ['gɑ:bld] *adj* (*distorted*) adulterado, deturpado.
garden ['gɑ:dn] *n* jardim *m*; ~**er** *n* jardineiro; ~**ing** *n* jardinagem *f*.
gargle ['gɑ:gl] *vi* gargarejar.
gargoyle ['gɑ:gɔil] *n* gárgula.
garish ['gɛəriʃ] *adj* espalhafatoso.
garland ['gɑ:lənd] *n* guirlanda.
garlic ['gɑ:lik] *n* alho.
garment ['gɑ:mənt] *n* peça de roupa.
garnish ['gɑ:niʃ] *vt* adornar; (*CULIN*) enfeitar.
garrison ['gærisn] *n* guarnição *f* // *vt* guarnecer.
garrulous ['gærjuləs] *adj* tagarela.
garter ['gɑ:tə*] *n* liga; ~ **belt** *n* cinta-liga.
gas [gæs] *n* gás *m*; (*US: gasoline*) gasolina // *vt* asfixiar com gás; ~ **cooker** *n* fogão *m* a gás; ~ **cylinder** *n* bujão *m* de gás; ~ **fire** *n* aquecedor *m* a gás.
gash [gæʃ] *n* talho; (*on face*) corte *m* // *vt* (*gen*) talhar; (*with knife*) cortar.
gasket ['gæskit] *n* (*AUT*) junta, gaxeta.
gas: ~**mask** *n* máscara antigás; ~ **meter** *n* medidor *m* de gás.
gasoline ['gæsəli:n] *n* (*US*) gasolina.
gasp [gɑ:sp] *n* arfada // *vi* arfar; (*pant*) esforçar-se para respirar; **to ~ out** *vt* (*say*) dizer com voz entrecortada.
gas: ~ **ring** *n* boca de gás; ~ **station** *n* (*US*) posto de gasolina; ~ **stove** *n* fogão *m* a gás; ~**sy** *adj* gasoso; ~ **tap** *n* torneira do gás.
gastric ['gæstrik] *adj* gástrico; ~ **ulcer** *n* úlcera gástrica.
gate [geit] *n* portão *m*; (*RAIL*) barreira; ~**crash** *vt* entrar de penetra em; ~**way** *n* portão *m*, passagem *f*.
gather ['gæðə*] *vt* (*flowers, fruit*) colher; (*assemble*) reunir; (*pick up*) colher; (*SEWING*) franzir; (*understand*) compreender // *vi* (*assemble*) reunir-se; ~**ing** *n* reunião *f*, assembleia.
gauche [gəuʃ] *adj* desajeitado.
gaudy ['gɔ:di] *adj* ostentoso, de mau gosto.

gauge [geɪdʒ] *n* padrão *m*, medida, medidor *m*; (RAIL) bitola; (instrument) indicador *m* // *vt* medir.

gaunt [gɔːnt] *adj* descarnado; (grim, desolate) desolado.

gauntlet ['gɔːntlɪt] *n* (fig): **to run the ~** expôr-se (à crítica); **to throw down the ~** lançar um desafio.

gauze [gɔːz] *n* gaze *f*.

gave [geɪv] *pt of* **give**.

gay [geɪ] *adj* (person) alegre; (colour) vistoso, vivo; (homosexual) gay.

gaze [geɪz] *n* olhar fixo; **to ~ at sth** fitar algo.

, gazelle [gə'zɛl] *n* gazela.

gazetteer [gæzə'tɪə*] *n* dicionário geográfico.

G.B. *abbr of* **Great Britain.**

gear [gɪə*] *n* equipamento; (TECH) engrenagem *f*; (AUT) marcha (Br), mudança (Pt); **top/low ~** quarta/primeira (marcha); **in ~** engrenado; **~ box** *n* caixa de mudança (Br), caixa de velocidades (Pt); **~ lever**, **~ shift** (US) *n* alavanca de (Pt: das) mudança; **~ wheel** *n* roda de engrenagem.

geese [giːs] *pl of* **goose.**

gelatin(e) ['dʒɛlətiːn] *n* gelatina.

gelignite ['dʒɛlɪgnaɪt] *n* gelignite *f*.

gem [dʒɛm] *n* jóia, gema.

Gemini ['dʒɛmɪnaɪ] *n* Gêminis *m*, Gêmeos *mpl*.

gender ['dʒɛndə*] *n* gênero.

general ['dʒɛnərl] *n* general *m* // *adj* geral; **in ~** em geral; **~ election** *n* eleições *fpl* gerais; **~ization** [-aɪ'zeɪʃən] *n* generalização *f*; **~ize** *vi* generalizar; **~ly** *adv* geralmente; **~ practitioner (G.P.)** *n* clínico geral *m*.

generate ['dʒɛnəreɪt] *vt* (ELEC) gerar; (fig) produzir.

generation [dʒɛnə'reɪʃən] *n* geração *f*.

generator ['dʒɛnəreɪtə*] *n* gerador *m*.

generosity [dʒɛnə'rɔsɪtɪ] *n* generosidade *f*; **generous** ['dʒɛnərəs] *adj* generoso; (helping etc) abundante.

genetics [dʒɪ'nɛtɪks] *n* genética.

Geneva [dʒɪ'niːvə] *n* Genebra.

genial ['dʒiːnɪəl] *adj* jovial, simpático.

genitals ['dʒɛnɪtlz] *npl* órgãos *mpl* genitais.

genius ['dʒiːnɪəs] *n* gênio.

genocide ['dʒɛnəusaɪd] *n* genocídio.

gent [dʒɛnt] *n abbr of* **gentleman.**

genteel [dʒɛn'tiːl] *adj* fino, elegante.

gentle ['dʒɛntl] *adj* (sweet) amável, doce; (touch etc) leve, suave; (animal) manso.

gentleman ['dʒɛntlmən] *n* senhor *m*; (well-bred man) cavalheiro.

gentleness ['dʒɛntlnɪs] *n* doçura, meiguice *f*; (of touch) suavidade *f*; (of animal) brandura.

gently ['dʒɛntlɪ] *adv* devagar, suavemente.

gentry ['dʒɛntrɪ] *n* gente *f* de nobreza.

gents [dʒɛnts] *n* banheiro de homens (Br), casa de banho dos homens (Pt).

genuine ['dʒɛnjuɪn] *adj* autêntico; (person) sincero.

geographic(al) [dʒɪə'græfɪk(l)] *adj* geográfico; **geography** [dʒɪ'ɔgrəfɪ] *n* geografia.

geological [dʒɪə'lɔdʒɪkl] *adj* geológico; **geologist** [dʒɪ'ɔlədʒɪst] *n* geólogo/a; **geology** [dʒɪ'ɔlədʒɪ] *n* geologia.

geometric(al) [dʒɪə'mɛtrɪk(l)] *adj* geométrico; **geometry** [dʒɪ'ɔmətrɪ] *n* geometria.

geranium [dʒɪ'reɪnjəm] *n* gerânio.

germ [dʒɜːm] *n* (gen) micróbio, bacilo; (BIO, fig) germe *m*.

German ['dʒɜːmən] *adj* alemão/mã // *n* alemão/mã *m/f*; (LING) alemão *m*; **~ measles** *n* rubéola.

Germany ['dʒɜːmənɪ] *n* Alemanha.

germination [dʒɜːmɪ'neɪʃən] *n* germinação *f*.

gesticulate [dʒɛs'tɪkjuleɪt] *vi* gesticular.

gesture ['dʒɛstjə*] *n* gesto.

get [gɛt], *pt*, *pp* **got**, *pp* **gotten** (US) *vt* (obtain) obter, arranjar; (receive) receber; (achieve) conseguir; (find) encontrar; (catch) pegar; (fetch) ir buscar; (understand) compreender // *vi* (become) ficar, tornar-se; **to ~ old** envelhecer; **to ~ to** (place) chegar a; **he got under the fence** passou por baixo da cerca; **to ~ ready** preparar-se; **to ~ washed** lavar-se; **to ~ sb to do sth** convencer alguém a fazer algo; **to ~ sth out of sth** tirar proveito de algo; **to ~ about** vi sair muito, viajar muito; (news) espalhar-se; **to ~ along** *vi* (agree) entender-se; (depart) pôr-se a andar, ir embora; (manage) = **to get by**; **to ~ at** *vt fus* (attack) atacar; (reach) chegar a; (the truth) descobrir; **to ~ away** *vi* partir; (on holiday) ir-se de férias; (escape) escapar; **to ~ away with** *vt fus* conseguir fazer impunemente; **to ~ back** *vi* (return) regressar, voltar // *vt* receber de volta; **to ~ by** *vi* (pass) passar; (manage) arranjar-se; **to ~ down** *vi* abaixar-se // *vt* (object) abaixar, descer; (depress) deprimir; **to ~ down to** *vt fus* (work) pôr-se a (fazer); **to ~ in** *vi* (train) chegar; (arrive home) voltar para casa // *vt fus* (car etc) subir a; **to ~ off** *vi* (from train etc) saltar (Br), descer (Pt); (depart: person, car) sair // *vt fus* (train, bus) saltar de (Br), sair de (Pt); **to ~ on** *vi* (at exam etc) ter sucesso; (agree) entender-se // *vt* (train etc) subir em (Br), subir para (Pt); **to ~ out** *vi* sair; (of vehicle) sair; (news) vir a público // *vt* (take out) tirar; **to ~ out of** *vt fus* sair de; (duty etc) escapar de; **to ~ over** *vt* (illness) restabelecer-se de; (put across) fazer compreender; **to ~ round** *vt fus* rodear; (fig: person) convencer; **to ~ through to** *vt fus* (TEL) comunicar-se com; **to ~ together** *vi* reunir-se; **to ~ up** *vi* (rise) levantar-se // *vt fus* levantar; **to ~ up to** *vt fus* (reach) chegar a; (prank etc) fazer; **~away** *n* fuga, escape *m*.

geyser ['giːzə*] n aquecedor m de água; (GEO) gêiser m.

Ghana ['gɑːnə] n Ghana.

ghastly ['gɑːstlɪ] adj horrível; (pale) pálido.

gherkin ['gəːkɪn] n pepino em vinagre.

ghetto ['gɛtəʊ] n gueto.

ghost [gəʊst] n fantasma m; ~ly adj fantasmal.

giant ['dʒaɪənt] n gigante m // adj gigantesco, gigante.

gibberish ['dʒɪbərɪʃ] n algaravia.

gibe [dʒaɪb] n deboche m.

giblets ['dʒɪblɪts] npl miúdos mpl.

giddiness ['gɪdɪnɪs] n vertigem f; **giddy** adj (dizzy) tonto; (speed) vertiginoso; (frivolous) frívolo; **it makes me giddy** me dá vertigem.

gift [gɪft] n (gen) presente m; (offering) oferta; (ability) dom m, talento; ~ed adj dotado.

gigantic [dʒaɪˈgæntɪk] adj gigantesco.

giggle ['gɪgl] vi dar risadinha boba // n risadinha boba.

gill [dʒɪl] n (measure) = 0.14 l // n [gɪl] (of fish) guelra, brânquia.

gilt [gɪlt] adj, n dourado; ~-edged adj (COMM) do Estado.

gimmick ['gɪmɪk] n truque m (publicitário).

gin [dʒɪn] n (liquor) gim m, genebra.

ginger ['dʒɪndʒə*] n gengibre m; ~ ale n cerveja de gengibre; ~bread n pão m de gengibre; ~-haired adj ruivo.

gingerly ['dʒɪndʒəlɪ] adv cuidadosamente.

gipsy ['dʒɪpsɪ] n cigano.

giraffe [dʒɪˈrɑːf] n girafa.

girder ['gəːdə*] n viga, trave f.

girdle ['gəːdl] n (corset) cinta // vt cintar.

girl [gəːl] n (small) menina (Br); rapariga (Pt); (young woman) jovem f, moça; **an English** ~ uma moça inglesa; ~friend n (of girl) amiga; (of boy) namorada; ~ish adj amenizado, de menina.

girth [gəːθ] n circunferência; (stoutness) gordura.

gist [dʒɪst] n o essencial m.

give [gɪv], pt **gave**, pp **given** vt (gen) dar; (deliver) entregar; (as gift) oferecer // vi (break) dar folga; (stretch: fabric) dar de si; **to** ~ **sb sth**, ~ **sth to sb** dar algo a alguém; **to** ~ **away** vt (give free) dar de graça; (betray) traiçoar; (disclose) revelar; **to** ~ **back** vt devolver; **to** ~ **in** vi ceder // vt entregar; **to** ~ **off** vt soltar; **to** ~ **out** vt distribuir; **to** ~ **up** vi renunciar, dar-se por vencido // vt renunciar a; **to** ~ **up smoking** deixar de fumar; **to** ~ **way** vi ceder; (AUT) deixar passar.

glacier ['glæsɪə*] n glaciar m, geleira.

glad [glæd] adj contente; ~den vt alegrar.

gladioli [glædɪˈəʊlaɪ] npl gladíolos mpl.

gladly ['glædlɪ] adv com muito prazer.

glamorous ['glæmərəs] adj encantador(a), glamoroso; **glamour** n encanto, glamour m.

glance [glɑːns] n relance m, vista // vi: **to** ~ **at** olhar (de relance); **to** ~ **off** (bullet) resvalar; **glancing** adj (blow) oblíquo.

gland [glænd] n glândula.

glare [glɛə*] n luz f, brilho // vi deslumbrar; **to** ~ **at** olhar furiosamente para; **glaring** adj (mistake) notório.

glass [glɑːs] n vidro, cristal m; (for drinking) copo; (:with stem) cálice m; (also: **looking** ~) espelho; ~es npl óculos mpl; ~house n estufa; ~ware n objetos de cristal; ~y adj (eyes) vidrado.

glaze [gleɪz] vt (door) envidraçar; (pottery) vitrificar // n verniz m; ~d adj (eye) vidrado; (pottery) vitrificado.

glazier ['gleɪzɪə*] n vidraceiro.

gleam [gliːm] n brilho // vi brilhar; ~ing adj brilhante.

glee [gliː] n alegria, regozijo.

glen [glɛn] n vale m.

glib [glɪb] adj loquaz, tagarela; ~ness n verbosidade f.

glide [glaɪd] vi deslizar; (AVIAT, birds) planar // n deslizamento; (AVIAT) vôo planado; **glider** n (AVIAT) planador m; **gliding** n (AVIAT) vôo sem motor.

glimmer ['glɪmə*] n luz f trêmula.

glimpse [glɪmps] n olhar m de relance, vislumbre m // vt vislumbrar, ver de relance.

glint [glɪnt] n brilho; (in the eye) cintilação f // vi cintilar.

glisten ['glɪsn] vi cintilar, resplandecer.

glitter ['glɪtə*] vi reluzir, brilhar // n brilho.

gloat [gləʊt] vi: **to** ~ **(over)** exultar (com).

global ['gləʊbl] adj mundial; (sum) global.

globe [gləʊb] n globo, esfera.

gloom [gluːm] n escuridão f; (sadness) tristeza; ~y adj (dark) escuro; (sad) triste; (pessimistic) pessimista.

glorify ['glɔːrɪfaɪ] vt glorificar; (praise) adorar.

glorious ['glɔːrɪəs] adj glorioso; **glory** n glória.

gloss [glɒs] n (shine) brilho; (paint) pintura brilhante, esmalte m; **to** ~ **over** vt fus encobrir.

glossary ['glɒsərɪ] n glossário.

glossy ['glɒsɪ] adj lustroso.

glove [glʌv] n luva; ~ **compartment** n (AUT) porta-luvas m inv.

glow [gləʊ] vi (shine) brilhar; (fire) arder // n brilho.

glower ['glaʊə*] vi: **to** ~ **at** olhar de modo ameaçador.

glucose ['gluːkəʊs] n glicose f.

glue [gluː] n cola // vt colar.

glum [glʌm] adj (mood) abatido; (person, tone) triste.

glut [glʌt] n abundância, fartura.

glutton ['glʌtn] n glutão/ona m/f; **a** ~

for work um trabalhador incansável; ~y n gula.

glycerin(e) ['glɪsəriːn] n glicerina.

gnarled [nɑːld] adj nodoso.

gnat [næt] n mosquito.

gnaw [nɔː] vt roer.

gnome [nəʊm] n gnomo.

go [gəʊ], pt **went**, pp **gone** vi ir; (travel) viajar; (depart) partir, ir-se; (work) funcionar, trabalhar; (be sold) vender; (time) passar; (become) ficar; (break etc) romper-se; (fit, suit): **to ~ with** acompanhar, combinar com // n, pl **~es: to have a ~ at** tentar a sorte com; **to be on the ~** ter muito para fazer; **whose ~ is it?** de quem é a vez?; **he's going to do it** ele vai fazê-lo; **to ~ for a walk** ir passear; **to ~ dancing** ir dançar; **how did it ~?** como foi?; **to ~ about** vi (rumour) espalhar-se // vt fus: **how do I ~ about this?** como é que eu faço isso?; **to ~ ahead** vi (make progress) progredir; (get going) continuar; **to ~ along** vi (go too) ir também; (continue) continuar, prosseguir // vt fus ladear; **to ~ along with** acompanhar; **to ~ away** vi ir-se, ir embora; **to ~ back** vi voltar; (fall back) retroceder; **to ~ back on** vt fus (promise) faltar com; **to ~ by** vi (years, time) passar // vt fus guiar-se por; **to ~ down** vi descer, baixar; (ship) afundar; (sun) pôr-se // vt fus descer; **to ~ for** vt fus (fetch) ir buscar; (like) gostar de; (attack) atacar; **to ~ in** vi entrar; **to ~ in for** vt fus (competition) apresentar-se em; **to ~ into** vt fus entrar em; (investigate) investigar; (embark on) embarcar em; **to ~ off** vi ir-se; (food) estragar, apodrecer; (explode) explodir; (event) realizar-se // vt fus deixar de gostar de; **to ~ on** vi seguir, continuar; (happen) acontecer, ocorrer; **to ~ on doing sth** continuar a fazer algo; **to ~ out** vi sair; (fire, light) apagar-se; **to ~ over** vi (ship) soçobrar // vt fus (check) revisar; **to ~ through** vt fus (town etc) atravessar; **to ~ up** vi subir; **to ~ without** vt fus passar sem.

goad [gəʊd] vt aguilhoar.

go-ahead ['gəʊəhɛd] adj empreendedor(a) // n luz f verde, permissão f para prosseguir.

goal [gəʊl] n meta, alvo; (in sport) gol m (Br), golo (Pt); (in sport) goleiro (Br), guarda-redes m (Pt); ~**post** n trave f.

goat [gəʊt] n cabra; (male) bode m.

gobble ['gɔbl] vt (also: ~ **down**, ~ **up**) engolir rapidamente, devorar.

goblet ['gɔblɪt] n cálice m.

goblin ['gɔblɪn] n duende m.

go-cart ['gəʊkɑːt] n carrinho de mão.

god [gɔd] n deus m; G~ n Deus m; ~**child** n afilhado; ~**dess** n deusa; ~**father** n padrinho; ~**forsaken** adj miserável, abandonado; ~**mother** n madrinha; ~**send** n dádiva do céu; ~**son** n afilhado.

goggles ['gɔglz] npl óculos mpl de proteção (Pt: -cç-).

going ['gəʊɪŋ] adj: **the ~ rate** tarifa corrente or em vigor.

gold [gəʊld] n ouro // adj de ouro; ~**en** adj (made of ~) de ouro, dourado; (~ in colour) dourado; ~**fish** n peixe-dourado m; ~**mine** n mina de ouro.

golf [gɔlf] n golfe m; ~ **club** n clube m de golfe; (stick) taco; ~ **course** n campo de golfe; ~**er** n jogador(a) m/f de golfe, golfista m/f.

gondola ['gɔndələ] n gôndola.

gone [gɔn] pp of **go**.

gong [gɔŋ] n gongo.

gonorrhea [gɔnə'rɪə] n gonorréia.

good [gʊd] adj (gen) bom/boa; (kind) bom, bondoso; (well-behaved) educado; (useful) útil // n bem m, proveito; ~**s** npl bens mpl; (COMM) mercadorias fpl; **to be ~ at** ser bom em; **to be ~ for** servir para; **it's ~ for you** faz-lhe bem; **would you be ~ enough to...?** podia fazer-me o favor de...?, poderia me fazer a gentileza de...?; **a ~ deal (of)** muito; **a ~ many** muitos; **to make ~** reparar; **for ~** para sempre, definitivamente; ~ **morning/afternoon!** bom dia/boa tarde!; ~ **evening!** boa tarde!, boa noite!; ~ **night!** boa noite!; ~**bye!** até logo! (Br), adeus! (Pt); **to say ~bye** despedir-se; G~ **Friday** n Sexta-Feira Santa; ~-**looking** adj bonito; ~**ness** n (of person) bondade f; **for ~ness sake!** pelo amor de Deus!; ~**ness gracious!** meu Deus!; ~**will** n boa vontade f.

goose [guːs], pl **geese** n ganso.

gooseberry ['gʊzbərɪ] n groselha.

gooseflesh ['guːsflɛʃ] n, **goose pimples** npl pele f arrepiada.

gore [gɔː*] vt escornar // n sangue m.

gorge [gɔːdʒ] n desfiladeiro // vr: **to ~ o.s. (on)** empanturrar-se de.

gorgeous ['gɔːdʒəs] adj magnífico, maravilhoso.

gorilla [gə'rɪlə] n gorila m.

gorse [gɔːs] n tojo.

gory ['gɔːrɪ] adj sangrento.

go-slow ['gəʊ'sləʊ] n greve f de trabalho lento, operação f tartaruga.

gospel ['gɔspl] n evangelho.

gossip ['gɔsɪp] n (scandal) fofocas fpl (Br), mexericos mpl (Pt); (a piece of ~) fofoca (Br), mexerico (Pt); (chat) conversa; (scandalmonger) fofoqueiro (Br), mexeriqueiro (Pt) // vi (spread scandal) fofocar (Br), mexericar (Pt); (chat) bater (um) papo (Br), cavaquear (Pt).

got [gɔt] pt, pp of **get**; ~**ten** (US) pp of **get**.

gout [gaʊt] n gota.

govern ['gʌvən] vt (gen) governar; (dominate) dominar.

governess ['gʌvənɪs] n governanta.

government ['gʌvnmənt] n governo; ~**al** [-'mɛntl] adj governamental.

governor [ˈgʌvənə*] n governador m; (of jail) diretor(a) (Pt: -ct-) m/f.

gown [gaun] n vestido; (of teacher, judge) toga.

G.P. n abbr of **general practitioner**.

GPO n abbr of **General Post Office**.

grab [græb] vt agarrar, apanhar.

grace [greis] n (REL) graça; (gracefulness) elegância, fineza // vt (favour) honrar; (adorn) adornar; **5 days'** ~ um prazo de 5 dias; **to say** ~ dar graças (antes de comer); ~**ful** adj elegante, gracioso; **gracious** [ˈgreiʃəs] adj gracioso, afável.

grade [greid] n (quality) classe f, qualidade f; (degree) grau m; (US: SCOL) classe; ~ **crossing** n (US) passagem f de nível // vt classificar.

gradient [ˈgreidiənt] n declive m.

gradual [ˈgrædjuəl] adj gradual, suave; ~**ly** adv gradualmente.

graduate [ˈgrædjut] n graduado, licenciado // vi [ˈgrædjueit] formar-se, licenciar-se; **graduation** [-ˈeiʃən] n graduação f.

graft [grɑ:ft] n (AGR, MED) enxerto; (bribery) suborno // vt enxertar.

grain [grein] n grão m; (corn) grãos mpl, cereais mpl; (in wood) veio, fibra.

gram [græm] n grama m.

grammar [ˈgræmə*] n gramática; **grammatical** [grəˈmætikl] adj gramatical.

gramme [græm] n = **gram**.

gramophone [ˈgræməfəun] n toca-discos m inv (Br), gira-discos m inv (Pt).

granary [ˈgrænəri] n celeiro.

grand [grænd] adj grande, magnífico; ~**children** npl netos mpl; ~**dad** n vovô m; ~**daughter** n neta; ~**eur** [ˈgrændjə*] n grandeza, magnificência; ~**father** n avô m; ~**iose** [ˈgrændiəuz] adj grandioso; (pej) pomposo; ~**ma** n vovó f; ~**mother** n avó f; ~**pa** n = ~**dad**; ~ **piano** n piano de cauda; ~**son** n neto; ~**stand** n (SPORT) tribuna principal.

granite [ˈgrænit] n granito.

granny [ˈgræni] n avó f, vovó f.

grant [grɑ:nt] vt (concede) conceder; (admit) admitir // n (SCOL) bolsa; **to take sth for** ~**ed** dar algo por certo.

granulated sugar [ˈgrænjuleitid-] n açúcar m granulado.

granule [ˈgrænju:l] n grânulo.

grape [greip] n uva; **sour** ~**s** (fig) inveja.

grapefruit [ˈgreipfru:t] n toranja, grapefruit m (Br).

graph [grɑ:f] n gráfico; ~**ic** adj gráfico.

grapple [ˈgræpl] vi: **to** ~ **with sth** estar às voltas com algo.

grasp [grɑ:sp] vt agarrar, segurar; (understand) compreender, entender // n (grip) agarramento; (reach) alcance m; (understanding) compreensão f; ~**ing** adj avaro.

grass [grɑ:s] n grama (Br), relva (Pt); (lawn) gramado (Br), relvado (Pt);

~**hopper** n gafanhoto; ~**land** n pradaria; ~-**roots** adj popular; ~ **snake** n serpente f; ~**y** adj coberto de grama (Br), coberto de relva (Pt).

grate [greit] n (fireplace) lareira; (of iron) grelha // vi ranger // vt (CULIN) ralar.

grateful [ˈgreitful] adj agradecido.

grater [ˈgreitə*] n ralador m, ralo.

gratify [ˈgrætifai] vt gratificar; (whim) satisfazer; ~**ing** adj gratificante.

grating [ˈgreitiŋ] n (iron bars) grade f // adj (noise) áspero.

gratitude [ˈgrætitju:d] n agradecimento.

gratuity [grəˈtju:iti] n gratificação f, gorjeta.

grave [greiv] n sepultura // adj sério, grave; ~**digger** n coveiro.

gravel [ˈgrævl] n cascalho.

grave: ~**stone** n lápide f; ~**yard** n cemitério.

gravity [ˈgræviti] n gravidade f; (seriousness) seriedade f.

gravy [ˈgreivi] n molho.

gray [grei] adj = **grey**.

graze [greiz] vi pastar // vt (touch lightly) roçar; (scrape) raspar // n (MED) esfoladura, arranhadura.

grease [gri:s] n (fat) gordura; (lubricant) lubrificante m // vt engordurar; ~**proof** adj à prova de gordura; (paper) papel m de cera (vegetal); **greasy** adj gorduroso.

great [greit] adj grande; (col) ótimo (Pt: -pt-); **G**~ **Britain** n Grã-Bretanha; ~-**grandfather** n bisavô m; ~-**grandmother** n bisavó f; ~**ly** adv imensamente, muito; ~**ness** n grandeza.

Greece [gri:s] n Grécia.

greed [gri:d] n (also: ~**iness**) avidez f, cobiça; (for food) gula; ~**ily** adv com avidez; ~**y** adj avarento; (for food) guloso.

Greek [gri:k] adj grego // n grego/a; (LING) grego.

green [gri:n] adj verde; (inexperienced) inexperiente // n verde m; (stretch of grass) gramado (Br), relvado (Pt); ~**s** npl verduras fpl; ~**gage** n rainha-cláudia; ~**grocer** n verdureiro; ~**house** n estufa; ~**ish** adj esverdeado.

Greenland [ˈgri:nlənd] n Groenlândia.

greet [gri:t] vt saudar; (welcome) dar as boas vindas a; ~**ing** n (gen) cumprimento; (welcome) acolhimento.

gregarious [grəˈgɛəriəs] adj gregário.

grenade [grəˈneid] n granada.

grew [gru:] pt of **grow**.

grey [grei] adj cinzento; ~-**haired** adj grisalho; ~**hound** n galgo.

grid [grid] n grade f; (ELEC) rede f.

grief [gri:f] n dor f, pena.

grievance [ˈgri:vəns] n motivo de queixas, agravo.

grieve [gri:v] vi afligir-se, sofrer // vt dar pena a; **to** ~ **for** chorar por.

grievous [ˈgri:vəs] adj penoso.

grill [gril] n (on cooker) grelha // vt

grelhar; (question) interrogar cerradamente.

grille [grɪl] n grade f.

grim [grɪm] adj sinistro; (fam) horrível.

grimace [grɪ'meɪs] n careta // vi fazer caretas.

grime [graɪm] n sujeira (Br), sujidade f (Pt); **grimy** adj sujo.

grin [grɪn] n sorriso largo // vi sorrir abertamente.

grind [graɪnd], pt, pp **ground** vt (coffee, pepper etc) moer; (make sharp) afiar // n (work) trabalho pesado e aborrecido; **to ~ one's teeth** ranger os dentes.

grip [grɪp] n (hands) aperto; (handle) punho; (of racquet etc) cabo; (holdall) valise f; (understanding) compreensão f // vt agarrar; **to come to ~s with** atacar; **~ping** adj absorvente.

grisly ['grɪzlɪ] adj horrendo, medonho.

gristle ['grɪsl] n cartilagem f.

grit [grɪt] n areia, grão m de areia; (courage) coragem f // vt (road) pôr areia em; **to ~ one's teeth** ranger os dentes.

groan [grəun] n gemido // vi gemer.

grocer ['grəusə*] n dono de mercearia; **~ies** npl comestíveis mpl; **~'s (shop)** n mercearia.

groggy ['grɔgɪ] adj cambaleante; (BOXING) grogue.

groin [grɔɪn] n virilha.

groom [gru:m] n cavalariço; (also: **bride~**) noivo // vt (horse) tratar; **well-~ed** bem-posto.

groove [gru:v] n ranhura, entalhe m.

grope [grəup] vi tatear; **to ~ for** vt fus procurar às cegas.

gross [grəus] adj grosso; (COMM) bruto; **~ly** adv (greatly) enormemente, gritantemente.

grotesque [grə'tɛsk] adj grotesco.

grotto ['grɔtəu] n gruta.

ground [graund] pt, pp of **grind** // n terreno, chão m; (SPORT) campo, terreno; (reason: gen pl) causa, razão f // vt (plane) manter em terra; (US: ELEC) ligar à terra // vi (ship) encalhar; **~s** npl (of coffee etc) borra; (gardens etc) jardins mpl, parque m; **on the ~** no chão; **to the ~** por terra; **~ floor** n andar m térreo (Br), rés-do-chão m (Pt); **~ing** n (in education) conhecimentos mpl básicos; **~less** adj infundado; **~sheet** n capa impermeável; **~ staff** n pessoal m de terra; **~work** n base f, preparação f.

group [gru:p] n grupo; (musical) conjunto // (vb: also: **~ together**) vt agrupar // vi agrupar-se.

grouse [graus] n, pl inv (bird) tetraz m, galo-silvestre m // vi (complain) queixar-se.

grove [grəuv] n arvoredo.

grovel ['grɔvl] vi (fig) humilhar-se.

grow [grəu], pt **grew**, pp **grown** vi (gen) crescer; (plants) cultivar; (increase) aumentar; (spread) espalhar-se,

estender-se; (become) tornar-se; **to ~ rich/weak** enriquecer(-se)/enfraquecer-se // vt cultivar, deixar crescer; **to ~ up** vi crescer, fazer-se homem/mulher; **~er** n cultivador(a) m/f, produtor(a) m/f; **~ing** adj crescente.

growl [graul] vi rosnar.

grown [grəun] pp of **grow**; **~-up** n adulto, pessoa mais velha.

growth [grəuθ] n crescimento, desenvolvimento; (what has grown) aumento; (MED) abcesso, tumor m.

grub [grʌb] n larva, lagarta; (col: food) comida, bóia (Br).

grubby ['grʌbɪ] adj sujo, porco.

grudge [grʌdʒ] n motivo de rancor // vt: **to ~ sb sth** dar algo a alguém de má vontade, invejar algo a alguém; **to bear sb a ~** guardar rancor a alguém por algo; **he ~s (giving) the money** ele dá dinheiro de má vontade.

gruelling ['gruəlɪŋ] adj duro, árduo.

gruesome ['gru:səm] adj horrível.

gruff [grʌf] adj (voice) rouca; (manner) brusco.

grumble ['grʌmbl] vi resmungar, queixar-se.

grumpy ['grʌmpɪ] adj rabujento.

grunt [grʌnt] vi grunhir // n grunhido.

guarantee [gærən'ti:] n garantia // vt garantir.

guarantor [gærən'tɔ:*] n fiador(a) m/f.

guard [gɑ:d] n guarda; (RAIL) guarda-freio m // vt guardar; **~ed** adj (fig) cauteloso; **~ian** n protetor (Pt: -ct-) m/f; (of minor) tutor(a) m/f.

guerrilla [gə'rɪlə] n guerrilheiro/a; **~ warfare** n guerrilha.

guess [gɛs] vt/i (gen) adivinhar; (suppose) supor // n suposição f, conjetura (Pt: -ct-); **to take or have a ~** adivinhar; **~work** n conjeturas (Pt: -ct-) fpl.

guest [gɛst] n convidado; (in hotel) hóspede m/f; **~-house** n pensão f; **~-room** n quarto de hóspedes.

guffaw [gʌ'fɔ:] n gargalhada // vi dar gargalhadas.

guidance ['gaɪdəns] n (gen) orientação f; (advice) conselhos mpl.

guide [gaɪd] n (person) guia m/f; (fig) guia m // vt guiar; (girl) **~** n escoteira; **~book** n guia m; **~ dog** n cão m de guia; **~ lines** npl (fig) princípios mpl gerais, diretrizes fpl.

guild [gɪld] n grêmio; **~hall** n (Brit) sede f da prefeitura.

guile [gaɪl] n astúcia; **~less** adj ingênuo, cândido.

guillotine ['gɪləti:n] n guilhotina.

guilt [gɪlt] n culpa; **~y** adj culpado.

guinea pig ['gɪnɪpɪg] n porquinho-da-índia m, cobaia.

guise [gaɪz] n: **in or under the ~ of** sob a aparência de.

guitar [gɪ'tɑ:*] n violão m; **~ist** n violonista m/f.

gulf [gʌlf] *n* golfo; (*abyss*) abismo.

gull [gʌl] *n* gaivota.

gullet ['gʌlit] *n* esôfago; (*fam*) garganta.

gullible ['gʌlibl] *adj* crédulo.

gully ['gʌli] *n* barranco.

gulp [gʌlp] *vi* engolir em seco // *vt* (*also*: ~ **down**) engolir // *n*: **at one ~** de um gole só.

gum [gʌm] *n* (ANAT) gengiva; (*glue*) goma; (*sweet*) chiclete *m* (*Br*), pastilha elástica (*Pt*) // *vt* colar; ~**boots** *npl* botas *fpl* de borracha, galochas *fpl*.

gun [gʌn] *n* (*gen*) arma de fogo; (*small*) pistola; (*shotgun*) espingarda de caça; (*rifle*) espingarda; (*cannon*) canhão *m*; ~**boat** *n* canhoneira; ~**fire** *n* fogo, tiroteio; ~**man** *n* pistoleiro; ~**ner** *n* artilheiro; **at** ~**point** sob a ameaça de uma arma; ~**powder** *n* pólvora; ~**shot** *n* tiro de arma de fogo; ~**smith** *n* armeiro.

gurgle ['gɔːgl] *vi* gorgolejar.

gush [gʌʃ] *vi* jorrar; (*fig*) alvoroçar-se.

gusset ['gʌsit] *n* nesga.

gust [gʌst] *n* (*of wind*) rajada.

gusto ['gʌstəu] *n* entusiasmo.

gut [gʌt] *n* intestino, tripa; (MUS etc) corda de tripa; ~**s** *npl* (*courage*) coragem *f*.

gutter ['gʌtə*] *n* (*of roof*) calha; (*in street*) sarjeta.

guttural ['gʌtərl] *adj* gutural.

guy [gai] *n* (*also*: ~**rope**) corda; (*col: man*) cara *m* (*Br*), tipo (*Pt*).

guzzle ['gʌzl] *vi* comer *or* beber com gula // *vt* engolir.

gym [dʒim] *n* (*also*: **gymnasium**) ginásio; (*also*: **gymnastics**) ginástica; ~**nast** *n* ginasta *m/f*; ~**nastics** *n* ginástica; ~**shoes** *npl* tênis *m(pl)* (*Br*), ténis *mpl* (*Pt*); ~ **slip** *n* uniforme *m* escolar.

gynaecologist, gynecologist (US) [gainɪˈkɔlədʒist] *n* ginecologista *m/f*; **gynaecology, gynecology** (US) [-nɔˈkɔlədʒi] *n* ginecologia.

gypsy ['dʒipsi] *n* = **gipsy**.

gyrate [dʒaiˈreit] *vi* girar.

H

haberdashery ['hæbəˈdæʃəri] *n* armarinho.

habit ['hæbit] *n* hábito, uso, costume *m*; (*costume*) hábito.

habitable ['hæbitəbl] *adj* habitável.

habitual [həˈbitjuəl] *adj* habitual, costumeiro; (*drinker, liar*) inveterado; ~**ly** *adv* habitualmente.

hack [hæk] *vt* (*cut*) cortar; (*slice*) talhar // *n* corte *m*; (*axe blow*) talho.

hackneyed ['hæknid] *adj* corriqueiro, batido.

had [hæd] *pt, pp* of **have**.

haddock ['hædɔk], *pl* ~ *or* ~**s** *n* hadoque *m* (*Br*), eglefim *m* (*Pt*).

hadn't ['hædnt] = **had not**.

haemorrhage, hemorrhage (US) ['hɛməridʒ] *n* hemorragia.

haemorrhoids, hemorrhoids (US) ['hɛmərɔidz] *npl* hemorróidas *fpl*.

haggard ['hægəd] *adj* emaciado, macilento.

haggle ['hægl] *vi* (*argue*) discutir; (*bargain*) pechinchar, regatear.

Hague [heig] *n*: **The** ~ a Haia.

hail [heil] *n* (*weather*) granizo // *vt* cumprimentar, saudar; (*call*) chamar // *vi* chover granizo; ~**stone** *n* pedra de granizo.

hair [hɛə*] *n* (*of human*) cabelo; (*of animal*) pêlo; (*one* ~) fio de cabelo, pêlo; (*head of* ~) cabeleira; (*on legs*) pêlo; **grey** ~ cabelo grisalho; ~**brush** *n* escova de cabelo; ~**cut** *n* corte *m* de cabelo; ~**do** *n* penteado; ~**dresser** *n* cabeleireiro/a; ~**dresser's** *n* cabeleireiro; ~**drier** *n* secador *m* de cabelo; ~**net** *n* rede *f* de cabelo; ~**piece** *n* aplique *m*; ~**pin** *n* grampo, pinça; ~**pin bend** *n* curva fechada; ~**raising** *adj* horripilante, de arrepiar os cabelos; ~ **remover** *n* (creme *m*) depilatório; ~ **spray** *n* spray *m* para o cabelo; ~**style** *n* penteado; ~**y** *adj* cabeludo, peludo.

half [hɑːf], *pl* **halves** *n* metade *f* // *adj* meio // *adv* meio, pela metade; ~**-an-hour** meia hora; **two and a** ~ dois e meio; ~ **a pound** meia libra; **to cut sth in** ~ cortar algo ao meio; ~ **asleep** meio adormecido; ~**-price** pela metade do preço; ~**-back** *n* (SPORT) meio-de-campo; ~**-breed**, ~**-caste** *n* mestiço; ~**-hearted** *adj* irresoluto, indiferente; ~**-hour** *n* meia hora; ~**-time** *n* meio tempo; ~**way** *adv* a meio caminho.

halibut ['hælibət] *n*, *pl inv* hipoglosso.

hall [hɔːl] *n* (*for concerts*) sala; (*entrance way*) hall *m*, vestíbulo; **town** ~ prefeitura (*Br*), câmara municipal (*Pt*); ~ **of residence** *n* residência universitária.

hallmark ['hɔːlmɑːk] *n* (*mark*) marca; (*seal*) selo.

hallo [həˈləu] *excl* = **hello**.

hallucination [həluːsɪˈneiʃən] *n* alucinação *f*.

halo ['heiləu] *n* (*of saint*) auréola.

halt [hɔːlt] *n* (*stop*) parada (*Br*), paragem *f* (*Pt*); (RAIL) pequena parada; (MIL) alto // *vi* parar // *vt* deter; (*process*) interromper.

halve [hɑːv] *vt* dividir ao meio.

halves [hɑːvz] *pl* of **half**.

ham [hæm] *n* presunto, fiambre *m* (*Pt*); (*actor*) canastrão *m*.

hamburger ['hæmbɔːgə*] *n* hambúrguer *m*.

hamlet ['hæmlit] *n* aldeola, lugarejo.

hammer ['hæmə*] *n* martelo // *vt* martelar // *vi* (*on door*) bater insistentemente.

hammock ['hæmək] *n* rede *f*.

hamper ['hæmpə*] vt dificultar, atrapalhar // n cesto.

hand [hænd] n mão f; (of clock) ponteiro; (writing) letra; (applause) aplauso; (worker) trabalhador m; (measure) palmo // vt (give) dar, transmitir; (deliver) entregar; **to give sb a ~** dar uma mão a alguém, ajudar alguém; **at ~** à mão, disponível; **in ~** sob controle; (COMM) em caixa, à disposição; **on the one ~ .... on the other ~ ...** por um lado ..., por outro (lado) ...; **to ~ in** vt entregar; **to ~ out** vt distribuir; **to ~ over** vt (deliver) entregar; (surrender) ceder; **~bag** n bolsa; **~basin** n pia (Br), lavatório (Pt); **~book** n manual m; **~brake** n freio de mão (Br), travão m de mão (Pt); **~cuffs** npl algemas fpl; **~ful** n punhado.

handicap ['hændɪkæp] n (MED) incapacidade f; (disadvantage) desvantagem f // vt prejudicar; **mentally/physically ~ped** deficiente mental/físico.

handicraft ['hændɪkrɑːft] n artesanato, trabalho manual.

handkerchief ['hæŋkətʃɪf] n lenço.

handle ['hændl] n (of door etc) maçaneta; (of cup etc) asa; (of knife etc) cabo; (for winding) manivela; (fam: name) título // vt (touch) manusear; (deal with) tratar de; (treat: people) lidar com; '**~ with care**' 'cuidado — frágil'; **to fly off the ~** perder as estribeiras; **~bar(s)** n(pl) guidom (Pt: -dão) m.

hand-luggage ['hændlʌgɪdʒ] n bagagem f de mão.

handmade ['hændmeɪd] adj feito a mão.

handout ['hændaut] n (distribution) distribuição f; (charity) doação f, esmola; (leaflet) folheto; (university) apostila.

handshake ['hændʃeɪk] n aperto de mão.

handsome ['hænsəm] adj bonito.

handwriting ['hændraɪtɪŋ] n letra, caligrafia.

handy ['hændɪ] adj (close at hand) à mão; (convenient) prático (Pt: -ct-); (skilful) habilidoso, hábil; **~man** n biscateiro, faz-tudo m.

hang [hæŋ], pt, pp **hung** vt pendurar; (criminal: pt, pp **hanged**) enforcar; (head) baixar // vi estar pendurado; **to ~ about** vi rondar, ficar perto; **to ~ on** vi (wait) esperar; **to ~ up** vi (TEL) desligar.

hangar ['hæŋə*] n hangar m.

hanger ['hæŋə*] n cabide m; **~-on** n parasita m/f, filão/filona m/f.

hangover ['hæŋəuvə*] n (after drinking) ressaca.

hang-up ['hæŋʌp] n mania, grilo.

hanker ['hæŋkə*] vi: **to ~ after** (miss) sentir saudade de; (long for) ansiar por.

hankie, hanky ['hæŋkɪ] n abbr of **handkerchief**.

haphazard [hæp'hæzəd] adj (random) fortuito; (disorganized) desorganizado.

happen ['hæpən] vi ocorrer, suceder; (take place) acontecer, realizar-se; **to ~ upon** encontrar por acaso; **~ing** n acontecimento, ocorrência.

happily ['hæpɪlɪ] adv (luckily) felizmente; (cheerfully) alegremente.

happiness ['hæpɪnɪs] n (gen) felicidade f; (joy) alegria.

happy ['hæpɪ] adj feliz, contente; **to be ~ (with)** estar contente (com); **to be ~** ser feliz.

harass ['hærəs] vt atormentar, hostilizar; **~ment** n perseguição f; (worry) preocupação f.

harbour, harbor (US) ['hɑːbə*] n porto; (fig) refúgio // vt (hope etc) abrigar; (hide) esconder.

hard [hɑːd] adj (gen) duro; (difficult) difícil; (work) árduo; (person) severo, cruel // adv (work) muito, diligentemente; (think, try) seriamente; **to look ~ (at)** olhar firme or fixamente (para); **no ~ feelings!** sem ressentimentos!; **to be ~ of hearing** ser surdo; **to be ~ done by** ser tratado injustamente; **~back** n livro de capa dura; **~board** n madeira compensada; **~en** vt endurecer; (fig) tornar insensível // vi endurecer-se; **~-headed** adj prático (Pt: -ct-), pouco sentimental; **~ labour** n trabalhos mpl forçados.

hardly ['hɑːdlɪ] adv (scarcely) apenas, mal; **that can ~ be true** dificilmente pode ser verdade; **~ ever** quase nunca.

hardness ['hɑːdnɪs] n dureza.

hardship ['hɑːdʃɪp] n (troubles) sofrimento; (financial) privação f.

hard-up [hɑːd'ʌp] adj (col) duro (Br), liso (Pt).

hardware ['hɑːdwɛə*] n ferragens fpl, maquinaria; (COMPUTERS) hardware m; **~ shop** n loja de ferragens.

hard-wearing [hɑːd'wɛərɪŋ] adj resistente, duradouro.

hard-working [hɑːd'wɔːkɪŋ] adj trabalhador(a).

hardy ['hɑːdɪ] adj forte; (plant) resistente.

hare [hɛə*] n lebre f; **~-brained** adj estonteado, desatinado.

harem [hɑː'riːm] n harém m.

harm [hɑːm] n mal m, dano // vt (person) fazer mal a, prejudicar; (thing) danificar; **out of ~'s way** a salvo; **~ful** adj prejudicial; (pest) daninho; **~less** adj inofensivo.

harmonica [hɑː'mɔnɪkə] n gaita de boca, harmônica.

harmonious [hɑː'məunɪəs] adj harmonioso; **harmonize** ['hɑːmənaɪz] vt/i harmonizar; **harmony** ['hɑːmənɪ] n harmonia.

harness ['hɑːnɪs] n arreios mpl // vt (horse) arrear, pôr arreios em; (resources) aproveitar.

harp [hɑːp] n harpa // vi: **to ~ on about** bater sempre na mesma tecla sobre; **~ist** n harpista m/f.

harpoon [haː'puːn] *n* arpão *m*.

harrowing ['hærəuɪŋ] *adj* doloroso, pungente.

harsh [haːʃ] *adj* (*hard*) duro, cruel; (*severe*) severo; (*unpleasant*) desagradável; (: *colour*) dissonante; (*contrast*) violento; ～**ness** *n* dureza.

harvest ['haːvɪst] *n* colheita; (*of grapes*) vindima // *vt/i* colher; ～**er** *n* (*machine*) segadora.

has [hæz] *vb see* **have**.

hash [hæʃ] *n* (CULIN) picadinho; (*fig: mess*) confusão *f*, bagunça.

hashish ['hæʃɪʃ] *n* haxixe *m*.

hasn't ['hæznt] = **has not**.

hassle ['hæsl] *n* briga, dificuldade *f* // *vt* molestar, chatear.

haste [heɪst] *n* pressa; **hasten** ['heɪsn] *vt* acelerar // *vi* apressar-se; **hastily** *adv* depressa; **hasty** *adj* apressado.

hat [hæt] *n* chapéu *m*.

hatch [hætʃ] *n* (NAUT. *also*: ～**way**) escotilha // *vi* sair do ovo, chocar // *vt* incubar; (*plot*) tramar, maquinar.

hatchback ['hætʃbæk] *n* (AUT) camionete *f*.

hatchet ['hætʃɪt] *n* machadinha.

hate [heɪt] *vt* odiar, detestar // *n* ódio; ～**ful** *adj* odioso; **hatred** *n* ódio.

hat trick ['hættrɪk] *n* (SPORT, *also fig*) três vitórias consecutivas.

haughty ['hɔːtɪ] *adj* soberbo, arrogante.

haul [hɔːl] *vt* puxar; (*by lorry*) carregar, fretar // *n* (*of fish*) redada; (*of stolen goods etc*) pilhagem *f*, presa; ～**age** *n* transporte *m*; (*costs*) gasto com transporte; ～**ier** *n* contratador *m* de frete, fretador *m*.

haunch [hɔːntʃ] *n* anca, quadril *m*; (*of meat*) quarto traseiro.

haunt [hɔːnt] *vt* (*subj: ghost*) assombrar; (*frequent*) freqüentar; (*obsess*) obcecar // *n* lugar *m* freqüentado; ～**ed house** casa mal-assombrada.

have [hæv], *pt*, *pp* **had** *vt* (*gen*) ter; (*possess*) possuir; (*shower*) tomar; (*meal*) comer; **to** ～ **sth done** mandar fazer algo; **she has to do it** ela tem que fazê-lo; **I had better leave** é melhor que eu vá embora; **I won't** ～ **it** não vou agüentar isso; **he has gone** foi embora; **to** ～ **it out with sb** ajustar as contas com alguém; **to** ～ **a baby** dar à luz, ter um nenê (*Br*), ter um bebé (*Pt*).

haven ['heɪvn] *n* porto; (*fig*) abrigo, refúgio.

haven't ['hævnt] = **have not**.

haversack ['hævəsæk] *n* mochila.

havoc ['hævək] *n* destruição *f*.

hawk [hɔːk] *n* falcão *m*.

hay [heɪ] *n* feno; ～ **fever** *n* febre *f* do feno; ～**stack** *n* palheiro.

haywire ['heɪwaɪə*] *adj* (*col*): **to go** ～ (*person*) ficar maluco; (*plan*) desorganizar-se, degringolar.

hazard ['hæzəd] *n* risco, acaso // *vt* aventurar; ～**ous** *adj* (*dangerous*) perigoso; (*risky*) arriscado.

haze [heɪz] *n* névoa, neblina.

hazelnut ['heɪzlnʌt] *n* avelã *f*.

hazy ['heɪzɪ] *adj* nublado; (*idea*) confuso.

he [hiː] *pron* ele; ～ **who** `...` **quem** ..., aquele que ...; ～**-man** *n* macho.

head [hɛd] *n* cabeça; (*leader*) chefe *m/f*, líder *m/f* // *vt* (*list*) encabeçar; (*group*) liderar; ～**s** (**or tails**) cara (ou coroa); ～ **first** de cabeça; ～ **over heels de pernas para o ar**; **to** ～ **the ball** cabecear a bola; **to** ～ **for** *vt fus* dirigir-se a; ～**ache** *n* dor *f* de cabeça; ～**ing** *n* título, cabeçalho; ～**lamp** *n* farol *m* (de veículo); ～**land** *n* promontório; ～**light** = ～**lamp**; ～**line** *n* manchete *f*, título; ～**long** *adv* (*fall*) de cabeça; (*rush*) precipitadamente; ～**master** *n* diretor (*Pt*: -ct-) *m* (de escola); ～ **mistress** *n* diretora (*Pt*: -ct-) *f* (de escola); ～ **office** *n* matriz *f*; ～**-on** *adj* (*collision*) de frente; ～**phones** *npl* fones *mpl* de ouvido; ～**quarters** (**HQ**) *npl* sede *f*; (MIL) quartel *m* general; ～**-rest** *n* apoio para a cabeça; ～**room** *n* (*in car*) espaço (para a cabeça); (*under bridge*) vão m livre; ～**scarf** *n* lenço de cabeça; ～**stone** *n* lápide *f* de ponta cabeça; ～**strong** *adj* voluntarioso, teimoso; ～ **waiter** *n* maitre *m* (*Br*), chefe de mesa (*Pt*); ～**way** *n* progresso; **to make** ～**way** avançar; ～**wind** *n* vento contrário.

heal [hiːl] *vt* curar // *vi* cicatrizar.

health [hɛlθ] *n* saúde *f*; **good** ～**!** saúde!; ～ **food** *n* comida natural *or* saudável; **H**～ **Service** *n* Previdência Social; ～**y** *adj* (*gen*) são/sã, sadio.

heap [hiːp] *n* pilha, montão *m* // *vt* amontoar, empilhar; (*plate*) encher.

hear [hɪə*], *pt*, *pp* **heard** [hɜːd] *vt* ouvir; (*listen to*) escutar; (*lecture*) assistir // *vi* ouvir; **to** ～ **about** ouvir falar de; **to** ～ **from sb** ter notícias de alguém; ～**ing** *n* (*sense*) audição *f*, ouvido; (LAW) audiência; ～**ing aid** *n* aparelho para a surdez; ～**say** *n* boato, ouvir-dizer *m*.

hearse [hɜːs] *n* carro fúnebre.

heart [haːt] *n* coração *m*; ～**s** *npl* (CARDS) copas *fpl*; **at** ～ no fundo; **by** ～ (*learn*, *know*) de cor; ～ **attack** *n* ataque *m* de coração; ～**beat** *n* batida do coração; ～**breaking** *adj* desolador(a); **to be** ～**broken** estar desolado; ～**burn** *m* azia; ～ **failure** *n* parada cardíaca; ～**felt** *adj* (*cordial*) cordial; (*deeply felt*) sincero.

hearth [haːθ] *n* (*gen*) lar *m*; (*fireplace*) lareira.

heartily ['haːtɪlɪ] *adv* sinceramente, cordialmente; (*laugh*) a gargalhadas, com vontade; (*eat*) apetitosamente.

heartless ['haːtlɪs] *adj* cruel.

hearty ['haːtɪ] *adj* cordial, sincero.

heat [hiːt] *n* (*gen*) calor *m*; (*ardour*) ardor *m*; (SPORT. *also*: **qualifying**) (*prova*) eliminatória // *vt* esquentar; (*fig*) acalorar; **to** ～ **up** *vi* (*gen*) aquecer-se; ～**ed** *adj* quente; (*fig*) acalorado; ～**er** *n* aquecedor *m*.

heath [hi:θ] n (Brit) charneca.

heathen ['hi:ðn] adj, n pagão/paga m/f.

heather ['hɛðə*] n urze f.

heating ['hi:tɪŋ] n aquecimento.

heatstroke ['hi:tstrəuk] n insolação f.

heatwave ['hi:tweɪv] n onda de calor.

heave [hi:v] vt (pull) puxar; (push) empurrar (com esforço); (lift) levantar (com esforço) // vi (water) agitar-se // n puxão m; empurrão m; (effort) esforço; (throw) arremesso.

heaven ['hɛvn] n céu m; (REL) paraíso; ~ly adj celestial; (REL) divino.

heavily ['hɛvɪlɪ] adv pesadamente; (drink, smoke) excessivamente; (sleep, sigh) profundamente.

heavy ['hɛvɪ] adj pesado; (work) duro; (sea) violento; (rain, meal) forte; (drinker, smoker) grande; (eater) comilão/lona; ~weight n (SPORT) peso-pesado.

Hebrew ['hi:bru:] adj hebreu/hebréia; (LING) hebraico.

heckle ['hɛkl] vt interromper.

hectic ['hɛktɪk] adj febril, agitado.

he'd [hi:d] = he would; he had.

hedge [hɛdʒ] n cerca-viva, sebe f // vt cercar (com uma sebe) // vi dar evasivas; **to ~ one's bets** (fig) resguardar-se.

hedgehog ['hɛdʒhɔg] n ouriço.

heed [hi:d] vt (also: **take ~ of**) (attend to) prestar atenção a; (bear in mind) levar em consideração; ~less adj desatento, negligente.

heel [hi:l] n (of shoe) salto; (of foot) calcanhar m // vt (shoe) pôr salto em.

hefty ['hɛftɪ] adj (person) robusto; (piece) grande; (price) alto.

heifer ['hɛfə*] n novilha, bezerra.

height [haɪt] n (of person) estatura; (of building) altura; (high ground) monte m; (altitude) altitude f; ~en vt elevar; (fig) aumentar.

heir [ɛə*] n herdeiro; ~ess n herdeira; ~loom n relíquia de família.

held [hɛld] pt, pp of hold.

helicopter ['hɛlɪkɔptə*] n helicóptero.

hell [hɛl] n inferno; ~! diabos!

he'll [hi:l] = he will, he shall.

hellish ['hɛlɪʃ] adj infernal; (fam) terrível.

hello [hə'ləu] excl oi! (Br), olá! (Pt); (on phone) alô! (Br), está (Pt); (surprise) nossa!

helm [hɛlm] n (NAUT) timão m, leme m.

helmet ['hɛlmɪt] n capacete m.

help [hɛlp] n ajuda; (charwoman) faxineira; (assistant etc) auxiliar m/f // vt ajudar; ~! socorro!; ~ **yourself** sirva-se; **he can't ~ it** não tem culpa; ~er n ajudante m/f; ~ful adj útil, benéfico; ~ing n porção f; ~less adj (incapable) incapaz; (defenceless) indefeso.

hem [hɛm] n bainha; **to ~ in** vt cercar, encurralar.

hemisphere ['hɛmɪsfɪə*] n hemisfério.

hen [hɛn] n galinha.

hence [hɛns] adv (therefore) daí, portanto; **2 years ~** daqui a 2 anos;

~**forth** adv de agora em diante, doravante.

henchman ['hɛntʃmən] n jagunço, capanga m.

henpecked ['hɛnpɛkt] adj dominado pela esposa.

her [hə:*] pron (direct) a; (indirect) lhe; (stressed, after prep) ela // adj seu/sua or dela; ~ **name** o nome dela.

herald ['hɛrəld] n (forerunner) precursor(a) m/f // vt anunciar.

heraldry ['hɛrəldrɪ] n heráldica.

herb [hə:b] n erva.

herd [hə:d] n rebanho.

here [hɪə*] adv aqui; ~! (present) presente!; ~ **she is** aqui está ela; ~**after** adv daqui por diante // n: **the** ~**after** a vida de além-túmulo; ~**by** adv (in letter) por este meio.

hereditary [hɪ'rɛdɪtrɪ] adj hereditário; **heredity** [-tɪ] n hereditariedade f, herança.

heresy ['hɛrəsɪ] n heresia.

heretic ['hɛrətɪk] n herege m/f; ~**al** [hɪ'rɛtɪkl] adj herético.

heritage ['hɛrɪtɪdʒ] n (gen) herança; (fig) patrimônio.

hermit ['hə:mɪt] n eremita.

hernia ['hə:nɪə] n hérnia.

hero ['hɪərəu], pl ~**es** n herói m; (in book, film) protagonista m; ~**ic** [hɪ'rəuɪk] adj heróico.

heroin ['hɛrəuɪn] n heroína.

heroine ['hɛrəuɪn] n heroína; (in book, film) protagonista.

heroism ['hɛrəuɪzm] n heroísmo.

heron ['hɛrən] n garça.

herring ['hɛrɪŋ] n arenque m.

hers [hə:z] pron (o) seu/(a) sua, (o/a) dela.

herself [hə:'sɛlf] pron (reflexive) se; (emphatic) ela mesma; (after prep) si (mesma).

he's [hi:z] = he is; he has.

hesitant ['hɛzɪtənt] adj hesitante, indeciso.

hesitate ['hɛzɪteɪt] vi hesitar, duvidar; **hesitation** [-'teɪʃən] n hesitação f, indecisão f.

hew [hju:] vt cortar (com machado).

hexagon ['hɛksəgən] n hexágono; ~**al** [-'sægənl] adj hexagonal.

hi [haɪ] excl oi!

hibernate ['haɪbəneɪt] vi hibernar.

hiccough, hiccup ['hɪkʌp] vi estar com soluço; ~**s** n pl soluço sg.

hid [hɪd] pt of hide.

hidden ['hɪdn] pp of hide.

hide [haɪd] n (skin) pele f // (vb: pt hid, pp hidden) vt esconder, ocultar // vi: **to ~** (from sb) esconder-se or ocultar-se (de alguém); ~**-and-seek** n esconde-esconde m; ~**away** n refúgio, esconderijo.

hideous ['hɪdɪəs] adj horrível.

hiding ['haɪdɪŋ] n (beating) surra; **to be in ~** (concealed) estar escondido; ~ **place** n esconderijo.

hierarchy ['haɪərɑːkɪ] *n* hierarquia.

high [haɪ] *adj* (*gen, speed*) (*number*) grande; (*price*) alto, elevado; (*wind*) forte; (*voice*) agudo // *adv* alto, a grande altura; **it is 20 m** ~ tem 20 m de altura; ~ **in the air** nas alturas; ~**brow** *adj* culto, metido a intelectual; ~**chair** *n* cadeira alta (para criança); ~**handed** *adj* despótico; ~**heeled** *adj* de salto alto; ~**jack** = **hijack**; ~ **jump** *n* (*SPORT*) salto em altura; ~**light** *n* (*fig: of event*) ponto alto // *vt* realçar; ~**ly** *adv* altamente; ~**ly strung** *adj* tenso, irritadiço; **H**~ **Mass** *n* missa cantada; ~**ness** *n* altura; **Her H**~**ness** Sua Alteza; ~**pitched** *adj* agudo; ~**rise block** *n* edifício alto, espigão *m*; ~ **school** *n* escola secundária; ~ **street** *n* rua principal; ~**way** *n* estrada, rodovia.

hijack ['haɪdʒæk] *vt* seqüestrar; ~**er** *n* seqüestrador(a) *m/f*.

hike [haɪk] *vi* (*go walking*) caminhar; (*tramp*) vagar // *n* caminhada; **hiker** *n* caminhante *m/f*, andarilho.

hilarious [hɪˈlɛərɪəs] *adj* (*behaviour, event*) hilariante, alegre.

hill [hɪl] *n* colina; (*high*) montanha; (*slope*) ladeira, rampa; ~**side** *n* vertente *f*; ~**y** *adj* montanhoso; (*uneven*) acidentado.

hilt [hɪlt] *n* (*of sword*) punho, guarda; **to the** ~ plenamente.

him [hɪm] *pron* (*direct*) o; (*indirect*) lhe; (*stressed, after prep*) ele; ~**self** *pron* (*reflexive*) se; (*emphatic*) ele mesmo; (*after prep*) si (mesmo).

hind [haɪnd] *adj* traseiro // *n* corça.

hinder ['hɪndə*] *vt* impedir, estorvar; **hindrance** ['hɪndrəns] *n* impedimento, estorvo.

Hindu ['hɪnduː] *n* hindu *m/f*.

hinge [hɪndʒ] *n* dobradiça // *vi* (*fig*): **to** ~ **on** depender de.

hint [hɪnt] *n* insinuação *f*; (*advice*) palpite *m*, dica // *vt*: **to** ~ **that** insinuar que // *vi* dar indiretas (*Pt*: -ct-); **to** ~ **at** fazer alusão a.

hip [hɪp] *n* quadril *m*; ~ **pocket** *n* bolso traseiro.

hippopotamus [hɪpəˈpɒtəməs], *pl* ~**es** *or* ~**mi** [-maɪ] *n* hipopótamo.

hire ['haɪə*] *vt* (*car, equipment*) alugar; (*worker*) contratar // *n* aluguel *m*; (*of person*) contratação *f*; **for** ~ aluga-se; (*taxi*) livre; ~ **purchase** (**H.P.**) *n* compra a prazo.

his [hɪz] *pron* (o) seu/(a) sua, (o/a) dele // *adj* seu/sua *or* dele; ~ **name** o nome dele.

Hispanic [hɪsˈpænɪk] *adj* hispânico.

hiss [hɪs] *vi* silvar; (*boo*) vaiar // *n* silvo, vaia.

historian [hɪˈstɔːrɪən] *n* historiador(a) *m/f*.

historic(al) [hɪˈstɒrɪk(l)] *adj* histórico.

history ['hɪstərɪ] *n* história.

hit [hɪt] *pt, pp* **hit** *vt* (*strike*) bater em, golpear; (*reach: target*) acertar, alcançar; (*collide with: car*) bater em,

colidir com // *n* golpe *m*, colisão *f*; (*success*) sucesso, grande êxito; **to** ~ **it off with sb** dar-se bem com alguém.

hitch [hɪtʃ] *vt* (*fasten*) atar, amarrar; (*also:* ~ **up**) levantar // *n* (*difficulty*) dificuldade *f*; **to** ~ **a lift** pegar carona (*Br*), arranjar uma boleia (*Pt*).

hitch-hike ['hɪtʃhaɪk] *vi* pegar carona (*Br*), andar à boleia (*Pt*); **hitch-hiker** *n* pessoa que pega carona (*Br*), pessoa que anda à boleia (*Pt*).

hive [haɪv] *n* colméia.

hoard [hɔːd] *n* provisão *f* // *vt* acumular; ~**ing** *n* acumulação *f*; (*for posters*) tapume *m*.

hoarfrost ['hɔːfrɒst] *n* geada.

hoarse [hɔːs] *adj* rouco.

hoax [həʊks] *n* trote *m*.

hobble ['hɒbl] *vi* coxear // *vt* (*horse*) pear, estar peado.

hobby ['hɒbɪ] *n* hobby *m*, passatempo predileto (*Pt*: -ct-); ~**horse** *n* (*fig*) tema *m* favorito.

hobo ['həʊbəʊ] *n* (*US*) vagabundo.

hockey ['hɒkɪ] *n* hóquei *m*.

hoe [həʊ] *n* enxada // *vt* trabalhar com enxada, capinar.

hog [hɒg] *n* porco; (*person*) glutão *m* // *vt* (*fig*) monopolizar; **to go the whole** ~ ir até o fim.

hoist [hɔɪst] *n* (*lift*) guincho; (*crane*) guindaste *m*.

hold [həʊld], *pt, pp* **held** *vt* ter; (*contain*) conter; (*keep back*) reter; (*believe*) sustentar; (*take* ~ *of*) segurar; (*take weight*) agüentar; (*meeting*) realizar // *vi* (*withstand pressure*) resistir; (*be valid*) ser válido; (*stick*) colar-se // *n* (*handle*) apoio (para a mão); (*fig: grasp*) influência, domínio; (*NAUT*) porão *m* de navio; ~ **the line!** (*TEL*) não desligue!; **to one's own** (*fig*) sair-se bem; **to catch** *or* **get (a)** ~ **of** agarrar-se a; **to** ~ **back** *vt* conter-se; (*secret*) manter, guardar; **to** ~ **down** *vt* (*person*) oprimir; (*job*) manter; **to** ~ **off** *vt* (*enemy*) afastar, repelir; **to** ~ **on** *vi* agarrar-se; (*wait*) esperar; ~ **on!** (*TEL*) não desligue!; **to** ~ **on to** *vt fus* agarrar-se a; (*keep*) guardar; **to** ~ **out** *vt* estender // *vi* (*resist*) resistir; **to** ~ **up** *vt* (*raise*) levantar; (*support*) apoiar; (*delay*) atrasar; (*rob*) assaltar; ~**all** *n* bolsa de viagem; ~**er** *n* (*of ticket*) portador *m*; (*of record*) detentor *m*; (*of office, title etc*) titular *m/f*; ~**ing** *n* (*share*) títulos, ações *fpl*; ~**up** *n* (*robbery*) assalto; (*delay*) demora; (*in traffic*) engarrafamento.

hole [həʊl] *n* buraco // *vt* esburacar.

holiday ['hɒlədɪ] *n* férias *fpl*; (*day off*) feriado; ~**maker** *n* pessoa (que está) de férias; ~ **resort** *n* local *m* de férias.

holiness ['həʊlɪnɪs] *n* santidade *f*.

Holland ['hɒlənd] *n* Holanda.

hollow ['hɒləʊ] *adj* oco, vazio; (*eyes*) fundo; (*sound*) surdo; (*doctrine*) falso // *n*

holly ['hɒlɪ] n azevinho; ~**hock** n malvarosa.

holster ['həulstə*] n coldre m.

holy ['həulɪ] adj (gen) santo, sagrado; (water) bento; **H~ Ghost** or **Spirit** n Espírito Santo.

homage ['hɒmɪdʒ] n homenagem f; **to pay ~** to prestar homenagem a.

home [həum] n casa, lar m; (country) pátria; (institution) asilo // adj (domestic) caseiro, doméstico; (ECON, POL) nacional, interno // adv (direction) para casa; **at ~** em casa; **to go/come ~** ir/vir para casa; **make yourself at ~** fique à vontade; ~ **address** n endereço residencial; ~**land** n terra (natal); ~**less** adj sem casa, sem teto (Pt: -ct-); ~**ly** adj (domestic) caseiro; (simple) simples; ~-**made** adj caseiro; ~ **rule** n autonomia; **H~ Secretary** n (Brit) Ministro do Interior; ~**sick** adj: **to be ~sick** estar com saudade or saudoso (do lar); ~ **town** n cidade f natal; ~**ward** ['həumwəd] adj (journey) para casa, para a terra natal; ~**work** n dever m de casa.

homicide ['hɒmɪsaɪd] n (US) homicídio.

homosexual [hɒməu'sɛksjuəl] adj, n homossexual m.

honest ['ɒnɪst] adj honesto; (sincere) sincero, franco; ~**ly** adv honestamente, francamente; ~**y** n honestidade f, sinceridade f.

honey ['hʌnɪ] n mel m; ~**comb** n favo de mel; (pattern) em forma de favo; ~**moon** n lua-de-mel f; (trip) viagem f de lua-de-mel.

honk [hɒŋk] vi (AUT) buzinar.

honorary ['ɒnərərɪ] adj não remunerado; (duty, title) honorário.

honour, honor (US) ['ɒnə*] vt honrar // n honra, fama; ~**able** adj honrado; ~**s degree** n (SCOL) diploma m com distinção.

hood [hud] n capuz m, touca; (Brit: AUT) capota; (US: AUT) capô m.

hoodlum ['hu:dləm] n pinta-braba m.

hoof [hu:f], pl **hooves** n casco, pata.

hook [huk] n gancho; (on dress) colchete m; (for fishing) anzol m // vt enganchar, fisgar.

hooligan ['hu:lɪgən] n desordeiro, bagunceiro.

hoop [hu:p] n arco.

hoot [hu:t] vi (AUT) buzinar; (siren) tocar // n buzinada, toque m de sirena; **to ~ with laughter** morrer de rir; ~**er** n (AUT) buzina; (NAUT) sirena.

hooves [hu:vz] pl of **hoof**.

hop [hɒp] vi saltar, pular; (on one foot) pular num pé só // n salto, pulo.

hope [həup] vi esperar // n esperança; **I ~ so/not** espero que sim/não; ~**ful** adj (person) otimista (Pt: -pt-), esperançoso; (situation) promissor(a);

~**fully** adv espera-se or esperamos que; ~**less** adj desesperado, irremediável.

hops [hɒps] npl lúpulo sg.

horde [hɔ:d] n horda, bando.

horizon [hə'raɪzn] n horizonte m; ~**tal** [hɔrɪ'zɒntl] adj horizontal.

hormone ['hɔ:məun] n hormônio.

horn [hɔ:n] n corno, chifre m; (MUS) trompa; (AUT) buzina; ~**ed** adj (animal) com chifres, chifrudo.

hornet ['hɔ:nɪt] n vespão m.

horn-rimmed ['hɔ:n-rɪmd] adj com aro de chifre or de tartaruga.

horny ['hɔ:nɪ] adj (material) córneo; (hands) calejado.

horoscope ['hɒrəskəup] n horóscopo.

horrible ['hɒrɪbl] adj horrível.

horrid ['hɒrɪd] adj hórrido, horrível.

horrify ['hɒrɪfaɪ] vt horrorizar.

horror ['hɒrə*] n horror m; ~ **film** n filme m de terror.

hors d'œuvre [ɔ:'də:vrə] n antepasto, entrada.

horse [hɔ:s] n cavalo; **on ~back** a cavalo; ~**man** n cavaleiro; (skilled) ginete m; ~**woman** n amazona; ~**power** (h.p.) n cavalo-vapor m; ~-**racing** n corrida de cavalo; ~**radish** n rábano-bastardo; ~**shoe** n ferradura.

horticulture ['hɔ:tɪkʌltʃə*] n horticultura.

hose [həuz] n (also: ~**pipe**) mangueira.

hosiery ['həuzɪərɪ] n meias e roupa de baixo.

hospitable ['hɒspɪtəbl] adj hospitaleiro.

hospital ['hɒspɪtl] n hospital m.

hospitality [hɒspɪ'tælɪtɪ] n hospitalidade f.

host [həust] n anfitrião m; (in hotel etc) hospedeiro; (REL) hóstia; (large number): **a ~ of** uma multidão de.

hostage ['hɒstɪdʒ] n refém m.

hostel ['hɒstl] n hospedaria; **youth ~** n albergue m para jovens.

hostess ['həustɪs] n anfitriã f; (air ~) aeromoça (Br), hospedeira de bordo (Pt).

hostile ['hɒstaɪl] adj hostil; **hostility** [-'stɪlɪtɪ] n hostilidade f.

hot [hɒt] adj quente; (as opposed to only warm) muito quente, ardente; (spicy) picante; (fig) ardente, veemente; ~ **dog** n cachorro-quente m.

hotel [həu'tɛl] n hotel m; ~**ier** n hoteleiro/a.

hot: ~-**headed** adj impetuoso, fogoso; ~**house** n estufa; ~**ly** adv ardentemente, apaixonadamente; ~-**water bottle** n bolsa de água quente.

hound [haund] vt acossar, perseguir // n cão m de caça, sabujo.

hour ['auə*] n hora; ~**ly** adv de hora em hora.

house [haus, pl: 'hauz z] n (also: firm) casa; (POL) câmara; (THEATRE) assistência, platéia // vt [hauz] (person) alojar; **on the ~** (fig) por conta da casa; ~ **arrest** n prisão f domiciliar; ~**boat** n casa flutuante; ~**breaking** n arrombamento de domicílio; ~**coat** n roupão m; ~**hold** n pessoas fpl da casa, família; ~**keeper** n governanta; ~**keeping** n (work) trabalhos mpl domésticos; ~**keeping** (money) economia doméstica; ~ **trailer** n (US) reboque m; ~**warming party** n festa de inauguração de uma casa; ~**wife** n dona de casa; ~**work** n trabalhos mpl domésticos.

housing ['hauzıŋ] n (act) alojamento; (houses) residências fpl; ~ **estate** n conjunto residencial.

hovel ['hɔvl] n choupana, casebre m.

hover ['hɔvə*] vi pairar; ~**craft** n aerobarco.

how [hau] adv como; ~ **are you?** como vai?; ~ **long have you been here?** quanto tempo faz que você está aqui?; ~ **lovely!** que lindo!; ~ **many/much?** quantos/quanto?; ~ **old are you?** quantos anos você tem?; ~**ever** adv de qualquer modo; (+ adjective) por mais ... que; (in questions) como // conj no entanto, contudo, todavia.

howl [haul] n uivo // vi uivar.

h.p., **H.P.** abbr of hire purchase; horse power.

HQ abbr of headquarters.

hub [hʌb] n (of wheel) centro.

hubbub ['hʌbʌb] n algazarra, vozerio.

hubcap ['hʌbkæp] n calota.

huddle ['hʌdl] vi: to ~ **together** aconchegar-se.

hue [hju:] n cor f, matiz m; ~ **and cry** n alarme m, gritaria.

huff [hʌf] n: in a ~ com raiva.

hug [hʌg] vt abraçar // n abraço.

huge [hju:dʒ] adj enorme, imenso.

hulk [hʌlk] n (wreck) navio velho; (hull) casco, carcaça.

hull [hʌl] n (of ship) casco.

hullo [hə'ləu] excl = hello.

hum [hʌm] vt cantarolar, zunir // vi fazer 'hum'; (insect) zumbir // n zumbido.

human ['hju:mən] adj n, humano.

humane [hju:'meın] adj humano, humanitário.

humanity [hju:'mænıtı] n humanidade f.

humble ['hʌmbl] adj humilde // vt humilhar; **humbly** adv humildemente.

humbug ['hʌmbʌg] n fraude f, embuste m; (sweet) bala de hortelã.

humdrum ['hʌmdrʌm] adj (boring) monótono, enfadonho; (routine) rotineiro.

humid ['hju:mıd] adj úmido; ~**ity** [-'mıdıtı] n umidade f.

humiliate [hju:'mılıeıt] vt humilhar; **humiliation** [-'eıʃən] n humilhação f.

humility [hju:'mılıtı] n humildade f.

humorist ['hju:mərıst] n humorista m/f.

humorous ['hju:mərəs] adj engraçado, divertido.

humour, **humor** (US) ['hju:mə*] n humorismo, senso de humor; (mood)

humor m // vt (person) fazer a vontade de.

hump [hʌmp] n (in ground) elevação f; (camel's) corcova, giba.

hunch [hʌntʃ] n (premonition) pressentimento; ~**back** n corcunda; ~**ed** adj corcunda.

hundred ['hʌndrəd] num cem; (before lower numbers) cento; (collective) centena; ~**weight** n (Brit) = 50.8 kg; 112 lb; (US) = 45.3 kg; 100 lb.

hung [hʌŋ] pt, pp of **hang**.

Hungarian [hʌŋ'gɛərıən] adj, n húngaro/a.

Hungary ['hʌŋgərı] n Hungria.

hunger ['hʌŋgə*] n fome f // vi: to ~ **for** (gen) ter fome de; (desire) desejar ardentemente; ~ **strike** n greve f de fome; **hungrily** [-grəlı] adv avidamente, com fome; **hungry** [-grı] adj faminto, esfomeado; **to be hungry** estar com fome.

hunt [hʌnt] vt (seek) buscar, perseguir; (SPORT) caçar // vi caçar // n caça, caçada; ~**er** n caçador m; ~**ing** n caça.

hurdle ['hə:dl] n (SPORT) barreira; (fig) obstáculo.

hurl [hə:l] vt arremessar, lançar.

hurrah [hu'rɑ:], **hurray** [hu'reı] n viva!, hurra!

hurricane ['hʌrıkən] n furacão m.

hurried ['hʌrıd] adj (fast) apressado; (rushed) feito às pressas; ~**ly** adv depressa, apressadamente.

hurry ['hʌrı] n pressa // vi apressar-se // vt (person) apressar; (work) acelerar; **to be in a** ~ estar com pressa.

hurt [hə:t], pt, pp **hurt** vt machucar, ferir; (pain) doer; (fig) magoar // vi doer // adj machucado, ferido; ~**ful** adj (gen) que dói; (harmful) prejudicial; (remark) que magoa, ofensivo.

hurtle ['hə:tl] vi: to ~ **past** passar como um raio; to ~ **down** cair com violência.

husband ['hʌzbənd] n marido, esposo.

hush [hʌʃ] n silêncio, quietude f // vt fazer calar; (cover up) abafar, encobrir; ~! silêncio!

husk [hʌsk] n (of wheat) casca.

husky ['hʌskı] adj rouco; (burly) robusto // n cão m esquimó.

hustle ['hʌsl] vt (push) empurrar; (hurry) apressar // n agitação f, atividade (Pt: -ct-) f febril; ~ **and bustle** n vaivém m.

hut [hʌt] n cabana, choupana; (shed) alpendre m.

hutch [hʌtʃ] n coelheira.

hyacinth ['haıəsınθ] n jacinto.

hybrid ['haıbrıd] adj, n híbrido.

hydrant ['haıdrənt] n (also: fire ~) hidrante m.

hydraulic [haı'drɔ:lık] adj hidráulico.

hydroelectric [haıdrəu'lɛktrık] adj hidroelétrico (Pt: -ct-).

hydrogen ['haıdrədʒən] n hidrogênio.

hyena [haı'i:nə] n hiena.

hygiene ['haɪdʒiːn] n higiene f; **hygienic** [-'dʒiːnɪk] adj higiênico.
hymn [hɪm] n hino.
hyphen ['haɪfn] n hífen m.
hypnosis [hɪp'nəʊsɪs] n hipnose f; **hypnotic** [-'nɒtɪk] adj hipnótico; **hypnotism** ['hɪpnətɪzm] n hipnotismo; **hypnotist** ['hɪpnətɪst] n hipnotizador(a) m/f; **hypnotize** ['hɪpnətaɪz] vt hipnotizar.
hypocrisy [hɪ'pɒkrɪsɪ] n hipocrisia; **hypocrite** ['hɪpəkrɪt] n hipócrita m/f; **hypocritical** [hɪpə'krɪtɪkl] adj hipócrita.
hypothesis [haɪ'pɒθɪsɪs], pl -ses [-siːz] n hipótese f; **hypothetic(al)** [-pəʊ'θetɪk(l)] adj hipotético.
hysteria [hɪ'stɪərɪə] n histeria; **hysterical** [-'sterɪkl] adj histérico. **hysterics** [-'sterɪks] npl histeria sg, histerismo sg.

I

I [aɪ] pron eu.
ice [aɪs] n gelo // vt (cake) cobrir com glacê; (drink) gelar // vi (also: ~ over, ~ up) gelar; ~ age n era glacial; ~ axe n picareta para o gelo; ~berg n iceberg m; ~box n (US) geladeira; ~-cold adj gelado; ~ cream n sorvete m (Br), gelado (Pt); ~ cube n cubo or pedra de gelo; ~ hockey n hóquei m sobre o gelo.
Iceland ['aɪslənd] n Islândia; ~er n islandês/esa m/f; ~ic [-'lændɪk] adj islandês/esa.
ice: ~ rink n pista de gelo; ~ skating n patinação f no gelo.
icicle ['aɪsɪkl] n pingente m de gelo.
icing ['aɪsɪŋ] n (CULIN) glacê m; (AVIAT etc) formação f de gelo; ~ sugar n açúcar m glacê.
icon ['aɪkɔn] n ícone m.
icy ['aɪsɪ] adj (road) gelado; (fig) glacial, indiferente.
I'd [aɪd] = I would; I had.
idea [aɪ'dɪə] n idéia f.
ideal [aɪ'dɪəl] n ideal m // adj ideal; ~ist n idealista m/f.
identical [aɪ'dentɪkl] adj idêntico.
identification [aɪdentɪfɪ'keɪʃən] n identificação f; ~ means of documentos mpl pessoais.
identify [aɪ'dentɪfaɪ] vt identificar.
identikit picture [aɪ'dentɪkɪt-] n retrato falado.
identity [aɪ'dentɪtɪ] n identidade f.
ideological [aɪdɪə'lɒdʒɪkəl] adj ideológico; **ideology** [-dɪ'ɒlədʒɪ] n ideologia.
idiocy ['ɪdɪəsɪ] n idiotice f; (stupid act) estupidez f.
idiom ['ɪdɪəm] n expressão f idiomática; (style of speaking) idioma m, linguagem f.
idiosyncrasy [ɪdɪəʊ'sɪŋkrəsɪ] n idiossincrasia; (col) mania.
idiot ['ɪdɪət] n (gen) idiota m/f; (fool) tolo, imbecil; ~ic [-'ɒtɪk] adj idiota, néscio.

idle ['aɪdl] adj (gen) ocioso; (lazy) preguiçoso; (unemployed) desempregado; (pointless) inútil, vão/vã // vi (machine) funcionar com a transmissão desligada // vt: to ~ away the time perder or desperdiçar tempo; ~ness n ociosidade f; preguiça; inutilidade f.
idol ['aɪdl] n ídolo; ~ize vt idolatrar.
if [ɪf] conj se.
igloo ['ɪgluː] n iglu m.
ignite [ɪg'naɪt] vt acender; (set fire to) incendiar // vi acender.
ignition [ɪg'nɪʃən] n (AUT) ignição f; to switch on/off the ~ ligar/desligar o motor; ~ key n (AUT) chave f de ignição.
ignorance ['ɪgnərəns] n ignorância; **ignorant** [-ənt] adj ignorante; to be ignorant of ignorar.
ignore [ɪg'nɔː*] vt (person) não fazer caso de; (fact) não levar em consideração, ignorar.
I'll [aɪl] = I will, I shall.
ill [ɪl] adj doente; (slightly) indisposto; (bad) mau/má // n mal m; (fig) desgraça // adv mal; to take or be taken ~ ficar doente; ~-advised adj pouco recomendado; (misled) mal aconselhado; ~-at-ease adj constrangido, pouco à vontade.
illegal [ɪ'liːgl] adj ilegal, ilegítimo.
illegible [ɪ'ledʒɪbl] adj ilegível.
illegitimate [ɪlɪ'dʒɪtɪmət] adj ilegítimo.
ill: ~-fated adj malfadado, azarento; ~ feeling n má vontade f, rancor m.
illicit [ɪ'lɪsɪt] adj ilícito.
illiterate [ɪ'lɪtərət] adj analfabeto.
ill-mannered [ɪl'mænəd] adj mal-educado, grosseiro.
illness ['ɪlnɪs] n doença.
illogical [ɪ'lɒdʒɪkl] adj ilógico.
ill-treat [ɪl'triːt] vt maltratar.
illuminate [ɪ'luːmɪneɪt] vt (room, street) iluminar, clarear; (subject) esclarecer; **illumination** [-'neɪʃən] n iluminação f; **illuminations** npl luminárias fpl.
illusion [ɪ'luːʒən] n ilusão f; to be under the ~ that... estar com a ilusão de que...; **illusory** [-sərɪ] adj ilusório.
illustrate ['ɪləstreɪt] vt (gen) ilustrar; (subject) esclarecer; (point) exemplificar; **illustration** [-'streɪʃən] n (example) exemplo; (explanation) esclarecimento; (in book) gravura, ilustração f.
illustrious [ɪ'lʌstrɪəs] adj ilustre.
ill will [ɪl'wɪl] n animosidade f, má vontade f.
I'm [aɪm] = I am.
image ['ɪmɪdʒ] n imagem f.
imaginary [ɪ'mædʒɪnərɪ] adj imaginário; **imagination** [-'neɪʃən] n imaginação f; (inventiveness) inventividade f; (illusion) fantasia; **imaginative** [-nətɪv] adj imaginativo; **imagine** vt imaginar; (delude o.s.) fantasiar.
imbalance [ɪm'bæləns] n (gen) desequilíbrio; (inequality) desigualdade.

imbecile ['ɪmbəsiːl] n imbecil m/f.
imbue [ɪm'bjuː] vt: to ~ sth with imbuir or impregnar algo de.
imitate ['ɪmɪteɪt] vt imitar; **imitation** [-'teɪʃən] n imitação f; (copy) cópia; (mimicry) mímica.
immaculate [ɪ'mækjulət] adj impecável; (REL) imaculado.
immaterial [ɪmə'tɪərɪəl] adj imaterial; it is ~ whether... é indiferente se...
immature [ɪmə'tjuə*] adj (person) imaturo; (of one's youth) juvenil.
immediate [ɪ'miːdɪət] adj imediato; (pressing) urgente, premente; ~ly adv (at once) imediatamente; ~ly next to bem junto a.
immense [ɪ'mɛns] adj imenso, enorme.
immerse [ɪ'mɜːs] vt (submerge) submergir; (sink) imergir, mergulhar; to be ~d in (fig) estar absorto em.
immersion heater [ɪ'mɜː-] n aquecedor m de imersão.
immigrant ['ɪmɪgrənt] n imigrante m/f; **immigrate** [-greɪt] vi imigrar; **immigration** [-'greɪʃən] n imigração f.
imminent ['ɪmɪnənt] adj iminente.
immobile [ɪ'məubaɪl] adj imóvel; **immobilize** [-bɪlaɪz] vt imobilizar
immoral [ɪ'mɔrl] adj imoral; ~ity [-'rælɪtɪ] n imoralidade f.
immortal [ɪ'mɔːtl] adj imortal; ~ize vt imortalizar.
immune [ɪ'mjuːn] adj: ~ to imune a, imunizado contra; **immunity** n (MED) imunidade f; (COMM) isenção f.
immunization [ɪmjunaɪ'zeɪʃən] n imunização f; **immunize** ['ɪmjunaɪz] vt imunizar.
imp [ɪmp] n diabinho, criança levada.
impact ['ɪmpækt] n (gen) impacto (Pt: impacte m).
impair [ɪm'pɛə*] vt prejudicar.
impale [ɪm'peɪl] vt perfurar, empalar.
impart [ɪm'pɑːt] vt dar, comunicar.
impartial [ɪm'pɑːʃl] adj imparcial; ~ity [ɪmpɑː'ʃælɪtɪ] n imparcialidade f.
impassable [ɪm'pɑːsəbl] adj (barrier, river) intransponível; (road) intransitável.
impatience [ɪm'peɪʃns] n impaciência; **impatient** [-ənt] adj impaciente; to get or grow impatient impacientar-se.
impeccable [ɪm'pɛkəbl] adj impecável.
impede [ɪm'piːd] vt impedir, estorvar.
impediment [ɪm'pɛdɪmənt] n obstáculo, impedimento; (also: speech ~) defeito (de fala).
impending [ɪm'pɛndɪŋ] adj (near) iminente, próximo.
impenetrable [ɪm'pɛnɪtrəbl] adj (gen) impenetrável; (unfathomable) incompreensível.
imperative [ɪm'pɛrətɪv] adj (tone) imperioso, obrigatório; (necessary) indispensável; (pressing) premente // n (LING) imperativo.
imperceptible [ɪmpə'sɛptɪbl] adj imperceptível.

imperfect [ɪm'pɜːfɪkt] adj imperfeito; (goods etc) defeituoso; ~ion [-'fɛkʃən] n (blemish) defeito; (state) imperfeição f.
imperial [ɪm'pɪərɪəl] adj imperial; ~ism n imperialismo.
imperil [ɪm'pɛrɪl] vt pôr em perigo, arriscar.
impersonal [ɪm'pɜːsənl] adj impessoal.
impersonate [ɪm'pɜːsəneɪt] vt fazer-se passar por, personificar; (THEATRE) representar o papel de.
impertinent [ɪm'pɜːtɪnənt] adj impertinente, insolente.
impervious [ɪm'pɜːvɪəs] adj impenetrável; (fig): ~ to insensível a.
impetuous [ɪm'pɛtjuəs] adj impetuoso, precipitado.
impetus ['ɪmpətəs] n ímpeto; (fig) impulso.
impinge [ɪm'pɪndʒ]: to ~ on vt fus impressionar, impingir em; (affect) afetar (Pt: -ct-).
implausible [ɪm'plɔːzɪbl] adj inverossímil (Pt: -osí-).
implement ['ɪmplɪmənt] n instrumento, ferramenta // vt ['ɪmplɪmɛnt] efetivar (Pt: -ct-); (carry out) realizar, executar.
implicate ['ɪmplɪkeɪt] vt (compromise) comprometer; (involve) implicar, envolver; **implication** [-'keɪʃən] n implicação f, consequência.
implicit [ɪm'plɪsɪt] adj (gen) implícito; (complete) absoluto.
implore [ɪm'plɔː*] vt (person) implorar, suplicar.
imply [ɪm'plaɪ] vt (involve) implicar; (mean) significar; (hint) dar a entender que; **it is implied** se subentende.
impolite [ɪmpə'laɪt] adj indelicado.
import [ɪm'pɔːt] vt importar // n ['ɪmpɔːt] (COMM) importação f; (: article) mercadoria importada; (meaning) significado, sentido.
importance [ɪm'pɔːtəns] n importância; **important** [-ənt] adj importante; it's not important não tem importância.
importer [ɪm'pɔːtə*] n importador(a) m/f.
impose [ɪm'pəuz] vt impor // vi: to ~ on sb abusar de alguém; **imposing** adj imponente.
impossible [ɪm'pɔsɪbl] adj impossível; (person) insuportável.
impostor [ɪm'pɔstə*] n impostor(a) m/f.
impotence ['ɪmpətəns] n impotência; **impotent** [-ənt] adj impotente.
impound [ɪm'paund] vt confiscar.
impoverished [ɪm'pɔvərɪʃt] adj empobrecido; (land) esgotado.
impracticable [ɪm'præktɪkəbl] adj impraticável, inexequível.
impractical [ɪm'præktɪkl] adj (person) pouco prático.
imprecise [ɪmprɪ'saɪs] adj impreciso, vago.
impregnable [ɪm'prɛgnəbl] adj invulnerável; (castle) inexpugnável.
impregnate ['ɪmprɛgneɪt] vt (gen)

impregnar; (*soak*) embeber; (*fertilize*) fecundar.

impresario [ɪmprɪˈsɑːrɪəu] *n* empresário.

impress [ɪmˈprɛs] *vt* impressionar; (*mark*) imprimir // *vi* causar boa impressão; to ~ sth on sb inculcar algo em alguém; it ~ed itself on me fiquei com isso gravado (na memória).

impression [ɪmˈprɛʃən] *n* impressão *f*; (*footprint etc*) marca; (*print run*) edição *f*; to be under the ~ that estar com a impressão de que; ~able *adj* impressionável; (*sensitive*) sensível; ~ist *n* impressionista *m/f.*

impressive [ɪmˈprɛsɪv] *adj* impressionante, imponente.

imprint [ˈɪmprɪnt] *n* impressão *f*; marca.

imprison [ɪmˈprɪzn] *vt* encarcerar; ~ment *n* encarceramento.

improbable [ɪmˈprɔbəbl] *adj* improvável, duvidoso.

impromptu [ɪmˈprɔmptjuː] *adj* improvisado // *adv* de improviso.

improper [ɪmˈprɔpə*] *adj* (*incorrect*) impróprio; (*unseemly*) indecoroso; (*indecent*) indecente.

impropriety [ɪmprəˈpraɪətɪ] *n* falta de decoro, inconveniência; (*indecency*) indecência; (*of language*) impropriedade *f.*

improve [ɪmˈpruːv] *vt* melhorar // *vi* melhorar; (*pupils*) progredir; ~ment *n* melhoria; aperfeiçoamento; progresso.

improvise [ˈɪmprəvaɪz] *vt/i* improvisar.

imprudent [ɪmˈpruːdnt] *adj* imprudente.

impudent [ˈɪmpjudnt] *adj* insolente, impudente.

impulse [ˈɪmpʌls] *n* impulso, ímpeto; to act on ~ agir sem pensar; **impulsive** [-ˈpʌlsɪv] *adj* impulsivo.

impunity [ɪmˈpjuːnɪtɪ] *n*: with ~ impunemente.

impure [ɪmˈpjuə*] *adj* (*adulterated*) adulterado; (*not pure*) impuro; **impurity** *n* (*gen*) impureza.

in [ɪn] *prep* em; (*within*) dentro de; (*with time: during, within*): ~ 2 days em or dentro de 2 dias; (: *after*): ~ 2 weeks (*within*) dentro de 2 semanas; (*after*) daqui a 2 semanas; (*with town, country*): it's ~ France é or fica na França // *adv* dentro, para dentro; (*fashionable*) na moda; is he ~? ele está?; ~ the country no campo; ~ town no centro (da cidade); ~ the distance ao longe; ~ the sun ao/sob o sol; ~ the rain na chuva; ~ French em francês; 1 ~ 10 1 em cada 10; ~ hundreds às centenas; the best pupil ~ the class o melhor aluno da classe; written ~ pencil escrito a lápis; ~ saying this ao dizer isto; their party is ~ seu partido chegou ao poder; to ask sb ~ convidar alguém para entrar; to run/limp ~ entrar correndo/mancando; the ~s and outs os cantos e recantos, os pormenores *mpl.*

in., ins *abbr of* **inch(es).**

inability [ɪnəˈbɪlɪtɪ] *n* incapacidade *f.*

inaccessible [ɪnəkˈsɛsɪbl] *adj* inacessível.

inaccuracy [ɪnˈækjurəsɪ] *n* inexatidão (*Pt*: -ct-) *f*, imprecisão *f*; **inaccurate** [-rət] *adj* inexato (*Pt*: -ct-).

inactivity [ɪnækˈtɪvɪtɪ] *n* inatividade (*Pt*: -ct-) *f.*

inadequate [ɪnˈædɪkwət] *adj* (*insufficient*) insuficiente; (*unsuitable*) inadequado; (*person*) impróprio.

inadvertently [ɪnədˈvɜːtntlɪ] *adv* inadvertidamente, sem querer.

inadvisable [ɪnədˈvaɪzəbl] *adj* não aconselhável, inoportuno.

inane [ɪˈneɪn] *adj* tolo; (*fatuous*) vazio.

inanimate [ɪnˈænɪmət] *adj* inanimado.

inapplicable [ɪnˈæplɪkəbl] *adj* inaplicável.

inappropriate [ɪnəˈprəuprɪət] *adj* inadequado, inconveniente; (*word, expression*) impróprio.

inapt [ɪnˈæpt] *adj* inapto; ~itude *n* incapacidade *f*, inaptidão *f.*

inarticulate [ɪnɑːˈtɪkjulət] *adj* (*person*) incapaz de expressar-se (bem); (*speech*) inarticulado.

inasmuch as [ɪnəzˈmʌtʃæz] *adv* (*given that*) visto que; (*since*) desde que, já que.

inattentive [ɪnəˈtɛntɪv] *adj* desatento.

inaudible [ɪnˈɔːdɪbl] *adj* inaudível.

inaugural [ɪˈnɔːgjurəl] *adj* (*speech*) inaugural; (: *of president*) de posse; **inaugurate** [-reɪt] *vt* inaugurar; **inauguration** [-ˈreɪʃən] *n* inauguração *f.*

in-between [ɪnbɪˈtwiːn] *adj* intermediário, entre dois extremos.

inborn [ɪnˈbɔːn] *adj* (*feeling*) inato.

inbred [ɪnˈbrɛd] *adj* inato; (*family*) de procriação consanguínea.

incalculable [ɪnˈkælkjuləbl] *adj* incalculável.

incapable [ɪnˈkeɪpəbl] *adj* incapaz.

incapacitate [ɪnkəˈpæsɪteɪt] *vt*: to ~ sb incapacitar alguém.

incapacity [ɪnkəˈpæsɪtɪ] *n* (*inability*) incapacidade *f.*

incarcerate [ɪnˈkɑːsəreɪt] *vt* encarcerar.

incarnate [ɪnˈkɑːnɪt] *adj* encarnado, personificado // *vt* [ˈɪnkɑːneɪt] encarnar; **incarnation** [-ˈneɪʃən] *n* encarnação *f.*

incendiary [ɪnˈsɛndɪərɪ] *adj* incendiário.

incense [ˈɪnsɛns] *n* incenso // *vt* [ɪnˈsɛns] (*anger*) exasperar, enraivecer.

incentive [ɪnˈsɛntɪv] *n* incentivo, estímulo.

incessant [ɪnˈsɛsnt] *adj* incessante, contínuo; ~ly *adv* constantemente.

incest [ˈɪnsɛst] *n* incesto.

inch [ɪntʃ] *n* polegada; to be within an ~ of estar a um passo de; he didn't give an ~ ele não cedeu nem um milímetro; to ~ forward avançar palmo a palmo.

incidence [ˈɪnsɪdns] *n* (*of crime, disease*) incidência.

incident ['ɪnsɪdnt] n incidente m, evento; (in book) episódio.

incidental [ɪnsɪ'dɛntl] adj acessório, não essencial; (unplanned) acidental, casual; ~ly [-'dɛntəlɪ] adv (by the way) a propósito.

incinerator [ɪn'sɪnəreɪtə*] n incinerador m.

incipient [ɪn'sɪpɪənt] adj incipiente.

incision [ɪn'sɪʒən] n incisão f.

incisive [ɪn'saɪsɪv] adj (mind) penetrante, perspicaz; (tone) mordaz, sarcástico; (remark etc) incisivo.

incite [ɪn'saɪt] vt incitar, provocar.

inclination [ɪnklɪ'neɪʃən] n (tendency) tendência, inclinação f.

incline ['ɪnklaɪn] n inclinação f, ladeira // (vb: [ɪn'klaɪn]) vt (slope) inclinar; (head) curvar, inclinar // vi inclinar-se; to be ~d to (tend) tender a, ser propenso a; (be willing) estar disposto a.

include [ɪn'kluːd] vt incluir, conter; including prep inclusive.

inclusion [ɪn'kluːʒən] n inclusão f; **inclusive** [-sɪv] adj incluído, incluso // adv inclusive.

incognito [ɪnkɔg'niːtəu] adv incógnito.

incoherent [ɪnkəu'hɪərənt] adj incoerente.

income ['ɪŋkʌm] n (salary) salário; (earnings) renda, rendimentos; (unearned) renda; (profit) lucro; ~ tax n imposto de renda (Br), imposto complementar (Pt); ~ tax inspector n fiscal m/f do imposto de renda; ~ tax return n declaração f do imposto de renda.

incoming ['ɪnkʌmɪŋ] adj: ~ flight chegada.

incomparable [ɪn'kɔmpərəbl] adj incomparável.

incompatible [ɪnkəm'pætɪbl] adj incompatível.

incompetence [ɪn'kɔmpɪtəns] n incompetência; **incompetent** [-ənt] adj incompetente.

incomplete [ɪnkəm'pliːt] adj incompleto; (unfinished) por terminar.

incomprehensible [ɪnkɔmprɪ'hɛnsɪbl] adj incompreensível.

inconceivable [ɪnkən'siːvəbl] adj inconcebível.

inconclusive [ɪnkən'kluːsɪv] adj inconclusivo; (argument) pouco convincente.

incongruous [ɪn'kɔŋgruəs] adj (foolish) ridículo, absurdo; (remark, act) incongruente, ilógico.

inconsiderate [ɪnkən'sɪdərət] adj sem consideração; how ~ of him! que falta de consideração (de sua parte)!

inconsistent [ɪnkən'sɪstnt] adj inconsistente, incompatível; ~ with (que) não está de acordo com.

inconspicuous [ɪnkən'spɪkjuəs] adj insignificante, modesto; to make o.s. ~ não chamar a atenção.

inconstant [ɪn'kɔnstnt] adj inconstante.

incontinent [ɪn'kɔntɪnənt] adj incontinente.

inconvenience [ɪnkən'viːnjəns] n (gen) inconveniência; (problem) inconveniente m // vt incomodar; **inconvenient** [-ənt] adj inconveniente, incômodo; (time, place) inoportuno.

incorporate [ɪn'kɔːpəreɪt] vt incorporar; (contain) compreender; (add) incluir; ~d adj: ~d company (US: abbr Inc.) Sociedade f Anônima.

incorrect [ɪnkə'rɛkt] adj incorreto (Pt: -ct-).

incorruptible [ɪnkə'rʌptɪbl] adj (gen) incorruptível; (not open to bribes) insubornável.

increase ['ɪnkriːs] n aumento // vi [ɪn'kriːs] aumentar; (grow) crescer; (price) subir; **increasing** adj (number) crescente, em aumento; **increasingly** adv cada vez mais, mais e mais.

incredible [ɪn'krɛdɪbl] adj incrível.

incredulous [ɪn'krɛdjuləs] adj incrédulo, cético (Pt: -ct-).

increment ['ɪnkrɪmənt] n aumento, incremento.

incriminate [ɪn'krɪmɪneɪt] vt incriminar.

incubation [ɪnkju'beɪʃən] n incubação f; **incubator** ['ɪnkjubeɪtə*] n incubadora; (for eggs) chocadeira.

incumbent [ɪn'kʌmbənt] n titular m/f // adj: it is ~ on him to... cabe a ele...

incur [ɪn'kəː*] vt (gen) incorrer em; (expenses) contrair.

incurable [ɪn'kjuərəbl] adj incurável; (fig) irremediável.

incursion [ɪn'kəːʃən] n incursão f.

indebted [ɪn'dɛtɪd] adj: to be ~ to sb estar em dívida, dever obrigação a alguém.

indecent [ɪn'diːsnt] adj indecente; ~ assault n atentado contra o pudor; ~ exposure n exibição f obscena.

indecisive [ɪndɪ'saɪsɪv] adj indeciso; (discussion) inconcludente, sem resultados.

indeed [ɪn'diːd] adv de fato (Pt: -ct-), realmente; yes ~! claro que sim!

indefinite [ɪn'dɛfɪnɪt] adj indefinido; (uncertain) impreciso; ~ly adv (wait) indefinidamente.

indelible [ɪn'dɛlɪbl] adj indelével.

indemnify [ɪn'dɛmnɪfaɪ] vt indenizar (Pt: -emn-), compensar.

indentation [ɪndɛn'teɪʃən] n entalhe m, recorte m; (TYP) parágrafo, recuo.

independence [ɪndɪ'pɛndns] n independência; **independent** [-ənt] adj independente; to become independent tornar-se independente.

index ['ɪndɛks] n (pl: ~es: in book) índice m; (: in library etc) catálogo; (pl: **indices** ['ɪndɪsiːz]: ratio, sign) expoente m; ~ card n ficha de arquivo; ~ finger n dedo indicador; ~-linked adj vinculado ao índice (do custo de vida).

India ['ɪndɪə] n Índia; ~n adj, n indiano/a; Red ~n pele vermelha m/f.

indicate ['ındıkeıt] vt indicar; **indication** [-'keıʃən] n indício, sinal m; **indicator** n (gen) indicador m.

indices ['ındısi:z] pl of **index**.

indict [ın'daıt] vt acusar; **~ment** n acusação f, denúncia.

indifference [ın'dıfrəns] n indiferença; **indifferent** [-ənt] adj indiferente; (poor) regular, medíocre.

indigenous [ın'dıdʒınəs] adj indígena m/f, nativo.

indigestion [ındı'dʒɛstʃən] n indigestão f.

indignant [ın'dıgnənt] adj: **to be ~ about sth** estar indignado com algo, indignar-se de algo; **indignation** [-'neıʃən] n indignação f.

indignity [ın'dıgnıtı] n indignidade f; (insult) ultraje m, afronta.

indigo ['ındıgəʊ] adj cor de anil // n anil m.

indirect [ındı'rɛkt] adj indireto (Pt: -ct-); **~ly** adv indire(c)tamente.

indiscreet [ındı'skri:t] adj indiscreto; (rash) imprudente; **indiscretion** [-'skrɛʃən] n indiscrição f; imprudência.

indiscriminate [ındı'skrımınət] adj indiscriminado.

indispensable [ındı'spɛnsəbl] adj indispensável, imprescindível.

indisposed [ındı'spəʊzd] adj (unwell) indisposto.

indisputable [ındı'spju:təbl] adj incontestável.

indistinct [ındı'stıŋkt] adj indistinto; (memory, noise) confuso, vago.

individual [ındı'vıdjʊəl] n indivíduo, pessoa // adj individual; (personal) pessoal; (for/of one only) particular; **~ist** n individualista m/f; **~ity** [-'ælıtı] n individualidade f; **~ly** adv individualmente, particularmente.

indoctrinate [ın'dɒktrıneıt] vt doutrinar; **indoctrination** [-'neıʃən] n doutrinação f.

indolent ['ındələnt] adj indolente, preguiçoso.

indoor ['ındɔ:*] adj (inner) interno, interior; (inside) dentro de casa; (swimming pool) coberto; (games, sport) de salão; **~s** [ın'dɔ:z] adv em lugar fechado; (at home) em casa.

induce [ın'dju:s] vt induzir; (bring about) causar, produzir; (provoke) provocar; **~ment** n (incentive) incentivo, estímulo.

induction [ın'dʌkʃən] n (MED: of birth) indução f; **~ course** n curso de indução.

indulge [ın'dʌldʒ] vt (desire) satisfazer; (whim) condescender com; (person) comprazer; (child) fazer a vontade de // vi: **to ~ in** entregar-se a, satisfazer-se com; **indulgence** n (of desire) satisfação f; (leniency) indulgência, tolerância; **indulgent** adj indulgente.

industrial [ın'dʌstrıəl] adj industrial; **~ action** n greve f; **~ estate** n zona industrial; **~ist** n industrial m/f; **~ize** vt industrializar.

industrious [ın'dʌstrıəs] adj (gen) trabalhador(a); (student) aplicado.

industry ['ındəstrı] n indústria; (diligence) aplicação f, diligência.

inebriated [ı'ni:brıeıtıd] adj embriagado, bêbado.

inedible [ın'ɛdıbl] adj não-comestível.

ineffective [ını'fɛktıv] adj ineficaz, inútil.

inefficiency [ını'fıʃənsı] n ineficiência; **inefficient** [-ənt] adj ineficiente.

ineligible [ın'ɛlıdʒıbl] adj (candidate) inelegível; **to be ~ for sth** não estar qualificado para algo.

inept [ı'nɛpt] adj inepto.

inequality [ını'kwɒlıtı] n desigualdade f.

inert [ı'nɜ:t] adj inerte; (immobile) imóvel; **~ia** [ı'nɜ:ʃə] n inércia; (laziness) lerdeza.

inescapable [ını'skeıpəbl] adj inevitável.

inestimable [ın'ɛstıməbl] adj inestimável, incalculável.

inevitable [ın'ɛvıtəbl] adj inevitável; (necessary) forçoso, necessário.

inexcusable [ınıks'kju:zəbl] adj imperdoável, indesculpável.

inexhaustible [ınıg'zɔ:stıbl] adj inesgotável, inexaurível.

inexorable [ın'ɛksɔrəbl] adj inexorável.

inexpensive [ınık'spɛnsıv] adj barato, econômico.

inexperience [ınık'spıərıəns] n inexperiência, falta de experiência; **~d** adj inexperiente.

inexplicable [ınık'splıkəbl] adj inexplicável.

inextricable [ınık'strıkəbl] adj inextricável.

infallible [ın'fælıbl] adj infalível.

infamous ['ınfəməs] adj infame, abominável; **infamy** [-mı] n infâmia.

infancy ['ınfənsı] n infância.

infant ['ınfənt] n (baby) bebê m; (young child) criança; **~ile** adj infantil; (pej) acriançado; **~ school** n escola primária.

infantry ['ınfəntrı] n infantaria; **~man** n soldado de infantaria.

infatuated [ın'fætjʊeıtıd] adj: **~ with** (gen) gamado por; (in love) apaixonado por; **infatuation** [-'eıʃən] n gamação f, paixão f louca.

infect [ın'fɛkt] vt (wound) infeccionar; (person) contagiar; (fig: pej) corromper, contaminar; **~ed with** (illness) contagiado por; **~ion** [ın'fɛkʃən] n infecção f; (fig) contágio; **~ious** [ın'fɛkʃəs] adj contagioso; (also: fig) infeccioso.

infer [ın'fɜ:*] vt deduzir, inferir; **~ence** ['ınfərəns] n dedução f, inferência.

inferior [ın'fıərıə*] adj, n inferior m/f; **~ity** [-rı'ɔrətı] n inferioridade f; **~ity complex** n complexo de inferioridade.

infernal [ın'fɜ:nl] adj infernal.

inferno [ın'fɜ:nəʊ] n inferno; (fig) inferno de chamas.

infertile [ın'fɜ:taıl] adj infértil, estéril;

infertility [-'tɪlɪtɪ] n infertilidade f, esterilidade f.

infested [ɪn'fɛstɪd] adj: ~ (with) infestado (de), assolado (por).

infidelity [ɪnfɪ'dɛlɪtɪ] n infidelidade f.

in-fighting ['ɪnfaɪtɪŋ] n (fig) lutas fpl internas, conflitos mpl internos.

infiltrate ['ɪnfɪltreɪt] vt (troops etc) infiltrar-se em // vi infiltrar-se.

infinite ['ɪnfɪnɪt] adj infinito.

infinitive [ɪn'fɪnɪtɪv] n infinitivo.

infinity [ɪn'fɪnɪtɪ] n (also MATH) infinito; (an ~) infinidade f.

infirm [ɪn'fɜːm] adj enfermo, fraco; ~ary n enfermaria, hospital m; ~ity n fraqueza; (illness) enfermidade f, achaque m.

inflame [ɪn'fleɪm] vt inflamar.

inflammable [ɪn'flæməbl] adj inflamável; (explosive) explosivo.

inflammation [ɪnflə'meɪʃən] n inflamação f.

inflate [ɪn'fleɪt] vt (tyre, balloon) inflar, encher; (fig) inchar; ~d adj (style) empolado, pomposo; (value) excessivo; **inflation** [ɪn'fleɪʃən] n (ECON) inflação f; **inflationary** [ɪn'fleɪʃnərɪ] adj inflacionário.

inflexible [ɪn'flɛksɪbl] adj inflexível.

inflict [ɪn'flɪkt] vt: to ~ on infligir em; (tax etc) impor a; ~ion [ɪn'flɪkʃən] n imposição f, inflição f.

inflow ['ɪnfləu] n afluência.

influence ['ɪnfluəns] n influência // vt influir em, influenciar; (persuade) persuadir; **under the ~ of alcohol** sob o efeito do álcool; **influential** [-'ɛnʃl] adj influente.

influenza [ɪnflu'ɛnzə] n gripe f.

influx ['ɪnflʌks] n afluxo, influxo.

inform [ɪn'fɔːm] vt: to ~ sb of sth informar alguém de algo; (warn) avisar alguém de algo; (communicate) comunicar algo a alguém // vi denunciar; **to ~ on sb** delatar alguém.

informal [ɪn'fɔːml] adj (person, manner) sem formalidade; (tone) informal; (visit, discussion) extra-oficial; (intimate) familiar; ~ity [-'mælɪtɪ] n falta de cerimônia; (intimacy) intimidade f; (familiarity) familiaridade f; (ease) informalidade f.

information [ɪnfə'meɪʃən] n informação f, informações fpl; (news) notícias fpl; (knowledge) conhecimento m; (LAW) denúncia; **a piece of ~** um dado, uma informação.

informative [ɪn'fɔːmətɪv] adj informativo.

informer [ɪn'fɔːmə*] n delator(a) m/f; (also: police ~) informante m/f, dedo-duro m/f (Br).

infra-red [ɪnfrə'rɛd] adj infravermelho.

infrequent [ɪn'friːkwənt] adj infreqüente.

infringe [ɪn'frɪndʒ] vt infringir, transgredir // vi: to ~ on invadir, violar; ~ment n transgressão f; (of rights) violação f; (SPORT) infração (Pt: -cç-) f.

infuriate [ɪn'fjuərɪeɪt] vt enfurecer, enraivecer; **infuriating** adj de dar raiva, enfurecedor(a).

ingenious [ɪn'dʒiːnjəs] adj engenhoso; **ingenuity** [-dʒɪ'njuːɪtɪ] n engenho, habilidade f.

ingenuous [ɪn'dʒɛnjuəs] adj ingênuo.

ingot ['ɪŋgət] n lingote m, barra.

ingrained [ɪn'greɪnd] adj arraigado, enraizado.

ingratiate [ɪn'greɪʃɪeɪt] vt: to ~ o.s. with cair nas (boas) graças de.

ingratitude [ɪn'grætɪtjuːd] n ingratidão f.

ingredient [ɪn'griːdɪənt] n ingrediente m.

inhabit [ɪn'hæbɪt] vt habitar, viver em; (occupy) ocupar; ~ant n habitante m/f.

inhale [ɪn'heɪl] vt inalar // vi (in smoking) aspirar.

inherent [ɪn'hɪərənt] adj: ~ in or to inerente a.

inherit [ɪn'hɛrɪt] vt herdar; ~ance n herança; (fig) patrimônio.

inhibit [ɪn'hɪbɪt] vt inibir, reprimir; **to ~ sb from doing sth** impedir alguém de fazer algo; ~ion [-'bɪʃən] n inibição f.

inhospitable [ɪnhəs'pɪtəbl] adj (person) inospitaleiro; (place) inóspito.

inhuman [ɪn'hjuːmən] adj inumano, desumano.

inimitable [ɪ'nɪmɪtəbl] adj inimitável.

iniquity [ɪ'nɪkwɪtɪ] n iniqüidade f; (injustice) injustiça.

initial [ɪ'nɪʃl] adj inicial; (first) primeiro // n inicial f // vt marcar com iniciais; ~s npl iniciais fpl; (abbreviation) abreviatura, sigla; ~ly adv inicialmente, em primeiro lugar.

initiate [ɪ'nɪʃɪeɪt] vt (start) iniciar, começar; **to ~ sb into a secret** revelar um segredo a alguém; **to ~ proceedings against sb** (LAW) abrir um processo contra alguém; **initiation** [-'eɪʃən] n (into secret etc) iniciação f; (beginning) começo.

initiative [ɪ'nɪʃətɪv] n iniciativa.

inject [ɪn'dʒɛkt] vt (liquid) injetar (Pt: -ct-); (fig) introduzir; ~ion [ɪn'dʒɛkʃən] n injeção (Pt: -cç-) f.

injunction [ɪn'dʒʌŋkʃən] n injunção f, ordem f.

injure ['ɪndʒə*] vt ferir, lesar; (fig) prejudicar; (offend) ofender, magoar; **injury** n ferida, lesão f; (wrong) dano, prejuízo; **injury time** n (SPORT) desconto.

injustice [ɪn'dʒʌstɪs] n injustiça.

ink [ɪŋk] n tinta.

inkling ['ɪŋklɪŋ] n suspeita, insinuação f; (idea) idéia vaga.

inlaid ['ɪnleɪd] adj embutido, marchetado.

inland ['ɪnlənd] adj interior, interno // adv [ɪn'lænd] para o interior; **I~ Revenue** n (Brit) fisco, receita federal (Br).

in-laws ['ɪnlɔːz] npl sogros mpl.

inlet ['ınlɛt] n (GEO) enseada, angra; (TECH) entrada.

inmate ['ınmeıt] n (in prison) presidiário/a; (in asylum) internado/a.

inn [ın] n hospedaria, taberna.

innate [ı'neıt] adj inato.

inner ['ınə*] adj interno, interior; ~ **city** n centro da cidade; ~ **tube** n (of tyre) câmara.

innocence ['ınəsns] n ● inocência; **innocent** [-nt] adj inocente.

innocuous [ı'nɔkjuəs] adj inócuo.

innovation [ınəu'veıʃən] n inovação f, novidade f.

innuendo [ınju'ɛndəu], pl ~**es** n insinuação f, indireta (Pt: -ct-).

innumerable [ı'nju:mrəbl] adj inumerável.

inoculation [ınɔkju'leıʃən] n inoculação f, vacinação f.

inopportune [ın'ɔpətju:n] adj inoportuno.

inordinately [ı'nɔ:dınətlı] adv desmedidamente, excessivamente.

inorganic [ınɔ:'gænık] adj inorgânico.

in-patient ['ınpeıʃənt] n paciente m/f interno/a.

input ['ınput] n (ELEC) entrada; (COMM) investimento.

inquest ['ınkwɛst] n inquérito policial; (coroner's) inquérito judicial.

inquire [ın'kwaıə*] vi pedir informação // vt (ask) perguntar; (seek information about) pedir informações sobre; **to ~ about** vt fus (person) perguntar por; (fact) informar-se sobre; **to ~ into** vt fus investigar, indagar; **inquiring** adj (mind) inquiridor(a); (look) interrogativo; **inquiry** n pergunta; (LAW) investigação f, pesquisa; (commission) comissão f de inquérito; **inquiry office** n seção (Pt :-cç-) f de informações.

inquisitive [ın'kwızıtıv] adj (curious) curioso, perguntador(a); (prying) indiscreto, intrometido.

inroad ['ınrəud] n incursão f; (fig) invasão f.

insane [ın'seın] adj louco, doido; (MED) demente, maluco.

insanitary [ın'sænıtərı] adj insalubre.

insanity [ın'sænıtı] n insanidade f, demência.

insatiable [ın'seıʃəbl] adj insaciável.

inscribe [ın'skraıb] vt inscrever; (book etc) **to ~ (to sb)** dedicar (a alguém).

inscription [ın'skrıpʃən] n (gen) inscrição f; (in book) dedicatória.

inscrutable [ın'skru:təbl] adj inescrutável, impenetrável.

insect ['ınsɛkt] n inseto (Pt: -ct-); ~**icide** [ın'sɛktısaıd] n inse(c)ticida m.

insecure [ınsı'kjuə*] adj inseguro; **insecurity** n insegurança.

insensible [ın'sɛnsıbl] adj impassível, insensível; (unconscious) inconsciente.

insensitive [ın'sɛnsıtıv] adj insensível.

inseparable [ın'sɛprəbl] adj inseparável;

they were ~ friends eles eram amigos inseparáveis.

insert [ın'sə:t] vt (between things) intercalar; (into sth) introduzir, inserir; (in paper) publicar; (: advert) pôr // n ['ınsə:t] folha solta; ~**ion** [ın'sə:ʃən] n inserção f; (publication) publicação f; (of pages) matéria inserida.

inshore [ın'ʃɔ:*] adj perto da costa, costeiro // adv (be) perto da costa; (move) em direção à costa.

inside ['ın'saıd] n interior m; (lining) forro // adj interior, interno; (secret) secreto // adv (within) (por) dentro; (with movement) para dentro; (fam: in prison) na prisão // prep dentro de; (of time): ~ **10 minutes** em menos de 10 minutos; ~**s** npl (col) entranhas fpl; ~ **forward** n (SPORT) centro avante; ~ **lane** n (AUT: in Britain) pista da direita; ~ **out** adv (turn) às avessas, ao revés; (know) perfeitamente, a fundo.

insidious [ın'sıdıəs] adj insidioso; (underground) clandestino.

insight ['ınsaıt] n (quality) discernimento; **an ~ into sth** uma idéia de algo.

insignificant [ınsıg'nıfıknt] adj insignificante.

insincere [ınsın'sıə*] adj insincero; **insincerity** [-'sɛrıtı] n insinceridade f.

insinuate [ın'sınjueıt] vt insinuar, sugerir; **insinuation** [-'eıʃən] n insinuação f; (hint) indireta (Pt: -ct-).

insipid [ın'sıpıd] adj insípido, insosso; (person) sem graça.

insist [ın'sıst] vi insistir; **to ~ on doing** teimar em fazer; **to ~ that** insistir em que; (claim) cismar que; ~**ence** n insistência; (stubbornness) teimosia; ~**ent** adj insistente, pertinaz.

insole ['ınsəul] n palmilha.

insolence ['ınsələns] n insolência, atrevimento; **insolent** [-ənt] adj insolente, atrevido.

insoluble [ın'sɔljubl] adj insolúvel.

insolvent [ın'sɔlvənt] adj insolvente.

insomnia [ın'sɔmnıə] n insônia.

inspect [ın'spɛkt] vt inspecionar (Pt: -cc-), examinar; (troops) passar revista em; ~**ion** [ın'spɛkʃən] n inspeção (Pt: -cç-) f, exame m; ~**or** n inspetor(a) (Pt: -ct-) m/f; (RAIL) fiscal m.

inspiration [ınspə'reıʃən] n inspiração f; **inspire** [ın'spaıə*] vt inspirar.

instability [ınstə'bılıtı] n instabilidade f.

install [ın'stɔ:l] vt instalar; ~**ation** [ınstə'leıʃən] n instalação f.

instalment, installment (US) [ın'stɔ:lmənt] n prestação f; (of story) fascículo; (of TV serial etc) capítulo.

instance ['ınstəns] n exemplo, caso; **for ~** por exemplo; **in the first ~** em primeiro lugar.

instant ['ınstənt] n instante m, momento // adj instantâneo, imediato; (coffee) instantâneo; ~**ly** adv imediatamente.

instead [ɪn'stɛd] *adv* em vez disso; ~ **of** em vez de, em lugar de.

instep ['ɪnstɛp] *n* peito do pé.

instigation [ɪnstɪ'geɪʃən] *n* instigação *f.*

instil [ɪn'stɪl] *vt:* to ~ **into** infundir em, incutir em.

instinct ['ɪnstɪŋkt] *n* instinto; ~**ive** [-'stɪŋktɪv] *adj* instintivo; ~**ively** [-'stɪŋktɪvlɪ] *adv* por instinto, instintivamente.

institute ['ɪnstɪtjuːt] *n* instituto; (*professional body*) associação *f //* *vt* (*inquiry*) começar, iniciar; (*proceedings*) instituir, estabelecer.

institution [ɪnstɪ'tjuːʃən] *n* (*gen*) instituição *f*; (*beginning*) início; (*organization*) instituto; (*MED: home*) asilo; (*asylum*) manicômio; (*custom*) costume *m.*

instruct [ɪn'strʌkt] *vt:* to ~ **sb in sth** instruir alguém em *or* sobre algo; to ~ **sb to do sth** dar instruções a alguém para fazer algo; ~**ion** [ɪn'strʌkʃən] *n* (*teaching*) instrução *f*; ~**ions** *npl* ordens *fpl*; ~**ions (for use)** modo sg de usar; ~**ive** *adj* instrutivo; ~**or** *n* instrutor(a) *m/f.*

instrument ['ɪnstrumənt] *n* instrumento; ~**al** [-'mɛntl] *adj* (*MUS*) instrumental; to be ~**al in** contribuir para; ~ **panel** *n* painel *m* de instrumentos.

insubordinate [ɪnsə'bɔːdənɪt] *adj* insubordinado; **insubordination** [-'neɪʃən] *n* insubordinação *f*; (*disobedience*) desobediência.

insufferable [ɪn'sʌfrəbl] *adj* insuportável.

insufficient [ɪnsə'fɪʃənt] *adj* insuficiente.

insular ['ɪnsjulə*] *adj* insular; (*outlook*) de mente limitada.

insulate ['ɪnsjuleɪt] *vt* isolar; **insulating tape** *n* fita isolante; **insulation** [-'leɪʃən] *n* isolamento.

insulin ['ɪnsjulɪn] *n* insulina.

insult ['ɪnsʌlt] *n* insulto; (*offence*) ofensa *// vt* [ɪn'sʌlt] insultar, ofender; ~**ing** *adj* insultante, ofensivo.

insuperable [ɪn'sjuːprəbl] *adj* insuperável.

insurance [ɪn'ʃuərəns] *n* seguro; **fire** ~ seguro contra incêndio; **life** ~ seguro de vida; ~ **agent** *n* agente *m/f* de seguros; ~ **policy** *n* apólice *f* de seguro.

insure [ɪn'ʃuə*] *vt* assegurar, pôr no seguro.

insurrection [ɪnsə'rɛkʃən] *n* insurreição *f.*

intact [ɪn'tækt] *adj* intacto, íntegro; (*unharmed*) ileso, são e salvo.

intake ['ɪnteɪk] *n* (*TEC*) entrada, tomada; (: *pipe*) tubo de entrada; (*of food*) quantidade *f* ingerida; (*SCOL*): **an** ~ **of 200 a year** 200 matriculados por ano.

intangible [ɪn'tændʒɪbl] *adj* intangível.

integral ['ɪntɪgrəl] *adj* (*whole*) integral, total; (*part*) integrante.

integrate ['ɪntɪgreɪt] *vt* integrar *// vi* integrar-se.

integrity [ɪn'tɛgrɪtɪ] *n* integridade *f*, honestidade *f*, retidão (*Pt:* -ct-) *f.*

intellect ['ɪntəlɛkt] *n* intelecto; ~**ual** [-'lɛktjuəl] *adj*, *n* intelectual *m/f.*

intelligence [ɪn'tɛlɪdʒəns] *n* inteligência; (*MIL etc*) informações *fpl*; **I~ Service** *or* **Intelligencia**; **intelligent** [-ənt] *adj* inteligente.

intelligible [ɪn'tɛlɪdʒɪbl] *adj* inteligível, compreensível.

intend [ɪn'tɛnd] *vt* (*gift etc*): to ~ **sth for** destinar algo a; to ~ **to do sth** tencionar *or* pretender fazer algo; ~**ed** *adj* (*effect*) desejado *// n* noivo/a.

intense [ɪn'tɛns] *adj* intenso; (*person*) muito emotivo *// adv* intensamente; (*very*) extremamente.

intensify [ɪn'tɛnsɪfaɪ] *vt* intensificar; (*increase*) aumentar.

intensity [ɪn'tɛnsɪtɪ] *n* intensidade *f*; (*strength*) força, veemência.

intensive [ɪn'tɛnsɪv] *adj* intensivo; ~ **care unit** *n* unidade *f* de tratamento intensivo.

intent [ɪn'tɛnt] *n* intenção *f // adj* (*absorbed*) absorto; (*attentive*) atento; **to all ~s and purposes** para todos os efeitos; **to be ~ on doing sth** estar resolvido a fazer algo.

intention [ɪn'tɛnʃən] *n* intenção *f*, propósito; (*plan*) projeto (*Pt:* -ct-); ~**al** *adj* intencional, premeditado; ~**ally** *adv* de propósito.

intently [ɪn'tɛntlɪ] *adv* atentamente, decididamente.

inter [ɪn'tɜː*] *vt* enterrar.

interact [ɪntər'ækt] *vi* interagir; ~**ion** [-'ækʃən] *n* interação (*Pt:* -cç-) *f*, ação (*Pt:* -cç-) *f* recíproca.

intercede [ɪntə'siːd] *vi:* to ~ (**with**) interceder (junto a).

intercept [ɪntə'sɛpt] *vt* interceptar; (*stop*) deter; ~**ion** [-'sɛpʃən] *n* interceptação *f*; detenção *f.*

interchange ['ɪntətʃeɪndʒ] *n* intercâmbio; (*exchange*) troca, permuta; (*on motorway*) trevo *// vt* [ɪntə'tʃeɪndʒ] intercambiar, trocar; ~**able** *adj* permutável.

intercom ['ɪntəkɔm] *n* interfone *m.*

interconnect [ɪntəkə'nɛkt] *vt* interligar.

intercourse ['ɪntəkɔːs] *n* (*sexual*) relações *fpl*; (*social*) relacionamento.

interest ['ɪntrɪst] *n* interesse *m*; (*COMM*) juros *mpl // vt* interessar; **to be ~ed in** estar interessado em; ~**ing** *adj* interessante, curioso.

interfere [ɪntə'fɪə*] *vi:* to ~ **in** (*quarrel, other people's business*) interferir *or* intrometer-se em; to ~ **with** (*hinder*) impedir; (*damage*) danificar; (*radio*) interferir com.

interference [ɪntə'fɪərəns] *n* (*gen*) intromissão *f*; (*RADIO, TV*) interferência.

interim ['ɪntərɪm] *n:* **in the** ~ neste ínterim, nesse meio tempo.

interior [ɪn'tɪərɪə*] *n* interior *m // adj* interior.

interject [ɪntəˈdʒɛkt] *vt* inserir, interpor; ~**ion** [-ˈdʒɛkʃən] *n* interjeição *f*, exclamação *f*.

interlock [ɪntəˈlɔk] *vi* entrelaçar-se; (*wheels etc*) engatar-se, engrenar-se.

interloper [ˈɪntələʊpə*] *n* intruso/a.

interlude [ˈɪntəluːd] *n* interlúdio; (*rest*) descanso; (*THEATRE*) intervalo.

intermarry [ɪntəˈmærɪ] *vi* ligar-se por casamento.

intermediary [ɪntəˈmiːdɪərɪ] *n* intermediário.

intermediate [ɪntəˈmiːdɪət] · *adj* intermédio, intermediário.

intermission [ɪntəˈmɪʃən] *n* (*THEATRE*) intervalo.

intermittent [ɪntəˈmɪtnt] *adj* intermitente.

intern [ɪnˈtəːn] *vt* internar; (*enclose*) encerrar // *n* [ˈɪntəːn] (*US*) médico-interno.

internal [ɪnˈtəːnl] *adj* interno, interior; ~**ly** *adv* interiormente; 'not to be taken ~**ly**' 'uso externo'; ~ **revenue** *n* (*US*) fisco, receita federal (*Br*).

international [ɪntəˈnæʃənl] *adj* internacional; ~ **game** jogo internacional; ~ **player** jogador(a) *m/f* internacional.

interplay [ˈɪntəpleɪ] *n* interação (*Pt*: -cç-) *f*.

interpret [ɪnˈtəːprɪt] *vt* interpretar; (*translate*) traduzir; (*understand*) compreender // *vi* interpretar; ~**ation** [-ˈteɪʃən] *n* interpretação *f*; tradução *f*; entendimento; ~**er** *n* intérprete *m/f*, tradutor(a) *m/f*.

interrelated [ɪntərɪˈleɪtɪd] *adj* inter-relacionado.

interrogate [ɪnˈtɛrəʊgeɪt] *vt* interrogar; **interrogation** [-ˈgeɪʃən] *n* interrogatório; **interrogative** [ɪntəˈrɔgətɪv] *adj* interrogativo.

interrupt [ɪntəˈrʌpt] *vt/i* interromper; ~**ion** [-ˈrʌpʃən] *n* interrupção *f*.

intersect [ɪntəˈsɛkt] *vt* cruzar // *vi* (*roads*) cruzar-se; ~**ion** [-ˈsɛkʃən] *n* interseção *f*; (*of roads*) cruzamento.

intersperse [ɪntəˈspəːs] *vt* intercalar, entremear.

intertwine [ɪntəˈtwaɪn] *vt* entrelaçar // *vi* entrelaçar-se.

interval [ˈɪntəvl] *n* pausa; (*SCOL*) recreio, intervalo; (*THEATRE*, *SPORT*) intervalo; at ~**s** de vez em quando, de tempo em tempo.

intervene [ɪntəˈviːn] *vi* (*gen*) intervir, interceder; (*take part*) participar; (*occur*) ocorrer; **intervention** [-ˈvɛnʃən] *n* intervenção *f*.

interview [ˈɪntəvjuː] *n* (*RADIO*, *TV etc*) entrevista // *vt* entrevistar; ~**ee** [-ˈiː] *n* entrevistado/a; ~**er** *n* entrevistador(a) *m/f*.

intestine [ɪnˈtɛstɪn] *n*: **large/small** ~ intestino grosso/delgado.

intimacy [ˈɪntɪməsɪ] *n* intimidade *f*; (*relations*) relações *fpl* sexuais.

intimate [ˈɪntɪmət] *adj* íntimo; (*friendship*, *knowledge*) profundo // *vt* [ˈɪntɪmeɪt] (*announce*) insinuar, sugerir.

intimidate [ɪnˈtɪmɪdeɪt] *vt* intimidar, amedrontar; **intimidation** [-ˈdeɪʃən] *n* intimidação *f*.

into [ˈɪntu] *prep* (*gen*) em; (*towards*) para; (*inside*) para dentro de; ~ **3 pieces/French** em 3 pedaços/para o francês.

intolerable [ɪnˈtɔlərəbl] *adj* intolerável, insuportável; **intolerance** [-rəns] *n* intolerância; **intolerant** [-rənt] *adj*: **intolerant of** intolerante com *or* para com.

intonation [ɪntəʊˈneɪʃən] *n* entonação *f*, inflexão *f*.

intoxicate [ɪnˈtɔksɪkeɪt] *vt* embriagar; ~**d** *adj* embriagado; **intoxication** [-ˈkeɪʃən] *n* intoxicação *f*, embriaguez *f*.

intractable [ɪnˈtræktəbl] *adj* (*child*) intratável; (*material*) difícil de trabalhar; (*problem*) espinhoso.

intransigent [ɪnˈtrænsɪdʒənt] *adj* intransigente.

intransitive [ɪnˈtrænsɪtɪv] *adj* intransitivo.

intravenous [ɪntrəˈviːnəs] *adj* intravenoso.

intrepid [ɪnˈtrɛpɪd] *adj* intrépido.

intricate [ˈɪntrɪkət] *adj* intricado; (*complex*) complexo, complicado.

intrigue [ɪnˈtriːg] *n* intriga // *vt* interessar, deixar intrigado // *vi* fazer intriga; **intriguing** *adj* intrigante.

intrinsic [ɪnˈtrɪnsɪk] *adj* intrínseco.

introduce [ɪntrəˈdjuːs] *vt* introduzir, inserir; **to** ~ **sb (to sb)** apresentar alguém (a outrem); **to** ~ **sb to** (*pastime*, *technique*) iniciar *or* introduzir alguém em; **introduction** [-ˈdʌkʃən] *n* introdução *f*; (*of person*) apresentação *f*; **introductory** [-ˈdʌktərɪ] *adj* introdutório, preliminar.

introspective [ɪntrəʊˈspɛktɪv] *adj* introspectivo.

introvert [ˈɪntrəʊvəːt] *adj*, *n* introvertido/a.

intrude [ɪnˈtruːd] *vi* (*person*) intrometer-se; **to** ~ **on** *or* **into** intrometer-se em; **intruder** *n* intruso/a, intrometido/a; **intrusion** [-ʒən] *n* intromissão *f*; **intrusive** [-sɪv] *adj* intruso.

intuition [ɪntjuːˈɪʃən] *n* intuição *f*; **intuitive** [-ˈtjuːɪtɪv] *adj* intuitivo.

inundate [ˈɪnʌndeɪt] *vt*: **to** ~ **with** inundar de.

invade [ɪnˈveɪd] *vt* invadir; **invader** *n* invasor(a) *m/f*.

invalid [ˈɪnvəlɪd] *n* inválido/a // *adj* [ɪnˈvælɪd] (*not valid*) inválido, nulo; ~**ate** [ɪnˈvælɪdeɪt] *vt* invalidar, anular.

invaluable [ɪnˈvæljuəbl] *adj* inestimável, impagável.

invariable [ɪnˈvɛərɪəbl] *adj* invariável.

invasion [ɪnˈveɪʒən] *n* invasão *f*.

invent [ɪnˈvɛnt] *vt* inventar; ~**ion** [ɪnˈvɛnʃən] *n* invenção *f*; (*inventiveness*) engenho; (lie) ficção f, mentira; ~ive adj engenhoso; ~iveness n engenhosidade f, inventiva; ~or n inventor(a) m/f.

inventory ['ɪnvəntrɪ] n inventário, relação f.

inverse [ɪn'vɜːs] adj, n inverso; ~ly adv inversamente.

invert [ɪn'vɜːt] vt inverter, transpor; ~ed commas npl aspas fpl.

invertebrate [ɪn'vɜːtɪbrət] n invertebrado.

invest [ɪn'vest] vt/i investir.

investigate [ɪn'vestɪgeɪt] vt investigar; (study) estudar, examinar; **investigation** [-'geɪʃən] n investigação f, pesquisa; **investigator** n investigador(a) m/f.

investiture [ɪn'vestɪtʃə*] n investidura.

investment [ɪn'vestmənt] n investimento.

investor [ɪn'vestə*] n investidor(a) m/f.

inveterate [ɪn'vetərət] adj inveterado.

invigorating [ɪn'vɪgəreɪtɪŋ] adj revigorante.

invincible [ɪn'vɪnsɪbl] adj invencível.

inviolate [ɪn'vaɪələt] adj inviolado.

invisible [ɪn'vɪzɪbl] adj invisível; ~ ink n tinta invisível.

invitation [ɪnvɪ'teɪʃən] n convite m.

invite [ɪn'vaɪt] vt (gen, drink, food) convidar; (opinions etc) solicitar, pedir; (trouble) provocar; **inviting** adj tentador(a), atraente; (look) convidativo, sedutor(a); (food) apetitoso.

invoice ['ɪnvɔɪs] n fatura (Pt: -ct-) // vt fa(c)turar.

invoke [ɪn'vəuk] vt invocar; (aid) implorar; (law) apelar para.

involuntary [ɪn'vɔləntrɪ] adj involuntário.

involve [ɪn'vɔlv] vt (entail) implicar; to ~ sb (in) envolver alguém (em); ~d adj envolvido; (emotionally) comprometido; ~ment n (gen) envolvimento; (obligation) compromisso; (difficulty) apuro.

invulnerable [ɪn'vʌlnərəbl] adj invulnerável.

inward ['ɪnwəd] adj (movement) interior, interno; (thought, feeling) íntimo; ~ly adv (feel, think etc) para si, para dentro; ~(s) adv para dentro.

iodine ['aɪəudiːn] n iodo.

iota [aɪ'əutə] n (fig) pouquinho, tiquinho.

IOU n abbr of I owe you vale m.

IQ n abbr of **intelligence quotient** quociente m intelectual or de inteligência.

Iran [ɪ'rɑːn] n Irã (Pt: Irão) m; ~ian [ɪ'reɪnɪən] adj, n iraniano/a m/f.

Iraq [ɪ'rɑːk] n Iraque m; ~i adj, n iraquiano/a m/f.

irascible [ɪ'ræsɪbl] adj irascível.

irate [aɪ'reɪt] adj irado, enfurecido.

Ireland ['aɪələnd] n Irlanda.

iris ['aɪrɪs], pl ~es n íris f.

Irish ['aɪrɪʃ] adj irlandês/esa // npl: the

~ os irlandeses; ~man n irlandês m; ~woman n irlandesa.

irk [ɜːk] vt aborrecer; ~some adj aborrecido.

iron ['aɪən] n ferro; (for clothes) ferro de passar roupa // adj de ferro // vt (clothes) passar; ~s npl (chains) grilhões mpl; to ~ out vt (crease) tirar; (fig) resolver.

ironic(al) [aɪ'rɔnɪk(l)] adj irônico.

ironing ['aɪənɪŋ] n (ironed clothes) roupa passada; (to be ironed) roupa a ser passada; ~ board n tábua de passar roupa.

ironmonger ['aɪənmʌngə*] n ferreiro; ~'s (shop) n loja de ferragens.

iron ore ['aɪən'ɔː*] n minério de ferro.

irony ['aɪrənɪ] n ironia; the ~ of it is that... o irônico é que...

irrational [ɪ'ræʃənl] adj irracional.

irreconcilable [ɪrekən'saɪləbl] adj irreconciliável, incompatível.

irrefutable [ɪrɪ'fjuːtəbl] adj irrefutável.

irregular [ɪ'regjulə*] adj irregular; (surface) desigual; (illegal) ilegal; ~ity [-'lærɪtɪ] n irregularidade f; desigualdade f.

irrelevant [ɪ'reləvənt] adj irrelevante, descabido.

irreparable [ɪ'repərəbl] adj irreparável.

irreplaceable [ɪrɪ'pleɪsəbl] adj insubstituível.

irrepressible [ɪrɪ'presəbl] adj irreprimível, irrefreável.

irreproachable [ɪrɪ'prəutʃəbl] adj irrepreensível.

irresistible [ɪrɪ'zɪstɪbl] adj irresistível.

irresolute [ɪ'rezəluːt] adj irresoluto.

irrespective [ɪrɪ'spektɪv]: ~ of prep independente de, sem considerar.

irresponsible [ɪrɪ'sponsɪbl] adj (act, person) irresponsável.

irreverent [ɪ'revərnt] adj irreverente, desrespeitoso.

irrevocable [ɪ'revəkəbl] adj irrevogável.

irrigate ['ɪrɪgeɪt] vt irrigar; **irrigation** [-'geɪʃən] n irrigação f.

irritable ['ɪrɪtəbl] adj irritável; (mood) de mal humor, nervoso.

irritate ['ɪrɪteɪt] vt irritar; **irritation** [-'teɪʃən] n irritação f.

is [ɪz] vb see **be**.

Islam ['ɪzlɑːm] n islamismo.

island ['aɪlənd] n ilha; (also: traffic ~) abrigo; ~er n ilhéu/ilhoa m/f.

isle [aɪl] n ilhota, ilha.

isn't ['ɪznt] = **is not**.

isolate ['aɪsəleɪt] vt isolar; ~d adj isolado; **isolation** [-'leɪʃən] n isolamento.

isotope ['aɪsəutəup] n isótopo.

Israel ['ɪzreɪl] n (Estado de) Israel m; ~i [ɪz'reɪlɪ] adj, n israelense m/f.

issue ['ɪsjuː] n questão f, tema m; (outcome) resultado; (of banknotes etc) emissão f; (of newspaper etc) número; (offspring) sucessão f, descendência // vt (rations, equipment) distribuir; (orders) dar; (certificate) emitir; (decree) promulgar; (*book*) publicar; (*cheques, banknotes, stamps*) emitir.

isthmus ['ɪsməs] *n* istmo.

it [ɪt] *pron* (*subject*) ele/ela; (*direct object*) o/a; (*indirect object*) lhe; (*impersonal*) isto, isso; (*after prep*) ele, ela; **~'s raining** está chovendo (*Br*), está a chover (*Pt*); **where is ~?** onde está?; **he's proud of ~** ele orgulha-se disso; **he agreed to ~** ele está de acordo com isso.

Italian [ɪ'tæljən] *adj* italiano // *n* italiano/a; (*LING*) italiano.

italic [ɪ'tælɪk] *adj* itálico, cursivo; **~s** *npl* itálico *sg*.

Italy ['ɪtəlɪ] *n* Itália.

itch [ɪtʃ] *n* comichão *f*, coceira; (*fig*) desejo ardente // *vi* (*person*) sentir or estar com comichão or coceira; (*part of body*) comichar, coçar; **I'm ~ing to do sth** estou louco para fazer algo; **~ing** *n* comichão *f*, coceira; **~y** *adj*: **to be ~y** sentir comichão or coceira.

it'd ['ɪtd] = **it would; it had.**

item ['aɪtəm] *n* (*gen*) item *m*; (*detail*) detalhe *m*; (*on agenda*) assunto; (*in programme*) número; (*also*: **news ~**) notícia; **~ize** *vt* detalhar, especificar.

itinerant [ɪ'tɪnərənt] *adj* itinerante.

itinerary [aɪ'tɪnərərɪ] *n* itinerário.

it'll ['ɪtl] = **it will, it shall.**

its [ɪts] *adj* seu/sua // *pron* (o) seu/(a) sua.

it's [ɪts] = **it is; it has.**

itself [ɪt'sɛlf] *pron* (*reflexive*) si mesmo/a; (*emphatic*) ele mesmo/ela mesma.

ITV *n abbr of* **Independent Television.**

I.U.D. *n abbr of* **intra-uterine device.**

I've [aɪv] = **I have.**

ivory ['aɪvərɪ] *n* marfim *m*; **~ tower** *n* (*fig*) torre *f* de marfim.

ivy ['aɪvɪ] *n* hera.

J

jab [dʒæb] *vt* (*elbow*) acotovelar; (*punch*) esmurrar, socar; **to ~ sth into sth** cravar algo em algo // *n* cotovelada, murro; (*MED: col*) injeção (*Pt*: -cç-) *f*.

jabber ['dʒæbə*] *vi/t* tagarelar.

jack [dʒæk] *n* (*AUT*) macaco; (*BOWLS*) bola branca; (*CARDS*) valete *m*; **to ~ up** *vt* (*AUT*) levantar com macaco.

jackdaw ['dʒækdɔ:] *n* gralha.

jacket ['dʒækɪt] *n* jaqueta, casaco curto; (*of boiler etc*) capa, forro; (*of book*) sobrecapa; **potatoes in their ~s** batatas com casca.

jack-knife ['dʒæknaɪf] *n* canivete *m*.

jackpot ['dʒækpɔt] *n* bolada, sorte *f* grande.

jade [dʒeɪd] *n* (*stone*) jade *m*.

jaded ['dʒeɪdɪd] *adj* (*tired*) cansado; (*fed-up*) aborrecido, amolado.

jagged ['dʒægɪd] *adj* dentado, denteado.

jail [dʒeɪl] *n* prisão *f*, cadeia; **~break** *n* fuga da prisão; **~er** *n* carcereiro.

jam [dʒæm] *n* geléia; (*also*: **traffic ~**) engarrafamento; (*difficulty*) apuro // *vt* (*passage etc*) obstruir, atravancar; (*mechanism*) emperrar; (*RADIO*) interferir // *vi* (*mechanism, drawer etc*) emperrar; **to ~ sth into sth** forçar algo dentro de algo.

Jamaica [dʒə'meɪkə] *n* Jamaica.

jangle ['dʒæŋgl] *vi* soar estridentemente, desafinar.

janitor ['dʒænɪtə*] *n* (*caretaker*) zelador *m*, porteiro.

January ['dʒænjuərɪ] *n* janeiro (*Pt*: J-).

Japan [dʒə'pæn] *n* Japão *m*; **~ese** [dʒæpə'ni:z] *adj* japonês/esa // *n, pl inv* japonês/esa *m/f*; (*LING*) japonês *m*.

jar [dʒɑ:*] *n* (*glass*: *large*) jarro; (*: small*) pote *m* // *vi* (*sound*) ranger, chiar; (*colours*) destoar.

jargon ['dʒɑ:gən] *n* jargão *m*, gíria.

jasmin(e) ['dʒæzmɪn] *n* jasmim *m*.

jaundice ['dʒɔ:ndɪs] *n* icterícia; **~d** *adj* (*fig: embittered*) amargurado, despeitado; (*: disillusioned*) desiludido.

jaunt [dʒɔ:nt] *n* excursão *f*; **~y** *adj* alegre, jovial.

javelin ['dʒævlɪn] *n* dardo de arremesso.

jaw [dʒɔ:] *n* mandíbula, maxilar *m*.

jaywalker ['dʒeɪwɔ:kə*] *n* pedestre *m/f* imprudente (*Br*), peão imprudente (*Pt*).

jazz [dʒæz] *n* jazz *m*; **to ~ up** *vt* (*liven up*) animar, avivar; **~y** *adj* de cor berrante.

jealous ['dʒɛləs] *adj* (*gen*) ciumento; (*envious*) invejoso; **to be ~** estar com ciúmes; **~y** *n* ciúmes *mpl*; (*envy*) inveja.

jeans [dʒi:nz] *npl* jeans *msg* (*Br*), jeans *mpl* (*Pt*).

jeep [dʒi:p] *n* jipe *m*.

jeer [dʒɪə*] *vi*: **to ~ (at)** (*boo*) vaiar; (*mock*) zombar (de).

jelly ['dʒɛlɪ] *n* geléia, gelatina; **~fish** *n* água-viva.

jeopardize ['dʒɛpədaɪz] *vt* arriscar, pôr em perigo; **jeopardy** [-dɪ] *n*: **to be in jeopardy** estar em perigo or correndo risco.

jerk [dʒɔ:k] *n* (*jolt*) sacudida; (*wrench*) puxão *m* // *vt* sacudir, empurrar // *vi* (*vehicle*) mover-se aos solavancos.

jerkin ['dʒɔ:kɪn] *n* jaqueta.

jerky ['dʒɔ:kɪ] *adj* espasmódico, aos arrancos.

jersey ['dʒɔ:zɪ] *n* suéter *m/f* (*Br*), camisola (*Pt*).

jest [dʒɛst] *n* gracejo, brincadeira.

jet [dʒɛt] *n* (*of gas, liquid*) jato (*Pt*: -ct-), forro; (*AVIAT*) avião *m* a ja(c)to; **~-black** *adj* da cor do azeviche; **~ engine** *n* motor *m* a ja(c)to.

jettison ['dʒɛtɪsn] *vt* alijar.

jetty ['dʒɛtɪ] *n* quebra-mar *m*, cais *m*.

Jew [dʒu:] *n* judeu; **~ess** *n* judia.

jewel ['dʒu:əl] *n* jóia; (*in watch*) rubi *m*; **~ler** *n* joalheiro; **~ler's (shop)** *n* joalheria; **~lery** *n* jóias *fpl*, pedrarias *fpl*.

Jewish ['dʒu:ɪʃ] *adj* judeu/judia.

jibe [dʒaɪb] *n* zombaria.

jiffy ['dʒɪfɪ] n (col): in a ~ num instante.

jig [dʒɪg] n jiga.

jigsaw ['dʒɪgsɔ:] n (also: ~ puzzle) quebra-cabeça m.

jilt [dʒɪlt] vt dar o fora em.

jingle ['dʒɪŋgl] n (advert) música de propaganda // vi tilintar, retinir.

jinx [dʒɪŋks] n (col) caipora, pé m frio.

jitters ['dʒɪtəz] npl (col): to get the ~ ficar muito nervoso.

job [dʒɔb] n (gen) trabalho; (task) tarefa; (duty) dever m; (post) emprego; (fam: difficulty) dificuldade f; it's a good ~ that... ainda bem que...; just the ~! justo o que queria!; ~less adj desempregado.

jockey ['dʒɔkɪ] n jóquei m // vi: to ~ for position manobrar or trapacear para conseguir uma posição.

jocular ['dʒɔkjulə*] adj (humorous) jocoso, divertido; (merry) alegre.

jog [dʒɔg] vt empurrar, sacudir // vi (run) fazer jogging or cooper; to ~ along ir levando; to ~ sb's memory refrescar a memória de alguém; ~ging n jogging m.

join [dʒɔɪn] vt (things) juntar, unir; (become member of) associar-se a, afiliar-se a; (meet: people) reunir-se or encontrar-se com // vi (roads, rivers) confluir // n junção f; to ~ up vi unir-se; (MIL) alistar-se.

joiner ['dʒɔɪnə*] n carpinteiro, marceneiro; ~y n carpintaria.

joint [dʒɔɪnt] n (TEC) junta, união f; (wood) encaixe m; (ANAT) articulação f; (CULIN) quarto; (col: place) espelunca // adj (common) comum; (combined) combinado; (committee) misto; by ~ agreement por comum acordo; ~ly adv (gen) junto, em comum; (collectively) coletivamente (Pt: -ect-); (together) conjuntamente.

joke [dʒəuk] n piada; (also: practical ~) brincadeira // vi brincar; to play a ~ on pregar uma peça em; joker n piadista m/f, brincalhão/lhona m/f; (CARDS) curingão m.

jolly ['dʒɔlɪ] adj (merry) alegre; (enjoyable) divertido // adv (col) muito, extremamente.

jolt [dʒəult] n (shake) sacudida, solavanco; (blow) golpe m; (shock) susto // vt sacudir.

Jordan ['dʒɔːdən] n Jordânia.

jostle ['dʒɔsl] vt acotovelar, empurrar.

jot [dʒɔt] n: not one ~ nem um pouquinho; to ~ down vt anotar, apontar; ~ter n bloco (de anotações); (SCOL) caderno.

journal ['dʒəːnl] n (paper) jornal m; (magazine) revista; (diary) diário; ~ese [-'liːz] n (pej) linguagem f jornalística; ~ism n jornalismo; ~ist n jornalista m/f.

journey ['dʒəːnɪ] n viagem f; (distance covered) trajeto (Pt: -ct-) // vi viajar; return ~ viagem de volta.

joy [dʒɔɪ] n alegria; ~ful, ~ous adj alegre; ~ ride n passeio de carro; (illegal) passeio (com veículo roubado).

J.P. n abbr of Justice of the Peace.

Jr, Jun., Junr abbr of junior.

jubilant ['dʒuːbɪlnt] adj jubilante; **jubilation** [-'leɪʃən] n júbilo, regozijo.

jubilee ['dʒuːbɪliː] n jubileu m.

judge [dʒʌdʒ] n juiz m, árbitro // vt (gen) julgar; (estimate) considerar; **judg(e)ment** n juízo; (punishment) decisão f, sentença.

judicial [dʒuː'dɪʃl] adj judicial.

judicious [dʒuː'dɪʃəs] adj judicioso.

judo ['dʒuːdəu] n judô m.

jug [dʒʌg] n jarro.

juggernaut ['dʒʌgənɔːt] n (huge truck) jamanta.

juggle ['dʒʌgl] vi fazer malabarismos; **juggler** n malabarista m/f.

Jugoslav ['juːgəu'slaːv] adj, n = Yugoslav.

juice [dʒuːs] n suco (Br), sumo (Pt); **juicy** adj suculento.

jukebox ['dʒuːkbɔks] n juke-box m.

July [dʒuː'laɪ] n julho (Pt: J-).

jumble ['dʒʌmbl] n confusão f, mixórdia // vt (also: ~ up: mix up) misturar confusamente; (: disarrange) desorganizar; ~ sale n (Brit) venda de objetos usados, bazar m.

jumbo (jet) ['dʒʌmbəu(dʒɛt)] n avião m jumbo.

jump [dʒʌmp] vi saltar, pular; (start) sobressaltar-se; (increase) aumentar // vt pular, saltar // n pulo, salto; (increase) alta; to ~ the queue furar fila (Br), pôr-se à frente (Pt).

jumper ['dʒʌmpə*] n suéter m/f (Br), pulôver m (Br), camisola (Pt).

jumpy ['dʒʌmpɪ] adj nervoso.

junction ['dʒʌŋkʃən] n (of roads) cruzamento, trevo; (RAIL) entroncamento.

juncture ['dʒʌŋktʃə*] n: at this ~ neste momento, nesta conjuntura.

June [dʒuːn] n junho (Pt: J-).

jungle ['dʒʌŋgl] n selva, mato.

junior ['dʒuːnɪə*] adj (in age) mais novo or moço; (competition) juvenil; (position) subalterno // n jovem m/f; ~ school n escola primária.

junk [dʒʌŋk] n (cheap goods) tranqueira, velharias fpl; (lumber) traste m; (rubbish) lixo; (ship) junco; ~shop n loja de objetos usados.

jurisdiction [dʒuərɪs'dɪkʃən] n jurisdição f.

jurisprudence [dʒuərɪs'pruːdəns] n jurisprudência.

jury ['dʒuərɪ] n júri m, jurados mpl.

just [dʒʌst] adj justo // adv (exactly) exatamente (Pt: -ct-); (only) apenas, somente; he's ~ done it/left ele acaba de fazê-lo/ir; ~ right perfeito; ~ two o'clock duas (horas) em ponto; ~ as well that... ainda bem que...; ~ as he was leaving no momento em que ele saía; ~ **before/enough** justo antes/o suficiente; ~ **here** bem aqui; **he** ~ **missed** falhou por pouco; ~ **listen** escute aqui!

justice ['dʒʌstɪs] n justiça; **J**~ **of the Peace (J.P.)** n juiz m de paz.

justifiable [dʒʌstɪ'faɪəbl] adj justificável; **justifiably** adv justificadamente.

justification [dʒʌstɪfɪ'keɪʃən] n justificativa, justificação f; **justify** ['dʒʌstɪfaɪ] vt justificar.

justly ['dʒʌstlɪ] adv (gen) justamente; (with reason) com razão.

justness ['dʒʌstnɪs] n justiça, justeza.

jut [dʒʌt] vi (also: ~ **out**) sobressair.

juvenile ['dʒu:vənaɪl] adj juvenil; (court) de menores; (books) juvenil // n jovem m/f, menor m/f de idade.

juxtapose ['dʒʌkstəpəuz] vt justapor.

K

kaleidoscope [kə'laɪdəskəup] n calidoscópio, caleidoscópio.

kangaroo [kæŋgə'ru:] n canguru m.

keel [ki:l] n quilha; **on an even** ~ (fig) em equilíbrio.

keen [ki:n] adj (interest, desire) grande, vivo; (eye, intelligence) penetrante; (competition) intenso; (edge) afiado; (eager) entusiasmado; **to be** ~ **to do or on doing sth** sentir muita vontade de fazer algo; **to be** ~ **on sth/sb** gostar de algo/alguém; ~**ness** n (eagerness) entusiasmo, interesse m.

keep [ki:p], pt, pp **kept** vt (retain, preserve) reter; (hold back) guardar, ficar com; (shop, diary) ter; (feed: family etc) manter; (promise) cumprir; (chickens, bees etc) criar // vi (food) conservar-se; (remain) continuar // n (of castle) torre f de menagem; **to** ~ **doing sth** continuar fazendo algo; **to** ~ **sb from doing sth** impedir alguém de fazer algo; **to** ~ **sth from happening** impedir que algo aconteça; **to** ~ **sb happy** fazer alguém feliz; **to** ~ **a place tidy** manter um lugar limpo; **to** ~ **sth to o.s.** guardar algo para si mesmo; **to** ~ **sth (back) from sb** ocultar algo de alguém; **to** ~ **time** (clock) marcar a hora exata (Pt: -ct-); **to** ~ **on** vi persistir, continuar; **to** ~ **out** vi (stay out) permanecer fora; ''~ **out**'' "entrada proibida"; **to** ~ **up** vt manter // vi não atrasar-se, acompanhar; **to** ~ **up with** (pace) acompanhar; (level) manter-se ao nível de; ~**er** n guarda m, guardião/diã m/f; ~**ing** n (care) cuidado; **in** ~**ing with** de acordo com; ~**sake** n lembrança.

keg [kɛg] n barrilete m, barril m pequeno.

kennel ['kɛnl] n casa de cachorro; ~**s** npl canil msg.

Kenya ['kɛnjə] n Quênia f.

kept [kɛpt] pt, pp of **keep**.

kerb [kə:b] n meio-fio.

kernel ['kə:nl] n amêndoa.

kerosene ['kɛrəsi:n] n querosene m.

ketchup ['kɛtʃəp] n molho de tomate, ketchup m.

kettle ['kɛtl] n chaleira.

key [ki:] n (gen) chave f; (MUS) clave f; (of piano, typewriter) tecla; ~**board** n teclado; ~**hole** n buraco da fechadura; ~**note** n (MUS) tônica; ~**ring** n chaveiro; ~**stone** n pedra angular.

khaki ['ka:kɪ] adj cáqui.

kick [kɪk] vt (person) dar um pontapé em; (ball) chutar // vi (horse) dar coices // n pontapé m, chute m; (of rifle) recuo; (thrill): **he does it for** ~**s** faz isso para divertir-se; **to** ~ **off** vi (SPORT) dar o pontapé inicial; ~-**off** n (SPORT) pontapé m inicial.

kid [kɪd] n (child) criança; (animal) cabrito; (leather) pelica // vi (col) brincar.

kidnap ['kɪdnæp] vt seqüestrar; ~**per** n seqüestrador(a) m/f; ~**ping** n seqüestro.

kidney ['kɪdnɪ] n rim m.

kill [kɪl] vt (gen) matar; (murder) assassinar; (destroy) destruir; (finish off) acabar com, aniquilar // n ato (Pt: -ct-) de matar; ~**er** n assassino/a; ~**ing** n (one) assassinato; (several) matança // adj (funny) divertido, engraçado.

kiln [kɪln] n forno.

kilo ['ki:ləu] n quilo; ~**gram(me)** ['kɪləugræm] n quilograma m; ~**metre**, ~**meter** (US) ['kɪləmi:tə*] n quilômetro; ~**watt** ['kɪləwɔt] n quilowatt m.

kilt [kɪlt] n saiote m escocês.

kimono [kɪ'məunəu] n quimono.

kin [kɪn] n parentela.

kind [kaɪnd] adj (generous) generoso; (good) bom, bondoso, amável // n espécie f, classe f; (species) gênero; **in** ~ (COMM) em espécie; **a** ~ **of** uma espécie de; **two of a** ~ dois da mesma espécie.

kindergarten ['kɪndəga:tn] n jardim m de infância.

kind-hearted [kaɪnd'ha:tɪd] adj de bom coração.

kindle ['kɪndl] vt acender.

kindly ['kaɪndlɪ] adj (gen) bondoso; (good) bom/boa; (gentle) gentil, carinhoso // adv bondosamente, amavelmente; **will you** ~... você pode fazer o favor de...

kindness ['kaɪndnɪs] n bondade f, amabilidade f.

kindred ['kɪndrɪd] n parentela, parentesco // adj: ~ **spirit** pessoa com os mesmos gostos.

king [kɪŋ] n rei m; ~**dom** n reino; ~**fisher** n martim-pescador m; ~-**size** adj tamanho grande.

kink [kɪŋk] n (of rope) dobra, coca.

kinky ['kɪŋkɪ] adj (odd) excêntrico, esquisito; (pej) pervertido.

kiosk ['ki:ɔsk] n banca de jornais; (TEL) cabine f.

kipper ['kıpə*] n tipo de arenque m defumado.

kiss [kıs] n beijo // vt beijar; **to ~ (each other)** beijar-se.

kit [kıt] n (gen) apetrechos mpl; (equipment) equipamento; (set of tools etc) caixa de ferramentas; (for assembly) kit m para montar.

kitchen ['kıtʃın] n cozinha; **~ garden** n horta; **~ sink** n pia (de cozinha); **~ware** n bateria de cozinha.

kite [kaıt] n (toy) papagaio, pipa.

kitten ['kıtn] n gatinho.

kitty ['kıtı] n (pool of money) fundo comum, vaquinha; (CARDS) bolo.

kleptomaniac [klɛptəu'meınıæk] n cleptomaníaco/a.

knack [næk] n: **to have the ~ of doing sth** ter um jeito or queda para fazer algo.

knapsack ['næpsæk] n mochila.

knead [ni:d] vt amassar.

knee [ni:] n joelho; **~cap** n rótula.

kneel [ni:l], pt, pp **knelt** vi ajoelhar-se.

knell [nɛl] n dobre m de finados.

knelt [nɛlt] pt, pp of **kneel**.

knew [nju:] pt of **know**.

knickers ['nıkəz] npl calcinha fsg (Br), cuecas fpl (Pt).

knife [naıf], pl **knives** n faca // vt esfaquear.

knight [naıt] n cavaleiro; (CHESS) cavalo; **~hood** n cavalaria; (title): **to get a ~hood** receber o título de sir.

knit [nıt] vt tricotar (Br), fazer malha (Pt); (brows) franzir // vi tricotar (Br), fazer malha (Pt); (bones) consolidar-se; **to ~ together** (fig) unir, juntar; **~ting** n trabalho de tricô (Br), malha (Pt); **~ting machine** n máquina de tricotar; **~ting needle** n agulha de tricô (Br), agulha de malha (Pt); **~wear** n roupa de malha.

knives [naıvz] pl of **knife**.

knob [nɔb] n (of door) maçaneta; (of drawer) puxador m; (of stick) castão m; (lump) calombo; (fig): **a ~ of butter** uma porção de manteiga.

knock [nɔk] vt (strike) bater; (bump into) colidir com; (fig: col) criticar, malhar // n pancada, golpe m; (on door) batida; **to ~ at** or **on the door** bater à porta; **to ~ down** vt derrubar; **to ~ off** vi (col: finish) parar // vt (col: steal) roubar; **to ~ out** vt derrotar; (remove) remover; (BOXING) nocautear; **~er** n (on door) aldrava; **~-kneed** adj cambaio; **~out** n (BOXING) nocaute m.

knot [nɔt] n (gen) nó m // vt dar nó em; **~ty** adj (fig) complicado.

know [nəu], pt **knew**, pp **known** vt (gen) saber; (person, author, place) conhecer; **to ~ that...** saber que...; **to ~ how to swim** saber nadar; **~-all** n sabichão/chona m/f; **~-how** n know-how m, experiência; **~ing** adj (look: of complicity) de cumplicidade; (: spiteful)

malicioso; **~ingly** adv (purposely) de propósito; (spitefully) maliciosamente.

knowledge ['nɔlıdʒ] n (gen) conhecimento; (range of learning) saber m, conhecimentos mpl; (learning) erudição f, ciência; **~able** adj entendido, versado.

known [nəun] pp of **know**.

knuckle ['nʌkl] n nó m.

K.O. n abbr of **knockout**.

Koran [kɔ'rɑːn] n Alcorão m.

L

l. abbr of **litre**.

lab [læb] n abbr of **laboratory**.

label ['leıbl] n etiqueta, rótulo; (brand: of record) marca // vt etiquetar, rotular.

laboratory [lə'bɔrətərı] n laboratório.

laborious [lə'bɔːrıəs] adj laborioso.

labour, labor (US) ['leıbə*] n (task) trabalho; (~ force) mão-de-obra f; (workers) trabalhadores mpl; (MED) (trabalho de) parto // vi: **to ~ (at)** trabalhar (em) // vt insistir em; **in ~** (MED) em trabalho de parto; **L~, the L~ party** o partido trabalhista; **hard ~** trabalhos mpl forçados; **~ed** adj (movement) forçado; (style) elaborado; **~er** n operário; (on farm) trabalhador m rural, peão m; (day ~er) diarista m.

labyrinth ['læbırınθ] n labirinto.

lace [leıs] n renda; (of shoe etc) cordão m // vt (shoe) amarrar.

lack [læk] n (absence) falta; (scarcity) escassez f // vt carecer de; **through** or **for ~ of** por falta de; **to be ~ing** faltar.

lackadaisical [lækə'deızıkl] adj (careless) descuidado; (indifferent) apático, aéreo.

laconic [lə'kɔnık] adj lacônico.

lacquer ['lækə*] n laca, verniz m.

lad [læd] n menino, rapaz m, moço; (in stable etc) empregado.

ladder ['lædə*] n escada-de-mão f; (in tights) defeito (em forma de escada) // vt (tights) desfiar.

laden ['leıdn] adj: **~ (with)** carregado (de).

ladle ['leıdl] n concha (de sopa).

lady ['leıdı] n senhora; (distinguished, noble) dama; **young ~** senhorita; **'ladies' (toilets)** 'senhoras'; **~bird, ~bug** (US) n joaninha; **~-in-waiting** n dama de companhia; **~like** adj elegante, refinado.

lag [læg] vi (also: **~ behind**) atrasar-se, ficar atrás // vt (pipes) revestir com isolante térmico.

lager ['lɑːgə*] n cerveja leve e clara.

lagging ['lægıŋ] n revestimento.

lagoon [lə'guːn] n lagoa.

laid [leıd] pt, pp of **lay**.

lain [leın] pp of **lie**.

lair [lɛə*] n covil m, toca.

lake [leık] n lago.

lamb [læm] *n* cordeiro; (*meat*) carne *f* de cordeiro; ~ **chop** *n* costeleta de cordeiro; **lambswool** *n* lã *f* de cordeiro.

lame [leɪm] *adj* coxo, manco; (*weak*) pouco convincente, fraco.

lament [lə'mɛnt] *n* lamento, queixa // *vt* lamentar-se de; ~**able** ['læməntəbl] *adj* lamentável.

laminated ['læmɪneɪtɪd] *adj* laminado.

lamp [læmp] *n* lâmpada.

lampoon [læm'puːn] *vt* satirizar.

lamp: ~**post** *n* poste *m*; ~**shade** *n* abajur *m*, quebra-luz *m*.

lance [lɑːns] *n* lança // *vt* (*MED*) lancetar; ~ **corporal** *n* cabo.

lancet ['lɑːnsɪt] *n* lanceta.

land [lænd] *n* (*gen*) terra; (*country*) país *m*; (*piece of* ~) terreno; (*estate*) terras *fpl*, propriedades *fpl*; (*AGR*) solo // *vi* (*from ship*) desembarcar; (*AVIAT*) aterrissar (*Br*), aterrar (*Pt*); (*fig: fall*) cair, terminar // *vt* (*obtain*) conseguir; (*passengers, goods*) desembarcar; **to** ~ **up in/at** ir parar em; ~**ing** *n* desembarque *m*, aterrissagem *f* (*Br*), aterragem *f* (*Pt*); (*of staircase*) patamar *m*; ~**ing craft** *n* navio para desembarque; ~**ing gear** *n* trem de aterrissagem (*Br*), trem *m* de aterragem (*Pt*); ~**ing stage** *n* cais *m* de desembarque; ~**ing strip** *n* pista de aterrissagem (*Br*), pista de aterragem (*Pt*); ~**lady** *n* (*of boarding house*) senhoria; (*owner*) proprietária; ~**locked** *adj* cercado de terra; ~**lord** *n* senhorio, locador *m*; (*of pub etc*) dono, proprietário; ~**lubber** *n* pessoa desacostumada ao mar; ~**mark** *n* lugar *m* conhecido; (*fig*) marco; **to be a** ~**mark** (*fig*) marcar uma época; ~**owner** *n* latifundiário/a *m/f*.

landscape ['lænskeɪp] *n* paisagem *f*; ~**d** *adj* projetado paisagisticamente, urbanizado.

landslide ['lændslaɪd] *n* (*GEO*) desmoronamento, desabamento; (*fig: POL*) vitória esmagadora.

lane [leɪn] *n* (*in country*) senda; (*in town*) ruela; (*AUT*) pista; (*in race*) raia; (*for air or sea traffic*) rota.

language ['læŋgwɪdʒ] *n* linguagem *f*; (*national tongue*) idioma *m*, língua; **bad** ~ linguagem indecente or grosseira.

languid ['læŋgwɪd] *adj* lânguido.

languish ['læŋgwɪʃ] *vi* elanguescer, debilitar-se.

lank [læŋk] *adj* (*hair*) liso.

lanky ['læŋkɪ] *adj* magricela.

lantern ['læntn] *n* lanterna.

lap [læp] *n* (*of track*) volta; (*of body*): **to sit on sb's** ~ sentar-se no colo de alguém // *vt* (*also*: ~ **up**) lamber // *vi* (*waves*) marulhar; ~**dog** *n* cãozinho de estimação.

lapel [lə'pɛl] *n* lapela.

Lapland ['læplænd] *n* Lapônia; **Lapp** [læp] *adj, n* lapão/ona *m/f*.

lapse [læps] *n* lapso, engano; (*moral*) decadência // *vi* (*expire*) caducar; (*LAW*) prescrever; (*morally*) decair; (*time*) passar, transcorrer; **to** ~ **into bad habits** adquirir maus hábitos; ~ **of time** lapso, intervalo.

larceny ['lɑːsənɪ] *n* furto; **petty** ~ delito leve.

lard [lɑːd] *n* banha de porco.

larder ['lɑːdə*] *n* despensa.

large [lɑːdʒ] *adj* (*gen*) grande; (*fat*) gordo; **at** ~ (*free*) em liberdade; (*generally*) em geral; ~**ly** *adv* em grande parte; ~-**scale** *adj* (*map*) em grande escala; (*fig*) importante.

lark [lɑːk] *n* (*bird*) cotovia; (*joke*) brincadeira, peça; **to** ~ **about** *vi* divertir-se, brincar.

larva ['lɑːvə], *pl* -**vae** [-viː] *n* larva.

laryngitis [lærɪn'dʒaɪtɪs] *n* laringite *f*.

larynx ['lærɪŋks] *n* laringe *f*.

lascivious [lə'sɪvɪəs] *adj* lascivo.

laser ['leɪzə*] *n* laser *m*.

lash [læʃ] *n* chicote *m*, açoite *m*; (*punishment*) chicotada; (*gen*: **eyelash**) pestana, cílio // *vt* chicotear, açoitar; (*tie*) atar; **to** ~ **out** *vi*: **to** ~ **out at** or **against sb** atacar alguém violentamente; **to** ~ **out** (*col: spend*) esbanjar.

lass [læs] *n* moça.

lasso [læ'suː] *n* laço // *vt* laçar.

last [lɑːst] *adj* (*gen*) último; (*final*) derradeiro // *adv* em último lugar // *vi* (*endure*) durar; (*continue*) continuar; ~ **week** na semana passada; ~ **night** ontem à noite; **at** ~ finalmente; ~ **but one** penúltimo; ~**ing** *adj* durável, duradouro; ~-**minute** *adj* de última hora.

latch [lætʃ] *n* trinco, fecho, tranca; ~**key** *n* chave *f* de trinco.

late [leɪt] *adj* (*not on time*) atrasado; (*far on in day etc*) tardio; (*hour*) avançado; (*recent*) recente; (*former*) antigo, ex-, anterior; (*dead*) falecido // *adv* tarde; (*behind time, schedule*) atrasado; **of** ~ recentemente; **in** ~ **May** no final de maio; **the** ~ **Mr X** o falecido Sr. X; ~**comer** *n* retardatário/a; ~**ly** *adv* ultimamente; ~**ness** *n* (*of person*) atraso; (*of event*) demora.

latent ['leɪtnt] *adj* latente.

later ['leɪtə*] *adj* (*date etc*) posterior; (*version etc*) mais recente // *adv* mais tarde, depois.

lateral ['lætərl] *adj* lateral.

latest ['leɪtɪst] *adj* último; **at the** ~ no mais tardar.

lathe [leɪð] *n* torno.

lather ['lɑːðə*] *n* espuma (de sabão) // *vt* ensaboar // *vi* fazer espuma.

Latin ['lætɪn] *n* latim *m* // *adj* latino; ~ **America** *n* América Latina; ~-**American** *adj, n* latino-americano/a.

latitude ['lætɪtjuːd] *n* latitude *f*.

latrine [lə'triːn] *n* latrina.

latter ['lætə*] *adj* último; (*of two*)

segundo // n: the ~ o último, este; ~ly adv ultimamente.

lattice ['lætɪs] n treliça; (on window) gelosia, rótula.

laudable ['lɔːdəbl] adj louvável.

laugh [lɑːf] n riso, risada; (loud) gargalhada // vi rir, dar risada or gargalhada; **to ~ at** vt fus rir de; ridicularizar; **to ~ off** vt disfarçar sorrindo; ~**able** adj risível, ridículo; **to be the ~ing stock of the town** ser o alvo de ridículo da cidade; ~**ter** n riso, risada.

launch [lɔːntʃ] n (boat) lancha; see also ~ing // vt (ship, rocket, plan) lançar; ~**ing** n (of rocket etc) lançamento; (inauguration) estréia; ~**(ing) pad** n plataforma de lançamento.

launder ['lɔːndə*] vt lavar e passar.

launderette [lɔːn'drɛt] n lavanderia automática.

laundry ['lɔːndrɪ] n lavanderia; (clothes) roupa para lavar; **to do the ~** lavar a roupa.

laureate ['lɔːrɪət] adj see **poet.**

laurel ['lɔrl] n louro; (BOT) loureiro.

lava ['lɑːvə] n lava.

lavatory ['lævətərɪ] n privada (Br), casa de banho (Pt); **lavatories** npl sanitários mpl (Br), lavabos mpl (Pt).

lavender ['lævəndə*] n lavanda.

lavish ['lævɪʃ] adj profuso, perdulário; (giving freely): ~ **with** pródigo em or generoso com // vt: **to ~ sth on sb** encher or cobrir alguém de algo.

law [lɔː] n lei f; (study) direito; (of game) regra; ~-**abiding** adj obediente à lei; ~ **and order** n ordem f pública; ~**breaker** n infrator(a) (Pt: -ct-) m/f (da lei); ~ **court** n tribunal m de justiça; ~**ful** adj legal, lícito; ~**fully** adv legalmente; ~**less** adj (act) ilegal; (person) rebelde; (country) sem lei, desordenado.

lawn [lɔːn] n gramado (Br), relvado (Pt); ~**mower** n cortador m de grama (Br), cortador m de relva (Pt); ~ **tennis** [-'tɛnɪs] n tênis m de gramado (Br), ténis m de relvado (Pt).

law: ~ **school** n faculdade f de direito; ~ **student** n estudante m/f de direito.

lawsuit ['lɔːsuːt] n ação (Pt: -çç-) f judicial, processo.

lawyer ['lɔːjə*] n advogado/a; (for sales, wills etc) notário, tabelião/liã m/f.

lax [læks] adj frouxo; (negligent) negligente, descuidado.

laxative ['læksətɪv] n laxante m.

laxity ['læksɪtɪ] n frouxidão f; (moral) complacência; (negligence) negligência.

lay [leɪ] pt of **lie** // adj leigo; (not expert) profano // vt, pt, pp **laid** (place) colocar; (eggs, table) pôr; (trap) armar; **to ~ aside** or **by** vt pôr de lado; **to ~ down** vt (pen etc) depositar; (~ flat) deitar; (arms) depor; (policy) estabelecer; **to ~ down the law** impor regras; **to ~ off** vt (workers) dispensar; **to ~ on** vt

(water, gas) instalar; (provide) prover; **to ~ out** vt (design) planejar; (display) expor; (spend) esbanjar; **to ~ up** vt (store) estocar; (ship) pôr fora de serviço; (subj: illness) acometer; ~**about** n vadio, preguiçoso; ~-**by** n acostamento.

layer ['leɪə*] n camada.

layette [leɪ'ɛt] n enxoval m de bebê.

layman ['leɪmən] n pessoa não entendida or não especializada; (REL) leigo.

layout ['leɪaut] n (design) leiaute m, esquema m; (disposition) disposição f; (PRESS) composição f.

laze [leɪz] vi viver na ociosidade; (pej) vadiar, malandrar; **laziness** n preguiça; **lazy** adj preguiçoso, indolente.

lb. abbr of **pound** (weight).

lead [liːd] n (front position) dianteira; (SPORT) liderança; (distance, time ahead) vantagem f; (clue) pista; (ELEC) fio; (for dog) correia; (THEATRE) papel m principal // n [lɛd] chumbo; (in pencil) grafite f // (vb: pt, pp **led**) vt conduzir; (induce) levar, induzir; (be leader of) dirigir; (SPORT) liderar // vi encabeçar; **to ~ to** levar a, conduzir a; **to ~ astray** vt desencaminhar; **to ~ away** vt levar; **to ~ back** vt fazer voltar, levar de volta; **to ~ on** vt (tease) provocar; **to ~ on to** vt (induce) incitar a; **to ~ up to** conduzir a.

leader ['liːdə*] n (gen) líder m, chefe m/f; (of union etc) dirigente m/f; (of gang) cabeça m; (guide) guia m/f; (of newspaper) artigo de fundo; ~**ship** n liderança, direção (Pt: -çç-) f; (quality) poder m de liderança.

leading ['liːdɪŋ] adj (main) principal; (outstanding) destacado, notável; (first) primeiro; (front) dianteiro; ~ **lady** n (THEATRE) primeira atriz f; ~ **light** n (person) figura principal.

leaf [liːf], pl **leaves** n folha // vi: **to ~ through** folhear; **to turn over a new ~** começar vida nova.

leaflet ['liːflɪt] n folheto.

league [liːg] n associação f; (FOOTBALL) liga; **to be in ~ with** estar de comum acordo com.

leak [liːk] n (of liquid, gas) escape m, vazamento; (hole) buraco, rombo; (in roof) goteira; (of money) desfalque m // vi (ship) fazer água; (shoe) deixar entrar água; (pipe) vazar; (roof) gotejar; (container) vazar; (gas) escapar; (fig: news) transpirar // vt (gen) deixar escapar; (exude) escoar; **the information was** ~**ed to the enemy** as informações foram passadas para o inimigo; **the news** ~**ed out** a notícia veio a público.

lean [liːn] adj magro // (vb: pt, pp **leaned** or **leant** [lɛnt]) vt: **to ~ sth on** apoiar algo em // vi (slope) inclinar-se; (rest): **to ~ against** apoiar-se contra; **to ~ on** apoiar-se em; (fig: rely on) contar com (o apoio de); **to ~ back/forward** vi inclinar-se para trás/frente; **to ~**

over vt/i inclinar-se (sobre); ~**ing** adj inclinação f, tendência // n: ~**ing (towards)** inclinação f (para); ~**-to** n alpendre m.

leap [li:p] n salto, pulo // vi, pt, pp **leaped** or **leapt** [lεpt] saltar; ~**frog** n carniça; ~ **year** n ano bissexto.

learn [lɜ:n], pt, pp **learned** or **learnt** vt (gen) aprender; (come to know of) informar-se de, ficar sabendo // vi aprender; **to** ~ **how to do sth** aprender a fazer algo; ~**ed** ['lɜ:nɪd] adj erudito; ~**er** n principiante m/f; ~**ing** n (process) aprendizagem f, (quality) erudição f.

lease [li:s] n arrendamento, locação f // vt arrendar, alugar.

leash [li:ʃ] n trela, correia.

least [li:st] adj menor; (smallest amount of) mínimo // adv o menos // n: **the** ~ mínimo; **the** ~ **possible effort** o menor esforço possível; **at** ~ pelo menos; **not in the** ~ de maneira nenhuma.

leather ['lεðə*] n couro.

leave [li:v], pt, pp **left** vt deixar; (go away from) abandonar // vi ir-se; (train) sair // n permissão f, licença f; **to be left** sobrar; **there's some milk left over** sobrou um pouco de leite; **on** ~ de licença; **to take one's** ~ **of** despedir-se de; **to** ~ **out** vt omitir, excluir.

leaves [li:vz] pl of **leaf**.

Lebanon ['lεbənən] n Líbano m.

lecherous ['lεtʃərəs] adj lascivo.

lecture ['lεktʃə*] n conferência; (SCOL) aula // vi dar uma aula // vt (scold) passar um sermão em; **to give a** ~ on dar uma conferência sobre; **lecturer** n conferencista m/f; (at university) professor(a) m/f.

led [lεd] pt, pp of **lead**.

ledge [lεdʒ] n (of window, on wall) saliência, borda; (of mountain) proeminência.

ledger ['lεdʒə*] n livro-razão m.

lee [li:] n sotavento.

leek [li:k] n alho-poró m.

leer [lɪə*] vi: **to** ~ **at sb** olhar maliciosamente para alguém.

leeway ['li:weɪ] n (fig): **to have some** ~ ter certa liberdade de ação (Pt: -çç-).

left [lεft] pt, pp of **leave** // adj esquerdo; (POL) de esquerda // n esquerda // adv à esquerda; **the L**~ (POL) a Esquerda; ~**-handed** adj canhoto; **the** ~**-hand side** a esquerda; ~ **luggage (office)** n depósito de bagagem; ~**-overs** npl sobras fpl; ~**-wing** adj (POL) de extrema esquerda, esquerdista.

leg [lεg] n perna; (of animal) pata; (of chair) pé m; (CULIN: of meat) perna; (of journey) etapa; **lst/2nd** ~ (SPORT) partida de ida/de volta; **to pull sb's** ~ brincar or mexer com alguém.

legacy ['lεgəsɪ] n legado.

legal ['li:gl] adj (gen) lícito; (of law) legal; (enquiry etc) jurídico; ~**ize** vt legalizar;

~**ly** adv legalmente; ~ **tender** n moeda corrente.

legend ['lεdʒənd] n lenda; ~**ary** adj legendário.

legible ['lεdʒəbl] adj legível.

legion ['li:dʒən] n legião f.

legislate ['lεdʒɪsleɪt] vi legislar; **legislation** [-'leɪʃən] n legislação f; **legislative** [-lətɪv] adj legislativo; **legislature** [-lətʃə*] n legislatura.

legitimacy [lɪ'dʒɪtɪməsɪ] n legitimidade f; **legitimate** [-mət] adj legítimo.

leg-room ['lεgru:m] n espaço para as pernas.

leisure ['lεʒə*] n lazer m, ócio; **at** ~ desocupado, livre; ~ **centre** n centro de lazer; ~**ly** adj calmo, vagaroso.

lemon ['lεmən] n limão m; ~**ade** [-'neɪd] n (fruit juice) limonada; (fizzy) refresco de limão.

lend [lεnd], pt, pp **lent** vt: **to** ~ **sth to sb** emprestar algo a alguém; ~**er** n emprestador(a) m/f; ~**ing library** n biblioteca volante.

length [lεŋθ] n comprimento, extensão f; (section: of road, pipe etc) trecho; **at** ~ (at last) finalmente, afinal; (lengthily) por extenso; ~**en** vt encompridar // vi encompridar-se; ~**ways** adv longitudinalmente; ~**y** adj comprido, prolixo; (meeting) prolongado.

leniency ['li:nɪənsɪ] n indulgência; **lenient** [-ənt] adj indulgente, clemente.

lens [lεnz] n (of spectacles) lente f; (of camera) objetiva (Pt: -ct-).

lent [lεnt] pt, pp of **lend**.

Lent [lεnt] n Quaresma.

lentil ['lεntl] n lentilha.

Leo ['li:əu] n Leão m.

leopard ['lεpəd] n leopardo.

leotard ['li:ətɑ:d] n collant m.

leper ['lεpə*] n leproso/a; **leprosy** [-prəsɪ] n lepra.

lesbian ['lεzbɪən] n lésbica.

less [lεs] det adj (in size, degree etc) menor; (in quantity) menos // pron, adv menos; ~ **than half** menos da metade; ~ **and** ~ cada vez menos; **the** ~ **he works...** quanto menos trabalha...

lessen ['lεsn] vi diminuir, minguar // vt diminuir, reduzir.

lesson ['lεsn] n lição f; **a maths** ~ uma aula or uma lição de matemática.

lest [lεst] conj: ~ **it happen** para que não aconteça.

let [lεt] pt, pp **let** vt (allow) deixar, permitir; (lease) alugar; ~'**s go** vamos!; ~ **him come** deixa-le vir!; **"to** ~" "aluga-se"; **to** ~ **down** vt (lower) abaixar; (dress) encompridar; (tyre) esvaziar; (hair) soltar; (disappoint) desapontar; **to** ~ **go** vt/i soltar; **to** ~ **in** vt deixar entrar; (visitor etc) fazer entrar; **to** ~ **off** vt deixar livre; (firework etc) disparar; **to** ~ **on** vt (col) divulgar (that que); **to** ~ **out** vt deixar sair; (dress) alargar; **to** ~ **up** vi cessar, afrouxar.

lethal ['li:θl] adj letal; (wound) mortal.

lethargic [lɛˈθɑːdʒɪk] *adj* letárgico;
lethargy [ˈlɛθədʒɪ] *n* letargia.

letter [ˈlɛtə*] *n* (*of alphabet*) letra;
(*correspondence*) carta; ~ **bomb** *n* carta
com bomba; ~**box** *n* caixa do correio;
~**ing** *n* letras *fpl*.

lettuce [ˈlɛtɪs] *n* alface *f*.

let-up [ˈlɛtʌp] *n* pausa, trégua.

leukaemia, leukemia (*US*) [luːˈkiːmɪə]
n leucemia.

level [ˈlɛvl] *adj* (*flat*) plano; (*flattened*)
nivelado; (*uniform*) uniforme // *adv* no
mesmo nível // *n* nível *m*; (*flat place*)
plano // *vt* nivelar, aplanar; **to be** ~
with estar no mesmo nível que; **on the**
~ (*fig: honest*) a sério, sincero; **to** ~ **off**
or **out** *vi* (*prices etc*) estabilizar-se; ~
crossing *n* passagem *f* de nível;
~**-headed** *adj* sensato.

lever [ˈliːvə*] *n* alavanca // *vt*: **to** ~ **up**
levantar com alavanca, ~**age** *n* (*fig:
influence*) influência.

levity [ˈlɛvɪtɪ] *n* leviandade *f*, frivolidade
f.

levy [ˈlɛvɪ] *n* arrecadação *f*, tributo // *vt*
arrecadar, exigir.

lewd [luːd] *adj* obsceno, lascivo.

liability [laɪəˈbɪlətɪ] *n* responsabilidade *f*;
(*handicap*) desvantagem *f*; (*risk*) risco;
liabilities *npl* obrigações *fpl*; (*COMM*)
dívidas *fpl*, passivo *sg*.

liable [ˈlaɪəbl] *adj* (*subject*): ~ **to** sujeito
a; **to be** ~ **for** ser responsável por; **to
be** ~ **to** (*likely*) ter uma tendência
para.

liaison [liːˈeɪzɔn] *n* (*coordination*) ligação
f; (*affair*) relação *f* amorosa.

liar [ˈlaɪə*] *n* mentiroso/a.

libel [ˈlaɪbl] *n* libelo, calúnia // *vt*
caluniar, difamar.

liberal [ˈlɪbərl] *adj* (*gen*) liberal;
(*generous*): ~ **with** generoso com.

liberate [ˈlɪbəreɪt] *vt* liberar; **liberation**
[-ˈreɪʃən] *n* liberação *f*.

liberty [ˈlɪbətɪ] *n* liberdade *f*; **to be at** ~
to ter permissão para; **to take the** ~
of doing sth tomar a liberdade de fazer
algo.

Libra [ˈliːbrə] *n* Libra.

librarian [laɪˈbrɛərɪən] *n* bibliotecário/a;
library [ˈlaɪbrərɪ] *n* biblioteca.

libretto [lɪˈbrɛtəu] *n* libreto.

Libya [ˈlɪbɪə] *n* Líbia; ~**n** *adj*, *n* líbio/a.

lice [laɪs] *pl of* **louse**.

licence, license (*US*) [ˈlaɪsns] *n* (*gen*)
licença; (*permit*) permissão *f*; (*also:
driving* ~) carteira de motorista (*Br*),
carta de condução (*Pt*); (*excessive
freedom*) libertinagem *f*; ~ **number** *n*
número da placa; ~ **plate** *n* placa (do
carro).

license [ˈlaɪsns] *n* (*US*) = **licence** // *vt*
autorizar, licenciar; ~**d** *adj* (*for alcohol*)
autorizado para vender bebida
alcoólica.

licensee [laɪsənˈsiː] *n* (*in a pub*) dono/a
m/f.

licentious [laɪˈsɛnʃəs] *adj* licencioso.

lichen [ˈlaɪkən] *n* líquem *m*.

lick [lɪk] *vt* lamber // *n* lambida; **a** ~ **of
paint** uma mão de pintura.

licorice [ˈlɪkərɪs] *n* = **liquorice**.

lid [lɪd] *n* (*of box, case, of pan*) tampa.

lido [ˈlaɪdəu] *n* piscina pública ao ar livre.

lie [laɪ] *n* mentira // *vi* mentir // *vi*, *pt* **lay**,
pp **lain** (*act*) deitar-se; (*state*) estar
deitado; (*of object: be situated*) estar,
encontrar-se; **to** ~ **low** (*fig*) esconder-
se; **to** ~ **about** *vi* (*things*) estar
espalhado; (*people*) vadiar; **to have a**
~**-down** descansar, tirar uma soneca;
to have a ~**-in** dormir até tarde.

lieu [luː]: **in** ~ **of** *prep* em vez de.

lieutenant [lɛfˈtɛnənt] *n* lugar-tenente
m; (*MIL*) tenente *m*.

life [laɪf] *pl* **lives** *n* (*gen*) vida; (*way of* ~)
modo de viver; (*of licence etc*) vigência;
~ **assurance** *n* seguro de vida; ~**belt**
n cinto salva-vidas; ~**boat** *n* barco
salva-vidas; ~**guard** *n* guarda *m* salva-
vidas; ~ **jacket** *n* colete *m* salva-vidas;
~**less** *adj* sem vida; (*dull*) sem graça;
~**like** *adj* natural; ~**line** *n* corda salva-
vidas; ~**long** *adj* vitalício, perpétuo; ~
preserver *n* (*US*) colete *m* salva-vidas;
~**-saver** *n* guarda *m* salva-vidas; ~
sentence *n* prisão *f* perpétua; ~**-sized**
adj de tamanho natural; ~ **span** *n* vida,
duração *f*; ~ **support system** *n* (*MED*)
sistema *m* de respiração artificial;
~**time** *n*: **in his** ~**time** durante a sua
vida; **once in a** ~**time** uma vez na
vida.

lift [lɪft] *vt* levantar; (*steal*) roubar // *vi*
(*fog*) dispersar-se, dissipar-se // *n*
(*elevator*) elevador *m*; **to give sb a** ~
dar uma carona para alguém (*Br*), dar
uma boleia a alguém (*Pt*); ~**-off** *n*
decolagem *f*.

ligament [ˈlɪgəmənt] *n* ligamento.

light [laɪt] *n* (*gen*) luz *f*; (*flame*) chama,
lume *m*; (*lamp*) luz, lâmpada; (*daylight*)
luz do dia; (*headlight*) farol *m*; (*rear* ~)
luz traseira; (*for cigarette etc*): **have you
got a** ~? (você) tem fogo? // *vt*, *pt*, *pp*
lighted *or* **lit** (*candle, cigarette, fire*)
acender; (*room*) iluminar // *adj* (*colour*)
claro; (*not heavy, also fig*) leve; (*room*)
iluminado; **to** ~ **up** *vi* (*smoke*) acender
um cigarro; (*face*) iluminar-se // *vt*
(*illuminate*) iluminar, acender; ~ **bulb** *n*
lâmpada; ~**en** *vi* (*grow* ~) clarear // *vt*
(*give light to*) iluminar; (*make lighter*)
clarear; (*make less heavy*) tornar mais
leve; ~**er** *n* (*also: cigarette* ~**er**)
isqueiro, acendedor *m*; ~**-headed** *adj*
(*dizzy*) aturdido, tonto; (*excited*)
exaltado; (*by nature*) estouvado;
~**-hearted** *adj* alegre, despreocupado;
~**house** *n* farol *m*; ~**ing** *n* (*act, system*)
iluminação *f*; ~**ly** *adv* (*touch*)
ligeiramente; (*thoughtlessly*) des-
preocupadamente; (*slightly*) levemente;
(*not seriously*) levianamente; **to get off**
~**ly** não ser castigado o suficiente; ~
meter *n* (*PHOT*) fotômetro; ~**ness** *n*
claridade *f*; (*in weight*) leveza.

lightning ['laɪtnɪŋ] n relâmpago, raio; ~ **conductor** n pára-raios m inv.

light: ~**weight** adj (suit) leve // n (BOXING) peso-leve m; ~ **year** n ano-luz m.

like [laɪk] vt (person) gostar de, simpatizar-se com; (things) gostar de // prep como // adj parecido, semelhante // n: **the** ~ coisas parecidas; **his** ~**s and dislikes** seus gostos e aversões; **I would** ~, **I'd** ~ (eu) gostaria de; **would you** ~ **a coffee?** você quer um café?; **to be** or **look** ~ sb/sth assemelhar-se a or parecer-se com alguém/algo; **that's just** ~ **him** é típico dele; **it is nothing** ~... não se parece nada com ...; ~**able** adj simpático, agradável.

likelihood ['laɪklɪhud] n probabilidade f; **likely** [-lɪ] adj provável; **he's likely to leave** é provável que ele se vá.

like-minded [laɪk'maɪndɪd] adj da mesma opinião.

liken ['laɪkən] vt: **to** ~ **sth to sth** comparar algo com algo.

likewise ['laɪkwaɪz] adv igualmente.

liking ['laɪkɪŋ] n: **to his** ~ ao seu gosto.

lilac ['laɪlək] n lilás m // adj (colour) de cor lilás.

lily ['lɪlɪ] n lírio, açucena; ~ **of the valley** n lírio-do-vale m.

limb [lɪm] n membro.

limber ['lɪmbə*]: **to** ~ **up** vi (fig) tornar-se flexível; (SPORT) fazer aquecimento.

limbo ['lɪmbəu] n: **to be in** ~ (fig) cair no ostracismo.

lime [laɪm] n (tree) limeira; (fruit) lima; (GEO) cal f.

limelight ['laɪmlaɪt] n: **to be in the** ~ (fig) ser o centro das atenções.

limerick ['lɪmərɪk] n quintilha humorística.

limestone ['laɪmstəun] n pedra calcária.

limit ['lɪmɪt] n limite m // vt limitar; ~**ation** [-'teɪʃən] n limitação f; ~**ed** adj limitado; **to be** ~**ed** to limitar-se a; ~**ed (liability) company (Ltd)** n sociedade f anônima; ~**less** adj ilimitado.

limousine ['lɪməziːn] n limusine f.

limp [lɪmp] n: **to have a** ~ mancar, ser coxo // vi mancar // adj frouxo.

limpet ['lɪmpɪt] n lapa.

limpid ['lɪmpɪd] adj límpido, cristalino.

line [laɪn] n (gen) linha; (straight ~) reta; (rope) corda; (for fishing) linha; (US: queue) fila (Br), bicha (Pt); (wire) arame m; (row) fila, fileira; (of writing) linha; (on face) ruga; (speciality) ramo de negócio // vt (SEWING) forrar (with de); **to** ~ **the streets** ocupar as ruas; **in** ~ **with** de acordo com; **to** ~ **up** vi fazer fila // vt alinhar, pôr em fila; ~**d** adj (face) enrugado; (paper) pautado.

linear ['lɪnɪə*] adj linear.

linen ['lɪnɪn] n roupa branca or de cama; (cloth) linho.

liner ['laɪnə*] n navio de linha regular.

linesman ['laɪnzmən] n (SPORT) juiz m de linha.

line-up ['laɪnʌp] n formação f em linha, alinhamento; (players) escalação f.

linger ['lɪŋgə*] vi demorar-se, retardar-se; (smell, tradition) persistir.

lingerie ['lænʒəriː] n lingerie f, roupa de baixo (de mulher).

lingering ['lɪŋgərɪŋ] adj persistente; (death) lento, vagaroso.

lingo ['lɪŋgəu], pl ~**es** n (pej) língua.

linguist ['lɪŋgwɪst] n linguista m/f; ~**ic** adj linguístico; ~**ics** nsg linguística.

lining ['laɪnɪŋ] n forro.

link [lɪŋk] n (of a chain) elo; (connection) conexão f; (bond) vínculo, laço // vt vincular, unir; ~**s** npl campo sg de golfe; **to** ~ **up** vt acoplar // vi unir-se; ~**-up** n (gen) união f; (in space) acoplamento.

lino ['laɪnəu], **linoleum** [lɪ'nəulɪəm] n linóleo.

lintel ['lɪntl] n verga.

lion ['laɪən] n leão m; ~**ess** n leoa.

lip [lɪp] n lábio; (of jug) bico; (of cup etc) borda; ~**read** vi ler os lábios; ~ **service** n: **to pay** ~ **service to sth** devotar-se a or elogiar algo falsamente; ~**stick** n batom m.

liquefy ['lɪkwɪfaɪ] vt liquefazer.

liqueur [lɪ'kjuə*] n licor m.

liquid ['lɪkwɪd] adj, n líquido.

liquidate ['lɪkwɪdeɪt] vt liquidar; **liquidation** [-'deɪʃən] n liquidação f; **liquidator** n liquidador(a) m/f.

liquidize ['lɪkwɪdaɪz] vt (CULIN) liquidificar, passar no liquidificador.

liquor ['lɪkə*] n licor m, bebida alcoólica.

liquorice ['lɪkərɪs] n alcaçuz m.

lisp [lɪsp] n ceceio // vi cecear, falar com a língua presa.

list [lɪst] n lista; (of ship) inclinação f // vt (write down) fazer uma lista or relação de; (enumerate) enumerar // vi (ship) inclinar-se.

listen ['lɪsn] vi escutar, ouvir; (pay attention) prestar atenção; ~**er** n ouvinte m/f.

listless ['lɪstlɪs] adj apático, indiferente.

lit [lɪt] pt, pp of **light**.

litany ['lɪtənɪ] n ladainha, litania.

literacy ['lɪtərəsɪ] n capacidade f de ler e escrever; ~ **campaign** campanha de alfabetização.

literal ['lɪtərl] adj literal; ~**ly** adv literalmente.

literary ['lɪtərərɪ] adj literário.

literate ['lɪtərət] adj alfabetizado, instruído; (fig) culto, letrado.

literature ['lɪtərɪtʃə*] n literatura; (brochures etc) folhetos mpl.

lithe [laɪð] adj ágil, flexível.

litigation [lɪtɪ'geɪʃən] n litígio.

litre, liter (US) ['liːtə*] n litro.

litter ['lɪtə*] n (rubbish) lixo; (paper) papel m jogado; (young animals) ninhada; (stretcher) maca, padiola; ~ **bin** n lata de lixo; ~**ed** adj: ~**ed with** (scattered) semeado de; (covered with) coberto de.

little ['lɪtl] *adj* (*small*) pequeno; (*not much*) pouco; *often translated by suffix: eg* ~ **house** casinha // *adv* pouco; **a** ~ um pouco (de); ~ **by** ~ pouco a pouco.

liturgy ['lɪtədʒɪ] *n* liturgia.

live [lɪv] *vi* viver; (*reside*) morar // *vt* (*a life*) levar; (*experience*) viver // *adj* [laɪv] (*animal*) vivo; (*wire*) eletrizado (*Pt:* -ct-); (*broadcast*) ao vivo; (*shell*) carregado; **to** ~ **down** *vt* redimir; **to** ~ **on** *vt fus* (*food*) viver de, alimentar-se de; **to** ~ **up to** *vt fus* (*fulfil*) cumprir; (*justify*) justificar.

livelihood ['laɪvlɪhud] *n* meio de vida, subsistência.

lively ['laɪvlɪ] *adj* (*gen*) vivo; (*talk*) animado; (*pace*) rápido; (*party, tune*) alegre.

liver ['lɪvə*] *n* (*ANAT*) fígado; ~**ish** *adj* (*fig*) rabugento, mal-humorado.

lives [laɪvz] *pl of* **life.**

livestock ['laɪvstɔk] *n* gado.

livid ['lɪvɪd] *adj* lívido; (*furious*) furioso.

living ['lɪvɪŋ] *adj* (*alive*) vivo // *n*: **to earn** *or* **make a** ~ ganhar a vida; ~ **conditions** *npl* condições *fpl* de vida; ~ **room** *n* sala de estar; ~ **standards** *npl* padrão *m* or nível *m* de vida; ~ **wage** *n* salário de subsistência.

lizard ['lɪzəd] *n* lagarto, lagartixa.

llama ['lɑːmə] *n* lhama.

load [ləud] *n* (*gen*) carga; (*weight*) peso // *vt*: **to** ~ (**with**) carregar (de); (*fig*) cumular (de), encher (de); **a** ~ **of,** ~**s of** (*fig*) (grande) quantidade de, um monte de; ~**ed** *adj* (*dice*) viciado; (*question, word*) intencionado; (*col: rich*) cheio da nota; (: *drunk*) de porre.

loaf [ləuf], *pl* **loaves** *n* (bisnaga de) pão *m* // *vi* (*also:* ~ **about,** ~ **around**) vadiar, vagabundar.

loan [ləun] *n* (*gen, COMM*) empréstimo // *vt* emprestar; **on** ~ emprestado.

loath [ləuθ] *adj:* **to be** ~ **to do sth** estar pouco inclinado a fazer algo.

loathe [ləuð] *vt* aborrecer; (*person*) odiar; **loathing** *n* aversão *f*; ódio; **it fills me with loathing** me dá (um) ódio.

loaves [ləuvz] *pl of* **loaf.**

lobby ['lɔbɪ] *n* vestíbulo, saguão *m*; (*POL: pressure group*) grupo de pressão // *vt* pressionar.

lobe [ləub] *n* lóbulo.

lobster ['lɔbstə*] *n* lagostim *m*; (*large*) lagosta.

local ['ləukl] *adj* local // *n* (*Brit: col: pub*) bar *m* (local); **the** ~**s** *npl* os moradores *mpl* locais; ~**ity** [-'kælɪtɪ] *n* localidade *f*; ~**ly** [-kəlɪ] *adv* nos arredores, na vizinhança.

locate [ləu'keɪt] *vt* (*find*) localizar, situar; (*situate*) colocar.

location [ləu'keɪʃən] *n* local *m*, posição *f*; **on** ~ (*CINEMA*) externas.

loch [lɔx] *n* lago.

lock [lɔk] *n* (*of door, box*) fechadura; (*of canal*) eclusa, comporta; (*stop*) tranca; (*of hair*) anel *m*, mecha // *vt* (*with key*)

fechar à chave; (*immobilize*) imobilizar // *vi* (*door etc*) fechar-se à chave; (*wheels*) travar-se.

locker ['lɔkə*] *n* compartimento com chave.

locket ['lɔkɪt] *n* medalhão *m*.

lockout ['lɔkaut] *n* greve *f* de patrões.

locomotive [ləukə'məutɪv] *n* locomotiva.

locum ['ləukəm] *n* (*MED*) (médico) interino.

locust ['ləukəst] *n* gafanhoto.

lodge [lɔdʒ] *n* casa do guarda; (*porter's*) portaria; (*FREEMASONRY*) loja // *vi* (*person*): **to** ~ (**with**) alojar-se (na casa de) // *vt* (*complaint*) apresentar; **lodger** *n* inquilino/a *m/f*, hóspede *m/f*.

lodgings ['lɔdʒɪŋz] *npl* alojamento *sg*; (*house*) casa *sg* de hóspedes.

loft [lɔft] *n* sótão *m*.

lofty ['lɔftɪ] *adj* alto; (*fig*) sublime; (*haughty*) altivo, arrogante.

log [lɔg] *n* (*of wood*) tronco, lenho; (*book*) = **logbook.**

logarithm ['lɔgərɪðəm] *n* logaritmo.

logbook ['lɔgbuk] *n* (*NAUT*) diário de bordo; (*AVIAT*) diário de vôo; (*of car*) documentação *f* (do carro).

loggerheads ['lɔgəhedz] *npl:* **at** ~ (**with**) em desacordo (com).

logic ['lɔdʒɪk] *n* lógica; ~**al** *adj* lógico.

logistics [lɔ'dʒɪstɪks] *n* logística.

loin [lɔɪn] *n* (*CULIN*) (carne de) lombo; ~**s** *npl* lombo *sg*, dorso *sg*; ~ **cloth** *n* tanga.

loiter ['lɔɪtə*] *vi* perder tempo; (*pej*) vadiar, vagabundar.

loll [lɔl] *vi* (*also:* ~ **about**) refestelar-se, reclinar-se.

lollipop ['lɔlɪpɔp] *n* pirulito (*Br*), chupa-chupa *m* (*Pt*); (*iced*) picolé *m*; ~ **man/lady** *n* pessoa que ajuda as crianças a atravessarem a rua.

London ['lʌndən] *n* Londres; ~**er** *n* londrino/a.

lone [ləun] *adj* solitário; (*deserted*) ermo.

loneliness ['ləunlɪnɪs] *n* solidão *f*, isolamento; **lonely** [-lɪ] *adj* solitário, isolado.

loner ['ləunə*] *n* solitário.

long [lɔŋ] *adj* longo, comprido // *adv* muito tempo, longamente // *vi:* **to** ~ **for sth** ansiar *or* suspirar por algo; **in the** ~ **run** no final de contas; **so** *or* **as** ~ **as** contanto que; **don't be** ~**!** não demore!, volte logo!; **how** ~ **is the street?** qual é a extensão da rua?; **how** ~ **is the lesson?** quanto dura a lição?; **6 metres** ~ de 6 metros de extensão, que mede 6 metros; **6 months** ~ de 6 meses de duração, que dura 6 meses; **all night** ~ a noite inteira; ~ **before** muito antes; **before** ~ (+ *future*) dentro de pouco; (+ *past*) pouco tempo depois; **at** ~ **last** por fim, no final; ~**-distance** *adj* (*race*) de longa distância; (*call*) interurbano; ~**-haired** *adj* cabeludo; ~**hand** *n* escrita usual; ~**ing** *n* desejo, anseio; (*nostalgia*) saudade *f* // *adj* saudoso.

longitude [ˈlɔŋgɪtjuːd] *n* longitude *f*.

long: ~ **jump** *n* salto em distância; ~**-lost** *adj* perdido há muito (tempo); ~**-playing record** *n* elepê (*Pt*: LP) *m*; ~**-range** *adj* de longo alcance; ~**-sighted** *adj* (*fig*) previdente; ~**-standing** *adj* de muito tempo; ~**-suffering** *adj* paciente, resignado; ~**-term** *adj* a longo prazo; ~ **wave** *adj* de onda longa; ~**-winded** *adj* prolixo, cansativo.

loo [luː] *n* (*col*) banheiro (*Br*), casa de banho (*Pt*).

loofah [ˈluːfə] *n* tipo de esponja.

look [luk] *vi* olhar; (*seem*) parecer; (*building etc*): to ~ **south/on** to the sea dar para o sul/o mar // *n* olhar *m*; (*glance*) olhada, vista de olhos; (*appearance*) aparência, aspecto; ~s *npl* físico, aparência; to ~ **like sb** parecer-se com alguém; to ~ **after** *vt fus* cuidar de; to ~ **at** *vt fus* olhar (para); (*consider*) considerar; to ~ **back** *vi* recordar, rever o passado; to ~ **down on** *vt fus* (*fig*) desdenhar, desprezar; to ~ **for** *vt fus* procurar; to ~ **forward to** *vt fus* aguardar com prazer, ansiar por; to ~ **into** *vt* investigar; to ~ **on** *vi* assistir; to ~ **out** *vi* (*beware*): to ~ **out (for)** tomar cuidado (com); to ~ **out for** *vt fus* procurar; (*await*) esperar; to ~ **round** *vi* virar a cabeça; to ~ **to** *vt fus* cuidar de; (*rely on*) contar com; to ~ **up** *vi* levantar os olhos; (*improve*) melhorar // *vt* (*word*) procurar; (*friend*) visitar; to ~ **up to** *vt fus* admirar, respeitar; ~**-out** *n* (*tower etc*) posto de observação, guarita; (*person*) vigia *m*; to **be on the** ~**-out for sth** estar na expectativa de algo.

loom [luːm] *n* tear *m* // *vi* assomar-se; (*threaten*) ameaçar.

loony [ˈluːnɪ] *n* (*col*) lunático/a; ~ **bin** *n* (*col*) hospício, manicômio.

loop [luːp] *n* laço; (*bend*) volta, curva; (*contraceptive*) D.I.U. *m*; ~**hole** *n* escapatória.

loose [luːs] *adj* (*gen*) solto; (*not tight*) frouxo; (*wobbly etc*) bambo; (*clothes*) folgado; (*morals, discipline*) relaxado; to **be at a** ~ **end** não ter o que fazer; ~**ly** *adv* livremente, folgadamente; **loosen** *vt* (*free*) soltar; (*untie*) desatar; (*slacken*) afrouxar.

loot [luːt] *n* saque *m*, despojo// *vt* saquear, pilhar; ~**ing** *n* saque *m*, pilhagem *f*.

lop [lɔp]: to ~ **off** *vt* cortar; (*branches*) podar.

lop-sided [ˈlɔpˈsaɪdɪd] *adj* desequilibrado, torto.

lord [lɔːd] *n* senhor *m*; **L**~ **Smith** Lord Smith; **the L**~ o Senhor; **the (House of) L**~**s** a Câmara dos Lordes; ~**ly** *adj* senhorial; (*arrogant*) arrogante; ~**ship** *n*: **your L**~**ship** Vossa senhoria.

lore [lɔː*] *n* sabedoria popular, tradições *fpl*.

lorry [ˈlɔrɪ] *n* caminhão *m* (*Br*), camião *m* (*Pt*); ~ **driver** *n* caminhoneiro (*Br*), camionista *m/f* (*Pt*).

lose [luːz], *pt*, *pp* **lost** *vt* perder // *vi* perder, ser vencido; to ~ (*time*) (*clock*) atrasar-se; **loser** *n* perdedor/a *m/f*.

loss [lɔs] *n* perda; to **be at a** ~ estar perplexo; to **be a dead** ~ ser totalmente inútil.

lost [lɔst] *pt*, *pp of* **lose** // *adj* perdido; ~ **property** *n* objetos (*Pt*: -ct-) perdidos e achados.

lot [lɔt] *n* (*at auctions*) lote *m*; (*destiny*) destino, sorte *f*; **the** ~ o todo, todos/as; **a** ~ muito, bastante; **a** ~ **of**, ~**s of** muito(s) (*pl*); to **draw** ~**s** tirar à sorte; **I read a** ~ leio bastante.

lotion [ˈləuʃən] *n* loção *f*.

lottery [ˈlɔtərɪ] *n* loteria.

loud [laud] *adj* (*voice*) alto; (*shout*) forte; (*noisy*) barulhento; (*gaudy*) berrante // *adv* (*speak etc*) em voz alta; ~**hailer** *n* megafone *m*; ~**ly** *adv* (*noisily*) ruidosamente; (*aloud*) em voz alta; ~**speaker** *n* alto-falante *m*.

lounge [laundʒ] *n* sala de estar *f*, salão *m* // *vi* recostar-se, espreguiçar-se; ~ **suit** *n* terno (*Br*), fato (*Pt*).

louse [laus], *pl* **lice** *n* piolho.

lousy [ˈlauzɪ] *adj* (*fig*) desprezível, vil.

lout [laut] *n* rústico, grosseiro.

lovable [ˈlʌvəbl] *adj* adorável, simpático.

love [lʌv] *n* amor *m* // *vt* amar, adorar; to ~ **to do** gostar muito de fazer; to **be in** ~ **with** estar apaixonado por; to **make** ~ fazer amor; to ~ **of** pelo amor de; '**15** ~' (*TENNIS*) 15 a zero; **I** ~ **coffee** adoro o café; '**with** ~' com carinho; ~ **affair** *n* aventura (amorosa), caso (de amor); ~ **letter** *n* carta de amor; ~ **life** *n* vida sentimental.

lovely [ˈlʌvlɪ] *adj* (*delightful*) encantador(a), delicioso; (*beautiful*) lindo, belo.

lover [ˈlʌvə*] *n* amante *m/f*; (*amateur*): **a** ~ **of** um apreciador de *or* um amante de.

lovesong [ˈlʌvsɔŋ] *n* canção *f* de amor.

loving [ˈlʌvɪŋ] *adj* carinhoso, afetuoso (*Pt*: -ct-).

low [ləu] *adj*, *adv* baixo // *n* (*METEOROLOGY*) área de baixa pressão // *vi* (*cow*) mugir; to **feel** ~ sentir-se deprimido; to **turn (down)** ~ *vt* baixar, diminuir; ~**-cut** *adj* (*dress*) decotado.

lower [ˈləuə*] *vt* abaixar; (*reduce*) reduzir, diminuir // *vr*: to ~ **o.s. to** (*fig*) rebaixar-se a.

low: ~**-grade** *adj* de baixa qualidade; ~**ly** *adj* humilde; ~**-lying** *adj* de baixo nível.

loyal [ˈlɔɪəl] *adj* leal; ~**ty** *n* lealdade *f*.

lozenge [ˈlɔzɪndʒ] *n* (*MED*) pastilha.

L.P. *n abbr of* **long-playing record**.

L-plates [ˈɛlpleɪts] *npl* placa de aprendiz de motorista.

Ltd abbr of limited company.
lubricant ['lu:brɪkənt] n lubrificante m; **lubricate** [-keɪt] vt lubrificar.
lucid ['lu:sɪd] adj lúcido; ~ity [-'sɪdɪtɪ] n lucidez f.
luck [lʌk] n sorte f; **bad** ~ azar m; **good** ~! boa sorte!; ~ily adv por sorte, felizmente; ~y adj feliz, felizardo.
lucrative ['lu:krətɪv] adj lucrativo.
ludicrous ['lu:dɪkrəs] adj ridículo.
ludo ['lu:dəu] n ludo m.
lug [lʌg] vt (drag) arrastar; (pull) puxar.
luggage ['lʌgɪdʒ] n bagagem f; ~ **rack** n (in train) rede f para bagagem; (on car) porta-bagagem m, bagageiro.
lukewarm ['lu:kwɔ:m] adj morno, tépido; (fig) indiferente.
lull [lʌl] n trégua, calmaria // vt (child) embalar, acalentar; (person, fear) acalmar.
lullaby ['lʌləbaɪ] n canção f de ninar.
lumbago [lʌm'beɪgəu] n lumbago.
lumber ['lʌmbə*] n (junk) trastes velhos mpl; (wood) madeira serrada, tábua; ~**jack** n madeireiro, lenhador m.
luminous ['lu:mɪnəs] adj luminoso.
lump [lʌmp] n torrão m; (fragment) pedaço; (in sauce) caroço; (in throat) nó m; (swelling) caroço // vt (also: ~ **together**) amontoar; **a** ~ **sum** soma total, montante m; ~**y** adj (sauce) encaroçado.
lunacy ['lu:nəsɪ] n loucura.
lunar ['lu:nə*] adj lunar.
lunatic ['lu:nətɪk] adj, n louco/a; ~ **asylum** n manicômio, hospício.
lunch [lʌntʃ] n almoço, comida // vi almoçar; ~ **time** n hora do almoço or da comida.
luncheon ['lʌntʃən] n almoço formal; ~ **meat** n bolo de carne.
lung [lʌŋ] n pulmão m; ~ **cancer** n câncer m de pulmão.
lunge [lʌndʒ] vi (also: ~ **forward**) dar estocada or bote; **to** ~ **at** arremeter-se contra.
lurch [lɜ:tʃ] vi guinar // n sacudida, solavanco; **to leave sb in the** ~ deixar alguém em dificuldades.
lure [luə*] n (bait) isca; (decoy) chamariz m, engodo // vt atrair, seduzir.
lurid ['luərɪd] adj (light) avermelhado; (dress) berrante; (account) sensacional; (detail) horrível.
lurk [lɜ:k] vi (hide) esconder-se; (wait) estar à espreita.
luscious ['lʌʃəs] adj delicioso.
lush [lʌʃ] adj exuberante.
lust [lʌst] n luxúria; (greed) cobiça; **to** ~ **after** vt fus cobiçar; ~**ful** adj lascivo, sensual.
lustre, luster (US) ['lʌstə*] n lustre m, brilho.
lusty ['lʌstɪ] adj robusto, forte.
lute [lu:t] n alaúde m.
Luxembourg ['lʌksəmbɔ:g] n Luxemburgo.

luxuriant [lʌg'zjuərɪənt] adj luxuriante, exuberante.
luxurious [lʌg'zjuərɪəs] adj luxuoso; **luxury** ['lʌkʃərɪ] n luxo // cmp de luxo.
lying ['laɪɪŋ] n mentiras fpl // adj mentiroso, falso.
lynch [lɪntʃ] vt linchar; ~**ing** n linchamento.
lynx [lɪŋks] n lince m.
lyre ['laɪə*] n lira.
lyric ['lɪrɪk] adj lírico; ~**s** npl (of song) letra sg; ~**al** adj lírico.

M

m. abbr of **metre; mile; million.**
M.A. abbr of **Master of Arts** licenciado/a em letras.
mac [mæk] n capa impermeável.
macaroni [mækə'rəunɪ] n macarrão m.
mace [meɪs] n (BOT) macis m.
machine [mə'ʃi:n] n máquina // vt (dress etc) trabalhar or coser à máquina; ~**gun** n metralhadora; ~**ry** n maquinaria; (fig) mecanismo; **machinist** n operário (de máquina); (RAIL) maquinista m.
mackerel ['mækrl] n, pl inv cavala.
mackintosh ['mækɪntɔʃ] n capa impermeável.
mad [mæd] adj (gen) louco; (crazed) demente; (angry) furioso.
madam ['mædəm] n senhora, madame f.
madden ['mædn] vt enlouquecer; (irritate) irritar.
made [meɪd] pt, pp of **make**; ~-**to-measure** adj feito sob medida.
madly ['mædlɪ] adv loucamente.
madman ['mædmən] n louco.
madness ['mædnɪs] n loucura, demência.
magazine [mægə'zi:n] n revista; (MIL: store) depósito; (of firearm) câmara.
maggot ['mægət] n larva de inseto (Pt: -ct-).
magic ['mædʒɪk] n magia // adj mágico; ~**al** adj mágico; ~**ian** [mə'dʒɪʃən] n mago, mágico; (conjurer) prestidigitador m.
magistrate ['mædʒɪstreɪt] n magistrado, juiz/juíza m/f.
magnanimous [mæg'nænɪməs] adj magnânimo.
magnate ['mægneɪt] n magnata m.
magnet ['mægnɪt] n ímã (Pt: íman) m; ~**ic** [-'nɛtɪk] adj magnético; ~**ism** n magnetismo.
magnification [mægnɪfɪ'keɪʃən] n aumento.
magnificence [mæg'nɪfɪsns] n magnificência; **magnificent** [-nt] adj magnífico.
magnify ['mægnɪfaɪ] vt aumentar; (fig) exagerar; ~**ing glass** n lupa, lente f de aumento.
magnitude ['mægnɪtju:d] n magnitude f.
magnolia [mæg'nəulɪə] n magnólia.
magpie ['mægpaɪ] n pega.

mahogany ['mə'hɔgənɪ] n mogno // cmp de mogno.

maid [meɪd] n empregada; old ~ (pej) solteirona.

maiden ['meɪdn] n moça, donzela // adj (aunt etc) solteirona; (speech, voyage) inaugural; ~ **name** n nome m de solteira.

mail [meɪl] n correio; (letters) cartas fpl // vt (post) pôr no correio; (send) mandar pelo correio; ~**box** n (US) caixa do correio; ~-**order** n pedido por reembolso postal; (business) venda por correspondência.

maim [meɪm] vt mutilar, aleijar.

main [meɪn] adj principal // n (pipe) cano or esgoto principal; the ~**s** (ELEC) a rede elétrica (Pt: -ct-); **in the** ~ na maior parte; ~**land** n continente m; ~**stay** n (fig) suporte m, esteio; ~**stream** n corrente f principal.

maintain [meɪn'teɪn] vt manter; (keep up) conservar (em bom estado); (affirm) afirmar; **maintenance** ['meɪntənəns] n manutenção f.

maize [meɪz] n milho.

majestic [mə'dʒestɪk] adj majestoso; **majesty** ['mædʒɪstɪ] n majestade f.

major ['meɪdʒə*] n (MIL) major m // adj principal; (MUS) maior.

Majorca [mə'jɔːkə] n Maiorca.

majority [mə'dʒɔrɪtɪ] n maioria.

make [meɪk], pt, pp **made** n marca // vt fazer; (manufacture) fabricar, produzir; (cause to be): **to** ~ **sb sad** entristecer alguém or fazer alguém ficar triste; (force): **to** ~ **sb do sth** fazer com que alguém faça algo; (equal): **2 and 2** ~ **4** dois e dois são quatro; **to** ~ **do with** contentar-se com; **to** ~ **for** vt fus (place) dirigir-se a; **to** ~ **out** vt (decipher) descifrar; (understand) compreender; (see) divisar, avistar; **to** ~ **up** vt (invent) inventar; (parcel) embrulhar // vi reconciliar-se; (with cosmetics) maquilar-se; **to** ~ **up for** vt fus compensar; ~-**believe** adj fingido, simulado; **maker** n fabricante m/f; ~-**shift** adj provisório; ~-**up** n maquilagem f.

making ['meɪkɪŋ] n (fig): **in the** ~ em vias de formação.

malaise [mæ'leɪz] n mal-estar m, indisposição f.

malaria [mə'lɛərɪə] n malária.

Malay ['mə'leɪ] adj, n malaio/a.

Malaysia [mə'leɪzɪə] n Malásia.

male [meɪl] n (BIOL, ELEC) macho // adj (sex, attitude) masculino; (child etc) menino.

malevolent [mə'lɛvələnt] adj malévolo.

malfunction [mæl'fʌŋkʃən] n funcionamento defeituoso.

malice ['mælɪs] n (ill will) malícia; (rancour) rancor m; **malicious** [mə'lɪʃəs] adj malicioso, mal-intencionado.

malign [mə'laɪn] vt caluniar, difamar // adj maligno.

malignant [mə'lɪgnənt] adj (MED) maligno.

malingerer [mə'lɪŋgərə*] n doente m fingido.

malleable ['mælɪəbl] adj maleável.

mallet ['mælɪt] n maço, marreta.

malnutrition [mælnjuː'trɪʃən] n desnutrição f.

malpractice [mæl'præktɪs] n falta profissional.

malt [mɔːlt] n malte m; ~ **whisky** uísque m de malte.

Malta ['mɔːltə] n Malta; **Maltese** [-'tiːz] adj, n, pl inv maltês/esa m/f.

maltreat [mæl'triːt] vt maltratar.

mammal ['mæml] n mamífero.

mammoth ['mæməθ] n mamute m // adj gigantesco, imenso.

man [mæn], pl **men** n homem m; (CHESS) peça // vt (NAUT) tripular; (MIL) guarnecer; **an old** ~ um velho; ~ **and wife** marido e mulher; **a young** ~ um jovem.

manacle ['mænəkl] n algema; ~**s** npl grilhões mpl.

manage ['mænɪdʒ] vi arranjar-se // vt (be in charge of) dirigir, administrar; (person etc) influenciar, saber lidar com; ~**able** adj manejável; ~**ment** n direção (Pt: -cç-) f, gerência; **manager**/**ess** n gerente m/f; (SPORT) treinador(a) m/f; **managerial** [-ə'dʒɪərɪəl] adj administrativo; **managing director** n diretor m geral (Pt: -ct-), diretor-gerente (Pt: -ct-) m.

mandarin ['mændərɪn] n (also: ~ **orange**) tangerina; (person) mandarim m.

mandate ['mændeɪt] n mandato.

mandatory ['mændətərɪ] adj obrigatório.

mandolin(e) ['mændəlɪn] n bandolim m.

mane [meɪn] n (of horse) crina; (of lion) juba.

manfully ['mænfəlɪ] adv virilmente.

mangle ['mæŋgl] vt mutilar, estropiar // n calandra.

mango ['mæŋgəu], pl ~**es** n manga.

mangy ['meɪndʒɪ] adj sarnento, esfarrapado.

manhandle ['mænhændl] vt maltratar.

manhole ['mænhəul] n poço de inspeção (Pt: -cç-).

manhood ['mænhud] n idade f adulta, virilidade f.

man-hour ['mæn'auə*] n hora-homem f.

manhunt ['mænhʌnt] n caça ao homem.

mania ['meɪnɪə] n mania; **maniac** ['meɪnɪæk] n maníaco/a; (fig) louco/a.

manicure ['mænɪkjuə*] n manicure (Pt: -cura) f // vt (person) fazer as unhas a; ~ **set** n estojo de manicure (Pt: -cura).

manifest ['mænɪfest] vt manifestar, mostrar // adj manifesto, evidente; ~**ation** [-'teɪʃən] n manifestação f.

manifesto [mænɪ'festəu] n manifesto.

manipulate [mə'nɪpjuleɪt] vt manipular, manejar.

mankind [mæn'kaɪnd] *n* humanidade *f*, raça humana.

manly ['mænlɪ] *adj* másculo, viril.

man-made ['mæn'meɪd] *adj* sintético, artificial.

manner ['mænə*] *n* modo, maneira; (*behaviour*) conduta, comportamento; (*type*) espécie *f*, gênero; ~s *npl* modos *mpl*, educação *f*; **bad** ~s falta de educação; ~ism *n* maneirismo, hábito.

manoeuvre, maneuver (*US*) [mə'nu:və*] *vt/i* manobrar // *n* manobra.

manor ['mænə*] *n* (*also:* ~ **house**) casa senhorial, solar *m.*

manpower ['mænpauə*] *n* potencial *m* humano, mão-de-obra *f.*

mansion ['mænʃən] *n* mansão *f*, palacete *m.*

manslaughter ['mænslɔ:tə*] *n* homicídio involuntário.

mantelpiece ['mæntlpi:s] *n* consolo da lareira.

mantle ['mæntl] *n* manto; (*fig*) camada.

manual ['mænjuəl] *adj* manual // *n* manual *m*; (*MUS*) teclado.

manufacture [mænju'fæktʃə*] *vt* manufaturar (*Pt:* -ct-), fabricar // *n* fabricação *f*; **manufacturer** *n* fabricante *m/f.*

manure [mə'njuə*] *n* estrume *m*, adubo.

manuscript ['mænjuskrɪpt] *n* manuscrito.

many ['menɪ] *det* muitos/as // *pron* muitos/as; **a great** ~ muitíssimos; ~ **a time** muitas vezes.

map [mæp] *n* mapa *m* // *vt* fazer o mapa de; **to** ~ **out** *vt* planejar cuidadosamente.

maple ['meɪpl] *n* bordo.

mar [mɑ:*] *vt* estragar.

marathon ['mærəθən] *n* maratona.

marauder [mə'rɔ:də*] *n* saqueador *m*; (*intruder*) intruso.

marble ['mɑ:bl] *n* mármore *m*; (*toy*) bola de gude.

March [mɑ:tʃ] *n* março (*Pt:* M-).

march [mɑ:tʃ] *vi* (*MIL*) marchar // *n* marcha; (*fig*) curso; (*demonstration*) manifestação *f*, (*procession*) passeata; ~-**past** *n* desfile *m.*

mare [mɛə*] *n* égua.

margarine [mɑ:dʒə'ri:n] *n* margarina.

margin ['mɑ:dʒɪn] *n* margem *f*; ~**al** *adj* marginal.

marigold ['mærɪgəuld] *n* malmequer *m.*

marijuana [mærɪ'wɑ:nə] *n* maconha.

marina [mə'ri:nə] *n* marina.

marine [mə'ri:n] *adj* marinho, marítimo // *n* fuzileiro naval.

marital ['mærɪtl] *adj* matrimonial, marital; ~ **status** estado civil.

maritime ['mærɪtaɪm] *adj* marítimo.

marjoram ['mɑ:dʒərəm] *n* manjerona.

mark [mɑ:k] *n* marca, sinal *m*; (*imprint*) impressão *f*; (*stain*) mancha; (*SCOL*) nota; (*currency*) marco; **to hit the** ~ acertar no alvo // *vt* marcar; (*stain*) manchar; (*SCOL*) dar nota em; **to** ~ **time** marcar

passo; **to** ~ **out** *vt* traçar; ~**ed** *adj* marcado; ~**er** *n* (*sign*) marcador *m*, marca; (*bookmark*) marcador.

market ['mɑ:kɪt] *n* mercado // *vt* (*COMM*) vender; **black** ~ mercado negro *or* paralelo; **Common M**~ Mercado Comum; ~ **day** *n* dia *m* de mercado; ~ **garden** *n* (*Brit*) horta; ~**ing** *n* compra e venda, marketing *m*; ~-**place** *n* mercado; ~ **research** *n* pesquisa de mercado.

marksman ['mɑ:ksmən] *n* bom atirador *m*; ~**ship** *n* boa pontaria.

marmalade ['mɑ:məleɪd] *n* geléia de laranja.

maroon [mə'ru:n] *vt*: **to be** ~**ed** ficar abandonado (numa ilha) // *adj* de cor castanho-avermelhado.

marquee [mɑ:'ki:] *n* toldo, tenda.

marquess, marquis ['mɑ:kwɪs] *n* marquês *m.*

marriage ['mærɪdʒ] *n* (*state*) matrimônio; (*wedding*) núpcias *fpl*, boda; (*act*) casamento; ~ **bureau** *n* agência matrimonial; ~ **certificate** *n* certidão *f* de casamento.

married ['mærɪd] *adj* casado; (*life, love*) conjugal; **to get** ~ casar-se.

marrow ['mærəu] *n* medula; (*vegetable*) abobrinha.

marry ['mærɪ] *vt* casar-se com; (*subj: father, priest etc*) casar, unir // *vi* (*also:* **get married**) casar-se.

marsh [mɑ:ʃ] *n* pântano; (*salt* ~) marisma.

marshal ['mɑ:ʃl] *n* (*MIL*) marechal *m*; (*at sports meeting etc*) oficial *m* // *vt* (*facts*) dispor, ordenar; (*soldiers*) formar.

marshmallow [mɑ:ʃ'mæləu] *n* espécie de doce de malvavisco.

marshy ['mɑ:ʃɪ] *adj* pantanoso.

martial ['mɑ:ʃl] *adj* marcial; ~ **law** *n* lei *f* marcial.

martyr ['mɑ:tə*] *n* mártir *m/f* // *vt* martirizar; ~**dom** *n* martírio.

marvel ['mɑ:vl] *n* maravilha, prodígio // *vi*: **to** ~ **(at)** maravilhar-se (de/com); ~**lous**, ~**ous** (*US*) *adj* maravilhoso, incrível.

Marxism ['mɑ:ksɪzəm] *n* marxismo; **Marxist** [-sɪst] *adj*, *n* marxista *m/f.*

marzipan ['mɑ:zɪpæn] *n* maçapão *m.*

mascara [mæs'kɑ:rə] *n* rímel *m.*

mascot ['mæskət] *n* mascote *m.*

masculine ['mæskjulɪn] *adj* masculino; **masculinity** [-'lɪnɪtɪ] *n* masculinidade *f.*

mash [mæʃ] *n* (*mix*) mistura; (*pulp*) pasta, papa; ~**ed potatoes** purê *m* de batatas.

mask [mɑ:sk] *n* máscara // *vt* mascarar.

masochist ['mæsəukɪst] *n* masoquista *m/f.*

mason ['meɪsn] *n* (*also:* **stone**~) pedreiro; (*also:* **free**~) maçom *m*; ~**ic** [mə'sɔnɪk] *adj* maçônico; ~**ry** *n* maçonaria; (*building*) alvenaria.

masquerade [mæskə'reɪd] *n* baile *m* de máscaras; (*fig*) farsa, embuste *m* // *vi*:

to ~ **as** disfarçar-se de, fazer-se passar por.

mass [mæs] *n* (*people*) multidão *f*; (*PHYSICS*) massa; (*REL*) missa; (*great quantity*) montão *m* // *vi* reunir-se; (*MIL*) concentrar-se; **the ~es** as massas.

massacre ['mæsəkə*] *n* massacre *m*, carnificina *f* // *vt* massacrar.

massage ['mæsɑːʒ] *n* massagem *f* // *vt* fazer massagem em, massagear.

masseur [mæ'sə:*] *n* massagista *m*; **masseuse** [-'sə:z] *n* massagista *f*.

massive ['mæsɪv] *adj* (*solid*) sólido; (*head etc*) enorme; (*support, intervention*) massivo.

mass media ['mæs'miːdɪə] *npl* meios *mpl* de comunicação de massa.

mass-production ['mæsprə'dʌkʃən] *n* produção *f* em massa *or* em série.

mast [mɑːst] *n* (*NAUT*) mastro; (*RADIO etc*) antena.

master ['mɑːstə*] *n* mestre *m*; (*landowner*) senhor *m*, dono; (*in secondary school*) professor *m*; (*title for boys*): **M~ X** o menino X // *vt* dominar; (*learn*) conhecer a fundo; ~ **key** *n* chave *f* mestra; ~**ly** *adj* magistral; ~**mind** *n* (*fig*) cabeça // *vt* dirigir, planejar; **M~ of Arts** *n* Licenciado/a em Letras; ~**piece** *n* obra-prima; ~ **plan** *n* plano piloto; ~ **stroke** *n* golpe *m* de mestre; ~**y** *n* domínio.

masturbate ['mæstəbeɪt] *vi* masturbar-se; **masturbation** [-'beɪʃən] *n* masturbação *f*.

mat [mæt] *n* esteira; (*also*: **door~**) capacho // *adj* = **matt**.

match [mætʃ] *n* fósforo; (*game*) jogo, partida; (*fig*) igual *m/f* // *vt* casar, emparelhar; (*go well with*) combinar com; (*equal*) igualar // *vi* casar-se, combinar; **to be a good ~** formar um bom casal; (*colours*) combinar; ~**box** *n* caixa de fósforos; ~**ing** *adj* que combina (com); ~**less** *adj* sem igual, incomparável.

mate [meɪt] *n* companheiro/a; (*assistant*) ajudante *m/f*; (*CHESS*) mate *m*; (*in merchant navy*) imediato *m* // *vi* acasalar-se // *vt* acasalar.

material [mə'tɪərɪəl] *n* (*substance*) matéria; (*equipment*) material *m*; (*cloth*) pano, tecido; (*data*) dados *mpl* // *adj* material; (*important*) importante; ~**s** *npl* materiais *mpl*; ~**istic** [-ə'lɪstɪk] *adj* materialista; ~**ize** *vi* materializar-se, concretizar-se.

maternal [mə'tə:nl] *adj* maternal.

maternity [mə'tə:nɪtɪ] *n* maternidade *f*; ~ **dress** *n* vestido de gestante; ~ **hospital** *n* maternidade *f*.

mathematical [mæθə'mætɪkl] *adj* matemático; **mathematician** [-mə'tɪʃən] *n* matemático/a; **mathematics** [-tɪks], **maths** [mæθs] *n* matemática *sg*.

matinée ['mætɪneɪ] *n* matinê *f*.

mating ['meɪtɪŋ] *n* acasalamento; ~ **call**

n chamado do macho; ~ **season** *n* época de cio.

matriarchal [meɪtrɪ'ɑːkl] *adj* matriarcal.

matrices ['meɪtrɪsiːz] *pl of* **matrix**.

matriculation [mətrɪkju'leɪʃən] *n* matrícula.

matrimonial [mætrɪ'məunɪəl] *adj* matrimonial.

matrimony ['mætrɪmənɪ] *n* matrimônio, casamento.

matrix ['meɪtrɪks], *pl* **matrices** *n* matriz *f*.

matron ['meɪtrən] *n* (*in hospital*) enfermeira-chefe; (*in school*) inspetora (*Pt*: -ct-); ~**ly** *adj* matronal; (*fig*: *figure*) corpulento.

matt [mæt] *adj* fosco, sem brilho.

matted ['mætɪd] *adj* emaranhado.

matter ['mætə*] *n* questão *f*, assunto; (*PHYSICS*) matéria, substância; (*content*) conteúdo; (*MED*: *pus*) pus *m* // *vi* importar; **it doesn't ~** não importa; **what's the ~?** o que (é que) há?, qual o problema?; **no ~ what** aconteça o que acontecer; **as a ~ of course** como se é de esperar; (*routine*) por rotina; **as a ~ of fact** na realidade, de fato (*Pt*: -ct-); ~**-of-fact** *adj* prosaico, prático.

mattress ['mætrɪs] *n* colchão *m*.

mature [mə'tjuə*] *adj* maduro // *vi* amadurecer; **maturity** *n* maturidade *f*.

maudlin ['mɔːdlɪn] *adj* piegas *inv*, chorão/rona.

maul [mɔːl] *vt* machucar, maltratar.

mausoleum [mɔːsə'lɪəm] *n* mausoléu *m*.

mauve [məuv] *adj* cor de malva.

maxim ['mæksɪm] *n* máxima.

maxima ['mæksɪmə] *pl of* **maximum**.

maximum ['mæksɪməm] *adj* máximo // *n*, *pl* **maxima** máximo.

May [meɪ] *n* maio (*Pt*: M-).

may [meɪ] *vi* (*conditional*: **might**) (*indicating possibility*): **he ~ come** pode ser que ele venha; (*be allowed to*): ~ **I smoke?** posso fumar?; (*wishes*): ~ **God bless you!** que Deus lhe abençoe.

maybe ['meɪbɪ] *adv* talvez.

mayday ['meɪdeɪ] *n* S.O.S. *m* (*chamada de socorro internacional*).

mayhem ['meɪhɛm] *n* caos *m*.

mayonnaise [meɪə'neɪz] *n* maionese *f*.

mayor [mɛə*] *n* prefeito (*Br*), presidente *m* do município (*Pt*); ~**ess** *n* prefeita.

maypole ['meɪpəul] *n* mastro usado no dia primeiro de maio.

maze [meɪz] *n* labirinto.

M.D. *abbr of* **Doctor of Medicine**.

me [miː] *pron* me; (*stressed, after prep*) mim; **with ~** comigo; **it's ~** sou eu.

meadow ['mɛdəu] *n* prado, campina.

meagre, meager (*US*) ['miːgə*] *adj* escasso, pobre.

meal [miːl] *n* refeição *f*; (*flour*) farinha; ~**time** *n* hora da refeição.

mean [miːn] *adj* (*with money*) sovina, avarento, pão-duro (*Br*); (*unkind*) mesquinho; (*shabby*) surrado, miserável; (*of poor quality*) inferior; (*average*) médio

// vt, pt, pp **meant** (signify) significar, querer dizer; (intend): **to ~ to do sth** pretender or tencionar fazer algo // n meio, meio termo; **~s** npl meio sg, método sg; (resource) recursos mpl, meios mpl; **by ~s of** por meio de, mediante; **by all ~s!** claro que sim!, evidentemente!; **do you ~ it?** você está falando sério?; **what do you ~?** o que você quer dizer?

meander [mɪ'ændə*] vi (river) serpentear; (person) vadiar, perambular.

meaning ['mi:nɪŋ] n sentido, significado; **~ful** adj significativo; **~less** adj sem sentido.

meanness ['mi:nnɪs] n (with money) avareza, sovinice f; (shabbiness) vileza, baixeza; (unkindness) maldade f, mesquinharia.

meant [mɛnt] pt, pp of **mean**.

meantime ['mi:ntaɪm], **meanwhile** ['mi:nwaɪl] adv (also: **in the ~**) entretanto, enquanto isso.

measles ['mi:zlz] n sarampo sg; **German ~** rubéola.

measly ['mi:zlɪ] adj (col) miserável.

measure ['mɛʒə*] vt medir; (for clothes etc) tirar as medidas de; (consider) avaliar, ponderar // vi medir // n medida; (ruler) régua; **~d** adj medido, calculado; (tone) ponderado; **~ments** npl medidas fpl.

meat [mi:t] n carne f; **cold ~** frios mpl; **~ball** n almôndega; **~ pie** n bolo de carne; **~y** adj carnudo; (fig) substancial.

mechanic [mɪ'kænɪk] n mecânico; **~s** n mecânica sg // npl mecanismo sg; **~al** adj mecânico.

mechanism ['mɛkənɪzəm] n mecanismo.

mechanization [mɛkənaɪ'zeɪʃən] n mecanização f.

medal ['mɛdl] n medalha, condecoração f; **~lion** [mɪ'dælɪən] n medalhão m; **~list, ~ist** (US) n (SPORT) ganhador(a) m/f.

meddle ['mɛdl] vi: **to ~ in** meter-se em, intrometer-se em; **to ~ with sth** mexer em algo; **~some** adj intrometido.

media ['mi:dɪə] npl meios mpl de comunicação.

mediaeval [mɛdɪ'i:vl] adj = **medieval**.

mediate ['mi:dɪeɪt] vi mediar; **mediation** [-'eɪʃən] n mediação f; **mediator** n mediador(a) m/f, árbitro.

medical ['mɛdɪkl] adj médico // n exame m médico.

medicated ['mɛdɪkeɪtɪd] adj medicinal, higienizado.

medicinal [mɛ'dɪsɪnl] adj medicinal.

medicine ['mɛdsɪn] n medicina; (drug) remédio, medicamento; **~ chest** n armário de remédios.

medieval [mɛdɪ'i:vl] adj medieval.

mediocre [mi:dɪ'əukə*] adj medíocre; **mediocrity** [-'ɔkrɪtɪ] n mediocridade f.

meditate ['mɛdɪteɪt] vi meditar; **meditation** [-'teɪʃən] n meditação f.

Mediterranean [mɛdɪtə'reɪnɪən] adj mediterrâneo; **the ~ (Sea)** o (mar) Mediterrâneo.

medium ['mi:dɪəm] adj médio, regular // n (pl **media**: means) meio; (pl **mediums**: person) médium m/f.

medley ['mɛdlɪ] n mistura; (MUS) potpourri m.

meek [mi:k] adj manso, dócil.

meet [mi:t], pt, pp **met** vt (gen) encontrar; (accidentally) dar com, dar de cara com; (by arrangement) encontrar-se com, ir ao encontro de; (for the first time) conhecer; (go and fetch) ir buscar; (opponent) enfrentar; (obligations) cumprir // vi encontrar-se; (in session) reunir-se; (join: objects) unir-se; (get to know) conhecer-se; **to ~ with** vt fus reunir-se com; (face: difficulty) encontrar; **~ing** n encontro; (session: of club etc) reunião f; (interview) entrevista; (COMM) junta, sessão f; (POL) assembléia.

megalomaniac [mɛgələʊ'meɪnɪæk] adj, n megalomaníaco/a.

megaphone ['mɛgəfəʊn] n megafone m.

melancholy ['mɛlənkəlɪ] n melancolia // adj melancólico.

mellow ['mɛləʊ] adj (sound) melodioso, suave; (colour) suave; (fruit) maduro // vi (person) amadurecer.

melodious [mɪ'ləʊdɪəs] adj melodioso.

melodrama ['mɛləʊdrɑːmə] n melodrama m.

melody ['mɛlədɪ] n melodia.

melon ['mɛlən] n melão m.

melt [mɛlt] vi (metal) fundir-se; (snow) derreter; (fig) desvanecer-se // vt (also: **~ down**) fundir; **to ~ away** vi desaparecer; **~ing point** n ponto de fusão; **~ing pot** n (fig) cadinho, mistura de raças.

member ['mɛmbə*] n (gen) membro; (of club) sócio; **M~ of Parliament (M.P.)** deputado; **~ship** n (members) número de sócios; **to seek ~ship of** candidatar-se a sócio de; **~ship card** n carteira de sócio.

membrane ['mɛmbreɪn] n membrana.

memento [mə'mɛntəʊ] n lembrança.

memo ['mɛməʊ] n memorando, nota.

memoirs ['mɛmwɑːz] npl memórias fpl.

memorable ['mɛmərəbl] adj memorável.

memorandum [mɛmə'rændəm], pl **-da** [-də] n memorando, lembrete m; (POL) memorando.

memorial [mɪ'mɔːrɪəl] n memorial m, monumento comemorativo // adj comemorativo.

memorize ['mɛməraɪz] vt decorar, aprender de cor.

memory ['mɛmərɪ] n memória; (recollection) lembrança.

men [mɛn] pl of **man**.

menace ['mɛnəs] n ameaça // vt ameaçar; **menacing** adj ameaçador(a).

mend [mɛnd] vt consertar, reparar; (darn) remendar; **to ~ one's ways** corrigir-se // vi restabelecer-se // n (gen) remendo; **to be on the ~** estar melhorando; **~ing** n reparação f; (clothes) roupas fpl por consertar.

menial ['mi:nɪəl] adj doméstico; (pej) baixo // n empregado/a.

meningitis [mɛnɪn'dʒaɪtɪs] n meningite f.

menopause ['mɛnəupɔ:z] n menopausa.

menstruate ['mɛnstrueɪt] vi menstruar; **menstruation** [-'eɪʃən] n menstruação f.

mental ['mɛntl] adj mental; **~ity** [-'tælɪtɪ] n mentalidade f.

mention ['mɛnʃən] n menção f // vt mencionar; (speak of) falar de; **don't ~ it!** não tem de quê!, de nada!

menu ['mɛnju:] n (set ~) menu m; (printed) cardápio (Br), ementa (Pt).

mercenary ['mɜːsɪnərɪ] adj, n mercenário.

merchandise ['mɜːtʃəndaɪz] n mercadorias fpl.

merchant ['mɜːtʃənt] n comerciante m/f; **~ bank** n banco mercantil; **~ navy** n marinha mercante.

merciful ['mɜːsɪful] adj piedoso, misericordioso; (fortunate) afortunado.

merciless ['mɜːsɪlɪs] adj desapiedado, impiedoso.

mercury ['mɜːkjurɪ] n mercúrio.

mercy ['mɜːsɪ] n piedade f; (REL) misericórdia; **at the ~ of** à mercê de.

mere [mɪə*] adj mero, simples; **~ly** adv simplesmente, somente, apenas.

merge [mɜːdʒ] vt (join) unir; (mix) misturar; (fuse) fundir // vi unir-se; (COMM) fundir-se; **merger** n (COMM) fusão f.

meridian [mə'rɪdɪən] n meridiano.

meringue [mə'ræŋ] n suspiro, merengue m.

merit ['mɛrɪt] n mérito // vt merecer.

mermaid ['mɜːmeɪd] n sereia.

merriment ['mɛrɪmənt] n alegria.

merry ['mɛrɪ] adj alegre; **M~ Christmas!** Feliz Natal; **~-go-round** n carrossel.

mesh [mɛʃ] n malha; (TECH) engrenagem f // vi (gears) engrenar.

mesmerize ['mɛzməraɪz] vt hipnotizar.

mess [mɛs] n (gen) confusão f; (of objects) desordem f; (tangle) bagunça; (MIL) rancho; **to ~ about** vi (col) perder tempo; (pass the time) vadiar; **to ~ about with** vt fus (col) (play with) divertir-se com; (handle) manusear; **to ~ up** vt (disarrange) desarrumar; (spoil) estragar; (dirty) sujar.

message ['mɛsɪdʒ] n recado, mensagem f.

messenger ['mɛsɪndʒə*] n mensageiro/a.

messy ['mɛsɪ] adj (dirty) sujo; (untidy) desarrumado.

met [mɛt] pt, pp of **meet**.

metabolism [mɛ'tæbəlɪzəm] n metabolismo.

metal ['mɛtl] n metal m; **~lic** [-'tælɪk] adj metálico; **~lurgy** [-'tælədʒɪ] n metalurgia.

metamorphosis [mɛtə'mɔːfəsɪs] pl **-ses** [-si:z] n metamorfose f.

metaphor ['mɛtəfə*] n metáfora.

metaphysics [mɛtə'fɪzɪks] n metafísica sg.

mete [mi:t]: **to ~ out** vt fus (gen) distribuir; (punishment) infligir.

meteor ['mi:tɪə*] n meteoro.

meteorological [mi:tɪərə'lɒdʒɪkl] adj meteorológico; **meteorology** [-'rɒlədʒɪ] n meteorologia.

meter ['mi:tə*] n (instrument) medidor m; (US) = **metre**.

method ['mɛθəd] n método; **~ical** [mɪ'θɒdɪkl] adj metódico.

Methodist ['mɛθədɪst] adj, n metodista m/f.

meths [mɛθs], **methylated spirits** ['mɛθɪleɪtɪd] n álcool m metílico or desnaturado.

meticulous [mɛ'tɪkjuləs] adj meticuloso.

metre, meter (US) ['mi:tə*] n metro.

metric ['mɛtrɪk] adj métrico.

metronome ['mɛtrənəum] n metrônomo.

metropolis [mɪ'trɒpəlɪs] n metrópole f.

mettle ['mɛtl] n (spirit) caráter (Pt: -ct-) m, têmpera; (tone) índole f.

mew [mju:] vi (cat) miar.

Mexican ['mɛksɪkən] adj, n mexicano/a.

Mexico ['mɛksɪkəu] n México m.

mezzanine ['mɛtsəni:n] n sobreloja, mezanino.

miaow [mi:'au] vi miar.

mice [maɪs] pl of **mouse**.

microbe ['maɪkrəub] n micróbio.

micro... [maɪkrəu] pref micro...; **~film** n microfilme m; **~phone** n microfone m; **~processor** n micro-processador m; **~scope** n microscópio; **~scopic** [-'skɒpɪk] adj microscópico; **~wave** adj de microondas.

mid [mɪd] adj: **in ~ May** em meados de maio; **in ~ afternoon** no meio da tarde; **in ~ air** em pleno ar; **~day** n meio-dia m.

middle ['mɪdl] n meio, centro; (half) metade f; (waist) cintura // adj meio; (quantity, size) médio, mediano; **~-aged** adj de meia idade; **M~ Ages** npl Idade Média sg; **~-class** adj de classe média; **M~ East** n Oriente m Médio; **~man** n intermediário; (COMM) atravessador m; **~ name** n segundo nome.

middling ['mɪdlɪŋ] adj mediano.

midge [mɪdʒ] n mosquito.

midget ['mɪdʒɪt] n anão/anã m/f // adj minúsculo, miniatura.

midnight ['mɪdnaɪt] n meia-noite f.

midriff ['mɪdrɪf] n diafragma m.

midst [mɪdst] n: **in the ~ of** no meio de, entre.

midsummer [mɪd'sʌmə*] *n*: a ~ day um dia em pleno verão.

midway [mɪd'weɪ] *adj*, *adv*: ~ (between) no meio do caminho (entre).

midweek [mɪd'wiːk] *adv* no meio da semana.

midwife ['mɪdwaɪf], *pl* -wives [-waɪvz] *n* parteira; ~ry [-wɪfərɪ] *n* trabalho de parteira.

midwinter [mɪd'wɪntə*] *n*: in ~ em pleno inverno.

might [maɪt] *vb*: he ~ be there pode ser que ele esteja ali; I ~ as well go mais vale que eu vá; you ~ like to try você poderia tentar // *n* poder *m*, força; ~y *adj* poderoso, forte.

migraine ['miːgreɪn] *n* enxaqueca.

migrant ['maɪgrənt] *n* (*bird*) ave *f* de arribação; (*person*) emigrante *m/f*; (*fig*) nômade *m/f* // *adj* migratório; (*worker*) emigrante.

migrate [maɪ'greɪt] *vi* emigrar; **migration** [-'greɪʃən] *n* emigração *f*.

mike [maɪk] *n* *abbr of* microphone microfone *m*.

mild [maɪld] *adj* (*character*) pacífico; (*climate*) temperado; (*slight*) ligeiro; (*taste*) suave; (*illness*) leve, benigno.

mildew ['mɪldjuː] *n* mofo; (*BOT*) míldio.

mildness ['maɪldnɪs] *n* (*softness*) suavidade *f*; (*gentleness*) doçura; (*quiet character*) brandura.

mile [maɪl] *n* milha (1609 metros); ~age *n* número de milhas; (*AUT*) quilometragem *f*; **mileometer** *n* conta-quilômetros *m inv*; ~stone *n* marco miliário; (*event*) fato que marca época.

milieu ['miːljəː] *n* meio, meio social.

militant ['mɪlɪtnt] *adj*, *n* militante *m/f*.

military ['mɪlɪtərɪ] *adj* militar.

militate ['mɪlɪteɪt] *vi*: to ~ against militar contra.

militia [mɪ'lɪʃə] *n* milícia.

milk [mɪlk] *n* leite *m* // *vt* (*cow*) ordenhar; (*fig*) explorar, chupar; ~man *n* leiteiro; ~ shake *n* leite batido com sorvete; ~y *adj* leitoso; M~y Way *n* Via Láctea.

mill [mɪl] *n* (*windmill etc*) moinho; (*coffee* ~) moedor *m* de café; (*factory*) moinho, engenho; (*spinning* ~) fábrica de tecelagem // *vt* moer // *vi* (*also*: ~ about) aglomerar-se, mover-se em círculos.

millennium [mɪ'lɛnɪəm], *pl* ~s *or* -ia [-nɪə] *n* milênio, milenário.

miller ['mɪlə*] *n* moleiro.

millet ['mɪlɪt] *n* milhete *m*.

milli... ['mɪlɪ] *pref*: ~gram(me) *n* miligrama *m*; ~litre, ~liter (*US*) *n* mililitro; ~metre, ~meter (*US*) *n* milímetro.

milliner ['mɪlɪnə*] *n* chapeleiro/a de senhoras; ~y *n* chapelaria de senhoras.

million ['mɪljən] *n* milhão *m*; a ~ times um milhão de vezes; ~aire *n* milionário.

millstone ['mɪlstəun] *n* mó *f*, pedra (de moinho).

milometer [maɪ'lɔmɪtə*] *n* marcador *m* de quilômetros.

mime [maɪm] *n* mimo; (*actor*) mímico, comediante *m/f* // *vt* imitar // *vi* fazer mímica.

mimic ['mɪmɪk] *n* mímico, imitador(a) *m/f* // *adj* mímico, simulado // *vt* imitar, parodiar; ~ry *n* imitação *f*.

min. *abbr of* **minute(s)**; **minimum**.

minaret [mɪnə'rɛt] *n* minarete *m*.

mince [mɪns] *vt* moer // *vi* (*in walking*) andar com afetação (*Pt*: -ct-) // *n* (*CULIN*) carne *f* moída; ~meat *n* recheio de sebo e frutas picadas; ~ pie *n* pastel *m* com recheio de sebo e frutas picadas; **mincer** *n* moedor *m* de carne.

mind [maɪnd] *n* (*gen*) mente *f*; (*intellect*) inteligência; (*contrasted with matter*) espírito // *vt* (*attend to, look after*) tomar conta de, cuidar de; (*be careful of*) ter cuidado com; (*object to*): **I don't** ~ **the noise** não me importa o ruído; **it is on my** ~ não me sai da cabeça; **to my** ~ a meu ver; **to be out of one's** ~ estar fora de si; **never** ~! não faz mal!, não importa!; (*don't worry*) não se preocupe!; **to bear sth in** ~ levar algo em consideração, não esquecer-se de algo; **to change one's** ~ mudar de opinião; **to make up one's** ~ decidir-se; '~ **the step**' 'cuidado com o degrau'; ~ful *adj*: ~ful of consciente de; ~less *adj* estúpido, insensato.

mine [maɪn] *pron* (o) meu/(a) minha *etc* // *adj*: **this book is** ~ este livro é meu // *n* mina // *vt* (*coal*) extrair, explorar; (*ship, beach*) minar; ~field *n* campo minado; **miner** *n* mineiro.

mineral ['mɪnərəl] *adj* mineral // *n* mineral *m*; ~s *npl* (*soft drinks*) águas *fpl* minerais *or* gasificadas.

minesweeper ['maɪnswiːpə*] *n* caça-minas *m inv*.

mingle ['mɪŋgl] *vi*: to ~ with misturar-se com.

mingy ['mɪndʒɪ] *adj* (*col*) pão-duro.

miniature ['mɪnətʃə*] *adj* em miniatura // *n* miniatura.

minibus ['mɪnɪbʌs] *n* micro-ônibus *m*.

minicab ['mɪnɪkæb] *n* mini-táxi *m*.

minim ['mɪnɪm] *n* (*MUS*) mínima.

minimal ['mɪnɪml] *adj* mínimo.

minimize ['mɪnɪmaɪz] *vt* minimizar.

minimum ['mɪnɪməm] *n*, *pl* **minima** ['mɪnɪmə] mínimo // *adj* mínimo.

mining ['maɪnɪŋ] *n* exploração *f* de minas // *adj* mineiro.

miniskirt ['mɪnɪskəːt] *n* minissaia.

minister ['mɪnɪstə*] *n* (*POL*) ministro; (*REL*) pastor *m* // *vi* prestar assistência; ~ial [-'tɪərɪəl] *adj* (*POL*) ministerial.

ministry ['mɪnɪstrɪ] *n* ministério.

mink [mɪŋk] *n* marta; ~ coat *n* casaco de marta.

minnow ['mɪnəu] *n* peixinho (de água doce).

minor ['maɪnə*] adj menor; (unimportant) de pouca importância; (inferior) inferior; (MUS) menor // n (LAW) menor m/f de idade.

minority [maɪ'nɔrɪtɪ] n minoria; (age) menoridade f.

minster ['mɪnstə*] n catedral f.

minstrel ['mɪnstrəl] n menestrel m.

mint [mɪnt] n (plant) hortelã f; (sweet) bala de hortelã // vt (coins) cunhar; **the (Royal) M~** a Real Casa da Moeda; **in ~ condition** em perfeito estado.

minuet [mɪnju'ɛt] n minueto.

minus ['maɪnəs] n (also: ~ sign) sinal m de subtração (Pt: -cç-) // prep menos; (without) sem.

minute ['mɪnɪt] n minuto; (fig) momento, instante m; ~**s** npl atas fpl // adj [maɪ'njuːt] miúdo, diminuto; (search) minucioso; **at the last ~** no último momento.

miracle ['mɪrəkl] n milagre m; **miraculous** [mɪ'rækjuləs] adj milagroso.

mirage ['mɪrɑːʒ] n miragem f.

mirror ['mɪrə*] n espelho; (in car) retrovisor m // vt refletir (Pt: -ct-).

mirth [mɜːθ] n alegria; (laughter) risada.

misadventure [mɪsəd'vɛntʃə*] n desgraça, infortúnio.

misanthropist [mɪ'zænθrəpɪst] n misântropo.

misapprehension ['mɪsæprɪ'hɛnʃən] n mal-entendido, engano.

misbehave [mɪsbɪ'heɪv] vi comportar-se mal; **misbehaviour** n mau comportamento.

miscalculate [mɪs'kælkjuleɪt] vt calcular mal; **miscalculation** [-'leɪʃən] n erro de cálculo.

miscarriage ['mɪskærɪdʒ] n (MED) aborto; (failure) fracasso; **~ of justice** erro judicial.

miscellaneous [mɪsɪ'leɪnɪəs] adj variado, diverso.

mischance [mɪs'tʃɑːns] n fatalidade f, azar m.

mischief ['mɪstʃɪf] n (naughtiness) travessura; (harm) dano, prejuízo; (maliciousness) malícia; **mischievous** [-ʃɪvəs] adj malicioso; (playful) travesso.

misconception ['mɪskən'sɛpʃən] n concepção f errada, conceito errado.

misconduct [mɪs'kɒndʌkt] n comportamento impróprio; **professional ~** má conduta profissional.

miscount [mɪs'kaʊnt] vt/i contar mal.

misdeed [mɪs'diːd] n delito, ofensa.

misdemeanour, misdemeanor (US) [mɪsdɪ'miːnə*] n má ação (Pt: -cç-) f.

misdirect [mɪsdɪ'rɛkt] vt (person) orientar or informar mal; (letter) endereçar mal.

miser ['maɪzə*] n avaro/a m/f, sovina m/f.

miserable ['mɪzərəbl] adj (unhappy) triste, sorumbático; (wretched) miserável; (despicable) desprezível.

miserly ['maɪzəlɪ] adj avarento, mesquinho.

misery ['mɪzərɪ] n (unhappiness) tristeza, angústia; (wretchedness) miséria, penúria.

misfire [mɪs'faɪə*] vi falhar.

misfit ['mɪsfɪt] n (person) inadaptado/a, deslocado/a.

misfortune [mɪs'fɔːtʃən] n desgraça, infortúnio.

misgiving(s) [mɪs'gɪvɪŋ(z)] n(pl) (mistrust) desconfiança, receio; (apprehension) mau pressentimento.

misguided [mɪs'gaɪdɪd] adj enganado.

mishandle [mɪs'hændl] vt (treat roughly) maltratar; (mismanage) manejar mal.

mishap ['mɪshæp] n desgraça, contratempo.

mishear [mɪs'hɪə*] (irr: like hear) vt ouvir mal.

misinform [mɪsɪn'fɔːm] vt informar mal.

misinterpret [mɪsɪn'tɜːprɪt] vt interpretar mal.

misjudge [mɪs'dʒʌdʒ] vt fazer um juízo errado de, julgar mal.

mislay [mɪs'leɪ] (irr: like lay) vt extraviar, perder.

mislead [mɪs'liːd] (irr: like lead) vt induzir em erro, enganar; **~ing** adj enganoso, errôneo.

mismanage [mɪs'mænɪdʒ] vt administrar mal; **~ment** n má administração f.

misnomer [mɪs'nəʊmə*] n termo impróprio or errado.

misogynist [mɪ'sɒdʒɪnɪst] n misógino.

misplace [mɪs'pleɪs] vt (lose) extraviar, perder; (wrongly) colocar em lugar errado.

misprint ['mɪsprɪnt] n erro tipográfico.

mispronounce [mɪsprə'naʊns] vt pronunciar mal.

misread [mɪs'riːd] (irr: like read) vt interpretar or ler mal.

misrepresent [mɪsrɛprɪ'zɛnt] vt desvirtuar, deturpar.

miss [mɪs] vt (train etc) perder; (fail to hit) errar, não acertar em; (regret the absence of): **I ~ him** sinto a falta dele or sinto a sua falta // vi falhar // n (shot) tiro perdido or errado; (fig): **that was a near ~** (near accident) por pouco não batemos; **to ~ out** vt omitir.

Miss [mɪs] n senhorita.

missal ['mɪsl] n missal m.

misshapen [mɪs'ʃeɪpən] adj disforme.

missile ['mɪsaɪl] n (AVIAT) míssil m; (object thrown) projétil (Pt: -ct-) m.

missing ['mɪsɪŋ] adj (pupil) ausente; (thing) perdido; (MIL) desaparecido; **to go ~** desaparecer.

mission ['mɪʃən] n missão f; **~ary** n missionário/a.

misspent ['mɪs'spɛnt] adj: **his ~ youth** sua juventude desperdiçada.

mist [mɪst] n (light) neblina; (heavy) névoa; (at sea) bruma // vi (also: ~ over, ~ up) embaciar.

mistake [mɪs'teɪk] n erro // vt (irr: like take) entender or interpretar mal; to ~ A for B confundir A com B; mistaken adj (idea etc) errado; to be mistaken enganar-se, equivocar-se.

mister ['mɪstə*] n (col) senhor m; see Mr.

mistletoe ['mɪsltəʊ] n visco.

mistook [mɪs'tuk] pt of mistake.

mistreat [mɪs'triːt] vt maltratar; ~ment n mau trato.

mistress ['mɪstrɪs] n (lover) amante f; (of house) dona (da casa); (school) professora, mestra; see Mrs.

mistrust [mɪs'trʌst] vt desconfiar de, duvidar de.

misty ['mɪstɪ] adj enevoado, nebuloso; (day) nublado; (glasses) embaciado.

misunderstand [mɪsʌndə'stænd] (irr: like understand) vt/i entender or interpretar mal; ~ing n mal-entendido.

misuse [mɪs'juːs] n mal uso; (of power) abuso // vt [mɪs'juːz] abusar de; (funds) desviar.

mitigate ['mɪtɪgeɪt] vt mitigar, atenuar.

mitre, miter (US) ['maɪtə*] n mitro; (CARPENTRY) meia-esquadria.

mitt(en) ['mɪt(n)] n mitene f.

mix [mɪks] vt (gen) misturar; (combine) combinar // vi misturar-se; (people) entrosar-se // n mistura; to ~ up vt misturar; (confuse) confundir; ~ed adj (assorted) sortido, variado; (school etc) misto; ~ed-up adj (confused) confuso; ~er n (for food) batedeira; (person) pessoa sociável; ~ture n mistura; ~up n trapalhada, confusão f.

moan [məʊn] n gemido, lamento // vi gemer; (col: complain): to ~ (about) queixar-se (de).

moat [məʊt] n fosso.

mob [mɒb] n multidão f; (pej): the ~ chusma, povinho // vt atacar, cercar.

mobile ['məʊbaɪl] adj móvel // n móvel m; ~ home n trailer m, casa móvel.

mobility [məʊ'bɪlɪtɪ] n mobilidade f.

mobilize ['məʊbɪlaɪz] vt mobilizar.

moccasin ['mɒkəsɪn] n mocassim m.

mock [mɒk] vt (make ridiculous) ridicularizar; (laugh at) zombar de, gozar de // adj falso, fingido; ~ery n zombaria; ~ing adj zombeteiro; ~-up n maqueta, modelo.

mode [məʊd] n modo; (fashion) moda.

model ['mɒdl] n (gen) modelo; (ARCH) maqueta; (person: for fashion, ART) modelo m/f // adj modelar // vt modelar // vi servir de modelo; ~ railway trenzinho de brinquedo; to ~ clothes desfilar apresentando modelos.

moderate ['mɒdərət] adj, n moderado/a // (vb: [-reɪt]) vi moderar-se, acalmar-se // vt moderar; moderation [-'reɪʃən] n moderação f.

modern ['mɒdən] adj moderno; ~ize vt modernizar, atualizar (Pt: -ct-).

modest ['mɒdɪst] adj modesto; ~y n modéstia.

modicum ['mɒdɪkəm] n: a ~ of um mínimo de.

modification [mɒdɪfɪ'keɪʃən] n modificação f; modify ['mɒdɪfaɪ] vt modificar.

modulation [mɒdju'leɪʃən] n modulação f.

mohair ['məʊhɛə*] n angorá m.

moist [mɔɪst] adj úmido (Pt: hú-), molhado; ~en ['mɔɪsn] vt (h)umedecer; ~ure ['mɔɪstʃə*] n (h)umidade f; ~urizer ['mɔɪstʃəraɪzə*] n creme m hidratante.

molar ['məʊlə*] n molar m.

molasses [məʊ'læsɪz] n melaço sg, melado sg.

mole [məʊl] n (animal) toupeira; (spot) sinal m, lunar m.

molecule ['mɒlɪkjuːl] n molécula.

molehill ['məʊlhɪl] n montículo (feito por uma toupeira).

molest [məʊ'lɛst] vt molestar, importunar.

mollusc ['mɒləsk] n molusco.

mollycoddle ['mɒlɪkɔdl] vt mimar.

molten ['məʊltən] adj fundido; (lava) liquefeito.

moment ['məʊmənt] n momento; ~ary adj momentâneo; ~ous [-'mɛntəs] adj importantíssimo.

momentum [məʊ'mɛntəm] n momento; (fig) ímpeto; to gather ~ ganhar ímpeto.

monarch ['mɒnək] n monarca m/f; ~y n monarquia.

monastery ['mɒnəstərɪ] n mosteiro, convento.

monastic [mə'næstɪk] adj monástico.

Monday ['mʌndɪ] n segunda-feira f.

monetary ['mʌnɪtərɪ] adj monetário.

money ['mʌnɪ] n dinheiro; to make ~ ganhar dinheiro; ~lender n agiota m/f; ~ order n vale (postal) m.

mongol ['mɒŋgəl] adj, n (MED) mongoloide m/f.

mongrel ['mʌŋgrəl] n (dog) cão cruzado, vira-lata m.

monitor ['mɒnɪtə*] n (SCOL) monitor m; (also: television ~) visor m // vt controlar.

monk [mʌŋk] n monge m.

monkey ['mʌŋkɪ] n macaco; ~ nut n amendoim m; ~ wrench n chave f inglesa.

mono... [mɒnəʊ] pref: ~chrome adj monocromático.

monocle ['mɒnəkl] n monóculo.

monogram ['mɒnəgræm] n monograma m.

monologue ['mɒnəlɔg] n monólogo.

monopoly [mə'nɒpəlɪ] n monopólio.

monorail ['mɒnəʊreɪl] n monotrilho.

monosyllabic [mɒnəʊsɪ'læbɪk] adj monossilábico.

monotone ['mɒnətəʊn] n monotonia; to speak in a ~ falar num tom monótono.

monotonous [mə'nɒtənəs] adj monótono; monotony [-nɪ] n monotonia.

monsoon [mɔn'suːn] *n* monção *f.*

monster ['mɔnstə*] *n* monstro.

monstrosity [mɔns'trɔsɪtɪ] *n* monstruosidade *f.*

monstrous ['mɔnstrəs] *adj* (*huge*) descomunal; (*atrocious*) monstruoso.

montage [mɔn'tɑːʒ] *n* montagem *f.*

month [mʌnθ] *n* mês *m;* ~ly *adj* mensal // *adv* mensalmente // *n* (*magazine*) revista mensal.

monument ['mɔnjumənt] *n* monumento; ~al [-'mɛntl] *adj* monumental.

moo [muː] *vi* mugir.

mood [muːd] *n* humor *m;* **to be in a good/bad** ~ estar de bom/mal humor; ~y *adj* (*variable*) caprichoso, de veneta; (*sullen*) melancólico.

moon [muːn] *n* lua; ~beam *n* raio de lua; ~light *n* luar *m;* ~lit *adj:* **a** ~lit **night** uma noite de lua.

moor [muə*] *n* charneca // *vt* (*ship*) amarrar // *vi* fundear, atracar.

Moor [muə*] *n* mouro/a.

moorings ['muərɪŋz] *npl* (*chains*) amarras *fpl;* (*place*) ancoradouro *sg.*

Moorish ['muərɪʃ] *adj* mouro; (*architecture*) mourisco.

moorland ['muələnd] *n* charneca.

moose [muːs] *n, pl inv* alce *m.*

mop [mɔp] *n* esfregão *m;* (*of hair*) grenha // *vt* esfregar; **to** ~ **up** *vt* limpar.

mope [məup] *vi* estar or andar deprimido or desanimado.

moped ['məuped] *n* (*Brit*) lambreta (*Br*), motorizada (*Pt*).

moral ['mɔrl] *adj* moral // *n* moral *f;* ~s *npl* moralidade *f,* costumes *mpl.*

morale [mɔ'rɑːl] *n* moral *f,* estado de espírito.

morality [mə'rælɪtɪ] *n* moralidade *f.*

morass [mə'ræs] *n* pântano, brejo.

morbid ['mɔːbɪd] *adj* (*depressed*) doentio; (*MED*) mórbido; **don't be** ~! não seja mórbido!

more [mɔː*] *det, adv* mais; **once** ~ outra vez; **I want** ~ quero mais; ~ **dangerous than** mais perigoso que; ~ **or less** mais ou menos; ~ **than ever** mais do que nunca.

moreover [mɔː'rəuvə*] *adv* além do mais, além disso.

morgue [mɔːg] *n* necrotério.

moribund ['mɔrɪbʌnd] *adj* moribundo, agonizante.

Mormon ['mɔːmən] *n* mórmon *m/f.*

morning ['mɔːnɪŋ] *n* (*gen*) manhã *f;* (*early* ~) madrugada; **good** ~ bom dia; **in the** ~ de manhã; **7 o'clock in the** ~ (as) 7 da manhã; **tomorrow** ~ amanhã de manhã.

Moroccan [mə'rɔkən] *adj, n* marroquino/a.

Morocco [mə'rɔkəu] *n* Marrocos *msg.*

moron ['mɔːrɔn] *n* débil mental *m/f,* idiota *m/f;* ~ic [mə'rɔnɪk] *adj* mentecapto.

morose [mə'rəus] *adj* taciturno, rabugento.

morphine ['mɔːfiːn] *n* morfina.

Morse [mɔːs] *n* (*also:* ~ **code**) código Morse.

morsel ['mɔːsl] *n* (*of food*) bocado.

mortal ['mɔːtl] *adj, n* mortal *m/f;* ~ity [-'tælɪtɪ] *n* mortalidade *f.*

mortar ['mɔːtə*] *n* argamassa; (*dish*) pilão *m,* almofariz *m.*

mortgage ['mɔːgɪdʒ] *n* hipoteca // *vt* hipotecar.

mortify ['mɔːtɪfaɪ] *vt* humilhar, mortificar.

mortuary ['mɔːtjuərɪ] *n* necrotério.

mosaic [məu'zeɪɪk] *n* mosaico.

Moscow ['mɔskəu] *n* Moscou *m.*

Moslem ['mɔzləm] *adj, n* = **Muslim.**

mosque [mɔsk] *n* mesquita.

mosquito [mɔs'kiːtəu], *pl* ~es *n* mosquito.

moss [mɔs] *n* musgo.

most [məust] *det* a maior parte de, a maioria de // *pron* a maior parte, a maioria // *adv* o mais; (*very*) muito; **the** ~ (*also:* + *adjective*) o mais; ~ **of them** a maioria deles; **I saw the** ~ vi mais; **at the** (*very*) ~ quando muito, no máximo; **to make the** ~ **of** aproveitar ao máximo; ~ly *adv* principalmente, na maior parte; **a** ~ **interesting book** um livro interessantíssimo.

motel [məu'tɛl] *n* motel *m.*

moth [mɔθ] *n* mariposa; (*clothes* ~) traça; ~ball *n* bola de naftalina; ~-eaten *adj* roído pelas traças.

mother ['mʌðə*] *n* mãe *f,* mamãe *f* // *adj* materno // *vt* (*care for*) cuidar de (*como uma mãe*); ~hood *n* maternidade *f;* ~-in-law *n* sogra; ~ly *adj* maternal; ~-of-pearl *n* madrepérola; ~-to-be *n* futura mamãe; ~ **tongue** *n* língua materna or pátria.

motif [məu'tiːf] *n* motivo; (*theme*) tema *m.*

motion ['məuʃən] *n* movimento; (*gesture*) gesto, sinal *m;* (*at meeting*) moção *f* // *vt/i:* **to** ~ (**to**) **sb to do sth** fazer sinal a alguém para que faça algo; ~less *adj* imóvel; ~ **picture** *n* filme *m* (cinematográfico).

motivated ['məutɪveɪtɪd] *adj* motivado; **motivation** [-'veɪʃən] *n* motivação *f.*

motive ['məutɪv] *n* motivo // *adj* motor/motriz.

motley ['mɔtlɪ] *adj* variado, heterogêneo.

motor ['məutə*] *n* motor *m;* (*col: vehicle*) carro, automóvel *m* // *adj* motor/motriz; ~bike *n* motocicleta; ~boat *n* barco a motor; ~car *n* carro, automóvel *m;* ~cycle *n* motocicleta; ~cyclist *n* motociclista *m/f;* ~ing *n* automobilismo; ~ist *n* automobilista *m/f,* motorista *m/f;* ~ **oil** *n* óleo de motor; ~ **racing** *n* corrida de carros, automobilismo; ~ **scooter** *n* moto *f,* Lambretta; ~ **vehicle** *n* automóvel *m;* ~way *n* (*Brit*) auto-estrada.

mottled ['mɔtld] *adj* mosqueado, em furta-cores.

motto ['mɔtəu], pl ~es n lema m; (watchword) senha.

mould, mold (US) [məuld] n molde m; (mildew) mofo, bolor m // vt moldar; (fig) modelar, plasmar; ~er vi (decay) desfazer-se; ~ing n moldura; ~y adj mofado.

moult, molt (US) [məult] vi mudar (de penas etc).

mound [maund] n montão m, montículo.

mount [maunt] n monte m; (horse) montaria; (for jewel etc) engaste m; (for picture) moldura // vt montar em, subir a // vi (also: ~ up) subir, aumentar.

mountain ['mauntin] n montanha // cmp de montanha; ~eer [-'niə*] n alpinista m/f, montanhista m/f; ~eering [-'niəriŋ] n alpinismo; to go ~eering praticar o alpinismo; ~ous adj montanhoso; ~side n lado da montanha.

mourn [mɔ:n] vt chorar, lamentar // vi: to ~ for chorar or lamentar a morte de; ~er n parente/a m/f or amigo/a do defunto; ~ful adj desolado, triste; ~ing n luto // cmp (dress) de luto; (to be) in ~ing (estar) de luto.

mouse [maus], pl mice n camundongo (Br), rato (Pt); ~trap n ratoeira.

moustache [məs'tɑ:ʃ] n bigode m.

mousy ['mausi] adj (person) tímido; (hair) pardacento.

mouth [mauθ], pl ~s [-ðz] n boca; (of river) desembocadura; ~ful n bocado; ~ organ n gaita; ~piece n (of musical instrument) bocal m; (spokesman) portavoz m; ~wash n líquido para limpeza bucal; ~-watering adj de dar água na boca.

movable ['mu:vəbl] adj móvel.

move [mu:v] n (movement) movimento; (in game) jogada; (: turn to play) turno, vez f; (change of house) mudança // vt mover; (emotionally) comover; (POL: resolution etc) propor // vi (gen) moverse, mexer-se; (traffic) circular; (also: ~ house) mudar-se; to ~ sb to do sth convencer alguém a fazer algo; to get a ~ on apressar-se; to ~ about vi ir de um lado para o outro; (travel) viajar; to ~ along vi avançar; to ~ away vi afastar-se; to ~ back vi recuar; to ~ forward vi avançar // vt adiantar; to ~ in vi (to a house) instalar-se (numa casa); to ~ on vi ir andando; to ~ out vi (of house) abandonar (uma casa); to ~ up vi subir; (employee) ser promovido.

movement ['mu:vmənt] n movimento; (TECH) mecanismo.

movie ['mu:vi] n filme m; to go to the ~s ir ao cinema; ~ camera n câmara cinematográfica.

moving ['mu:viŋ] adj (emotional) comovente; (that moves) móvel.

mow [məu], pt mowed, pp mowed or mown vt (grass) cortar; (corn: also: ~ down) ceifar; ~er n ceifeira; (for lawn) cortador m de grama (Br), cortador m de relva (Pt).

M.P. (Brit) n abbr of **Member of Parliament.**

m.p.h. abbr of miles per hour.

Mr ['mistə*] n: ~ Smith (o) Sr. Smith.

Mrs ['misiz] n: ~ Smith (a) Sra. Smith.

Ms [miz] n = Miss or Mrs: ~ X (a) Sa X.

M.Sc. (Brit) abbr of **Master of Science.**

much [mʌtʃ] det, adv, pron muito // n muito, grande parte; how ~ is it? quanto é?, quanto custa?; too ~ demais, demasiado; it's not ~ não é muito; as ~ as tanto como; however ~ he tries por mais que tente.

muck [mʌk] n (dirt) sujeira (Br), sujidade f (Pt); (manure) estrume m; (fig) porcaria; to ~ about vi (col) perder o tempo; (enjoy o.s.) divertir-se; to ~ up vt (col: ruin) estragar; ~y adj (dirty) sujo.

mucus ['mju:kəs] n muco.

mud [mʌd] n lama, lodo.

muddle ['mʌdl] n confusão f, desordem f; (mix-up) trapalhada // vt (also: ~ up) confundir, misturar; to ~ through vi sair-se bem.

mud: ~dy adj (road) lamacento; (person, clothes) enlameado ~guard n pára-lama m; ~pack n máscara (de beleza); ~-slinging n difamação f, injúria.

muff [mʌf] n regalo // vt (chance) desperdiçar, perder; (lines) estropiar.

muffle ['mʌfl] vt (sound) abafar; (against cold) agasalhar; ~d adj abafado, surdo; ~r n (US) silencioso (Br), panela de escape (Pt).

mufti ['mʌfti] n: in ~ vestido à paisana.

mug [mʌg] n (cup) caneca; (: for beer) caneco, canecão m; (col: face) careta; (: fool) bobo // vt (assault) assaltar; ~ging n assalto.

muggy ['mʌgi] adj abafado.

mule [mju:l] n mula.

mull [mʌl]: to ~ over vt meditar sobre.

mulled [mʌld] adj: ~ wine quentão m.

multi- [mʌlti] pref multi...; ~coloured, ~colored (US) adj multicolor.

multifarious [mʌlti'fɛəriəs] adj variado.

multiple ['mʌltipl] adj, n múltiplo; ~ sclerosis n esclerose f múltipla; ~ store n cadeia de lojas.

multiplication [mʌltipli'keiʃən] n multiplicação f; **multiply** ['mʌltiplai] vt multiplicar // vi multiplicar-se.

multitude ['mʌltitju:d] n multidão f.

mum [mʌm] n mamãe f // adj: to keep ~ ficar calado.

mumble ['mʌmbl] vt/i resmungar, murmurar.

mummy ['mʌmi] n (mother) mamãe f; (embalmed) múmia.

mumps [mʌmps] n caxumba sg.

munch [mʌntʃ] vt/i mascar.

mundane [mʌn'dein] adj mundano.

municipal [mju:'nisipl] adj municipal; ~ity [-'pæliti] n municipalidade f.

munitions [mju:'niʃənz] npl munições fpl.

mural ['mjuərl] n mural m.

murder ['mɔːdə*] n assassinato; (in law) homicídio // vt assassinar; (spoil) estragar; ~er n assassino; ~ess n assassina; ~ous adj homicida.

murky ['mɔːkɪ] adj escuro; (fig) sombrio.

murmur ['mɔːmə*] n murmúrio // vt/i murmurar.

muscle ['mʌsl] n músculo; (fig: strength) força (muscular); to ~ in vi abrir caminho à força; muscular ['muskjulə*] adj muscular; (person) musculoso.

muse [mjuːz] vi meditar // n musa.

museum [mjuːˈzɪəm] n museu m.

mushroom ['mʌʃrum] n (gen) cogumelo, fungo; (food) cogumelo // vi (fig) crescer da noite para o dia.

mushy ['mʌʃɪ] adj mole; (pej) piegas inv.

music ['mjuːzɪk] n música; ~al adj melodioso; (person) musical // n (show) musical m; ~al instrument n instrumento musical; ~ hall n teatro de variedades; ~ian [-ˈzɪʃən] n músico/a.

musket ['mʌskɪt] n mosquete m.

Muslim ['mʌzlɪm] adj, n muçulmano/a m/f.

muslin ['mʌzlɪn] n musselina.

mussel ['mʌsl] n mexilhão m.

must [mʌst] auxiliary vb (obligation): I ~ do it tenho que or devo fazer isso; (probability): he ~ be there by now ele já deve estar lá agora // n (wine) mosto; (necessity): it's a ~ é imprescindível.

mustard ['mʌstəd] n mostarda.

muster ['mʌstə*] vt reunir, juntar.

mustn't ['mʌsnt] = must not.

musty ['mʌstɪ] adj mofado, com cheiro de bolor.

mute [mjuːt] adj, n mudo/a.

muted ['mjuːtɪd] adj calado; (MUS) abafado.

mutilate ['mjuːtɪleɪt] vt mutilar; mutilation [-ˈleɪʃən] n mutilação f.

mutinous ['mjuːtɪnəs] adj (troops) amotinado; (attitude) rebelde.

mutiny ['mjuːtɪnɪ] n motim m, rebelião f // vi amotinar-se.

mutter ['mʌtə*] vt/i resmungar, murmurar.

mutton ['mʌtn] n carne f de carneiro.

mutual ['mjuːtʃuəl] adj mútuo; (gen: shared) comum; ~ly adv reciprocamente.

muzzle ['mʌzl] n focinho; (protective device) focinheira; (of gun) boca // vt amordaçar; (dog) pôr focinheira em.

my [maɪ] adj meu/minha // interj: ~! meu Deus!

mynah bird ['maɪnə-] n mainá m.

myopic [maɪˈɔpɪk] adj míope.

myself [maɪˈsɛlf] pron (reflexive) me; (emphatic) eu mesmo; (after prep) mim mesmo, mim próprio.

mysterious [mɪsˈtɪərɪəs] adj misterioso; **mystery** ['mɪstərɪ] n mistério.

mystic ['mɪstɪk] adj, n místico/a; ~al adj místico.

mystify ['mɪstɪfaɪ] vt (perplex) mistificar, confundir; (disconcert) desconcertar.

myth [mɪθ] n mito; ~ical adj mítico; ~ological [mɪθəˈlɔdʒɪkl] adj mitológico; ~ology [mɪˈθɔlədʒɪ] n mitologia.

N

nab [næb] vt (col: grab) pegar, prender; (: catch out) pegar (em flagrante).

nag [næg] n (pej: horse) rocim m // vt (scold) ralhar; (annoy) aborrecer; ~ging adj (doubt) persistente; (pain) contínuo // n queixas fpl, censuras fpl.

nail [neɪl] n (human) unha; (metal) prego // vt pregar, cravar; (fig: catch) agarrar, pegar; to ~ sb down to doing sth comprometer alguém para que faça algo; ~brush n escova de unhas; ~file n lixa de unhas; ~ polish n esmalte m de unhas; ~ scissors npl tesourinha de unhas; ~ varnish n = ~ polish.

naïve [naɪˈiːv] adj ingênuo; (simple) simples.

naked ['neɪkɪd] adj (nude) nu/nua; (fig) desprotegido; (flame) exposto ao ar; with the ~ eye a olho nu; ~ness n nudez f.

name [neɪm] n (gen) nome m; (surname) sobrenome m; (reputation) reputação f, fama // vt (child) pôr nome em; (criminal) dar o nome de; (appoint) nomear; by ~ de nome; in the ~ of em nome de; what's your ~? como (você) se chama?; to give one's ~ and address dar o nome e o endereço; ~less adj sem nome, anônimo; ~ly adv a saber, isto é; ~sake n xará m/f (Br); homônimo/a (Pt).

nanny ['nænɪ] n babá f; ~ goat n cabra.

nap [næp] n (sleep) soneca, soninho; (cloth) felpa.

napalm ['neɪpɑːm] n napalm m.

nape [neɪp] n: the ~ of the neck nuca.

napkin ['næpkɪn] n (also: table ~) guardanapo; (Brit: for baby) fralda.

nappy ['næpɪ] n fralda; ~ liner n gaze f; ~ rash n assadura.

narcissus [nɑːˈsɪsəs], pl -si [-saɪ] n narciso.

narcotic [nɑːˈkɔtɪk] adj, n narcótico.

narrate [nəˈreɪt] vt narrar, contar; **narrative** ['nærətɪv] n narrativa // adj narrativo; **narrator** n narrador(a) m/f.

narrow ['nærəu] adj estreito; (shoe) apertado; (fig) intolerante, limitado // vi estreitar-se; (diminish) diminuir-se; to ~ down the possibilities to restringir as possibilidades a; ~ly adv (miss) por pouco; ~-minded adj de visão limitada, bitolado.

nasal ['neɪzl] adj nasal.

nastiness ['nɑːstɪnɪs] n (malice) maldade f; (rudeness) grosseria.

nasty ['nɑːstɪ] adj (unpleasant: remark) desagradável; (: person) mau, ruim; (malicious) maldoso; (rude) grosseiro, obsceno; (*revolting: taste, smell*) repugnante, asqueroso; (*wound, disease etc*) grave, sério.

nation ['neɪʃən] n nação f.

national ['næʃənl] adj, n nacional m/f; ~**ism** n nacionalismo; ~**ist** adj, n nacionalista m/f; ~**ity** [-'nælɪtɪ] n nacionalidade f; ~**ization** [-aɪ'zeɪʃən] n nacionalização f; ~**ize** vt nacionalizar; ~**ly** adv (*nationwide*) de âmbito nacional; (*as a nation*) nacionalmente, como nação.

nationwide ['neɪʃənwaɪd] adj de âmbito or a nível nacional.

native ['neɪtɪv] n (*local inhabitant*) natural m/f, nativo/a; (*in colonies*) indígena m/f, nativo/a // adj (*indigenous*) indígena; (*of one's birth*) natal; (*innate*) inato, natural.

NATO ['neɪtəu] n abbr of **North Atlantic Treaty Organization** OTAN, Organização do Tratado do Atlântico Norte.

natter ['nætə*] vi conversar fiado.

natural ['nætʃrəl] adj natural; (*unaffected: manner*) sem afetação (Pt: -ct-); ~**ist** n naturalista m/f; ~**ize** vt: **to become** ~**ized** (*person*) naturalizar-se; (*plant*) aclimatar-se; ~**ly** adv naturalmente; (*of course*) claro, evidentemente; (*instinctively*) por instinto, espontaneamente; ~**ness** n naturalidade f.

nature ['neɪtʃə*] n natureza; (*group, sort*) tipo, espécie f; (*character*) caráter (Pt: -ct-) m, índole f; **by** ~ por natureza.

naughty ['nɔːtɪ] adj (*child*) travesso, levado; (*story, film*) picante.

nausea ['nɔːsɪə] n náusea; **nauseate** [-sɪeɪt] vt dar náuseas a; (*fig*) repugnar; **nauseating** [-sɪeɪtɪŋ] adj nauseabundo, enjoativo; (*fig*) nojento, repugnante.

nautical ['nɔːtɪkl] adj náutico; (*mile*) marítimo.

naval ['neɪvl] adj naval; ~ **officer** n oficial m de marinha.

nave [neɪv] n nave f.

navel ['neɪvl] n umbigo.

navigable ['nævɪgəbl] adj navegável.

navigate ['nævɪgeɪt] vt (*guide*) pilotar; (*sail along*) navegar; (*fig*) dirigir // vi navegar; **navigation** [-'geɪʃən] n (*action*) navegação f; (*science*) náutica; **navigator** n navegante m/f, navegador(a) m/f.

navvy ['nævɪ] n trabalhador m braçal, cavouqueiro.

navy ['neɪvɪ] n marinha de guerra; (*ships*) armada, frota; ~(**-blue**) adj azul-marinho.

Nazi ['nɑːtsɪ] n nazista m/f; **Nazism** n nazismo.

neap tide [niːp-] n maré f.

near [nɪə*] adj (*place*) vizinho, perto; (*time*) próximo; (*relation*) íntimo // adv perto // prep (*also*: ~ **to**) (*space*) perto de, junto de; (*time*) perto de, quase // vt aproximar-se de, abeirar-se de; ~**by** [nɪə'baɪ] adj próximo, vizinho // adv à mão, perto; **N**~ **East** n Oriente m

Próximo; ~**ly** adv quase, por pouco; **I** ~**ly fell** quase que caí; ~ **miss** n tiro que passou de raspão; ~**ness** n proximidade f; (*relationship*) intimidade f, familiaridade f; ~**side** n (AUT: *right-hand drive*) lado esquerdo (: *left-hand drive*) lado direito; ~**sighted** adj míope.

neat [niːt] adj (*place*) arrumado, em ordem; (*person*) asseado, arrumado; (*skilful*) hábil; (: *plan*) engenhoso, bem bolado; (*spirits*) puro.

nebulous ['nɛbjuləs] adj nebuloso; (*fig*) vago, confuso.

necessarily ['nɛsɪsrɪlɪ] adv necessariamente.

necessary ['nɛsɪsrɪ] adj necessário; **he did all that was** ~ fez tudo o que foi necessário.

necessitate [nɪ'sɛsɪteɪt] vt exigir, tornar necessário.

necessity [nɪ'sɛsɪtɪ] n (*thing needed*) necessidade f, requisito; (*compelling circumstances*) a necessidade; **necessities** npl artigos mpl de primeira necessidade.

neck [nɛk] n (ANAT) pescoço; (*of garment*) gola // vi ficar de agarramento; ~ **and** ~ emparelhados; **to stick one's** ~ **out** arriscar-se.

necklace ['nɛklɪs] n colar m.

neckline ['nɛklaɪn] n decote m.

necktie ['nɛktaɪ] n gravata.

née [neɪ] adj: ~ **Scott** em solteira Scott.

need [niːd] n (*lack*) falta, carência; (*necessity*) necessidade f; (*thing needed*) requisito, necessidade // vt (*require*) necessitar; **I** ~ **to do it** tenho que or devo fazê-lo; **you don't** ~ **to go** você não precisa ir.

needle ['niːdl] n agulha // vt (*fig: fam*) provocar, picar, alfinetar.

needless ['niːdlɪs] adj inútil, desnecessário; ~ **to say** é claro que

needlework ['niːdlwɔːk] n (*activity*) trabalho de agulha, costura.

needy ['niːdɪ] adj necessitado.

negation [nɪ'geɪʃən] n negação f.

negative ['nɛgətɪv] n (PHOT) negativo; (*answer*) negativa // adj negativo.

neglect [nɪ'glɛkt] vt (*one's duty*) negligenciar, não cumprir com; (*child*) descuidar, esquecer-se de // n (*gen*) descuido, desatenção f; (*personal*) desleixo; (*of duty*) negligência.

negligee ['nɛglɪʒeɪ] n négligé m.

negligence ['nɛglɪdʒəns] n negligência, descuido; **negligent** [-ənt] adj (*careless*) negligente, desleixado; (*forgetful*) esquecido.

negligible ['nɛglɪdʒɪbl] adj insignificante, desprezível, ínfimo.

negotiable [nɪ'gəuʃɪəbl] adj (*cheque*) negociável; (*road*) transitável.

negotiate [nɪ'gəuʃɪeɪt] vi negociar // vt (*treaty*) negociar; (*transaction*) efetuar (Pt: -ct-), fazer; (*obstacle*) contornar; **negotiation** [-'eɪʃən] n negociação f, transação f; **negotiator** n negociador(a) m/f.

Negress ['ni:grɪs] n negra.

Negro ['ni:grəʊ] adj, n negro/a.

neigh [neɪ] n relincho // vi relinchar.

neighbour, neighbor (US) ['neɪbə*] n vizinho/a; **~hood** n (place) vizinhança, bairro; (people) vizinhos mpl; **~ing** adj vizinho; **~ly** adj amistoso, prestativo.

neither ['naɪðə*] adj nem // conj: **I didn't move an ~ did he** não me movi nem ele // pron nenhum (dos dois), nem um nem outro // adv: **~ good nor bad** nem bom nem mau.

neo... ['ni:əʊ] pref neo-.

neon ['ni:ɔn] n neônio, néon m; **~ light** n luz f de neônio.

nephew ['nevju:] n sobrinho.

nerve [nə:v] n (ANAT) nervo; (courage) coragem f; (impudence) descaramento, atrevimento; **~-racking** adj exasperante, enervante; **~s** npl (fig: anxiety) nervosismo.

nervous ['nə:vəs] adj (anxious, ANAT) nervoso; (timid) tímido, acanhado; **~ breakdown** n esgotamento nervoso; **~ly** adv nervosamente, timidamente; **~ness** n nervosismo; (timidity) timidez f.

nest [nɛst] n (of bird) ninho; (of wasp) vespeiro // vi aninhar-se.

nestle ['nɛsl] vi: **to ~ up to sb** aconchegar-se a alguém.

net [nɛt] n (gen) rede f; (fig) armadilha // adj (COMM) líquido // vt pegar or cobrir com rede; (SPORT) atirar na rede; **~ball** n (espécie de) basquetebol m.

Netherlands ['nɛðələndz] npl: **the ~** os Países Baixos.

nett [nɛt] adj = **net**.

netting ['nɛtɪŋ] n rede f, redes fpl.

nettle ['nɛtl] n urtiga.

network ['nɛtwə:k] n rede f, cadeia.

neurosis [njuə'rəʊsɪs], pl **-ses** [-si:z] n neurose f; **neurotic** [-'rɔtɪk] adj, n neurótico/a.

neuter ['nju:tə*] adj (sexless) assexuado, castrado; (LING) neutro // vt castrar, capar.

neutral ['nju:trəl] adj neutro // n (AUT) ponto morto; **~ity** [-'trælɪtɪ] n neutralidade f.

neutron ['nju:trɔn] n nêutron (Pt: neutrão) m; **~ bomb** n bomba de nêutrons (Pt: neutrões).

never ['nɛvə*] adv nunca; **I ~ went** nunca fui; **~ in my life** nunca na minha vida; **~-ending** adj sem fim, interminável; **~theless** [nɛvəðə'lɛs] adv todavia, contudo.

new [nju:] adj (brand ~) novo (em folha); (recent) recente; (different) diferente; (inexperienced) inexperiente, principiante; **~ born** adj recém-nascido; **~comer** ['nju:kʌmə*] n recém-chegado; **~ly** adv recém, novamente; **~ moon** n lua nova; **~ness** n novidade f; (fig) inexperiência.

news [nju:z] n notícias fpl; **a piece of ~** uma notícia; **the ~** (RADIO, TV) o noticiário; **~ agency** n agência de notícias; **~agent, ~dealer** (US) n jornaleiro/a m/f; **~caster** n noticiarista m/f; **~ flash** n notícia de última hora; **~letter** n boletim m informativo; **~paper** n jornal m; (material) papel m de jornal; **~reel** n jornal m cinematográfico, atualidades (Pt: -ct-) fpl; **~stand** n banca de jornais.

New Year ['nju:'jɪə*] n ano novo; **~'s Day** n dia m de ano novo; **~'s Eve** n véspera de ano novo.

New York ['nju:'jɔ:k] n Nova Iorque.

New Zealand [nju:'zi:lənd] n Nova Zelândia.

next [nɛkst] adj (in space) próximo, vizinho; (in time) seguinte, próximo // adv (place) depois; (time) depois, logo; **~ time** na próxima vez; **~ year** (n)o ano que vem, (n)o próximo ano; **~ door** adv na casa do lado // adj vizinho, seguinte; **~-of-kin** n parentes mpl mais próximos; **~ to** prep junto a, ao lado de.

N.H.S. (Brit) n abbr of **National Health Service.**

nib [nɪb] n ponta or bico da pena.

nibble ['nɪbl] vt mordiscar, beliscar; (ZOOL) roer.

nice [naɪs] adj (likeable) simpático; (kind) amável, atencioso; (pleasant) agradável; (attractive) atraente, bonito; (subtle) sutil, fino; **~-looking** adj bonito; **~ly** adv agradavelmente, bem.

niche [ni:ʃ] n nicho.

nick [nɪk] n (wound) corte m, arranhão m; (cut, indentation) entalhe m, incisão f // vt (col) furtar; **in the ~ of time** na hora H, no momento exato (Pt: -ct-).

nickel ['nɪkl] n níquel m.

nickname ['nɪkneɪm] n apelido (Br), alcunha (Pt) // vt apelidar de (Br), alcunhar de (Pt).

nicotine ['nɪkəti:n] n nicotina.

niece [ni:s] n sobrinha.

Nigeria [naɪ'dʒɪərɪə] n Nigéria; **~n** adj, n nigeriano/a.

niggardly ['nɪgədlɪ] adj (person) avarento, sovina; (amount) miserável.

niggling ['nɪglɪŋ] adj (trifling) insignificante, mesquinho; (annoying) irritante.

night [naɪt] n (gen) noite f; (evening) noitinha, anoitecer m; **last ~** ontem à noite; **the ~ before last** anteontem à noite; **good ~!** boa noite!; **at or by ~** à or de noite; **~cap** n (drink) bebida tomada antes de dormir; **~ club** n boate f, cabaré m; **~dress** n camisola m, camisa de noite (Pt); **~fall** n cair m da noite, anoitecer m; **~gown** n, **~ie** ['naɪtɪ] n camisola (Br), camisa de noite (Pt).

nightingale ['naɪtɪŋgeɪl] n rouxinol m.

nightly ['naɪtlɪ] adj noturno (Pt: -ct-), de noite // adv todas as noites, cada noite.

night: **~mare** n pesadelo; **~ school** n escola no(c)turna; **~ shift** n turno no(c)turno or da noite; ~-time n noite f; ~ watchman n vigia m, guarda-no(c)turno.

nil [nɪl] n nada, zero.

nimble ['nɪmbl] adj (agile) ágil, ligeiro; (skilful) hábil, esperto.

nine [naɪn] num nove; ~teen num dezenove (Br), dezanove (Pt); ~ty num noventa.

ninth [naɪnθ] adj nono.

nip [nɪp] vt (pinch) beliscar; (bite) morder // n (drink) gole m, trago.

nipple ['nɪpl] n (ANAT) bico do seio, mamilo; (of bottle) bocal m, bico; (TECH) bocal (roscado).

nippy ['nɪpɪ] adj (person) rápido, ágil; (taste) picante; (cold) frio.

nitrate ['naɪtreɪt] n nitrato.

nitrogen ['naɪtrədʒən] n nitrogênio.

no [nəʊ] adv não // adj nenhum, não ... algum; I have ~ money não tenho dinheiro algum // n não m, negativa.

nobility [nəʊ'bɪlɪtɪ] n nobreza.

noble ['nəʊbl] adj (person) nobre; (title) de nobreza; (generous) magnânimo; ~man n nobre m, fidalgo.

nobody ['nəʊbədɪ] pron ninguém.

nod [nɔd] vi cumprimentar com a cabeça; (in agreement) acenar (que sim) com a cabeça; (doze) cochilar, dormitar // vt inclinar (a cabeça) // n inclinação f; to ~ off vi cochilar.

noise [nɔɪz] n barulho, ruído; (din) algazarra, gritaria; noisily adv ruidosamente; noisy adj barulhento.

nomad ['nəʊmæd] n nômade m/f; ~ic [-'mædɪk] adj nômade.

nominal ['nɔmɪnl] adj nominal.

nominate ['nɔmɪneɪt] vt (propose) propor; (appoint) nomear; nomination [-'neɪʃən] n nomeação f; (proposal) proposta.

nominee [nɔmɪ'niː] n candidato/a, pessoa nomeada.

non... [nɔn] pref não-, des..., in..., anti-...; ~-alcoholic adj não-alcoólico; ~-aligned adj não-alinhado; ~chalant adj despreocupado; ~-committal ['nɔn-kə'mɪtl] adj (reserved) reservado; (uncommitted) evasivo; ~conformist adj não-conformista, dissidente; ~descript ['nɔndɪskrɪpt] adj indeterminado; (pej) medíocre.

none [nʌn] pron (person) ninguém; (thing) nenhum, nada // adv de modo algum.

nonentity [nɔ'nentɪtɪ] n nulidade f, zero à esquerda m; (person) João Ninguém.

nonetheless [nʌnðə'les] adv no entanto, apesar disso, contudo.

non: ~-fiction n literatura de não-ficção; ~plussed adj perplexo, pasmado.

nonsense ['nɔnsəns] n disparate m, asneira, ninharia.

non-stop ['nɔn'stɔp] adj ininterrupto; (RAIL) direto (Pt: -ct-); (AER) sem escala // adv sem parar.

noodles ['nuːdlz] npl talharim msg.

nook [nuk] n canto, recanto; ~s and crannies esconderijos mpl.

noon [nuːn] n meio-dia m.

no-one ['nəʊwʌn] pron = nobody.

noose [nuːs] n laço corrediço; (hangman's) corda da forca.

nor [nɔː*] conj = neither // adv see neither.

norm [nɔːm] n norma, regra.

normal ['nɔːml] adj (usual) normal; (ordinary) comum, regular; ~ly adv normalmente.

north [nɔːθ] n norte m // adj do norte, setentrional // adv ao or para o norte; N~ America n América do Norte; ~-east n nordeste m; ~ern ['nɔːðən] adj do norte, setentrional; N~ern Ireland n Irlanda do Norte; N~ Pole n Polo Norte; N~ Sea n Mar m do Norte; ~ward(s) ['nɔːθwəd(z)] adv em direção (Pt: -cç-) norte; ~-west n noroeste m.

Norway ['nɔːweɪ] n Noruega; Norwegian [-'wiːdʒən] adj, n norueguês/esa.

nose [nəʊz] n (ANAT) nariz m; (ZOOL) focinho; (sense of smell) olfato; to turn up one's ~ at desdenhar // vi: to ~ about bisbilhotar; ~bleed n hemorragia nasal; ~-dive n (deliberate) vôo picado; (involuntary) parafuso; ~y adj intrometido, abelhudo.

nostalgia [nɔs'tældʒɪə] n nostalgia, saudades fpl; nostalgic adj nostálgico, saudoso.

nostril ['nɔstrɪl] n narina; ~s npl focinho, fuça.

nosy ['nəʊzɪ] adj = nosey.

not [nɔt] adv não; ~ at all não ... de modo nenhum; ~ that he knows não é que ele o saiba; ~ yet ainda não; ~ now agora não; why ~? porque não?

notable ['nəʊtəbl] adj notável.

notary ['nəʊtərɪ] n tabelião m.

notch [nɔtʃ] n entalhe m, corte m.

note [nəʊt] n (MUS, bank~) nota; (letter) nota, bilhete m; (record) nota, anotação f; (fame) fama, reputação f; (tone) tom m // vt (observe) observar, reparar em; (write down) anotar, tomar nota de; ~book n caderno (de notas), agenda; ~-case n carteira; ~d ['nəʊtɪd] adj célebre, conhecido; ~paper n papel m de carta.

nothing ['nʌθɪŋ] n nada; (zero) zero; for ~ (free) de graça, grátis; (in vain) em vão, por nada.

notice ['nəʊtɪs] n (announcement) notícia, anúncio; (attention) atenção f, interesse m; (warning) aviso; (dismissal) demissão f; (resignation) pedido de demissão; (period of time) prazo // vt (observe) observar, notar; to take ~ of prestar atenção a, fazer caso de; at short ~ a curto prazo, com pouca antecipação; until further ~ até nova ordem; ~able adj evidente, óbvio; ~ board n (Brit) quadro de avisos.

notification [nəʊtɪfɪ'keɪʃən] n aviso,

notificação f; **notify** ['nəutifai] vt avisar, notificar.

notion ['nəuʃən] n noção f, idéia; (opinion) opinião f; **~s** npl (US) miudezas fpl.

notorious [nəu'tɔ:rɪəs] adj célebre, notório.

notwithstanding [nɔtwið'stændɪŋ] adv no entanto, não obstante; **~ this** apesar disto.

nougat ['nu:gɑ:] n torrone m, nugá m.

nought [nɔ:t] n zero, nada m.

noun [naun] n substantivo, nome m.

nourish ['nʌrɪʃ] vt nutrir, alimentar; (fig) fomentar, alentar; **~ing** adj nutritivo, alimentício; **~ment** n alimento, nutrimento.

novel ['nɔvl] n romance m; (short) novela // adj (new) novo, recente; (unexpected) insólito; **~ist** n romancista m/f, novelista m/f; **~ty** n novidade f.

November [nəu'vembə*] n novembro (Pt: N-).

novice ['nɔvɪs] n principiante m/f, novato/a; (REL) noviço/a.

now [nau] adv (at the present time) agora; (these days) atualmente (Pt: act-), hoje em dia; **right ~** agora mesmo; **~ and then, ~ and again** de vez em quando; **from ~ on** de agora em diante; **~adays** ['nauədeiz] adv a(c)tualmente, hoje em dia.

nowhere ['nəuweə*] adv (direction) a lugar nenhum; (location) em parte alguma.

nozzle ['nɔzl] n (gen) bico, bocal m; (TECH) tubeira; (: hose) agulheta.

nuance ['nju:ɑ:ns] n nuança, matiz m.

nuclear ['nju:klɪə*] adj nuclear.

nucleus ['nju:klɪəs], pl **-lei** [-lɪaɪ] n núcleo.

nude [nju:d] adj, n nu/nua; **in the ~** nu, pelado.

nudge [nʌdʒ] vt acotovelar.

nudist ['nju:dɪst] n nudista m/f.

nudity ['nju:dɪtɪ] n nudez f.

nuisance ['nju:sns] n amolação f, aborrecimento; (person) chato; **what a ~!** que amolação! (Br), que chatice! (Pt).

null [nʌl] adj: **~ and void** írrito e nulo; **~ify** ['nʌlɪfaɪ] vt anular, invalidar.

numb [nʌm] adj dormente, entorpecido; (fig) insensível // vt adormecer, entorpecer.

number ['nʌmbə*] n número; (numeral) algarismo // vt (pages etc) numerar; **to be ~ed among** achar-se entre; **a ~ of** vários, muitos; **they were ten in ~** eram em número de dez; **~ plate** n placa (do carro).

numbness ['nʌmnɪs] n torpor m, dormência; (fig) insensibilidade f.

numeral ['nju:mərəl] n numeral m, algarismo.

numerical ['nju:merɪkl] adj numérico.

numerous ['nju:mərəs] adj numeroso.

nun [nʌn] n freira, monja.

nurse [nə:s] n enfermeiro/a; (nanny)

ama-seca, babá f // vt (patient) cuidar de, tratar de; (baby) criar, amamentar; (fig) alimentar; **wet ~** ama de leite.

nursery ['nə:sərɪ] n (institution) creche f; (room) quarto das crianças; (for plants) viveiro; **~ rhyme** n poesia infantil; **~ school** n (escola) maternal; **~ slope** n (SKI) rampa para principiantes.

nursing ['nə:sɪŋ] n (profession) enfermagem f; (care) cuidado, assistência; **~ home** n sanatório, clínica de repouso.

nut [nʌt] n (TECH) porca; (BOT) noz f; **~s** adj (col) maluco, biruta; **~case** n (col) doido, biruta m/f; **~crackers** npl quebra-nozes m inv; **~meg** ['nʌtmeg] n noz-moscada f.

nutrient ['nju:trɪənt] n nutrimento.

nutrition [nju:'trɪʃən] n nutrição f, alimentação f; **nutritious** [-ʃəs] adj nutritivo.

nutshell ['nʌtʃel] n casca de noz; **in a ~** em poucas palavras.

nylon ['naɪlɔn] n nylon m // adj de nylon; **~s** npl meias fpl (de nylon).

nymph [nɪmf] n ninfa.

O

oaf [əuf] n imbecil m/f.

oak [əuk] n carvalho // adj de carvalho.

O.A.P. abbr of **old-age pensioner**.

oar [ɔ:*] n remo; **oarsman** n remador m.

oasis [əu'eɪsɪs], pl **-ses** [-si:z] n oásis m.

oath [əuθ] n (juramento); (swear word) palavrão f; (curse) praga; **on ~** sob juramento; **to take an ~** prestar juramento.

oatmeal ['əutmi:l] n farinha or mingau m de aveia.

oats [əuts] n aveia sg.

obedience [ə'bi:dɪəns] n obediência; **in ~ to** em conformidade f com; **obedient** [-ənt] adj obediente.

obesity [əu'bi:sɪtɪ] n obesidade f.

obey [ə'beɪ] vt obedecer; (instructions, regulations) cumprir.

obituary [ə'bɪtjuərɪ] n necrológio.

object ['ɔbdʒɪkt] n (gen, LING) objeto (Pt: -ct-); (purpose) obje(c)tivo // vi [əb'dʒekt]: **to ~ to** (attitude) desaprovar, objetar (Pt: -ct-) a; (proposal) opor-se a; **I ~!** protesto!; **~ion** [əb'dʒekʃən] n objeção (Pt: -çç-) f; **I have no ~ion to...** não tenho nada contra...; **~ionable** [əb'dʒekʃənəbl] adj (gen) desagradável; (conduct) censurável; **~ive** adj, n obje(c)tivo; **~ivity** [ɔbdʒɪk'tɪvɪtɪ] n obje(c)tividade f; **~or** n opositor(a) m/f.

obligation [ɔblɪ'geɪʃən] n obrigação f; (debt) dever m; **without ~** sem compromisso.

obligatory [ə'blɪgətərɪ] adj obrigatório.

oblige [ə'blaɪdʒ] vt (force): **to ~ sb to do sth** obrigar or forçar alguém a fazer algo; (do a favour for) obsequiar, fazer um favor a; **I should be ~d if...** agradeceria muito se...; **obliging** *adj* amável, prestativo.

oblique [ə'bli:k] *adj* oblíquo; *(allusion)* indireto *(Pt: -ct-)*.

obliterate [ə'blitəreit] *vt (erase)* apagar; *(destroy)* destruir.

oblivion [ə'bliviən] *n* esquecimento; **oblivious** [-iəs] *adj:* **oblivious of** inconsciente de, esquecido de.

oblong ['ɔbləŋ] *adj* oblongo, retangular *(Pt: -ct-) // n* re(c)tângulo.

obnoxious [əb'nɔkʃəs] *adj* odioso, detestável; *(smell)* enjoativo.

oboe ['əubəu] *n* oboé *m.*

obscene [əb'si:n] *adj* obsceno; **obscenity** [-'sɛniti] *n* obscenidade *f.*

obscure [əb'skjuə*] *adj* obscuro, pouco claro // *vt* escurecer; *(hide: sun)* esconder; **obscurity** *n* obscuridade *f*, escuridão *f.*

obsequious [əb'si:kwiəs] *adj* obsequioso, servil.

observance [əb'zə:vns] *n* observância, cumprimento; *(ritual)* prática, hábito.

observant [əb'zə:vnt] *adj* atento.

observation [əbzə'veiʃən] *n* observação *f; (by police etc)* vigilância; *(MED)* exame *m.*

observatory [əb'zə:vətri] *n* observatório.

observe [əb'zə:v] *vt (gen)* observar; *(rule)* cumprir; **observer** *n* observador(a) *m/f.*

obsess [əb'sɛs] *vt* obsedar, obcecar; **~ion** [əb'sɛʃən] *n* obsessão *f*, idéia fixa; **~ive** *adj* obsessivo.

obsolescence [ɔbsə'lɛsns] *n* obsolescência; **obsolete** ['ɔbsəli:t] *adj* obsoleto; **to become ~** cair em desuso.

obstacle ['ɔbstəkl] *n* obstáculo; *(nuisance)* estorvo, impedimento; **~ race** *n* corrida de obstáculos.

obstetrician [ɔbstə'triʃən] *n* obstetra *m/f;* **obstetrics** [ɔb'stɛtriks] *n* obstetrícia *sg.*

obstinate ['ɔbstinit] *adj* teimoso, obstinado; *(determined)* pertinaz.

obstruct [əb'strʌkt] *vt* obstruir; *(block)* entupir; *(hinder)* estorvar; **~ion** [əb'strʌkʃən] *n* obstrução *f; (hindrance)* estorvo, obstáculo.

obtain [əb'tein] *vt (get)* obter; *(achieve)* conseguir; **~able** *adj* alcançável.

obtrusive [əb'tru:siv] *adj (person)* intrometido, intruso; *(building etc)* que dá muito na vista.

obvious ['ɔbviəs] *adj (clear)* óbvio, evidente; *(unsubtle)* nada sutil; **~ly** *adv* evidentemente.

occasion [ə'keiʒən] *n (gen)* ocasião *f; (chance)* oportunidade *f*, ensejo; *(reason)* motivo; *(time)* momento, vez *f; (event)* acontecimento // *vt* ocasionar, causar; **~ally** *adv* de vez em quando.

occult [ɔ'kʌlt] *adj (gen)* oculto.

occupant ['ɔkjupənt] *n (of house)* inquilino/a; *(of car)* ocupante *m/f.*

occupation [ɔkju'peiʃən] *n (of house)* posse *f; (job)* emprego; (: *calling)* ofício; **unfit for ~** *(house)* inabitável; **~al hazard** *n* risco profissional.

occupier ['ɔkjupaiə*] *n* inquilino/a.

occupy ['ɔkjupai] *vt (gen)* ocupar; *(house)* morar em; *(time)* encher, tomar; *(attention)* entreter; **to ~ o.s. with** *or* **by doing** *(as job)* dedicar-se a fazer; *(to pass time)* preencher o tempo fazendo.

occur [ə'kə:*] *vi* ocorrer, acontecer; **to ~ to** vir à mente de; **it ~s to me that...** ocorre-me que...; **~rence** *n (event)* acontecimento; *(existence)* existência.

ocean ['əuʃən] *n* oceano; **~-going** *adj* de longo curso; **~ liner** *n* transatlântico.

o'clock [ə'klɔk] *adv:* **it is 5 ~** são cinco horas.

octagonal [ɔk'tægənl] *adj* octogonal.

octane ['ɔktein] *n* octano.

octave ['ɔktiv] *n* oitava.

October [ɔk'təubə*] *n* outubro *(Pt: O-) m.*

octopus ['ɔktəpəs] *n* polvo.

odd [ɔd] *adj (strange)* estranho, esquisito; *(number)* ímpar; *(left over)* avulso, de sobra; **60-~** 60 e tantos; **at ~ times** às vezes, de vez em quando; **to be the ~ one out** ficar sobrando; **~ity** *n* coisa estranha, esquisitice *f; (person)* excêntrico; **~-job man** *n* faz-tudo *m;* **~ jobs** *npl* biscates *mpl*, bicos; **~ly** *adv* curiosamente; **~ments** *npl (COMM)* retalhos *mpl;* **~s** *npl (in betting)* pontos *mpl* de vantagem; **it makes no ~s** dá no mesmo; **at ~s** brigados/as, de mal.

ode [əud] *n* ode *f.*

odious ['əudiəs] *adj* odioso.

odometer [ɔu'dɔmitə*] *n (US)* conta-quilômetros *m inv.*

odour, odor *(US)* ['əudə*] *n* odor *m; (perfume)* fragrância, perfume *m;* **~less** *adj* inodoro.

of [ɔv, əv] *prep* de; **a friend ~ ours** um amigo nosso; **3 ~ them** 3 deles; **the 5th ~ July** dia 5 de julho; **a boy ~ 10** um menino de 10 anos; **made ~ wood** feito de madeira.

off [ɔf] *adj, adv (engine)* desligado; *(light)* apagado; *(tap)* fechado; *(food: bad)* passado; *(milk)* talhado; *(cancelled)* anulado // *prep* de; **to be ~** *(to leave)* ir(-se) embora; **to be 5 km ~** estar a 5 km de distância; **a day ~** um dia de folga *or* livre; **today I had an ~ day** hoje não foi o meu dia; **he had his coat ~** ele havia tirado o casaco; **10 % ~** *(COMM)* 10% de abatimento *or* desconto; **5 km ~ (the road)** a 5 km (da estrada); **~ the coast** em frente à costa; **on the ~ chance** ao acaso.

offal ['ɔfl] *n (CULIN)* sobras *fpl*, restos *mpl.*

off-colour ['ɔf'kʌlə*] *adj (ill)* indisposto.

offence, offense *(US)* [ə'fɛns] *n (crime)* delito; *(insult)* insulto, ofensa; **to take ~ at** ofender-se com, melindrar-se com.

offend [ə'fɛnd] *vt (person)* ofender; **~er**

n delinqüente *m/f*; (*against regulations*) infrator(a) (*Pt*: -ct-).

offensive [əˈfɛnsɪv] *adj* ofensivo, chocante; (*smell etc*) repugnante // *n* (*MIL*) ofensiva.

offer [ˈɔfə*] *n* (*gen*) oferta; (*proposal*) proposta // *vt* oferecer; (*opportunity*) proporcionar; 'on ~' (*COMM*) 'em oferta'; ~ing *n* oferenda; ~tory *n* (*REL*) ofertório.

offhand [ɔfˈhænd] *adj* informal // *adv* de improviso.

office [ˈɔfɪs] *n* (*place*) escritório; (*room*) gabinete *m*; (*position*) cargo, função *f*; **to take** ~ tomar posse; ~ **block** *n* conjunto de escritórios; ~ **boy** *n* contínuo; **officer** *n* (*MIL etc*) oficial *m*; (*of organization*) diretor (*Pt*: -ct-) *m*; (*also:* **police officer**) agente *m/f* policial or de polícia; ~ **worker** *n* empregado/a or funcionário de escritório.

official [əˈfɪʃl] *adj* (*authorized*) autorizado, oficial // *n* funcionário/a (público/a); ~**dom** *n* burocracia.

officious [əˈfɪʃəs] *adj* intrometido.

offing [ˈɔfɪŋ] *n*: **in the** ~ (*fig*) em perspectiva.

off: ~-**licence** *n* (*Brit*: *shop*) loja de bebidas alcoólicas; ~-**peak** *adj* de temporada de pouco consumo or pouca atividade (*Pt*: act-); ~-**putting** *adj* desconcertante; ~-**season** *adj*, *adv* fora de estação or temporada.

offset [ˈɔfsɛt] (*irr: like* **set**) *vt* (*counteract*) compensar, contrabalançar // *n* (*also:* ~ **printing**) ofsete *m*.

offshore [ɔfˈʃɔː*] *adv* a pouca distância da costa.

offside [ˈɔfˈsaɪd] *adj* (*SPORT*) impedido.

offspring [ˈɔfsprɪŋ] *n* descendência, prole *f*.

off: ~**stage** *adv* nos bastidores; ~-**the-peg** *adv* pronto; ~-**white** *adj* quase branco.

often [ˈɔfn] *adv* muitas vezes, freqüentemente.

ogle [ˈəʊgl] *vt* comer com os olhos.

oil [ɔɪl] *n* óleo; (*petroleum*) petróleo; (*CULIN*) azeite *m* // *vt* (*machine*) lubrificar; ~**can** *n* almotolia; ~**field** *n* campo petrolífero; ~-**fired** *adj* que usa óleo combustível; ~ **painting** *n* pintura a óleo; ~ **refinery** *n* refinaria de petróleo; ~ **rig** *n* torre *f* de perfuração; ~**skins** *npl* capa *sg* de oleado; ~ **tanker** *n* petroleiro; ~ **well** *n* poço petrolífero; ~**y** *adj* oleoso; (*food*) gorduroso.

ointment [ˈɔɪntmənt] *n* pomada.

O.K., okay [ˈəʊˈkeɪ] *excl* está bem, está bom; (*col*) tá (bem or bom), OK // *adj* bom; (*correct*) certo // *vt* aprovar.

old [əʊld] *adj* velho; (*former*) antigo, anterior; **how** ~ **are you?** quantos anos você tem?; **he's 10 years** ~ ele tem 10 anos; ~**er brother** irmão *m* mais velho; ~ **age** *n* velhice *f*; ~-**age pensioner** (**O.A.P.**) *n* aposentado/a

(*Br*), reformado/a (*Pt*); ~-**fashioned** *adj* antiquado, fora de moda.

olive [ˈɔlɪv] *n* (*fruit*) azeitona; (*tree*) oliveira // *adj* (*also:* ~-**green**) verde-oliva; ~ **oil** *n* azeite *m* de oliva.

Olympic [əʊˈlɪmpɪk] *adj* olímpico; **the** ~ **Games, the** ~**s** os Jogos Olímpicos, as Olimpíadas.

omelet(te) [ˈɔmlɪt] *n* omelete *f*.

omen [ˈəʊmən] *n* presságio, agouro.

ominous [ˈɔmɪnəs] *adj* ameaçador(a), de mau agouro.

omission [əʊˈmɪʃən] *n* omissão *f*; (*error*) descuido, negligência.

omit [əʊˈmɪt] *vt* omitir; (*by mistake*) esquecer.

on [ɔn] *prep* sobre, em (cima de) // *adv* (*machine*) em funcionamento; (*light*) aceso; (*radio*) ligado; (*tap*) aberto; **is the meeting still** ~? ainda vai haver reunião?; **when is this film** ~? quando vão passar este filme?; ~ **the wall** (pendurado) na parede; ~ **television** na televisão; ~ **horseback** a cavalo; ~ **seeing this** ao ver isto; ~ **arrival** ao chegar; ~ **the left** à esquerda; ~ **Friday** na sexta-feira; **a week** ~ **Friday** daqui a uma semana a partir de sexta-feira; **to have one's coat** ~ estar de casaco; **to go** ~ continuar (em frente); **it's not** ~! isso não se faz!

once [wʌns] *adv* uma vez; (*formerly*) outrora // *conj* uma vez que; **at** ~ imediatamente; (*simultaneously*) ao mesmo tempo; ~ **a week** uma vez por semana; ~ **more** mais uma vez; ~ **and for all** definitivamente; ~ **upon a time** era uma vez.

oncoming [ˈɔnkʌmɪŋ] *adj* (*traffic*) que vem de frente.

one [wʌn] *det, num* um/uma // *pron* um/uma; (*impersonal*) a gente; (+ *verb*: *impersonal*) se // *adj* (*sole*) único; (*same*) mesmo; **this** ~ este/esta; **that** ~ esse/essa, aquele/aquela; ~ **by** ~ um por um; ~ **never knows** nunca se sabe; ~ **another** um ao outro; ~ **day excursion** *n* (*US*) bilhete *m* de ida e volta; ~-**man** *adj* (*business*) individual; ~-**man band** *n* um homem-orquestra; ~**self** *pron* se; (*after prep, also emphatic*) si (mesmo/a); '~-**way**' 'mão única' (*Br*), 'sentido único' (*Pt*).

ongoing [ˈɔngəʊɪŋ] *adj* contínuo, em andamento.

onion [ˈʌnjən] *n* cebola.

onlooker [ˈɔnlʊkə*] *n* espectador(a) *m/f*.

only [ˈəʊnlɪ] *adv* somente, apenas // *adj* único, só // *conj* só que, porém; **an** ~ **child** um filho único; **not** ~ ... **but also**... não só ... mas também...

onset [ˈɔnsɛt] *n* (*beginning*) começo; (*attack*) ataque *m*.

onslaught [ˈɔnslɔːt] *n* ataque *m* violento, arremetida.

onto [ˈɔntu] *prep* = **on to**.

onus [ˈəʊnəs] *n* responsabilidade *f*.

onward(s) [ˈɔnwəd(z)] *adv* (*move*) para

diante, para a frente; **from this time ~** de (ag)ora em diante.

onyx ['ɒnɪks] n ônix m.

ooze [u:z] vi ressumar, filtrar-se.

opal ['əupl] n opala.

opaque [əu'peɪk] adj opaco, fosco.

open ['əupn] adj (gen) aberto; (road) livre; (meeting) público; (admiration) declarado // vt abrir // vi (flower, eyes, door, debate) abrir-se; (book etc: commence) começar; **to ~ on to** vt fus (subj: room, door) dar para, ter vista para; **to ~ up** vt abrir; (blocked road) desobstruir // vi abrir-se, começar; **in the ~ (air)** ao ar livre; **~ing** n abertura; (start) início; (opportunity) oportunidade f; (job) vaga; **~ly** adv abertamente; **~-minded** adj aberto, imparcial; **~-necked** adj aberto no colo.

opera ['ɒpərə] n ópera; **~ glasses** npl binóculo sg de teatro; **~ house** n teatro lírico or de ópera.

operate ['ɒpəreɪt] vt (machine) fazer funcionar, pôr em funcionamento; (company) dirigir // vi funcionar; (drug) fazer efeito; **to ~ on sb** (MED) operar alguém.

operatic [ɒpə'rætɪk] adj lírico, operístico.

operating ['ɒpəreɪtɪŋ]: **~ table** n mesa de operações; **~ theatre** n sala de operações.

operation [ɒpə'reɪʃən] n (gen) operação f; (of machine) funcionamento; **to be in ~** estar em vigor or funcionando; **~al** adj operacional.

operative ['ɒpərətɪv] adj (measure) em vigor.

operator ['ɒpəreɪtə*] n (of machine) operador(a) m/f, manipulador(a) m/f; (TEL) telefonista m/f.

operetta [ɒpə'rɛtə] n opereta.

ophthalmic [ɒf'θælmɪk] adj oftálmico.

opinion [ə'pɪnɪən] n (gen) opinião f; (point of view) parecer m, juízo; **in my ~** a meu ver; **~ated** adj teimoso, opinioso; **~ poll** n pesquisa.

opium ['əupɪəm] n ópio.

opponent [ə'pəunənt] n adversário/a, oponente m/f.

opportune ['ɒpətju:n] adj oportuno; **opportunist** [-'tju:nɪst] n oportunista m/f.

opportunity [ɒpə'tju:nɪtɪ] n oportunidade f.

oppose [ə'pəuz] vt opor-se a; **to be ~d to sth** opor-se a algo, estar contra algo; **opposing** adj (side) oposto, contrário.

opposite ['ɒpəzɪt] adj oposto, (house etc) em frente // adv (lá) em frente // prep em frente de, defronte de // n o oposto, o contrário.

opposition [ɒpə'zɪʃən] n oposição f.

oppress [ə'prɛs] vt oprimir; **~ion** [ə'prɛʃən] n opressão f; **~ive** adj opressivo.

opt [ɒpt] vi: **to ~ for** escolher; **to ~**

do optar por fazer; **to ~ out of doing sth** optar por não fazer algo.

optical ['ɒptɪkl] adj ótico (Pt: -pt-).

optician [ɒp'tɪʃən] n oculista m/f.

optimism ['ɒptɪmɪzəm] n otimismo (Pt: -pt-).

optimist ['ɒptɪmɪst] n o(p)timista m/f; **~ic** [-'mɪstɪk] adj o(p)timista.

optimum ['ɒptɪməm] adj ó(p)timo.

option ['ɒpʃən] n opção f; **to keep one's ~s open** (fig) manter as opções em aberto; **~al** adj opcional, facultativo.

opulent ['ɒpjulənt] adj opulento.

or [ɔ:*] conj ou; (with negative): **he hasn't seen ~ heard anything** ele não viu nem ouviu nada; **~ else** senão.

oracle ['ɒrəkl] n oráculo.

oral ['ɔ:rəl] adj oral // n exame m oral.

orange ['ɒrɪndʒ] n (fruit) laranja // adj cor de laranja, alaranjado.

oration [ɔ:'reɪʃən] n oração f; **orator** ['ɒrətə*] n orador(a) m/f.

orbit ['ɔ:bɪt] n órbita // vt/i orbitar.

orchard ['ɔ:tʃəd] n pomar m.

orchestra ['ɔ:kɪstrə] n orquestra; **orchestral** [-'kɛstrəl] adj orquestral.

orchid ['ɔ:kɪd] n orquídea.

ordain [ɔ:'deɪn] vt (REL) ordenar, decretar; (decide) decidir, mandar.

ordeal [ɔ:'di:l] n experiência penosa, provação f.

order ['ɔ:də*] n (gen) ordem f; (type, kind) tipo; (state) estado; (COMM) pedido, encomenda // vt (also: **put in ~**) pôr em ordem, arrumar; (in restaurant) pedir; (COMM) encomendar, pedir; (command) mandar, ordenar; **in ~** (of document) em ordem; **in ~ to do** a fim de fazer; **to ~ sb to do sth** mandar alguém fazer algo; **~ly** n (MIL) ordenança m; (MED) servente m/f // adj (room) arrumado, ordenado; (person) metódico.

ordinary ['ɔ:dnrɪ] adj comum, usual; (pej) ordinário, medíocre; **out of the ~** fora do comum.

ordnance ['ɔ:dnəns] n (MIL: unit) artilharia; **O~ Survey** (Brit) n serviço oficial de topografia e cartografia.

ore [ɔ:*] n minério.

organ ['ɔ:gən] n (gen) órgão m; **~ic** [ɔ:'gænɪk] adj orgânico.

organism ['ɔ:gənɪzəm] n organismo.

organist ['ɔ:gənɪst] n organista m/f.

organization [ɔ:gənaɪ'zeɪʃən] n organização f; **organize** ['ɔ:gənaɪz] vt organizar; **organizer** ['ɔ:gənaɪzə*] n organizador(a) m/f.

orgasm ['ɔ:gæzəm] n orgasmo.

orgy ['ɔ:dʒɪ] n orgia.

Orient ['ɔ:rɪənt] n Oriente m; **oriental** [-'ɛntl] adj oriental.

orientate ['ɔ:rɪənteɪt] vt orientar.

origin ['ɒrɪdʒɪn] n origem f; (point of departure) procedência.

original [ə'rɪdʒɪnl] adj original; (first) primeiro, (earlier) primitivo // n original m; **~ity** [-'nælɪtɪ] n originalidade f; **~ly**

adv (*at first*) originalmente; (*with originality*) com originalidade.

originate [ə'rɪdʒɪneɪt] *vi*: **to ~ from** *or* **in** originar-se de, surgir de.

ornament ['ɔːnəmənt] *n* ornamento; (*trinket*) quinquilharia; **~al** [-'mɛntl] *adj* decorativo, ornamental.

ornate [ɔː'neɪt] *adj* enfeitado, requintado.

ornithologist [ɔːnɪ'θɔlədʒɪst] *n* ornitólogo; **ornithology** [-dʒɪ] *n* ornitologia.

orphan ['ɔːfn] *n* órfão/órfã // *vt*: **to be ~ed** ficar orfão; **~age** *n* orfanato.

orthodox ['ɔːθədɔks] *adj* ortodoxo; **~y** *n* ortodoxia.

orthopaedic, orthopedic (*US*) [ɔːθə'piːdɪk] *adj* ortopédico; **~s** *n* ortopedia *sg*.

oscillate ['ɔsɪleɪt] *vi* oscilar; (*person*) vacilar, hesitar.

ostensibly [ɔs'tɛnsɪblɪ] *adv* aparentemente.

ostentatious [ɔstɛn'teɪʃəs] *adj* aparatoso, pomposo; (*person*) ostentoso.

osteopath ['ɔstɪəpæθ] *n* osteopata *m/f*.

ostracize ['ɔstrəsaɪz] *vt* condenar ao ostracismo.

ostrich ['ɔstrɪtʃ] *n* avestruz *m/f*.

other ['ʌðə*] *adj* outro; **~ than** (*in another way*) de outro modo que; (*apart from*) senão; **~wise** *adv*, *conj* de outra maneira; (*if not*) senão.

otter ['ɔtə*] *n* lontra.

ought [ɔːt] *pt* **ought** *auxiliary vb*: **I ~ to do it** eu deveria fazê-lo; **this ~ to have been corrected** isto deveria ter sido corrigido; **he ~ to win** (*probability*) ele deve ganhar.

ounce [auns] *n* onça (*28.35g*).

our ['auə*] *adj* nosso; **~s** *pron* (o) nosso/(a) nossa *etc*; **~selves** *pron pl* (*reflexive, after prep*) nós; (*emphatic*) nós mesmos/as.

oust [aust] *vt* desalojar, expulsar.

out [aut] *adv* fora; (*not at home*) fora (de casa); (*light, fire*) apagado; **~ there** lá, lá fora; **he's ~** (*absent*) não está, está fora; **get ~!** fora!; **to be ~ in one's calculations** enganar-se nos cálculos; **to run ~** sair correndo; **~ loud** em voz alta; **~ of** (*outside*) fora de; (*because of: anger etc*) por; **~ of petrol** sem gasolina; "**~ of order**" "não funciona", "avariado"; **~-of-the-way** (*fig*) fora do comum; (*place*) remoto.

outback ['autbæk] *n* interior *m*.

outboard ['autbɔːd] *adj*: **~ motor** motor *m* de popa.

outbreak ['autbreɪk] *n* (*of war*) deflagração *f*; (*of disease*) surto, epidêmico; (*of violence etc*) explosão *f*.

outburst ['autbɔːst] *n* explosão *f*.

outcast ['autkɑːst] *n* pária *m/f*.

outcome ['autkʌm] *n* resultado.

outcry ['autkraɪ] *n* manifestação *f* de protesto, gritaria.

outdated [aut'deɪtɪd] *adj* antiquado, fora de moda.

outdo [aut'duː] (*irr: like* **do**) *vt* ultrapassar, exceder.

outdoor [aut'dɔː*] *adj*, **~s** *adv* ao ar livre.

outer ['autə*] *adj* exterior, externo; **~ space** *n* o espaço (exterior).

outfit ['autfɪt] *n* equipamento; (*clothes*) roupa, traje *m*; **~ter's** *n* fornecedor *m* de roupas.

outgoing ['autgəuɪŋ] *adj* (*character*) extrovertido; sociável; **~s** *npl* despesas *fpl*.

outgrow [aut'grəu] (*irr: like* **grow**) *vt*: **he has ~n his clothes** a roupa ficou pequena para ele.

outing ['autɪŋ] *n* excursão *f*; passeio.

outlandish [aut'lændɪʃ] *adj* estranho, bizarro.

outlast [aut'lɑːst] *vt* sobreviver a.

outlaw ['autlɔː] *n* fora-da-lei *m/f* // *vt* (*person*) declarar fora da lei; (*practice*) declarar ilegal.

outlay ['autleɪ] *n* despesa.

outlet ['autlɛt] *n* saída; (*of pipe*) desagüe *m*, escoadouro; (*for emotion*) desabafo; (*US: ELEC*) tomada; (*also: retail ~*) posto de venda.

outline ['autlaɪn] *n* (*shape*) contorno, perfil *m*; (*plan*) traçado; (*sketch*) esboço, linhas *fpl* gerais.

outlive [aut'lɪv] *vt* sobreviver a.

outlook ['autluk] *n* perspectiva; (*opinion*) ponto de vista.

outlying ['autlaɪɪŋ] *adj* afastado, remoto.

outmoded [aut'məudɪd] *adj* antiquado, fora de moda, obsoleto.

outnumber [aut'nʌmbə*] *vt* exceder em número.

outpatient ['autpeɪʃənt] *n* paciente *m/f* externo/a *or* de ambulatório.

outpost ['autpəust] *n* posto avançado.

output ['autput] *n* (volume *m* de) produção *f*; (*TEC*) rendimento.

outrage ['autreɪdʒ] *n* (*scandal*) escândalo; (*atrocity*) atrocidade *f* // *vt* ultrajar; **~ous** [-'reɪdʒəs] *adj* ultrajante, escandaloso.

outright [aut'raɪt] *adv* completamente // *adj* ['autraɪt] completo.

outset ['autsɛt] *n* início, princípio.

outside [aut'saɪd] *n* exterior *m*; (*surface*) superfície *f*; (*aspect*) aspecto (exterior) // *adj* exterior, externo // *adv* (lá) fora // *prep* fora de; (*beyond*) além (dos limites) de; **at the ~** (*fig*) no máximo; **~ lane** *n* (*AUT: in Britain*) pista da direita; **~-left** *n* (*FOOTBALL*) ponta esquerda; (*player*) ponta *m* esquerda; **outsider** *n* (*stranger*) estranho, forasteiro.

outsize ['autsaɪz] *adj* (*clothes*) de tamanho extra-grande.

outskirts ['autskɔːts] *npl* arredores *mpl*, subúrbios *mpl*.

outspoken [aut'spəukən] *adj* franco, sem rodeios.

outstanding [aut'stændɪŋ] *adj*

excepcional, saliente; (unfinished) pendente.

outstay [aut'steɪ] vt: **to ~ one's welcome** abusar da hospitalidade (demorando mais tempo).

outstretched [aut'stretʃt] adj (hand) estendido, esticado.

outward ['autwəd] adj (sign, appearances) externo; (journey) de ida; **~ly** adv aparentemente, para fora.

outweigh [aut'weɪ] vt pesar mais que.

outwit [aut'wɪt] vt superar, ser mais esperto que.

oval ['əuvl] adj ovalado // n oval m.

ovary ['əuvərɪ] n ovário.

ovation [əu'veɪʃən] n ovação f.

oven ['ʌvn] n forno; **~proof** adj refratário (Pt: -ct-).

over ['əuvə*] adj (or adv) (finished) acabado // prep por cima de; (above) sobre; (on the other side of) do outro lado de; (more than) mais de; (during) durante; **~ here** por aqui, cá; **~ there** por ali, lá; **all ~** (everywhere) por todos os lados; (finished) acabado; **~ and ~** (again) repetidamente; **~ and above** além de; **to ask sb ~** convidar alguém; **to bend ~** inclinar-se (sobre).

over... [əuvə*] pref sobre..., super...; **~abundant** adj superabundante.

overall ['əuvərɔːl] adj (length) total; (study) global // adv [əuvər'ɔːl] globalmente; **~s** npl macacão msg (Br), (fato) macaco msg (Pt).

overbalance [əuvə'bæləns] vi perder o equilíbrio, desequilibrar-se.

overbearing [əuvə'bɛərɪŋ] adj autoritário, dominador(a); (arrogant) arrogante.

overboard ['əuvəbɔːd] adv (NAUT) ao mar; **man ~!** homem ao mar!

overcast ['əuvəkɑːst] adj nublado.

overcharge [əuvə'tʃɑːdʒ] vt: **to ~ sb** cobrar alguém em excesso.

overcoat ['əuvəkəut] n sobretudo, casaco.

overcome [əuvə'kʌm] (irr: like come) vt (gen) vencer, dominar; (difficulty) superar.

overcrowded [əuvə'kraudɪd] adj superlotado, apinhado de gente; (country) superpovoado.

overdo [əuvə'duː] (irr: like do) vt exagerar, exceder; (overcook) cozinhar demais.

overdose ['əuvədəus] n dose f excessiva.

overdraft ['əuvədrɑːft] n saldo negativo.

overdrawn [əuvə'drɔːn] adj (account) sem fundos, a descoberto.

overdue [əuvə'djuː] adj atrasado; (COMM) vencido; (recognition) tardio.

overestimate [əuvər'estɪmeɪt] vt sobrestimar.

overexcited [əuvərɪk'saɪtɪd] adj superexcitado.

overexpose [əuvərɪk'spəuz] vt (PHOT) expor demasiado (à luz).

overflow [əuvə'fləu] vi transbordar // n

['əuvəfləu] (excess) excesso; (of river) inundação f; (also: **~ pipe**) tubo de descarga, ladrão m.

overgrown [əuvə'grəun] adj (garden) coberto de vegetação.

overhaul [əuvə'hɔːl] vt examinar, revisar // n ['əuvəhɔːl] revisão f.

overhead [əuvə'hɛd] adv por cima, em cima // adj ['əuvəhɛd] aéreo, elevado; (railway) suspenso // n **~** (US), **~s** npl despesas fpl gerais.

overhear [əuvə'hɪə*] (irr: like hear) vt ouvir por acaso.

overjoyed [əuvə'dʒɔɪd] adj maravilhado, cheio de alegria.

overland ['əuvəlænd] adj, adv por terra.

overlap [əuvə'læp] vi coincidir or sobrepor-se em parte // n ['əuvəlæp] sobreposição f.

overleaf [əuvə'liːf] adv no verso.

overload [əuvə'ləud] vt sobrecarregar.

overlook [əuvə'luk] vt (have view on) dar para; (miss: by mistake) deixar passar; (: deliberately) fazer vista grossa a; (forgive) perdoar.

overnight [əuvə'naɪt] adv durante a noite; (fig) da noite para o dia // adj noturno (Pt: -ct-); **to stay ~** passar a noite, pernoitar.

overpass ['əuvəpɑːs] n passagem f elevada.

overpower [əuvə'pauə*] vt dominar, subjugar; **~ing** adj (heat, stench) sufocante.

overrate [əuvə'reɪt] vt sobrestimar, supervalorizar; (cost) cotar acima do preço.

override [əuvə'raɪd] (irr: like ride) vt (order, objection) não fazer caso de, ignorar; **overriding** adj primordial.

overrule [əuvə'ruːl] vt (decision) anular; (claim) indeferir.

overseas [əuvə'siːz] adv ultra-mar; (abroad) no estrangeiro, no exterior // adj (trade) exterior; (visitor) estrangeiro.

overseer ['əuvəsɪə*] n (in factory) superintendente m/f; (foreman) capataz m.

overshadow [əuvə'ʃædəu] vt (fig) eclipsar, ofuscar.

overshoot [əuvə'ʃuːt] (irr: like shoot) vt passar.

oversight ['əuvəsaɪt] n descuido.

oversleep [əuvə'sliːp] (irr: like sleep) vi dormir além da hora.

overspend [əuvə'spɛnd] (irr: like spend) vi gastar demais.

overspill ['əuvəspɪl] n excesso (de população).

overstate [əuvə'steɪt] vt exagerar; **~ment** n afirmação f exagerada.

overt [əu'vɜːt] adj aberto, indissimulado.

overtake [əuvə'teɪk] (irr: like take) vt superar, exceder; (AUT) ultrapassar; **overtaking** n (AUT) ultrapassagem m.

overthrow [əuvə'θrəu] (irr: like throw) vt (government) derrubar.

overtime ['əuvətaɪm] n horas fpl extras.

overtone ['ǝuvǝtǝun] *n* (*fig*) insinuação *f*, alusão *f*.

overture ['ǝuvǝtʃuǝ*] *n* (*MUS*) abertura; (*fig*) proposta, oferta.

overturn [ǝuvǝ'tǝːn] *vt/i* virar; (*car*) capotar.

overweight [ǝuvǝ'weit] *adj* gordo demais, com excesso de peso.

overwhelm [ǝuvǝ'wɛlm] *vt* esmagar; ~**ing** *adj* (*victory*, *defeat*) esmagador(a); (*desire*) irresistível.

overwork [ǝuvǝ'wǝːk] *n* excesso de trabalho // *vt* sobrecarregar de trabalho // *vi* trabalhar demais.

overwrought [ǝuvǝ'rɔːt] *adj* extenuado, superexcitado.

owe [ǝu] *vt* dever; to ~ sb sth, to ~ sth to sb dever algo a alguém; owing to *prep* devido a, por causa de.

owl [aul] *n* coruja.

own [ǝun] *vt* possuir, ter // *adj* próprio; a room of my ~ meu próprio quarto; to get one's ~ back ir à forra; on one's ~ sozinho; (*unaided*) sem auxílio; to ~ up *vi* confessar; ~**er** *n* dono, proprietário/a; (*possessor*) possuidor(a) *m/f*; ~**ership** *n* posse *f*.

ox [ɔks], *pl* ~**en** [ɔksn] *n* boi *m*.

oxide ['ɔksaid] *n* óxido.

oxtail ['ɔksteil] *n*: ~ **soup** rabada.

oxygen ['ɔksidʒǝn] *n* oxigênio; ~ **mask / tent** máscara/tenda de oxigênio.

oyster ['ɔistǝ*] *n* ostra.

oz. *abbr of* **ounce(s)**.

ozone ['ǝuzǝun] *n* ozônio.

P

p [piː] *abbr of* **penny**, **pence**.

p.a. *abbr of* **per annum**.

pa [pɑː] *n* (*col*) papai *m*, paizinho.

pace [peis] *n* (*step*) passo; (*rhythm*) ritmo // *vi*: to ~ **up and down** andar de um lado para o outro; to **keep** ~ **with** acompanhar o passo de; (*events*) manter-se inteirado de ou atualizado com; ~**maker** *n* (*MED*) regulador *m* cardíaco, marca-passo *m*.

pacific [pǝ'sifik] *adj* pacífico // *n*: the P~ (Ocean) o (Oceano) Pacífico.

pacifier ['pæsifaiǝ*] *n* (*US*) chupeta.

pacifist ['pæsifist] *n* pacifista *m/f*.

pacify ['pæsifai] *vt* (*soothe*) acalmar, serenar; (*country*) pacificar.

pack [pæk] *n* (*gen*) pacote *m*, embrulho; (*US: packet*) maço; (*of hounds*) matilha; (*of thieves etc*) bando, quadrilha; (*of cards*) baralho; (*bundle*) trouxa; (*back* ~) mochila // *vi* fazer as malas // *vt* (*wrap*) empacotar, embrulhar; (*fill*) encher; (*in suitcase etc*) arrumar (na mala); (*cram*) entupir, entulhar; (*fig: meeting etc*) encher de partidários; to ~ **sb off** despachar alguém; ~ **it in!** (*col*) pára com isso!; to ~ **one's cases** fazer as malas.

package ['pækidʒ] *n* pacote *m*; (*bulky*)

embrulho, fardo; (*also*: ~ **deal**) pacote de acordo; ~ **tour** *n* excursão *f* organizada.

packet ['pækit] *n* pacote *m*, maço; (*NAUT*) paquete *m*.

packing ['pækiŋ] *n* embalagem *f*; (*external*) envoltório; (*internal*) enchimento; ~ **case** *n* caixa de embalagem.

pact [pækt] *n* pacto; (*COMM*) convênio.

pad [pæd] *n* (*of paper*) bloco; (*cushion*) almofada; (*launching* ~) plataforma (de lançamento); (*foot*) pata; (*col: flat*) casa // *vi* caminhar sem ruído; ~**ding** *n* enchimento, recheio; (*fig*) palavreado inútil.

paddle ['pædl] *n* (*oar*) remo curto // *vt* remar // *vi* (*with feet*) patinhar; ~ **steamer** *n* vapor *m* movido a rodas; **paddling pool** *n* lago de recreação.

paddock ['pædǝk] *n* cercado, paddock *m*.

paddy field ['pædi-] *n* arrozal *m*.

padlock ['pædlɔk] *n* cadeado // *vt* fechar com cadeado.

padre ['pɑːdri] *n* capelão *m*, padre *m*.

paediatrics, pediatrics (*US*) [piːdi'ætriks] *n* pediatria *sg*.

pagan ['peigǝn] *adj*, *n* pagão/pagã *m/f*.

page [peidʒ] *n* página; (*also*: ~ **boy**) mensageiro // *vt* (*in hotel etc*) mandar chamar.

pageant ['pædʒǝnt] *n* (*procession*) cortejo suntuoso; (*show*) desfile alegórico; ~**ry** *n* pompa, fausto.

pagoda [pǝ'gǝudǝ] *n* pagode *m*.

paid [peid] *pt*, *pp of* **pay** // *adj* (*work*) remunerado; (*official*) assalariado; to **put** ~ **to** acabar com.

pail [peil] *n* balde *m*.

pain [pein] *n* dor *f*; to **be in** ~ sofrer, sentir dor; **on** ~ **of death** sob pena de morte; to **take** ~**s to do sth** dar-se ao trabalho de fazer algo; ~**ed** *adj* (*expression*) magoado, aflito; ~**ful** *adj* doloroso; (*difficult*) penoso; (*disagreeable*) desagradável; ~**fully** *adv* (*fig: very*) terrivelmente; ~**killer** *n* analgésico, calmante *m*; ~**less** *adj* sem dor, indolor; **painstaking** ['peinzteikiŋ] *adj* (*person*) esmerado, meticuloso.

paint [peint] *n* pintura // *vt* pintar; to ~ **one's face** pintar-se, maquilar-se; to ~ **the town red** (*fig*) cair na farra; to ~ **the door blue** pintar a porta de azul; ~**brush** (*artist's*) pincel *m*; (*decorator's*) broxa; ~**er** *n* pintor(a) *m/f*; ~**ing** *n* pintura.

pair [pɛǝ*] *n* (*of shoes*, *gloves etc*) par *m*; (*of people*) casal *m*; **a** ~ **of scissors** uma tesoura; **a** ~ **of trousers** uma calça.

pajamas [pi'dʒɑːmǝz] *npl* (*US*) pijama *msg*.

Pakistan [pɑːki'stɑːn] *n* Paquistão *m*; ~**i** *adj*, *n* paquistanês/esa *m/f*.

pal [pæl] *n* (*col*) camarada *m/f*, companheiro/a.

palace ['pælǝs] *n* palácio.

palatable ['pælɪtəbl] *adj* saboroso, apetitoso; (*acceptable*) aceitável.

palate ['pælɪt] *n* paladar *m*.

palaver [pə'lɑːvə*] *n* (*fuss*) confusão *f*; (*hindrances*) complicação *f*.

pale [peɪl] *adj* (*gen*) pálido; (*colour*) claro; **to grow ~** empalidecer; **to be beyond the ~** passar dos limites; **~ness** *n* palidez *f*.

Palestine ['pælɪstaɪn] *n* Palestina; **Palestinian** [-'tɪnɪən] *adj*, *n* palestino/a.

palette ['pælɪt] *n* palheta.

paling ['peɪlɪŋ] *n* (*stake*) estaca; (*fence*) cerca.

palisade [pælɪ'seɪd] *n* paliçada.

pall [pɔːl] *n* (*of smoke*) manto // *vi* tornar-se insípido; (*fig*) perder a graça.

pallid ['pælɪd] *adj* pálido, descorado.

palm [pɑːm] *n* (*hand*) palma; (*also:* **~ tree**) palmeira // *vt*: **to ~ sth off on sb** (*col*) impingir algo a alguém; **~ist** *n* quiromante *m/f*; **P~ Sunday** *n* Domingo de Ramos.

palpable ['pælpəbl] *adj* palpável.

palpitation [pælpɪ'teɪʃən] *n* palpitação *f*; **to have ~s** sentir palpitações.

paltry ['pɔːltrɪ] *adj* (*insignificant*) insignificante, fútil; (*miserable*) vil, reles *inv*.

pamper ['pæmpə*] *vt* mimar.

pamphlet ['pæmflət] *n* panfleto.

pan [pæn] *n* (*also:* **sauce~**) panela (*Br*), caçarola (*Pt*); (*also:* **frying ~**) frigideira; (*of lavatory*) vaso // *vi* (*CINEMA*) tomar uma panorâmica.

panacea [pænə'sɪə] *n* panacéia.

Panama ['pænəmɑː] *n* Panamá *m*.

pancake ['pænkeɪk] *n* panqueca.

panda ['pændə] *n* panda *m/f*; **~ car** *n* patrulhinha.

pandemonium [pændɪ'məʊnɪəm] *n* (*noise*) pandemônio; (*mess*) caos *m*.

pander ['pændə*] *vi*: **to ~** to favorecer.

pane [peɪn] *n* vidraça, vidro.

panel ['pænl] *n* (*of wood*) painel *m*; (*of cloth*) pano; (*RADIO, TV*) júri *m*; **~ling**, **~ing** (*US*) *n* painéis *mpl*.

pang [pæŋ] *n*: **~s of conscience** dor *f* de consciência; **~s of hunger** fome *f* aguda.

panic ['pænɪk] *n* pânico // *vi* entrar em pânico; **~ky** *adj* (*person*) assustadiço, apavorado; **~-stricken** *adj* tomado de pânico.

pannier ['pænɪə*] *n* (*on bicycle*) cesta; (*on mule etc*) cesto, alcofa.

panorama [pænə'rɑːmə] *n* panorama *m*.

pansy ['pænzɪ] *n* (*BOT*) amor-perfeito; (*col*) bicha (*Br*), maricas *m* (*Pt*).

pant [pænt] *vi* arquejar, ofegar.

panther ['pænθə*] *n* pantera.

panties ['pæntɪz] *npl* (*Brit*) calcinha *sg* (*Br*), cuecas *fpl* (*Pt*).

pantomime ['pæntəmaɪm] *n* pantomima, *revista musical representada no Natal, baseada em contos de fada*.

pantry ['pæntrɪ] *n* despensa.

pants [pænts] *n* (*man's*) cueca *sg* (*Br*),

cuecas *fpl* (*Pt*); (*US: trousers*) calça *sg* (*Br*), calças *fpl* (*Pt*); (*woman's*) calcinha *sg* (*Br*), cuecas *fpl* (*Pt*); **panty hose** *n* (*US*) meia-calça (*Br*), collants *mpl* (*Pt*).

papal ['peɪpəl] *adj* papal.

paper ['peɪpə*] *n* papel *m*; (*also:* **news~**) jornal *m*; (*study, article*) artigo, dissertação *f*; (*exam*) exame *m*, prova // *adj* de papel // *vt* empapelar; (*identity*) **~s** *npl* documentos *mpl*; **~back** *n* livro de capa mole; **~ bag** *n* saco de papel; **~ clip** *n* clipe *m*; **~ hankie** *n* lenço de papel; **~ money** *n* papel-moeda *m*; **~weight** *n* pesa-papéis *m inv*; **~work** *n* trabalho burocrático; (*pej*) papelada.

papier-mâché ['pæpɪeɪ'mæʃeɪ] *n* papel *m* machê.

paprika ['pæprɪkə] *n* páprica, pimentão-doce *m*.

par [pɑː*] *n* par *m*; (*GOLF*) média *f*; **to be on a ~ with** estar em igualdade de condições com.

parable ['pærəbl] *n* parábola.

parachute ['pærəʃuːt] *n* pára-quedas *m inv* // *vi* saltar de pára-quedas; **~ jump** *n* salto de pára-quedas.

parade [pə'reɪd] *n* desfile *m* // *vt* (*gen*) desfilar; (*show off*) exibir // *vi* desfilar; (*MIL*) passar revista.

paradise ['pærədaɪs] *n* paraíso.

paradox ['pærədɒks] *n* paradoxo; **~ical** [-'dɒksɪkl] *adj* paradoxal.

paraffin ['pærəfɪn] *n*: **~** (**oil**) petróleo.

paragraph ['pærəgrɑːf] *n* parágrafo.

parallel ['pærəlɛl] *adj* paralelo; (*fig*) correspondente // *n* (*line*) paralela; (*fig, GEO*) paralelo.

paralysis [pə'rælɪsɪs] *n* paralisia; **paralyze** ['pærəlaɪz] *vt* paralisar.

paramount ['pærəmaunt] *adj*: **of ~ importance** de suma importância, primordial.

paranoia [pærə'nɔɪə] *n* paranóia; **paranoiac** *adj* paranóico.

paraphernalia [pærəfə'neɪlɪə] *n* (*gear*) acessórios *mpl*, equipamento.

paraplegic [pærə'pliːdʒɪk] *n* paraplégico/a.

parasite ['pærəsaɪt] *n* parasito/a.

parasol [pærə'sɒl] *n* guarda-sol *m*, sombrinha.

paratrooper ['pærətruːpə*] *n* pára-quedista *m/f*.

parcel ['pɑːsl] *n* pacote *m* // *vt* (*also:* **~ up**) embrulhar, empacotar.

parch [pɑːtʃ] *vt* secar, ressecar; **~ed** *adj* (*person*) morto de sede.

parchment ['pɑːtʃmənt] *n* pergaminho.

pardon ['pɑːdn] *n* perdão *m*; (*LAW*) indulto // *vt* perdoar; (*LAW*) indultar; **~!** desculpe!, **~ me!, I beg your ~!** desculpe-me; (**I beg your**) **~?** como?, como disse?

parent ['pɛərənt] *n* pai *m*/mãe *f*; **~s** *npl* pais *mpl*; **~al** [pə'rɛntl] *adj* paternal/maternal, dos pais.

parenthesis [pə'rɛnθɪsɪs], *pl* **-theses** [-θɪsiːz] *n* parêntese *m*.

Paris ['pærɪs] n Paris m.
parish ['pærɪʃ] n paróquia, freguesia;
~**ioner** [pə'rɪʃənə*] n paroquiano/a.
Parisian [pə'rɪzɪən] adj, n parisiense m/f.
parity ['pærɪtɪ] n paridade f, igualdade f.
park [pɑːk] n parque m // vt estacionar
// vi estacionar; ~**ing** n
estacionamento; '**no** ~**ing**'
'estacionamento proibido'; ~**ing lot** n
(US) (parque de) estacionamento; ~**ing
meter** n parquímetro.
parliament ['pɑːləmənt] n parlamento,
assembléia; ~**ary** [-'mɛntərɪ] adj
parlamentar.
parlour, parlor (US) ['pɑːlə*] n sala de
visitas, salão m, saleta.
parochial [pə'rəukɪəl] adj paroquial;
(pej) provinciano.
parody ['pærədɪ] n paródia // vt
parodiar.
parole [pə'rəul] n: **on** ~ em liberdade
condicional, sob promessa.
parquet ['pɑːkeɪ] n: ~ **floor(ing)**
parquete m, assoalho de tacos.
parrot ['pærət] n papagaio; ~ **fashion**
adv mecanicamente.
parry ['pærɪ] vt aparar, desviar.
parsimonious [pɑːsɪ'məunɪəs] adj
parco.
parsley ['pɑːslɪ] n salsa.
parsnip ['pɑːsnɪp] n cherivia, pastinaga.
parson ['pɑːsn] n (parish) pároco, (gen)
padre m, clérigo.
part [pɑːt] n (gen, MUS) parte f; (bit)
pedaço; (of machine) peça; (THEATRE etc)
papel m; (of serial) capítulo; (US: in hair)
risca, repartido // adv = **partly** // vt
dividir; (break) partir // vi (people)
separar-se; (roads) bifurcar-se; (crowd)
dispersar-se; (break) partir-se; **to take
~ in** participar de, tomar parte em; **to
take sth in good** ~ não se ofender
com algo; **to take sb's** ~ defender
alguém; **for my** ~ de minha parte; **for
the most** ~ na maior parte; **to** ~
with vt fus ceder, entregar; (money)
pagar; (get rid of) desfazer-se de; **in** ~
exchange como parte do pagamento; ~
spare ~ peça sobressalente.
partial ['pɑːʃl] adj parcial; **to be** ~ **to**
gostar de, ser apreciador de; ~**ly** adv
parcialmente.
participant [pɑː'tɪsɪpənt] n (in competition) participante m/f; **participate**
[-peɪt] vi: **to participate in** participar
de; **participation** [-'peɪʃən] n
participação f.
participle ['pɑːtɪsɪpl] n particípio.
particle ['pɑːtɪkl] n partícula; (of dust)
grão m; (fig) bocadinho.
particular [pə'tɪkjulə*] adj (special)
especial; (specific) específico; (given)
determinado; (detailed) detalhado,
minucioso; (fussy) exigente, minucioso;
~**s** npl (information) dados mpl, detalhes
mpl; (details) pormenores mpl; ~**ly** adv
em particular, especialmente.
parting ['pɑːtɪŋ] n (act of) separação f;

(farewell) despedida; (in hair) risca,
repartido // adj de despedida.
partisan [pɑːtɪ'zæn] adj, n partidário/a.
partition [pɑː'tɪʃn] n (POL) divisão f;
(wall) tabique m, divisória // vt separar
com tabique; (fig) dividir.
partly ['pɑːtlɪ] adv em parte.
partner ['pɑːtnə*] n (COMM) sócio/a;
(SPORT) parceiro/a; (at dance) par m;
(spouse) cônjuge m/f; (friend etc)
companheiro/a // vt acompanhar;
~**ship** n (gen) associação f; (COMM)
sociedade f.
partridge ['pɑːtrɪdʒ] n perdiz f.
part-time ['pɑːt'taɪm] adj, adv de meio
expediente.
party ['pɑːtɪ] n (POL) partido; (celebration)
festa; (group) grupo; (LAW) parte f
interessada, litigante m/f // adj (POL) do
partido; (dress etc) de gala, de luxo.
pass [pɑːs] vt (time, object) passar;
(exam) passar em; (place) passar por;
(overtake, surpass) ultrapassar; (approve)
aprovar // vi (SCOL) ser aprovado, passar
// n (permit) passe m; (membership card)
carteira; (in mountains) garganta,
desfiladeiro; (SPORT) passe; (SCOL: also: ~
mark): **to get a** ~ in ser aprovado em;
to ~ **sth through sth** passar algo por
algo; **to** ~ **away** vi falecer; **to** ~ **by** vi
passar // vt (ignore) passar por cima de;
to ~ **for** passar por; **to** ~ **out** vi
desmaiar; **to** ~ **up** vt rejeitar; ~**able**
adj (road) transitável; (work) aceitável.
passage ['pæsɪdʒ] n (also: ~**way**)
corredor m; (act of passing) trânsito; (in
book) passagem f, trecho; (fare)
passagem f (Br), bilhete m (Pt); (by boat)
travessia; (MECH, MED) conduto.
passenger ['pæsɪndʒə*] n passageiro/a,
viajante m/f.
passer-by [pɑːsə'baɪ] n transeunte m/f.
passing ['pɑːsɪŋ] adj (fleeting)
passageiro, fugaz; **in** ~ de passagem.
passion ['pæʃən] n paixão f; (anger)
cólera; ~**ate** adj apaixonado, irado.
passive ['pæsɪv] adj (also LING) passivo.
Passover ['pɑːsəuvə*] n Páscoa (dos
judeus).
passport ['pɑːspɔːt] n passaporte m.
password ['pɑːswɔːd] n senha, contra-
senha.
past [pɑːst] prep (further than) para além
de; (later than) depois de // adj passado;
(president etc) ex-, anterior // n o
passado; (antecedents) antecedentes mpl;
he's ~ **forty** ele tem mais de quarenta
anos; **for the** ~ **few days** nos últimos
dias; **to run** ~ passar correndo por.
pasta ['pæstə] n macarrão m, massa.
paste [peɪst] n (gen) pasta; (glue) grude
m, cola // vt (stick) grudar; (glue) colar.
pastel ['pæstl] adj pastel; (painting) a
pastel.
pasteurized ['pæstəraɪzd] adj
pasteurizado.
pastille ['pæstl] n pastilha.
pastime ['pɑːstaɪm] n passatempo.

pastor ['pɑːstə*] n pastor m.

pastoral ['pɑːstərl] adj pastoral.

pastry ['peɪstrɪ] n massa; (cakes) bolos mpl.

pasture ['pɑːstʃə*] n (grass) pasto; (land) pastagem f, pasto.

pasty ['pæstɪ] n empadão m de carne // adj ['peɪstɪ] pastoso; (complexion) pálido.

pat [pæt] vt dar palmadinhas em; (dog etc) fazer festa em // n (of butter) porção f; **to give sb a ~ on the back** animar alguém.

patch [pætʃ] n (of material) retalho; (piece) pedaço; (mend) remendo; (of land) lote m, terreno // vt (clothes) remendar; **to ~ up** vt (mend temporarily) consertar provisoriamente; (quarrel) resolver; **~work** adj (feito de) retalhos; **~y** adj desigual.

pâté ['pæteɪ] n patê m.

patent ['peɪtnt] n patente f // vt patentear // adj patente, evidente; **~ leather** n verniz m.

paternal [pə'tɜːnl] adj paternal; (relation) paterno; **paternity** [-nɪtɪ] n paternidade f.

path [pɑːθ] n caminho; (trail, track) trilha, pista; (of missile) trajetória (Pt: -ct-).

pathetic [pə'θetɪk] adj (pitiful) patético, digno de pena; (very bad) péssimo; (moving) comovente.

pathologist [pə'θɒlədʒɪst] n patologista m/f; **pathology** [-dʒɪ] n patologia.

pathos ['peɪθɒs] n patos msg, patético.

pathway ['pɑːθweɪ] n caminho, trilha.

patience ['peɪʃns] n paciência.

patient ['peɪʃnt] n paciente m/f // adj paciente, resignado.

patio ['pætɪəʊ] n pátio.

patriot ['peɪtrɪət] n patriota m/f; **~ic** [pætrɪ'ɒtɪk] adj patriótico.

patrol [pə'trəʊl] n patrulha // vt patrulhar; **~ car** n carro de patrulha, radiopatrulha f; **~man** n (US) guarda m, policial m (Br), polícia (Pt).

patron ['peɪtrən] n (in shop) cliente m/f; (of charity) benfeitor/a m/f; **~ of the arts** mecenas msg; **~age** ['pætrənɪdʒ] n patrocínio m; **~ize** ['pætrənaɪz] vt (shop) ser cliente de; (business) patrocinar; (look down on) tratar com ar de superioridade; **~ saint** n (santo) padroeiro.

patter ['pætə*] n tamborilada; (of feet) passos miúdos mpl; (sales talk) jargão m profissional // vi correr dando passinhos; (rain) tamborilar.

pattern ['pætən] n modelo, padrão m; (SEWING) molde m; (design) desenho; (sample) amostra.

paunch [pɔːntʃ] n pança, barriga.

pauper ['pɔːpə*] n pobre m/f.

pause [pɔːz] n pausa; (interval) intervalo // vi fazer uma pausa.

pave [peɪv] vt pavimentar; **to ~ the way for** preparar o terreno para.

pavement ['peɪvmənt] n (Brit) calçada, passeio.

pavilion [pə'vɪlɪən] n pavilhão m; (for band etc) coreto; (SPORT) barraca.

paving ['peɪvɪŋ] n pavimento, calçamento; **~ stone** n laje f, paralelepípedo.

paw [pɔː] n pata; (of cat) garra // vt passar a pata; (touch) manusear; (amorously) apalpar.

pawn [pɔːn] n (CHESS) peão m; (fig) títere m // vt empenhar; **~broker** n agiota m/f; **~shop** n loja de penhores.

pay [peɪ] n paga, pagamento; (wage etc) salário // (vb: pt, pp **paid**) vt pagar; (debt) liquidar, saldar; (visit) fazer; (respect) apresentar // vi pagar; (be profitable) valer a pena, render; **to ~ attention (to)** prestar atenção (a); **to ~ back** vt (money) devolver; (person) pagar; **to ~ for** vt pagar; **to ~ in** vt depositar; **to ~ off** vt saldar; **to ~ up** vt pagar, liquidar; **~able** adj pagável; **~ day** n dia m do pagamento; **~ee** n pessoa a quem se paga; **~ing** adj remunerador(a); **~ment** n pagamento; **advance ~ment** pagamento adiantado; **monthly ~ment** mensalidade f; **~ packet** n envelope m com o pagamento; **~roll** n folha de pagamento; **~ slip** n contracheque m.

p.c. abbr of **per cent**.

pea [piː] n ervilha; **sweet ~** ervilha-de-cheiro f.

peace [piːs] n paz f; (calm) tranquilidade f, quietude f; **~able** adj pacato; **~ful** adj (gentle) pacífico; (calm) tranquilo, sossegado; **~-keeping** n pacificação f; **~ offering** n proposta de paz.

peach [piːtʃ] n pêssego.

peacock ['piːkɒk] n pavão m.

peak [piːk] n (of mountain: top) cume m; (: point) pico; (of cap) pala, viseira; (fig) apogeu m, máximo; **~ hours** npl horário de maior movimento.

peal [piːl] n (of bells) repique m, toque m de sinos; **~ of laughter** gargalhada.

peanut ['piːnʌt] n amendoim m; **~ butter** n manteiga de amendoim.

pear [peə*] n pêra; **~ tree** n pereira.

pearl [pɜːl] n pérola.

peasant ['peznt] n camponês/esa m/f.

peat [piːt] n turfa.

pebble ['pebl] n seixo, calhau m.

peck [pek] vt (also: ~ **at**) bicar, dar bicadas em; (food) beliscar // n bicada; (kiss) beijoca; **~ing order** n ordem f de hierarquia; **~ish** adj (col) faminto.

peculiar [pɪ'kjuːlɪə*] adj (odd) estranho, esquisito; (typical) próprio, característico; (marked) especial; **~ to** próprio de; **~ity** [pɪkjuːlɪ'ærɪtɪ] n peculiaridade f; (feature) característica; (oddity) excentricidade f, singularidade f.

pedal ['pedl] n pedal m // vi pedalar.

pedantic [pɪ'dæntɪk] adj pedante.

peddle ['pedl] vt vender nas ruas, mascatear; **peddler** n mascate m/f, camelô m.

pedestal ['pedəstl] n pedestal m.

pedestrian [pɪ'dɛstrɪən] n pedestre m/f // adj pedestre; ~ **crossing** n faixa para pedestres (Br), passadeira (Pt).

pedigree ['pɛdɪgriː] n genealogia; (of animal) raça // cmp (animal) de raça.

peek [piːk] vi espiar, espreitar.

peel [piːl] n casca // vt descascar // vi (paint etc) descascar; (wallpaper) desprender-se.

peep [piːp] n (look) espiadela; (sound) pio // vi (look) espreitar; (sound) piar; to ~ out vi mostrar-se, surgir; ~ hole n vigia.

peer [pɪə*] vi: to ~ at perscrutar, fitar // n (noble) par m; (equal) igual m; ~ age n nobreza; ~ less adj sem igual.

peeved [piːvd] adj irritado.

peevish ['piːvɪʃ] adj rabugento.

peg [pɛg] n cavilha; (for coat etc) cabide m; (also: **clothes** ~) pregador m; (tent ~) estaca // vt (prices) fixar; **off the** ~ adv pronto.

pejorative [pɪ'dʒɔrətɪv] adj pejorativo.

pekingese [piːkɪ'niːz] n pequinês/esa m/f.

pelican ['pɛlɪkən] n pelicano.

pellet ['pɛlɪt] n bolinha; (bullet) pelota de chumbo.

pelmet ['pɛlmɪt] n sanefa.

pelt [pɛlt] vt: to ~ **sb with sth** atirar algo em alguém // vi (rain) chover a cântaros // n pele f (não curtida).

pelvis ['pɛlvɪs] n pelvis f, bacia.

pen [pɛn] n caneta; (for sheep) redil m, cercado; ~ **pal** n (US) amigo/a por correspondência, correspondente m/f; ~ **name** n pseudônimo.

penal ['piːnl] adj penal; ~ **ize** vt impor penalidade a; (SPORT) penalizar.

penalty ['pɛnltɪ] n (gen) pena, penalidade f; (fine) multa; (SPORT) punição f; ~ (**kick**) n (FOOTBALL) pênalti m.

penance ['pɛnəns] n penitência.

pence [pɛns] pl of **penny**.

pencil ['pɛnsl] n lápis m; (for eyebrows) lápis de sombrancelha; **propelling** ~ n lapiseira; ~ **sharpener** n apontador m.

pendant ['pɛndnt] n pingente m.

pending ['pɛndɪŋ] prep (during) durante; (until) até // adj pendente.

pendulum ['pɛndjuləm] n pêndulo.

penetrate ['pɛnɪtreɪt] vt penetrar; **penetrating** adj penetrante; **penetration** [-'treɪʃən] n penetração f.

penfriend ['pɛnfrɛnd] n amigo/a por correspondência, correspondente m/f.

penguin ['pɛŋgwɪn] n pingüim m.

penicillin [pɛnɪ'sɪlɪn] n penicilina.

peninsula [pə'nɪnsjulə] n península.

penis ['piːnɪs] n pênis m.

penitence ['pɛnɪtns] n penitência; **penitent** [-nt] adj (gen) arrependido; (REL) penitente.

penitentiary [pɛnɪ'tɛnʃərɪ] n (US) penitenciária, presídio.

penknife ['pɛnnaɪf] n canivete m.

pennant ['pɛnənt] n flâmula.

penniless ['pɛnɪlɪs] adj sem dinheiro; (col) sem um tostão.

penny ['pɛnɪ], pl **pennies** ['pɛnɪz] or **pence** [pɛns] n pêni m.

pension ['pɛnʃən] n (gen) pensão f; (old-age) aposentadoria f; (MIL) reserva; ~ **er** n aposentado/a (Br), reformado/a (Pt); ~ **fund** n fundo da aposentadoria.

pensive ['pɛnsɪv] adj pensativo; (withdrawn) absorto.

pentagon ['pɛntəgən] n pentágono.

Pentecost ['pɛntɪkɔst] n Pentecostes m.

penthouse ['pɛnthaus] n cobertura.

pent-up ['pɛntʌp] adj (feelings) reprimido.

penultimate [pɛ'nʌltɪmət] adj penúltimo.

people ['piːpl] npl gente f, pessoas fpl; (citizens) povo sg, cidadãos mpl // n (nation, race) nação f, raça // vt povoar; **several** ~ **came** vieram várias pessoas; ~ **say that...** dizem que...

pep [pɛp] n (col) energia, dinamismo; to ~ **up** vt animar.

pepper ['pɛpə*] n pimenta; (vegetable) pimentão m // vt (fig) salpicar; ~ **mint** n hortelã-pimenta; (sweet) bala de hortelã.

peptalk ['pɛptɔːk] n (col) conversa para levantar o espírito.

per [pɜː*] prep por; ~ **day** / **person** por dia/pessoa; ~ **cent** por cento; ~ **annum** por ano.

perceive [pə'siːv] vt perceber; (realize) compreender.

percentage [pə'sɛntɪdʒ] n percentagem f.

perception [pə'sɛpʃən] n percepção f; (insight) perspicácia; **perceptive** [-'sɛptɪv] adj perceptivo.

perch [pɜːtʃ] n (fish) perca; (for bird) poleiro // vi empoleirar-se, pousar.

percolator ['pɜːkəleɪtə*] n cafeteira de filtro.

percussion [pə'kʌʃən] n percussão f.

peremptory [pə'rɛmptərɪ] adj peremptório, decisivo; (person: imperious) autoritário.

perennial [pə'rɛnɪəl] adj perene.

perfect ['pɜːfɪkt] adj perfeito // n (also: ~ **tense**) perfeito // vt [pə'fɛkt] aperfeiçoar; ~ **ion** [-'fɛkʃən] n perfeição f; ~ **ionist** n perfeccionista m/f.

perforate ['pɜːfəreɪt] vt perfurar; ~ **d** adj (stamp) picotado; **perforation** [-'reɪʃən] n perfuração f.

perform [pə'fɔːm] vt (carry out) realizar, fazer; (concert etc) executar; (piece of music) interpretar // vi (animal) fazer truques de amestramento; (THEATRE) representar; (TECH) funcionar; ~ **ance** n (of task) cumprimento, realização f; (of an artist, of player etc) atuação (Pt: -ct-) f; (of car, engine, of function) desempenho; ~ **er** n (actor) artista m/f, ator/atriz (Pt: -ct-) m/f; (MUS) intérprete m/f; ~ **ing** adj (animal) amestrado, adestrado.

perfume [pə'fju:m] *n* perfume *m* // *vt* perfumar.

perhaps [pə'hæps] *adv* talvez.

peril ['pεrɪl] *n* perigo, risco.

perimeter [pə'rɪmɪtə*] *n* perímetro.

period ['pɪərɪəd] *n* período; (*HISTORY*) época, era; (*time limit*) prazo; (*SCOL*) aula; (*full stop*) ponto final; (*MED*) menstruação *f*, regra // *adj* (*costume, furniture*) da época; ~**ic** [-'ɔdɪk] *adj* periódico; ~**ical** [-'ɔdɪkl] *n* periódico; ~**ically** [-'ɔdɪklɪ] *adv* periodicamente, de vez em quando.

peripheral [pə'rɪfərəl] *adj, n* periférico; **periphery** [-rɪ] *n* periferia.

periscope ['pərɪskəup] *n* periscópio.

perish ['pεrɪʃ] *vi* perecer; (*decay*) deteriorar-se, estragar; ~**able** *adj* perecível, deteriorável; ~**ing** *adj* (*col: cold*) gelado, glacial.

perjure ['pə:dʒə*] *vt*: to ~ **o.s.** prestar falso testemunho; **perjury** *n* (*LAW*) perjúrio.

perk [pə:k] *n* mordomia, regalia; to ~ **up** *vi* (*cheer up*) animar-se; (*in health*) recuperar-se; ~**y** *adj* (*cheerful*) animado, alegre.

perm [pə:m] *n* permanente *f*.

permanent ['pə:mənənt] *adj* permanente.

permissible [pə'mɪsɪbl] *adj* permissível, lícito.

permission [pə'mɪʃən] *n* permissão *f*; (*authorization*) autorização *f*.

permissive [pə'mɪsɪv] *adj* permissivo.

permit ['pə:mɪt] *n* permissão *f*, licença // *vt* [pə'mɪt] permitir; (*authorize*) autorizar; (*accept*) consentir em.

permutation [pə:mju'teɪʃən] *n* permutação *f*.

pernicious [pə:'nɪʃəs] *adj* nocivo; (*MED*) pernicioso, maligno.

perpendicular [pə:pən'dɪkjulə*] *adj* perpendicular.

perpetrate ['pə:pɪtreɪt] *vt* cometer.

perpetual [pə'pεtjuəl] *adj* perpétuo.

perpetuate [pə'pεtjueɪt] *vt* perpetuar.

perplex [pə'plεks] *vt* deixar perplexo.

persecute ['pə:sɪkju:t] *vt* (*pursue*) perseguir; (*harass*) importunar; **persecution** [-'kju:ʃən] *n* perseguição *f*.

persevere [pə:sɪ'vɪə*] *vi* perseverar.

Persian ['pə:ʃən] *adj, n* persa *m/f*.

persist [pə'sɪst] *vi*: to ~ (**in doing sth**) persistir (em fazer algo); ~**ence** *n* persistência; (*of disease*) insistência; ~**ent** *adj* persistente; (*determined*) teimoso; (*disease*) insistente, persistente.

person ['pə:sn] *n* pessoa; ~**able** *adj* atraente, bem apessoado; ~**al** *adj* pessoal; (*private*) particular; (*visit*) em pessoa, pessoal; (*TEL*) particular, pessoa a pessoa; (*column*) de anúncios pessoais; ~**ality** [-'nælɪtɪ] *n* personalidade *f*; ~**ally** *adv* pessoalmente; ~**ify** [-'sɔnɪfaɪ] *vt* personificar.

personnel [pə:sə'nεl] *n* pessoal *m*.

perspective [pə'spεktɪv] *n* perspectiva.

perspiration [pə:spɪ'reɪʃən] *n* transpiração *f*, suor *m*; **perspire** [-'spaɪə*] *vi* transpirar, suar.

persuade [pə'sweɪd] *vt* persuadir; **persuasion** [-'sweɪʒən] *n* persuasão *f*; (*persuasiveness*) poder *m* de persuasão; (*creed*) convicção *f*, crença; **persuasive** [-'sweɪsɪv] *adj* persuasivo.

pert [pə:t] *adj* atrevido, descarado.

pertaining [pə:'teɪnɪŋ]: ~ **to** *prep* relativo a, próprio de.

pertinent ['pə:tɪnənt] *adj* pertinente, a propósito.

perturb [pə'tə:b] *vt* perturbar.

Peru [pə'ru:] *n* Peru *m*.

peruse [pə'ru:z] *vt* ler com atenção, examinar.

Peruvian [pə'ru:vjən] *adj, n* peruano/a.

pervade [pə'veɪd] *vt* impregnar, penetrar em.

perverse [pə'və:s] *adj* perverso; (*stubborn*) teimoso; (*wayward*) caprichoso; **perversion** [-'və:ʃən] *n* perversão *f*.

pervert ['pə:və:t] *n* pervertido/a // *vt* [pə'və:t] perverter, corromper.

pessary ['pεsərɪ] *n* pessário.

pessimism ['pεsɪmɪzəm] *n* pessimismo; **pessimist** [-mɪst] *n* pessimista *m/f*; **pessimistic** [-'mɪstɪk] *adj* pessimista.

pest [pεst] *n* peste *f*, praga; (*insect*) inseto (*Pt*: -ct-) nocivo; (*fig*) peste *f*, chato.

pester ['pεstə*] *vt* incomodar.

pesticide ['pεstɪsaɪd] *n* pesticida *m*.

pet [pεt] *n* animal *m* de estimação; (*favourite*) preferido/a // *vt* acariciar // *vi* (*col*) acariciar-se, emburrar.

petal ['pεtl] *n* pétala.

peter ['pi:tə*]: to ~ **out** *vi* esgotar-se, acabar-se.

petite [pə'ti:t] *adj* delicado, frágil.

petition [pə'tɪʃən] *n* petição *f*.

petrified ['pεtrɪfaɪd] *adj* (*fig*) petrificado, paralisado; **petrify** *vt* paralisar; (*frighten*) petrificar.

petrol ['pεtrəl] *n* (*Brit*) gasolina; (*for lighter*) fluido.

petroleum [pə'trəuliəm] *n* petróleo.

petrol: ~ **pump** *n* bomba de gasolina; ~ **station** *n* posto de gasolina (*Br*), bomba de gasolina (*Pt*); ~ **tank** *n* tanque *m* de gasolina.

petticoat ['pεtɪkəut] *n* anágua; (*slip*) combinação *f*.

pettiness ['pεtɪnɪs] *n* mesquinharia *f*.

petty ['pεtɪ] *adj* (*mean*) mesquinho; (*unimportant*) insignificante; ~ **cash** *n* fundo para despesas miúdas; ~ **officer** *n* suboficial *m* da marinha.

petulant ['pεtjulənt] *adj* irascível.

pew [pju:] *n* banco de igreja.

pewter ['pju:tə*] *n* peltre *m*.

phallic ['fælɪk] *adj* fálico.

phantom ['fæntəm] *n* fantasma *m*.

Pharaoh ['fεərəu] *n* faraó *m*.

pharmacist ['fɑ:məsɪst] *n* farmacêutico/a; **pharmacy** [-sɪ] *n* farmácia.

phase [feɪz] n fase f // vt: **to ~ sth in/out** introduzir/retirar algo por etapas.

Ph.D. abbr of **Doctor of Philosophy**.

pheasant ['feznt] n faisão m.

phenomenon [fə'nɔmɪnɔn], pl **-mena** [-mɪnə] n fenômeno.

phial ['faɪəl] n frasco.

philanthropist [fɪ'lænθrəpɪst] n filantropo/a.

philately [fɪ'lætəlɪ] n filatelia.

Philippines ['fɪlɪpi:nz] npl (also: **Philippine Islands**) Filipinas fpl.

philosopher [fɪ'lɔsəfə*] n filósofo/a; **philosophical** [fɪlə'sɔfɪkl] adj filosófico; **philosophy** [-fɪ] n filosofia.

phlegm [flɛm] n fleuma; **~atic** [flɛg'mætɪk] adj fleumático.

phobia ['fəubjə] n fobia.

phone [fəun] n telefone m // vt telefonar a, ligar para; **to be on the ~** ter telefone; (be calling) estar no telefone; **to ~ back** vt/i ligar de volta.

phonetics [fə'nɛtɪks] n fonética sg.

phoney ['fəunɪ] adj falso; (person) fingido // n (person) impostor(a) m/f.

phosphate ['fɔsfeɪt] n fosfato.

phosphorus ['fɔsfərəs] n fósforo.

photo ['fəutəu] n foto f.

photo... ['fəutəu] pref: **~copier** n fotocopiadora f; **~copy** n fotocópia // vt fotocopiar; **~genic** [-'dʒɛnɪk] adj fotogênico; **~graph** n fotografia // vt fotografar; **~grapher** [fə'tɔgrəfə*] n fotógrafo/a; **~graphic** [-'græfɪk] adj fotográfico; **~graphy** [fə'tɔgrəfɪ] n fotografia; **~stat** ['fəutəustæt] n cópia fotostática.

phrase [freɪz] n frase f, expressão f // vt expressar; **~book** n livro de expressões idiomáticas.

physical ['fɪzɪkl] adj físico.

physician [fɪ'zɪʃən] n médico/a.

physicist ['fɪzɪsɪst] n físico/a.

physics ['fɪzɪks] n física sg.

physiology [fɪzɪ'ɔlədʒɪ] n fisiologia.

physiotherapy [fɪzɪəu'θɛrəpɪ] n fisioterapia.

physique [fɪ'zi:k] n físico.

pianist ['pi:ənɪst] n pianista m/f.

piano [pɪ'ænəu] n piano; **grand ~** piano de cauda.

pick [pɪk] n (tool: also: **~-axe**) picareta, picão m // vt (select) escolher, selecionar (Pt: -cc-); (gather) colher; (lock) forçar; **take your ~** escolha o que quiser; **the ~ of** o melhor de; **to ~ one's teeth** palitar os dentes; **to ~ pockets** roubar or bater carteira; **to ~ off** vt (kill) matar de um tiro; **to ~ on** vt fus (person) azucrinar, aporrinhar; **to ~ out** vt escolher; (distinguish) distinguir; **to ~ up** vi (improve) melhorar // vt (from floor) apanhar; (telephone) atender, tirar do gancho; (buy) comprar; (find) encontrar; (learn) aprender com facilidade; **to ~ up**

speed acelerar; **to ~ o.s. up** levantar-se.

picket ['pɪkɪt] n (in strike) piquete m // vt formar piquete; **~ line** n fileira de grevistas, piquete m.

pickle ['pɪkl] n (also: **~s**: as condiment) picles mpl; (fig: mess) apuro // vt (in vinegar) conservar em vinagre.

pickpocket ['pɪkpɔkɪt] n batedor(a) m/f de carteira (Br), carteirista m/f (Pt).

pickup ['pɪkʌp] n (on record player) pick-up m; (small truck) camioneta.

picnic ['pɪknɪk] n piquenique m // vi fazer um piquenique.

pictorial [pɪk'tɔ:rɪəl] adj pictórico; (magazine etc) ilustrado.

picture ['pɪktʃə*] n quadro; (painting) pintura; (photograph) fotografia; (film) filme m // vt pintar; **the ~s** o cinema; **~ book** n livro de figuras.

picturesque [pɪktʃə'rɛsk] adj pitoresco.

pidgin ['pɪdʒɪn] adj: **~ English** forma achinesada do inglês usada entre comerciantes.

pie [paɪ] n pastelão m; (open) torta; (of meat) empadão m.

piebald ['paɪbɔ:ld] adj malhado.

piece [pi:s] n pedaço, parte f; (of land) lote m; (of cake) porção f; (item): **a ~ of furniture/advice** um móvel/um conselho // vt: **to ~ together** unir, juntar; (TECH) montar; **to take to ~s** desmontar; **~meal** adv pouco a pouco; **~work** n trabalho por empreitada.

pier [pɪə*] n cais m; (jetty) embarcadouro, molhe m.

pierce [pɪəs] vt penetrar, romper; (puncture) furar, perfurar.

piercing ['pɪəsɪŋ] adj (cry) penetrante, agudo.

piety ['paɪətɪ] n piedade f.

pig [pɪg] n porco; (fig) porcalhão/lhona m/f.

pigeon ['pɪdʒən] n pombo/a; **~hole** n escaninho.

piggy bank ['pɪgɪbæŋk] n cofre m em forma de porquinho.

pigheaded ['pɪg'hɛdɪd] adj teimoso, cabeçudo.

pigment ['pɪgmənt] n pigmento; **~ation** [-'teɪʃən] n pigmentação f.

pigmy ['pɪgmɪ] n = **pygmy**.

pigsty ['pɪgstaɪ] n chiqueiro.

pigtail ['pɪgteɪl] n (girl's) trança; (Chinese) rabicho, rabo-de-cavalo.

pike [paɪk] n (spear) lança, pique m; (fish) lúcio.

pilchard ['pɪltʃəd] n sardinha.

pile [paɪl] n (heap) pilha, monte m; (of carpet) pêlo; (of cloth) lado felpudo // (vb: also: **~ up**) vt amontoar; (fig) acumular // vi amontoar-se.

piles [paɪlz] npl (MED) hemorróidas fpl.

pile-up ['paɪlʌp] n (AUT) acidente m com vários carros.

pilfer ['pɪlfə*] vt furtar, afanar; **~ing** n furto.

pilgrim ['pɪlgrɪm] *n* peregrino/a; ~**age** *n* peregrinação *f*, romaria.

pill [pɪl] *n* pílula; **the** ~ a pílula.

pillage ['pɪlɪdʒ] *n* pilhagem *f*, saque *m*.

pillar ['pɪlə*] *n* (*gen*) pilar *m*; (*concrete*) coluna; ~ **box** *n* (*Brit*) caixa coletora (do correio) (*Br*), marco do correio (*Pt*).

pillion ['pɪljən] *n* (*of motor cycle*) garupa.

pillory ['pɪlərɪ] *vt* expor ao ridículo.

pillow ['pɪləu] *n* travesseiro (*Br*), almofada (*Pt*); ~**case** *n* fronha.

pilot ['paɪlət] *n* piloto // *adj* (*scheme etc*) piloto // *vt* pilotar; (*fig*) guiar; ~ **light** *n* piloto.

pimp [pɪmp] *n* cafetão *m* (*Br*), cáften *m* (*Pt*).

pimple ['pɪmpl] *n* espinha.

pin [pɪn] *n* alfinete *m*; (*TECH*) cavilha; (*wooden*) pino // *vt* alfinetar; ~**s and needles** comichão *f sg*, sensação *f* de formigamento; **rolling** ~ rolo de cozinha; **safety** ~ alfinete de segurança; **to** ~ **sb down** (*fig*) conseguir que alguém assuma uma posição; **to** ~ **sth on sb** (*fig*) culpar alguém de algo.

pinafore ['pɪnəfɔ:*] *n* avental *m*; ~ **dress** *n* avental *m*.

pinball ['pɪnbɔ:l] *n* fliper *m*, fliperama *m*.

pincers ['pɪnsəz] *npl* alicate *msg*, pinça *sg*, tenaz *fsg*.

pinch [pɪntʃ] *n* beliscão *m*; (*of salt etc*) pitada // *vt* beliscar; (*col: steal*) furtar; (*: arrest*) deter, dar uma batida em // *vi* (*shoe*) apertar; **to feel the** ~ passar por um aperto.

pincushion ['pɪnkuʃən] *n* alfineteira.

pine [paɪn] *n* (*also:* ~ **tree**) pinho // *vi*: **to** ~ **for** ansiar por; ~ **away** consumir-se, estar definhando.

pineapple ['paɪnæpl] *n* abacaxi *m* (*Br*), ananás *m* (*Pt*).

ping [pɪŋ] *n* (*noise*) silvo, sibilo; (*of bullet through air*) zumbido; ~-**pong** *n* pingue-pongue *m*.

pink [pɪŋk] *adj* rosa, cor de rosa // *n* (*colour*) cor *m* de rosa; (*BOT*) cravo, cravina.

pinnacle ['pɪnəkl] *n* cume *m*; (*fig*) auge *m*.

pinpoint ['pɪnpɔɪnt] *vt* localizar com precisão.

pint [paɪnt] *n* pinta (*0.57 litros*), quartilho; **to go for a** ~ ir tomar uma cerveja.

pin-up ['pɪnʌp] *n* pin-up *f*, retrato de mulher atraente.

pioneer [paɪə'nɪə*] *n* pioneiro.

pious ['paɪəs] *adj* piedoso, devoto.

pip [pɪp] *n* (*seed*) caroço, semente *f*; (*time signal on radio*) sinal *m*.

pipe [paɪp] *n* cano, tubo; (*for smoking*) cachimbo // *vt* canalizar, encanar; ~**s** *npl* (*gen*) canalização *fsg*; (*also:* **bag**~**s**) gaita *fsg* de foles; **to** ~ **down** *vi* (*col*) calar o bico, meter a viola no saco; ~ **dream** *n* sonho impossível, castelo no ar; ~**line** *n* encanamento; (*for oil*) oleoduto; (*for gas*) gaseoduto; **piper** *n*

pilgrim ['pɪlgrɪm] *n* peregrino/a;

(*gen*) flautista *m/f*; (*with bagpipes*) gaiteiro.

piping ['paɪpɪŋ] *adv*: ~ **hot** chiando de quente.

piquant ['pi:kənt] *adj* picante.

pique [pi:k] *n* ressentimento, melindre *m*.

pirate ['paɪərət] *n* pirata *m*; ~ **radio** *n* rádio pirata *or* ilegal.

pirouette [pɪru'ɛt] *n* pirueta // *vi* fazer piruetas.

Pisces ['paɪsi:z] *n* Pisces *m*, peixes *mpl*.

piss [pɪs] *vi* (*col*) mijar; ~**ed** *adj* (*col: drunk*) bêbado, de porre.

pistol ['pɪstl] *n* pistola.

piston ['pɪstən] *n* pistão *m*, êmbolo.

pit [pɪt] *n* cova, fossa; (*also:* **coal** ~) mina de carvão; (*in garage*) poço de inspeção (*Pt:* -çç-); (*also:* **orchestra** ~) fosso; (*quarry*) canteira, pedreira // *vt*: **to** ~ **A against B** opor A a B; ~**s** *npl* (*AUT*) box *m*.

pitch [pɪtʃ] *n* (*throw*) arremesso, lance *m*; (*MUS*) tom *m*; (*SPORT*) campo; (*tar*) piche *m*, breu *m*; (*in market etc*) barraca // *vt* (*throw*) arremessar, lançar // *vi* (*fall*) tombar, cair; (*NAUT*) jogar, arfar; **to** ~ **a tent** armar uma tenda; ~-**black** *adj* escuro como o breu; ~**ed battle** *n* batalha campal.

pitcher ['pɪtʃə*] *n* jarro, cântaro; (*US: baseball*) arremessador *m*.

pitchfork ['pɪtʃfɔ:k] *n* forcado.

piteous ['pɪtɪəs] *adj* lastimável.

pitfall ['pɪtfɔ:l] *n* perigo (imprevisto), armadilha.

pith [pɪθ] *n* (*of orange*) casca interna e branca; (*fig*) essência, parte *f* essencial.

pithy ['pɪθɪ] *adj* substancial, rico.

pitiable ['pɪtɪəbl] *adj* deplorável.

pitiful ['pɪtɪful] *adj* (*touching*) comovente, tocante; (*contemptible*) desprezível, lamentável.

pitiless ['pɪtɪlɪs] *adj* impiedoso.

pittance ['pɪtns] *n* ninharia, miséria.

pity ['pɪtɪ] *n* (*compassion*) compaixão *f*, piedade *f*; (*shame*) pena // *vt* ter pena de, compadecer-se de; **what a** ~! que pena!

pivot ['pɪvət] *n* pino, eixo; (*fig*) pivô *m* // *vi*: **to** ~ **on** girar sobre; (*fig*) depender de.

pixie ['pɪksɪ] *n* duende *m*.

placard ['plækɑ:d] *n* (*sign*) placar *m*; (*in march etc*) cartaz *m*.

placate [plə'keɪt] *vt* apaziguar, aplacar.

place [pleɪs] *n* lugar *m*; (*rank*) posição *f*; (*seat*) assento, lugar *m*; (*post*) posto; (*home*): **at/to his** ~ em/para a casa dele // *vt* (*object*) pôr, colocar, botar; (*identify*) identificar, situar; (*find a post for*) colocar; **to take** ~ realizar-se, ocorrer; **to be** ~**d** (*in race, exam*) classificar-se; **out of** ~ (*not suitable*) fora de lugar; **in the first** ~ em primeiro lugar; **to change** ~**s with sb** trocar de lugar com alguém.

placid ['plæsɪd] *adj* plácido, sereno.

plagiarism ['pleɪdʒərɪzm] *n* plágio.

plague [pleɪg] n praga; (MED) peste f // vt (fig) atormentar, importunar; **to ~ sb** amofinar alguém.

plaice [pleɪs] n, pl inv solha.

plaid [plæd] n (material) tecido enxadrezado; (pattern) xadrez m escocês.

plain [pleɪn] adj (clear) claro, evidente; (simple) simples, despretensioso; (frank) franco, sem rodeios; (not handsome) sem atrativos (Pt: -cti-); (pure) puro, natural // adv claramente, com franqueza // n planície f, campina; **in ~ clothes** (police) à paisana; **~ly** adv claramente, obviamente; (frankly) francamente; **~ness** n clareza; simplicidade f; franqueza.

plaintiff ['pleɪntɪf] n querelante m/f, queixoso/a.

plait [plæt] n trança, dobra // vt trançar.

plan [plæn] n (drawing) plano; (scheme) esquema m, projeto (Pt: -ct-); (schedule) programa m // vt (think in advance) idear, proje(c)tar; (prepare) planejar (Pt: planear), programar // vi fazer planos; **to ~ to do** tencionar fazer, propor-se fazer.

plane [pleɪn] n (AVIAT) avião m; (tree) plátano; (tool) plaina; (MATH) plano.

planet ['plænɪt] n planeta m; **~arium** [-'tɛərɪəm] n planetário.

plank [plæŋk] n tábua; (POL) item m da plataforma política.

planner ['plænə*] n projetista (Pt: -ect-) m/f.

planning ['plænɪŋ] n planejamento (Pt: planeamento); **family ~** planejamento familiar.

plant [plɑːnt] n planta; (machinery) maquinaria; (factory) fábrica // vt plantar; (field) semear; (bomb) colocar, pôr; (fam) pôr às escondidas.

plantation [plæn'teɪʃən] n plantação f, roça; (estate) fazenda.

plaque [plæk] n placa, insígnia.

plasma ['plæzmə] n plasma m.

plaster ['plɑːstə*] n (for walls) reboco; (also: sticking ~) esparadrapo, band-aid m; **~ of Paris** gesso // vt rebocar; (cover): **to ~ with** encher or cobrir de; **~ed** adj (col) bêbado, de porre; **~er** n rebocador m, caiador m.

plastic ['plæstɪk] n plástico // adj de plástico.

plasticine ['plæstɪsiːn] n plasticina.

plastic surgery n ['plæstɪk'sɔːdʒərɪ] n cirurgia or operação f plástica.

plate [pleɪt] n (dish) prato; (metal) placa, chapa; (PHOT) chapa; (dental) dentadura.

plateau ['plætəʊ], pl **~s** or **~x** [-z] n planalto, platô m.

plateful ['pleɪtful] n pratada.

plate glass [pleɪt'glɑːs] n vidro laminado.

platform ['plætfɔːm] n (RAIL) plataforma (Br), cais m (Pt); (stage) estrado; (at meeting) tribuna; (POL) programa m

partidário; **~ ticket** n bilhete m de plataforma.

platinum ['plætɪnəm] n platina.

platitude ['plætɪtjuːd] n lugar m comum, chavão m.

platoon [plə'tuːn] n pelotão m.

platter ['plætə*] n travessa.

plausible ['plɔːzɪbl] adj plausível, aceitável; (person) convincente.

play [pleɪ] n (gen) jogo; (also: **~time**) recreio; (THEATRE) obra, peça // vt (game) jogar; (instrument) tocar; (THEATRE) representar; (: part) fazer o papel de; (fig) desempenhar // vi jogar; (amuse o.s.) divertir-se; (frolic) brincar; **to ~ down** vt não ligar para; **to ~ up** vt (cause trouble to) importunar, incomodar; **~-acting** n teatro; **~er** n jogador(a) m/f; (THEATRE) ator/atriz (Pt: -ct-) m/f; (MUS) músico/a; **~ful** adj brincalhão/lhona; **~ground** n pátio de recreio; **~group** n espécie de jardim de infância; **~ing card** n carta de baralho; **~ing field** n campo de esportes (Br), campo de jogos (Pt); **~mate** n companheiro de brincadeira; **~-off** n (SPORT) partida de desempate; **~pen** n cercado para crianças; **~thing** n brinquedo; **~wright** n dramaturgo/a.

plea [pliː] n (request) apelo, petição f; (excuse) justificativa, pretexto; (LAW: defence) defesa.

plead [pliːd] vt (LAW) defender, advogar; (give as excuse) alegar, argumentar // vi (LAW) declarar-se; (beg): **to ~ with sb** suplicar or rogar a alguém; **to ~ guilty** confessar-se culpado; **to ~ not guilty** negar a acusação.

pleasant ['plɛznt] adj agradável; (surprise) grato; (person) simpático; **~ness** n (of person) amabilidade f, simpatia; (of place) encanto; **~ries** npl (polite remarks) amenidades fpl (na conversa).

please [pliːz] vt (give pleasure to) agradar, dar prazer a; (get on well with) dar-se bem com // vi (think fit): **do as you ~** faça o que or como quiser; **~!** por favor!; **~ yourself!** como queira!; **~d** adj (happy) satisfeito, contente; **~d (with)** satisfeito (com); **pleasing** adj (gen) agradável; (surprise) grato; (flattering) lisonjeiro.

pleasure ['plɛʒə*] n prazer m; (delight) deleite m; (will) vontade f // cmp de recreio; **~ trip** n viagem f de recreio; **'it's a ~'** o prazer é (todo) meu; **it's a ~ to see him** é um prazer vê-lo.

pleat [pliːt] n prega.

plebs [plɛbz] npl (pej) plebe fsg.

plectrum ['plɛktrəm] n plectro.

pledge [plɛdʒ] n (object) garantia, penhor m; (promise) promessa, voto // vt (pawn) empenhar, pôr no prego; (promise) prometer.

plentiful ['plɛntɪful] adj abundante, profuso.

plenty ['plɛntɪ] *n* abundância; ~ **of** (*enough*) bastante; (*many*) muitos/as.

pleurisy ['pluərɪsɪ] *n* pleurisia.

pliable ['plaɪəbl] *adj* flexível; (*fig*) adaptável, influenciável.

pliers ['plaɪəz] *npl* alicate *msg*.

plight [plaɪt] *n* situação *f* difícil, apuro.

plimsolls ['plɪmsɔlz] *npl* tênis *mpl*, calçado *sg* de lona.

plod [plɔd] *vi* caminhar pesadamente; (*fig*) trabalhar laboriosamente; ~**der** *n* (*col*) cu-de-ferro, cê-dê-efe *m/f*; ~**ding** *adj* caminhador(a); (*in work*) mourejador(a).

plonk [plɔŋk] (*col*) *n* (*wine*) vinho de segunda (categoria) // *vt*: **to ~ sth down** deixar cair algo (pesadamente).

plot [plɔt] *n* (*scheme*) trama, conspiração *f*, complô *m*; (*of story, play*) enredo; (*of land*) lote *m* // *vt* (*mark out*) traçar; (*conspire*) tramar, planejar (*Pt*: planear) // *vi* conspirar; ~**ter** *n* conspirador(a) *m/f*.

plough, plow (*US*) [plau] *n* arado // *vt* (*earth*) arar; **to ~ back** *vt* (*COMM*) reinvestir; **to ~ through** *vt fus* (*crowd*) abrir caminho por.

ploy [plɔɪ] *n* estratagema *m*.

pluck [plʌk] *vt* (*fruit*) colher; (*musical instrument*) dedilhar; (*bird*) depenar // *n* coragem *f*, puxão *m*; **to ~ up courage** reunir coragem; ~**y** *adj* corajoso, valente.

plug [plʌg] *n* tampão *m*; (*ELEC*) tomada (*Br*), ficha (*Pt*); (*AUT: also:* **sparking ~**) vela (de ignição) // *vt* (*hole*) tapar; (*col: advertise*) fazer (insistente) propaganda de; **to ~ in** (*ELEC*) ligar.

plum [plʌm] *n* (*fruit*) ameixa // *adj* (*col: job*) vantajoso.

plumage ['plu:mɪdʒ] *n* plumagem *f*.

plumb [plʌm] *adv* (*exactly*) exatamente (*Pt*: -act-) // *vt* sondar.

plumber ['plʌmə*] *n* bombeiro (*Br*), encanador *m* (*Br*), canalizador *m* (*Pt*); **plumbing** [-mɪŋ] *n* (*trade*) ofício de encanador; (*piping*) encanamento.

plume [plu:m] *n* (*gen*) pluma; (*on helmet*) penacho.

plummet ['plʌmɪt] *vi*: **to ~ (down)** cair verticalmente.

plump [plʌmp] *adj* roliço, rechonchudo // *vt*: **to ~ sth (down) on** deixar cair algo em; **to ~ for** (*col: choose*) optar por.

plunder ['plʌndə*] *n* saque *m*, pilhagem *f*; (*loot*) despojo // *vt* pilhar, espoliar; (*tomb*) saquear.

plunge [plʌndʒ] *n* (*dive*) salto; (*submersion*) mergulho; (*bath*) imersão *f*, banho // *vt* mergulhar, afundar // *vi* (*fall*) cair; (*dive*) mergulhar; (*person*) lançar-se; (*sink*) afundar-se; **to take the ~** decidir-se; **plunger** *n* êmbolo; **plunging** *adj* (*neckline*) decotado.

pluperfect [plu:'pə:fɪkt] *n* mais-que-perfeito.

plural ['pluərl] *n* plural *m*.

plus [plʌs] *n* (*also:* **~ sign**) sinal *m* de adição // *prep* mais, e; **ten / twenty ~** dez / vinte e tantos.

plush [plʌʃ] *adj* de pelúcia.

ply [plaɪ] *vt* (*a trade*) exercer // *vi* (*ship*) ir e vir; (*for hire*) oferecer-se para alugar; **three ~** (*wool*) de três fios; **to ~ sb with drink** insistir para que alguém beba; **to ~ sb with questions** bombardear alguém com perguntas; ~**wood** *n* madeira compensada.

P.M. *abbr of* **Prime Minister**.

p.m. *adv abbr of* **post meridiem** da tarde, da noite.

pneumatic [nju:'mætɪk] *adj* pneumático.

pneumonia [nju:'məunɪə] *n* pneumonia.

poach [pəutʃ] *vt* (*cook*) escaldar, escalfar; (*eggs*) fazer pochê (*Br*), escalfar (*Pt*); (*steal*) furtar // *vi* caçar / pescar em propriedade alheia; ~**ed** *adj* (*egg*) pochê (*Br*), escalfado (*Pt*); ~**er** *n* caçador *m* furtivo; ~**ing** *n* caça furtiva.

pocket ['pɔkɪt] *n* bolso; (*of air, GEO, fig*) bolsa; (*BILLIARDS*) caçapa, ventanilha // *vt* embolsar, meter no bolso; (*steal*) apropriar-se de; (*BILLIARDS*) encaçapar; **to be out of ~** perder, ter prejuízo; ~**book** *n* (*US: wallet*) carteira; ~ **knife** *n* canivete *m*; ~ **money** *n* dinheiro para despesas miúdas.

pod [pɔd] *n* vagem *f*.

podgy ['pɔdʒɪ] *adj* nédio, mole.

podiatrist *n* (*US*) pedicuro.

poem ['pəuɪm] *n* poema *m*.

poet ['pəuɪt] *n* poeta *m/f*; ~**ess** *n* poetisa; ~**ic** [-'ɛtɪk] *adj* poético; ~ **laureate** *n* poeta laureado; ~**ry** *n* poesia.

poignant ['pɔɪnjənt] *adj* comovente; (*sharp*) agudo.

point [pɔɪnt] *n* (*gen*) ponto; (*tip*) ponta; (*purpose*) finalidade *f*, objetivo (*Pt*: -ct-); (*use*) utilidade *f*; (*significant part*) relevância; (*characteristic*) característica; (*also:* **decimal ~**): **2 ~ 3 (2.3)** dois ponto três; **to the ~** pertinente // *vt* (*show*) mostrar, indicar; (*gun etc*): **to ~ sth at sb** apontar algo para alguém // *vi* indicar com o dedo; ~**s** *npl* (*AUT*) platinado, contato (*Pt*: -ct-) *sg*; (*RAIL*) agulhas *fpl*; **to make a ~ of** fazer questão de, insistir em; **to get the ~** compreender; **to come to the ~** ir ao que interessa, falar sem rodeios; **there's no ~ (in doing)** não adianta nada (fazer); **to ~ out** *vt* mostrar, realçar; **to ~ to** indicar com o dedo; (*fig*) indicar; ~-**blank** *adv* (*also:* **at ~-blank range**) à queima-roupa; ~**ed** *adj* (*shape*) pontudo, aguçado; (*remark*) mordaz, intencional; ~**edly** *adv* mordazmente; ~**er** *n* (*stick*) indicador *m*, ponteiro; (*needle*) agulha; ~**less** *adj* (*useless*) inútil; (*senseless*) sem sentido; (*motiveless*) sem razão; ~ **of view** *n* ponto de vista.

poise [pɔɪz] *n* (*balance*) equilíbrio; (*of*

head, *body*) porte *m*; (*calmness*) serenidade *f*.

poison ['pɔɪzn] *n* veneno // *vt* envenenar; ~**ing** *n* envenenamento; ~**ous** *adj* venenoso; (*fumes etc*) tóxico; (*fig*) pernicioso.

poke [pəuk] *vt* (*fire*) atiçar; (*jab with finger, stick etc*) cutucar; (*put*): **to ~ sth in(to)** meter algo em // *n* (*to fire*) remexida; (*push*) empurrão *m*; (*with elbow*) cotovelada; **to ~ about** *vi* escarafunchar, espionar; **to ~ one's nose into** meter o nariz em.

poker ['pəukə*] *n* atiçador *m*; (*CARDS*) pôquer *m*; ~-**faced** *adj* com rosto impassível.

poky ['pəukɪ] *adj* acanhado, apertado.

Poland ['pəulənd] *n* Polônia.

polar ['pəulə*] *adj* polar; ~ **bear** *n* urso polar.

polarize ['pəuləraɪz] *vt* polarizar.

pole [pəul] *n* vara; (*GEO*) pólo; (*TEL*) poste *m*; (*flag* ~) mastro; (*tent* ~) estaca.

Pole [pəul] *n* polonês/esa *m/f*.

pole vault ['pəulvɔːlt] *n* salto com vara.

police [pə'liːs] *n* polícia // *vt* policiar; ~ **car** *n* rádio-patrulha *f*; ~**man** *n* policial *m* (*Br*), polícia *m* (*Pt*); ~ **state** *n* estado policial; ~ **station** *n* delegacia (de polícia) (*Br*), esquadra (*Pt*); ~**woman** *n* policial *f* (feminina) (*Br*), mulher *f* polícia (*Pt*).

policy ['pɔlɪsɪ] *n* política; (*also:* **insurance** ~) apólice *f*.

polio ['pəulɪəu] *n* poliomielite *f*, polio *f*.

Polish ['pəulɪʃ] *adj, n* polonês/esa *m/f*.

polish ['pɔlɪʃ] *n* (*for shoes*) graxa; (*for floor*) cera (para encerar); (*for nails*) esmalte *m*; (*shine*) verniz *m*, polimento; (*fig: refinement*) refinamento, cultura // *vt* (*shoes*) engraxar; (*make shiny*) lustrar, dar brilho a; (*fig: improve*) refinar, polir; **to ~ off** *vt* (*work*) dar os arremates a; (*food*) raspar; ~**ed** *adj* (*fig: person*) culto; (*: manners*) refinado.

polite [pə'laɪt] *adj* gentil, bem educado; (*formal*) cortês; ~**ness** *n* gentileza, cortesia.

politic ['pɔlɪtɪk] *adj* prudente; ~**al** [pə'lɪtɪkl] *adj* político; ~**ian** [-'tɪʃən] *n* político; ~**s** *npl* política *sg*.

polka ['pɔlkə] *n* polca; ~ **dot** *n* bolinha.

poll [pəul] *n* (*votes*) votação *f*; (*also:* **opinion** ~) pesquisa, sondagem *f* // *vt* (*votes*) receber, obter.

pollen ['pɔlən] *n* pólen *m*.

pollination [pɔlɪ'neɪʃən] *n* polinização *f*.

polling ['pəulɪŋ]: ~ **booth** *n* cabine *f* de votar; ~ **day** *n* dia *m* de eleição; ~ **station** *n* centro eleitoral.

pollute [pə'luːt] *vt* poluir; **pollution** [-'luːʃən] *n* poluição *f*, contaminação *f*.

polo ['pəuləu] *n* (*sport*) pólo; ~-**neck** *adj* de gola rolê.

polyester [pɔlɪ'ɛstə*] *n* poliéster *m*.

polygamy [pə'lɪgəmɪ] *n* poligamia.

polytechnic [pɔlɪ'tɛknɪk] *n* politécnico, escola politécnica.

polythene, polyethylene (*US*) ['pɔlɪθiːn, pɔlɪ'ɛθɪliːn] *n* politeno.

pomegranate ['pɔmɪgrænɪt] *n* (*fruit*) romã *f*.

pommel ['pɔml] *n* botão *m*; (*saddle*) maçaneta // *vt* esmurrar.

pomp [pɔmp] *n* pompa.

pompous ['pɔmpəs] *adj* pomposo.

pond [pɔnd] *n* (*natural*) lago pequeno; (*artificial*) tanque *m*.

ponder ['pɔndə*] *vt* ponderar, meditar (sobre); ~**ous** *adj* pesado.

pontiff ['pɔntɪf] *n* pontífice *m*.

pontificate [pɔn'tɪfɪkeɪt] *vi* (*fig*): **to ~ (about)** pontificar (sobre).

pontoon [pɔn'tuːn] *n* pontão *m*; (*card game*) vinte-e-um *m*.

pony ['pəunɪ] *n* pônei *m*; ~**tail** *n* rabo-de-cavalo; ~ **trekking** *n* excursão *f* em pônei.

poodle ['puːdl] *n* cão-d'água *m*.

pool [puːl] *n* (*of rain*) poça, charco; (*pond*) lago; (*also:* **swimming** ~) piscina; (*billiards*) sinuca // *vt* reunir; (*football*) ~**s** loteria esportiva (*Br*), totobola (*Pt*).

poor [puə*] *adj* pobre; (*bad*) inferior, mau // *npl:* **the** ~ os pobres *mpl*; ~**ly** *adj* adoentado, indisposto.

pop [pɔp] *n* bum!; (*sound*) ruído seco, estouro; (*MUS*) pop *m*; (*US: col: father*) papai *m*; (*lemonade*) bebida gasosa // *vt* (*put*) pôr // *vi* estourar; (*cork*) saltar; **to ~ in** *vi* entrar de repente; (*visit*) dar um pulo; **to ~ out** *vi* sair de repente; **to ~ up** *vi* aparecer inesperadamente; ~ **concert** *n* concerto pop; ~**corn** *n* pipoca.

pope [pəup] *n* Papa *m*.

poplar ['pɔplə*] *n* álamo, choupo.

poplin ['pɔplɪn] *n* popeline *f*.

poppy ['pɔpɪ] *n* papoula.

populace ['pɔpjuləs] *n* populaça, povão *m*.

popular ['pɔpjulə*] *adj* popular; (*fashionable*) na moda; ~**ity** [-'lærɪtɪ] *n* popularidade *f*; ~**ize** *vt* popularizar; (*disseminate*) vulgarizar.

populate ['pɔpjuleɪt] *vt* povoar; **population** [-'leɪʃən] *n* população *f*.

populous ['pɔpjuləs] *adj* populoso.

porcelain ['pɔːslɪn] *n* porcelana.

porch [pɔːtʃ] *n* pórtico; (*US*) varanda.

porcupine ['pɔːkjupaɪn] *n* porco-espinho.

pore [pɔː*] *n* poro // *vi:* **to ~ over** examinar com atenção.

pork [pɔːk] *n* carne *f* de porco.

pornographic [pɔːnə'græfɪk] *adj* pornográfico; **pornography** [-'nɔgrəfɪ] *n* pornografia.

porous ['pɔːrəs] *adj* poroso.

porpoise ['pɔːpəs] *n* golfinho, boto.

porridge ['pɔrɪdʒ] *n* mingau *m* de aveia.

port [pɔːt] *n* (*harbour*) porto; (*NAUT. left side*) bombordo; (*wine*) vinho do Porto.

portable ['pɔːtəbl] *adj* portátil.

portend [pɔː'tɛnd] *vt* pressagiar; **portent** [pɔːtɛnt] *n* presságio, portento.

porter ['pɔːtə*] n (for luggage) carregador; (doorkeeper) porteiro.

porthole ['pɔːthəul] n vigia.

portion ['pɔːʃən] n porção f, quinhão m; (helping) ração f.

portly ['pɔːtlı] adj corpulento.

portrait ['pɔːtreıt] n retrato.

portray [pɔː'treı] vt retratar; (in writing) descrever; ~al n representação f.

Portugal [pɔː'tjugl] n Portugal m.

Portuguese [pɔːtju'giːz] adj português/esa // n, pl inv português/esa m/f; (LING) português m.

pose [pəuz] n postura, pose f; (pej) pose, afetaçao (Pt: -ct-) f // vi posar; (pretend): to ~ as fazer-se passar por // vt (question) pôr.

posh [pɔʃ] adj (col) fino, elegante.

position [pə'zıʃən] n posição f; (job) cargo // vt colocar, situar.

positive ['pɔzıtıv] adj positivo; (certain) certo; (definite) definitivo.

posse ['pɔsı] n (US) pelotão m de civis armados.

possess [pə'zɛs] vt possuir; ~ion [pə'zɛʃən] n posse f, possessão f; ~ive adj possessivo.

possibility [pɔsı'bılıtı] n possibilidade f; **possible** ['pɔsıbl] adj possível; **as big as possible** o maior possível; **possibly** ['pɔsıblı] adv (perhaps) possivelmente, talvez; **I cannot possibly come** estou impossibilitado de vir.

post [pəust] n (letters, delivery) correio; (job, situation) posto; (pole) poste m // vt (send by post) pôr no correio; (MIL) nomear; (bills) afixar, pregar; (appoint): **to ~** destinar a; ~**age** n porte m, franquia; ~**al** adj postal; ~**al order** n vale m postal; ~**box** n caixa do correio; ~**card** n cartão m postal.

postdate [pəust'deıt] vt (cheque) pós-datar.

poster ['pəustə*] n cartaz m.

posterior [pɔs'tıərıə*] n (col) traseiro, nádegas fpl; (col) bunda.

posterity [pɔs'tɛrıtı] n posteridade f.

postgraduate ['pəust'grædjuət] n pós-graduado/a.

posthumous ['pɔstjuməs] adj póstumo.

post: ~**man** n carteiro; ~**mark** n carimbo do correio; ~**master** n agente m/f do correio (Br), chefe m/f do correio (Pt).

post-mortem [pəust'mɔːtəm] n autópsia.

post office ['pəustɔfıs] n (building) agência do correio, correio; (organization) Departamento dos Correios e Telégrafos (Br), C.T.T. (Correios, Telégrafos e Telefones) (Pt); ~ **box** (P.O. box) n caixa postal.

postpone [pəs'pəun] vt adiar; ~**ment** n adiamento.

postscript ['pəustskrıpt] n pós-escrito.

postulate ['pɔstjuleıt] vt postular.

posture ['pɔstʃə*] n postura, atitude f.

postwar [pəust'wɔː*] adj de após-guerra.

posy ['pəuzı] n ramalhete m.

pot [pɔt] n (for cooking) panela; (for flowers) vaso; (for jam) pote m; (col: marijuana) maconha // vt (plant) plantar em vaso; (conserve) pôr em conserva.

potato [pə'teıtəu] pl ~**es** n batata.

potent ['pəutnt] adj potente, poderoso; (drink) forte.

potential [pə'tɛnʃl] adj potencial, latente // n potencial m.

pothole ['pɔthəul] n (in road) buraco; (underground) caldeirão m, cova; **potholer** n espeleologista f; **potholing** n: **to go potholing** dedicar-se à espeleologia.

potion ['pəuʃən] n poção f.

potluck [pɔt'lʌk] n: **to take ~** contentar-se com o que houver.

potshot ['pɔtʃɔt] n: **to take a ~ at sth** atirar em algo a esmo.

potted ['pɔtıd] adj (food) em conserva; (plant) de vaso.

potter ['pɔtə*] n (artistic) ceramista m/f; (artisan) oleiro // vi: **to ~ around, ~ about** desperdiçar tempo com ninharias; ~**y** n cerâmica, olaria.

potty ['pɔtı] adj (col: mad) maluco, doido // n urinol m (de criança).

pouch [pautʃ] n (ZOOL) bolsa; (for tobacco) tabaqueira.

pouf(fe) [puːf] n pufe m.

poultice ['pəult s] n cataplasma.

poultry ['pəultrı] n aves fpl domésticas; ~ **farm** n granja avícola.

pounce [pauns] vi: **to ~ on** lançar-se sobre // n salto, arremetida.

pound [paund] n (gen) libra; (for dogs) canil m; (for cars) depósito // vt (beat) socar, esmurrar; (crush) triturar // vi (beat) dar pancadas; ~ **sterling** n libra esterlina.

pour [pɔː*] vt despejar; (tea) servir // vi fluir, correr; (rain) chover a cântaros; **to ~ away or off** vt esvaziar, decantar; **to ~ in** vi (people) entrar em enxurrada; **to ~ out** vi (people) sair aos borbotões // vt (drink) servir; ~**ing** adj: ~**ing rain** chuva torrencial.

pout [paut] vi fazer beicinho or biquinho.

poverty ['pɔvətı] n pobreza; (fig) falta, escassez f; ~-**stricken** adj indigente, necessitado.

powder ['paudə*] n pó m; (face ~) pó-de-arroz m; (gun~) pólvora // vt pulverizar; (face) empoar, passar pó em; ~ **compact** n estojo (de pó-de-arroz); ~ **room** n toucador m; ~**y** adj poeirento.

power ['pauə*] n (gen) poder m; (strength) força; (nation) potência; (ability, POL: of party, leader) poder, poderio; (drive) propulsão f; (TECH) potência; (ELEC) força, energia // vt (ELEC) alimentar; ~ **cut** n corte m de energia; ~**ed** adj: ~**ed by** com propulsão a; ~**ful** adj poderoso; (engine) potente; (build) vigoroso; (emotion) intenso; ~**less** adj impotente; ~ **line** n fio de alta tensão; ~ point *n* tomada; ~ station *n* central *f* elétrica (*Pt*: -ct-).

practicable ['præktɪkəbl] *adj* (*scheme*) praticável, viável.

practical ['præktɪkl] *adj* prático; ~ **joke** *n* brincadeira, peça; ~**ly** *adv* (*almost*) praticamente.

practice ['præktɪs] *n* (*habit*) costume *m*, hábito; (*exercise*) prática, exercício; (*training*) treinamento; (*MED*) consultório // *vt/i* (*US*) = **practise**; **in** ~ (*in reality*) na prática; **out of** ~ destreinado.

practise, practice (*US*) ['præktɪs] *vt* (*carry out*) praticar; (*be in the habit of*) ter por costume; (*profession*) exercer; (*train at*) fazer exercícios de // *vi* exercer (*profissão*); (*train*) treinar, exercitar-se; **practising** *adj* (*Christian etc*) praticante; (*lawyer*) que exerce.

practitioner [præk'tɪʃənə*] *n* praticante *m/f*; (*MED*) médico/a.

pragmatic [præg'mætɪk] *adj* pragmático.

prairie ['prɛərɪ] *n* campina, pradaria.

praise [preɪz] *n* louvor *m*, elogio; ~**worthy** *adj* louvável, digno de elogio.

pram [præm] *n* carrinho de bebê.

prance [prɑːns] *vi* (*horse*) curvetear, fazer cabriolas.

prank [præŋk] *n* travessura, peça.

prattle ['prætl] *vi* tagarelar; (*child*) balbuciar.

prawn [prɔːn] *n* pitu *m*; (*small*) camarão *m*.

pray [preɪ] *vi* rezar; ~**er** *n* oração *f*, prece *f*; (*entreaty*) súplica, rogo; ~**er book** *n* missal *m*, livro de orações.

preach [priːtʃ] *vi* pregar; ~**er** *n* pregador(a) *m/f*; (*US*) pastor *m*.

preamble [prɪ'æmbl] *n* preâmbulo.

prearranged [priːə'reɪndʒd] *adj* combinado de antemão.

precarious [prɪ'kɛərɪəs] *adj* precário.

precaution [prɪ'kɔːʃən] *n* precaução *f*.

precede [prɪ'siːd] *vt/i* preceder.

precedence ['prɛsɪdəns] *n* precedência; (*priority*) prioridade *f*; **precedent** [-ənt] *n* precedente *m*.

preceding [prɪ'siːdɪŋ] *adj* precedente.

precept ['priːsɛpt] *n* preceito.

precinct ['priːsɪŋkt] *n* recinto; ~**s** *npl* arredores *mpl*; **pedestrian** ~ área de pedestres; **shopping** ~ zona comercial.

precious ['prɛʃəs] *adj* precioso; (*stylized*) afetado (*Pt*: -ct-).

precipice ['prɛsɪpɪs] *n* precipício.

precipitate [prɪ'sɪpɪt] *adj* (*hasty*) precipitado, apressado // *vt* [prɪ'sɪpɪteɪt] (*hasten*) precipitar, acelerar; (*bring about*) causar; **precipitation** [-'teɪʃən] *n* precipitação *f*.

precipitous [prɪ'sɪpɪtəs] *adj* (*steep*) íngreme, escarpado.

precise [prɪ'saɪs] *adj* exato (*Pt*: -ct-), preciso; (*person*) escrupuloso, meticuloso; ~**ly** *adv* exa(c)tamente; **precision** [-'sɪʒən] *n* precisão *f*.

preclude [prɪ'kluːd] *vt* excluir.

precocious [prɪ'kəʊʃəs] *adj* precoce.

preconceived [priːkən'siːvd] *adj* (*idea*) preconcebido.

precursor [priː'kɜːsə*] *n* precursor(a) *m/f*.

predator ['prɛdətə*] *n* predador *m*; ~**y** *adj* predatório, rapace.

predecessor ['priːdɪsɛsə*] *n* predecessor(a) *m/f*, antepassado/a.

predestination [priːdɛstɪ'neɪʃən] *n* predestinação *f*, destino.

predetermine [priːdɪ'tɜːmɪn] *vt* predeterminar, predispor.

predicament [prɪ'dɪkəmənt] *n* predicamento, apuro.

predict [prɪ'dɪkt] *vt* predizer, prognosticar; ~**ion** [-'dɪkʃən] *n* prognóstico.

predominant [prɪ'dɒmɪnənt] *adj* predominante, preponderante; **predominate** [-neɪt] *vi* predominar.

pre-eminent [priː'ɛmɪnənt] *adj* preeminente.

pre-empt [priː'ɛmt] *vt* adquirir por preempção *or* de antemão.

preen [priːn] *vt*: **to** ~ **itself** (*bird*) limpar e alisar as penas (com o bico); **to** ~ **o.s.** enfeitar-se, envaidecer-se.

prefab ['priːfæb] *n* casa pré-fabricada.

prefabricated [priː'fæbrɪkeɪtɪd] *adj* pré-fabricado.

preface ['prɛfəs] *n* prefácio.

prefect ['priːfɛkt] *n* (*Brit: SCOL*) monitor *m*, tutor *m*.

prefer [prɪ'fɜː*] *vt* preferir; ~**able** ['prɛfrəbl] *adj* preferível; ~**ably** ['prɛfrəblɪ] *adv* de preferência; ~**ence** ['prɛfrəns] *n* preferência, prioridade *f*; ~**ential** [prɛfə'rɛnʃəl] *adj* preferencial.

prefix ['priːfɪks] *n* prefixo.

pregnancy ['prɛgnənsɪ] *n* gravidez *f*; **pregnant** [-ənt] *adj* grávida; **to be pregnant** estar grávida; **pregnant with** rico de, cheio de.

prehistoric ['priːhɪs'tɒrɪk] *adj* pré-histórico.

prejudge [priː'dʒʌdʒ] *vt* fazer um juízo antecipado de, prejulgar.

prejudice ['prɛdʒudɪs] *n* (*bias*) preconceito; (*harm*) prejuízo // *vt* (*predispose*) predispor; (*harm*) prejudicar; ~**d** *adj* (*person*) predisposto, preconceituoso; (*view*) parcial, preconcebido.

prelate ['prɛlət] *n* prelado.

preliminary [prɪ'lɪmɪnərɪ] *adj* preliminar, prévio.

prelude ['prɛljuːd] *n* prelúdio.

premarital ['priː'mærɪtl] *adj* pré-nupcial.

premature ['prɛmətʃuə*] *adj* prematuro, precoce.

premeditated [priː'mɛdɪteɪtɪd] *adj* premeditado.

premier ['prɛmɪə*] *adj* primeiro, principal // *n* (*POL*) primeiro-ministro.

première ['prɛmɪɛə*] *n* estréia.

premise ['prɛmɪs] *n* premissa; ~**s** *npl*

local *msg*; (*house*) casa *sg*; (*shop*) loja *sg*; on the ~s no local.

premium ['priːmɪəm] *n* prêmio, recompensa; (*COMM*) prêmio; **to be at a** ~ ser difícil de obter.

premonition [prɛmə'nɪʃən] *n* presságio, pressentimento.

preoccupation [priːɔkju'peɪʃən] *n* preocupação *f*; **preoccupied** [-'ɔkjupaɪd] *adj* (*worried*) preocupado, apreensivo; (*absorbed*) absorto.

prep [prɛp] *n* (*SCOL: study*) deveres *mpl*; ~ **school** *n* = **preparatory school.**

prepaid [priː'peɪd] *adj* com porte pago.

preparation [prɛpə'reɪʃən] *n* preparação *f*; ~s *npl* preparativos *mpl*.

preparatory [prɪ'pærətərɪ] *adj* preparatório, introdutório; ~ **to** antes de; ~ **school** *n* escola preparatória.

prepare [prɪ'pɛə*] *vt* preparar, aprontar // *vi*: **to** ~ **for** preparar-se *or* aprontar-se para; (*make preparations*) fazer preparativos para; ~**d to** preparado *or* pronto para.

preponderance [prɪ'pɔndərns] *n* preponderância, predomínio.

preposition [prɛpə'zɪʃən] *n* preposição *f*.

preposterous [prɪ'pɔstərəs] *adj* absurdo, disparatado.

prerequisite [priː'rɛkwɪzɪt] *n* pré-requisito, condição *f* prévia.

prerogative [prɪ'rɔgətɪv] *n* prerrogativa, privilégio.

presbyterian [prɛzbɪ'tɪərɪən] *adj, n* presbiteriano/a.

preschool ['priː'skuːl] *adj* pré-escolar.

prescribe [prɪ'skraɪb] *vt* prescrever; (*MED*) receitar.

prescription [prɪ'skrɪpʃən] *n* prescrição *f*, ordem *f*; (*MED*) receita.

presence ['prɛzns] *n* presença; (*attendance*) assistência; ~ **of mind** *n* presença de espírito.

present ['prɛznt] *adj* (*in attendance*) presente; (*current*) atual (*Pt:* -ct-) // *n* (*gift*) presente *m*; (*actuality*) (*a*(*c*)tualidade *f*, momento; **for the** ~ por enquanto // *vt* [prɪ'zɛnt] (*introduce*) apresentar; (*expound*) expor; (*give*) presentear, oferecer; (*THEATRE*) representar; **at** ~ no momento, agora; ~**able** [prɪ'zɛntəbl] *adj* apresentável; ~**ation** [-'teɪʃən] *n* apresentação *f*; (*gift*) presente; (*of case*) exposição *f*; (*THEATRE*) representação *f*; ~**-day** *adj* atual (*Pt:* -ct-); ~**ly** *adv* (*soon*) logo, em breve.

preservation [prɛzə'veɪʃən] *n* conservação *f*, preservação *f*.

preservative [prɪ'zɔːvətɪv] *n* preservativo.

preserve [prɪ'zɔːv] *vt* (*keep safe*) preservar, proteger; (*maintain*) conservar, manter; (*food*) pôr em conserva; (*in salt*) conservar em sal, salgar // *n* (*for game*) reserva de caça, coutada; (*often pl: jam*) compota, conserva.

preside [prɪ'zaɪd] *vi* presidir.

presidency ['prɛzɪdənsɪ] *n* presidência; **president** [-ənt] *n* presidente *m/f*; **presidential** [-'dɛnʃl] *adj* presidencial.

press [prɛs] *n* (*tool, machine, newspapers*) prensa; (*printer's*) imprensa, prelo; (*crowd*) turba, apinhamento; (*of hand*) aperto *m* // *vt* (*push*) empurrar; (*squeeze*) apertar, espremer; (*clothes: iron*) passar; (*TECH*) prensar; (*harry*) assediar; **to** ~ **down** (*button*) apertar; (*insist*): **to** ~ **sth on sb** insistir para que alguém aceite algo // *vi* (*squeeze*) apertar; (*pressurize*) fazer pressão, pressionar; **we are** ~**ed for time** estamos com pouco tempo; **to** ~ **on** *vi* avançar; (*hurry*) apertar o passo; ~ **agency** *n* agência (de imprensa); ~ **conference** *n* entrevista coletiva (para a imprensa); ~ **cutting** *n* recorte m de jornal; ~**ing** *adj* urgente; ~ **stud** *n* botão *m* de pressão.

pressure ['prɛʃə*] *n* pressão *f*; (*urgency*) premência, urgência; (*influence*) coação (*Pt:* -cç-) *f*; (*MED*) pressão *f* sanguínea; ~ **cooker** *n* panela de pressão; ~ **gauge** *n* manômetro; ~ **group** *n* grupo de pressão; **pressurized** *adj* pressurizado.

prestige [prɛs'tiːʒ] *n* prestígio; **prestigious** [-'tɪdʒəs] *adj* de prestígio.

presumably [prɪ'zjuːməblɪ] *adv* presumivelmente, provavelmente.

presume [prɪ'zjuːm] *vt* presumir, supor; **to** ~ **to do** (*dare*) ousar, atrever-se a; (*set out to*) pretender.

presumption [prɪ'zʌmpʃən] *n* suposição *f*; (*pretension*) presunção *f*; (*boldness*) atrevimento, audácia.

presuppose [prɪsə'pəuz] *vt* pressupor, implicar.

pretence, pretense (*US*) [prɪ'tɛns] *n* (*claim*) pretensão *f*; (*display*) ostentação *f*; (*pretext*) pretexto; (*make-believe*) fingimento; **on the** ~ **of** sob o pretexto de.

pretend [prɪ'tɛnd] *vt* (*feign*) fingir; // *vi* (*feign*) fingir; (*claim*): **to** ~ **to sth** aspirar a *or* pretender a algo.

pretension [prɪ'tɛnʃən] *n* (*presumption*) presunção *f*; (*claim*) pretensão *f*.

pretentious [prɪ'tɛnʃəs] *adj* pretensioso, presunçoso; (*ostentatious*) exibicionista, ostentativo.

pretext ['priːtɛkst] *n* pretexto.

pretty ['prɪtɪ] *adj* (*gen*) lindo; (*person*) bonito; (*dress*) lindo; (*sum*) considerável // *adv* (*quite*) bastante; (*nearly*) quase.

prevail [prɪ'veɪl] *vi* (*win*) triunfar; (*be current*) imperar; (*be in fashion*) estar na moda; (*be usual*) prevalecer, vigorar; (*persuade*): **to** ~ **(up)on sb to do sth** persuadir alguém a fazer algo; ~**ing** *adj* (*dominant*) predominante; (*usual*) corrente.

prevalent ['prɛvələnt] *adj* (*dominant*) predominante; (*usual*) corrente; (*fashionable*) dominante, da moda; (*present-day*) atual (*Pt:* -ct-).

prevent [pri'vɛnt] vt: to ~ (sb) from doing sth impedir (alguém) de fazer algo; ~able adj evitável; ~ative adj preventivo; ~ion [-'vɛnʃən] n prevenção f, impedimento; ~ive adj preventivo.

preview ['pri:vju:] n (of film) pré-estréia; (fig) antecipação f.

previous ['pri:vɪəs] adj prévio, anterior; (hasty) apressado; ~ly adv previamente, antecipadamente; (in earlier times) antes, anteriormente.

prewar [pri:'wɔ:*] adj anterior à guerra.

prey [preɪ] n presa f // vi: to ~ on viver às custas de; (feed on) alimentar-se de; (plunder) saquear, pilhar; it was ~ing on his mind preocupava-o, atormentava-o.

price [praɪs] n preço // vt (goods) fixar o preço de; ~less adj inestimável.

prick [prɪk] n picada; (with pin) alfinetada; (sting) picada, ferroada // vt picar, furar; to ~ up one's ears aguçar os ouvidos.

prickle ['prɪkl] n (sensation) comichão, ardência; (BOT) espinho; (ZOOL) acúleo; **prickly** adj espinhoso; (fig: person) irritadiço; (: touchy) susceptível, melindroso.

pride [praɪd] n orgulho; (pej) soberba // vt: to ~ o.s. on orgulhar-se de, vangloriar-se de.

priest [pri:st] n sacerdote m, padre m; ~ess n sacerdotisa; ~hood n (practice) sacerdócio; (priests) clero.

prig [prɪg] n pedante m/f.

prim [prɪm] adj (formal) empertigado; (affected) afetado (Pt: -ct-); (prudish) que afe(c)ta recato.

primarily ['praɪmərɪlɪ] adv (above all) fundamentalmente, antes de nada; (firstly) em primeiro lugar.

primary ['praɪmərɪ] adj primário; (first in importance) principal; ~ school n escola primária.

primate ['praɪmɪt] n (REL) primaz m // n ['praɪmeɪt] (ZOOL) primata m.

prime [praɪm] adj primeiro, principal; (basic) fundamental, primário; (excellent) superior // vt (gun, pump) escorvar; (fig) aprontar, preparar; in the ~ of life na primavera da vida; ~ minister n primeiro-ministro; primer n (book) livro de leitura; (paint) pintura de base.

primitive ['prɪmɪtɪv] adj primitivo; (crude) rudimentar; (uncivilized) grosseiro, inculto.

primrose ['prɪmrəuz] n prímula, primavera.

primus (stove) ['praɪməs] n fogão m portátil a petróleo.

prince [prɪns] n príncipe m.

princess [prɪn'sɛs] n princesa.

principal ['prɪnsɪpl] adj principal, fundamental // n diretor(a) (Pt: -ct-) m/f.

principality [prɪnsɪ'pælɪtɪ] n principado.

principle ['prɪnsɪpl] n princípio.

print [prɪnt] n (impression) impressão f,

marca; (letters) letra de forma; (fabric) estampado; (ART) estampa, gravura; (PHOT) cópia // vt (gen) imprimir; (on mind) gravar; (write in capitals) escrever em letra de imprensa; out of ~ esgotado; ~ed matter n impressos mpl; ~er n impressor(a) m/f; ~ing n (art) imprensa; (act) impressão f; (quantity) tiragem f; ~ing press n prelo, máquina impressora.

prior ['praɪə*] adj anterior, prévio // n prior m; ~ to doing antes de or até fazer.

priority [praɪ'ɔrɪtɪ] n prioridade f.

prise [praɪz] vt: to ~ open abrir com alavanca, arrombar.

prism ['prɪzəm] n prisma m.

prison ['prɪzn] n prisão f, cárcere m // adj carcerário; ~er n (in prison) preso, prisioneiro; (under arrest) detido; (in dock) acusado, réu m.

privacy ['prɪvəsɪ] n (seclusion) isolamento, solidão f; (intimacy) intimidade f, privacidade f.

private ['praɪvɪt] adj (personal) particular; (confidential) confidencial, reservado; (intimate) privado, íntimo; (sitting etc) a portas fechadas // n soldado raso; '~' (on envelope) 'confidencial'; (on door) 'particular'; in ~ em particular; ~ enterprise n a iniciativa privada; ~ eye n detetive (Pt: -ct-) m particular; ~ly adv em particular; (in o.s.) no fundo.

privet ['prɪvɪt] n alfena.

privilege ['prɪvɪlɪdʒ] n privilégio; (prerogative) prerrogativa; ~d adj privilegiado.

privy ['prɪvɪ] adj: to be ~ to estar inteirado de; P~ Council n Conselho Privado.

prize [praɪz] n prêmio // adj premiado; (first class) de primeira classe // vt estimar, apreciar; ~-giving n distribuição f dos prêmios; ~winner n premiado/a.

pro [prəu] n (SPORT) profissional m/f; the ~s and cons os prós e os contras.

probability [prɔbə'bɪlɪtɪ] n probabilidade f; **probable** ['prɔbəbl] adj provável; (plausible) verossímil; **probably** ['prɔbəblɪ] adv provavelmente.

probation [prə'beɪʃən] n: on ~ (employee) em estágio probatório; (LAW) em liberdade condicional.

probe [prəub] n (MED, SPACE) sonda; (enquiry) pesquisa // vt sondar; (investigate) investigar, esquadrinhar.

problem ['prɔbləm] n problema m; ~atic [-'mætɪk] adj problemático.

procedure [prə'si:dʒə*] n (ADMIN, LAW) procedimento; (method) método, processo; (bureaucratic) protocolo.

proceed [prə'si:d] vi proceder; (continue) to ~ (with) continuar or prosseguir (com); ~ings npl ato (Pt: -ct-) sg, procedimento sg; (LAW) processo sg; (meeting) reunião fsg; (records) atas

(Pt: -ct-) fpl; **~s** ['prəusi:dz] *npl* produto *sg.*

process ['prəusɛs] *n* processo; *(method)* método, sistema *m; (proceeding)* procedimento *// vt* processar, elaborar; **in ~** em andamento; **~ing** *n* processamento.

procession [prə'sɛʃən] *n* procissão *f;* **funeral ~** cortejo fúnebre.

proclaim [prə'kleɪm] *vt* proclamar; *(announce)* anunciar; **proclamation** [prɔklə'meɪʃən] *n* proclamação *f; (written)* promulgação *f.*

procreation [prəukrɪ'eɪʃən] *n* procriação *f.*

procure [prə'kjuə*] *vt* obter.

prod [prɔd] *vt (push)* empurrar; *(with elbow)* cutucar, acotovelar; *(jab)* espetar *// n* empurrão *m;* cotovelada; espetada.

prodigal ['prɔdɪgl] *adj* pródigo.

prodigious [prə'dɪdʒəs] *adj* prodigioso, extraordinário.

prodigy ['prɔdɪdʒɪ] *n* prodígio.

produce ['prɔdju:s] *n (AGR)* produtos *mpl* agrícolas *// vt* [prə'dju:s] *(gen)* produzir; *(profit)* render; *(show)* apresentar, exibir; *(THEATRE)* pôr em cena *or* em cartaz; *(offspring)* dar a luz; **producer** *n (THEATRE)* diretor(a) *(Pt: -ct-) m/f; (AGR, CINEMA)* produtor(a) *m/f.*

product ['prɔdʌkt] *n (thing)* produto; *(result)* fruto, resultado.

production [prə'dʌkʃən] *n (act)* produção *f; (thing)* produto; *(THEATRE)* representação *f,* encenação *f;* **~ line** *n* linha de produção *or* de montagem.

productive [prə'dʌktɪv] *adj* produtivo; **productivity** [prɔdʌk'tɪvɪtɪ] *n* produtividade *f.*

profane [prə'feɪn] *adj* profano; *(language etc)* irreverente, sacrílego.

profess [prə'fɛs] *vt* professar; *(regret)* manifestar.

profession [prə'fɛʃən] *n* profissão *f;* **~al** *n* profissional *m/f; (expert)* experto, versado *// adj* perito; *(by profession)* de carreira, por profissão.

professor [prə'fɛsə*] *n* catedrático/a.

proficiency [prə'fɪʃənsɪ] *n* proficiência, capacidade *f;* **proficient** [-ənt] *adj* proficiente, capaz.

profile ['prəufaɪl] *n* perfil *m.*

profit ['prɔfɪt] *n (COMM)* lucro; *(fig)* vantagem *f // vi:* **to ~ by** *or* **from** aproveitar-se de, tirar proveito de; **~ability** [-ə'bɪlɪtɪ] *n* rentabilidade *f;* **~able** *adj (ECON)* lucrativo, rendoso; *(useful)* proveitoso; **~eering** [-'tɪərɪŋ] *n (pej)* lucros *mpl* excessivos.

profound [prə'faund] *adj* profundo.

profuse [prə'fju:s] *adj* profuso, pródigo; **~ly** *adv* abundantemente; **profusion** [-'fju:ʒən] *n* profusão *f,* abundância.

progeny ['prɔdʒɪnɪ] *n* prole *f,* progênie *f.*

programme, program *(US)* ['prəugræm] *n* programa *m // vt* programar; **programming, programing** *(US) n* programação *f.*

progress ['prəugrɛs] *n* progresso; *(development)* desenvolvimento *// vi* [prə'grɛs] progredir, avançar; **in ~** em andamento; **~ion** [-'grɛʃən] *n* progressão *f,* avanço; **~ive** [-'grɛsɪv] *adj* progressivo *// n (person)* progressista *m/f.*

prohibit [prə'hɪbɪt] *vt* proibir; **to ~ sb from doing sth** proibir alguém de fazer algo; **~ion** [prəuɪ'bɪʃən] *n (US)* lei *f* seca; **~ive** *adj (price etc)* proibitivo, excessivo.

project ['prɔdʒɛkt] *n* projeto *(Pt: -ct-) // (vb:* [prə'dʒɛkt]*) vt* proje(c)tar *// vi (stick out)* ressaltar, sobressair.

projectile [prə'dʒɛktaɪl] *n* projétil *(Pt: -ct-) m.*

projection [prə'dʒɛkʃən] *n* projeção *(Pt: -cç-) f; (overhang)* saliência.

projector [prə'dʒɛktə*] *n* projetor *(Pt: -ct-) m.*

proletarian [prəulɪ'tɛərɪən] *adj, n* proletário/a; **proletariat** [-rɪət] *n* proletariado.

proliferate [prə'lɪfəreɪt] *vi* proliferar, multiplicar-se; **proliferation** [-'reɪʃən] *n* proliferação *f.*

prolific [prə'lɪfɪk] *adj* prolífico.

prologue ['prəulɔg] *n* prólogo.

prolong [prə'lɔŋ] *vt* prolongar, estender.

promenade [prɔmə'na:d] *n (by sea)* passeio (à orla marítima).

prominence ['prɔmɪnəns] *n (fig)* eminência, importância; **prominent** [-ənt] *adj (standing out)* proeminente; *(important)* eminente, notório.

promiscuous [prə'mɪskjuəs] *adj (sexually)* promíscuo, libertino.

promise ['prɔmɪs] *n* promessa *// vt/i* prometer; **promising** *adj* prometedor(a).

promontory ['prɔməntrɪ] *n* promontório.

promote [prə'məut] *vt (gen)* promover; *(new product)* fazer propaganda de; *(MIL)* promover; **promoter** *n (of sporting event)* patrocinador(a) *m/f;* **promotion** [-'məuʃən] *n (gen, MIL)* promoção *f.*

prompt [prɔmpt] *adj* pronto, rápido *// adv (punctually)* pontualmente *// vt (urge)* incitar, impelir; *(THEATRE)* servir de ponto a; **to ~ sb to do sth** induzir alguém a fazer algo; **~er** *n (THEATRE)* ponto; **~ly** *adv (punctually)* pontualmente; *(rapidly)* rapidamente; **~ness** *n* pontualidade *f;* rapidez *f.*

prone [prəun] *adj (lying)* inclinado, de bruços; **~ to** propenso a, predisposto a.

prong [prɔŋ] *n* dente *m,* ponta.

pronoun ['prəunaun] *n* pronome *m.*

pronounce [prə'nauns] *vt* pronunciar; *(declare)* declarar, afirmar *// vi:* **to ~ (up)on** pronunciar-se sobre; **~d** *adj (marked)* marcado, nítido; **~ment** *n* pronunciamento.

pronunciation [prənʌnsɪ'eɪʃən] *n* pronúncia.

proof [pru:f] *n* prova; *(of alcohol)* teor *m*

alcoólico // adj: ~ **against** à prova de; ~**reader** n revisor(a) m/f de provas.

prop [prɔp] n suporte m, escora; (fig) amparo, apoio // vt (also: ~ **up**) apoiar, escorar; (lean): **to ~ sth against** apoiar algo contra.

propaganda [prɔpə'gændə] n propaganda.

propagate ['prɔpəgeɪt] vt propagar.

propel [prə'pel] vt propelir, propulsionar; ~**ler** n hélice f; ~**ling pencil** n lapiseira.

proper ['prɔpə*] adj (suited, right) próprio; (exact) preciso; (apt) apropriado, conveniente; (timely) oportuno; (seemly) decente, respeitável; (authentic) genuíno; (col: real) autêntico; ~**ly** adv corre(c)tamente; (well) bem.

property ['prɔpətɪ] n (gen) propriedade f; (goods) posses fpl, bens mpl; (estate) propriedade f, fazenda; **it's their ~** é seu, pertence a eles.

prophecy ['prɔfɪsɪ] n profecia; **prophesy** [-saɪ] vt profetizar; (fig) predizer.

prophet ['prɔfɪt] n profeta m/f; ~**ic** [prə'fɛtɪk] adj profético.

proportion [prə'pɔ:ʃən] n proporção f; (share) parte f, porção f; ~**al** adj proporcional; ~**ate** adj proporcionado.

proposal [prə'pəuzl] n proposta; (offer) oferta; (plan) plano; (of marriage) pedido; (suggestion) sugestão f.

propose [prə'pəuz] vt propor; (offer) oferecer // vi declarar-se; **to ~ to do** propor-se fazer.

proposition [prɔpə'zɪʃən] n proposta, proposição f.

proprietor [prə'praɪətə*] n proprietário/a, dono/a.

propulsion [prə'pʌlʃən] n propulsão f.

pro rata [prəu'rɑ:tə] adv pro rata, proporcionalmente.

prosaic [prəu'zeɪɪk] adj prosaico.

prose [prəuz] n prosa.

prosecute ['prɔsɪkju:t] vt (LAW) processar, acionar (Pt: -cc-); **prosecution** [-'kju:ʃən] n acusação f; (accusing side) autor m da demanda; **prosecutor** n promotor(a) m/f; (also: **public prosecutor**) promotor(a) m/f público/a.

prospect ['prɔspɛkt] n (view) vista; (chance) probabilidade f; (outlook) perspectiva; (hope) esperança // (vb: [prə'spɛkt]) vt explorar // vi procurar; ~**s** npl (for work etc) probabilidades fpl; ~**ing** n inspecção f; ~**ive** adj (possible) provável, esperado; (certain) futuro; (heir) presumível; (legislation) em perspectiva; ~**or** n explorador(a) m/f.

prospectus [prə'spɛktəs] n prospecto, programa m.

prosper ['prɔspə*] vi prosperar; ~**ity** [-'spɛrɪtɪ] n prosperidade f; ~**ous** adj próspero, bem sucedido.

prostitute ['prɔstɪtju:t] n prostituta.

prostrate ['prɔstreɪt] adj prostrado; (fig) abatido, aniquilado.

protagonist [prə'tægənɪst] n protagonista m/f.

protect [prə'tɛkt] vt proteger; ~**ion** n proteção (Pt: -cç-) f; ~**ive** adj prote(c)tor(a); ~**or** n prote(c)tor(a) m/f.

protégé ['prəutɛʒeɪ] n protegido/a.

protein ['prəuti:n] n proteína.

protest ['prəutɛst] n protesto // (vb: [prə'tɛst]) vi protestar // vt (affirm) afirmar, declarar; ~**er** n manifestante m/f.

Protestant ['prɔtɪstənt] adj, n protestante m/f.

protocol ['prəutəkɔl] n protocolo.

prototype ['prəutətaɪp] n protótipo.

protracted [prə'træktɪd] adj prolongado, demorado.

protrude [prə'tru:d] vi projetar-se (Pt: -ct-), sobressair, ressaltar.

proud [praud] adj orgulhoso; (pej) vaidoso, soberbo; (imposing) imponente, magnífico.

prove [pru:v] vt provar; (verify) comprovar; (show) demonstrar // vi: **to ~ correct** vir a ser or mostrar estar correto (Pt: -ct-); **to ~ o.s.** pôr-se à prova.

proverb ['prɔvə:b] n provérbio; ~**ial** [prə'və:bɪəl] adj proverbial.

provide [prə'vaɪd] vt proporcionar, providenciar; **to ~ sb with sth** munir alguém de algo; **to ~ for** vt (person) prover à subsistência de; (emergency) prevenir; ~**d (that)** conj contanto que, sob condição de (que).

providing [prə'vaɪdɪŋ] conj contanto que, desde que.

province ['prɔvɪns] n província; (fig) esfera; **provincial** [prə'vɪnʃəl] adj provincial; (pej) provinciano.

provision [prə'vɪʒən] n (gen) provisão f; (supply) fornecimento; (supplying) abastecimento; ~**s** npl (food) mantimentos mpl; ~**al** adj provisório; (temporary) interino, temporário.

proviso [prə'vaɪzəu] n condição f; (LAW) cláusula.

provocation [prɔvə'keɪʃən] n provocação f, estímulo.

provocative [prə'vɔkətɪv] adj provocante; (stimulating) sugestivo.

provoke [prə'vəuk] vt (arouse) provocar; (cause) causar, motivar; (anger) irritar, exasperar.

prow [prau] n proa.

prowess ['prauɪs] n (skill) destreza, perícia; (courage) coragem f; (deed) proeza.

prowl [praul] vi (also: ~ **about**, ~ **around**) rondar, andar à espreita // n: **on the ~** de ronda, rondando; ~**er** n o que faz a ronda; (thief) gatuno/a m/f.

proximity [prɔk'sɪmɪtɪ] n proximidade f.

proxy ['prɔksɪ] n procuração f; (person)

procurador(a) *m/f*; **by ~ por**
procuração.

prudence ['pru:dns] *n* prudência,
cautela; **prudent** [-ənt] *adj* prudente.

prudish ['pru:dɪʃ] *adj* melindroso,
puritano.

prune [pru:n] *n* ameixa seca // *vt* podar,
aparar.

pry [praɪ] *vi*: **to ~ into** (intro)meter-se
em.

psalm [sɑ:m] *n* salmo.

pseudo- [sju:dəu] *pref* pseudo-; **~nym** *n*
pseudônimo.

psychiatric [saɪkı'ætrık] *adj*
psiquiátrico; **psychiatrist** [-'kaɪətrɪst] *n*
psiquiatra *m/f*; **psychiatry** [-'kaɪətrɪ] *n*
psiquiatria.

psychic ['saɪkık] *adj* (*also*: **~al**)
paranormal // *n* médium *m/f*.

psychoanalyse [saɪkəu'ænəlaɪz] *vt*
psicanalisar; **psychoanalysis** [-kəuə-
'nælɪsɪs] *n* psicanálise *f*; **psychoanalyst**
[-'ænəlɪst] *n* psicanalista *m/f*.

psychological [saɪkə'lɔdʒıkl] *adj*
psicológico.

psychologist [saɪ'kɔlədʒıst] *n*
psicólogo/a; **psychology** [-dʒɪ] *n*
psicologia.

psychopath ['saɪkəupæθ] *n* psicopata
m/f.

psychosomatic ['saɪkəusə'mætık] *adj*
psicossomático.

psychotic [saɪ'kɔtık] *adj*, *n* psicótico/a.

pub [pʌb] *n abbr of* **public house** bar *m*,
botequim *m*.

puberty ['pju:bətɪ] *n* puberdade *f*.

public ['pʌblɪk] *adj*, *n* público.

publican ['pʌblɪkən] *n* taberneiro.

publication [pʌblɪ'keɪʃən] *n* publicação *f*.

public: ~ convenience *n* banheiro
público; **~ house** *n* bar *m*, taberna.

publicity [pʌb'lɪsıtɪ] *n* publicidade *f*.

publicly ['pʌblɪklɪ] *adv* publicamente,
abertamente.

public: ~ opinion *n* opinião *f* pública;
~ relations *npl* relações *fpl* públicas; **~
school** *n* (*Brit*) escola particular;
~-spirited *adj* zeloso pelo bem-estar
público.

publish ['pʌblɪʃ] *vt* publicar; **~er** *n*
editor(a) *m/f*; **~ing** *n* (*industry*) a
indústria editorial.

puce [pju:s] *adj* marrom arroxeado.

pucker ['pʌkə*] *vt* (*pleat*) enrugar,
preguear; (*brow etc*) franzir.

pudding ['pudɪŋ] *n* sobremesa; (*sweet*)
pudim *m*, doce *m*; **black ~** morcela.

puddle ['pʌdl] *n* poça.

puff [pʌf] *n* sopro; (*from mouth*) baforada;
(*gust*) rajada, lufada; (*sound*) sopro; (*also*:
powder ~) pompom *m* // *vt*: **to ~
one's pipe** tirar baforadas do cachimbo
// *vi* (*gen*) soprar; (*pant*) arquejar; **to ~
out smoke** lançar uma baforada; **to ~
up** *vt* inflar; **~ed** *adj* (*col*: *out of breath*)
sem fôlego.

puffin ['pʌfɪn] *n* papagaio-do-mar *m*.

puffy ['pʌfɪ] *adj* inchado, entumecido.

pull [pul] *n* (*fig*: *advantage*) vantagem *f*;
(: *influence*) influência; (*tug*): **to give sth
a ~** dar um puxão em algo // *vt* puxar;
(*tug*) rebocar; (*muscle*) distender; (*haul*)
puxar, arrastar // *vi* puxar, dar um
puxão; **to ~ a face** fazer careta; **to ~
to pieces** picar em pedacinhos; **to ~
one's punches** não usar toda a força;
to ~ one's weight fazer a sua parte;
to ~ o.s. together recompor-se; **to ~
sb's leg** fazer hora com alguém, caçoar
de alguém; **to ~ apart** *vt* (*break*)
romper; **to ~ down** *vt* (*house*) demolir;
to ~ in *vi* (*AUT*: *at the kerb*) parar,
encostar; (*RAIL*) chegar (na plataforma);
to ~ off *vt* (*deal etc*) concluir *or* realizar
com sucesso; **to ~ out** *vi* ir(-se)
embora, partir; (*AUT*: *from kerb*) afastar-
se // *vt* tirar, arrancar; **to ~ through** *vi*
sair-se bem (de um aperto); (*MED*)
restabelecer-se; **to ~ up** *vi* (*stop*) deter-
se, parar // *vt* (*uproot*) desarraigar,
arrancar; (*stop*) parar.

pulley ['pulɪ] *n* roldana.

pullover ['puləuvə*] *n* pulôver *m*.

pulp [pʌlp] *n* (*of fruit*) polpa; (*for paper*)
pasta, massa.

pulpit ['pulpɪt] *n* púlpito.

pulsate [pʌl'seɪt] *vi* pulsar, palpitar.

pulse [pʌls] *n* (*ANAT*) pulso; (*of music,
engine*) cadência *f*; (*BOT*) legumes *mpl*.

pulverize ['pʌlvəraɪz] *vt* pulverizar; (*fig*)
esmagar, aniquilar.

puma ['pju:mə] *n* puma, onça-parda.

pummel ['pʌml] *vt* esmurrar, socar.

pump [pʌmp] *n* bomba; (*shoe*) sapatilha
(de dança) // *vt* bombear; (*fig*: *col*)
sondar; **to ~ up** *vt* encher (pneu).

pumpkin ['pʌmpkɪn] *n* abóbora.

pun [pʌn] *n* jogo de palavras.

punch [pʌntʃ] *n* (*blow*) soco, murro; (*tool*)
punção *m*; (*for tickets*) furador *m*; (*drink*)
ponche *m* // *vt* (*hit*): **to ~ sb/sth**
esmurrar *or* socar alguém/algo; (*make a
hole in*) perfurar, picotar; **~card** *n*
cartão *m* perfurado; **~-up** *n* (*col*) briga.

punctual ['pʌŋktjuəl] *adj* pontual; **~ity**
[-'ælɪtɪ] *n* pontualidade *f*.

punctuate ['pʌŋktjueɪt] *vt* pontuar;
(*interrupt*) interromper; **punctuation**
[-'eɪʃən] *n* pontuação *f*.

puncture ['pʌŋktʃə*] *n* picada, furo // *vt*
picar, furar.

pundit ['pʌndɪt] *n* erudito, sábio.

pungent ['pʌndʒənt] *adj* pungente, acre.

punish ['pʌnɪʃ] *vt* punir, castigar;
~ment *n* castigo, punição *f*.

punt [pʌnt] *n* (*boat*) chalana.

punter ['pʌntə*] *n* (*gambler*) jogador(a)
m/f.

puny ['pju:nɪ] *adj* débil, fraco.

pup [pʌp] *n* filhote *m* de cachorro (*Br*),
cachorro (*Pt*).

pupil ['pju:pl] *n* aluno/a.

puppet ['pʌpɪt] *n* marionete *f*.

puppy ['pʌpɪ] *n* cachorrinho (*Br*),
cachorro (*Pt*).

purchase ['pɔ:tʃɪs] *n* compra; (*grip*)

ponto de apoio // vt comprar; purchaser n comprador(a) m/f.
pure [pjuə*] adj puro.
purée ['pjuəreɪ] n purê m.
purge [pə:dʒ] n (MED) purgante m; (POL) expurgo // vt purgar; (POL) expurgar.
purification [pjuərɪfɪ'keɪʃən] n purificação f, depuração f; purify ['pjuərɪfaɪ] vt purificar, depurar.
purist ['pjuərɪst] n purista m/f.
puritan ['pjuərɪtən] n puritano/a; ~ical [-'tænɪkl] adj puritano.
purity ['pjuərɪtɪ] n pureza, limpeza.
purl [pə:l] n ponto reverso.
purple ['pə:pl] adj roxo, purpúreo.
purport [pə:'pɔ:t] vi: to ~ to be/do dar a entender que é/faz.
purpose ['pə:pəs] n propósito; on ~ de propósito; ~ful adj decidido, resoluto.
purr [pə:*] n ronrom m // vi ronronar.
purse [pə:s] n carteira; (bag) bolsa // vt enrugar, franzir.
purser ['pə:sə*] n (NAUT) comissário de bordo.
pursue [pə'sju:] vt perseguir, seguir; (profession) exercer; pursuer n perseguidor(a) m/f.
pursuit [pə'sju:t] n (chase) caça; (persecution) perseguição f; (occupation) ocupação f, atividade (Pt: -ct-) f; (pastime) passatempo.
purveyor [pə'veɪə*] n fornecedor(a) m/f.
pus [pʌs] n pus m.
push [puʃ] n (gen) empurrão m; (shove) impulso; (attack) ataque m, arremetida; (advance) avanço // vt empurrar; (button) apertar; (promote) promover; (thrust): to ~ sth (into) introduzir algo à força // vi empurrar; (fig) esforçar-se; to ~ aside vt afastar com a mão; to ~ off vi (col) ir embora; to ~ on vi (continue) prosseguir; to ~ through vt (measure) forçar a aceitação de; to ~ up vt (total, prices) forçar a alta de; ~chair n carrinho; ~ing adj empreendedor(a); ~ over n (col): it's a ~over está de bandeja or de graça; ~y adj (pej) intrometido, agressivo.
puss [pus], pussy(-cat) ['pusi(kæt)] n gatinho.
put [put], pt, pp put vt (place) pôr, colocar; (~ into) meter; (say) dizer, expressar; (a question) fazer; (estimate) avaliar, calcular; to ~ about vt (NAUT) mudar de rumo // vt (rumour) espalhar; to ~ across vt (ideas etc) expressar, comunicar; to ~ away vt (store) guardar; to ~ back vt (replace) repor; (postpone) adiar; to ~ by vt (money) poupar, pôr de lado; to ~ down vt (on ground) pôr no chão; (animal) sacrificar; (in writing) anotar, inscrever; (suppress: revolt etc) sufocar; to ~ down to vt atribuir a; to ~ forward vt (ideas) apresentar, propor; (date) adiantar; to ~ in vt (application, complaint) apresentar; to ~ off vt (postpone) adiar, protelar; (discourage) desencorajar; to

~ on vt (clothes, lipstick etc) pôr; (light etc) acender; (play etc) encenar; (weight) ganhar; (brake) aplicar; (attitude) simular; to ~ out vt (fire, light) apagar; (one's hand) estender; (news) anunciar; (rumour) espalhar; (tongue etc) mostrar; (person: inconvenience) incomodar; to ~ right consertar; to ~ up vt (raise) levantar, erguer; (hang) alçar, içar; (build) construir, edificar; (increase) aumentar; (accommodate) hospedar; to ~ up with vt fus suportar, aguentar.
putrid ['pju:trɪd] adj pútrido, podre.
putt [pʌt] vt (golf) dar uma tacada de leve // n tacada leve; ~er n (GOLF) taco; ~ing green n campo de golfe em miniatura.
putty ['pʌtɪ] n massa de vidraceiro, betume m.
puzzle ['pʌzl] n (riddle) charada; (jigsaw) quebra-cabeça m; (crossword) palavras cruzadas fpl; (mystery) enigma m // vt desconcertar, confundir // vi estar perplexo; puzzling adj enigmático, misterioso.
pygmy ['pɪgmɪ] n pigmeu m.
pyjamas [pɪ'dʒɑ:məz] npl pijama msg.
pylon ['paɪlən] n pilono, poste m, torre f.
pyramid ['pɪrəmɪd] n pirâmide f.
python ['paɪθən] n pitão m.

Q

quack [kwæk] n (of duck) grasnido; (pej: doctor) curandeiro, charlatão/tã m/f // vi grasnar.
quad [kwɔd] abbr of quadrangle; quadruplet.
quadrangle ['kwɔdræŋgl] n (courtyard: abbr: quad) pátio quadrangular.
quadruple [kwɔ'drupl] adj quádruplo // n quádruplo // vt/i quadruplicar.
quadruplets [kwɔ'dru:plɪts] npl quadrigêmeos mpl, quádruplos mpl.
quagmire ['kwægmaɪə*] n lamaçal m, atoleiro.
quail [kweɪl] n (bird) codorniz f, codorna (Br) // vi acovardar-se.
quaint [kweɪnt] adj curioso, esquisito; (picturesque) pitoresco.
quake [kweɪk] vi tremer, estremecer // n abbr of earthquake.
Quaker ['kweɪkə*] n quacre m/f.
qualification [kwɔlɪfɪ'keɪʃən] n (reservation) restrição f; (modification) modificação f; (act) qualificação f; (degree) título; qualified ['kwɔlɪfaɪd] adj (trained) habilitado, qualificado; (fit) apto, capaz; (limited) limitado; (professionally) diplomado.
qualify ['kwɔlɪfaɪ] vt qualificar; (capacitate) capacitar; (modify) modificar; (limit) restringir, limitar; to ~ (as) classificar (como) // vi (SPORT) classificar-se; to ~ (as) formar-se (em); to ~ (for) reunir os requisitos (para).

quality ['kwɔlɪtɪ] n qualidade f; (moral) valor m.

qualm [kwɑːm] n escrúpulo.

quandary ['kwɒndərɪ] n: **to be in a ~** estar num dilema.

quantity ['kwɒntɪtɪ] n quantidade f; **unknown ~** (MATH) incógnita.

quarantine ['kwɒrəntiːn] n quarentena.

quarrel ['kwɔrl] n (argument) discussão f, querela; (fight) briga // vi brigar, discutir; **~some** adj brigão/gona.

quarry ['kwɔrɪ] n (for stone) pedreira; (animal) presa, caça.

quart [kwɔːt] n quarto de galão = 1.136 litros.

quarter ['kwɔːtə*] n quarto, quarta parte f; (of year) trimestre m; (district) bairro // vt dividir em quatro; (MIL: lodge) aquartelar; **~s** npl (barracks) quartel msg; (living ~s) alojamento sg; **a ~ of an hour** um quarto de hora; **~ final** n quarta de final; **~ly** adj trimestral // adv trimestralmente; **~master** n (MIL) quartel-mestre m; (NAUT) contramestre m.

quartet(te) [kwɔːˈtɛt] n quarteto.

quartz [kwɔːts] n quartzo.

quash [kwɒʃ] vt (verdict) anular.

quasi- ['kweɪzaɪ] pref quase-, semi-.

quaver ['kweɪvə*] n (MUS) colcheia // vi tremer; (trill) trinar, gorjear.

quay [kiː] n (also: **~side**) cais m.

queasy ['kwiːzɪ] adj (sickly) enjoado.

queen [kwiːn] n (gen) rainha; (CARDS etc) dama; **~ mother** n rainha-mãe f.

queer [kwɪə*] adj (odd) esquisito, estranho; (suspect) suspeito, duvidoso // n (col) bicha m (Br), maricas m (Pt).

quell [kwɛl] vt abrandar, acalmar; (put down) sufocar.

quench [kwɛntʃ] vt apagar; (thirst) matar.

query ['kwɪərɪ] n (question) pergunta; (doubt) dúvida; (fig) incerteza // vt questionar.

quest [kwɛst] n busca; (journey) expedição f.

question ['kwɛstʃən] n pergunta; (matter) questão f, assunto, problema m // vt (gen) perguntar; (doubt) duvidar, questionar; (interrogate) interrogar, inquirir; **it is a ~ of** é questão de; **beyond ~** sem dúvida; **out of the ~** fora de cogitação, impossível; **~able** adj discutível, questionável; (doubtful) duvidoso; **~ mark** n ponto de interrogação; **~naire** [-'nɛə*] n questionário.

queue [kjuː] n fila (Br), bicha (Pt) // vi fazer fila (Br), fazer bicha (Pt).

quibble ['kwɪbl] vi usar de evasivas, tergiversar.

quick [kwɪk] adj rápido; (temper) vivo; (agile) ágil; (mind) sagaz, despachado; (eye) agudo; (ear) apurado; **be ~!** ande depressa!; **~en** vt apressar // vi apressar-se; **~ly** adv rapidamente, depressa; **~ness** n rapidez f; (agility)

agilidade f; (liveliness) vivacidade f; **~sand** n areia movediça; **~tempered** adj irascível; **~-witted** adj perspicaz, vivo.

quid [kwɪd] n, pl inv (Brit: col) libra.

quiet ['kwaɪət] adj (tranquil) tranqüilo, calmo; (still) quieto; (silent) silencioso; (: person) calado; (ceremony) discreto // n sossego, quietude f; **keep ~!** cale-se!, fique quieto!; **~en** (also: **~en down**) vi (grow calm) acalmar-se; (grow silent) calar-se // vt tranqüilizar, fazer calar; **~ly** adv (gen) tranqüilamente; (silently) silenciosamente; **~ness** n (silence) quietude f; (calm) tranqüilidade f.

quilt [kwɪlt] n acolchoado, colcha; (continental) n edredão m.

quin [kwɪn] abbr of **quintuplet**.

quince [kwɪns] n (fruit) marmelo.

quinine [kwɪˈniːn] n quinina.

quintet(te) [kwɪnˈtɛt] n quinteto.

quintuplets [kwɪnˈtjuːplɪts] npl quíntuplos mpl.

quip [kwɪp] n escárnio, dito espirituoso.

quirk [kwɔːk] n peculiaridade f.

quit [kwɪt], pt, pp **quit** or **quitted** vt deixar, desistir de; (premises) abandonar // vi parar; (give up) desistir; (go away) ir(-se) embora; (resign) renunciar, demitir-se; (stop work) deixar o emprego; **to be ~ of** ficar livre de.

quite [kwaɪt] adv (rather) bastante; (entirely) totalmente; **~ a few of them** um bom número deles; **~ (so)!** exatamente! (Pt: -ct-), isso mesmo!

quits [kwɪts] adj: **~ with** quite (com).

quiver ['kwɪvə*] vi estremecer // n (for arrows) carcás m, aljava.

quiz [kwɪz] n (game) concurso (de cultura geral); (questioning) questionário, teste m // vt interrogar; **~zical** adj zombeteiro.

quoits [kwɔɪts] npl jogo de malha.

quorum ['kwɔːrəm] n quorum m.

quota ['kwəʊtə] n cota, quota.

quotation [kwəʊˈteɪʃən] n citação f; (estimate) orçamento, cotação f; **~ marks** npl aspas fpl.

quote [kwəʊt] n citação f; (COMM) cotação f // vt (sentence) citar; (price) cotar, fixar // vi: **to ~ from** citar de, transcrever de.

quotient ['kwəʊʃənt] n quociente m.

R

rabbi ['ræbaɪ] n rabino.

rabbit ['ræbɪt] n coelho; **~ hole** n toca, lura; **~ hutch** n coelheira.

rabble ['ræbl] n (pej) plebe f, povinho, ralé f.

rabies ['reɪbiːz] n raiva, hidrofobia.

RAC n abbr of **Royal Automobile Club**.

raccoon [rəˈkuːn] n espécie de mão-pelada ou guaxinim.

race [reɪs] n (gen) corrida; (species) raça,

espécie f // vt (*horse*) fazer correr; (*engine*) acelerar // vi (*compete*) competir; (*run*) correr; (*pulse*) bater rapidamente; ~**course** n. hipódromo; ~**horse** n cavalo de corridas; ~**track** n pista de corridas; (*for cars*) autódromo.

racial ['reɪʃl] adj racial; ~**ism** n racismo; ~**ist** adj, n racista m/f.

racing ['reɪsɪŋ] n corrida; ~ **car** n carro de corrida; ~ **driver** n piloto de corrida.

racist ['reɪsɪst] adj, n (*pej*) racista m/f.

rack [ræk] n (*also*: **luggage** ~) bagageiro; (*shelf*) estante f; (*also*: **roof** ~) xalmas fpl, porta-bagagem m; (*clothes* ~) cabide m // vt (*cause pain to*) atormentar.

racket ['rækɪt] n (*for tennis*) raquete f (*Br*), raqueta (*Pt*); (*noise*) barulheira, zoeira; (*swindle*) negócio ilegal, fraude f.

racoon [rə'ku:n] n = **raccoon**.

racquet ['rækɪt] n raquete f (*Br*), raqueta (*Pt*).

racy ['reɪsɪ] adj vivo, espirituoso, picante.

radar ['reɪdɑ:*] n radar m.

radiance ['reɪdɪəns] n brilho, esplendor m; **radiant** [-ənt] adj radiante, brilhante.

radiate ['reɪdɪeɪt] vt (*heat*) irradiar; (*emit*) emitir // vi (*lines*) difundir-se, estender-se.

radiation [reɪdɪ'eɪʃən] n radiação f.

radiator ['reɪdɪeɪtə*] n radiador m; ~ **cap** n tampa do radiador.

radical ['rædɪkl] adj radical.

radio ['reɪdɪəu] n rádio; **on the** ~ no rádio; ~ **station** n emissora, estação f de rádio.

radio... [reɪdɪəu] pref: ~**active** adj radioativo (Pt: -ct-); ~**activity** n radioatividade (Pt: -ct-) f; ~**-controlled** adj controlado por rádio; ~**graphy** [-'ɔgrəfi] n radiografia; ~**logy** [-'ɔlədʒɪ] n radiologia; ~**telephone** n radiotelefone m; ~**therapy** n radioterapia.

radish ['rædɪʃ] n rabanete m.

radius ['reɪdɪəs], pl **radii** [-ɪaɪ] n raio.

raffia ['ræfɪə] n ráfia.

raffle ['ræfl] n rifa, sorteio // vt rifar, sortear.

raft [rɑ:ft] n (*also*: **life** ~) balsa.

rafter ['rɑ:ftə*] n viga, caibro.

rag [ræg] n (*piece of cloth*) trapo; (*torn cloth*) farrapo; (*pej: newspaper*) jornaleco; (*for charity*) atividades estudantis beneficentes // vt encarnar em, zombar de; ~**s** npl trapos mpl, farrapos mpl; ~**-and-bone man** n negociante m/f de trastes; ~ **doll** n boneca de trapo.

rage [reɪdʒ] n (*fury*) raiva, furor m; (*fashion*) voga, moda // vi (*person*) estar furioso; (*storm*) bramar; **to fly into a** ~ enfurecer-se.

ragged ['rægɪd] adj (*edge*) irregular, desigual; (*cuff*) puído, gasto; (*appearance*) esfarrapado, andrajoso; (*coastline*) acidentado.

raid [reɪd] n (*MIL*) incursão f; (*criminal*) assalto; (*attack*) ataque m; (*by police*)

batida // vt invadir, atacar, assaltar; ~**er** n atacante m/f; (*criminal*) assaltante m/f.

rail [reɪl] n (*on stair*) corrimão m; (*on bridge, balcony*) parapeito, anteparo; (*of ship*) amurada; (*for train*) trilho (*Br*), carril m (*Pt*); ~**s** npl : **off the** ~**s** descarrilado; **by** ~ de trem (*Br*), por caminho de ferro (*Pt*); ~ **ing(s)** n(pl) grade fsg, balaustrada sg; ~**road** (*US*), ~**way** n estrada de ferro (*Br*), caminho de ferro (*Pt*); ~**wayman** n ferroviário; ~**way station** n estação f ferroviária (*Br*), estação f de caminho de ferro (*Pt*).

rain [reɪn] n chuva // vi chover; **in the** ~ na chuva; **it's** ~**ing** está chovendo (*Br*), está a chover (*Pt*); ~**bow** n arco-íris m inv; ~**coat** n impermeável m, capa de chuva; ~**drop** n gota de chuva; ~**fall** n chuva, pluviosidade f; ~**y** adj chuvoso.

raise [reɪz] n aumento // vt (*lift*) levantar; (*build*) erguer, edificar; (*increase*) aumentar; (*doubts*) suscitar, despertar; (*a question*) fazer, expor; (*cattle, family*) criar; (*crop*) cultivar, plantar; (*army*) recrutar, alistar; (*funds*) angariar; (*loan*) levantar, obter; **to** ~ **one's voice** levantar a voz.

raisin ['reɪzn] n passa, uva seca.

rake [reɪk] n (*tool*) ancinho; (*person*) libertino // vt (*garden*) revolver or limpar com o ancinho; (*fire*) remover as cinzas; (*with machine gun*) varrer.

rakish ['reɪkɪʃ] adj (*suave*) elegante; **at a** ~ **angle** de banda, inclinado.

rally ['rælɪ] n (*POL etc*) reunião f, comício, (*AUT*) rally m, rali m; (*TENNIS*) rebatida // vt reunir; (*encourage*) animar, encorajar // vi reorganizar-se; (*sick person, Stock Exchange*) recuperar-se; **to** ~ **round** vt fus (*fig*) dar apoio a.

ram [ræm] n (*carneiro*); (*TECH*) êmbolo, aríete m // vt (*crash into*) colidir com; (*tread down*) pisar, calcar.

ramble ['ræmbl] n caminhada, excursão f a pé // vi (*pej: also:* ~ **on**) divagar; ~**bler** n caminhante m/f; (*BOT*) trepadeira; **rambling** adj (*speech*) desconexo, incoerente // n excursionismo.

ramp [ræmp] n rampa.

rampage [ræm'peɪdʒ] n: **to be on the** ~ alvoroçar-se // vi: **they went rampaging through the town** correram feito loucos pela cidade.

rampant ['ræmpənt] adj (*disease etc*) violento, implacável.

rampart ['ræmpɑ:t] n baluarte m; (*wall*) muralha.

ramshackle ['ræmʃækl] adj prestes a desmoronar, em ruínas.

ran [ræn] pt of **run**.

ranch [rɑ:ntʃ] n rancho, fazenda, estância; ~**er** n rancheiro, fazendeiro.

rancid ['rænsɪd] adj rançoso, râncio.

rancour, rancor (*US*) ['ræŋkə*] n rancor m, ódio.

random ['rændəm] *adj* ao acaso, casual, fortuito // *n*: **at** ~ a esmo, aleatoriamente.

randy ['rændɪ] *adj* (col) de fogo.

rang [ræŋ] *pt of* **ring.**

range [reɪndʒ] *n* (of mountains) cadeia, cordilheira; (of missile) alcance *m*; (of voice) extensão *f*; (series) série *f*; (of products) sortimento; (MIL: also: **shooting** ~) campo de alcance; (also: **kitchen** ~) fogão *m* // *vt* (place) colocar; (arrange) arrumar, ordenar // *vi*: **to** ~ **over** (wander) percorrer; (extend) estender-se por; **to** ~ **from ... to...** variar de ... a ..., oscilar entre ... e ...; **ranger** *n* guarda-florestal *m*.

rank [ræŋk] *n* (row) fila, fileira; (MIL) posto; (status) categoria, posição *f*; (also: **táxi** ~) ponto de táxi // *vi*: **to** ~ **among** figurar entre // *adj* (stinking) fétido, malcheiroso; **the** ~ **and file** (fig) a gente *f* comum.

rankle ['ræŋkl] *vi* (insult) doer, magoar.

ransack ['rænsæk] *vt* (search) revistar; (plunder) saquear, pilhar.

ransom ['rænsəm] *n* resgate *m*; **to hold sb to** ~ (fig) encostar alguém contra a parede.

rant [rænt] *vi* falar em tom declamatório; ~**ing** *n* palavreado oco.

rap [ræp] *n* batida breve e seca // *vt* bater de leve.

rape [reɪp] *n* violação *f*, estupro *f* // *vt* violentar, estuprar.

rapid ['ræpɪd] *adj* rápido; ~**s** *npl* (GEO) cachoeira *sg*; ~**ity** [rə'pɪdɪtɪ] *n* rapidez *f*.

rapist ['reɪpɪst] *n* estuprador *m*.

rapport [ræ'pɔ:*] *n* harmonia, afinidade *f*.

rapture ['ræptʃə*] *n* êxtase *m*, arrebatamento; **rapturous** *adj* extático; (applause) entusiasta.

rare [rɛə*] *adj* raro, fora do comum; (CULIN: steak) mal passado.

rarely ['rɛəlɪ] *adv* raramente.

rarity ['rɛərɪtɪ] *n* raridade *f*.

rascal ['rɑ:skl] *n* maroto, malandro.

rash [ræʃ] *adj* impetuoso, precipitado // *n* (MED) exantema *m*, erupção *f* cutânea.

rasher ['ræʃə*] *n* fatia fina.

rashness ['ræʃnɪs] *n* impetuosidade *f*.

rasp [rɑ:sp] *n* (tool) lima, raspadeira.

raspberry ['rɑ:zbərɪ] *n* framboesa; ~ **bush** *n* framboeseira.

rasping ['rɑ:spɪŋ] *adj*: **a** ~ **noise** ruído áspero *or* irritante.

rat [ræt] *n* rato (Br), ratazana (Pt).

ratchet ['rætʃɪt] *n* (TECH) roquete *m*, catraca.

rate [reɪt] *n* (ratio) razão *f*; (percentage) percentagem *f*, proporção *f*; (price) preço, taxa; (: of hotel) diária; (of interest) taxa; (speed) velocidade *f* // *vt* (value) taxar; (estimate) avaliar; **at any** ~ de qualquer modo; ~ **of exchange** taxa de câmbio; **to** ~ **as** ser considerado como; ~**s** *npl* (Brit) imposto *sg* municipal; (fees) taxa *sg*; ~**able value** *n*

valor *m* tributável; ~**payer** *n* contribuinte *m/f*.

rather ['rɑ:ðə*] *adv* antes, preferivelmente; (in speech) melhor dito; **it's** ~ **expensive** é um pouco caro; (too much) é caro demais; **there's** ~ **a lot** há bastante *or* muito; **I would** *or* **I'd** ~ **go** preferiria ir.

ratify ['rætɪfaɪ] *vt* ratificar.

rating ['reɪtɪŋ] *n* (valuation) avaliação *f*; (value) valor *m*; (standing) posição *f*; (NAUT. category) posto; (: sailor) marinheiro.

ratio ['reɪʃɪəu] *n* razão *f*, proporção *f*; **in the** ~ **of 100 to 1** na proporção de 100 para 1.

ration ['ræʃən] *n* ração *f*; ~**s** *npl* mantimentos *mpl*, víveres *mpl* // *vt* racionar.

rational ['ræʃənl] *adj* racional; (solution, reasoning) lógico; (person) sensato, razoável; **rationale** [-'nɑ:l] *n* razão *f* fundamental; ~**ize** *vt* racionalizar, organizar logicamente; ~**ly** *adv* racionalmente; (logically) logicamente.

rationing ['ræʃnɪŋ] *n* racionamento.

rattle ['rætl] *n* batida, rufar *m*; (of train etc) chocalhada; (of hail) saraivada; (object: of baby) chocalho; (: of sports fan) matraca; (of snake) guizo // *vi* chocalhar; (small objects) tamborilar // *vt* sacudir, fazer bater; (person) desconcertar; ~**snake** *n* cascavel *f*.

raucous ['rɔ:kəs] *adj* áspero, rouco.

ravage ['rævɪdʒ] *vt* devastar, estragar; ~**s** *npl* estragos *mpl*.

rave [reɪv] *vi* (in anger) encolerizar-se; (with enthusiasm) falar com entusiasmo; (MED) delirar, desvairar.

raven ['reɪvən] *n* corvo.

ravenous ['rævənəs] *adj* morto de fome, esfaimado.

ravine [rə'vi:n] *n* ravina, barranco.

raving ['reɪvɪŋ] *adj*: ~ **lunatic** doido/a varrido/a.

ravioli [rævɪ'əulɪ] *n* ravióli *m*.

ravish ['rævɪʃ] *vt* arrebatar; (delight) encantar; ~**ing** *adj* encantador(a).

raw [rɔ:] *adj* (uncooked) cru; (not processed) bruto; (sore) vivo; (inexperienced) inexperiente, novato; ~ **material** *n* matéria-prima.

ray [reɪ] *n* raio; ~ **of hope** raio de esperança.

rayon ['reɪɔn] *n* raiom *m*.

raze [reɪz] *vt* arrasar, aniquilar.

razor ['reɪzə*] *n* (open) navalha; (safety ~) aparelho de barbear; ~ **blade** *n* gilete *m* (Br), lâmina de barbear (Pt).

Rd *abbr of* **road.**

re [ri:] *prep* referente a.

reach [ri:tʃ] *n* alcance *m*; (BOXING) campo de ação; (of river etc) braço do rio entre duas voltas // *vt* alcançar, atingir; (achieve) conseguir; (stretch out) estender, esticar // *vi* alcançar; (stretch) estender-se; **within** ~ (object) ao alcance (da mão); **out of** ~ fora de

alcance; **to ~ out for sth** estender or
esticar a mão para pegar (em) algo.

react [ri:'ækt] vi reagir; **~ion** [-'ækʃən] n
reação (Pt: -çç-) f; **~ionary** [-'ækʃənrı]
adj, n reacionário/a (Pt: -cc-).

reactor [ri:'æktə*] n reator (Pt: -ct-) m.

read [ri:d], pt, pp **read** [rɛd] vi ler // vt
ler; (understand) compreender; (study)
estudar; **to ~ out** vt ler em voz alta;
~able adj (writing) legível; (book) que
merece ser lido; **~er** n leitor(a) m/f;
(book) livro de leituras; (at university)
professor(a) adjunto/a m/f; **~ership** n
(of paper etc) número de leitores.

readily ['rɛdılı] adv (willingly) de boa
vontade; (easily) facilmente; (quickly)
sem demora, prontamente.

readiness ['rɛdınıs] n boa vontade f,
prontidão f; (preparedness) preparação f;
in ~ (prepared) preparado, pronto.

reading ['ri:dıŋ] n leitura; (understanding)
compreensão f; (on instrument) indicação
f.

readjust [ri:ə'dʒʌst] vt reajustar // vi
(person): **to ~ to** reorientar-se para.

ready ['rɛdı] adj pronto, preparado;
(willing) disposto; (available) disponível;
to get ~ preparar-se // vt:
~-cooked pronto para comer // n: **at
the ~** (MIL) pronto para atirar;
~-made adj (já) feito; (clothes) pronto;
~ reckoner n tabela de cálculos feitos.

reaffirm [ri:ə'fə:m] vt reafirmar.

real [rıəl] adj verdadeiro, autêntico; **in ~
terms** em termos reais; **~ estate** n
bens mpl imobiliários or de raiz; **~ism** n
(also ART) realismo; **~ist** n realista m/f;
~istic [-'lıstık] adj realista.

reality [ri:'ælıtı] n realidade f; **in ~** na
verdade.

realization [rıəlaı'zeıʃən] n realização f;
(understanding) compreensão f; (COMM)
conversão f em dinheiro, realização.

realize ['rıəlaız] vt (understand) perceber,
compreender; (a project, COMM: asset)
realizar.

really ['rıəlı] adv realmente, na verdade;
~? é mesmo?

realm [rɛlm] n reino; (fig) domínio.

realtor ['rıəltə] n (US) imobiliária.

reap [ri:p] vt segar, ceifar; (fig) colher;
~er n segador/a m/f, ceifeiro/a.

reappear [ri:ə'pıə*] vi reaparecer;
~ance n reaparição f.

reapply [ri:ə'plaı] vi: **to ~ for** requerer
de novo.

rear [rıə*] adj traseiro, posterior // n
traseira, retaguarda // vt (cattle, family)
criar // vi (also: **~ up**) (animal)
empinar-se; **~-engined** adj (AUT) com
motor traseiro; **~guard** n retaguarda.

rearm [ri:'ɑ:m] vt/i rearmar; **~ament** n
rearmamento m.

rearrange [ri:ə'reındʒ] vt arrumar de
novo, reorganizar.

rear-view ['rıəvju:] adj: **~ mirror** (AUT)
espelho retrovisor.

reason ['ri:zn] n (gen) razão f; (cause)

motivo, causa; (sense) sensatez f // vi: **to
~ with sb** argumentar com alguém,
persuadir alguém; **it stands to ~ that**
é razoável or lógico que; **~able** adj
razoável; (sensible) sensato; **~ably** adv
razoavelmente; **~ed** adj (argument)
fundamentado; **~ing** n raciocínio,
argumentação f.

reassemble [ri:ə'sɛmbl] vt (machine)
montar de novo // vi reunir-se de novo.

reassert [ri:ə'sə:t] vt reafirmar.

reassure [ri:ə'ʃuə*] vt tranqüilizar,
animar; **to ~ sb of** reafirmar a
confiança de alguém acerca de;
reassuring adj animador(a).

rebate ['ri:beıt] n (on product)
abatimento; (on tax etc) desconto,
devolução f.

rebel ['rɛbl] n rebelde m/f // vi [rı'bɛl]
rebelar-se, sublevar-se; **~lion** n rebelião
f, revolta; **~lious** adj insurreto (Pt: -ct-);
(child) rebelde.

rebirth [ri:'bə:θ] n renascimento.

rebound [rı'baund] vi (ball) ressaltar //
n ['ri:baund] ressalto.

rebuff [rı'bʌf] n repulsa, recusa // vt
repelir.

rebuild [ri:'bıld] (irr: like **build**) vt
reconstruir.

rebuke [rı'bju:k] n reprimenda, censura
// vt repreender.

recalcitrant [rı'kælsıtrənt] adj
recalcitrante, teimoso.

recall [rı'kɔ:l] vt (remember) recordar,
lembrar; (ambassador etc) mandar voltar
// n chamada (de volta); (memory)
recordação f.

recant [rı'kænt] vi retratar-se (Pt: -act-).

recap ['ri:kæp] vt/i recapitular.

recapture [ri:'kæptʃə*] vt (town)
retomar, recobrar; (atmosphere) recriar.

recede [rı'si:d] vi retroceder; **receding**
adj (forehead, chin) metido/puxado para
dentro.

receipt [rı'si:t] n (document) recibo; (act
of receiving) recepção f; **~s** npl (COMM)
rendimentos mpl; **on ~ of** ao receber.

receive [rı'si:v] vt receber; (guest)
acolher; (wound) sofrer; **receiver** n
(TEL) fone m (Br), auscultador m (Pt);
(rádio) receptor m; (of stolen goods)
receptador(a) m/f; (COMM) curador(a)
m/f or síndico/a de massa falida.

recent ['ri:snt] adj recente; **~ly** adv
recentemente, ultimamente.

receptacle [rı'sɛptıkl] n receptáculo,
recipiente m.

reception [rı'sɛpʃən] n (gen) recepção f;
(welcome) acolhida; **~ desk** n mesa de
recepção; **~ist** n recepcionista m/f.

receptive [rı'sɛptıv] adj receptivo.

recess [rı'sɛs] n (in room) recesso, vão
m; (for bed) nicho; (secret place)
esconderijo; (POL etc: holiday) férias fpl;
~ion n recessão f.

recharge [ri:'tʃɑ:dʒ] vt (battery)
recarregar.

recipe ['rɛsıpı] n receita.

recipient [rɪ'sɪpɪənt] n recipiente m/f, recebedor(a) m/f; (of letter) destinatário/a.

reciprocal [rɪ'sɪprəkl] adj recíproco.

recital [rɪ'saɪtl] n recital m.

recite [rɪ'saɪt] vt (poem) recitar; (complaints etc) enumerar.

reckless ['rɛkləs] adj temerário, estouvado; (speed) imprudente, excessivo; ~ly adv temerariamente, sem prudência.

reckon ['rɛkən] vt (count) calcular, contar; (consider) considerar, crer; (think): I ~ that... acho que ..., suponho que ...; ~ing n (calculation) cálculo; the day of ~ing o dia do Juízo Final.

reclaim [rɪ'kleɪm] vt recuperar; (land) desbravar; (: from sea) aterrar; (demand back) reivindicar; **reclamation** [rɛklə'meɪʃən] n recuperação f.

recline [rɪ'klaɪn] vi reclinar-se; (lean) apoiar-se, recostar-se; **reclining** adj (seat) reclinável.

recluse [rɪ'kluːs] n recluso/a.

recognition [rɛkəg'nɪʃən] n reconhecimento; **transformed beyond** ~ tão transformado que está irreconhecível.

recognizable ['rɛkəgnaɪzəbl] adj reconhecível.

recognize ['rɛkəgnaɪz] vt reconhecer; (accept) aceitar; **to** ~ **by/as** reconhecer por/como.

recoil [rɪ'kɔɪl] vi (gun) retroceder, recuar, dar coice; (person): **to** ~ **from doing sth** recusar-se a fazer algo.

recollect [rɛkə'lɛkt] vt lembrar, recordar; ~ion [-'lɛkʃən] n recordação f, lembrança.

recommend [rɛkə'mɛnd] vt recomendar, aconselhar; ~ation [-'deɪʃən] n recomendação f.

recompense ['rɛkəmpɛns] vt recompensar // n recompensa.

reconcile ['rɛkənsaɪl] vt (two people) reconciliar; (two facts) conciliar, harmonizar; **to** ~ **o.s. to sth** resignar-se a or conformar-se com algo; **reconciliation** [-sɪlɪ'eɪʃən] n reconciliação f.

reconnaissance [rɪ'kɔnɪsns] n (MIL) reconhecimento.

reconnoitre, reconnoiter (US) [rɛkə'nɔɪtə*] vt (MIL) reconhecer.

reconsider [riːkən'sɪdə*] vt reconsiderar.

reconstitute [riː'kɔnstɪtjuːt] vt reconstituir.

reconstruct [riːkən'strʌkt] vt reconstruir; ~ion [-kʃən] n reconstrução f.

record ['rɛkɔːd] n (MUS) disco; (of meeting etc) ata (Pt: -ct-), minuta; (register) registro (Br), registo (Pt); (file) arquivo; (also: **police** ~) antecedentes mpl; (written) história; (SPORT) recorde m // vt [rɪ'kɔːd] (set down) assentar, registrar (Br), registar (Pt); (relate) relatar, referir; (MUS: song etc) gravar; **in** ~ **time**

num tempo recorde; **off the** ~ adj confidencial // adv confidencialmente; ~ **card** n (in file) ficha; ~**er** n (MUS) flauta; (TECH) indicador m mecânico; (official) escrivão m; ~ **holder** n (SPORT) detentor(a) m/f de recorde; ~**ing** n (MUS) gravação f; ~ **player** n toca-discos m inv (Br), gira-discos m inv (Pt).

recount [rɪ'kaunt] vt relatar.

re-count ['riː'kaunt] n (POL: of votes) nova contagem f, recontagem f // vt [riː'kaunt] recontar.

recoup [rɪ'kuːp] vt: **to** ~ **one's losses** ser indenizado (Pt: imn-) pelas perdas.

recourse [rɪ'kɔːs] n recurso; **to have** ~ **to** recorrer a.

recover [rɪ'kʌvə*] vt recuperar, reconquistar; (rescue) resgatar // vi (from illness) restabelecer-se; (from shock) refazer-se; ~**y** n recuperação f, restabelecimento; (MED) melhora.

recreate [riː'kriː'eɪt] vt recriar.

recreation [rɛkrɪ'eɪʃən] n recreação f; (play) recreio; ~**al** adj recreativo.

recrimination [rɪkrɪmɪ'neɪʃən] n recriminação f.

recruit [rɪ'kruːt] n recruta m/f // vt recrutar; ~**ment** n recrutamento.

rectangle ['rɛktæŋgl] n retângulo (Pt: -ct-); **rectangular** [-'tæŋgjulə*] adj retangular (Pt: -ct-).

rectify ['rɛktɪfaɪ] vt retificar (Pt: -ct-).

rector ['rɛktə*] n (REL) pároco; (SCOL) reitor(a) m/f; ~**y** n residência paroquial.

recuperate [rɪ'kuːpəreɪt] vi restabelecer-se, recuperar-se.

recur [rɪ'kəː*] vi repetir-se, ocorrer outra vez; (opportunity) surgir de novo; ~**rence** n repetição f; ~**rent** adj repetido, periódico.

red [rɛd] n vermelho // adj vermelho; **to be in the** ~ estar em situação deficitária; **R~ Cross** n Cruz f Vermelha; ~**currant** n groselha; ~**den** vt avermelhar // vi corar, ruborizar-se; ~**dish** adj (hair) avermelhado.

redecorate [riː'dɛkəreɪt] vt decorar de novo, redecorar; **redecoration** [-'reɪʃən] n remodelação f.

redeem [rɪ'diːm] vt (gen) redimir; (sth in pawn) tirar do prego; (fig, also REL) resgatar; ~**ing** adj: ~**ing feature** lado bom or que salva.

redeploy [riːdɪ'plɔɪ] vt (resources, troops) redistribuir.

red: ~-**haired** adj ruivo; ~-**handed** adj: **to be caught** ~-**handed** ser apanhado em flagrante; ~**head** n ruivo/a; ~-**hot** adj incandescente.

redirect [riːdaɪ'rɛkt] vt (mail) endereçar de novo.

redness ['rɛdnɪs] n rubor m, avermelhado; (of hair) vermelhidão f.

redo [riː'duː] (irr: like do) vt refazer.

redouble [riː'dʌbl] vt: **to** ~ **one's efforts** redobrar os esforços.

redress [rɪ'drɛs] n reparação f // vt retificar (Pt: -ct-), remediar.

red tape n (fig) formalidades fpl, papelada, rotina burocrática.

reduce [rɪ'djuːs] vt reduzir; (lower) rebaixar; '~ **speed now**' (AUT) 'diminua a velocidade agora'; **at a ~d price** (of goods) a preço remarcado; **reduction** [rɪ'dʌkʃən] n redução f; (of price) abatimento; (discount) desconto.

redundancy [rɪ'dʌndənsɪ] n redundância; (unemployment) desemprego.

redundant [rɪ'dʌndnt] adj (worker) desempregado; (detail, object) redundante, supérfluo; **to be made ~** ficar sem trabalho or desempregado.

reed [riːd] n (BOT) junco; (MUS: of clarinet etc) palheta.

reef [riːf] n (at sea) recife m.

reek [riːk] vi: **to ~ (of)** cheirar (a), feder (a).

reel [riːl] n (gen) carretel m, bobina; (of film) rolo, filme m // vt (TECH) bobinar, enrolar // vi (sway) cambalear, oscilar.

re-election [riːɪ'lɛkʃən] n reeleição f.

re-enter [riː'ɛntə*] vt reentrar; **re-entry** n reentrada.

ref [rɛf] n (col) abbr of **referee**.

refectory [rɪ'fɛktərɪ] n refeitório.

refer [rɪ'fəː*] vt (send) remeter, encaminhar; (ascribe) referir, atribuir // vi: **to ~ to** (allude to) referir-se a, aludir a; (apply to) aplicar-se a; (consult) recorrer a.

referee [rɛfə'riː] n árbitro; (for job application) pessoa que dá referência // vt arbitrar.

reference ['rɛfrəns] n (mention) referência, menção f; (sending) envio, indicação f; (relevance) relação f; (for job application: letter) referência, carta de recomendação; **with ~ to** com relação a; (COMM: in letter) com referência a; **~ book** n livro de consulta.

referendum [rɛfə'rɛndəm], pl **-da** [-də] n referendum m, plebiscito.

refill [riː'fɪl] vt reencher, reabastecer // n ['riːfɪl] peça sobressalente, carga nova.

refine [rɪ'faɪn] vt (sugar, oil) refinar; **~d** adj (person, taste) refinado, culto; **~ment** n (of person) cultura, refinamento, requinte m; **~ry** n refinaria.

reflect [rɪ'flɛkt] vt (light, image) refletir (Pt: -ct-) // vi (think) refle(c)tir, meditar; **it ~s badly/well on him** prejudica-o/lhe dá crédito; **~ion** [-'flɛkʃən] n (act) reflexão f; (image) reflexo; **on ~ion** depois de refle(c)tir bem; **~or** n (also AUT) refle(c)tor m; **~ stud** n (US: AUT) olho de gato.

reflex ['riːflɛks] adj, n reflexo; **~ive** [rɪ'flɛksɪv] adj (LING) reflexivo.

reform [rɪ'fɔːm] n reforma // vt reformar; **the R~ation** [rɛfə'meɪʃən] n a Reforma; **~er** n reformador(a) m/f; **~ist** n reformista m/f.

refrain [rɪ'freɪn] vi: **to ~ from doing** abster-se de fazer // n estribilho, refrão m.

refresh [rɪ'frɛʃ] vt refrescar; **~er course** n curso de atualização (Pt: -ct-); **refreshing** adj refrescante; **~ments** npl (drinks) refrescos mpl.

refrigeration [rɪfrɪdʒə'reɪʃən] n refrigeração f; **refrigerator** [-'frɪdʒəreɪtə*] n refrigerador m, geladeira (Br), frigorífico (Pt).

refuel [riː'fjuəl] vi reabastecer (de combustível).

refuge ['rɛfjuːdʒ] n refúgio, asilo; **to take ~ in** refugiar-se em.

refugee [rɛfju'dʒiː] n refugiado/a.

refund ['riːfʌnd] n reembolso // vt [rɪ'fʌnd] devolver, reembolsar.

refurbish [riː'fəːbɪʃ] vt renovar.

refusal [rɪ'fjuːzəl] n recusa, negativa; **first ~** primeira opção f.

refuse ['rɛfjuːs] n refugo, lixo // (vb: [rɪ'fjuːz]) vt (reject) rejeitar; (say no to) negar-se a, recusar // vi negar-se; (horse) recusar; **~ bin** n lata de lixo; **~ tip** n depósito.

refute [rɪ'fjuːt] vt refutar, contradizer.

regain [rɪ'geɪn] vt recuperar, recobrar, readquirir.

regal ['riːgl] adj real, régio.

regalia [rɪ'geɪlɪə] n, npl insígnias fpl reais.

regard [rɪ'gɑːd] n (gaze) olhar m; (aspect) respeito; (attention) atenção f; (esteem) estima, consideração f // vt (consider) considerar; (look at) olhar; '**with kindest ~s**' 'atenciosamente'; **~ing, as ~s, with ~ to** com relação a, com respeito a, quanto a; **~less** adv sem considerar as conseqüências; **~less of** apesar de.

regatta [rɪ'gætə] n regata.

regent ['riːdʒənt] n regente m/f.

régime [reɪ'ʒiːm] n regime m.

regiment ['rɛdʒɪmənt] n regimento // vt regulamentar; **~al** [-'mɛntl] adj regimental; **~ation** [-'teɪʃən] n organização f.

region ['riːdʒən] n região f; **in the ~ of** (fig) por volta de, ao redor de; **~al** adj regional.

register ['rɛdʒɪstə*] n (gen) registro (Pt: registo); (list) lista // vt registrar (Pt: registar); (subj: instrument) marcar, indicar // vi (at hotel) registrar-se (Pt: registar-se); (sign on) inscrever-se; (make impression) causar impressão; **~ed** adj (design, letter) registrado (Pt: registado).

registrar ['rɛdʒɪstrɑː*] n oficial m de registro (Pt: registo), escrivão/vã m/f.

registration [rɛdʒɪs'treɪʃən] n (act) registro (Pt: registo), inscrição f; (AUT: also: **~ number**) número da placa.

registry ['rɛdʒɪstrɪ] n registro (Pt: registo), arquivo; **~ office** n regist(r)o civil, cartório; **to get married in a ~ office** casar-se no civil.

regret [rɪ'grɛt] n desgosto, pesar m; (remorse) remorso // vt sentir, lamentar;

(repent of) arrepender-se de; ~**fully** adv com pesar, pesarosamente; ~**table** adj deplorável; (loss) lamentável.

regroup [ri:'gru:p] vt reagrupar // vi reagrupar-se.

regular ['rɛgjulə*] adj (gen) regular; (usual) normal, habitual; (soldier) de linha; (intensive) verdadeiro, completo // n (client etc) cliente m/f, habitual m/f; ~**ity** [-'læriti] n regularidade f; ~**ly** adv regularmente.

regulate ['rɛgjuleit] vt regular; (TECH) ajustar; **regulation** [-'leiʃən] n (rule) regra, regulamento; (adjustment) ajuste m.

rehabilitation ['ri:həbili'teiʃən] n reabilitação f.

rehearsal [ri'hə:səl] n ensaio; **rehearse** vt ensaiar.

reign [rein] n reinado; (fig) domínio // vi reinar; (fig) imperar; ~**ing** adj (monarch) reinante atual (Pt: -ct-); (predominant) imperante, predominante.

reimburse [ri:im'bə:s] vt reembolsar; ~**ment** n reembolso.

rein [rein] n (for horse) rédea; **to give ~ to** dar rédeas a, dar rédea larga a.

reincarnation [ri:inkɑ:'neiʃən] n reencarnação f.

reindeer ['reindiə*] n, pl inv rena.

reinforce [ri:in'fɔ:s] vt reforçar; ~**d** adj (concrete) armado; ~**ment** n (action) reforço; ~**ments** npl (MIL) reforços mpl.

reinstate [ri:in'steit] vt (worker) reintegrar ao seu posto, reempossar.

reiterate [ri:'itəreit] vt reiterar, repetir.

reject ['ri:dʒɛkt] n (COMM) artigo defeituoso // vt [ri'dʒɛkt] rejeitar; (plan) recusar; (solution) descartar; ~**ion** [ri'dʒɛkʃən] n rejeição f.

rejoice [ri'dʒɔis] vi: **to ~ at** or **over** regozijar-se or alegrar-se de.

rejuvenate [ri'dʒu:vəneit] vt rejuvenescer.

rekindle [ri:'kindl] vt reacender; (fig) despertar, reanimar.

relapse [ri'læps] n (MED) recaída; (into crime) reincidência.

relate [ri'leit] vt (tell) contar, relatar; (connect) relacionar // vi relacionar-se; ~**d** adj afim, ligado; (person) aparentado; ~**d to** com referência a; **relating to** prep relativo a, acerca de.

relation [ri'leiʃən] n (person) parente m/f; (link) relação f, conexão f; ~**ship** n relacionamento; (personal ties) relações fpl; (also: **family ~ship**) parentesco.

relative ['rɛlətiv] n parente/a m/f, familiar m/f // adj relativo.

relax [ri'læks] vi descansar; (person: unwind) descontrair-se // vt relaxar; (mind, person) descansar; ~**ation** [ri:læk'seiʃən] n (rest) descanso; (ease) relaxamento, alívio m; (amusement) passatempo; (entertainment) diversão f; ~**ed** adj relaxado; (tranquil) tranquilo; ~**ing** adj calmante, relaxante.

relay ['ri:lei] n (race) (corrida de)

revezamento // vt (message) retransmitir.

release [ri'li:s] n (from prison) libertação f; (from obligation) liberação f; (of shot) disparo; (of gas etc) escape m; (of film etc) estréia // vt (prisoner) pôr em liberdade; (book, film) lançar, estrear; (report, news) publicar; (gas etc) escapar; (free: from wreckage etc) soltar; (TECH: catch, spring etc) desengatar, desapertar; (let go) soltar, afrouxar.

relegate ['rɛləgeit] vt relegar, afastar; (SPORT): **to be ~d** descer.

relent [ri'lɛnt] vi abrandar-se; (yield) ceder; ~**less** adj implacável.

relevance ['rɛləvəns] n relevância, pertinência; **relevant** [-ənt] adj (fact) relevante, pertinente; (apt) apropriado.

reliable [ri'laiəbl] adj (person, firm) digno de confiança; (method, machine) seguro; (news) fidedigno; **reliably** adv: **to be reliably informed that...** saber de fonte segura que... .

reliance [ri'laiəns] n: ~ (**on**) confiança (em), esperança (em).

relic ['rɛlik] n (REL) relíquia; (of the past) vestígio.

relief [ri'li:f] n (from pain, anxiety) alívio; (help, supplies) ajuda, socorro; (ART, GEO) relevo.

relieve [ri'li:v]' vt (pain, patient) aliviar; (bring help to) ajudar, socorrer; (burden) abrandar, mitigar; (take over from: gen) substituir, revezar; (: guard) render; **to ~ sb of sth** tirar algo de alguém; **to ~ o.s.** fazer as necessidades.

religion [ri'lidʒən] n religião f; **religious** adj religioso.

relinquish [ri'liŋkwiʃ] vt abandonar; (plan, habit) renunciar a.

relish ['rɛliʃ] n (CULIN) condimento, tempero; (enjoyment) entusiasmo; (flavour) sabor m, gosto // vt (food etc) saborear; **to ~ doing** gostar de fazer.

reload [ri:'ləud] vt recarregar.

reluctance [ri'lʌktəns] n relutância; **reluctant** [-ənt] adj relutante; **reluctantly** [-əntli] adv relutantemente, de má vontade.

rely [ri'lai]: **to ~ on** vt fus confiar em, contar com; (be dependent on) depender de.

remain [ri'mein] vi (survive) ficar; (be left) sobrar; (continue) continuar, manter-se; ~**der** n resto, restante m; ~**ing** adj restante; ~**s** npl (mortal) restos mpl mortais; (leftovers) sobras fpl.

remand [ri'mɑ:nd] n: **on ~** sob prisão preventiva // vt: **to ~ in custody** recolocar em prisão preventiva, manter sob custódia; ~ **home** n instituição f do juizado de menores.

remark [ri'mɑ:k] n observação f // vt comentar, reparar; (notice) observar; ~**able** adj notável; (outstanding) extraordinário.

remarry [ri:'mæri] vi casar-se de novo, contrair segundas núpcias.

remedial [rɪ'miːdɪəl] adj (tuition, classes) de reforço.

remedy ['rɛmədɪ] n remédio, cura // vt remediar, curar.

remember [rɪ'mɛmbə*] vt lembrar-se de, recordar-se de; (bear in mind) ter presente; **remembrance** n (memory) memória; (souvenir) lembrança, recordação f.

remind [rɪ'maɪnd] vt: **to ~ sb to do sth** lembrar a alguém que tem de fazer algo; **to ~ sb of sth** lembrar algo a alguém; **she ~s me of her mother** ela me lembra a mãe dela; **~er** n aviso, lembrete m; (souvenir) lembrança.

reminisce [rɛmɪ'nɪs] vi relembrar velhas histórias; **reminiscent** adj: **to be reminiscent of sth** lembrar algo.

remiss [rɪ'mɪs] adj remisso, desleixado; **it was ~ of him** foi um descuido seu.

remission [rɪ'mɪʃən] n remissão f; (of debt, sentence) perdão m.

remit [rɪ'mɪt] vt (send: money) remeter, enviar, mandar; **~tance** n remessa, envio.

remnant ['rɛmnənt] n resto; (of cloth) retalho.

remorse [rɪ'mɔːs] n remorso; **~ful** adj arrependido; **~less** adj (fig) desapiedado, implacável.

remote [rɪ'məut] adj (distant) remoto, distante; (person) reservado, afastado; **~ control** n controle m remoto; **~ly** adv remotamente; (slightly) levemente; **~ness** n afastamento, isolamento.

remould ['riːməuld] vt (tyre) recauchutar.

removable [rɪ'muːvəbl] adj (detachable) removível, desmontável.

removal [rɪ'muːvəl] n (taking away) remoção f; (from house) mudança; (from office: sacking) afastamento, demissão f; (MED) extração (Pt: -cç-) f; **~ van** n caminhão (Pt: camião) m de mudanças.

remove [rɪ'muːv] vt tirar; (employee) afastar, demitir; (name: from list) eliminar, remover; (doubt, abuse) afastar; (TECH) retirar, separar; (MED) extrair, extirpar; **removers** npl (company) companhia de mudanças.

remuneration [rɪmjuːnə'reɪʃən] n remuneração f.

rend [rɛnd], pt, pp **rent** vt rasgar, despedaçar.

render ['rɛndə*] vt (give) dar, prestar; (hand over) entregar; (reproduce) reproduzir; (make) fazer, tornar; (return) devolver; (translate) traduzir; **~ing** n (MUS etc) interpretação f.

rendez-vous ['rɔndɪvuː] n encontro; (place) ponto de encontro.

renegade ['rɛnɪgeɪd] n renegado.

renew [rɪ'njuː] vt vt renovar; (resume) retomar, recomeçar; (loan etc) prorrogar; (negotiations, acquaintance) reatar; **renewable** adj renovável; **~al** n renovação f; (loan) prorrogação f.

renounce [rɪ'nauns] vt renunciar a; (disown) repudiar, rejeitar.

renovate ['rɛnəveɪt] vt renovar; **renovation** [-'veɪʃən] n renovação f.

renown [rɪ'naun] n renome m; **~ed** adj renomado, famoso.

rent [rɛnt] pt, pp of **rend** // n aluguel m (Br), aluguer m (Pt) // vt alugar; **~al** n (for television, car) aluguel m (Br), aluguer m (Pt).

renunciation [rɪnʌnsɪ'eɪʃən] n renúncia.

reorganize [riː'ɔːgənaɪz] vt reorganizar.

rep [rɛp] n abbr of **representative; repertory.**

repair [rɪ'pɛə*] n reparação f, conserto; (patch) remendo // vt reparar, remediar; (shoes) consertar; **in good/bad ~** em bom/mau estado; **~ kit** n (tool box) caixa de ferramentas.

repartee [rɛpɑː'tiː] n resposta arguta e engenhosa; (skill) presteza em replicar.

repay [riː'peɪ] (irr: like **pay**) vt (money) reembolsar, restituir; (person) pagar de volta; (debt) saldar, liquidar; (sb's efforts) corresponder, retribuir; **~ment** n reembolso, retribuição f; (of debt) pagamento.

repeal [rɪ'piːl] n (of law) revogação f; (of sentence) anulação f // vt revogar, anular.

repeat [rɪ'piːt] n (RADIO, TV) repetição f // vt repetir // vi repetir-se; **~edly** adv repetidamente.

repel [rɪ'pɛl] vt (lit, fig) repelir, repugnar; **~lent** adj repelente, repugnante // n: **insect ~lent** repelente m de insetos (Pt: -ct-).

repent [rɪ'pɛnt] vi: **to ~ (of)** arrepender-se (de); **~ance** n arrependimento.

repercussion [riːpə'kʌʃən] n (consequence) repercussão f; **to have ~s** repercutir.

repertoire ['rɛpətwɑː*] n repertório.

repertory ['rɛpətərɪ] n (also: **~ theatre**) teatro de repertório.

repetition [rɛpɪ'tɪʃən] n repetição f.

repetitive [rɪ'pɛtɪtɪv] adj (movement, work) repetitivo, reiterativo; (speech) prolixo, redundante.

replace [rɪ'pleɪs] vt (put back) repor, devolver; (take the place of) substituir, ocupar o lugar de; **~ment** n (gen) substituição f; (act) reposição f; (person) substituto/a.

replenish [rɪ'plɛnɪʃ] vt (glass) reencher; (stock etc) completar, prover; (with fuel) reabastecer.

replete [rɪ'pliːt] adj repleto; (well- fed) cheio, empanturrado.

replica ['rɛplɪkə] n réplica, cópia, reprodução f.

reply [rɪ'plaɪ] n resposta, réplica // vi responder, replicar.

report [rɪ'pɔːt] n relatório; (PRESS etc) reportagem f; (also: **school ~**) boletim m escolar; (of gun) estampido, detonação f; **weather ~** boletim m meteorológico

// vt informar sobre; (PRESS etc) fazer uma reportagem sobre; (bring to notice: occurrence) comunicar, anunciar // vi (make a report) apresentar um relatório; (present o.s.): to ~ (to sb) apresentar-se (a), comparecer; ~er n jornalista m/f, repórter m/f.

reprehensible [reprɪ'hensɪbl] adj repreensível, censurável, condenável.

represent [reprɪ'zent] vt representar; (fig) falar em nome de; (COMM) ser representante de; ~ation [-'teiʃən] n representação f; (petition) petição f; ~ations npl (protest) reclamação fsg, protesto sg; ~ative n representante m/f // adj representativo.

repress [rɪ'pres] vt reprimir, subjugar; ~ion [-'preʃən] n repressão f; ~ive adj repressivo.

reprieve [rɪ'priːv] n (LAW) suspensão f temporária; (fig) alívio // vt suspender temporariamente, aliviar.

reprimand ['reprɪmɑːnd] n reprimenda // vt repreender, censurar.

reprint ['riːprɪnt] n reimpressão f // vt [riː'prɪnt] reimprimir, reeditar.

reprisal [rɪ'praɪzl] n represália.

reproach [rɪ'prəʊtʃ] n repreensão f, censura // vt: to ~ sb with sth repreender alguém por algo; beyond ~ irrepreensível, impecável; ~ful adj repreensivo, acusatório.

reproduce [riːprə'djuːs] vt reproduzir // vi reproduzir-se; **reproduction** [-'dʌkʃən] n reprodução f; **reproductive** [-'dʌktɪv] adj reprodutivo.

reprove [rɪ'pruːv] vt: to ~ sb for sth repreender alguém por algo.

reptile ['reptaɪl] n réptil m.

republic [rɪ'pʌblɪk] n república; ~an adj, n republicano/a.

repudiate [rɪ'pjuːdɪeɪt] vt (accusation) rejeitar, negar; (friend) repudiar; (obligation) desconhecer.

repugnant [rɪ'pʌgnənt] adj repugnante, repulsivo.

repulse [rɪ'pʌls] vt rejeitar, repelir; **repulsive** adj repulsivo.

reputable ['repjutəbl] adj (make etc) bem conceituado, de confiança; (person) honrado, respeitável.

reputation [repju'teɪʃən] n reputação f.

repute [rɪ'pjuːt] n reputação f, renome m; ~d adj suposto, pretenso; ~dly adv segundo se diz, supostamente.

request [rɪ'kwest] n pedido; (formal) petição f; on ~ a pedido // vt: to ~ sth of or from sb pedir algo a alguém; (formally) solicitar algo a alguém.

requiem ['rekwɪəm] n réquiem m.

require [rɪ'kwaɪə*] vt (need: subj: person) precisar de, necessitar; (: thing, situation) requerer, exigir; (want) pedir; (order) mandar, ordenar; ~ment n requisito; (need) necessidade f.

requisite ['rekwɪzɪt] n requisito // adj

necessário, indispensável; **toilet** ~s artigos mpl de toalete pessoal.

requisition [rekwɪ'zɪʃən] n: ~ (for) requerimento (para) // vt (MIL) requisitar, confiscar.

reroute [riː'ruːt] vt (train etc) desviar.

resale ['riː'seɪl] n revenda.

rescue ['reskjuː] n salvamento, resgate m // vt salvar, livrar; **to** ~ **from** livrar de; ~ **party** n grupo or expedição f de salvamento; **rescuer** n salvador(a) m/f, libertador(a) m/f.

research [rɪ'səːtʃ] n pesquisa, investigação f // vt pesquisar; ~er n pesquisador(a) m/f; ~ **work** n trabalho de pesquisa.

resell [riː'sel] vt revender.

resemblance [rɪ'zembləns] n parecença, semelhança; **to bear a** ~ **to** assemelhar-se a; **resemble** vt parecer-se com.

resent [rɪ'zent] vt ressentir-se de; ~ful adj ressentido; ~ment n ressentimento.

reservation [rezə'veɪʃən] n (gen) reserva; (on road: also: **central** ~) canteiro central.

reserve [rɪ'zəːv] n (gen) reserva; (SPORT) suplente m/f // vt (seats etc) reservar; ~s npl (MIL) (tropas da) reserva sg; **in** ~ de reserva; ~d adj reservado.

reservoir ['rezəvwɑː*] n (large) represa; (small) depósito.

reshape [riː'ʃeɪp] vt (policy) reformar, remodelar.

reshuffle [riː'ʃʌfl] n: **Cabinet** ~ (POL) reforma ministerial.

reside [rɪ'zaɪd] vi residir, viver.

residence ['rezɪdəns] n residência; (formal: home) domicílio; (length of stay) permanência, estadia; **resident** [-ənt] n residente m/f; (in hotel) hóspede m/f // adj (population) permanente; (doctor) interno, residente; **residential** [-'denʃəl] adj residencial.

residue ['rezɪdjuː] n resíduo, resto; (COMM) montante m líquido.

resign [rɪ'zaɪn] vt (one's post) renunciar a // vi demitir-se; **to** ~ **o.s. to** (endure) resignar-se a; ~ation [rezɪg'neɪʃən] n renúncia; (state of mind) resignação f, submissão f; ~ed adj resignado.

resilience [rɪ'zɪlɪəns] n (of material) elasticidade f; (of person) resistência; **resilient** [-ənt] adj (person) resistente.

resin ['rezɪn] n resina.

resist [rɪ'zɪst] vt resistir; ~ance n resistência.

resolute ['rezəluːt] adj resoluto, firme.

resolution [rezə'luːʃən] n (gen) resolução f; (purpose) propósito.

resolve [rɪ'zɔlv] n resolução f; (purpose) intenção f // vt resolver // vi resolver-se; **to** ~ **to do** resolver-se a fazer; ~d adj decidido.

resonant ['rezənənt] adj ressonante.

resort [rɪ'zɔːt] n (town) local m turístico, estação f de veraneio; (recourse) recurso // vi: **to** ~ **to** recorrer a, fazer uso de;

in the last ~ em último caso, em última instância.

resound [rɪ'zaund] *vi* ressoar, retumbar; **the room ~ed with shouts** os gritos ressoaram no quarto; **~ing** *adj* retumbante.

resource [rɪ'sɔ:s] *n* recurso; **~s** *npl* recursos *mpl*, meios *mpl*; **~ful** *adj* desembaraçado, engenhoso, expedito.

respect [rɪs'pɛkt] *n* (*consideration*) respeito, consideração *f*; (*relation*) respeito; **~s** *npl* saudações *fpl*, cumprimentos *mpl* // *vt* respeitar; **with ~ to** com respeito a; **in this ~** a este respeito; **~ability** [-ə'bɪlɪtɪ] *n* respeitabilidade *f*; **~able** *adj* respeitável; (*large*) considerável; (*passable*) aceitável; **~ful** *adj* atencioso, respeitador(a).

respective [rɪs'pɛktɪv] *adj* respectivo; **~ly** *adv* respectivamente.

respiration [rɛspɪ'reɪʃən] *n* respiração *f*.

respiratory [rɛs'pɪrətərɪ] *adj* respiratório.

respite ['rɛspaɪt] *n* pausa, folga; (*LAW*) adiamento, suspensão *f*.

resplendent [rɪs'plɛndənt] *adj* resplandecente, brilhante.

respond [rɪs'pɔnd] *vi* responder; (*react*) reagir; **response** [-'pɔns] *n* resposta, reação (*Pt*: -cç-) *f*.

responsibility [rɪspɔnsɪ'bɪlɪtɪ] *n* responsabilidade *f*.

responsible [rɪs'pɔnsɪbl] *adj* (*liable*): **~ (for)** responsável por; (*character*) sério, respeitável; (*job*) de responsabilidade.

responsive [rɪs'pɔnsɪv] *adj* sensível.

rest [rɛst] *n* descanso, repouso; (*MUS*) pausa; (*break*) intervalo; (*support*) apoio; (*remainder*) resto // *vi* descansar; (*be supported*): **to ~ on** apoiar-se em // *vt* (*lean*): **to ~ sth on/against** apoiar algo em *or* sobre/apoiar algo contra.

restart [ri:'stɑ:t] *vt* (*engine*) arrancar de novo; (*work*) reiniciar, recomeçar.

restaurant ['rɛstərɔŋ] *n* restaurante *m*; **~ car** *n* vagão-restaurante *m*.

restful ['rɛstful] *adj* sossegado, tranqüilo, repousante.

rest home *n* asilo, casa de repouso.

restitution [rɛstɪ'tju:ʃən] *n*: **to make ~ to sb for sth** restituir *or* indenizar (*Pt*: -mn-) alguém de algo.

restive ['rɛstɪv] *adj* inquieto, impaciente; (*horse*) rebelão, teimoso.

restless ['rɛstlɪs] *adj* desassossegado, irrequieto; **~ly** *adv* inquietamente.

restoration [rɛstə'reɪʃən] *n* restauração *f*; **restore** [rɪ'stɔ:*] *vt* (*building*) restaurar; (*sth stolen*) restituir, repor; (*health*) restabelecer.

restrain [rɪs'treɪn] *vt* (*feeling*) reprimir, refrear; (*person*): **to ~ (from doing)** impedir (de fazer); **~ed** *adj* (*style*) moderado, comedido; **~t** *n* (*restriction*) limitação *f*, coibição *f*; (*moderation*) moderação *f*, comedimento *f*; (*of style*) sobriedade *f*.

restrict [rɪs'trɪkt] *vt* restringir, limitar; **~ion** [-kʃən] *n* restrição *f*, limitação *f*; **~ive** *adj* restritivo.

rest room *n* (*US*) banheiro (*Br*), lavabo (*Pt*).

result [rɪ'zʌlt] *n* resultado // *vi*: **to ~ in** resultar em; **as a ~ of** como conseqüência de.

resume [rɪ'zju:m] *vt*, *vi* (*work, journey*) retomar, recomeçar.

résumé ['reɪzju:meɪ] *n* resumo.

resumption [rɪ'zʌmpʃən] *n* reatamento, recomeço.

resurgence [rɪ'sɔ:dʒəns] *n* ressurgimento.

resurrection [rɛzə'rɛkʃən] *n* ressurreição *f*.

resuscitate [rɪ'sʌsɪteɪt] *vt* (*MED*) ressuscitar, reanimar; **resuscitation** [-'teɪʃn] *n* ressuscitação *f*.

retail ['ri:teɪl] *n* varejo (*Br*), venda a retalho (*Pt*) // *cmp* a varejo (*Br*), a retalho (*Pt*) // *vt* vender a varejo (*Br*), vender a retalho (*Pt*); **~er** *n* varejista *m/f* (*Br*), retalhista *m/f* (*Pt*).

retain [rɪ'teɪn] *vt* (*keep*) reter, conservar; (*employ*) contratar; **~er** *n* (*servant*) empregado; (*fee*) adiantamento.

retaliate [rɪ'tælɪeɪt] *vi*: **to ~ (against)** fazer represália (contra); **retaliation** [-'eɪʃən] *n* represália, vingança.

retarded [rɪ'tɑ:dɪd] *adj* retardado.

retch [rɛtʃ] *vi* fazer esforço para vomitar.

retentive [rɪ'tɛntɪv] *adj* (*memory*) retentivo, fiel.

reticent ['rɛtɪsnt] *adj* reservado.

retina ['rɛtɪnə] *n* retina.

retinue ['rɛtɪnju:] *n* séquito, comitiva; (*escort*) escolta.

retire [rɪ'taɪə*] *vi* (*give up work*) aposentar-se; (*withdraw*) retirar-se; (*go to bed*) deitar-se; **~d** *adj* (*person*) aposentado (*Br*), reformado (*Pt*); **retiree** *n* (*US*) aposentado/a (*Br*), reformado/a (*Pt*); **~ment** *n* (*state, act*) aposentadoria; **retiring** *adj* (*leaving*) de saída; (*shy*) acanhado, retraído.

retort [rɪ'tɔ:t] *n* (*reply*) réplica // *vi* replicar, retorquir.

retrace [ri:'treɪs] *vt*: **to ~ one's steps** voltar sobre (os) seus passos, refazer o mesmo caminho.

retract [rɪ'trækt] *vt* (*statement*) retirar, retratar (*Pt*: -act-); (*claws*) encolher; (*undercarriage, aerial*) recolher // *vi* retratar-se (*Pt*: -act-); **~able** *adj* retrátil (*Pt*: -áct-); revogável.

retrain [ri:'treɪn] *vt* reeducar, retreinar; **~ing** *n* readaptação *f* profissional.

retreat [rɪ'tri:t] *n* (*place*) retiro; (*act*) retraimento; (*MIL*) retirada // *vi* retirar-se; (*flood*) retroceder.

retribution [rɛtrɪ'bju:ʃən] *n* desforra, revide *m*, vingança.

retrieve [rɪ'tri:v] *vt* (*gen*) reaver, recuperar; (*situation, honour*) salvar;

(*error, loss*) reparar; **retriever** *n* cão *m* de busca, perdigueiro.

retrospect ['rɛtrəspɛkt] *n*: **in ~** retrospectivamente, em retrospecto; **~ive** [-'spɛktɪv] *adj* (*law*) retrospectivo, retroativo (*Pt*: -act-).

return [rɪ'tə:n] *n* (*going or coming back*) regresso, volta; (*of sth stolen etc*) devolução *f*; (*recompense*) recompensa; (FINANCE: *from land, shares*) rendimento, lucro; (*report*) relatório // *cmp* (*journey*) de regresso, de volta; (*ticket*) de ida e volta; (*match*) de revanche // *vi* (*person etc: come or go back*) voltar, regressar; (*symptoms etc*) voltar // *vt* devolver; (*favour, love etc*) retribuir; (*verdict*) proferir, anunciar; (POL: *candidate*) eleger; **~s** *npl* (COMM) receita *sg*; **in ~** em troca; **many happy ~s (of the day)!** parabéns! *mpl*.

reunion [ri:'ju:nɪən] *n* reunião *f*.

reunite [ri:ju:'naɪt] *vt* reunir; (*reconcile*) reconciliar.

rev [rɛv] *n abbr of* **revolution** (AUT) // (*vb: also*: **~ up**) *vt* aumentar a velocidade (do motor) // *vi* acelerar.

reveal [rɪ'vi:l] *vt* (*make known*) revelar; **~ing** *adj* revelador(a).

reveille [rɪ'vælɪ] *n* (MIL) toque *m* de alvorada.

revel ['rɛvl] *vi*: **to ~ in sth/in doing sth** deleitar-se com algo/em fazer algo.

revelation [rɛvə'leɪʃən] *n* revelação *f*.

reveller ['rɛvlə*] *n* farrista *m/f*, folião/liã *m/f*; **revelry** [-rɪ] *n* festança, folia.

revenge [rɪ'vɛndʒ] *n* vingança, desforra; (*in sport*) revanche *f*; **to take ~ on** vingar-se de.

revenue ['rɛvənju:] *n* receita, renda; (*on investment*) rendimento; (*profit*) lucro.

reverberate [rɪ'və:bəreɪt] *vi* (*sound*) ressoar, repercutir, ecoar; **reverberation** [-'reɪʃən] *n* reverberação *f*, repercussão *f*.

revere [rɪ'vɪə*] *vt* reverenciar, venerar; **reverence** ['rɛvərəns] *n* reverência; **reverent** ['rɛvərənt] *adj* reverente.

reverie ['rɛvərɪ] *n* devaneio, sonho.

reversal [rɪ'və:sl] *n* (*of order*) reversão *f*; (*of direction*) mudança em sentido contrário; (*of decision*) revogação *f*.

reverse [rɪ'və:s] *n* (*opposite*) contrário; (*back: of cloth*) avesso; (: *of coin*) reverso; (: *of paper*) dorso; (AUT: *also*: **~ gear**) marcha à ré (*Br*), marcha atrás (*Pt*) // *adj* (*order*) inverso, oposto; (*direction*) contrário // *vt* (*turn over*) virar do lado do avesso; (*invert*) inverter; (*change*) mudar (totalmente); *vi* (AUT) dar (marcha à) ré (*Br*), fazer marcha atrás (*Pt*); **reversible** *adj* reversível.

revert [rɪ'və:t] *vi*: **to ~ to** voltar a.

review [rɪ'vju:] *n* (*magazine*, MIL) revista; (*of book, film*) crítica, resenha; (*examination*) recapitulação *f*, exame *m* // *vt* rever, examinar; (MIL) passar em revista; (*book, film*) fazer a crítica *or* resenha de; **~er** *n* crítico/a.

revile [rɪ'vaɪl] *vt* ultrajar, injuriar, vilipendiar.

revise [rɪ'vaɪz] *vt* (*manuscript*) corrigir; (*opinion*) alterar, modificar; (*study: subject*) recapitular; (*look over*) revisar, rever; **revision** [rɪ'vɪʒən] *n* correção (*Pt*: -cç-) *f*, modificação *f*, revisão *f*.

revitalize [ri:'vaɪtəlaɪz] *vt* revitalizar, revivificar.

revival [rɪ'vaɪvəl] *n* (*recovery*) restabelecimento; (*of interest*) renascença, renascimento; (THEATRE) reestréia; (*of faith*) despertar *m*.

revive [rɪ'vaɪv] *vt* (*gen*) ressuscitar; (*custom*) restabelecer, restaurar; (*hope, courage*) despertar, reanimar; (*play*) reapresentar // *vi* (*person*) voltar a si; (*from faint*) recuperar os sentidos; (*activity*) renascer.

revoke [rɪ'vəuk] *vt* revogar.

revolt [rɪ'vəult] *n* revolta, rebelião *f*, insurreição *f* // *vi* revoltar-se // *vt* causar aversão a, repugnar; **~ing** *adj* revoltante, repulsivo.

revolution [rɛvə'lu:ʃən] *n* revolução *f*; **~ary** *adj, n* revolucionário/a; **~ize** *vt* revolucionar.

revolve [rɪ'vɔlv] *vi* revolver, girar.

revolver [rɪ'vɔlvə*] *n* revólver *m*.

revolving [rɪ'vɔlvɪŋ] *adj* (*chair etc*) giratório; **~ door** *n* porta giratória.

revue [rɪ'vju:] *n* (THEATRE) revista.

revulsion [rɪ'vʌlʃən] *n* aversão *f*, repugnância.

reward [rɪ'wɔ:d] *n* prêmio, recompensa // *vt*: **to ~ (for)** recompensar *or* premiar (por); **~ing** *adj* (*fig*) gratificante, compensador(a) *m/f*.

rewire [ri:'waɪə*] *vt* (*house*) renovar a instalação elétrica (*Pt*: -ct-) de.

reword [ri:'wɔ:d] *vt* reformular, exprimir em outras palavras.

rewrite [ri:'raɪt] (*irr: like* **write**) *vt* reescrever, escrever de novo.

rhapsody ['ræpsədɪ] *n* (MUS) rapsódja; (*fig*) elocução *f* exagerada *or* empolada.

rhetoric ['rɛtərɪk] *n* retórica; **~al** [rɪ'tɔrɪkl] *adj* retórico.

rheumatic [ru:'mætɪk] *adj* reumático; **rheumatism** ['ru:mətɪzəm] *n* reumatismo.

Rhine [raɪn] *n*: **the ~** o (rio) Reno.

rhinoceros [raɪ'nɔsərəs] *n* rinoceronte *m*.

rhododendron [rəudə'dɛndrn] *n* rododendro.

Rhone [rəun] *n*: **the ~** o (rio) Ródano.

rhubarb ['ru:ba:b] *n* ruibarbo.

rhyme [raɪm] *n* rima; (*verse*) verso(s) rimado(s), poesia.

rhythm ['rɪðm] *n* ritmo, cadência; **~ method** método anticoncepcional por tabelinha; **~ic(al)** *adj* rítmico, compassado.

rib [rɪb] *n* (ANAT) costela // *vt* (*mock*) zombar de, encarnar em.

ribald ['rɪbəld] *adj* vulgarmente engraçado, irreverente.

ribbon ['rɪbən] n fita; (strip) faixa, tira; **in ~s** (torn) em tirinhas, esfarrapado.

rice [raɪs] n arroz m; **~field** n arrozal m; **~ pudding** n arroz doce.

rich [rɪtʃ] adj rico; (banquet) suntuoso, opulento; (soil) fértil; (food) suculento, forte; (: sweet) rico; **the ~** os ricos; **~es** npl riquezas fpl, bens mpl; **~ness** n riqueza, opulência; (soil, etc) fertilidade f.

rickets ['rɪkɪts] n raquitismo.

rickety ['rɪkɪtɪ] adj raquítico; (shaky) sem firmeza, vacilante.

rickshaw ['rɪkʃɔː] n jinriquixá m.

ricochet ['rɪkəʃeɪ] n ricochete m // vi ricochetear.

rid [rɪd], pt, pp **rid** vt: **to ~ sb of sth** livrar alguém de algo; **to get ~ of** livrar-se or desembaraçar-se de.

ridden ['rɪdn] pp of **ride**.

riddle ['rɪdl] n (conundrum) adivinhação f; (mystery) enigma m, charada; (sieve) crivo, peneira // vt: **to be ~d with** estar cheio or crivado de.

ride [raɪd] n (gen) passeio; (on horse) passeio a cavalo; (distance covered) percurso, trajeto (Pt: -ct-) // (vb: pt **rode**, pp **ridden**) vi (as sport) cavalgar, montar; (go somewhere: on horse, bicycle) passear or andar (a cavalo, de bicicleta); (journey: on bicycle, motor cycle, bus) viajar // vt (a horse) montar a; (distance) viajar; **to ~ a bicycle** andar de bicicleta; **to ~ at anchor** (NAUT) estar ancorado; **to take sb for a ~** (fig) enganar alguém; **rider** n (on horse: male) cavaleiro; (: female) amazona; (on bicycle) ciclista m/f; (on motorcycle) motociclista m/f.

ridge [rɪdʒ] n (of hill) cume m, topo; (of roof) cumeeira; (wrinkle) ruga.

ridicule ['rɪdɪkjuːl] n escárnio, zombaria, mofa // vt ridicularizar, zombar de; **ridiculous** [-'dɪkjuləs] adj ridículo, absurdo.

riding ['raɪdɪŋ] n equitação f, passeio a cavalo; **~ school** n escola de equitação.

rife [raɪf] adj: **to be ~** ser comum; **to be ~ with** estar repleto de, abundar em.

riffraff ['rɪfræf] n plebe f, ralé f, povinho.

rifle ['raɪfl] n rifle m, fuzil m // vt saquear; **~ range** n campo de tiro; (at fair) tiro ao alvo.

rift [rɪft] n (fig: disagreement: between friends) desentendimento; (: in party) rompimento, divergência.

rig [rɪg] n (also: **oil ~**) torre f de perfuração // vt (election etc) adulterar or falsificar os resultados de; **to ~ out** vt ataviar, vestir; **to ~ up** vt instalar, montar, improvisar; **~ging** n (NAUT) cordame m.

right [raɪt] adj (true, correct) certo, correto; (suitable) adequado, conveniente; (proper) apropriado, próprio; (just) justo; (morally good) honrado, bom; (not left) direito; **it serves you ~!** bem feito! // n (title, claim) direito; (not left) direita // adv

(correctly) bem, corretamente (Pt: -ct-); (straight) diretamente (Pt: -ct-), direto (Pt: -ct-); (not on the left) à direita; (to the ~) para a direita // vt endireitar // excl muito bem!, certo!, bom!; **to be ~** (person) ter razão; **all ~!** tudo bem!, está bem; (enough) chega!, basta!; **~ now** agora mesmo; **~ in the middle** bem no meio; **~ away** imediatamente, logo, já; **by ~s** por direito; **on the ~** à direita; **~ angle** n ângulo reto (Pt: -ct-); **~eous** ['raɪtʃəs] adj justo, honrado; (anger) justificado; **~eousness** ['raɪtʃəsnɪs] n justiça; **~ful** adj (heir) legítimo; **~-hand** adj à direita; **~-handed** adj (person) destro; **~ly** adv corre(c)tamente, devidamente; (with reason) com razão; **~-wing** adj (POL) de direita.

rigid ['rɪdʒɪd] adj rígido; (principle) inflexível; **~ity** [rɪ'dʒɪdɪtɪ] n rigidez f, inflexibilidade f.

rigorous ['rɪɡərəs] adj rigoroso.

rigour, rigor (US) ['rɪɡə*] n rigor m, severidade f.

rig-out ['rɪɡaʊt] n (col) roupa, traje m.

rile [raɪl] vt irritar, aborrecer.

rim [rɪm] n borda, beira, orla; (of spectacles, wheel) aro.

rind [raɪnd] n (of bacon) couro, pele f; (of lemon etc) casca; (of cheese) crosta, casca.

ring [rɪŋ] n (of metal) aro; (on finger) anel m; (of people, objects) círculo, grupo; (of spies) grupo; (for boxing) ringue m; (of circus) pista, picadeiro; (bull~) picadeiro, arena; (sound of bell) toque m, badalada; (telephone call) chamada (telefônica), telefonema m // (vb: pt **rang**, pp **rung**) vi (on telephone) telefonar; (large bell) tocar, badalar; (also: **~ out**: voice, words) soar; (ears) zumbir // vt (TEL; also: **~ up**) telefonar a, ligar para; (bell etc) badalar; (doorbell) tocar; **to ~ back** vt/i (TEL) telefonar or ligar de volta; **to ~ off** vi (TEL) desligar; **~ing** n (of large bell) repicar m; (in ears) zumbido; **~leader** n (of gang) cabeça m/f, cérebro.

ringlets ['rɪŋlɪts] npl caracóis mpl, argolinhas fpl.

ring road n estrada periférica or perimetral.

rink [rɪŋk] n (also: **ice ~**) pista de patinação, ringue m.

rinse [rɪns] n enxaguada // vt enxaguar.

riot ['raɪət] n distúrbio, motim m, desordem f // vi provocar distúrbios, amotinar-se; **to run ~** desenfrear-se; **~er** n desordeiro, amotinado(a) m/f; **~ous** adj (gen) desordeiro; (party) tumultuado, barulhento; (uncontrolled) desenfreado.

rip [rɪp] n rasgão m; (opening) abertura // vt rasgar, romper // vi correr; **~cord** n corda de abertura (de pára-quedas); **~ off** n: **this is a ~ off** isto custa os olhos da cara.

ripe [raɪp] adj (fruit) maduro; (ready)

pronto; ~n vt/i amadurecer; ~ness n maturidade f, amadurecimento.

ripple ['rɪpl] n ondulação f, encrespação f; (sound) murmúrio // vi encrespar-se // vt ondular.

rise [raɪz] n (slope) elevação f, ladeira; (hill) colina, rampa; (increase: in wages) aumento; (: in prices, temperature) subida; (fig: to power etc) ascensão f // vi, pt rose, pp risen ['rɪzn] (gen) levantar-se, erguer-se; (prices, waters) subir; (river) encher; (sun) nascer; (person: from bed etc) levantar(-se); (also: ~ up: rebel) sublevar-se; (in rank) ascender, subir; **to give ~ to** ocasionar, dar origem a; **to ~ to the occasion** mostrar-se à altura da situação.

risk [rɪsk] n risco, perigo // vt (gen) arriscar; (dare) atrever-se a; **to take or run the ~ of** doing correr o risco de fazer; **at ~** em perigo; **at one's own ~** por sua própria conta e risco; ~y adj arriscado, perigoso.

risqué ['ri:skeɪ] adj (joke) malicioso, picante, indecente.

rissole ['rɪsəʊl] n rissole m.

rite [raɪt] n rito; **funeral ~s** exéquias fpl, cerimônia fúnebre.

ritual ['rɪtjʊəl] adj ritual // n ritual m, rito, cerimonial m.

rival ['raɪvl] n rival m/f; (in business) concorrente m/f // adj rival, adversário, competidor/a // vt rivalizar, competir com; ~ry n rivalidade f, concorrência.

river ['rɪvə*] n rio; **up/down ~** rio acima/abaixo; ~**bank** n margem f (do rio); ~**bed** n leito (do rio); ~**side** n beira, orla (do rio) // cmp (port, traffic) do rio, fluvial.

rivet ['rɪvɪt] n rebite m, cravo // vt rebitar; (fig) cravar.

Riviera [rɪvɪ'ɛərə] n: **the (French) ~** a Costa Azul (francesa), a Riviera francesa.

road [rəʊd] n (gen) caminho, via; (motorway etc) estrada (de rodagem); (in town) rua; ~**block** n barricada; ~**hog** n dono da estrada; ~ **map** n mapa m rodoviário; ~**side** n beira da estrada // cmp ao lado da estrada; ~**sign** n sinal m (da estrada), placa de sinalização; ~**user** n usuário da via pública; ~**way** n pista, estrada; ~**worthy** adj (car) pronto para ser usado or dirigido.

roam [rəʊm] vi vagar, perambular, errar // vt vagar por, vadiar por.

roar [rɔ:*] n (of animal) rugido, urro; (of crowd) bramido; (of vehicle, storm) estrondo; (of laughter) barulho // vi rugir, bramar, bradar; **to ~ with laughter** rir ruidosamente or espalhafatosamente; **to do a ~ing trade** fazer um bom negócio.

roast [rəʊst] n carne f assada, assado // vt (meat) assar; (coffee) torrar.

rob [rɔb] vt roubar; **to ~ sb of sth** roubar algo de alguém; (fig: deprive) despojar alguém de algo; ~**ber** n ladrão/ladra m/f; ~**bery** n roubo.

robe [rəʊb] n (for ceremony etc) toga, beca; (also: **bath ~**) roupão m (de banho).

robin ['rɔbɪn] n pisco-de-peito-ruivo (Br), pintarroxo (Pt).

robot ['rəʊbɔt] n robô m, autômato.

robust [rəʊ'bʌst] adj robusto, forte.

rock [rɔk] n (gen) rocha, pedra; (boulder) penhasco, rochedo; (sweet) pirulito // vt (swing gently: cradle) balançar, oscilar; (: child) embalar, acalentar; (shake) sacudir // vi balançar-se; (child) embalar-se; (shake) sacudir-se; **on the ~s** (drink) com gelo; (marriage etc) arruinado, em dificuldades; **to ~ the boat** (fig) criar confusão; ~ **and roll** n rock-and-roll m; ~-**bottom** adj (fig) mínimo, ínfimo; ~**ery** n jardim m de plantas rasteiras entre pedras.

rocket ['rɔkɪt] n foguete m.

rocking ['rɔkɪŋ]: ~ **chair** n cadeira de balanço; ~ **horse** n cavalo de balanço.

rocky ['rɔkɪ] adj (gen) rochoso, pedregoso; (unsteady: table) bambo, instável.

rod [rɔd] n vara, varinha; (TECH) haste f; (also: **fishing ~**) vara de pescar.

rode [rəʊd] pt of **ride**.

rodent ['rəʊdnt] n roedor m.

rodeo ['rəʊdɪəʊ] n rodeio.

roe [rəʊ] n (species: also: ~ **deer**) corça, cerva; (of fish): **hard/soft ~** ova/esperma m de peixe.

rogue [rəʊg] n velhaco, maroto; **roguish** adj brincalhão/lhona.

role [rəʊl] n papel m.

roll [rəʊl] n rolo; (of banknotes) maço; (also: **bread ~**) pãozinho; (register) rol m, lista; (sound: of drums etc) rufar m; (movement: of ship) jogo // vt rolar; (also: ~ **up**: string) enrolar; (: sleeves) arregaçar; (cigarettes) enrolar; (also: ~ **out**: pastry) esticar, alisar // vi (gen) rolar, rodar; (drum) rufar; (in walking) gingar; (ship) balançar, jogar; **to ~ by** vi (time) passar; **to ~ in** vi (mail, cash) chegar em grande quantidade; **to ~ over** vi dar uma volta; **to ~ up** vi (col: arrive) chegar, aparecer // vt (carpet) enrolar; ~ **call** n chamada, toque m de chamada; ~**er** n rolo; (wheel) roda, roldana; ~**er skates** npl patins mpl de roda.

rollicking ['rɔlɪkɪŋ] adj alegre, brincalhão/lhona, divertido.

rolling ['rəʊlɪŋ] adj (landscape) ondulado; ~ **pin** n rolo de pastel; ~ **stock** n (RAIL) material m rodante.

Roman ['rəʊmən] adj, n romano/a; ~ **Catholic** adj, n católico (romano).

romance [rə'mæns] n (love affair) aventura amorosa, romance m; (charm) romantismo.

Romanesque [rəʊmə'nɛsk] adj românico, romanesco.

Romania [rəʊ'meɪnɪə] n = **Rumania**.

romantic [rə'mæntɪk] adj romântico; **romanticism** [-tɪsɪzəm] n romantismo.

romp [rɔmp] *n* brincadeira, travessura // *vi* (*also*: ~ **about**) brincar, jogar.

rompers ['rɔmpəz] *npl* roupa de bebê.

roof [ru:f], *pl* ~**s** *n* (*gen*) teto (*Pt*: -ct-); (*of house*) telhado; (*of car*) capota, teto // *vt* telhar, cobrir com telhas; **the** ~ **of the mouth** o céu da boca; ~**ing** *n* cobertura; ~ **rack** *n* (*AUT*) porta-bagagem *m inv*, xalmas *fpl*.

rook [ruk] *n* (*bird*) gralha; (*CHESS*) torre *f*.

room [ru:m] *n* (*in house*) quarto, sala, aposento; (*also*: **bed**~) dormitório, quarto; (*in school etc*) sala; (*space*) espaço, lugar *m*; ~**s** *npl* (*lodging*) alojamento *sg*; '~**s to let**' 'alugam-se quartos *or* apartamentos'; **single** ~ quarto individual; **double** ~ quarto duplo/de casal/para duas pessoas; ~**mate** *n* companheiro/a de quarto; ~ **service** *n* serviço de quarto; ~**y** *adj* espaçoso.

roost [ru:st] *n* poleiro // *vi* empoleirar-se, pernoitar.

rooster ['ru:stə*] *n* galo.

root [ru:t] *n* (*BOT, MATH*) raiz *f* // *vi* (*plant, belief*) enraizar, arraigar; **to** ~ **about** *vi* (*fig*) revirar ao buscar; **to** ~ **for** *vt fus* torcer para; **to** ~ **out** *vt* desarraigar, extirpar.

rope [rəup] *n* corda; (*NAUT*) cabo // *vt* (*box*) atar *or* amarrar com uma corda; (*climbers: also*: ~ **together**) ligar-se (uns aos outros) com cordas; **to** ~ **sb in** (*fig*) persuadir alguém a tomar parte de; **to know the** ~**s** (*fig*) estar por dentro (do assunto); ~ **ladder** *n* escada de corda.

rosary ['rəuzərɪ] *n* rosário.

rose [rəuz] *pt of* **rise** // *n* rosa; (*also*: ~**bush**) roseira; (*on watering can*) crivo // *adj* rosado, cor de rosa.

rosé ['rəuzeɪ] *n* rosado, rosé *m*.

rose: ~**bed** *n* roseiral *m*; ~**bud** *n* botão *m* de rosa; ~**bush** *n* roseira.

rosemary ['rəuzmərɪ] *n* alecrim *m*.

rosette [rəu'zɛt] *n* rosácea, roseta.

roster ['rɔstə*] *n*: **duty** ~ lista de tarefas, escala de serviço.

rostrum ['rɔstrəm] *n* tribuna.

rosy ['rəuzɪ] *adj* rosado, rosáceo; **a** ~ **future** um futuro promissor.

rot [rɔt] *n* (*decay*) putrefação (*Pt*: -cç-) *f*, podridão *f*; (*fig: pej*) decadência // *vt/i* apodrecer.

rota ['rəutə] *n* rodízio.

rotary ['rəutərɪ] *adj* rotativo.

rotate [rəu'teɪt] *vt* (*revolve*) fazer girar, dar voltas em; (*change round: crops*) alternar; (: *jobs*) alternar, revezar // *vi* (*revolve*) girar, dar voltas; **rotating** *adj* (*movement*) rotativo; **rotation** [-'teɪʃən] *n* rotação *f*; **in rotation** por turnos.

rotor ['rəutə*] *n* rotor *m*.

rotten ['rɔtn] *adj* (*decayed*) podre; (*wood*) carcomido; (*fig*) corrupto; (*col: bad*) detestável, miserável; **to feel** ~ (*ill*) sentir-se péssimo.

rotting ['rɔtɪŋ] *adj* podre.

rotund [rəu'tʌnd] *adj* rotundo.

rouble, ruble (*US*) ['ru:bl] *n* rublo.

rouge [ru:ʒ] *n* rouge *m*, blush *m*, carmim *m*.

rough [rʌf] *adj* (*skin, surface*) áspero; (*terrain*) acidentado; (*road*) desigual; (*voice*) áspero, rouco; (*person, manner: coarse*) grosseiro, grosso; (*weather*) tempestuoso; (*treatment*) brutal, mau; (*sea*) agitado; (*cloth*) grosseiro; (*plan*) preliminar; (*guess*) aproximado; (*violent*) violento // *n* (*person*) grosseirão *m*; (*GOLF*): **in the** ~ na grama crescida; **to** ~ **it** passar aperto; **to sleep** ~ dormir na rua; ~**-and-ready** *adj* improvisado, feito às pressas; ~**en** *vt* (*surface*) tornar áspero; ~**ly** *adv* (*handle*) bruscamente; (*make*) toscamente; (*approximately*) aproximadamente; ~**ness** *n* aspereza; (*rudeness*) grosseria; (*suddenness*) brusquidão *f*.

roulette [ru:'lɛt] *n* roleta.

Roumania [ru:'meɪnɪə] *n* = **Rumania**.

round [raund] *adj* redondo // *n* círculo; (*of toast*) rodela; (*of policeman*) ronda; (*of milkman*) trajeto (*Pt*: -ct-); (*of doctor*) visitas *fpl*; (*game: of cards, in competition*) partida; (*of ammunition*) cartucho; (*BOXING*) rounde *m*, assalto; (*of talks*) ciclo // *vt* (*corner*) virar // *prep* ao/em redor de, em/à volta de // *adv*: **all** ~ por todos os lados; **the long way** ~ o caminho mais comprido; **all the year** ~ durante todo o ano; **it's just** ~ **the corner** (*fig*) está logo depois de virar a esquina; **to go** ~ **to sb's** (*house*) dar um pulinho na casa de alguém; **to go** ~ **the back** passar por detrás; **to go** ~ **a house** visitar uma casa; **to go the** ~**s** (*story*) divulgar-se; **to** ~ **off** *vt* (*speech etc*) terminar, completar; **to** ~ **up** *vt* (*cattle*) encurralar; (*people*) reunir; (*prices*) arredondar; ~**about** *n* (*AUT*) cruzamento circular, balão *m*; (*at fair*) carrossel *m* // *adj* (*route, means*) indireto (*Pt*: -ct-); **a** ~ **of applause** uma salva de palmas; **a** ~ **of drinks** uma rodada de bebidas; ~**ed** *adj* arredondado; (*style*) expressivo; ~**ly** *adv* (*fig*) energicamente, totalmente; ~**-shouldered** *adj* encurvado; ~ **trip** *n* viagem *f* de ida e volta; ~**up** *n* rodeio; (*of criminals*) batida.

rouse [rauz] *vt* (*wake up*) despertar, acordar; (*stir up*) suscitar; **rousing** *adj* emocionante, vibrante.

rout [raut] *n* (*MIL*) derrota; (*flight*) fuga, debandada // *vt* derrotar.

route [ru:t] *n* caminho, rota; (*of bus*) trajeto; (*of shipping*) rumo, rota; ~ **map** *n* (*for journey*) mapa *m* rodoviário.

routine [ru:'ti:n] *adj* (*work*) rotineiro // *n* rotina; (*THEATRE*) número.

roving ['rəuvɪŋ] *adj* (*wandering*) errante; (*salesman*) ambulante.

row [rəu] *n* (*line*) fila, fileira; (*KNITTING*) carreira, fileira; ~ **boat** *n* (*US*) barco a remo // *n* [rau] (*noise, racket*) barulho, balbúrdia; (*dispute*) discussão *f*, briga;

(fuss) confusão f, bagunça; **(scolding)** repreensão f // vi **[rɔu]** (in boat) remar // vi **[rau]** brigar // vt **[rɔu]** (boat) remar.

rowdy ['raudɪ] adj (person: noisy) barulhento; (: quarrelsome) brigão; (occasion) tumultuado // n encrenqueiro, criador m de caso.

rowing ['rouɪŋ] n remo; ~ **boat** n barco a remo.

royal ['rɔɪəl] adj real; ~**ist** adj, n monárquico; ~**ty** n (~ persons) família real, realeza; (payment to author) direitos mpl autorais.

R.S.V.P. abbr of **répondez s'il vous plaît** Q.R.P.G., Queira Responder Por Gentileza.

rub [rʌb] vt (gen) esfregar; (hard) friccionar; (polish) polir, lustrar // n (gen) esfregadela, fricção f; (touch) roçar m; **to ~ sb up the wrong way** irritar alguém; **to ~ off** vi tirar esfregando; **to ~ off on** transmitir-se para, influir sobre; **to ~ out** vt apagar.

rubber ['rʌbə*] n borracha; (Brit: eraser) borracha; ~ **band** n elástico, fita elástica; ~ **plant** (tree) seringueira; (plant) figueira; ~**y** adj elástico.

rubbish ['rʌbɪʃ] n (from household) lixo; (waste) rebotalho, resto; (fig: pej) disparates mpl, asneiras fpl; (trash) refugo; ~ **bin** n lata de lixo; ~ **dump** n (in town) depósito (de lixo).

rubble ['rʌbl] n escombros mpl.

ruby ['ru:bɪ] n rubi m.

rucksack ['rʌksæk] n mochila.

ructions ['rʌkʃɔnz] npl confusão fsg, tumulto sg.

rudder ['rʌdə*] n leme m.

ruddy ['rʌdɪ] adj (face) corado, avermelhado; (col: damned) maldito, desgraçado.

rude [ru:d] adj (impolite: person) grosso, mal-educado; (: word, manners) grosseiro; (sudden) brusco; (shocking) obsceno, chocante; ~**ly** adv grosseiramente; ~**ness** n falta de educação.

rudiment ['ru:dɪmənt] n rudimento; ~**s** npl primeiras noções fpl; ~**ary** [-'mɛntərɪ] adj rudimentar.

rue [ru:] vt arrepender-se de; ~**ful** adj arrependido.

ruffian ['rʌfɪən] n brigão m, desordeiro.

ruffle ['rʌfl] vt (hair) despentear, desmanchar; (clothes) enrugar, amarrotar; (fig: person) perturbar, irritar.

rug [rʌg] n tapete m; (for knees) manta (de viagem).

rugby ['rʌgbɪ] n (also: ~ **football**) rúgbi m (Br), râguebi m (Pt).

rugged ['rʌgɪd] adj (landscape) acidentado, irregular; (features) marcado; (character) severo, austero.

rugger ['rʌgə*] n (col) rúgbi m (Br), râguebi m (Pt).

ruin ['ru:ɪn] n ruína // vt arruinar; (spoil) estragar; ~**s** npl escombros mpl, destroços mpl; ~**ous** adj desastroso.

rule [ru:l] n (norm) norma, regulamento; (regulation) regra; (government) governo, domínio; (ruler) régua // vt (country, person) governar; (decide) decidir; (draw: lines) traçar // vi reger; (LAW) decretar; **to ~ out** excluir; **as a ~** via de regra; ~**d** adj (paper) pautado; **ruler** n (sovereign) soberano/a; (for measuring) régua; **ruling** adj (party) dominante; (class) dirigente // n (LAW) parecer m, decisão f.

rum [rʌm] n rum m.

Rumania [ru:'meɪnɪə] n Romênia; ~**n** adj, n romeno/a.

rumble ['rʌmbl] n ruído surdo, barulho; (of thunder) estrondo, ribombo // vi ribombar, ressoar; (stomach) roncar; (pipe) fazer barulho.

rummage ['rʌmɪdʒ] vi esquadrinhar, remexer, revistar.

rumour, rumor (US) ['ru:mə*] n rumor m, boato // vt: **it is** ~**ed that...** corre o boato de que ...

rump [rʌmp] n (of animal) anca, garupa; ~**steak** n alcatra.

rumpus ['rʌmpəs] n (col) barulho, confusão f, zorra; (quarrel) rixa, discussão f.

run [rʌn] n (gen) corrida; (outing) passeio, excursão f; (distance travelled) trajecto (Pt: -ct-), percurso; (series) série f; (THEATRE) temporada; (SKI) pista // (vb: pt ran, pp run) vt (operate: business) dirigir; (: competition, course) organizar; (: hotel, house) administrar; (to pass: hand) passar; (water) deixar correr; **to ~ the bath** correr a água para o banho // vi (gen) correr; (work: machine) funcionar; (bus, train: operate) circular, fazer o percurso; (: travel) ir; (continue: play) continuar; (: contract) ser válido; (flow: river, bath) fluir, correr; (colours, washing) desbotar; (in election) candidatar-se; **there was a ~ on** (meat, tickets) houve muita procura de; **in the long ~** no final das contas, mais cedo ou mais tarde; **on the ~** em fuga, fugindo; **I'll ~ you to the station** vou lhe dar uma carona até a estação (Br), dou-lhe uma boleia até à estação (Pt); **to ~ a risk** correr um risco; **to ~ about** vi (children) correr por todos os lados; **to ~ across** vt fus (find) encontrar por acaso, topar com, cruzar com; **to ~ away** vi fugir; **to ~ down** vi (clock) parar // vt (AUT) atropelar; (criticize) falar mal de, criticar; **to be ~ down** estar enfraquecido or exausto; **to ~ off** vt (water) deixar correr // vi partir correndo; **to ~ out** vi (person) sair correndo; (liquid) escorrer, esgotar-se; (lease) caducar, vencer; (money) acabar; **to ~ out of** vt fus ficar sem; **to ~ over** vt sep (AUT) atropelar // vt fus (revise) recapitular; **to ~ through** vt fus (instructions) examinar, recapitular; **to ~ up** vt (debt) acumular; **to ~ up against** (difficulties) tropeçar em; ~**away** adj (*horse*) desembestado; (*truck*) sem freios; (*person*) fugitivo.

rung [rʌŋ] *pp* of **ring** // *n* (*of ladder*) degrau *m*.

runner ['rʌnə*] *n* (*in race: person*) corredor(a) *m/f*; (: *horse*) cavalo de corrida; (*on sledge*) patim *m*, lâmina; (*on curtain*) anel *m*; (*wheel*) roldana, roda; ~ **bean** *n* (BOT) vagem *f* (*Br*), feijão *m* verde (*Pt*); ~**-up** *n* segundo/a colocado/a *m/f*.

running ['rʌnɪŋ] *n* (*sport, race*) corrida // *adj* (*water*) corrente; (*commentary*) contínuo, seguido; **6 days** ~ **6** dias seguidos; ~ **board** *n* estribo.

runny ['rʌnɪ] *adj* derretido, gotejante.

run-of-the-mill ['rʌnəvðə'mɪl] *adj* comum, normal.

runt [rʌnt] *n* (*also: pej*) nanico, anão/anã *m/f*.

runway ['rʌnweɪ] *n* (AVIAT) pista de decolagem.

rupee [ru:'pi:] *n* rupia.

rupture ['rʌptʃə*] *n* (MED) hérnia // *vt*: **to** ~ **o.s.** provocar-se uma hérnia.

rural ['ruərl] *adj* rural, campestre.

ruse [ru:z] *n* ardil *m*, manha.

rush [rʌʃ] *n* ímpeto, investida; (*hurry*) pressa; (COMM) grande procura or demanda; (BOT) junco; (*current*) corrente *f* forte, torrente *f* // *vt* apressar; (*work*) fazer depressa; (*attack: town etc*) assaltar // *vi* apressar-se, precipitar-se; ~ **hour** *n* rush *m* (*Br*), hora de ponta (*Pt*).

rusk [rʌsk] *n* rosca, biscoito.

Russia ['rʌʃə] *n* Rússia; ~**n** *adj*, *n* russo/a.

rust [rʌst] *n* ferrugem *f*; (BOT) mofo, bolor *m* // *vi* enferrujar.

rustic ['rʌstɪk] *adj* rústico, camponês/esa.

rustle ['rʌsl] *vi* sussurrar // *vt* (*paper*) farfalhar; (*US: cattle*) roubar, afanar.

rustproof ['rʌstpru:f] *adj* inoxidável, à prova de ferrugem.

rusty ['rʌstɪ] *adj* enferrujado.

rut [rʌt] *n* sulco, trilho; (ZOOL) cio; **to be in a** ~ ser escravo da rotina.

ruthless ['ru:θlɪs] *adj* desapiedado, cruel; ~**ness** *n* crueldade *f*, desumanidade *f*, insensibilidade *f*.

rye [raɪ] *n* centeio; ~ **bread** *n* pão *m* de centeio.

S

sabbath ['sæbəθ] *n* domingo; (*Jewish*) sábado.

sabbatical [sə'bætɪkl] *adj*: ~ **year** ano sabático or de licença.

sabotage ['sæbətɑːʒ] *n* sabotagem *f* // *vt* sabotar.

saccharin(e) ['sækərɪn] *n* sacarina, adoçante *m*.

sack [sæk] *n* (*bag*) saco, saca // *vt* (*dismiss*) despedir; (*plunder*) saquear; **to get**

the ~ ser demitido; ~**ing** *n* (*dismissal*) demissão *f*; (*material*) aniagem *f*.

sacrament ['sækrəmənt] *n* sacramento.

sacred ['seɪkrɪd] *adj* sagrado.

sacrifice ['sækrɪfaɪs] *n* sacrifício // *vt* sacrificar, renunciar.

sacrilege ['sækrɪlɪdʒ] *n* sacrilégio.

sacrosanct ['sækrəusæŋkt] *adj* sacrossanto.

sad [sæd] *adj* (*unhappy*) triste; (*deplorable*) deplorável; ~**den** *vt* entristecer.

saddle ['sædl] *n* sela; (*of cycle*) selim *m* // *vt* (*horse*) selar; **to be** ~**d with sth** (*col*) estar sobrecarregado com algo; ~**bag** *n* alforje *m*.

sadism ['seɪdɪzm] *n* sadismo; **sadist** *n* sadista *m/f*; **sadistic** [sə'dɪstɪk] *adj* sádico.

sadly ['sædlɪ] *adv* tristemente; ~ **lacking (in)** muito carente (de).

sadness ['sædnɪs] *n* tristeza.

safari [sə'fɑ:rɪ] *n* safári *m*.

safe [seɪf] *adj* (*out of danger*) fora de perigo; (*not dangerous*) seguro; (*unharmed*) ileso, incólume; (*trustworthy*) digno de confiança // *n* cofre *m*, caixa-forte *f*; ~ **and sound** são e salvo; (*just*) **to be on the** ~ **side** por via das dúvidas; ~**guard** *n* salvaguarda, proteção (*Pt*: -cç-) *f* // *vt* proteger, defender; ~**keeping** *n* custódia, prote(c)ção *f*; ~**ly** *adv* com segurança, a salvo; (*without mishap*) sem perigo.

safety ['seɪftɪ] *n* segurança // *adj* de segurança; ~ **first!** cuidado!; ~ **belt** *n* cinto de segurança; ~ **pin** *n* alfinete *m* de segurança.

saffron ['sæfrən] *n* açafrão *m*.

sag [sæg] *vi* afrouxar.

sage [seɪdʒ] *n* (*herb*) salva; (*man*) sábio.

Sagittarius [sædʒɪ'teərɪəs] *n* Sagitário.

sago ['seɪgəu] *n* sagu *m*.

said [sɛd] *pt, pp* of **say**.

sail [seɪl] *n* (*on boat*) vela; (*trip*): **to go for a** ~ ir dar um passeio de barco a vela // *vt* (*boat*) governar // *vi* (*travel: ship*) navegar, velejar; (: *passenger*) passear de barco; (*set off*) zarpar; **to** ~ **through** *vt/i fus* (*fig*) fazer com facilidade; ~**boat** *n* (*US*) barco a vela; ~**ing** *n* (SPORT) navegação *f* a vela, vela; **to go** ~**ing** ir velejar; ~**ing ship** *n* veleiro; ~**or** *n* marinheiro, marujo.

saint [seɪnt] *n* santo/a; **S** ~ **John** São João; ~**ly** *adj* santo, santificado.

sake [seɪk] *n*: **for the** ~ **of** por (causa de), em consideração a; **for my** ~ por mim.

salad ['sæləd] *n* salada; ~ **bowl** *n* saladeira; ~ **cream** *n* maionese *m*; ~ **dressing** *n* tempero or molho da salada; ~ **oil** *n* azeite *m* de mesa.

salami [sə'lɑ:mɪ] *n* salame *m*.

salary ['sælərɪ] *n* salário.

sale [seɪl] *n* venda; (*at reduced prices*) liquidação *f*, saldo; "**grand** ~" "grande liquidação"; "**for** ~" "à venda", "vende-se"; **on** ~ à venda; ~**room** *n* sala de vendas; **salesman/woman** n vendedor(a) m/f; (in shop) balconista m/f; (representative) vendedor(a) m/f viajante; **salesmanship** n arte f de vender.

saliva [sə'laɪvə] n saliva.

sallow ['sæləʊ] adj amarelado.

salmon ['sæmən] n, pl inv salmão m.

saloon [sə'lu:n] n (US) bar m, botequim m; (AUT) sedã; (ship's lounge) salão m.

salt [sɔlt] n sal m // vt salgar; (put ~ on) pôr sal em; ~ **cellar** n saleiro; ~**water** adj de água salgada; ~**y** adj salgado.

salutary ['sæljʊtərɪ] adj salutar.

salute [sə'lu:t] n saudação f; (of guns) salva; (MIL) continência // vt saudar; (guns) receber com salvas; (MIL) fazer continência a.

salvage ['sælvɪdʒ] n (saving) salvamento, recuperação f; (things saved) salvados mpl // vt salvar.

salvation [sæl'veɪʃən] n salvação f; **S~ Army** n Exército da Salvação.

salve [sælv] n (cream etc) ungüento, pomada.

salver ['sælvə*] n bandeja, salva.

same [seɪm] adj mesmo // adv do mesmo modo, igualmente // pron: the ~ o mesmo/a mesma; the ~ **book as** o mesmo livro que; **all** or **just the** ~ apesar de tudo, mesmo assim; **it's all the** ~ dá no mesmo, tanto faz; **to do the** ~ **(as sb)** fazer o mesmo (que alguém); **the** ~ **to you!** igualmente!

sample ['sɑ:mpl] n amostra // vt (food, wine) provar, experimentar.

sanatorium [sænə'tɔ:rɪəm], pl **-ria** [-rɪə] n sanatório.

sanctify ['sæŋktɪfaɪ] vt santificar.

sanctimonious [sæŋktɪ'məʊnɪəs] adj santarrão/rona, sacripanta.

sanction ['sæŋkʃən] n sanção f, pena // vt sancionar, ratificar.

sanctity ['sæŋktɪtɪ] n (gen) santidade f, divindade f; (inviolability) inviolabilidade f.

sanctuary ['sæŋktjʊərɪ] n (gen) santuário; (refuge) refúgio, asilo.

sand [sænd] n areia; (beach) praia // vt arear, jogar areia em.

sandal ['sændl] n sandália; (wood) sândalo.

sand: ~**bag** n saco de areia; ~**bank** n banco de areia; ~**castle** n castelo de areia; ~ **dune** n duna (de areia); ~**paper** n lixa; ~**pit** n (for children) caixa de areia; ~**stone** n arenito, grés m.

sandwich ['sændwɪtʃ] n sanduíche m (Br), sandes f (Pt) // vt (also: ~ **in**) intercalar; ~**ed between** encaixado entre; **cheese/ham** ~ sanduíche de queijo/presunto (Br), sandes de queijo/presunto (Pt); ~ **board** n cartaz m ambulante; ~ **course** n curso de teoria e prática alternadas.

sandy ['sændɪ] adj arenoso; (colour) vermelho amarelado.

sane [seɪn] adj são/sã do juízo; (sensible) ajuizado, sensato.

sang [sæŋ] pt of **sing**.

sanitarium [sænɪ'tɛərɪəm] (US) = **sanatorium**.

sanitary ['sænɪtərɪ] adj (system, arrangements) sanitário; (clean) higiênico; ~ **towel**, ~ **napkin** (US) n toalha higiênica or absorvente.

sanitation [sænɪ'teɪʃən] n (in house) higiene f; (in town) saneamento.

sanity ['sænɪtɪ] n sanidade f, equilíbrio mental; (common sense) juízo, sensatez f.

sank [sæŋk] pt of **sink**.

Santa Claus [sæntə'klɔ:z] n Papai Noel m.

sap [sæp] n (of plants) seiva // vt (strength) esgotar, minar.

sapling ['sæplɪŋ] n árvore f nova.

sapphire ['sæfaɪə*] n safira.

sarcasm ['sɑ:kæzm] n sarcasmo; **sarcastic** [-'kæstɪk] adj sarcástico.

sardine [sɑ:'di:n] n sardinha.

Sardinia [sɑ:'dɪnɪə] n Sardenha.

sari ['sɑ:rɪ] n sári m.

sash [sæʃ] n faixa, banda; (belt) cinto.

sat [sæt] pt, pp of **sit**.

Satan ['seɪtn] n Satanás m, Satã m.

satchel ['sætʃl] n bolsa; (child's) sacola escolar a tiracolo.

satellite ['sætəlaɪt] n satélite m.

satin ['sætɪn] n cetim m // adj acetinado.

satire ['sætaɪə*] n sátira; **satirical** [sə'tɪrɪkl] adj satírico; **satirize** ['sætɪraɪz] vt satirizar.

satisfaction [sætɪs'fækʃən] n satisfação f; (of debt) liquidação f, pagamento; **satisfactory** [-'fæktərɪ] adj satisfatório.

satisfy ['sætɪsfaɪ] vt satisfazer; (pay) liquidar, saldar; (convince) convencer, persuadir; ~**ing** adj satisfatório.

saturate ['sætʃəreɪt] vt: **to** ~ **(with)** saturar or embeber (de); **saturation** [-'reɪʃən] n saturação f.

Saturday ['sætədɪ] n sábado.

sauce [sɔ:s] n molho; (sweet) creme m, calda; (fig: cheek) atrevimento; ~**pan** n panela (Br), caçarola (Pt).

saucer ['sɔ:sə*] n pires msg.

saucy ['sɔ:sɪ] adj atrevido, descarado; (flirtatious) flertivo, provocante.

sauna ['sɔ:nə] n sauna.

saunter ['sɔ:ntə*] vi caminhar devagar, perambular.

sausage ['sɒsɪdʒ] n salsicha, lingüiça; (cold meat) frios mpl; ~ **roll** n folheado de salsicha.

sauté ['səʊteɪ] adj sauté, frito rapidamente.

savage ['sævɪdʒ] adj (cruel, fierce) cruel, feroz; (primitive) selvagem // n selvagem m/f // vt (attack) atacar ferozmente; ~**ry** n selvageria, ferocidade f.

save [seɪv] vt (rescue) salvar, resgatar; (money, time) poupar, economizar; (put by) guardar; (SPORT) impedir; (avoid: trouble) evitar // vi (also: ~ **up**) poupar

// n (SPORT) salvamento // prep salvo, exceto (Pt: -pt-).

saving ['seɪvɪŋ] n (on price etc) economia // adj: **the ~ grace of** o único mérito de; **~s** npl economias fpl; **~s bank** n caixa econômica, caderneta de poupança.

saviour ['seɪvjə*] n salvador(a) m/f.

savour, savor (US) ['seɪvə*] n sabor m // vt saborear; **~y** adj saboroso; (dish: not sweet) não doce; (: salted) salgado.

saw [sɔː] pt of **see** // n (tool) serra // vt, pt **sawed**, pp **sawed** or **sawn** serrar; **~dust** n serragem f, pó m de serra; **~mill** n serraria.

saxophone ['sæksəfəun] n saxofone m.

say [seɪ] n: **to have one's ~** exprimir sua opinião; **to have a** or **some ~ in sth** opinar sobre algo, ter que ver com algo // vt, pt, pp **said** dizer; **to ~ yes/no** dizer (que) sim/não; **that is to ~** ou seja; **that goes without ~ing** é óbvio, nem é preciso dizer; **~ing** n ditado, provérbio.

scab [skæb] n casca, crosta (de ferida); (pej) canalha m/f, fura-greves m/f inv; **~by** adj cheio de casca or cicatrizes.

scaffold ['skæfəuld] n (for execution) cadafalso, patíbulo; **~ing** n andaime m.

scald [skɔːld] n escaldadura // vt escaldar, queimar; **~ing** adj (hot) escaldante.

scale [skeɪl] n (gen, MUS) escala; (of fish) escama; (of salaries, fees etc) tabela; (of map, also size, extent) escala // vt (mountain) escalar; (tree) trepar em, subir em; **~s** npl balança sg; **on a large ~** em grande escala; **~ of charges** tarifa, lista de preços; **social ~** escala social; **~ drawing** n desenho em escala; **~ model** n maquete m em escala.

scallop ['skɔləp] n (ZOOL) vieira, venera; (SEWING) barra, arremate m.

scalp [skælp] n escalpo, couro cabeludo // vt escalpar.

scalpel ['skælpl] n escalpelo, bisturi m.

scamp [skæmp] n moleque m, malandro, patife m.

scamper ['skæmpə*] vi: **to ~ away, ~ off** sair correndo, fugir precipitadamente.

scan [skæn] vt (examine) esquadrinhar, perscrutar; (glance at quickly) passar uma vista de olhos por; (TV, RADAR) explorar.

scandal ['skændl] n escândalo; (gossip) mexerico; **~ize** vt escandalizar; **~ous** adj escandaloso; (libellous) difamatório, calunioso.

Scandinavia [skændɪ'neɪvɪə] n Escandinávia; **~n** adj, n escandinavo/a.

scant [skænt] adj escasso, insuficiente; **~y** adj escasso.

scapegoat ['skeɪpgəut] n bode m expiatório.

scar [skaː] n cicatriz f // vt marcar (com uma cicatriz) // vi cicatrizar.

scarce [skɛəs] adj escasso, raro; **~ly** adv

mal, quase não; **scarcity** n escassez f; (shortage) falta, carência.

scare [skɛə*] n susto, espanto; (panic) pânico // vt assustar, espantar; **to ~ sb stiff** deixar alguém morrendo de medo; **bomb ~** ameaça de bomba; **~crow** n espantalho; **~d** adj: **to be ~d** estar assustado or apavorado.

scarf [skaːf], pl **scarves** n (long) cachecol m; (square) lenço (de cabeça).

scarlet ['skaːlɪt] adj escarlate; **~ fever** n escarlatina.

scarves [skaːvz] pl of **scarf**.

scary ['skɛərɪ] adj (col) assustador(a), medroso.

scathing ['skeɪðɪŋ] adj mordaz, severo.

scatter ['skætə*] vt (spread) espalhar; (put to flight) dispersar // vi espalhar-se, debandar; **~brained** adj desmiolado, avoado; (forgetful) esquecido.

scavenger ['skævəndʒə*] n (refuse collector) varredor m de rua, gari m; (ZOOL) animal m/ave f que se alimenta de carniça.

scene [siːn] n (THEATRE, fig etc) cena; (of crime, accident) cenário; (sight, view) vista, panorama m; (fuss) escândalo; **~ry** n (THEATRE) cenário; (landscape) paisagem f; **scenic** adj (picturesque) pitoresco.

scent [sɛnt] n perfume m; (smell) aroma; (fig: track) pista, rastro; (sense of smell) olfato // vt perfumar; (smell) cheirar; (sniff out) farejar; (suspect) suspeitar, pressentir.

sceptic, skeptic (US) ['skɛptɪk] n cético/a (Pt: -pt-); **~al** adj cético (Pt: -pt-); **~ism** ['skɛptɪsɪzm] n ceticismo (Pt: -pt-).

sceptre, scepter (US) ['sɛptə*] n cetro; (fig) autoridade f real.

schedule ['ʃɛdjuːl] n (of trains) horário; (of events) programa m; (plan) plano; (list) lista // vt (timetable) planejar, estabelecer; (list) catalogar, fazer lista de; (visit) marcar (a hora de); **on ~** na hora, sem atraso; **to be ahead of/behind ~** estar adiantado/atrasado.

scheme [skiːm] n (plan) plano, esquema m; (method) método; (plot) conspiração f; (trick) ardil m; (arrangement) disposição f // vt projetar (Pt: -ct-) // vi (plan) planejar, tramar; (intrigue) conspirar; **scheming** adj intrigante.

schism ['skɪzəm] n cisma m.

schizophrenia [skɪtsəu'friːnɪə] n esquizofrenia; **schizophrenic** [-sə-'frɛnɪk] adj esquizofrênico.

scholar ['skɔlə*] n (pupil) aluno/a, estudante m/f; (learned person) sábio/a, erudito/a; **~ly** adj erudito, douto; **~ship** n erudição f; (grant) bolsa de estudo.

school [skuːl] n (gen) escola, colégio; (in university) faculdade f // vt (animal) adestrar, treinar; **~ age** n idade f escolar; **~book** n livro de textos or escolar; ~**boy** n aluno; ~**days** npl anos mpl escolares; ~**girl** n aluna; ~**ing** n educação f, ensino; ~**master/ mistress** n (primary, secondary) professor(a) m/f; ~**room** n sala de aula; ~**teacher** n professor(a) m/f.

schooner ['sku:nə*] n (ship) escuna; (glass) caneca, canecão m.

sciatica [saɪ'ætɪkə] n ciática.

science ['saɪəns] n ciência; ~ **fiction** n ficção f científica; **scientific** [-'tɪfɪk] adj científico; **scientist** n cientista m/f.

scimitar ['sɪmɪtə*] n cimitarra.

scintillating ['sɪntɪleɪtɪŋ] adj cintilante, brilhante.

scissors ['sɪzəz] npl tesoura; **a pair of** ~ uma tesoura.

scoff [skɔf] vt (col: eat) engolir // vi: **to** ~ **(at)** (mock) zombar (de).

scold [skəuld] vt ralhar, xingar.

scone [skɔn] n bolinho.

scoop [sku:p] n colherona; (for flour etc) pá f; (PRESS) furo (jornalístico); **to** ~ **out** vt escavar; **to** ~ **up** vt juntar.

scooter ['sku:tə*] n (motor cycle) moto f, lambreta; (toy) patinete m.

scope [skəup] n (of plan, undertaking) âmbito; (reach) alcance m; (of person) alçada, esfera de ação (Pt: -cç-); (opportunity) oportunidade f.

scorch [skɔːtʃ] vt (clothes) chamuscar; (earth, grass) secar, queimar; ~**er** n (col: hot day) dia m quente or abafado; ~**ing** adj ardente.

score [skɔː*] n (points etc) escore m, contagem f; (MUS) partitura; (reckoning) conta; (twenty) jogo de vinte, vintena // vt (goal, point) fazer; (mark) marcar, entalhar // vi ganhar; (FOOTBALL) marcar or fazer um gol; (keep score) marcar o escore; **on that** ~ a esse respeito, por esse motivo; **to** ~ **6 out of 10** conseguir um escore de 6 num total de 10; ~**board** n marcador m, placar m; ~**card** n (SPORT) cartão m de marcação; **scorer** n marcador m.

scorn [skɔːn] n desprezo // vt desprezar, rejeitar; ~**ful** adj desdenhoso, zombador(a).

Scorpio ['skɔːpɪəu] n Escorpião m.

scorpion ['skɔːpɪən] n escorpião m.

Scot [skɔt] n escocês/esa m/f.

scotch [skɔtʃ] vt (rumour) desmentir; (plan) estragar; **S**~ n uísque m (Pt: whisky) m escocês; **S**~ **tape** n = sellotape.

Scotland ['skɔtlənd] n Escócia f; **Scotsman/woman** n escocês/esa m/f; **Scottish** ['skɔtɪʃ] adj escocês/esa.

scoundrel n ['skaundrl] n canalha m/f, patife m.

scour ['skauə*] vt (clean) limpar, esfregar; (search) percorrer, procurar em; ~**er** n esponja de aço, bombril ® m (Br).

scourge [skɜːdʒ] n açoite m, flagelo.

scout [skaut] n (also: **boy** ~) escoteiro; (MIL) explorador m, batedor m; **to** ~

around explorar, fazer reconhecimento.

scowl [skaul] vi franzir a testa; **to** ~ **at sb** olhar alguém carrancudamente.

scraggy ['skrægɪ] adj magricela, descarnado.

scram [skræm] vi (col) dar o fora, safar-se.

scramble ['skræmbl] n (climb) escalada (difícil); (struggle) luta // vi: **to** ~ **out/through** conseguir sair com dificuldade; **to** ~ **for** lutar por; ~**d eggs** npl ovos mpl mexidos.

scrap [skræp] n (bit) pedacinho; (fig) pouquinho; (fight) rixa, luta; (also: ~ **iron**) ferro velho, sucata // vt reduzir a ferro velho, jogar no ferro velho; (discard) desfazer-se de, descartar // vi brigar, armar uma briga; ~**s** npl (waste) sobras fpl, restos mpl; ~**book** n álbum m de recortes.

scrape [skreɪp] n (fig) aperto, enrascada // vt raspar; (skin etc) arranhar; (~ against) roçar // vi: **to** ~ **together** juntar com dificuldade; **scraper** n raspador m.

scrap: ~ **heap** n (fig): **on the** ~ **heap** rejeitado, jogado fora; ~ **merchant** n sucateiro; ~ **paper** n papel m de rascunho; ~**py** adj (poor) pobre; (speech) incoerente, desconexo; (bitty) fragmentário.

scratch [skrætʃ] n arranhão m; (from claw) arranhadura // adj: ~ **team** time m improvisado, escrete m // vt (record) marcar, riscar; (with claw, nail) arranhar, unhar // vi coçar(-se); **to start from** ~ começar do princípio, partir do zero; **to be up to** ~ estar à altura (das circunstâncias).

scrawl [skrɔːl] n garrancho, garatujas fpl // vi garatujar, rabiscar.

scream [skriːm] n grito // vi gritar.

screech [skriːtʃ] vi guinchar.

screen [skriːn] n (CINEMA, TV) tela (Br), écran m (Pt); (movable) biombo; (wall) tapume m; (also: **wind**~) pára-brisa m; (fig) cortina // vt (conceal) esconder, tapar; (from the wind etc) proteger; (film) projetar (Pt: -ct-); (candidates etc) examinar, checar; ~**ing** n (MED) exame m médico; ~ **test** n teste m cinematográfico.

screw [skruː] n parafuso; (propeller) hélice f // vt aparafusar; (also: ~ **in**) apertar, atarraxar; ~**driver** n chave f de fenda or de parafuso; ~**y** adj (col) maluco, estranho.

scribble ['skrɪbl] n garrancho // vt escrevinhar, rabiscar.

script [skrɪpt] n (CINEMA etc) roteiro, script m; (writing) escrita, caligrafia.

Scripture ['skrɪptʃə*] n Sagrada Escritura.

scriptwriter ['skrɪptraɪtə*] n roteirista m/f.

scroll [skrəul] n rolo de pergaminho.

scrounge [skraundʒ] vt (col): **to** ~ **sth**

off *or* **from sb** filar algo de alguém // *vi*: **to ~ on sb** viver às custas de alguém; **scrounger** *n* filão/lona *m/f*.

scrub [skrʌb] *n* (*clean*) esfregação *f*, limpeza; (*land*) mato, cerrado // *vt* esfregar; (*reject*) cancelar, eliminar.

scruff [skrʌf] *n*: **by the ~ of the neck** pelo cangote.

scruffy ['skrʌfɪ] *adj* sujo, desmazelado.

scruple ['skru:pl] *n* escrúpulo; **scrupulous** *adj* escrupuloso.

scrutinize ['skru:tɪnaɪz] *vt* examinar minuciosamente; (*votes*) escrutinar; **scrutiny** [-nɪ] *n* escrutínio, exame *m* cuidadoso.

scuff [skʌf] *vt* desgastar.

scuffle ['skʌfl] *n* luta confusa.

scullery ['skʌlərɪ] *n* copa.

sculptor ['skʌlptə*] *n* escultor *m*; **sculptress** [-trɪs] *n* escultora; **sculpture** [-tʃə*] *n* escultura.

scum [skʌm] *n* (*on liquid*) espuma; (*pej: people*) ralé *f*, gentinha; (*fig*) escória.

scurry ['skʌrɪ] *vi*: **to ~ off** sair correndo, dar no pé.

scurvy ['skɜːvɪ] *n* escorbuto.

scuttle ['skʌtl] *n* (*also:* **coal ~**) balde *m* para carvão // *vt* (*ship*) afundar voluntariamente, fazer ir a pique // *vi* (*scamper*): **to ~ away, ~ off** sair em disparada.

scythe [saɪð] *n* segadeira, foice *f* grande.

sea [si:] *n* mar *m*; **on the ~** (*boat*) no mar; (*town*) junto ao mar; **to be all at ~** (*fig*) estar confuso or desorientado; **out to** *or* **at ~** em alto mar; **~ bird** *n* ave *f* marinha; **~board** *n* costa, litoral *m*; **~ breeze** *n* brisa marítima, viração *f*; **~farer** *n* marinheiro, homem *m* do mar; **~food** *n* marisco; **~ front** *n* (*beach*) praia; (*prom*) passeio *or* avenida à beira-mar; **~going** *adj* (*ship*) de longo curso; **~gull** *n* gaivota.

seal [si:l] *n* (*animal*) foca; (*stamp*) selo *m* // *vt* (*close*) fechar; (*: with ~*) selar; **to ~ off** vedar, lacrar; **it ~ed his fate** decidiu seu destino.

sea level ['si:lɛvl] *n* nível *m* do mar.

sealing wax ['si:lɪŋwæks] *n* lacre *m*.

sea lion ['si:laɪən] *n* leão-marinho *m*.

seam [si:m] *n* costura; (*of metal*) junta, junção *f*; (*of coal*) veio, filão *m*.

seaman ['si:mən] *n* marinheiro.

seamless ['si:mlɪs] *adj* sem costura.

seamstress ['sɛmstrɪs] *n* costureira.

seance ['seɪɔns] *n* sessão *f* espírita.

sea: ~plane *n* hidroavião *m*; **~port** *n* porto de mar.

search [sɜːtʃ] *n* (*for person, thing*) busca, procura; (*of drawer, pockets*) revista; (*inspection*) exame *m*, investigação *f* // *vt* (*look in*) procurar em; (*examine*) examinar; (*person, place*) revistar // *vi*: **to ~ for** procurar; **to ~ through** *vt fus* dar busca em; **in ~ of** à procura de; **~ing** *adj* penetrante, perscrutador(a); **~light** *n* holofote *m*; **~ party** *n* equipe

f de salvamento; **~ warrant** *n* mandado de busca.

sea: ~shore *n* praia, beira-mar *f*, litoral *m*; **~sick** *adj* enjoado, mareado; **~side** *n* costa, litoral *m*; **~side resort** *n* balneário.

season ['si:zn] *n* (*gen*) época, período; (*of year*) estação *f*; (*sporting etc*) temporada // *vt* (*food*) temperar; **~al** *adj* sazonal, periódico; **~ing** *n* condimento, tempero; **~ ticket** *n* entrada *or* ticket *m* de assinatura.

seat [si:t] *n* (*in bus, train: place*) assento; (*chair*) cadeira; (*POL*) lugar *m*, cadeira; (*bicycle*) selim *m*; (*buttocks*) traseiro, nádegas *fpl*; (*of government*) sede *f* // *vt* sentar; (*have room for*) ter capacidade para; **to be ~ed** estar sentado; **~ belt** *n* cinto de segurança.

sea: ~ water *n* água do mar; **~weed** *n* alga marinha; **~ worthy** *adj* em condições de navegar, resistente.

sec. *abbr of* **second(s)**.

secede [sɪ'si:d] *vi* separar-se.

secluded [sɪ'klu:dɪd] *adj* retirado; (*place*) afastado; **seclusion** [-'klu:ʒən] *n* reclusão *f*, isolamento.

second ['sɛkənd] *adj* segundo // *adv* (*in race etc*) em segundo lugar // *n* (*gen*) segundo; (*AUT: also:* **~ gear**) segunda; (*COMM*) artigo defeituoso // *vt* (*motion*) apoiar, secundar; **~ary** *adj* secundário; **~ary school** *n* escola secundária; **~-class** *adj* de segunda classe; **~hand** *adj* de (*Pt:* em) segunda mão, usado; **~ hand** *n* (*on clock*) ponteiro de segundos; **~ly** *adv* em segundo lugar; **~ment** [sɪ'kɔndmənt] *n* substituição *f* temporária; **~-rate** *adj* de segunda categoria.

secrecy ['si:krəsɪ] *n* segredo, sigilo; **secret** [-krɪt] *adj* secreto // *n* segredo.

secretarial [sɛkrɪ'tɛərɪəl] *adj* de secretário/a, secretarial.

secretariat [sɛkrɪ'tɛərɪət] *n* secretaria, secretariado.

secretary ['sɛkrətərɪ] *n* secretário/a; **S~ of State** (*Brit: POL*) Ministro de Estado.

secretive ['si:krətɪv] *adj* sigiloso, reservado, secretório.

sect [sɛkt] *n* seita; **~arian** [-'tɛərɪən] *adj* sectário.

section ['sɛkʃən] *n* seção (*Pt:* -cç-) *f*; (*part*) parte *f*, porção *f*; (*of document*) parágrafo, artigo; (*of opinion*) setor (*Pt:* -ct-) *m*; **~al** *adj* (*drawing*) transversal, secional (*Pt:* -cc-).

sector ['sɛktə*] *n* setor (*Pt:* -ct-) *m*.

secular ['sɛkjulə*] *adj* secular, leigo.

secure [sɪ'kjuə*] *adj* (*free from anxiety*) seguro; (*firmly fixed*) firme, rígido // *vt* (*fix*) assegurar, garantir; (*get*) conseguir, obter.

security [sɪ'kjurɪtɪ] *n* segurança; (*for loan*) fiança, garantia; (*: object*) penhor *m*.

sedan [sɪ'dæn] *n* (*US*) sedã *m*.

sedate [sɪˈdeɪt] adj (calm) sossegado, tranqüilo; (formal) sério, ponderado // vt sedar; tratar com calmantes.

sedation [sɪˈdeɪʃən] n (MED) sedação f; **sedative** [ˈsɛdɪtɪv] n calmante m, sedativo.

sedentary [ˈsɛdntrɪ] adj sedentário.

sediment [ˈsɛdɪmənt] n sedimento.

seduce [sɪˈdjuːs] vt (gen) seduzir; **seduction** [ˈdʌkʃən] n sedução f; **seductive** [-ˈdʌktɪv] adj sedutor(a).

see [siː], pt **saw**, pp **seen** vt (gen) ver; (understand) compreender, entender; (look at) olhar (para); (accompany): to ~ sb to the door acompanhar or levar alguém até a porta // vi ver // n sé f, sede f; to ~ that (ensure) assegurar que; to ~ about vi tratar de, encarregar-se de; to ~ off vt despedir-se de; to ~ through vt enxergar através de // vt fus realizar, terminar; (help) ajudar em momento difícil; to ~ to vt fus providenciar.

seed [siːd] n semente f; (in fruit) caroço; (sperm) sêmen m, esperma; (fig) germe m; (TENNIS) pré-selecionado/a (Pt: -cc-); ~**ling** n planta brotada da semente, muda; ~**y** adj (shabby) gasto, surrado; (person) maltrapilho.

seeing [ˈsiːɪŋ] conj: ~ (that) visto (que), considerando (que).

seek [siːk], pt, pp **sought** vt (gen) procurar, buscar; (post) solicitar.

seem [siːm] vi parecer; ~**ingly** adv aparentemente, pelo que aparenta.

seen [siːn] pp of **see**.

seep [siːp] vi filtrar-se, penetrar.

seesaw [ˈsiːsɔː] n gangorra, balanço.

seethe [siːð] vi ferver; to ~ with anger estar danado (da vida).

segment [ˈsɛgmənt] n segmento.

segregate [ˈsɛgrɪgeɪt] vt segregar; **segregation** [-ˈgeɪʃən] n segregação f.

seismic [ˈsaɪzmɪk] adj sísmico.

seize [siːz] vt (grasp) agarrar, pegar; (take possession of) apoderar-se de, confiscar; (: territory) tomar posse de; (opportunity) aproveitar; to ~ (up)on vt fus valer-se de; to ~ up vi (TECH) gripar.

seizure [ˈsiːʒəˣ] n (MED) ataque m, acesso; (LAW) confisco, embargo.

seldom [ˈsɛldəm] adv raramente.

select [sɪˈlɛkt] adj seleto (Pt: -ct-), escolhido // vt escolher, selecionar (Pt: -cc-); (SPORT) sele(c)cionar, escalar; ~**ion** [-ˈlɛkʃən] n seleção (Pt: -çç-) f, escolha; (COMM) sortimento; ~**ive** adj seletivo (Pt: -ct-); ~**or** n (person) sele(c)cionador(a) m/f, sele(c)tor(a) m/f.

self [sɛlf], pl **selves** pron see **myself**, **yourself**, **himself**, **herself**, **itself**, **oneself**, **ourselves**, **themselves** // n: the ~ o eu.

self... pref auto...; ~**-appointed** adj auto-nomeado; ~**-assured** adj seguro de si, ~**-catering** adj sem pensão; ~**-centred** adj egocêntrico; ~**-coloured** adj de cor natural; (of one

colour) de uma só cor; ~**-confidence** n auto-confiança, confiança em si; ~**-conscious** adj inibido, constrangido; ~**-contained** adj (gen) independente; (flat) completo, autônomo; ~**-control** n autocontrole m, autodomínio; ~**-defence** n legítima defesa, autodefesa; ~**-discipline** n auto-disciplina; ~**-employed** adj autônomo; ~**-evident** adj patente; ~**-governing** adj autônomo; ~**-important** adj presunçoso, que se dá muita importância; ~**-indulgent** adj que se permite excessos; ~**-interest** n egoísmo; ~**ish** adj egoísta; ~**ishness** n egoísmo; ~**lessly** adv des-interessadamente; ~**-pity** n pena de si mesmo; ~**-portrait** n auto-retrato; ~**-possessed** adj calmo, senhor de si mesmo; ~**-preservation** n auto-preservação f; ~**-reliant** adj seguro de si, independente; ~**-respect** n amor em próprio; ~**-righteous** adj farisaico, santarrão/rona; ~**-sacrifice** n abnegação f, altruísmo; ~**-satisfied** adj satisfeito consigo mesmo; ~**-service** adj de auto-serviço; ~**-sufficient** adj auto-suficiente; ~**-taught** adj autodidata (Pt: -acta).

sell [sɛl], pt, pp **sold** vt vender // vi vender-se; to ~ at or for £10 vender a or por 10 libras; to ~ off vt liquidar; to ~ out vi vender todo o estoque; ~**er** n vendedor(a) m/f; ~**ing price** n preço de venda.

sellotape [ˈsɛləuteɪp] ® n (fita) durex ® (Br), fita cola (Pt).

sellout [ˈsɛlaut] n traição f; (of tickets): it was a ~ foi um sucesso de bilheteria (Pt: -teira).

selves [sɛlvz] pl of **self**.

semaphore [ˈsɛməfɔːˣ] n semáforo.

semen [ˈsiːmən] n sêmen m.

semi... [ˈsɛmɪ] pref semi..., meio...; ~**circle** n semicírculo; ~**colon** n ponto e vírgula; ~**conscious** adj semi-consciente; ~**detached (house)** n (casa) geminada; ~**final** n semifinal f.

seminar [ˈsɛmɪnɑːˣ] n seminário.

semitone [ˈsɛmɪtəun] n (MUS) semitom m.

semolina [sɛməˈliːnə] n sêmola, semolina.

senate [ˈsɛnɪt] n senado; **senator** n senador(a) m/f.

send [sɛnd], pt, pp **sent** vt mandar, enviar; (dispatch) expedir, remeter; (telegram) passar; to ~ away vt (letter, goods) expedir, mandar; to ~ away for vt fus encomendar; to ~ back vt devolver; to ~ for vt fus mandar buscar; to ~ off vt (goods) despachar, expedir; (SPORT: player) expulsar; to ~ out vt (invitation) distribuir; (signal) emitir; to ~ up vt (person, price) fazer subir; (parody) parodiar; ~**er** n remetente m/f; ~**-off** n: a good ~**-off** uma boa despedida.

senile ['si:naıl] adj senil; **senility** [sı'nılıtı] n senilidade f.

senior ['si:nıə*] adj (older) mais velho or idoso; (: on staff) mais antigo; (of higher rank) superior // n sênior m/f; **~ity** [-'ɔrıtı] n antiguidade f.

sensation [sɛn'seıʃən] n sensação f; **~al** adj sensacional; **~alism** n sensacionalismo.

sense [sɛns] n sentido; (feeling) sensação f; (good ~) bom senso; (sentiment) opinião f // vt sentir, perceber; **it makes ~** faz sentido; **~less** adj insensato, estúpido; (unconscious) sem sentidos, inconsciente.

sensibility [sɛnsı'bılıtı] n sensibilidade f; **sensibilities** npl suscetibilidade (Pt: -pt-) fsg.

sensible ['sɛnsıbl] adj sensato, de bom senso; (cautious) cauteloso, prudente; (reasonable) lógico, razoável; (perceptible) sensível.

sensitive ['sɛnsıtıv] adj sensível, impressionável; (touchy) suscetível (Pt: -pt-); **sensitivity** [-'tıvıtı] n sensibilidade f; susce(p)tibilidade f.

sensual ['sɛnsjuəl] adj sensual.

sensuous ['sɛnsjuəs] adj sensual.

sent [sɛnt] pt, pp of **send**.

sentence ['sɛntns] n (LING) frase f, oração f; (LAW) sentença, decisão f // vt: **to ~ sb to death/to 5 years** condenar alguém à morte/a 5 anos de prisão.

sentiment ['sɛntımənt] n sentimento; (opinion) opinião f; **~al** [-'mɛntl] adj sentimental; **~ality** [-'tælıtı] n sentimentalismo.

sentry ['sɛntrı] n sentinela f.

separate ['sɛprıt] adj separado; (distinct) diferente // (vb: ['sɛpəreıt]) vt separar; (part) dividir // vi separar-se; **~ly** adv separadamente; **~s** npl (clothes) roupas que fazem jogo; **separation** [-'reıʃən] n separação f.

September [sɛp'tɛmbə*] n setembro.

septic ['sɛptık] adj sético (Pt: -pt-).

sequel ['si:kwl] n consequência, resultado; (of story) continuação f.

sequence ['si:kwəns] n série f, seqüência; (CINEMA) série.

sequin ['si:kwın] n lantejoula.

serenade [sɛrə'neıd] n serenata // vt fazer serenata para.

serene [sı'ri:n] adj sereno, tranqüilo; **serenity** [sə'rɛnıtı] n serenidade f, tranqüilidade f.

sergeant ['sɑ:dʒənt] n sargento.

serial ['sıərıəl] n seriado, história em folhetim; **~ize** vt publicar em folhetim; **~ number** n número de série.

series ['sıərı:s] n série f.

serious ['sıərıəs] adj sério; (grave) grave; **~ly** adv a sério, com seriedade; (gravely) gravemente; **~ness** n seriedade f; gravidade f.

sermon ['sə:mən] n sermão m.

serrated [sı'reıtıd] adj serrado, dentado.

serum ['sıərəm] n soro.

servant ['sə:vənt] n (gen) servidor(a) m/f; (house ~) empregado/a m/f; **civil ~** funcionário (público).

serve [sə:v] vt (gen) servir; (in shop: goods) vender, servir; (: customer) atender; (subj: train) passar por; (treat) tratar; (apprenticeship) fazer; (prison term) cumprir // vi (also TENNIS) sacar; (be useful): **to ~ as/for/to do** servir como/para/para fazer // n (TENNIS) saque m; **to ~ out, ~ up** vt (food) servir.

service ['sə:vıs] n (gen) serviço; (REL) cerimônia religiosa, culto; (AUT) revisão f; (of dishes) aparelho; (silver) baixela // vt (car, washing machine) fazer a revisão de; (: repair) consertar; **the S~s** as Forças Armadas; **to be of ~ to** sb ser útil a alguém; **~able** adj aproveitável, prático, durável; **~ area** n (on motorway) posto de gasolina com bar, restaurante etc; **~man** n militar m; **~ station** n posto de gasolina, manutenção etc; (petrol station) posto de gasolina (Br), estação f de serviço (Pt).

serviette [sə:vı'ɛt] n guardanapo.

servile ['sə:vaıl] adj servil.

session ['sɛʃən] n (sitting) sessão f; **to be in ~** estar celebrando uma sessão.

set [sɛt] n jogo, coleção (Pt: -cç-) f; (RADIO) (aparelho de) rádio; (TV) televisão f; (of utensils) bateria de cozinha; (of cutlery) talher m; (of books) cole(c)ção; (group of people) grupo; (TENNIS, CINEMA) set m; (THEATRE) cenário; (HAIRDRESSING) penteado // adj (fixed) marcado, fixo; (ready) pronto; (resolved) decidido, estabelecido // (vb: pt, pp set) vt (place) pôr, colocar, botar; (fix) fixar; (: a time) marcar; (adjust) ajustar, consertar; (decide: rules etc) estabelecer, decidir // vi (sun) pôr-se; (jam, jelly, concrete) endurecer, solidificar-se; **to be ~ on doing sth** estar decidido a fazer algo; **to ~ to music** musicar, pôr música em; **to ~ on fire** botar fogo em, incendiar; **to ~ free** libertar; **to ~ sth going** botar algo para funcionar, pôr algo em movimento; **to ~ sail** zarpar, alçar velas; **to ~ about vt fus** (task) começar a; **to ~ aside** vt pôr à parte, deixar de lado; **to ~ back** vt (in time) atrasar (por); **to ~ off** vi partir, ir indo // vt (bomb) fazer explodir; (cause to start) colocar em funcionamento; (show up well) ressaltar; **to ~ out** vi: **to ~ out to do sth** começar or pôr-se a fazer algo // vt (arrange) colocar em ordem, arrumar, providenciar; (state) expor, explicar; **to ~ up** vt (organization, record) estabelecer; **to ~ up shop** (fig) estabelecer-se; **~back** n (hitch) revés m, contratempo.

settee [sɛ'ti:] n sofá m.

setting ['sɛtıŋ] n (frame) moldura; (placing) colocação f; (of sun) pôr-(do-sol) *m*; (*of jewel*) engaste *m*; (*location*) cenário.

settle ['setl] *vt* (*argument, matter*) resolver, esclarecer; (*accounts*) ajustar, liquidar; (*land*) colonizar; (*MED: calm*) acalmar, tranqüilizar // *vi* (*dust etc*) assentar; (*weather*) firmar, melhorar; (*also:* ~ **down**) instalar-se, estabilizar-se; **to** ~ **for sth** concordar em aceitar algo; **to** ~ **in** *vi* instalar-se; **to** ~ **on sth** decidir algo; **to** ~ **up with sb** ajustar as contas com alguém; ~**ment** *n* (*payment*) liquidação *f*; (*agreement*) acordo, convênio; (*village etc*) povoado, povoação *f*; **settler** *n* colono/a, colonizador(a) *m/f*.

setup ['setʌp] *n* (*arrangement*) sistema *m*, organização *f*; (*situation*) situação *f*.

seven ['sevn] *num* sete; ~**teen** *num* dezessete (*Br*), dezassete (*Pt*); ~**th** *adj* sétimo; ~**ty** *num* setenta.

sever ['sevə*] *vt* cortar, separar; (*relations*) romper.

several ['sevərl] *adj, pron* vários *mpl*, diversos *mpl*; ~ **of us** vários de nós.

severance ['sevərəns] *n* (*of relations*) rompimento; ~ **pay** *n* indenização *f* pela demissão.

severe [sɪ'vɪə*] *adj* severo; (*serious*) austero, grave; (*hard*) duro; (*pain*) intenso; **severity** [sɪ'verɪtɪ] *n* severidade *f*; austeridade *f*; intensidade *f*.

sew [səu], *pt* **sewed**, *pp* **sewn** *vt/i* coser, costurar; **to** ~ **up** *vt* coser, cerzir.

sewage ['suːɪdʒ] *n* (*effluence*) detritos *mpl*; (*system*) esgoto.

sewer ['suːə*] *n* (*cano do*) esgoto, bueiro.

sewing ['səuɪŋ] *n* costura; ~ **machine** *n* máquina de costura.

sewn [səun] *pp* of **sew.**

sex [seks] *n* sexo; **to have** ~ **with sb** fazer sexo com alguém; ~ **act** *n* ato (*Pt*: -ct-) sexual.

sextet [seks'tet] *n* sexteto.

sexual ['seksjuəl] *adj* sexual.

sexy ['seksɪ] *adj* sexy.

shabby ['ʃæbɪ] *adj* (*person*) esfarrapado, maltrapilho; (*clothes*) usado, surrado.

shack [ʃæk] *n* choupana, barraco.

shackles ['ʃæklz] *npl* algemas *fpl*, grilhões *mpl*.

shade [ʃeɪd] *n* sombra; (*for lamp*) quebra-luz *m*; (*for eyes*) viseira; (*of colour*) tom *m*, tonalidade *f*; (*window*) estore *m* // *vt* sombrear, dar sombra a; **in the** ~ à sombra.

shadow ['ʃædəu] *n* sombra // *vt* (*follow*) seguir de perto (sem ser visto); ~ **cabinet** *n* (*POL*) gabinete *m* paralelo formado pelo partido da oposição; ~**y** *adj* escuro; (*dim*) vago, indistinto.

shady ['ʃeɪdɪ] *adj* sombreado, à sombra; (*fig: dishonest*) suspeito, duvidoso; (: *deal*) desonesto.

shaft [ʃɑːft] *n* (*of arrow, spear*) haste *f*; (*column*) fuste *m*; (*AUT, TECH*) eixo,

manivela; (*of mine, of lift*) poço; (*of light*) raio.

shaggy ['ʃægɪ] *adj* peludo, felpudo.

shake [ʃeɪk], *pt* **shook**, *pp* **shaken** *vt* sacudir; (*building*) fazer tremer; (*perturb*) perturbar, inquietar; (*weaken*) enfraquecer; (*surprise*) surpreender // *vi* estremecer(-se); (*tremble*) tremer // *n* (*movement*) sacudidela; (*violent*) safanão *m*; **to** ~ **hands with sb** apertar a mão de alguém; **to** ~ **off** *vt* sacudir; (*fig*) livrar-se de; **to** ~ **up** *vt* reorganizar; **shaky** *adj* (*hand, voice*) trêmulo; (*person : in shock*) abalado; (: *old*) frágil; (*chair*) bambo.

shall [ʃæl] *auxiliary vb*: **I** ~ **go** irei.

shallot [ʃə'lɔt] *n* cebolinha.

shallow ['ʃæləu] *adj* raso; (*fig*) superficial, leviano.

sham [ʃæm] *n* fraude *f*, fingimento // *adj* falso, simulado // *vt* fingir, simular.

shambles ['ʃæmblz] *n* confusão *fsg*.

shame [ʃeɪm] *n* vergonha; (*pity*) pena // *vt* envergonhar; **it is a** ~ **that/to do** é (uma) pena que/fazer; **what a** ~! que pena!; ~**faced** *adj* envergonhado; ~**ful** *adj* indecente, vergonhoso; ~**less** *adj* sem vergonha, descarado; (*immodest*) cínico, impudico.

shampoo [ʃæm'puː] *n* xampu *m* (*Br*), champô *m* (*Pt*) // *vt* lavar o cabelo (com xampu).

shamrock ['ʃæmrɔk] *n* trevo.

shandy ['ʃændɪ] *n* mistura de cerveja com refresco gaseificado.

shan't [ʃɑːnt] = **shall not.**

shanty town ['ʃæntɪ-] *n* favela.

shape [ʃeɪp] *n* forma // *vt* formar, modelar; (*sb's ideas*) moldar; (*sb's life*) determinar // *vi* (*also:* ~ **up**) (*events*) desenrolar-se; (*person*) amadurecer, tomar jeito; **to take** ~ tomar forma; -**shaped** *suff*: **heart-shaped** em forma de coração; ~**less** *adj* informe, sem forma definida; ~**ly** *adj* bem proporcionado *or* talhado, escultural.

share [ʃeə*] *n* (*part*) parte *f*, porção *f*; (*contribution*) cota; (*COMM*) ação (*Pt*: -çç-) *f* // *vt* dividir; (*have in common*) compartilhar; **to** ~ **out** (*among or between*) distribuir (entre); ~**holder** *n* acionista (*Pt*: -cç-) *m/f*.

shark [ʃɑːk] *n* tubarão *m*.

sharp [ʃɑːp] *adj* (*razor, knife*) afiado; (*point*) pontiagudo; (*outline*) definido, bem marcado; (*pain*) agudo; (*MUS*) desafinado; (*contrast*) marcado; (*voice*) agudo; (*person: quick-witted*) perspicaz; (*dishonest*) desonesto // *n* (*MUS*) sustenido // *adv*: **at 2 o'clock** ~ às 2 (horas) em ponto; ~**en** *vt* afiar; (*pencil*) apontar, fazer a ponta de; (*fig*) aguçar; ~**ener** *n* (*also:* **pencil** ~**ener**) apontador *m* (*Br*), apara-lápis *m inv* (*Pt*); ~-**eyed** *adj* de vista aguda; ~-**witted** *adj* perspicaz, observador(a).

shatter ['ʃætə*] *vt* despedaçar, esmigalhar; (*fig: ruin*) destruir, acabar //

vi despedaçar-se; **I feel** ~**ed** estou morto de cansaço.

shave [ʃeɪv] *vt* barbear, fazer a barba // *vi* fazer a barba, barbear-se // *n*: **to have a** ~ fazer a barba; **shaver** *n* aparelho de barbear, barbeador *m*; **electric shaver** *m* elétrico.

shaving [ˈʃeɪvɪŋ] *n*: ~ **brush** *n* pincel *m* de barba; ~ **cream** *n* creme *m* de barbear; ~**s** *npl (of wood etc)* aparas *fpl*.

shawl [ʃɔːl] *n* xale *m*.

she [ʃiː] *pron* ela; ~**-cat** *n* gata.

sheaf [ʃiːf], *pl* **sheaves** *n (of corn)* gavela; *(of arrows)* feixe *m*; *(of papers)* maço.

shear [ʃɪə*], *pt* **sheared**, *pp* **sheared** *or* **shorn** *vt (sheep)* tosquiar, tosar; **to** ~ **off** *vt* cercear; ~**s** *npl (for hedge)* tesoura *sg* de jardim.

sheath [ʃiːθ] *n* bainha; *(contraceptive)* camisa-de-vênus *f*, camisinha.

sheaves [ʃiːvz] *pl of* **sheaf**.

shed [ʃed] *n* alpendre *m*, galpão *m* // *vt*, *pt, pp* **shed** *(gen)* desprender-se de; *(skin)* mudar; *(tears)* derramar.

she'd [ʃiːd] = **she had; she would**.

sheep [ʃiːp] *n, pl inv* ovelha; ~**dog** *n* cão *m* pastor; ~**ish** *adj* tímido, acanhado; ~**skin** *n* pele *f* de carneiro, pelego.

sheer [ʃɪə*] *adj (utter)* puro, completo; *(steep)* íngreme, empinado; *(almost transparent)* fino, translúcido // *adv* a pique.

sheet [ʃiːt] *n (on bed)* lençol *m*; *(of paper)* folha; *(of glass, metal)* lâmina, chapa.

sheik(h) [ʃeɪk] *n* xeque *m*.

shelf [ʃelf], *pl* **shelves** *n* estante *f*, prateleira.

shell [ʃɛl] *n (on beach)* concha; *(of egg, nut etc)* casca; *(explosive)* obus *m*, granada; *(of building)* armação *f*, esqueleto // *vt (peas)* descascar; *(MIL)* bombardear.

she'll [ʃiːl] = **she will; she shall**.

shellfish [ˈʃɛlfɪʃ] *n, pl inv* crustáceo, molusco; *(pl: as food)* frutos *mpl* do mar, marisco.

shelter [ˈʃɛltə*] *n* abrigo, refúgio // *vt (aid)* amparar, proteger; *(give lodging to)* abrigar; *(hide)* esconder // *vi* abrigar-se, refugiar-se; ~**ed** *adj (life)* protegido; *(spot)* abrigado, protegido.

shelve [ʃɛlv] *vt (fig)* pôr de lado, engavetar; ~**s** *pl of* **shelf**.

shepherd [ˈʃɛpəd] *n* pastor *m* // *vt (guide)* guiar, conduzir; ~**ess** *n* pastora; ~'**s pie** *n* empadão *m* de carne e batata.

sheriff [ˈʃɛrɪf] *n* xerife *m*.

sherry [ˈʃɛrɪ] *n (vinho de)* Xerez *m*.

she's [ʃiːz] = **she is; she has**.

shield [ʃiːld] *n* escudo; *(TECH)* blindagem *f* // *vt*: **to** ~ *(from)* proteger contra.

shift [ʃɪft] *n (change)* mudança; *(of place)* transferência; *(of workers)* turno // *vt* transferir; *(remove)* tirar // *vi* mudar; *(change place)* mudar de lugar; ~ **work** *n* trabalho por turno; ~**y** *adj* esperto, trapaceiro; *(eyes)* velhaco, maroto.

shilling [ˈʃɪlɪŋ] *n* xelim *m*.

shimmer [ˈʃɪmə*] *n* reflexo trêmulo // *vi* cintilar, tremeluzir.

shin [ʃɪn] *n* canela *(da perna)*.

shine [ʃaɪn] *n* brilho, lustre *m* // *(vb: pt, pp* **shone**) *vi* brilhar, reluzir // *vt (shoes)* lustrar; **to** ~ **a torch on sth** apontar uma lanterna para algo.

shingle [ˈʃɪŋgl] *n (on beach)* pedrinhas *fpl*, seixinhos *mpl*; ~**s** *n (MED)* herpes-zoster *m*.

shiny [ˈʃaɪnɪ] *adj* brilhante, lustroso.

ship [ʃɪp] *n* navio, barco // *vt (goods)* embarcar; *(oars)* desarmar, guardar; *(send)* transportar *or* mandar *(por via marítima)*; ~**building** *n* construção *f* naval; ~**ment** *n (act)* embarque *m*; *(goods)* carregamento; ~**per** *n* exportador(a) *m/f*; ~**ping** *n (act)* embarque *m*; *(traffic)* transporte *m*; ~**shape** *adj* em ordem; ~**wreck** *n* naufrágio; ~**yard** *n* estaleiro.

shire [ˈʃaɪə*] *n* condado.

shirk [ʃəːk] *vt* eludir, esquivar-se; *(obligations)* não cumprir, faltar a.

shirt [ʃəːt] *n* camisa, blusa; **in** ~ **sleeves** em manga de camisa.

shiver [ˈʃɪvə*] *n* tremor *m*, arrepio // *vi* tremer, estremecer, tiritar.

shoal [ʃəul] *n (of fish)* cardume *m*.

shock [ʃɔk] *n (impact)* choque *m*; *(ELEC)* descarga; *(emotional)* comoção *f*, abalo; *(start)* susto, sobressalto; *(MED)* trauma *m* // *vt* dar um susto em, chocar; *(offend)* escandalizar; ~ **absorber** *n* amortecedor *m*; ~**ing** *adj (awful)* chocante, lamentável; *(improper)* escandaloso; ~**proof** *adj* à prova de choque.

shod [ʃɔd] *pt, pp of* **shoe** // *adj* calçado.

shoddy [ˈʃɔdɪ] *adj* ordinário, de má qualidade.

shoe [ʃuː] *n* sapato; *(for horse)* ferradura; *(brake* ~) sapata // *vt, pt, pp* **shod** *(horse)* ferrar; ~**brush** *n* escova de sapato; ~**horn** *n* calçadeira; ~**lace** *n* cadarço, cordão *m (de sapato)*; ~**maker** *n* sapateiro; ~ **polish** *n* graxa de sapato; ~**shop** *n* sapataria.

shone [ʃɔn] *pt, pp of* **shine**.

shook [ʃuk] *pt of* **shake**.

shoot [ʃuːt] *n (on branch, seedling)* rebento, broto // *(vb: pt, pp* **shot**) *vt* disparar; *(kill)* matar à bala; *(wound)* ferir à bala; *(execute)* fuzilar; *(film)* filmar, rodar // *vi (with gun, bow)*: **to** ~ *(at)* atirar *(em)*; *(FOOTBALL)* chutar; **to** ~ **down** *vt (plane)* derrubar, abater; **to** ~ **in/out** *vi* entrar correndo/sair em disparada; **to** ~ **up** *vi (fig)* subir vertiginosamente; ~**ing** *n (shots)* tiros *mpl*, tiroteio; *(HUNTING)* caçada *(com espingarda)*; ~**ing star** *n* estrela cadente.

shop [ʃɔp] *n* loja; *(workshop)* oficina // *vi (also:* **go** ~**ping**) ir fazer compras; ~ **assistant** *n* vendedor(a) *m/f*, empregado/a; ~ **floor** *n (fig)* que veio de baixo; ~**keeper** *n* lojista *m/f*;

~lifter n larápio de loja; ~lifting n furto (em lojas); ~per n comprador(a) m/f; ~ping (goods) compras fpl; ~ping bag n bolsa (de compras); ~ping centre, ~ping center (US) n shopping (center) m; ~-soiled adj manuseado; ~ steward n (INDUSTRY) representante m/f sindical; ~ window n vitrine f (Br), montra (Pt); ~worn adj (US) = ~-soiled.

shore [ʃɔ:ʲ] n (of sea) costa, praia; (lake) margem f // vt: to ~ (up) reforçar, escorar.

shorn [ʃɔ:n] pp of **shear**.

short [ʃɔ:t] adj (not long) curto; (in time) breve, de curta duração; (person) baixo; (curt) seco, brusco; (insufficient) insuficiente, em falta // vi (ELEC) dar um curto-circuito // n (also: ~ film) curta-metragem m; (a pair of) ~s (um) short m; to be ~ of sth estar em falta de algo; in ~ em resumo; it is ~ for é a abreviação de; to cut ~ (speech, visit) encurtar, interromper; to fall ~ ser deficiente; to stop ~ parar de repente; to stop ~ of chegar quase a; ~age n escassez f, falta; ~-circuit n curto-circuito // vt provocar um curto-circuito // vi entrar em curto-circuito; ~coming n defeito, imperfeição f, falha; ~(crust) pastry n massa amanteigada; ~cut n atalho; ~en vt encurtar, reduzir; (visit) abreviar, interromper; ~hand n taquigrafia; ~hand typist n estenodatilógrafa (Pt: -act-); ~ list n (for job) lista dos candidatos escolhidos; ~-lived adj efêmero, fugaz; ~ly adv em breve, dentro em pouco; ~ness n (of distance) curteza; (of time) brevidade f; (manner) maneira brusca, secura; ~-sighted adj míope; (fig) imprevidente; ~ story n conto; ~-tempered adj irritadiço; ~-term adj (effect) a curto prazo; ~wave n (RADIO) onda curta.

shot [ʃɔt] pt, pp of **shoot** // n (sound) tiro, disparo; (cannon) bala; (person) atirador(a) m/f; (try) tentativa; (injection) injeção (Pt: -cç-) f; (PHOT) fotografia; ~gun n espingarda.

should [ʃud] auxiliary vb: I ~ go now devo ir embora agora; he ~ be there now ele já deve ter chegado; I ~ go if I were you se eu fosse você eu iria; I ~ like to eu gostaria de.

shoulder [ˈʃouldəʲ] n ombro; (of road): hard ~ acostamento (Br), berma (Pt) // vt (fig) arcar com; ~ blade n omoplata m.

shouldn't [ˈʃudnt] = **should not**.

shout [ʃaut] n grito // vt gritar // vi gritar, berrar; to ~ down vt fazer calar com gritos; ~ing n gritaria, berreiro.

shove [ʃʌv] n empurrão m // vt empurrar; (col: put): to ~ sth in fazer algo entrar à força; to ~ off vi (NAUT) zarpar, partir; (fig: col) dar o fora.

shovel [ˈʃʌvl] n pá f; (mechanical) escavadeira // vt cavar com pá.

show [ʃou] n (of emotion) demonstração f; (semblance) aparência; (exhibition) exibição f; (THEATRE) espetáculo, (Pt: -ct-), representação f // (vb: pt showed, pp shown) vt mostrar; (courage etc) demonstrar, dar prova de; (exhibit) exibir, expor; (film) passar // vi mostrar-se; (appear) aparecer; to ~ sb in mandar alguém entrar; to ~ off vi (pej) mostrar-se, exibir-se // vt (display) exibir, mostrar; (pej) fazer ostentação de; to ~ sb out acompanhar alguém até a porta; to ~ up vi (stand out) destacar-se; (col: turn up) aparecer // vt descobrir; (unmask) desmascarar; ~ business n a vida artística; ~down n confrontação f.

shower [ˈʃauəʲ] n (rain) pancada de chuva; (of stones etc) chuva, enxurrada; (also: ~bath) banho de chuveiro // vi chover // vt: to ~ sb with sth cumular alguém de algo; ~proof adj impermeável; ~y adj (weather) chuvoso.

showing [ˈʃouiŋ] n (of film) projeção (Pt: -cç-) f, exibição f.

show jumping [ˈʃoudʒʌmpiŋ] n exibição f de hipismo.

shown [ʃoun] pp of **show**.

show: ~-off n (col: person) exibicionista m/f, faroleiro; ~piece n (of exhibition etc) obra mais importante; ~room n sala de exposição.

shrank [ʃræŋk] pt of **shrink**.

shrapnel [ˈʃræpnl] n estilhaços mpl.

shred [ʃred] n (gen pl) tira, pedaço // vt rasgar em tiras, retalhar; (CULIN) desfiar, picar.

shrewd [ʃru:d] adj astuto, perspicaz, sutil; ~ness n astúcia.

shriek [ʃri:k] n guincho, grito // vt/i guinchar, berrar.

shrill [ʃril] adj agudo, estridente.

shrimp [ʃrimp] n camarão m.

shrine [ʃrain] n santuário, relicário.

shrink [ʃriŋk], pt shrank, pp shrunk vi encolher; (be reduced) reduzir-se // vt fazer encolher; to ~ from doing sth não se atrever a fazer algo; ~age n encolhimento, redução f.

shrivel [ˈʃrivl] (also: ~ up) vt (dry) secar; (crease) enrugar // vi secar-se, enrugar-se, murchar.

shroud [ʃraud] n mortalha // vt: ~ed in mystery envolto em mistério.

Shrove Tuesday [ˈʃrouvˈtju:zdi] n terça-feira gorda.

shrub [ʃrʌb] n arbusto; ~bery n arbustos mpl.

shrug [ʃrʌg] n encolhimento dos ombros // vt/i: to ~ (one's shoulders) encolher os ombros, dar de ombros (Br); to ~ off vt negar a importância de.

shrunk [ʃrʌŋk] pp of **shrink**.

shudder [ˈʃʌdəʲ] n estremecimento, tremor m // vi estremecer, tremer de medo.

shuffle ['ʃʌfl] vt (cards) embaralhar; **to ~ (one's feet)** arrastar os pés.

shun [ʃʌn] vt evitar, afastar-se de.

shunt [ʃʌnt] vt (RAIL) manobrar, desviar // vi: **to ~ to and fro** mandar daqui para lá.

shut [ʃʌt], pt, pp **shut** vt fechar // vi fechar-se; **to ~ down** vt/i fechar, encerrar; **to ~ off** vt (supply etc) cortar, interromper; **to ~ up** vi (col: keep quiet) calar-se, calar a boca // vt (close) fechar; (silence) calar; **~ter** n veneziana; (PHOT) obturador m.

shuttle ['ʃʌtl] n lançadeira; (also: **~ service**) (plane) ponte f aérea.

shuttlecock ['ʃʌtlkɔk] n peteca.

shy [ʃaɪ] adj tímido; (reserved) reservado, esquivo; (unsociable) insociável; **~ness** n timidez f; acanhamento.

Siamese [saɪə'miːz] adj: **~ cat** gato siamês.

Sicily ['sɪsɪlɪ] n Sicília.

sick [sɪk] adj (ill) doente; (nauseated) enjoado, indisposto; (humour) negro; (vomiting): **to be ~** vomitar; **to feel ~** estar enjoado; **to be ~ of** (fig) estar cheio or farto de; **~ bay** n enfermaria; **~en** vt dar náuseas a // vi adoecer; **~ening** adj (fig) repugnante.

sickle ['sɪkl] n foice f.

sick: ~ leave n licença por doença; **~ly** adj doentio; (causing nausea) nauseante; **~ness** n doença, indisposição f; (vomiting) náusea, enjôo; **~ pay** n auxílio-doença m.

side [saɪd] n (gen) lado; (of body) flanco; (of lake) margem f; (aspect) aspeto; (team) time m (Br), equipa (Pt); (of hill) declive m // adj (door, entrance) lateral // vi: **to ~ with sb** tomar o partido de alguém; **by the ~ of** ao lado de; **~ by ~** lado a lado, juntos; **from all ~s** de todos os lados; **to take ~s** with pôr-se ao lado de; **~board** n aparador m; **~boards, ~burns** npl suíças fpl, costeletas fpl; **~ effect** n efeito colateral; **~light** n (AUT) luz f lateral; **~line** n (SPORT) linha lateral; (fig) linha adicional de produtos; (: job) emprego suplementar; **~long** adj de soslaio; **~ road** n rua lateral; **~saddle** adv de silhão; **~ show** n (stall) barraca; (fig) exibição f suplementar; **~step** vt (fig) evitar, esquivar-se de; **~track** vt (fig) desviar (do seu propósito); **~walk** n (US) calçada; **~ways** adv de lado.

siding ['saɪdɪŋ] n (RAIL) desvio, ramal m.

sidle ['saɪdl] vi: **to ~ up (to)** aproximar-se furtivamente (de).

siege [siːdʒ] n sítio, assédio, cerco.

sieve [sɪv] n peneira // vt peneirar.

sift [sɪft] vt peneirar; (fig: information) esquadrinhar, analisar minuciosamente.

sigh [saɪ] n suspiro // vi suspirar.

sight [saɪt] n (faculty) vista, visão f; (spectacle) espetáculo (Pt: -ct-); (on gun) alça, mira // vt avistar, mirar; **in ~** à vista; **out of ~** longe dos olhos;

~seeing n turismo; **to go ~seeing** visitar lugares turísticos.

sign [saɪn] n (with hand) sinal m, aceno; (indication) indício; (trace) rastro, vestígio; (notice) letreiro, tabuleta; (written) signo // vt assinar; **to ~ sth over to sb** assinar a transferência de algo para alguém; **to ~ up** vi (MIL) alistar-se // vt (contract) firmar contrato com.

signal ['sɪgnl] n sinal m, aviso; (US: TEL) ruído discal // vi (AUT) sinalizar // vt (person) fazer sinais para; (message) transmitir.

signature ['sɪgnətʃə*] n assinatura.

signet ring ['sɪgnətrɪŋ] n anel m com o sinete or a chancela.

significance [sɪg'nɪfɪkəns] n significado; (importance) importância; **significant** [-ənt] adj significativo, importante.

signify ['sɪgnɪfaɪ] vt significar.

sign: ~ language n mímica, linguagem f através de sinais; **~post** n indicador m; (traffic) placa de sinalização.

silence ['saɪləns] n silêncio // vt silenciar, impor silêncio a; (guns) silenciar; **silencer** n (on gun) silenciador m; (AUT) silencioso.

silent ['saɪlnt] adj (gen) silencioso; (not speaking) calado; (film) mudo; **to remain ~** manter-se em silêncio.

silhouette [sɪluː'et] n silhueta; **~d against** em silhueta contra.

silicon chip ['sɪlɪkən'tʃɪp] n placa or chip m de silicone.

silk [sɪlk] n seda // adj de seda; **~y** adj sedoso.

silly ['sɪlɪ] adj (person) bobo, idiota, imbecil; (idea) absurdo, ridículo.

silt [sɪlt] n sedimento, aluvião m.

silver ['sɪlvə*] n prata; (money) moedas fpl // adj de prata; **~ paper** n papel m de prata; **~-plated** adj prateado, banhado a prata; **~smith** n ourives m de prata; **~y** adj prateado.

similar ['sɪmɪlə*] adj: **~ to** parecido com, semelhante a; **~ity** [-'lærɪtɪ] n semelhança, similitude f; **~ly** adv da mesma maneira.

simmer ['sɪmə*] vi cozer em fogo lento, ferver lentamente.

simpering ['sɪmpərɪŋ] adj afetado (Pt: -ct-); (foolish) bobo, idiota, bobalhão/lhona m/f.

simple ['sɪmpl] adj (easy) fácil; (mere, COMM) simples inv; (foolish) ingênuo, humilde; **~ton** n simplório, pateta m/f; **simplicity** [-'plɪsɪtɪ] n simplicidade f; (foolishness) ingenuidade f; **simplify** ['sɪmplɪfaɪ] vt simplificar.

simulate ['sɪmjuleɪt] vt simular; **simulation** [-'leɪʃən] n simulação f.

simultaneous [sɪməl'teɪnɪəs] adj simultâneo; **~ly** adv simultaneamente.

sin [sɪn] n pecado // vi pecar.

since [sɪns] adv desde então, depois // prep desde // conj (time) desde que;

(*because*) porque, visto que, já que; ~ **then** desde então.

sincere [sɪn'sɪə*] *adj* sincero; **yours** ~**ly** atenciosamente; **sincerity** [-'sɛrɪtɪ] *n* sinceridade *f.*

sinful ['sɪnful] *adj* (*thought*) pecaminoso; (*person*) pecador(a).

sing [sɪŋ], *pt* **sang**, *pp* **sung** *vt* cantar // *vi* (*gen*) cantar; (*bird*) gorjear; (*ears*) zumbir.

singe [sɪndʒ] *vt* chamuscar.

singer ['sɪŋə*] *n* cantor(a) *m/f.*

singing ['sɪŋɪŋ] *n* (*gen*) canto; (*songs*) canções *fpl*; (*in the ears*) zumbido.

single ['sɪŋgl] *adj* único, só; (*unmarried*) solteiro; (*not double*) simples *inv*; (*bed, room*) individual // *n* (*also*: ~ **ticket**) passagem *f* de ida; (*record*) compacto; ~**s** *npl* (*TENNIS*) individual *fsg*; **to** ~ **out** *vt* (*choose*) escolher; (*point out*) distinguir, preferir; ~ **bed** *n* cama de solteiro; **in** ~ **file** em fila indiana; ~**-handed** *adv* sem ajuda, sozinho; ~**-minded** *adj* determinado; ~ **room** *n* quarto individual.

singular ['sɪŋgjulə*] *adj* (*odd*) esquisito, peculiar; (*LING*) singular // *n* (*LING*) singular *m.*

sinister ['sɪnɪstə*] *adj* sinistro.

sink [sɪŋk] *n* pia // (*vb*: *pt* **sank**, *pp* **sunk**) *vt* (*ship*) afundar; (*foundations*) escavar; (*piles etc*): **to** ~ **sth** enterrar algo // *vi* (*gen*) afundar-se, ir a pique; **to** ~ **in** *vi* (*fig*) penetrar, entranhar-se; **a** ~**ing feeling** um vazio no estômago.

sinner ['sɪnə*] *n* pecador(a) *m/f.*

sinus ['saɪnəs] *n* (*ANAT*) seio (nasal).

sip [sɪp] *n* gole *m* // *vt* tomar um golinho de, sorver, bebericar.

siphon ['saɪfən] *n* sifão *m*; **to** ~ **off** *vt* extrair com sifão.

sir [sə*] *n* senhor *m*; **S**~ **John Smith** Sir John Smith; **yes** ~ sim, senhor.

siren ['saɪərn] *n* sirena; (*mermaid*) sereia.

sirloin ['sɜ:lɔɪn] *n* lombo de vaca.

sister ['sɪstə*] *n* irmã *f*; (*nurse*) enfermeira-chefe *f*; (*nun*) freira; ~**-in-law** *n* cunhada.

sit [sɪt], *pt*, *pp* **sat** *vi* sentar-se; (*be sitting*) estar sentado; (*assembly*) reunir-se // *vt* (*exam*) prestar; **to** ~ **down** *vi* sentar-se; **to** ~ **in on** assistir a; **to** ~ **up** *vi* endireitar-se; (*not go to bed*) aguardar acordado, velar.

site [saɪt] *n* local *m*, sítio; (*also*: **building** ~) lote *m* (de terreno) // *vt* situar, localizar.

sit-in ['sɪtɪn] *n* (*demonstration*) ocupação *f* de um local como forma de protesto, manifestação *f* pacífica.

sitting ['sɪtɪŋ] *n* (*of assembly etc*) sessão *f*; (*in canteen*) turno; ~ **room** *n* sala de estar.

situated ['sɪtjueɪtd] *adj* situado.

situation [sɪtju'eɪʃən] *n* situação *f.*

six [sɪks] *num* seis; ~**teen** *num* dezesseis (*Pt*: -ass-); ~**th** *adj* sexto; ~**ty** *num* sessenta.

size [saɪz] *n* (*gen*) tamanho; (*extent*) dimensão *f*, proporção *f*; (*of clothing*) tamanho, medida; (*of shoes*) número; (*glue*) goma; **to** ~ **up** *vt* avaliar, formar uma opinião sobre; ~**able** *adj* considerável, importante.

sizzle ['sɪzl] *vi* chiar.

skate [skeɪt] *n* patim *m*; (*fish*: *pl inv*) arraia // *vi* patinar; ~**board** *n* skate *m*, patim-tábua *m*; ~**skater** *n* patinador(a) *m/f*; **skating** *n* patinação *f*; **skating rink** *n* ringue *m* de patinação.

skeleton ['skɛlɪtn] *n* esqueleto; (*TECH*) armação *f*; (*outline*) esquema *m*, esboço; ~ **key** *n* chave *f* mestra; ~ **staff** *n* pessoal *m* reduzido (ao mínimo).

sketch [skɛtʃ] *n* (*drawing*) desenho; (*outline*) esboço, croqui *m*; (*THEATRE*) pequena peça teatral, esquete *m* // *vt* desenhar, esboçar; ~ **book** *n* caderno de rascunho; ~ **pad** *n* bloco de desenho; ~**y** *adj* incompleto, esboçado.

skewer ['skju:ə*] *n* espetinho.

ski [ski:] *n* esqui *m* // *vi* esquiar; ~ **boot** *n* bota de esquiar.

skid [skɪd] *n* derrapagem *f* // *vi* derrapar, deslizar; ~**mark** *n* marca da derrapagem.

ski: ~**er** *n* esquiador(a) *m/f*; ~**ing** *n* esqui *m*; ~ **jump** *n* pista para saltos de esqui.

skilful ['skɪlful] *adj* habilidoso, jeitoso.

ski lift *n* ski lift *m.*

skill [skɪl] *n* habilidade *f*, perícia; ~**ed** *adj* hábil, perito; (*worker*) especializado, qualificado.

skim [skɪm] *vt* (*milk*) desnatar; (*glide over*) roçar // *vi*: **to** ~ **through** (*book*) folhear.

skimp [skɪmp] *vt* (*work*) atamancar; (*cloth etc*) economizar, regatear; ~**y** *adj* (*meagre*) escasso, insuficiente; (*skirt*) sumário.

skin [skɪn] *n* (*gen*) pele *f*; (*complexion*) cútis *f* // *vt* (*fruit etc*) pelar, descascar; (*animal*) tirar a pele a; ~**-deep** *adj* superficial; ~ **diving** *n* caça-submarina; ~**ny** *adj* magro, descarnado; ~**tight** *adj* (*dress etc*) justo, grudado (no corpo).

skip [skɪp] *n* salto, pulo; (*container*) balde *m* // *vi* saltar; (*with rope*) pular (corda) // *vt* (*pass over*) omitir, saltar.

ski pants *npl* calça *sg* de esquiar.

skipper ['skɪpə*] *n* (*NAUT, SPORT*) capitão *m.*

skipping rope ['skɪpɪŋ-] *n* corda (de pular).

skirmish ['skɜ:mɪʃ] *n* escaramuça.

skirt [skɜ:t] *n* saia // *vt* (*surround*) rodear; (*go round*) orlar, circundar; ~**ing board** *n* rodapé *m.*

skit [skɪt] *n* paródia, sátira.

skittle ['skɪtl] *n* pau *m*; ~**s** *n* (*game*) espécie de boliche *m.*

skive [skaɪv] *vi* (*Brit*: *col*) evitar trabalhar.

skull [skʌl] *n* caveira; (*ANAT*) crânio.

skunk [skʌŋk] n gambá m; (fig: person) cafajeste m/f, pessoa vil.

sky [skaɪ] n céu m; ~-**blue** adj azul celeste; ~**light** n clarabóia, escotilha; ~**scraper** n arranha-céu m.

slab [slæb] n (stone) bloco; (flat) laje f; (of cake) fatia grossa.

slack [slæk] adj (loose) frouxo, bambo; (slow) lerdo; (careless) descuidoso, desmazelado; ~**s** npl calça sg comprida; ~**en** (also: ~**en off**) vi afrouxar-se // vt afrouxar; (speed) diminuir.

slag [slæg] n escória, escombros mpl; ~ **heap** n monte m de escória or de escombros.

slalom ['slɑːləm] n slalom m.

slam [slæm] vt (door) bater or fechar (com violência); (throw) atirar violentamente; (criticize) malhar, criticar // vi fechar-se (com violência).

slander ['slɑːndə*] n calúnia, difamação f // vt caluniar, difamar; ~**ous** adj calunioso, difamatório.

slang [slæŋ] n gíria; (jargon) jargão m.

slant [slɑːnt] n declive m, inclinação f; (fig) ponto de vista; ~**ed**, ~**ing** adj inclinado, de esguelha.

slap [slæp] n palmada, tapa m; (in face) bofetada; (fig) repulsa, fora // vt dar um tapa or uma bofetada em // adv (directly) diretamente (Pt: -ct-), exatamente (Pt: -ct-); ~**dash** adj impetuoso, descuidado; ~**stick** n (comedy) palhaçada vulgar.

slash [slæʃ] vt cortar, talhar; (fig: prices) cortar.

slate [sleɪt] n lousa, ardósia // vt (fig: criticize) criticar duramente, arrasar.

slaughter ['slɔːtə*] n (of animals) matança; (of people) carnificina // vt matar; ~**house** n matadouro.

Slav [slɑːv] adj, m/f eslavo/a.

slave [sleɪv] n escravo // vi (also: ~ away) trabalhar como escravo; ~**ry** n escravidão f; **slavish** adj servil.

Slavonic [slə'vɔnɪk] adj eslavo.

slay [sleɪ] vt matar.

sleazy ['sliːzɪ] adj (fig: place) abandonado, maltratado.

sledge [slɛdʒ], **sled** (US) n trenó m; ~**hammer** n marreta, malho.

sleek [sliːk] adj (gen) macio, lustroso; (neat) limpo.

sleep [sliːp] n sono // vi, pt, pp **slept** dormir; **to go to ~** ir dormir, adormecer; **to ~ in** vi (oversleep) dormir demais; ~**er** n (person) dorminhoco/a m/f; (RAIL: on track) dormente; (: train) carro-dormitório; ~**ily** adv sonolentamente; ~**ing bag** n saco de dormir; ~**ing car** n carro-dormitório; ~**ing pill** n pílula para dormir; ~**lessness** n insônia; ~**walker** n sonâmbulo; ~**y** adj sonolento.

sleet [sliːt] n chuva com neve or granizo.

sleeve [sliːv] n manga; (TECH) camisa de cilindro; ~**less** adj (garment) sem manga.

sleigh [sleɪ] n trenó m.

sleight [slaɪt] n: ~ **of hand** prestidigitação f.

slender ['slɛndə*] adj magro, delgado; (means) escasso, insuficiente.

slept [slɛpt] pt, pp of **sleep**.

slice [slaɪs] n (of meat) fatia; (of bread) pedaço; (of lemon) rodela; (of fish) posta; (utensil) pá f or espátula de bolo // vt cortar em fatias, partir.

slick [slɪk] adj (skilful) jeitoso, ágil, engenhoso; (quick) rápido; (astute) astuto // n (also: **oil ~**) mancha de óleo.

slid [slɪd] pt, pp of **slide**.

slide [slaɪd] n (in playground) escorregador m; (PHOT) slide m; (also: **hair ~**) passador m // (vb: pt, pp **slid**) vt deslizar, patinar // vi (slip) escorregar; (glide) deslizar; **sliding** adj (door) corrediço.

slight [slaɪt] adj (slim) fraco, franzino; (frail) delicado; (pain etc) leve; (trifling) insignificante; (small) pequeno // n desfeita, desconsideração f // vt (offend) desdenhar, menosprezar; **not in the ~est** em absoluto, de maneira alguma; ~**ly** adv ligeiramente, um pouco.

slim [slɪm] adj magro, esbelto // vi emagrecer, tornar-se esbelto.

slime [slaɪm] n lodo, limo, lama; **slimy** adj viscoso, pegajoso.

slimming ['slɪmɪŋ] n emagrecimento; **a ~ diet** um regime or uma dieta para emagrecer.

sling [slɪŋ] n (MED) tipóia; (weapon) estilingue m, funda // vt, pt, pp **slung** atirar, arremessar, lançar.

slip [slɪp] n (slide) tropeção m; (fall) escorregão m; (mistake) erro, lapso; (underskirt) combinação f; (of paper) tira // vt (slide) deslizar // vi (slide) escorregar; (stumble) tropeçar; (decline) decair; **to give sb the ~** esgueirar-se or escapar de alguém; **to ~ away** vi escapulir; **to ~ in** vt meter // vi meter-se; **to ~ out** vi (go out) sair (um momento).

slipper ['slɪpə*] n chinelo.

slippery ['slɪpərɪ] adj escorregadio.

slip: ~**shod** adj descuidoso, desmazelado; ~-**up** n (error) equívoco, mancada; (by neglect) descuido; ~**way** n carreira.

slit [slɪt] n fenda; (cut) corte m // vt, pt, pp **slit** rachar, cortar, fender.

slither ['slɪðə*] vi escorregar, deslizar.

slob [slɔb] n (col) desmazelado, lambão m.

slog [slɔg] vi mourejar; **it was a ~** deu um trabalho louco.

slogan ['sləugən] n lema m, slogan m.

slop [slɔp] vi (also: ~ **over**) transbordar, derramar // vt transbordar, entornar.

slope [sləup] n (up) ladeira, rampa; (down) declive m; (side of mountain) encosta, vertente f // vi: **to ~ down** estar em declive; **to ~ up** inclinar-se; **sloping** adj inclinado, em declive.

sloppy ['slɔpɪ] *adj* (*work*) descuidado; (*appearance*) relaxado.

slot [slɔt] *n* ranhura, abertura; ~ **machine** *n* máquina caça-níqueis.

slouch [slautʃ] *vi*: **to** ~ **about** (*laze*) vadiar, viver na ociosidade.

slovenly ['slʌvənlɪ] *adj* (*dirty*) desalinhado, sujo; (*careless*) desmazelado.

slow [sləu] *adj* lento, vagaroso; (*watch*): **to be** ~ atrasar // *adv* lentamente, devagar // *vi* (*also*: ~ **down**, ~ **up**) ir mais devagar; '~' (*road sign*) 'devagar'; ~**down** *n* (*US*) = go-slow; ~**ly** *adv* lentamente, devagar; **in** ~ **motion** em câmara lenta; ~**ness** *n* lentidão *f*.

sludge [slʌdʒ] *n* lama, lodo.

slug [slʌg] *n* lesma; (*bullet*) bala, metralha; ~**gish** *adj* (*slow*) lerdo; (*lazy*) preguiçoso.

sluice [sluːs] *n* (*gate*) comporta, eclusa; (*channel*) canal *m*.

slum [slʌm] *n* (*area*) favela; (*house*) cortiço, barraco.

slumber ['slʌmbə*] *n* sono, soneca.

slump [slʌmp] *n* (*economic*) depressão *f* // *vi* baixar repentinamente.

slung [slʌŋ] *pt, pp of* sling.

slur [sləː*] *n* calúnia // *vt* difamar, caluniar; (*word*) pronunciar indistintamente.

slush [slʌʃ] *n* neve *f* meio derretida; ~**y** *adj* (*snow*) meio derretido; (*street*) lamacento; (*fig*) sentimentalóide.

slut [slʌt] *n* mulher *f* desmazelada; (*whore*) prostituta.

sly [slaɪ] *adj* (*clever*) astuto; (*nasty*) malicioso, velhaco.

smack [smæk] *n* (*slap*) palmada; (*blow*) tabefe *m*; (*kiss*) beijoca // *vt* dar uma palmada ou um tabefe em // *vi*: **to** ~ **of** cheirar a, saber a.

small [smɔːl] *adj* pequeno; ~**holder** *n* pequeno proprietário; ~**ish** *adj* de pequeno porte; ~ **pox** *n* varíola; ~ **talk** *n* conversa fiada.

smart [smɑːt] *adj* elegante; (*clever*) inteligente, astuto; (*quick*) vivo, esperto // *vi* arder, coçar; **to** ~**en up** *vi* arrumar-se, melhorar // *vt* arrumar.

smash [smæʃ] *n* (*also*: ~-up) colisão *f*, choque *m* // *vt* (*break*) escangalhar, despedaçar; (*car etc*) chocar-se com; (*SPORT: record*) quebrar // *vi* (*collide*) colidir; (*against wall etc*) espatifar-se; ~**ing** *adj* (*col*) genial, excelente.

smattering ['smætərɪŋ] *n*: **a** ~ **of** conhecimento superficial de.

smear [smɪə*] *n* mancha, nódoa; (*MED*) esfregação *f* // *vt* untar, lambuzar; (*fig*) caluniar, difamar.

smell [smɛl] *n* cheiro; (*sense*) olfato *f* (*vb: pt, pp* smelt *or* smelled) *vt/i* cheirar; **it** ~**s good/of garlic** cheira bem/a alho; ~**y** *adj* fedorento, malcheiroso.

smile [smaɪl] *n* sorriso // *vi* sorrir; **smiling** *adj* sorridente, risonho.

smirk [sməːk] *n* sorriso falso *or* afetado (*Pt*: -ct-).

smith [smɪθ] *n* ferreiro; ~**y** ['smɪðɪ] *n* forja, oficina de ferreiro.

smock [smɔk] *n* guarda-pó *m*; (*children's*) avental *m*.

smoke [sməuk] *n* fumaça (*Br*), fumo (*Pt*) // *vi* fumar; (*chimney*) fumegar // *vt* (*cigarettes*) fumar; ~**d** *adj* (*bacon*) defumado; (*glass*) fumeé; **smoker** *n* (*person*) fumante *m/f*; (*RAIL*) vagão *m* para fumantes; ~ **screen** *n* cortina de fumaça; ~ **shop** *n* (*US*) tabacaria; **smoking** *n*: 'no smoking' (*sign*) 'proibido fumar'; **smoky** *adj* (*gen*) fumegante; (*room*) cheio de fumaça (*Br*), cheio de fumo (*Pt*).

smooth [smuːð] *adj* (*gen*) liso, macio; (*sea*) tranqüilo, calmo; (*flat*) plano; (*flavour, movement*) suave; (*person*) culto, refinado; (: *pej*) meloso // *vt* alisar; (*also*: ~ **out**) (*difficulties*) acalmar, aplainar.

smother ['smʌðə*] *vt* sufocar, suprimir; (*repress*) reprimir.

smoulder ['sməuldə:] *vi* arder sem chamas, estar latente.

smudge [smʌdʒ] *n* mancha // *vt* manchar, sujar.

smug [smʌg] *adj* metido, convencido.

smuggle ['smʌgl] *vt* contrabandear; **smuggler** *n* contrabandista *m/f*; **smuggling** *n* contrabando.

smutty ['smʌtɪ] *adj* (*fig*) obsceno, indecente, manchado.

snack [snæk] *n* lanche *m* (*Br*), merenda (*Pt*); ~ **bar** *n* lanchonete *f* (*Br*), snackbar *m* (*Pt*).

snag [snæg] *n* dificuldade *f*, obstáculo.

snail [sneɪl] *n* caramujo, lesma.

snake [sneɪk] *n* cobra.

snap [snæp] *n* (*sound*) estalo; (*of whip*) estalido; (*click*) clique *m*; (*photograph*) foto *f* // *adj* repentino // *vt* (*fingers, whip*) estalar; (*break*) quebrar; (*photograph*) tirar uma foto de // *vi* (*break*) despedaçar-se; (*fig: person*) retrucar asperamente; (*sound*) fazer um clique; **to** ~ **shut** fechar ruidosamente; **to** ~ **at** *vt fus* (*subj: dog*) tentar morder; **to** ~ **off** *vi* (*break*) partir-se; **to** ~ **up** *vt* arrebatar, comprar rapidamente; ~**shot** *n* foto *f* (instantânea).

snare [snɛə*] *n* armadilha, laço // *vt* apanhar no laço ou na armadilha; (*fig*) enganar.

snarl [snɑːl] *n* grunhido // *vi* grunhir.

snatch [snætʃ] *n* (*fig*) roubo; (*small amount*): ~**es of** pedacinhos *mpl* de // *vt* (~ **away**) arrebatar; (*grasp*) agarrar, tirar à força.

sneak [sniːk] *vi*: **to** ~ **in/out** entrar/sair furtivamente // *n* (*fam*) pessoa covarde *or* vil; ~**y** *adj* sorrateiro.

sneer [snɪə*] *n* sorriso de desprezo // *vi* rir-se com desdém; (*mock*) zombar de, escarnecer de.

sneeze [sniːz] *n* espirro // *vi* espirrar.

sniff [snɪf] *n* (*of dog*) farejada; (*of person*)

fungadela // vi fungar, farejar.

snigger ['snɪgə*] n riso dissimulado // vi rir-se com dissimulação.

snip [snɪp] n tesourada; (piece) pedaço, retalho; (bargain) pechincha // vt cortar com tesoura.

sniper ['snaɪpə*] n franco-atirador(a) m/f.

snippet ['snɪpɪt] n pedacinho.

snivelling ['snɪvlɪŋ] adj (whimpering) chorão/rona, lamuriento.

snob [snɔb] n esnobe m/f; **~bery** n esnobismo; **~bish** adj esnobe.

snooker ['snu:kə*] n sinuca.

snoop [snu:p] vi: **to ~ about** bisbilhotar; **~er** n bisbilhoteiro/a m/f.

snooty ['snu:tɪ] adj arrogante.

snooze [snu:z] n soneca, sesta // vi tirar uma soneca, dormitar.

snore [snɔ:*] vi roncar // n ronco.

snorkel ['snɔ:kl] n tubo snorkel.

snort [snɔ:t] n bufo, bufido // vi bufar.

snout [snaut] n focinho, nariz m.

snow [snəu] n neve f // vi nevar; **~ball** n bola de neve // vt acumular-se; **~bound** adj bloqueado pela neve; **~drift** n monte m de neve (formado pelo vento); **~drop** n campainha branca; **~fall** n nevada; **~flake** n floco de neve; **~man** n boneco de neve; **~plough**, **~plow** (US) n máquina limpa-neve; **~storm** n nevasca, tempestade f de neve; **S~ White** n Branca de Neve.

snub [snʌb] vt desdenhar, menosprezar // n desdém m, repulsa.

snuff [snʌf] n rapé m.

snug [snʌg] adj (sheltered) abrigado, protegido; (fitted) justo, cômodo.

snuggle ['snʌgl] vi: **to ~ up to sb** aconchegar-se or aninhar-se a alguém.

so [səu] adv (degree) tão; (manner: thus) assim, deste modo // conj (purpose) para que, a fim de que; (result) de modo que; **~ that** consequentemente, portanto; **~ do I** eu também; **if ~** se for assim, se assim é; **I hope ~** espero que sim; **10 or ~** 10 mais ou menos; **~ far** até aqui; **~ long!** tchau!; **~ many** tantos; **~ much** adv, det tanto; **~ and ~** n fulano/a.

soak [səuk] vt (drench) embeber, ensopar; (put in water) pôr de molho // vi estar de molho, impregnar-se; **to ~ in** vi infiltrar; **to ~ up** vt absorver.

soap [səup] n sabão m; **~flakes** npl flocos mpl de sabão; **~ powder** n sabão m em pó; **~y** adj ensaboado.

soar [sɔ:*] vi (on wings) elevar-se em vôo; (building etc) levantar-se.

sob [sɔb] n soluço // vi soluçar.

sober ['səubə*] adj (serious) sério; (sensible) sensato; (moderate) moderado; (not drunk) sóbrio; (colour, style) discreto; **to ~ up** vi tornar-se sóbrio.

Soc. abbr of **society.**

so-called ['səu'kɔ:ld] adj chamado.

soccer ['sɔkə*] n futebol m.

sociable ['səuʃəbl] adj sociável.

social ['səuʃl] adj (gen) social; (sociable) sociável // n reunião f social; **~ climber** n arrivista m/f; **~ club** n clube m; **~ism** n socialismo; **~ist** adj, n socialista m/f; **~ly** adv socialmente; **~ science** n ciências fpl sociais; **~ security** n previdência social; **~ work** n assistência social, serviço social; **~ worker** n assistente m/f social.

society [sə'saɪətɪ] n sociedade f; (club) associação f; (also: **high ~**) alta sociedade.

sociologist [səusɪ'ɔlədʒɪst] n sociólogo/a; **sociology** [-dʒə] n sociologia.

sock [sɔk] n meia (Br), peúga (Pt).

socket ['sɔkɪt] n (ELEC) tomada.

sod [sɔd] n (of earth) gramado, torrão m; (person) idiota m/f // vt: **~ it!** (col!) droga.

soda ['səudə] n (CHEM) soda; (also: **~ water**) água com gás.

sodden ['sɔdn] adj encharcado.

sodium ['səudɪəm] n sódio.

sofa ['səufə] n sofá m.

soft [sɔft] adj (gen) macio; (gentle, not loud) suave; (kind) meigo, bondoso; (weak) fraco; (stupid) idiota; **~ drink** n refrigerante m; **~en** ['sɔfn] vt amolecer, amaciar, enternecer // vi abrandar-se, enternecer-se, suavizar-se; **~-hearted** adj bondoso, caridoso; **~ly** adv suavemente; (gently) delicadamente, devagarinho; **~ness** n suavidade f, afabilidade f; (sweetness) doçura; (tenderness) ternura.

soggy ['sɔgɪ] adj ensopado, encharcado.

soil [sɔɪl] n (earth) terra, solo // vt sujar, manchar; **~ed** adj sujo.

solace ['sɔlɪs] n consolo.

solar ['səulə*] adj solar.

sold [səuld] pt, pp of **sell**; **~ out** (COMM) esgotado.

solder ['səuldə*] vt soldar // n solda.

soldier ['səuldʒə*] n (gen) soldado; (army man) militar m.

sole [səul] n (of foot, of shoe) sola; (fish: pl inv) solha, linguado // adj único; **~ly** adv somente, unicamente.

solemn ['sɔləm] adj solene.

solicitor [sə'lɪsɪtə*] n (for wills etc) tabelião m; (in court) advogado em causas simples.

solid ['sɔlɪd] adj (not hollow) sólido; (gold etc) maciço; (person) sério // n sólido.

solidarity [sɔlɪ'dærɪtɪ] n solidariedade f.

solidify [sə'lɪdɪfaɪ] vi solidificar-se.

solitaire [sɔlɪ'tɛə*] n (gem) solitário; (game) solitário, jogo de paciência.

solitary ['sɔlɪtərɪ] adj solitário, só; (isolated) isolado, retirado; (only) único; **~ confinement** n prisão f solitária.

solitude ['sɔlɪtju:d] n solidão f.

solo ['səuləu] n solo; **~ist** n solista m/f.

soluble ['sɔljubl] adj solúvel.

solution [sə'lu:ʃən] n solução f.

solve [sɔlv] vt resolver, solucionar.

solvent ['sɔlvənt] adj (COMM) solvente // n (CHEM) solvente m.

sombre, somber (US) ['sɔmbə*] adj sombrio, escuro, lúgubre.

some [sʌm] det (a few) alguns/algumas; (certain) algum(a); (a certain number or amount) see phrases below; (unspecified) um pouco de // pron alguns/algumas; (a bit) um pouco // adv: ~ 10 people umas 10 pessoas; ~ children came algumas crianças vieram; have ~ tea tome um pouco de chá; there's ~ milk in the fridge há leite na geladeira; ~ was left ficou um pouco; I've got ~ (books etc) tenho alguns; (milk, money etc) tenho um pouco; ~body pron alguém; ~ day adv algum dia; ~how adv de alguma maneira; (for some reason) por uma razão ou outra; ~one pron ~ ~body.

somersault ['sʌməsɔːlt] n (deliberate) salto mortal; (accidental) cambalhota // vi dar um salto mortal or uma cambalhota.

something ['sʌmθɪŋ] pron alguma coisa, algo (Br).

sometime ['sʌmtaɪm] adv (in future) algum dia, em outra oportunidade; (in past): ~ last month durante o mês passado.

sometimes ['sʌmtaɪmz] adv às vezes, de vez em quando.

somewhat ['sʌmwɔt] adv um tanto.

somewhere ['sʌmwɛə*] adv (be) em algum lugar; (go) para algum lugar; ~ else (be) em outro lugar; (go) para outro lugar.

son [sʌn] n filho.

song [sɔŋ] n canção f; ~writer n compositor(a) m/f de canções.

sonic ['sɔnɪk] adj (boom) sônico.

son-in-law ['sʌnɪnlɔː] n genro.

sonnet ['sɔnɪt] n soneto.

soon [suːn] adv logo, brevemente; (early) cedo; ~ afterwards pouco depois; see also as; ~er adv (time) antes, mais cedo; (preference): I would ~er do that preferia fazer isso; ~er or later mais cedo ou mais tarde.

soot [sut] n fuligem f.

soothe [suːð] vt acalmar, sossegar; (pain) aliviar, suavizar.

sophisticated [sə'fɪstɪkeɪtɪd] adj sofisticado, cosmopolita.

soporific [sɔpə'rɪfɪk] adj soporífico.

sopping ['sɔpɪŋ] adj: ~ wet totalmente encharcado e molhado.

soppy ['sɔpɪ] adj (pej) sentimentalóide.

soprano [sə'prɑːnəʊ] n soprano m/f.

sorcerer ['sɔːsərə*] n feiticeiro.

sordid ['sɔːdɪd] adj (dirty) imundo, sórdido; (wretched) miserável.

sore [sɔː*] adj (painful) doloroso, doído; (offended) magoado, ofendido // n chaga, ferida; ~ly adv: I am ~ly tempted estou muito tentado.

sorrow ['sɔrəʊ] n tristeza, mágoa, dor f; ~ful adj triste, aflito, magoado.

sorry ['sɔrɪ] adj (regretful) arrependido; (condition, excuse) lamentável; ~! desculpe!, perdão!, sinto muito!; to feel ~ for sb sentir pena de alguém; I feel ~ for him estou com pena dele.

sort [sɔːt] n espécie f, gênero, tipo // vt (also: ~ out: papers) classificar; (: problems) solucionar, resolver; ~ing office n departamento de distribuição.

so-so ['səʊsəʊ] adv mais ou menos, regular.

soufflé ['suːfleɪ] n suflê m.

sought [sɔːt] pt, pp of seek.

soul [səʊl] n alma; ~-destroying adj embrutecedor(a); ~ing n (sleep) profundamente; (beat) completamente; ~proof adj à prova de som; ~track n (of film) trilha sonora.

sound [saʊnd] adj (healthy) saudável, sadio; (safe, not damaged) sólido, completo; (secure) seguro; (reliable, not superficial) digno de confiança; (sensible) sensato // adv: ~ asleep dormindo profundamente // n (noise) som m, ruído, barulho; (GEO) estreito, braço (de mar) // vt (alarm) soar; (also: ~ out: opinions) sondar // vi soar, tocar; (fig: seem) parecer; to ~ like soar como; ~ barrier n barreira do som; ~ effects npl efeitos mpl sonoros; ~ing n (NAUT etc) sondagem f; ~ly adv (sleep) profundamente; (beat) completamente; ~proof adj à prova de som; ~track n (of film) trilha sonora.

soup [suːp] n (thick) sopa; (thin) caldo; in the ~ (fig) numa encrenca; ~spoon n colher f de sopa.

sour ['saʊə*] adj azedo, ácido; (milk) talhado; (fig) mal-humorado, rabugento.

source [sɔːs] n fonte f.

south [saʊθ] n sul m // adj do sul, meridional // adv ao or para o sul; S~ Africa n África do Sul; S~ African adj, n sul-africano/a; S~ America n América do Sul; S~ American adj, n sul-americano/a; ~-east n sudeste m; ~erly ['sʌðəlɪ] adj meridional; (from the ~) do sul; ~ern ['sʌðən] adj do sul, sulista; S~ Pole n Pólo Sul; ~ward(s) adv para o sul; ~-west n sudoeste m.

souvenir [suːvə'nɪə*] n lembrança.

sovereign ['sɔvrɪn] adj, n soberano/a; ~ty n soberania.

soviet ['səʊvɪət] adj soviético; the S~ Union n a União Soviética.

sow [saʊ] n porca // vt [səʊ], pt sowed, pp sown [səʊn] (gen) semear; (spread) disseminar, espalhar.

soy [sɔɪ] n: ~ sauce molho de soja.

soya bean ['sɔɪəbiːn] n semente f de soja.

spa [spɑː] n (spring) fonte f de água mineral; (town) estância hidro-mineral.

space [speɪs] n (gen) espaço; (room) lugar m // vt (also: ~ out) espaçar; ~craft n nave f espacial; ~man/woman n astronauta m/f, cosmonauta m/f; spacing n espacejamento, espaçamento.

spacious ['speɪʃəs] adj espaçoso.

spade [speɪd] n (tool) pá f; ~s npl (CARDS) espadas fpl.

spaghetti [spəˈgɛtɪ] n espaguete m.

Spain [speɪn] n Espanha.

span [spæn] n (of bird, plane) envergadura; (of hand) palma; (of arch) vão m; (in time) lapso, espaço // vt estender-se sobre, atravessar; (fig) abarcar.

Spaniard [ˈspænjəd] n espanhol(a) m/f.

spaniel [ˈspænjəl] n spaniel m.

Spanish [ˈspænɪʃ] adj espanhol(a) // n (LING) espanhol m, castelhano.

spank [spæŋk] vt bater, dar palmadas.

spanner [ˈspænə*] n chave f inglesa.

spar [spɑː*] n mastro, verga // vi (BOXING) boxear.

spare [spɛə*] adj (free) vago, desocupado; (surplus) de sobra, a mais; (available) disponível, de reserva // n (part) peça sobressalente // vt (do without) dispensar, passar sem; (afford to give) dispor de, ter de sobra; (refrain from hurting) perdoar, poupar; (be grudging with) dar frugalmente; ~ part n peça sobressalente; ~ time n tempo livre.

sparing [ˈspɛərɪŋ] adj: to be ~ with ser econômico com; ~ly adv escassamente.

spark [spɑːk] n chispa, faísca; (fig) centelha; ~(ing) plug n vela de ignição.

sparkle [ˈspɑːkl] n cintilação f, brilho // vi cintilar; (shine) brilhar, faiscar; **sparkling** adj cintilante; (wine) espumante.

sparrow [ˈspærəu] n pardal m.

sparse [spɑːs] adj escasso; (hair) ralo.

spasm [ˈspæzəm] n (MED) espasmo; (fig) acesso, ataque m; ~odic [-ˈmɔdɪk] adj espasmódico.

spastic [ˈspæstɪk] n espástico/a.

spat [spæt] pt, pp of spit.

spate [speɪt] n (fig) jorro, fluxo; in ~ (river) em cheia.

spatter [ˈspætə*] vt borrifar, salpicar.

spatula [ˈspætjulə] n espátula.

spawn [spɔːn] vi desovar, procriar // n ovas fpl.

speak [spiːk] pt spoke, pp spoken vt (language) falar; (truth) dizer // vi falar; (make a speech) discursar; to ~ to sb/of or about sth falar com alguém/de or sobre algo; ~ up! fale alto!; ~er n (in public) orador(a) m/f; (also: loud~er) alto-falante m; (POL): the S~er o Presidente da Câmara.

spear [spɪə*] n lança; (for fishing) arpão m // vt lancear, arpoar; ~head n ponta-de-lança.

special [ˈspɛʃl] adj especial; (edition etc) extra; (delivery) rápido; take ~ care tome muito cuidado; ~ist n especialista m/f; ~ity [spɛʃɪˈælɪtɪ] n especialidade f; ~ize vi: to ~ize (in) especializar-se (em); ~ly adv sobretudo, especialmente.

species [ˈspiːʃiːz] n espécie f.

specific [spəˈsɪfɪk] adj específico; ~ally adv especificamente.

specification [spɛsɪfɪˈkeɪʃən] n especificação f; ~s npl detalhes mpl, características fpl; **specify** [ˈspɛsɪfaɪ] vt/i especificar, pormenorizar.

specimen [ˈspɛsɪmən] n espécime m, amostra; (fig) exemplar m.

speck [spɛk] n mancha, pinta.

speckled [ˈspɛkld] adj manchado.

specs [spɛks] npl (col) óculos mpl.

spectacle [ˈspɛktəkl] n espetáculo (Pt: -ct-); ~s npl óculos mpl; **spectacular** [-ˈtækjulə*] adj espetacular (Pt: -ct-); (success) impressionante, tremendo.

spectator [spɛkˈteɪtə*] n espectador(a) m/f.

spectre, specter (US) [ˈspɛktə*] n espectro m, aparição f.

spectrum [ˈspɛktrəm] pl -tra [-trə] n espectro.

speculate [ˈspɛkjuleɪt] vi especular; (try to guess): to ~ about especular sobre; **speculation** [-ˈleɪʃən] n especulação f.

speech [spiːtʃ] n (faculty) fala, palavra; (formal talk) discurso; (talk) conversa; (language) idioma m, linguagem f; ~less adj estupefato (Pt: -cto), emudecido.

speed [spiːd] n velocidade f, rapidez f; (haste) pressa; (promptness) prontidão f; at full or top ~ a toda velocidade; to ~ up vi acelerar // vt acelerar; ~boat n lancha; ~ily adv depressa, rapidamente; ~ing n (AUT) excesso de velocidade; ~ limit n limite m de velocidade, velocidade f máxima; ~ometer [spɪˈdɔmɪtə*] n velocímetro; ~way n (SPORT) pista de corrida, rodovia de alta velocidade; ~y adj (fast) veloz, rápido; (prompt) pronto, imediato.

spell [spɛl] n (also: magic ~) encanto, feitiço; (period of time) período breve, intervalo; (turn) turno, temporada // vt, pt, pp spelt or spelled (also: ~ out) soletrar; (fig) pressagiar, ser sinal de; to cast a ~ on sb enfeitiçar alguém; he can't ~ não sabe escrever bem, comete erros de ortografia; ~bound adj enfeitiçado, fascinado; ~ing n ortografia.

spend [spɛnd] pt, pp spent [spɛnt] vt (money) gastar; (time) passar; (life) passar, dedicar; ~thrift n esbanjador(a) m/f, perdulário/a.

sperm [spɔːm] n esperma; ~ whale n cachalote m.

spew [spjuː] vt vomitar, lançar.

sphere [sfɪə*] n esfera; **spherical** [ˈsfɛrɪkl] adj esférico.

sphinx [sfɪŋks] n esfinge f.

spice [spaɪs] n especiaria // vt condimentar; **spicy** adj condimentado; (fig) picante.

spider [ˈspaɪdə*] n aranha.

spike [spaɪk] n (point) ponta, espigão m; (BOT) espiga.

spill [spɪl] pt, pp spilt or spilled vt entornar, derramar // vi derramar-se; to ~ over transbordar-se.

spin [spɪn] n (revolution of wheel) volta,

rotação f; (AVIAT) parafuso; (trip in car) volta or passeio de carro // (vb: pt, pp **spun**) vt (wool etc) fiar, tecer; (wheel) girar // vi girar, rodar; **to ~ out** vt prolongar, alargar.

spinach ['spɪnɪtʃ] n espinafre m.

spinal ['spaɪnl] adj espinhal; **~ cord** n coluna vertebral, espinha dorsal.

spindly ['spɪndlɪ] adj alto e magro, espigado.

spin-drier [spɪn'draɪə*] n máquina de secar centrífuga.

spine [spaɪn] n espinha dorsal; (thorn) espinho; **~less** adj (fig) fraco, covarde.

spinning ['spɪnɪŋ] n (of thread, art) fiação f; **~ top** n pião m; **~ wheel** n roca de fiar.

spinster ['spɪnstə*] n solteira; (pej) solteirona.

spiral ['spaɪərl] n espiral f // adj em espiral, helicoidal; **~ staircase** n escada em caracol.

spire ['spaɪə*] n flecha, agulha.

spirit ['spɪrɪt] n (gen) espírito; (soul) alma; (ghost) fantasma m; (humour) humor m; (courage) coragem f, ânimo; **~s** npl (drink) álcool msg, bebida alcoólica sg; **in good ~s** alegre, de bom humor; **~ed** adj animado, espirituoso; **~ level** n nível m de bolha.

spiritual ['spɪrɪtjuəl] adj espiritual // n (also: **Negro ~**) canto religioso dos negros; **~ism** n espiritualismo.

spit [spɪt] n (for roasting) espeto; (NAUT) restinga // vi, pt, pp **spat** cuspir; (sound) escarrar.

spite [spaɪt] n rancor m, ressentimento // vt mortificar, contrariar; **in ~ of** apesar de, a despeito de; **~ful** adj rancoroso, malévolo.

spittle ['spɪtl] n saliva, cuspe m.

splash [splæʃ] n (sound) borrifo, respingo; (of colour) mancha // vt salpicar (with de) // vi (also: **~ about**) borrifar, respingar.

spleen [spli:n] n (ANAT) baço.

splendid ['splendɪd] adj esplêndido; **splendour, splendor** (US) [-də*] n esplendor m; (of achievement) pompa, glória.

splint [splɪnt] n tala, lasca.

splinter ['splɪntə*] n (of wood) lasca; (in finger) farpa // vi lascar-se, estilhaçar-se, despedaçar-se.

split [splɪt] n fenda, brecha; (fig) rompimento; (POL) divisão f // (vb: pt, pp **split**) vt partir, fender; (party) dividir; (work, profits) rachar, repartir // vi (divide) dividir-se, repartir-se; **to ~ up** vi (couple) separar-se, romper; (meeting) terminar.

splutter ['splʌtə*] vi crepitar; (person) balbuciar, gaguejar.

spoil [spɔɪl], pt, pp **spoilt** or **spoiled** vt (damage) danificar; (mar) estragar, arruinar; (child) mimar, estragar; **~s** npl despojo sg, saque m; **~sport** n desmancha-prazeres m/f inv.

spoke [spəuk] pt of **speak** // n (of wheel) raio.

spoken ['spəukn] pp of **speak**.

spokesman ['spəuksmən] n porta-voz m/f.

sponge [spʌndʒ] n esponja; (cake) pão-de-ló m // vt (wash) lavar com esponja // vi: **to ~ on sb** viver às custas de alguém; **~ bag** n bolsa de toalete; **~ cake** n pão-de-ló m; **spongy** adj esponjoso, absorvente.

sponsor ['spɒnsə*] n (RADIO, TV) patrocinador(a) m/f; (for membership) padrinho m, madrinha f; (COMM) fiador(a) m/f, financiador m // vt patrocinar; apadrinhar; fiar; (idea etc) promover; **~ship** n patrocínio.

spontaneous [spɒn'teɪnɪəs] adj espontâneo.

spool [spu:l] n carretel m; (of sewing machine) bobina, novelo.

spoon [spu:n] n colher f; **~-feed** vt dar de comer com colher; (fig) dar tudo mastigado a; **~ful** n colherada.

sporadic [spə'rædɪk] adj esporádico.

sport [spɔ:t] n esporte m (Br), desporto (Pt); (person) bom perdedor(a) m/f; **~ing** adj esportivo (Br), desportivo (Pt); **~s car** n carro esporte (Br), carro de sport (Pt); **~(s) jacket** n casaco (d)esportivo; **sportsman** n (d)esportista m/f; **sportsmanship** n espírito (d)esportivo; **sportswear** n roupa (d)esportiva or esporte; **sportswoman** n (d)esportista; **~y** adj (d)esportivo.

spot [spɒt] n lugar m, local m; (dot: on pattern) mancha, ponto; (pimple) espinha; (freckle) sarda, pinta; (small amount): **a ~ of** um pouquinho de // vt (notice) localizar, notar; **on the ~** (at once) no ato (Pt: -ct-), ali mesmo; (in difficulty) em apuros; **~ check** n fiscalização f de surpresa; **~less** adj sem mancha, imaculado; **~light** n holofote m, refletor (Pt: -ct-) m; **~ted** adj (pattern) com bolinhas; **~ty** adj (face) manchado.

spouse [spauz] n cônjuge m/f.

spout [spaut] n (of jug) bico; (pipe) cano // vi jorrar.

sprain [spreɪn] n distensão f, torcedura // vt: **to ~ one's ankle** torcer o tornozelo.

sprang [spræŋ] pt of **spring**.

sprawl [sprɔ:l] vi esparramar-se.

spray [spreɪ] n spray m, borrifador m; (of sea) borrifo; (container) atomizador m; (of paint) pistola borrifadora; (of flowers) ramalhete m // vt pulverizar; (crops) borrifar, regar.

spread [spred] n extensão f; (distribution) expansão f, difusão f; (col: food) mesa coberta de comida, banquete m // (vb: pt, pp **spread**) vt espalhar; (butter) untar, passar; (wings, sails) abrir, desdobrar; (scatter) disseminar // vi espalhar-se, alastrar-se, difundir-se.

spree [spri:] *n*: **to go on a ~** fazer uma farra.

sprightly ['spraɪtlɪ] *adj* vivo, esperto, desembaraçado.

spring [sprɪŋ] *n* (*leap*) salto, pulo; (*coiled metal*) mola; (*season*) primavera; (*of water*) fonte *f*, nascente *f* // *vi*, *pt* **sprang**, *pp* **sprung** (*arise*) brotar, nascer; (*leap*) pular, saltar; **to ~ up** *vi* nascer *or* aparecer de repente; **~board** *n* trampolim *m*; **~-clean** *n* (*also*: **~-cleaning**) limpeza total, faxina (geral); **~time** *n* primavera; **~y** *adj* elástico, flexível; (*grass*) macio.

sprinkle ['sprɪŋkl] *vt* (*pour*) salpicar, borrifar; **to ~ water on, ~ with water** borrifar *or* salpicar de água; **~d with** (*fig*) salpicado *or* polvilhado de.

sprint [sprɪnt] *n* corrida de pequena distância // *vi* (*gen*) correr a toda velocidade; **~er** *n* corredor(a) *m/f*; (*horse*) sprinter *m*.

sprite [spraɪt] *n* duende *m*, elfo.

sprout [spraut] *vi* brotar, germinar; **(Brussels) ~s** *npl* couve-de-Bruxelas *fsg*.

spruce [spru:s] *n* (*BOT*) abeto // *adj* arrumado, limpo, elegante.

sprung [sprʌŋ] *pp* of **spring**.

spry [spraɪ] *adj* vivo, ativo, ágil.

spun [spʌn] *pt*, *pp* of **spin**.

spur [spə:*] *n* espora; (*fig*) estímulo // *vt* (*also*: **~ on**) incitar, estimular; **on the ~ of the moment** de improviso, de repente.

spurn [spə:n] *vt* desdenhar, desprezar.

spurt [spə:t] *n* esforço supremo; (*of energy*) acesso, acometida; (*water*) jorro // *vi* fazer um esforço supremo; (*water*) jorrar.

spy [spaɪ] *n* espião/espiã *m/f* // *vi*: **to ~ on** espiar, espionar // *vt* (*see*) enxergar, avistar; **~ing** *n* espionagem *f*.

sq. *abbr* of **square**.

squabble ['skwɔbl] *n* briga, bate-boca *m* // *vi* brigar, altercar, discutir.

squad [skwɔd] *n* (*MIL*, *POLICE*) pelotão *m*, esquadra *f*.

squadron ['skwɔdrn] *n* (*MIL*) esquadrão *m*; (*AVIAT*) esquadrilha; (*NAUT*) esquadra.

squalid ['skwɔlɪd] *adj* esquálido, sórdido.

squall [skwɔ:l] *n* (*storm*) tempestade *f*; (*wind*) pé *m* (de vento), rajada.

squalor ['skwɔlə*] *n* sordidez *f*.

squander ['skwɔndə*] *vt* (*money*) esbanjar, dissipar; (*chances*) desperdiçar.

square [skwɛə*] *n* quadrado; (*in town*) praça; (*MATH. instrument*) esquadro // *adj* quadrado; (*col*: *ideas*, *tastes*) quadrado, antiquado // *vt* (*arrange*) ajustar, acertar; (*MATH*) elevar ao quadrado; **all ~** igual, quite; **a ~ meal** uma refeição substancial; **2 metres ~** um quadrado de dois metros de lado; **1 ~ metre** um metro quadrado; **~ly** *adv* em forma quadrada; (*fully*) em cheio.

squash [skwɔʃ] *n* (*drink*):

lemon/orange ~ suco (*Pt*: sumo) de limão/laranja; (*SPORT*) squash *m*, jogo de raquetes // *vt* esmagar; **to ~ together** apinhar.

squat [skwɔt] *adj* agachado; (*short*) atarracado // *vi* agachar-se, acocorar-se; **~ter** *n* posseiro/a.

squawk [skwɔ:k] *vi* grasnar.

squeak [skwi:k] *n* grunhido, chiado; (*of shoe*) rangido; (*of mouse*) guincho // *vi* grunhir, chiar; ranger; guinchar.

squeal [skwi:l] *vi* guinchar, gritar agudamente; (*tell on*) delatar.

squeamish ['skwi:mɪʃ] *adj* melindroso, delicado.

squeeze [skwi:z] *n* (*gen*) aperto, compressão *f*; (*of hand*) apertão *m*; (*in bus etc*) apinhamento // *vt* comprimir, socar; (*hand*, *arm*) apertar; **to ~ out** *vt* espremer; (*fig*) extorquir; **to ~ through** abrir caminho.

squelch [skwɛltʃ] *vt* esmagar // *vi* fazer ruído de passos na lama.

squid [skwɪd] *n* lula.

squint [skwɪnt] *vi* olhar *or* ser vesgo // *n* (*MED*) estrabismo; **to ~ at sth** olhar algo de soslaio *or* de esguelha.

squirm [skwə:m] *vi* retorcer-se, mexer-se, contorcer-se.

squirrel ['skwɪrəl] *n* esquilo.

squirt [skwə:t] *vi* jorrar, esguichar.

Sr *abbr of* **senior**.

St *abbr of* **saint**; **street**.

stab [stæb] *n* (*with knife etc*) punhalada; (*of pain*) pontada; (*col*: *try*): **to have a ~ at (doing) sth** tentar (fazer) algo // *vt* apunhalar.

stability [stə'bɪlɪtɪ] *n* estabilidade *f*.

stabilize ['steɪbəlaɪz] *vt* estabilizar // *vi* estabilizar-se; **stable** ['steɪbl] *adj* estável // *n* estábulo, cavalariça.

stack [stæk] *n* montão *m*, pilha // *vt* amontoar, empilhar.

stadium ['steɪdɪəm] *n* estádio.

staff [stɑ:f] *n* (*work force*) pessoal *m*, corpo administrativo; (*stick*) cajado, bastão *m* // *vt* prover de pessoal.

stag [stæg] *n* veado, cervo.

stage [steɪdʒ] *n* cena, cenário; (*profession*): **the ~** palco, teatro; (*point*) etapa, fase *f*; (*platform*) plataforma, estrado // *vt* (*play*) pôr em cena, representar; (*demonstration*) montar, organizar; (*fig*: *perform*: *recovery etc*) realizar; **~coach** *n* diligência; **~ door** *n* entrada dos artistas; **~ manager** *n* diretor(a) (*Pt*: -ct-) *m/f* de cena.

stagger ['stægə*] *vi* cambalear // *vt* (*amaze*) surpreender, chocar; (*hours*, *holidays*) escalonar; **~ing** *adj* (*amazing*) surpreendente, chocante.

stagnant ['stægnənt] *adj* estagnado; **stagnate** [-'neɪt] *vi* estagnar-se.

stag party *n* despedida de solteiro.

staid [steɪd] *adj* sério, sóbrio.

stain [steɪn] *n* mancha; (*colouring*) tinta, tintura // *vt* manchar; (*wood*) tingir;

~ed glass window n janela com vitral; **~less** adj (steel) inoxidável.

stair [stɛə*] n (step) degrau m; **~s** npl escada sg; **~case**, **~way** n escadaria, escada.

stake [steik] n estaca, poste m; (BETTING) aposta // vt apostar; **to be at** ~ estar em jogo ou em perigo.

stalactite ['stælǝktait] n estalactite f.

stalagmite ['stælǝgmait] n estalagmite f.

stale [steil] adj (bread) amanhecido; (food) passado, estragado.

stalemate ['steilmeit] n empate m; (fig) impasse m, beco sem saída.

stalk [stɔːk] n caule m, talo, haste f // vt caçar de tocaia; **to** ~ **off** andar com arrogância.

stall [stɔːl] n (in market) barraca; (in stable) baia // vt (AUT) fazer morrer // vi (AUT) morrer; (fig) esquivar-se, ganhar tempo; **~s** npl (in cinema, theatre) platéia sg.

stallion ['stælıǝn] n garanhão m.

stalwart ['stɔːlwǝt] n (in build) robusto, rijo; (in spirit) valente, leal.

stamina ['stæmınǝ] n resistência.

stammer ['stæmǝ*] n gagueira // vi gaguejar, balbuciar.

stamp [stæmp] n selo, estampilha; (mark, also fig) marca, impressão f; (on document) timbre m, sinete m // vi pisar, esmagar // vt bater com o pé; (in dance) sapatear; (letter) selar; (with rubber ~) carimbar; ~ **album** n álbum m de selos; ~ **collecting** n filatelia.

stampede [stæm'piːd] n debandada, estouro (da boiada).

stance [stæns] n postura, posição f.

stand [stænd] n (position) posição f, postura; (for taxis) ponto, (hall ~) pedestal m; (music ~) estante f; (SPORT) tribuna, palanque m; (news ~) banca de jornais // (vb: pt, pp **stood**) vi (be) estar, encontrar-se; (be on foot) estar em pé; (rise) levantar-se; (remain) ficar em pé // vt (place) pôr, colocar; (tolerate, withstand) agüentar, suportar; (cost) pagar; (invite) convidar; **to make a** ~ resistir; (fig) ater-se a um princípio; **to** ~ **for parliament** apresentar-se como candidato ao parlamento; **to** ~ **by** vi (be ready) estar a postos // vt fus (opinion) aferrar-se a; **to** ~ **for** vt fus (defend) apoiar; (signify) significar; (tolerate) tolerar, permitir; **to** ~ **in for** vt fus substituir; **to** ~ **out** vi (be prominent) destacar-se; **to** ~ **up** vi (rise) levantar-se; **to** ~ **up for** vt fus defender; **to** ~ **up to** vt fus enfrentar.

standard ['stændǝd] n padrão m, critério; (flag) estandarte m; (degree) grau m // adj (size etc) padronizado, regular, normal; **~s** npl (morals) valores mpl morais; **~ize** vt padronizar, uniformizar; **~ lamp** n abajur m de pé; ~ **of living** n padrão de vida.

stand-by ['stændbai] n (alert) alerta,

aviso; **to be on** ~ estar de sobreaviso; ~ **ticket** n (AVIAT) passagem f stand-by or de lista de espera.

stand-in ['stændın] n suplente m/f; (CINEMA) dublê m/f.

standing ['stændıŋ] adj (upright) ereto (Pt: -ct-), vertical; (on foot) em pé // n posição f, reputação f; **of many years'** ~ que leva muito tempo; ~ **order** n (at bank) instrução f permanente; ~ **orders** npl (MIL) regulamento sg geral; ~ **room** n lugar m em pé.

stand: ~-**offish** adj incomunicativo, reservado; ~**point** n ponto de vista; ~**still**: **at a** ~**still** paralisado, parado; **to come to a** ~**still** ficar or estar paralisado.

stank [stæŋk] pt of **stink**.

staple ['steipl] n (for papers) grampo // adj (food etc) básico // vt grampear; **stapler** n grampeador m.

star [stɑː*] n estrela; (celebrity) astro, estrela // vi: **to** ~ **in** ser a estrela em.

starboard ['stɑːbǝd] n estibordo.

starch [stɑːtʃ] n amido, fécula, goma; ~**ed** adj (collar) engomado; ~**y** adj amiláceo.

stardom ['stɑːdǝm] n estrelato, qualidade f de estrela.

stare [stɛə*] n olhar m fixo // vt: **to** ~ **at** olhar fixamente, fitar.

starfish ['stɑːfıʃ] n estrela-do-mar f.

stark [stɑːk] adj (bleak) severo, áspero // adv: ~ **naked** completamente nu, em pêlo.

starlight ['stɑːlait] n: **by** ~ à luz das estrelas.

starling ['stɑːlıŋ] n estorninho.

starry ['stɑːrı] adj estrelado; ~-**eyed** adj (innocent) deslumbrado.

start [stɑːt] n (beginning) princípio, começo, (departure) partida, (sudden movement) sobressalto, ímpeto; (advantage) vantagem f // vt começar, iniciar; (cause) causar; (found) fundar; (engine) ligar // vi (begin) começar, iniciar; (with fright) sobressaltar-se, assustar-se; (train etc) sair; **to** ~ **off** vi começar, principiar; (leave) sair, pôr-se a caminho; **to** ~ **up** vi começar; (car: motor) pegar, pôr-se em marcha // vt começar; (car) pôr em marcha; ~**er** n (AUT) arranque m; (SPORT: official) juiz(a) m/f da partida; (: runner) corredor(a) m/f; (CULIN) entrada; ~**ing point** n ponto de partida.

startle ['stɑːtl] vt assustar, aterrar; **startling** adj surpreendente.

starvation [stɑː'veiʃǝn] n fome f; (MED) inanição f; **starve** vi passar fome; (to death) morrer de fome // vt fazer passar fome; (fig) privar (of de); **I'm starving** estou morrendo de fome, estou com fome.

state [steit] n estado // vt (say, declare) afirmar, declarar; (a case) expor, apresentar; **the S~s** os Estados Unidos; **to be in a** ~ estar agitado; ~**ly**

adj majestoso, imponente; **~ment** *n* afirmação *f*; (*LAW*) declaração *f*, balanço; **statesman** *n* estadista *m*.

static ['stætɪk] *n* (*RADIO*) interferência // *adj* estático; **~ electricity** *n* eletricidade *f* estática.

station ['steɪʃən] *n* (*gen*) estação *f*; (*place*) posto, lugar *m*; (*RADIO*) emissora; (*rank*) posição *f* social // *vt* colocar, botar; (*MIL*) designar para um posto.

stationary ['steɪʃnərɪ] *adj* estacionário.

stationer's (**shop**) ['steɪʃənəz] *n* papelaria; **stationery** [-nərɪ] *n* artigos *mpl* de papelaria or para escrever.

station master *n* (*RAIL*) chefe *m* da estação.

station wagon *n* (*US*) perua (*Br*), canadiana *f* (*Pt*).

statistic [stə'tɪstɪk] *n* estatística; **~s** *npl* (*science*) estatística *sg*; **~al** *adj* estatístico.

statue ['stætju:] *n* estátua.

stature ['stætʃə*] *n* estatura, altura; (*fig*) tamanho.

status ['steɪtəs] *n* posição *f*, categoria; (*reputation*) reputação *f*, status *m*; **the ~ quo** o status quo; **~ symbol** *n* símbolo de prestígio.

statute ['stætju:t] *n* estatuto, lei *f*; **statutory** *adj* estatutário.

staunch [stɔ:ntʃ] *adj* firme, constante.

stave [steɪv] *vt*: **to ~ off** (*attack*) repelir; (*threat*) evitar, protelar.

stay [steɪ] *n* (*period of time*) estadia, estada // *vi* (*remain*) ficar; (*as guest*) hospedar-se; (*spend some time*) demorar-se; **to ~ put** não se mexer; **to ~ the night** pernoitar; **to ~ behind** *vi* ficar atrás; **to ~ in** *vi* (*at home*) ficar em casa; **to ~ on** *vi* ficar; **to ~ out** *vi* (*of house*) ficar fora de casa; **to ~ up** *vi* (*at night*) velar, ficar acordado; **~ing power** *n* resistência, "raça".

steadfast ['stedfɑ:st] *adj* firme, estável, resoluto.

steadily ['stedɪlɪ] *adv* (*firmly*) firmemente; (*unceasingly*) sem parar; (*fixedly*) fixamente; (*walk*) normalmente; (*drive*) a uma velocidade constante.

steady ['stedɪ] *adj* (*constant*) constante, fixo; (*unswerving*) firme; (*regular*) regular; (*person, character*) sensato, equilibrado; (*diligent*) trabalhador(a); (*calm*) calmo, sereno // *vt* (*hold*) manter firme; (*stabilize*) estabilizar; (*nerves*) acalmar; **to ~ o.s. on** or **against sth** firmar-se em algo.

steak [steɪk] *n* (*gen*) filé *m*; (*beef*) bife *m*.

steal [sti:l], *pt* **stole**, *pp* **stolen** *vt/i* roubar.

stealth [stelθ] *n*: **by ~** furtivamente, às escondidas; **~y** *adj* furtivo, secreto.

steam [sti:m] *n* vapor *m*; (*mist*) névoa *f* // *vt* (*CULIN*) cozinhar no vapor // *vi* exalar vapor; (*ship*): **to ~ along** avançar or mover-se (a vapor); **~ engine** *n* máquina a vapor; **~er** *n* vapor *m*, navio (a vapor); **~roller** *n* rolo compressor (a

vapor); **~y** *adj* vaporoso; (*room*) cheio de vapor, úmido (*Pt*: hu-); (*window*) embaçado.

steel [sti:l] *n* aço // *adj* de aço; **~works** *n* siderurgia.

steep [sti:p] *adj* íngreme, escarpado; (*stair*) empinado; (*price*) exorbitante // *vt* ensopar, embeber, impregnar.

steeple ['sti:pl] *n* campanário, torre *f*; **~chase** *n* corrida de obstáculos; **~jack** *n* consertador *m* de torres or de chaminés altas.

steer [stɪə*] *vt* guiar, dirigir, pilotar // *vi* conduzir; **~ing** *n* (*AUT*) direção (*Pt*: -cç-) *f*; **~ing wheel** *n* volante *m*.

stellar ['stelə*] *adj* estelar.

stem [stem] *n* (*of plant*) caule *m*, haste *f*; (*of glass*) pé *m*; (*of pipe*) tubo // *vt* deter, reter; (*blood*) estancar; **to ~ from** *vt fus* originar-se de.

stench [stentʃ] *n* fedor *m*.

stencil ['stensl] *n* (*typed*) estêncil *m*; (*lettering*) gabarito de letra // *vt* imprimir com estêncil.

stenographer [ste'nɔgrəfə*] *n* (*US*) estenodatilógrafa, estenógrafa.

step [step] *n* passo; (*sound*) passada, pisada; (*stair*) degrau *m* // *vi*: **to ~ forward** avançar, dar um passo em frente; **~s** *npl* = **~ladder**; **to ~ down** *vi* (*fig*) retirar-se; **to ~ off** *vt fus* descer de; **to ~ on** *vt fus* pisar, calcar; **to ~ over** *vt fus* passar por cima de; **to ~ up** *vt* (*increase*) aumentar; **~brother** *n* meio-irmão *m*; **~daughter** *n* enteada; **~father** *n* padrasto; **~ladder** *n* escada portátil or de abrir; **~mother** *n* madrasta; **~ping stone** *n* pedra utilizada em passarelas; (*fig*) trampolim *m*; **~sister** *n* meia-irmã *f*; **~son** *n* enteado.

stereo ['stɛrɪəu] *n* estéreo // *adj* (*also*: **~phonic**) estereofônico.

stereotype ['stɪərɪətaɪp] *n* estereótipo // *vt* estereotipar.

sterile ['stɛraɪl] *adj* estéril; **sterility** [-'rɪlɪtɪ] *n* esterilidade *f*; **sterilization** [-'zeɪʃən] *n* esterilização *f*; **sterilize** ['stɛrɪlaɪz] *vt* esterilizar.

sterling ['stɔ:lɪŋ] *adj* esterlino; (*silver*) de lei; (*fig*) genuíno, puro.

stern [stɔ:n] *adj* severo, austero // *n* (*NAUT*) popa, ré *f*.

stethoscope ['stɛθəskəup] *n* estetoscópio.

stew [stju:] *n* guisado, ensopado; (*fig*: *mess*) apuro, confusão *f* // *vt/i* guisar, ensopar; (*fruit*) cozinhar.

steward ['stju:əd] *n* (*AVIAT*) comissário de bordo; **~ess** *n* aeromoça (*Br*), hospedeira de bordo (*Pt*).

stick [stɪk] *n* pau *m*; (*as weapon*) cacete *m*; (*walking ~*) bengala, cajado // (*vb*: *pt*, *pp* **stuck**) *vt* (*glue*) colar; (*thrust*): **to ~ sth into** cravar or enfiar algo em; (*col*: *put*) meter; (*col*: *tolerate*) agüentar, suportar, aturar // *vi* colar-se, aderir-se; (*come to a stop*) ficar parado; (*in mind etc*)

gravar-se; (pin etc) pregar-se; **to ~ out,
~ up** vi estar saliente, projetar-se (Pt:
-ct-); **to ~ up for** vt fus defender; **~er** n
etiqueta adesiva, adesivo.
stickler ['stɪklə*] n: **to be a ~ for** ser
um defensor ferrenho de.
stick-up ['stɪkʌp] n assalto armado.
sticky ['stɪkɪ] adj pegajoso; (label)
adesivo; (fig) difícil.
stiff [stɪf] adj rígido, forte; (hard) duro;
(difficult) difícil; (person) inflexível,
obstinado; (price) exorbitante; **~en** vt
endurecer; (limb) entumecer // vi
enrijecer-se; (grow stronger) fortalecer-
se; **~ness** n rigidez f, inflexibilidade f;
(character) indiferença.
stifle ['staɪfl] vt sufocar-se, abafar-se;
stifling adj (heat) sufocante, abafado.
stigma ['stɪgmə], pl (BOT, MED, REL) **~ta**
[-tə], (fig) **~s** n estigma m.
stile [staɪl] n degraus para passar por sobre
uma cerca ou muro.
stiletto [stɪ'lɛtəu] n estilete m; (also: **~
heel**) salto (de sapato) fino.
still [stɪl] adj imóvel, quieto // adv (up to
this time) ainda; (even) ainda;
(nonetheless) entretanto, contudo;
~born adj nascido morto, natimorto; **~
life** n natureza morta.
stilt [stɪlt] n perna de pau; (pile) estaca,
suporte m.
stilted ['stɪltɪd] adj afetado (Pt: -ct-).
stimulant ['stɪmjulənt] n estimulante m.
stimulate ['stɪmjuleɪt] vt estimular;
stimulating adj estimulante; **stimu-
lation** [-'leɪʃən] n estímulo.
stimulus ['stɪmjuləs], pl **-li** [-laɪ] n
estímulo, incentivo.
sting [stɪŋ] n (wound) picada; (pain)
ferroada, dor f forte; (of insect) ferrão m
// (vb: pt, pp **stung**) vt picar // vi arder,
doer.
stingy ['stɪndʒɪ] adj pão-duro, sovina.
stink [stɪŋk] n fedor m, catinga // vi, pt
stank, pp **stunk** feder, cheirar mal;
~ing adj fedorento, fétido.
stint [stɪnt] n tarefa, parte f; **to do one's
~** fazer a sua parte // vi: **to ~ on**
restringir.
stipend ['staɪpɛnd] n (of vicar etc)
estipêndio, remuneração f.
stipulate ['stɪpjuleɪt] vt estipular,
estabelecer; **stipulation** [-'leɪʃən] n
estipulação f, cláusula.
stir [stə:*] n (fig: agitation) comoção f,
rebuliço // vt (tea etc) mexer; (fire)
atiçar; (move) mover; (fig: emotions)
comover // vi mover-se, remexer-se; **to
~ up** vt excitar; (trouble) provocar;
~ring adj comovedor(a).
stirrup ['stɪrəp] n estribo.
stitch [stɪtʃ] n (SEWING, KNITTING, MED)
ponto; (pain) pontada // vt costurar;
(MED) dar pontos.
stoat [stəut] n arminho.
stock [stɔk] n (COMM: reserves) estoque
m, provisão f; (: selection) sortimento;
(AGR) gado; (CULIN) caldo; (fig: lineage)

estirpe f, linhagem f; (FINANCE) fundo,
capital m; (: shares) ações (Pt: -çç-) fpl;
~s npl tronco sg, canga sg; **~s and
shares** ações (Pt: -çç-) e valores // adj
(fig: reply etc) trivial, comum // vt (have
in ~) ter em estoque, estocar; (supply)
prover, sortir; **to take ~ of** (fig) fazer
um balanço de, examinar; **to ~ up
with** vt abastecer-se de.
stockade [stɔ'keɪd] n estacada.
stockbroker ['stɔkbrəukə*] n
corretor(a) (Pt: -ct-) m/f de valores or da
Bolsa.
stock exchange n Bolsa de Valores.
stock holder n (US) acionista (Pt: -cc-)
m/f.
stocking ['stɔkɪŋ] n meia.
stock market n Bolsa de Valores.
stockpile ['stɔkpaɪl] n reserva // vt
acumular reservas, estocar.
stocktaking ['stɔkteɪkɪŋ] n (COMM)
inventário, balanço.
stocky ['stɔkɪ] adj (strong) robusto;
(short) atarracado.
stodgy ['stɔdʒɪ] adj maçante, enfadonho.
stoical ['stəuɪkəl] adj estóico.
stoke [stəuk] vt atiçar, alimentar.
stole [stəul] pt of **steal** // n estola.
stolen ['stəuln] pp of **steal**.
stomach ['stʌmək] n (ANAT) estômago;
(belly) barriga, ventre m; (appetite)
apetite m // vt suportar, tolerar; **~
ache** n dor f de estômago.
stone [stəun] n (in fruit) caroço; (in
weight) medida de peso (6.348kg) // adj de
pedra, pétreo // vt apedrejar; **~-cold**
adj gelado; **~-deaf** adj totalmente surdo;
~work n (art) cantaria; (stones) pedras
fpl; **stony** adj pedregoso; (glance) glacial.
stood [stud] pt, pp of **stand**.
stool [stu:l] n tamborete m, banco.
stoop [stu:p] vi (also: **have a ~**) ser
corcunda; (bend) debruçar-se, curvar-se.
stop [stɔp] n parada, interrupção f; (de
ônibus etc) parada (Br), ponto (Br),
paragem f (Pt); (in punctuation) ponto //
vt parar, deter; (break off) paralisar,
cessar; (block) tapar, obstruir; (also: put
a ~ to) terminar, pôr fim a // vi parar-
se, deter-se; (end) acabar-se; **to ~
doing sth** deixar de fazer algo; **to ~
dead** vi parar de repente; **to ~ off** vi
fazer pausa; **to ~ up** vt (hole) tapar,
obstruir; **~gap** n substituto provisório;
~lights npl (AUT) luzes fpl do freio (Br),
faróis mpl de stop (Pt); **~over** n escala.
stoppage ['stɔpɪdʒ] n (strike) greve f;
(temporary stop) paralisação f; (of pay)
suspensão f; (blockage) obstrução f.
stopper ['stɔpə*] n tampa, rolha.
stopwatch ['stɔpwɔtʃ] n cronômetro.
storage ['stɔ:rɪdʒ] n armazenagem f.
store [stɔ:*] n (stock) suprimento; (depot,
large shop) armazém m; (reserve)
estoque m; **~s** npl víveres mpl,
provisões fpl // vt armazenar; (keep)
guardar; **to ~ up** vt acumular; **~room**
n depósito, almoxarifado.

storey, story (*US*) ['stɔːrɪ] *n* andar *m*.
stork [stɔːk] *n* cegonha.
storm [stɔːm] *n* tempestade *f*; (*wind*) borrasca, vendaval *m*; (*fig*) tumulto // *vi* (*fig*) enfurecer-se // *vt* tomar de assalto, assaltar; ~ **cloud** *n* nuvem *f* de tempestade; ~**y** *adj* tempestuoso.
story ['stɔːrɪ] *n* história, estória; (*LIT*) narrativa; (*joke*) anedota, piada; (*plot*) enredo; (*lie*) mentira, conto; (*US*) = **storey**; ~**book** *n* livro de contos; ~**teller** *n* contador(a) *m/f* de estórias; (*: liar*) mentiroso/a.
stout [staut] *adj* (*strong*) sólido, forte; (*fat*) gordo, corpulento // *n* cerveja preta.
stove [stəuv] *n* (*for cooking*) fogão *m*; (*for heating*) estufa, fogareiro.
stow [stəu] *vt* guardar, meter; (*NAUT*) estivar; ~**away** *vi* viajar como clandestino.
straddle ['strædl] *vi* escarranchar-se // *vt* cavalgar.
straggle ['strægl] *vi* (*wander*) vagar, perambular; (*lag behind*) ficar atrás, extraviar-se; **straggler** *n* pessoa extraviada; **straggling**, **straggly** *adj* (*hair*) rebelde, emaranhado.
straight [streit] *adj* reto (*Pt*: -ct-), correto (*Pt*: -ct-); (*honest*) honrado; (*frank*) franco, direto (*Pt*: -ct-); (*simple*) simples *inv*; (*in order*) em ordem // *adv* direito, diretamente (*Pt*: -ct-); (*drink*) puro; **to put** *or* **get sth** ~ falar com toda franqueza; ~ **away**, ~ **off** (*at once*) imediatamente; ~**en** *vt* (*also*: ~**en out**) endireitar, pôr em ordem; ~**-faced** *adj* inexpressivo, solene; ~**forward** *adj* (*simple*) simples, direto (*Pt*: -ct-); (*honest*) honesto, franco.
strain [strein] *n* (*gen*) tensão *f*; (*TECH*) esforço; (*MED*) distensão *f*, luxação *f*; (*breed*) raça, estirpe *f* // *vt* (*back etc*) forçar, torcer, distender; (*tire*) extenuar; (*stretch*) puxar, estirar; (*filter*) filtrar // *vi* esforçar-se; ~**s** *npl* (*MUS*) sons *mpl* musicais; ~**ed** *adj* (*muscle*) distendido; (*laugh*) forçado; (*relations*) tenso; ~**er** *n* coador *m*, peneira.
strait [streit] *n* (*GEO*) estreito; ~**jacket** *n* camisa-de-força; ~**-laced** *adj* puritano, austero.
strand [strænd] *n* (*of thread*) fio; (*of hair*) madeixa; (*of rope*) cordão *m*; (*shore*) praia; ~**ed** *adj* abandonado (*sem recursos*), desamparado.
strange [streindʒ] *adj* (*not known*) desconhecido; (*odd*) estranho, esquisito; **stranger** *n* desconhecido; (*from another area*) forasteiro/a.
strangle ['stræŋgl] *vt* estrangular; (*sobs etc*) sufocar; ~**hold** *n* (*fig*) domínio total; **strangulation** [-'leɪʃən] *n* estrangulação *f*.
strap [stræp] *n* correia; (*of slip, dress*) alça // *vt* prender com correia, apertar; (*punish*) açoitar.

strapping ['stræpiŋ] *adj* corpulento, robusto, forte.
strata ['strɑːtə] *pl of* **stratum**.
stratagem ['strætidʒəm] *n* estratagema *m*.
strategic [strə'tiːdʒɪk] *adj* estratégico.
strategy ['strætidʒɪ] *n* estratégia.
stratum ['strɑːtəm], *pl* **-ta** *n* estrato, camada.
straw [strɔː] *n* palha; (*drinking* ~) canudo.
strawberry ['strɔːbərɪ] *n* morango; (*plant*) morangueiro.
stray [strei] *adj* (*animal*) extraviado; (*bullet*) perdido; (*scattered*) disperso // *vi* extraviar-se, perder-se.
streak [striːk] *n* listra, traço; (*fig: of madness etc*) sinal *m* // *vt* listrar // *vi*: **to** ~ **past** passar como um raio; ~**y** *adj* listrado.
stream [striːm] *n* riacho, córrego; (*jet*) jato (*Pt*: -ct-); (*current*) fluxo, corrente *f*; (*of people*) fluxo // *vt* (*SCOL*) classificar // *vi* correr, fluir; **to** ~ **in/out** (*people*) entrar/sair em massa.
streamer ['striːmə*] *n* serpentina; (*pennant*) flâmula.
streamlined ['striːmlaind] *adj* aerodinâmico.
street [striːt] *n* rua // *adj* da rua; ~**car** *n* (*US*) bonde *m* (*Br*), eléctrico (*Pt*); ~ **lamp** *n* poste *m*.
strength [streŋθ] *n* força; (*of girder, knot etc*) firmeza, resistência; ~**en** *vt* fortalecer, intensificar.
strenuous ['strenjuəs] *adj* (*tough*) árduo, estrênuo; (*energetic*) enérgico; (*determined*) tenaz.
stress [stres] *n* (*force, pressure*) pressão *f*; (*mental strain*) tensão *f*; (*accent*) ênfase *f*, acento; (*TECH*) tensão // *vt* realçar, dar ênfase a.
stretch [stretʃ] *n* (*of sand etc*) trecho // *vi* esticar-se; (*extend*): **to** ~ **to** *or* **as far as** estender-se até (a) // *vt* estirar, esticar; (*make demands of*) exigir o máximo de; **to** ~ **out** *vi* deitar-se // *vt* (*arm etc*) esticar; (*spread*) estirar.
stretcher ['stretʃə*] *n* maca, padiola.
strewn [struːn] *adj*: ~ **with** coberto *or* cheio de.
stricken ['strikən] *adj* (*wounded*) ferido; (*ill*) doente.
strict [strikt] *adj* (*person*) severo, rigoroso; (*precise*) exato (*Pt*: -ct-), preciso; ~**ly** *adv* (*exactly*) estritamente; (*totally*) terminantemente; (*severely*) rigorosamente; ~**ness** *n* exatidão (*Pt*: -ct-) *f*; rigor *m*, severidade *f*.
stride [straid] *n* passo largo // *vi*, *pt* **strode**, *pp* **stridden** ['stridn] andar a passos largos.
strident ['straidnt] *adj* estridente; (*colour*) berrante.
strife [straif] *n* luta, conflito.
strike [straik] *n* greve *f*; (*of oil etc*) descoberta; (*attack*) ataque *m*; (*SPORT*) golpe *m* // (*vb: pt*, *pp* **struck**) *vt* bater,

golpear; (*oil etc*) descobrir; (*obstacle*) chocar-se com // *vi* entrar em greve; (*attack*) atacar; (*clock*) bater, dar (as horas); **to ~ a match** acender um fósforo; **to ~ down** *vt* derrubar; **to ~ out** *vt* cancelar, rasurar; **to ~ up** *vt* (*MUS*) começar a tocar; (*conversation, friendship*) travar; **~breaker** *n* furagreve *m/f inv*; **striker** *n* grevista *m/f*; (*SPORT*) atacante *m/f*; **striking** *adj* impressionante; (*nasty*) chocante; (*colour*) chamativo.

string [strɪŋ] *n* (*gen*) fio, corda; (*row*) série *f*, fileira // *vt, pt, pp* **strung: to ~ together** enfiar // *vi*: **to ~ out** estender-se; **the ~s** *npl* (*MUS*) os instrumentos de corda; **to pull ~s** (*fig*) usar pistolão; **~ bean** *n* vagem *f*; **~(ed) instrument** *n* (*MUS*) instrumento de corda.

stringent ['strɪndʒənt] *adj* severo, estrito.

strip [strɪp] *n* tira; (*of land*) faixa; (*of metal*) lâmina, tira // *vt* despir; (*also:* **~ down:** *machine*) desmontar // *vi* despirse; **~ cartoon** *n* história em quadrinhos (*Br*), banda desenhada (*Pt*).

stripe [straɪp] *n* listra, faixa; (*MIL*) galão *m*; **~d** listrado, com listras.

stripper ['strɪpə*] *n* artista *m/f* de striptease.

striptease ['strɪptiːz] *n* striptease *m*.

strive [straɪv], *pt* **strove**, *pp* **striven** ['strɪvn] *vi*: **to ~ to do sth** esforçar-se por *or* batalhar para fazer algo.

strode [strəud] *pt of* **stride**.

stroke [strəuk] *n* (*blow*) pancada, golpe *m*; (*MED*) ataque *m* apoplético (*Pt*: -ct-); (*caress*) carícia; (*of pen*) traço // *vt* acariciar, afagar; **at a ~** de repente, de golpe.

stroll [strəul] *n* volta, passeio // *vi* passear, dar uma volta; **stroller** *n* (*US*) carrinho.

strong [strɒŋ] *adj* forte; **they are 50 ~** são 50; **~box** *n* cofre-forte *f*; **~hold** *n* fortaleza; (*fig*) baluarte *m*; **~ly** *adv* fortemente, vigorosamente; (*believe*) firmemente; **~room** *n* caixa-forte *f*.

strove [strəuv] *pt of* **strive**.

struck [strʌk] *pt, pp of* **strike**.

structural ['strʌktʃərəl] *adj* estrutural; **structure** *n* estrutura; (*building*) construção *f*.

struggle ['strʌgl] *n* luta, contenda // *vi* lutar, brigar.

strum [strʌm] *vt* (*guitar*) dedilhar.

strung [strʌŋ] *pt, pp of* **string**.

strut [strʌt] *n* escora, suporte *m* // *vi* pavonear-se, empertigar-se.

stub [stʌb] *n* (*of ticket etc*) canhoto; (*of cigarette*) toco, ponta; **to ~ out** *vt* apagar; **to ~ one's toe** tropeçar, dar topada.

stubble ['stʌbl] *n* restolho; (*on chin*) barba por fazer.

stubborn ['stʌbən] *adj* teimoso, cabeçudo, obstinado.

stuck [stʌk] *pt, pp of* **stick** // *adj* (*jammed*) emperrado; **~-up** *adj* convencido, metido, esnobe.

stud [stʌd] *n* (*shirt ~*) botão *m*; (*of boot*) cravo; (*of horses*) haras *msg*; (*also:* **~ horse**) garanhão *m* // *vt* (*fig*): **~ded with** salpicado de.

student ['stjuːdənt] *n* estudante *m/f* // *adj* estudantil; **~ driver** *n* (*US*) principiante *m/f*.

studio ['stjuːdɪəu] *n* estúdio; (*sculptor's*) ateliê *m*.

studious ['stjuːdɪəs] *adj* estudioso, aplicado; (*studied*) calculado; **~ly** *adv* (*carefully*) com esmero.

study ['stʌdɪ] *n* (*gen*) estudo // *vt* estudar; (*examine*) examinar, investigar // *vi* estudar.

stuff [stʌf] *n* matéria; (*cloth*) tecido; (*substance*) material *m*, substância // *vt* encher; (*CULIN*) rechear; (*animals*) empalhar; **~ing** *n* recheio; **~y** *adj* (*room*) abafado, mal ventilado; (*person*) rabujento, melindroso.

stumble ['stʌmbl] *vi* tropeçar, dar topada; **to ~ across** (*fig*) topar com; **stumbling block** *n* obstáculo, impedimento.

stump [stʌmp] *n* (*of tree*) toco; (*of limb*) coto // *vt*: **to be ~ed** ficar perplexo.

stun [stʌn] *vt* aturdir, pasmar.

stung [stʌŋ] *pt, pp of* **sting**.

stunk [stʌŋk] *pp of* **stink**.

stunning ['stʌnɪŋ] *adj* (*fig*) atordoante.

stunt [stʌnt] *n* façanha sensacional; (*AVIAT*) vôo acrobático; (*publicity* ~) truque *m* publicitário; **~ed** *adj* atrofiado, retardado; **~man** *n* dublê *m*.

stupefy ['stjuːpɪfaɪ] *vt* deixar estupefato (*Pt*: -ct-).

stupendous [stjuːˈpɛndəs] *adj* assombroso, prodigioso, monumental.

stupid ['stjuːpɪd] *adj* estúpido, idiota; **~ity** [-ˈpɪdɪtɪ] *n* estupidez *f*; **~ly** *adv* estupidamente.

stupor ['stjuːpə*] *n* estupor *m*.

sturdy ['stɜːdɪ] *adj* robusto; (*firm*) resoluto.

stutter ['stʌtə*] *n* gagueira, gaguez *f* // *vi* gaguejar.

sty [staɪ] *n* (*for pigs*) chiqueiro.

stye [staɪ] *n* (*MED*) terçol *m*.

style [staɪl] *n* estilo; **stylish** *adj* elegante, da moda.

stylus ['staɪləs] *n* (*of record player*) agulha.

suave [swɑːv] *adj* suave, melífluo.

sub... [sʌb] *pref* sub...; **~conscious** *adj* do subconsciente // *n* subconsciente *m*; **~divide** *vt* subdividir; **~division** *n* subdivisão *f*.

subdue [səbˈdjuː] *vt* subjugar; (*passions*) dominar; **~d** *adj* (*light*) tênue; (*person*) submisso, subjugado.

subject ['sʌbdʒɪkt] *n* súdito (*Pt*: -bd-); (*theme*) assunto, tópico; (*SCOL*) matéria // *vt* [səbˈdʒɛkt]: **to ~ sb to sth** submeter alguém a algo; **to be ~ to**

(*law*) estar sujeito a; ~**ion** [-'dʒɛkʃən] *n* submissão *f*, dependência; ~**ive** *adj* subjetivo (*Pt*: -ct-); ~ **matter** *n* assunto; (*content*) conteúdo.

subjugate ['sʌbdʒugeɪt] *vt* subjugar, submeter.

sublet [sʌb'lɛt] *vt* sublocar.

sublime [sə'blaɪm] *adj* sublime.

submachine gun ['sʌbmə'ʃiːn-] *n* metralhadora de mão.

submarine [sʌbmə'riːn] *n* submarino.

submerge [səb'mɜːdʒ] *vt* submergir; (*flood*) inundar // *vi* submergir-se.

submission [səb'mɪʃən] *n* submissão *f*; **submissive** [-'mɪsɪv] *adj* submisso.

submit [səb'mɪt] *vt* submeter // *vi* submeter-se.

subnormal [sʌb'nɔːməl] *adj* anormal, subnormal; (*backward*) atrasado.

subordinate [sə'bɔːdɪnət] *adj*, *n* subordinado/a.

subpoena [səb'piːnə] (*LAW*) *n* intimação *f* judicial // *vt* intimar a comparecer judicialmente.

subscribe [səb'skraɪb] *vi* subscrever; **to ~ to** (*opinion*) concordar com; (*fund*) contribuir para; (*newspaper*) assinar; **subscriber** *n* (*to periodical, telephone*) assinante *m/f*.

subscription [səb'skrɪpʃən] *n* subscrição (*Pt*: -pç-) *f*, assinatura.

subsequent ['sʌbsɪkwənt] *adj* subseqüente, posterior; ~**ly** *adv* mais tarde, depois.

subside [səb'saɪd] *vi* baixar; (*flood*) descer; (*wind*) acanhar-se; **subsidence** [-'saɪdns] *n* baixa.

subsidiary [səb'sɪdɪərɪ] *n* subsidiário, sucursal *f*.

subsidize ['sʌbsɪdaɪz] *vt* subsidiar; **subsidy** [-dɪ] *n* subsídio.

subsistence [səb'sɪstəns] *n* subsistência; (*allowance*) subsídio, ajuda de custo.

substance ['sʌbstəns] *n* substância; (*fig*) essência.

substandard [sʌb'stændəd] *adj* inferior ao padrão.

substantial [səb'stænʃl] *adj* substancial, essencial; (*fig*) importante; ~**ly** *adv* substancialmente.

substantiate [səb'stænʃɪeɪt] *vt* comprovar, justificar.

substitute ['sʌbstɪtjuːt] *n* substituto; (*person*) suplente *m/f* // *vt*: **to ~ A for B** substituir B por A; **substitution** [-'tjuːʃən] *n* substituição *f*, troca.

subterfuge ['sʌbtəfjuːdʒ] *n* subterfúgio.

subterranean [sʌbtə'reɪnɪən] *adj* subterrâneo.

subtitle ['sʌbtaɪtl] *n* subtítulo.

subtle ['sʌtl] *adj* sutil; ~**ty** *n* sutileza.

subtract [səb'trækt] *vt* subtrair, deduzir; ~**ion** [-'trækʃən] *n* subtração (*Pt*: -cç-) *f*, dedução *f*.

suburb ['sʌbɜːb] *n* subúrbio; ~**an** [sə'bɜːbən] *adj* suburbano; (*train etc*) de subúrbio.

subversive [səb'vɜːsɪv] *adj* subversivo.

subway ['sʌbweɪ] *n* (*Brit*) passagem *f* subterrânea; (*US*) metrô (*Pt*: -o) *m*.

succeed [sək'siːd] *vi* (*person*) ser bem sucedido, ter êxito; (*plan*) sair bem // *vt* suceder a; **to ~ in doing** conseguir fazer; ~**ing** *adj* (*following*) sucessivo, posterior.

success [sək'sɛs] *n* sucesso, êxito; (*gain*) triunfo; ~**ful** *adj* (*venture*) bem sucedido; **to be** ~**ful (in doing)** conseguir (fazer); ~**fully** *adv* com sucesso, com êxito.

succession [sək'sɛʃən] *n* (*series*) sucessão *f*, série *f*; (*descendants*) descendência; **successive** [-'sɛsɪv] *adj* sucessivo, consecutivo; **successor** [-'sɛsə*] *n* sucessor(a) *m/f*.

succinct [sək'sɪŋkt] *adj* sucinto.

succulent ['sʌkjulənt] *adj* suculento.

succumb [sə'kʌm] *vi* sucumbir.

such [sʌtʃ] *adj*, *det* tal, semelhante; (*of that kind*): ~ **a book** um livro parecido; ~ **books** tais livros; (*so much*): ~ **courage** tanta coragem; ~ **a long trip** uma viagem tão longa; ~ **a lot of** tanto; ~ **as** (*like*) tal como; **a noise** ~ **as** to um ruído tal que; **as** ~ *adv* como tal // *pron* os/as que; ~**-and-~** *det* tal e qual; **until** ~ **time** as até que.

suck [sʌk] *vt* chupar; (*bottle*) tragar, tomar; (*breast*) mamar; ~**er** *n* (*BOT*) rebento; (*ZOOL*) ventosa; (*col*) trouxa *m/f*, otário.

suckle ['sʌkl] *vt* amamentar.

suction ['sʌkʃən] *n* sucção *f*.

sudden ['sʌdn] *adj* (*rapid*) repentino, súbito; (*unexpected*) imprevisto; **all of a** ~, ~**ly** *adv* de repente; (*unexpectedly*) inesperadamente.

suds [sʌdz] *npl* água de sabão, espuma.

sue [suː] *vt* processar.

suede [sweɪd] *n* camurça.

suet ['suːt] *n* sebo.

suffer ['sʌfə*] *vt* sofrer, padecer; (*bear*) agüentar; (*allow*) permitir // *vi* sofrer, padecer; ~**er** *n* sofredor(a) *m/f*; (*MED*) doente *m/f*, paciente *m/f*; ~**ing** *n* sofrimento, padecimento; (*pain*) dor *f*.

suffice [sə'faɪs] *vi* bastar, ser suficiente.

sufficient [sə'fɪʃənt] *adj* suficiente, bastante.

suffix ['sʌfɪks] *n* sufixo.

suffocate ['sʌfəkeɪt] *vi* sufocar-se, asfixiar-se; **suffocation** [-'keɪʃən] *n* sufocação *f*, asfixia.

suffrage ['sʌfrɪdʒ] *n* sufrágio; (*vote*) direito de voto.

sugar ['ʃugə*] *n* açúcar *m* // *vt* pôr açúcar em; ~ **beet** *n* beterraba; ~ **cane** *n* cana-de-açúcar *f*; ~**y** *adj* açucarado.

suggest [sə'dʒɛst] *vt* sugerir; (*advise*) aconselhar; ~**ion** [-'dʒɛstʃən] *n* sugestão *f*; ~**ive** *adj* sugestivo; (*pej*) indecente.

suicidal [suɪ'saɪdl] *adj* suicida; **suicide** ['suɪsaɪd] *n* suicídio; (*person*) suicida *m/f*.

suit [suːt] *n* (*man's*) terno (*Br*); fato (*Pt*); (*woman's*) conjunto; (*LAW*) processo;

(CARDS) naipe *m* // *vt* *(gen)* convir a; *(clothes)* ficar bem a; *(adapt)*: **to ~ sth to** adaptar *or* acomodar algo a; **~able** *adj* conveniente; *(apt)* apropriado; **~ably** *adv* convenientemente, apropriadamente.

suitcase ['su:tkeɪs] *n* mala, maleta.

suite [swi:t] *n (of rooms)* conjunto de salas; *(MUS)* suite *f*; *(furniture)*: **bedroom/dining room ~** conjunto de quarto/de sala de jantar.

suitor ['su:tə*] *n* pretendente *m*.

sulk [sʌlk] *vi* ficar emburrado; **~y** *adj* emburrado.

sullen ['sʌlən] *adj* rabujento, teimoso.

sulphur, sulfur *(US)* ['sʌlfə*] *n* enxofre *m*.

sultan ['sʌltən] *n* sultão *m*.

sultana [sʌl'tɑ:nə] *n (fruit)* passa.

sultry ['sʌltrɪ] *adj (weather)* abafado, mormacento; *(seductive)* sedutor(a).

sum [sʌm] *n (gen)* soma; *(total)* total *m*; **to ~ up** *vt* sumariar, fazer um resumo de // *vi* resumir.

summarize ['sʌmǝraɪz] *vt* resumir.

summary ['sʌmǝrɪ] *n* resumo, sumário // *adj (justice)* sumário.

summer ['sʌmə*] *n* verão *m* // *adj* de verão; **~house** *n (in garden)* pavilhão *m*; **~time** *n (season)* verão *m*; **~ time** *n (by clock)* horário de verão.

summit ['sʌmɪt] *n* topo, cume *m*; *(fig)* apogeu *m*; **~ (conference)** *n* (conferência de) cúpula.

summon ['sʌmən] *vt (person)* mandar chamar; *(meeting)* convocar; *(LAW)* citar; **to ~ up** *vt (forces)* concentrar; *(courage)* criar; **~s** *n* citação *f*, intimação *f* // *vt* citar, intimar.

sump [sʌmp] *n (AUT)* cárter *m*.

sumptuous ['sʌmptjuǝs] *adj* suntuoso, magnífico, esplêndido.

sun [sʌn] *n* sol *m*; **~bathe** *vi* tomar sol; **~burn** *n (painful)* queimadura; *(tan)* bronzeado; **~burnt** *adj (tanned)* bronzeado; *(painfully)* queimado.

Sunday ['sʌndɪ] *n* domingo.

sundial ['sʌndaɪǝl] *n* relógio de sol.

sundry ['sʌndrɪ] *adj* vários, diversos; **all and ~** todos; **sundries** *npl* gêneros *mpl* diversos.

sunflower ['sʌnflauǝ*] *n* girassol *m*.

sung [sʌŋ] *pp of* **sing.**

sunglasses ['sʌnglɑ:sɪz] *npl* óculos *mpl* de sol.

sunk [sʌŋk] *pp of* **sink.**

sun: ~light *n* luz *f* do sol; **~lit** *adj* iluminado pelo sol; **~ny** *adj* cheio de sol; *(day)* ensolarado; *(fig)* alegre; **~rise** *n* nascer *m* do sol; **~set** *n* pôr *m* do sol; **~shade** *n (over table)* pára-sol *m*; **~shine** *n* luz *f* do sol; **~spot** *n* mancha solar; **~stroke** *n* insolação *f*; **~tan** *n* bronzeado; **~tan oil** *n* óleo de bronzear, bronzeador *m*.

super ['su:pə*] *adj (col)* bacana *(Br)*, muito giro *(Pt)*.

superannuation [su:pərænju'eɪʃǝn] *n* aposentadoria, pensão *f*.

superb [su:'pə:b] *adj* soberbo, magnífico, excelente.

supercilious [su:pǝ'sɪlɪǝs] *adj (disdainful)* arrogante, desdenhoso; *(haughty)* altivo.

superficial [su:pǝ'fɪʃǝl] *adj* superficial.

superfluous [su'pǝ:fluǝs] *adj* supérfluo, desnecessário.

superhuman [su:pǝ'hju:mǝn] *adj* sobre-humano.

superimpose ['su:pǝrɪm'pǝuz] *vt* sobrepor.

superintendent [su:pǝrɪn'tɛndǝnt] *n* superintendente *m/f*; *(POLICE)* chefe *m* de polícia.

superior [su'pɪǝrɪǝ*] *adj* superior; *(smug)* desdenhoso // *n* superior *m*; **~ity** [-'ɔrɪtɪ] *n* superioridade *f*; desdém *m*.

superlative [su'pǝ:lǝtɪv] *adj*, *n* superlativo.

superman ['su:pǝmæn] *n* super-homem *m*.

supermarket ['su:pǝmɑ:kɪt] *n* supermercado.

supernatural [su:pǝ'nætʃǝrǝl] *adj* sobrenatural.

superpower ['su:pǝpauǝ*] *n (POL)* superpotência.

supersede [su:pǝ'si:d] *vt* suplantar.

supersonic ['su:pǝ'sɔnɪk] *adj* supersônico.

superstition [su:pǝ'stɪʃǝn] *n* superstição *f*; **superstitious** [-ʃǝs] *adj* supersticioso.

supertanker ['su:pǝtæŋkǝ*] *n* superpetroleiro.

supervise ['su:pǝvaɪz] *vt* supervisar, supervisionar; **supervision** [-'vɪʒǝn] *n* supervisão *f*; **supervisor** *n* supervisor(a) *m/f*; *(academic)* orientador(a) *m/f*.

supper ['sʌpǝ*] *n* jantar *m*; **to have ~** jantar.

supple ['sʌpl] *adj* flexível.

supplement ['sʌplɪmǝnt] *n* suplemento // *vt* [sʌplɪ'mɛnt] suprir; **~ary** [-'mɛntǝrɪ] *adj* suplementar.

supplier [sǝ'plaɪǝ*] *n* abastecedor(a) *m/f*, fornecedor(a) *m/f*; *(COMM)* distribuidor(a) *m/f*.

supply [sǝ'plaɪ] *vt (provide)* abastecer, fornecer; *(equip)*: **to ~ (with)** suprir de // *n* fornecimento, provisão *f*; *(supplying)* abastecimento // *adj (teacher etc)* suplente; **supplies** *npl (food)* víveres *mpl*; *(MIL)* apetrechos *mpl*; **~ and demand** oferta e procura.

support [sǝ'pɔ:t] *n (moral, financial etc)* apoio; *(TECH)* suporte *m* // *vt* apoiar; *(financially)* manter; *(uphold)* sustentar; **~er** *n (POL etc)* partidário; *(SPORT)* torcedor(a) *m/f*.

suppose [sǝ'pǝuz] *vt/i (gen)* supor; *(imagine)* imaginar; **to be ~d to do sth** dever fazer algo; **~dly** [sǝ'pǝuzɪdlɪ] *adv* supostamente, pretensamente; **supposing** *conj* se, supondo-se que; **supposition** [sʌpǝ'zɪʃǝn] *n* suposição *f*.

suppository [sǝ'pɔzɪtǝr] *n* supositório.

suppress [sə'prɛs] vt suprimir, reprimir; (yawn) conter; ~ion [sə'prɛʃən] n repressão f.

supremacy [su'prɛməsɪ] n supremacia; **supreme** [-'priːm] adj supremo.

surcharge ['sɜːtʃɑːdʒ] n sobrecarga; (extra tax) sobretaxa.

sure [ʃuə*] adj (gen) seguro; (definite, convinced) certo, firme; (aim) certeiro; ~! (of course) claro que sim!; ~-footed adj de andar seguro; ~ly adv (certainly) certamente.

surety ['ʃuərətɪ] n garantia, fiança; (person) fiador(a) m/f.

surf [sɜːf] n surfe m.

surface ['sɜːfɪs] n superfície f // vt (road) revestir // vi vir à superfície or à tona.

surfboard ['sɜːfbɔːd] n prancha de surfe.

surfeit ['sɜːfɪt] n: a ~ of um excesso de.

surfing ['sɜːfɪŋ] n surfe m.

surge [sɜːdʒ] n onda, vaga // vi encapelar-se, crescer de repente; to ~ forward avançar em tropel.

surgeon ['sɜːdʒən] n cirurgião m; dental ~ cirurgião-dentista m.

surgery ['sɜːdʒərɪ] n cirurgia; (room) consultório; to undergo ~ operar-se; ~ hours npl horas fpl de consulta.

surgical ['sɜːdʒɪkl] adj cirúrgico; ~ spirit n álcool m.

surly ['sɜːlɪ] adj malcriado, rude.

surmount [sɜː'maunt] vt superar, sobrepujar, vencer.

surname ['sɜːneɪm] n sobrenome m (Br), apelido (Pt).

surpass [sɜː'pɑːs] vt superar, exceder, ultrapassar.

surplus ['sɜːpləs] n (gen) excedente m; (COMM) superávit m // adj excedente, de sobra.

surprise [sə'praɪz] n (gen) surpresa; (astonishment) assombro // vt surpreender, assombrar; **surprising** adj surpreendente, inesperado.

surrealist [sə'rɪəlɪst] adj, n surrealista m/f.

surrender [sə'rɛndə*] n rendição f, entrega // vi render-se, entregar-se.

surreptitious [sʌrəp'tɪʃəs] adj clandestino, furtivo.

surround [sə'raund] vt circundar, rodear; (MIL etc) cercar; ~ing adj circundante, adjacente; ~ings npl arredores mpl, cercanias fpl.

surveillance [sɜː'veɪləns] n vigilância.

survey ['sɜːveɪ] n inspeção (Pt: -cç-) f, vistoria; (inquiry) pesquisa, levantamento // vt [sɜː'veɪ] (gen) inspecionar (Pt: -cç-), vistoriar; (look at) observar, contemplar; (make inquiries about) pesquisar, fazer um levantamento de; ~or n agrimensor m.

survival [sə'vaɪvl] n sobrevivência; **survive** vi sobreviver; (custom etc) perdurar // vt sobreviver a; **survivor** n sobrevivente m/f.

susceptible [sə'sɛptəbl] adj: ~ (to) suscetível (Pt: -pt-) or sensível a.

suspect ['sʌspɛkt] adj, n suspeito/a // vt [səs'pɛkt] suspeitar, desconfiar.

suspend [səs'pɛnd] vt suspender; ~er belt n cinta-liga; ~ers npl ligas fpl; (US) suspensórios mpl.

suspense [səs'pɛns] n incerteza, ansiedade f; (in film etc) suspense m.

suspension [səs'pɛnʃən] n (gen) suspensão f; ~ bridge n ponte f pênsil.

suspicion [səs'pɪʃən] n (gen) suspeita; (distrust) receio; (trace) traço, vestígio; **suspicious** [-ʃəs] adj (suspecting) suspeitoso; (causing ~) suspeito.

sustain [səs'teɪn] vt sustentar, manter; (suffer) sofrer, agüentar; ~ed adj (effort) contínuo.

sustenance ['sʌstɪnəns] n sustento.

swab [swɔb] n (MED) mecha de algodão.

swagger ['swægə*] vi andar com arrogância.

swallow ['swɔləu] n (bird) andorinha; (of food etc) bocado, trago // vt engolir, tragar; to ~ up vt (savings etc) consumir.

swam [swæm] pt of **swim**.

swamp [swɔmp] n pântano, brejo // vt atolar, inundar, sobrecarregar; ~y adj pantanoso.

swan [swɔn] n cisne m.

swap [swɔp] n troca, permuta // vt: to ~ (for) trocar (por).

swarm [swɔːm] n (of bees) enxame m; (gen) multidão f // vi formigar, aglomerar-se.

swarthy ['swɔːðɪ] adj moreno.

swastika ['swɔstɪkə] n suástica.

swat [swɔt] vt esmagar, bater.

sway [sweɪ] vi balançar-se, oscilar, inclinar-se // vt (influence) influenciar, ter influência sobre.

swear [swɛə*], pt **swore**, pp **sworn** vi jurar, xingar; to ~ to sth afirmar algo sob juramento; ~word n palavrão m.

sweat [swɛt] n suor m // vi suar.

sweater ['swɛtə*] n suéter m/f (Br), camisola (Pt).

sweaty ['swɛtɪ] adj suado.

swede [swiːd] n tipo de nabo.

Swede [swiːd] n sueco/a; **Sweden** n Suécia; **Swedish** adj sueco // n (LING) sueco.

sweep [swiːp] n (act) varredura; (of arm) movimento circular; (range) extensão f, alcance m; (also: chimney ~) limpador m de chaminés // (vb: pt, pp **swept**) vt/i varrer; to ~ away vt varrer; (rub out) apagar; to ~ past vi passar rapidamente; (brush by) roçar; to ~ up vi recolher o lixo; ~ing adj (gesture) abarcador(a); (victory) arrasador(a); (generalized) generalizado.

sweet [swiːt] n (candy) doce m, bombom m; (pudding) sobremesa // adj doce; (sugary) açucarado; (fresh) fresco; (fig) meigo, agradável; ~corn n milho; ~en vt adoçar; (add sugar to) pôr açúcar em; ~heart n namorado/a; (in speech) amor m; ~ly adv docemente; (gently) suavemente; ∼**ness** n (gen) doçura; (amount of sugar) o doce; ∼ **pea** n ervilha-de-cheiro f.

swell [swɛl] n (of sea) vaga, onda // adj (col: excellent) excelente, elegante // (vb: pt **swelled**, pp **swollen** or **swelled**) vt inchar, inflar // vi inchar-se, dilatar-se; ∼**ing** n (MED) inchação f.

sweltering ['swɛltərɪŋ] adj sufocante, mormacento; (burning) abrasador(a).

swept [swɛpt] pt, pp of **sweep**.

swerve [swɔːv] vi desviar-se bruscamente, dar uma guinada.

swift [swɪft] n (bird) andorinhão m // adj rápido, veloz; ∼**ness** n rapidez f, ligeireza.

swig [swɪg] n (col: drink) trago, gole m.

swill [swɪl] n água de lavagem // vt (also: ∼ **out**, ∼ **down**) lavar, limpar com água.

swim [swɪm] n: to go for a ∼ ir nadar // (vb: pt **swam**, pp **swum**) vi nadar; my head/the room is ∼ming estou com a cabeça zonza/sinto o quarto rodar // vt atravessar a nado; ∼**mer** n nadador(a) m/f; ∼**ming** n natação f; ∼**ming baths** npl piscina sg; ∼**ming cap** n touca de natação; ∼**ming costume** n (woman) maiô m (Br), fato de banho (Pt); (man) calção m de banho (Br), calções mpl de banho (Pt); ∼**ming pool** n piscina; ∼**suit** n = ∼**ming costume**.

swindle ['swɪndl] n fraude f // vt defraudar; **swindler** n vigarista m/f.

swine [swaɪn] n, pl inv porcos mpl; (col!) canalha sg, calhorda sg.

swing [swɪŋ] n (in playground) balanço; (movement) balanceio, oscilação f; (change of direction) virada; (rhythm) ritmo // (vb: pt, pp **swung**) vt fazer girar; (on a ∼) balançar; (also: ∼ **round**) girar, rodar // vi balançar-se, mover-se; (also: ∼ **round**) voltar-se bruscamente; to be in full ∼ estar em plena atividade (Pt: -ct-); ∼ **bridge** n ponte f giratória; ∼ **door** n porta giratória.

swipe [swaɪp] n pancada violenta // vt (hit) bater com violência; (col: steal) afanar, roubar.

swirl [swɔːl] vi redemoinhar.

Swiss [swɪs] adj, n, pl inv suíço/a.

switch [swɪtʃ] n (for light, radio etc) interruptor m; (change) mudança; (of hair) trança postiça // vt (change) mudar de; to ∼ **off** vt apagar; (engine) desligar; to ∼ **on** vt acender; (engine, machine) ligar; ∼**board** n (TEL) mesa telefônica.

Switzerland ['swɪtsələnd] n Suíça.

swivel ['swɪvl] vi (also: ∼ **round**) girar (sobre um eixo), fazer pião.

swollen ['swəulən] pp of **swell**.

swoon [swuːn] vi desmaiar, desfalecer, ter uma síncope.

swoop [swuːp] n (by police etc) batida // vi (also: ∼ **down**) precipitar-se, cair.

swop [swɔp] = **swap**.

sword [sɔːd] n espada; ∼**fish** n peixe-espada m.

swore [swɔː*] pt of **swear**.

sworn [swɔːn] pp of **swear**.

swot [swɔt] vt, vi trabalhar or estudar arduamente.

swum [swʌm] pp of **swim**.

swung [swʌŋ] pt, pp of **swing**.

sycamore ['sɪkəmɔː*] n sicômoro.

syllable ['sɪləbl] n sílaba.

syllabus ['sɪləbəs] n programa m de estudos.

symbol ['sɪmbl] n símbolo; ∼**ic(al)** [-'bɔlɪk(l)] adj simbólico; ∼**ism** n simbolismo; ∼**ize** vt simbolizar.

symmetrical [sɪ'mɛtrɪkl] adj simétrico; **symmetry** ['sɪmɪtrɪ] n simetria.

sympathetic [sɪmpə'θɛtɪk] adj solidário; (pleasant) simpático; ∼**ally** adv solidariamente.

sympathize ['sɪmpəθaɪz] vi: to ∼ **with** **sb** compadecer-se de alguém; **sympathizer** n (POL) simpatizante m/f.

sympathy ['sɪmpəθɪ] n (pity) compaixão f; (liking) simpatia; **with our deepest** ∼ com nossos mais profundos pêsames; ∼ **strike** n greve f de solidariedade.

symphony ['sɪmfənɪ] n sinfonia; ∼ **orchestra** n orquestra sinfônica.

symposium [sɪm'pəuzɪəm] n simpósio.

symptom ['sɪmptəm] n sintoma m; (sign) indício; ∼**atic** [-'mætɪk] adj sintomático.

synagogue ['sɪnəgɔg] n sinagoga.

synchronize ['sɪŋkrənaɪz] vt sincronizar // vi: to ∼ **with** sincronizar-se com.

syndicate ['sɪndɪkɪt] n (gen) sindicato; (of newspapers) cadeia.

syndrome ['sɪndrəum] n síndrome f.

synonym ['sɪnənɪm] n sinônimo; ∼**ous** [sɪ'nɔnɪməs] adj: ∼**ous (with)** sinônimo (de).

synopsis [sɪ'nɔpsɪs], pl -**ses** [-siːz] n sinopse f.

syntax ['sɪntæks] n sintaxe f.

synthesis ['sɪnθəsɪs], pl -**ses** [-siːz] n síntese f.

synthetic [sɪn'θɛtɪk] adj sintético.

syphilis ['sɪfɪlɪs] n sífilis f.

syphon ['saɪfən] = **siphon**.

Syria ['sɪrɪə] n Síria; ∼**n** adj, n sírio/a.

syringe [sɪ'rɪndʒ] n seringa.

syrup ['sɪrəp] n xarope m, melado, melaço.

system ['sɪstəm] n (gen) sistema m; (method) método; (ANAT) organismo; ∼**atic** [-'mætɪk] adj sistemático; ∼**s** **analyst** n analista m/f de sistemas.

T

ta [taː] excl (Brit: col) obrigado/a.

tab [tæb] n (gen) lingüeta, aba; (label) etiqueta; to **keep** ∼**s on** (fig) vigiar.

tabby ['tæbɪ] n (also: ∼ **cat**) gato malhado or listrado.

table ['teɪbl] n mesa; (of statistics etc) quadro, tabela // vt (motion etc) apresentar; to **lay** or **set the** ∼ pôr a mesa; ∼**cloth** n toalha de mesa; ∼

d'hôte [ta:bl'dɔut] *n* refeição *f* comercial; ~**mat** *n* descanso; ~**spoon** *n* colher *f* de sopa; (*also:* ~**spoonful:** *as measurement*) colherada.

tablet ['tæblɪt] *n* (*MED*) comprimido; (*for writing*) bloco; (*of stone*) lápide *f.*

table: ~ **tennis** *n* pingue-pongue *m*, tênis *m* de mesa; ~ **wine** *n* vinho de mesa.

taboo [tə'bu:] *n* tabu *m* // *adj* tabu.

tacit ['tæsɪt] *adj* tácito, implícito.

taciturn ['tæsɪtə:n] *adj* taciturno.

tack [tæk] *n* (*nail*) tachinha, percevejo; (*stitch*) alinhavo; (*NAUT*) amura // *vt* (*nail*) prender com tachinha; (*stitch*) alinhavar // *vi* virar de bordo.

tackle ['tækl] *n* (*gear*) equipamento; (*also: fishing* ~) apetrechos *mpl*; (*for lifting*) guincho; (*FOOTBALL*) ato de tirar a bola de adversário // *vt* (*difficulty*) enfrentar; (*grapple with*) atracar-se com; (*FOOTBALL*) tirar a bola de.

tacky ['tækɪ] *adj* pegajoso, grudento.

tact [tækt] *n* tato (*Pt:* -ct-), diplomacia; ~**ful** *adj* com ta(c)to, diplomático; ~**fully** *adv* discretamente, com ta(c)to.

tactical ['tæktɪkl] *adj* tático (*Pt:* -ct-); **tactics** [-tɪks] *n*, *npl* tá(c)tica *sg.*

tactless ['tæktlɪs] *adj* sem ta(c)to, sem diplomacia; ~**ly** *adv* indiscretamente.

tadpole ['tædpəul] *n* girino.

tag [tæg] *n* (*label*) etiqueta; (*loose end*) rabo, penduricalho; **to** ~ **along with** sb acompanhar alguém.

tail [teɪl] *n* (*gen*) rabo; (*of bird, comet etc*) cauda; (*of shirt, coat*) aba // *vt* (*follow*) seguir bem de perto; **to** ~ **away, ~ off** *vi* (*in size, quality etc*) diminuir gradualmente; ~ **coat** *n* fraque *m*; ~**end** *n* cauda, parte *f* final; ~**gate** *n* tampa traseira.

tailor ['teɪlə*] *n* alfaiate *m*; ~**ing** *n* (*cut*) feitio; (*craft*) ofício de alfaiate; ~**-made** *adj* feito sob medida; (*fig*) especial.

tailwind ['teɪlwɪnd] *n* vento de popa *or* de cauda.

tainted ['teɪntɪd] *adj* (*food*) estragado, passado; (*water, air*) poluído; (*fig*) manchado.

take [teɪk], *pt* **took**, *pp* **taken** *vt* (*gen*) tomar; (*grab*) pegar (em); (*gain: prize*) ganhar; (*require: effort, courage*) requerer, exigir; (*tolerate*) agüentar; (*hold: passengers etc*): **it** ~**s 50 people** cabem 50 pessoas; (*accompany, bring, carry*) levar; (*exam*) prestar; **to** ~ **sth from** (*drawer etc*) tirar algo de; (*person*) pegar algo de; **l** ~ **it that...** suponho que...; **to** ~ **after** *vt fus* parecer-se com; **to** ~ **apart** *vt* desmontar; **to** ~ **away** *vt* (*remove*) tirar; (*carry off*) levar; **to** ~ **back** *vt* (*return*) devolver; (*one's words*) retirar; **to** ~ **down** *vt* (*building*) demolir; (*letter etc*) tomar por escrito; **to** ~ **in** *vt* (*deceive*) enganar; (*understand*) compreender; (*include*) abranger; (*lodger*) acolher, receber; **to** ~ **off** *vi* (*AVIAT*) decolar // *vt* (*remove*) tirar;

(*imitate*) imitar; **to** ~ **on** *vt* (*work*) empreender; (*employee*) empregar; (*opponent*) desafiar; **to** ~ **out** *vt* tirar; (*remove*) extrair; **to** ~ **over** *vt* (*business*) tomar posse de // *vi*: **to** ~ **over from sb** suceder a alguém; **to** ~ **to** *vt fus* (*person*) simpatizar com; (*activity*) devotar-se a, viciar-se em; **to** ~ **up** *vt* (*a dress*) encurtar; (*occupy: time, space*) ocupar; (*engage in: hobby etc*) dedicar-se a; ~**away** *adj* (*food*) para levar; ~**-home pay** *n* salário líquido; ~**off** *n* (*AVIAT*) decolagem *f*; ~**over** *n* (*COMM*) absorção *f*, fusão *f*; ~**over bid** *n* oferta de compra.

takings ['teɪkɪŋz] *npl* (*COMM*) receita, renda.

talc [tælk] *n* (*also:* ~**um powder**) talco.

tale [teɪl] *n* (*story*) conto; (*account*) narrativa; **to tell** ~**s** (*fig: lie*) dizer mentiras.

talent ['tælnt] *n* talento, gênio; ~**ed** *adj* talentoso.

talk [tɔ:k] *n* (*gen*) conversa, fala; (*gossip*) mexerico, fofoca; (*conversation*) conversa, conversação *f* // *vi* (*speak*) falar; (*chatter*) bater papo, conversar; **to** ~ **about** falar sobre; **to** ~ **sb into doing sth** persuadir alguém de que deve fazer algo; **to** ~ **sb out of doing sth** dissuadir alguém de fazer algo; **to** ~ **shop** falar de assuntos profissionais; **to** ~ **over** *vt* discutir; ~**ative** *adj* loquaz, tagarela.

tall [tɔ:l] *adj* (*gen*) alto; (*tree*) grande; **to be 6 feet** ~ medir 6 pés, ter 6 pés de altura; ~**boy** *n* cômoda alta; ~**ness** *n* altura; ~ **story** *n* estória inverossímil.

tally ['tælɪ] *n* conta // *vi*: **to** ~ (**with**) conferir (com).

talon ['tælən] *n* garra.

tambourine [tæmbə'ri:n] *n* tamborim *m*, pandeiro.

tame [teɪm] *adj* (*mild*) manso; (*tamed*) domesticado; (*fig: story, style*) sem graça, insípido.

tamper ['tæmpə*] *vi*: **to** ~ **with** intrometer-se em.

tampon ['tæmpən] *n* tampão *m.*

tan [tæn] *n* (*also:* **sun**~) bronzeado // *vt* bronzear // *vi* bronzear-se // *adj* (*colour*) bronzeado, marrom claro.

tandem ['tændəm] *n* tandem *m.*

tang [tæŋ] *n* sabor *m* forte.

tangerine [tændʒə'ri:n] *n* tangerina, mexerica.

tangible ['tændʒəbl] *adj* tangível.

tangle ['tæŋgl] *n* emaranhado; **to get in(to) a** ~ meter-se num rolo.

tango ['tæŋgəu] *n* tango.

tank [tæŋk] *n* (*water* ~) tanque *m*; (*for fish*) aquário; (*MIL*) tanque *m.*

tanker ['tæŋkə*] *n* (*ship*) navio-tanque *m*; (*truck*) caminhão-tanque *m.*

tanned [tænd] *adj* (*skin*) moreno, bronzeado.

tantalizing   ['tæntəlaɪzɪŋ]   *adj* tentador(a).

tantamount ['tæntəmaunt] *adj:* ~ **to** equivalente a.

tantrum ['tæntrəm] *n* chilique *m*, acesso de raiva.

tap [tæp] *n* (*on sink etc*) torneira; (*gentle blow*) palmadinha; (*gas* ~) chave *f* // *vt* dar palmadinha em, bater de leve; (*resources*) utilizar, explorar; ~**-dancing** *n* sapateado.

tape [teɪp] *n* fita; (*also:* **magnetic** ~) fita magnética; (*sticky* ~) fita adesiva // *vt* (*record*) gravar (em fita); ~ **measure** *n* fita métrica, trena.

taper ['teɪpə*] *n* círio // *vi* afilar-se, estreitar-se.

tape recorder ['teɪprɪkɔːdə*] *n* gravador *m*.

tapered ['teɪpəd], **tapering** ['teɪpərɪŋ] *adj* afilado.

tapestry ['tæpɪstrɪ] *n* (*object*) tapete *m* de parede; (*art*) tapeçaria.

tapioca [tæpɪˈəukə] *n* tapioca.

tar [tɑː] *n* alcatrão *m*; (*on road*) piche *m*.

tarantula [təˈræntjulə] *n* tarântula.

target ['tɑːgɪt] *n* (*gen*) alvo, mira; ~ **practice** tiro ao alvo.

tariff ['tærɪf] *n* tarifa.

tarmac ['tɑːmæk] *n* (*on road*) macadame *m*; (*AVIAT*) pista de aterrissagem.

tarnish ['tɑːnɪʃ] *vt* perder o brilho.

tarpaulin [tɑːˈpɔːlɪn] *n* lona encerada *or* alcatroada.

tarragon ['tærəgon] *n* estragão *m*.

tart [tɑːt] *n* (*CULIN*) torta; (*col: pej: woman*) prostituta // *adj* (*flavour*) ácido, azedo.

tartan ['tɑːtn] *n* pano escocês axadrezado, tartan *m* // *adj* axadrezado.

tartar ['tɑːtə*] *n* (*on teeth*) tártaro; ~(**e**) **sauce** *n* molho tártaro.

task [tɑːsk] *n* tarefa, dever *m*; **to take to** ~ repreender; ~ **force** *n* (*MIL, POLICE*) força-tarefa.

tassel ['tæsl] *n* borla, pendão *m*.

taste [teɪst] *n* sabor *m*, gosto; (*also: after*~) gosto residual; (*sip*) golinho; (*fig: glimpse, idea*) amostra, idéia // *vt* provar // *vi:* **to** ~ **of** *or* **like** (*fish etc*) ter gosto de, saber a; **you can** ~ **the garlic (in it)** sente-se o gosto de alho; **can I have a** ~ **of this wine?** posso provar o vinho?; **to have a** ~ **for** sentir predileção por; **in good/bad** ~ de bom/mau gosto; ~**ful** *adj* de bom gosto; ~**fully** *adv* com bom gosto; ~**less** *adj* (*food*) insípido, insosso; (*remark*) de mau gosto; **tasty** *adj* saboroso, delicioso.

tattered ['tætəd] *adj see* **tatters**.

tatters ['tætəz] *npl:* **in** ~ (*also:* **tattered**) esfarrapado.

tattoo [təˈtuː] *n* tatuagem *f*; (*spectacle*) espetáculo (*Pt:* -ct-) militar // *vt* tatuar.

tatty ['tætɪ] *adj* (*col: worn*) surrado; (*: dirty*) enxovalhado.

taught [tɔːt] *pt, pp of* **teach**.

taunt [tɔːnt] *n* zombaria, escárnio // *vt* zombar de, mofar de.

Taurus ['tɔːrəs] *n* Touro.

taut [tɔːt] *adj* esticado, retesado.

tawdry ['tɔːdrɪ] *adj* de mau gosto, espalhafatoso, berrante.

tawny ['tɔːnɪ] *adj* moreno, trigueiro.

tax [tæks] *n* imposto // *vt* lançar imposto sobre, tributar; (*fig: test*) sobrecarregar; (*: patience*) esgotar; **direct** ~ contribuição *f* direta (*Pt:* -ct-); ~**ation** [-ˈseɪʃən] *n* impostos *mpl*; ~ **collector** *n* cobrador(a) *m/f* de impostos; ~**-free** *adj* isento de imposto.

taxi ['tæksɪ] *n* táxi *m* // *vi* (*AVIAT*) taxiar.

taxidermist ['tæksɪdəːmɪst] *n* taxidermista *m/f.*

taxi: ~ **driver** *n* motorista *m/f* de táxi; ~ **rank,** ~ **stand** *n* ponto de táxi.

tax: ~ **payer** *n* contribuinte *m/f*; ~ **return** *n* declaração *f* de rendimentos.

TB *abbr of* **tuberculosis**.

tea [tiː] *n* chá *m*; (*snack*) lanche *m*; **high** ~ jantar-lanche *m*; ~ **bag** *n* saquinho de chá; ~ **break** *n* pausa para o chá; ~**cake** *n* bolo para o chá.

teach [tiːtʃ], *pt, pp* **taught** *vt:* **to** ~ **sb sth,** ~ **sth to sb** ensinar algo a alguém // *vi* ensinar; (*be a teacher*) lecionar (*Pt:* -cc-); ~**er** *n* professor(a) *m/f*; ~**ing** *n* ensino.

tea: ~ **cosy** *n* coberta do bule, abafador *m*; ~**cup** *n* xícara de chá.

teak [tiːk] *n* (*madeira de*) teca.

tea leaves *npl* folhas *fpl* de chá.

team [tiːm] *n* (*SPORT*) time *m* (*Br*), equipa (*Pt*); (*group*) equipe *f* (*Br*), equipa (*Pt*); (*of animals*) parelha; ~**work** *n* trabalho de equipe.

teapot ['tiːpɔt] *n* bule *m* de chá.

tear [tɛə*] *n* rasgão *m*, ruptura // *n* [tɪə*] lágrima // (*vb: pt* **tore***, pp* **torn**) *vt* rasgar // *vi* rasgar-se, despedaçar-se; **in** ~**s** chorando, em lágrimas; **to burst into** ~**s** romper em lágrimas; **to** ~ **along** *vi* (*rush*) precipitar-se; ~**ful** *adj* choroso; ~ **gas** *n* gás *m* lacrimogênio.

tearoom ['tiːruːm] *n* salão *m* de chá.

tease [tiːz] *n* gozador(a) *m/f* // *vt* gozar (de).

tea: ~**spoon** *n* colher *f* de chá; (*also:* ~**spoonful:** *as measurement*) (*conteúdo de*) colher de chá.

teat [tiːt] *n* (*of bottle*) bico (de mamadeira).

tea: ~**time** *n* hora do chá; ~ **towel** *n* pano de prato.

technical ['tɛknɪkl] *adj* técnico; ~**ity** [-ˈkælɪtɪ] *n* detalhe *m* técnico; ~**ly** *adv* tecnicamente.

technician [tɛkˈnɪʃn] *n* técnico/a.

technique [tɛkˈniːk] *n* técnica.

technological [tɛknəˈlɔdʒɪkl] *adj* tecnológico; **technology** [-ˈnɔlədʒɪ] *n* tecnologia.

teddy (bear) ['tɛdɪ] *n* ursinho de pelúcia.

tedious ['tiːdɪəs] *adj* maçante, chato.

tee [tiː] *n* (*GOLF*) montículo.

teem [tiːm] *vi* abundar, pulular; **to** ~

with abundar em; **it is** ~**ing (with rain)** está chovendo a cântaros.

teenage ['ti:neɪdʒ] adj (fashions etc) de or para adolescentes; **teenager** n adolescente m/f or jovem m/f.

teens [ti:nz] npl: **to be in one's** ~ estar entre os 13 e 19 anos or na adolescência.

tee-shirt ['ti:ʃəːt] n = **T-shirt**.

teeter ['ti:tə*] vi balançar-se.

teeth [ti:θ] pl of **tooth**.

teethe [ti:ð] vi começar a ter dentes.

teething ['ti:ðɪŋ]: ~ **ring** n mastigador m para a dentição; ~ **troubles** npl (fig) dificuldades fpl iniciais.

teetotal ['ti:'təutl] adj (person) abstêmio.

telecommunications ['tɛlɪkəmju:nɪ'keɪʃənz] n telecomunicações fpl.

telegram ['tɛlɪgræm] n telegrama m.

telegraph ['tɛlɪgrɑːf] n telégrafo; ~**ic** [-'græfɪk] adj telegráfico; ~ **pole** n poste m de telégrafos.

telepathic [tɛlɪ'pæθɪk] adj telepático; **telepathy** [tə'lɛpəθɪ] n telepatia.

telephone ['tɛlɪfəun] n telefone m // vt (person) telefonar para, chamar ao telefone; (message) telefonar; ~ **booth**, ~ **box** n cabine f telefônica; ~ **call** n telefonema; ~ **directory** n lista telefônica; ~ **exchange** n centro telefônico; ~ **number** n número de telefone; **telephonist** [tə'lɛfənɪst] n telefonista m/f.

telephoto ['tɛlɪ'fəutəu] adj: ~ **lens** teleobjetivo (Pt: -ct-).

teleprinter ['tɛlɪprɪntə*] n teletipo.

telescope ['tɛlɪskəup] n telescópio; **telescopic** [-'skɔpɪk] adj telescópico.

televise ['tɛlɪvaɪz] vt televisar.

television ['tɛlɪvɪʒən] n televisão f; ~ **set** n (aparelho de) televisão f, televisor m.

telex ['tɛlɛks] n telex m.

tell [tɛl], pt, pp **told** vt dizer; (relate: story) contar; (distinguish): **to** ~ **sth from** distinguir algo de // vi (have effect) produzir efeito; **to** ~ **sb to do sth** mandar alguém fazer algo; **to** ~ **sb off** repreender or dar bronca em alguém; ~**er** n (in bank) caixa m/f; ~**ing** adj (impressive) impressionante; (remark, detail) revelador(a); ~**tale** adj (sign) denunciador(a), revelador(a).

telly ['tɛlɪ] n (col) abbr of **television**.

temerity [tə'mɛrɪtɪ] n temeridade f.

temper ['tɛmpə*] n (nature) temperamento; (mood) humor m; (bad ~) mau gênio; (fit of anger) cólera; (of child) birra // vt (moderate) moderar; **to be in a** ~ estar de mau humor; **to lose one's** ~ perder a paciência or a calma.

temperament ['tɛmprəmənt] n (nature) temperamento; ~**al** [-'mɛntl] adj temperamental.

temperance ['tɛmpərns] n moderação f; (in drinking) sobriedade f.

temperate ['tɛmprət] adj moderado; (climate) temperado.

temperature ['tɛmprətʃə*] n temperatura; **to have** or **run a** ~ ter febre.

tempered ['tɛmpəd] adj (steel) temperado.

tempest ['tɛmpɪst] n tempestade f.

temple ['tɛmpl] n (building) templo; (ANAT) têmpora.

tempo ['tɛmpəu], pl ~**s** or **tempi** [-pi:] n tempo; (fig: of life etc) ritmo.

temporal ['tɛmpərl] adj temporal.

temporarily ['tɛmpərərɪlɪ] adv temporariamente.

temporary ['tɛmpərəri] adj temporário, efêmero; (passing) transitório; (worker) provisório.

tempt [tɛmpt] vt tentar; **to** ~ **sb into doing sth** tentar or induzir alguém a fazer algo; ~**ation** [-'teɪʃən] n tentação f; ~**ing** adj tentador(a).

ten [tɛn] num dez.

tenable ['tɛnəbl] adj sustentável.

tenacious [tə'neɪʃəs] adj tenaz; **tenacity** [-'næsɪtɪ] n tenacidade f.

tenancy ['tɛnənsɪ] n aluguel m; (of house) locação f; **tenant** n (rent-payer) inquilino/a, locatário/a; (occupant) ocupante m/f.

tend [tɛnd] vt cuidar de // vi: **to** ~ **to do sth** tender a fazer algo.

tendency ['tɛndənsɪ] n tendência.

tender ['tɛndə*] adj macio, tenro; (delicate) delicado, meigo; (gentle) terno; (sore) sensível, dolorido; (affectionate) carinhoso, afetuoso (Pt: -ct-); (meat) tenro // n (COMM: offer) oferta, proposta; (money): **legal** ~ moeda corrente or legal // vt oferecer; ~**ize** vt (CULIN) amaciar; ~**ness** n ternura; (of meat) maciez f.

tendon ['tɛndən] n tendão m.

tenement ['tɛnəmənt] n conjunto habitacional.

tennis ['tɛnɪs] n tênis m; ~ **ball** n bola de tênis; ~ **court** n quadra de tênis; ~ **racket** n raquete f de tênis.

tenor ['tɛnə*] n (MUS) tenor m.

tenpin bowling ['tɛnpɪn-] n boliche m com 10 paus.

tense [tɛns] adj tenso; (stretched) estirado, esticado; (stiff) rígido, teso // n (LING) tempo; ~**ness** n tensão f.

tension ['tɛnʃən] n tensão f.

tent [tɛnt] n tenda, barraca.

tentacle ['tɛntəkl] n tentáculo.

tentative ['tɛntətɪv] adj (conclusion) provisório, experimental.

tenterhooks ['tɛntəhuks] npl: **on** ~ em suspense.

tenth [tɛnθ] adj décimo.

tent: ~ **peg** n estaca; ~ **pole** n pau m.

tenuous ['tɛnjuəs] adj tênue.

tenure ['tɛnjuə*] n posse f; (time) ocupação f.

tepid ['tɛpɪd] adj tépido, morno.

term [təːm] n (limit) limite m; (COMM) prazo; (word) termo; (period) período; (SCOL) trimestre m // vt denominar; ~**s** npl (conditions) condições fpl; (COMM) cláusulas *fpl*, termos *mpl*; **in the short/long ~** a curto/longo prazo; **to be on good ~s with sb** dar-se bem com alguém; **to come to ~s with** (*person*) chegar a um acordo com; (*problem*) adaptar-se a.

terminal ['tɔːmɪnl] *adj* terminal; (*disease*) mortal, letal // *n* (ELEC) borne *m*; (*also:* **air ~**) terminal *m*; (*also:* **coach ~**) estação *f* terminal.

terminate ['tɔːmɪneɪt] *vt* terminar, pôr fim a // *vi:* **to ~ in** acabar em; **termination** [-'neɪʃən] *n* término; (*of contract*) conclusão *f*.

terminology [tɔːmɪ'nɔlədʒɪ] *n* terminologia, nomenclatura.

terminus ['tɔːmɪnəs], *pl* **-mini** [-mɪnaɪ] *n* término, terminal *m*.

termite ['tɔːmaɪt] *n* cupim *m*.

terrace ['tɛrəs] *n* terraço; (*row of houses*) renque *m* de casas; **the ~s** (SPORT) a geral; **~ed** *adj* (*house*) ladeado por outras casas; (*garden*) em dois níveis.

terrain [tɛ'reɪn] *n* terreno.

terrible ['tɛrɪbl] *adj* terrível, horroroso; **terribly** *adv* terrivelmente; (*very badly*) pessimamente.

terrier ['tɛrɪə*] *n* terrier *m*.

terrific [tɔ'rɪfɪk] *adj* terrível, magnífico; (*wonderful*) maravilhoso.

terrify ['tɛrɪfaɪ] *vt* aterrorizar.

territorial [tɛrɪ'tɔːrɪəl] *adj* territorial.

territory ['tɛrɪtərɪ] *n* território.

terror ['tɛrə*] *n* terror *m*; **~ism** *n* terrorismo; **~ist** *n* terrorista *m/f*; **~ize** *vt* aterrorizar.

terse [tɔːs] *adj* (*style*) conciso, sucinto; (*reply*) brusco.

test [tɛst] *n* (*trial, check*) prova, ensaio; (: *of goods in factory*) controle *m*; (*of courage etc, CHEM*) prova; (MED) exame *m*; (*exam*) teste *m*, prova; (*also:* **driving ~**) exame de motorista // *vt* testar, pôr à prova.

testament ['tɛstəmənt] *n* testamento; **the Old/New T~** o Velho/Novo Testamento.

testicle ['tɛstɪkl] *n* testículo.

testify ['tɛstɪfaɪ] *vi* (LAW) prestar declaração, testemunhar; **to ~ to sth** afirmar or asseverar algo.

testimonial [tɛstɪ'məunɪəl] *n* (*reference*) carta de recomendação; (*gift*) obséquio, tributo.

testimony ['tɛstɪmənɪ] *n* (LAW) testemunho, depoimento.

test: ~ match *n* (CRICKET, RUGBY) jogo internacional; **~ pilot** *n* piloto de prova; **~ tube** *n* proveta, tubo de ensaio.

testy ['tɛstɪ] *adj* rabugento, irritável.

tetanus ['tɛtənəs] *n* tétano.

tether ['tɛðə*] *vt* prender com corda // *n:* **at the end of one's ~** a ponto de perder a paciência or as estribeiras.

text [tɛkst] *n* texto; **~book** *n* livro didático (*Pt:* -ct-), compêndio.

textiles ['tɛkstaɪlz] *npl* têxteis *mpl*, tecidos *mpl*.

texture ['tɛkstʃə*] *n* textura.

Thai [taɪ] *adj, n* tailandês/esa *m/f*; **~land** *n* Tailândia.

Thames [tɛmz] *n:* **the ~** o Tâmisa *m*.

than [ðæn, ðən] *conj* (*do*) que; (*with numerals*): **more ~ 10/once** mais de 10/uma vez; **I have more/less ~ you** tenho mais/menos (do) que você.

thank [θæŋk] *vt* agradecer; **~ you (very much)** muito obrigado/a; **~s** *npl* agradecimento, graças *fpl*; **~s to** *prep* graças a; **~ful** *adj:* **~ful (for)** agradecido (por); **~less** *adj* ingrato; **Thanksgiving (Day)** *n* dia *m* de ação (*Pt:* -çç-) de graças.

that [ðæt, ðət] *conj* que // *det* esse/essa; (*more remote*) aquele/aquela // *pron* esse/essa, aquele/aquela; (*neuter*) isso, aquilo; (*relative*) que, quem, o qual/a qual *etc*; (*with time*): **on the day ~ he came** no dia em que ele veio // *adv:* **~ high** dessa altura, até dessa altura; **it's about ~ high** é mais ou menos dessa altura; **~ one** esse/essa; **what's ~?** o que é isso?; **who's ~?** quem é?; **is ~ you?** é você?; (*formal*) é o/a senhor(a)?; **~'s what he said** foi isso o que ele disse; **all ~** tudo isso; **I can't work ~ much** não posso trabalhar tanto.

thatched [θætʃt] *adj* (*roof*) de sapê; **~ cottage** chalé *m* com telhado de sapê or de colmo.

thaw [θɔː] *n* degelo // *vi* (*ice*) derreter-se; (*food*) descongelar-se // *vt* (*food*) descongelar.

the [ðiː, ðə] *def art* o/a; (*pl*) os/as; **~ sooner ~ better** quanto mais cedo, melhor.

theatre, theater (US) ['θɪətə*] *n* teatro; **~-goer** *n* freqüentador(a) *m/f* de teatro.

theatrical [θɪ'ætrɪkl] *adj* teatral.

theft [θɛft] *n* roubo.

their [ðɛə*] *adj* seu/sua; **~s** *pron* (o) seu/(a) sua; **a friend of ~s** um amigo seu/deles.

them [ðɛm, ðəm] *pron* (*direct*) os/as; (*indirect*) lhes; (*stressed, after prep*) a eles/a elas; **I see ~** eu os vejo; **give ~ the book** dê o livro a eles.

theme [θiːm] *n* tema *m*; **~ song** tema musical.

themselves [ðəm'sɛlvz] *pl pron* (*subject*) eles mesmos/elas mesmas; (*complement*) se; (*after prep*) si (mesmos/as).

then [ðɛn] *adv* (*at that time*) então; (*next*) em seguida; (*later*) logo, depois; (*and also*) além disso // *conj* (*therefore*) então, nesse caso, portanto // *adj:* **the ~ president** o então presidente; **from ~ on** a partir de então.

theological [θɪə'lɔdʒɪkl] *adj* teológico; **theology** [θɪ'ɔlədʒɪ] *n* teologia.

theorem ['θɪərəm] *n* teorema *m*.

theoretical [θɪə'rɛtɪkl] *adj* teórico; **theorize** ['θɪəraɪz] *vi* teorizar, elaborar uma teoria; **theory** ['θɪərɪ] *n* teoria.

therapeutic(al) [θɛrə'pju:tɪk(l)] *adj* terapêutico.

therapist [ˈθɛrəpɪst] *n* terapeuta *m/f*; **therapy** *n* terapia.

there [ðɛə*] *adv* aí, ali, lá; ~, ~! calma!; it's ~ está aí; ~ is, ~ are há; ~ he is lá está ele; on/in ~ lá *or* aí encima/dentro; ~abouts *adv* por aí; ~after *adv* depois disso; ~fore *adv* portanto; ~'s = ~ is; ~ has.

thermal [ˈθə:ml] *adj* termal, térmico.

thermometer [θəˈmɒmɪtə*] *n* termômetro.

Thermos [ˈθə:mɒs] *n* garrafa térmica (*Br*), termo (*Pt*).

thermostat [ˈθə:məʊstæt] *n* termostato.

thesaurus [θɪˈsɔ:rəs] *n* tesouro.

these [ði:z] *pl det, pron* estes/estas.

thesis [ˈθi:sɪs], *pl* **-ses** [-si:z] *n* tese *f*.

they [ðeɪ] *pl pron* eles/elas; (*stressed*) eles (mesmos)/elas (mesmas); ~ **say that...** (*it is said that*) diz-se que..., dizem que...; ~'d = **they had; they would**; ~'ll = **they shall, they will**; ~'re = **they are**; ~'ve = **they have**.

thick [θɪk] *adj* espesso, grosso; (*fat*) gordo; (*dense*) denso, compacto; (*stupid*) estúpido, bronco // *n*: in the ~ of the battle em plena batalha; it's 20 cm ~ tem 20 cm de espessura; ~en *vi* espessar-se // *vt* (*sauce etc*) engrossar; ~ness *n* espessura, grossura; ~set *adj* troncudo; ~skinned *adj* (*fig*) insensível, indiferente.

thief [θi:f], *pl* **thieves** [θi:vz] *n* ladrão/ladra *m/f*.

thieving [ˈθi:vɪŋ] *n* roubo, furto.

thigh [θaɪ] *n* coxa.

thimble [ˈθɪmbl] *n* dedal *m*.

thin [θɪn] *adj* (*gen*) magro; (*watery*) aguado; (*light*) tênue; (*hair, crowd*) escasso, ralo; (*fog*) pouco denso // *vt*: to ~ (**down**) (*sauce, paint*) diluir.

thing [θɪŋ] *n* (*gen*) coisa; (*object*) objeto (*Pt*: -ct-), artigo; (*matter*) assunto, negócio; (*mania*) mania; ~s *npl* (*belongings*) pertences *mpl*; the best ~ would be to... o melhor seria...; how are ~s? como vai?, tudo bem?

think [θɪŋk], *pt, pp* **thought** *vi* pensar // *vt* pensar, achar, supor; (*imagine*) imaginar; what did you ~ of them? o que você achou deles?; to ~ about sth/sb pensar em algo/alguém; I'll ~ about it vou pensar sobre isso; to ~ of doing sth pensar em fazer algo; I ~ so/not acho que sim/não; to ~ well of sb fazer bom juízo de alguém; to ~ over *vt* refletir (*Pt*: -ct-) sobre, meditar sobre; to ~ up *vt* engendrar; ~ing *adj* pensativo.

thinly [ˈθɪnlɪ] *adv* (*cut*) em fatias finas; (*spread*) numa camada fina.

thinness [ˈθɪnnɪs] *n* magreza.

third [θə:d] *adj* terceiro/a // *n* terceiro/a; (*fraction*) terço; (*SCOL: degree*) terceira categoria; ~ly *adv* em terceiro lugar; ~ party insurance *n* seguro contra

terceiros; ~-rate *adj* ordinário, reles *inv*; the T~ World *n* o Terceiro Mundo.

thirst [θə:st] *n* sede *f*; ~y *adj* (*person*) sedento, com sede; to be ~y estar com sede.

thirteen [ˈθə:'ti:n] *num* treze.

thirty [ˈθə:tɪ] *num* trinta.

this [ðɪs] *det* este/esta // *pron* este/esta; (*neuter*) isto; ~ is what he said foi isto o que ele disse; ~ high dessa altura.

thistle [ˈθɪsl] *n* cardo.

thong [θɒŋ] *n* correia, tira de couro.

thorn [θɔ:n] *n* espinho; ~y *adj* espinhoso.

thorough [ˈθʌrə] *adj* (*search*) minucioso; (*knowledge, research*) profundo; ~bred *adj* (*horse*) de puro sangue; ~fare *n* via, passagem *f*; "no ~fare" "passagem proibida"; ~ly *adv* minuciosamente, profundamente, a fundo.

those [ðəʊz] *pl pron, det* esses/essas; (*more remote*) aqueles/aquelas.

though [ðəʊ] *conj* embora, se bem que // *adv* no entanto.

thought [θɔ:t] *pt, pp of* **think** // *n* pensamento; (*opinion*) opinião *f*; (*intention*) intenção *f*; ~ful *adj* pensativo; (*considerate*) atencioso; ~less *adj* descuidado, desatento.

thousand [ˈθaʊzənd] *num* mil; **two ~** dois mil; ~s (of) milhares *mpl* (de); ~th *adj* milésimo.

thrash [θræʃ] *vt* surrar, malhar; (*defeat*) derrotar; to ~ **about** *vi* debater-se; to ~ **out** *vt* discutir exaustivamente.

thread [θrɛd] *n* fio, linha; (*of screw*) rosca // *vt* (*needle*) enfiar; ~bare *adj* surrado, puído.

threat [θrɛt] *n* ameaça; ~en *vi* ameaçar // *vt*: to ~en sb with sth/to do ameaçar alguém com algo/de fazer.

three [θri:] *num* três; ~-dimensional *adj* tridimensional, em três dimensões; ~fold *adv*: to increase ~fold triplicar; ~-piece suit *n* terno (3 peças) (*Bt*), fato de 3 peças (*Pt*); ~-piece suite *n* conjunto de sofá e duas poltronas; ~-ply *adj* (*wool*) triple, com três fios; ~-wheeler *n* (*car*) carro de três rodas.

thresh [θrɛʃ] *vt* (*AGR*) debulhar.

threshold [ˈθrɛʃhəʊld] *n* limiar *m*.

threw [θru:] *pt of* **throw**.

thrift [θrɪft] *n* economia, poupança; ~y *adj* econômico, frugal.

thrill [θrɪl] *n* (*excitement*) emoção *f*; (*shudder*) estremecimento // *vt* emocionar, vibrar; to be ~ed (*with gift etc*) estar emocionado; ~er *n* novela/filme *m* de suspense.

thrive [θraɪv], *pt* **thrived** *or* **throve** [θrəʊv], *pp* **thrived** *or* **thriven** [ˈθrɪvn] *vi* (*grow*) crescer; (*do well*) prosperar, florescer; **thriving** *adj* próspero.

throat [θrəʊt] *n* garganta; to have a sore ~ estar com dor de garganta.

throb [θrɒb] *n* (*of heart*) batida; (*of*

engine) vibração f // vi bater, palpitar; (*pain*) dar pontadas.

throes [θrəuz] *npl*: **in the ~ of** no meio de.

thrombosis [θrɔm'bəusɪs] *n* trombose f.

throne [θrəun] *n* trono.

throttle ['θrɔtl] *n* (*AUT*) acelerador m // vt estrangular.

through [θru:] *prep* por, através de; (*time*) durante; (*by means of*) por meio de, por intermédio de; (*owing to*) devido a // *adj* (*ticket, train*) direto (*Pt*: -ct-) // *adv* completamente, do começo ao fim; **to put sb ~ to sb** (*TEL*) ligar alguém com alguém; **to be ~** (*TEL*) estar na linha; (*have finished*) acabar; "**no ~ way**" "rua sem saída"; **~out** *prep* (*place*) por todas as partes; (*time*) durante todo, todo // *adv* por ou em todas as partes.

throw [θrəu] *n* arremesso, tiro; (*SPORT*) lançamento // vt, pt **threw**, pp **thrown** jogar, atirar; (*SPORT*) lançar; (*rider*) derrubar; (*fig*) desconcertar; **to ~ a party** dar uma festa; **to ~ away** vt desperdiçar; **to ~ in** vt (*SPORT*) pôr em jogo; **to ~ off** vt desfazer-se de; **to ~ out** vt expulsar; **to ~ up** vi vomitar; **~away** *adj* descartável, para jogar fora.

thru [θru:] (*US*) = **through**.

thrush [θrʌʃ] *n* tordo; (*MED*: *in mouth*) sapinho; (: *in vagina*) infecção f vaginal.

thrust [θrʌst] *n* impulso; (*TECH*) empuxo // vt, pt, pp **thrust** empurrar; (*push in*) enfiar, meter.

thud [θʌd] *n* baque m, som m surdo.

thug [θʌg] *n* (*criminal*) criminoso/a m/f; (*pej*) facínora m/f.

thumb [θʌm] *n* (*ANAT*) polegar m; (*col*) dedão m // vt (*book*) folhear; **to ~ a lift** pegar carona (*Br*), arranjar uma boleia (*Pt*); **~tack** *n* (*US*) percevejo.

thump [θʌmp] *n* murro, pancada; (*sound*) baque m // vt dar um murro em, golpear.

thunder ['θʌndə*] *n* (*gen*) trovão m; (*sudden noise*) trovoada; (*of applause etc*) estrondo // vi trovejar; (*train etc*): **to ~ past** passar como um raio; **~bolt** *n* raio; **~clap** *n* estampido do trovão; **~storm** *n* tempestade f com trovoada, temporal m; **~struck** *adj* estupefato (*Pt*: -ct-); **~y** *adj* tempestuoso.

Thursday ['θə:zdɪ] *n* quinta-feira.

thus [ðʌs] *adv* assim, desta maneira.

thwart [θwɔ:t] vt frustrar.

thyme [taɪm] *n* tomilho.

thyroid ['θaɪrɔɪd] *n* tireóide f.

tiara [tɪ'ɑːrə] *n* tiara, diadema m.

tic [tɪk] *n* tic m.

tick [tɪk] *n* (*sound: of clock*) tique-taque m; (*mark*) tique m, marca; (*ZOOL*) carrapato; (*col*): **in a ~** num instante // vi fazer tique-taque // vt marcar; **to ~ off** vt assinalar; (*person*) censurar.

ticket ['tɪkɪt] *n* passagem f, bilhete m; (*for cinema*) entrada; (*in shop: on goods*) etiqueta; (*for library*) cartão m; **~**

collector *n* revisor m; **~ office** *n* bilheteria (*Br*), bilheteira (*Pt*).

tickle ['tɪkl] *n* cócegas fpl // vt fazer cócegas; **ticklish** *adj* coceguento.

tidal ['taɪdl] *adj* de maré; **~ wave** *n* macaréu m, onda gigantesca.

tiddlywinks ['tɪdlɪwɪŋks] *n* jogo de fichas.

tide [taɪd] *n* maré f; (*fig*: *of events*) marcha, curso.

tidiness ['taɪdɪnɪs] *n* (*good order*) ordem f; (*neatness*) asseio, limpeza.

tidy ['taɪdɪ] *adj* (*room*) arrumado; (*dress, work*) limpo; (*person*) bem arrumado // vt (*also*: **~ up**) pôr em ordem, arrumar.

tie [taɪ] *n* (*string etc*) fita, corda; (*also*: **neck~**) gravata; (*fig*: *link*) vínculo, laço; (*SPORT*: *draw*) empate m // vt (*gen*) amarrar, atar // vi (*SPORT*) empatar; **to ~ in a bow** dar um laço; **to ~ a knot in sth** dar um nó em algo; **to ~ down** vt amarrar; **to ~ sb down to** obrigar alguém a; **to ~ up** vt (*parcel*) embrulhar; (*dog*) prender; (*boat*) amarrar; (*arrangements*) concluir; **to be ~d up** (*busy*) estar ocupado; **~-up** *n* (*US*) engarrafamento.

tier [tɪə*] *n* fileira; (*of cake*) camada.

tiger ['taɪgə*] *n* tigre m.

tight [taɪt] *adj* (*rope*) esticado, firme; (*money*) escasso; (*clothes*) justo; (*budget, programme*) apertado; (*col*: *drunk*) bêbado // *adv* (*squeeze*) bem forte; (*shut*) hermeticamente; **~s** *npl* meia-calça sg; (*for gym*) malha sg; **~en** vt (*rope*) esticar; (*screw*) apertar // vi apertar-se, esticar-se; **~-fisted** *adj* pão-duro; **~ly** *adv* (*grasp*) firmemente; **~-rope** *n* corda esticada para acrobacias.

tile [taɪl] *n* (*on roof*) telha; (*on floor*) ladrilho; (*on wall*) azulejo, ladrilho; **~d** *adj* ladrilhado.

till [tɪl] *n* caixa (registradora) // vt (*land*) cultivar // *prep, conj* = **until**.

tiller ['tɪlə*] *n* (*NAUT*) cana do leme.

tilt [tɪlt] vt inclinar // vi inclinar-se.

timber ['tɪmbə*] *n* (*material*) madeira; (*trees*) mata, floresta.

time [taɪm] *n* tempo; (*epoch: often pl*) época; (*by clock*) hora; (*moment*) momento; (*occasion*) vez f; (*MUS*) compasso // vt (*gen*) calcular ou medir o tempo de; (*race*) cronometrar; (*remark etc*) escolher o momento para; **a long ~** muito tempo; **for the ~ being** por enquanto; **from ~ to ~** de vez em quando; **in ~** (*soon enough*) a tempo; (*after some time*) com o tempo; (*MUS*) no compasso; **in a week's ~** dentro de uma semana; **on ~** na hora; **5 ~s 5 is 25** 5 vezes 5 são 25; **what ~ is it?** que horas são?; **to have a good ~** divertir-se, distrair-se; **~ bomb** *n* bomba de ação retardada; **~keeper** *n* (*SPORT*) cronometrista m/f; **~less** *adj* eterno; **limit** *n* (*gen*) limite m de tempo; (*COMM*) prazo; **~ly** *adj* oportuno; **~ off** *n* tempo livre; **timer** *n* (*in kitchen*) relógio programador, timer m; **~ switch** *n*

interruptor m; ~**table** n horário; ~
zone n fuso horário.

timid ['tımıd] adj tímido.

timing ['taımıŋ] n (SPORT)
cronometragem f; (gen) escolha do
momento; **the ~ of his resignation** o
momento que escolheu para se demitir.

timpani ['tımpənı] npl tímbalos mpl.

tin [tın] n estanho; (also: ~ **plate**) folha-
de-flandres f; (can) lata; ~ **foil** n papel
m de estanho.

tinge [tındʒ] n matiz m, toque m // vt:
~**d with** tingido de.

tingle ['tıŋgl] n comichão f // vi sentir
comichão.

tinker ['tıŋkə*] n funileiro; (gipsy)
cigano; **to ~ with** vt mexer com.

tinkle ['tıŋkl] vi tilintar, tinir // n (col):
to give sb a ~ dar uma ligada para
alguém.

tinned [tınd] adj (food) em lata, em
conserva.

tin opener ['tınəupnə*] n abridor m de
latas (Br), abre-latas m inv (Pt).

tinsel ['tınsl] n ouropel m.

tint [tınt] n matiz m; (for hair) tonalidade
f, tom m.

tiny ['taını] adj pequenino, diminuto.

tip [tıp] n (end) ponta; (gratuity) gorjeta;
(for rubbish) depósito; (advice) dica // vt
(waiter) dar uma gorjeta a; (tilt) inclinar;
(overturn: also: ~ **over**) virar,
emborcar; (empty: also: ~ **out**) esvaziar,
entornar; ~**-off** n (hint) aviso; ~**ped**
adj (cigarette) com filtro.

tipsy ['tıpsı] adj embriagado, tocado, alto,
alegre.

tiptoe ['tıptəu] n: **on ~** na ponta dos
pés.

tiptop ['tıp'tɔp] adj: **in ~ condition** em
perfeitas condições.

tire ['taıə*] n (US) = **tyre** // vt cansar //
vi (gen) cansar-se; (become bored)
chatear-se; ~**d** adj cansado; **to be ~d
of sth** estar farto or cheio de algo;
tiredness n cansaço; ~**less** adj
incansável; ~**some** adj enfadonho,
chato; **tiring** adj cansativo.

tissue ['tıʃu:] n tecido; (paper
handkerchief) lenço de papel; ~ **paper** n
papel m de seda.

tit [tıt] n (bird) passarinho; **to give ~
for tat** pagar na mesma moeda.

titbit ['tıtbıt] n (food) guloseima; (news)
boato, rumor m.

titillate ['tıtıleıt] vt titilar, excitar.

titivate ['tıtıveıt] vt arrumar.

title ['taıtl] n título; ~ **deed** n (LAW)
título de propriedade; ~ **role** n papel m
principal.

titter ['tıtə*] vi rir-se com riso sufocado.

titular ['tıtjulə*] adj (in name only)
nominal, titular.

to [tu:, tə] prep a, para; (towards) para; (of
time) até; (of) de; **give it ~ me** me dá
isso; **the key ~ the front door** a
chave da porta da frente; **the main
thing is ~...** o principal é...; **to go ~**

France/school ir à França/ao colégio;
a quarter ~ 5 quinze para as 5 (Br), 5
minos um quarto (Pt); **pull/push the
door ~** puxar/empurrar a porta; **to go
~ and fro** ir de um lado para outro.

toad [təud] n sapo; ~**stool** n chapéu-de-
cobra m, cogumelo venenoso.

toast [təust] n (CULIN: also: **piece of ~**)
torrada; (drink, speech) brinde m // vt
(CULIN) torrar; (drink to) brindar; ~**er** n
torradeira.

tobacco [tə'bækəu] n tabaco, fumo;
~**nist** n vendedor(a) m/f de tabaco;
~**nist's (shop)** n charutaria; (Pt)
tabacaria.

toboggan [tə'bɔgən] n tobogã m.

today [tə'deı] adv, n (also fig) hoje m.

toddler ['tɔdlə*] n criança que começa a
andar.

toddy ['tɔdı] n ponche m quente.

toe [təu] n dedo do pé; (of shoe) bico; **to
~ the line** (fig) conformar-se, cumprir
as obrigações; ~**nail** n unha do pé.

toffee ['tɔfı] n puxa-puxa m, bala "tofee";
~ **apple** n maçã f do amor.

toga ['təugə] n toga.

together [tə'gɛðə*] adv juntos; (at same
time) ao mesmo tempo; ~ **with** prep
junto com; ~**ness** n companheirismo,
camaradagem f.

toil [tɔıl] n faina, labuta // vi labutar,
trabalhar arduamente.

toilet ['tɔılət] n (lavatory) banheiro (Br),
casa de banho (Pt) // cmp (bag, soap etc)
de toalete; ~ **bowl** n vaso sanitário; ~
paper n papel m higiênico; ~**ries** npl
artigos mpl de toalete; (make-up etc)
artigos de toucador; ~ **roll** n rolo de
papel higiênico; ~ **water** n água de
colônia.

token ['təukən] n (sign) sinal m, símbolo,
prova; (souvenir) lembrança; (voucher)
cupom m; **book/record ~** vale m para
comprar livros/discos.

told [təuld] pt, pp of **tell**.

tolerable ['tɔlərəbl] adj (bearable)
suportável; (fairly good) passável.

tolerance ['tɔlərns] n (also: TECH)
tolerância; **tolerant** adj: **tolerant of**
tolerante com.

tolerate ['tɔləreıt] vt tolerar; **toleration**
[-'reıʃən] n tolerância.

toll [təul] n (of casualties) número de
baixas; (tax, charge) pedágio (Br),
portagem f (Pt) // vi (bell) dobrar,
tanger; ~**bridge** n ponte f de pedágio
(Br), ponte de portagem (Pt).

tomato [tə'mɑːtəu], pl ~**es** n tomate m.

tomb [tu:m] n tumba.

tombola [tɔm'bəulə] n tômbola.

tomboy ['tɔmbɔı] n menina moleque f.

tombstone ['tu:mstəun] n lápide f.

tomcat ['tɔmkæt] n gato.

tomorrow [tə'mɔrəu] adv, n (also fig)
amanhã; **the day after ~** depois de
amanhã; ~ **morning** amanhã de
manhã.

ton [tʌn] n tonelada; **~s of** (col) um monte de, uma pá de.

tone [təun] n tom m // vi dar o tom, harmonizar; **to ~ down** vt (colour, criticism) suavizar; (sound) baixar; (MUS) entoar; **to ~ up** vt (muscles) fortalecer; **~-deaf** adj que não tem ouvido.

tongs [tɔŋz] npl (for coal) tenaz fsg; (for hair) pinças fpl.

tongue [tʌŋ] n língua; **~ in cheek** adv ironicamente; **~-tied** adv (fig) calado; **~-twister** n expressão f difícil de pronunciar.

tonic ['tɔnɪk] n (MED) tônico; (MUS) tônica; (also: **~ water**) (água) tônica.

tonight [tə'naɪt] adv, n esta noite, hoje à noite.

tonnage ['tʌnɪdʒ] n (NAUT) tonelagem f.

tonsil ['tɔnsl] n amígdala, amídala; **~litis** [-'laɪtɪs] n amigdalite f, amidalite f.

too [tu:] adv (excessively) demasiado, demais; (very) muito; (also) também; **~ much** adv demais; **~ many** det demasiados/as; **~ good** demasiado bom, bom demais.

took [tuk] pt of **take**.

tool [tu:l] n ferramenta; **~ box** n caixa de ferramentas.

toot [tu:t] n (of horn) buzinada; (of whistle) apito // vi (with car-horn) buzinar, tocar a buzina.

tooth [tu:θ], pl **teeth** n (ANAT, TECH) dente m; (molar) molar m; **~ache** n dor f de dente; **~brush** n escova de dente; **~paste** n pasta de dente; **~pick** n palito.

top [tɔp] n (of mountain) cume m, cimo; (of head) cocuruto; (of ladder) o alto; (of cupboard, table) superfície f, topo; (lid: of box, jar, bottle) tampa; (of list etc) cabeça m; (toy) pião m // adj mais alto, máximo; (in rank) principal, superior; (best) melhor // vt (exceed) exceder; (be first in) estar à cabeça de; **on ~ of** sobre, em cima de; **from ~ to toe** da cabeça aos pés; **to ~ up** vt encher; **~coat** n sobretudo; **~ hat** n cartola; **~-heavy** adj (object) desequilibrado.

topic ['tɔpɪk] n tópico, assunto; **~al** adj atual (Pt: -ct-).

top: ~less adj (bather etc) topless, sem a parte superior do biquíni; **~-level** adj (talks) de alto nível; **~most** adj supremo, o mais alto.

topple ['tɔpl] vt derrubar, desabar // vi cair para frente, ruir.

topsy-turvy ['tɔpsɪ'tə:vɪ] adj, adv de pernas para o ar, confuso, às avessas.

torch [tɔ:tʃ] n tocha, archote m; (electric) lanterna.

tore [tɔ:*] pt of **tear**.

torment n ['tɔ:mɛnt] n tormento, suplício // vt [tɔ:'mɛnt] atormentar; (fig: annoy) chatear, aborrecer.

torn [tɔ:n] pp of **tear**.

tornado [tɔ:'neɪdəu], pl **~es** n tornado.

torpedo [tɔ:'pi:dəu], pl **~es** n torpedo.

torrent ['tɔrnt] n torrente f, corrente f; **~ial** [-'rɛnʃl] adj torrencial.

torso ['tɔ:səu] n torso.

tortoise ['tɔ:təs] n tartaruga; **~shell** ['tɔ:təʃɛl] adj de tartaruga.

tortuous ['tɔ:tjuəs] adj tortuoso.

torture ['tɔ:tʃə*] n tortura // vt torturar; (fig) atormentar.

Tory ['tɔ:rɪ] adj, n conservador(a) m/f.

toss [tɔs] vt atirar, arremessar; (head) sacudir, lançar para trás; **to ~ a coin** tirar cara ou coroa; **to ~ up for sth** jogar cara ou coroa por algo; **to ~ and turn in bed** virar de um lado para o outro na cama.

tot [tɔt] n (drink) copinho, golinho; (child) criancinha f.

total ['təutl] adj total, inteiro // n total m, soma f // vt (add up) somar; (amount to) montar a.

totalitarian [təutælɪ'tɛərɪən] adj totalitário.

totem pole ['təutəm-] n mastro totêmico.

totter ['tɔtə*] vi cambalear-se.

touch [tʌtʃ] n (gen) toque m, tato (Pt: -ct-); (contact) contato (Pt: -ct-); (FOOTBALL): **in ~** fora do campo // vt (gen) tocar, apalpar; (emotionally) comover; **a ~ of** (fig) uma pitada de, um pouquinho de; **to get in ~ with sb** entrar em conta(c)to com alguém; **to lose ~** (friends) perder o conta(c)to; **to ~ on** vt fus (topic) aludir a, fazer menção de; **to ~ up** vt (paint) retocar; **~-and-go** adj arriscado; **~down** n aterrissagem f (Br), aterragem f (Pt); (on sea) amerissagem f (Br), amaragem f (Pt); **~ed** adj comovido; (col) tocado, muito louco; **~ing** adj comovedor(a); **~line** n (SPORT) linha de fundo; **~y** adj (person) suscetível, sensitivo.

tough [tʌf] adj (gen) duro, forte; (difficult) difícil; (resistant) resistente; (person) tenaz, obstinado; (: pej) rude // n (gangster etc) bandido, capanga m; **~en** vt endurecer; **~ness** n dureza, dificuldade f; resistência, tenacidade f.

toupee ['tu:peɪ] n peruca.

tour ['tuə*] n viagem f, excursão f; (also: **package ~**) excursão organizada; (of town, museum) visita // vt excursionar por; **~ing** n viagens fpl turísticas, turismo.

tourism ['tuərɪzm] n turismo.

tourist ['tuərɪst] n turista m/f // cmp turístico; **~ office** n agência de turismo.

tournament ['tuənəmənt] n torneio.

tousled ['tauzld] adj (hair) despenteado.

tout [taut] vi: **to ~ for** angariar clientes para // n: **ticket ~** cambista m/f.

tow [təu] vt rebocar; **'on ~'** (AUT) rebocado.

toward(s) [tə'wɔ:d(z)] prep para; (of attitude) com respeito a, para com; (of purpose) para.

towel ['tauəl] n toalha; ~**ling** n (fabric) tecido para toalhas; ~ **rail** n toalheiro.

tower ['tauə*] n torre f; ~ **block** n arranha-céu m; ~**ing** adj elevado, eminente.

town [taun] n cidade f; **to go to** ~ ir à cidade; (fig) fazer com entusiasmo; ~ **clerk** n administrador(a) m/f municipal; ~ **council** n câmara municipal; ~ **hall** n prefeitura (Br), concelho (Pt); ~ **planning** n urbanismo.

towrope ['touroup] n cabo de reboque; **tow truck** n = **breakdown lorry.**

toxic ['tɔksɪk] adj tóxico.

toy [tɔɪ] n brinquedo; **to** ~ **with** vt fus jogar com; (idea) andar com; ~**shop** n loja de brinquedos.

trace [treɪs] n traço, rasto // vt (draw) traçar, esboçar; (follow) seguir a pista de; (locate) encontrar.

track [træk] n (mark) pegada, vestígio; (path: gen) caminho, vereda; (: of bullet etc) trajetória (Pt: -ct-); (: of suspect, animal) pista, rasto; (RAIL) trilhos (Br), carris mpl (Pt); (on tape) trilha; (SPORT) pista // vt seguir a pista de; **to keep** ~ **of** não perder de vista, manter-se informado sobre; **to** ~ **down** vt (prey) seguir a pista de; (sth lost) procurar e encontrar; ~ **suit** n roupa de jogging.

tract [trækt] n (GEO) região f; (pamphlet) folheto.

tractor ['træktə*] n trator (Pt: -ct-) m.

trade [treɪd] n comércio, negócio; (skill, job) ofício, emprego // vi negociar, comerciar; **to** ~ **in** vt (old car etc) dar como parte do pagamento; ~-**in price** n valor de um objeto usado que se desconta do preço do outro novo; ~**mark** n marca de indústria or comércio; ~ **name** n nome m comercial; **trader** n comerciante m/f; **tradesman** n (shopkeeper) lojista m; ~ **union** n sindicato; ~ **unionism** n sindicalismo; **trading** n comércio; **trading estate** n zona comercial.

tradition [trə'dɪʃən] n tradição f; ~**al** adj tradicional.

traffic ['træfɪk] n (gen, AUT) trânsito, tráfico; (air ~ etc) tráfego // vi: **to** ~ **in** (pej: liquor, drugs) traficar com, fazer tráfico com; ~ **circle** n (US) cruzamento circular, balão m; ~ **jam** n engarrafamento, congestionamento; ~ **lights** npl sinal msg luminoso; ~ **warden** n guarda m/f de trânsito.

tragedy ['trædʒədɪ] n tragédia.

tragic ['trædʒɪk] adj trágico.

trail [treɪl] n (tracks) rasto, pista; (path) caminho, trilha; (wake) esteira // vt (drag) arrastar; (follow) seguir a pista de; (follow closely) vigiar // vi arrastar-se; **to** ~ **behind** vi atrasar-se; ~**er** n (AUT) trailer m; (US) carro-reboque m; (CINEMA) trailer.

train [treɪn] n trem m (Br), comboio (Pt); (of dress) cauda; (series) sequência, série f; (followers) séquito, comitiva // vt (educate) ensinar; (teach skills to) instruir,

treinar; (sportsman) treinar; (dog) adestrar, amestrar; (point: gun etc): **to** ~ **on** apontar para // vi (SPORT) ser treinado; (be educated) ser instruído; ~**ed** adj (worker) instruído; (teacher) formado; (animal) adestrado; ~**ee** [treɪ'niː] n aluno; (in trade) aprendiz m; ~**er** n (SPORT) treinador(a) m/f; (of animals) adestrador(a) m/f; ~**ing** n instrução f, preparo; **in** ~**ing** (SPORT) em treinamento; ~**ing college** n (for teachers) Escola Normal.

traipse [treɪps] vi arrastar os pés.

trait [treɪt] n traço.

traitor ['treɪtə*] n traidor(a) m/f.

tram [træm] n (also: ~**car**) bonde m (Br), eléctrico (Pt).

tramp [træmp] n (person) vagabundo/a // vi caminhar pesadamente.

trample ['træmpl] vt: **to** ~ (underfoot) calcar aos pés.

trampoline ['træmpəliːn] n trampolim m.

trance [trɑːns] n estupor m; (MED) transe m hipnótico.

tranquil ['træŋkwɪl] adj tranqüilo; ~**lity** n tranqüilidade f; ~**lizer** n (MED) tranqüilizante m.

transact [træn'zækt] vt (business) negociar; ~**ion** [-'zækʃən] n transação (Pt: -çç-) f, negócio.

transatlantic ['trænzət'læntɪk] adj transatlântico.

transcend [træn'sɛnd] vt transcender, exceder.

transcript ['trænskrɪpt] n cópia, traslado; ~**ion** [-'skrɪpʃən] n transcrição f.

transept ['trænsɛpt] n transepto.

transfer ['trænsfə*] n (gen) transferência; (picture, design) decalcomania // vt [træns'fə:*] transferir, trasladar; **to** ~ **the charges** (TEL) ligar a cobrar; ~**able** [-'fɔːrəbl] adj transferível; **not** ~**able** intransferível.

transform [træns'fɔːm] vt transformar; ~**ation** [-'meɪʃən] n transformação f; ~**er** n (ELEC) transformador m.

transfusion [træns'fjuːʒən] n transfusão f.

transient ['trænzɪənt] adj transitório.

transistor [træn'zɪstə*] n (ELEC) transistor m; ~ **radio** n rádio transistor.

transit ['trænzɪt] n: **in** ~ em trânsito, de passagem.

transition [træn'zɪʃən] n transição f; ~**al** adj transitório.

transitive ['trænzɪtɪv] adj (LING) transitivo.

transitory ['trænzɪtərɪ] adj transitório.

translate [trænz'leɪt] vt traduzir; **translation** [-'leɪʃən] n tradução f; **translator** n tradutor(a) m/f.

transmission [trænz'mɪʃən] n transmissão f.

transmit [trænz'mɪt] vt transmitir; ~**ter** n transmissor m; (station) emissora.

transparency [træns'pɛɔrnsɪ] n (PHOT) transparência, diapositivo.

transparent [træns'pærnt] adj transparente.

transplant [træns'plɑːnt] vt transplantar // n ['trænsplɑːnt] (MED) transplante m.

transport ['trænspɔːt] n (gen) transporte m; (also: road/rail ~) transporte rodoviário/ferroviário // vt [-'pɔːt] transportar; (carry) acarretar; ~ation [-'teɪʃən] n transporte m; ~ café n bar m de estrada.

transverse ['trænzvɔːs] adj transversal.

transvestite [trænz'vɛstaɪt] n travesti m/f.

trap [træp] n (snare, trick) armadilha, cilada; (carriage) aranha, charrete f // vt pegar em armadilha; (immobilize) bloquear; (jam) emperrar; ~ door n alçapão m.

trapeze [trɔ'piːz] n trapézio.

trappings ['træpɪŋz] npl adornos mpl, enfeites mpl.

trash [træʃ] n (pej: goods) refugo, escória; (: nonsense) besteira; ~ can n (US) lata de lixo.

trauma ['trɔːmɔ] n trauma m; ~tic [-'mætɪk] adj traumático.

travel ['trævl] n viagem f // vi viajar // vt (distance) percorrer; ~ agency n agência de viagens; ~ler, ~er (US) n viajante m/f; ~ler's cheque n cheque m de viagem; ~ling, ~ing (US) n as viagens fpl, viajar m; ~ sickness n enjôo.

traverse ['trævɔs] vt atravessar.

travesty ['trævɔstɪ] n paródia.

trawler ['trɔːlɔ*] n traineira.

tray [treɪ] n bandeja.

treacherous ['trɛtʃɔrɔs] adj traiçoeiro; **treachery** n traição f.

treacle ['triːkl] n melado.

tread [trɛd] n (step) passo, pisada; (sound) passada; (of tyre) banda de rodagem // vi, pt trod, pp trodden pisar, esmagar com os pés; to ~ on vt fus pisar sobre.

treason ['triːzn] n traição f.

treasure ['trɛʒɔ*] n tesouro // vt (value) apreciar, estimar; ~ hunt n caça ao tesouro.

treasurer ['trɛʒɔrɔ*] n tesoureiro.

treasury ['trɛʒɔrɪ] n: the T~ (POL) Ministério da Fazenda.

treat [triːt] n (present) regalo, deleite m; (pleasure) prazer m // vt tratar; to ~ sb to sth convidar alguém para algo.

treatise ['triːtɪz] n tratado.

treatment ['triːtmɔnt] n tratamento, trato.

treaty ['triːtɪ] n tratado, acordo.

treble ['trɛbl] adj tríplice // n (MUS) soprano // vt triplicar // vi triplicar-se.

tree [triː] n árvore f; ~ trunk n tronco de árvore.

trek [trɛk] n (long journey) viagem penosa e comprida; (tiring walk) caminhada; (as holiday) excursão f.

trellis ['trɛlɪs] n grade f de ripas, latada.

tremble ['trɛmbl] vi tremer; **trembling** n tremor m // adj trêmulo, trepidante.

tremendous [trɪ'mɛndɔs] adj tremendo; (enormous) enorme; (excellent) formidável, fantástico.

tremor ['trɛmɔ*] n tremor m; (also: **earth** ~) tremor de terra.

trench [trɛntʃ] n trincheira.

trend [trɛnd] n (tendency) inclinação f; (of events) curso; (fashion) tendência; ~y adj (idea) de acordo com a tendência atual (Pt: -ct-); (clothes) da última moda.

trepidation [trɛpɪ'deɪʃɔn] n trepidação f; (fear) apreensão f.

trespass ['trɛspɔs] vi: to ~ on invadir; "no ~ing" "passagem proibida".

tress [trɛs] n trança.

trestle ['trɛsl] n cavalete m; ~ table n mesa de cavaletes.

trial ['traɪɔl] n (LAW) julgamento, processo; (test: of machine etc) prova, teste m; (hardship) provação f; **by** ~ **and error** por ensaio e erro.

triangle ['traɪæŋgl] n (MATH, MUS) triângulo; **triangular** [-'æŋgjulɔ*] adj triangular.

tribal ['traɪbɔl] adj tribal.

tribe [traɪb] n tribo f; **tribesman** n membro do tribo.

tribulation [trɪbju'leɪʃɔn] n tribulação f, aflição f.

tribunal [traɪ'bjuːnl] n tribunal m.

tributary ['trɪbjuːtɔrɪ] n (river) afluente m.

tribute ['trɪbjuːt] n homenagem f; (payment) tributo; **to pay** ~ **to** prestar homenagem a.

trice [traɪs] n: **in a** ~ num instante.

trick [trɪk] n truque m; (deceit) fraude f, trapaça; (joke) brincadeira; (CARDS) vaza // vt enganar; **to play a** ~ **on sb** pregar uma peça em alguém; ~ery n trapaça.

trickle ['trɪkl] n (of water etc) fio de água // vi gotejar, pingar.

tricky ['trɪkɪ] adj difícil, complicado.

tricycle ['traɪsɪkl] n triciclo.

trifle ['traɪfl] n bagatela; (CULIN) tipo de bolo com fruta e creme // adv: **a** ~ **long** um pouquinho longo; **trifling** adj insignificante.

trigger ['trɪgɔ*] n (of gun) gatilho; **to** ~ **off** vt desencadear.

trigonometry [trɪgɔ'nɔmɔtrɪ] n trigonometria.

trill [trɪl] n (of bird) trinado, trilo.

trim [trɪm] adj (elegant) elegante; (house) arrumado; (garden) bem cuidado; (figure) bem vestido, esbelto // n (haircut etc) aparada; (on car) estofamento // vt arrumar; (cut) aparar, cortar; (decorate) enfeitar; (NAUT: a sail) ajustar; ~mings npl decoração fsg; (cuttings) aparas fpl.

Trinity ['trɪnɪtɪ] n: the ~ a Trindade.

trinket ['trɪŋkɪt] n bugiganga; (piece of jewellery) berloque m, bijuteria.

trio ['triːəu] n trio, terceto.

trip [trɪp] n viagem f; (excursion) excursão f; (stumble) tropeção m // vi (also: ~ up) tropeçar; (go lightly) andar com passos ligeiros // vt fazer tropeçar.

tripe [traɪp] n (CULIN) bucho, tripa; (pej: rubbish) bobagem f.

triple ['trɪpl] adj triplo, tríplice.

triplets ['trɪplɪts] npl trigêmeos/as.

triplicate ['trɪplɪkət] n: in ~ em triplicata.

tripod ['traɪpɔd] n tripé m.

trite [traɪt] adj vulgar, gasto.

triumph ['traɪʌmf] n triunfo // vi: to ~ (over) triunfar (sobre); ~ant [-'ʌmfənt] adj triunfante.

trivia ['trɪvɪə] npl trivialidades fpl.

trivial ['trɪvɪəl] adj insignificante; (commonplace) trivial; ~ity [-'ælɪtɪ] n trivialidade f.

trod [trɔd], **trodden** ['trɔdn] pt, pp of tread.

trolley ['trɔlɪ] n carrinho; ~ bus n ônibus m elétrico (Br), trólei m (Pt).

trombone [trɔm'bəun] n trombone m.

troop [truːp] n bando, grupo; ~s npl (MIL) tropa fsg; to ~ in/out vi entrar/sair em bando; ~er n (MIL) soldado de cavalaria.

trophy ['trəufɪ] n troféu m.

tropic ['trɔpɪk] n trópico; ~al adj tropical.

trot [trɔt] n trote m // vi trotar; on the ~ (fig: col) atarefado.

trouble ['trʌbl] n problema m, dificuldade f; (worry) preocupação f; (bother, effort) incômodo, esforço; (unrest) inquietude f; (MED): stomach ~ problemas mpl gástricos // vt perturbar; (worry) preocupar, incomodar // vi: to ~ to do sth incomodar-se or preocupar-se de fazer algo; ~s npl (POL etc) distúrbios mpl; to be in ~ estar num aperto; to go to the ~ of doing sth dar-se ao trabalho de fazer algo; what's the ~? qual é o problema?; ~d adj (person) preocupado; (epoch, life) agitado; ~maker n criador-de-casos m; (child) encrenqueiro; ~shooter n (in conflict) conciliador m; ~some adj incômodo, importuno.

trough [trɔf] n (also: drinking ~) bebedouro, cocho; (also: feeding ~) gamela; (channel) canal m.

troupe [truːp] n companhia teatral.

trousers ['trauzəz] npl calça fsg (Br), calças fpl (Pt).

trousseau ['truːsəu], pl ~x or ~s [-z] n enxoval m.

trout [traut] n, pl inv truta.

trowel ['trauəl] n colher f de jardineiro or de pedreiro.

truant ['truənt] n: to play ~ matar aula (Br), fazer gazeta (Pt).

truce [truːs] n trégua, armistício.

truck [trʌk] n caminhão m (Br), camião m (Pt); (RAIL) vagão m; ~ driver n caminhoneiro (Br), camionista m/f (Pt);

~ **farm** n (US) horta; ~ **stop** n (US) bar m de estrada.

truculent ['trʌkjulənt] adj agressivo.

trudge [trʌdʒ] vi andar com dificuldade, arrastar-se.

true [truː] adj verdadeiro; (accurate) exato (Pt: -ct-); (genuine) autêntico; (faithful) fiel, leal.

truffle ['trʌfl] n trufa.

truly ['truːlɪ] adv exatamente (Pt: -act-); (truthfully) verdadeiramente; (faithfully) fielmente; **yours** ~ (in letter) atenciosamente.

trump [trʌmp] n trunfo; ~ed-up adj inventado, forjado.

trumpet ['trʌmpɪt] n trombeta.

truncheon ['trʌntʃən] n cassetete m.

trundle ['trʌndl] vt/i: to ~ along rolar or rodar fazendo ruído.

trunk [trʌŋk] n (of tree, person) tronco; (of elephant) tromba; (case) baú m, mala grande; (US: AUT) mala; ~s npl (also: swimming ~s) calção m (de banho) (Br), calções mpl de banho (Pt); ~ call n (TEL) ligação f interurbana.

truss [trʌs] n (MED) funda; to ~ (up) vt atar, amarrar.

trust [trʌst] n confiança; (COMM) truste m, monopólio; (obligation) responsabilidade f; (LAW) fideicomisso // vt (rely on) confiar em; (entrust): to ~ sth to sb confiar algo a alguém; ~ed adj de confiança; ~ee [trʌs'tiː] n (LAW) fideicomissário, depositário; (of school etc) administrador(a) m/f; ~ful, ~ing adj confiante; ~worthy adj digno de confiança; ~y adj fidedigno, fiel.

truth [truːθ], pl ~s [truːðz] n verdade f; ~ful adj (person) sincero, honesto; ~fully adv sinceramente, honestamente; ~fulness n veracidade f.

try [traɪ] n tentativa, experimento; (RUGBY) ensaio // vt (LAW) julgar; (test: sth new) provar, pôr à prova; (attempt) tentar; (strain) cansar // vi provar; to ~ to do sth tentar fazer algo; to ~ on vt (clothes) experimentar, provar; to ~ out vt experimentar // n; ~ing adj penoso, árduo.

tsar [zɑː*] n czar m.

T-shirt ['tiːʃɔːt] n camiseta (Br), T-shirt f (Pt).

tub [tʌb] n balde m; (bath) tina, banheira.

tuba ['tjuːbə] n tuba.

tubby ['tʌbɪ] adj gorducho.

tube [tjuːb] n tubo, cano; (underground) metrô m (Br), metro(-politano) (Pt); (for tyre) câmara-de-ar f; ~less adj sem câmara.

tuberculosis [tjubəːkju'ləusɪs] n tuberculose f.

tube station n estação f do metrô.

tubing ['tjuːbɪŋ] n tubulação f, encanamento; a piece of ~ um pedaço de tubo.

tubular ['tjuːbjulə*] adj tubular; (furniture) tubiforme.

TUC *n abbr of* **Trades Union Congress.**

tuck [tʌk] *n* (SEWING) prega, dobra // *vt* (*put*) enfiar, meter; **to ~ away** *vt* esconder; **to ~ in** *vt* enfiar a beirada de; (*child*) cobrir bem // *vi* (*eat*) comer com apetite; **to ~ up** *vt* (*child*) cobrir bem; **~ shop** *n* loja de balas.

Tuesday ['tju:zdɪ] *n* terça-feira.

tuft [tʌft] *n* penacho; (*of grass etc*) tufo.

tug [tʌg] *n* (*ship*) rebocador *m* // *vt* rebocar; **~-of-war** *n* cabo-de-guerra *m*; (*fig*) disputa.

tuition [tjuː'ɪʃn] *n* ensino; (*private* **~**) aulas *fpl* particulares.

tulip ['tjuːlɪp] *n* tulipa.

tumble ['tʌmbl] *n* (*fall*) queda // *vi* cair, tropeçar // *vt* tombar, desabar; **~down** *adj* em ruínas *fpl*; **~ dryer** *n* máquina de secar roupa.

tumbler ['tʌmblə*] *n* copo.

tummy ['tʌmɪ] *n* (*col: belly*) barriga; (: *stomach*) estômago.

tumour ['tjuːmə*] *n* tumor *m*.

tumult ['tjuːmʌlt] *n* tumulto; **~uous** [-'mʌltjuəs] *adj* tumultuado.

tuna ['tjuːnə] *n, pl inv* (*also:* **~ fish**) atum *m*.

tune [tjuːn] *n* (*melody*) melodia // *vt* (MUS) afinar; (RADIO, TV) sintonizar; (AUT) ajustar; **to be in/out of ~** (*instrument*) estar afinado/desafinado; (*singer*) cantar bem/mal; **to be in/out of ~ with** (*fig*) harmonizar-se com/desentoar de; **to ~ up** *vi* (*musician*) afinar (seu instrumento); **~ful** *adj* melodioso; **tuner** *n* (*radio set*) sintonizador *m*; **piano tuner** afinador *m* de pianos.

tunic ['tjuːnɪk] *n* túnica.

tuning ['tjuːnɪŋ] *n* sintonização *f*; (MUS) afinação *f*; **~ fork** *n* diapasão *m*.

Tunisia [tjuː'nɪzɪə] *n* Tunísia.

tunnel ['tʌnl] *n* túnel *m*; (*in mine*) galeria // *vi* abrir um túnel/uma galeria.

tunny ['tʌnɪ] *n* atum *m*.

turban ['təːbən] *n* turbante *m*.

turbine ['təːbaɪn] *n* turbina.

turbulence ['təːbjuləns] *n* (AVIAT) turbulência; **turbulent** *adj* turbulento.

tureen [tə'riːn] *n* terrina.

turf [təːf] *n* torrão *m*, turfa; (*clod*) gramado // *vt* relvar, gramar; **to ~ out** *vt* (*col*) pôr no olho da rua.

turgid ['təːdʒɪd] *adj* (*speech*) pomposo.

Turk [təːk] *n* turco/a.

turkey ['təːkɪ] *n* peru/perua *m/f*.

Turkey ['təːkɪ] *n* Turquia; **Turkish** *adj, n* turco/a; **Turkish bath** *n* banho turco.

turmoil ['təːmɔɪl] *n* tumulto, distúrbio, agitação *f*.

turn [təːn] *n* volta, turno; (*in road*) curva; (*go*) vez *f*, turno; (*tendency: of mind, events*) propensão *f*, tendência; (THEATRE) número; (MED) choque *m* // *vt* dar volta a, fazer girar; (*collar*) virar; (*steak*) virar; (*change*): **to ~ sth into** converter algo em // *vi* voltar; (*person:*

look back) voltar-se; (*reverse direction*) mudar de direção (Pt: -cç-); (*milk*) azedar; (*change*) mudar; (*become*) converter-se em; **a good ~** um favor; **it gave me quite a ~** me deu um susto enorme; 'no left ~' (AUT) 'proibido dobrar à esquerda'; **it's your ~** é a sua vez; **in ~** por sua vez; **to take ~s** revezar; **to ~ about** *vi* dar uma volta completa; **to ~ away** *vi* virar a cabeça; **to ~ back** *vi* voltar atrás; **to ~ down** *vt* (*refuse*) recusar; (*reduce*) baixar; (*fold*) dobrar, virar para baixo; **to ~ in** *vi* (*col: go to bed*) ir dormir // *vt* (*fold*) dobrar para dentro; **to ~ off** *vi* (*from road*) desviar-se // *vt* (*light, radio etc*) apagar; (*engine*) desligar; **to ~ on** *vt* (*light, radio etc*) acender; (*engine*) ligar; **to ~ out** *vt* (*light, gas*) apagar // *vi:* **to ~ out to be...** revelar-se (ser)..., resultar (ser)...; **to ~ up** *vi* (*person*) chegar, apresentar-se; (*lost object*) aparecer // *vt* (*gen*) subir; **~ing** *n* (*in road*) volta, curva; **~ing point** *n* (*fig*) momento decisivo, virada.

turnip ['təːnɪp] *n* nabo.

turnout ['təːnaut] *n* assistência.

turnover ['təːnəuvə*] *n* (COMM: amount of money) volume *m* de negócios; (: of goods) movimento *m*.

turnpike ['təːnpaɪk] *n* (US) estrada *e* rodovia com pedágio (Pt: com portagem).

turnstile ['təːnstaɪl] *n* borboleta (Br), torniquete *m* (Pt).

turntable ['təːnteɪbl] *n* (*on record player*) prato.

turn-up ['təːnʌp] *n* (*on trousers*) volta, dobra.

turpentine ['təːpəntaɪn] *n* (*also:* **turps**) terebentina, aguarrás *f*.

turquoise ['təːkwɔɪz] *n* (*stone*) turquesa // *adj* cor turquesa.

turret ['tʌrɪt] *n* torre *f* pequena.

turtle ['təːtl] *n* tartaruga, cágado.

tusk [tʌsk] *n* presa, colmilho.

tussle ['tʌsl] *n* (*fight*) luta; (*scuffle*) contenda, rixa.

tutor ['tjuːtə*] *n* (*gen*) professor(a) *m/f*; **~ial** [-'tɔːrɪəl] *n* (SCOL) seminário.

T.V. [tiː'viː] *n abbr of* **television.**

twaddle ['twɔdl] *n* bobagens *fpl*, disparates *mpl*.

twang [twæŋ] *n* (*of instrument*) dedilhado; (*of voice*) timbre *m* nasal or fanhoso // *vi* vibrar // *vt* (*guitar*) dedilhar.

tweed [twiːd] *n* tweed *m*, pano grosso de lã.

tweezers ['twiːzəz] *npl* pinça (pequena).

twelfth [twelfθ] *adj* décimo-segundo; **T~ Night** *n* noite *f* de Reis, Epifania.

twelve [twelv] *num* doze.

twentieth ['twentɪɪθ] *adj* vigésimo.

twenty ['twentɪ] *num* vinte.

twerp [twəːp] *n* (*col*) imbecil *m/f*.

twice [twaɪs] *adv* duas vezes; **~ as much** duas vezes mais.

twig [twɪg] n graveto, varinha // vi (col) perceber.

twilight ['twaɪlaɪt] n crepúsculo, meia-luz f.

twin [twɪn] adj, n gêmeo/a // vt irmanar-se, emparelhar.

twine [twaɪn] n barbante m (Br), cordel m (Pt) // vi (plant) enroscar-se, enrolar-se.

twinge [twɪndʒ] n (of pain) pontada; (of conscience) remorso.

twinkle ['twɪŋkl] n cintilação f // vi cintilar; (eyes) pestanejar.

twirl [twəːl] n giro, volta // vt fazer girar // vi girar rapidamente.

twist [twɪst] n (action) torção f; (in road, coil) curva; (in wire, flex) virada; (in story) mudança imprevista // vt torcer, retorcer; (weave) entrelaçar; (roll around) enrolar; (fig) deformar // vi serpentear.

twit [twɪt] n (col) idiota, bobo.

twitch [twɪtʃ] n puxão m; (nervous) tique m nervoso // vi contrair-se, puxar bruscamente, contorcer-se.

two [tuː] num dois; **to put ~ and ~ together** (fig) concluir pela evidência dos fatos (Pt: -ct-); **~-door** adj (AUT) de duas portas; **~-faced** adj (pej: person) falso; **~fold** adv: **to increase ~fold** duplicar; **~-piece (suit)** n traje m de duas peças; **~-piece (swimsuit)** n maiô m de duas peças, biquíni m; **~-seater** n (plane) avião m de dois lugares; (car) carro de dois lugares; **~some** n (people) casal m; **~-way** adj: **~-way traffic** trânsito em mão dupla.

tycoon [taɪˈkuːn] n: (business) **~** magnata m, ricaço.

type [taɪp] n (category) tipo, espécie f; (model) modelo; (TYP) tipo, letra // vt (letter etc) datilografar (Pt: -ct-); **~script** n texto da(c)tilografado; **~writer** n máquina de escrever; **~written** adj da(c)tilografado.

typhoid ['taɪfɔɪd] n febre f tifóide.

typhoon [taɪˈfuːn] n tufão m.

typhus ['taɪfəs] n tifo.

typical ['tɪpɪkl] adj típico; **typify** [-faɪ] vt tipificar, simbolizar.

typing ['taɪpɪŋ] n datilografia (Pt: -ct-); **typist** n datilógrafo/a (Pt: -ct-) m/f.

tyranny ['tɪrənɪ] n tirania.

tyrant ['taɪərnt] n tirano/a.

tyre, tire (US) ['taɪə*] n pneu m, pneumático.

tzar [zɑː*] n = **tsar**.

U

U-bend ['juːbend] n (in pipe) curva em U.

ubiquitous [juːˈbɪkwɪtəs] adj ubíquo, onipresente (Pt: -mn-).

udder ['ʌdə*] n ubre f.

UFO ['juːfəu] n abbr of **unidentified flying object** O.V.N.I. m (objeto voador não identificado).

ugliness ['ʌglɪnɪs] n feiúra; **ugly** adj feio; (dangerous) perigoso.

U.K. n abbr of **United Kingdom** Reino Unido.

ulcer ['ʌlsə*] n úlcera.

Ulster ['ʌlstə*] n Ulster m, Irlanda do Norte.

ulterior [ʌlˈtɪərɪə*] adj ulterior; **~ motive** segundas intenções fpl.

ultimate ['ʌltɪmət] adj último, final; (authority) máximo; **~ly** adv (in the end) no final, por último; (fundamentally) no fundo.

ultimatum [ʌltɪˈmeɪtəm] n ultimato.

ultraviolet ['ʌltrəˈvaɪəlɪt] adj ultravioleta.

umbilical cord [ʌmbɪˈlaɪkl-] n cordão m umbilical.

umbrella [ʌmˈbrelə] n guarda-chuva m.

umpire ['ʌmpaɪə*] n árbitro // vt arbitrar.

umpteen [ʌmpˈtiːn] adj inúmeros; **for the ~th time** pela enegésima vez.

UN, UNO abbr of **United Nations (Organization)** O.N.U. f (Organização f das) Nações Unidas fpl.

unable [ʌnˈeɪbl] adj: **to be ~ to do sth** ser incapaz de or não poder fazer algo.

unabridged [ʌnəˈbrɪdʒd] adj integral.

unaccompanied [ʌnəˈkʌmpənɪd] adj desacompanhado.

unaccountably [ʌnəˈkauntəblɪ] adv inexplicavelmente.

unaccustomed [ʌnəˈkʌstəmd] adj: **to be ~ to** não estar acostumado a.

unaided [ʌnˈeɪdɪd] adj sem ajuda, por si só.

unanimous [juːˈnænɪməs] adj unânime; **~ly** adv unanimemente.

unarmed [ʌnˈɑːmd] adj (without a weapon) desarmado; (defenceless) indefeso.

unassuming [ʌnəˈsjuːmɪŋ] adj modesto, despretencioso.

unattached [ʌnəˈtætʃt] adj (person) livre; (part etc) solto, separado.

unattended [ʌnəˈtendɪd] adj (car, luggage) sem vigilância, abandonado.

unattractive [ʌnəˈtræktɪv] adj sem atrativos (Pt: -ct-), pouco atraente.

unauthorized [ʌnˈɔːθəraɪzd] adj não autorizado, proibido.

unavoidable [ʌnəˈvɔɪdəbl] adj inevitável.

unaware [ʌnəˈwɛə*] adj: **to be ~ of** ignorar, não perceber; **~s** adv improvisadamente, de surpresa.

unbalanced [ʌnˈbælənst] adj desequilibrado; (mentally) desajustado.

unbearable [ʌnˈbɛərəbl] adj insuportável.

unbeatable [ʌnˈbiːtəbl] adj (team) invencível; (price) sem igual.

unbeaten [ʌnˈbiːtn] adj invicto.

unbeknown(st) [ʌnbɪˈnəun(st)] adv: **~ to me** desconhecido por mim.

unbelievable [ʌnbɪ'li:vəbl] *adj* inacreditável, incrível.

unbend [ʌn'bɛnd] (*irr: like* **bend**) *vi* relaxar-se // *vt* (*wire*) desentortar.

unblock [ʌn'blɔk] *vt* (*pipe*) desentupir.

unborn [ʌn'bɔ:n] *adj* por nascer, futuro.

unbounded [ʌn'baundɪd] *adj* ilimitado, infinito, imenso.

unbreakable [ʌn'breɪkəbl] *adj* inquebrável.

unbridled [ʌn'braɪdld] *adj* (*fig*) desenfreado.

unbroken [ʌn'brəukən] *adj* (*seal*) intacto; (*series*) ininterrupto; (*record*) mantido; (*spirit*) indômito.

unburden [ʌn'bɜ:dn] *vr*: **to ~ o.s.** desabafar.

unbutton [ʌn'bʌtn] *vt* desabotoar.

uncalled-for [ʌn'kɔ:ldfɔ:*] *adj* desnecessário, gratuito.

uncanny [ʌn'kænɪ] *adj* (*strange*) estranho; (*mysterious*) sobrenatural.

unceasing [ʌn'si:sɪŋ] *adj* ininterrupto.

uncertain [ʌn'sɜ:tn] *adj* incerto; (*character*) indeciso; **~ty** *n* incerteza.

unchanged [ʌn'tʃeɪndʒd] *adj* sem mudar, inalterado.

uncharitable [ʌn'tʃærɪtəbl] *adj* sem caridade.

uncharted [ʌn'tʃɑ:tɪd] *adj* inexplorado.

unchecked [ʌn'tʃɛkt] *adj* desenfreado, livre.

uncivil [ʌn'sɪvɪl] *adj* grosseiro, rude.

uncle ['ʌŋkl] *n* tio.

uncomfortable [ʌn'kʌmfətəbl] *adj* incômodo; (*uneasy*) pouco à vontade.

uncommon [ʌn'kɔmən] *adj* raro, incomum, excepcional.

unconcerned [ʌnkən'sɜ:nd] *adj* indiferente, despreocupado.

unconditional [ʌnkən'dɪʃənl] *adj* incondicional.

unconscious [ʌn'kɔnʃəs] *adj* sem sentidos, desacordado; (*unaware*) inconsciente // *n*: **the ~** o inconsciente; **~ly** *adv* inconscientemente.

uncontrollable [ʌnkən'trəuləbl] *adj* (*temper*) ingovernável; (*laughter*) incontrolável.

uncouth [ʌn'ku:θ] *adj* rude, grosseiro, inculto.

uncover [ʌn'kʌvə*] *vt* (*gen*) descobrir; (*take lid off*) destapar, destampar.

undecided [ʌndɪ'saɪdɪd] *adj* (*character*) indeciso; (*question*) não respondido, pendente.

undeniable [ʌndɪ'naɪəbl] *adj* inegável.

under ['ʌndə*] *prep* embaixo de (*Br*), debaixo de (*Pt*); (*fig*) sob; (*less than*) menos de, inferior a; (*according to*) segundo, de acordo com; **~ there** ali embaixo; **~ repair** em conserto // *adv* embaixo.

under... [ʌndə*] *pref* sub-; **~-age** *adj* menor de idade; **~carriage** *n* trem *m* de aterrissagem; **~clothes** *npl* roupa *sg* de baixo; **~coat** *n* (*paint*) primeira mão

f; **~cover** *adj* secreto, furtivo; **~current** *n* corrente f submarina; (*fig*) tendência oculta; **~cut** *vt irr* rebaixar o preço para competir com; **~developed** *adj* subdesenvolvido; **~dog** *n* o mais fraco; **~done** *adj* (*CULIN*) mal passado; **~estimate** *vt* subestimar; **~exposed** *adj* (*PHOT*) sem exposição suficiente; **~fed** *adj* subnutrido; **~foot** *adv* sob os pés; **~go** *vt irr* sofrer; (*treatment*) receber; **~graduate** *n* estudante *m/f* universitário/a; **~ground** *n* (*RAILWAY*) metrô *m*; (*Pt*) metro (-politano) (*POL*) organização f clandestina // *adj* subterrâneo; **~growth** *n* vegetação f rasteira; **~hand(ed)** *adj* (*fig*) desleal; **~lie** *vt irr* estar debaixo de; (*fig*) ser a base de; **~line** *vt* sublinhar; **~ling** ['ʌndəlɪŋ] *n* (*pej*) subalterno/a; **~mine** *vt* minar, solapar; **~neath** [ʌndə'ni:θ] *adv* embaixo, debaixo, por baixo // *prep* embaixo de (*Br*), debaixo de (*Pt*); **~paid** *adj* mal pago; **~pants** *npl* (*Brit*) cueca(s) f(*pl*); **~pass** *n* passagem f inferior; **~price** *vt* vender abaixo do preço; **~privileged** *adj* menos favorecido; **~rate** *vt* depreciar, subestimar; **~side** *n* parte f inferior; **~skirt** *n* anágua.

understand [ʌndə'stænd] (*irr: like* **stand**) *vt/i* entender, compreender; (*assume*) subentender; **~able** *adj* compreensível; **~ing** *adj* compreensivo // *n* compreensão f, entendimento; (*agreement*) acordo.

understatement [ʌndə'steɪtmənt] *n* descrição f atenuada; (*quality*) modéstia (excessiva).

understood [ʌndə'stud] *pt, pp of* **understand** // *adj* entendido; (*implied*) subentendido, implícito.

understudy ['ʌndəstʌdɪ] *n* ator (*Pt*: -ct-) *m* substituto.

undertake [ʌndə'teɪk] (*irr: like* **take**) *vt* empreender; **to ~ to do sth** comprometer-se a fazer algo.

undertaker ['ʌndəteɪkə*] *n* agente *m* funerário; (*col*) papa-defuntos *m inv*.

undertaking [ʌndə'teɪkɪŋ] *n* empreendimento; (*promise*) promessa.

underwater [ʌndə'wɔ:tə*] *adv* sob a água // *adj* subaquático.

underwear ['ʌndəwɛə*] *n* roupa de baixo, roupa íntima.

underweight [ʌndə'weɪt] *adj* de peso inferior ao normal; (*person*) magro.

underworld ['ʌndəwɜ:ld] *n* (*of crime*) submundo.

underwriter ['ʌndəraɪtə*] *n* (*INSURANCE*) subscritor(a) *m/f* (que faz resseguro).

undesirable [ʌndɪ'zaɪərəbl] *adj* indesejável.

undies ['ʌndɪz] *npl* (*col*) roupa de baixo.

undignified [ʌn'dɪgnɪfaɪd] *adj* sem dignidade, indecoroso.

undisputed [ʌndɪ'spju:tɪd] *adj* incontestável, evidente.

undo [ʌn'duː] (*irr: like* do) *vt* desfazer;
~ing *n* ruína, desgraça.

undoubted [ʌn'dautɪd] *adj* indubitável;
~ly *adv* sem dúvida, indubitavelmente.

undress [ʌn'drɛs] *vi* despir-se.

undue [ʌn'djuː] *adj* indevido, excessivo.

undulating ['ʌndjuleɪtɪŋ] *adj* ondulante.

unduly [ʌn'djuːlɪ] *adv* indevidamente,
impropriamente.

unearth [ʌn'ɔːθ] *vt* desenterrar.

unearthly [ʌn'ɔːθlɪ] *adj*: **at an ~ hour
of the night** na calada da noite.

uneasy [ʌn'iːzɪ] *adj* inquieto,
desassossegado; (*worried*) preocupado.

uneconomic(al) [ʌniːkə'nɔmɪk(l)] *adj*
antieconômicos.

uneducated [ʌn'ɛdjukeɪtɪd] *adj* inculto,
sem instrução, não escolarizado.

unemployed [ʌnɪm'plɔɪd] *adj*
desempregado // *n*: **the ~** os
desempregados; **unemployment**
[-'plɔɪmənt] *n* desemprego.

unending [ʌn'ɛndɪŋ] *adj* interminável.

unenthusiastic [ʌnɪnθuːzɪ'æstɪk] *adj*
sem entusiasmo.

unerring [ʌn'ɔːrɪŋ] *adj* infalível.

uneven [ʌn'iːvn] *adj* desigual; (*road etc*)
irregular, acidentado.

unexpected [ʌnɪk'spɛktɪd] *adj*
inesperado.

unfair [ʌn'fɛə*] *adj*: ~ **(to)** injusto
(com); ~**ly** *adv* injustamente.

unfaithful [ʌn'feɪθful] *adj* infiel.

unfamiliar [ʌnfə'mɪlɪə*] *adj* pouco
familiar, desconhecido.

unfashionable [ʌn'fæ∫nəbl] *adj* fora da
moda.

unfasten [ʌn'faːsn] *vt* desatar.

unfavourable, unfavorable (*US*)
[ʌn'feɪvərəbl] *adj* desfavorável.

unfeeling [ʌn'fiːlɪŋ] *adj* insensível.

unfinished [ʌn'fɪnɪ∫t] *adj* incompleto,
inacabado.

unfit [ʌn'fɪt] *adj* sem preparo físico *or*
mental; (*incompetent*) incompetente,
incapaz; ~ **for work** inapto para
trabalhar.

unflagging [ʌn'flægɪŋ] *adj* incansável.

unfold [ʌn'fəuld] *vt* desdobrar; (*fig*)
revelar // *vi* abrir-se, desdobrar-se.

unforeseen ['ʌnfɔː'siːn] *adj* imprevisto.

unforgettable [ʌnfə'gɛtəbl] *adj*
inesquecível.

unforgivable [ʌnfə'gɪvəbl] *adj*
imperdoável.

unfortunate [ʌn'fɔːt∫nət] *adj* infeliz;
(*event, remark*) inoportuno; ~**ly** *adv*
infelizmente.

unfounded [ʌn'faundɪd] *adj* infundado.

unfriendly [ʌn'frɛndlɪ] *adj* hostil,
antipático.

unfurnished [ʌn'fɔːnɪ∫t] *adj*
desmobiliado, sem mobília.

ungainly [ʌn'geɪnlɪ] *adj* desalinhado.

unhappiness [ʌn'hæpɪnɪs] *n* tristeza;
unhappy *adj* (*sad*) triste; (*unfortunate*)
desventurado; (*childhood*) infeliz;

unhappy with (*arrangements etc*)
descontente com, insatisfeito com.

unharmed [ʌn'haːmd] *adj* ileso; (*col*) são
e salvo.

unhealthy [ʌn'hɛlθɪ] *adj* (*gen*) insalubre;
(*person*) doentio, doente.

unheard-of [ʌn'hɔːdɔv] *adj*
(*extraordinary*) inaudito, insólito;
(*unknown*) desconhecido.

unhook [ʌn'huk] *vt* desenganchar; (*from
wall*) despendurar; (*dress*) abrir, soltar.

unhurt [ʌn'hɔːt] *adj* ileso.

unidentified [ʌnaɪ'dɛntɪfaɪd] *adj* não-
identificado.

uniform ['juːnɪfɔːm] *n* uniforme *m* // *adj*
uniforme; ~**ity** [-'fɔːmɪtɪ] *n*
uniformidade *f*.

unify ['juːnɪfaɪ] *vt* unificar, unir.

unilateral [juːnɪ'lætərəl] *adj* unilateral.

unintentional [ʌnɪn'tɛn∫ənəl] *adj*
involuntário, não intencional.

union ['juːnjən] *n* união *f*; (*also*: **trade ~**)
sindicato (de trabalhadores) // *adj*
sindical; **U~ Jack** *n* bandeira britânica.

unique [juː'niːk] *adj* único, sem igual.

unison ['juːnɪsn] *n*: **in ~** em harmonia,
em uníssono.

unit ['juːnɪt] *n* unidade *f*; (*team, squad*)
grupo; **kitchen ~** móvel *m* de cozinha.

unite [juː'naɪt] *vt* unir // *vi* unir-se; ~**d**
adj unido; **U~d Kingdom (U.K.)** *n* (o)
Reino Unido; **U~d Nations
(Organization) (UN, UNO)** *n*
(Organização *f* das) Nações Unidas *fpl*
(O.N.U.); **U~d States (of America)
(US, USA)** *n* (os) Estados Unidos *mpl*
(da América) (E.U.A.).

unity ['juːnɪtɪ] *n* unidade *f*.

universal [juːnɪ'vɔːsl] *adj* universal.

universe ['juːnɪvɔːs] *n* universo.

university [juːnɪ'vɔːsɪtɪ] *n* universidade *f*.

unjust [ʌn'dʒʌst] *adj* injusto.

unkempt [ʌn'kɛmpt] *adj* desleixado,
descuidado; (*hair*) despenteado.

unkind [ʌn'kaɪnd] *adj* descortês,
indelicado; (*comment etc*) cruel.

unknown [ʌn'nəun] *adj* desconhecido.

unladen [ʌn'leɪdn] *adj* (*ship, weight*) sem
carga.

unleash [ʌn'liː∫] *vt* soltar; (*fig*)
desencadear.

unless [ʌn'lɛs] *conj* a menos que, a não
ser que; ~ **he comes** a menos que ele
venha; ~ **otherwise stated** salvo
indicação contrária.

unlike [ʌn'laɪk] *adj* diferente // *prep*
diferentemente de, ao contrário de.

unlikely [ʌn'laɪklɪ] *adj* improvável,
inverossímil.

unlimited [ʌn'lɪmɪtɪd] *adj* ilimitado.

unload [ʌn'ləud] *vt* descarregar.

unlock [ʌn'lɔk] *vt* destrancar.

unlucky [ʌn'lʌkɪ] *adj* infeliz; (*object, number*) de mau agouro; **to be ~** ser
azarado.

unmarried [ʌn'mærɪd] *adj* solteiro.

unmask [ʌn'maːsk] *vt* desmascarar.

unmistakable [ˌʌnmɪsˈteɪkəbl] *adj*
inconfundível.

unmitigated [ʌnˈmɪtɪgeɪtɪd] *adj* não
mitigado, absoluto.

unnatural [ʌnˈnætʃrəl] *adj* (*gen*)
antinatural, artificial; (*manner*) afetado
(*Pt: -ct-*); (*habit*) depravado.

unnecessary [ʌnˈnɛsəsərɪ] *adj*
desnecessário, inútil.

unnoticed [ʌnˈnəʊtɪst] *adj*: **to go** ~
passar despercebido.

unobtainable [ʌnəbˈteɪnəbl] *adj*
inalcançável.

unoccupied [ʌnˈɔkjupaɪd] *adj* (*seat etc*)
desocupado, livre.

unofficial [ʌnəˈfɪʃl] *adj* não-oficial,
informal; (*strike*) desautorizado.

unorthodox [ʌnˈɔːθədɔks] *adj* pouco
ortodoxo, heterodoxo.

unpack [ʌnˈpæk] *vi* desfazer as malas,
desembrulhar.

unpalatable [ʌnˈpælətəbl] *adj* não
apetecível; (*truth*) desagradável.

unparalleled [ʌnˈpærəleld] *adj*
(*unequalled*) sem paralelo; (*unique*) único,
incomparável.

unpleasant [ʌnˈplɛznt] *adj* (*disagreeable*)
desagradável; (*person, manner*)
antipático.

unplug [ʌnˈplʌg] *vt* desligar.

unpopular [ʌnˈpɔpjʊlə*] *adj* impopular.

unprecedented [ʌnˈprɛsɪdəntɪd] *adj*
sem precedentes.

unpredictable [ʌnprɪˈdɪktəbl] *adj*
imprevisível.

unproductive [ʌnprəˈdʌktɪv] *adj*
improdutivo.

unqualified [ʌnˈkwɔlɪfaɪd] *adj* leigo;
(*teacher*) não qualificado, inabilitado;
(*success*) irrestrito, absoluto.

unravel [ʌnˈrævl] *vt* desemaranhar.

unreal [ʌnˈrɪəl] *adj* irreal, ilusório.

unrealistic [ʌnrɪəˈlɪstɪk] *adj* pouco
realista.

unreasonable [ʌnˈriːznəbl] *adj*
despropositado; (*demand*) absurdo,
injusto.

unrelated [ʌnrɪˈleɪtɪd] *adj* sem relação;
(*family*) sem parentesco.

unrelenting [ʌnrɪˈlɛntɪŋ] *adj* implacável.

unreliable [ʌnrɪˈlaɪəbl] *adj* (*person*)
indigno de confiança; (*machine*) incerto,
perigoso.

unrelieved [ʌnrɪˈliːvd] *adj* (*monotony*)
monótono.

unrepeatable [ʌnrɪˈpiːtəbl] *adj* (*offer*)
irrepetível.

unrepresentative [ʌnrɛprɪˈzɛntətɪv]
adj pouco representativo or
característico.

unrest [ʌnˈrɛst] *n* inquietação *f*,
desassossego; (*POL*) distúrbios *mpl*.

unroll [ʌnˈrəʊl] *vt* desenrolar.

unruly [ʌnˈruːlɪ] *adj* indisciplinado.

unsafe [ʌnˈseɪf] *adj* (*journey*) perigoso;
(*car etc*) inseguro.

unsaid [ʌnˈsɛd] *adj*: **to leave sth** ~
deixar algo sem dizer.

unsatisfactory [ˈʌnsætɪsˈfæktərɪ] *adj*
insatisfatório.

unsavoury, unsavory (*US*) [ʌnˈseɪvərɪ]
adj (*fig*) repugnante, vil.

unscathed [ʌnˈskeɪðd] *adj* ileso.

unscrew [ʌnˈskruː] *vt* desparafusar.

unscrupulous [ʌnˈskruːpjʊləs] *adj*
inescrupuloso, imoral.

unsettled [ʌnˈsɛtld] *adj* incerto,
duvidoso; (*weather*) variável, instável.

unshaven [ʌnˈʃeɪvn] *adj* com a barba por
fazer.

unsightly [ʌnˈsaɪtlɪ] *adj* feio, disforme.

unskilled [ʌnˈskɪld] *adj*: ~ **worker**
operário não-especializado.

unspeakable [ʌnˈspiːkəbl] *adj* indizível;
(*bad*) inqualificável.

unsteady [ʌnˈstɛdɪ] *adj* instável.

unstuck [ʌnˈstʌk] *adj*: **to come** ~
despregar-se; (*fig*) fracassar.

unsuccessful [ʌnsəkˈsɛsful] *adj* (*attempt*) frustrado, vão/vã; (*writer, proposal*) sem êxito; **to be** ~ (*in attempting
sth*) ser mal sucedido; ~**ly** *adv* em vão,
debalde.

unsuitable [ʌnˈsuːtəbl] *adj* inadequado,
inconveniente.

unsure [ʌnˈʃuə*] *adj* inseguro, incerto.

unsuspecting [ʌnsəˈspɛktɪŋ] *adj*
confiante, insuspeitado.

unswerving [ʌnˈswɜːvɪŋ] *adj* inabalável,
firme, resoluto.

untangle [ʌnˈtæŋgl] *vt* desemaranhar,
desenredar.

untapped [ʌnˈtæpt] *adj* (*resources*)
inexplorado.

unthinkable [ʌnˈθɪŋkəbl] *adj*
impensável, inconcebível, incalculável.

untidy [ʌnˈtaɪdɪ] *adj* (*room*)
desarrumado, desleixado; (*appearance*)
desmazelado, desalinhado.

untie [ʌnˈtaɪ] *vt* desatar, desfazer.

until [ənˈtɪl] *prep* até (a) // *conj* até que;
~ **he comes** até que ele venha; ~
then até então.

untimely [ʌnˈtaɪmlɪ] *adj* inoportuno,
intempestivo; (*death*) prematuro.

untold [ʌnˈtəʊld] *adj* (*story*) inédito;
(*suffering*) incalculável; (*wealth*)
inestimável.

untoward [ʌntəˈwɔːd] *adj* desfavorável,
inconveniente.

unused [ʌnˈjuːzd] *adj* novo, sem uso.

unusual [ʌnˈjuːʒʊəl] *adj* incomum,
extraordinário, insólito.

unveil [ʌnˈveɪl] *vt* (*statue*) desvelar,
descobrir.

unwavering [ʌnˈweɪvərɪŋ] *adj* firme,
inabalável.

unwelcome [ʌnˈwɛlkəm] *adj* (*at a bad
time*) inoportuno, indesejável;
(*unpleasant*) desagradável.

unwell [ʌnˈwɛl] *adj*: **to feel** ~ estar
indisposto; **to be** ~ estar adoentado.

unwieldy [ʌnˈwiːldɪ] *adj* difícil de
manejar, pesado.

unwilling [ʌnˈwɪlɪŋ] *adj*: **to be** ~ **to do**

sth estar relutante em fazer algo; ~ly adv de má vontade.

unwind [ʌn'waɪnd] (irr: like wind) vt desenrolar // vi (relax) relaxar-se.

unwitting [ʌn'wɪtɪŋ] adj inconsciente, involuntário.

unworthy [ʌn'wɔːðɪ] adj indigno.

unwrap [ʌn'ræp] vt desembrulhar.

up [ʌp] prep: to go/be ~ sth subir algo/estar em cima de algo // adv em cima, para cima; ~ there lá em cima; ~ above em cima; to be ~ (out of bed) estar levantado; it is ~ to you você é quem sabe, você decide; what is he ~ to? o que ele está querendo?, o que ele está tramando?; he is not ~ to it ele não é capaz de fazê-lo; ~-and-coming adj prometedor(a); ~s and downs npl (fig) altos e baixos mpl.

upbringing ['ʌpbrɪŋɪŋ] n educação f, criação f.

update [ʌp'deɪt] vt atualizar (Pt: -ct-), pôr em dia; (contract etc) a(c)tualizar.

upgrade [ʌp'greɪd] vt promover.

upheaval [ʌp'hiːvl] n transtorno; (unrest) convulsão f.

uphill [ʌp'hɪl] adj ladeira acima; (fig: task) trabalhoso, árduo // adv: to go ~ ir morro acima.

uphold [ʌp'həʊld] (irr: like hold) vt suster, sustentar.

upholstery [ʌp'həʊlstərɪ] n estofamento, tapeçaria.

upkeep ['ʌpkiːp] n manutenção f.

upon [ə'pɒn] prep sobre.

upper ['ʌpə*] adj superior, de cima // n (of shoe) gáspea, parte f superior; ~-class adj da classe alta; ~most adj o mais elevado; what was ~most in my mind o que me preocupava mais.

upright ['ʌpraɪt] adj vertical; (fig) honrado, honesto.

uprising ['ʌpraɪzɪŋ] n revolta, rebelião f, sublevação f.

uproar ['ʌprɔː*] n tumulto, algazarra; (col) fuzuê m.

uproot [ʌp'ruːt] vt desarraigar, arrancar.

upset ['ʌpsɛt] n (to plan etc) revés m, reviravolta; (MED) indisposição f // vt [ʌp'sɛt] (irr: like set) (glass etc) virar; (spill) derramar; (plan) perturbar; (person) aborrecer, perturbar // adj [ʌp'sɛt] aborrecido, contrariado; (stomach) indisposto.

upshot ['ʌpʃɒt] n resultado.

upside-down ['ʌpsaɪddaʊn] adv de cabeça para baixo.

upstairs [ʌp'stɛəz] adv em cima, lá em cima // adj (room) de cima // n andar m de cima.

upstart ['ʌpstaːt] n novo-rico, pessoa sem classe.

upstream [ʌp'striːm] adv rio acima.

uptake ['ʌpteɪk] n: he is quick on the ~ ele vê longe; he is slow on the ~ ele tem raciocínio lento.

up-to-date ['ʌptə'deɪt] adj moderno, atualizado.

upturn ['ʌptɔːn] n (in luck) virada.

upward ['ʌpwəd] adj ascendente, para cima; ~(s) adv para cima.

uranium [juə'reɪnɪəm] n urânio.

urban ['ɔːbən] adj urbano, da cidade.

urbane [ɔː'beɪn] adj gentil, urbano.

urchin ['ɔːtʃɪn] n moleque m, criança maltrapilha.

urge [ɔːdʒ] n (force) impulso; (desire) desejo // vt: to ~ sb to do sth incitar alguém a fazer algo.

urgency ['ɔːdʒənsɪ] n urgência; (of tone) insistência; **urgent** adj urgente.

urinal ['juərɪnl] n urinol m, mictório.

urinate ['juərɪneɪt] vi urinar; **urine** n urina.

us [ʌs] pron nos; (after prep) nós.

US, USA n abbr of **United States (of America)** E.U.A., Estados Unidos (da América) mpl.

usage ['juːzɪdʒ] n uso, costume m.

use [juːs] n uso, emprego; (usefulness) utilidade f // vt [juːz] usar, empregar; **she ~d to do it** (ela) costumava fazê-lo; **in ~** em uso; **out of ~** fora de uso, antiquado; **to be of ~** servir; **it's no ~** (pointless) é inútil; (not useful) não serve; **to be ~d to** estar acostumado a; **to ~ up** vt esgotar, consumir; **~d** adj (car) usado; **~ful** adj útil; **to be ~ful** servir, ser útil; **~less** adj inútil; **user** n usuário.

usher ['ʌʃə*] n porteiro; (LAW) oficial m de justiça; **~ette** [-'rɛt] n (in cinema) lanterninha m/f (Br), arrumador(a) m/f (Pt).

USSR n: the ~ (a) U.R.S.S.

usual ['juːʒʊəl] adj usual, habitual; ~ly adv normalmente.

usurp [juː'zɔːp] vt usurpar.

utensil [juː'tɛnsl] n utensílio; **kitchen ~s** utensílios de cozinha.

uterus ['juːtərəs] n útero.

utilitarian [juːtɪlɪ'tɛərɪən] adj utilitário.

utility [juː'tɪlɪtɪ] n utilidade f; ~ **room** n copa.

utilize ['juːtɪlaɪz] vt utilizar.

utmost ['ʌtməʊst] adj maior // n: to do one's ~ fazer todo o possível.

utter ['ʌtə*] adj completo, total // vt proferir, pronunciar; ~**ance** n declaração f; ~**ly** adv completamente, totalmente.

U-turn ['juː'tɔːn] n curva em U.

V

v. abbr of **verse; versus; volt.**

vacancy ['veɪkənsɪ] n (job) vaga; (room) quarto livre; **vacant** adj desocupado, livre; (expression) distraído; **vacate** [və'keɪt] vt (house) desocupar; (job) deixar; (throne) renunciar a.

vacation [və'keɪʃən] n férias fpl; ~**er** n (US) pessoa de férias.

vaccinate ['væksɪneɪt] vt vacinar; **vaccination** [-'neɪʃən] n vacinação f.

vaccine ['væksi:n] *n* vacina.
vacuum ['vækjum] *n* vácuo *m*; ~ **cleaner** *n* aspirador *m* de pó; ~ **flask** *n* garrafa térmica (*Br*), termo (*Pt*).
vagabond ['vægəbɔnd] *n* vagabundo/a.
vagina [və'dʒaɪnə] *n* vagina.
vagrant ['veɪgrnt] *n* vagabundo/a.
vague [veɪg] *adj* vago; (*blurred: memory*) fraco; (*uncertain*) incerto, impreciso; (*person*) que divaga; ~**ly** *adv* vagamente.
vain [veɪn] *adj* (*conceited*) vaidoso; (*useless*) vão/vã, inútil; **in** ~ em vão.
vale [veɪl] *n* vale *m*.
valentine ['væləntaɪn] *n*: **V** ~'**s Day** dia *m* dos namorados.
valid ['vælɪd] *adj* válido; (*ticket, law*) vigente; ~**ity** [-'lɪdɪtɪ] *n* validade *f*; vigência.
valley ['vælɪ] *n* vale *m*.
valour, valor (*US*) ['vælə*] *n* valor *m*, valentia.
valuable ['væljuəbl] *adj* (*jewel*) de valor; (*time*) valioso; ~**s** *npl* objetos (*Pt*: -ct-) *mpl* de valor.
valuation [vælju'eɪʃən] *n* avaliação *f*, estimativa.
value ['vælju:] *n* valor *m*; (*importance*) importância // *vt* (*fix price of*) avaliar, calcular; (*esteem*) estimar; (*cherish*) apreciar; ~ **added tax** (**VAT**) *n* imposto sobre valor aduzido (IVA); ~**d** *adj* (*appreciated*) apreciado, estimado.
valve [vælv] *n* (*gen*) válvula.
vampire ['væmpaɪə*] *n* vampiro/a *m/f*.
van [væn] *n* (*AUT*) camionete *f* (*Br*), camioneta (*Pt*).
vandal ['vændl] *n* vândalo; ~**ism** *n* vandalismo; ~**ize** *vt* destruir, depredar.
vanilla [və'nɪlə] *n* baunilha.
vanish ['vænɪʃ] *vi* desaparecer, sumir.
vanity ['vænɪtɪ] *n* vaidade *f*; ~ **case** *n* bolsa de maquilagem.
vantage point ['vɑ:ntɪdʒ-] *n* posição *f* estratégica.
vapour, vapor (*US*) ['veɪpə*] *n* vapor *m*.
variable ['vɛərɪəbl] *adj* variável.
variance ['vɛərɪəns] *n*: **to be at** ~ (**with**) estar em desacordo (com).
variation [vɛərɪ'eɪʃən] *n* variação *f*, variante *f*; (*in opinion*) variedade *f*.
varicose ['værɪkous] *adj*: ~ **veins** varizes *fpl*.
varied ['vɛərɪd] *adj* variado.
variety [və'raɪətɪ] *n* variedade *f*, diversidade *f*; (*quantity*) sortimento; ~ **show** *n* espetáculo de variedades.
various ['vɛərɪəs] *adj* vários/as, diversos/as.
varnish ['vɑ:nɪʃ] *n* (*gen*) verniz *m*; (*nail* ~) esmalte *m* // *vt* (*gen*) envernizar; (*nails*) pintar (com esmalte).
vary ['vɛərɪ] *vt* variar; (*change*) mudar // *vi* variar; (*disagree*) divergir, discrepar; (*deviate*) desviar-se; ~**ing** *adj* variado.
vase [vɑ:z] *n* vaso.
vaseline ['væsɪli:n] *n* vaselina.

vast [vɑ:st] *adj* vasto, enorme; (*success*) imenso; ~**ness** *n* imensidão *f*.
vat [væt] *n* tina, cuba.
VAT [væt] *n abbr of* **Value Added Tax.**
Vatican ['vætɪkən] *n*: **the** ~ o Vaticano.
vault [vɔ:lt] *n* (*of roof*) abóbada; (*tomb*) sepulcro; (*in bank*) caixa-forte *f* // *vt* (*also*: ~ **over**) saltar (por cima de).
veal [vi:l] *n* carne *f* de vitela.
veer [vɪə*] *vi* virar, mudar de direção (*Pt*: -cç-).
vegetable ['vedʒtəbl] *n* (*BOT*) vegetal *m*; (*edible plant*) legume *m*, hortaliça; ~**s** *npl* (*cooked*) verduras *fpl* // *adj* vegetal; ~ **garden** *n* horta.
vegetarian [vedʒɪ'tɛərɪən] *adj*, *n* vegetariano.
vegetate ['vedʒɪteɪt] *vi* vegetar.
vegetation [vedʒɪ'teɪʃən] *n* vegetação *f*.
vehement ['vi:mənt] *adj* veemente; (*impassioned*) apaixonado.
vehicle ['vi:ɪkl] *n* veículo.
veil [veɪl] *n* véu *m* // *vt* velar.
vein [veɪn] *n* veia; (*of ore etc*) filão *m*.
velocity [vɪ'lɔsɪtɪ] *n* velocidade *f*.
velvet ['velvɪt] *n* veludo // *adj* aveludado.
vendetta [vɛn'detə] *n* vendeta.
vending machine ['vendɪŋ-] *n* vendedor *m* automático.
vendor ['vendə*] *n* vendedor(a) *m/f*.
veneer [və'nɪə*] *n* capa exterior, folheado; (*wood*) compensado; (*fig*) verniz *m*, aparência.
venereal [vɪ'nɪərɪəl] *adj*: ~ **disease** (**VD**) doença venérea.
Venetian blind [vɪ'ni:ʃən-] *n* persiana.
Venezuela [venɛ'zweɪlə] *n* Venezuela; ~**n** *adj*, *n* venezuelano/a.
vengeance ['vendʒəns] *n* vingança; **with a** ~ (*fig*) com fúria, com violência.
venison ['venɪsn] *n* carne *f* de veado.
venom ['venəm] *n* veneno; ~**ous** *adj* venenoso.
vent [vent] *n* (*opening*) abertura; (*air-hole*) respiradouro; (*in wall*) abertura para ventilação // *vt* (*fig: feelings*) desabafar, descarregar.
ventilate ['ventɪleɪt] *vt* ventilar; **ventilation** [-'leɪʃən] *n* ventilação *f*; **ventilator** *n* ventilador *m*.
ventriloquist [ven'trɪləkwɪst] *n* ventríloquo.
venture ['ventʃə*] *n* empreendimento // *vt* aventurar; (*opinion*) arriscar // *vi* arriscar-se, ousar.
venue ['venju:] *n* local *m*; (*meeting place*) ponto de encontro.
veranda(h) [və'rændə] *n* varanda; (*with glass*) jardim *m* de inverno.
verb [və:b] *n* verbo; ~**al** *adj* verbal.
verbatim [və:'beɪtɪm] *adj*, *adv* palavra por palavra, literalmente.
verbose [və:'bəus] *adj* prolixo.
verdict ['və:dɪkt] *n* veredicto, decisão *f*; (*fig*) opinião *f*, parecer *m*.
verge [və:dʒ] *n* limite *m*, margem *f*; **to**

be on the ~ of doing sth estar a ponto de fazer algo; **to ~ on** vt fus beirar em.

verify ['vɛrɪfaɪ] vt verificar.

vermin ['vɜːmɪn] npl (animals) bichos mpl; (insects, fig) insetos (Pt: -ct-) mpl nocivos; (fig) canalha, gente f vil.

vermouth ['vɜːməθ] n vermute m.

vernacular [vəˈnækjʊlə*] n vernáculo, língua materna.

versatile ['vɜːsətaɪl] adj (person) versátil; (machine, tool etc) polivalente; (mind) ágil, flexível.

verse [vɜːs] n verso, poesia; (stanza) estrofe f; (in bible) versículo.

versed [vɜːst] adj: (well-)~ in versado em, especialista em.

version ['vɜːʃən] n versão f.

versus ['vɜːsəs] prep contra, versus.

vertebra ['vɜːtɪbrə] pl ~e [-briː] n vértebra; **vertebrate** [-brɪt] n vertebrado.

vertical ['vɜːtɪkl] adj vertical.

vertigo ['vɜːtɪɡəʊ] n vertigem f.

very ['vɛrɪ] adv muito // adj: **the ~ book which** o mesmo livro que; **the ~ last** o último (de todos), bem o último; **at the ~ least** no mínimo; **~ much** muitíssimo.

vespers ['vɛspəz] npl vésperas fpl.

vessel ['vɛsl] n (ANAT) vaso; (NAUT) navio, barco; (container) vaso, vasilha.

vest [vɛst] n camiseta (Br), camisola interior (Pt); (US: waistcoat) colete m; ~**ed interests** npl (COMM) interesses mpl ocultos.

vestibule ['vɛstɪbjuːl] n vestíbulo.

vestige ['vɛstɪdʒ] n vestígio, rasto.

vestry ['vɛstrɪ] n sacristia.

vet [vɛt] n abbr of **veterinary surgeon** // vt examinar.

veteran ['vɛtərn] n veterano/a; ~ **car** n carro antigo.

veterinary ['vɛtrɪnərɪ] adj veterinário; ~ **surgeon** n veterinário/a.

veto ['viːtəʊ] pl ~**es** n veto // vt vetar, proibir.

vex [vɛks] vt (irritate) irritar, apoquentar; (make impatient) impacientar; ~**ed** adj (question) controvertido, discutido.

via ['vaɪə] prep por, por via de.

viable ['vaɪəbl] adj viável.

viaduct ['vaɪədʌkt] n viaduto.

vibrate [vaɪˈbreɪt] vi vibrar; **vibration** [-ˈbreɪʃən] n vibração f.

vicar ['vɪkə*] n vigário; ~**age** n vicariato.

vice [vaɪs] n (evil) vício; (TECH) torno mecânico.

vice- [vaɪs] pref vice-; ~**chairman** n vice-presidente m/f.

vice versa ['vaɪsɪ'vɜːsə] adv vice-versa.

vicinity [vɪˈsɪnɪtɪ] n (area) vizinhança; (nearness) proximidade f.

vicious ['vɪʃəs] adj (violent) violento; (depraved) depravado, vicioso; (cruel) cruel; (bitter) rancoroso; ~**ness** n

violência; depravação f; crueldade f; rancor m.

victim ['vɪktɪm] n vítima f; ~**ization** [-ˈzeɪʃən] n (gen) perseguição f; (in strike) represálias fpl; ~**ize** vt (strikers etc) fazer represália contra.

victor ['vɪktə*] n vencedor(a) m/f.

Victorian [vɪkˈtɔːrɪən] adj vitoriano.

victorious [vɪkˈtɔːrɪəs] adj vitorioso.

victory ['vɪktərɪ] n vitória.

video ['vɪdɪəʊ] cmp vídeo; ~**(-tape) recorder** n gravador m de vídeoteipe, vídeo-cassete m.

vie [vaɪ] vi: **to ~ with** competir com.

Vienna [vɪˈɛnə] n Viena.

view [vjuː] n vista, perspectiva; (landscape) paisagem f; (opinion) opinião f, parecer m // vt (look at) olhar; (examine) examinar; **on ~** (in museum etc) em exposição; **in full ~ (of)** à plena vista (de); **in ~ of the fact that** em vista do fato (Pt: -ct-) de que; ~**er** n (small projector) visor m; (TV) telespectador(a) m/f; ~**finder** n visor m; ~**point** n ponto de vista.

vigil ['vɪdʒɪl] n vigília; **to keep ~** velar; ~**ance** n vigilância; ~**ant** adj vigilante.

vigorous ['vɪɡərəs] adj enérgico, vigoroso; **vigour**, **vigor** (US) n energia, vigor m.

vile [vaɪl] adj (action) vil, infame; (smell) repugnante, repulsivo.

vilify ['vɪlɪfaɪ] vt vilipendiar.

villa ['vɪlə] n (country house) casa de campo; (suburban house) vila, quinta.

village ['vɪlɪdʒ] n aldeia, povoado; **villager** n aldeão/aldeã m/f.

villain ['vɪlən] n (scoundrel) patife m; (criminal) marginal m/f.

vindicate ['vɪndɪkeɪt] vt vingar, desagravar.

vindictive [vɪnˈdɪktɪv] adj vingativo.

vine [vaɪn] n vinha, videira.

vinegar ['vɪnɪɡə*] n vinagre m.

vineyard ['vɪnjɑːd] n vinha, vinhedo.

vintage ['vɪntɪdʒ] n vindima; (year) safra, colheita; ~ **wine** n vinho velho.

vinyl ['vaɪnl] n vinil m.

violate ['vaɪəleɪt] vt violar; **violation** [-ˈleɪʃən] n violação f.

violence ['vaɪələns] n violência; **violent** adj (gen) violento; (intense) intenso.

violet ['vaɪələt] adj violeta // n (plant) violeta.

violin [vaɪəˈlɪn] n violino; ~**ist** n violinista m/f.

viper ['vaɪpə*] n víbora.

virgin ['vɜːdʒɪn] n virgem m/f // adj virgem; **the Blessed V~** a Virgem Santíssima; ~**ity** [-ˈdʒɪnɪtɪ] n virgindade f.

Virgo ['vɜːɡəʊ] n Virgem f.

virile ['vɪraɪl] adj viril; **virility** [vɪˈrɪlɪtɪ] n virilidade f; (fig) machismo.

virtually ['vɜːtjʊəlɪ] adv (almost) virtualmente.

virtue ['vɜːtjuː] n virtude f; **by ~ of** em virtude de.

virtuoso [vɔːtjuˈəuzəu] n virtuoso/a.

virtuous [ˈvɔːtjuəs] adj virtuoso.

virulent [ˈvɪrulənt] adj virulento.

virus [ˈvaɪərəs] n vírus m.

visa [ˈviːzə] n visto.

vis-à-vis [viːzəˈviː] prep com relação a.

visibility [vɪzɪˈbɪlɪtɪ] n visibilidade f.

visible [ˈvɪzəbl] adj visível; **visibly** adv visivelmente.

vision [ˈvɪʒən] n (sight) vista, visão f; (foresight, in dream) visão f; ~**ary** n visionário/a.

visit [ˈvɪzɪt] n visita // vt (person) visitar, fazer uma visita a; (place) ir a, ir conhecer; ~**or** n (gen) visitante m/f; (to one's house) visita; (tourist) turista m/f; (tripper) excursionista m/f; ~**ors' book** n livro de visitas.

visor [ˈvaɪzə*] n viseira.

vista [ˈvɪstə] n vista, perspectiva.

visual [ˈvɪzjuəl] adj visual; ~**ize** vt visualizar; (foresee) prever.

vital [ˈvaɪtl] adj (essential) essencial, indispensável; (important) de importância vital; (crucial) crucial; (person) vivo, animado; (of life) vital; ~**ity** [-ˈtælɪtɪ] n energia, vitalidade f; ~**ly** adv: ~**ly important** de importância vital.

vitamin [ˈvɪtəmɪn] n vitamina.

vivacious [vɪˈveɪʃəs] adj vivaz, espirituoso.

vivid [ˈvɪvɪd] adj (account) vívido; (light) claro, brilhante; (imagination) vivo.

vivisection [vɪvɪˈsɛkʃən] n vivissecção f.

V-neck [ˈviːnɛk] n gola em V.

vocabulary [vəuˈkæbjulərɪ] n vocabulário.

vocal [ˈvəukl] adj vocal; (noisy) clamoroso; ~ **chords** npl cordas fpl vocais; ~**ist** n vocalista m/f, cantor(a) m/f.

vocation [vəuˈkeɪʃən] n vocação f; ~**al** adj vocacional.

vociferous [vəˈsɪfərəs] adj vociferante.

vodka [ˈvɔdkə] n vodca.

vogue [vəug] n voga, moda.

voice [vɔɪs] n voz f; **in a low/loud** ~ em voz baixa/alta // vt (opinion) expressar.

void [vɔɪd] n vazio; (hole) oco // adj (gen) vazio; (vacant) vago; (null) nulo, inútil.

volatile [ˈvɔlətaɪl] adj volátil.

volcanic [vɔlˈkænɪk] adj vulcânico; **volcano** [-ˈkeɪnəu], pl **-es** n vulcão m.

volley [ˈvɔlɪ] n (of gunfire) descarga, salva; (of stones etc) chuva; (TENNIS etc) voleio; ~**ball** n voleibol m.

volt [vəult] n volt m; ~**age** n voltagem f.

voluble [ˈvɔljubl] adj tagarela, loquaz.

volume [ˈvɔljuːm] n (gen) volume m.

voluntarily [ˈvɔləntrɪlɪ] adv livremente, voluntariamente.

voluntary [ˈvɔləntərɪ] adj voluntário, intencional; (unpaid) (a título) gratuito.

volunteer [vɔlənˈtɪə*] n voluntário/a m/f // vi oferecer-se voluntariamente.

voluptuous [vəˈlʌptjuəs] adj voluptuoso.

vomit [ˈvɔmɪt] n vômito // vt/i vomitar.

vote [vəut] n voto; (votes cast) votação f; (right to ~) direito de votar; (franchise) título de eleitor // vt (chairman) eleger // vi votar; **voter** n votante m/f, eleitor(a) m/f; **voting** n votação f.

vouch [vautʃ]: **to** ~ **for** vt garantir, responder por.

voucher [ˈvautʃə*] n (for meal, petrol) vale m.

vow [vau] n voto // vi fazer votos.

vowel [ˈvauəl] n vogal f.

voyage [ˈvɔɪdʒ] n (journey) viagem f; (crossing) travessia.

vulgar [ˈvʌlgə*] adj (rude) grosseiro, ordinário; (in bad taste) vulgar, baixo; ~**ity** [-ˈgærɪtɪ] n grosseria, vulgaridade f.

vulnerable [ˈvʌlnərəbl] adj vulnerável.

vulture [ˈvʌltʃə*] n abutre m.

W

wad [wɔd] n (of cotton wool) chumaço; (of paper) bola; (of banknotes etc) maço.

waddle [ˈwɔdl] vi gingar, bambolear.

wade [weɪd] vi: **to** ~ **through** vadear; (fig: a book) ler com dificuldade; (river) atravessar (a vau).

wafer [ˈweɪfə*] n (biscuit) bolacha; (REL) hóstia.

waffle [ˈwɔfl] vi ficar de conversa fiada.

waft [wɔft] vt levar // vi flutuar.

wag [wæg] vt sacudir, menear // vi acenar, abanar.

wage [weɪdʒ] n (also: ~s) salário, ordenado // vt: **to** ~ **war** empreender guerra; ~ **claim** n pedido de aumento salarial; ~ **earner** n assalariado/a; ~ **freeze** n congelamento de salários.

wager [ˈweɪdʒə*] n aposta, parada // vt apostar.

waggle [ˈwægl] vt sacudir, agitar.

wag(g)on [ˈwægən] n (horse-drawn) carroça; (truck) caminhão m; (: Pt) camião m; (RAIL) vagão m.

wail [weɪl] n lamento, gemido // vi lamentar-se, gemer.

waist [weɪst] n cintura; ~**coat** n colete m; ~**line** n cintura.

wait [weɪt] n espera; (interval) pausa // vi esperar; **to lie in** ~ **for** aguardar em emboscada; **I can't** ~ **to** (fig) mal posso esperar para; **to** ~ **for** esperar, aguardar; **to** ~ **on** vt fus servir; "**no** ~**ing**" (AUT) "proibido estacionar"; ~**er** n garçom m (Br), empregado (Pt); ~**ing list** n lista de espera; ~**ing room** n sala de espera; ~**ress** n garçonete f (Br), empregada (Pt).

waive [weɪv] vt renunciar a.

wake [weɪk], pt **woke** or **waked**, pp **woken** or **waked** vt (also: ~ **up**) acordar, despertar // vi (also: ~ **up**) despertar-se // n (for dead person) velório; (NAUT) esteira; **waken** vt/i = **wake**.

Wales [weɪlz] n País m de Gales.

walk [wɔːk] n passeio; (hike) excursão f a pé, caminhada; (gait) passo, modo de andar; (in park etc) alameda, passeio // vi andar; (for pleasure, exercise) passear // vt (distance) percorrer a pé, andar; (dog) levar para passear; **it's 10 minutes'** ~ **from here** daqui são 10 minutos a pé; **people from all** ~**s of life** pessoas de todos os níveis; ~**er** n (person) caminhante m/f; ~**ie-talkie** ['wɔːkɪ'tɔːkɪ] n transmissor-receptor portátil m, walkie-talkie m; ~**ing** n o andar m; ~**ing shoes** npl sapatos para andar; ~**ing stick** n bengala; ~**out** n (of workers) greve f branca; ~**over** n (col) barbada; ~**way** n passeio.

wall [wɔːl] n parede f; (exterior) muro; (city ~ etc) muralha; ~**ed** adj (city) cercado por muralhas; (garden) murado, cercado.

wallet ['wɔlɪt] n carteira.

wallflower ['wɔːlflauə*] n goivo-amarelo; **to be a** ~ (fig) tomar chá de cadeira.

wallop ['wɔləp] vt (col) surrar, espancar.

wallow ['wɔləu] vi chafurdar.

wallpaper ['wɔːlpeɪpə*] n papel m de parede.

walnut ['wɔːlnʌt] n noz f; (tree) nogueira.

walrus ['wɔːlrəs], pl ~ or ~**es** n morsa, vaca marinha.

waltz [wɔːlts] n valsa // vi valsar.

wand [wɔnd] n (also: **magic** ~) varinha de condão.

wander ['wɔndə*] vi (person) vagar, perambular; (thoughts) divagar; (get lost) extraviar-se // vt percorrer; ~**er** n vagabundo; ~**ing** adj errante; (thoughts) distraído.

wane [weɪn] vi diminuir; (moon) minguar.

wangle ['wæŋgl] vt (col): **to** ~ **sth** conseguir algo através de pistolão.

want [wɔnt] vt (wish for) querer, desejar; (demand) exigir; (need) precisar (de), necessitar; (lack) carecer de // n: **for** ~ **of** por falta de; ~**s** npl (needs) necessidades fpl; **to** ~ **to do** querer fazer; **to** ~ **sb to do sth** querer que alguém faça algo; ~**ing** adj falto, deficiente; **to be found** ~**ing** não estar à altura da situação.

wanton ['wɔntn] adj (playful) brincalhão/lhona; (licentious) libertino, lascivo.

war [wɔː*] n guerra; **to make** ~ fazer guerra.

ward [wɔːd] n (in hospital) ala, enfermaria; (POL) distrito eleitoral; (LAW: child) tutelado, pupilo; **to** ~ **off** vt desviar, aparar; (attack) repelir.

warden ['wɔːdn] n (of institution) diretor(a) (Pt: -ct-) m/f; (of park, game reserve) administrador m; (also: **traffic** ~) guarda m/f.

warder ['wɔːdə*] n carcereiro.

wardrobe ['wɔːdrəub] n (cupboard) armário; (clothes) guarda-roupa.

warehouse ['wɛəhaus] n armazém m, depósito.

wares [wɛəz] npl artigos mpl, mercadorias fpl.

war: ~**fare** n guerra, combate m; ~**head** n ogiva (de combate).

warily ['wɛərɪlɪ] adv cautelosamente, com precaução.

warlike ['wɔːlaɪk] adj guerreiro, bélico.

warm [wɔːm] adj quente, morno, cálido; (thanks, welcome) cordial; (clothes, day) quente; **it's** ~ está quente; **I'm** ~ estou com calor; **to** ~ **up** vi (person, room) aquecer, esquentar; (athlete) fazer aquecimento; (discussion) esquentar-se // vt esquentar; ~**-hearted** adj afetuoso (Pt: -ct-); ~**ly** adv calorosamente, afetuosamente (Pt: -ct-); ~**th** n calor m.

warn [wɔːn] vt prevenir, avisar; ~**ing** n advertência, aviso; ~**ing light** n luz f de advertência.

warp [wɔːp] vt deformar // vi empenar, deformar-se.

warrant ['wɔrnt] n (guarantee) garantia, fiança; (LAW) ordem f judicial.

warranty ['wɔrəntɪ] n garantia.

warren ['wɔrən] n (of rabbits) lura; (house) coelheira.

warrior ['wɔrɪə*] n guerreiro.

warship ['wɔːʃɪp] n navio de guerra.

wart [wɔːt] n verruga.

wartime ['wɔːtaɪm] n: **in** ~ em tempo de guerra.

wary ['wɛərɪ] adj cauteloso, precavido.

was [wɔz] pt of **be**.

wash [wɔʃ] vt lavar // vi lavar-se // n (clothes etc) lavagem f; (bath) banho; (of ship) esteira; **to have a** ~ lavar-se; **to** ~ **away** vt (stain) tirar ao lavar; (subj: river etc) levar, arrastar; (fig) purificar; **to** ~ **off** vt tirar lavando; **to** ~ **up** vi lavar a louça; (US) lavar-se; ~**able** adj lavável; ~**basin** n, ~**bowl** (US) n pia (Br), lavatório (Pt); ~**er** n (TECH) arruela, anilha; ~**ing** n (dirty) roupa suja; (clean) roupa lavada; ~**ing machine** n máquina de lavar; ~**ing powder** n sabão m em pó; ~**ing-up** n lavagem f da louça; ~**-out** n (col) fracasso, fiasco; ~**room** n banheiro (Br), casa de banho (Pt).

wasn't ['wɔznt] = **was not.**

wasp [wɔsp] n vespa.

wastage ['weɪstɪdʒ] n desgaste m, desperdício; (loss) perda; **natural** ~ desgaste natural.

waste [weɪst] n desperdício, esbanjamento; (wastage) desperdício; (of time) perda; (food) sobras fpl; (rubbish) lixo // adj (material) de refugo; (left over) de sobra; (land) baldio // vt (squander) esbanjar, dissipar; (time) perder; (opportunity) desperdiçar; (use up) consumir; **to** ~ **away** vi consumir-se; ~**bin** n lata de lixo; ~ **disposal unit** n triturador m de lixo; ~**ful** adj esbanjador(a); (process) anti-econômico; ~ **ground** n terreno baldio; ~**paper**

basket *n* cesta de papel; ~ **pipe** *n* cano de esgoto.

watch [wɔtʃ] *n* relógio; (*act of watching*) vigia; (*vigilance*) vigilância; (*guard:* MIL) sentinela *f*; (NAUT: *spell of duty*) quarto // *vt* (*look at*) observar, olhar; (*programme*) ver; (*go and see*) assistir a; (*spy on, guard*) vigiar; (*be careful of*) tomar cuidado com // *vi* ver, olhar; (*keep guard*) montar guarda; **to** ~ **out** *vi* cuidar-se, ter cuidado; ~**dog** *n* cão *m* de guarda; ~**ful** *adj* vigilante, atento; ~**maker** *n* relojoeiro; ~**man** *n* vigia *m*; (*also:* **night** ~**man**) guarda *m* noturno; (*in factory*) vigia *m* noturno; ~ **strap** *n* pulseira (do relógio); ~**word** *n* lema *m*, divisa.

water ['wɔ:tə*] *n* água // *vt* (*plant*) regar; **to** ~ **down** *vt* (*milk*) aguar; ~**colour** *n* aquarela; ~**cress** *n* agrião *m*; ~**fall** *n* cascata, cachoeira; ~ **hole** *n* bebedouro, poço; ~**ing can** *n* regador *m*; ~ **level** *n* nível *m* d'água; ~ **lily** *n* nenúfar *m*; ~**line** *n* (NAUT) linha d'água; ~**logged** *adj* alagado; ~ **main** *n* adutora; ~**mark** *n* (*on paper*) filigrana; ~**melon** *n* melancia; ~ **polo** *n* polo-aquático; ~**proof** *adj* impermeável; (*watch*) à prova d'água; ~**shed** *n* (fig) momento crítico; ~**skiing** *n* esqui *m* aquático; ~ **tank** *n* depósito d'água; ~**tight** *adj* hermético, à prova d'água; ~**works** *npl* sistema hidráulico; ~**y** *adj* (*colour*) pálido; (*coffee*) aguado; (*eyes*) húmido.

watt [wɔt] *n* watt *m*.

wave [weiv] *n* onda; (*of hand*) aceno, sinal *m*; (RADIO) onda, vaga; (*in hair*) onda, ondulação *f*; (fig: *series*) série *f* // *vi* acenar com a mão; (*flag*) tremular, flutuar // *vt* (*handkerchief*) acenar com; (*weapon*) brandir; (*hair*) ondular; ~**length** *n* comprimento de onda.

waver ['weivə*] *vi* vacilar; (*person*) hesitar.

wavy ['weivi] *adj* ondulado, ondulante.

wax [wæks] *n* cera // *vt* encerar // *vi* (*moon*) crescer; ~**works** *npl* museu *msg* de cera.

way [wei] *n* (*gen*) caminho; (*distance*) percurso; (*direction*) direção (Pt: -cç-) *f*, sentido; (*manner*) maneira, modo; (*habit*) costume *m*; (*condition*) estado; **which** ~? em qual dire(c)ção?, qual é o caminho?; **to be on one's** ~ estar a caminho; **to be in the** ~ estorvar; **to go out of one's** ~ **to do sth** dar-se ao trabalho de fazer algo; **to lose one's** ~ perder-se; **in a** ~ de certo modo, até certo ponto; **by the** ~ a propósito; "~ **out**" "saída"; **the** ~ **back** o caminho de volta; "**give** ~" (AUT) "via preferencial".

waylay [wei'lei] (*irr: like* lay) *vt* armar uma cilada para.

wayward ['weiwəd] *adj* (*wilful*) voluntarioso, teimoso; (*capricious*) caprichoso; (*naughty*) travesso.

W.C. ['dʌblju'si:] *n* banheiro (Br), casa de banho (Pt).

we [wi:] *pl pron* nós.

weak [wi:k] *adj* (*gen*) fraco, débil; (*tea*) aguado, ralo; ~**en** *vi* enfraquecer-se; (*give way*) ceder // *vt* atenuar; (*lessen*) diminuir; ~**ling** *n* pessoa fraca *or* delicada; ~**ness** *n* fraqueza; (*fault*) ponto fraco.

wealth [wεlθ] *n* (*money, resources*) riqueza; (*of details*) abundância; ~**y** *adj* rico, abastado.

wean [wi:n] *vt* desmamar.

weapon ['wεpən] *n* arma.

wear [wεə*] *n* (*use*) uso; (*deterioration through use*) desgaste *m*; (*clothing*): **sports/baby** ~ roupa de esporte/infantil // (*vb: pt* **wore**, *pp* **worn**) *vt* (*clothes*) usar; (*shoes*) usar, calçar; (*put on*) vestir; (*damage: through use*) desgastar // *vi* (*last*) durar; (*rub through etc*) gastar-se; ~ **and tear** *n* desgaste *m* natural; **to** ~ **away** *vt* gastar // *vi* desgastar-se; **to** ~ **down** *vt* gastar; (*strength*) esgotar; **to** ~ **off** *vi* (*pain etc*) passar; **to** ~ **out** *vt* desgastar; (*person, strength*) esgotar.

weariness ['wiərinis] *n* cansaço, fadiga; (*boredom*) aborrecimento.

weary ['wiəri] *adj* (*tired*) cansado; (*dispirited*) deprimido // *vt* aborrecer // *vi:* **to** ~ **of** cansar-se de.

weasel ['wi:zl] *n* (ZOOL) doninha.

weather ['wεðə*] *n* tempo // *vt* (*storm, crisis*) resistir a; ~-**beaten** *adj* curtido; ~ **cock** *n* cata-vento; ~ **forecast** *n* boletim *m* meteorológico; ~ **vane** *n see* ~ **cock**.

weave [wi:v], *pt* **wove**, *pp* **woven** *vt* (*cloth*) tecer; (fig) compor, criar; **weaver** *n* tecelão/loa *m/f*; **weaving** *n* tecelagem *f*.

web [wεb] *n* (*of spider*) teia; (*on foot*) membrana; (*network*) rede *f*; ~**bed** *adj* (*foot*) palmípede; ~**bing** *n* (*on chair*) tira de tecido forte.

wed [wεd], *pt, pp* **wedded** *vt* casar // *vi* casar-se // *n:* **the newly-**~**s** os recém-casados *mpl*.

we'd [wi:d] = **we had; we would**.

wedded ['wεdid] *pt, pp of* **wed**.

wedding ['wεdiŋ] *n* casamento, núpcias *fpl*; **silver/golden** ~ bodas *fpl* de prata/de ouro; ~ **day** *n* dia *m* do casamento; ~ **night** noite *f* de núpcias; ~ **dress** *n* vestido de noiva; ~ **present** *n* presente *m* de casamento; ~ **ring** *n* anel *m* or aliança de casamento.

wedge [wεdʒ] *n* (*of wood etc*) cunha, calço; (*of cake*) fatia // *vt* (*pack tightly*) socar, apertar.

wedlock ['wεdlɔk] *n* matrimônio, casamento.

Wednesday ['wεdnzdi] *n* quarta-feira.

wee [wi:] *adj* (*Scottish*) pequeno, pequenino.

weed [wi:d] *n* erva daninha // *vt* capinar; ~-**killer** *n* herbicida *m*.

week [wi:k] *n* semana; ~**day** *n* dia *m* da semana; ~**end** *n* fim *m* de semana; ~**ly**

adv semanalmente // *adj* semanal // *n* semanário.

weep [wi:p] *pt, pp* **wept** *vt/i* chorar; ~**ing willow** *n* salgueiro chorão.

weigh [weɪ] *vt/i* pesar; **to** ~ **down** *vt* sobrecarregar; (*fig: with worry*) deprimir, acabrunhar; **to** ~ **up** *vt* ponderar, avaliar; ~**bridge** *n* báscula automática.

weight [weɪt] *n* peso; **to lose / put on** ~ emagrecer/engordar; ~**lessness** *n* ausência de peso; ~ **lifter** *n* levantador *m* de pesos; ~**y** *adj* pesado, importante.

weir [wɪə*] *n* represa, açude *m*.

weird [wɪəd] *adj* misterioso, estranho.

welcome ['wɛlkəm] *adj* bem-vindo // *n* acolhimento, recepção *f* // *vt* dar as boas-vindas a; (*be glad of*) receber com alegria; **you're** ~ de nada; **welcoming** *adj* acolhedor(a); (*speech*) de boas-vindas.

weld [wɛld] *n* solda // *vt* soldar, unir; ~**er** *n* (*person*) soldador *m*; ~**ing** *n* soldagem *f*, solda.

welfare ['wɛlfɛə*] *n* bem-estar *m*; (*social aid*) assistência social; ~ **state** *n* país auto-financiador da sua assistência social.

well [wɛl] *n* poço; (*pool*) nascente *f* // *adv* bem // *adj*: **to be** ~ estar bem (de saúde) // *excl* bem!, então!; **as** ~ também; **as** ~ **as** assim como; ~ **done!** muito bem!; **get** ~ **soon!** melhoras!; **to do** ~ ir *or* sair-se bem; **to** ~ **up** *vi* brotar, manar.

we'll [wi:l] = **we will, we shall.**

well: ~-**behaved** *adj* bem educado, bem comportado; ~-**being** *n* bem-estar *m*; ~-**built** *adj* (*person*) robusto; ~-**deserved** *adj* bem merecido; ~-**developed** *adj* bem desenvolvido; ~-**dressed** *adj* bem vestido; ~-**heeled** *adj* (*col: wealthy*) rico; ~-**informed** *adj* bem informado, versado.

wellingtons ['wɛliŋtənz] *n* (*also:* **wellington boots**) botas *fpl* de plástico até os joelhos.

well: ~-**known** *adj* (*person*) conhecido, famoso; ~-**mannered** *adj* bem-educado; ~-**meaning** *adj* bem intencionado; ~-**off** *adj* próspero, rico; ~-**read** *adj* lido, versado; ~-**to-do** *adj* abastado; ~-**wisher** *n* simpatizante *m/f*.

Welsh [wɛlʃ] *adj* galês/galesa // *n* (*LING*) galês *m*; ~**man/woman** *n* galês/galesa *m/f*.

went [wɛnt] *pt of* **go.**

wept [wɛpt] *pt, pp of* **weep.**

were [wə:*] *pt of* **be.**

we're [wɪə*] = **we are.**

weren't [wə:nt] = **were not.**

west [wɛst] *n* oeste *m* // *adj* ocidental, do oeste // *adv* para o oeste *or* ao oeste; **the W**~ *n* o Oeste, o Ocidente; ~**erly** *adj* (*situation*) ocidental; (*wind*) oeste; ~**ern** *adj* ocidental // *n* (*CINEMA*) western *m*; **W**~ **Germany** *n* Alemanha Ocidental; **W**~ **Indies** *npl* Antilhas *fpl*; ~**ward(s)** *adv* para o oeste.

wet [wɛt] *adj* (*damp*) úmido; (~ *through*) molhado, encharcado; (*rainy*) chuvoso; **to get** ~ molhar-se; "~ **paint**" "tinta fresca"; **to be a** ~ **blanket** (*fig*) ser um desmancha-prazeres; ~**ness** *n* umidade *f*; ~ **suit** *n* roupa de mergulho.

we've [wi:v] = **we have.**

whack [wæk] *vt* bater; ~**ed** *adj* (*col: tired*) morto, esgotado.

whale [weɪl] *n* (*ZOOL*) baleia.

wharf [wɔ:f], *pl* **wharves** [wɔ:vz] *n* cais *m inv.*

what [wɔt] *excl* quê!, como! // *det* que // *pron* (*interrogative*) que, o que; (*relative, indirect: object, subject*) o que, a que; ~ **are you doing?** o que é que você está fazendo?; **I saw** ~ **you did** eu vi o que você fez; ~ **a mess!** que bagunça!; ~ **is it called?** como se chama?; ~ **about me?** e eu?; ~**ever** *det*: ~**ever book you choose** qualquer livro que você escolha // *pron*: **do** ~**ever is necessary** faça tudo o que for preciso; **no reason** ~**ever** *or* ~**soever** nenhuma razão seja qual for, em absoluto; **nothing** ~**ever** nada em absoluto.

wheat [wi:t] *n* trigo.

wheel [wi:l] *n* roda; (*AUT: also:* **steering** ~) volante *m*; (*NAUT*) roda do leme // *vt* (*pram etc*) empurrar // *vi* (*also:* ~ **round**) girar, dar voltas, virar-se; ~**barrow** *n* carrinho de mão; ~**chair** *n* cadeira de rodas; ~**house** *n* casa do leme.

wheeze [wi:z] *n* respiração *f* difícil, chiado // *vi* respirar ruidosamente.

when [wɛn] *adv* quando // *conj* quando; (*whereas*) ao passo que; **on the day** ~ **I met him** no dia em que o conheci; ~**ever** *conj* quando, quando quer que; (*every time that*) sempre que.

where [wɛə*] *adv* onde // *conj* onde, aonde; **this is** ~ aqui é onde; ~**abouts** *adv* (por) onde // *n*: **nobody knows his** ~**abouts** ninguém sabe o seu paradeiro; ~**as** *conj* uma vez que, ao passo que; **wherever** [-'ɛvə*] *adv* onde quer que; (*interrogative*) onde?; ~**withal** *n* recursos *mpl*, meios *mpl*.

whet [wɛt] *vt* afiar; (*appetite*) abrir; (*desire*) despertar.

whether ['wɛðə*] *conj* se; **I don't know** ~ **to accept or not** não sei se aceito ou não; ~ **you go or not** quer você vá quer não.

which [wɪtʃ] *det* (*interrogative*) que, qual; ~ **one of you?** qual de vocês?; ~ **picture do you want?** que quadro você quer? // *pron* (*interrogative*) qual; (*relative: subject, object*) que, o que, o qual, *etc*; **I don't mind** ~ não me importa qual; **the apple** ~ **is on the table** a maçã que está sobre a mesa; **the chair on** ~ **you are sitting** a cadeira na qual você está sentado; **he said he knew,** ~ **is true** ele disse que sabia, o que é verdade; **in** ~ **case** em cujo caso; ~**ever** *det*: **take** ~**ever book you prefer** pegue o livro que preferir; **~ever book you take** qualquer livro que você pegue.

whiff [wɪf] n baforada, cheiro.

while [waɪl] n tempo, momento // conj durante; (as long as) enquanto; (although) embora; **for a ~** durante algum tempo.

whim [wɪm] n capricho, veneta.

whimper ['wɪmpə*] n (weeping) choradeira; (moan) lamúria // vi choramingar, soluçar.

whimsical ['wɪmzɪkl] adj (person) caprichoso, de veneta; (look) excêntrico.

whine [waɪn] n (of pain) gemido; (of engine) zunido // vi gemer, zunir; (dog) ganir.

whip [wɪp] n açoite m; (for riding) chicote m; (Brit: POL) líder m da bancada // vt chicotear; (snatch) apanhar de repente; **~ped cream** n creme m batido, chantilly m; **~-round** n coleta (Pt: -ct-), vaquinha.

whirl [wə:l] n remoinho // vt fazer rodar, rodopiar // vi girar; (leaves, water etc) fazer um remoinho; **~pool** n remoinho; **~wind** n furacão m, remoinho.

whirr [wə:*] vi zumbir.

whisk [wɪsk] n (CULIN) batedeira // vt bater; **to ~ sth away** from sb arrebatar algo de alguém; **to ~ sb away** or off levar rapidamente alguém.

whisker [wɪskə*] n: **~s** (of animal) bigodes mpl; (of man) suíças fpl.

whisk(e)y ['wɪskɪ] n uísque (Pt: whisky) m.

whisper ['wɪspə*] n sussurro, murmúrio; (rumour) rumor m; (fig) confidência // vi sussurrar, murmurar; (fig) segredar.

whist [wɪst] n uíste (Pt: whist) m.

whistle ['wɪsl] n (sound) assobio; (object) apito // vi assobiar.

white [waɪt] adj branco; (pale) pálido // n branco; (of egg) clara; **~-collar worker** n empregado de escritório; **~ lie** n mentira inofensiva or social; **~ness** n brancura; **~ paper** n (POL) livro branco; **~wash** n (paint) cal f // vt caiar; (fig) encobrir.

whiting ['waɪtɪŋ] n, pl inv (fish) pescada-marlonga.

Whitsun ['wɪtsn] n Pentecostes m.

whittle ['wɪtl] vt aparar; **to ~ away, ~ down** reduzir gradualmente.

whizz [wɪz] vi zunir; **to ~ past** or **by** passar a toda velocidade; **~ kid** n (col) prodígio.

who [hu:] pron (relative) que, o qual etc, quem; (interrogative) quem?; **~ever** pron: **~ever finds it** quem quer que or seja quem for que o encontre; **ask ~ever you like** pergunte a quem quiser; **~ever he marries** não importa com quem se case.

whole [həul] adj (complete) todo, inteiro; (not broken) intacto // n (total) total m; (sum) conjunto; **the ~ of the town** toda a cidade, a cidade inteira; **on the ~, as a ~** como um todo, no conjunto; **~hearted** adj sincero; **~sale** n venda

por atacado // adj por atacado; (destruction) em grande escala; **~saler** n atacadista m/f; **~some** adj saudável, sadio; **wholly** adv totalmente, completamente.

whom [hu:m] pron que, o qual, quem; (interrogative) quem?

whooping cough ['hu:pɪŋkɔf] n coqueluche f, tosse f terrível.

whopper ['wɔpə*] n (lie) lorota; **it was a ~** era enorme; **whopping** adj (col: big) imenso.

whore [hɔ:*] n (pej) puta.

whose [hu:z] det: **~ book is this?** de quem é este livro?; **the man ~ son you rescued** o homem cujo filho você salvou; **the girl ~ sister you were speaking to** a menina com cuja irmã você estava falando or/ pron: **~ is this?** de quem é isto?; **I know ~ it is** eu sei de quem é.

why [waɪ] adv porque; (interrogative) por quê?, por que razão? // excl ora essa!, bem!; **tell me ~** diga-me (o) porquê.

wick [wɪk] n mecha, pavio.

wicked ['wɪkɪd] adj malvado, perverso.

wicker ['wɪkə*] n (also: **~work**) (trabalho de) vime m.

wicket ['wɪkɪt] n (CRICKET) arco.

wide [waɪd] adj largo; (broad) extenso, amplo; (region, knowledge) vasto; (choice) variado; **it is 4 metres ~** tem 4 metros de largura // adv: **to open ~** abrir totalmente; **to shoot ~** atirar longe do alvo; **~-awake** adj bem acordado; (fig) vivo, esperto; **~ly** adv (different) extremamente; **it is ~ly believed that...** há uma convicção generalizada de que...; **widen** vt alargar; **~ness** n largura; (breadth) extensão f; **~ open** adj (eyes) arregalado; (door) escancarado; **~spread** adj (belief etc) difundido, comum.

widow ['wɪdəu] n viúva; **~ed** adj viúvo; **~er** n viúvo.

width [wɪdθ] n largura.

wield [wi:ld] vt (sword) brandir, empunhar; (power) exercer.

wife [waɪf], pl **wives** [waɪvz] n mulher f, esposa.

wig [wɪg] n peruca.

wiggle ['wɪgl] vt menear, agitar // vi menear, agitar-se.

wild [waɪld] adj (animal) selvagem; (plant) silvestre; (rough) violento, furioso; (idea) disparatado, extravagante; (person) louco, insensato; **~s** npl regiões fpl selvagens, terras fpl virgens; **~erness** ['wɪldənɪs] n ermo, sertão m; **~life** n animais e plantas selvagens; **~ly** adv (roughly) violentamente; (foolishly) loucamente; (rashly) desenfreadamente.

wilful ['wɪlful] adj (person) teimoso, voluntarioso; (action) deliberado, intencional; (obstinate) obstinado; (child) teimoso.

will [wɪl] auxiliary vb: **he ~ come** ele

virá // vt, pt, pp **willed: to ~ sb to do
sth** desejar que alguém faça algo; **he
~ed himself to go on** reuniu grande
força de vontade para continuar // n
vontade f; (testament) testamento; **~ing**
adj (with goodwill) disposto, pronto;
(submissive) complacente; **~ingly** adv de
bom grado, de boa vontade; **~ingness**
n boa vontade f, prontidão f.

willow ['wɪləu] n salgueiro.

will power n força de vontade.

wilt [wɪlt] vi murchar, definhar.

wily ['waɪlɪ] adj esperto, astuto.

win [wɪn] n (in sports etc) vitória // (vb:
pt, pp **won**) vt ganhar, vencer; (obtain)
conseguir, obter // vi ganhar; **to ~
over, ~ round** vt conquistar.

wince [wɪns] vi encolher-se, estremecer.

winch [wɪntʃ] n guincho.

wind [wɪnd] n vento; (MED) gases mpl,
flatulência; (breath) fôlego // (vb:
[waɪnd], pt, pp **wound**) vt enrolar,
bobinar; (wrap) envolver; (clock, toy) dar
corda a // vi (road, river) serpentear //
vt (take breath away from) deixar
sem fôlego; **to ~ up** vt (clock) dar
corda em; (debate) rematar, concluir;
~break n quebra-ventos msg; **~fall** n
golpe m de sorte; **~ing** ['waɪndɪŋ] adj
(road) sinuoso, tortuoso; **~instrument**
n (MUS) instrumento de sopro; **~mill** n
moinho de vento.

window ['wɪndəu] n janela; (in shop etc)
vitrine f (Br), montra (Pt); **~ box** n
jardineira (no peitoril da janela); **~
cleaner** n (person) limpador m de
janelas; **~ ledge** n peitoril m da janela;
~ pane n vidraça, vidro; **~sill** n
peitoril m, soleira.

windpipe ['wɪndpaɪp] n traquéia.

windscreen ['wɪndskri:n] n, **windshield** ['wɪndʃi:ld] (US) n pára-brisa m;
~ washer n lavador m de pára-brisa;
~ wiper n limpador m de pára-brisa.

windswept ['wɪndswept] adj varrido
pelo vento.

windy ['wɪndɪ] adj com muito vento,
batido pelo vento; **it's ~** está ventando
(Br), faz vento (Pt).

wine [waɪn] n vinho; **~ cellar** n adega;
~ glass n cálice m (de vinho); **~ list** n
lista de vinhos; **~ merchant** n
vinhateiro; **~ tasting** n degustação f de
vinhos.

wing [wɪŋ] n (gen) asa; (of building) ala;
(AUT) aleta, pára-lamas m inv; **~s** npl
(THEATRE) bastidores mpl; **~er** n
(SPORT) ponta, extremo.

wink [wɪŋk] n piscadela // vi piscar o
olho; (light etc) piscar.

winner ['wɪnə*] n vencedor(a) m/f.

winning ['wɪnɪŋ] adj (team) vencedor(a);
(goal) decisivo; **~s** npl lucros mpl,
ganhos mpl; **~ post** n meta de chegada.

winter ['wɪntə*] n inverno // vi hibernar;
~ sports npl esportes (Pt: desportos)
mpl de inverno.

wintry ['wɪntrɪ] adj glacial, invernal.

wipe [waɪp] n: **to give sth a ~** limpar
algo com um pano // vt limpar; **to ~
off** vt remover esfregando; **to ~ out** vt
(debt) liquidar; (memory) apagar;
(destroy) exterminar.

wire ['waɪə*] n arame m; (ELEC) fio
(elétrico); (TEL) telegrama m // vt
(house) instalar a rede elétrica (Pt: -ct-)
em; (also: **~ up**) conectar; (TEL)
telegrafar para // vi passar um
telegrama.

wireless ['waɪəlɪs] n rádio.

wiring ['waɪərɪŋ] n instalação f elétrica
(Pt: -ct-).

wiry ['waɪərɪ] adj nervoso.

wisdom ['wɪzdəm] n sabedoria,
sagacidade f; (good sense) bom senso;
(care) prudência; **~ tooth** n dente m do
siso.

wise [waɪz] adj sábio; (sensible) sensato;
(careful) prudente.

...wise [waɪz] suff: **time~** com relação
ao tempo.

wisecrack ['waɪzkræk] n piada.

wish [wɪʃ] n (desire) desejo // vt desejar;
(want) querer; **best ~es** (on birthday
etc) parabéns mpl, felicidades fpl; **with
best ~es** (in letter) cumprimentos; **to
~ sb goodbye** despedir-se de alguém;
he ~ed me well me desejou boa sorte;
to ~ to do/sb to do sth querer
fazer/que alguém faça algo; **to ~ for**
desejar; **it's ~ful thinking** é mais
desejo do que realidade.

wisp [wɪsp] n mecha, tufo; (of smoke) fio.

wistful ['wɪstful] adj pensativo.

wit [wɪt] n (wittiness) presença de
espírito, engenho; (intelligence)
entendimento; (person) espirituoso/a.

witch [wɪtʃ] n bruxa; **~craft** n bruxaria.

with [wɪð, wɪθ] prep com; **red ~ anger**
vermelho de raiva; **the man ~ the
grey hat** o homem do chapéu cinza; **to
be ~ it** (fig: aware) estar a par da
situação; (: fashionable) estar na moda; **I
am ~ you** (I understand) compreendo.

withdraw [wɪð'drɔ:] (irr: like **draw**) vt
tirar, remover // vi retirar-se; (go back on
promise) voltar atrás; **to ~ money
(from the bank)** retirar dinheiro (do
banco); **~al** n retirada; **~n** adj (person)
reservado, introvertido.

wither ['wɪðə*] vi murchar; **~ed** adj
murcho.

withhold [wɪð'həuld] (irr: like **hold**)
vt (money) reter; (decision) adiar;
(permission) negar; (information) esconder.

within [wɪð'ɪn] prep dentro de // adv
dentro; **~ reach** ao alcance da mão; **~
sight** à vista; **~ the week** antes do fim
da semana.

without [wɪð'aut] prep sem.

withstand [wɪð'stænd] (irr: like **stand**)
vt resistir a, opor-se a.

witness ['wɪtnɪs] n (person) testemunha;
(evidence) testemunho // vt (event)
testemunhar, presenciar; (document)

legalizar; ~ **box**, ~ **stand** (*US*) *n* banco das testemunhas.

witticism ['wɪtɪsɪzm] *n* observação *f* espirituosa, chiste *m*.

witty ['wɪtɪ] *adj* espirituoso, engenhoso.

wives [waɪvz] *pl of* **wife**.

wizard ['wɪzəd] *n* feiticeiro, mago.

wk *abbr of* **week**.

wobble ['wɔbl] *vi* oscilar; (*chair*) balançar.

woe [wəu] *n* dor *f*, mágoa.

woke [wəuk], **woken** ['wəukən] *pt*, *pp of* **wake**.

wolf [wulf], *pl* **wolves** [wulvz] *n* lobo.

woman ['wumən], *pl* **women** *n* mulher *f*; ~**ly** *adj* feminino.

womb [wu:m] *n* (*ANAT*) matriz *f*, útero.

women ['wɪmɪn] *pl of* **woman**.

won [wʌn] *pt*, *pp of* **win**.

wonder ['wʌndə*] *n* maravilha, prodígio; (*feeling*) espanto // *vi*: to ~ **whether** perguntar-se a si mesmo se; to ~ **at** admirar-se de; to ~ **about** pensar sobre or em; it's no ~ **that** não é de admirar que; ~**ful** *adj* maravilhoso; ~**fully** *adv* esplendidamente.

won't [wəunt] = **will not**.

woo [wu:] *vt* (*woman*) namorar, cortejar.

wood [wud] *n* (*timber*) madeira; (*forest*) floresta, bosque *m*; ~ **carving** *n* escultura em madeira, entalhe *m*; ~**ed** *adj* arborizado; ~**en** *adj* de madeira; (*fig*) inexpressivo; ~**pecker** *n* pica-pau *m*; ~**wind** *n* (*MUS*) instrumentos *mpl* de sopro de madeira; ~**work** *n* carpintaria; ~**worm** *n* carcoma, caruncho.

wool [wul] *n* lã *f*; to pull the ~ over sb's eyes (*fig*) enganar alguém, vender a alguém gato por lebre; ~**len**, ~**en** (*US*) *adj* de lã; ~**lens** *npl* artigos *mpl* de lã; ~**ly**, ~**y** (*US*) *adj* de lã; (*fig*: *ideas*) confuso.

word [wə:d] *n* palavra; (*news*) notícia; (*message*) aviso // *vt* (*express*) expressar; (*document*) redigir, in other ~**s** em outras palavras; to **break**/**keep** one's ~ faltar à palavra/cumprir a promessa; ~**ing** *n* redação (*Pt*: -cç-) *f*.

wore [wɔ:*] *pt of* **wear**.

work [wə:k] *n* (*gen*) trabalho; (*job*) emprego, trabalho; (*ART*, *LITERATURE*) obra // *vi* trabalhar; (*mechanism*) funcionar; (*medicine*) surtir efeito, ser eficaz // *vt* (*wood etc*) talhar; (*mine etc*) explorar; (*machine*) fazer trabalhar, manejar; (*cause*) fazer, produzir; to be out of ~ estar desempregado; ~**s** *n* (*factory*) fábrica *sg* // *npl* (*of clock*, *machine*) mecanismo *sg*; to ~ **loose** *vi* (*part*) soltar-se, desprender-se; (*knot*) afrouxar-se; to ~ **on** *vt fus* trabalhar em, dedicar-se a; (*principle*) basear-se em; to ~ **out** *vi* (*plans etc*) dar certo, surtir efeito // *vt* (*problem*) resolver; (*plan*) elaborar, formular; **does it** ~ **out?** está dando resultado?; **it** ~**s out at £100** monta *or* soma a 100 libras; to

get ~**ed up** ficar exaltado; ~**able** *adj* (*solution*) viável; ~**er** *n* trabalhador(a) *m/f*, operário/a; ~**ing class** *n* proletariado, classe *f* operária; ~**ing-class** *adj* do proletariado, da classe operária; **in** ~**ing order** em funcionamento; ~**man** *n* operário, trabalhador *m*; ~**manship** *n* (*art*) acabamento; (*skill*) habilidade *f*, ~**shop** *n* oficina; ~**-to-rule** *n* paralisação *f* de trabalho extraordinário.

world [wə:ld] *n* mundo // *cmp* mundial; to think the ~ of sb (*fig*) ter alguém em alto conceito; ~**ly** *adj* mundano; ~**-wide** *adj* mundial, universal.

worm [wə:m] *n* verme *m*; (*earth*~) minhoca, lombriga.

worn [wɔ:n] *pp of* **wear** // *adj* usado; ~**-out** *adj* (*object*) gasto; (*person*) esgotado, exausto.

worried ['wʌrɪd] *adj* preocupado.

worry ['wʌrɪ] *n* preocupação *f* // *vt* preocupar, inquietar // *vi* preocupar-se, afligir-se; ~**ing** *adj* inquietante, preocupante.

worse [wə:s] *adj*, *adv* pior, inferior // *n* o pior; **a change for the** ~ uma mudança para pior; **worsen** *vt/i* piorar; ~ **off** *adj* (*fig*): **you'll be** ~ **off this way** assim você ficará pior que nunca.

worship ['wə:ʃɪp] *n* culto; (*act*) adoração *f* // *vt* adorar, venerar; **Your W**~ (*to mayor*) vossa Excelência; (*to judge*) senhor Juiz; ~**per** *n* devoto/a, venerador(a) *m/f*.

worst [wə:st] *adj* (*of a*) pior // *adv* pior // *n* o pior; **at** ~ na pior das hipóteses.

worth [wə:θ] *n* valor *m*, mérito // *adj*: to be ~ valer; **it's** ~ **it** vale a pena; ~**less** *adj* sem valor; (*useless*) inútil; ~**while** *adj* (*activity*) que vale a pena; (*cause*) de mérito, louvável.

worthy [wə:ðɪ] *adj* (*person*) merecedor(a), respeitável; (*motive*) justo; ~ **of** digno de.

would [wud] *auxiliary vb*: **she** ~ **come** ela viria; **he** ~ **have come** ele teria vindo; ~ **you like a biscuit?** você quer um biscoito?; **he** ~ **go on Mondays** costumava ir às segundas-feiras; ~**-be** *adj* (*pej*) aspirante, que pretende ser.

wound [waund] *pt*, *pp of* **wind** // *n* [wu:nd] ferida // *vt* [wu:nd] ferir.

wove [wəuv], **woven** ['wəuvən] *pt*, *pp of* **weave**.

wrangle ['ræŋgl] *n* briga // *vi* brigar.

wrap [ræp] *n* (*stole*) xale *m*; (*cape*) capa // *vt* (*also*: ~ **up**) embrulhar; ~**per** *n* envoltório, invólucro; (*of book*) capa; ~**ping paper** *n* papel *m* de embrulho.

wrath [rɔθ] *n* cólera, ira.

wreath [ri:θ], *pl* ~**s** [ri:ðz] *n* (*funeral* ~) coroa; (*of flowers*) grinalda.

wreathe [ri:ð] *vt* trançar, cingir.

wreck [rɛk] *n* naufrágio; (*ship*) restos *mpl* do naufrágio; (*pej*: *person*) ruína, caco // *vt* destruir, danificar; (*fig*) arruinar, arrasar; **~age** n restos mpl; (of building) escombros mpl.

wren [rɛn] n (ZOOL) carriça.

wrench [rɛntʃ] n (TECH) chave f inglesa; (tug) puxão m // vt arrancar; to ~ sth from sb arrancar algo de alguém.

wrestle ['rɛsl] vi: to ~ (with sb) lutar (com or contra alguém); **wrestler** n lutador m; **wrestling** n luta romana; **wrestling match** n partida de luta romana.

wretched ['rɛtʃɪd] adj desventurado, infeliz.

wriggle ['rɪgl] n (gen) contorção f // vi (gen) retorcer-se, contorcer-se.

wring [rɪŋ], pt, pp **wrung** vt torcer, espremer; (wet clothes) torcer; (fig): to ~ sth out of sb arrancar à força algo de alguém.

wrinkle ['rɪŋkl] n ruga, prega // vt franzir // vi enrugar-se.

wrist [rɪst] n pulso; ~ **watch** n relógio m de pulso.

writ [rɪt] n mandado judicial; to issue a ~ **against sb** demandar judicialmente alguém.

write [raɪt], pt **wrote**, pp **written** vt/i escrever; to ~ **down** vt escrever; (note) anotar; to ~ **off** vt (debt) cancelar; (depreciate) reduzir; to ~ **out** vt escrever por extenso; to ~ **up** vt redigir; **~-off** n perda total; **the car is a ~-off** o carro virou sucata or está destroçado; **writer** n escritor(a) m/f.

writhe [raɪð] vi contorcer-se.

writing ['raɪtɪŋ] n escrita; (hand-~) caligrafia, letra; (of author) obra; **in ~** por escrito; ~ **paper** n papel m para escrever.

written ['rɪtn] pp of **write**.

wrong [rɔŋ] adj (bad) errado, mau; (unfair) injusto; (incorrect) errado, equivocado; (not suitable) impróprio, inconveniente // adv mal, erroneamente // n mal m; (injustice) injustiça // vt ser injusto com; (hurt) ofender; **you are ~ to do it** você se engana ao fazê-lo; **you are ~ about that, you've got it ~** você está enganado sobre isso; **to be in the ~** não ter razão; **what's ~?** que se passa com você?, o quê que há?; **to go ~** (person) desencaminhar-se; (plan) dar errado; (machine) sofrer uma avaria; **~ful** adj injusto; **~ly** adv injustamente.

wrote [rəʊt] pt of **write**.

wrought [rɔːt] adj: ~ **iron** ferro forjado.

wrung [rʌŋ] pt, pp of **wring**.

wry [raɪ] adj (smile) irônico; to make a ~ **face** fazer uma careta.

wt. abbr of **weight**.

X

Xmas ['ɛksməs] n abbr of **Christmas**.

X-ray [ɛks'reɪ] n radiografia; ~**s** npl raios mpl X // vt radiografar, tirar uma chapa de.

xylophone ['zaɪləfəʊn] n xilofone m.

Y

yacht [jɔt] n iate m; ~**ing** n (sport) iatismo; **yachtsman** n iatista m/f.

Yank [jæŋk] n (pej) ianque m/f.

yap [jæp] vi (dog) ganir.

yard [jɑːd] n pátio, quintal m; (measure) jarda; ~**stick** n (fig) critério, padrão m.

yarn [jɑːn] n fio; (tale) história inverossímil.

yawn [jɔːn] n bocejo // vi bocejar.

yd. abbr of **yard(s)**.

year [jɪə*] n ano; to be 8 ~**s old** ter 8 anos; ~**ly** adj anual // adv anualmente.

yearn [jɔːn] vi: to ~ **for sth** ansiar or suspirar por algo; ~**ing** n ânsia, desejo ardente.

yeast [jiːst] n levedura, levedo.

yell [jɛl] n grito, berro // vi gritar, berrar.

yellow ['jɛləʊ] adj, n amarelo.

yelp [jɛlp] n latido // vi latir.

yes [jɛs] adv, n sim m.

yesterday ['jɛstədɪ] adv, n ontem m; **the day before ~** anteontem.

yet [jɛt] adv ainda // conj porém, no entanto; **it is not finished ~** ainda não está acabado; **the best ~** o melhor até agora; **as ~** até agora, ainda.

yew [juː] n teixo.

Yiddish ['jɪdɪʃ] n (i)ídiche m.

yield [jiːld] n produção f; (AGR) colheita; (COMM) rendimento // vt (gen) produzir; (profit) render // vi render-se, ceder; (US: AUT) ceder.

yoga ['jəʊgə] n ioga.

yog(h)ourt, yog(h)urt ['jəʊgət] n iogurte m.

yoke [jəʊk] n canga, cangalha; (pair of oxen) junta; (on shoulders) balancim m; (fig) jugo // vt unir, ligar.

yolk [jəʊk] n gema (do ovo).

yonder ['jɔndə*] adv além, acolá.

you [juː] pron (subject) tu, você; (: pl) vós, vocês; (direct object) te, o/a; (: pl) vos, os/as; (indirect object) te, lhe; (: pl) vos, lhes; (after preposition) ti, você; (: pl) vós, vocês; (polite form) o senhor/a senhora; (: pl) os senhores/as senhoras; **with ~** contigo, com você; convosco, com vocês; com o senhor etc; (one): ~ **never know** a gente nunca sabe; (impersonal): **can't do that** isso não se faz.

you'd [juːd] = **you had; you would.**

you'll [juːl] = **you will; you shall.**

young [jʌŋ] adj jovem, moço (Br), novo (Pt) // npl (of animal) filhotes mpl, crias fpl; (people): **the ~** a mocidade fsg, a juventude fsg; ~**er** adj (brother etc) mais novo; ~**ish** adj bem novo; ~**ster** n jovem m/f, moço/a.

your [jɔː*] adj teu/tua, seu/sua; (pl) vosso, seu/sua; (formal) do senhor/da senhora.

you're [juə*] = **you are.**

yours [jɔːz] pron teu/tua, seu/sua; (pl)

vosso, seu/sua; (*formal*) do senhor/da
senhora; ~ **is blue** o teu/a tua é azul; **is
it** ~? é teu *etc*?; ~ **sincerely** or
faithfully atenciosamente.
yourself [jɔː'sɛlf] *pron* (*subject*)
tu mesmo, você mesmo; (*direct/indirect
object*) te, se; (*after prep*) ti mesmo, si
mesmo; (*formal*) o senhor mesmo/a
senhora mesma; **yourselves** *pl pron*
(*subject*) vós mesmos, vocês mesmos;
(*direct/indirect object*) vos, se; (*formal*) os
senhores mesmos/as senhoras mesmas.
youth [juːθ] *n* mocidade *f*, juventude *f*;
(*young man*: *pl* ~**s** [juːðz]) jovem *m*;
~**ful** *adj* juvenil; ~ **hostel** *n* albergue *m*
da juventude.
you've [juːv] = **you have.**
Yugoslav ['juːgəu'slɑːv] *adj*, *n*
iugoslavo/a; ~**ia** *n* Iugoslávia.
Yuletide ['juːltaɪd] *n* época natalina or
do Natal.

Z

zany ['zeɪnɪ] *adj* tolo, bobo.
zeal [ziːl] *n* zelo, fervor *m*; ~**ous** ['zɛləs]

adj zeloso, entusiasta.
zebra ['ziːbrə] *n* zebra; ~ **crossing** *n*
faixa (para pedestres) (*Br*), passadeira
(*Pt*).
zenith ['zɛnɪθ] *n* zênite *m*, apogeu *m*.
zero ['zɪərəu] *n* zero.
zest [zɛst] *n* vivacidade *f*, entusiasmo.
zigzag ['zɪgzæg] *n* ziguezague *m* // *vi*
ziguezaguear.
zinc [zɪŋk] *n* zinco.
Zionism ['zaɪənɪzm] *n* sionismo; **Zionist**
n sionista *m/f*.
zip [zɪp] *n* (*also*: ~ **fastener**, ~**per**)
fecho ecler (*Pt*: éclair) // *vt* (*also*: ~
up) fechar o fecho ecler de, subir o
fecho ecler de; ~ **code** *n* (*US*) código
postal.
zodiac ['zəudiæk] *n* zodíaco.
zombie ['zɔmbɪ] *n* (*fig*): **like a** ~ como
um zumbi.
zone [zəun] *n* zona, região *f*.
zoo [zuː] *n* (jardim *m*) zoológico.
zoological [zuə'lɔdʒɪkl] *adj* zoológico.
zoologist [zuː'ɔlədʒɪst] *n* zoólogo/a.
zoology [zuː'ɔlədʒɪ] *n* zoologia.
zoom [zuːm] *vi*: **to** ~ **past** passar
zunindo; ~ **lens** *n* zoom *m*, zum *m*.

PORTUGUESE VERB TABLES

1 Gerund. **2** Imperative. **3** Present. **4** Imperfect. **5** Preterite. **6** Future. **7** Present subjunctive. **8** Imperfect subjunctive. **9** Future subjunctive. **10** Past participle. **11** Pluperfect. **12** Personal infinitive.

Etc indicates that the irregular root is used for all persons of the tense, e.g. **ouvir**: **7** ouça, ouças, ouça, ouçamos, ouçais, ouçam.

abrir 10 aberto
acudir 2 acode **3** acudo, acodes, acode, acodem
aderir 3 adiro **7** adira
aduzir 2 aduz **3** aduzo, aduzes, aduz
advertir 3 advirto **7** advirta *etc*
afear 2 afeia **3** afeio, afeias, afeia, afeiam **7** afeie *etc*
agir 3 ajo **7** aja *etc*
agradecer 3 agradeço **7** agradeça *etc*   •
agredir 2 agride **3** agrido, agrides, agride, agridem **7** agrida *etc*
AMAR 1 amando **2** ama, amai **3** amo, amas, ama, amamos, amais, amam **4** amava, amavas, amava, amávamos, amáveis, amavam **5** amei, amaste, amou, amamos (*Pt*: amá-), amastes, amaram **6** amarei, amarás, amará, amaremos, amareis, amarão **7** ame, ames, ame, amemos, ameis, amem **8** amasse, amasses, amasse, amássemos, amásseis, amassem **9** amar, amares, amar, ámarmos, amardes, amarem **10** amado **11** amara, amaras, amara, amáramos, amáreis, amaram **12** amar, amares, amar, amarmos, amardes, amarem
ansiar 2 anseia **3** anseio, anseias, anseia, anseiam **7** anseie *etc*
aprazer 2 apraz **3** aprazo, aprazes, apraz **5** aprouve *etc* **8** aprouvesse *etc* **9** aprouver *etc* **11** aprouvera *etc*
apreçar 7 aprece *etc*
arrancar 7 arranque *etc*
arruinar 2 arruína **3** arruíno, arruínas, arruína, arruínam **7** arruíne, arruínes, arruíne, arruínem
aspergir 3 aspirjo **7** aspirja *etc*
averiguar 7 averigúe, averigúes, averigúe, averigúem
boiar 2 bóia **3** bóio, bóias, bóia, bóiam **7** bóie, bóies, bóie, bóiem
bulir 2 bole **3** bulo, boles, bole, bolem
caber 3 caibo **5** coube *etc* **7** caiba *etc* **8** coubesse *etc* **9** couber *etc*
cair 2 cai **3** caio, cais, cai, caímos, caís, caem **4** caía *etc* **5** caí, caíste **7** caia *etc* **8** caísse *etc*
cobrir 3 cubro **7** cubra *etc* **10** coberto
colorir 3 coluro **7** colura *etc*
compelir 3 compilo **7** compila *etc*
crer 2 crê **3** creio, crês, crê, cremos, credes, crêem **5** cri, creste, creu, cremos, crestes, creram **7** creia *etc*
cuspir 2 cospe **3** cuspo, cospes, cospe, cospem

dar 2 dá 3 dou, dás, dá, damos, dais, dão 5 dei, deste, deu, demos, destes, deram 7 dê, dês, dê, demos, deis, dêem 8 desse *etc* 9 der *etc* 11 dera *etc*

delir 3 dilo 7 dila *etc*

demolir 3 demulo 7 demula *etc*

denegrir 2 denigre 3 denigro, denigres, denigre, denigrem 7 denigra *etc*

despir 3 dispo 7 dispa *etc*

dizer 2 diz (dize) 3 digo, dizes, diz, dizemos, dizeis, dizem 5 disse *etc* 6 direi *etc* 7 diga *etc* 8 dissesse *etc* 9 disser *etc* 10 dito

doer 2 dói 3 doo, dóis, dói

dormir 3 durmo 7 durma *etc*

escrever 10 escrito

ESTAR 2 está 3 estou, estás, está, estamos, estais, estão 4 estava *etc* 5 estive, estiveste, esteve, estivemos, estivestes, estiveram 7 esteja *etc* 8 estivesse *etc* 9 estiver *etc* 11 estivera *etc*

explodir 3 expludo 7 expluda *etc*

extorquir 3 exturco 7 exturca *etc*

FAZER 3 faço 5 fiz, fizeste, fez, fizemos, fizestes, fizeram 6 farei *etc* 7 faça *etc* 8 fizesse *etc* 9 fizer *etc* 10 feito 11 fizera *etc*

ferir 3 firo 7 fira *etc*

flectir 3 flito 7 flita *etc*

fluir 3 fluo, fluis, flui, fluímos, fluís, fluem

fremir 3 frimo 7 frima *etc*

fruir 3 fruo, fruis, frui, fruímos, fruís, fruem

fugir 2 foge 3 fujo, foges, foge, fogem 7 fuja *etc*

ganhar 10 ganho

gastar 10 gasto

gerir 3 giro 7 gira *etc*

haver 2 há 3 hei, hás, há, havemos, haveis, hão 4 havia *etc* 5 houve, houveste, houve, houvemos, houvestes, houveram 7 haja *etc* 8 houvesse *etc* 9 houver *etc* 11 houvera *etc*

ir 1 indo 2 vai 3 vou, vais, vai, vamos, ides, vão 4 ia *etc* 5 fui, foste, foi, fomos, fostes, foram 7 vá, vás, vá, vamos, vades, vão 8 fosse, fosses, fosse, fôssemos, fôsseis, fossem 9 for *etc* 10 ido 11 fora *etc*

jazer 3 jazo, jazes, jaz

ler 2 lê 3 leio, lês, lê, lemos, ledes, lêem 5 li, leste, leu, lemos, lestes, leram 7 leia *etc*

medir 3 meço 7 meça *etc*

mentir 3 minto 7 minta *etc*

ouvir 3 ouço 7 ouça *etc*

pagar 10 pago

parar 2 pára 3 paro, paras, pára

parir 7 pára, paras, pára

pecar 7 peque *etc*

pedir 3 peço 7 peça *etc*

perder 3 perco 7 perca *etc*

poder 3 posso 5 pude, pudeste, pôde, pudemos, pudestes, puderam 7 possa *etc* 8 pudesse *etc* 9 puder *etc* 11 pudera *etc*

polir 2 pule **3** pulo, pules, pule, pulem **7** pula *etc*

pôr 1 pondo **2** põe **3** ponho, pões, põe, pomos, pondes, põem **4** punha *etc* **5** pus, puseste, pôs, pusemos, pusestes, puseram **6** porei *etc* **7** ponha *etc* **8** pusesse *etc* **9** puser *etc* **10** posto **11** pusera *etc*

premir 2 prime **3** primo, primes, prime, primem **7** prima *etc*

preferir 3 prefiro **7** prefira *etc*

prevenir 2 previne **3** previno, prevines, previne, previnem **7** previna *etc*

prover 2 provê **3** provejo, provês, provê, provemos, provedes, provêem **5** provi, proveste, proveu, provemos, provestes, proveram **7** proveja *etc* **8** provesse *etc* **9** prover *etc*

provir 2 provém **3** provenho, provéns, provém, provimos, provindes, provêm **4** provinha *etc* **5** provim, provieste, proveio, proviemos, proviestes, provieram **7** provenha *etc* **8** proviesse *etc* **9** provier **10** provindo **11** proviera *etc*

querer 3 quero, queres, quer **5** quis, quiseste, quis, quisemos, quisestes, quiseram **7** queira *etc* **8** quisesse *etc* **9** quiser *etc* **11** quisera *etc*

repetir 3 repito **7** repita *etc*

requerer 3 requeiro, requeres, requer **7** requeira *etc*

retorquir 3 returco **7** returca *etc*

reunir 2 reúne **3** reúno, reúnes, reúne, reúnem **7** reúna *etc*

rir 2 ri **3** rio, ris, ri, rimos, rides, riem **5** ri, riste, riu, rimos, ristes, riram **7** ria *etc*

saber 3 sei, sabes, sabe, sabemos, sabeis, sabem **5** soube, soubeste, soube, soubemos, soubestes, souberam **7** saiba *etc* **8** soubesse *etc* **9** souber *etc* **11** soubera *etc*

seguir 3 sigo **7** siga *etc*

sentir 3 sinto **7** sinta *etc*

ser 2 sê **3** sou, és, é, somos, sois, são **4** era *etc* **5** fui, foste, foi, fomos, fostes, foram **7** seja *etc* **8** fosse *etc* **9** for *etc* **11** fora *etc*

servir 3 sirvo **7** sirva *etc*

subir 2 sobe **3** subo, sobes, sobe, sobem

suster 2 sustém **3** sustenho, sustens, sustém, sustemos, sustendes, sustêm **5** sustive, sustiveste, sustive, sustivemos, sustivestes, sustiveram **7** sustenha *etc*

ter 2 tem **3** tenho, tens, tem, temos, tendes, têm **4** tinha *etc* **5** tive, tiveste, teve, tivemos, tivestes, tiveram **6** terei *etc* **7** tenha *etc* **8** tivesse *etc* **9** tiver *etc* **11** tivera *etc*

torcer 3 torço **7** torça *etc*

tossir 3 tusso **7** tussa *etc*

trair 2 trai **3** traio, trais, trai, traímos, traís, traem **7** traia *etc*

trazer 2 (traze) traz **3** trago, trazes, traz **5** trouxe, trouxeste, trouxe, trouxemos, trouxestes, trouxeram **6** trarei *etc* **7** traga *etc* **8** trouxesse *etc* **9** trouxer *etc* **11** trouxera *etc*

UNIR 1 unindo **2** une, uni **3** uno, unes, une, unimos, unis, unem **4** unia, unias, unia, uníamos, uníeis, uniam **5** uni, uniste, uniu, unimos, unistes, uniram **6** unirei, unirás, unirá, uniremos, unireis, unirão **7** una, unas, una, unamos, unais, unam **8** inisse, unisses, unisse, uníssemos, unísseis, unissem **9** unir, unires, unir, unirmos, unirdes, unirem **10** unido **11** unira, uniras, unira, uníramos, uníreis, uniram **12** unir, unires, unir, unirmos, unirdes, unirem

valer 3 valho **7** valha *etc*

ver 2 vê **3** vejo, vês, vê, vemos, vedes, vêem **4** via *etc* **5** vi, viste, viu, vimos, vistes, viram **7** veja *etc* **8** visse *etc* **9** vir *etc* **10** visto **11** vira

vir 1 vindo **2** vem **3** venho, vens, vem, vimos, vindes, vêm **4** vinha *etc* **5** vim, vieste, veio, viemos, viestes, vieram **7** venha *etc* **8** viesse *etc* **9** vier *etc* **10** vindo **11** viera *etc*

VIVER 1 vivendo **2** vive, vivei **3** vivo, vives, vive, vivemos, viveis, vivem **4** vivia, vivias, vivia, vivíamos, vivíeis, viviam **5** vivi, viveste, viveu, vivemos, vivestes, viveram **6** viverei, viverás, viverá, viveremos, vivereis, viverão **7** viva, vivas, viva, vivamos, vivais, vivam **8** vivesse, vivesses, vivesse, vivêssemos, vivêsseis, vivessem **9** viver, viveres, viver, vivermos, viverdes, viverem **10** vivido **11** vivera, viveras, vivera, vivêramos, vivêreis, viveram **12** viver, viveres, viver, vivermos, viverdes, viverem

VERBOS IRREGULARES EM INGLÊS

present	pt	pp	present	pt	pp
arise	arose	arisen	eat	ate	eaten
awake	awoke	awaked	fall	fell	fallen
be (am, is, are; being)	was, were	been	feed	fed	fed
			feel	felt	felt
			fight	fought	fought
bear	bore	born(e)	find	found	found
beat	beat	beaten	flee	fled	fled
become	became	become	fling	flung	flung
befall	befell	befallen	fly	flew	flown
begin	began	begun	forbid	forbade	forbidden
behold	beheld	beheld	forecast	forecast	forecast
bend	bent	bent	forget	forgot	forgotten
beset	beset	beset	forgive	forgave	forgiven
bet	bet, betted	bet, betted	forsake	forsook	forsaken
			freeze	froze	frozen
bid	bid	bid	get	got	got, (US) gotten
bind	bound	bound			
bite	bit	bitten	give	gave	given
bleed	bled	bled	go (goes)	went	gone
blow	blew	blown			
break	broke	broken	grind	ground	ground
breed	bred	bred	grow	grew	grown
bring	brought	brought	hang	hung, hanged	hung, hanged
build	built	built			
burn	burnt, burned	burnt, burned	have	had	had
			hear	heard	heard
burst	burst	burst	hide	hid	hidden
buy	bought	bought	hit	hit	hit
can	could	(been able)	hold	held	held
cast	cast	cast	hurt	hurt	hurt
catch	caught	caught	keep	kept	kept
choose	chose	chosen	kneel	knelt, kneeled	knelt, kneeled
cling	clung	clung			
come	came	come	know	knew	known
cost	cost	cost	lay	laid	laid
creep	crept	crept	lead	led	led
cut	cut	cut	lean	leant, leaned	leant, leaned
deal	dealt	dealt			
dig	dug	dug	leap	leapt, leaped	leapt, leaped
do (3rd person; he/she/it does)	did	done	learn	learnt, learned	learnt, learned
			leave	left	left
draw	drew	drawn	lend	lent	lent
dream	dreamed, dreamt	dreamed, dreamt	let	let	let
			lie (lying)	lay	lain
drink	drank	drunk	light	lit, lighted	lit, lighted
drive	drove	driven			
dwell	dwelt	dwelt			

404

present	pt	pp	present	pt	pp
lose	lost	lost	speed	sped,	sped,
make	made	made		speeded	speeded
may	might	—	spell	spelt,	spelt,
mean	meant	meant		spelled	spelled
meet	met	met	spend	spent	spent
mistake	mistook	mistaken	spill	spilt,	spilt,
mow	mowed	mown,		spilled	spilled
		mowed	spin	spun	spun
must	(had to)	(had to)	spit	spat	spat
pay	paid	paid	split	split	split
put	put	put	spoil	spoiled,	spoiled,
quit	quit,	quit,		spoilt	spoilt
	quitted	quitted	spread	spread	spread
read	read	read	spring	sprang	sprung
rend	rent	rent	stand	stood	stood
rid	rid	rid	steal	stole	stolen
ride	rode	ridden	stick	stuck	stuck
ring	rang	rung	sting	stung	stung
rise	rose	risen	stink	stank	stunk
run	ran	run	stride	strode	stridden
saw	sawed	sawn	strike	struck	struck,
say	said	said			stricken
see	saw	seen	strive	strove	striven
seek	sought	sought	swear	swore	sworn
sell	sold	sold	sweep	swept	swept
send	sent	sent	swell	swelled	swollen,
set	set	set			swelled
shake	shook	shaken	swim	swam	swum
shall	should	—	swing	swung	swung
shear	sheared	shorn,	take	took	taken
		sheared	teach	taught	taught
shed	shed	shed			
shine	shone	shone	tear	tore	torn
shoot	shot	shot	tell	told	told
show	showed	shown	think	thought	thought
shrink	shrank	shrunk	throw	threw	thrown
shut	shut	shut	thrust	thrust	thrust
sing	sang	sung	tread	trod	trodden
sink	sank	sunk	wake	woke,	woken,
sit	sat	sat		waked	waked
slay	slew	slain			
sleep	slept	slept	wear	wore	worn
slide	slid	slid	weave	wove,	woven,
sling	slung	slung		weaved	weaved
slit	slit	slit	wed	wedded,	wedded,
smell	smelt,	smelt,		wed	wed
	smelled	smelled	weep	wept	wept
sow	sowed	sown,	win	won	won
		sowed	wind	wound	wound
speak	spoke	spoken	wring	wrung	wrung
			write	wrote	written

NOTES TO THE USER OF THIS DICTIONARY

I   **Using the dictionary**

     1. The wordlist: where to look for a word   408
     2. Entry layout and 'signposting'   411
     3. Using the translations   412

II   **Notes on Portuguese grammar**

     1. Nouns and noun groups   414
       1.1 Gender
       1.2 Articles
       1.3 Adjectives
       1.4 Possessives
       1.5 Demonstratives
       1.6 Comparative and superlative

     2. Verbs   417
       2.1 Verb forms
       2.2 Negatives and questions
       2.3 Tenses
       2.4 The verb 'to be'

     3. Prepositions   420

     4. Adverbs   421

     5. Pronouns   421

III   **Portuguese verb conjugations**   422

IV   **The sounds of Portuguese**   428

V   **The time, dates and numbers**   435

I. Using the dictionary

In using this book, you will either want to check the meaning of a Portuguese word you don't know, or find the Portuguese for an English word. These two operations are quite different, and so are the problems you may face when using one side of the dictionary or the other. In order to help you, we have tried to explain below the main features of this book.

The 'wordlist' is the alphabetical list of all the items in large bold type, i.e. all the 'headwords'. Each 'entry', or article, is introduced by a headword, and may contain additional 'references' in smaller bold type, such as phrases, derivatives, and compound words. Section 1. below deals with the way references are listed.

The typography distinguishes between three broad categories of text within the dictionary. All items in bold type, large or small, are 'source language' references, for which an equivalent in the other language is provided. All items in standard type are translations. Items in italics are information about the words being translated, i.e. either labels, or 'signposts' pinpointing the appropriate translation, or explanations.

1. *Where to look for a word*

1.1   Derivatives

In order to save space, a number of derivatives have been listed within entries, provided this does not break alphabetical order. Thus, **gracejar**, **gracejo**, and **gracioso** are listed under the entry for **graça**, and **caller** and **calling** under **call**. You must remember this when looking for a word you don't find listed as a headword. These derivatives are always listed last within an entry (see I.2 on entry layout).

1.2 Homographs

Homographs are words which are spelt in exactly the same way, like **sede** (thirst) and **sede** (headquarters). As a rule, in order to save space, such words have been treated under one headword only. However, words which differ only in the written accent have separate entries, like **se** (if), **sé** (cathedral), and **sê** (*vb* **ser**).

1.3 Regional variants

There are some fairly regular spelling differences between Brazilian and European Portuguese. The most important of these are the cases where Brazilian spelling simplifies the combinations -ct-, -pt- and -cç- to -t-, -t- and -ç- respectively while European Portuguese retains the longer forms. Words are listed in this dictionary according to their Brazilian spelling, but you will find an indication of the European spelling in brackets after the Brazilian form. See the entries for **batismo**, **seção** and **teto**.

1.4 Phrases

Because of the constraints of space, there can only be a limited number of idiomatic phrases in a pocket dictionary like this one. Particular emphasis is given to verbal phrases like **dar à luz, dar uma volta, estar de volta** etc., and also to basic constructions (see the entries for **apply, agree, ficar, dever, dar**). Verbal phrases with the basic verbs (**andar, dar, estar, fazer, ficar, ir, levar, pôr, ser, ter**) are listed under the noun. Other phrases and idioms are listed under the first key word, for instance **de antemão** under **antemão**, **não obstante** under **obstante**.

1.5 Abbreviations and proper names

For easier reference, abbreviations, acronyms and proper names have been listed alphabetically in the wordlist, as opposed to being relegated to the appendices. **M.O.T.** is used in every way like **certificate** or **permit**, **OTAN** like **organização**, and these words are treated like other nouns.

1.6 Compounds

Housewife, smoke screen, caixa econômica and **motor de arranque** are all compounds. One-word compounds like 'housewife' are not a problem when consulting the dictionary, since they can appear only in one place and in strict alphabetical order. When it comes to other compounds, however - hyphenated compounds and compounds made up of separate words - each language presents its own peculiar problems.

1.6.1   Portuguese compounds

There are many compounds made up of two or more 'words'. When checking a Portuguese compound, you might not be aware that you are dealing with a compound and not a string of autonomous words, and there may inevitably be some toing and froing between entries.

Though there is some variation in the use of the hyphen in Portuguese (you may see 'dona-de-casa' as well as 'dona de casa'), most compounds of this type are normally written without hyphens and are therefore listed under the first word and grouped alphabetically within that entry. For instance, **cama de solteiro** is within the entry for **cama** and comes before the headword **camada. Caixa postal** comes before the headword **caixão,** in the entry for **caixa.** Remember that the meaning of a phrase or of a compound can be quite different from that of its elements taken separately, so be prepared to check through an entry thoroughly before giving up.

1.6.2   English compounds

Here there is a problem of where to find a compound because of less predictable spelling than is the case with Portuguese: is it **airgun, air-gun** or **air gun**? This is why we choose to list them according to strict alphabetical order. Thus **coalfield** and **coalman** are separated by **coalition.** The entries between **tax** and **technical** will provide a good illustration of the system of listing. It has drawbacks, for instance in that **tax-free** and **tax payer** are separated by **taxi, taxidermist** and three 'taxi' compounds, However, in a short dictionary used by beginners, it has the merits of simplicity and consistency.

1.6.3   English 'phrasal verbs'

'Phrasal verbs' are verbs like **go off, blow up, cut down** etc. Here you have the advantage of knowing that these words belong together, whereas it will take the foreign user some time before he can identify these verbs immediately. They have been listed under the entry for the basic verb (e.g. **go, blow, cut**), grouped alphabetically before any other derivative or compound - for instance, **pull up** comes before **pulley.** (See also **to back out, to look up** (a word), **to look out.**)

1.7   Irregular forms

When looking up a Portuguese word, you may not immediately find the form you are looking for, although the word in question has been duly entered in the dictionary. This is possibly because you are looking up an irregular noun or verb form, and these are not always given as entries in their own right.

We have assumed that you know basic Portuguese grammar. Thus you will be expected to know that 'cantam' is a form of the verb **cantar**, 'jornais' the plural of **jornal** and so on. However, in order to help you, we have included the main irregular forms as entries in their own right with a cross-reference to the basic form. Thus, if you come across the word 'fui' and attempt to look up a verb 'fuir', you won't find it, but what you will find between **fuga** and **fulano** is the entry **fui** *vb ver ir ou* **ser**. Similarly **fez, feito** etc.

With past participles, it sometimes happens that in addition to the purely verbal form there is an adjectival or noun use, for instance **feito** or **pago**. These usages are translated as autonomous words, but they are also cross-referred to the verb whenever appropriate (see for instance entries for **aberto** or **morto**).

2. *Entry layout*

All entries, however long or complex, are arranged systematically. But it may be a little difficult at first to find one's way through an entry like Portuguese **parte**, or English **back, round** or **run** because homographs are grouped under the same entry (see 1.2) and the text is run on without any breakdown into paragraphs, in order to save space. Ease of reference comes with practice, but the guidelines below will make it easier for you.

2.1 'Signposting'

If you look up a Portuguese word and find a string of quite different English translations, you are unlikely to have much trouble finding out which is the relevant one for the context, because you know what the English words mean, and the context will almost automatically rule out unsuitable translations. It is quite a different matter when you want to find the Portuguese for, say, **lock**, in the context 'we got to the lock around lunchtime', and are faced with an entry that reads 'lock: fechadura; eclusa; tranca; anel, mecha.' You can of course go to the other side and check what each translation means. But this is time-consuming, and it doesn't always work. This is why we have provided the user with signposts which pinpoint the relevant translation. For instance with **lock**, the entry reads: ... (*of door, box*) fechadura; (*of canal*) eclusa, comporta; (*stop*) tranca; (*of hair*) anel *m*, mecha ... For the context suggested above, it is now clear that 'eclusa' or 'comporta' is the right word.

2.2 Grammatical categories and meaning categories

Complex entries are first broken down into grammatical categories, e.g.: **lock** *n // vt // vi*. Be prepared to go through entries like **run** or **back** carefully, and you will find how useful all these 'signposts' are. Each grammatical category is then split where appropriate into the various meanings, e.g.:

lock n (*of door, box*) fechadura; (*of canal*) eclusa, comporta; (*stop*) tranca; (*of hair*) anel m, mecha // vt (*with key*) fechar à chave; (*immobilize*) imobilizar // vi (*door etc*) fechar-se à chave; (*wheels*) travar-se.

3. Using the translations

3.1 Gender

Feminine endings for Portuguese adjectives ending in -o have not been given on the English-Portuguese side, but endings for other adjectives are shown. When an -a is simply added to the masculine form it is shown in brackets after the masculine form: **charming** *adj* encantador(a) (feminine = encantadora). When the feminine is formed by adding an -a and by deleting an accent, the vowel which loses the accent is also shown: **French** *adj* francês/esa (feminine = francesa). Finally, if there is a change of vowels from masculine to feminine, this is shown, together with the preceding consonant: **German** *adj* alemão/mã (feminine = alemã). This may appear to duplicate information given in the Portuguese-English side of the dictionary, but we feel it is a useful reminder where and when it matters. The feminine form is also given for words like **teacher**, **researcher** etc.

3.2 Plurals

Most plural forms in Portuguese are regular and are not shown, but where a problem could arise, the plural is shown beside the headword on the Portuguese side, e.g. **pão** m, pl **pães**. We have shown when a translation in the plural is given for a word used in the singular; see for instance **jealousy, offal**.

3.3 Verb forms

Irregular Portuguese verbs appearing as translations have not been marked as such, and the user should refer to the Portuguese verb tables when in doubt (pp. 400-403).

3.4 Regional labels

In many cases, European Portuguese uses a different spelling or a completely different word from Brazilian Portuguese to denote a certain concept. Words used in Brazil only are labelled (*Br*) while those used in Portugal only are labelled (*Pt*). Where the difference is merely one of spelling, the European form is indicated in brackets immediately after the Brazilian form. See the entries for **tram**, **clutch** (*AUT*) and **direct**. If there is no regional label you can assume that the Portuguese word given is used in both Brazil and Portugal.

3.5 Colloquial language

You should as a rule proceed with great caution when handling foreign language which has a degree of informality. When an English word or phrase has been labelled (*col*), i.e. colloquial, you must assume that the translation belongs to a similar level of informality. If the translation is followed by (*col!*) you should use it with extreme care, or better still avoid it unless you are with close friends!

3.6 'Grammatical words'

It is exceedingly difficult to give adequate treatment for words like **for, away, whose, which, out, off,** etc. in a short dictionary such as this one. We have tried to go some way towards providing as much relevant information as possible about the most frequent uses of these words. However, for further information use a good monolingual dictionary of Portuguese, and a good modern Portuguese grammar.

3.7 'Approximate' translations and cultural equivalents

It is not always possible to give a genuine translation, when for instance an English word denotes an object or institution which either doesn't exist in Brazil or Portugal, or is quite different. Therefore, only an approximate equivalent can be given, sometimes indicated by the sign ≈, or else an explanation. See for instance **shadow cabinet,** and on the Portuguese side **caipirinha, carioca.**

3.8 Alternative translations

As a rule, translations separated by commas can be regarded as broadly interchangeable for the meaning indicated. Translations separated by a semi-colon are not interchangeable and when in doubt you should consult a good monolingual Portuguese dictionary. You will find however that there are very few cases of translations separated by a semi-colon without an intervening 'signpost'.

II. Notes on Portuguese grammar

When you are first confronted with Portuguese, it may seem to you that it is very different from English. On the other hand, if you stand back and consider a wide range of related and unrelated languages, Portuguese can come to look very close to English.

We have tried here to show some of the main differences, especially with the beginner and the dictionary user in mind, without dwelling on subtleties or aspects of Portuguese grammar that are broadly similar to English. Among the greatest obstacles for the beginner are gender, verb forms and tenses, the position of adjectives, the use of object pronouns and prepositions, and of course the sounds of Portuguese.

1. *Nouns and 'satellite' words (articles, adjectives)*

1.1   Gender

Note the basic difference: 'the table and the plate', but '*a* mes*a* e *o* prato'. Gender can often be determined by the ending of the word: 'mesa' ends in *a* and is feminine; 'prato' ends in *o* and is masculine. But in many cases it is not possible to tell the gender of a word by its ending and you just have to learn the gender in each case. It is most important to get the article right, and of course the agreement of adjectives and past participles: '*um* homen alt*o* e *uma* mulher bonit*a*'. See also 1.4 (possessive adjectives).

1.2   Articles: '*o, a; um; do, dos*' etc.

Apart from the problem of gender, there is the question of whether the article is used or not, and Portuguese does not always follow the English pattern. For instance, you say 'salmon is expensive', but Portuguese speakers say '*o* salmão é caro'. Conversely, 'my father is **a** teacher', but 'meu pai é professor'.

1.2.1. *'o, a; os, as'*

(a) In general statements where 'the' is not used in English, the article must be used in Portuguese. For instance:

apples are good for you   **as** maçãs fazem bem à saúde
patience is a virtue   **a** paciência é uma virtude

The article is also used with most names of countries, e.g.: **a** França, **o** Brasil. A notable exception to this rule is 'Portugal' which has no article.

(b) Use of *'o/a'* with parts of the body and family

Where the possessive is used in English, *'o/a'* tends to be used in Portuguese:

I've twisted **my** ankle   torci **o** tornozelo
put up **your** hand   levante **a** mão
he looks a lot like **his** father   ele se parece muito com **o** pai

(c) *'a + o, de + o, em + o, por + o'* etc.

Remember the contracted forms (shown in the dictionary under **a**, **de**, **em** and **por**). For instance: 'vou ao cinema', 'a porta da casa' etc.

1.2.2 *'um, uma; uns, umas'*

(a) In structures like 'my father is a postman' (i.e. expressing occupation, nationality or rank), Portuguese does not use the indefinite article:

my brother is **a** doctor   meu irmão é médico
he's **a** Frenchman   ele é francês

(b) After negatives, the article 'um/uma' is not used with unspecified nouns:

I don't have **a** car   não tenho carro
you can't write without **a** pen   sem caneta não se pode escrever

(c) *'uns/umas'*

Remember to use the plural of the article, even though there may be no article in English:

friends from Brazil arrived   chegaram **uns** amigos do Brasil

(d) *'em + um/uma; de + um/uma'*

Remember the contracted forms **num/numa** and, in Portugal only, **dum/duma**.

1.2.3 'some/any'

Unless 'some/any' expresses something specific, it is not normally translated in Portuguese, especially after a negative:

alguns dias depois **some** (= a few) days later

BUT: você quer batatas? do you want *some/any* potatoes?
       quero pão I want *some* bread
       não tenho cigarros I haven't *any* cigarettes

1.3 Adjectives

Apart from the question of gender, the main difficulty is the position of adjectives. As a general rule, they follow the noun (uma comida gostosa, uns sapatos azuis). Some adjectives or types of adjectives will *always* go after the noun, especially if their meaning can only be literal (um carro italiano, um vestido vermelho). Others can also go before the noun in a figurative sense or for stylistic purposes (a gostosa comida de Portugal).

Adjectives, however, which 'limit' rather than 'describe' (muito, pouco, tanto, primeiro, último) always come in front of the noun.

1.4 Possessives

1.4.1 *o meu, a minha/os meus, as minhas, o nosso, a nossa/os nossos, as nossas* etc. *vs* my, our.

Unlike English, the possessive varies in Portuguese according to the gender and number of the noun it qualifies. Remember that the word for 'my, your' etc. is usually preceded by the definite article.

1.4.2 'his/her/your/their'

In Brazilian Portuguese, 'o seu/a sua' etc. are generally used to mean 'your'. 'His/her/their' are usually expressed using 'o,a ... dele/dela/deles/delas' in colloquial speech, and by 'seu/sua' *without* the definite article in written and more formal contexts. However, usage is not fixed on this point. In European Portuguese, 'o seu/a sua' is used in all the above cases and never without the article:

eu falei com **o** pai **dele**   I spoke to his father
eu falei com **o** **seu** pai   I spoke to your father (*or* his/her/their)

1.5   Demonstratives: *'este, esse, aquele'* etc.

Demonstrative adjectives agree in gender and number with the noun
they qualify. Portuguese also has a neuter form for the pronouns
'this' and 'that'.

o que é **isso**?   what's that?

The main problem, however, is choosing between the three forms of
demonstrative: the 'este' forms are straightforward and mean 'this';
the 'esse' forms mean 'that' in the sense of 'that nearby or near you';
the 'aquele' forms mean 'that over there':

este livro   **this** book
o que é **isso** que você tem na mão?   what is **that** you have (*there*)
in your hand?
como se chamam **aquelas** montanhas?   what are **those** mountains
called (*over there*)?

1.6   Comparative and superlative: *'mais ... do que'* etc.

Generally you use 'mais' + *adjective* or *adverb* to form the
comparative; the superlative is slightly more complicated because
you use the definite article with the 'mais' and the article must agree
in gender and number with the adjective.

ele é **mais** alto do que eu   he's taller than me
esta casa é **a mais** velha da cidade   this house is the oldest in the
town

2. *Verbs*

This is one of the main areas of difficulty for English-speaking
learners. There are four major problems. First, the variety of
endings (falo, falamos etc.) and the number of irregular or
'semi-irregular' forms. Second, the difference in the formation of
negative or interrogative phrases (no equivalent of 'do', 'did' etc., as
in 'I didn't go; did you?'). Third, the difference in the use of tenses
(e.g. two past tenses, imperfect and preterite). Fourth, the use of two
verbs meaning 'to be' (ser, estar).

2.1 Verb forms

The verb tables on pp. 425–427 will give you the patterns for the main verb groups; irregular verb forms are shown on page 400. There is no substitute for practice on this, but try not to look on these forms as a vast array of separate items to be learnt: there are two basic combining patterns, one relating to the person doing the action (*I* speak vs *you* speak: falo/fal*as*) and one relating to the tense (I *speak*/I *spoke*: falo/fal*ei*). The present, imperfect, future, preterite and conditional will cater for most of your needs at first.

2.2 Negatives and questions

Although the use of 'não' to negate a verb causes few problems, it is important to remember that when 'negative' words such as 'nunca' follow the verb, 'não' is inserted before the verb:

não saio   I do *not* go out
não saía **nunca**   I *never* went out

The way Portuguese forms questions is really a matter of the tone of voice in which the sentence is said and presents no real problem because we often use the same tone in English:

ele é louco   he's mad
ele é louco?   is he mad?

Remember that question words are often followed by the phrase ' ... é que ...':

quando **é que** ela volta?   when's she coming back?
o que **é que** você falou?   what did you say?

Note that when answering a yes/no question affirmatively, Portuguese speakers often simply repeat the verb contained in the question:

você fala português?   **falo** (sim)   do you speak Portuguese? yes (I do)
vocês vão com a gente?   **vamos** (sim)   are you coming with us?   yes (we are)

2.3 Tenses

2.3.1 There are two continuous tenses in Portuguese corresponding to English '-ing' forms. Remember that the continuous tenses are formed differently in Brazil and Portugal:

(Br) estou trabalh*ando*,   (Pt) estou a trabalhar   I am work*ing*
(Br) estava trabalh*ando*,   (Pt) estava a trabalhar   I was work*ing*

2.3.2 When translating the past tenses of English (I went there, he has taken it, etc.) you have to decide between the imperfect and the preterite in Portuguese. Basically it is a question of 'when' and 'how often'.

2.3.2.1 The imperfect

The 'imperfect' describes an action done repeatedly in the past or which went on for some time (often being a replacement for the continuous tense), e.g. *faziam-no* means 'they *used* to do it' or 'they *were* doing it', which is what the English preterite implies in a sentence such as 'they *did* it *all the time*'.

2.3.2.2 The preterite

The preterite denotes completed actions in the past and often translates the English perfect tense:

você leu o livro todo?   did you read *or* have you read the whole book?

The idea of the English perfect tense can be made clearer in Portuguese by inserting the word 'já' (= already):

você **já** viu esse filme? – Já   have you (already) seen that film? – Yes

Notice how the 'já' is picked up to give the answer 'yes'.

2.3.3 The future tense is often avoided in the spoken language by using either the verb 'ir' followed by an infinitive or a simple present tense:

eu **vou falar** com você amanhã   I'll talk to you tomorrow
ele **viaja** amanhã   he's going away tomorrow

Remember that the Portuguese continuous present tense 'estou trabalhando' NEVER refers to the future.

2.3.4 The subjunctive: 'quero que você faça' *vs* 'sei que você faz'

Good command of the present, future and imperfect subjunctive is necessary in order to speak good Portuguese, but you would probably be understood without it. It is not possible here to give you all the rules governing the use of the subjunctive, but with practice you will gain a feeling for when it is required.

2.3.5 The personal infinitive

A feature peculiar to Portuguese is the personal infinitive. Once again, it is beyond the scope of this book to give rules for its use but it is well worth mastering as it is extremely common and very useful. Here are some examples of its uses:

pedi para eles **virem** amanhã   I asked them to come tomorrow
comprei um carro para nós **podermos** sair nos fins de semana
I('ve) bought a car so (that) we can go out at the weekends
eles não trabalharam por **estarem** doentes   they didn't work because they were ill

2.4 Portuguese has two verbs 'to be': ser, estar.

2.4.1   *ser*

Ser means 'to exist' but it also covers the meanings of 'to be' which express qualities or permanent states: 'é inteligente'   he's clever (always); 'é professora'   she's a teacher. It is also used to form the passive: 'fui ferido'   I was wounded.

2.4.2   *estar*

Estar means 'to be (temporarily in a place or state)': 'a comida está na mesa'   the food is on the table; 'você está linda hoje'   you're looking very nice today;   'ele está sentado'   he's sitting down.

2.4.3   The verb 'ficar' is often used in Portuguese to translate the English verb 'to be' in the sense of 'to be situated' or 'to become':

onde **fica** o banco?   where's the bank?
ele vai **ficar** surpreso quando souber disso   he'll be surprised when he hears about this

3. *Prepositions*

Most prepositions present no problems. The main confusion will be about when to use 'por' and when to use 'para' when translating English 'for'. Essentially, 'por' expresses *cause* or *reason* and 'para' expresses *purpose*:

nós o admiramos **por** sua coragem   we admire him *for* his courage
para que você quer isso?   what do you want it *for*?

'por' also expresses *exchange*:
quanto você me dá **por** isto?   how much will you give me *for* this?

3.1 Don't forget that many verbs in English are followed by prepositions which are contained in the Portuguese verb: to go *up* 'subir'; to sit *down* 'sentar-se' etc.

4. Adverbs

Adverbs can be formed from most adjectives by taking the feminine form and adding '-mente': quick-ly rapida-mente; easi-ly facil-mente. Portuguese often uses a prepositional phrase to translate an adverb, such as 'com cuidado' (carefully).

5. Pronouns

5.1 Subject pronouns need not be used in Portuguese except for emphasis, though it is quite common to hear them, especially 'ele' and 'ela' where the verb form alone would be ambiguous.

5.2 Pronoun table

	SUBJECT	REFLEX.	INDIRECT OBJECT	OBJECT	PREPOSITIONAL
I	eu	me	me	me	para mim/comigo
you	tu	te	te	te	para ti/contigo
he	ele	se	lhe	o	para ele
she	ela	se	lhe	a	para ela
you	você	se	lhe	o/a	para você
we	nós	nos	nos	nos	para nós/conosco
they	eles	se	lhes	os	para eles
they	elas	se	lhes	as	para elas
you	vocês	se	lhes	os/as	para vocês

5.3 The rules for the position, combination (e.g. lhe + o = lho) and usage of the object pronouns are so complicated that even native speakers have difficulty! Colloquial Brazilian speech tends to avoid the problematic third person object pronouns either by leaving them out altogether, or by using the subject/prepositional forms after the verb:

você entregou o livro a ele?   vou entregar (a ele) amanhã
did you give him the book?   I'll give *it* to him tomorrow
eu vi ele ontem   I saw him yesterday
gostou do livro?   eu li, mas não gostei   did you like the book?
I read *it* but I didn't like *it*

III. Portuguese verb conjugations

1. The table of irregular verbs on p. 400 is self-explanatory. In many cases all six singular and plural forms are shown. Where only one form is given it is either the first person or the third person singular, according to the type of verb; if two forms are given, they are the first and second person singular; if three forms are shown they are the first, second and third person singular; if four forms are shown, they are the first, second and third person singular plus the third person plural. The imperatives given are the second person singular and, in a few cases, also the second person plural. Any forms not shown are regular and can be found by consulting the model verb tables below: table A for an infinitive ending in '-ar', table B for an infinitive ending in '-er', and table C for an infinitive ending in '-ir'.

2. Do not forget to use the appropriate pronoun with reflexive verbs:
   eu *me* lavo, nós *nos* lavamos, eles *se* lavam

3. 'Semi-irregular' verbs

   Some verbs appear to be irregular but they are in fact predictable with reference to the following guidelines:

3.1 Because a 'c' or a 'g' in Portuguese is pronounced differently depending on the vowel which follows, these letters will change in certain cases in order to maintain the original root sound:
   Roots ending in 'c': fic-ar, fi*qu*-ei; venc-er, ven*ç*-o
   Roots ending in 'g': pag-ar, pa*gu*-ei; proteg-er, prote*j*-o
   Roots ending in 'ç': coç-ar, coc-ei
   Verbs ending in '-guer': er*gu*-er, erg-o
   Verbs ending in '-guir': distin*gu*-ir, disting-o

3.2 With verbs ending in '-ear', the '-e-' is strengthened with an 'i' when it takes the stress:

passear: passeio, passeia, passeamos, passeiam

Verbs ending in '-iar' are regular except for **ansiar, incendiar, odiar** and **remediar** where the '-i-' is strengthened with an 'e' when it takes the stress:

odiar: odeio, odeia, odeamos, odeiam

3.3 Portuguese also has what are called 'radical-changing' verbs. With '-ar' and '-er' verbs, there is no change of spelling although there is a difference in the pronunciation of the root vowel depending on whether it is stressed or unstressed. However, with '-ir' verbs, the following spelling changes often take place:

u>o subir: subo, sobe, subimos, sobem

e>i sentir: sinto, sente, sentimos, sentem
    agredir: agrido, agride, agredimos, agridem

o>u dormir: durmo, dorme, dormimos, dormem
    polir: pulo, pule, polimos, pulem

4. The 'compound tenses' are formed as follows:

Indicative:

(a) 'perfect': *present* of 'ter' or 'haver' + *past participle* (tenho/hei falado)
(b) 'pluperfect': *imperfect* of 'ter' or 'haver' + *past participle* (tinha/havia falado)
(c) 'future perfect': *future* of 'ter' or 'haver' + *past participle* (terei/haverei falado)
(d) 'conditional perfect': *conditional* of 'ter' or 'haver' + *past participle* (teria/haveria falado)

Subjunctive:

(a) 'perfect': *present subjunctive* of 'ter' or 'haver' + *past participle* (tenha/haja falado)
(b) 'pluperfect': *imperfect subjunctive* of 'ter' or 'haver' + *past participle* (tivesse/houvesse falado)
(c) 'future perfect': *future subjunctive* of 'ter' or 'haver' + *past participle* (tiver/houver falado)

The forms with 'ter' are much more common in everyday speech.

5. The passive is formed by using the verb 'ser' + *past participle*. The past participle agrees in number and gender with the subject: a televisão foi inventada em...   television was invented in...

6. Remember that there is a simple pluperfect tense (falara/vendera/partira) which you may encounter when reading Portuguese.

7. Imperative forms:

The familiar imperative form is found in the verb tables (tu). The formal imperative (você, vocês) adopts the form of the subjunctive. Note that the familiar (tu) imperative is much used in Brazil even though other 'tu' forms are not.

A. A regular '-ar' verb: 'falar'

PRESENT: Indicative		Subjunctive	
	o		e
	as		es
fal	a	fal	e
	amos		emos
	am		em

IMPERFECT: Indicative		Subjunctive	
	ava		asse
	avas		asses
fal	ava	fal	asse
	ávamos		ássemos
	avam		assem

PRETERITE		FUTURE SUBJUNCTIVE	
	ei		ar
	aste		ares
fal	ou	fal	ar
	amos		armos
	aram		arem

FUTURE		CONDITIONAL	
	ei		ia
	ás		ias
falar	á	falar	ia
	emos		íamos
	ão		iam

IMPERATIVE: fala

PAST PARTICIPLE: falado

GERUND: falando

INFINITIVE: falar
PERSONAL INFINITIVE: falar (-, -es, -, -mos, -em)

425

B. A regular '-er' verb: 'vender'

PRESENT: Indicative		Subjunctive	
	o		a
	es		as
vend	e	vend	a
	emos		amos
	em		am

IMPERFECT: Indicative		Subjunctive	
	ia		esse
	ias		esses
vend	ia	vend	esse
	íamos		êssemos
	iam		essem

PRETERITE		FUTURE SUBJUNCTIVE	
	i		er
	este		eres
vend	eu	vend	er
	emos		ermos
	eram		erem

FUTURE		CONDITIONAL	
	ei		ia
	ás		ias
vender	á	vender	ia
	emos		íamos
	ão		iam

IMPERATIVE: vende

PAST PARTICIPLE: vendido

GERUND: vendendo

INFINITIVE: vender
PERSONAL INFINITIVE: vender (-, -es, -, -mos, -em)

C. A regular '-ir' verb: 'partir'

PRESENT: Indicative			Subjunctive	
		o		a
		es		as
	part	e	part	a
		imos		amos
		em		am

IMPERFECT: Indicative			Subjunctive	
		ia		isse
		ias		isses
	part	ia	part	isse
		íamos		íssemos
		iam		issem

PRETERITE			FUTURE SUBJUNCTIVE	
		i		ir
		iste		ires
	part	iu	part	ir
		imos		irmos
		iram		irem

FUTURE			CONDITIONAL	
		ei		ia
		ás		ias
	partir	á	partir	ia
		emos		íamos
		ão		iam

IMPERATIVE: parte

PAST PARTICIPLE: partido

GERUND: partindo

INFINITIVE: partir
PERSONAL INFINITIVE: partir (-, -es, -, -mos, -em)

IV. The sounds of Portuguese

Portuguese, particularly Brazilian Portuguese, is not difficult to pronounce for English speakers though it may sound quite odd when you first hear it. What is more difficult is knowing how to pronounce a given word when you see it written down but even this becomes quite straightforward if you learn a few basic principles.

The main problem for the foreigner learning Portuguese is the nasal sounds. The production of nasal vowels can scarcely be explained without the help of a teacher or a recording of the sound quality. As a guide, however, the vowel is pronounced by allowing air to come partly down the nose and partly through the mouth. Best tip: ask a native Portuguese speaker to say and repeat for you the contrasting pairs 'pais' *vs* 'pães', 'pois' *vs* 'pões', and 'maus' *vs* 'mãos'.

Pronunciation of the sounds of Portuguese

The examples given here and on the following pages reflect pronunciation in Rio de Janeiro. For notes on pronunciation in Portugal, see p. 433.

1. Vowel Sounds

	as in:	Hints on pronunciation
[i]	*id*a, ond*e*	Like the sound in English '*bea*t'
[e]	m*e*sa, gên*e*ro	Like 'e' in 'they' but without the 'y' sound
[ɛ]	*e*la, p*é*rola	Like 'e' in English 'pet'
[a]	f*a*do, *a*ba	Like 'a' in English 'father' but shorter
[ɔ]	id*o*sa, p*ó*	Like 'o' in English 'pot'
[o]	id*o*so, f*ô*lego	Like 'o' in English 'hope' without the 'w' sound

428

| [u] | urna, prato | Like 'u' in English 'rule' |

Nasal Vowels:

[ĩ]	sim, pinto	Similar to the sound in English 'sing'
[ẽ]	vem, lento	Similar to the sound in the name 'Cheng'
[ã]	maçã, canto	Similar to the sound in English 'hung'
[õ]	som, ponto	Similar to the sound in English 'song'
[ũ]	um, junto	Similar to Northern English 'lung'

Diphthongs:

[ai]	baile	Like the 'i' in English 'ride'
[au]	fraude	Like the 'ow' in English 'cow'
[ej]	inteiro	Like the 'ey' in English 'they'
[ew]	seu	Like the vowel sound in English 'sale' followed by a 'w' sound
[ɛw]	céu	Like the vowel sound in English 'sell' followed by a 'w' sound
[oj]	noite	Like the 'oy' in English 'boy'

Nasal Diphthongs:

[ãj]	mãe	Similar to the sound in English 'tying'
[ãw]	mão, falam	Similar to the sound in English 'cow' + 'ng'
[õj]	põe	Similar to the sound in English 'boing'
[ẽj]	bem	Similar to the sound in English 'saying'

Semivowels:

| [j] | quiabo | Like the 'y' in English 'yacht' |
| [w] | água | Like the 'w' in English 'water' |

2. Consonants

The consonant sounds [b, p, t, d, k, g, f, v, s, z, m, n, l] are pronounced more or less as in English. The following sounds also have an equivalent in English:

[ʃ]	chamar	Like the 'sh' in English 'ship'
[ʒ]	jeito	Like the 's' in English 'measure'
[tʃ]	noite	Like the 'ch' in English 'chin'
[dʒ]	pode	Like the 'j' in English 'Jim'

The following sounds have no equivalent in English:

[x]	rua, carro	Very similar to the 'h' in English 'house' pronounced quite emphatically
[r]	caro	A single 'roll' of a rolled 'r', as in the Scottish pronunciation of 'very'
[ʎ]	filho	'lh' is pronounced like the 'lli' in English 'million'
[ɲ]	sonho	'nh' is pronounced like the 'ni' in English 'onion'

3. Stress

In English a difference in meaning between two words which are spelt identically can be indicated by a difference in stress - for instance, the two different stress patterns for the word 'escort' produce two different words, one a noun and one a verb (*an escort bureau; may I escort you*). This does not happen in Portuguese because each word can only be stressed in one way, the rules for which are as follows:

(a) when a word ends in *a, e, o, m* (except *im, um*) or *s* (except *ns*), the *next to last* syllable is stressed: bat*a*ta, bat*a*tas, p*a*rte, p*a*rtem

(b) when a word ends in *ã, i, u, im, um, ns* or a consonant other than *m* or *s*, the stress falls on the *last* syllable: vend*i*, alg*u*m, alg*u*ns, fal*a*r (c)　When the rules set out in (a) and (b) are not applied, an acute or circumflex accent appears over the stressed vowel: ótica, ânimo, inglês

(d)　the same syllable is stressed in the plural forms and in the feminine singular form as in the masculine singular form so that accents may disappear accordingly: inglês, BUT inglesa, ingleses, inglesas; mês BUT meses.

From Spelling to Sounds

1. Portuguese is an *almost* 'phonetic' language, by which we mean that every vowel and consonant has a fixed sound value. In other words, if you see a word written down, you can be fairly sure how it should be pronounced. The only thing you cannot tell from the spelling of a Portuguese word is whether a stressed 'e' or 'o' is 'open' or 'closed', i.e. whether 'e' should be pronounced [e] or [ɛ] and whether 'o' should be pronounced [o] or [ɔ]. This need hardly worry the beginner since there is little danger of being misunderstood.

Another important thing to remember is that when the letters 'm' and 'n' appear immediately after a vowel and before another consonant or at the end of a word, they are merely the written markers of nasality and should not be pronounced as [m, n]. Thus, 'limpo' and 'tom' are pronounced [lĩpu] and [tõ]. When 'm' and 'n' appear before another vowel, they are pronounced as normal but still have a slight nasalizing effect on a preceding vowel. Thus, 'ano' and 'uma' are pronounced [anu] and [uma].

2. Here is a brief guide to the pronunciation of each letter or combination of letters:

a　　　　[a], or when nasal [ã]. Note that the verbal ending '-am' is pronounced [ãw]: *casa, angra, falam*

b　　　　[b] *bicho*

c　　　　before i, e : [s] *cesta, cinto*
　　　　before a, o, u : [k] *casa, cobra, cubo*

ç　　　　[s] *maçã*

ch　　　　[ʃ] *chato*

d　　　　before i and before e in word final position: [dʒ] *disse, pode*
　　　　everywhere else: [d] *duro, gado*

431

e	unstressed: [e] v*e*rmelho
	word final: [i] vontad*e*
	stressed: [e] or [ɛ]. 'ê' is pronounced [e], 'é' is pronounced [ɛ].
	Nasal 'e' is pronounced [ẽ] within words and [ẽj] at the end of
	words.

f   [f] *f*ilme

g   before i, e : [ʒ] *g*íria, *g*eral
       before a, o, u : [g] *g*asolina, *g*ole, *g*uri

gu   before a, o : [gw] á*gu*a, averi*gu*ou
       before i, e : [g] *gu*indaste, *gu*eto

h   always silent: *h*ora, *h*umor. Remember that lh, nh and ch
       represent the sounds [ʎ], [ɲ] and [ʃ] respectively.

i   [i] f*i*lho

j   [ʒ] *j*eito

k   [k] *k*art

l   before a vowel: [l] *l*onge, pe*l*o
       at the end of a word or before a consonant: [w] sa*l*, sa*l*to

lh   [ʎ] fi*lh*a

m   before a vowel: [m] *m*ato, a*m*o
       at the end of a word or before a consonant: shows that
       preceding vowel is nasal: fala*m*, sa*m*ba

n   before a vowel: [n] *n*ariz, a*n*o
       at the end of a word or before a consonant: shows that
       preceding vowel is nasal: Nelso*n*, ho*n*ra, ca*n*to

nh   [ɲ] dese*nh*o

o   unstressed: [o] positiv*o*
       word final: [u] carr*o*
       stressed: [o] or [ɔ]. 'ô' is pronounced [o], 'ó' is pronounced [ɔ]
       nasal 'o' is pronounced [õ]

p [p] *p*ai

qu before a, o : [kw] a*qu*ático, *qu*ota
before i, e : [k] *qu*ilo, *qu*em

r single 'r' between vowels: [r] ca*r*o
single 'r' elsewhere: [x] *r*ua, ma*r*, pa*r*te, hon*r*a
double 'r' : [x] ca*rr*o

s single 's' between vowels: [z] ro*s*a
single 's' at the beginning of a word: [s] *s*al
single 's' before c (=[k]), f, p, t or at the end of a word: [ʃ]
e*s*ta, pire*s*
single 's' before other consonants: [ʒ] me*s*mo
double 's' : [s] se*ss*enta

t before i and before e in word final position: [tʃ] *t*io, noi*t*e
everywhere else: [t] *t*udo, a*t*o

u [u] j*u*sto
when nasal: [ũ] f*u*ndo

v [v] *v*erdade

w [w] *w*indsurfe

x [ʃ], [ʒ], [ks], [s] or [z]. There are no fixed rules, so consult
the dictionary if in doubt.

z between vowels: [z] a*z*ar
at the end of a word: [ʒ] lu*z*

The pronunciation described here is that of Rio de Janeiro. The
Portuguese of Portugal is very similar, though there are some
important differences. For instance:

Unstressed 'a' and 'e', including word final 'e', are pronounced [ə] like
'er' in English 'bett*er*'.
Unstressed 'o' is pronounced [u].
't' and 'd' are pronounced [t] and [d] in all positions.
The [x] sound is realized as a rolled 'r' between vowels and in word
initial position in many parts of Portugal.
The [ej] sound of Brazilian is replaced in most cases by an [aj] sound
as in English 'p*ie*'. The nasal [ẽj] is replaced by [ãj].

3. The letters of the Portuguese alphabet

When a Brazilian wishes to spell out a word he pronounces the letters like this:

a [a]	b [be]	c [se]	d [de]	e [ɛ]	f [ˈɛfi]
g [ʒe]	h [aˈga]	i [i]	j [ˈʒɔta]	k [ka]	l [ˈɛli]
m [ˈemi]	n [ˈeni]	o [ɔ]	p [pe]	q [ke]	r [ˈɛxi]
s [ˈɛsi]	t [te]	u [u]	v [ve]	w [ˈdabʎu]	x [ʃiʃ]
y [ˈipsilõ]	z [ze]				

A Portuguese will spell out the following letters very differently:

k [ˈkapɔ]   r [ˈɛrrə]   w [veˈduplu]

The letters are masculine and you therefore talk of 'um a' or 'o a':
o meu nome se escreve com dois ms [emiʃ]

V. The time

what is the time?	que horas são?
it's...	é... (*midnight, noon, 1 o'clock*), são... (*other times*)
00.00	meia-noite
01.00	uma hora (da noite)
01.10	uma e dez
01.15	(*Br*) uma e quinze, (*Pt*) uma e um quarto
01.30	uma e meia
01.45	(*Br*) quinze para as duas, (*Pt*) duas menos um quarto
01.50	(*Br*) dez para as duas, (*Pt*) duas menos dez
02.00	duas
12.00	meio-dia
13.00	uma (hora) treze horas
18.00	seis dezoito horas
22.30	dez e meia vinte e duas horas e trinta
at what time?	a qué horas?
at one	à uma hora
at 2.15	(*Br*) às duas e quinze, (*Pt*) às duas e um quarto
just after 3.00	às três e pouco
about 4.30	por volta das quatro e meia
from 6.00 to 8.00	das seis às oito
it's nearly 9.00	são quase nove horas
at 4.00 sharp	às quatro em ponto

Dates and numbers

1. The date

what is the date today?	que dia é hoje?
the first of May	dia primeiro de maio
the 2nd of March	dia dois de março (*cardinals are used from 2nd to 31st*)
today is the 14th	hoje é dia catorze
on the 10th of June	no dia dez de junho
on Tuesday	na terça(-feira)
on Tuesdays	nas terças(-feiras)

Letter headings: dates on Portuguese letters are normally written thus:

22nd October, 1949	22 de outubro de 1949

Years:		
	1981	mil novecentos e oitenta e um
	2000 B.C	2000 a.C (= antes de Cristo)
	70 A.D.	70 d.C. (= depois de'Cristo)
	in the 12th century	no século doze
	in the 1940's	nos anos 40

2. Notes on numbers

Cardinals

(a) 'um' (+ 'vinte e um' etc.) and 'dois' (+ 'vinte e dois' etc.) agree in gender with their noun: trinta e uma pessoas, quarenta e duas horas

(b) 'cem' is used when it is not followed by a lower number: cem mil, cem mulheres, etc. 'cento e' is used when a lower number follows: cento e vinte dias

(c) Remember that the hundreds (duzentos, trezentos etc.) agree in gender with a following noun: mil duzentas e trinta páginas. Note that 2,000 is '*duas* mil' before a feminine noun.

436

Ordinals

(a) They are adjectives and therefore agree in gender and number.

(b) They are not commonly used above 10, except for 100th and 1,000th.

(c) The ordinals are used for fractions:
a third   um terço
three quarters   três quartos

(d) Portuguese abbreviations for 1st, 2nd, 3rd etc. depend on gender and are written thus:
1st 1º (masculine), 1ª (feminine)
4th 4º, 4ª

Decimals

Where English uses a point, Portuguese uses a comma:

101.7   101,7 (cento e um *vírgula* sete)
0.031   0,031 (zero *vírgula* zero três um)

Calculations

$4 + 7 = 11$	quatro *mais* sete *são* onze
$12 - 3 = 9$	doze *menos* três *são* nove
$3 \times 7 = 21$	tres *vezes* sete *são* vinte e um
$16 \div 4 = 4$	dezesseis *dividido por* quatro *dá* quatro

Telephone numbers

When saying telephone numbers, Brazilians use 'meia' for 'six':

704 5678   sete zero quatro cinco meia sete oito

Numbers

1	um, uma	1st	primeiro/a
2	dois, duas	2nd	segundo/a
3	três	3rd	terceiro/a
4	quatro	4th	quarto/a
5	cinco	5th	quinto/a
6	seis	6th	sexto/a
7	sete	7th	sétimo/a
8	oito	8th	oitavo/a
9	nove	9th	nono/a
10	dez	10th	décimo/a
11	onze	11th	décimo primeiro
12	doze	12th	décimo segundo
13	treze	13th	décimo terceiro
14	catorze	14th	décimo quarto
15	quinze	15th	décimo quinto
16	(Br) dezesseis, (Pt) dezasseis	16th	décimo sexto
17	(Br) dezesete, (Pt) dezassete	17th	décimo sétimo
18	dezoito	18th	décimo oitavo
19	(Br) dezenove, (Pt) dezanove	19th	décimo nono
20	vinte	20th	vigésimo/a
21	vinte e um (uma)*	21st	vigésimo primeiro
22	vinte e dois (duas)*	22nd	vigésimo segundo
30	trinta	30th	trigésimo/a
40	quarenta	40th	quadragésimo/a
50	(Br) cinqüenta, (Pt) cinquenta	50th	(Br) qüinquagésimo/a, (Pt) quinquagésimo/a
60	sessenta	60th	sexagésimo/a
70	setenta	70th	(Br) setuagésimo/a, (Pt) septuagésimo/a
80	oitenta	80th	octagésimo/a
90	noventa	90th	nonagésimo/a
100	cem (cento)**	100th	centésimo/a
101	cento e um (uma)*		
102	cento e dois (duas)*	5½	cinco e meio
146	cento e quarenta e seis	0.3	zero vírgula três
200	duzentos/as	10%	dez por cento
300	trezentos/as		
500	quinhentos/as		
1,000	mil	1000th	milésimo/a
1,003	mil e três		
1,203	mil duzentos/as e três	2m²	dois metros
2,000	dois (duas) mil***		quadrados
1,000,000	um milhão	1,000,000th	milionésimo/a

*,**,*** See notes on p.436

438